ECDL3

The Complete Coursebook

Brendan Munnelly and Paul Holden

An imprint of Pearson Education
London · New York · Toronto · Sydney · Tokyo · Singapore
Madrid · Mexico City · Munich · Paris

PEARSON EDUCATION LIMITED

Head Office:
Edinburgh Gate
Harlow CM20 2JE
Tel: +44 (0)1279 623623
Fax: +44 (0)1279 431059

London Office:
128 Long Acre
London WC2E 9AN
Tel: +44 (0)20 7447 2000
Fax: +44 (0)20 7240 5771

First published in Great Britain in 2000

ISBN 0-130-90837-1

British Library Cataloguing in Publication Data
A CIP catalogue record for this book can be obtained from the British Library

Rédacteurs Software Documentation Limited is at http://www.redact.ie

Brendan Munnelly is at http://www.munnelly.com

10 9 8 7 6 5 4 3

Typeset by the authors.

Printed and bound in Great Britain by Ashford Colour Press, Gosport, Hampshire.

The Publishers' policy is to use paper manufactured from sustainable forests.

Contents

Module 1: Basic Concepts of Information Technology 1

Module 2: Using a Computer and Managing Files 53

Module 6: Presentations 393

1 Basic Concepts of Information Technology

Learning about computers for the first time is rather like learning about a foreign country. A land where words like 'megabyte' and 'peripheral' are part of the everyday conversation. The only crop grown and harvested is something called 'data'. And it is important not only to be faster than your neighbour, but smaller too!

But you need to learn about this country. It was once an out-of-the-way place that attracted only handfuls of scientists to its shores. Now no other destination is more popular.

Like all good tourist guides, this Module introduces you gently to the more commonly spoken words of the computer dialect. It points out the major landmarks (the hard disk, memory and processor are all places you need to take in). And it steers you away from the pitfalls that most offend native computer speakers – such as confusing an 'operating system' with an 'application program'.

Have a pleasant trip. And good luck!

Section 1.1: A Short History of Computing

In This Section

This Section gives you a brief overview of the history of commercial computing, and paints a picture of the role of computers in the world today.

New Skills

At the end of this Section, you should know that computers:

- Have been developed relatively recently
- Become faster, more reliable, and cheaper every year
- Are being used widely in business and education

A Long Line of Machines

From earliest times, people have counted things, measured things, kept records of things, and told other people about things. The 'things' could have been the number of sheep in a flock, the weight of a child, the size of a field, the length of time since the last drought, or the intensity of an earthquake.

From earliest times, people used tools and techniques to help them count more reliably, measure more accurately, record more indelibly, transmit more clearly – they used, for example, measuring tapes, slide rules, sextants, weighing scales, and clocks.

The computer is simply the latest in this long line of calculating and recording machines. That's all it is. Everything we see computers doing today – and we see them doing a lot – they are doing because they can calculate and they can store the results of their calculations.

However, this principle is masked by one outstanding fact: what computers do may be simple, but they do an incredible amount of work, quickly and reliably. The speed of computers today is measured in millions of operations per second. The operations may be simple, but they can be combined in all sorts of ways to yield a vast array of useful functions.

This has almost all come about within the last thirty or forty years, which is the entire history of commercial computers.

In the 1960s, a commercial computer occupied a large air-conditioned room; it needed a team of specialists to operate it; it consumed vast amounts of electricity; and it frequently broke down.

Today's computers are typically much smaller and faster: what previously took up a full room fits into a small box. They can store more information; they consume less power; and they have become far easier to operate.

To give you some idea of the speed of advance, the first personal computers (PCs) were launched in 1979, with a clock speed (don't worry about it – it's just how we measure the speed of computers) of about 5 megahertz (MHz). Today, if you go out to buy a new PC, it is unlikely that you will be offered anything less than 400 MHz or even 500 MHz – eighty or one hundred times as fast. Similar progress has been made in the other main measure of computer power – storage capacity.

You don't need to understand how this has been achieved, and you don't need to know all the details. However, you should be aware of the speed of progress and the main ways in which it is measured. So, if you go out to buy a computer, you will at least know what questions to ask, and will understand the answers.

Every year, computers are becoming smaller, faster, cheaper, more reliable, and easier to use. They are being used in all sorts of situations where it would previously have been impossible to use them: not only in business and government, but also in education, entertainment, health care, sport, art and design. You see computers in homes, clubs, and restaurants; you don't see them (but they are there) in car engines, in bank automatic teller machines, in supermarket checkouts, in washing machines, in telephone systems, in video recorders. You are probably wearing one at this moment, on your wrist, buried inside your watch.

You're surrounded.

But you're *not* under threat: computers are machines, tools. They are designed by people to meet people's needs; they are operated by people. People turn them on. People turn them off.

People like you.

The ECDL is designed to take the fear out of computing, to give you the knowledge and the skills you need to use this technology. With this book, you will learn about the most common PC applications. You won't learn everything: it is not necessary to know everything – it's not even possible. What this book aims to do is to teach you *enough* – enough to perform most of the tasks that most people do most of the time, and to give you enough confidence to tackle the unknown, and to learn from experience.

Self-Test 1.1: History of Computing

1) Today's PCs are approximately how much faster than the first PCs?

    a) Five times as fast
    b) Ten times as fast
    c) A hundred times as fast
    d) A thousand times as fast

2) Which of the following devices may incorporate a computer? (Pick as many as you think, and for each, say what the computer might do.)

    a) A car engine
    b) A video recorder
    c) A bank cash machine
    d) A bicycle

3) True or false: In the 1960s, computers were built by hand from stronger materials. As a result, they were more reliable than today's computers, which are mass-produced, smaller and more delicate.

4) Because of the tiny size of modern computers, they are very hard to make, virtually impossible to repair, and as a result, very expensive.

Section Summary: So Now You Know

The computer is the latest in a long line of tools used to perform calculations and store the results. As they have developed, they have become faster, more reliable, and capable of storing more information. These developments have enabled them to be applied in many areas of commercial life, administration, education, and entertainment.

Section 1.2: What Exactly Is a Computer?

In This Section

In this Section you will learn what distinguishes a computer from other machines. You will also learn about the different types of computer in use today.

New Skills

At the end of this Section you should know:

- What a computer is
- The difference between hardware and software
- The various categories of computers

New Words

At the end of this Section you should be able to explain the following terms:

- Hardware
- Software
- PC
- Mainframe
- Dumb terminal
- Intelligent terminal

The Trouble with Definitions

It is relatively easy to define a washing machine, or a motor car, or a telephone: these devices may be complicated and technologically advanced, but we can talk about them in terms of what they do. They wash clothes, transport people from A to B, enable people to hold conversations with one another over a distance.

As we saw in the previous Section, a computer can be used for almost anything – including controlling the different washing cycles in a washing machine.

In fact, the first part of our definition of a computer recognises this fact: computers are *general purpose* machines. The same computer can operate over a few hours as a typewriter, desktop publishing studio, sound editor, video editor, accounts tracker, e-mail sender, Internet browser, etc.

When you flick the light switch, the light comes on: you could say that the light has obeyed your instruction. Well, computers respond in the same way to instructions: these instructions are called *programs*. And programs are written to make computers behave in specific ways: to act as word processors or to control generating stations. Computers are *programmable*.

Different programs enable the same computer to operate under different guises. We could leave our definition at that, but it will help to add two other ideas: computers can *calculate*, and they can *store* the results of their calculations.

Computer

A computer is a general-purpose, programmable device that is capable of calculating and storing results.

One way of thinking about a computer is as a 'black box' that accepts input on one side, processes it in some way, and then produces output on the other side.

The input might be a mathematical problem, the supplier invoices for the month, a search for a good restaurant in Tullamore, or the temperature of a furnace. The output might be the answer to the mathematical problem, the cheques to pay the invoices, the name and address of the restaurant, or the instructions to shut the control valves on the fuel supply.

What goes on inside the black box is called *processing*: the manipulation of the input necessary to produce the output.

However, the black box is not magic: everything – *everything* – going into a computer is first converted into numbers, and all forms of output – including text on the page, graphics on the screen, music, even telephone conversations – have to be converted into their final form from numbers. In the middle – inside the black box – the numbers are added together in various ways and combinations, under a set of rules called a program. The only magic is the fact that these calculations take place at a rate of millions per second – and, of course, the human ingenuity in the design and the programming.

Computer systems consist of two very different types of elements: *hardware* and *software*.

- Hardware includes all the physical things that you can touch, feel, weigh, and, on rare occasions, kick
- Software is the intangible information component – the instructions, or programs that tell the hardware how to behave.

Hardware

Hardware is the term used to describe the physical parts of a computer system.

Software

Software is the term used to describe the instructions that cause the computer system to behave in a given way.

Types of Computer

Computers fall into a number of different categories, although the dividing line between the categories is not always clear. At one end of the spectrum are *mainframes*. These are big, expensive machines, typically used by large corporations, governmental organisations, and scientific research establishments. They are expected to run continuously, 24 hours a day, 365 days a year. They are capable of processing huge numbers of transactions, and performing extremely complex calculations.

At the other end of the spectrum are the computers most of us are familiar with – the *PC (personal computer)*, formerly known as the *microcomputer*. Today, PCs can be bought for less than £1,000.

PCs come in various shapes and sizes. *Desktop* computers are the most common: they generally include a system unit, a screen, and a keyboard, as separate components. *Laptop* or *notebook* computers are more portable: the screen is a flat *liquid crystal display* (LCD), which forms a lid hinged to cover the keyboard and system unit. Laptops are somewhat more expensive than desktop PCs.

In between these two ends of the computer spectrum lie *minicomputers*, which are typically used by medium-sized enterprises, or by departments within larger organizations. Like mainframes, they offer greater processing power, storage capacity and reliability than PCs.

Network computers (*network servers*) are computers that administer, support, and protect the security of a computer network. Users on a network are able to use the resources (data, software, hardware) on the network server. In the past, such users mainly used *dumb terminals* – devices that simply accepted input from the user and displayed results. All the processing and storage was done by the server. Nowadays, most users have *intelligent terminals* – PCs that have their own 'local' processing and storage capacity.

Self-Test 1.2: A Computer Is...?

1) Distinguish between a computer and a pocket calculator.
   a) Because the calculator is purpose-built, it is more accurate.
   b) There is no difference: the calculator contains a computer.
   c) The computer includes a word-processor; the calculator doesn't.
   d) The computer has a bigger screen.
2) Which of the following statements is/are true?
   a) Cables and other flexible parts of a computer are called software; all the solid parts are called hardware.
   b) Hardware is the term used to describe the physical parts of a computer system.
   c) Diskettes and CDs are software; the screen and keyboard are hardware.
   d) Software is another word for programs.

3) Which of the following statements is/are true?

   a) A mainframe is a large computer built in the 1960s or 1970s that is now obsolete.
   b) A mainframe is a large computer typically used by a big company or governmental organisation.
   c) A mainframe is a metal framework inside the plastic casing of a computer.
   d) A mainframe is another word for hardware.

4) A microcomputer is often called a PC. The abbreviation PC stands for:

   a) Personal computer
   b) Portable computer
   c) Politically correct
   d) Personal calculator
   e) Professional capacity

5) Which of the following is/are portable computer(s)?

   a) Minicomputer
   b) Microcomputer
   c) Laptop
   d) Notebook

6) Which of the following statements is/are true?

   a) A network server is another name for a dumb terminal.
   b) A dumb terminal is useless without a network server.
   c) A network server is useless without a dumb terminal.
   d) A dumb terminal is a computer without any loudspeakers.
   e) An intelligent terminal is a computer used for military or industrial espionage.
   f) An intelligent terminal is another name for a bank cash machine.

Section Summary: So Now You Know

Computers are general-purpose machines. What distinguishes a computer calculating a payroll from one forecasting the weather is the program it is running. And in fact the *same* computer could be programmed to do both tasks.

Computers accept information from the outside (input), do something to it (processing), and display or print out the results (output). The two main elements in a computer system are *hardware*, which is the term used for the physical parts, and *software*, which describes the instructions or programs that cause the computer to behave in a given way.

The most familiar computers are called PCs or microcomputers. The biggest and most expensive – used by large organisations – are called mainframes. In between are minicomputers.

A computer network is controlled by a network computer, or network server. The devices connected to the server are called terminals. These may be dumb terminals – with no processing or storage power of their own – or intelligent terminals – with their own processing and storage capability.

Section 1.3: Computer Hardware

In This Section

When you go out to buy a computer, you are immediately faced with a range of options that even experienced computer people find bewildering. To make a sensible choice, you need to know the function of the main components in a computer system, and the criteria upon which you should base your decision.

A typical PC system is made up of a number of components. Some of these are essential, and some optional. In some cases, a number of alternatives are available, from which you have to choose.

This Section takes you on a tour of the typical computer system, and identifies all the hardware components. We look first at the components that are normally inside the main '*system unit*' ('In the Box'), and then at the other components in a typical system ('Outside the Box').

New Skills

At the end of this Section, you should be able to:

- Name the hardware components in a computer system
- Say what each component is for
- Describe some of the 'optional extras'
- Describe how to look after your computer

New Words

At the end of this Section, you should be able to explain the following terms:

- Processor
- Memory
- Hard Disk
- Diskette
- Keyboard
- Screen
- Mouse
- Printer
- Modem
- Multimedia

Unfortunately, when talking about computer hardware, a certain amount of jargon is unavoidable. Other new terms in this Section are in *italics* and explained in their context.

In the Box

The system unit – usually a beige or grey box – is the most essential part of the computer. It houses the processor (the 'brain'), the various kinds of memory (described below), and the electronics to control all the other components. It also usually includes a fan, designed to keep the whole unit cool. The fan is responsible for the hum from the computer when you turn it on. The system unit may stand vertically on the floor (a *tower*), or horizontally on the desk, usually with the screen on top (a *desktop* unit). In a *laptop* or *notebook* computer, the system unit is usually built underneath the keyboard.

Processor

The length of time it takes a computer to perform a task depends on a number of factors. The first of these is the speed of the processor – the chip at the heart of the computer. This is measured in megahertz (MHz), and the bigger the number, the faster the processor (the more calculations it can perform per second). This measure of the computer's performance is so critical that it is usually included in the name of the computer. So the Dell Dimension R450, for example, includes the Intel Pentium II 450 MHz processor.

The processor chip and the electronics that support it are referred to as the *Central Processing Unit* (CPU).

Memory

The definition of a computer includes the idea of storage: the computer has to be able to store the results of its calculations. In practice, a computer has to store a huge amount of information. It has a number of different kinds of memory, two of which are regularly cited in the advertisements for computers: RAM and disk space.

Random Access Memory

Random Access Memory (RAM) is used by the computer as a sort of working area while it is carrying out a given task. (It is often called *working storage*.) Here it holds the list of instructions that it is currently working on, the data on which it is working, and the interim results of its calculations. The 'R' in RAM is its main advantage. It can be accessed randomly, which means that the computer can get at any piece of data directly – it does not have to look through the storage area from the start until it finds the piece of interest. This makes it fast. In general, the more RAM the better, and a certain minimum is required for many programs. RAM is often called *main memory*.

Memory capacity is measured in *bytes*. One byte consists of eight *bits*. You can think of a bit in electrical terms as a switch: on or off, or in mathematical terms as a single binary number: 0 or 1. Eight of these – a byte – can represent a letter of the alphabet, or a single number. You are likely to be offered a new computer with at least 64 megabytes (64 MB – 64 million bytes) or possibly 128 MB of RAM. (This is twice as much as you would have been offered for the same price last year, and probably half as much as you will be offered this time next year.)

Read-Only Memory

AM should not be confused with another kind of memory that you may occasionally hear of: ROM (Read-Only Memory). This is where the computer stores its low-level programs – the ones that tell it how to behave, how to check its own circuitry, how to treat various kinds of input devices, and so on. ROM differs from RAM in two ways: first, it is not changed after the computer is assembled (you can read it, but not write to it), and second, its contents remain unchanged even when the power is turned off. (RAM is *volatile* – its contents are erased if the power supply is cut off.)

It is relatively easy to upgrade the memory on your computer by buying additional memory chips. They are inexpensive and easy to install. Depending on what you are using your computer for, additional memory can make a huge difference to its performance. (Don't, however, attempt to install additional memory without expert guidance.)

Hard Disk

After processor speed and amount of RAM, the next major determinant of computer power is the amount of disk space. A disk is a device for storing information. It is very different from RAM, for a number of reasons:

- First, disks record information magnetically, in much the same way as music tapes or video tapes. They are not volatile: once the information is recorded, it remains on the disk until it is changed or deleted.
- Second, the process of getting information onto a disk or retrieving information from a disk involves mechanical movement. The disk revolves at a constant high speed, and a *read/write head* moves in and out just above the surface of the disk. The read/write head can change the polarisation of tiny magnetic particles on the surface of the disk, and can detect the polarisation of particles. Moving parts eventually wear out and

as a result, disks are more likely to malfunction than non-moving RAM. The moving parts also introduce delays into the processes of reading and writing, whereas reading from RAM is almost instantaneous.

Like memory capacity, disk capacity is measured in *bytes*. Disk capacity is bigger by several orders of magnitude: a new computer today will typically come with a 12-gigabyte disk (12 GB – 12 billion bytes) rising to 20 gigabytes.

Let's consider this slowly: 12,000,000,000 bytes. The 32 volumes of *Encyclopaedia Brittanica* contain approximately 44,000,000 words, or approximately 220,000,000 characters (bytes). A 12-GB disk could hold that text almost fifty-six times, yet it only weighs about 1 kilogram, and takes up less space than one of the encyclopaedia's volumes. The amount of information that a disk can hold is the third performance measure that you should consider when buying a computer.

Diskettes, CD-ROMs, DVDs, Zip Disks, Tapes

The disks described on the previous page are built in to the computer. They are often called *hard disks*. They remain in the computer, and are not (generally) transferred between computers. There is, however, a wide range of removable storage devices that can be transferred easily from one computer to another, or used as security backups in case of loss, damage, or theft of the computer.

Diskettes (Floppy Disks)

Another kind of disk is the so-called '*floppy disk*' or *diskette*. (Early removable disks were housed in flexible envelopes, which earned them the name 'floppy'. The more recent design, with which you are probably familiar, uses a hard plastic shell with a sliding metal cover.)

The most common type of diskette holds 1.4 MB. This is enough to easily hold many typical word processing documents, so that they can easily be passed from one person to another. You can use a diskette to transfer a document from your office computer to your home computer – simply copy the document to the diskette, and bring it home in your pocket. The entire text of this book (but not the graphics) fits onto a single diskette, with room to spare!

Just as RAM is often referred to as 'working storage' or 'main memory', disks and diskettes are often called 'backing storage', or 'secondary storage'.

CD-ROM and DVD

Until quite recently, diskettes were also the principal way of loading programs onto a computer. Nowadays, however, software is most often supplied on CD-ROM (Compact Disk Read-Only Memory). Physically, a CD-ROM is indistinguishable from a music CD, and in fact CD readers in computers are almost all capable of playing music CDs.

The move from diskette to CD-ROM as the favoured medium for distributing software has taken place mainly because of the size of modern software systems: they need more storage space. (More space is required because the programs have added functionality, because they are more graphic in design, and because they may include other multimedia elements.) A single CD-ROM can hold as much information as 460 diskettes – about 650 MB.

CD-ROM drives (the part of the computer that reads CD-ROMs) are now offered as standard on all new computers. The only performance measure to watch out for is the speed of the drive, always quoted as a multiple of the normal music CD-player speed: nowadays, 36x speed or 40x speed CD-ROM drives are normal.

CD-ROMs are now being overtaken by DVDs (Digital Versatile Disks), which look similar, but have a great deal more storage capacity – up to 3.9 gigabytes or GB.

To record information on a CD, you need a CD Writer (or 'burner'). Information is encoded on the surface of CDs as tiny holes, which are detected by a laser beam.

Remember, however, that CDs differ from magnetic disks (hard disks and diskettes) in that the holes burnt into the read/write surface of the CD are permanent: once burnt, they cannot be changed or erased (hence Read Only Memory). Magnetic media, on the other hand, can be changed at will. For this reason, hard disks will continue to be the favoured media for storing information in normal office applications.

Magnetic Tape

Magnetic tape – usually in cassettes not unlike music cassettes – is used for distributing software and for keeping backup copies of large volumes of data. It is less useful in normal everyday use, because it cannot be accessed randomly: the computer has to read it through from the beginning to find the part of interest.

Zip Disks, etc.

High-capacity removable diskettes are gaining favour for keeping backups and for transferring large files between computers. Some use magnetic technology, some laser technology. Among the most popular such devices is the *Zip drive*, which attaches to any computer's parallel port (printer connection) and provides storage on 100-MB or 250-MB removable disks.

Medium	Typical Capacity	Typical Cost of Medium (July 2000)
Hard Disk (Fixed)	12 to 20 Gigabytes,	£50 to £300
Diskette	1.4 Megabytes	Less than £1
CD	650 Megabytes	Less than £10
DVD	5.2 Gigabytes	£20 to £30
Zip	150 Megabytes	Less than £10
Tape	4 to 100 Gigabytes	£20 to £70

Out of the Box: The Essentials

Everything outside the grey box is peripheral, which is why all the other objects are called *peripherals*. (Here we're cheating a little: technically, all secondary storage, such as disks, CD-ROMs, etc. can be considered to be peripheral as well.) In most computer systems, the three *essential* peripherals are the keyboard and mouse (used for input), and the screen (used for output).

Keyboard

A keyboard is a set of typewriter-like keys that enables you, the user, to enter information and instructions into a computer. Keys on a computer keyboard are of three types:

- **Alphanumeric Keys:** Letters and numbers
- **Punctuation Keys:** Comma, full stop, semicolon, and so on
- **Special Keys:** Function keys, control keys, arrow keys, Caps Lock key, and so on.

Screen

The screen looks somewhat like a television. It is also called the *monitor* (because you use it to monitor what is going on in the computer) or the *visual display unit* (VDU). Most programs are designed in such a way that you appear to enter input directly from the keyboard onto the screen. In fact, you enter it into the processor, and the processor shows you what it has received by displaying it on the screen. Most programs also give you continuous feedback on their progress, and display their output on the screen.

Mouse

Many programs present themselves on the screen as *Graphical User Interfaces* (GUI – pronounced, believe it or not, 'gooey'). A GUI represents programs, files, and functions as pictures on the screen. The GUI includes a pointer that you can move around the screen until it is at the picture that represents what you want to do. You then indicate your intention, and the program responds accordingly.

The mouse is the tool that you use to move the pointer around the screen. The underside of the mouse houses a ball, and, as you move the mouse over your desk, this ball detects the movements, and converts them into movements of the pointer. Move the mouse left, the pointer moves left; right, and the pointer moves right; push the mouse away from you, and the pointer moves up the screen; pull it towards you, the pointer moves down. After a very short time it becomes second nature.

Note that the ball only moves (and therefore the pointer only moves) when the underside of the mouse is in contact with the desk. So you can move the pointer a long distance in one direction by making a series of short moves in that direction with the mouse, each time lifting the mouse so that the return journey does not affect the position of the pointer.

The mouse has two or three buttons on top: these are used to signal to the computer that the pointer has arrived where you want to go. You press one or other buttons once (called a *click*), or twice in quick succession (called a *double click*).

The mouse (or whatever pointing device you use – see *Other Pointing Devices* on the next page) makes operation of the computer easy, and even intuitive, but it is seldom absolutely necessary. Most programs allow you to move the pointer around the screen and choose your options using special keys or combinations of keys on the keyboard. Some users prefer this: it means they can do all their work from the keyboard – they don't have to switch back and forth between the keyboard and the mouse.

Other Pointing Devices

Mice are by far the most common pointing devices, but there are others.

Trackballs are like upside-down mice: you move the pointer by manipulating a ball in a special housing with your fingers. They are useful in situations where desk space is limited.

Joysticks and *Games Controllers* fulfil the same function, but are designed specially for games and simulation.

Most portable computers have a device built in to the keyboard for moving the pointer, either in the form of a miniature joystick, or a pressure-sensitive *touchpad* that detects movements of your finger.

Light Pens are pen-shaped devices that, when placed close to the screen, can be used both to draw and to control icons or choices shown on the screen.

Touch Screens are often seen in public information kiosks: the user simply touches the screen at the point of interest in order to exercise a choice from the options displayed.

Graphics Tablets are flat surfaces that detect the movement of a plastic stylus (pen) across them. They are typically used for art and design applications, but smaller versions are becoming common in 'pocket', 'hand-held' or 'palmtop' computers. These devices (known as *Personal Digital Assistants*, or *PDA*s) are too small to allow typing.

Out of the Box: Optional Extras

Without the components described in the previous section, it would be hard to get the computer to do anything useful. There are a number of other devices that, although they are not essential, are normal parts of the system in the home, school or office. These are a printer, a modem, and loudspeakers. Some others – scanners, digital cameras, microphones – would have been considered exotic a couple of years ago, but are increasingly considered 'normal'.

Printers

There are several kinds of printer on the market: the two most common are *laser printers* and *inkjet printers*.

Laser Printers

Laser printers use a technology similar to that used in photocopying to transfer the image of a page onto paper. The image is 'drawn' under instruction from the computer.

Inkjet Printers

Inkjet printers have a moving 'pen' (the *write head*) that holds an ink cartridge. This moves back and forth over the page and, under computer control, ejects a minute quantity of ink at the precise point where it is required on the page.

Other Kinds of Printer

You will occasionally come across a third category of printer: *impact printers*. These work like a typewriter: they hammer out the required characters onto the page through an ink-impregnated (or carbon-covered) ribbon. There are several kinds, using slightly different techniques for making the marks on the paper: dot matrix printers, daisy wheel printers, line printers. Nowadays their use is confined to specialist applications (printing receipts from cash registers, printing the time of arrival on a ticket in a car park), or high-volume printouts that do not use graphics (tax forms, electricity bills).

Plotters are used in specialist applications, such as producing architectural or engineering drawings. Most of them are designed to produce large drawings accurately. They are relatively expensive.

How to Choose a Printer

Some of the factors you should consider when buying a printer are:

- **Speed of Output:** Most laser printers can print 8 or 12 pages a minute. This speed may depend on what you are printing: graphics, or text pages with a variety of different fonts, tend to be slower. If you need a faster printer, be prepared to pay a lot more.

  Inkjet printers are generally a lot slower than laser printers, but their speed doesn't depend on what you are printing. The quality of the print tends to vary, because they rely on a moving write head.

- **Colour:** If you want colour output, you have to buy a colour printer. It's that simple. Colour laser printers are expensive; colour inkjet printers are only slightly more expensive than black-and-white printers.

  Some colour printers use three different inks to produce their output, some four. Some use a combined three- or four-colour cartridge, some a separate cartridge for each colour. Your choice depends on what you are using the printer for. If you are only occasionally using colour output, make sure you have a separate black cartridge: the density of the black printout from a black cartridge is much higher than that from a combination of colours. If you get a combined four-colour cartridge, you will be throwing out the almost-full colour inks just because you have run out of black.

- **Cost of Consumables:** The initial cost of the printer is only one of the cost factors that you need to consider: ink cartridges (for inkjet printers) and toner cartridges (for laser printers) have to be replaced regularly, and it is worthwhile calculating the cost per page of output before making your final decision.

Modem

A *modem* is used to connect your computer to the telephone network, so that you can send e-mail, or use the Internet. Most computers sold today include a modem already installed in the system unit, but they can also be obtained as external devices that are connected to the computer by a cable. Most modems can enable your computer to function as a fax machine (although, unless you have a scanner, you are limited to sending text-only faxes).

Multimedia

Computers can manipulate any kind of data that can be converted into numbers, including music, pictures, animated drawings, video, and speech. A range of applications has grown up around this capability, in which text, video, and sound are mixed to deliver instruction, information, or entertainment. These applications are called *multimedia applications*, and a computer that can run them is often called a *multimedia computer*. Most computers nowadays can run these applications. However, if this is your main interest, you may want to consider a computer with a larger screen, and more advanced sound generation and video display capabilities. In addition, a number of specialised peripherals are available.

Scanner

Think of a scanner as the first half of a photocopier – it copies a photograph, drawing, or page of text into the computer, where you can use a program to manipulate it, or print it out (like the second half of the photocopier). You can use the scanner to include a drawing or photograph in a newsletter, or use *Optical Character Recognition* software to decipher the text, and use all or part of it in a word-processing document (without having to re-type it).

Digital Camera

A digital camera works exactly like a standard camera, except that it does not use photographic film – the images are recorded digitally in the camera's memory. From there, you can transfer them to your computer and subsequently print them out, use graphics software to edit them, archive them for posterity, or e-mail them to your friends.

Loudspeakers

Loudspeakers are standard equipment on almost all new computers. They are used to play music and other sounds.

Sound Cards

Again, your system unit almost certainly includes a sound card, which is used to control all the audio output (music, speech, etc.). However, if the quality of music output is important to you, you may want to upgrade from the sound card supplied as standard equipment.

Microphone

Many software applications can be controlled by speech commands. These are spoken into a microphone.

Looking after Your Hardware

Modern computers are robust and reliable: once they start working, they tend to go on working. But remember that they are sensitive instruments, and avoid testing their tolerance.

DO give your computer room to breathe: it has to have access to fresh air so that the fan can keep the electronics cool.

DON'T block the air vents by stacking books or magazines or (worse) draping clothes over the back of the computer.

DO keep the computer dry. Excessive moisture can play havoc with electric circuitry.

DON'T eat or drink while using your computer: crumbs can clog up your keyboard. A spilt cup of coffee can wreck your computer and (probably worse) cause the loss of all your files stored on the computer.

DO keep your computer free of dust: you will notice that it tends to attract dust. Clean the air vents occasionally, and use an anti-static wipe on the screen.

DON'T expose your computer to extremes of temperature.

DO shut down the computer in an orderly fashion, by systematically closing the applications you have opened.

DON'T just switch it off or pull the plug from the socket.

DO keep diskettes away from the screen: the strong magnetic field generated by the screen may erase or change some of the data.

DON'T move the system unit while the computer is in operation – you risk damaging the hard disk drive.

When Something Goes Wrong

You are more likely to be a computer user than a computer engineer. Therefore respect your PC as a delicate instrument – if it seems to be malfunctioning, don't try to fix it. You risk destroying it or electrocuting yourself. Always call a person qualified to deal with the problem.

Self-Test 1.3: Hardware

1) Which of the following is/are essential pieces of hardware for a computer to work?
   a) Processor
   b) Scanner
   c) Hammer
   d) Word processor
2) The C in CPU stands for:
   a) Central
   b) Computer
   c) Complex
   d) Computing
   e) Commercial
3) What is a scanner used for?
4) What is a modem used for?
5) The speed of a computer is measured in:
   a) CPUs
   b) MHz
   c) MB
   d) K
   e) RAM
   f) GUIs

6) The R in ROM stands for:

   a) Random
   b) Read
   c) Regular
   d) Right

7) The R in RAM stands for:

   a) Random
   b) Read
   c) Regular
   d) Right

8) Correct any of the following statements that are wrong.

   a) There are exactly eight bytes in a bit.
   b) A megabyte is double the size of a normal byte.
   c) 100K bytes is equal to a GB.
   d) A gigabyte is approximately equal to 1,000,000,000 bytes.

9) Which of the following statements is/are true?

   a) Information stored in RAM is erased when the computer is turned off.
   b) Information stored in ROM is erased when the computer is turned off.
   c) The M in RAM stands for memory.
   d) The M in ROM stands for memory.
   e) Hard disks, diskettes, and CD-ROMs are all used to store computer programs.

10) Name three kinds of pointing device.

11) Name the two most common types of printer.

12) Which can store more information: a high-density diskette or a Zip disk?

Section Summary: So Now You Know

The basic PC consists of a system unit, a screen, and a keyboard. Virtually all PCs include a pointing device – most commonly a mouse.

Inside the system unit are the processor (CPU), main memory, hard disk, and some removable storage – usually a diskette drive.

Other items that are almost essential are a printer and a modem. A modem is used to connect the computer to the telephone network, so that you can send and receive e-mail or access the Internet.

Many – even most – PCs sold today are equipped for multimedia: they include loudspeakers, sound cards, and microphones.

To capture images, drawings, or photographs and include them in newsletters, project reports, or e-mails, you need a scanner or a digital camera.

Finally, you learnt how to look after your computer, so that it gives a long life of good service.

Section 1.4: Software and Data

In This Section

In this Section you will learn more about the different kinds of software and how they are made. You will also learn what the most valuable part of a computer system is – the data.

New Skills

At the end of this Section you should be able to:

- Distinguish between system software and application software
- Describe the process of software development
- Discuss software licensing and the different types of licence
- Describe how to protect software and data from unauthorised access, loss or damage, and computer viruses
- State the principles of data copyright
- State the principles of data protection and the main provisions of the European Data Protection Directive
- Describe the advantages of computer networking
- Describe the use of the telephone network in computing
- Describe the uses of e-mail, the Internet, and the World Wide Web
- Describe how e-commerce is changing business practices

New Words

At the end of this Section you should be able to explain the following terms:

- System software
- Application software
- Graphical user interface
- Systems analyst
- Programmer
- Backup
- Virus
- Copyright
- Data protection
- Network
- LAN
- WAN
- PSTN
- ISDN
- E-mail
- Internet
- World Wide Web
- Browser
- Search engine
- E-commerce

Software

Software is the intangible side of computing: it is the generic name given to all the programs – the sets of instructions – that determine how the computer behaves.

We distinguish between two kinds of software: *system software* and *applications software*.

- System software is concerned with the computer itself – what devices it can control, how it manages files and storage, and how it deals with exceptional conditions.
- Applications software is concerned with the world outside the computer – the world of business, entertainment, or education.

System Software

The main piece of system software that we are concerned with is the *Operating System* (OS). This is the driving program of the PC: without it, the PC would be virtually unusable. All other programs depend on the operating system to communicate with and control the hardware. The operating system also controls the timing of different events to make sure they happen in the correct sequence, and manages access to data to ensure security and integrity.

When you add a new piece of hardware to your system, you might have to load a special piece of software called a *driver* to enable the operating system to control the hardware. Older PCs use an operating system called DOS (Disk Operating System). To use DOS, you have to type in commands such as DIR, COPY, or REN.

Graphical User Interface

More recent computers present their operating system through a *Graphical User Interface* (GUI). The GUI represents all the computer's resources – the hardware resources such as disks and printers, the software resources, including both system software and application programs, and the data files on which you can work – as small pictures or symbols called *icons*. You use the mouse to move the pointer to the icon representing the object you want to use, and press (or *click*) the mouse button to signal your request. This is considerably easier than having to remember a command and typing it accurately. Examples of GUIs include Windows, MacOS, and SunOS.

Application Software

Nobody wants to use a lawnmower or a telephone or a satellite: what they want to do is cut the grass, talk to their friends, or predict the weather. Similarly, you don't really want to use a computer: you want to use a computer to do *something else*. That 'something else' is your application, and the program that enables you to do it is called the *application program*. By the time you have finished this book you will be able to use several application programs: word processing, spreadsheets, electronic mail, and so on. Some application programs are very common – it is hard to find an office that doesn't use Microsoft Word or Excel or various Internet browsers such as Netscape Navigator or Microsoft Explorer. Many computers are sold with these applications pre-loaded.

Other applications are developed for more specialised tasks. People and organisations purchase them in accordance with their particular needs. An architect might use a sophisticated drawing package to design houses; a submarine builder might purchase a piece of project management software to help keep track of the thousands of components. In Section 1.5 we will look in more detail at the types of applications in daily use in business, administration, education, entertainment, and communication.

How Software Is Made

The development of any software system involves a cycle of research, analysis, development, and testing, involving the following types of people:

- **Systems Analysts:** They study the business processes that the software is intended to support, and produce the design for the software. They decide what the software should do (but not necessarily how it should do it). You can think of the systems analyst as the software architect. Systems analysts are focused on the needs of the users and the application area.
- **Programmers:** They translate the design into a working program. They write instructions that tell the computer what to do in order to accomplish the task for which the system is intended. You can think of the programmer as the software builder. Programmers are focused on the computer, its capabilities and its limitations.

Software Copyright

In general, software is *licensed* rather than sold. When you buy a software package, you don't own the software: you gain the right to use it under specified conditions.

In general, software is easy to duplicate, so it is easy for unscrupulous people to make unauthorised copies: don't do it. It's piracy; it's illegal; and it deprives an individual developer or a company of their rightful income, which they need to produce the next version of that piece of software, or the next application that you will want to use.

Don't accept software from dubious sources, whether in person, by mail-order, or over the Internet. You are responsible for the legality of the software that you use.

Some software, called *freeware* is distributed without charge: you find it on disks given away with magazines, or download it from the Internet. Again, you should be clear about the terms of use: in most cases, you can use it, but you may not, for example, sell it for profit, change it in any way, or label it as if it was your own product.

Other software is called *shareware*. It is widely distributed in much the same way as freeware. You can try it out, but if you decide to use it you are expected to send a licence fee to the developer. In some cases, this is based on honour; in other cases, the shareware version will not function after a time period (typically 30 days), or certain functions are disabled in some way. When you register with the developer and send the licence fee, you are given a fully working copy of the software, or a password to unlock the disabled functions.

Problems with Software

Software – even the smallest piece of application software – is complex. It is difficult to test thoroughly, because it is difficult to imagine every possible input in every possible combination. Sometimes mistakes are made, or unusual circumstances are not adequately catered for by the designers or programmers.

When the software produces incorrect or unexpected results, it is said to have a *bug*. Bugs can range from minor irritations, where, for example, the screen displays are inconsistent, through significant errors, such as incorrect totals on invoices, to total collapse.

An example of a problem caused by short-sighted programming practices was the so-called 'Millennium Bug'. Many programs stored dates as six digits – two each for day, month and year. For most purposes, this was fine, but when you use these dates in calculations, difficulties can arise. For example, is someone born on 06 01 99 just over a year old or one hundred years old? Such ambiguities can be of critical importance in calculating interest payments, sell-by dates, eligibility for pensions, and so. Although this problem may seem trivial, putting it right costs businesses around the world many millions of pounds.

When the computer 'freezes' – it ceases to function, refuses to accept any input, won't produce any output – we say that it *hangs*. When this happens, you may be able to resort to an old trick: press three of the keyboard keys simultaneously – CTRL, ALT, and DEL. Most of the time, this will enable you to shut down the offending program, and continue working on something else. Pressing this key combination *twice* generally causes your computer to restart.

Infrequently, a bug will cause the whole system to *crash*. The only solution is to turn off the power, wait a minute, and then turn it on again. A quicker way to achieve the same end is to press the Reset button on your system unit. Treat this as a last resort, however – you will lose any work since you last saved in all the applications that you have open at the time.

Data

We haven't yet dealt in any detail with data. Data is another intangible in a computer system, but it is not generally built by the software developer. It's built by users – people like you.

So to write a letter, you need a keyboard, a screen, and a printer (hardware), and you need a word-processing program (software). The letter itself, and the name and address of the recipient, are *data*.

Data is held on a computer system in *files*. Files are organised into *directories* (otherwise known as *folders*). Files and directories are given *names*, so that you can find them and recognise them when you need them, and so that the operating system can find them and work on them when it needs to.

Looking After Your Data

In most computer systems, the data is the most important element. Hardware and software are easily replaced if they break down, or are lost or stolen. Data, on the other hand, can represent years of work, and may be irreplaceable. So it makes sense to look after it. Data can be lost, corrupted, damaged, or abused in a variety of ways, accidentally or deliberately.

Security and Passwords

You can protect your data against theft, corruption, and prying eyes by using a system of *passwords*. Depending on the application, you can use passwords to decide who can see the data and who can change it.

Most applications allow you to choose your own password, and encourage you to change it frequently. Choose a password that is not too obvious – if it is easy to guess, its purpose may be defeated. However, choose a password that is easy to remember. If you forget it, you may not be able to get at your own data, and if you write it down, it may be discovered and used by someone else. The best passwords include both numbers and letters, so that unauthorised persons will find them less easy to guess.

Backups

Files can be lost or destroyed accidentally. The hard disk may develop problems, or the whole office may be destroyed by fire. You can protect yourself against these nightmare scenarios by keeping backup copies of all your data files, on diskette or another removable medium, and storing it safely at home or at another location. That way, even in the worst situation, you can be up and running very quickly after a disaster.

Save Frequently

You should also save your work at regular intervals while you are working. Remember that the computer works on your data in working storage (RAM), which is volatile. If there is a power cut, or if someone accidentally unplugs your PC, everything you have done since you last saved will be lost. It is a good discipline to save after every paragraph of text, or after you have done any complex operation.

Viruses

Computer viruses are attempts at sabotage. They are clever but poisonous programs written by malicious software developers and amateur hackers. They attack the integrity of your files, and are designed to transfer easily and stealthily from one computer to another. Their effects vary from minor irritation (where a message is displayed on your screen, but no files are damaged), through inconvenience (where one or more files are affected), to total disaster (where the entire hard disk is rendered unusable).

Viruses are spread through e-mail attachments and the exchange of infected diskettes. So, never open an e-mail attachment if you are unsure of its origin, and always use virus scanning software to check any diskette that comes into your possession or organisation from outside.

Prevention is better than cure: make sure that you install reputable anti-virus software on your computer that will automatically scan your disks (hard drive and diskette), and detect and remove any viruses found. Anti-virus software must be kept up to date – new viruses are being concocted all the time, and the software used to detect them needs to be the very latest.

Data Copyright

Remember that computer data carries the same copyright rights and responsibilities as printed works or musical compositions: someone created it, and that person owns it. If you download information from the Internet, you may not have the right to include it in your own publications without the consent of the author or creator.

Data Protection

We all appear in numerous databases: banks, insurance companies, educational institutions, employers, and governments all hold files full of personal information. Our date of birth, address and marital status, our incomes, credit and educational records, our health, criminal and bill-paying histories are all known by various institutions. This information is sometimes general, sometimes special. It may be sensitive and, in the wrong hands, damaging or dangerous.

Marketing departments are willing to pay large sums of money for name and address databases of specific categories of people. This enables them to target products and services at precise sectors of the population.

It follows that the collection, maintenance, and protection of information is a responsibility that demands great respect. Wrong or misleading information could lead to a person being refused a mortgage, a job, an overseas work visa, or medical insurance. It could ruin their life. Holding personal information thus demands sensitivity and respect. This is reflected in the *data protection laws*.

The European Data Protection Directive

All EU countries either have already adopted laws to give effect to this EU Directive or will shortly do so.

The Directive requires that all computer-based data be:

- Processed fairly and lawfully
- Collected for specified and explicit purposes
- Adequate, relevant and not excessive
- Accurate and up-to-date where necessary
- Maintained in a form that means that the data subject (that is, the person about whom the data is gathered) cannot be identified once their identification is no longer necessary.

It is quite common for data to be gathered about Internet users – this enables online businesses to target their marketing more effectively. Such information is also subject to the rules on data protection. The EU Directive sets out the information that must be provided to web users when such details are collected, including the identity of the collecting body, the purposes for which the data is intended, the likely recipients of the data, and the right to access the information and correct it if it is inaccurate. Each EU Member State must ensure that controllers of information respect the above rules.

Hacking has worrying implications for data protection. Controllers are required to implement adequate security measures to protect data against accidental or malicious disclosure or access, in particular where the information is being transferred over a network, as in the case of the Internet.

One difficulty with the Internet is that it is transnational. Data can be transferred from an EU website to a US one at the click of a button. However, the EU Directive prohibits the transfer of information to countries outside the EU unless they have similar protections in place.

Self-Test 1.4: Software

1) Is a word processor systems software or application software?

2) Is Windows systems software or application software?

3) What is the difference between freeware and shareware?

4) Which of the following statements is/are true?

    a) A folder is another name for a diskette.

    b) A file can contain any number of folders.

    c) Records have been made obsolete by CDs

    d) Files contain records

5) What is a computer virus?

6) Say some of the ways to protect your data against loss or corruption.

7) You edit the newsletter for your local community. Are you entitled to sell the mailing list to a marketing company? Why/why not?

Networks

Computers can function quite happily on their own (*stand-alone computing*), but increasingly they are being connected together into *networks*.

The Advantages of Networking

When your computer is connected to other computers – whether they are in the same building or on the other side of the world – it is part of a computer network. You can still use it to do your own work as usual, but several new possibilities open up:

- **Sharing Hardware:** In a stand-alone world, people can print only if a printer is attached directly to their computer. By connecting one or more printers to a computer network, everyone whose computer is also attached to the same network can print their documents. Printer-sharing means that everyone can print (although not at the same time) without everyone having an individual printer. The same is true of other hardware resources, such as modems, scanners, and plotters.

- **File-sharing:** On a stand-alone computer, you can work with all the files stored on your computer's hard disk. On a network-connected computer, you may be able to work with files stored on other people's computers too. Rather than have network users rummaging through each other's hard disks, information that is needed by everyone in a particular department (in accounts, for example, or in a warehouse) is usually stored on a single, powerful, permanently switched-on computer called a *file server*.

- **E-mail:** Meetings, telephone conversations, letters and memos – typically, these are the ways in which people in an organisation communicate with one another. Computer networks make possible another form of communication called electronic mail, or e-mail for short. This is the exchange of (usually plain-text) messages between users of computers that are connected to a common network.

- **Data Exchange:** Users connected to a computer network can exchange files: one person can write an article for the newsletter, another can edit it, a third can lay it out, while a fourth can contribute a drawing or a scanned photograph. This kind of co-operative work over a network is known as *workgroup computing*, or *groupwork*.

Computer Network
Two or more computers that are connected together by some means to provide their users with such services as printer-sharing, file-sharing, and electronic mail.

LANs and WANs

Networks come in two sizes: big and small. A Local Area Network, or LAN, is the kind that connects the computers in a single office, building or group of adjoining buildings.

Local Area Network (LAN)
A network that connects computers located within a small area.

Large corporations operate computer networks that connect offices at locations within the same or different countries. Such Wide Area Networks, or WANs, can enable, for example:

- The Frankfurt office to exchange e-mails with the Sydney office
- The Tokyo office to read files that are stored on a computer in the New Orleans office
- The Cape Town office to print a report on a printer that is located in the Bombay office

Wide Area Network (WAN)
A network that connects computers over a wide area, typically across international boundaries.

In reality, most networks are bigger than LANs but smaller than WANs. But, for some reason, no one has thought up a name for them.

Computer networks can be open to everyone or restricted to the chosen few. An example of a *private access* network is one operated by a company or government agency for its own personnel only. An example of a *public access* network is the Internet.

Making the Connection

How do the computers in a network actually connect with one another? Well, in a LAN it's relatively simple: the computers (and printers) are connected together with a special cable. However, in a WAN, that isn't an option. It would be quite impractical to run cables from one side of the country to another, or from one continent to the next.

The Telephone Network

The solution is that WANs use cables already in place – the cables of the national and international telephone system (the PSTN, or Public Switched Telephone Network). They also use all the other technology of the telephone network – satellites, microwaves, optic fibres, and so on. This has advantages, and one major disadvantage too:

- **Advantages:** It's already in place (so there is no need to run WAN cables across rivers and over mountains), and its connection points are never far away (the phone system reaches into every workplace and virtually every home).
- **Disadvantage:** Computer signals (the ones that travel around inside a computer) are a different 'shape' from the signals accepted by the phone system (ones resulting from the sound of the human voice). Computer signals are 'digital'; voice signals are 'analog'.

We therefore have a problem: a *signal shape* problem. To connect a computer to a phone line, we need a device than can do two jobs. Which job it does at any particular time depends on the direction of the information transfer:

- **Outgoing Information:** When your computer sends data (such as an e-mail) down the phone line, the device must 'shape' the signal – convert it from computer-shape to phone-shape (digital to analog).
- **Incoming Information:** When you receive data (such as a file from a distant computer), the device must 'deshape' the signal – reconvert it back from phone-shape to its original computer-shape (analog to digital).

Another, rather poetic, word for the act of shaping anything in this way is *modulation*. A device that shapes (*mod*ulates) and deshapes (*dem*odulates) a signal is called – guess what? – a modem.

Modem

A device that enables computers to communicate over the telephone system. At the sending computer, the modem converts the outgoing data to the format acceptable to the phone system. At the receiving computer, another modem reconverts the data back to its original computer format.

Most modern computers have built-in modems. To connect such a computer to the telephone system, you plug the phone line into the socket at the back of the computer. If your modem is a separate unit, you plug the telephone line into the modem and use another cable to connect the modem to the serial port on the computer. The modem may be battery-powered or may need to be plugged into the mains.

Modems are rated according to the speed at which they can transmit and receive data. The *baud rate* is the number of times the signal changes in one second. However, each change in the signal can carry more than one bit of data, so the measure more commonly used nowadays is *bits per second* or *bps*. The top speed of current modems is around 56 kbps (kilobits per second, or thousands of bits per second).

ISDN

An alternative to using modems and the normal telephone network (PSTN) is to use ISDN, or Integrated Services Digital Network. As its name suggests, this network is designed to carry digital signals. In the past it has been used mainly by businesses that need frequent high-volume communication with other offices, and has been relatively expensive for low-volume users. This is beginning to change – the cost of ISDN is now within the reach of small businesses and home users.

ISDN gives access to two 64 kbps channels; these can be used separately or combined to exchange data at 128 kbps.

E-mail

Networks enable users to exchange personal messages with one another: this is the idea behind *e-mail*.

To send someone an e-mail message, you need to have a computer connected to a network, and the recipient has to have a computer connected (directly or indirectly) to the same network. You also need e-mail software, and the unique ‘address’ of the recipient. That’s the minimum.

In practice, this means that both of you have:

- A PC
- A modem
- A telephone line
- A subscription to an Internet Service Provider (ISP)

The ISP maintains a continuous connection to the Internet, and stores on its computer all e-mail that is sent, from anywhere in the world, to your *mailbox*, until you collect it after submitting a password to prove your entitlement to it.

This system means that you can send a message to your friend even when their computer is turned off: it is stored for them, by their ISP, until they collect it.

Thus, you can carry on an electronic conversation over a period of time, during which neither you nor your friend are ever talking at the same time. This is particularly useful if you live in different time zones.

E-mail

The exchange of (usually plain-text) messages between users of computers that are connected to a common network.

E-mail has largely taken over from two earlier technologies that used the telephone network to send and receive written messages:

- **Fax** can be thought of as remote photocopying. The sender used a fax machine to scan a letter, drawing, map, or whatever. The fax machine encoded it so that it could be sent down the telephone line. The recipient's fax machine decoded the message and provided a printout.
- **Telex** was a much more primitive technology, which acted like a remote typewriter. It accepted only text typed on a special Telex machine (no pictures). At the receiving end, the Telex machine responded by typing out the same letters and numbers.

The Internet

The *Internet* – everyone's talking about it. It may even be one of the main reasons you decided to learn about computers.

Internet

The Internet is a worldwide network of interconnected networks.

If you connect to the Internet, you can:

- Send e-mail to other users
- Access information stored on computers all around the world

Millions of users have access to the Internet; hundreds of thousands of computers are permanently connected to it – computers owned by governments, universities, companies, retailers, voluntary organisations, and private individuals. Any user, anywhere, can send a message to any other user, and can access files on the other computers. This rich resource can be used for research, news, entertainment, education, information, sports, current affairs, shopping, and art.

The Internet has become by far the most popular network for carrying e-mail, for a number of reasons:

- The network is already in place: there is no need to create a new physical network connecting all the people you want to communicate with.
- It has a huge population of already-connected users: the chances are high that the person you want to communicate with has an Internet connection.
- It is designed so that there is no single point of failure – if one computer on the network breaks down, or one phone line fails, the message is routed a different way to avoid the problem.
- It uses common standards: messages sent from one computer system in one country can be received and interpreted correctly by a different computer system in a different country.

The term *World Wide Web* is used to describe documents made available over the Internet which are in a particular graphic format. The documents can be linked together, irrespective of where they are physically located, and users can follow the links from document to document. This enables you to pursue a research topic from the general to the specific, from detail to 'big picture', from graphic to text, from text to sound. These links are called *hyperlinks*, and documents constructed with hyperlinks are called *hypertext*, or *hypermedia* if sound, graphics, or video are involved.

The software used to display World Wide Web documents (or *web pages*) is called a *browser*. The two most frequently used browsers are Microsoft Internet Explorer and Netscape Navigator.

World Wide Web

The range of documents published on the Internet in a format that enables them to be displayed using a browser.

Browser

A program that enables you to display web pages and follow links from one web page to another.

However, with hundreds of thousands of computers connected to the Internet, each with thousands of pages of information available to you, how do you find anything of value?

You use a *search engine* – a program that trawls the Internet looking for documents that contain information of interest to you: the share price of a company, flight times from Rome to Athens, comparisons of different brands of vacuum cleaner, the correct spelling of a word in German, the prognosis for a medical condition, tonight's TV listing ... it's all there – somewhere.

Search Engine

A program that searches the World Wide Web for documents that match your criteria.

Another term used to describe the Internet and the World Wide Web is *Information Superhighway*.

E-commerce

Businesses around the world are beginning to use the Internet as a way of developing their markets. They use the Internet to advertise their goods, to take orders, and, in many cases, to deliver their products and services. Obviously only certain kinds of goods can be delivered online, but this includes some that have traditionally been sold in shops, such as software, music, concert tickets, and books. Businesses are also using the Internet to find the cheapest or most efficient source of supply of raw materials, to track orders and deliveries, and to communicate with customers.

This move of business to the Internet is known as *e-commerce* (or electronic commerce).

The Internet can change the way you shop. You can compare prices from different suppliers, buy direct from the manufacturer, or from a supplier anywhere in the world, and communicate with other buyers to get their views on quality and suitability.

When you are making a trip, you can plan your itinerary, find the cheapest flights, look at alternative hotels and compare their facilities and prices, check out special offers, look at maps, and check event listings. You can book flights, hire cars, hotel or guest-house accommodation, concerts, sporting events, even meals in your favourite restaurant.

Self-Test 1.5: Networks

1) Name two reasons you might connect your computer in a network.
2) The L in LAN stands for:
   a) Leading
   b) Local
   c) Long
   d) Linked
3) The A in WAN stands for:
   a) Access
   b) Attached
   c) Area
   d) Aerial
4) Comment on each of the following statements, indicating whether each is true or false.
   a) Computer networks will shortly make the telephone system obsolete.
   b) Modems are used to increase the speed at which computers can communicate.
   c) The telephone system is ideally suited for communication between computers.
   d) E-mail is another name for the Internet.
5) What is the Internet? State two of the most common uses of the Internet.
6) What is the World Wide Web? What kind of software do you need to use it?
7) What is a search engine?
8) Give some examples of e-commerce.
9) What kinds of goods and services are most easily traded over the Internet?
10) For *one* of the following businesses, say how its business could be changed by e-commerce: travel agent, record company, supermarket, restaurant, hairdresser.

Section Summary: So Now You Know

A computer *is* hardware, but it *does* software. Software determines how the computer behaves – the particular problems it solves at any given time.

System software is inward looking – it is software that controls the computer itself.

Application software is software that addresses a 'real world' problem – it does something that you or I want done.

Software is developed by systems analysts and programmers in a process that involves detailed research, analysis, program development and testing. Testing is almost never comprehensive, so that errors and problems sometimes occur (bugs).

Software belongs to the authors, and, in general, copying it is illegal.

Data is often the most valuable part of a computer system, because it is the least easily replaced. For that reason, you should protect your data against loss or damage by using passwords and anti-virus software. You should also save your work frequently and make backups at regular intervals.

You should be especially careful with personal information. The EU Data Protection Directive imposes specific responsibilities on anyone who maintains databases of personal information.

Computer networking enables users to share resources such as hardware and data. They can also exchange messages. When the network covers a wide area (a Wide Area Network) the connection between the computers makes use of the telephone network. This requires the use of a modem.

To use e-mail, the sender and the receiver must each have a PC, a modem, access to a telephone line, and a subscription to an Internet Service Provider (or other e-mail carrier).

The Internet is a worldwide network of interconnected networks. It is by far the most common medium for e-mail, and also provides the infrastructure for the World Wide Web. The World Wide Web is a vast array of documents that are available over the Internet in a particular format – a format that enables them to be displayed with a browser. The browser enables you to display the document of your choice, and to follow hyperlinks from one document to another. The Internet is enabling many businesses to reach new markets and offer new services to customers around the world. This is known as e-commerce.

Section 1.5: What Computers Are Used for

In This Section

In this Section we take a look at some of the ways in which computers are used, and the effects they have on our lives. This isn't comprehensive – it can't be, as new uses are being found every day. However, by the end of the Section, you should appreciate that the range of applications is very wide indeed.

New Skills

At the end of this Section you should be able to:

- Discuss the widespread use of computers in modern society
- Offer examples of computer application in business, industry, schools, healthcare, and the home
- Discuss appropriate and inappropriate uses of computers
- Discuss the Information Society

Business and Administration

Most offices today depend on computers. Computers are used to keep accounts, to send invoices, to maintain records of customers and suppliers, to hold details of stock, to calculate payroll, to write and edit letters, memos and reports, to design sales presentations, to communicate with other companies, to collect market intelligence, to collaborate with others in research activities.

Computers are also used in more complex business processes such as resource planning, scheduling, route planning, customer relationship management, sales analysis, and simulation.

Computers are particularly useful where there are large volumes of data to be maintained, analysed, stored and filtered, or where complex or repetitive calculations have to be performed.

Industry

In manufacturing industry, the range of applications includes all of the administrative functions mentioned above, and a whole lot more besides. Computers are used to schedule production, to monitor raw material usage and finished product quality, to control machine tools, to design new products, to minimise waste, and to determine optimum stock levels.

In the most automated plants, computers are used to collect orders from customers, to issue instructions to build the required products to the customer's specifications, to order the parts and materials automatically from the relevant subsuppliers (having first checked that they can deliver on time), and to schedule the plant and personnel necessary for satisfying the customer's order.

Retailing

In supermarkets, and increasingly in smaller shops, computers are used at the checkout to scan the bar codes on your purchases, and to calculate your bill. In many stores the information on your purchases is passed immediately to the warehouse, and orders for replacement stock are generated automatically when stock falls below a given point. Instructions can also be generated for the personnel responsible for stacking the shelves, so that the products are always available. This technology enables the supermarket to keep its stock to the minimum necessary to satisfy its customers, instead of having money tied up unnecessarily in stock and storage space.

Computers can also be used to control moving-message advertising panels. These displays are made up of hundreds of *Light-Emitting Diodes* (LEDs) that are turned on and off rapidly to create text and pictures.

Home

In the home, computers have found a wide variety of uses – for playing games (most often), for keeping household accounts, for getting information over the Internet (to research ancient history for a homework project or for checking the scores in the Italian football league), for sending e-mail to friends and relatives abroad. The list grows every day, and the only limit is imagination.

Many people have established professional design studios and desktop publishing businesses at home using PCs. Others have managed to use their PC to offer desktop video or sound editing comparable to that offered by expensive and sophisticated dedicated equipment. Book-keepers and accountants, journalists and writers and database designers are also able to work from home nowadays, thanks to the PC and connectivity.

Schools

When you hear about young people using computers in schools, you may think they are doing something very technical, like programming, or electronics. They seldom are.

The main uses for computers in schools are in the traditional subject areas. There is a lot of educational software available that presents school subjects in a structured and entertaining way. Some students respond better to information presented this way, and computers also enable each student to progress at his or her own pace – the computer will repeat lessons as often as necessary, without losing patience!

In addition, the computer opens up the school to the outside world. Students can retrieve information from libraries, universities, government agencies, voluntary bodies, news organisations, and other sources. They can communicate with students in other countries, and co-operate with them on research projects. They can take lessons from world experts without leaving their classroom.

In some science subjects, computers can be used to simulate experiments that are either dangerous or expensive. This enables the students to learn without exposing themselves to the dangers, or without incurring the costs of the materials of equipment involved in the experiment.

Students can also use the computer to write reports, produce school newsletters, and design posters.

Health Care

The administration of hospitals depends more and more on computers. In fact, many of the applications are similar to manufacturing: scheduling expensive and scarce equipment, drawing up rosters, making appointments for patients, etc. In addition, computers are used for monitoring patients' conditions and alerting staff when abnormalities arise. Computers also allow doctors to keep comprehensive patient records, and to conduct research into the effectiveness of different treatments.

Research is also heavily dependent on computing power: most modern drugs are designed with the aid of computers and manufactured under computer control. The Human Genome Project, which promises major breakthroughs in the treatment of genetic disorders, would be impossible without powerful computers.

Computers and communications technology are also being used to deliver health services to remote regions: the patient can connect to a major centre (or a centre of specialist expertise) for diagnosis and, in some cases, for treatment. This development is expected to yield significant cost-savings and better treatment for patients in the coming years.

Government and Public Administration

Government agencies use computers for a wide range of purposes, in the same way as businesses – for accounting, stock control, project management, budgeting, forecasting, and so on. The main difference is one of scale: in general, governments need to maintain very large bodies of information – registers of births, marriages and deaths; tax and social welfare records; census of population data; voting registers, for example. It would be almost impossible to maintain these records in a usable condition without computers.

Everyday Life

You would recognise the computers used in the applications outlined so far. However, computer technology is also used in less visible ways. Computers control the cycles in your washing machine, the timer in your video recorder, the sequences of the traffic lights, the delivery of money through an automatic teller machine, and the supply of fuel to your car engine. Almost anywhere you see something happening 'automatically', there is a computer at its heart, monitoring the outside world and responding to it.

Speech synthesizers are programs that produce computer-generated speech in imitation of the human voice. They are increasingly used in telephone applications such as in directory enquiries, in voicemail systems, in telephone banking, and in travel information systems. They are also used to enable blind or partially sighted people to use computers: the speech synthesizer 'reads' aloud any text that appears on the screen.

Information Technology and Society

Some people find this proliferation of computers somewhat disturbing. Is there no aspect of our lives that is untouched by computers? Are computers replacing people, creating unemployment? Are all uses of computers good, or are computers being used to manipulate and control us? Are all computer-assisted services and all computer-manufactured goods better than their predecessors?

These questions don't have clear-cut answers.

From the discussion in this Section, you probably agree that the society we live in uses computers a lot, and that many of the goods we consume and many of the services we use would not be available without computers. Like it or not, we are living in the Computer Age, or the Information Age, or the Digital Age (take your pick), and our society can justifiably be called an *Information Society*. In essence this means that value in the society comes from information.

In the Age of Agriculture, most of the work, and most of the value, related to food production. In the Industrial Age, it was manufacturing that defined the society. The availability of food was almost taken for granted; proportionately less time and effort went into ensuring the food supply to the individual. Value, wealth and incomes depended more on manufactured goods.

In recent years, the balance has shifted again, this time towards service occupations – office-based occupations, in which information, knowledge, and intelligence play the key role. The emphasis has been transferred from brawn to brain. And in this new economy, computers play a critical, central role.

It is worth asking, however, whether all uses of computers are good. We can see the benefit of using computers, for example, to process bank transactions. Would we be equally happy to let computers decide loan approvals? Routine administration of, say, parking fines could usefully be delegated to computers, but what about putting computer systems in the role of judges in court? In medicine and health care, there are many obvious useful applications, and there are other applications that make many people uncomfortable.

In the world of art, there are also difficulties: does computer-generated 'art' deserve the name? Can a computer write poetry, make paintings, compose music? And should we judge these 'creations' by the same criteria that we judge work made by humans?

As we said, these questions do not have clear-cut answers. But it is worth thinking about them, because they are becoming increasingly relevant to everyday life.

Participation in the Information Society

Computers and related technologies are touching our lives from the time the electronic alarm clock wakes us up to the time we use the remote control to turn off the television at night. We can respond as passive consumers of entertainment and advertising, or by becoming active participants in this society.

Participation means exercising choice: choice about what information we get, when we get it, in what form we get it, and how we use it. It means analysing the information for relevance, salience, accuracy. It means deciding what to keep, and what to discard. It means deciding what to produce: what to publish, to whom you publish it, in what form, and at what time.

The idea of the ECDL – and the idea of this book – is to enable you to use some of the tools necessary for this kind of active participation in the Information Society.

However, you already have the most important tools, and you know how to use them: your natural intelligence, your critical faculties, the ability to judge whether or not something makes sense. No amount of technology can replace these, and you should never be blinded by technological wizardry so that you doubt these innate talents.

Self-Test 1.6: Computers in Society

1) Which of the following statements do you agree with, and why?
    a) Computers are faster than humans at mathematical calculations.
    b) Humans have more reliable long-term memory than computers.
    c) Computers can be programmed to write poetry.
    d) Computers can diagnose and treat medical conditions better than doctors.

2) Name some of the ways in which your local supermarket uses computers. Say how each of these affects the management, the staff, and the customers.

3) What does the term *Information Society* mean?

4) Who benefits from the transition to an Information Society? What problems might arise?

5) 'The Information Society will involve gross invasions of personal privacy.' Discuss.

Section Summary: So Now You Know

Computers are used in business, in industry, in retailing, in the home, in schools and colleges, in health care, in public administration, and in almost every aspect of everyday life.

It is worthwhile pausing every so often to consider whether every possible application of computers is necessarily a good one. Some things are best left to human beings, exercising human judgement, and bringing human values to bear.

And it is also worth considering what this proliferation of computers into every aspect of modern life means for society. There is a danger that society will be divided into those who have access to computers and know how to use them (the 'information rich'), and those that have no access to computers or don't know how to use them (the 'information poor').

The ECDL will equip you with the skills to participate in the Information Society, but you will increasingly need to exercise your critical faculties: remember that all the information available on the Internet, for example, was created and input by someone, somewhere. And that 'someone' could be biased, misguided, prejudiced, or just plain wrong.

Section 1.6: Looking after Number One: Health and Safety

In This Section

This Section deals with something even more valuable than hardware, software, or data. Something irreplaceable – you.

Just as we have accustomed ourselves to using safety belts and child-proof locks in cars, we need to adopt safe computing practices. Problems can arise in a number of areas, but sensible precautions can help you avoid them.

New Skills

At the end of this Section you should be able to:

- Describe some of the hazards associated with using a computer
- Describe sensible computing practices

New Words

At the end of this Section you should be able to explain the following term:

- Repetitive strain injury

Health Warning!

In general, computers are clean, quiet, and safe to use. You should be aware, however, of a number of potential dangers, and how to avoid them.

Repetitive Strain Injury

If you do any physical activity for a long time without a break, you risk straining or injuring yourself. Using a keyboard or mouse for a prolonged period can lead to the computer user's equivalent of tennis elbow. It can affect the fingers, hands, wrists, elbows, or even the back. The best way to avoid this problem is to take a break every fifteen or twenty minutes to allow your muscles to rest and recuperate.

You should also make sure your desk and chair are at a suitable height, and that your keyboard is at a comfortable angle (see below).

Eyesight

Extended periods of staring at a PC screen can lead to fatigue and ultimately to eye-strain. Avoid locking your eyes into a fixed screen stare. Look away frequently and focus your eyes on objects on the other side of the room, or out the window. Make sure that your work area is adequately lit and ventilated.

Posture

Simple ergonomics are often so obvious that they are overlooked. You should arrange the hardware elements of your PC in such a way as to provide the easiest and most physically comfortable access. Your desk should support your screen at the correct eye level. Your chair should be comfortable, adjustable, and provide adequate lumbar support

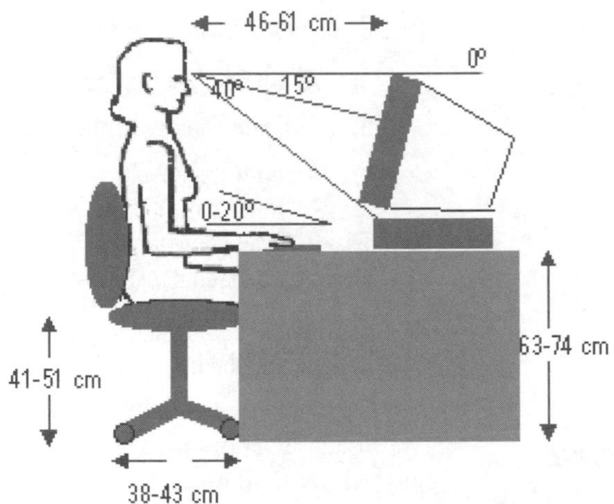

Accidents

Your computer system includes a number of different physical devices. They are all connected together by cables. The system unit is plugged into the mains electricity socket. On some models the screen takes its electricity supply from the system unit; in others it plugs directly into the mains. The loudspeakers are usually plugged into the mains. The modem is connected to the telephone socket.

That's a lot of cables and wires. Make sure that the cables connecting the components are kept tidy, secure, and out of the way, so that there is no danger of tripping over them. Also make sure that the mains electricity sockets you use are capable of handling the load safely: don't plug all the appliances into a single adaptor or you risk overloading the circuit.

Self-Test 1.7: Using Your Computer Safely

1) Which of the following is/are true?

   a) It is best to get all your data entry done in the morning, while you are fresh.

   b) You should sit as close to the screen as possible, so that you don't strain your eyes.

   c) If you sit too close to the screen, you can catch a computer virus.

   d) The best way to avoid repetitive strain injury (RSI) is to continue working after you feel pain. That way, your arm muscles develop faster.

2) If you are using a computer for a long time, the best kind of chair is:

   a) An office chair that can be adjusted for height

   b) A dining chair with arm supports

   c) A comfortable sofa

3) True or false: In winter, it is a good idea to cover the system unit with a blanket, so that it doesn't get cold.

4) State some of the dangers associated with using a computer, and how to minimise them.

Section Summary: So Now You Know

While using a computer is generally safe, there are a number of hazards, and all of them are avoidable. Most of them – in particular repetitive strain injury and eye strain – arise only if you use the computer for long periods without a break. Others arise from bad posture or inappropriate positioning of equipment. Cabling also presents a potential source of accidents: you should make sure that cables are tidy and out of the way.

2 Using a Computer and Managing Files

Module 1 was the tourist guidebook to prepare for your visit to computer land. Module 2 is where you get to meet the natives in the flesh.

And what exotic creatures they are! The citizens are called files. They reside in houses called folders. And folders are built on areas called drives. (Files inside folders, and folders on top of drives – you have learnt quite a lot already!)

And such obedient citizens too! You can change their names, move them to a different location, alter their appearance, get rid of ones you don't want anymore – you can even create new ones out of nothing.

But remember this: files are delicate. So treat them with care. You do this by saving them regularly and by making copies of them every so often – just in case something bad happens to the originals. It's always the files you like and need most that seem to disappear the quickest. Better to learn this lesson from the book than from real life in computer land.

Section 2.1: Starting Up, Clicking Around, Shutting Down

In This Section

Are you ready to take your first practical steps in computing?

This Section guides you through the basics. You will learn the correct ways of starting and shutting down a computer, discover the meaning of the various little pictures on the Windows screen, and find out how to start and close Word, Excel and other software applications that you will meet in later ECDL Modules.

New Skills

At the end of this Section you should be able to:

- Power up and power down a computer
- Use the Start menu to open software applications
- Switch between open applications
- Click, double-click, right-click and drag with the mouse
- Use the three control buttons at the top-right of a window
- Move, resize and scroll windows
- Restart a computer when problems occur

New Words

At the end of this Section you should be able to explain the following terms:

- Powering up/Booting
- Cursor
- Clicking
- Menu
- Taskbar
- Close button
- Restore button
- Folder
- Desktop window
- Application window
- Maximise button
- Minimise button
- Dragging
- Double-clicking
- Pop-up/Shortcut menu
- Dialog box

Starting Your Computer

Before you start your computer, check that it is plugged into the electricity socket. Now, press the button to switch on the computer.

- On some computers, a *single button* switches on both the computer and the computer's screen.
- Other computers have *two buttons*: one for the computer itself and a second for the screen.

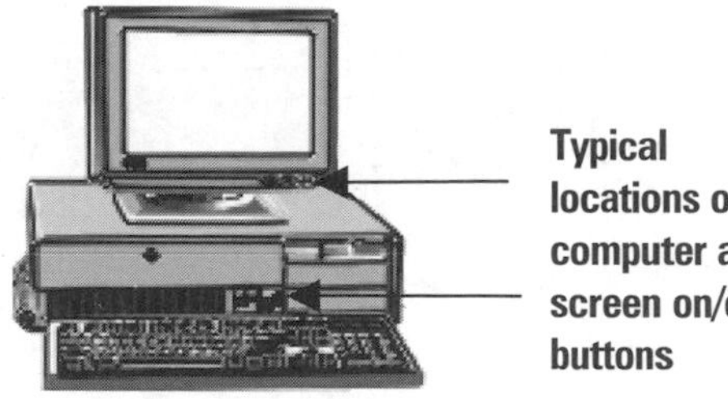

Typical locations of computer and screen on/off buttons

Your computer will make some humming noises and some messages will flicker on your screen. Don't worry: this is just your computer warming up and checking that everything is in working order.

The Windows Desktop

The Windows desktop appears – little pictures set against a coloured background. These pictures are called *icons*. Along the bottom of your screen you will see a grey bar, with a button named **Start** in its left corner and a clock in its right. This is called the *Taskbar*.

You will learn more about icons and the Taskbar later. You will also discover how you can change the appearance of your Windows desktop to suit your working needs and personal taste.

A sample Windows *desktop*

The little pictures are called *icons*

The grey bar along the bottom of the screen is called the *Taskbar*

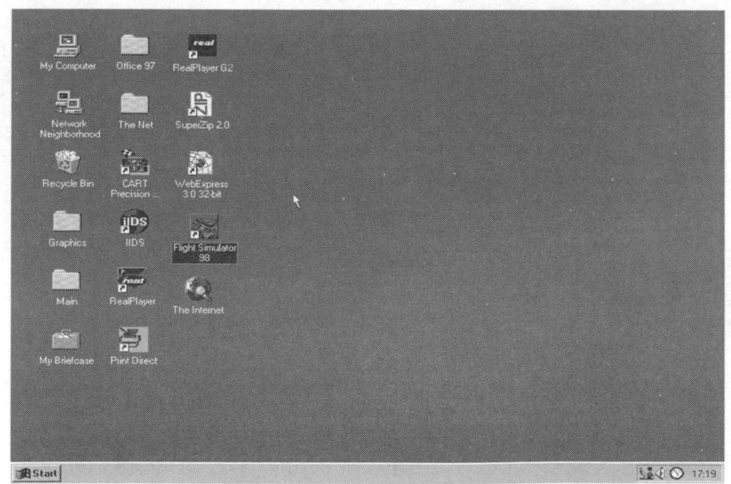

Congratulations. You have now powered up your computer.

Powering Up/Booting

The technical terms for starting a computer and displaying the Windows desktop on the screen. You don't 'switch on' a computer; you 'power it up' or 'boot' the computer.

Starting Applications

Software applications are useful programs such as Microsoft Word, Excel, Access and PowerPoint that enable you to create documents, spreadsheets, databases and presentations. You will learn a lot about these in Modules 3, 4, 5 and 6 of this ECDL course. Your first step in working with applications is to learn how to start them.

Using the Mouse

Place your hand over the mouse and move it around your (physical) desktop. As you move the mouse, the cursor moves around the Windows desktop, allowing you to point to the item you want to work with.

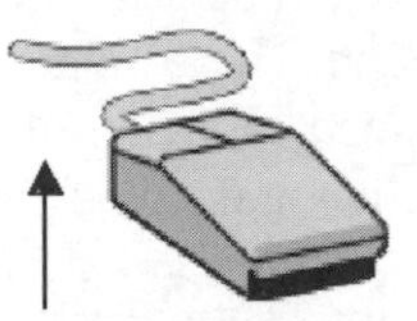

To move the cursor up the screen, move the mouse in the up direction

To move the cursor down the screen, move the mouse in the down direction

Cursor

A symbol, usually an arrow, that you move around the computer screen by moving the mouse across your (physical) desktop.

The Start Button

Move the cursor down to the bottom-left of your screen so that it is over the **Start** button. Now, press down the left mouse button and then release it. You don't need to hold down the button for more than a second. This is called clicking.

Clicking with the Mouse

Briefly holding down the left mouse button. By clicking on an item on the screen, you tell your computer: 'I want to select this item'.

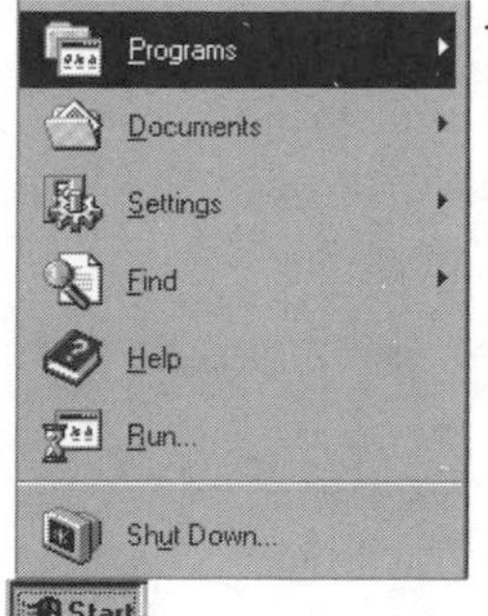

Windows start-up menu

Your mouse-click causes the **Start** button to display the start-up menu. Move the cursor up over the item called **Programs**. As you do, another menu appears to its right. On this second menu or submenu, move the cursor over the item called **Microsoft Word** and click on it. This opens the Microsoft Word application.

> **Menu**
>
> *A list of items displayed on the computer screen that allows you to work with applications and files, and get more information. Some menus offer submenus of further options.*

Multi-tasking with Windows

You can open more than one application at one time – this is called multi-tasking. Move the cursor back down over the **Start** button and click on it. Next, move the cursor over the menu item called **Programs**. On the next menu displayed, move the cursor over the item called **Microsoft Excel** and click on it. You have now started a second application.

Why stop at two applications? Exercise 2.1 takes you through the steps of starting a third application, Notepad.

Exercise 2.1: Opening the Notepad Application

1) Click on the **Start** button.
2) Click **Start | Programs** to display the start-up menu.
3) Click **Start | Programs | Accessories** to display the Accessories submenu.
4) Click **Start | Programs | Accessories | Notepad** to open the Notepad application.

Congratulations. You have now three applications open on your screen.

The expression **Start | Programs** is a shorthand way of saying ‘Open the start-up menu and select the option named Programs’. And **Start | Programs | Accessories | Notepad** means: ‘Open the start-up menu and select the option called Programs. Next, on the Programs menu, choose the option named Accessories, and on the Accessories menu, choose Notepad’.

Although you can have lots of applications open at one time, only one can be in the foreground; the others wait behind it in the background. How do you tell Windows which application you want to bring to the foreground?

Take a look at the Taskbar along the bottom of your Windows desktop. Notice how it displays the names of all your open applications.

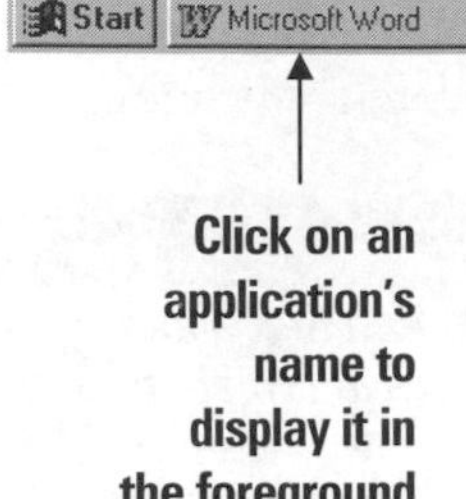

Click on an application's name to display it in the foreground

To select one, for example Word, click on Word. Or, to select Excel, click on Excel. You use the Taskbar to switch between open applications and display a particular one in foreground.

Taskbar
A horizontal bar across the bottom of the Windows desktop that displays the Start button, plus the names of any open applications. Click an application's name to display it in the foreground.

You will find Windows' ability to open several applications at one time very useful. For example, you could have the following open on your computer: a Word letter (see ECDL Module 3), an Excel spreadsheet (Module 4), and an e-mail (Module 7). As you will also learn, you can copy items from one application to another.

Multi-tasking
The ability of Windows to open several applications and files at one time.

The Control Buttons

Using the Taskbar, switch to Notepad. Notice the three buttons at the top-right? These are called *control buttons*. You can use these to perform various actions, as the following Exercises show.

Close button

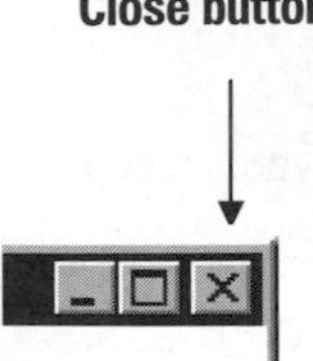

Exercise 2.2: Using the Close Button to Close a Notepad

1) Is Notepad in the foreground? If not, click its name on the Taskbar.
2) Move the mouse to the top-right of the Notepad screen, and click on the button that contains an X.

You have closed the Notepad application by clicking on one of the control buttons – the *Close button*.

Close Button

A button at the top right of an application window which, if selected, closes the application.

In the next two Exercises you will learn how to use the Restore and Maximise control buttons.

Exercise 2.3: Using the Restore Button to Reduce a Window's Size

1) Is Excel in the foreground? If not, click its name on the Taskbar.

2) Move the mouse to the top-right of the Excel screen, and click on the Restore button.

   This reduces the size of the Excel screen, so that it no longer fills the entire Windows desktop.

Restore button

3) Using the Taskbar, switch to Word. Click on Word's Restore button.

You should now be able to see both applications on your screen, with the currently selected application (Word) overlapping the other (Excel). Each application appears within its own *window*.

Overlapping application windows of Microsoft Word and Microsoft Excel

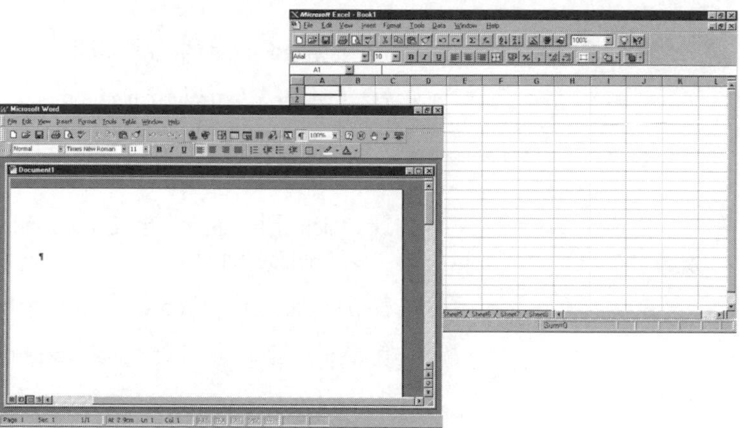

Restore Button

A button beside the Close button that reduces the size of the application screen area.

To bring Excel to the foreground, click on any part of its window. You do not need to click its name on the Taskbar. The Excel window now overlaps the Word window. To return the Word window to the foreground, click on any part of it.

Application Window

A rectangular area that can display a file or files from an application. All application windows, regardless of their content, share common components and features.

Maximise button

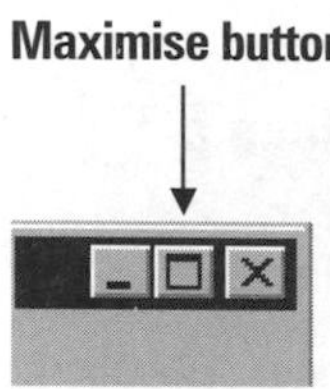

When you click on a Restore button to reduce the size of a window, the Restore button disappears and is replaced by another button, called the Maximise button.

Clicking on this button reverses the effect of Restore: that is, it increases the size of the window so that it again fills the Windows desktop.

Maximise Button

A button that increases the size of a previously reduced window so that it fills the entire Windows desktop.

Minimise button

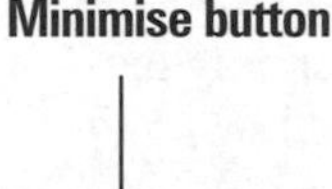

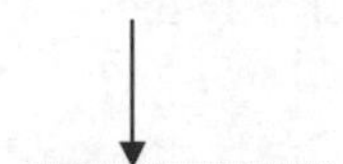

One control button remains: the Minimise button. Exercise 2.4 provides an example of the Minimise button in use.

Exercise 2.4: Shrinking a Window with the Minimise Button

1) Is Word in the foreground? If not, click on any part of its window.
2) Click on Word's Minimise button.

   This 'shrinks' Word so that it appears on the Taskbar and nowhere else.
3) Click on any part of the Excel window to select it, and then click its Minimise button.

Both applications now appear only on the Taskbar.

To display Word and Excel again, click on their names on the Taskbar.

Minimise Button

A button that shrinks an application window to remove it from the desktop to the Taskbar only.

Your will find the Close, Restore or Maximise, and Minimise buttons at the top-right corner of every window.

Moving Windows with the Title Bar

Another feature that every window shares is a title bar – the identifying bar that runs across the top of the window. You use the title bar to move a window to a different position on the desktop as follows:

- Click on the window's title bar – but do not release the mouse button.
- With your finger still on the mouse button, move the mouse to reposition the window.
- When you have positioned the window where you want it, release the mouse button.

Click on the title bar and drag to reposition a window

Microsoft Excel - Book1 

This series of click-move-release actions is called dragging.

> **Dragging with the Mouse**
>
> *Moving a selected item on the desktop by clicking on it with the left mouse button, and holding down the button as you move the item.*

Using the Close box, close Excel. You now have only the Word application open on your desktop.

Working with Desktop Windows

On the Windows desktop, move your cursor over the icon (little picture) named My Computer and click. Notice that the icon is highlighted. Your single-click selected it – but does not perform any action on it.

Now, click anywhere on the desktop to deselect the My Computer icon.

Once again, move the cursor over the My Computer icon. Now, click once and then, very quickly, click a second time on My Computer. This two-click action (called *double-clicking*) opens the My Computer icon so that you can see its contents.

A sample My Computer desktop window

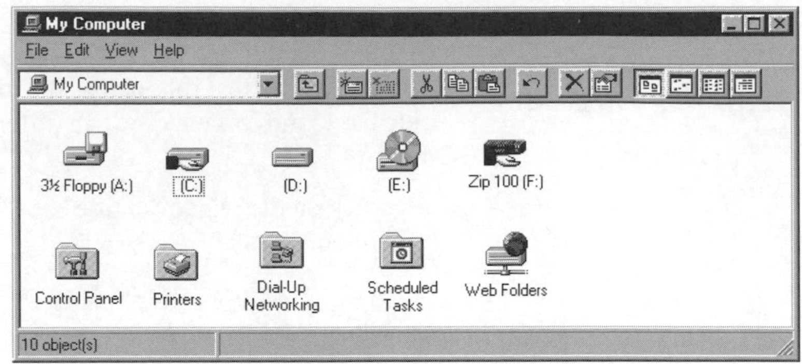

Double-Clicking with the Mouse

To tell Windows to perform an action on a selected item, press the left mouse button quickly twice in succession.

Click on the Close box at the top right of the My Computer window to close it. My Computer is an example of a desktop folder – an icon that represents a number of items grouped together.

Except for My Computer, every other folder on your desktop looks like a 'real' folder. Here are some examples.

Folder

An icon on the Windows desktop that contains within it one or more icons representing applications, files or physical devices.

A window opened when a folder is double-clicked is called a desktop window. Desktop windows look and can be used in a similar way to applications windows – so much so that the term 'window' is commonly used to describe either type.

Desktop Window

A window opened when a folder is double-clicked. Desktop windows contain similar components and features to application windows.

Practise opening folders on your desktop by double-clicking on them. Some folders, you may find, contain subfolders. (A subfolder is no different to a folder; it's just a folder that happens to be inside another folder.) Close any folders you open by using their Close box.

Changing the Shape and Size of a Window

You can change the shape and size of an application or desktop window by selecting it, and dragging any of its four sides.

To change the width of a window, click on its left or right edge. The cursor changes to a double-headed arrow. Then drag with the mouse. As you drag the window, its edges change to dashed lines.

To make a window taller or shorter, click on its top or bottom edge. Again, the cursor changes to a double-headed arrow. Drag the edge with the mouse.

To change both window height and width, click in the bottom right corner of the window. The cursor changes to a double-headed, diagonal arrow. Drag the corner with the mouse.

Practise your window resizing skills with the My Computer folder window.

Scrolling a Window

Sometimes a window may not be large enough to display all its contents. In such cases, scroll bars appear on the right and/or along the bottom of the window. To view a different part of the window:

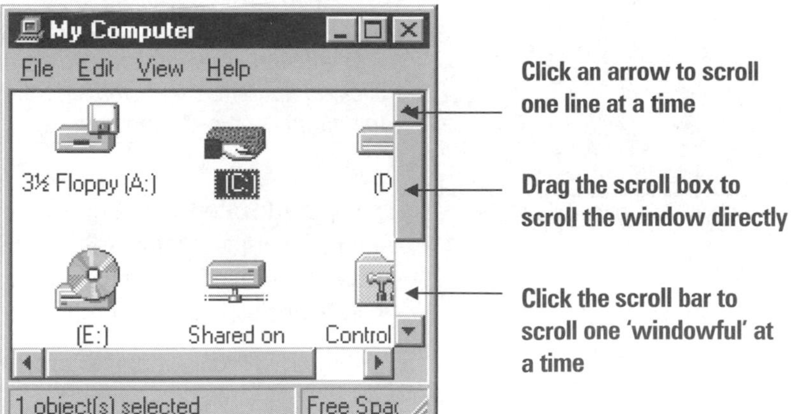

- The *position* of the scroll box in relation to the scroll bar indicates which area of the window you are viewing. When the scroll box is in the middle of the scroll bar, for example, the window is positioned halfway through its contents.

- The *size* of the scroll box indicates how much of the window's contents you can see at one time. For example, if the scroll box is half the length of the scroll bar, you can see half the contents.

Right-Clicking and Pop-Up Menus

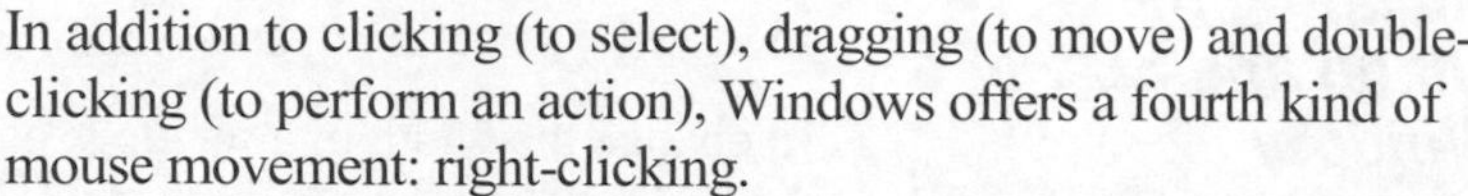

In addition to clicking (to select), dragging (to move) and double-clicking (to perform an action), Windows offers a fourth kind of mouse movement: right-clicking.

To right-click something is to click on it once with the right mouse button.

Right-clicking on anything – whether a folder, application or file icon, or even the desktop – displays a pop-up menu. The menu options shown depend on the item you right-click.

Right-Clicking with the Mouse
Briefly holding down the right mouse button. Windows responds by displaying a pop-up menu of options.

One option that a right-click always displays is called **Properties**. Select this option from the pop-up menu to view details about the item.

Practise right-clicking on icons and on the desktop background. In each case, click the **Properties** option on the pop-up menu.

Pop Up or Shortcut Menu
A small menu that appears temporarily, typically when you right-click on an item. When you select an option from a pop-up menu, the menu usually disappears.

Shutting Down

The opposite of powering up a computer is powering or shutting it down. Never just switch off your computer – you may lose unsaved information and damage your computer's hard disk drive (thereby losing saved information too!).

To shut down your computer properly, follow the steps in Exercise 2.5:

Exercise 2.5: Shutting Down Your Computer

1) Click the **Start** button.
2) Click **Shut Down**.
3) Select the 'Shut down the computer' option by clicking on it.

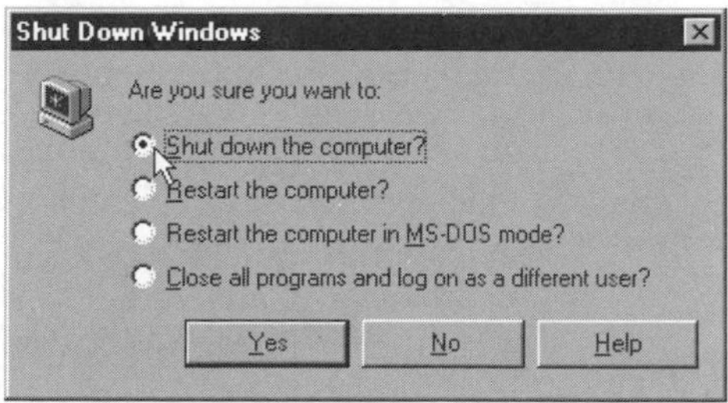

4) Click the **Yes** button to confirm your selection.

Some computers can switch themselves off automatically. On others, you need to press the on/off button after you see the message: 'It is now safe to turn off your computer'.

Now, power up your computer again – *but wait at least twenty seconds*. Otherwise, you may damage your computer's hard disk drive.

Restarting your Computer

The 'Restart the computer' option has the same effect as powering down the computer and powering it up again very quickly – but without the risk of damage to the computer hardware.

Exercise 2.6: Restarting Your Computer

1) Click **Start | Shut Down.**

2) Select the 'Restart the computer' option.

3) Click the **Yes** button.

When Your Computer Hangs

Sometimes an application open on a computer may 'hang' or 'freeze'. This means that it does not respond to the pressing of any keys or any clicking with the mouse. On other occasions Windows itself may fail to respond to any user action, with the result that the entire computer hangs. What do you do? This topic provides the answers.

Application Problems

When a particular application fails to respond to any action you take, press the following three keys simultaneously: CTRL, ALT and DELETE. Most computer users do this by holding down the CTRL and ALT keys with the fingers of their left hand, and then pressing the DELETE key with a finger of their right.

The shorthand way of writing 'Press the CTRL, ALT and DELETE keys simultaneously' is CTRL+ALT+DELETE.

You are then shown a window similar to the one below, which lists all the applications currently open on your computer. The frozen application is indicated by the message 'Not Responding'.

The Close Program dialog box showing a 'Not Responding' application

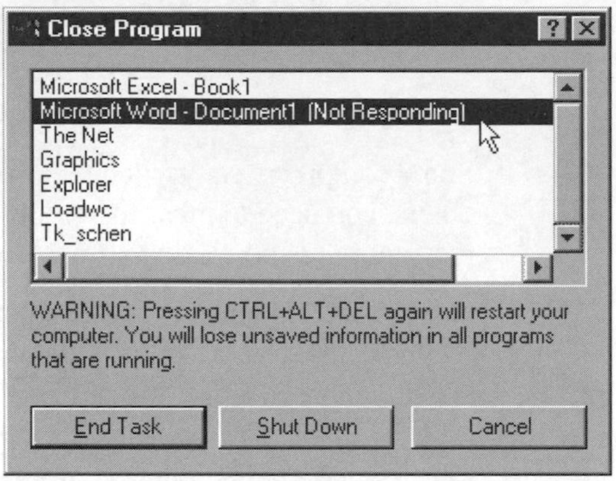

Click on the frozen application, and then click on the **End Task** button. The application closes, as does the Close Program window. You can then reopen the application in the usual way.

Windows Problems

If Windows hangs and your computer freezes, press CTRL+ALT+DELETE *twice* in quick succession. This has the effect of powering down the computer and powering it up again very quickly – but without the risk of damage to the computer hardware. In fact, it has the same effect as selecting the 'Restart the computer' option from the Shut Down Windows window.

Improper Shutdowns and ScanDisk

If you power down your computer in any way other than using **Start | Shut Down**, Windows will typically suggest that you run a program called ScanDisk when you next power up the computer. This checks your hard disk drive(s) for errors. Windows starts when ScanDisk finishes.

Dialog Boxes

The Close Program window described in the previous topic is an example of a Windows *dialog box*. You will meet many such dialog boxes when you use Windows Explorer, Word, Excel and other applications.

Dialog Box

A rectangular box that Windows displays when it needs further information before it can carry out a command, or when it needs to provide you with more information.

Dialog Box Components

Dialog boxes typically contain some or all of the following components:

- **Command Button:** A button that performs or cancels an action. **OK** and **Cancel** are the two most common buttons. Here are some more:

- **Drop-Down List Box:** A list of options from which you can select. Click the arrow on its right to view all the choices available.

  The example below is from the Print dialog box. It shows the printer choices available to you. You click to select the one you require.

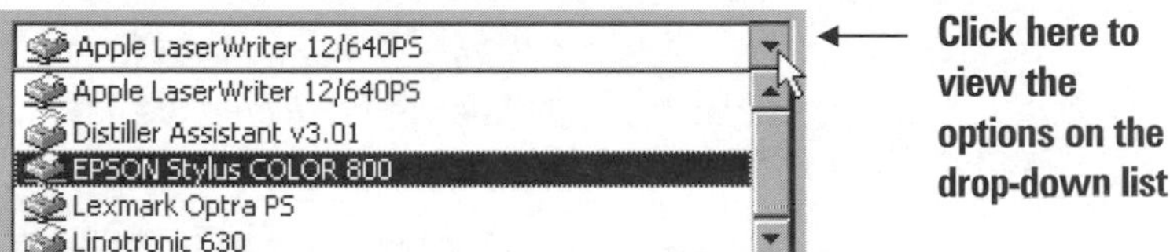

- **Option Buttons:** A group of *round buttons* indicating alternative choices. The example below is also from the Print dialog box.

- **Check Boxes:** A set of *square boxes* you can select or deselect to turn options on or off. More than one check box can be selected at one time.

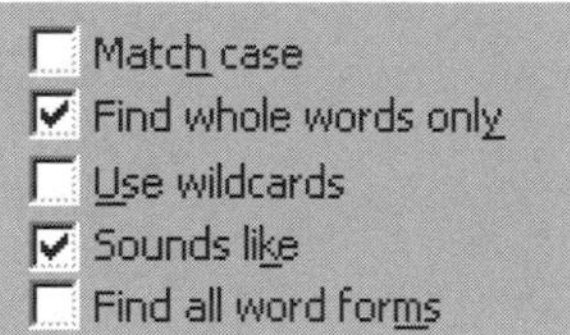

Default Options

Most dialog boxes offer preselected or default settings. Unless you choose otherwise, the default settings decide which options and actions are performed. When you choose **Start | Shut Down**, for example, the default option is 'Shut down the computer', and the default action is **Yes**. To accept the defaults offered by a dialog box, simply press the ENTER key.

Section Summary: So Now You Know

To power up a computer, switch on the system box. If the screen has a separate on/off switch, switch it on also. Windows starts and displays *icons* on the *desktop*.

Use the **Start | Programs** menu to start software applications such as Word or Excel, and the *Taskbar* to switch between open applications.

The *control buttons* at the top-left of a window enable you to restore (decrease the size of), *maximise*, *minimise* and *close* that window. To *move* a window across the desktop, drag it by its *title bar*. To *resize* a window, drag its edges.

Icons on the desktop represent drives, applications, files and folders.

Clicking an item selects it. *Double-clicking* performs an action on it. And *right-clicking* displays a small, *pop-up menu* of relevant options.

Where a window is too small to display all its contents, *scroll* to view different parts of that window. When Windows needs further information before carrying out an action, it displays a *dialog box*.

Always use the *shut down* procedure when switching off your computer. To restart a 'hung' application, press CTRL+ALT+DELETE. Press the three keys twice in quick succession if Windows itself hangs.

Section 2.2: Exploring Your Computer

In This Section

Ever wondered what information was stored on your computer? Or on someone else's computer? After reading this Section, you will be able to answer such questions as: what drives are installed on a computer, what are the names of its folders and files, and what processor chip and how much memory does it have?

You will also discover how to find a particular file without knowing its name, and how to use the Windows online help system.

New Skills

At the end of this Section you should be able to:

- Distinguish between files, folders and drives
- Use My Computer to view drives, folders and files
- Change the order in which folders and files are displayed in My Computer
- Explain file name extensions and recognise the most common types
- Search for folders and files
- Use Windows online help

New Words

At the end of this Section you should be able to explain the following terms:

- File
- Folder
- Subfolder
- Drive
- My Computer
- Recycle Bin
- File name extension
- Windows Find
- Wildcard

How Your Computer Stores Information

If you throw all your belongings in a heap together on the floor, you will have a difficult time finding anything. How much easier to sort your valuables beforehand, dividing them neatly between shelves or drawers. When you need to find something, you know exactly where it is.

As with your belongings, so with information stored on a computer. In this Section you will learn about files, folder and drives – the three levels at which information is organised on a computer.

Files

All the information and applications on your computer are stored in individual files. Think of a file as the computer's basic unit of storage.

File

The computer's basic unit of information storage. Everything on a computer is stored in a file of one type or another.

Folders

A computer may contain many thousands of files. To make it easier for you (and the computer) to find and keep track of files, you can group files together in folders.

Folder

A group of files. Files grouped into folders are easier to find and work with.

A folder can also contain one or more folders, thereby forming a tree-like hierarchy.

Subfolder

A folder located within another folder

A sample hierarchy of folders and files

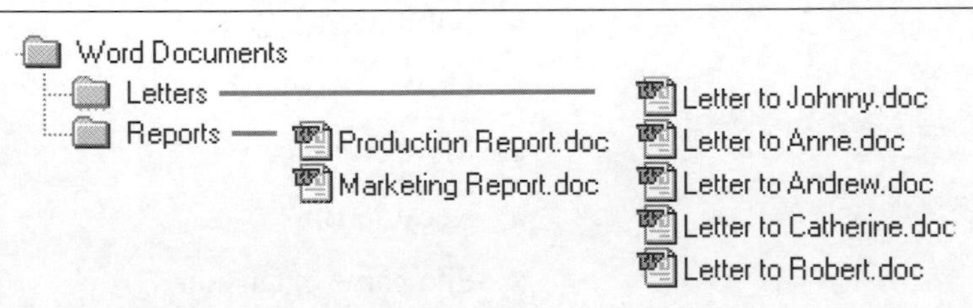

In the example above, the folder named Word Documents contains two subfolders: Letters and Reports.

Another advantage of placing files in a folder or subfolder is that you can work with the files as a group. For example, you can copy or delete all files in a folder in a single operation.

Drives

A drive is a device that stores folders and files. Typical PCs have a hard disk drive that is named the C: drive. On some computers, the hard disk is divided ('partitioned') into two – a C: drive and a D: drive.

The next available letter after the hard disk is given to the CD-ROM drive. This can be D: or E:, depending on whether your hard drive is partitioned or not. The floppy diskette drive is named the A: drive.

Drive

A physical storage device for holding files and folders. Typically, A: is the floppy diskette drive, C: the hard disk, and D: is the CD-ROM drive.

Where is the B: drive? Early personal computers had just two floppy diskette drives, A: and B:. The advent of hard disks, which were named as C: drives, eliminated the need for a second floppy drive.

Using My Computer

My Computer

Take a look at your Windows desktop. Can you see a folder named My Computer? If not, resize or minimise any open windows until the My Computer icon is visible.

My Computer displays icons showing the hard disk, floppy diskette and CD-ROM drives on your PC. You can also see folders called Control Panel (in which you can change your computer's settings), Printers (for changing printer's settings) and Dial-up Networking (for changing Internet connection settings).

My Computer

A desktop folder in which you view almost everything on your computer, including drive contents, and computer, printer and Internet settings.

Exploring Drives with My Computer

What disk drives does your computer contain? Find out in Exercise 2.7.

Exercise 2.7: Exploring Drives with My Computer

1) Double-click the My Computer icon on the Windows desktop. In the example below, you can see fives drives: a floppy diskette drive (A:), two hard disk drives (C: and D:), a CD-ROM drive (E:), and a Zip drive (F:).

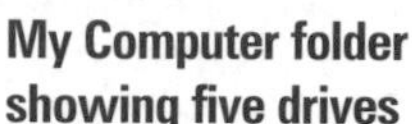

My Computer folder showing five drives

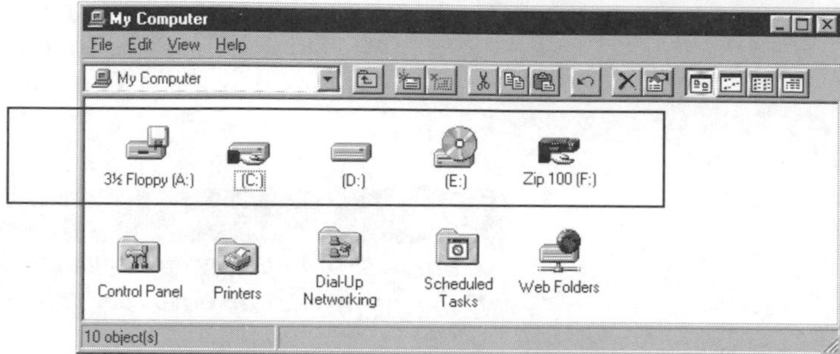

What drives are on your computer?

Now you know how to discover what drives are installed on your PC – or on any other PC you encounter. In Exercise 2.8 you will learn how to view basic information about an installed drive.

Exercise 2.8: Viewing Drive Properties

1) With the My Computer window open, right-click on the C: drive icon.

2) On the pop-up menu displayed, click the last option, **Properties**.

   You are now shown a dialog box similar to the one on the right.

   You can see how much space is occupied on your hard disk, and how much is still free. You can also use this dialog box to give a name ('label') to your hard disk drive.

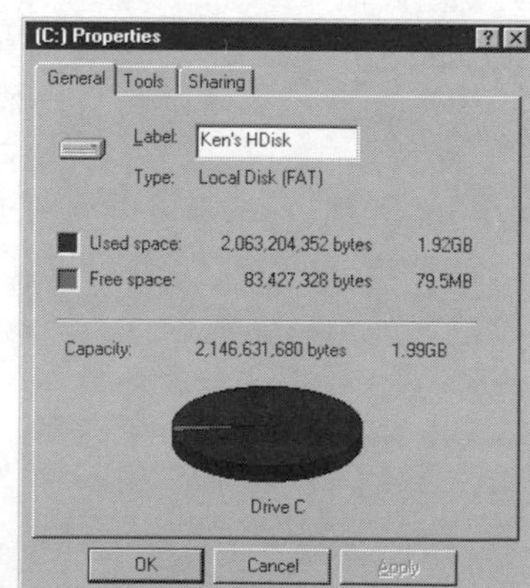

3) When finished, click **OK**.

As further practice, perform this Exercise on your other drives.

Leave the My Computer window open on your desktop. Note that an icon for the My Computer window is displayed on your Taskbar.

Exploring Folders and Files with My Computer

You can use My Computer to display the folders and files contained on any drive of your computer. Just double-click a drive icon – for example, the C: icon – and My Computer opens a second window showing the selected drives contents.

My Computer can display folders and files within a drive in a number of ways. Click the **View** menu to display the options available. Here are the main ones:

- **Large Icons:** Displays folders and files like this:

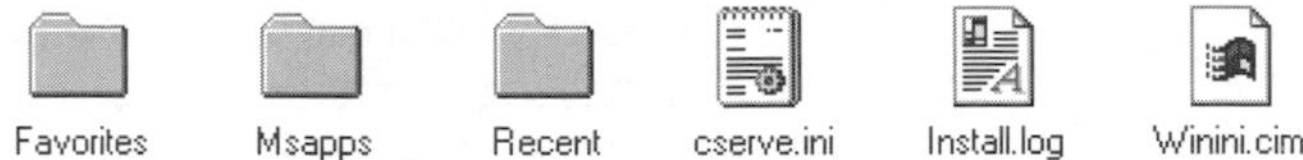

- **Small Icons:** Displays folders and files in columns, with folders at the top of each column and files underneath.

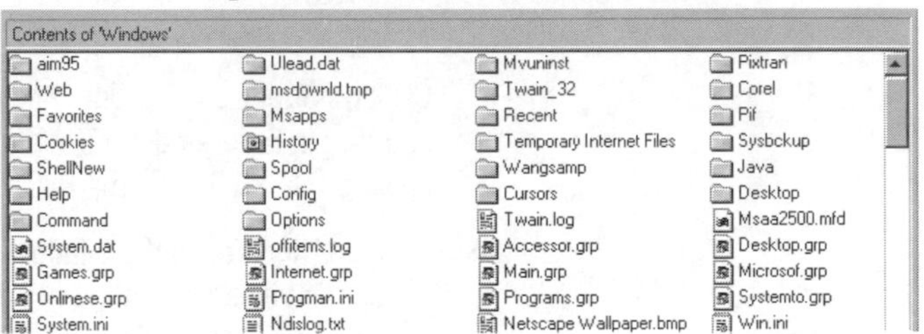

- **List:** Displays folders and files in columns, but lists all your folders before it shows the files.
- **Details:** Lists folders first and then files in a single column, and displays additional information about each item.

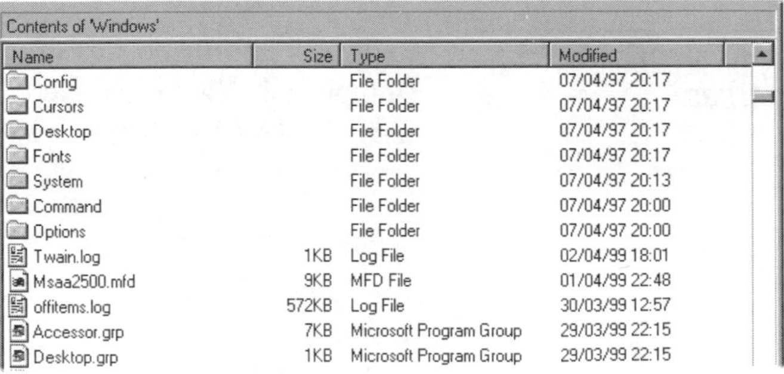

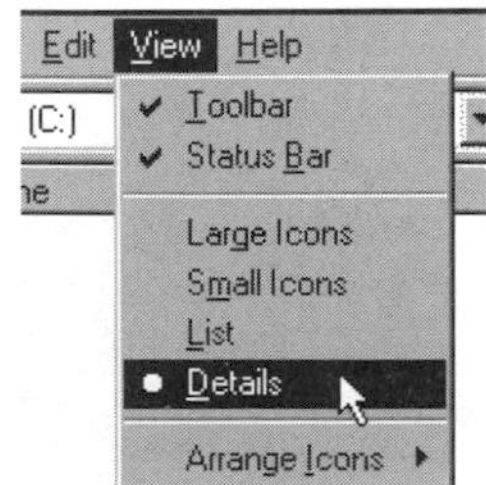

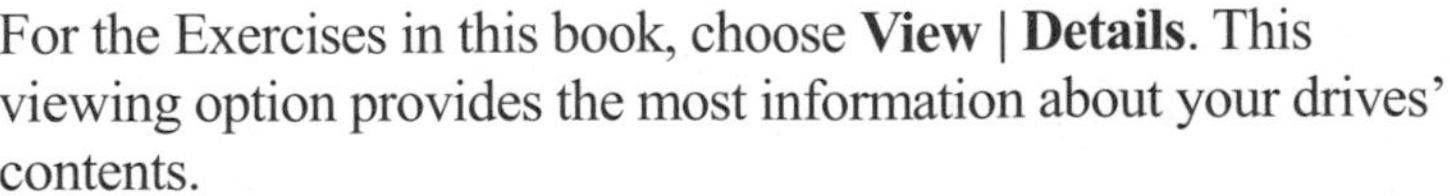

For the Exercises in this book, choose **View | Details**. This viewing option provides the most information about your drives' contents.

Along the bottom of the My Computer window, in the status bar, you can see the number of items in the window, and the disk space that they occupy. Can't see the status bar or toolbar? Click the relevant options on the **View** menu to display them.

Sorting Folders and Files

You can change the order in which My Computer displays your folders and files. By default, folders and files are listed alphabetically by name. To view them in order of size, for example, click on Size in the bar across the top of the window. Alternatively, you can sort them by Type or (date) Modified.

Exercise 2.9: Sorting Folders and Files in My Computer

1) Use My Computer to display the contents of your C: drive.
2) Click on Name in the window heading. My Computer sorts the folders and files in reverse alphabetical order. Click again on Name to resort them in their original order.

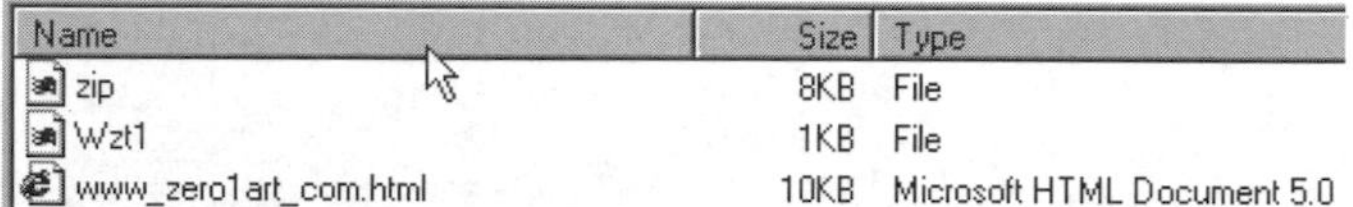

3) Click on Size in the window heading. My Computer sorts the folders and files in order of decreasing size, with the largest shown first. Click again on Size to resort them so that the smallest files are listed first.
4) Click on Modified in the window heading. My Computer sorts the folders and files so that the most recently created or changed are shown first. Click again on Modified to resort them so that the oldest are listed first.

You can make any column narrower or wider by clicking on the boundary line and holding down the mouse button. The cursor changes to a cross-wire. Next, drag the boundary left or right.

Looking at a Folder's Properties

To display information about a folder in My Computer – for example, the Windows folder – right-click on it. From the pop-up menu displayed, click the **Properties** option.

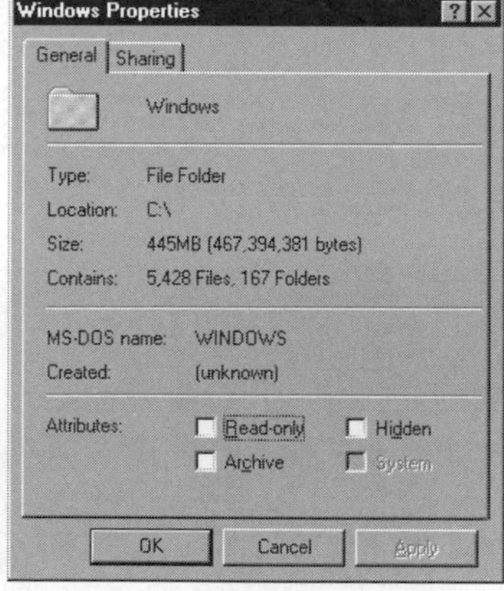

You are shown a dialog box similar to the one on the right.

Among other details, this tells you the number of folders and files within the Windows folder.

It also shows the drive where the folder is located (in this case, C:), and the size of the folder (in this case, 445 megabytes).

File Name Extensions and Icons

A file, as stated at the beginning of this Section, is the basic unit of information storage on a computer. When you look at files in My Computer windows, you can see that different files are represented by different icons.

The icon that Windows uses to represent a file depends on the file's three-letter *file name extension*. Application files have the extension .exe or .dll. A file name extension is separated from the remainder of the file name by a full stop.

When you name and save a file within an application (for example, a Word document within Microsoft Word), Windows automatically attaches the appropriate three-letter extension to that file.

File Name Extension

A three-letter addition to a file name that indicates the type of information stored in the file. A full stop separates the extension from the remainder of the file name.

Here are some common application file name extensions and their icons:

Application File Type	Extension	Icon
Microsoft Word document	.doc	
Microsoft Excel spreadsheet	.xls	
Microsoft Access database	.mdb	
Microsoft PowerPoint presentation	.ppt	
Plain text file	.txt	
Online help file	.hlp	
Web page file	.htm	

Searching for Folders and Files

The quickest way to locate a folder of file on your (or anyone else's) computer is to use the Windows Find feature. Most Find actions are based on all or part of the folder or file name. But Find also allows you perform sophisticated searches based on date ranges or content.

To find a folder or file on a drive, choose the **Start | Find | Files or Folders** command. This displays the dialog box below. Using the Look in: box, you can specify My Computer (all your drives), a particular drive or a folder within a drive. In the Named: box, type the file name. Next, click **Find Now**.

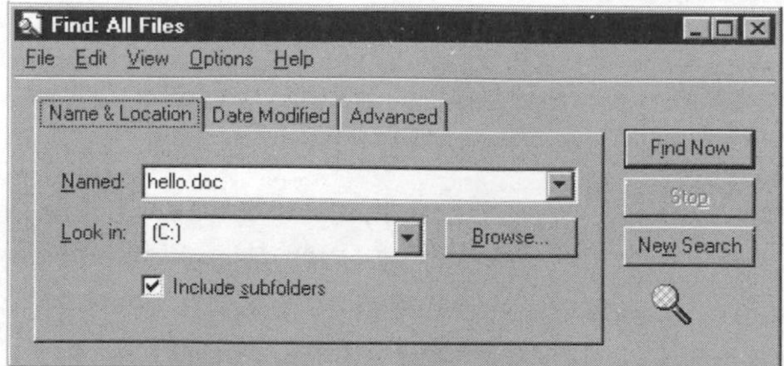

You can use the **Browse** button to display a My Computer-style view of the drives, folders and files of the computer on which you are searching.

Wildcard Searches

In folder and file names, an asterisk (*) is called a wildcard – it can represent one or several characters. If you cannot remember the full name of the item you want to search for, type the wildcard character in place of the missing letter(s).

For instance, report*.doc finds all files that begin with 'report' and have the .doc extension. Examples might be report3.doc, reportnew.doc and report-a.doc.

If you search for *.xls, Windows finds all files on your computer that have the Microsoft Excel file name extension. Try it and see!

Wildcard

The asterisk symbol (*) which can stand for one or a combination of characters when performing a search for a folder or file.

Exercise 2.10: Finding All Word Documents Using a Wildcard

1) Choose **Start | Find | Files or Folders**.
2) In the Named: box, type *.doc.
3) In the Look in: box, select the C: drive.
4) Click **Find Now**.

Windows displays all files ending in .doc in a My Computer-style window. You can open any listed file by double-clicking on it. To close the Find dialog box, click the Close button in the top-right corner.

Date-Based Searches

If you click on the Date Modified tab of the File Find dialog box, you can limit your search to only those folders or files created or changed between certain dates, or during a specified number of days or months.

Limiting your search by date

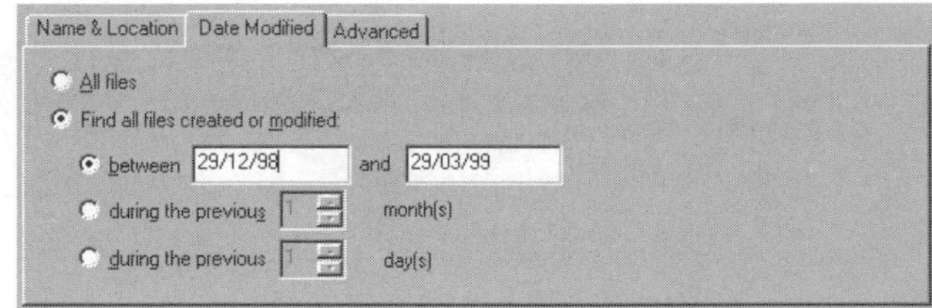

You can search by date or date range alone, if you don't know the file or folder name. Or if you just want to see what folders or files were created or modified on or between certain dates.

Content-Based Searches

If you have absolutely no idea of the name of the item that you are looking for, or when it was created or modified, you can search by content.

Click on the Advanced tab of the File Find dialog box and type one or more words you think are contained within the files you are searching for.

Searching by file content

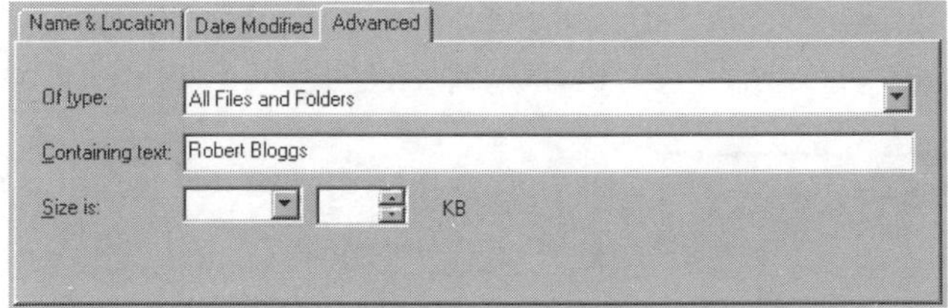

> **Windows Find**
>
> *A search feature that enables you to locate folders or files on any of the following bases: all or part of their name, date of creation or last modification, or their content.*

The Recycle Bin

Windows stores files that you delete in an area it calls the Recycle Bin. Can you see its icon on your Windows desktop? If not, resize or minimise some open windows.

Bin containing files marked for deletion

Empty bin

If you delete a file in error, double-click on the Recycle bin icon, click the file to select it, and choose **File | Restore**. You can empty your Recycle Bin by choosing **File | Empty Recycle Bin**. Emptying your Bin increases the free space available on your C: drive.

Recycle Bin

A storage area where Windows holds deleted files. You can retrieve items that you deleted in error, or empty the Bin to free more disk space.

What are your computer's specifications? To find out, follow these steps:

- Choose **Start | Settings | Control Panel** to display the Control Panel desktop folder.
- Alternatively, double-click the Control Panel icon within My Computer.
- Double-click the System icon.

You are now shown the System Properties dialog box. Its General tab displays your computer's operating system type, processor type, and amount of RAM.

System:
Microsoft Windows 95
4.00.950 B
IE 5 5.00.2314.1003
Registered to:
User 1
Rédacteurs
03697-OEM-0020372-54560
Dell Computer Corporation
Dell Windows 95 PC
Pentium(r)
32.0MB RAM

Online Help

Windows offers a searchable online help system:

- The 'help' means that the information is there to assist you understand and use the operating system.
- The 'online' means that the material is presented on the computer screen rather than as a traditional printed manual.

You can search through and read online help by choosing **Start | Help**. Alternatively, when using My Computer, choose **Help | Help Topics**.

You can search through and read online help in two ways: from the **Help** menu, or from dialog boxes.

Using Help Menu Options

Choose **Help | Contents and Index** to display the three tabs of the Help Topics dialog box. These are explained on the following page:

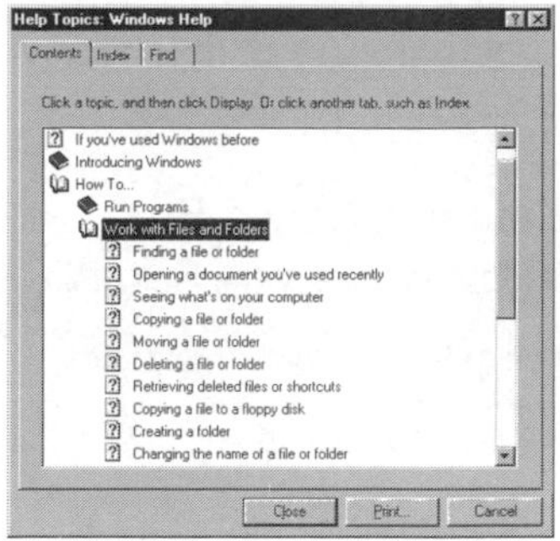

Contents Tab

This offers short descriptions of Windows' main features.

Where you see a heading with a book symbol, double-click to view the related sub-headings.

Double-click on a question-mark symbol to read the help text.

Click a Show me arrow for Windows to demonstrate how to perform a particular action.

Click a double arrow to view step-by-step instructions.

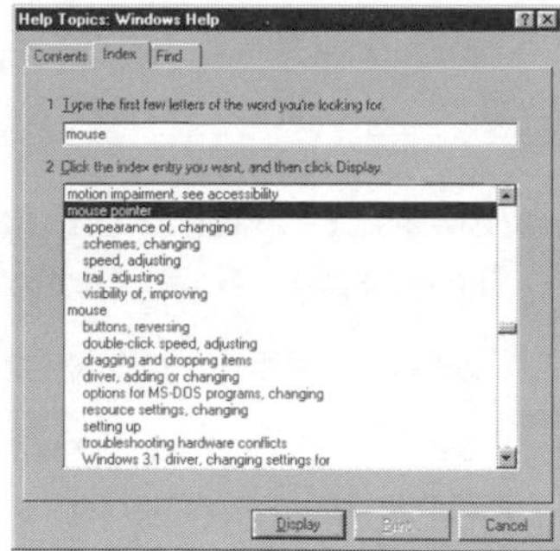

Index Tab

Reading the material displayed on this tab is like looking through the index of a printed book.

Just type the first letters of the word or phrase you are interested in.

Windows responds by displaying all matches from the online help in the lower half of the dialog box.

When you find the index entry that you are looking for, click the **Display** button.

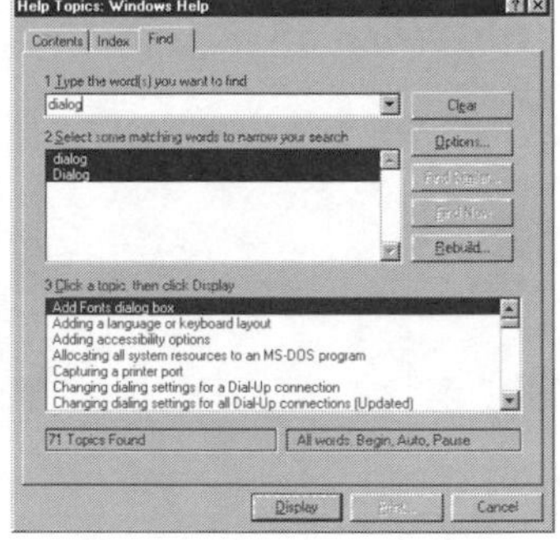

Find Tab

Can't find what you are looking for in the Contents or Index tabs? Try this tab.

When you type a word or phrase, Windows performs a deeper search of the online help.

Windows also displays some related words to help you narrow your search.

When you find the item you are looking for, double-click on it to display it.

As you search through and read online help topics, you will see the following buttons at the top of the online help window:

- **Help Topics:** Click this to return to the Contents tab.
- **Back:** Click this to return to the previous help topic.
- **Options:** Click this to perform such actions as copying the online help text to a document, or printing it on your printer.

Using Help from Dialog Boxes

You can also access online help directly from a dialog box, as Exercise 2.11 demonstrates.

Exercise 2.11: Using Online Help in a Dialog Box

1) Choose **Start | Find | Files or Folders** to display the Find dialog box.
2) Click on the Advanced tab, and then in the Containing text: box.
3) Press F1. Windows displays online help text telling you about the purpose of the selected box.

    > Provides a place for you to type some of the text a file contains. If you don't know a file's name, you may be able to find the file by typing some of its contents.

4) Click anywhere on the Find dialog box to remove the online help text.

Practise this Exercise with other dialog boxes in Windows.

Section Summary: So Now You Know

A *file* is the computer's basic unit of information storage. A *folder* is a group of files (and perhaps subfolders too). Grouping files into folders makes them easier to find and work with.

A *drive* is a physical storage device for holding files and folders. Typically, A: is the floppy drive, C: the hard disk, and D: is the CD-ROM drive.

Use *My Computer* to view the hierarchy of folders on your computer, and to see all the files and subfolders in any selected folder.

To display the details of a drive, folder or file, right-click on it and select the *Properties* option.

Windows adds a three-letter *file name extension* to every file, to indicate the file type. A full stop (.) separates the extension from the remainder of the file name. Common file name extensions are *.doc* (Word), *.xls* (Excel), *.mdb* (Access) and *.ppt* (PowerPoint).

To find a file on a drive, choose the **Start | Find | Files or Folders** command. Windows allows you to use *wildcards* to represent missing letters. You can also restrict your search to files of a certain date or date range, or that contain the specified keywords.

The Windows *online help* system provides a comprehensive and searchable guide to the system's features and procedures.

Section 2.3: Working With Folders and Files

In This Section

In the previous Section you used My Computer to explore the folders and files on your PC. Now you will learn how to perform actions on folders and files – how to create, name and rename, move and copy, and delete and undelete them – using the Windows Explorer application.

New Skills

At the end of this Section you should be able to:

- Create, save, rename and delete folders
- Create, save, rename and delete files
- Move and copy folders and files
- Select several folders or files, whether adjacent or non-adjacent

New Words

At the end of this Section you should be able to explain the following terms:

- Windows Explorer
- Clipboard
- Pull-down menu
- Toolbar

About Windows Explorer

Think of a Windows application and names such as Word, Excel and PowerPoint are probably the first to come to mind. But included with the Windows operating system is another, powerful application. It's called Windows Explorer and you can use to:

- *View* the folders on your computer, and the hierarchy of subfolders and files within any folder.
- *Perform operations* on various folders and files, such as renaming, copying, moving and deleting.

You can open Windows Explorer in either of two ways:

- Choose **Start | Programs | Windows Explorer**, or
- Right-click on the **Start** button, and click **Explore**.

The Two Panes of Windows Explorer

Windows Explorer differs from My Computer in that its window is divided into left and right subwindows called panes.

- You use the *left pane* to select a particular drive or folder. You cannot view files in the left pane.
- You use the *right pane* to view the folders and files in the drive or folder selected in the left pane.

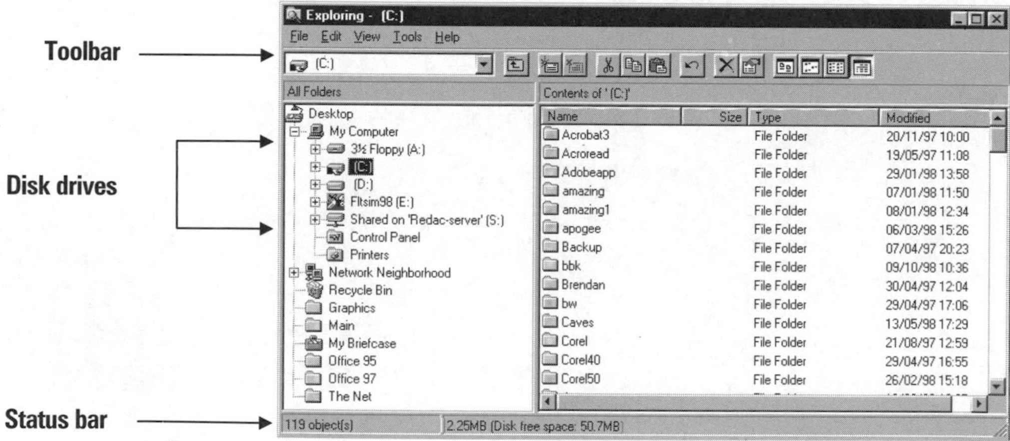

In the Windows Explorer left pane, you can see a hierarchical diagram of your computer's storage space:

- **Top Level:** The Windows Desktop.
- **Second Level:** System folders such as My Computer and Recycle Bin, and any user-created desktop folders.
- **Third Level:** Disk drives, Control Panel and Printers.

The right pane looks and works in a similar way to My Computer.

- Click on any drive in the left pane to display, in the right pane, the folders and files stored on that drive.
- Double click on any folder in the right pane to view any subfolders and files contained within that folder.

Windows Explorer

A Windows application for viewing the hierarchy of folders and files, and for performing such actions as renaming, moving and deleting.

Viewing Options

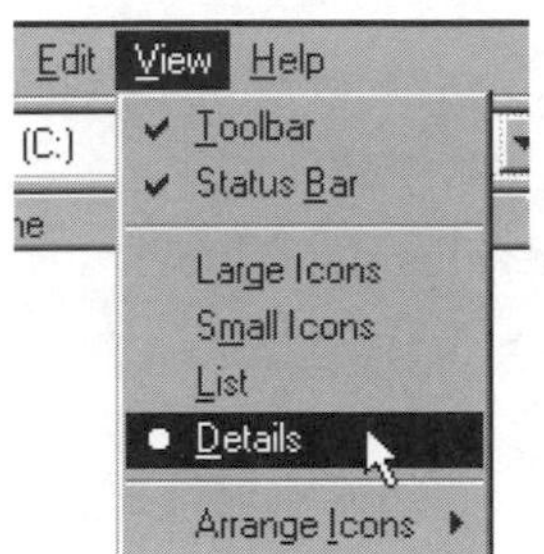

As with My Computer, Windows Explorer offers a number of options that let you control how you view your drives, folders and files. Choose **View | Details** – it's the option that provides the most information in the smallest screen space.

Along the bottom of the Windows Explorer window, in the status bar, you can see the number of items in the currently open folder (the one whose contents are shown in the right pane), the disk space occupied by the folder's contents, and the remaining free space on the drive.

Can't see the status bar or toolbar? Click the relevant options on the **View** menu to display them.

Follow Exercise 2.12 to practise your Windows Explorer skills.

Exercise 2.12: Viewing the Windows Folder

1) If Windows Explorer is not already open, open it now.
2) In the left pane, click on the C: drive icon.
3) In the right pane, scroll down until you see the Windows folder. Double-click on it.

You can now see the folders and files stored within it. Folders are listed first. Scroll down through the Windows folder to see what files are within it.

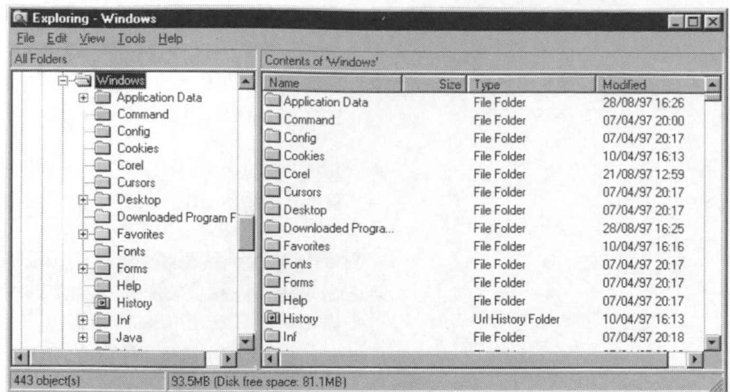

Explorer's Plus and Minus Signs

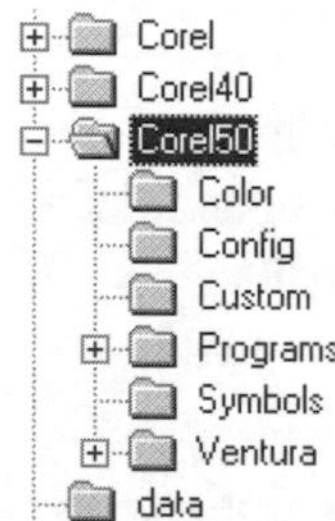

In Windows Explorer, a folder without a plus (+) or a minus (–) sign in front of it is either empty or has only files inside it.

A folder with a plus (+) sign has folders inside it, and perhaps files too. To open it, click on the folder name or the + sign.

A minus (–) sign in front of a folder indicates that the folder is open – its subfolders and files are currently displayed on the screen.

Click on a plus sign to display ('expand') or a minus sign to hide ('collapse') your view of a folder.

Working With Folders

In the next few Exercises you will use Windows Explorer to create folders and subfolders, and to rename, delete and restore (undelete) folders.

Exercise 2.13: Creating Two New Folders

1) In the left pane of the Windows Explorer window, click on the C: drive.

2) Choose **File | New | Folder**. Window displays a new folder at the bottom of the list in the right pane. It gives it the default name of New Folder.

3) Type a name for your new folder. If your initials are KB, for example, call it KB Folder 1.

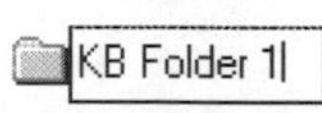

4) Repeat steps 1), 2) and 3). Name your second folder (say) KB Folder 2.

Exercise 2.14: Creating a Subfolder

1) In the right pane of the Windows Explorer window, double-click on the first folder that you created in Exercise 2.13 – in this example, the folder named KB Folder 1.
2) Choose **File | New | Folder**. Windows displays a new subfolder.

3) Type a name for your new folder. If your initials are KB, for example, call it KB Sub Folder 1.

Changing a Folder's Name

You can change a folder's name at any stage. Exercise 2.15 shows you how.

Exercise 2.15: Changing a Folder's Name

1) Right-click on one of your new folders to display a pop-up menu.
2) Choose **Rename**.
3) Type a new folder name. For example, KB New Folder.

Well done! You have given your folder a new name.

Deleting a Folder

Suppose that you don't need a folder any more? Here is how to delete an unwanted folder.

Delete button

Exercise 2.16: Deleting a Folder

1) In the left pane of the Windows Explorer window, click on the first folder that you created in Exercise 2.13. It should contain the subfolder you created in Exercise 2.14.
2) In the left pane of the Windows Explorer window, right-click on the subfolder. From the pop-up menu, select **Delete**.

   Alternatively, click once on the subfolder to select it, and click the Delete button on the Windows Explorer Toolbar.

Confirm Folder Delete
Are you sure you want to remove the folder 'KB Subfolder 1' and move all its contents to the Recycle Bin?
Yes
No

3) Click **Yes** to confirm that you want to remove the folder.

The folder is deleted, as are any subfolders and files it may have contained.

Restoring a Folder's Files

Where did your deleted folder go? If it contained no files, it has been deleted permanently by Windows. If it contained files, Windows moves the files to the Recycle Bin. Follow the steps in Exercise 2.17 to bring your deleted folder and files back to life.

Exercise 2.17: Restoring a Folder's Files

1) In the left pane of the Windows Explorer window, scroll down until you can see the Recycle Bin, and click on it.

   Windows Explorer now displays the contents of the Recycle Bin in the right pane.

2) Choose **Edit | Undo Delete** to restore the files and the folder that contained them.

Working With Files

A file, as you learnt in Section 2.2, is the basic unit of information storage on a computer. In the next few Exercises you will discover how to create, save and name, delete and restore a file.

Creating a File

Files are created by applications. For example, you can create a letter in Microsoft Word and a spreadsheet in Microsoft Excel.

The simplest type of file that you can create on a computer is a plain-text file. A file of this kind contains just words, numbers and punctuation marks – and no fancy formatting or graphics of any kind.

The Windows application for creating plain text files is called Notepad.

Exercise 2.18: Creating a File

1) Choose **Start | Programs | Accessories | Notepad**. A blank Notepad window appears on your screen, ready to accept text.
2) Type the following words: Just testing

You have now created a file and entered content in that file. But your file is not saved on your hard disk. It exists only in the computer's memory. If the computer were to switch off for any reason, your file would be lost.

Naming and Saving a File

The first time that you save a file, Windows asks you to give that file a name. Follow the steps in Exercise 2.19 to discover how.

Exercise 2.19: Naming and Saving a File

1) Choose **File | Save** to view the Save As dialog box. By displaying this dialog box, Windows is asking:
   - What *drive* do you want to save your folder in?
   - What *folder* (or subfolder) do you want to save your file in?
   - What *name* do you want to give your new file?
2) Click on the arrow at the right of the Save in: drop-down list box.

   Now, scroll up until you see the C: drive icon. Click on it.

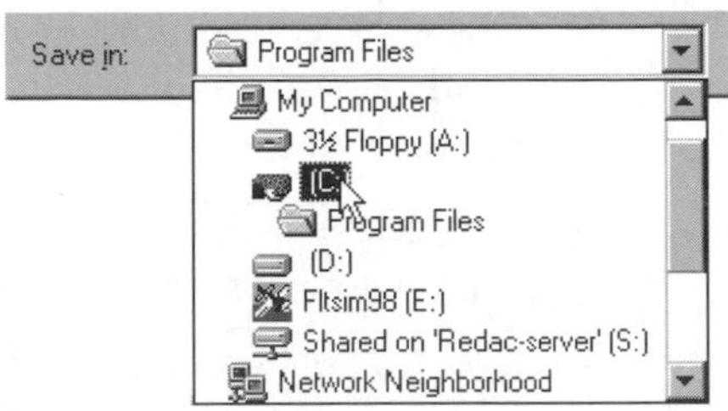

The Save As dialog box now displays a list of the folders on your C: drive.

3) Locate the folder that you renamed in Exercise 2.15. Double-click on it.

   You have now told Windows the drive and folder where you want to save your file. All that remains is for you to give your file a name.

4) Click in the File name: box, delete any text there, and type a name for your new file. If your initials are KB, for example, name it KB New File.

   When finished, click **Save**.

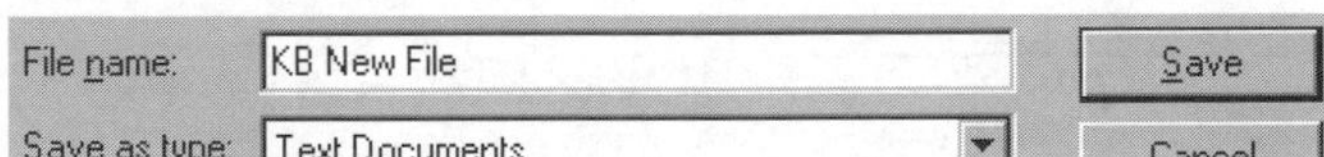

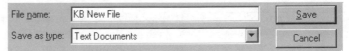

Windows automatically adds the three-letter file name extension of .txt to all plain-text files created with the Notepad application.

Well done! You have learnt how to name and save a file.

Move the mouse to the top-right of the Notepad window, and click on the Close box to close it.

Changing a File's Name

You can change a file's name at any stage. Exercise 2.20 shows you how.

Exercise 2.20: Changing a File's Name

1) Using Windows Explorer, open the folder containing the file you saved in Exercise 2.19.

2) Right-click on the file to display a pop-up menu.

3) Choose **Rename**.

4) Type a new file name. For example, KB Renamed File. Do not change or delete the file name extension (.txt).

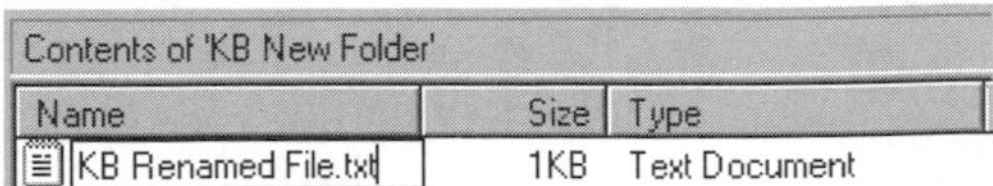

You have given your file a new name. Another Exercise completed!

Deleting a File

When you have been working on your computer for a while, you may find that its hard disk is taken up by files and folders you no longer use or need.

You can delete these files, but be careful not to delete any files that your computer needs to run programs! If in doubt, don't delete!

Exercise 2.21 shows you how to delete an unwanted file.

Exercise 2.21: Deleting a File

1) Using Windows Explorer, display and right-click on the file that you renamed in Exercise 2.20.
2) From the pop-up menu, select the **Delete** command.
3) Click **Yes** to confirm that you want to remove the file to the Recycle Bin.

   Alternatively, click once on the file in Windows Explorer, and click the Delete button on the toolbar.

Restoring a File

Follow the steps in Exercise 2.22 to restore your deleted file.

Exercise 2.22: Restoring a File

1) In the left pane of the Windows Explorer window, scroll until you can see the Recycle Bin, and click on it.

   Windows Explorer now displays the contents of the Recycle Bin in the right pane.
2) Click the file to select it, and then choose **File | Restore**.

The Windows Clipboard

Suppose you want to place a folder or file in a different location on your computer. Or reproduce a folder or file so that two copies of it appear in different locations. Can you do it? Yes. It is a two-step process:

- **Copy:** You select and then *copy* the folder or file to the Clipboard, a temporary storage area. The selected folder or file remains in its original location.

  -or-

  Cut: You select and then *cut* the folder or file to the Clipboard. The selected folder or file is no longer in its original location.
- **Paste:** You *paste* the folder or file from the Clipboard into a different part of your computer – into a different folder, or even a different drive.

Clipboard

A temporary storage area to which you can copy or cut folders or files. You can paste from the Clipboard to any location within the same or a different drive.

About the Clipboard

Three points you should remember about the Windows Clipboard:

- The Clipboard is temporary. Turn off your computer and the Clipboard contents are deleted.
- The Clipboard can hold only a single, copied item at a time. If you copy or cut a second item, the second overwrites the first.
- Items stay in the Clipboard after you paste from it, so you can paste the same folder or file into as many locations as you need.

Copying and Moving Folders

To copy a folder means to make a copy of it, and to place that copy in a new location. Exercise 2.23 takes you through the steps.

Copy button

Paste button

Exercise 2.23: Copying a Folder

1) In the left pane of Windows Explorer, click the folder that you renamed in Exercise 2.15.
2) Choose **Edit | Copy** or click the Copy button on the Windows Explorer Toolbar.
3) Scroll down the left pane until you can see the Windows folder. Click on it to display its contents in the right pane.
4) Choose **Edit | Paste** or click the Paste button on the toolbar.

This places a copy of your folder within the Windows folder.

To move a folder means to place it in a new location – and to *remove* it from its original location. Exercise 2.24 shows you how.

Cut button

Exercise 2.24: Moving a Folder

1) In the right pane, display the folder that you copied to the Windows folder in Exercise 2.23. Click on it to select it.
2) Choose **Edit | Cut** or click the Cut button on the toolbar.
3) Scroll back up the right pane to locate the folder named System.
4) Double-click on the System folder to open it.
5) Choose **Edit | Paste** or click the Paste button on the toolbar.

This places your folder within the System folder of the Windows folder.

Copying and Moving Files

In Exercise 2.25 you will make a copy of your plain-text file, and place that copy in a different folder on your hard disk. Following that, in Exercise 2.26, you will move the file from its current folder to a new one.

Exercise 2.25: Copying a File

1) In the left pane, display the folder containing the file that you created in Exercise 2.18. Double-click on the folder to display its contents in the right pane.
2) Choose **Edit | Copy** or click the Copy button on the toolbar.
3) In the left pane, scroll down to locate the folder called Windows.
4) Click on the Windows folder to open it. Its contents are now listed in the right pane.
5) Choose **Edit | Paste** or click the Paste button on the toolbar.

You have now placed a copy of your file within the Windows folder.

Exercise 2.26: Moving a File

1) In the right pane, display the file that you copied to the Windows folder in Exercise 2.25. Click on it to select it.
2) Choose **Edit | Cut** or click the Cut button on the toolbar.
3) Scroll back up the right pane to locate the folder named System.
4) Double-click the System folder to open it
5) Choose **Edit | Paste** or click the Paste button on the toolbar.

You have now moved the file to the System subfolder of the Windows folder.

Working with Multiple Files

Windows Explorer provides an easy method of copying or moving several files in a single operation. This method works only when:

- The files you want to copy or move are currently located in the *same* folder.
- The place you want to copy or move them to is also a single folder.

When you list the files to copy or move in Windows Explorer, two situations are possible:

- The files are *adjacent*. They are positioned immediately below or above one another.
- The files are *non-adjacent*. They are not positioned immediately below or above one another.

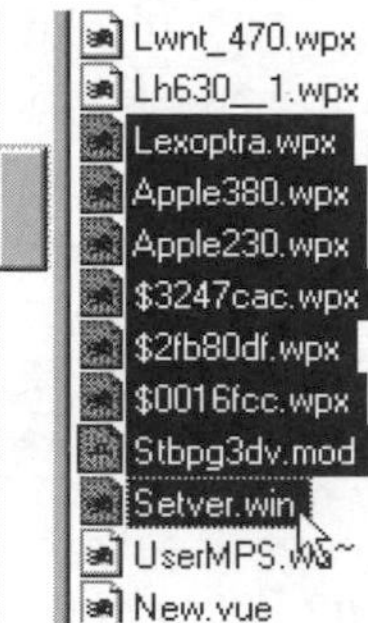

If the files are adjacent, follow these steps:

- Click on the first file
- Press and hold down the SHIFT key
- Click on the last file

All the files – the first, last and in-between – are now selected, and you can copy or cut them in a single operation.

If the files are non-adjacent, follow these steps:

- Click on the first file
- Press and hold down the CTRL key
- Click the relevant files, one after the other, to select them

Again, all the files are now selected, and you can copy or cut them in a single operation.

When selecting several files, you can scroll down or up as you make your selection. This methods works for folders as well as files. Another operation that you can perform on selected folders or files is deletion. Simply select the adjacent or non-adjacent files or folders, and click the Delete button on the toolbar.

Menubars, Toolbars and Shortcuts

In the final part of this Section you will discover the three ways that you perform actions in a Windows application: menu commands, toolbar buttons, and keyboard shortcuts.

Menubars

Start the Microsoft Word application. Take a look at the line of words that runs just under the title bar. Each of these words represents a pull-down menu.

Word's menubar

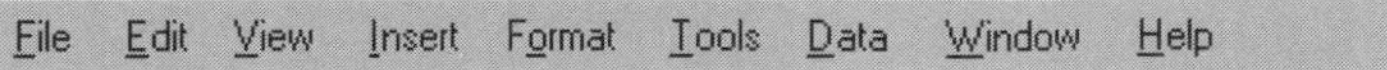

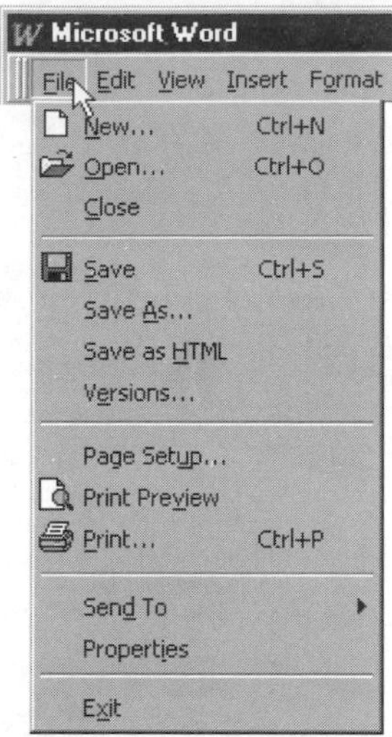

Word's pull-down File menu

Click the **File** menu name to display the commands (actions) available on this menu. You tell Word that you want to perform a particular action by clicking the action's name on the pull-down menu. Click the **Exit** command to close Word.

Pull-Down Menu
A list of options that appears when you click on a menu name. The menu name is generally on a menubar along the top of the window, and the menu appears below that bar, as if you pulled it down.

Whenever you see an arrow to the right of a menu option, selecting that option displays a further submenu of choices.

All Windows applications share a number of common menus. Understand their general purpose and you will be able to use most applications. The common menus are:

- **File:** Use the commands on this menu to create a new (blank) file, open an existing file, save the current file, save the current file with a new name (**Save as**), print the current file, and quit the application.
- **Edit:** Use the commands on this menu to copy and move selected files, or items (such as text or graphics) within files.
- **View:** Use the commands on this menu to display your file in different ways, including a zoomed-in (up close) view or zoomed-out (bird's eye) view.
- **Help:** Use the commands on this menu to display online help information about the application you are using.

Toolbars

A second way of performing an action is to click a button on a toolbar. Instead of choosing **File | Save** to save a file, for example, you could click the Save button on the toolbar. Not every menu command has a toolbar button equivalent, but the most commonly used commands do.

Toolbar
A collection of buttons that you can click to perform frequently used actions, such as creating, opening or saving files, and for Clipboard operations.

Here are the toolbar buttons that you will find on almost every Windows application:

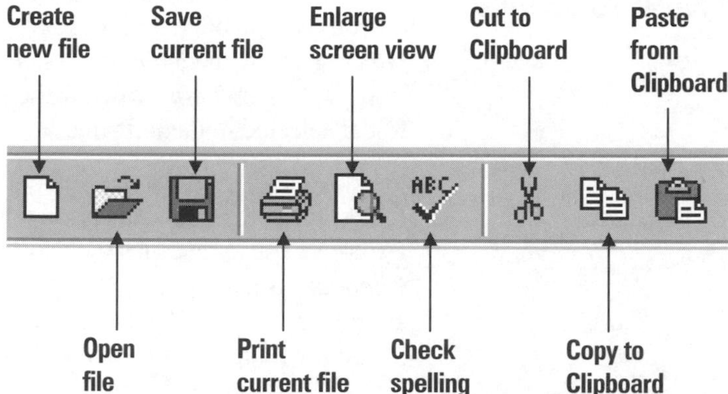

Keyboard Shortcuts

Keyboard shortcut for copying a selected item to the Clipboard

A third way of performing actions in Windows is to use keyboard shortcuts. You may find using these faster than either menu commands or toolbar buttons, as you need not take either hand away from the keyboard.

An example of a keyboard short cut is CTRL+c, which means 'Hold down the control key and press the letter c key'. This has the same effect as choosing **Edit | Copy** or clicking the Copy button on the toolbar.

Here are the most commonly used shortcut keys:

Keyboard Shortcut	Action Performed	Menu Command
CTRL+o	Opens an existing file	File | Open
CTRL+n	Opens a new file	File | New
CTRL+s	Saves the current file	File | Save
CTRL+c	Copies to the Clipboard	Edit | Copy
CTRL+x	Cuts to the Clipboard	Edit | Cut
CTRL+v	Pastes from the Clipboard	Edit | Paste

Section Summary: So Now You Know

Use *Windows Explorer* to view the hierarchy of folders on your computer, and to view and work with the drives, folders and files on your computer. Windows Explorer displays two subwindows or *panes*. You use the *left pane* to select a particular drive or folder. You use the *right pane* to view the folders and files in the drive or folder selected in the left pane.

Windows Explorer enables you to *copy*, *move*, *rename* and *delete* folders and files. You can also create folders with Windows Explorer. You create files with software applications. The *Clipboard* is a temporary storage area to which you can copy or cut folders or files. You can paste from the Clipboard to any location within the same or a different drive.

You can *select multiple files*, and then copy, cut, paste or delete them in a single operation. If the files are *adjacent*, click the first file, hold down the SHIFT key, and then click the last file. If *non-adjacent*, click the first file, hold down the CTRL key, and then click the individual files to select them.

A *pull-down* menu is a list of options that appears when you click a menu name on a menubar. When you see an arrow to the right of a menu option, selecting that option displays a further *submenu* of choices. You tell Word that you want to perform a particular action by clicking the action's name on the pull-down menu.

A second way of performing an action is to click a button on a toolbar. Most applications have toolbar buttons for creating, opening or saving files, and for Clipboard operations.

A third option is to press the CTRL key in combination with a particular letter key. Examples of such *keyboard shortcuts* include CTRL+c to copy to the Clipboard and CTRL+v to paste from it.

Section 2.4: Mastering Windows

In This Section

Now that you are familiar with Windows basics, you are ready to move on to the more advanced features.

You will discover how to take control of your Windows desktop, enabling you to customise it to reflect your working needs and your personal taste. You will also learn how to make backup copies of your files on diskettes.

New Skills

At the end of this Section you should be able to:

- Personalise your desktop by moving icons and creating folders to hold application and file icons
- Create shortcuts that take you directly to a particular application, file or folder
- Select a screen saver
- Customise your wallpaper, background pattern, scheme and screen resolution
- Change your computer's date and time settings
- Adjust your computer's sound volume
- Change your computer's regional settings
- Format a diskette
- Copy a file to a diskette
- Save a file to a diskette
- Use various print features and options

New Words

At the end of this Section you should be able to explain the following terms:

- Desktop shortcut
- Screen saver
- Print queue

Managing Your Desktop

You can arrange your Windows desktop to suit your working needs and personal taste:

- To reposition your icons, simply drag them to where you want them.
- To make your screen look tidier, create desktop folders and place application and file icons in them.

You create a desktop folder as follows:

- Right-click on the desktop to display a pop-up menu
- Choose **New | Folder**. Windows creates a desktop folder with the default name New Folder.

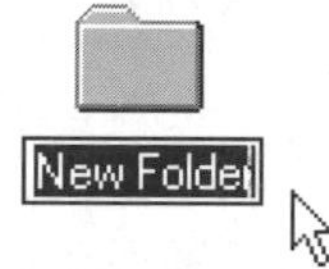

- Type your folder name, and press ENTER.

Next, double-click the folder to open it, and drag icons into it, either from the desktop or from other desktop folders.

Creating Desktop Shortcuts

You will use some applications more frequently than others. You can save yourself time by creating a shortcut to these programs from your desktop (or from a folder on your desktop). As a result, you won't have to go the **Start | Programs** route every time you want to start that application.

Follow the steps in Exercise 2.27 to create a desktop shortcut for Notepad.

Exercise 2.27: Creating a Desktop Shortcut for Notepad

1) Choose **Start | Programs | Windows Explorer**. If the Explorer window occupies the full Windows desktop, click on the Restore button (top-right).
2) Display the application for which you want to create a shortcut. You will find Notepad in the Windows folder.

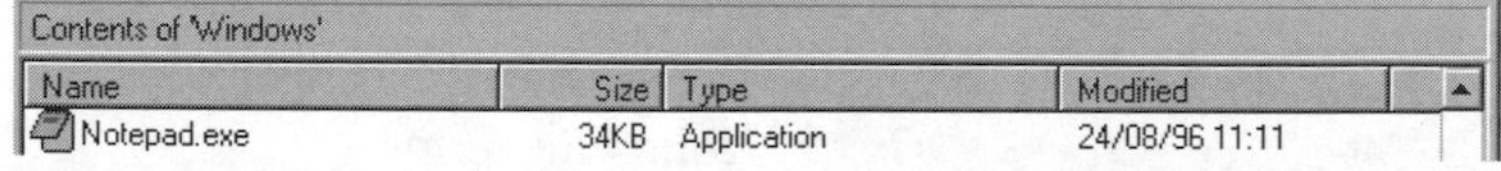

3) Right-click on the Notepad icon, drag it from Windows Explorer onto your desktop, and release the right mouse button.
4) On the pop-up menu displayed, choose **Select Create Shortcut(s) Here**.

If you don't like your shortcut's default name, right-click on it, choose Rename, type a new name, and press the ENTER key. You can also create shortcuts for frequently used folders and files. You can leave the Notepad icon on your desktop, or drag it to a desktop folder.

Desktop Shortcut

A user-created icon that, when clicked on, takes you directly to an application, folder or file. It is a fast, convenient alternative to using the Start menu.

In Exercise 2.28 you will create a desktop folder named Office 97, and create desktop shortcuts for three Office applications within it.

Exercise 2.28: Creating an Office 97 Desktop Folder Containing Shortcuts

1) Right-click on your desktop. On the pop-up menu displayed, choose **New | Folder**. Windows creates a folder with the default name New Folder.

2) Type the following folder name, and press ENTER: Office 97

3) Double-click your new folder to open it. You are now ready to create desktop shortcuts and place them within the folder.

4) Let's start with a shortcut to Microsoft Word. Choose **Start | Find | Files or Folders** to display the Find dialog box.

5) In the Named: box, type winword.exe, and click **Find Now**.

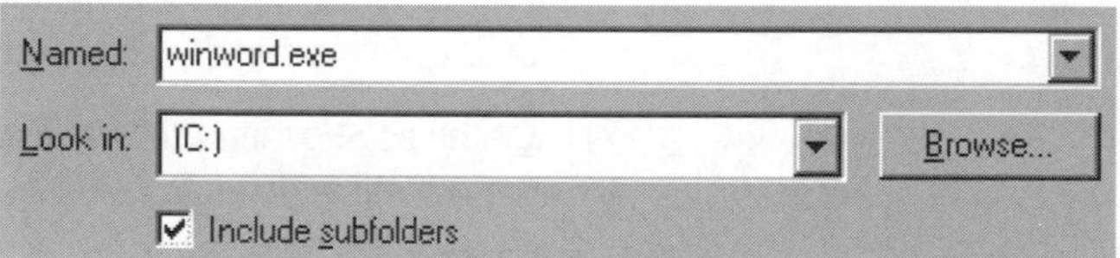

6) When winword.exe is found, right-click on its icon, and drag it from the Find dialog box into your Office 97 desktop folder.

7) Click on the Find dialog box again. Repeat steps 5) and 6) for the following other Office 97 application files: excel.exe, and powerpnt.exe.

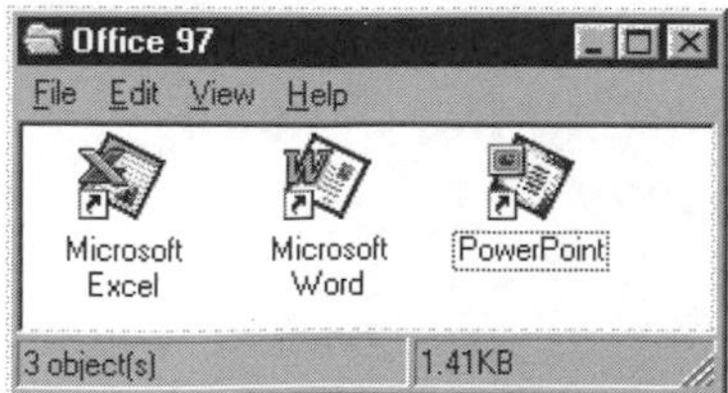

When finished, your Office 97 folder should look as shown.

Setting the Time and Date

Is your computer set to the correct date and time? If not, the files you create and edit, and e-mails you send, will show misleading dates or times. Exercise 2.29 shows you how to set the date and time on your computer.

Exercise 2.29: Setting Your Computer's Date and Time

1) Choose **Start | Settings | Control Panel**.
2) On the folder displayed, double-click the Date/Time icon.
3) Make the changes you want. Click **Apply** and then **OK**.

A small battery inside your computer ensures that Windows remembers the date and time settings, even when your computer is turned off.

Adjusting the Sound Volume

Modern PCs have the ability to play sound files through attached loudspeakers or headphones. Follow Exercise 2.30 to discover how to adjust the playback volume setting on your computer.

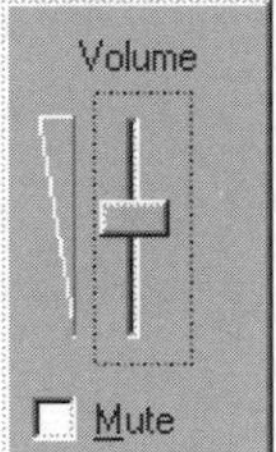

Exercise 2.30: Changing the Playback Volume

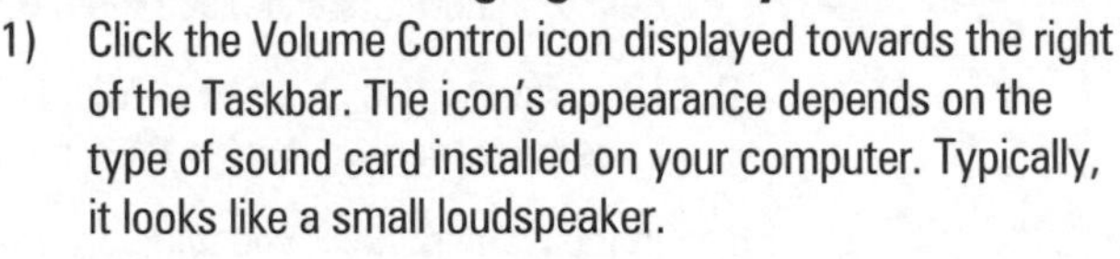

1) Click the Volume Control icon displayed towards the right of the Taskbar. The icon's appearance depends on the type of sound card installed on your computer. Typically, it looks like a small loudspeaker.

   Unsure which Taskbar icon is the Volume Control? Position the cursor over each icon until you see a text box telling you the icon's purpose.

2) On the pop-up menu shown, drag the Volume Control slider up to raise the volume or down to lower it.

   You can switch off sound completely by selecting the Mute box.

3) When finished, click on any other part of your screen to close the Volume Control.

Setting the Screen Saver

A screen saver is a program that takes over the computer's display screen if there are no keystrokes or mouse movements for a specified amount of time.

Screen savers were developed originally to prevent damage to monitors that could arise if one fixed image was displayed continuously over a long period – such as a weekend, for example. Screen savers prevented this by either blanking out the screen entirely or by displaying a series of constantly moving images.

Today's monitors are less likely to suffer from the problem that screen savers were designed to prevent, and they are now mostly an adornment.

Exercise 2.31 shows you how to set up or change your computer's screen saver.

Screen Saver

A program that takes over the computer's display screen if there are no keystrokes or mouse movements for a specified amount of time. They either blank out the screen entirely or display a series of continually moving images.

Exercise 2.31: Setting Up or Changing Your Screen Saver

1) Right-click on the Windows desktop, choose **Properties** from the pop-up menu, and select the Screen Saver tab.

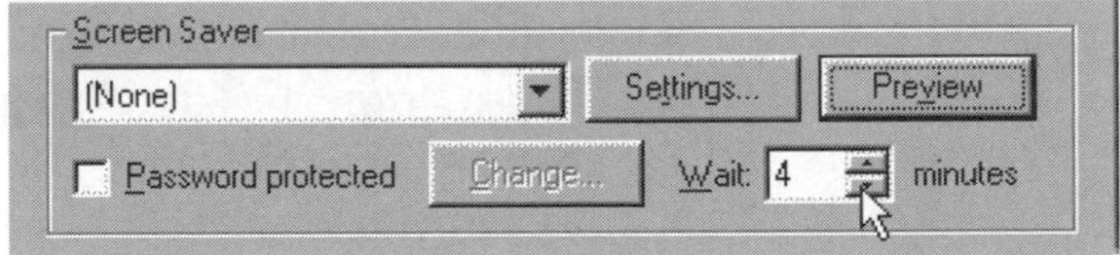

2) Click the arrow to the right of the Screen Saver drop-down list box to display a list of screen savers installed on your computer.

3) Click to select the screen saver you require from the list.

4) In the Wait: box enter the number of minutes before which the screen saver will activate, and click **OK**.

To clear the screen saver after it has started, move your mouse or press any key.

Customising Your Screen

The appearance of Windows on your computer is controlled by the setting of the following three items, each of which you can change to suit your working needs or personal taste:

- Background pattern
- Wallpaper
- Scheme

Background Pattern

By default, the Windows background is typically an area of one continuous colour. You can change this to one of a dozen or so patterns.

To view or adjust your background pattern setting:

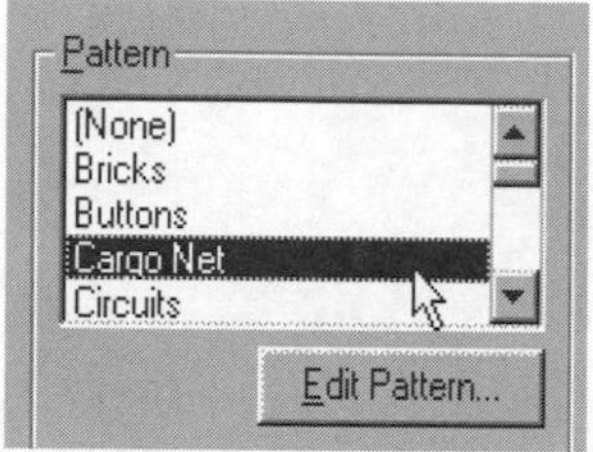

- Right-click on the desktop, choose **Properties** from the pop-up menu, and select the Background tab.
- Select your required pattern from the drop-down list box and click **OK**.

You can use the Edit Pattern button to edit an existing pattern or create a new one.

Wallpaper

You can insert an image, such as a scanned photograph or a picture downloaded from the Internet, on your desktop background. Follow these steps to do so:

- Right-click on the desktop, choose **Properties** from the pop-up menu, and select the Background tab.
- Select your required wallpaper from the drop-down list box.
- Select Centre to position the image in the middle of your desktop, or Tile to repeat the image horizontally and vertically until it fills the entire screen, and click **OK**.

Scheme

This is the combination of colours, fonts and spacing that controls the appearance of such items as title bars, scroll bars and icons. To view or adjust your scheme:

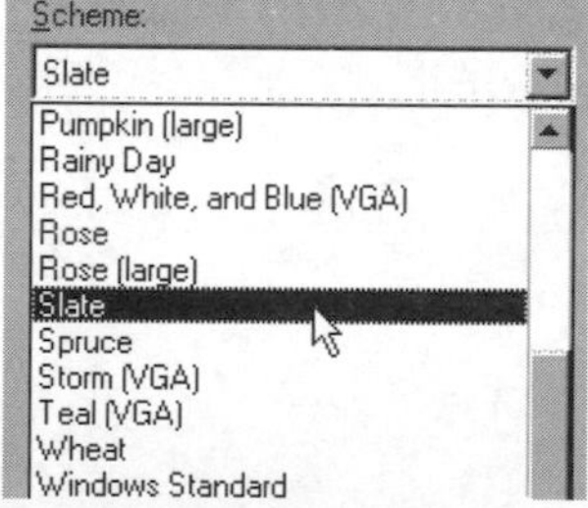

- Right-click on the desktop, choose **Properties** from the pop-up menu, and select the Appearance tab.
- Select your required scheme from the drop-down list box, and click **OK**.

You can change your background pattern, wallpaper and scheme as often as you wish. The relevant dialog boxes offer a preview area where you can view the effect of any changes before you apply them. Don't be afraid to experiment with different settings.

Changing Your Screen Resolution

Everything you view on your screen is composed of tiny square dots called pixels. The number of pixels displayed is determined by your screen resolution.

- Lower resolution settings (such as 640x480) result in fewer, larger pixels, so that everything on your screen appears bigger and blockier.
- Higher resolution settings (such as 1024x768) use more, smaller pixels, so that everything appears smaller and more defined.

To change your screen resolution:

- Right-click on the desktop, choose **Properties** from the pop-up menu, and select the Settings tab.

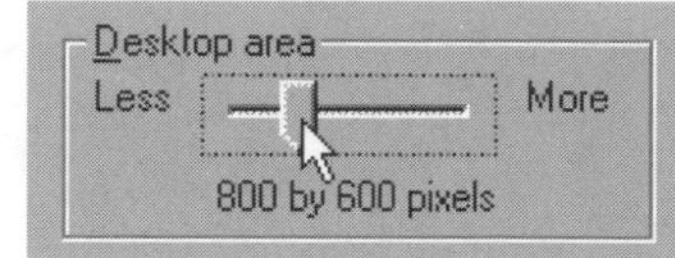

- Drag the Desktop area slider left to decrease the resolution or right to increase it.

You can see the effect of a new screen resolution in the preview area. When finished, click **OK** to save your new settings and close the dialog box.

Changing Your Regional Settings

The options you select in the Windows Regional Settings decide the default currency symbol shown in your applications, and which conventions Windows uses when displaying times, dates and numbers.

To change your regional settings:

- Choose **Start | Settings | Control Panel**, and click the Regional Settings icon.
- On the Regional Settings tab, select the relevant region from the drop-down list.
- To override the default conventions for your selected region, use the options on the Number, Currency, Time and Date tabs.
- When finished, click **OK** to save your new settings and to close the dialog box.

Working with Diskettes

You can copy files and folders from your hard disk to a floppy diskette to:

- Make a copy of your work that you can give to a colleague or friend.

- Have a second, backup copy of your work just in case your computer is somehow damaged and the files on it are 'lost'.

The more regularly you make backups, the more up-to-date your files will be if your computer fails.

Formatting a Diskette

You can only copy files to a diskette that is formatted. When Windows formats a floppy diskette, it:

- Sets up a 'table of contents' on the diskette which it later uses to locate files stored on the disk.
- Checks for any damaged areas, and, when it finds them, marks those areas as off-limits for file storage.

Most new diskettes come already formatted. But it is cheaper to buy unformatted ones and format them yourself. The ECDL Syllabus also specifies that you must know how to format a diskette. Exercise 2.32 shows you how.

Exercise 2.32: Formatting a Floppy Diskette

1) Insert the floppy diskette you want to format into the diskette drive.
2) Chose **Start | Programs | Windows Explorer** and right-click the A: drive icon in the left-hand pane.
3) Choose **Format** and select the following two options on the dialog box displayed:

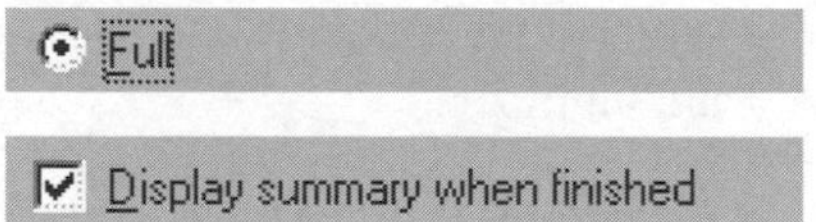

4) When Windows has formatted the disk, click **OK** to display the Format Results dialog box.
5) Click **Close**.

Formatting a disk overwrites any table of contents there may have been previously on the disk, so making it impossible for Windows to find files that were saved on the diskette before it was formatted.

For that reason, don't even think about formatting your computer's hard disk.

You cannot format a disk if there are files open on that disk.

Copying a File to a Diskette

You can copy a file to a diskette using the copy and paste option available with Windows Explorer. See Exercise 2.33.

Exercise 2.33: Copying a File to a Diskette

1) Place a formatted diskette in the A: drive of your computer.
2) Choose **Start | Programs | Windows Explorer** and, in the right-hand pane, display the file that you want to copy – for example, the Mouse.txt file from the Windows folder.
3) Click on the file and choose **Edit | Copy** or click the Copy button on the toolbar.

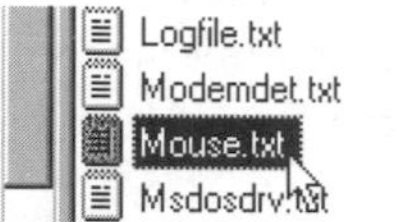

4) In the left pane, click on the A: drive icon.

   If there are currently any files on the diskette, Windows Explorer lists them in its right pane.

5) Choose **Edit | Paste** or click the Paste button to copy the file to the diskette.

Saving a File to a Diskette

A second way to copy a file to a diskette is to use the **File | Save As** command of the application in which you created and worked with the file. If you currently have the application open on your screen, this is faster than using Windows Explorer. See Exercise 2.34.

Exercise 2.34: Saving a File to a Diskette

1) Choose **Start | Programs | Accessories | Notepad.**
2) Choose **File | Open**, locate the file you saved in Exercise 2.19, and click **Open**.
3) Choose **File | Save As**, locate the A: drive, and click **Save** to save the file.

A copy of the Notepad file is now stored on the diskette.

Printing Files

Now that you can open and work with files, you will want to print copies of your work so you can see it on paper.

Exercise 2.35: Printing a File

1) Open the file, for example, a Word document.
2) Select **File | Print**.
3) Click **OK** in the Print dialog box.

If your printer is connected and set up correctly, your file should print.

The Print Queue

What happens to a file after you choose to print it with the Print command? The answer is that it goes to a file called a print queue, and is then taken from the print queue by the selected printer.

The print queue can store a number of files, which the printer then collects in turn as it becomes ready to print them. The time it takes to print a file depends on the number and size of the other print jobs in the print queue.

You can view your print queue to see what print jobs are waiting in it, delete print jobs from the queue, and reorder the sequence in which print jobs are listed.

Print Queue

A list of files (print jobs) that are waiting to be printed. The printer pulls the files off the queue one at a time.

Viewing the Print Queue

What jobs are currently in the print queue? See Exercise 2.36 to find out.

Exercise 2.36: Viewing the Print Queue

1) Choose **Start | Settings | Printers**.
2) Double-click on the icon for the printer you want to check.

Windows displays a list of all the print jobs in the queue.

Cancelling a Print Job in the Queue

There are many reasons why you may decide to cancel a print job – you may discover that the job is not printing correctly. You may realise that you already have a copy of the printout. Or you may simply change your mind about printing the file.

Follow the steps in Exercise 2.37 to cancel a job.

Exercise 2.37: Removing a Job from the Print Queue

1) Choose **Start | Settings | Printers**.
2) Double-click on the icon for the printer you want to look at. Windows displays a list of all the print jobs in the queue.
3) Select the document you want to cancel printing.
4) Choose **Document | Cancel Printing**.

Changing the Order of Jobs in the Print Queue

You can change the current sequence of jobs in the print queue. Here's how.

Exercise 2.38: Reordering the Jobs in a Print Queue

1) Choose **Start | Settings | Printers**.
2) Double-click on the icon for the printer you want to look at. Windows displays a list of all the print jobs in the queue.
3) Select the file you want to move, and drag it to the required place in the queue.

You can't move a file that is already in the process of printing.

Deleting All Documents from the Print Queue

Follow the steps in Exercise 2.39 to remove all pending print jobs from the print queue.

Exercise 2.39: Deleting All Jobs in the Print Queue

1) Choose **Start | Settings | Printers**.
2) Double-click on the icon for the printer you want to look at. Windows displays a list of all the print jobs in the queue.
3) Choose **Printer | Purge Jobs**.

The Print Dialog Box

When you choose the **File | Print** command within an application, you are shown a dialog box that typically offers the following options:

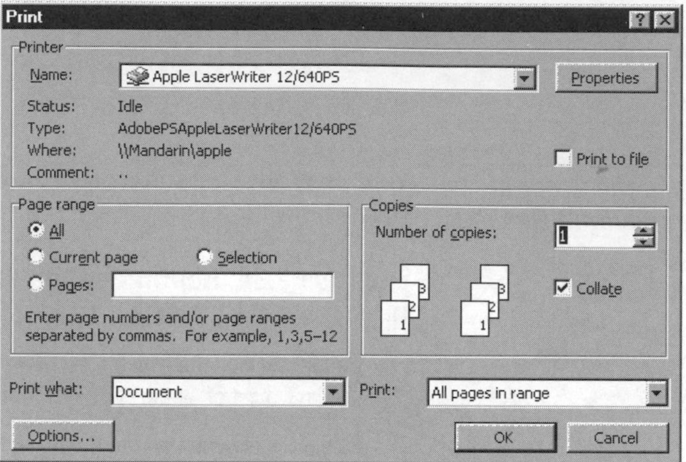

Name

To choose a different printer, click on the arrow on the right of the Name: drop-down list box, and then click the printer you require.

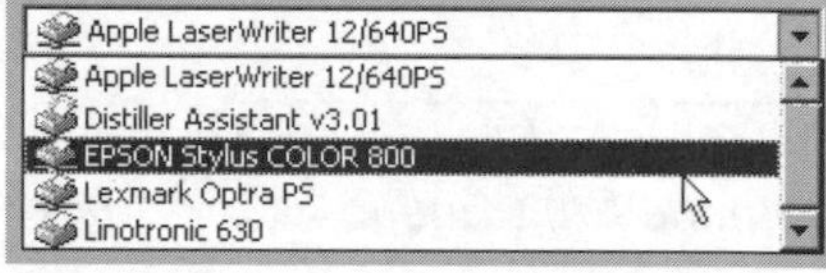

Print Range

You can choose to print all pages, the currently displayed page only or a range of pages.

To print a group of continuous pages, enter the first and last page number of the group, separated by a dash. For example, 2-6 or 12-13.

To print a non-continuous group of pages, enter their individual page numbers, separated by commas. For example, 3,5,9 or 12,17,34. You can combine continuous with non-continuous page selections.

Copies

You can specify how many copies of the file you want to print. For multiple copies, ensure that the Collate check box is selected.

The Properties Button

Clicking on the **Properties** button displays some further print choices that will vary with the type of printer selected – colour or black-and-white, inkjet or laser.

All printers offer choices about paper size (A4 is standard) and orientation (Portrait means 'standing up', Landscape means 'on its side').

When you have selected your options, click **OK** to print your file.

Print Preview

Most Windows applications have a **Print Preview** command on their **File** menu that lets you see on screen how the file contents will look when printed on paper.

Changing the Default Printer

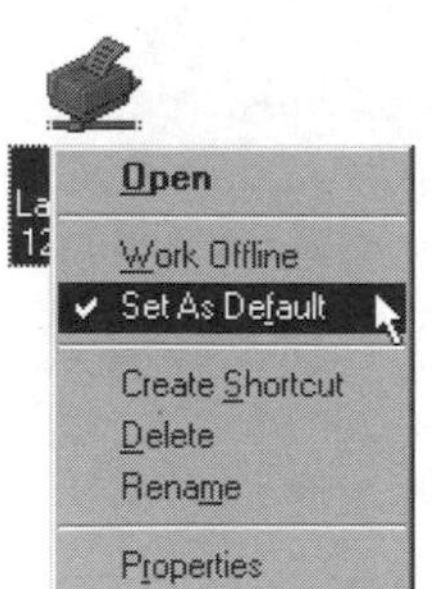

If your PC is attached to a network, you may have a number of printers available to you. It's a good idea to set the printer you use most often as the default printer. When you choose the **File | Print** command in Word or other Windows application, your file outputs on the default printer unless you specify otherwise.

Follow this procedure to set a printer as the default printer:

- Choose **Start | Settings | Printers**.
- Right-click on the icon of the printer you want to set as the default.
- Select the **Set As Default** command from the pop-up menu.

If there is a check mark beside this command, the printer is already selected as the default printer.

Section Summary: So Now You Know

You can *personalise* your Windows desktop by repositioning icons, creating new folders, and placing application and file icons in them. You can create desktop shortcuts – icons that take you directly to a particular application, file or folder. You can also customise your *wallpaper*, *background pattern*, *scheme* and *screen saver*.

You can adjust the *date and time* settings on your computer so that Windows attaches the correct date and time to the files you create and edit, and to e-mails you send. You can also adjust the *sound volume*.

By either blanking out the screen or showing a series of continually moving images, a *screen saver* program takes over the computer's display screen if there are no keystrokes or mouse movements for a specified amount of time.

Your *regional settings* decide the default currency symbol shown in your applications, and which conventions Windows uses when displaying times, dates and numbers.

Your *screen resolution* is the number of pixels its displays. Lower resolution settings make everything appear bigger and blockier. Higher resolution settings make everything appear smaller and more defined.

Before you can copy files to a floppy diskette, you must *format* the diskette. If you format a previously used diskette, any files that may have been on the disk are no longer accessible.

Anything you print goes first to a file called a *print queue* that can hold multiple print jobs. It is then taken from the print queue by the selected printer. You can view your print queue to see what jobs are waiting in it, delete jobs from the queue, and reorder the sequence in which jobs are listed.

3 Word Processing

Back in the days when people thought they could predict the future, someone came up with the phrase 'paperless office'.

As computers found their way into more and more workplaces, the theory was that paper-based communication would disappear. Forever.

But alongside affordable computers came affordable printers. Result: computerisation has led to more rather than less paper usage. The office-supplies people have never been busier.

In this Word Processing Module, you will learn how to add further to the world's output of computer-generated paperwork.

You will discover how to create formal business letters and reports, and produce stylish posters and restaurant menus. We will even share with you the secrets of generating personalised form letters, (un)popularly known as junk mail.

Good luck with it.

Section 3.1: Your First Letter in Word

In This Section

There is a lot more to word processing than just typing and editing words, but these are the two basics. Read the material and follow the examples in this Section and you will have the foundation skills to move on to more advanced tasks.

You will also learn how to access and search through Word's online help, which is a great place to find answers and advice on using any of the program's features.

New Skills

At the end of this Section you should be able to:

- Start and quit Word
- Enter and edit text
- Recognise Word's non-printing characters
- Use the SHIFT, BACKSPACE, DELETE, ARROW and TAB keys
- Type and print a standard letter
- Use Word's Insert Date feature
- Reverse typing and editing actions with Word's Undo feature
- Save, name, open, create and close Word documents
- Use online help to learn more about Word

New Words

At the end of this Section you should be able to explain the following terms:

- Document
- Paragraph mark
- Wrap around
- Non-printing characters

Starting Word

Double click on the Microsoft Word icon or choose **Start | Programs | Microsoft Word**. Word starts and displays a new window containing a new, blank document ready for you to type into.

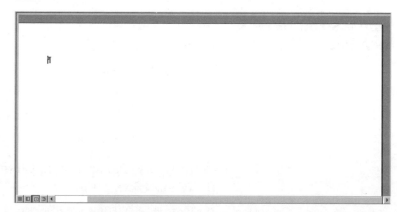

A blank Word document ready to accept your text

Word Document

A Microsoft Word file. For example, a letter or a report.

What? No New, Blank Document?

If starting Word did not automatically open a new, blank document, click on the New button at the top-left of your screen.

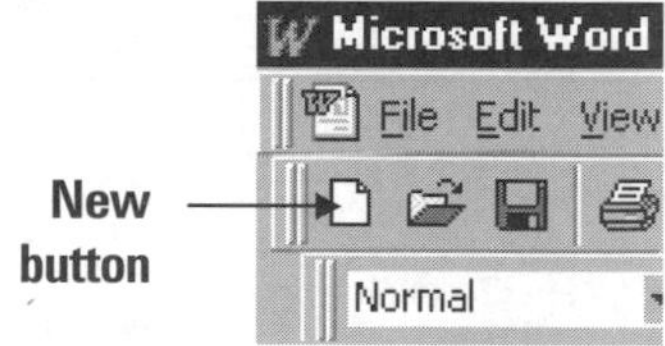

New button

Text Cursor and Paragraph Mark

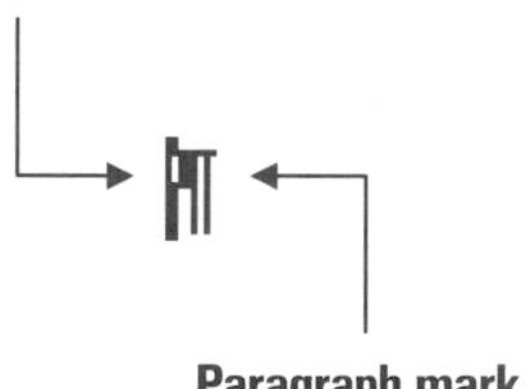

Near the top-left corner of your document you can see two items:

- **Text Cursor:** A blinking vertical line. Whenever you type text, Word places the text at the text cursor's location. Think of the cursor as a 'you are here' indicator, telling you where you are in a document.
- **Paragraph Mark:** Every new Word document contains one of these (it looks like a backwards letter P). Whenever you press the ENTER key to begin a new paragraph, Word inserts another one at that point. The paragraph mark appears on the screen only and not on printouts.

Paragraph Mark

Every document has at least one paragraph mark. Word displays another one each time you press the ENTER key.

Show/Hide Paragraph Mark button

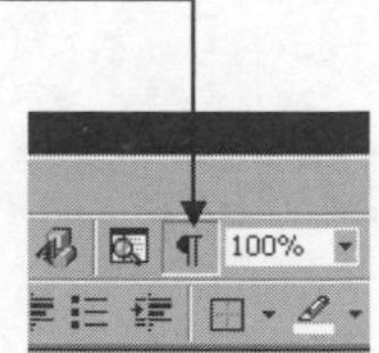

What? No Paragraph Mark?

If Word does not display the paragraph mark in your document, click on the Show/Hide Paragraph Mark button at the top of the screen, near the top-right corner of your Word window.

Actions You Need to Know

Here are the four basic operations in Word that you need to know:

- Typing text
- Editing (changing) text you previously typed
- Using the SHIFT key to type upper-case (capital) letters
- Using the ENTER key to type new paragraph marks

You will practise each one in the following four Exercises.

Exercise 3.1: Typing Text in Word

7·dwarfs¶

1) Type the following number: 7
2) Press the SPACEBAR. Word displays a dot on the screen. This is Word's way of telling that you have typed a space. Word will not print the dot.
3) Type the following six letters: dwarfs

That's it. Congratulations! You have typed your first text in Word.

Exercise 3.2: Editing Previously Typed Text

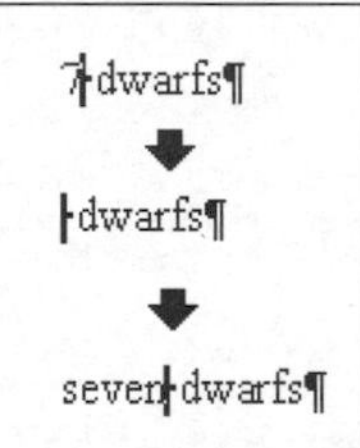

Often you will want to change – or, perhaps, remove completely – text that you have typed. This is called editing.

1) Using the mouse, click to the right of the 7.
2) Press the BACKSPACE key. (You will find it directly above the ENTER key.)
3) Type the following word: seven

You have completed the editing Exercise.

Exercise 3.3: Using the SHIFT Key

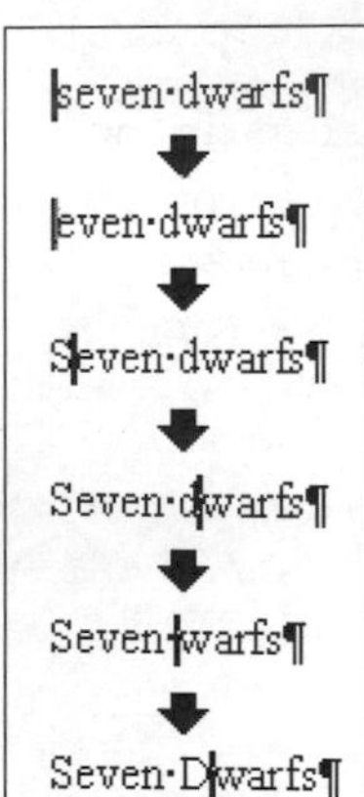

1) Click to the left of the letter s in seven.
2) Press the DELETE key to delete the letter s.
3) Hold down the SHIFT key and type the letter s. Word displays an upper-case S.
4) Move the cursor to the right of the letter d in dwarfs.
5) Press the BACKSPACE key to delete the letter d.
6) Hold down the SHIFT key and type the letter d. Word displays an upper-case D.

Well done! Another Exercise completed.

John¶
Paul¶
George¶
Ringo¶

Exercise 3.4: Using ENTER to Type New Paragraph Marks

1) Now you will use the ENTER key to end one paragraph and begin another.
2) Click to the right of the word Dwarfs, and press ENTER. This creates a new paragraph. Word places the cursor at the start of a new line.
3) Type: John.
4) Press ENTER.
5) Type: Paul.
6) Press ENTER.
7) Type George.
8) Press ENTER.
9) Type Ringo.

You will not need this text for future Exercises. So delete it as follows:

10) Click to the right of the word Ringo.
11) Press and hold down the BACKSPACE key until Word has removed all the text from the document.

Keys You Need to Know

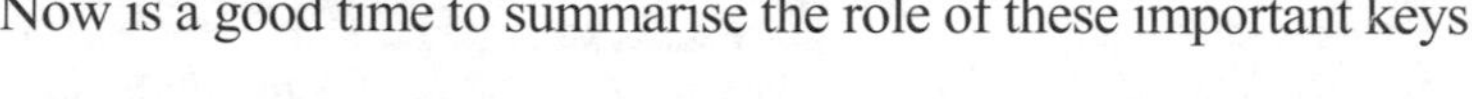

Now is a good time to summarise the role of these important keys:

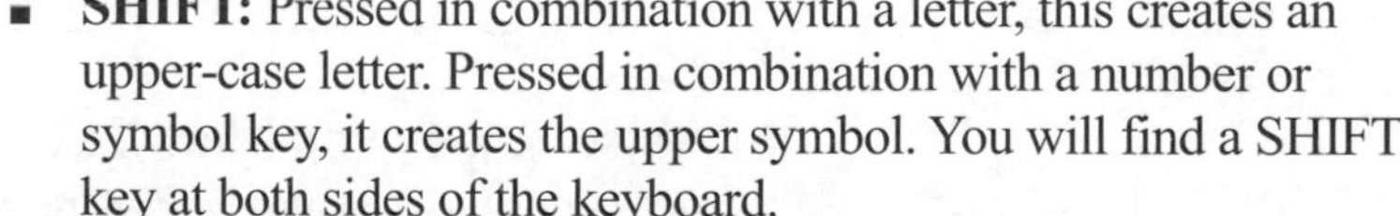

- **SHIFT:** Pressed in combination with a letter, this creates an upper-case letter. Pressed in combination with a number or symbol key, it creates the upper symbol. You will find a SHIFT key at both sides of the keyboard.

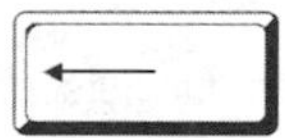

- **BACKSPACE:** Deletes the character to the *left* of the cursor. You will find the BACKSPACE key at the top-right of the keyboard, just above the ENTER key.

- **DELETE:** Deletes the character to the *right* of the cursor. You will find the DELETE key in a group of six keys to the right of the ENTER key.

- **ARROW:** Rather than use the mouse to move the cursor around your document, you can press any of the four ARROW keys, located to the right of the ENTER key. You may find this method faster than moving and clicking the mouse, because you need not take either hand away from the keyboard.

Typing a Letter

Now you are ready to type a longer piece of text, a letter.

Exercise 3.5: Typing a Paragraph of a Letter

1) Type the following text:

   I am writing to you in relation to our annual Sale of Work which will take place in our local Scout Hall 17 October next.

   Your screen should look as follows.

I·am·writing·to·you·in·relation·to·our·annual·Sale·of·Work·which·will·take·place·in·our·local·Scout·Hall·on·17·October·next.¶

Notice how Word moved the cursor to the beginning of the next line when the text you were typing reached the right-hand edge of the page.

On an old-style typewriter, you would have needed to press the ENTER (also called RETURN) key to move down to the next line. Word does this for you automatically. This feature is called wrap around, and Word is said to 'wrap' the text to a new line once the previous line is full.

Wrap Around

Word's automatic moving of the cursor to the beginning of a new line when the text reaches the end of the previous one.

Exercise 3.6: Typing More Text in Your Letter

In this Exercise, you will type your address at the top of the letter, type more text in the letter, and type your name at the bottom.

Click here

1) Click at the beginning of the first line, so that the cursor is just to the left of the letter I.

I·am·writing·to·you·in·relation·to·our·annual·Sale·of·Work·which·will·take·place·in·our·local·Scout·Hall·on·17·October·next.¶

2) Press the ENTER key to create a new line, and then the UP ARROW key to position the cursor at the start of the new line.
3) Type the following:
   24 Main Street,
4) Press ENTER and then type the following:
   Anytown.
5) Press ENTER and then type the following:
   333444

6) Press ENTER three times. Then type the following:
   Dear Ms Smith,

7) Press ENTER. Then click at the end of the last line, so that the cursor is just to the right of the full stop and to the left of the paragraph mark.

I·am·writing·to·you·in·relation·to·our·annual·Sale·of·Work·which·will·take·place·in·our·local·Scout·Hall·on·17·October·next.¶

Click here

8) Press ENTER twice. Then type the following:

   In previous years your company was kind enough to donate a prize for our wheel of fortune.

9) Press ENTER twice. Then type the following:

   Could we ask you to be as generous again this year?

The HYPHEN key (left of the EQUALS key)

10) Press ENTER twice. Then hold down the SHIFT key and press the HYPHEN key about twenty times. (The HYPHEN key is the second key to the left of the BACKSPACE key.)

    Release the SHIFT key. When you print the letter, you can write your signature on the line created by the repeated pressing of the hyphen.

11) Press ENTER and type the following:

    Ken Bloggs

That's it. You have completed the Exercise.

No letter is complete without a date. In Exercise 3.7 you will discover how you can use Word to insert today's date in a letter or other document.

Click here

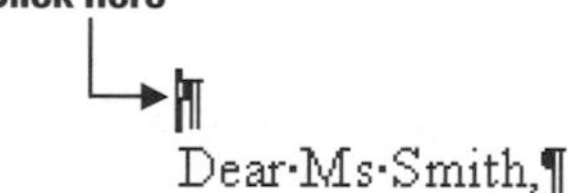

Exercise 3.7: Entering a Date

1) Click the paragraph mark on the empty line above 'Dear Ms Smith'.

2) Choose **Insert | Date and Time**.

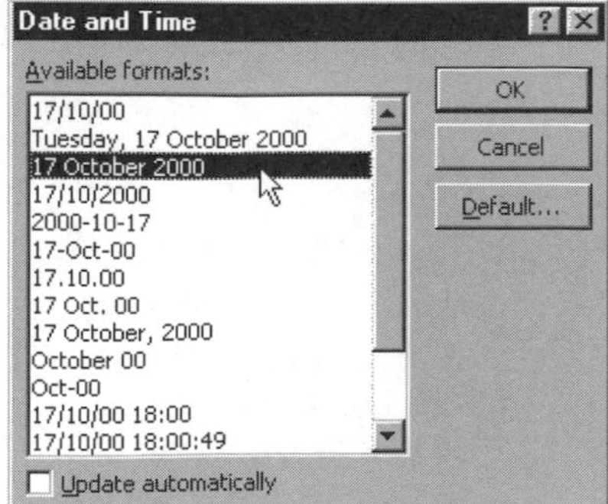

3) Word displays a dialog box that shows today's date in a variety of formats.

   Select the date format you want, and click **OK**. This inserts the date in your letter, and closes the dialog box.

4) Press ENTER twice to create two empty lines after the inserted date and before the 'Dear Ms Smith'.

Well done. You have typed your first letter in Word. It should look as shown below.

24·Main·Street,¶

Anytown.¶

333444¶

¶

17·October·2000¶

¶

¶

Dear·Ms·Smith,¶

¶

I·am·writing·to·you·in·relation·to·our·annual·Sale·of·Work·which·will·take·place·in·our·local· Scout·Hall·on·17·October·next.¶

¶

In·previous·years·your·company·was·kind·enough·to·donate·a·prize·for·our·wheel·of·fortune.¶

¶

Could·we·ask·you·to·be·as·generous·again·this·year?¶

¶

______________________¶

Ken·Bloggs¶

Moving Text with the TAB Key

There is a problem with your letter. The address, phone number and date at the top are in the wrong position. You need to move them to the right.

In Exercise 3.8 you learn how to use the TAB key to change the position of text on the page.

Click here

Exercise 3.8: Using the TAB Key

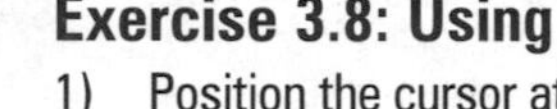

1) Position the cursor at the top-left of the page, just to the left of the 2.

|24·Main·Street,¶

Anytown.¶

333444¶

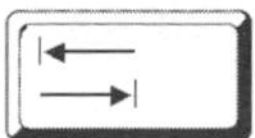

TAB key

2) Press the TAB key eight times. Word moves all text between the cursor and the paragraph mark to the right.

3) Repeat step 2) for the second address line, the phone number line, and the date line. Your screen should look as shown below.

```
→   →   →   →   →   →   →   →   24·Main·Street,¶
→   →   →   →   →   →   →   →   Anytown.¶
→   →   →   →   →   →   →   →   333444¶
¶
→   →   →   →   →   →   →   →   17·October·2000¶
¶
¶
Dear·Ms·Smith,¶
```

Non-Printing Characters and Wavy Underlines

Each time you press the TAB key, Word inserts an arrow symbol on the screen. Like the paragraph mark that indicates a paragraph ending, and the dot between words that represents a blank space, the tab symbol is a non-printing character.

Non-Printing Characters

Symbols that Word displays on the screen to help you type and edit your document, but that are not printed.

Ken·Bloggs¶

Wavy underlines indicate possible spelling or grammar problems

Depending on how Word is set up on your computer, you may see green and/or red wavy underlines beneath certain words or phrases. These have to do with Word's spell- and grammar-checking features, which are explained in Section 3.3. Until then, ignore them.

Printing Your Letter

Your letter is ready to be printed out. Choose **File | Print**. If your printer is set up correctly all you need to do is click **OK** on the Print dialog box. You will learn more about printing in Section 3.3.

Word's Toolbars

Above the document window you can see Word's two main toolbars: the Standard Toolbar and the Formatting Toolbar.

The Standard Toolbar includes buttons for managing files – that is, Word documents – and for working with tables.

Word's Standard Toolbar

The Formatting Toolbar includes buttons for changing the appearance of text, and for inserting bullets.

Word's Formatting Toolbar

Rather than introduce all these buttons at once, we will explain each one as it becomes relevant through this ECDL Word Processing Module.

Word's Undo Feature

Undo button

Redo Button

Enter the wrong text? Press the wrong key? Word's Undo feature enables you to reverse your most recent typing or editing action if it has produced unwanted results:

- Choose **Edit | Undo** or click the Undo button on the Standard Toolbar.

Pressing Undo repeatedly reverses your last series of actions. To view a list of recent actions that you can undo, click the arrow at the right of the Undo button. If you undo an action and then change your mind, click the Redo button (to the right of the Undo button).

Working with Word Documents

A Word document is a file containing text (and sometimes graphics too). The file names of Word documents end in .doc. This helps you to distinguish Word files from other file types.

Saving Your Document

Save button

In Word, as in other applications, always save your work as you go along. Don't wait until you are finished! To save a document:

- Choose **File | Save** or click the Save button on the Standard Toolbar.

The first time you save a document file, Word asks you to give the file a name. The following Exercise shows you how.

Exercise 3.9: Saving and Naming a New Document

1) Choose **File | Save**. Word displays a dialog box similar to the one shown.

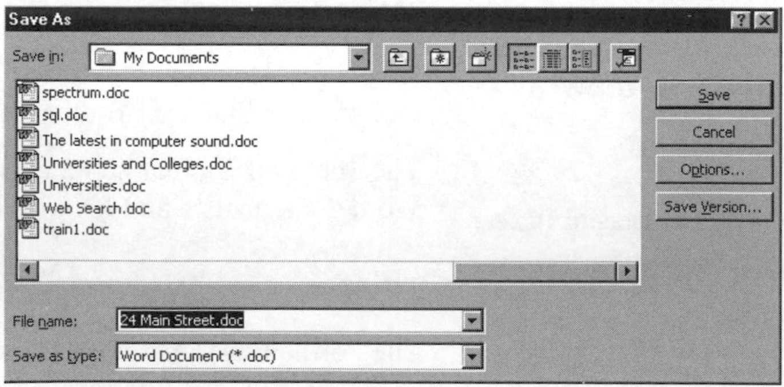

2) By default, Word suggests the first words of your document as the file name. Replace this file name with something that you will find easier to remember and recognise – such as your initials. If your name is Ken Bloggs, for example, name the document KBletter.doc. Click the **Save** button.

Word adds the file name extension of .doc automatically. You need not type it.

Creating a New Document

New button

To create a new Word file:

- Choose **File** | **New**.
  -or-
  Click the New button on the Standard Toolbar.

Opening an Existing Document

Open button

To open an existing Word file:

- Choose **File** | **Open**.
  -or-
  Click the Open button on the Standard Toolbar. Select the file you want from the dialog box.

Closing a Document

To close a Word document:

- Choose **File** | **Close** or click the Close button on the document window.

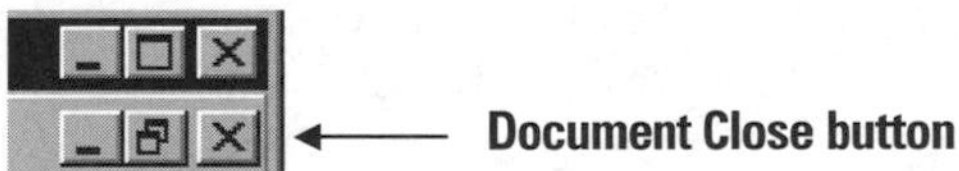

If you have made changes to your document since you last saved it, Word prompts you to save the changes before it closes the file.

Quitting Word

To leave Word:

- Choose **File** | **Exit** or click the Close button on the Word window.

If you have left open any files containing unsaved work, Word prompts you to save them.

Online Help

Like Excel, Access, PowerPoint and other Microsoft applications, Word offers a searchable online help system.

- The word 'help' means that the information is there to assist you understand and use the application.
- The word 'online' means that the material is presented on the computer screen rather than as a traditional printed manual.

You can search through and read online help in two ways: from the **Help** menu, or from dialog boxes.

Using Help Menu Options

Choose **Help | Contents and Index** to display the three tabs of the Help Topics dialog box. These are explained below.

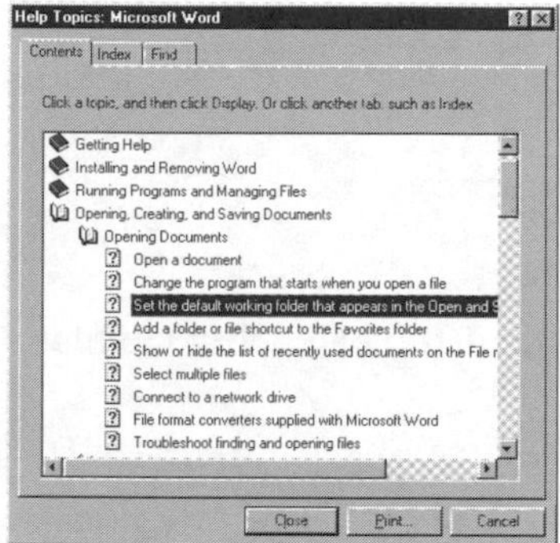

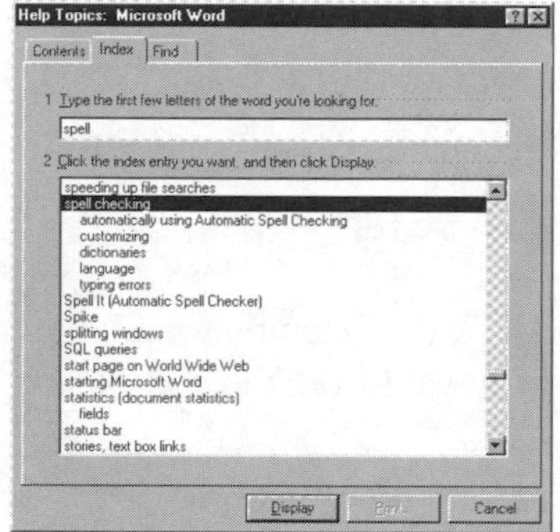

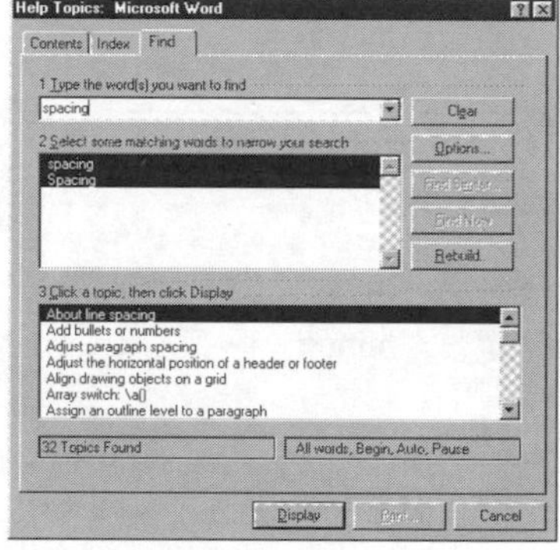

Contents Tab

This offers short descriptions of Word's main features.

Where you see a heading with a book symbol, double-click to view the related sub-headings.

Double-click on a question-mark symbol to read the help text.

Click a Show me arrow for Word to demonstrate how to perform a particular action.

Click a double arrow to view step-by-step instructions.

Index Tab

Reading the material displayed on this tab is like looking through the index of a printed book.

Just type the first letters of the word or phrase you are interested in.

Word responds by displaying all matches from the online help in the lower half of the dialog box.

When you find the index entry that you are looking for, click the **Display** button.

Find Tab

Can't find what you are looking for in the Contents or Index tabs? Try this tab.

When you type a word or phrase, Word performs a deeper search of the online help.

Word also displays some related words to help you narrow your search.

When you find the item you are looking for, double-click on it to display it.

As you search through and read online help topics, you will see the following buttons at the top of the online help window:

- **Help Topics:** Click this to return to the Contents tab.
- **Back:** Click this to return to the previous help topic.
- **Options:** Click this to perform such actions as copying the online help text to a document, or printing it on your printer.

Using Help from Dialog Boxes

You can also access online help directly from a dialog box, as Exercise 3.10 demonstrates.

Exercise 3.10: Using Online Help in a Dialog Box

1) Choose **Edit | Find** to display the Find and Replace dialog box.

2) Click on the question mark symbol near the top-right of the dialog box. Word displays a question mark to the right of the cursor.

3) Move the mouse down and right, and click anywhere in the Find what: box.

Word displays online help text telling you about the purpose of the Find what: box.

4) Click anywhere on the Word window to remove the online help text.

5) Practise this Exercise with other dialog boxes in Word.

When finished, you can close your letter document and close Microsoft Word. You have now completed this Section 3.1 of the ECDL Word-Processing Module.

Section Summary: So Now You Know

A Word *document* is a file containing text (and sometimes graphics too). Every new Word document contains a *text cursor*. Whenever you type text, Word places the text at the text cursor's location. You can move the text cursor with the mouse or with the ARROW keys.

Every new document also contains a *paragraph mark*. Whenever you press the ENTER key to type a new paragraph of text or insert a blank line, Word inserts another paragraph mark at that point.

You can edit text with the following two keys:

- BACKSPACE: Removes text to the *left* of the text cursor
- DELETE: Removes text to the *right* of the text cursor

Press the SHIFT key in combination with a letter, number or symbol key to type an *upper-case* (capital) character or symbol.

Press the TAB key repeatedly to move text to the right. When typing a letter, for example, use TAB to position the address and related details at the top-right of the letter.

Word's *Insert Date* feature inserts the current date in a document. You can choose from a wide range of date formats.

Word's *non-printing characters*, such as a single dot to represent a space, do not appear on printouts. They are displayed on the screen only as a guide to typing and editing.

Word's *Undo* feature enables you to reverse your most recent typing or editing actions if they have produced unwanted results.

In Word, as in other applications, always save your work as you go along. The first time you save a document file, Word prompts you to give it a *file name*. Word automatically adds the file name extension *.doc* to all saved documents.

Word offers a searchable *online help* system that you can access in two ways: from the Help menu, and from the question-mark button at the top-right of individual dialog boxes.

Section 3.2: Formatting, Positioning and Copying Text

In This Section

In addition to typing and editing text, you can use a word processor to:

- Change the *appearance* of the text. This is called formatting. It includes such actions as making text bolder (heavier), placing a line under it, and putting it in italics. You can also change the text font and font size, format text as bullets, and apply shading (coloured backgrounds) and borders to text.
- Change the *position* of text on the page. You have already learnt how to reposition text using the TAB key. Now you will discover two other methods: alignment and indenting.

Also in this Section you will learn how to copy text within and between documents, and how to insert symbols and special characters.

New Skills

At the end of this Section you should be able to:

- Select text
- Format text (bold, italic and underline)
- Copy, cut and paste text
- Indent text from the left and right page margins
- Align text (left, right, centre and justified)
- Create text bullets
- Explain fonts and font sizes, and super- and subscripts
- Add borders and shading to text
- Use Word's Zoom feature to enlarge and reduce the document display
- Save a Word document to a diskette
- Insert symbols and special characters
- Use Word's Format Painter feature to copy formatting

New Words

At the end of this Section you should be able to explain the following terms:

- Select
- Bulleted text
- Clipboard
- Font
- Indent
- Superscript
- Alignment
- Subscript
- Format Painter

Selecting Text

Typically, when you want to format or position some text, it is only a particular character, word, group of words or paragraph that you want to change.

You tell Word which part of the document you want to change by first selecting that text. Selecting a piece of text is sometimes called highlighting that text.

Selected text

In·previous·years·your·company·was·kind·enough·to·donate·a·prize·for·our·wheel·of·fortune.¶

When you select text, Word displays that text in reverse (white text on black background), rather like the negative of a photograph.

Selecting Text

Highlighting a piece of text in order to perform an action on it such as formatting or alignment.

Formatting and alignment are just two of the actions that you will learn how to perform on selected text. In later Sections, you will learn how to find and replace, and spell-check selected text.

To select text within a Word document, first position the mouse at the beginning of the text that you want to select:

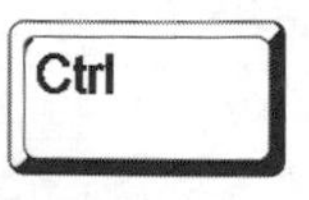

CTRL (Control) key

- To select text on a single line, drag the mouse to the right until you have selected the characters or words.
- To select a sentence or other piece of text that is on more than a single line, drag the mouse to the right and down the page.
- To select your whole document, hold down the CTRL key and click anywhere in the left margin.

Exercise 3.11: Selecting Text

In this Exercise you will learn how to select text – characters, words sentences and paragraphs.

Dear·Ms·Smith,¶

1) Open Word, and open the letter you saved in Exercise 3.9 of Section 3.1.
2) Position the cursor to the left of the letter D in Dear Ms Smith.
3) Drag the mouse to the right until you have selected the letter D. Release the mouse button.

Dear·Ms·Smith,¶

   You have learned how to select a single character. Now click anywhere on the page to deselect the letter D. Deselecting a piece of text does not remove the text; it just means that it is no longer selected.

Dear·Ms·Smith,¶

4) Again, position the mouse to the left of the letter D, but this time keep dragging with the mouse until you have selected the entire word Dear.

   Release the mouse button.

5) Finally, position the mouse to the left of the letter D. Now drag the mouse down and right until you have selected the first paragraph of the letter.

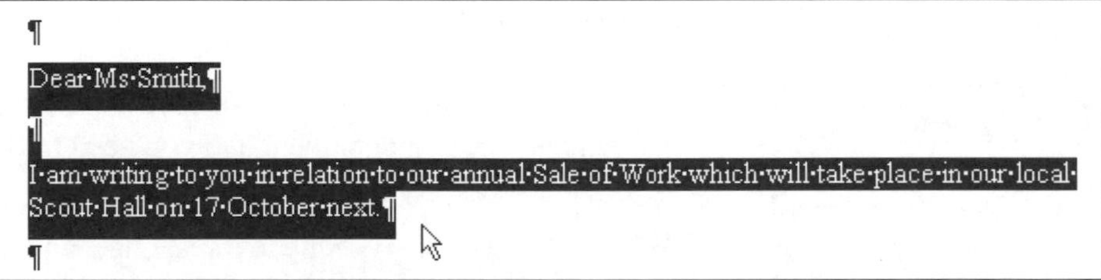

   You have learned how to select several lines of text. Click anywhere outside the selected area to deselect it.

That completes the Exercise. But practise your text-selection skills by clicking at any point in your document, and dragging the mouse in various directions.

Formatting Text

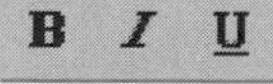

Format buttons

Word's most commonly used formatting features are:

- **Bold**: Heavy black text, often used for headings
- *Italic*: Slanted text, often used for emphasis or foreign words
- Underline: A single line under the text, often used in legal documents and beneath signatures on letters

You will find the relevant buttons on the Formatting Toolbar. In the next Exercises you will learn how to apply the bold and italic formats.

Exercise 3.12: Applying the Bold Format

1) Place the cursor at the start of the first line of the address.
2) Drag right and down with the mouse until you have selected the two address lines and the phone number.
3) Click the Bold button or press CTRL+b (hold down CTRL and type b).
4) Deselect the lines by clicking on any other area of the document.

Applying the bold format

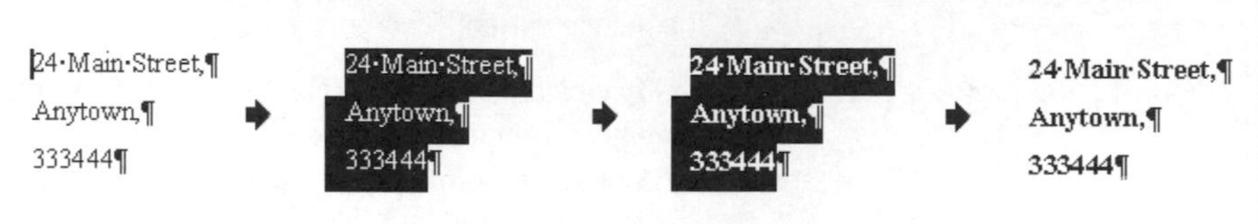

Exercise 3.13: Applying the Italic Format

1) Place the cursor at the start of the name, Ken Bloggs.
2) Drag right until you have selected the name.
3) Click the Italic button or press CTRL+i.
4) Deselect the name by clicking on any other area of the document.

Well done. Save your letter.

Copying and Pasting Text

Suppose you want to use the same text – words or paragraphs – more than once in a document. Do you need to retype it each time that you need it? No.

With Word, you can type the text just once, and then insert it as many times as you need. This is a two-step process:

- **Copy**: You select and then *copy* the text to the Clipboard, a temporary holding area.
- **Paste**: You insert or *paste* the text from the Clipboard into a different part of the same document, or even a different document.

Clipboard

A temporary storage area to which you can copy text (or graphics). You can paste to any location within the same or different documents.

Exercise 3.14: Copying and Pasting Text within a Document

1) Select the second paragraph of your letter.

In·previous·years·your·company·was·kind·enough·to·donate·a·prize·for·our·wheel·of·fortune.¶

Copy button

2) Click the Copy button on the Standard Toolbar, or choose **Edit | Copy**.

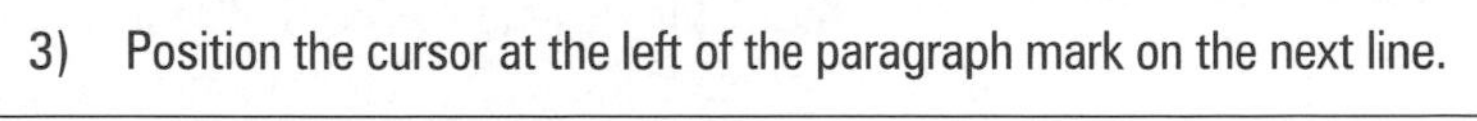

3) Position the cursor at the left of the paragraph mark on the next line.

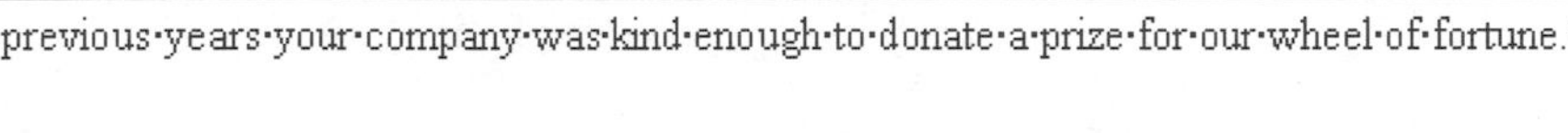

Paste button

4) Click the Paste button on the Standard Toolbar, or choose **Edit | Paste**

In·previous·years·your·company·was·kind·enough·to·donate·a·prize·for·our·wheel·of·fortune.¶
In·previous·years·your·company·was·kind·enough·to·donate·a·prize·for·our·wheel·of·fortune.¶

Select the line that you have pasted from the Clipboard, and press the DELETE key. You will not need it again.

About the Clipboard

Four points you should remember about the Clipboard:

- The Clipboard is temporary. Turn off your computer and the Clipboard contents are deleted.
- The same Clipboard is available to all Windows applications. For example, you can copy from Excel and paste into Word.
- The Clipboard can hold only a single, copied item at a time. If you copy a second piece of text, the second overwrites the first.
- Text stays in the Clipboard after you paste from it, so you can paste the same piece of text into as many locations as you need.

Exercise 3.15: Copying and Pasting Text between Documents

The line you copied in Exercise 3.14 is still in the Clipboard. In this Exercise you will copy it to a different document.

New button

1) Click the New button to create a new, blank Word document.
2) Word places the cursor at the beginning of the document.
3) Click the Paste button on the Standard Toolbar, or choose **Edit | Paste**.
4) Choose **File | Close** to close the new document. When Word asks you whether you want to save the new file, click **No**.

When you have more than one Word document open at a time, you can switch between them by choosing **Window | <document name>**.

Cutting and Pasting Text

Sometimes, you may want to remove text from one part of a document and place it in a different part.

Rather than deleting the text and then retyping it elsewhere, Word allows you to move the text by cutting it from its current location and pasting it to the new location.

Cut-and-paste differs from copy-and-paste in that Word removes the cut text, whereas copied text remains in its original location. You can cut selected text using the Cut button on the Standard Toolbar by choosing **Edit | Cut**.

Keyboard Shortcuts

You may find it quicker to use Word's keyboard shortcuts for copy, cut and paste operations as you need not take either hand away from the keyboard:

- To copy, press CTRL+c.
- To cut, press CTRL+x.
- To paste, press CTRL+v.

You can also right-click on your document to get a pop-up menu displaying the available commands for copying, cutting or pasting.

Formatted Documents

All Word documents are formatted, but some are more formatted than others. In the remainder of this Section you will discover the Word tools that enable you to design a highly formatted poster: indents, alignment, bullets, fonts, borders and shading.

Left and Right Indents

The term indent means 'in from the margin'. Word's indenting feature lets you push a paragraph of text a specified distance in from the left margin, right margin, or both.

To indent a selected paragraph, choose **Format | Paragraph**, and enter the required left and/or right distances on the Indents and Spacing tab of the Paragraph dialog box.

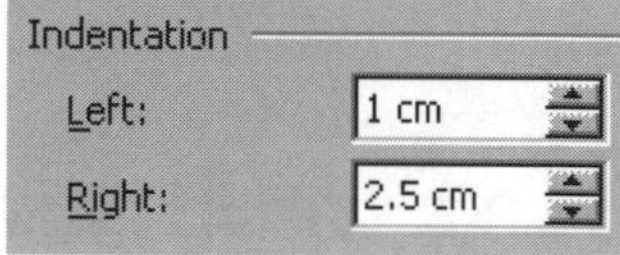

In long documents, you may sometimes see indenting used as a way of attracting attention to a particular part of the text. Here is an example that combines a left and right indent with italics:

> *Another successful year has seen revenues rise by 35% and profits by 47.5%. Our company is well placed to face the challenges of the future.*

Indent

The positioning of a paragraph of text a specified distance in from the left and/or right margin.

Aligning Text

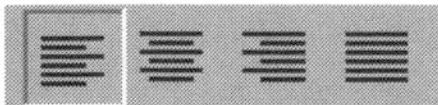

Alignment buttons

To align text means to 'line up' the text in a particular horizontal (left-right) way. Word gives you four choices:

- **Left:** The default, used for letters and business documents. Left-aligned text is generally the easiest to read.
- **Centre:** Places the text between the left and right margins. Used for headings.
- **Right:** Aligns the text against the right-hand margin of the page. Used by graphic designers for decorative purposes.
- **Justify:** Both left and right aligned at the same time! Used for narrow columns of text in newspapers and magazines.

Do not use justification when your text is in a single column across the width of the page (such as in letters), because it makes the text more difficult to read.

You can only align paragraphs. You cannot align selected characters or words within a paragraph.

To align a single paragraph, you don't need to select the text. You need only to position the cursor anywhere within the paragraph. The four alignment buttons are on the Formatting Toolbar.

Alignment

The horizontal positioning of lines in a paragraph in relation to one another. They can share a common centre-point, begin at the same point on the left, end at the same point on the right, or begin and end at the same points.

Bullets and Numbered Lists

Bullets button

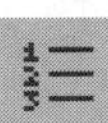

Numbering button

Lists are good ways to communicate a series of short statements or instructions. Lists are of two types:

- **Bulleted:** Used when the reading order is not critical. The bullet character is typically a dot, square, diamond, line or arrow. To make a bulleted list, select the paragraphs and click the Bullets button on the Formatting Toolbar.
- **Numbered:** Used when the order of reading is important. For example, in directions and instructions. Each item is assigned a sequentially increasing number. To make a numbered list,

select the paragraphs and click the Numbering button on the Formatting Toolbar.

You can also make lists by choosing **Format | Bullets and Numbering**. Word offers you a wide range of options, such as the style of bullet or number character, and the distance between the bullet or number character and the bulleted or numbered text.

Bulleted and Numbered Lists
A list of short statements. The statements can be bulleted (preceded by a dot or other symbol) or numbered (preceded by a sequentially increasing number).

Exercises 3.16, 3.17 and 3.18 take you through the steps of applying numbering and bullets to selected text.

Exercise 3.16: Applying Numbering to Text

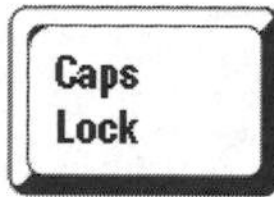

CAPS LOCK key

1) Open a new document, press the CAPS LOCK key once, type the following text, and press ENTER twice:

   MY FAVOURITE FRUIT

   (The CAPS LOCK key is to the left of the letter 'a' key. After you press it, every letter you type is displayed as a capital letter.)

2) Press the CAPS LOCK key again to turn off capitals.
3) Select the text by clicking in front of the 'M' in My, and dragging to the right with the mouse.

MY·FAVOURITE·FRUIT¶ MY·FAVOURITE·FRUIT¶

Click in front of the text... and drag to the right with the mouse.

4) Click the Underline button on the Formatting Toolbar to underline the selected text.
5) Click the paragraph mark right of the text, and press ENTER twice to create two new lines.
6) Type the following six fruit names, pressing ENTER after each one: Apples, Bananas, Grapes, Kiwis, Oranges and Peaches. Your text should look as shown on the right.

MY·FAVOURITE·FRUIT¶
¶
Apples¶
Bananas¶
Grapes¶
Kiwis¶
Oranges¶
Peaches¶

7) Select the six fruit names by clicking in front of the 'A' in Apples, and then dragging right and down with the mouse until you reach the final paragraph mark.

8) Click the Numbering button on the Formatting Toolbar to applying numbering to the selected text.

9) Click anywhere in your document outside the selected area to deselect the text. Your text should now look as shown on the right.

   (The arrows after the numbers are non-printing characters.)

MY·FAVOURITE·FRUIT¶
¶
1.→Apples¶
2.→Bananas¶
3.→Grapes¶
4.→Kiwis¶
5.→Oranges¶
6.→Peaches¶

10) Choose **File | Save** or press CTRL+s to save your document. If your initials are KB, for example, name it KBList.doc. Leave the document open.

In Exercise 3.17 you will replace the numbers in Exercise 3.16 with bullets.

Exercise 3.17: Applying Bullets to Text

1) Select the list of six fruit names that you entered in Exercise 3.16.

   (Notice that you cannot select the numbers. Why? Because they are not entered text – they are generated automatically by Word.)

2) Click the Bullets button on the Formatting Toolbar. Word replaces the numbers with bullets.

3) Choose **Format | Bullets and Numbering**, select the Bullets tab, and click **Customize**.

4) In the Text position area, increase the value in the Indent at: box from 0.63 cm (the default) to 1 cm, and click **OK**.

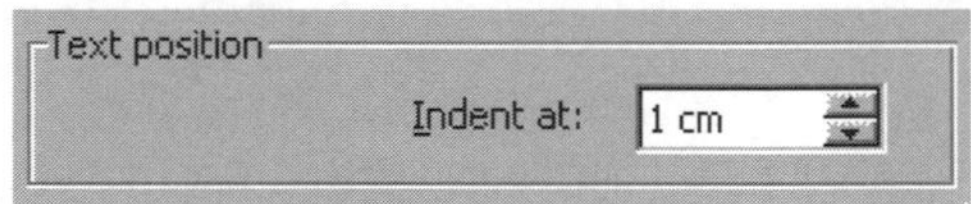

5) Click anywhere in your document outside the selected area to deselect the text.

   Your text should now look as shown on the right.

   (The arrows after the bullets are non-printing characters.)

MY·FAVOURITE·FRUIT¶
¶
• → Apples¶
• → Bananas¶
• → Grapes¶
• → Kiwis¶
• → Oranges¶
• → Peaches¶

Sometimes you want to apply bullets or numbering only to certain items in a list, and not to others. Exercise 3.18 provides an example.

Exercise 3.18: Applying Bullets to Selected Items in a List

1) Click at the paragraph mark after the word Kiwis, and press ENTER to create a new line. Notice that Word places a bullet in front of the line.

2) Type the following:

   (my absolute favourite)

3) You don't want this new line to have a bullet character in front of it.

4) Select the new line and click the Bullets button on the Formatting Toolbar. Word removes the bullet format from the selected line.

5) Your final task is to align the new line with the other, bulleted lines.

6) With the new line still selected, choose **Format | Paragraph**, type a Left: indent of 1 cm, and click **OK**.

7) Click anywhere in your document outside the selected line to deselect it. Your text should now look as shown on the right.

MY·FAVOURITE·FRUIT¶
¶
• → Apples¶
• → Bananas¶
• → Grapes¶
• → Kiwis¶
(my·absolute·favourite)¶
• → Oranges¶
• → Peaches¶

This completes the bullets and numbering exercises. Save and close your document.

Fonts

Viewing the fonts on your computer

A font or typeface is a particular style of text. What fonts are installed on your computer? Click the arrow on the drop-down Font box on the Formatting Toolbar to see.

Do you need to remember the names and characteristics of all these fonts? No. You need remember only two points about fonts:

- There are really just two kinds (families) of fonts: serif and sans serif. Sans serif just means without serifs.
- Serif fonts are good for long paragraphs of text (what is called body text). Sans serif fonts are good for short pieces of text such as headlines, headers, captions and maybe bulleted text.

You can recognise which family a font belongs to by asking: do its characters have serifs (tails or squiggles) at their edges?

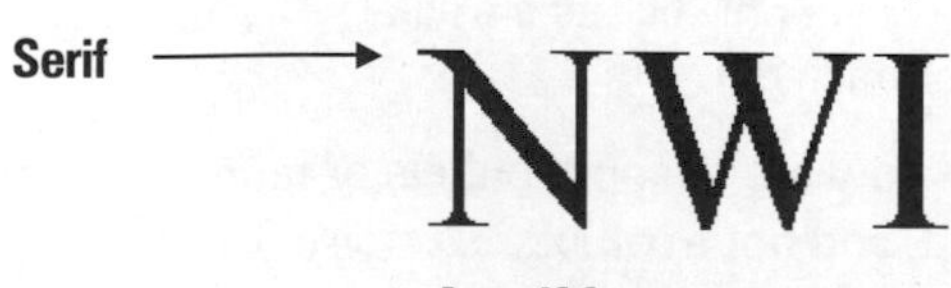

A serif font

Sans serif font

Serif Fonts

Word's default font is a serif font called Times New Roman. It takes its name from *The Times* newspaper of London, where it was developed in the 1930s.

Other popular serif fonts include Garamond and Century Schoolbook:

- This text is written in a font named Garamond.
- This text is written in a font named Century Schoolbook.

Sans Serif Fonts

Word's default sans serif font is Arial. It is based on another font, Helvetica, which is one of the most widely-used fonts in the world.

Other common sans serif fonts include Futura and Avant Garde:

- This text is written in a font named Futura.
- This text is written in a font named Avant Garde.

Font

A typeface: a particular style of text. The two main font families are serif and sans serif.

Font Sizes

Font size is measured in a non-metric unit called the point, with approximately 72 points equal to one inch.

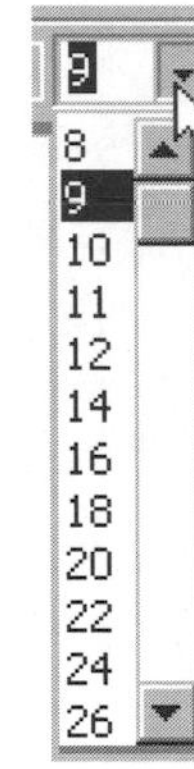

- For the body text of letters or longer business documents such as reports, 10, 11 or 12 points is a good choice. For headings, use larger font sizes in the range 14 to 28 points.
- Headers, footers, endnotes, footnotes and captions are often in 8 or 9 point font size.

To change the font size of selected text, click the required font size from the Font Size drop-down list box on the Formatting Toolbar.

Font Properties

Word's **Format | Font** dialog box enables you to apply a number of properties to fonts: style, effects, colour and spacing.

Font Style

You have already applied these options using the Bold and Italic buttons on the Formatting Toolbar.

Underline

A lot of choices here. Single is both the simplest and most commonly used. It is also the type of underline applied with the Underline button on the Formatting Toolbar.

Font Colour

Have you a colour printer? Then you may want to select a text colour other than Auto. Even without a colour printer, you may want to print your headings in grey.

What colour is Auto? Auto is black, unless the background is black or a dark grey, in which case Auto switches to white.

Font Effects

You can experiment with the various font effects by selecting any of the Effects check boxes and viewing the result in the Preview area at the bottom of the dialog box.

Effects

☐ Strikethrough	☐ Shadow	☐ Small caps
☐ Double strikethrough	☐ Outline	☐ All caps
☐ Superscript	☐ Emboss	☐ Hidden
☐ Subscript	☐ Engrave	

One important effect you need to know about is superscript.

This raises the selected text above the other text on the same line, and reduces its font size. It is used most commonly for mathematical symbols. For example: 2^2, x^8, 10^3.

Superscript

Text that is raised above other text on the same line and is reduced in font size. Commonly used in maths texts for indices.

The opposite of superscript is subscript. You will find subscripts used in typing chemical formulae, for example:

H_2SO_4

Subscript

Text that is lowered beneath other text on the same line and is reduced in font size. Commonly used in chemistry texts for formulae.

Font Spacing

You can expand or condense the space between characters by using the options on the Character Spacing tab of the Font dialog box.

Here is a line of text that is expanded by 1 point.

You may want to use this spacing effect for document headings.

Font Borders and Shading

You can brighten up your document with borders (decorative boxes) and shading (coloured backgrounds), using the options available with the **Format | Borders and Shading** command.

Word offers a range of border settings, with Box and Shadow the most common choices. Use the Preview section on the right of the dialog box to select the edges that you want bordered. The default is all four edges.

Pay attention to the Apply to: drop-down box at the bottom right. Your choice affects how Word draws the border. See the following example.

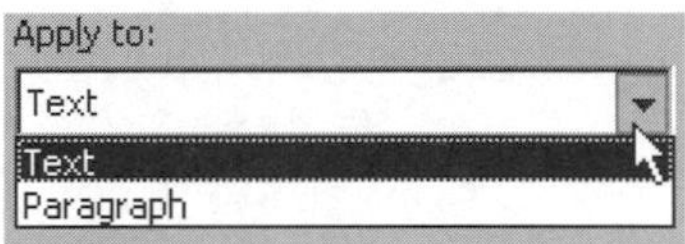

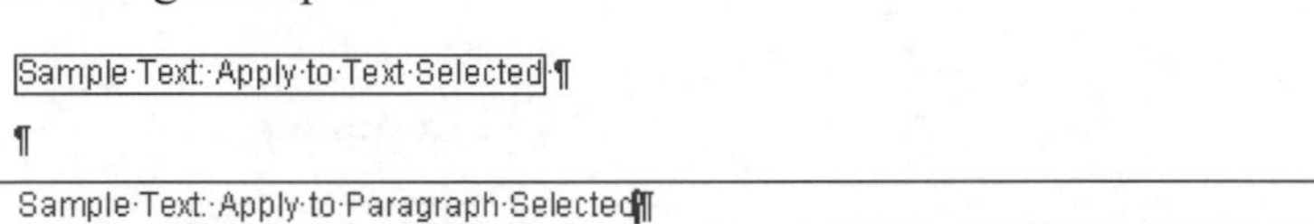

To apply shading, select the text, choose **Format | Borders and Shading**, and then select your required Fill, Style and Colour options from the Shading tab of the dialog box:

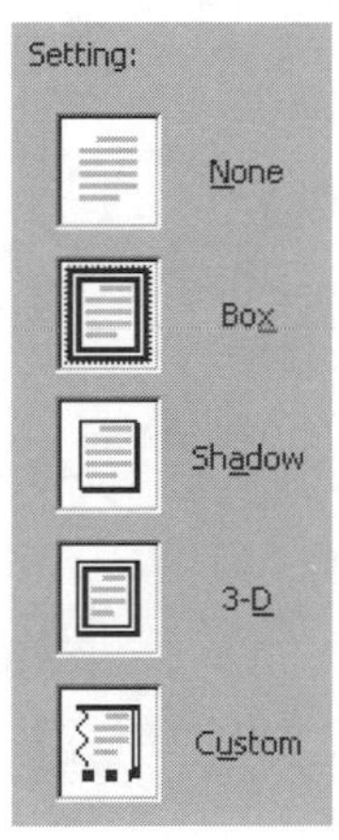

Border options

- **Fill:** This is the text background colour. If you are placing a grey shade behind black text, use 25% or less of grey. Otherwise, the text is difficult to read.
- **Style:** This allows you to apply tints (percentages of a colour) or patterns of a second colour (selected in the Colour box) on top of the selected Fill colour. Leave the Style: box at its default value of Clear if you do not want to apply a second colour.
- **Colour:** If you have selected a pattern in the Style box, select the colour of the lines and dots in the pattern here.

You can apply a border and shading to one or more characters, words or paragraphs. You need not apply both, but generally the border and shading features tend to be used together.

Exercise 3.19: Designing Your Poster

Practice makes perfect. In this Exercise you will apply the formatting (fonts, bullets, borders and shading) and text positioning (alignment and indenting) skills that you have learned in this Section. Your aim is to write and design a poster.

1) Open a new document and type the text shown.

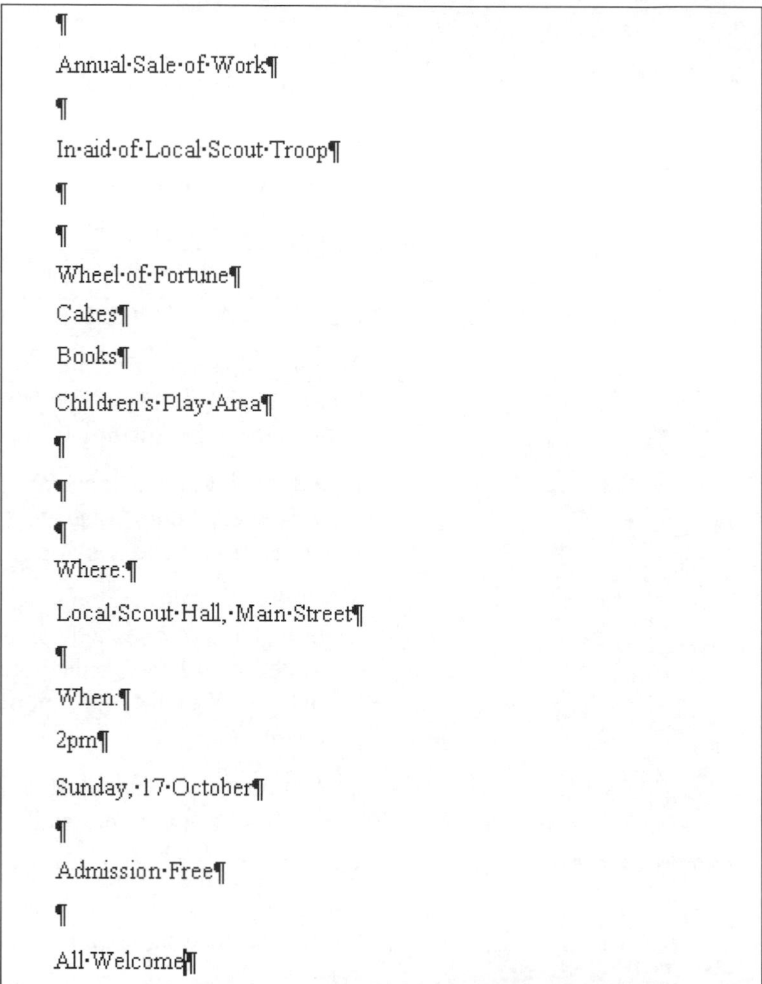

¶
Annual·Sale·of·Work¶
¶
In·aid·of·Local·Scout·Troop¶
¶
¶
Wheel·of·Fortune¶
Cakes¶
Books¶
Children's·Play·Area¶
¶
¶
¶
Where:¶
Local·Scout·Hall,·Main·Street¶
¶
When:¶
2pm¶
Sunday,·17·October¶
¶
Admission·Free¶
¶
All·Welcome¶

2) Select the text: Annual Sale of Work. Using **Format | Font**, make it Times New Roman, 28 point.

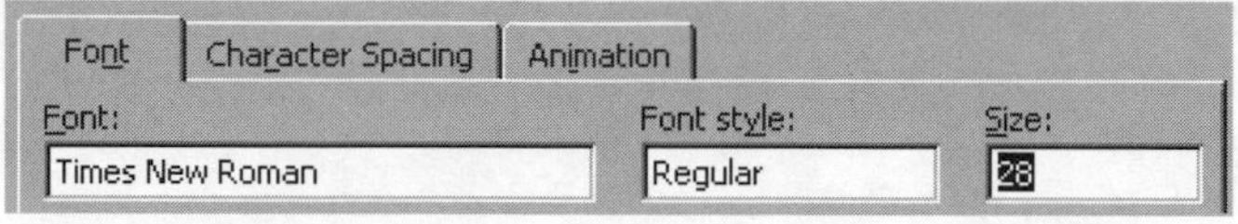

3) Choose **Format | Borders and Shading**, select a Setting: of Box and select Text as the Apply to: option.

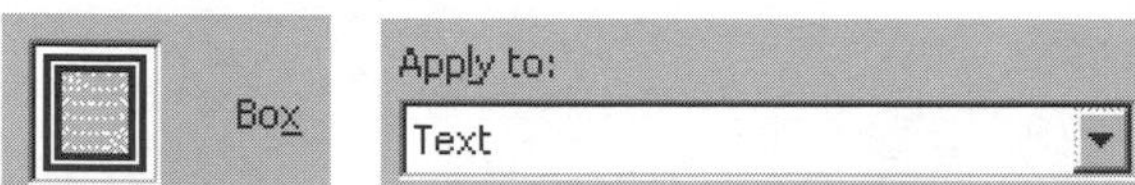

4) On the Shading tab, select a shading of 15% grey.

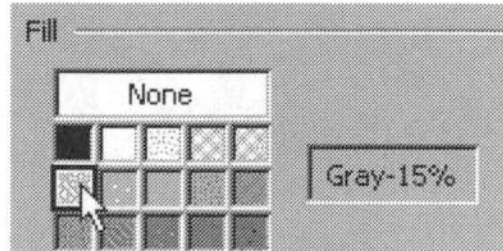

When finished, click **OK**.

5) Select the text: In aid of Local Scout Troop. Use the options on the Formatting Toolbar to centre align it, and make it Arial Black, 14 point.

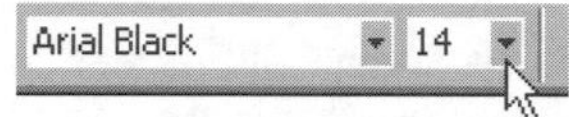

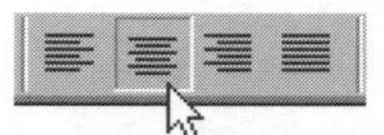

6) Select the four attractions: Wheel of Fortune, Cakes, Books and Children's Play Area. Make them Arial, 20 point.

(Ensure the paragraph mark after Children's Play Area is included in your selection.)

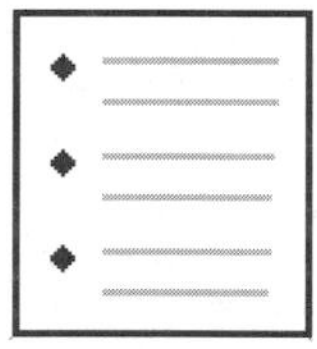

Diamond style bullet character

Choose **Format | Bullets and Numbering**. On the Bulleted tab, select the diamond bullet character style.

7) You want to place the bullets where they will get attention: in the centre of the page between the left and right page margins.

But do *not* apply centre alignment, as shown below, as the bullets are easier to read if they are left aligned.

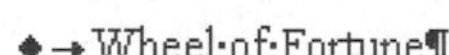

◆→Cakes¶

◆→Books¶

◆→Children's·Play·Area¶

8) With the four attractions still selected, select **Format | Paragraph** and apply a left indent of 4.5 cm.

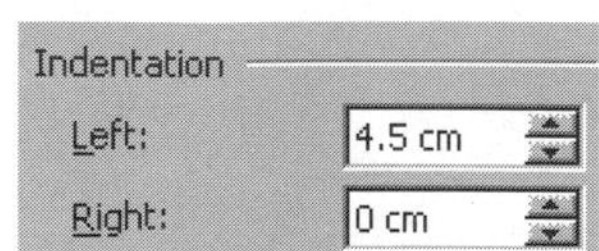

Your bulleted text remains left-aligned, but is now in the centre of the page.

9) Select the remainder of the text, and make it centre-aligned, Arial, Regular, 20 point.

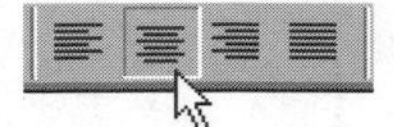

10) Select each of the following words in turn and click the Bold button on the Formatting Toolbar:

    Where:, When:, Admission Free.

11) Select the words All Welcome and click the Italics button on the Formatting Toolbar.

12) Finally, with the cursor positioned anywhere on the page, choose **Format | Borders and Shading**, and select the Page Border tab.

    Select a Setting: of Box and, in the Apply to: field, select Whole document, and click **OK**.

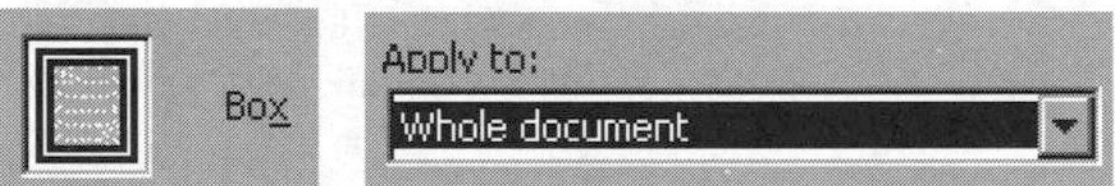

Your poster is now complete and should look like the sample shown.

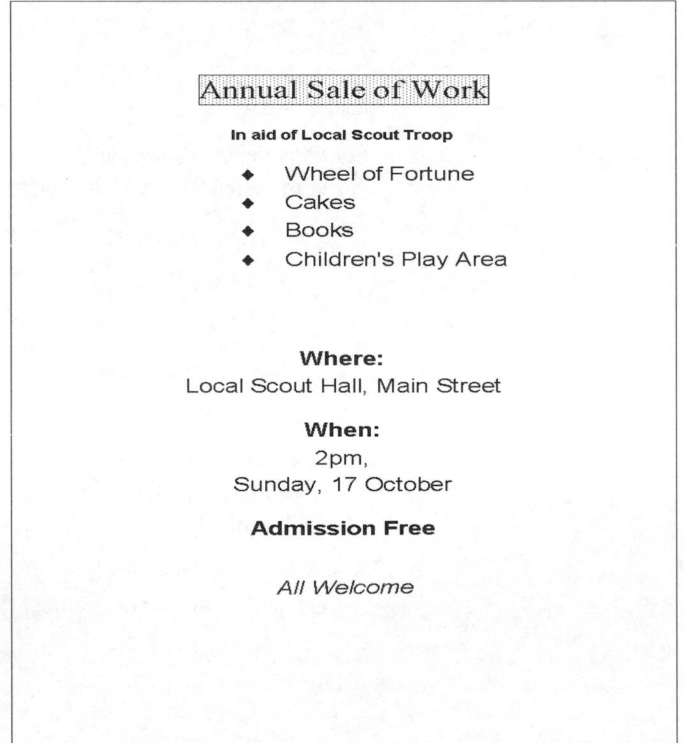

Save your poster with a name that you will find easy to remember and recognise. If your initials are KB, for example, save the poster document as KBposter.doc.

If you have a printer, print out your poster and inspect your work!

Word's Zoom Views

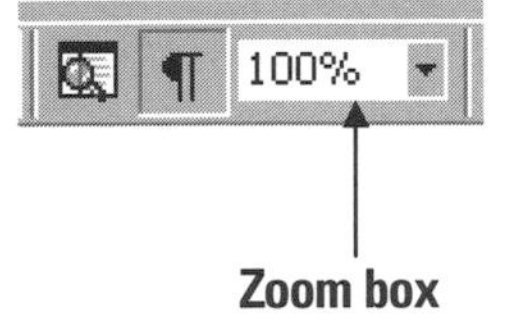

Zoom box

Word's Zoom feature enables you to magnify or reduce the document display. You can use Zoom in either of two ways:

- Click in the Zoom box on the Standard Toolbar, enter a number between 10% and 500%, and press ENTER.
- Choose **View | Zoom**, and select a magnification or reduction option from the Zoom dialog box.

To return from an enlarged or reduced view to normal view, select a magnification of 100% – or click the Undo button on the Standard Toolbar.

Zoom and Printing

The Zoom feature affects only the way that Word displays a document on-screen – and not how a document is printed. (You will learn about printing documents in Section 3.3.)

Saving to a Diskette

Have you been saving your documents as you went along? You should. It is also a good idea to save a copy of your document to a diskette. Follow the steps in Exercise 3.20 to learn how to save your poster to the A: drive.

Exercise 3.20: Saving a Word Document to a Diskette

1) Insert a diskette in the diskette drive of your computer:
   - If it is a new diskette, ensure that it is formatted.
   - If it is a previously used one, ensure that there is sufficient space on it to hold the Word document file. Your poster file should be around 60 KB in size.
2) Choose **File | Save As**, locate the A: drive, and click **Save** to save the file. Word suggests the default file name (in this example, KBposter.doc) for you to accept or amend.

When finished, use **File | Save As** again to resave the document to its original location on your computer.

If you do not, saving the file in future (by clicking the Save button on the Standard Toolbar or choosing **File | Save**) will save the document to the diskette – and not to your computer.

Symbols and Special Characters

Word allows you to insert symbols and special characters in your documents:

- **Symbols:** Among the symbols are foreign language letters with accents (such as á, é, ä, and ë), fractions, and characters used in science and mathematics.
- **Special Characters:** These include copyright (©), registered (®) and trademark (^{TM}), plus typographic characters such as the en dash (a short dash the width of the letter 'n'), the em dash (a longer dash the width of the letter 'm'), and various types of opening and closing quotes.

To insert a symbol or special character:

- Click where you want to insert the symbol.
- Choose **Insert | Symbol**, and then click the Symbols or Special Characters tab.
- Double-click the symbol or character you want to insert.
- Click **Close** to close the dialog box.

Format Painter

Format Painter button

Word's Format Painter provides a quick, convenient way to copy formatting from one piece of text to another. Follow these steps:

- Select the text that has the formatting you want to copy.
- Click the Format Painter button on the Standard Toolbar.
- Select the text to which you want to apply the formatting.

To copy the selected formatting to several locations, double-click Format Painter.

When you have finished copying the formatting, click the Format Painter button again or press the ESC key at the top-left of your keyboard.

Exercise 3.21: Copying Formatting

You begin this Exercise by removing the formatting from two lines of your Annual Sale of Work poster.

1) Is the poster document from Exercise 3.19 open? If not, open it now.
2) Select the text 'Where:', choose **Format | Font**, make it 10 point, Regular, Times New Roman, and click **OK**.

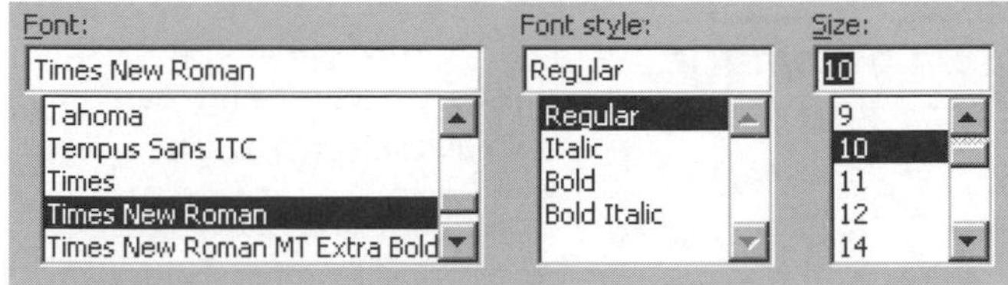

3) Select the text 'When:'. Also make it 10 point, Regular, Times New Roman.

In the next part of this Exercise, you will copy the formatting from another part of the poster to the two lines whose formatting you removed in steps 2) and 3) above.

4) Click anywhere within the words 'Admission Free'.

5) Double-click on the Format Painter button.

6) Select the text 'Where:', and click the Format Painter button.

7) Select the text 'When:', and click the Format Painter button.

8) Press the ESC key to switch off the Format Painter feature.

Your poster now looks as it did before this Exercise. Save the poster and close it. You can also close Microsoft Word. You have now completed this Section 3.2 of the ECDL Word-Processing Module.

Section Summary: So Now You Know

Before you format or align text, you must first select that text. You do so by clicking and then dragging with the mouse. Word displays selected text in reverse (white text on black background).

Bold, italic and underline are Word's most commonly used *formatting* features. Buttons for these options are provided on the Formatting Toolbar.

You can *copy* text from one part of a document and then *paste* it to another part (or even to a different document) using the *Clipboard*, a temporary storage area. You can also *cut* and paste text, in which case Word deletes the text from its original location.

Indenting is a way of moving text in a specified distance from the left or right margin of the page – or from both. *Alignment* is a way of positioning text in a paragraph so it lines up beside the left margin, beside the right margin, beside both left and right margins (justification) or away from both left and right margins (centering). Buttons for the alignment options are provided on the Formatting Toolbar.

Use lists to communicate short statements or instructions. *Bulleted lists*, in which each item is preceded by a symbol such as a square or diamond, are suitable when the reading order is not critical. *Numbered lists*, in which each item is preceded by a sequentially increasing number, are used for instructions and directions, where the order of reading is important.

Fonts (typefaces) are styles of text. Serif fonts are better for long paragraphs. Use sans serif fonts for shorter text items, such as headlines or captions. Two important font effects are *superscript* (used for writing mathematical indices) and *subscript* (used for writing chemical formulae).

You can brighten up your documents by adding decorative *borders* and background *shading*.

Word's *Zoom* feature enables you to magnify or reduce the document display – without affecting how the document is printed.

You can insert *symbols* and *special characters* in a document to represent such items as foreign language letters with accents, fractions, characters used in scientific and mathematical texts, and typographic characters such as dashes and quotes.

Word's *Format Painter* provides a quick, convenient way to copy formatting from one piece of text to another.

Section 3.3: Long Documents, Little Details

In This Section

Both for the writer and for the reader, long documents present problems that shorter ones do not. Word offers features to make life easier.

To help you edit long documents, Word includes a spell-checker, grammar-checker, and a find-and-replace feature.

You can help readers navigate their way through long documents by inserting page numbers and other details in the header or footer.

Also in this Section you will discover how to control vertical spacing between lines and paragraphs, how to create new types of indents to highlight breaks between paragraphs, and how to insert line and page breaks.

New Skills

At the end of this Section you should be able to:

- Change the spacing between lines and between paragraphs
- Apply a first line indent to a paragraph
- Apply a hanging indent to a paragraph
- Find and replace text, text with formatting, and special characters
- Adjust page margins and page orientation
- Create and format headers and footers
- Insert page numbers and document details in a header or footer
- Insert manual line breaks and page breaks
- Use Word's spell- and grammar-checkers
- Use Word's printing options

New Words

At the end of this Section you should be able to explain the following terms:

- Inter-line spacing
- Margin
- Inter-paragraph spacing
- A4
- First line indent
- Header and footer
- Hanging indent

Creating Your Long Document

To learn how to work with long documents in Word, you need a sample long document to practise on. You begin this Section by copying some text from Word's online help.

Exercise 3.22: Copying Text from Word Online Help

1) Open Word and choose **Help | Contents and Index**. On the Contents tab of the Help Topics dialog box, double-click the topic: Working with Long Documents.

2) Word displays a list of sub-topics. Double-click on: Automatically Summarizing a Document. You are shown a further sub-listing. Double-click on: Automatically summarize a document.

Automatically Summarizing a Document
- Automatically summarize a document
- Troubleshoot automatically summarizing a document

3) On the help screen displayed, select the two paragraphs of text shown below by dragging the mouse over them.

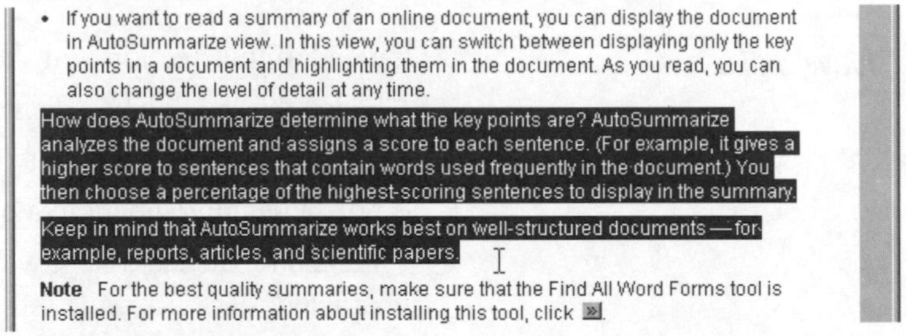

- If you want to read a summary of an online document, you can display the document in AutoSummarize view. In this view, you can switch between displaying only the key points in a document and highlighting them in the document. As you read, you can also change the level of detail at any time.

How does AutoSummarize determine what the key points are? AutoSummarize analyzes the document and assigns a score to each sentence. (For example, it gives a higher score to sentences that contain words used frequently in the document.) You then choose a percentage of the highest-scoring sentences to display in the summary.

Keep in mind that AutoSummarize works best on well-structured documents — for example, reports, articles, and scientific papers.

Note For the best quality summaries, make sure that the Find All Word Forms tool is installed. For more information about installing this tool, click .

4) Choose **Options | Copy**. Close the online help window by clicking on the close box in the top-right corner.

5) Click the New button on the Standard Toolbar to create a new Word document. The cursor is positioned at the start of the first line.

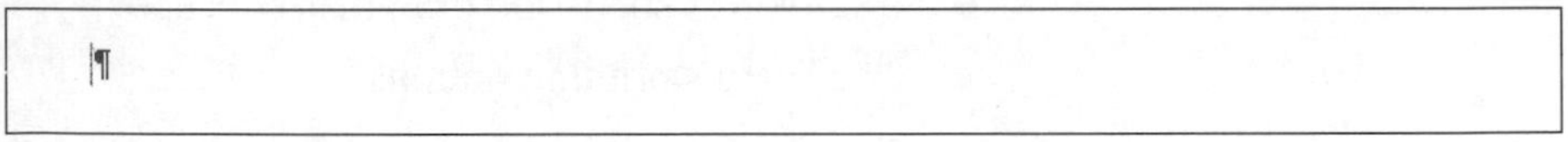

¶

6) Choose **Edit | Paste** to paste the online help text into the new document.

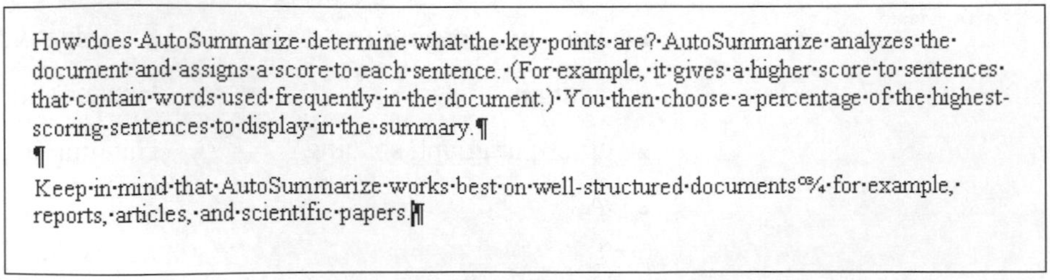

How·does·AutoSummarize·determine·what·the·key·points·are?·AutoSummarize·analyzes·the·document·and·assigns·a·score·to·each·sentence.·(For·example,·it·gives·a·higher·score·to·sentences·that·contain·words·used·frequently·in·the·document.)·You·then·choose·a·percentage·of·the·highest-scoring·sentences·to·display·in·the·summary.¶
¶
Keep·in·mind·that·AutoSummarize·works·best·on·well-structured·documents⁰³⁄₄·for·example,·reports,·articles,·and·scientific·papers.¶

7) Move the cursor to the start of the first line of the first paragraph. Press ENTER to create a new line, and move the cursor up to the start of that line.

¶
How·does·AutoSummarize·determine·what·the·key·points·are?·AutoSummarize·analyzes·the·
document·and·assigns·a·score·to·each·sentence.·(For·example,·it·gives·a·higher·score·to·sentences·

8) Type the following: Heading One

Heading·One¶
How·does·AutoSummarize·determine·what·the·key·points·are?·AutoSummarize·analyzes·the·
document·and·assigns·a·score·to·each·sentence.·(For·example,·it·gives·a·higher·score·to·sentences·

9) Hold down the CTRL key and click in the left margin of the page where there is no text. This selects all the text in the document.

Heading·One¶
How·does·AutoSummarize·determine·what·the·key·points·are?·AutoSummarize·analyzes·the·
document·and·assigns·a·score·to·each·sentence.·(For·example,·it·gives·a·higher·score·to·sentences·

10) Choose **Edit | Copy** to copy the text to the Clipboard. Deselect the text by clicking anywhere on the page outside the selected text.

11) Move the cursor down to the end of the second paragraph, and press ENTER twice to move down the cursor a further two lines.

reports,·articles,·and·scientific·papers.¶
¶
¶

12) The text you copied from Word's online help in step 4) is still in the Clipboard. Choose **Edit | Paste** to paste it again.

13) Repeat steps 11) and 12) fifteen times to create three pages of text.

14) Choose **File | Save** to save the document with a name that you will find easy to remember. If your initials are KB, for example, call it KBlong.doc.

Inter-Line Spacing

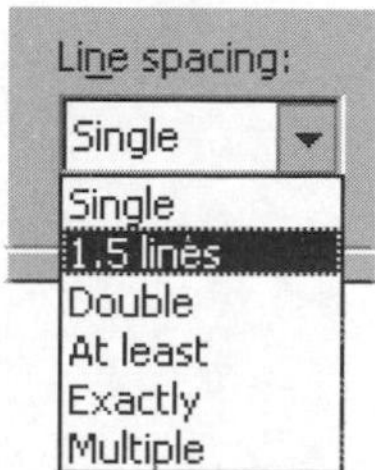

Inter-line spacing is the vertical space between lines within a paragraph of text. By default, Word applies single inter-line spacing. You can increase the inter-line spacing of a selected paragraph by choosing **Format | Paragraph**, and, in the Line spacing: box, selecting 1.5 or Double.

Alternatively, enter a font size in the At: box, and select At least: in the Line spacing: box. A good rule is to make inter-line spacing one point size larger than the font size. If your text is 10 points, for example, make inter-line spacing 11 points.

Inter-Line Spacing
The vertical space between lines within a paragraph of text. Word's default is single line spacing.

Examples of single, 1.5 and double inter-line spacing

Single	1.5	Double
How·does·AutoS document·and·as that·contain·worc scoring·sentence ¶ Keep·in·mind·thε reports,·articles,· ¶ How·does·AutoS document·and·as that·contain·worc scoring·sentence that·contain·worc scoring·sentence	How·does·AutoSu document·and·assi that·contain·words scoring·sentences· ¶ Keep·in·mind·that· reports,·articles,·aı ¶ How·does·AutoSu	How·does·AutoS document·and·as that·contain·worc scoring·sentence: ¶ Keep·in·mind·tha reports,·articles,·ε

Inter-Paragraph Spacing

Pressing the ENTER key to add a blank line between paragraphs of text is a crude – if effective – way of controlling the inter-paragraph spacing (spacing between paragraphs) in your documents.

For longer documents, you may instead wish to use the **Format | Paragraph** command, and enter an inter-paragraph space value in the Space Before: and/or Space After: boxes:

- For body text, enter a value in the Space After: box that is slightly larger than the text font size, to separate the next paragraph from the current one.
- For headings, enter a value in the Space Before: box to place an extra area of blank space above the headings. This helps your headings to stand out from the rest of the text.

Inter-paragraph spacing, created with and without extra paragraph marks

How·does·AutoSu document·and·ass that·contain·word scoring·sentences ¶ Keep·in·mind·that reports,·articles,·a ¶ How·does·AutoSu document·and·ass that·contain·word scoring·sentences	How·does·AutoSu document·and·ass that·contain·word scoring·sentences Keep·in·mind·that reports,·articles,·a How·does·AutoSu document·and·ass that·contain·word scoring·sentences

Inter-Paragraph Spacing

The spacing between successive paragraphs of text.

Another option for long documents is to set inter-paragraph spacing for body text to zero, and to use instead first line indenting as a way of indicating where each new paragraph begins. See the next topic.

First Line Indents

In Section 3.2 you learned how to indent a selected paragraph from the left and/or right margins of the page. Word also lets you indent the first line of a paragraph only, so that it is in a greater distance from the left margin than the other lines of the same paragraph.

Exercise 3.23: Creating a First Line Indent

Here you will use a first line indent to separate two paragraphs of body text.

1) Select the second paragraph of your sample text.

¶
Keep·in·mind·that·AutoSummarize·works·best·on·well-structured·documents%·for·example,·reports,·articles,·and·scientific·papers.¶
¶

2) Choose **Format | Paragraph**.

3) On the Indents and Spacing tab, in the Special: box, select First Line. In the By: box, enter a value of 1 cm. Click **OK**.

4) Delete the extra paragraph mark above the indented paragraph. Your text should now look as below.

scoring·sentences·to·display·in·the·summary.¶
Keep·in·mind·that·AutoSummarize·works·best·on·well-structured·documents%·for·example,·reports,·articles,·and·scientific·papers.¶

5) Undo the first line indent change and paragraph mark deletion by choosing **Edit | Undo** twice. Word's Undo reverses formatting and text positioning operations as well as typing and editing. Also, replace the extra paragraph mark to separate the two paragraphs.

Your sample text should look as it was before this Exercise.

First Line Indent

The positioning of the first line of a paragraph a greater distance in from the left margin than the remaining lines of the same paragraph.

If using first line indents to separate paragraphs, set inter-paragraph spacing to zero or to just 1 or 2 points. Do not use first line indents for the first paragraph after a heading.

Hanging Indents

A hanging indent is where all the lines of a paragraph are indented – except the first one. Hanging indents are sometimes used for lists such as bibliographies. Below is an example.

The·Memoirs·of·James·II·Translated·by·A.·Lytton·Sells·from·the·Bouillon·Manuscript.·Edited·and·collated·with·the·Clarke·Edition.·With·an·introduction·by·Sir·Arthur·Bryant.¶

The·History·of·England·from·the·Accession·of·James·II.·Lord·Macauley,·edited·by·Lady·Tevelyan.¶

Practise creating a hanging indent with the sample text by selecting a paragraph, choosing **Format | Paragraph**, selecting Hanging Indent from the Special: box, and entering a value in the By: box. Undo any changes that you make.

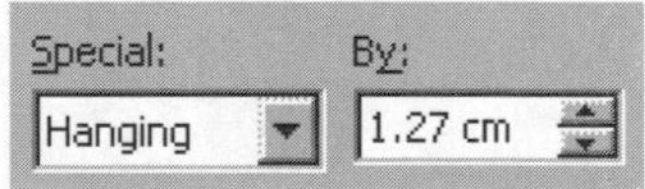

Hanging Indent

Where all the lines of a paragraph are indented – except the first one. Sometimes used for lists.

Finding Text

Need to locate quickly a particular word or phrase in a long document? Word's Find feature can take you straight to the text that you are looking for.

By default, Word searches the whole document. To limit the text that Word searches through, first select only that part of the document. When Word has finished searching the selected text, it asks whether you want to search the remainder of the document or not.

The Basics

Choose **Edit | Find** to display the Find and Replace dialog box. In the Find what: box, type (or paste in from the Clipboard) the text you want to find, and choose **Find Next**.

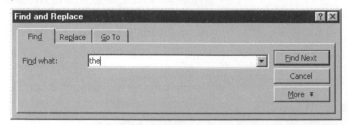

Word takes you to the first occurrence of the search text in your document. The dialog box stays open on your screen. Click **Find Next** to continue searching for further occurrences, or click **Cancel** to close the dialog box and end your search. Practise by searching for the word 'the' in your sample document.

Special Options

By default, Word finds parts of words as well as whole words. When you search for 'the', Word also finds 'then'. You can tell Word to find whole words only by clicking the **More** button, and then selecting the 'Find whole words only' check box.

Another option is to select the 'Match case' check box. So, for example, a search for 'The' does not find 'the' or 'THE'.

To find paragraph marks, tabs or other special or non-printing characters, choose the **Special** button and click on the relevant character.

Formats

You can tell Word to find only occurrences of text that is in a certain format. Click the **More** button, then the **Format** button, and select the formatting option that you require.

Finding and Replacing Text

Sometimes you will want to find and replace all occurrences of a word or phrase in a document with a different word or phrase. You might have misspelled a word consistently throughout a document, for example, or maybe you want to substitute 'person' for 'man' or 'woman'.

To replace text, choose **Edit | Replace**. On the Replace tab, enter the text you want to replace in the Find what: box, and the new text you want to substitute for the replaced text in the Replace with: box.

The Two Replace Methods

You are offered two options by the Replace tab of the Find and Replace dialog box.

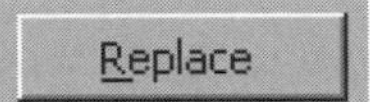

- Word replaces your text *one occurrence at a time.* At each occurrence, you are asked whether you want to make the replacement or not. This is the 'safe' option.

- Word replaces *all occurrences in a single operation*. Use this option only if you are certain that you want to replace every instance of the text you are searching for!

Special Options

Anything that you can locate with the **Find** command, you can replace with **Edit | Find and Replace** – including formatting, tabs and other special and non-printing characters.

Exercise 3.24: Finding and Replacing Text

In this Exercise you will practise finding and replacing text in your sample long document.

1) Look at the second of the two paragraphs that you pasted in from the online help text. Word pasted °¾ instead of a dash (–) after the word 'documents'.

2) Copy the following to the Clipboard: documents °¾

3) Move the cursor to the start of the first line of the document. Choose **Edit | Replace**.

4) On the Replace tab, paste the copied text in the Find what: box.

5) Type this in the Replace with: box: documents –

6) Choose the **Replace All** button.

Word performs the find-and-replace operation through the entire document. So much easier than correcting each occurrence of the error! Click **Close** to close the dialog box.

Exercise 3.25: Finding and Replacing Formatting

In this Exercise you will use Word's find-and-replace feature to reformat all occurrences of a heading in your sample long document.

1) Move the cursor to the start of the first line of the document. Choose **Edit | Replace**.
2) On the Replace tab, notice that the Find what: box still contains the text from Exercise 3.24. Click in the Find what: box, delete the previous text, and type the following: Heading One.
3) Click in the Replace with: box, delete the text from the previous Exercise 3.24, and type the following: Heading One.
4) Click the **More** button and then the **Format** button.
5) Select the Font option, and specify a Font of Arial, a Font Style of Bold, and a Font Size of 14. Then click **OK**.

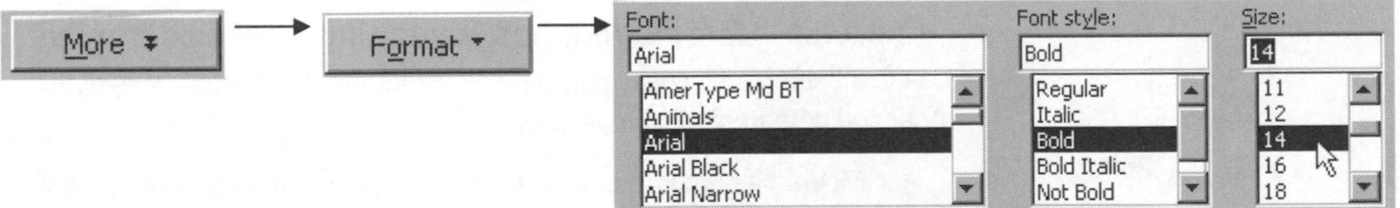

6) Click the **Replace All** button.

Word reformats every occurrence of the heading. Click **Close** to close the dialog box.

Exercise 3.26: Finding and Replacing Special Characters

In this Exercise you will remove the extra paragraph mark that separates the paragraphs of the sample text.

1) Move the cursor to the start of the first line of the document. Choose **Edit | Replace**.

2) On the Replace tab, click in the Find what: box and delete the text from Exercise 3.25.

3) With the cursor in the Find what: box, click the **Special** button and select Paragraph Mark from the pop-up menu. Click **Special** again and click Paragraph Mark.

   The Find what: box should contain Word's paragraph mark symbol twice (^ p ^ p).

4) Click in the Replace with: box and delete the text from Exercise 3.25. Also, click **No Formatting** to remove the formatting that you specified in Exercise 3.25.

5) With the cursor in the Replace with: box, click the **Special** button and select Paragraph Mark from the pop-up menu.

6) Click **Replace All**.

Word replaces all occurrences of two consecutive paragraph marks with a single paragraph mark. Click **Close** to close the dialog box.

Exercise 3.27: Finding and Replacing Text Positioning

In this Exercise you will apply a first line indent to all occurrences of the second paragraph of sample text.

1) Move the cursor to the start of the first line of the document. Choose **Edit | Replace**.

2) On the Replace tab, click in the Find what: box. Delete the text from Exercise 3.26 and type the first word of the second paragraph of the sample text: Keep.

3) Click in the Replace with: box, delete the text from Exercise 3.26 and type the same word as in the Find what: box.

4) With the cursor still in the Replace with: box, click the **Format** button, then the Paragraph option, and specify a First Line indent of 1 cm. Click **OK**.

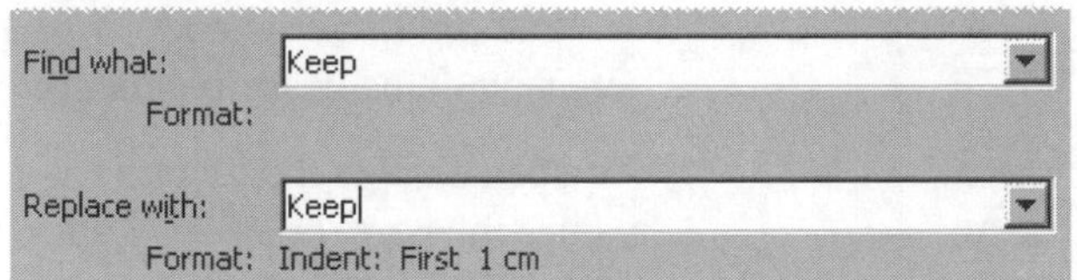

5) Click **Replace All**.

Word indents the first line of every occurrence of the second paragraph. Click **Close** to close the dialog box. Your document should look like the sample shown below.

Heading·One¶

How·does·AutoSummarize·determine·what·the·key·points·are?·AutoSummarize·analyzes·the· document·and·assigns·a·score·to·each·sentence.·(For·example,·it·gives·a·higher·score·to·sentences· that·contain·words·used·frequently·in·the·document.)·You·then·choose·a·percentage·of·the·highest-scoring·sentences·to·display·in·the·summary.¶

Keep·in·mind·that·AutoSummarize·works·best·on·well-structured·documents·-for·example,· reports,·articles,·and·scientific·papers.¶

You have completed the find-and-replace Exercises. Save your long document and leave it open.

Page Setup

You have learnt how to control where text appears on the printed page, using text alignment, indenting, inter-line spacing and inter-paragraph spacing.

But what about the page on which the text appears? What options does Word offer you?

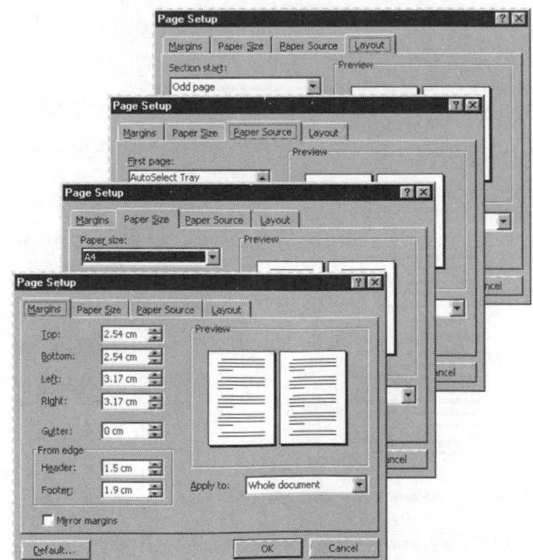

Choose **File | Page Setup** to view the four tabs of page setup options. Only two of these tabs are relevant at this stage: Margins and Paper Size.

The Margins Tab

Margins indicated by dashed lines

A margin is the distance that the text and graphics are positioned in from the edge of the printed page.

Word's default margin values – top and bottom, 1 inch (2.54 cm), left and right, 1.25 inches (3.17 cm) – are acceptable for most letters and business documents.

You can change the margins at any stage, and make your new values the new defaults by clicking the **Default** button.

Margin

The distance of the text and graphics from the edge of the printed page. Word lets you specify separate top, bottom, left and right margins.

Paper Size

For the Paper Size: box, accept the default of A4. This is the European standard paper size (21 cm wide and 29.7 cm high). A4 is used for almost all letters and other business documents.

A4

The standard page size for letters and most other business documents throughout Europe.

Orientation is the direction in which the page is printed. Your options are Portrait ('standing up') and Landscape ('on its side'). Letters and most other business documents are printed in portrait.

Headers and Footers

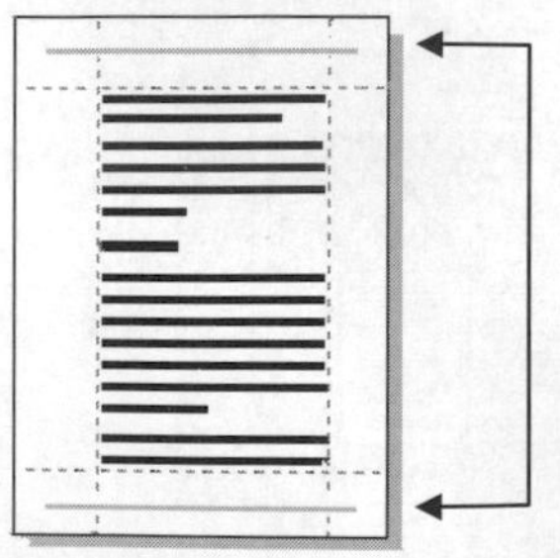

Word places headers and footers in the top and bottom page margins, set with the File | Page Setup command

Headers and footers are pieces of text that appear on the top and bottom of every page of a document (except the title and contents pages).

Looking at examples of published documents, you will see that headers and footers typically contain such details as document title, organisation name, author name, and perhaps a version or draft number. Usually, headers and footers also contain page numbers. You will learn about page numbering in the next topic.

With Word, you need only type in header and/or footer text once, and the program repeats the text on every page. Any formatting that you can apply to text in your document – such as bold, italics, alignment, borders and shading – you can also apply to text in the headers and footers. You can also insert graphics, such as a company logo, in a header and footer.

Headers and Footers

Standard text and graphics that are printed in the top and bottom margins of every page of a document.

Here are a few facts about headers and footers in Word:

- You insert them with the **View | Headers and Footers** command.
- This command displays the header or footer area (surrounded by a dashed border), the document text (which you cannot edit when working with headers and footers), and a Header and Footer Toolbar (giving you quick access to the commonly used commands).

Word's header area with Toolbar

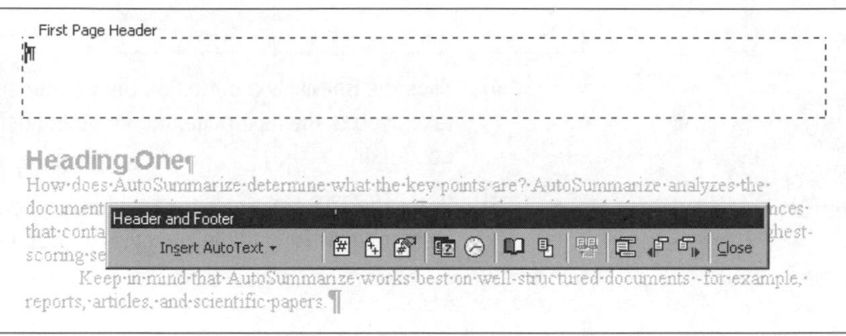

- Word positions the paragraph mark at the left of the header or footer area, ready for you to type text.
- Word inserts two preset tab stops to make it easy for you to centre-align or right-align headers or footers. Press TAB once to centre a header or footer, press TAB twice to line it up against the right margin.

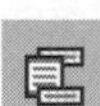

Switch Between Header and Footer button

- Click the Switch Between Header and Footer button to view the footer area when in the header area, and vice versa. The two areas are similar in appearance and operation.
- Place page numbers (discussed in the next topic) at the outside margin (left for left-hand side pages, right for right-hand pages) or at the centre of the header or footer area.
- Place text at the centre or at the inside margin of the header or footer area.

Exercise 3.28: Creating a Header

In this Exercise you will insert header text in your sample document.

1) Choose **File | Page Setup**, select the **Layout** tab, ensure that the Header and Footer checkboxes are as shown on the right, and click **OK**.

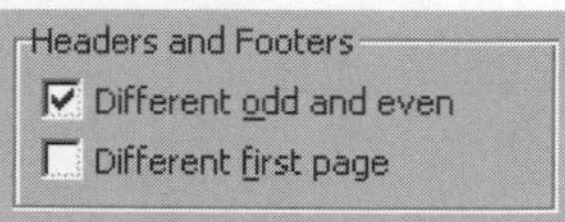

2) Choose **View | Header and Footer**. Word positions the paragraph mark at the left of the header area, ready for you to type text.

3) Type the following text: Annual Report

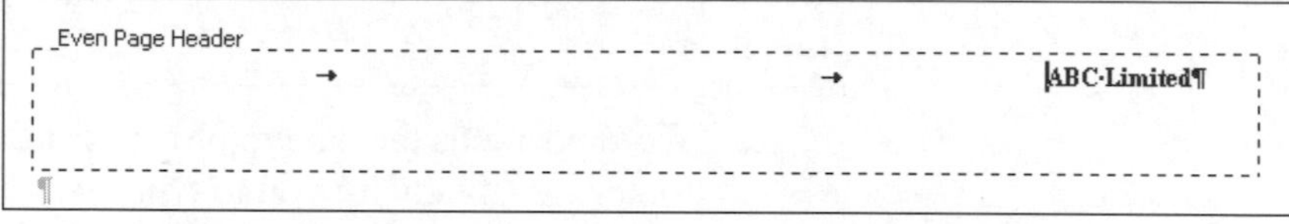

Show Next button

4) Click the Show Next button on the Header and Footer Toolbar. Word takes you to the next page, the first even (left-hand) page of the document.

5) Press the TAB key twice to move the paragraph mark against the right-hand margin. Type the following text: ABC Limited

Even Page Header

ABC·Limited¶

6) Click the Close button on the Header and Footer Toolbar.

Because you began this Exercise by selecting the 'Different odd and even' check box on **File | Setup**, Word allowed you to type separate headers for odd (right-hand) and even (left-hand) pages.

In the next Exercise you will place a border under the header text to help separate it from the main body of the document. You will also change the font and font size. Typically, the header font is 2 or 3 point sizes smaller than the body text. At that size, sans serif fonts such as Arial are easier to read than serif ones.

Exercise 3.29: Formatting a Header

1) Choose **View | Header and Footer**.

2) Select the header text on the first page of your document.

3) Chose **Format | Font**, and select Arial, Regular, 8 point.

4) With the text still selected, choose **Format | Borders and Shading**.

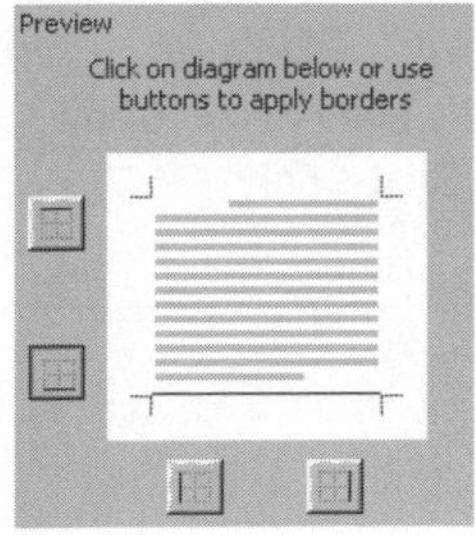

Apply a bottom border to the header text

5) On the Borders tab, select None for Setting:. Then, in the Preview area, select a bottom border. Select a Width: of 1 point, an Apply to: of Paragraph, and click **OK**.

6) Click the Show Next button on the Header and Footer Toolbar. Repeat steps 4) and 5) for the left-hand page.

7) Click the Close button on the Header and Footer Toolbar.

The top of your right-hand pages should now look as below.

Annual·Report¶

Heading·One¶

How·does·AutoSummarize·determine·what·the·key·points·are?·AutoSummarize·analyzes·the·

The top of your left-hand pages should now look as below.

→ → ABC·Limited¶

Heading·One¶

How·does·AutoSummarize·determine·what·the·key·points·are?·AutoSummarize·analyzes·the·

Notice that the header text is 'greyed out', indicating that you cannot edit it when working with the main body of the document.

Page Numbering

You can insert a page number in the header or footer of a document. Word updates the page numbers as you add or remove document pages. The same formatting options are available for the page number as for header and footer text. You can align a page number at the left or right margin, or in the centre of the header or footer area.

Exercise 3.30: Inserting a Page Number

In this Exercise you will insert a centre-aligned page number in the footer of the document.

1) Choose **View | Headers and Footers**.

2) Display the footer area of the first page. Press TAB to move the cursor to the centre-aligned position.

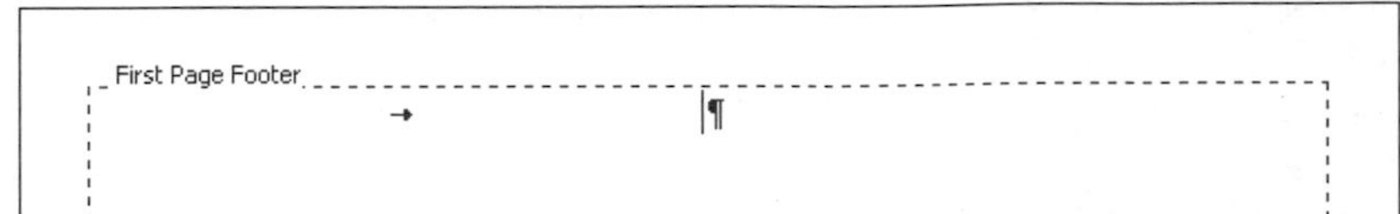

Insert Page Number button

3) Click the Insert Page Number button on the Header and Footer Toolbar. Word inserts the page number and displays it against a grey background.

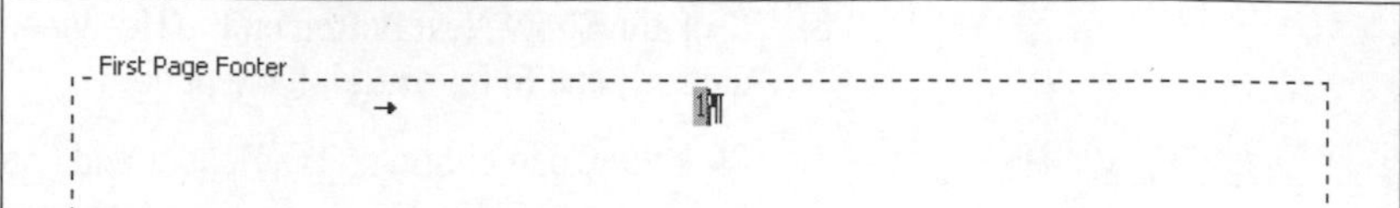

4) Click the Show Next button on the Header and Footer Toolbar to move to the second page, the first even (left-hand) page of your document.

5) Repeat steps 2) and 3) to insert the page number in the centre-aligned position.

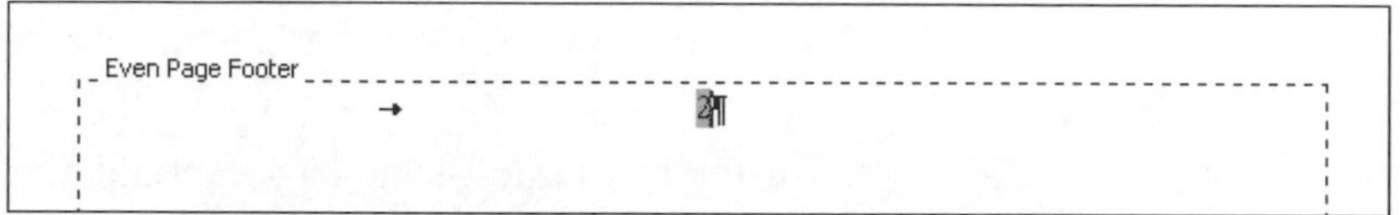

6) Click the Close button on the Header and Footer Toolbar. Save the document.

Page Numbering Options

Format Page Number button

Click on the Format Page Number button on the Header and Footer Toolbar to display the page numbering options.

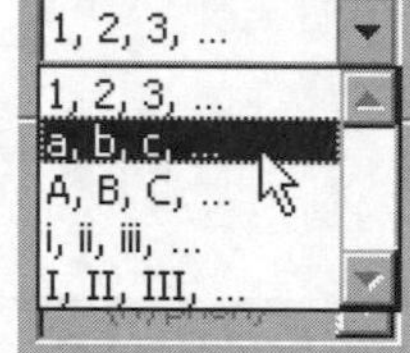

You can number the pages using numbers, letters, or Roman numerals. And you can start at a number other than one.

Document Date and Author Name

Word offers special features to make it easier for you to insert today's date and your name in a header or footer.

Document Creation Date

To insert today's date (as recorded on your computer) in a header or footer, follow these steps:

Date button

- Choose **View | Headers and Footers**.
- Position the cursor where you want to insert the current date.
- Click the Date button on the Header and Footer Toolbar.

Document Author Name

To insert the author's name (that is, your name), follow these steps:

- Choose **File | Properties**, and check that your name is displayed in the Author: box.

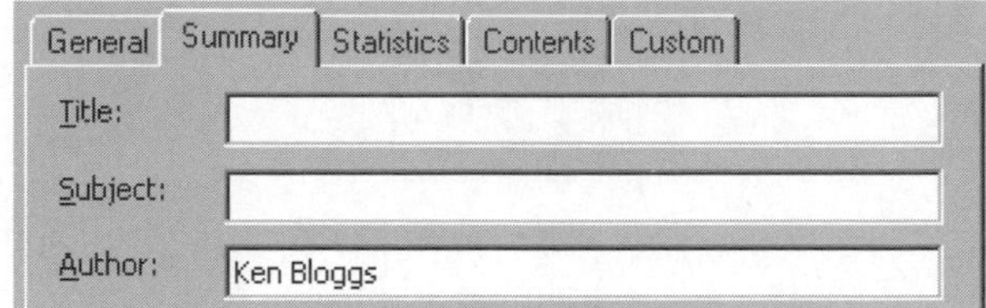

  Word displays in this box the user name entered when Windows was installed on your computer. If yours is not the name shown, delete the displayed name, type in your name, and select **OK**.

- Choose **View | Headers and Footers**.
- Position the cursor in the header or footer area where you want to insert the author name.
- Choose **Insert | Field** to display the Field dialog box.

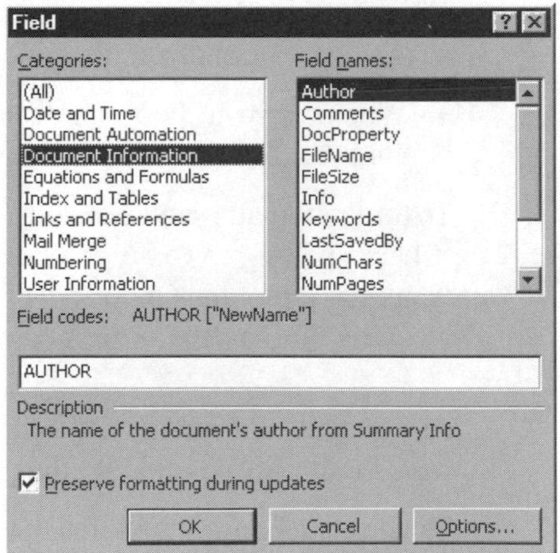

- In the Categories: list, select Document Information. In the Field names: list, select Author. Click **OK**.

Manual Line and Page Breaks

Pressing ENTER at any stage inserts a new paragraph mark, and causes Word to begin a new paragraph. To insert a line break within a paragraph, press SHIFT+ENTER.

Example of three line breaks

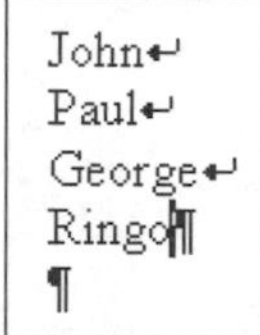

When text fills a page, Word automatically creates another page to hold the additional text.

You can insert a page break manually at any point in a document by pressing CTRL+ENTER. Alternatively, choose the **Insert | Breaks** command, select the Page Break option, and click **OK**.

Word's Manual Page Break Indicator

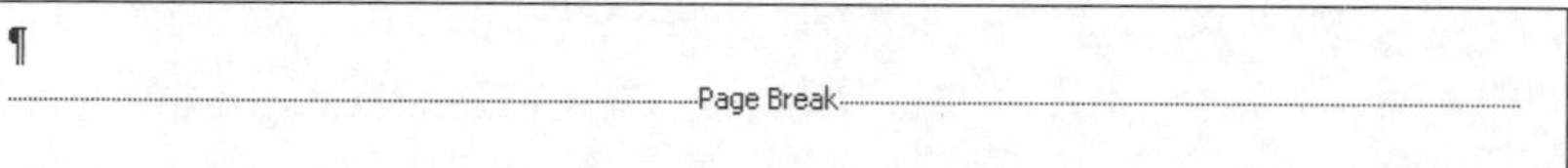

Checking Your Spelling

How's your spelling? Word can check your spelling and suggest corrections to errors in two ways:

- As you type and edit your document (the automatic option)
- Whenever you choose the **Tools | Spelling and Grammar** command (the on-request option)

☑ Check spelling as you type

To turn automatic spell-checking on or off, select or deselect the 'Check spelling as you type' check box on the Spelling & Grammar tab of the Options dialog box. You display this dialog box with the **Tools | Options** command.

Spell Checking: The Automatic Option

As you type and edit, a wavy red line under words indicates possible spelling errors.

To correct an error, right-click the word with a wavy underline, and then select the correction you want from the pop-up menu.

Selecting the last menu option, **Spelling**, displays Word's Spelling dialog box.

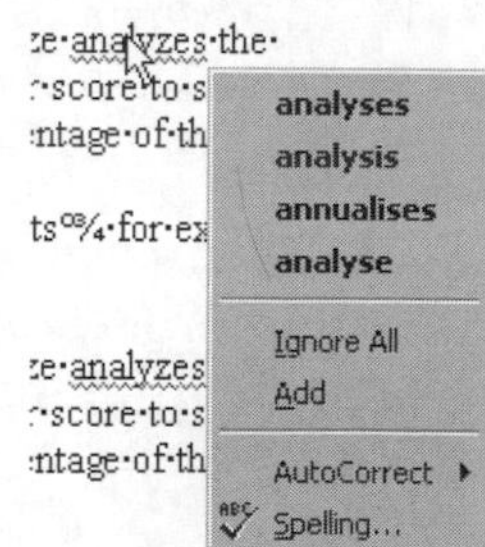

The Spell-Check Dialog Box

Whether automatic spell-checking is selected or not, you can spell-check your document at any stage by choosing the **Tools | Spelling and Grammar** command.

If Word's spell-checker finds no errors, it displays a box telling you that the spell-check is complete.

If Word finds something it does not recognise, it displays the Spelling dialog box, and shows the relevant word in red.

The Spelling and Grammar dialog box includes a Suggestions area that offers likely alternatives to queried words. Click on any suggested word to substitute it for the incorrect one.

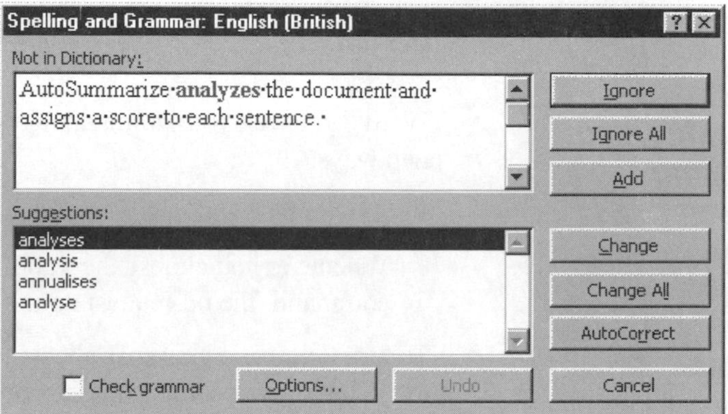

Whenever the spell-checker queries a word, your options include:

- **Ignore**: Leave this occurrence of the word unchanged.
- **Ignore All:** Leave this and all other occurrences of the word in the document unchanged.
- **Add:** Add the word to the spelling dictionary, so that Word will recognise it during future spell-checks of any document. Use this option for the names of people or places, or abbreviations or acronyms that you type regularly.
- **Change:** Correct this occurrence of the word, but prompt again on further occurrences.
- **Change All:** Correct this occurrence of the word – and all other occurrences without further prompting.

A word of caution: if the word that you have typed is correctly spelt but inappropriate – for example, 'their' instead of 'there' – your spell-checker will not detect it as an error. Therefore, you should always read over the final version of the document to ensure that it doesn't contain any errors.

Watch Your Language

Before spell-checking your documents, choose **Tools | Language | Set Language** to display the current dictionary language. If it is incorrect (perhaps US English instead of British), select your required language and choose **Default**.

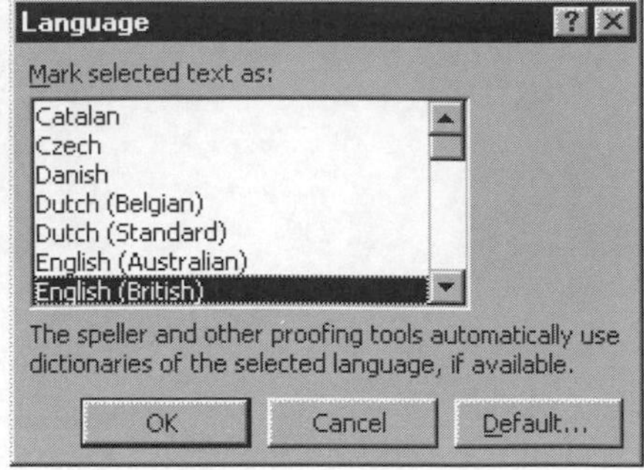

Checking Your Grammar

Word can check your grammar and suggest corrections to errors in two ways:

- As you type and edit your document (the automatic option).
- Whenever you choose the **Tools | Spelling and Grammar** command (the on-request option).

To turn automatic grammar-checking on or off, select or deselect the 'Check grammar as you type' or the 'Check grammar with spelling' check box on the Spelling & Grammar tab of the Options dialog box. You display this dialog box with the **Tools | Options** command.

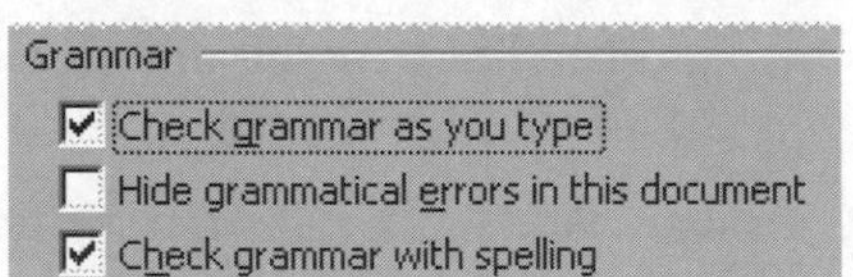

If automatic grammar-checking is turned on, a wavy green line under words indicates possible errors. You use Word's grammar checking features in the same way as its spell-checker.

Printing Options

Word offers a wide range of printing options. These include the ability to preview a document on your screen before you print it, and the choice of printing all your document, the current page, selected continuous or non-continuous pages, or the currently selected text.

Print Preview

Print Preview button

This displays each page as it will appear when it is printed on paper. To preview your document:

- Choose **File | Print Preview** or click the Print Preview button on the Standard Toolbar. Click Close to return to your document.

Print Range Options

When you choose **File | Print**, you have the following options regarding which pages of your document you may print:

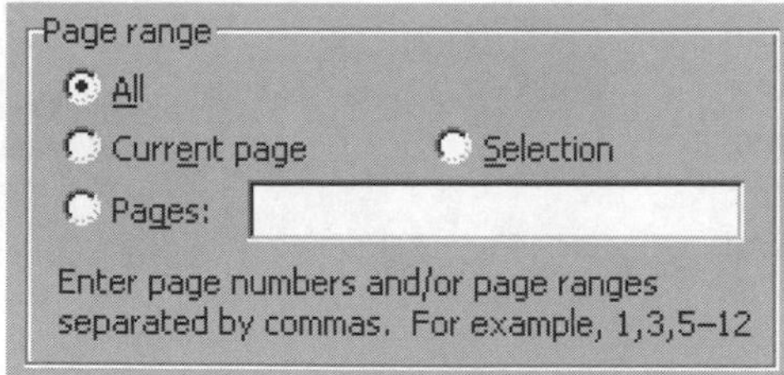

- **All:** Prints every page of your document.
- **Current Page:** Prints only the currently displayed page.
- **Selection:** Prints only the currently selected text (and/or graphic).
- **Pages:** To print any single page of your document, enter its page number here.

To print a group of continuous pages, enter the first and last page number of the group, separated by a dash. For example, 2-6 or 12-13.

To print a non-continuous group of pages, enter their individual page numbers, separated by commas. For example, 3,5,9 or 12,17,34. You can combine continuous with non-continuous page selections.

Other options on the Print dialog box allow you to specify how many copies you want to print of your selected pages, and indicate whether you want to print left or right pages only.

Save and close your long document, and close Microsoft Word.

Modifying the Toolbar

Word's toolbars give you convenient, one-click access to the commands that you use most often. Too many toolbars, however, reduce the area on your screen in which you write and edit.

Hiding and Displaying Toolbars

You can display or hide any of Word's toolbars, according to your personal preference.

- To display a particular toolbar, choose **View | Toolbars** and select the toolbar that you want to display. On the toolbar sub-menu, Word displays a check mark against the toolbar that you have selected.

- To hide a particular toolbar, choose **View | Toolbars** and select the toolbar that you want to hide. On the toolbar sub-menu, Word removes the check mark from the toolbar.

The check marks beside the Standard and Formatting toolbars indicate that they are already selected for display on screen

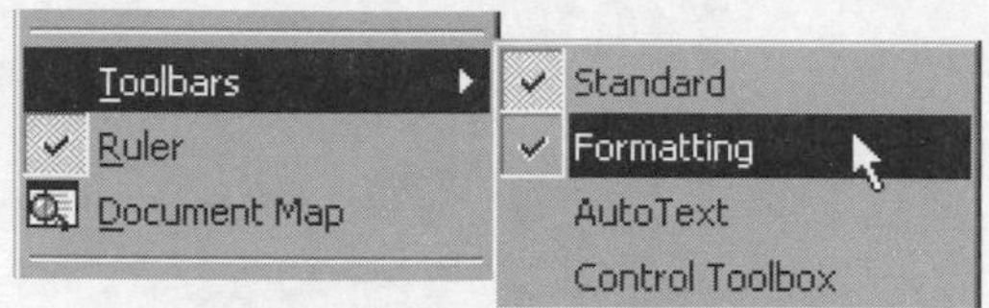

Hiding and Displaying Toolbar Buttons

You can remove one or more buttons from a toolbar. Follow these steps:

- Display the toolbar that you want to change.
- Hold down ALT key, and drag the button off the toolbar.

  Word removes the selected button from the toolbar.

Want the button back again? Follow this procedure:

- Display the toolbar.
- Choose **Tools | Customize**.

  Word displays the Customize dialog box. You do not need to use this dialog box, but it must remain open on your screen.

  Notice that any deleted buttons are again displayed on the toolbar.

- Right-click the button you that want to display again.
- From the pop-up menu displayed, choose **Reset**.

Word closes the Customise dialog box, and redisplays the button on the toolbar.

You have now completed this Section 3.3 of the ECDL Word-Processing Module.

Section Summary: So Now You Know

You can increase or decrease Word's default *inter-line spacing* and *inter-paragraph* spacing.

You can highlight the start of each new paragraph by typing an extra paragraph mark (crude, but effective), by increasing inter-paragraph spacing, or by applying a *first line indent*. The opposite of a first line indent is a *hanging indent*, which is sometimes used for lists.

Word's *find and replace* feature enables you quickly to locate a particular piece of text, and replace it with an alternative piece of text. You can also find and replace text with specific formatting, and special characters such as paragraph marks and tabs.

The standard page size is A4, and pages can be oriented in *portrait* or *landscape*. A *margin* is the distance of the text (and graphics) from a particular edge of the page.

Headers and footers are small text items that reoccur on every (or every second) page, and typically contain such details as the *document title* and *author name*. Either can also contain the automatically generated *page number*.

Word contains a *spell-checker* and a *grammar-checker*. You can set up these checkers so that they are permanently switched on, or you can run them only as you require.

Word's *print options* include a print preview feature and the ability to print one or a range of pages.

Section 3.4: Tables, Tabs and Graphics

In This Section

On most Word documents, you want text to flow left to right across the width of the page. Sometimes, however, you may want to create narrow, side-by-side columns of text, numbers and graphics.

In this Section you will learn about Word's two options for creating such side-by-side columns: tables and tabs.

You will also discover how to insert and manipulate graphics and AutoShapes in Word.

Finally, you are introduced to hyphenation – a way of splitting long words across lines to improve the appearance of text.

New Skills

At the end of this Section you should be able to:

- Create and format tables
- Insert and edit tabs
- Paste and insert graphics
- Create AutoShapes
- Move, reshape and resize graphics and AutoShapes
- Apply automatic and manual hyphenation to text

New Words

At the end of this Section you should be able to explain the following terms:

- Table
- Tab
- AutoShape
- Hyphenation

Using Tables in Word

A table consists of rectangular cells, arranged in rows and columns. Inside cells, text wraps just as it does on a page. As you type text into a cell, the cell expands vertically to hold each new line.

You can create a new, blank table, and enter text and graphics in its empty cells. Or you can convert existing paragraphs of text to a table.

Table

An array of cells arranged in rows and columns that can hold text and graphics.

Exercise 3.31: Creating a New Table

In this Exercise you create a table, and enter text in it.

1) Open Word and click on the New button on the Standard Toolbar to create a new document. Click the Save button to save it. Give your new document a name that you will find easy to remember. If your initials are KB, for example, name it KBtable.doc.

2) Choose **Table | Insert Table**. In the Insert Table dialog box, select 2 columns and 4 rows, and click **OK**. You can add or remove columns and rows later, as required.

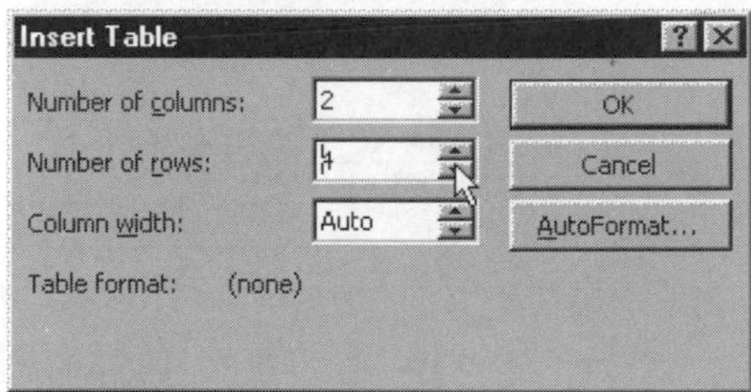

Accept the Column width default of Auto. This creates columns of equal size across the width of your page. Word displays a blank table as shown below.

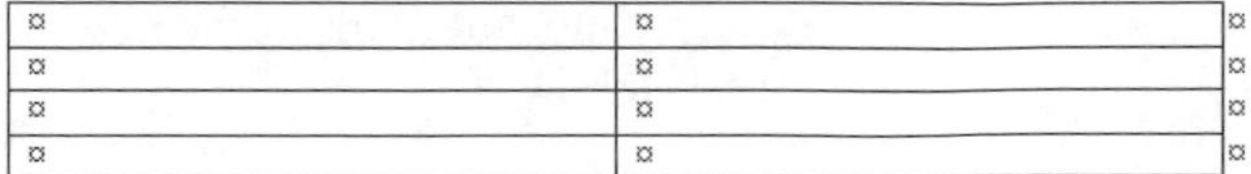

3) Click in the top-left cell, and type: Sales Region

4) Press the TAB key. In a table, pressing TAB does not insert a tab stop. Instead, it moves the cursor to the next cell. SHIFT+TAB moves the cursor back to the previous cell. You can also use the ARROW keys or the mouse to move the cursor between different cells. (To insert a tab in a table, press CTRL+TAB.)

With the cursor in the top-right cell, type the text: Number of Units Sold

5) Continue moving the cursor and typing text until your table looks like the one below.

Sales·Region¤	Number·of·Units·Sold¤	¤
Europe¤	1234¤	¤
Latin·America¤	5678¤	¤
China¤	4321¤	¤

Congratulations. You have created your first table in Word. Save your table document and leave the Word document open.

Selecting Table Cells

You can format and align table text in the same way as text outside a table. Here are the rules on selecting table text:

- To select text in a cell, drag the mouse across the text.
- To select a single cell, click at the left edge of the cell.

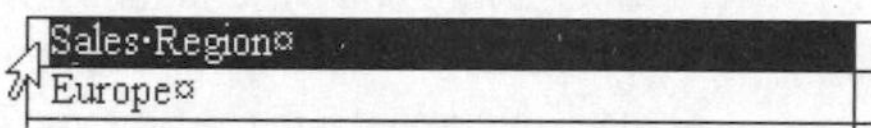

- To select a row, double-click at the left edge of the leftmost cell.
- To select a column, use the mouse to move the cursor to the top edge of the column, wait for the cursor to change to a thick, downward arrow, and then click to select the column.

Number·of·Units·Sold¤	¤
1234¤	¤
5678¤	¤
4321¤	¤

- To select the entire table, click in any cell and choose **Table | Select Table**.

Here are the rules for making changes to a table:

- To add a new row, select the row *beneath* the position where you want to insert the new row, and choose **Table | Insert Rows**.
- To add a new row at the bottom of a table, select the last end-of-row mark, and press ENTER.
- To add a new column, select the column to the *right* of where you want to insert the new column, and choose **Table | Insert Columns**.

- To add a new column at the right of a table, select all the end-of-row marks and choose **Table | Insert Column**.

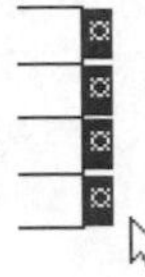

- To delete a row or column, select it, and choose **Table | Delete Rows** or **Table | Delete Columns**.
- To merge two or more selected cells from the same row into a single cell, choose **Table | Merge Cells**.
- To split a single, selected cell into two cells on the same row, choose **Table | Split Cells**.
- To apply borders and shading, select the cells, rows, columns or entire table, and apply the **Format | Borders and Shading** command.
- To turn off a table's default borders (called *gridlines*) so that they appear only on the screen and not on the printout, select the table and choose **Table | Hide Gridlines**.

Exercise 3.32: Formatting and Changing Your Table

1) Select the top row of the table you created in Exercise 3.31, choose **Format | Font**, select Arial, 12 pt, Bold, and click **OK**.
2) With the top row still selected, click on the Centre Align button on the Formatting Toolbar.

Sales·Region¤	Number·of·Units·Sold¤
Europe¤	1234¤

3) Place the cursor in the cell that contains Latin America. Choose **Table | Insert Row**. Type the following text into the new row.

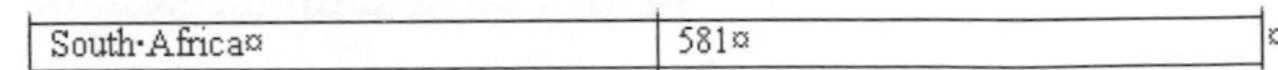
South·Africa¤ | 581¤

4) Select the top row of the table, and choose **Table | Insert Row**.
5) With the new, inserted top row still selected, choose **Table | Merge Cells**.
6) Type the following text in the merged row: Sales Figures.
7) Select the top, merged row, choose **Format | Font**, select Arial, 14 pt, Bold and Italic, and click **OK**.

8) By default, Word places a 1/2 pt black, single solid-line border around each cell. Select the top row, choose **Format | Borders and Shading** and place a double-line border under the first row.

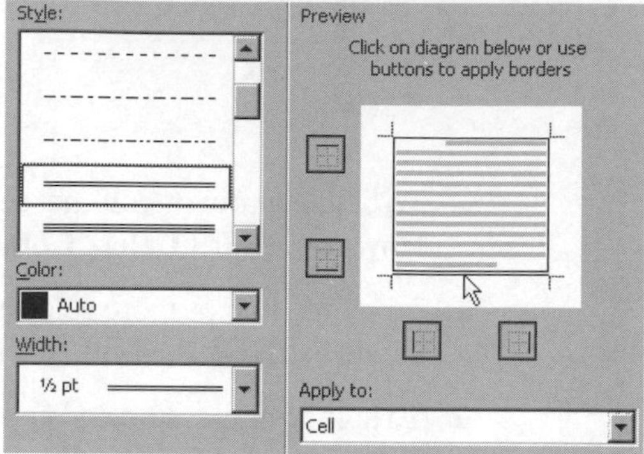

9) Select all rows except the top one, choose **Format | Borders and Shading**, click on the Shading tab, and select a 15% grey background.

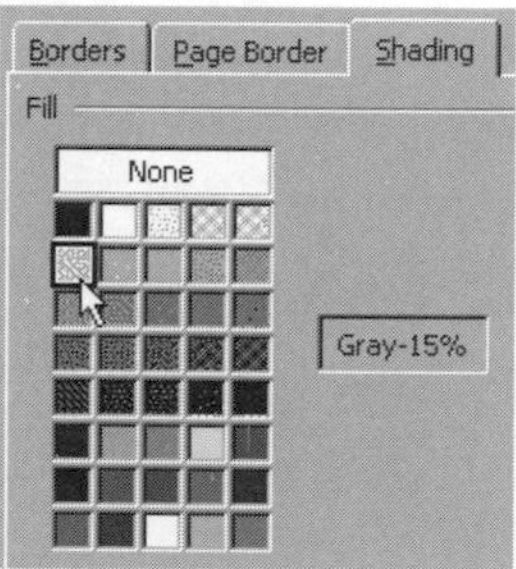

Your table should look as shown.

Save your table document again and leave it open.

Sales Figures	
Sales Region	**Number of Units Sold**
Europe	1234
South Africa	581
Latin America	5678
China	4321

Column Width, Spacing and Row Height

To change the width of a column, use the mouse to position the cursor over the left or right vertical edge of the column. Then drag with the mouse until the column is the width that you require.

As you make a column wider or narrower, Word adjusts the width of the other columns so that the overall table width stays the same. If you hold down the SHIFT key while dragging a column edge, Word changes the width of the whole table accordingly.

You can change the height of cells in a similar way.

The Table AutoFormat Option

Word's AutoFormat option offers a range of predefined formats for your table, including borders and shading. To apply AutoFormat, select your table and choose **Table | Table AutoFormat**. The

Table AutoFormat dialog box offers a preview area where you can view the formatting effects on your table.

Some examples of Word's AutoFormat options

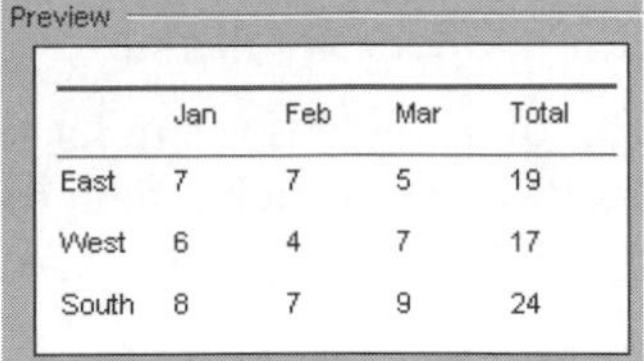

Preview

	Jan	Feb	Mar	Total
East	7	7	5	19
West	6	4	7	17
South	8	7	9	24

Preview

	Jan	*Feb*	*Mar*	*Total*
East	7	7	5	19
West	6	4	7	17
South	8	7	9	24

Preview

	Jan	***Feb***	***Mar***	***Total***
East	7	7	5	19
West	6	4	7	17
South	8	7	9	24

Preview

	Jan	Feb	Mar	Total
East	7	7	5	19
West	6	4	7	17
South	8	7	9	24

Practise by selecting your table and applying a series of AutoFormats. When finished, save and close your table document.

Introduction to Tabs

Old-style typewriters had a key called TAB that, when pressed, changed the position at which the letter keys struck the page and printed text. Typically, there were about ten tab positions – called tab stops – usually about half-an-inch apart.

Pressing the TAB key once advanced the text position to the first tab stop, pressing TAB again moved it to the second tab stop, and so on.

By typing text at the same tab position on successive lines, the typist could create vertical columns of text.

1	2	3	4	5	6	7	8	9	10
	Cajun·Heat·Fries				£1.45				
	Onion·Rings				£1.65				
	Bread·Sticks				£1.25				
	Fried·Cheese·Ravioli				£2.75				
	Primo·Mozzarella·Poppers				£3.25				
	Cream·Cheese·Poppers				£3.95				
	Breaded·Mushrooms				£2.95				
	Breaded·Zucchini·Sticks				£2.75				

The example above shows the second tab stop used to position menu items, and the sixth tab stop used to position menu prices.

As computers and word processing software replaced the typewriter, the idea of tabs continued. Computer keyboards include a TAB key, and Word, like other word-processing applications, offers a tab feature.

The effect of using tabs is similar to using tables: text appears in side-by-side columns rather than running continuously from the left to the right margin on the page.

Tabs

Predefined horizontal locations between the left and right page margins that determine where typed text is positioned. Using tabs on successive lines gives the effect of side-by-side columns of text.

If you want to position small amounts of text such as the address lines at the top of a letter, tabs are quicker to use than tables. Also, tabs have a feature called *leaders* that tables do not have, which can make it easier to read text that is separated into different columns.

Using Tabs in Word

To view the tab stops set up on your copy of Word, choose **Format | Tabs** to display the Tabs dialog box. By default, Word has ten preset tab stops, each one of which is a half-inch apart.

Word's default tab stops in centimetres and inches

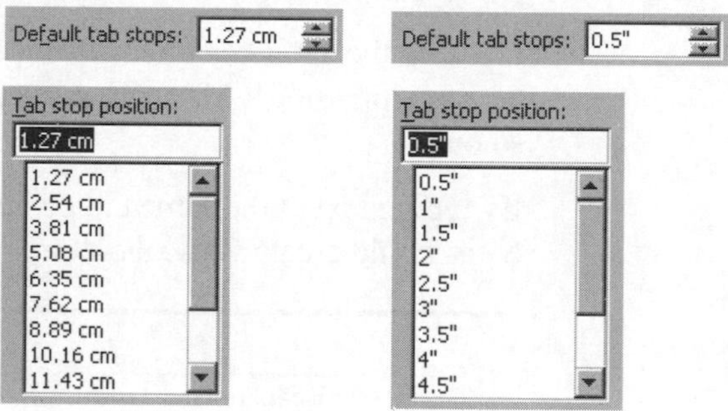

Exercise 3.33: Using Tab Stops

1) Open the letter that you created and saved in Section 3.1.

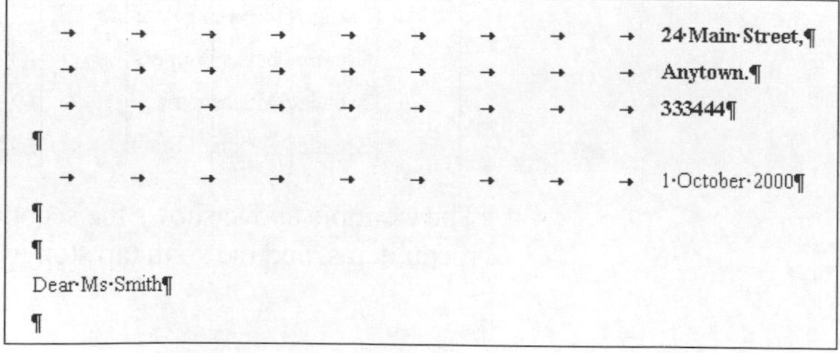

→ → → → → → → → → 24·Main·Street,¶
→ → → → → → → → → Anytown.¶
→ → → → → → → → → 333444¶
¶
→ → → → → → → → → 1·October·2000¶
¶
¶
Dear·Ms·Smith¶
¶

2) Move the cursor to the start of the first line and type: ABC Limited,

3) Move the cursor to the start of the second line and type: Unit 32A,

4) Move the cursor to the start of the third line and type: Smithstown Business Park.

   If your new text pushes any of the sender's address lines to the right or on to the next line, use the DELETE key to remove the tab stops from the line until that address line returns to its original position.

5) Your new text picks up the bold formatting of the sender's address. Change its formatting back to normal. Your letter should now look as below.

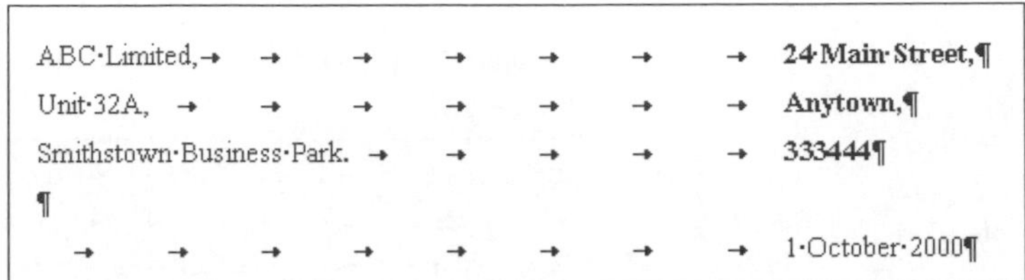

ABC·Limited,→ → → → → → → **24·Main·Street,¶**
Unit·32A, → → → → → → → **Anytown,¶**
Smithstown·Business·Park. → → → → → **333444¶**
¶
→ → → → → → → → 1·October·2000¶

   Save and close your letter document.

In the next Exercise you will use Word's tabs to create a restaurant menu.

Exercise 3.34: Creating a Restaurant Menu with Tabs

1) Open a new document and enter the following text:

Cajun·Heat·Fries·£1.45·Primo·Mozzarella·Poppers·£3.25¶
Onion·Rings·£1.65·Breaded·Zucchini·Sticks·£2.75¶
Bread·Sticks·£1.25·Fried·Cheese·Ravioli·£2.75¶
Cream·Cheese·Poppers·£3.95·Breaded·Mushrooms·£2.95¶

2) Are Word's tabs measured in centimetres or inches? Find out by choosing **Format | Tabs** to display the Tabs dialog box. Click **OK** to close the box.

   If inches, change the tabs to centimetres by choosing **Tools | Options**, selecting the General tab, and selecting centimetres.

3) On the first line of your document, position the cursor at the end of the word Fries, and press DELETE to remove the space between Fries and £1.45. Press TAB repeatedly to move the £1.45 rightwards to the 5.08 cm default tab stop.

4) Repeat step 3) for the other three lines. Your text should look as below.

```
Cajun·Heat·Fries →      →   £1.45·Primo·Mozzarella·Poppers·£3.25¶
Onion·Rings →   →       →   £1.65·Breaded·Zucchini·Sticks·£2.75¶
Bread·Sticks →  →       →   £1.25·Fried·Cheese·Ravioli·£2.75¶
Cream·Cheese·Poppers→   →   £3.95·Breaded·Mushrooms·£2.95¶
```

5) On the first line, position the cursor after £1.45, and press DELETE to remove the space before Primo. Press TAB twice to move the Primo Mozzarella Poppers rightwards to the 7.62 cm default tab stop.

6) Repeat step 5) for the remaining three lines.

7) On the first line, position the cursor after Poppers, and press DELETE to remove the space between Poppers and £3.25. Press TAB repeatedly to move the £3.25 rightwards to the 13.65 cm default tab stop.

8) Repeat step 7) for the remaining three lines. Your text should look as below.

```
Cajun·Heat·Fries·  →    →  £1.45→  →  Primo·Mozzarella·Poppers →  → £3.25¶
Onion·Rings →      →    →  £1.65→  →  Breaded·Zucchini·Sticks  →  → £2.75¶
Bread·Sticks →     →    →  £1.25→  →  Fried·Cheese·Ravioli →   →  → £2.75¶
Cream·Cheese·Poppers→   →  £3.95→  →  Breaded·Mushrooms →      →  → £2.95¶
```

Save your document with a memorable name, and close it. If your initials are KB, for example, call it KBtabsmenu.doc.

Tab Alignment

The tabs you have used so far have all been left-aligned; that is, a tab stop of 5 cm means that the relevant text or number is positioned so that it begins 5 cm in from the left margin. Word offers three other tab alignment options:

- **Centred:** The tabbed text or number is positioned so that its centre is (say) 5 cm from the left margin.
- **Right-aligned:** The tabbed text or number is positioned so that it ends (say) 5 cm from the left margin.
- **Decimal:** If the tabbed item is a number that contains a decimal point, the number is positioned so that the decimal point is (say) 5 cm from the left margin.

  If the tabbed item is a number that does not contain a decimal point, or is text, a decimal tab stop has the same effect as a right-aligned tab.

In the next Exercise you will practise using all four tab stop types – left, right, centre and decimal.

Exercise 3.35: Using All Four Tab Alignment Types

1) Create a new document, and type the text and numbers as shown. Make the text 'Unit Cost' bold.

Unit·Cost¶
.853 ¶
621¶
45¶
26.82¶

2) In turn, select each of the five lines (but not the paragraph mark), and copy and paste it three times to its right. Your document should now look as shown below.

Unit·CostUnit·CostUnit·CostUnit·Cost¶
.853.853.853.853¶
621621621621¶
45454545¶
26.8226.8226.8226.82¶

3) Insert four tab stops on each line as shown below. (The tab positions are Word's default ones.)

→ **Unit·Cost → Unit·Cost → Unit·Cost → Unit·Cost¶**
→ .853 → .853 → .853 → .853¶
→ 621 → 621 → 621 → 621¶
→ 45 → 45 → 45 → 45¶
→ 26.82 → 26.82 → 26.82→26.82¶

4) Select the five lines of text, choose **Format | Tab**, and click **Clear All** to remove all the default tabs.

5) Set the following tab positions and alignments:

Tab stop position	Alignment
2 cm	Left
6 cm	Centre
10 cm	Right
13 cm	Decimal

In each case, type the tab position, select the alignment, and click **Set**.

6) When finished, click **OK**. Your document should now look as shown.

→	**Unit·Cost**	→	**Unit·Cost**	→	**Unit·Cost**	→	**Unit·Cost¶**
→	.853	→	.853	→	.853	→	.853¶
→	621	→	621	→	621	→	621¶
→	45	→	45	→	45	→	45¶
→	26.82	→	26.82	→	26.82	→	26.82¶

Save your document with a memorable name, and close it. If your initials are KB, for example, call it KBunitcost.doc.

Using Tabs with the Ruler

You can display and amend Word's default tab stops by choosing **View | Ruler**. The ruler appears along the top of the document window. You can see the default tab stops at evenly spaced positions along the base of the ruler.

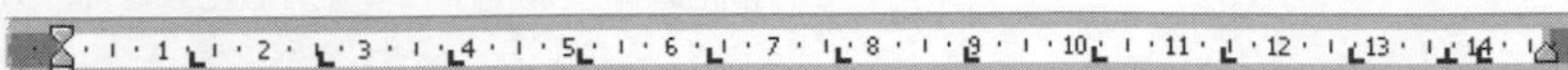

You can change the position of a tab stop by dragging it left or rightwards to a new location on the ruler.

The space between all default tab stops changes proportionately. As you drag a tab stop, Word displays a vertical, dashed line stretching down from the tab ruler to the document itself.

Left
Centre
Right
Decimal point

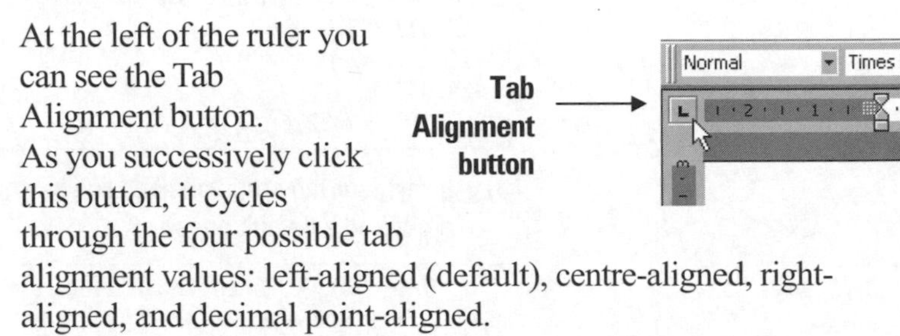

At the left of the ruler you can see the Tab Alignment button. As you successively click this button, it cycles through the four possible tab alignment values: left-aligned (default), centre-aligned, right-aligned, and decimal point-aligned.

To add a new tab stop, click the tab button to display the type of tab you want, and then click the ruler where you want to place the tab. To remove a tab stop, click on it and drag it to the right off the ruler.

Using Graphics in Word

You can illustrate your Word documents with graphics of various kinds. For example:

- Charts (graphs) created in a spreadsheet applications such as Excel.
- Drawings and photographs created or manipulated in graphics applications such as Paint Shop Pro or Adobe Photoshop.

  Word contains sixteen categories of standard or so-called clip art images that you can use and reuse in a wide range of documents. Examples of clip art would be Man Answering Phone, Woman Sitting at Desk, Handshake, Sunset and so on. Clip art is also available on CD-ROMs and on the Internet.

Clip Art

Standard or stock images that can be used and reused in a wide range of documents.

Importing Graphics: Two Options

You have two options for inserting graphics: copy and paste, and file insert. Let's look at these two in detail.

Graphics: Copy and Paste

This option is possible only if you can open the file containing the relevant graphic. To do so, you need to have installed on your computer a software application that can read that graphic format.

For example, to copy into Word a graphic created in Adobe Photoshop, you need Adobe Photoshop installed and open on your computer. Or, failing that, another graphics program capable of opening Adobe Photoshop (.psd) files.

When you have the graphic open in your graphics program, select it (or part of it, as you require), and choose **Edit | Copy** to copy it to the Clipboard. Then, switch to Word, position the cursor where you want the graphic to appear in your document, and choose **Edit | Paste**.

Graphics: File Insert

This option enables you to include a graphic in a Word document – even if you do not have installed the software package in which the graphic was created.

Position the cursor where you want the graphic to appear in your document, and choose **Insert | Picture | From File**. Locate the relevant graphic – it may be on your hard disk, on a diskette in the A: drive, or on a CD-ROM – and click **OK** to insert the image.

To include any of Word's own set of clip art images, choose the **Insert | File | Clip Art** command, select the clip art category, then the individual image, and click **Insert**.

Working With Graphics

There are a number of common operations that you can perform on imported graphics, regardless of their type.

Moving a Graphic

To move a graphic, first select it by clicking anywhere inside it. Next, hold down the mouse button. Word changes the cursor to a cross. Then drag the graphic to its new location.

To move a graphic between documents, use the **Cut** and **Paste** commands on the **Edit** menu.

Changing the Shape and Size of a Graphic

You can change the shape and size of a graphic by selecting it and clicking on any of its six handles.

Hold down the mouse button and drag the edge of the graphic to change its shape. As you drag the object, Word changes its border to a dashed line.

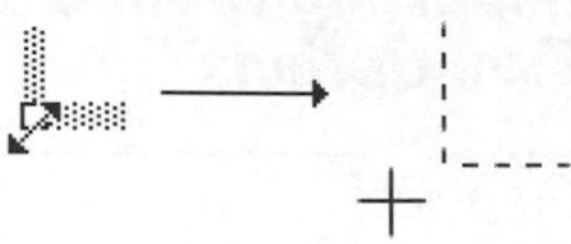

To change a graphic's size but not its shape, hold down the SHIFT key as you drag with the mouse.

Exercise 3.36: Inserting a Word Clip Art Image

1) Open the poster document that you created in Section 3.2.
2) Position the cursor at the end of the last line, All Welcome. Press ENTER to insert a new paragraph mark.
3) With the cursor positioned at the new paragraph mark, choose **Insert | Picture | Clip Art**, select the Pictures tab, scroll down to display the Signs category, and click on it.

4) Click on the No Smoking symbol, and click **OK**. Word creates a new, second page, and inserts the clip art image on it.

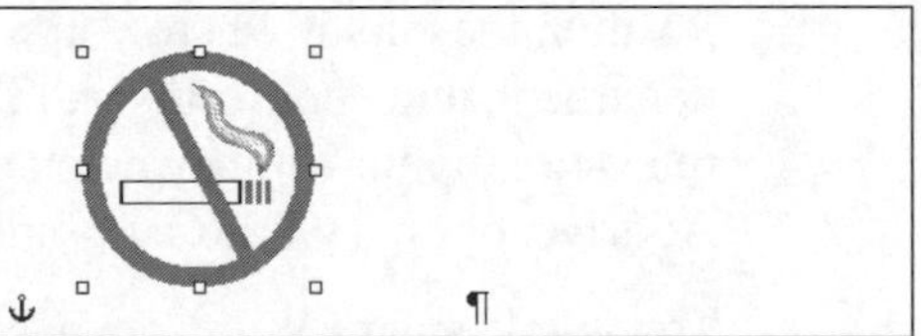

5) Select the graphic, reduce its size by a half, and drag it until it is under the All Welcome line. Delete the paragraph mark that you typed in step 2). The bottom of your poster should now look as shown below. Save your poster.

Inserting AutoShapes

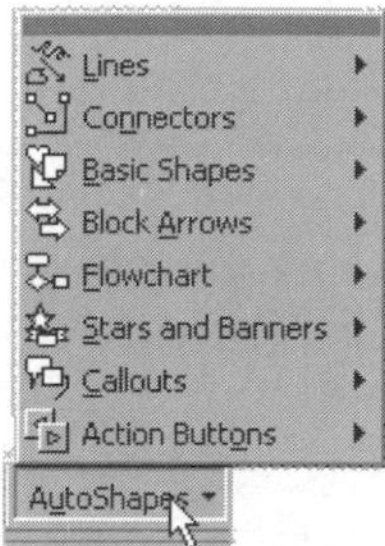

AutoShapes are categories of ready-made shapes that you can insert in your Word documents. They include lines, basic shapes, flowchart elements, stars and banners, and callouts.

When you insert an AutoShape in a document, you can reposition it, and change its size and colour, as required.

To select an AutoShape:

- Display Word's Drawing Toolbar by choosing **View | Toolbars | Drawing**.
- Click the AutoShapes button on the Drawing Toolbar.

You can then choose from the options offered by the pop-up menu.

AutoShapes
Categories of ready-made shapes, including lines, geometric shapes and flowchart elements, which you can use in your Word documents.

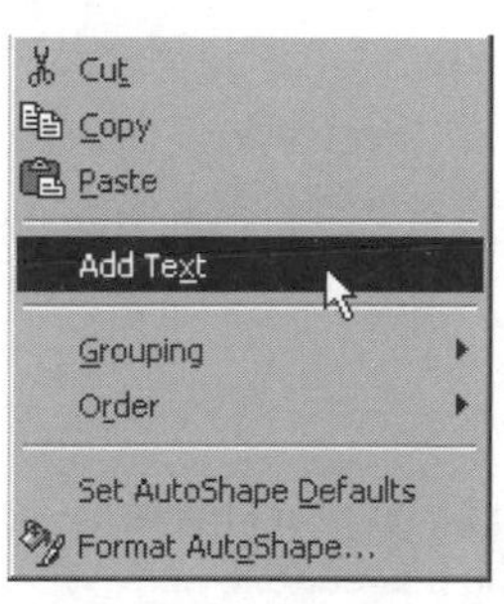

When you right-click on an AutoShape, Word offers a number of options including:

- **Add Text:** This enables you to type characters inside the circle, square, oval or other AutoShape. You can also paste text from the Clipboard into an AutoShape.
- **Format AutoShape:** This enables you to change the border (edge) and fill (background) colours of the AutoShape.

You move and resize AutoShapes in the same way that you can graphics.

Exercise 3.37 provides examples of creating AutoShapes and applying AutoShape features.

Exercise 3.37: Working with AutoShapes

1) If your poster document is not open after Exercise 3.36, open it now.
2) Select the text Admission Free (but not its accompanying paragraph mark).

   Admission·Free¶

3) Cut the selected text from the poster to the Clipboard.
4) With the cursor positioned at the paragraph mark of the cut text, press ENTER to insert a second paragraph mark.

5) With the cursor positioned at the first of the two paragraph marks, choose **View | Toolbars**, and select the Drawing Toolbar option.

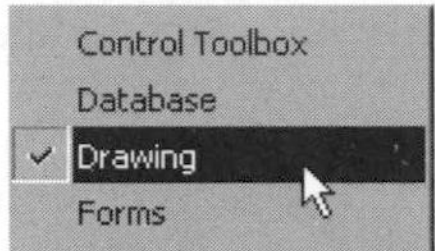

6) Click the AutoShapes button on the Drawing Toolbar. From the pop-up menu displayed, select **Basic Shapes**. Finally, select the Rounded Rectangle AutoShape.

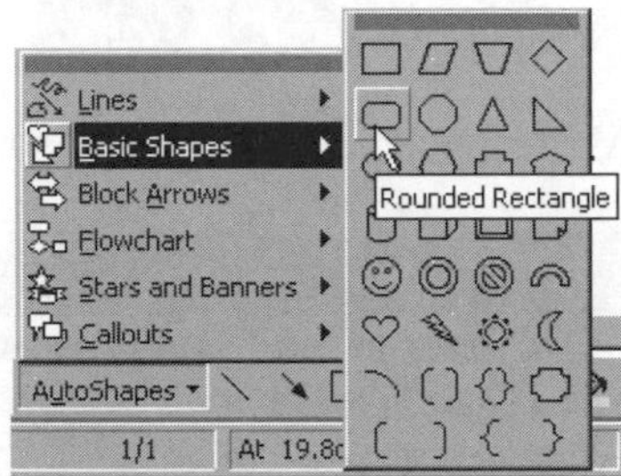

7) Draw the AutoShape so that it is big enough to hold the text in the Clipboard. Position it so that it is centered between the left and right page margins.

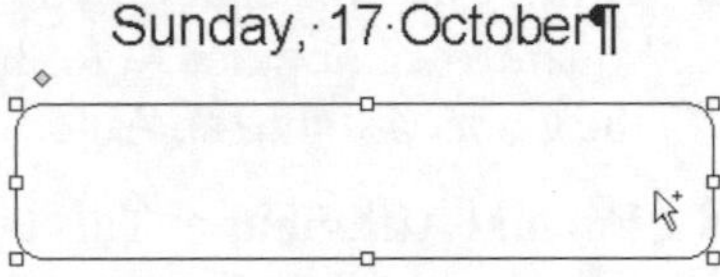

8) Right-click on the AutoShape, choose **Add Text**, and paste the text from the Clipboard to the AutoShape. Select the pasted text, and choose Centre-Align to centre it within the AutoShape. Make the text to Arial, 20 point, Bold.

9) Click any edge of the AutoShape to select it, right-click to display the pop-up menu, and choose **Format AutoShape**.

   On the Colours and Lines tab, select a Fill colour of Yellow. Also, change the Line Weight to 1.5 pt.

10) Select the text within the AutoShape, and, using the **Format | Paragraph** command, change the Spacing Before until the text is centred vertically between the top and bottom edges of the AutoShape. The new poster layout should now look as shown.

When:¶

2pm,¶

Sunday,·17·October¶

Admission·Free¶

All·Welcome¶

Save and close your poster document.

Hyphenating Justified Text

In Section 3.2 you learnt about an alignment option called justification, whereby text is aligned against both the left and right margins. Justification is typically used for the narrow columns of text found in newspapers and magazines.

Justified columns can contain a lot of white (that is, blank) space, because Word spreads out the text in order to align it with both margins simultaneously. This is particularly true when the text contains a lot of long words.

Hyphenation – the process of breaking up long words and splitting them across two lines – gives justified text a more professional appearance. Consider the following two examples:

Word spreads out the text in order to align it with both margins simultaneously. This is particularly true when the text contains a lot of long words.

Hyphenation Off

Word spreads out the text in order to align it with both margins simultane-ously. This is particularly true when the text con-tains a lot of long words.

Hyphenation On

Word applies two rules when hyphenating text: certain words are never hyphenated, and words that are hyphenated are split only in certain places. Word allows you to hyphenate both justified and unjustified text.

Hyphenation

The process of splitting a long word across two successive lines to avoid unsightly amounts of white space. Used mostly in narrow, justified columns of text.

You can hyphenate text in two ways: automatically or manually.

Automatic Hyphenation

Word can hyphenate your document automatically as you type. To use this option, choose **Tools | Language | Hyphenation**, select the 'Automatically hyphenate document' check box, and click **OK**.

☑ Automatically hyphenate document

Automatic Hyphenation Options

If you select automatic hyphenation, Word offers you a number of options that let you control how it applies hyphenation to your document.

- **Text in Capitals:** Typically, only headings are in capitals, so you can decide to turn automatic hyphenation off for capitalised text.
- **Hyphenation Zone:** The amount of space that Word leaves between the end of the last word in a line and the right margin. It applies only to unjustified text. Make the zone wider to reduce the number of hyphens, or narrower to reduce the raggedness of the right margin.
- **Consecutive Hyphens:** The number of consecutive lines that Word hyphenates.

Manual Hyphenation

If you don't want Word to insert hyphens in your text automatically, ensure that the 'Automatically hyphenate document' check box is deselected.

The better option is to turn automatic hyphenation off, and run manual hyphenation after you have finished writing and editing, and adding and removing text.

Running Manual Hyphenation

To hyphenate your document (or a selected part of it) manually, choose **Tools | Language | Hyphenation** and click **Manual**.

Word scans through your text, and when it finds a word it thinks it should hyphenate, it displays a dialog box similar to the one below.

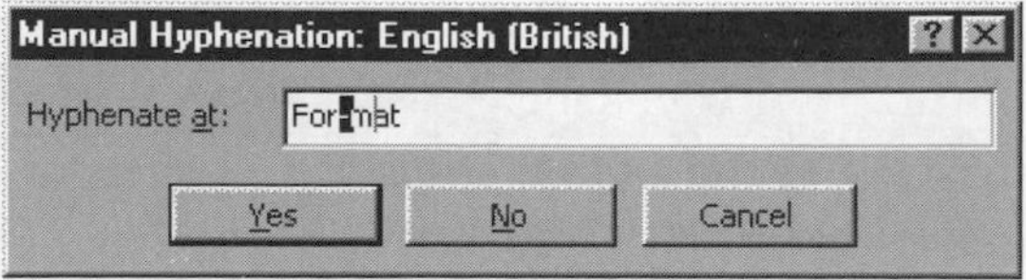

Click **Yes** if you want Word to insert a hyphen in the suggested location. If you prefer Word to insert the hyphen at a different location, move the cursor to that location, and then click **Yes**. Alternatively, click **No** to leave the word unbroken.

You can close any open documents and exit Microsoft Word. You have now completed Section 3.4 of the ECDL Word Processing Module.

Section Summary: So Now You Know

A Word *table* consists of rectangular cells arranged in rows and columns. As required, you can insert and delete rows and columns in a table, split a single cell into two cells, or merge multiple cells into a single cell.

You can also change row and column height and width, apply formatting, and add borders and shading. Word's *AutoFormat* option provides a quick way to improve the appearance of any table.

Tabs are predefined horizontal locations that, when used on successive lines, give the appearance of columns.

You can add *graphics* to a Word document in two ways: by copy and paste, or by inserting the graphic as a file. You can move, reposition, resize or change the shape of any graphic.

AutoShapes are ready-made shapes that you can insert in your Word documents. They include lines, basic shapes, flowchart elements, stars and banners, and callouts. You can manipulate AutoShapes in a similar way to graphics.

You can use Word's *hyphenation* feature to remove unsightly amounts of white space by splitting long words across successive lines. Hyphenation is applied mostly to narrow columns of justified text.

Section 3.5: Mail Merge and Templates

In This Section

Bulk mail is the name given to mass-produced letters that contain individual names and addresses (as in 'Dear Ms Murray') but have the same basic text (as in 'Allow us to introduce our Spring Promotion...'). A more commonly used term might be junk mail.

How is it done? Each letter is basically the same, but clearly no one letter is just a copy of another, as each is slightly different. Read this Section to find out.

Hint: each letter is the result of combining or merging two separate components: the form letter, which contains the basic text, and the data source, which holds a list of names, addresses and other details.

Also in this Section you will learn about templates and styles. These are quick, convenient ways to create documents that can contain ready-made text, images, formatting and page settings.

New Skills

At the end of this Section you should be able to:

- Create the two components of a merged letter: the form letter and the data source
- Select the appropriate merge fields and insert them in a form letter
- Merge a form letter with a data source to produce a mail merge
- Explain the two possible roles of a Word template: document model, and interface controller
- Choose an appropriate Word template for a document type
- Explain the relationship between styles and templates, and apply styles to selected text
- Attach a different template to a document, and create a new template
- Apply Word's document views – Normal, Page Layout and Outline

New Words

At the end of this Section you should be able to explain the following terms:

- Form letter
- Template
- Data source
- Style
- Merge field
- Normal view
- Page Layout view
- Outline view

Mail Merge: the Components

Think of a mail merge as composed of two components: a form letter and a data source. And think of merge fields as the glue that binds the two together. Read on to discover what these three terms mean.

Form Letter

The form letter holds the text that remains the same in every letter – plus punctuation, spaces and perhaps graphics.

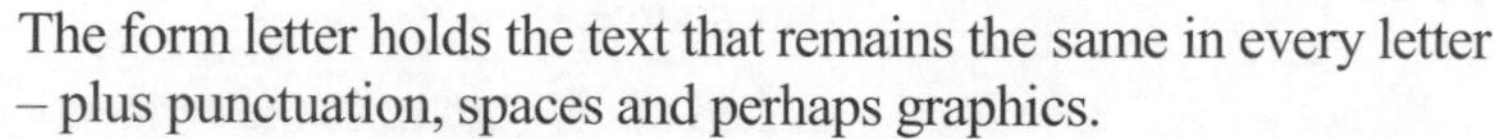

You never type the names or addresses in the form letter, because these will be different on each copy of the final, merged letter.

Form Letter

A Word document containing information (text, spaces, punctuation and graphics) that remains the same in each copy of the merged letter.

Data Source

The data source holds the information that changes for each copy of the final, merged letter – the names and addresses of the people that you want to send the merged letters to.

You can create a data source in Word, or in a spreadsheet (such as Excel) or database (such as Access). Whichever file type you use, its contents must be arranged in a table. Along the top row must be the titles identifying the information categories in the columns underneath, such as Title or Last Name.

Data Source

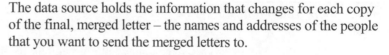

A file containing information (such as names and addresses) that will be different in each merged copy of the final letter.

Merge Fields

The merge fields are special instructions that you insert in your form letter. They tell Word which details you want to merge from your data source, and where Word is to position them in your merged letter.

«FirstName»¶

«Title»·«LastName»,¶

«Company».¶

Merge fields are enclosed within double angle brackets.

Merge fields have names such as Job Title, First Name and Town. When you merge the form letter and the data source, Word replaces the merge fields in the form letter with the associated details from the data source. For example, Word might replace the merge field called Town with Bristol, Carlisle or Derby on different copies of the merged letter.

Merge Field

An instruction to Word to insert a particular type of information, such as job title or a line of an address, in a specified location on the form letter.

Mail Merge: the Procedure

You can think of a mail merge as a five-step process. Steps one and two are about preparing the ingredients: the form letter and the data source.

In step three, you make the connection between the two by inserting the merge fields in your form letter – one merge field for every item of information that you want to merge to the form letter from the data source.

Step four is optional, but recommended. Before you produce your merged letters, take a preview of the first one or two to check that the merge worked successfully.

Finally in step five, print your merged letters.

One: Prepare Your Form Letter

This is simply a Word document. Using the **Tools | Mail Merge** command, you can do one of the following:

- Create a new letter especially for the merge operation.
- Select a letter you have already typed as the form letter.

Exercises 3.38 and 3.39 show you how to perform these steps.

Two: Prepare Your Data Source

Again, using the **Tools | Mail Merge** command, you can do one of the following:

- Create a new Word file and enter the names, addresses and other details of the people you plan to send the merged letter to

  -or-

- Select a file created in another software application.

You will learn how to create a Word data source in Exercise 3.40.

Three: Insert Merge Fields in Your Form Letter

When you open your form letter on screen, Word displays a special Mail Merge Toolbar. One of its buttons is called Insert Merge Field. This is the one you use to select and then position the merge fields in your form letter. Exercise 3.41 shows you how to insert the merge field codes.

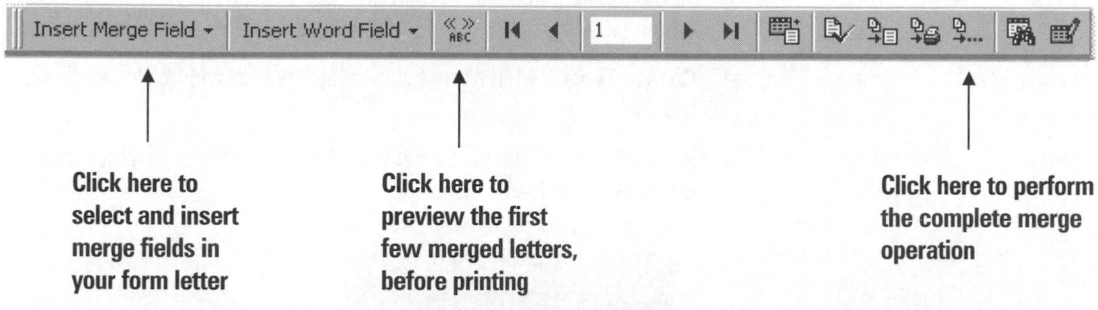
Insert Merge Field
Insert Word Field
1
Click here to select and insert merge fields in your form letter
Click here to preview the first few merged letters, before printing
Click here to perform the complete merge operation

Four: Preview Your Merged Letters

Before you produce your (perhaps hundreds or thousands!) of merged letters, click on the toolbar's View Merged Data button to preview the first one or two merged letters.

You will learn how to preview your merged letters in Exercise 3.42.

Five: Print Your Merged Letters

Merge to:
Printer

If you are happy with the preview, click on the Mail Merge button to perform the complete merge operation. Select the Merge to Printer option to output copies of your merged letters.

You will learn how to print your merged letters in Exercise 3.43.

Word gives you the option of saving all the merged letters in a single file. You don't need to do this, because you can quickly recreate them at any stage by rerunning the merge operation.

Your Mail Merge Exercises

Exercises 3.38 to 3.43 take you, step-by-step, through a complete, worked example of a mail merge operation.

For these Exercises, we will assume that the merged letters are produced on pre-printed paper that already contains the sender's name and address. Only the recipients' names and addresses need therefore be inserted.

Exercise 3.38: Using an Existing Document as a Form Letter

Do you still have the letter you saved from Exercise 3.33? If so, this Exercise shows you how to use that text as a basis for your form letter.

If not, proceed to Exercise 3.39 to create a new form letter from scratch.

1) Open the file that you saved in Exercise 3.33 of Section 3.4.

2) Remove the recipient's name and address from the top left of the letter, and remove the sender's address from the top right. Also delete the 'Ms Smith' after the word 'Dear'.

3) At the top left, type 'To:' and press TAB. Insert three new lines, each with a tab stop, under the 'To:'. Your letter should look like that shown.

4) Choose **Tools | Mail Merge** to display the Mail Merge Helper dialog box.

5) In the Main document area, click the **Create** button to display a drop-down list of options.

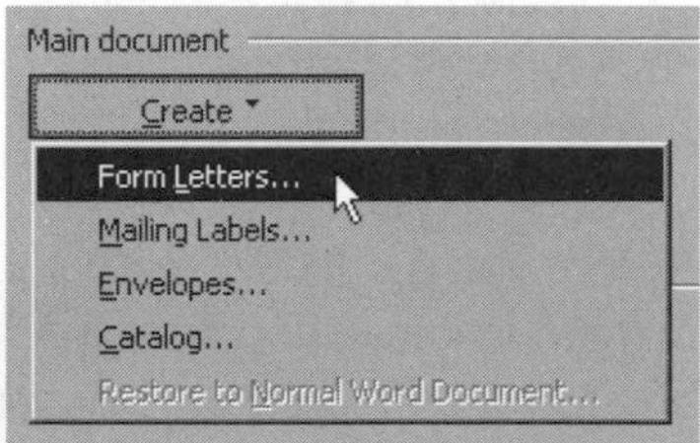

From this list, select the option named Form Letters.

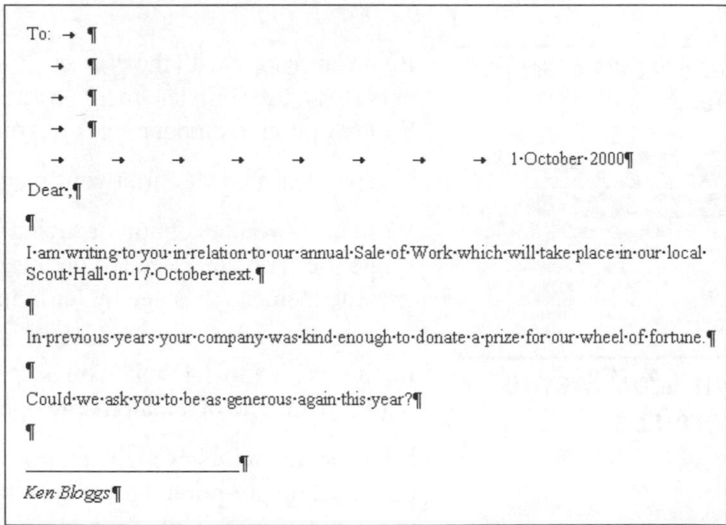
To: → ¶
→ ¶
→ ¶
→ ¶
→ → → → → → → → 1·October·2000¶
Dear,¶
¶
I·am·writing·to·you·in·relation·to·our·annual·Sale·of·Work·which·will·take·place·in·our·local·Scout·Hall·on·17·October·next.¶
¶
In·previous·years·your·company·was·kind·enough·to·donate·a·prize·for·our·wheel·of·fortune.¶
¶
Could·we·ask·you·to·be·as·generous·again·this·year?¶
¶
_____________________¶
Ken·Bloggs¶

6) On the next dialog box displayed, click the **Active Window** button.

7) Word next displays a dialog box that asks you to select or create a data source. Proceed to Exercise 3.40.

Exercise 3.39: Creating a New Form Letter

Follow this Exercise to create a new form letter for a mail merge operation.

1) Choose **Tools | Mail Merge** to display the Mail Merge Helper dialog box.

2) In the Main Document area, choose the **Create** button to display a drop-down list of options.

   From this list, select the option called Form Letters.

   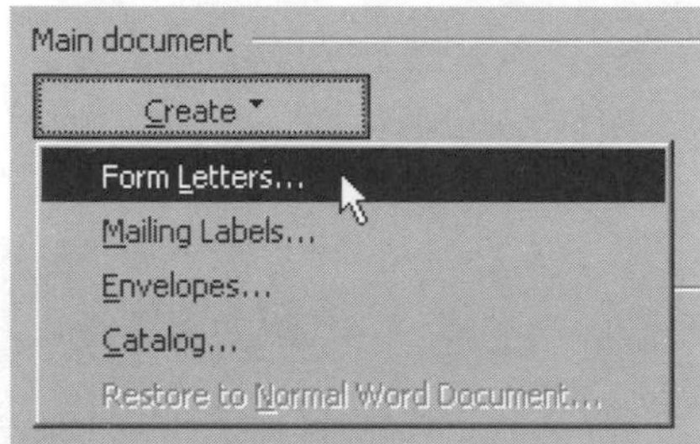

3) On the next dialog box displayed, click the **New Main Document** button, and click **Cancel**.

4) Word leaves a new document open on your screen for you to enter the text of your form letter. Type the text as shown in Exercise 3.38.

5) Click the File Save button and give your new document a name that you will find easy to remember. If your initials are KB, for example, name it KBformlet.doc.

Proceed to Exercise 3.40.

Exercise 3.40: Creating a Data Source

In this Exercise you create your data source to contain the names, addresses and other information that will vary on each copy of the final, merged letter.

Do not begin this Exercise until you have completed either Exercise 3.38 or 3.39.

1) If the Mail Merge Helper dialog box is not already open, choose **Tools | Mail Merge** to display it.

2) In the Data source area, choose the **Get Data** button to display a drop-down list of options.

   From this list, select the option called Create Data Source.

3) Word now displays the Create Data Source dialog box.

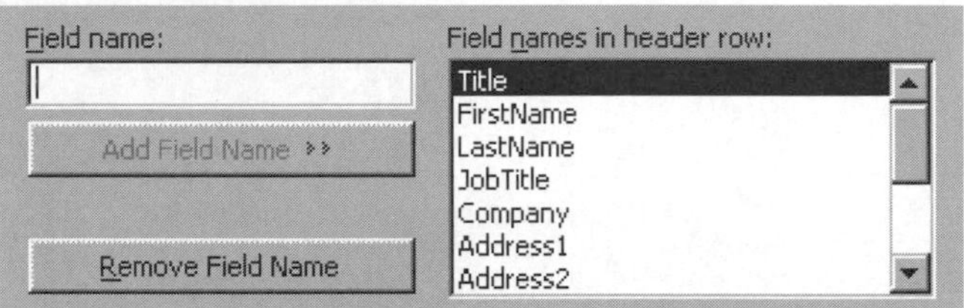

4) In the case of each of the following merge fields, click the field name in the list displayed then click the **Remove Field Name** button to delete them: JobTitle, City, State, PostalCode, Country, HomePhone and WorkPhone.

5) You now have all the merge fields that you need. Click **OK**.

6) Word next asks you to name and save your Data Source file. If your initials are KB, for example, name it KBDataSource and click **Save**.

7) You are now shown the dialog box below. Click **Edit Data Source**.

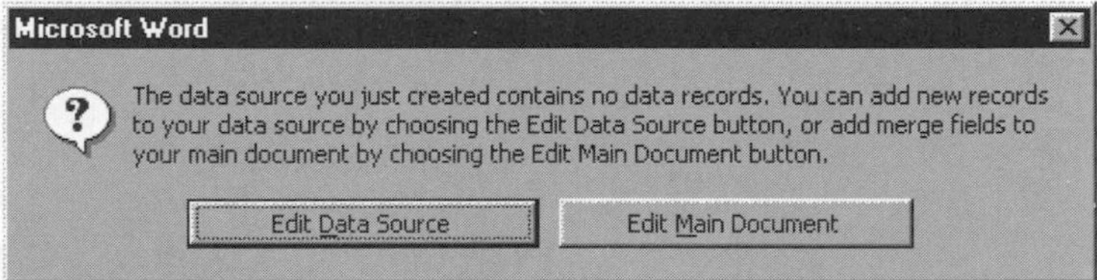

8) Word displays a Data Form dialog box. Enter the information as shown and click **Add New**.

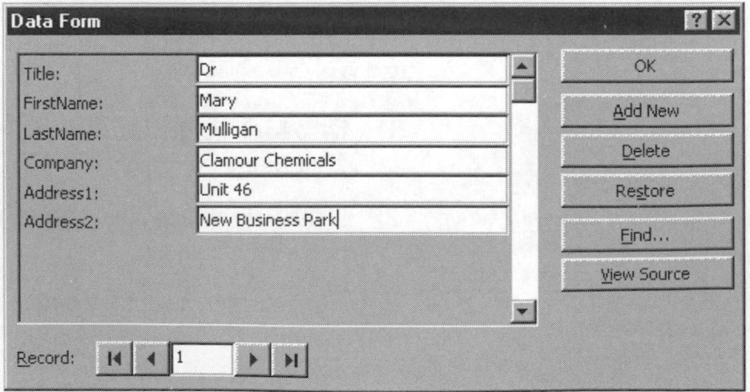

9) Enter a second set of details in the Data Form dialog box as shown below. Click **Add New** and then click **OK**.

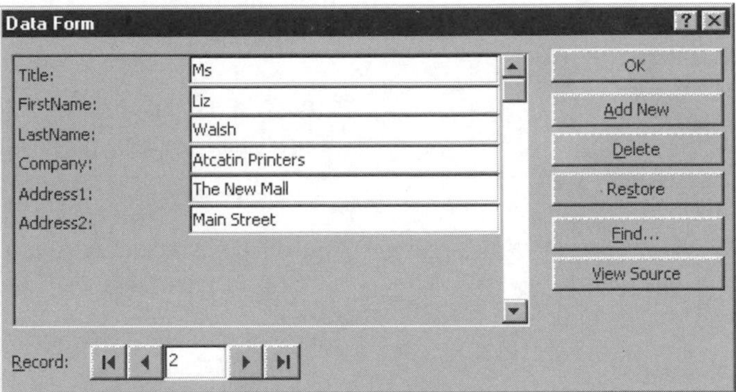

You have now created a Data Source with two records – enough for this Exercise. But you can easily imagine a Data Source with hundreds or thousands of records, each record holding the name, address and other information regarding a particular person or organisation.

Viewing Your Word Data Source

You can open, view and edit your data source file just as you can any other Word document. Open the data source you created in Exercise 3.40. It should look like the following:

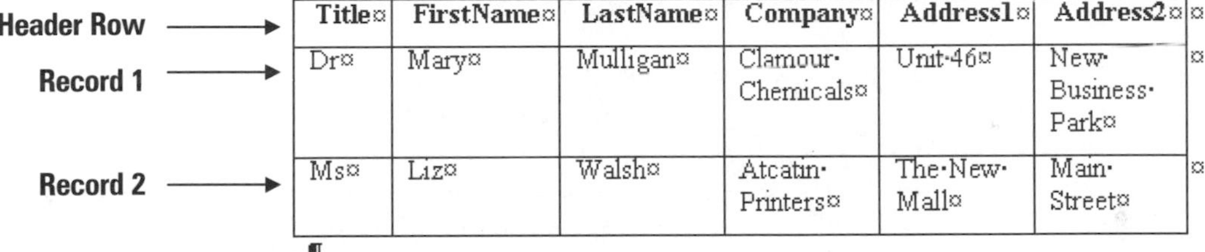

Title	FirstName	LastName	Company	Address1	Address2
Dr	Mary	Mulligan	Clamour Chemicals	Unit 46	New Business Park
Ms	Liz	Walsh	Atcatin Printers	The New Mall	Main Street

¶

You can see a header row containing the merge field names such as FirstName and LastName. And under the header row are the records themselves, each in a row of its own.

Using Non-Word Data Sources

Does your data source have to be a Word document? No. You can also use files created in a spreadsheet such as Excel or a database such as Access. The only requirement is that the information is arranged in the same type of table format: a single, top row of merge field titles, followed by other rows holding individual records.

Inserting Merge Codes in Your Form Letter

Before you move on to the mail merge operation, you need to perform one more step. You must insert the merge field codes in your form letter. Exercise 3.41 shows you how.

Exercise 3.41: Inserting the Merge Field Codes

1) Open your form letter document.

2) For each merge field:

   - Place the cursor in the appropriate position in your form letter
   - Click the Insert Merge Field button on the Mail Merge Toolbar, and
   - Click the relevant field title from the drop-down list.

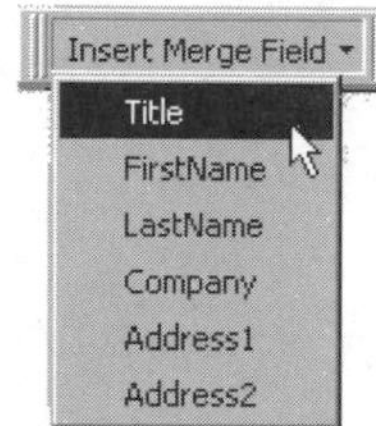

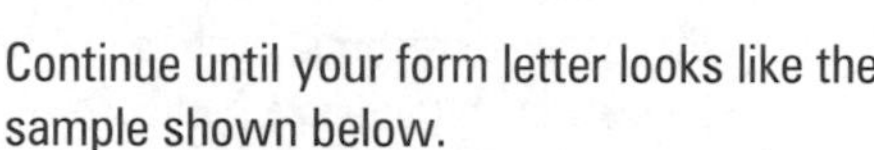

   Continue until your form letter looks like the sample shown below.

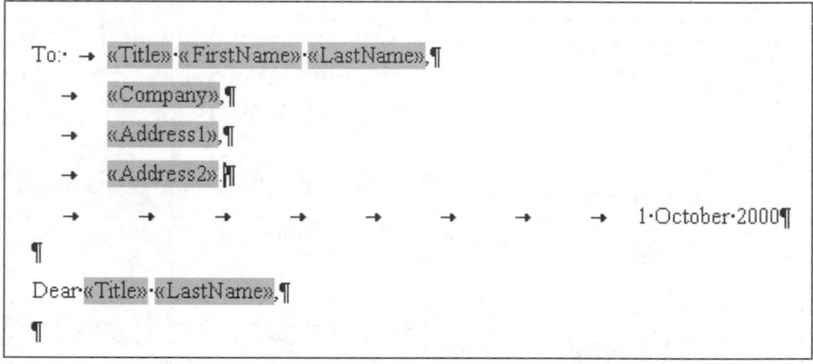

To: → «Title» «FirstName» «LastName»,¶
→ «Company»,¶
→ «Address1»,¶
→ «Address2».¶
→ → → → → → → → 1 October 2000¶
¶
Dear «Title» «LastName»,¶
¶

   Do not forget to type spaces between merge fields just as you would between ordinary text. Also, type commas or full stops at the end of lines.

   Save and name your form letter when finished.

Now everything is in place for the mail merge operation.

Exercise 3.42: Previewing the Mail Merge

View Merged Data button

1) If your form letter is not already open, open it now and make it the active window.

2) Click the View Merged Data button on the Mail Merge Toolbar. Word displays the first merged letter. It should look as shown on the next page.

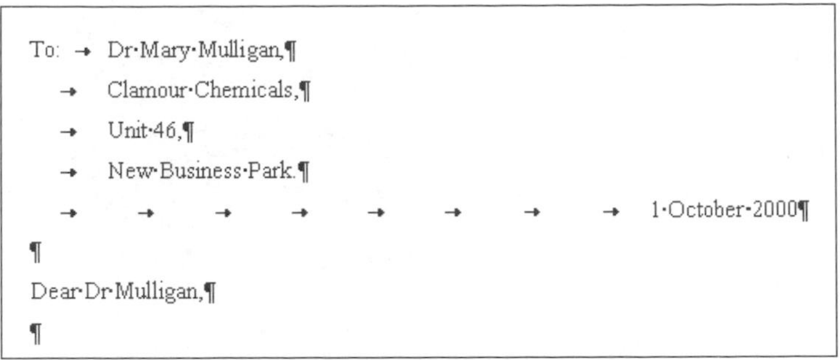

To: Dr Mary Mulligan,
Clamour Chemicals,
Unit 46,
New Business Park.
1 October 2000

Dear Dr Mulligan,

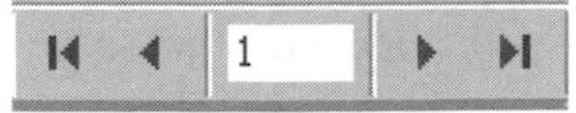

Arrow buttons

3) You can view the second merged letter by clicking the Forward Arrow button on the Mail Merge Toolbar.

You are now ready to perform the mail merge.

Exercise 3.43: Performing the Mail Merge

Mail Merge button

1) If your form letter is not already open, open it now and make it the active window.

2) Click the Mail Merge button on the Mail Merge Toolbar to display the Merge dialog box. Select the options as shown below and click **Merge**.

3) Word now displays the Printer dialog box. Click **OK**. Your form letter and the two records from the data source are now merged to the printer.

Congratulations! You have performed your first mail merge in Word.

Merging Addresses to Labels

You can use Word's mail merge features to print a list of names and addresses (or any other list or structured information) on adhesive labels. Exercise 3.44 shows you how.

Exercise 3.44: Merging to Address Labels

1) Click New to open a new Word document.

2) Chose **Tools | Mail Merge**.

3) Click **Create**, select the Mailing Labels option, and then click the **Active Window** button.

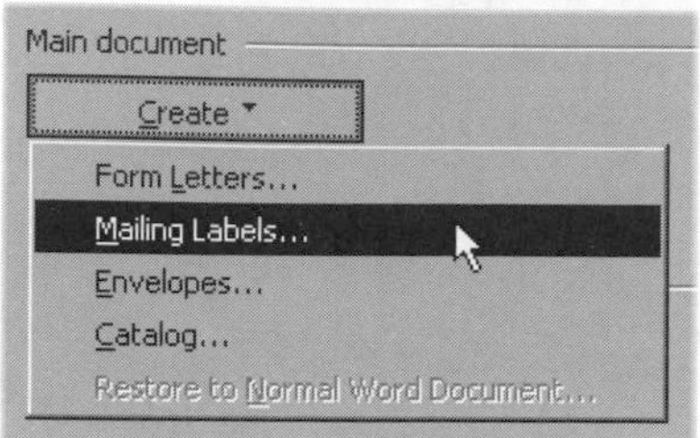

4) Click **Get Data** to select the source of the names and address that you want to use. Word offers three options:

- **Create Data Source:** Select this to enter the name and address information in Word.
- **Open Data Source:** Select this to use a list of names and addresses that is contained in an existing Word document (or in a spreadsheet, a database, or other list).
- **Use Address Book**: Select this to use names and addresses from an electronic address book such as that contained in Outlook Express.

For this Exercise, choose the **Open Data Source** option, and select the Word document that you created as a data source in Exercise 3.40.

5) Click **Set Up Main Document**.

In the Label Options dialog box, select the type of printer and the type of labels you want to use, and click **OK**.

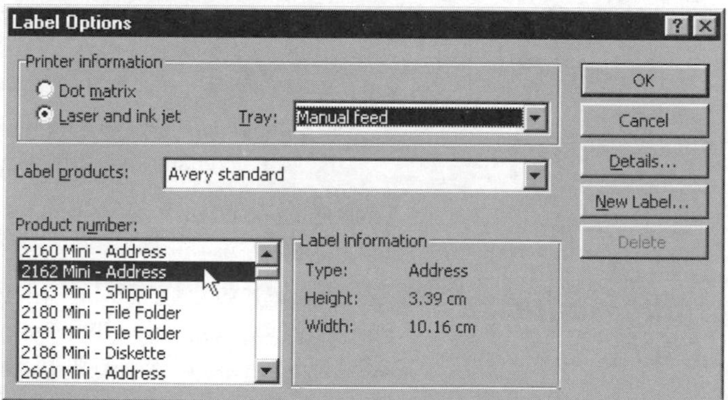

6) In the Create Labels dialog box, insert the merge fields for the address information.

7) In the Mail Merge Helper dialog box, click **Merge**.

8) In the Merge to box, click **Printer** to merge to the selected printer.

Well done! That completes your mail merge exercises.

Word Templates

Microsoft Word is made up of three components: the Word software application itself, the document files that Word produces, and a third component, which you now meet for the first time: templates.

- **Word Application:** This provides the standard Word menus, commands and toolbars – the things you use to create and work with documents.
- **Document Files:** Look in any of these and you will find the text, graphics, formatting, and settings such as margins and page layout for that particular document.
- **Word Templates:** These have two main purposes:
    - They can provide a model for creating documents.
    - They control Word's interface: the menus, commands and toolbars available to the user.

A Template as a Document Model

A template can act as a document model by storing:

- Built-in text and graphics such as your company's name and logo. These are sometimes called 'boilerplate' text and graphics.
- Preset formatting (such as font settings) and text positioning (such as alignment, indents, tab stops, and inter-line and inter-paragraph spacing settings).
- Preset page settings (such as margins and page orientation).

For example, you could save everyone in your organisation time by creating a memo template that contained preset margins, the company logo, and text for standard headings such as 'Memo', 'To:' and 'From:'. With much of the formatting and typing already done, users simply fill in the additional text.

A Template as an Interface Controller

A template can also store customised Word commands, menus and toolbar settings. This allows managers to remove unused and unnecessary features, and adapt Word to meet the needs of different levels of users.

For example, you could create a template that helped new Word users by displaying a customised toolbar with buttons and menus to lead them through everyday tasks.

Templates and Documents

Whether you realised it or not, every new Word document that you have created has been based on a template.

A single template can provide the basis for lots of documents. But each document can be based on only a single template at a time.

A template, like a document, is a Word file. Whereas document file names end in .doc, template file names end in .dot.

The Normal.dot Template

Unless you choose otherwise, every new Word document you create is based on a template called Normal.dot.

In addition to this standard, all-purpose template, Word provides templates for specific document types such as letters, memos and reports.

Word Template

A file that can contain ready-made text, formatting and page settings, and interface controls. Every Word document is based on, and takes its characteristics from, a template of one kind or another.

Templates and New Documents

New button

In Section 3.1 you learned two ways to create a new document:

- Clicking on the New button on the Standard Toolbar
- Choosing the **File | New** command.

If you click the New button, Word automatically bases your new document on the Normal.dot template.

Choose **File | New**, however, and Word presents you with a wide range of templates to choose from. You will find the various templates on different tabs of the New dialog box.

Exercise 3.45: Previewing Word's Templates

1) Choose **File | New** to display the New dialog box.

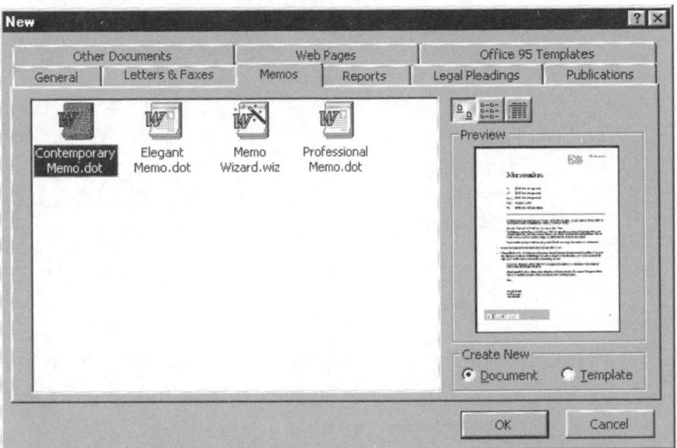

2) Click on the various tabs to view the available templates.

3) Click on the various templates to view a miniature of them in the Preview area on the right of the dialog box.

Templates and Styles

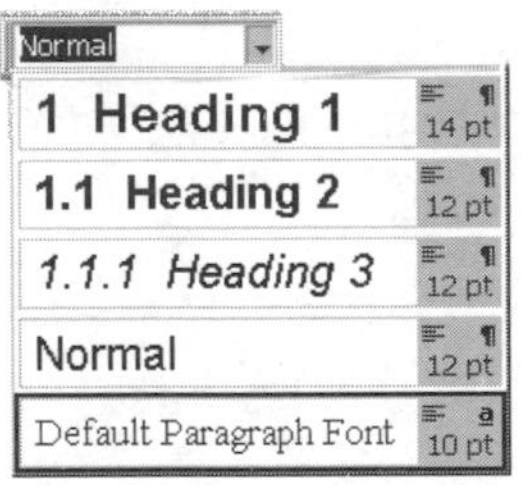

Style drop-down list box

At the top-left of the Standard Toolbar is a drop-down list box containing items called Normal, Heading 1, Heading 2 and so on. These items are termed *styles*.

For ECDL, you need know only four things about styles:

- A style is a bundle of formatting and text positioning settings.
- You apply a style by first positioning the cursor in the text, and then clicking on that style from the drop-down list.
- Unless you choose otherwise, Word applies the style called Normal to all text you type in a document.
- Styles are linked to templates. For example, in one template the style called Heading 3 might be centre-aligned, Times, 10 point, italic. In another, Heading 3 might be left-aligned, Arial, 12 point, bold.

Exercise 3.46: Applying a Style to Text

In this Exercise you will open a document that you previously created and saved, and apply a style to its headings.

1) Open the document that you saved in Exercise 3.30 of Section 3.3.

2) Choose **Edit | Replace**, and on the Replace tab, type the text Heading One in both the Find what: and Replace with: boxes.

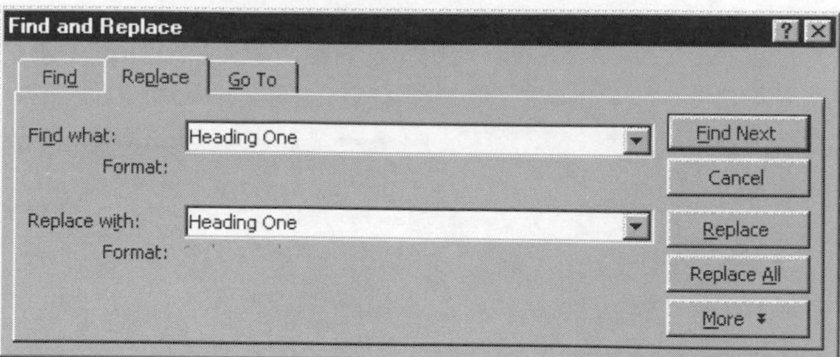

3) With the cursor in the Replace with: box, click the **More** button. Next, click the **No Formatting** button to remove the formatting left over from previous exercises.

4) Select the option **Style** from the pop-up menu, and then select the style Heading 1 from the list displayed. Click **OK**.

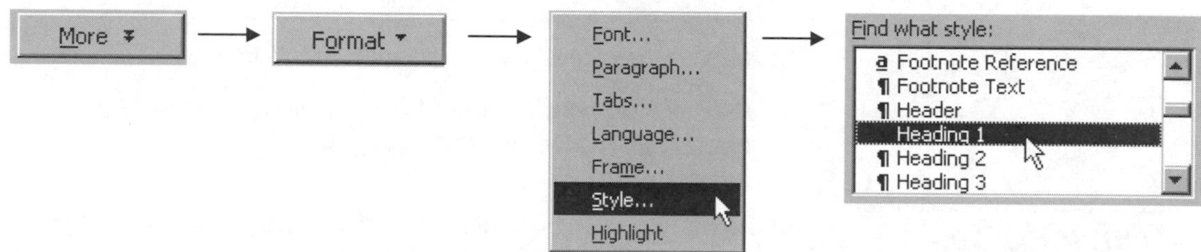

5) You are returned to the Find and Replace dialog box. Click **Replace All**.

Word now applies the style called Heading 1 to all the headings in your document. Unless you have at some stage changed the Heading 1 style that comes with Normal.dot, the Heading 1 font should be Arial 14 point, bold. Save the document.

Why Use Styles?

Using styles to control the appearance of a document has three advantages:

- You can apply a bundle of formatting and text positioning settings to a piece of selected text in a single, quick operation.
- By changing the settings of a particular style, Word can automatically apply your new settings to all occurrences of text in that style throughout the entire document.

  For example, by changing the Heading 1 style from bold to italic, all text with the Heading 1 style changes from bold to italic. This is so much faster than individually selecting and then changing every heading.
- If you change the template on which a document is based, the document takes its style settings from the new template.

You can therefore change the entire appearance of a document by linking it with a different template. Exercise 3.47 illustrates this point.

Style
A collection of formatting and positioning settings that you can apply to selected text in a single operation. Styles are linked to templates, and can have different settings in different templates.

Exercise 3.47: Attaching a Different Template to a Document

1) If the document you worked with in Exercise 3.46 is not already open, open it now. Select all the text in the document, and chose **Edit | Copy** (or CTRL+c). You can now close that document.

2) Choose **File | New** to display the New dialog box. Click the Reports tab, and then click the template called Professional Report.dot. Finally, click **OK**.

3) Word opens a new document that is based on Professional Report.dot.

   This contains instructions which you can ignore. Hold down the CTRL key and click in the left margin to select everything in the new document, and then press DELETE to delete the new document's contents.

Heading·One¶

How·does·AutoSummarize·determine·what·the·key·points·are?·AutoSummarize·analyzes·the·document·and·assigns·a·score·to·each·sentence.·(For·example,·it·gives·a·higher·score·to·sentences·that·contain·words·used·frequently·in·the·document.)·You·then·choose·a·percentage·of·the·highest-scoring·sentences·to·display·in·the·summary.¶

Keep·in·mind·that·AutoSummarize·works·best·on·well-structured·documents·-for·example,·reports,·articles,·and·scientific·papers.¶

4) Choose **Edit | Paste** (or press CTRL+v) to paste the text copied from your document into the new document. Save and name your new document.

Notice how all text in your document with the Normal and Heading 1 styles changes in appearance. This is because such text is now taking its settings from the Professional Report.dot template – and not from the Normal.dot template on which the document was originally based.

You can now close the document.

Creating a New Template

Word offers a number of ways of creating a new template. Here is the easiest way:

- Create a document that has the features you want in your template – some boilerplate text, perhaps, or a particular margin setting.
- With the document open on your screen, save it, not as a document, but as a template.

In future, whenever you use the **File | New** command to create a document, your new template appears as an option on the General tab of the New dialog box.

Exercise 3.48 takes you through an example of this procedure.

Exercise 3.48: Creating a New Template

1) Create a new document and enter the following:

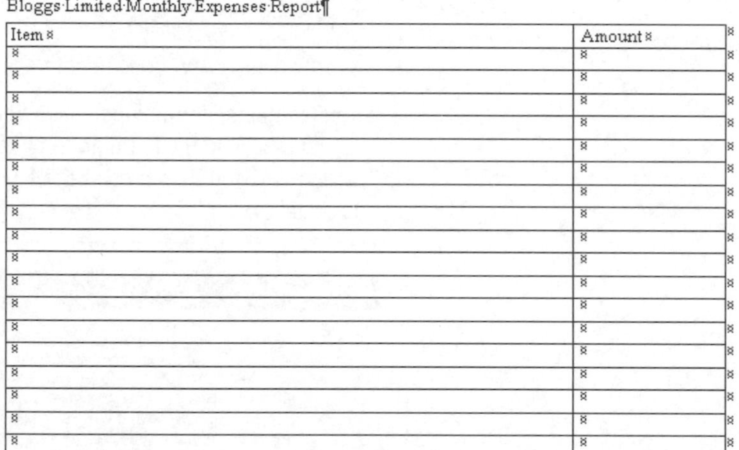

Bloggs·Limited·Monthly·Expenses·Report¶

Item	Amount

Apply the following settings:

- Page Orientation: Use the Paper Size tab displayed by the **File | Page Setup** command to change the page orientation to Landscape.
- Heading: Centre-align the heading, and make it Times New Roman, 20 point.
- Table: Create a 2-column, 19-row table. Select the table and, using the Row tab displayed by the **Table | Cell Height and Width** command, set the row height to 20 points.

2) Choose **File | Save As**, and save the file as a template.

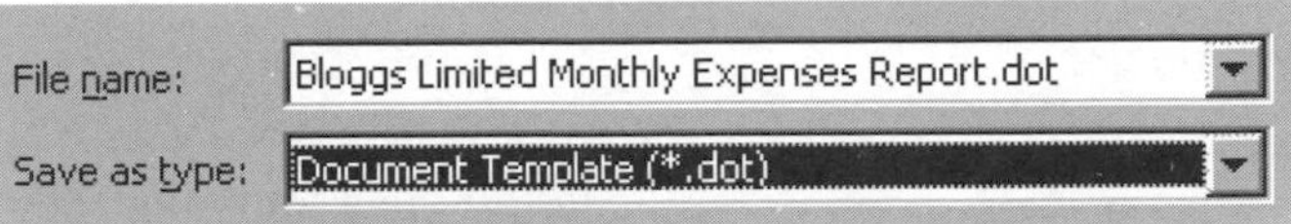

3) Choose **File | Close** to close your new template.

4) Choose **File | New** to display the General tab of the New dialog box, where you can see your new template as an option. Select your new template and then click **OK**.

Word creates a new document based on your template. You can close the template.

Styles and Outline View

Using styles in your Word documents offers another advantage: it allows you to display documents in a way that reflects their structure. Such a structured view of a document is called an Outline view.

To switch to outline view, choose **Views | Outline**. An Outline view of a document that is formatted using styles would typically look as follows:

- **This·is·Heading·One·Style¶**
  - This·is·body·text·(in·Normal)¶
  - **This·is·a·Heading·Two·Style¶**
    - This·is·body·text·(in·Normal)¶
- **This·is·Heading·One·Style¶**
  - This·is·body·text·(in·Normal)¶

In the above example, three styles are applied: Heading 1, Heading 2 and Normal (the default, used for body text).

Notice that Word progressively indents styled text according to its level of importance in the document, starting with Heading 1.

To change from Outline view, choose the **View** menu and select the option **Normal** view or **Page Layout** view. These are explained in the next topic.

Outline View
A view of a Word document that is formatted using styles. Outline view displays the structure of a document, with text indented progressively to reflect its level of importance.

Other Document Views

The two most common document views in Word are Normal and Page Layout.

Normal View

Normal view is Word's default view for all new documents. It is the fastest view for typing, editing and scrolling. Any graphics or AutoShapes in the document are not displayed in this view. To switch to Normal view, choose **View | Normal**.

Normal View
A view of a Word document that displays only text.

Page Layout View

If you insert a graphic or an AutoShape in a document, Word automatically switches to Page Layout view. While it is necessary for manipulating graphics and AutoShapes, Page Layout view may slow down such tasks as typing, editing and scrolling. To switch to Page Layout view, choose **View | Page Layout**.

If you are working with a long document that contains a small number of graphics or AutoShapes, you may want to switch to Normal view.

Page Layout View
A view of a Word document that displays any graphics or AutoShapes in that document.

You can close any open documents and exit Microsoft Word. You have now completed this Section 3.5 of the ECDL Word-Processing Module.

Section Summary: So Now You Know

Mail merge is the process of combining a *form letter* (which holds the unchanging letter text) and a *data source* (which holds the names, addresses and other details that are different in every merged letter).

The data source can be created in Word, or in a spreadsheet (such as Excel) or database (such as Access). Whichever the file type, the data source contents must be arranged in a table. Along the top row must be the titles identifying the information categories in the columns underneath, such as Title or Last Name.

Merge fields in the form letter indicate which details are taken from the data source, and where they are positioned on the final, merged letter.

A *template* can act as a *document model* by storing built-in text and graphics such as your company's name and logo, preset formatting and text positioning, and preset page settings. A template can also act as an *interface controller* by specifying which of Word's menus, commands and toolbars are available to the user.

A template, like a document, is a Word file. Whereas document file names end in .doc, template file names end in .dot.

Unless you choose otherwise, every new Word document you create is based on a template called *Normal.dot*. Word also provides templates for specific document types. You can create new templates, and change the template on which a document is based.

Styles, which are linked to templates, enable you to apply a bundle of formatting and text positioning settings to selected text in a single, quick operation.

In *Outline* view, you can display the structure of a document that has been formatted using styles. Use *Normal* view to display only the text in a document, and *Page Layout* view to display both text and any graphics or AutoShapes that it may contain.

Section 3.6: File Formats and Importing Spreadsheet Data

In This Section

In this Section you will learn how Word 97, as with all other applications, uses a particular file format. You will also discover how to convert your documents into other, non-Word 97 file formats, so that they can be opened and read by people who work with applications other than Word 97.

Copying and pasting within and between Word documents was covered in previous Sections of this Word-Processing Module. This Section takes you a step further, and shows you how to move data from a spreadsheet file to a word-processor document. As you will see, you can transfer the data in either of two ways: pasting or embedding.

New Skills

At the end of this Section you should be able to:

- Save Word 97 documents in the following file formats: earlier versions of Word, RTF, WordPerfect, Text-Only and HTML.
- Explain the difference between pasting and embedding spreadsheet data in Word.
- Paste spreadsheet data from Excel into a Word document.
- Embed spreadsheet data from Excel into a Word document.

New Words

At the end of this Section you should be able to explain the following term:

- File Format

File Formats

In Section 3.2 you met the term *format*, where it referred to items that affect the appearance of text in a Word document – italics, colours, bullets, and so on. When used alongside the word 'file', however, format has another, different meaning.

In ECDL Module 1 you learnt how all information stored on a computer consists ultimately of just two characters: 1 and 0. This raises two questions:

- When you open a file, how are these 1s and 0s translated into the text and graphics you see on your computer screen?
- And, when you save a file, how are the text and graphics converted back to 1s and 0s on your computer?

The answer is that the application developers apply a set of rules that translate between the 1s and 0s and the displayed text and graphics. Such a set of rules is called a file format.

File Format

A set of rules that translates 1s and 0s into text and graphics on computers screens and printouts, and vice versa.

A Word file, for example, is said to be in Word file format, an Excel file in Excel file format, and so on.

Different Applications, Different File Formats

Different software companies, however, use different rules for translating 1s and 0s into the text and graphics on screens and printouts.

Moreover, different versions of the one application often use different file formats. The Microsoft Word 97 file format, for example, is different from the file format in the two previous versions of Word.

These different file formats, as you can imagine, can create problems.

- In one company's file format, for example, the characters 10101010 might translate as the letter 'w' in Arial, 12 point italics, positioned 5 cm from the left page margin.
- In another, the same characters of 10101010 might convert to a thick blue line running down the left-hand side of the page.

File Name Extensions

The format of a file is revealed by its three-letter file name extension, which the software application adds to the file name when the user saves the file.

The file name extension of .doc, for example, indicates a Word file, and .xls an Excel one. If you have worked with graphics files, you have probably met files with extensions such as .bmp, .gif and .jpg.

The file format used in pages on the World Wide Web is HTML, which stands for HyperText Markup Language. HTML file names typically end in .htm.

Word's File Format Options

Word 97 offers you the ability to save your documents in a format other than its own. This feature is very useful when you want to provide a file you have created to someone who uses a word processor other than Word 97.

To view the file formats in which you can save your Word 97 documents:

- Open a document.
- Choose **File | Save As**.
- Click on the arrow to the right of the Save as type: box.

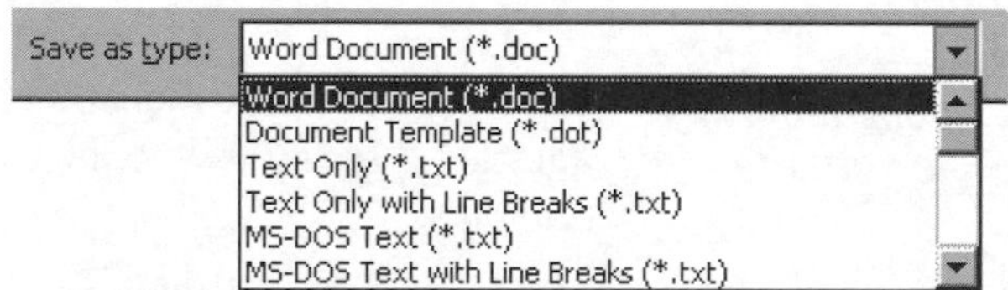

Only some of the listed options are relevant to this ECDL Word-Processing Module.

Previous Word Version

To save your Word 97 document in a previous Word file format, select either Word 6.0/95 or Word 2.x for Windows. Both file formats have the same file name extension as Word 97 (.doc).

Saving a Word 97 file in an earlier file format may result in some adjustment or loss of formatting.

Rich Text Format

This is the common format of all Microsoft Office applications, including Word. A Word 97 document saved in this file format looks just like one saved in Word 97's own file format. The file name extension that is added is .rtf.

WordPerfect Format

Select from these options to save your document so that it can be opened and read within WordPerfect, another word-processor application. Of the various WordPerfect options listed, the most commonly used is WordPerfect 5.x for Windows.

Converting a file from Word 97 to WordPerfect may result in some adjustment or loss of formatting. The file name extension of WordPerfect for Windows files is also .doc.

Text-Only Format

As its name suggests, this format saves only the text of a file. Any text formatting (such as bold or italics) or graphics contained in the Word 97 file are lost. The file name extension added is .txt. This format is also called plain-text or ASCII format.

Only two of the various plain-text options offered by Word are relevant:

- **Text-Only:** Each paragraph of the original Word document occupies a single line of the plain-text file, often resulting in very long lines of text that you can view only by scrolling horizontally.

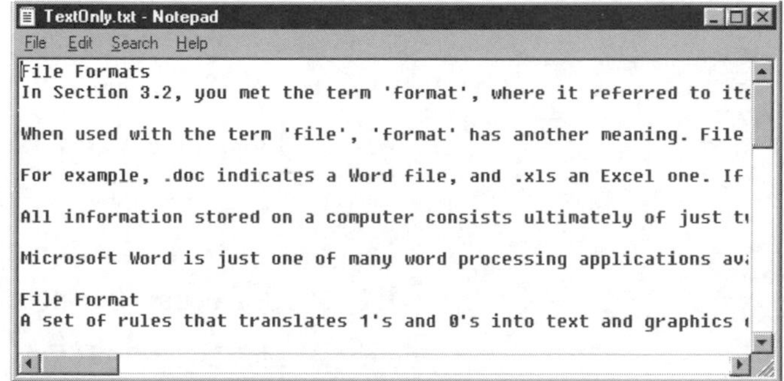

TextOnly.txt - Notepad
File Edit Search Help
File Formats
In Section 3.2, you met the term 'format', where it referred to ite
When used with the term 'file', 'format' has another meaning. File
For example, .doc indicates a Word file, and .xls an Excel one. If
All information stored on a computer consists ultimately of just t
Microsoft Word is just one of many word processing applications av
File Format
A set of rules that translates 1's and 0's into text and graphics

A Text-Only file, viewed in Notepad

- **Text-Only with Line Breaks:** A paragraph break is inserted everywhere a line ended in the original Word document, so that each line of the Word document becomes a separate paragraph in the plain-text file.

  The advantage of this file format is that line width remains the same as in the original Word document, so that the text is easier to read on screen.

  The disadvantage is that the plain-text file contains many more paragraph marks than the original Word file, and these can make editing the plain-text file awkward.

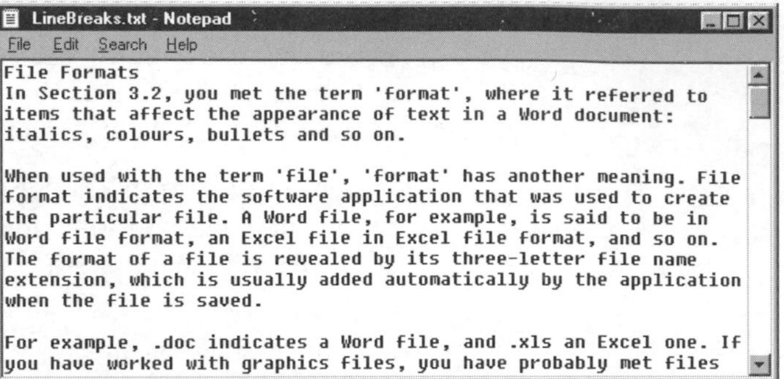

LineBreaks.txt - Notepad

File Edit Search Help

File Formats
In Section 3.2, you met the term 'format', where it referred to items that affect the appearance of text in a Word document: italics, colours, bullets and so on.

When used with the term 'file', 'format' has another meaning. File format indicates the software application that was used to create the particular file. A Word file, for example, is said to be in Word file format, an Excel file in Excel file format, and so on. The format of a file is revealed by its three-letter file name extension, which is usually added automatically by the application when the file is saved.

For example, .doc indicates a Word file, and .xls an Excel one. If you have worked with graphics files, you have probably met files

A Text-Only with Line Breaks file, viewed in Notepad

Because plain-text is such a 'basic', no-frills format, plain-text files can be opened and read correctly by just about all software applications on virtually every type of computer. Plain-text is the file format most commonly used in electronic mail messages on the Internet.

HTML (Web) Format

Web pages are created using the HTML file format. The file name extension of this format is .htm (or, sometimes, .html).

You can save a Word 97 file in HTML format in either of two ways:

- Choose **File | Save As HTML**.

  -or-

- Choose **File | Save As**, and select the HTML Document option.

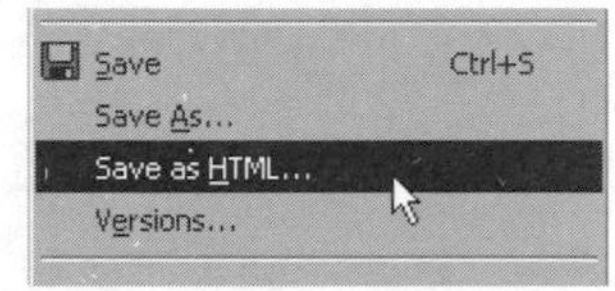

You can display and print HTML format files with a web browser application such as Microsoft Internet Explorer or Netscape Navigator.

Embedding or Pasting Spreadsheet Data

Microsoft Office applications (and most other Windows applications) allow you to transfer information between them. For this ECDL Module, you need only know how to insert data (text and numbers) into Word from the spreadsheet application, Microsoft Excel. In Excel, numbers and text are stored in little boxes called cells.

To transfer information from Excel to Word, follow these steps:

- Open the Excel file and select the required cells.
- Copy the selected Excel cells to the Clipboard.
- Open the Word file and insert the Excel cells in Word.

Pasting Special Options

The Word command you use for pasting Excel cells is **Edit | Paste Special**.

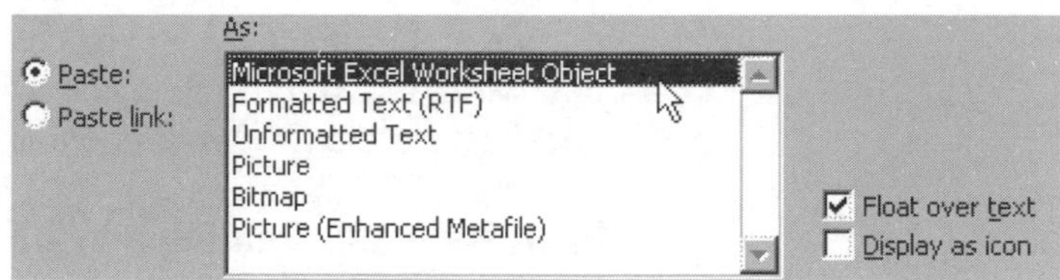

The Paste Special dialog box offers the following options:

- **Paste or Paste Link:** Leave this as the default of Paste.
- **Float Over Text/Display As Icon:** Leave this at its default of Float Over Text.
- **As:** Two options are relevant here: Formatted Text (RTF) and Microsoft Excel Worksheet Object. These options are explained in the next two topics.

Pasting from Excel

When you insert with the Formatted Text (RTF) option, the inserted spreadsheet data:

- Becomes fully part of Word
- Is displayed as a Word table
- Can be edited within Word itself

Pasting Excel data into Word in this way is similar to pasting from another Word document.

Embedding from Excel

When you select with the Microsoft Excel Worksheet Object option, the inserted spreadsheet data:

- Is positioned within Word, but remains part of Excel
- Behaves like an imported graphic – it can be repositioned and resized by selecting and dragging
- Cannot be edited within Word

If you try to edit the spreadsheet data in any way (to change a number, for example, or apply a different border style), Word's menu and toolbars disappear from your screen and are replaced by Excel's ones. Inserting data in this way brings with it the functionality of the application in which it was created. This is called *embedding*.

The following four Exercises demonstrate pasting and embedding from Excel to Word.

In Exercise 3.49 you create two copies of an identical Word document. In Exercise 3.50 you create the Excel data for inserting into Word. In Exercises 3.51 and 3.52 you embed and paste your Excel data in the two Word documents.

Exercise 3.49: Creating a Word Document that You Can Embed and Paste Data Into

1) Open Word and create a new document.
2) Type the following text and press ENTER twice:

   First Quarter Sales Figures
3) Select the text and make it Arial, Bold Italic, 22 point. Centre-align the text.
4) Type the following text and press ENTER three times:

   Congratulations Everyone!!!
5) Select the text you typed in step 4) and make it Times New Roman, Normal Italic, 24 point. Centre-align the text. Your document should now look as shown.

   First·Quarter·Sales·Figures¶

   ¶

   Congratulations·Everyone!!!¶

   ¶

   ¶
6) Save and name the Word document. If your initials are KB, for example, save it as KBsalesfigures1.doc.
7) Choose **File | Save As** to resave your Word document – but this time save it under a different name. For example, KBsalesfigures2.doc.
8) Choose **File | Open** and re-open the first saved version of your Word document.

You now have two Word documents, with identical content, open on your screen.

Exercise 3.50: Creating an Excel Data Source File

1) Choose **Start | Programs | Microsoft Excel** to open a new Excel file on your screen.
2) Click on the cell at location C3, type the word January, and press ENTER.

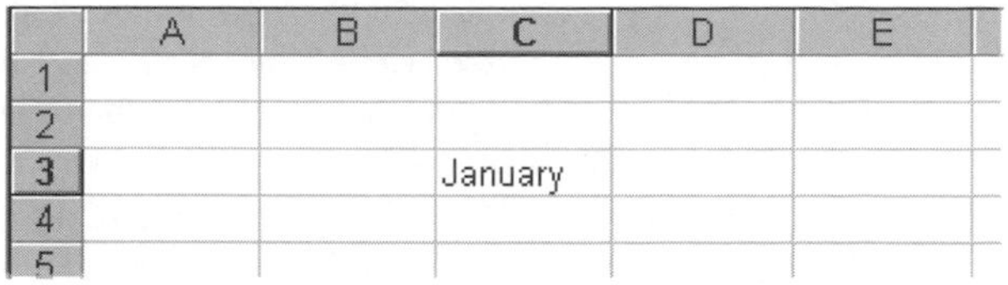

	A	B	C	D	E
1					
2					
3			January		
4					
5					

3) Enter more text and numbers to Excel as shown below.

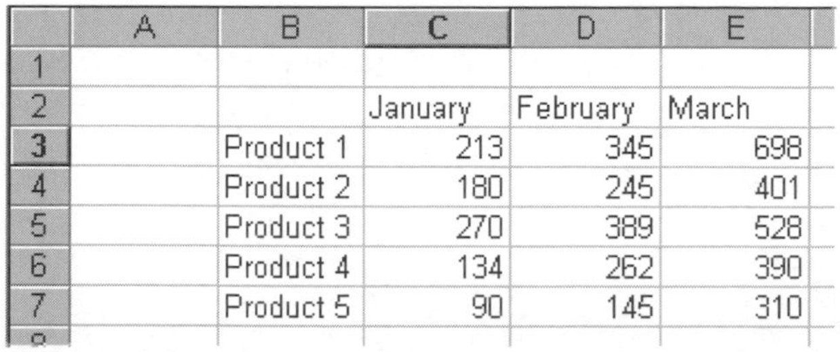

	A	B	C	D	E
1					
2			January	February	March
3		Product 1	213	345	698
4		Product 2	180	245	401
5		Product 3	270	389	528
6		Product 4	134	262	390
7		Product 5	90	145	310

4) When finished, save the Excel file. If your initials are KB, for example, save it as KBsalesfigures.xls. Leave the Excel file open on your screen.

5) Click on cell B2 and hold down the mouse button. Drag rightwards and down to cell E8.

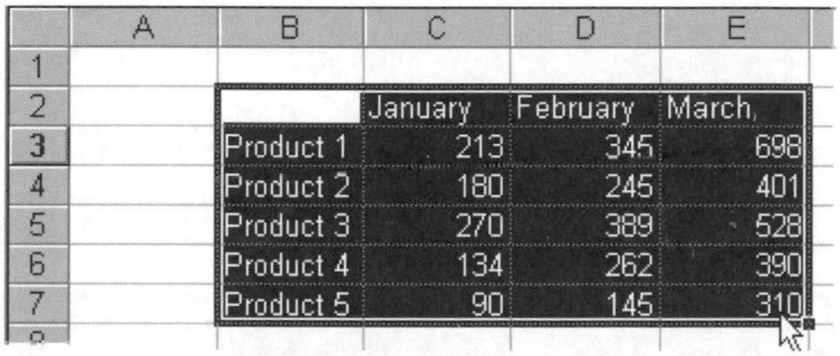

	A	B	C	D	E
1					
2			January	February	March
3		Product 1	213	345	698
4		Product 2	180	245	401
5		Product 3	270	389	528
6		Product 4	134	262	390
7		Product 5	90	145	310

6) Choose **Edit | Copy** to copy the selected Excel cells to the Clipboard.

You may now close the Excel file, but, for Exercise 3.51 to work, you must *not* exit the Excel application.

Exercise 3.51: Embedding the Excel Data in Word

1) Use the **Window | <document name>** command to display the first Word document that you saved (in this example, KBsalesfigures1.doc), and then click the last paragraph mark in that document.

2) Choose **Edit | Paste Special**, select the Microsoft Excel Worksheet Document option, and click **OK**.

   (The option is available *only* when the Excel application is open on your computer.)

   This embeds the Excel data from the Clipboard to the Word document.

3) Click on the bottom-right handle of the inserted data, and drag it until the inserted data is centred between the left and right page margins. Your Word document should now look like that shown.

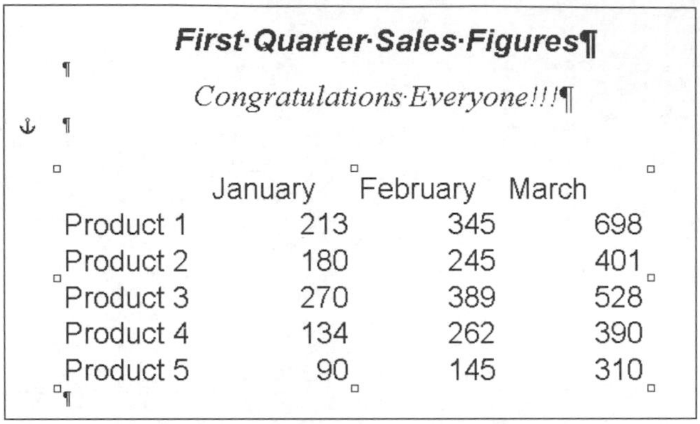

First·Quarter·Sales·Figures¶

¶

Congratulations·Everyone!!!¶

¶

	January	February	March
Product 1	213	345	698
Product 2	180	245	401
Product 3	270	389	528
Product 4	134	262	390
Product 5	90	145	310

¶

You can work with the embedded data area just as you can with a graphic: you select it and reposition and resize it. You cannot edit it, however, at least not in Word.

To change the embedded data in any way – edit a number, delete a row, or add a coloured border – you must first double-click on it. This action causes Word's menus and toolbars to be replaced by Excel ones. Try it and see. Your screen should look as shown.

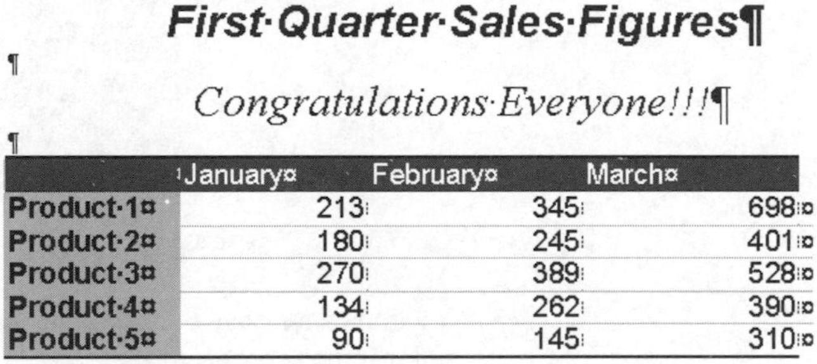

First·Quarter·Sales·Figures¶

¶

Congratulations·Everyone!!!¶

¶

	January¤	February¤	March¤
Product·1¤	213	345	698¤
Product·2¤	180	245	401¤
Product·3¤	270	389	528¤
Product·4¤	134	262	390¤
Product·5¤	90	145	310¤

To return to Word, click anywhere on the Word document, outside the embedded spreadsheet area. Save your Word document.

You can now exit Excel. You do not need it open for Exercise 3.52.

Exercise 3.52: Pasting the Excel Data in Word

1) Use the **Window | <document Name>** command to display the second Word document that you saved (in this example, KBsalesfigures2.doc), and then click the last paragraph mark in that document.

2) Choose **Edit | Paste Special**, select the Formatted Text (RTF) option, and click **OK**.

   (The option is available whether Excel is open or not.)

   This pastes the Excel data from the Clipboard to the Word document. The spreadsheet cells have the format of a Word table.

3) Click anywhere in the table, choose **Table | Table Autoformat**, select the Classic 2 option, and click **OK**.

4) Drag the vertical edges of the column borders until the table is centred evenly between the left and right margins of the page.

5) With the cursor anywhere in the table, choose **Select | Table**. On the Formatting Toolbar, change the font size to 14 point.

   Your Word document should now look like that shown.

First Quarter Sales Figures

Congratulations Everyone!!!

	January	February	March
Product 1	213	345	698
Product 2	180	245	401
Product 3	270	389	528
Product 4	134	262	390
Product 5	90	145	310

6) Save your Word document. You have finished the embedding and pasting Exercises, and you can close both Word documents.

You have now completed the final Section of the ECDL Word-Processing Module. Congratulations.

Section Summary: So Now You Know

A *file format* is a set of rules that translates between the 1s and 0s used by the computer to store information and the text and graphics displayed on screens and on printouts. Different applications – even different versions of the same application – can use different and incompatible file formats.

To help you share your files with others, Word 97 allows you save your documents in a file format other than its own. The options include: earlier versions of Microsoft Word, RTF (the common Microsoft Office file format), WordPerfect (another word processor), and HTML (the Web page file format).

You can also save a Word document as a *text-only* file, so that it can be opened and read by virtually all applications on all types of computers. Any formatting or graphics in the Word document are lost, however.

You can insert spreadsheet data from Excel to Word in either of two ways: pasting or embedding.

Pasted data becomes fully part of the Word document: it is displayed as a Word table, and can be edited within Word itself. Inserting Excel data into Word in this way is similar to pasting from another Word document.

Embedded spreadsheet data, while positioned within the Word document, remains part of Excel: it behaves like an imported graphic and cannot be edited within Word. If you try to edit the spreadsheet data in any way, Word's menu and toolbars are replaced on screen by Excel's ones. Embedded data brings with it the functionality of the application in which it was created.

Spreadsheets

Some things are easy to explain or describe – but difficult to use or operate. A spreadsheet is not one of those things. In fact, it's the very opposite.

At the end of this Module, you will able to build number-crunching spreadsheets for recording, analysing and graphing just about any kind of numbers you can think of.

Quarterly sales commission, annual rainfall, or the monthly household budget: if you can count it now, you will be able to spreadsheet it later.

Along the way we will show you the shortcuts that will help you get a lot of work done on long numbers, but with little typing, and in a very short time.

But you will be no closer to being able to give a one-sentence definition of what exactly a spreadsheet is.

Perhaps it's because spreadsheets are about processing numbers rather than words that makes them so hard to define.

Think of this Module as your chance to count rather be counted. Good luck with it.

Section 4.1: Your First Steps in Excel

In This Section

'Why do I need to know all this ... What is the point ?' You may find yourself asking such questions when reading this Section.

But first lessons are like that – whether you are learning the guitar, karate or spreadsheets.

In your first hour you usually have the hard work of remembering new activities and words – but rarely the pleasure of putting your new knowledge into practice.

There is nothing in this Section that you will find difficult or complex. We have included only the material that you absolutely need to know, and we have introduced it as gently as possible.

Halfway through Section 4.2, when you discover the power and convenience of spreadsheets, you will be asking a very different question: 'How did I ever manage to organise my work or life without Microsoft Excel!'

New Skills

At the end of this Section you should be able to:

- Start and quit Excel
- Explain the difference between a worksheet and a workbook
- Create and name Excel worksheets
- Enter numbers, text and cell references to a worksheet
- Edit and delete the contents of a cell
- Use Excel's Undo feature to reverse commands and cell entries
- Save, name, open, create and close Excel workbooks
- Use Excel's online help

New Words

At the end of this Section you should be able to explain the following terms:

- Worksheet
- Column
- Workbook
- Cell
- Cell reference
- Name Box
- Active cell
- Dependent cell
- Row

Starting Excel

Double click on the Microsoft Excel icon.

-or-

Choose **Start | Programs | Microsoft Excel**.

Excel starts and displays a new workbook with three worksheets ready for you to use.

Worksheets and Workbooks

This ECDL Module is about spreadsheets. But Excel does not use the word spreadsheet. Instead, it uses two other words – worksheet and workbook. Let's explain what these mean.

Worksheet

A page that is made up of little boxes arranged in rows and columns. Relationships can be created between the cells so that changing the contents of one cell affects the contents of the related cells.

In Excel, a worksheet is a spreadsheet. A worksheet is much larger than your screen. You can see only a very small part of it at one time.

Workbook

A file containing worksheets.

When you create a new workbook, Excel creates three blank worksheets inside that workbook. Excel calls the worksheets Sheet1, Sheet2 and Sheet3.

To move from one worksheet to another, click the tab that displays its name

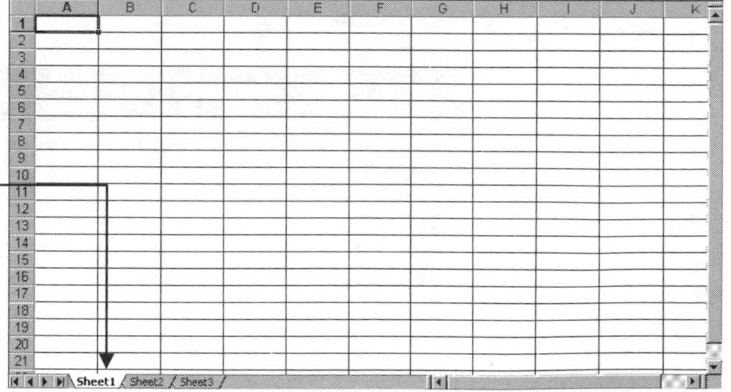

An Excel worksheet

If three worksheets are not enough, you can add more to your workbook – up to a maximum of 256. Think of worksheets as pages in a book, and the workbook as the book containing those pages.

Now you will learn the names of the important parts of a worksheet.

Cells

The little boxes that make up a worksheet.

Cells are arranged in (horizontal) rows and (vertical) columns.

Active Cell

The cell in which the cursor is currently located.

Only one cell on a worksheet can be the active cell at any one time. You will always know which cell is the active cell: Excel surrounds it with a thicker border. You can make a cell active by clicking on it with the mouse.

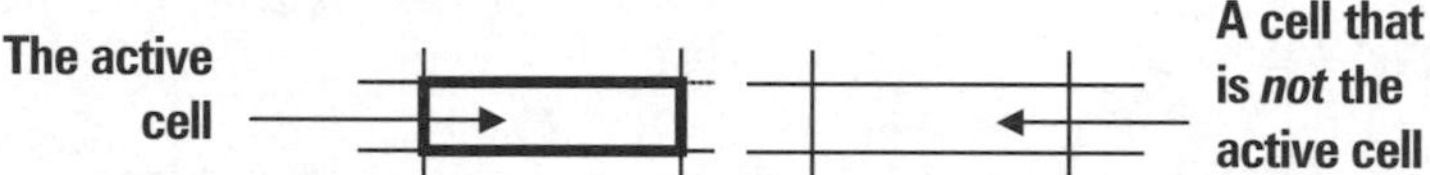

When you open a new workbook, Excel makes the top-left cell of the first worksheet, Sheet1, the active cell.

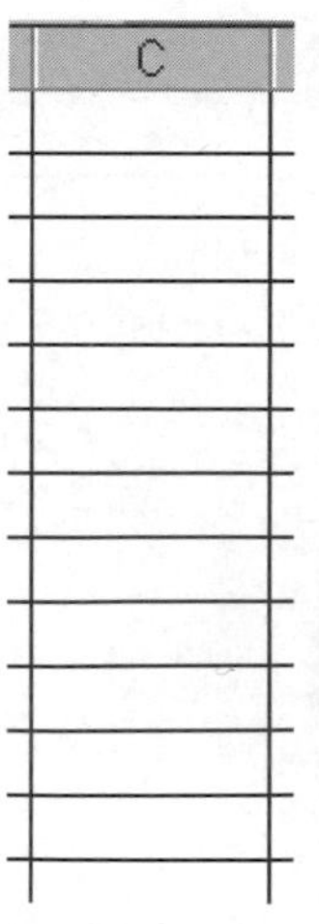

A worksheet column

Column

A vertical line of cells from the top of the worksheet to the bottom.

Each worksheet contains 256 columns. Excel names each column with a letter or group of letters. The first 26 are named A to Z. The remainder are AA to AZ, BA to BZ, and continuing through to IA through to IV.

Row

A horizontal line of cells that stretches left-to-right across a worksheet.

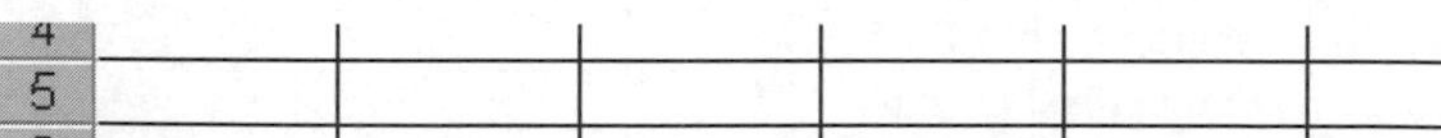

A worksheet row

Each worksheet contains 65,536 rows. Excel gives each row a number, from 1 to 65,536. The total number of cells in a worksheet is therefore 256 multiplied by 65,536 or 16,777,216!

Each cell in a worksheet has a unique address or location known as its cell reference.

Cell Reference

The location or 'address' of a cell on a worksheet.

A cell reference is made up of two parts:

- The column letter (A, B, C, ...)
- The row number (1, 2, 3, ...)

When you open a new workbook in Excel, the active cell is the one on Sheet1 with the cell reference A1.

Remember: column letter first, row number second. For example, B6, C8 and J12.

Column Letters: Upper- or Lower- Case?

You will always see cell references written with the column letters in upper-case letters (for example, A1, B10 and W90) rather than in lower-case ones (for example, a1, b10 and w90). This is true for Excel's online help – and this book.

However, when you type a cell reference into Excel, as you will in Exercise 4.1, it does not matter whether you type the column letter in upper- or lower-case. Excel accepts either. You may find it easier to enter column letters in lower-case, because you need to type only the letter key, and not the letter key in combination with the SHIFT key.

Name Box

The rectangular area above the top-left corner of a worksheet in which Excel displays the cell reference of the active cell.

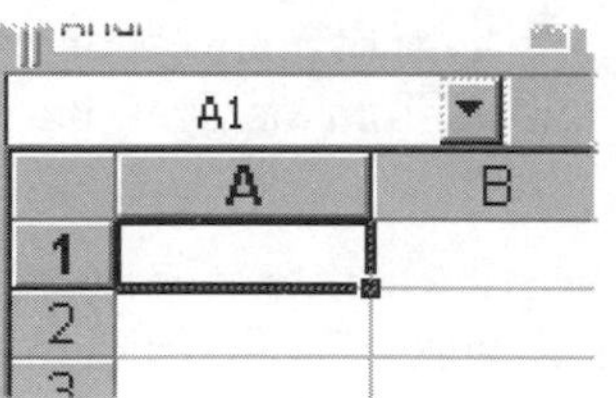

You can use the Name Box to move the cursor to any cell on the worksheet, making that cell the active cell.

To do so, type the cell reference in the Name Box and press ENTER.

Exercise 4.1: Name Box and Cell References

Perform this exercise to learn how to enter a cell reference in the Name Box.

1) Click in the Name Box.

2) Type B2 and press ENTER.

   Excel responds by making cell B2 the active cell.

As further practice, repeat these two steps for the following cells: D8, A3, H5 and I19.

Entering Numbers in Cells

When you type something into a cell and press ENTER, Excel looks at your entry and asks:

- Is this a number?
- Is this text?
- Is this a cell reference?
- Is this a calculation?

Excel treats each type of entry in a different way. In this Section you will deal with entering numbers, text and cell references.

Excel accepts two kinds of calculations: formulae (you will learn about these in Section 4.2) and functions (covered in Section 4.3).

Exercise 4.2: Entering a Number in a Cell

1) Click on B3, making it the active cell.
2) Type the number 1274.
3) Press ENTER.

	A	B
1		
2		
3		1274
4		

	A	B
1		
2		
3		1274
4		

Why Does Excel Right-Align Numbers?

In Exercise 4.2, Excel did two things after you pressed ENTER.

- It moved 1274 from the left of cell B3 to the right. This is because Excel assumes that you will want to perform addition or another arithmetic operation on the entered number. When you write a list of numbers on paper to add them, you line up the numbers from the right. Excel right-aligns numbers for the same reason.
- It moved down the cursor to cell B4, the cell under B3. Again, this is because of arithmetic. Excel assumes that you will want to enter another number beneath the previous one.

Entering Text to a Cell

	A	B
1		
2		Add
3		1274
4		

You can enter text to a worksheet as well as numbers. By using text to identify the meaning or source of numbers, you make your worksheet easier to read and understand.

Exercise 4.3: Entering Text in a Cell

1) Click on B2, making it the active cell.
2) Type the word: Add.
3) Press ENTER.

Notice how Excel responded after you pressed ENTER.

- 'Add' remained in the left of the cell B2. While Excel right-aligns numbers, it left-aligns text.
- It moved the cursor down to cell B3, the cell under B2. Excel assumes that this is the next cell you will want to use.

Text that describes a number on a worksheet is known as a label.

Label

A piece of text in a worksheet cell that provides information about the number in an accompanying cell, usually either below it or to its right.

Entering a Cell Reference in a Cell

The EQUALS key is to the left of the BACKSPACE key

Another type of entry you can make in a cell is a cell reference – that is, the address of another cell – preceded by the 'equal to' (=) sign. When you do so, Excel reproduces the content of the other cell to the active cell.

Exercise 4.4: Entering a Cell Reference in a Cell

If B3 does not contain the number 1274 from Exercise 4.2, enter it now.

1) Click on cell B10, type the following, and press ENTER:
2) =B3

   That is, an 'equal to' sign (=) followed by cell reference B3.

Excel responds by displaying the current content of B3 (that is, number 1274) in B10.

The ARROW Keys

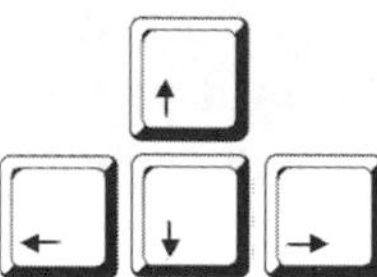

So far you have used the mouse and the Name Box to move the cursor around the worksheet.

Another way of moving the cursor is by pressing the ARROW keys. You may find this method faster than moving and clicking the mouse, because you need not take either hand away from the keyboard.

Editing the Content of a Cell

Sometimes, you will want to change the content of a cell. Exercise 4.5 shows you how.

Exercise 4.5: Editing the Content of a Cell

1) Double-click on B3.

   Excel makes the cell border thinner and displays a blinking cursor in the cell. (The location of the cursor within the cell depends on which part of the cell you double-clicked on.)

2) Using the ARROW keys, move the blinking cursor to the left of the 4.

3) Press DELETE once, deleting the 4.

4) Type 5.

5) Press ENTER.

   This moves the cursor out of B3 and down to B4. Excel has replaced 1274 with 1275. Notice that the number in B10 also changes.

Dependent Cells

Cell B10 is an example of a dependent cell – a cell whose content depends on the content of another cell. In this case, the other cell is B3.

When B3 changed from 1274 to 1275, so too did B10. That is because B10 contains the cell reference of =B3.

As you will learn in later Sections of this Module, cell relationships are the basis of spreadsheets.

	A	B
1		
2		Add
3		1275
4		
5		
6		
7		
8		
9		
10		1275

Content of B10 depends on content of B3

F2: Excel's EDIT Key

In Exercise 4.5 you double-clicked on cell B3. This made the cell editable – that is, you were able to move the cursor within the cell and change the cell content.

When a cell is already the active cell, you can make it editable by pressing F2. This is Excel's EDIT key. You may find this method faster than double-clicking with the mouse.

Deleting the Content of a Cell

Want to delete a number, text or cell reference from a cell? The following exercise shows you how.

Exercise 4.6: Deleting the Content of a Cell

1) Move the cursor to cell B10. From Exercises 4.4 and 4.5, this contains the cell reference =B3 and displays the number 1275.

2) Press BACKSPACE or DELETE.

Excel removes the content of the cell. B10 is now empty.

Deleting and the ENTER Key

When you enter something to a cell, you must press ENTER to confirm the new content of the cell. Similarly, when you edit a cell, Excel makes the change only after you press ENTER.

When deleting a cell's content, however, you do not need to press ENTER to confirm the deletion. Just pressing BACKSPACE or DELETE is enough.

Deleting Cell Content – Not the Cell

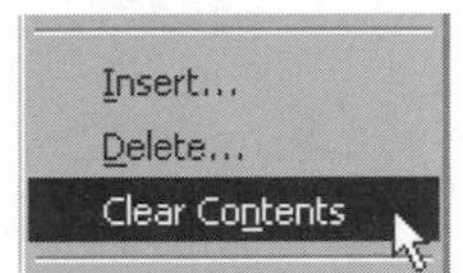

Another way to delete the content of a cell is to right-click on the cell and choose **Clear Contents** from the pop-up menu.

Do not choose **Delete** from this pop-up menu. This command not only deletes the cell contents – it also removes the cell itself from the worksheet! As a result, other cells must change their position to fill the space left empty.

Standard and Formatting Toolbars

Only two of Excel's toolbars are relevant to this ECDL Module: the Standard Toolbar and the Formatting Toolbar.

The Standard Toolbar includes buttons for managing files and working with numbers in cells.

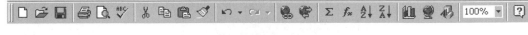

Excel's Standard Toolbar

The Formatting Toolbar includes buttons for changing the appearance of text and numbers in cells.

Excel's Formatting Toolbar

Rather than introduce all these buttons at once, we will explain the ones you need to know about as they become relevant through the remainder of this ECDL Spreadsheet Module.

Working with Toolbars

You can display or hide Excel's various toolbars by choosing the **View | Toolbars** command, and then selecting or deselecting the various toolbar options from the drop-down menu displayed.

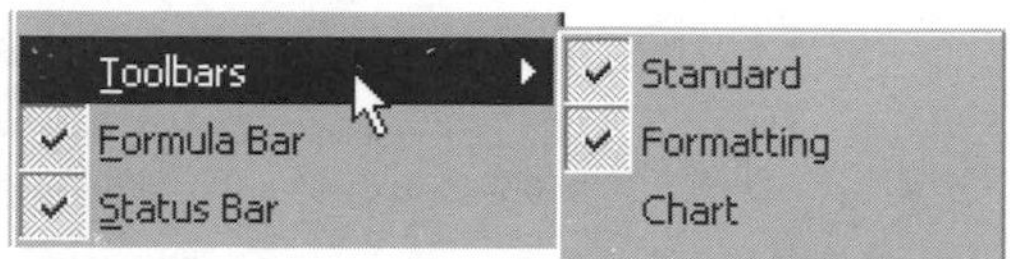

Excel's Undo

Undo button

Redo Button

Enter the wrong data? Press the wrong key? Don't panic. Excel allows you to undo your most recent cell entry or action if it has produced unwanted results. To undo a cell entry or action:

Choose **Edit | Undo**.
-or-
Click the Undo button on the Standard Toolbar.

Pressing Undo repeatedly reverses your last series of actions. To view a list of recent actions that you can undo, click the arrow at the right of the Undo button. If you undo an action and then change your mind, click the Redo button (to the right of the Undo button).

Exercise 4.7: Using the Undo Feature

Perform this Exercise to practise using Excel's Undo feature.

1) Click in cell B2, and press DELETE.
2) Click in cell B3, and press DELETE.

Everything that you entered in the worksheet is now deleted! But you can use Undo to get it all back by reversing your two delete actions.

3) Click the Undo button.

   This reverses your most recent action (in Step 2 above). B3 again contains the number 1275.

4) Click Undo a second time.

   This reverses your second most recent action (Step 1 above). B2 again contains the word Add.

Working with Excel Workbooks

An Excel workbook is a file containing a collection of worksheets. The file names of Excel workbooks end in .xls. This helps you to distinguish Excel files from other file types, such as Word files (ending in .doc).

Saving Your Workbook

Save button

In Excel, as in other applications, always save your work as you go along. Don't wait until you are finished!

To save a workbook:

Choose **File | Save**.
-or-
Click the Save button on the Standard Toolbar.

The first time that you save a workbook file, Excel asks you to give the file a name. Exercise 4.8 shows you how.

Exercise 4.8: Saving and Naming a New Workbook

1) Sheet1 of your workbook should contain the word 'Add' in cell B2 and the number 1275 in cell B3, as entered in this Section's Exercises.

   If not, enter that data now.

2) Choose **File | Save** or click the Save icon on the Standard Toolbar. Excel displays a dialog box with two boxes similar to the ones shown below.

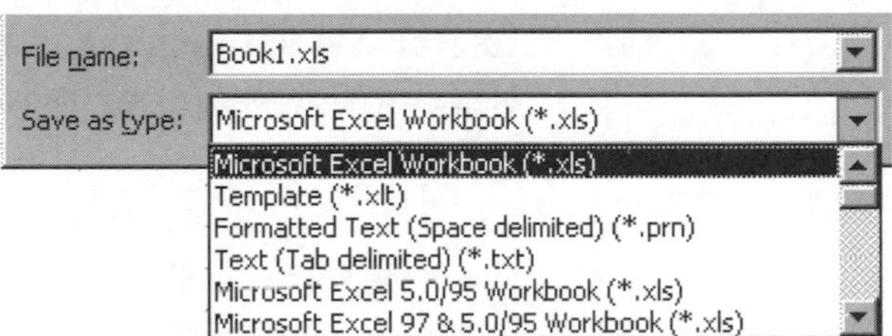

3) By default, Excel names the first workbook file you open and save as Book1.xls. Replace this file name with something that you will find easier to remember and recognise – such as your own name – and click the Save button.

   Excel adds the file name extension of .xls automatically. You need not type it.

Creating a New Workbook

New button

To create a new workbook file:

Choose **File | New**.
-or-
Click the New button on the Standard Toolbar.

Opening an Existing Workbook

Open button

To open an existing workbook file:

Choose **File | Open**.
-or-
Click the Open button on the Standard Toolbar. Select the file you want from the dialog box.

Closing a Workbook

To close a workbook file:

Choose **File | Close**.
-or-
Click the Close button on the workbook window.

Workbook Close button

If you have made changes to your workbook since you last saved it, Excel prompts you to save the changes before it closes the file.

Exercise 4.9: Closing and Reopening a Saved Workbook

In this Exercise you will close and then reopen the workbook you saved in Exercise 4.8.

1) Choose **File | Close** or click the Workbook Close button at the top-right of the workbook window.
2) Choose **File | Open** or click the Open button on the Standard Toolbar to display the File Open dialog box. Locate your workbook and open it.

Quitting Excel

To leave Excel:

Choose **File | Exit**.
-or-
Click the Close button on the Excel window.

Excel Close button

If you have left open any files containing unsaved work, Excel prompts you to save them.

Online Help

Like Word, Access, PowerPoint and other Microsoft Office applications, Excel offers a searchable online help system:

- The 'help' in online help means that the information is there to assist you understand and use Excel.
- The word 'online' means that the material is presented on the computer screen rather than as a traditional printed manual.

You can search through and read online help in two ways: from the **Help** menu, or from dialog boxes.

Using Help Menu Options

Choose **Help | Contents and Index** to display the three tabs of the Help Topics dialog box. These are explained below:

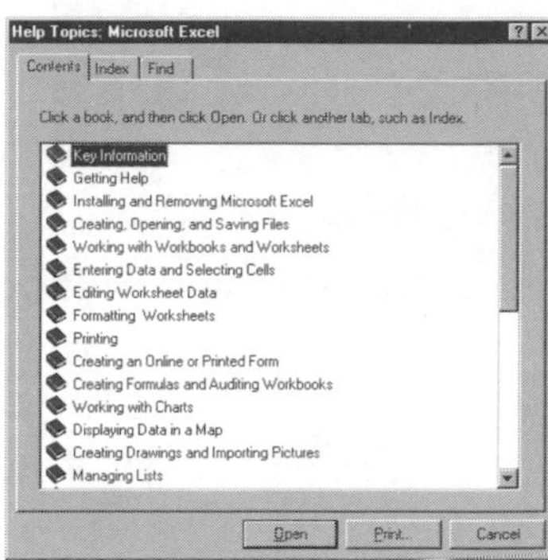

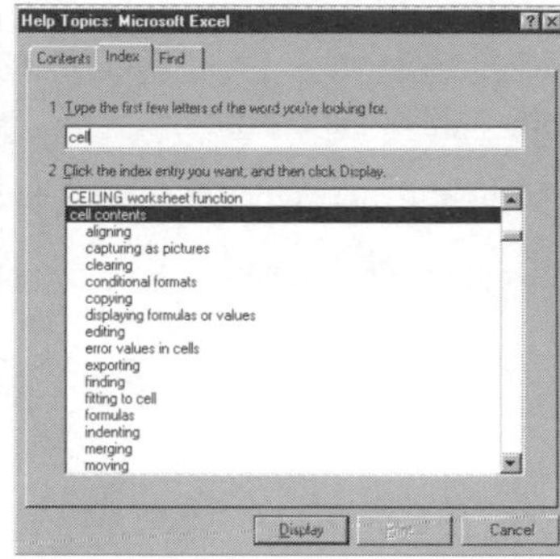

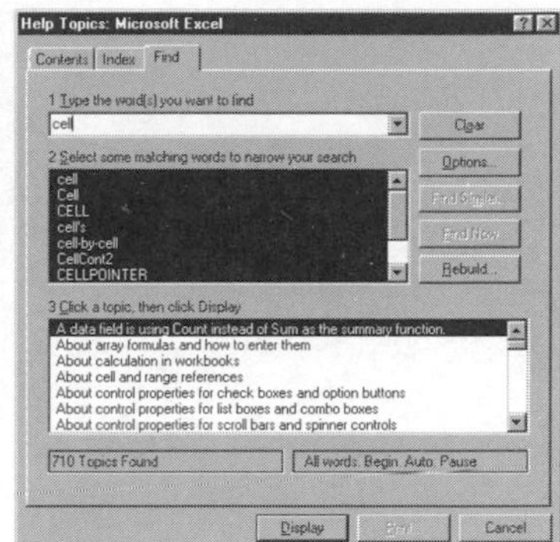

Contents Tab

This offers short descriptions of Excel's main features.

Where you see a heading with a book symbol, double-click to view the related sub-headings.

? Double-click on a question-mark symbol to read the help text.

Click a Show me arrow for Excel to demonstrate how to perform a particular action.

Click a double arrow to view step-by-step instructions.

Index Tab

Reading the material displayed on this tab is like looking through the index of a printed book.

Just type the first letters of the word or phrase you are interested in.

Excel responds by displaying all matches from the online help in the lower half of the dialog box.

When you find the index entry that you are looking for, click the **Display** button.

Find Tab

Can't find what you are looking for in the Contents or Index tabs? Try this tab.

When you type a word or phrase, Excel performs a deeper search of the online help.

Excel also displays some related words to help you narrow your search.

When you find the item you are looking for, double-click on it to display it.

As you search through and read online help topics, you will see the following buttons at the top of the online help window:

- **Help Topics**: Click this to return to the Contents tab.
- **Back:** Click this to return to the previous help topic.
- **Options:** Click this to perform such actions as copying the online help text to a document, or printing it on your printer.

Using Help from Dialog Boxes

You can also access online help directly from a dialog box, as Exercise 4.10 demonstrates.

Exercise 4.10: Using Online Help in a Dialog Box

1) Choose **View | Zoom** to display the Zoom dialog box.

2) Click on the question mark symbol near the top-right of the dialog box. Excel displays a question mark to the right of the cursor.

3) Move the mouse down and left, and click on the Custom option.

   Excel displays online help text that tells you about the Custom option.

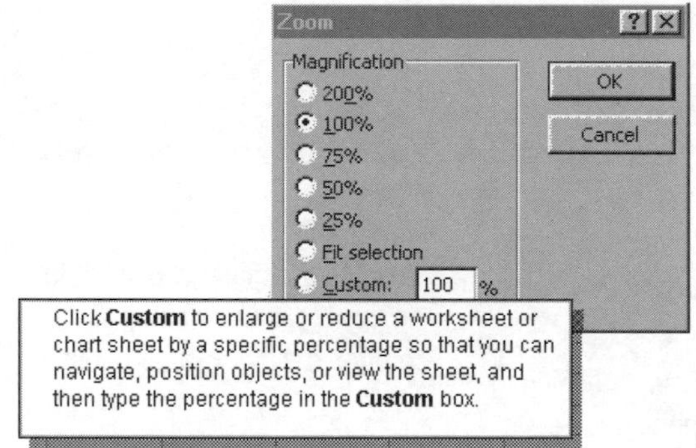

Practise this Exercise with other dialog boxes in Excel.

When finished, you can close your workbook and Excel. You have now completed this Section 4.1 of the ECDL Spreadsheet Module.

Section Summary: So Now You Know

An Excel *workbook* is a file containing spreadsheets, which Excel calls *worksheets*. Workbook file names end in *.xls*.

A worksheet is made up of *cells*, arranged in *columns* and *rows*. Each cell has a *unique cell reference*, consisting of its column letter and row number. For example, B3 and G47.

Only one cell is the *active cell* at any one time. You make a cell active by moving the cursor to it, using the mouse, ARROW keys or *Name Box*.

You can enter a number, text (to *label* a number) or a cell reference to any cell. Press ENTER to confirm your entry. Excel *left-aligns text* but *right-aligns numbers*.

To *edit* a cell, first make it editable. You do so by double-clicking it with the mouse. Alternatively, make it the active cell and then press Excel's EDIT key, F2.

You can *delete* the content of the active cell (but not the cell itself) by pressing DELETE or BACKSPACE.

Excel's *Undo* feature, available from a button on the Standard Toolbar, allows you to reverse your recent cell entries or actions if they have produced unwanted results.

You can hide and display Excel's various *toolbars*. The two most commonly used are the Standard and Formatting Toolbars.

Excel's online help system, available from the **Help** menu and from individual dialog boxes, provides a comprehensive and searchable guide to the program's features and procedures.

Section 4.2: Arithmetic with Excel

In This Section

Prepare to be impressed. In Section 4.1 you learnt the names for the important parts of an Excel worksheet, and practised the simple operations of entering numbers, text and cell references to cells.

Now you have the basics you need to discover the power of spreadsheets in this Section.

You will very quickly discover why people who work with numbers – such as accountants, statisticians, engineers and project managers – rely on spreadsheets to perform tedious calculations quickly, easily and accurately.

In the practical Exercises you will use fewer than a dozen numbers. These simple examples differ from the multi-page financial reports of a large corporation in size only. The principles are the same. Learn the principles here in Section 4.2 and you will never meet an amount of data too large or too complex for you to master with your spreadsheet skills.

New Skills

At the end of this Section you should be able to:

- Explain what an Excel formula is; and name its components
- Use Excel formulae to add, subtract, multiply and divide numbers
- Apply the rules of arithmetic to calculations in Excel
- Recognise Excel error messages
- Use Excel's Zoom feature to enlarge and reduce worksheet display
- Save a workbook to a diskette

New Words

At the end of this Section you should be able to explain the following terms:

- Formula
- Calculated cell
- Non-adjacent cells
- Argument
- Operator
- Constant

Formulae in Excel

In Section 4.1 you learnt how to enter numbers, text and cell references to worksheet cells. Now it's time to discover a fourth type of cell entry, called a calculation.

Calculations are the reason that you enter numbers to cells, because calculations enable you to perform arithmetic – addition, subtraction, multiplication and division – on your entered numbers.

Excel accepts two kinds of calculations: formulae and functions. This Section 4.2 shows you how to perform calculations using formulae. You will learn about functions in Section 4.3.

Exercise 4.11: Adding Two Numbers with an Excel Formula

1) Open the workbook that you saved in Exercise 4.8. If cells B2 and B3 do not contain the word 'Add' and the number 1275, enter that data now.
2) Click on B4, and type the number 25
3) Press ENTER.

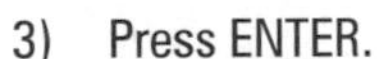

4) Click on B5, and type: =B3+B4

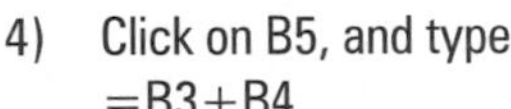

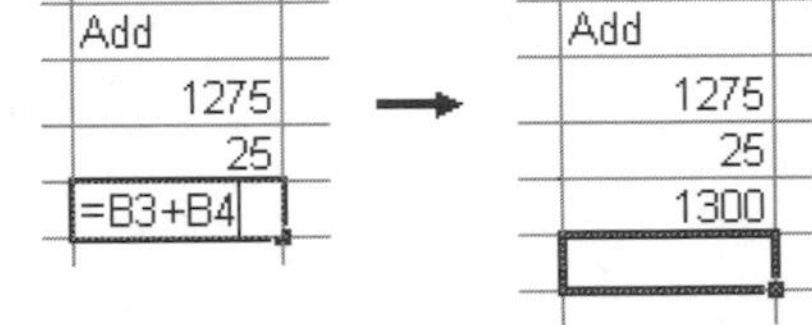

5) Press ENTER.

   Excel displays in B5 the sum of the contents of the two cells B3 and B4.

To type a plus (+), hold down the SHIFT key and press the EQUALS (=)

Congratulations! You have performed your first calculation in Excel.

Formulae and Arguments

Formula and argument are two words you will meet a lot when learning about spreadsheets. So it is important that you understand what they mean.

Formula
An equation that performs operations such as addition, subtraction, multiplication or division on data that is stored in a worksheet.

In Exercise 4.11 the formula you used was =B3+B4. Note the following about formulae:

- Always begin formulae with the equal to (=) sign.
- Always press ENTER to confirm your formula.

The components of a formula are called arguments. In the formula, =B3+B4, the arguments are B3 and B4. Both are cell references. As you will see, you can also use numbers as arguments.

Argument
The inputs to a calculation that generate the result.

Next, let's perform three other arithmetic operations using Excel formulae: subtraction, multiplication and division.

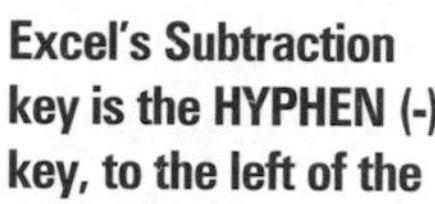

Excel's Subtraction key is the HYPHEN (-) key, to the left of the EQUALS key

Exercise 4.12: Subtracting with Excel

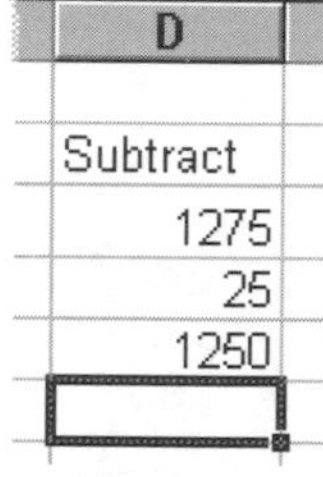

1) In cell D2, enter the word Subtract. (That is, type the word and press ENTER.)
2) In cell D3, enter the number 1275. (That is, type the number and press ENTER.)
3) In cell D4, enter the number 25.
4) In cell D5, enter the formula:
   =D3-D4
   (That is, type the formula and press ENTER.)

   D5 now shows the result of subtracting the contents of D4 from D3.

Excel's Multiplication key is the ASTERISK (*) key, typed by holding down the SHIFT key and pressing the 8 key

Exercise 4.13: Multiplying with Excel

1) In cell F2, enter the word Multiply.
2) In cell F3, enter the number 1275.
3) In cell F4, enter the number 25.
4) In cell F5, enter the formula:
   =F3*F4

   Excel displays in F5 the result of multiplying the contents of F3 by F4.

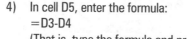

Excel's Division key is the FORWARD SLASH (/) key, to the right of the FULL STOP (.) key

Exercise 4.14: Dividing with Excel

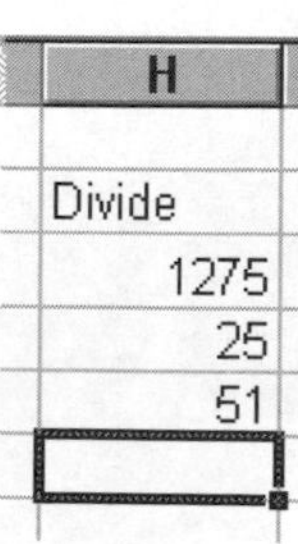

1) In cell H2, enter the word Divide.
2) In cell H3, enter the number 1275.
3) In cell H4, enter the number 25.
4) In cell H5, enter the formula:
   =H3/H4

Excel displays in H5 the result of dividing the contents of H3 by H4.

Calculated Cells

In Exercises 4.11 to 4.14, the cells B3 and B4, D3 and D4, F3 and F4, and H3 and H4 each:

- Contain a number, and
- Display a number.

In other words, what they contain and what they display are the same.

Cells B5, D5, F5 and H5, however, contain one thing (a formula) but display another (a number). These are examples of calculated cells.

Calculated Cell

A cell that contains a calculation but displays only the result of that calculation.

You can think of a calculated cell as an 'answer cell'.

In addition to arguments, the other type of component in a formula is the operator.

Operators

Symbols that specify the type of calculation you want to perform on the arguments of a formula. Excel's four main arithmetic operators are +,-, and /.*

Excel offers other, more complex, operators that are beyond the scope of this ECDL Spreadsheet Module.

Adding Down and Across

Two of the most common arithmetic operations in spreadsheets are the addition of numbers that are arranged in vertical or horizontal lists. Exercises 4.15 and 4.16 provide examples of each.

8		1234
9		4532
10		5693
11		3512
12		239
13	Total	15210
14		

Exercise 4.15: Adding a Vertical List of Numbers

1) In cells B8, B9, B10, B11 and B12, enter the numbers 1234, 4532, 5693, 3512 and 239.

2) In cell A13, enter the word: Total.

3) In cell B13, enter the formula:

   =B8+B9+B10+B11+B12

   Excel displays in B13 the result of adding the specified cells.

Exercise 4.16: Adding a Horizontal List of Numbers

1) In cells B16, C16, D16, E16 and F16, enter the numbers 1234, 4532, 5693, 3512 and 239. (The same numbers as in Exercise 4.15.)

	A	B	C	D	E	F	G
14							
15							Total
16		1234	4532	5693	3512	239	15210
17							
18							

2) In cell G15, enter the word Total.

3) In cell G16, enter the formula:

   =B16+C16+D16+E16+F16

   Excel displays in G16 the result of adding the specified cells.

Adding Non-Adjacent Cells

Excel can add cells even when they are not arranged in neat, vertical or horizontal lists, as Exercise 4.17 demonstrates. Cells that are not immediately adjoining one another are called 'non-adjacent cells'.

Exercise 4.17: Adding Non-Adjacent Cells

Enter the following numbers:

1) 1234 in B20, 4532 in C22, 5693 in D21, 3512 in E19 and 239 in F20.

   (The same numbers as in Exercises 4.15 and 4.16.)

2) In G19, enter the word Total.

3) In G20, enter the formula:

   =B20+C22+D21+E19+F20

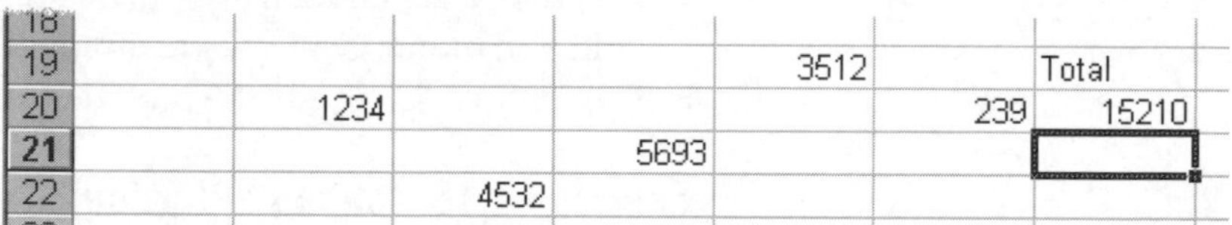

	A	B	C	D	E	F	G
18							
19					3512		Total
20		1234				239	15210
21				5693			
22			4532				

Excel displays in G20 the result of adding the specified cells.

Non-Adjacent Cells

Cells that are not located immediately beside, above or below one another.

Editing Formulae

In Exercise 4.5 of Section 4.1, you learnt how to edit a number in a cell. You can also edit a formula, as Exercise 4.18 demonstrates.

Exercise 4.18: Editing a Formula

1) Double-click on G20. (Alternatively, move the cursor to it with the ARROW keys, and then press Excel's EDIT key, F2.)

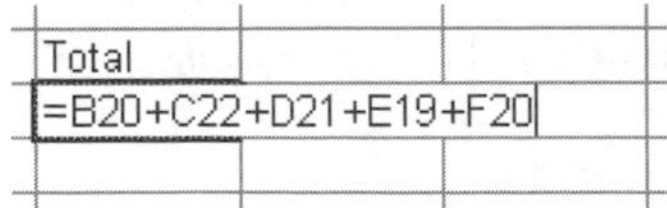

2) Using the BACKSPACE or DELETE key, delete from the formula the argument F20 and the plus operator (+) in front of it.

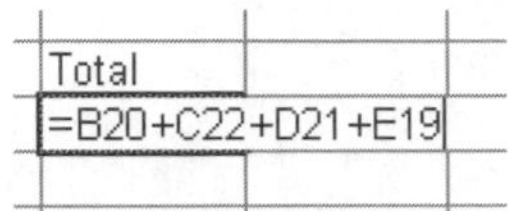

3) When finished press ENTER.

Excel now displays in G20 the result of adding B20, C22, D21 and E19 only.

Combining Operators

You can enter more than one type of operator in a single formula. In Exercise 4.19 you will enter formulae that contain both the addition and the subtraction operators.

Exercise 4.19: Formulae with Multiple Operators

Your company produces four products. They have fixed costs, variable costs, discounts and prices as set out in the cells shown below.

	B	C	D	E	F	G	H
24							
25	Name	Fixed	Variable	Total	Discount	Price	Profit
26	Product 1	12	2		2	21	
27	Product 2	34	6		8	56	
28	Product 3	56	28		12	112	
29	Product 4	127	92		19	290	
30							

Your task is to enter formulae to calculate the total costs for each product, and determine the profit for each product.

1) Enter the numbers and text in the cells as shown above.

2) Enter the formulae shown on the right in cells E26, E27, E28 and E29.

   When you press ENTER after typing each formula, Excel displays the calculated result.

E
Total
=C26+D26
=C27+D27
=C28+D28
=C29+D29

→

E
Total
14
40
84
219

3) Enter the formulae shown on the right in cells H26, H27, H28 and H29.

   When you press ENTER after typing each formula, Excel displays the calculated result as shown.

H
Profit
=G26-(E26+F26)
=G27-(E27+F27)
=G28-(E28+F28)
=G29-(E29+F29)

→

H
Profit
5
8
16
52

   That is, the profit on each product is its price minus the sum of the total cost and the discount.

Formulae: Using Constants

Excel formulae can contain numbers instead of (or as well as) cell references. Excel calls these numbers 'constants'.

Constant
An argument in a formula that is a fixed number.

Here are some examples of formulae containing both cell references and constants:

26*109 =45*(A12+3) =B2/100-B3/50

You can even enter formulae that contain only constants and no cell references, as shown in Exercise 4.20.

Exercise 4.20: Entering Constant-Only Formulae

Enter the following in cell B32:

1) =32/4

Excel displays the result (8) in B32.

Formulae: The Rules of Arithmetic

Excel allows you to combine addition, subtraction, multiplication and division in a single formula. For example:

=C5*(A4+A7)-(C4/C7)

Excel follows the rules of arithmetic in calculating such formulae:

- Operations are carried out in the following order: division, multiplication, addition and subtraction.

  For example, the following formula gives a result of 11 because Excel first multiplies 2 by 3 (resulting in 6) and then adds 5.

  =5+2*3

- You can use parentheses (brackets) to force Excel to calculate your formula in a particular order.

  For example, the following formula gives a result of 21 because Excel first adds 5 and 2 (because they are within parentheses) and then multiplies that result by 3 to give 21.

  =(5+2)*3

  Ensure that you follow every opening bracket that you type with a matching closing bracket.

If you have difficulty remembering that:

= (A1+A2)*B1

gives a different result from:

= A1+(A2*B1)

then, here's a way to help you remember the order of precedence among arithmetical operators:

Oh Dear! My Aunt Sally!

Fixed Factor Calculations

In some calculations, you need to apply the same number or factor several times to different numbers. The fixed factor may be a currency exchange rate, for example, or an employee tax rate or sales commission rate.

It is best to place such a fixed factor in a cell of its own, and enter its cell reference as needed in formulae. Exercise 4.21 provides an example.

Exercise 4.21: Sales Commission and Tax Calculations

Your company employs four sales representatives: Edgar, Sheila, Wallace and Deirdre. In addition to a basic salary, each receives commission of 20% on goods sold. All four are taxed at a rate of 15%.

Given the information displayed below, use Excel formulae to calculate the Net Income of each employee.

	B	C	D	E	F	G	H
34							
35	Comm. Rate		0.2				
36	Tax Rate		0.15				
37							
38							
39	Person	Basic	Sales	Comm.	Gross	Tax	Net Income
40	Edgar	1200	3000				
41	Sheila	1300	3100				
42	Wallace	1600	3500				
43	Deirdre	1700	3800				

1) Enter the numbers and text in the cells as shown above. You enter 20% as .2 and 15% as .15. Excel displays your entered numbers as 0.2 and 0.15.

2) To calculate each employee's sales commission, gross income, tax payment and net income, enter the formulae as shown below.

E	F	G	H
Comm.	Gross	Tax	Net Income
=D40*D35	=C40+E40	=F40*D36	=F40-G40
=D41*D35	=C41+E41	=F41*D36	=F41-G41
=D42*D35	=C42+E42	=F42*D36	=F42-G42
=D43*D35	=C43+E43	=F43*D36	=F43-G43

When you press ENTER after typing each formula, Excel displays the calculated result as shown below.

E	F	G	H
Comm.	Gross	Tax	Net Income
600	1800	270	1530
620	1920	288	1632
700	2300	345	1955
760	2460	369	2091

Exercise 4.22 provides an example of currency conversions, which are another type of fixed-factor type calculations.

Exercise 4.22: Currency Conversion Calculations

Your company sells a range of five products, priced at £100, £150, £200, £250 and £300, to the USA and Japan. The sterling-to-dollar exchange rate is 1.64, and the sterling-to-yen rate is 170.94.

Your task is to create a currency conversion table that shows the prices of your products in sterling, dollars and yen.

1) Enter the text labels and numbers as shown below.

	B	C	D
45			
46	GBP/USD	1.64	
47	GBP/JPY	170.94	
48			
49	Sterling	Dollars	Yen
50	100		
51	150		
52	200		
53	250		
54	300		

2) In cells C50 to C54, enter formulae to calculate the price of each product in dollars, obtained by multiplying its price in sterling by the exchange rate in cell C46.

   In cells D50 to D54, enter formulae to calculate the price of each product in yen, obtained by multiplying its price in sterling by the exchange rate in cell C47.

   The formulae are as shown on the right.

Dollars	Yen
=B50*C46	=B50*C47
=B51*C46	=B51*C47
=B52*C46	=B52*C47
=B53*C46	=B53*C47
=B54*C46	=B54*C47

   When you press ENTER after typing each formula, Excel displays the calculated result as shown below.

	B	C	D
45			
46	GBP/USD	1.64	
47	GBP/JPY	170.94	
48			
49	Sterling	Dollars	Yen
50	100	164	17094
51	150	246	25641
52	200	328	34188
53	250	410	42735
54	300	492	51282

Calculations and Recalculations

In Exercises 4.11 to 4.22 you learnt how to use your £1,000 computer as a £10 pocket calculator! You have performed calculations using handfuls of numbers but you can imagine how you could use the same methods to record and calculate hundreds or even thousands of numbers on a worksheet.

The power and convenience of a spreadsheet is not so much the ability to calculate as the ability to recalculate. Excel will recalculate the result of an addition (or other type of operation) whenever any of the numbers that make up the operation are changed.

Let's try it and see.

Exercise 4.23: Recalculating an Addition

In Exercise 4.11 you entered the number 25 in cell B4.

1) Click on B4, type 52, and press ENTER.

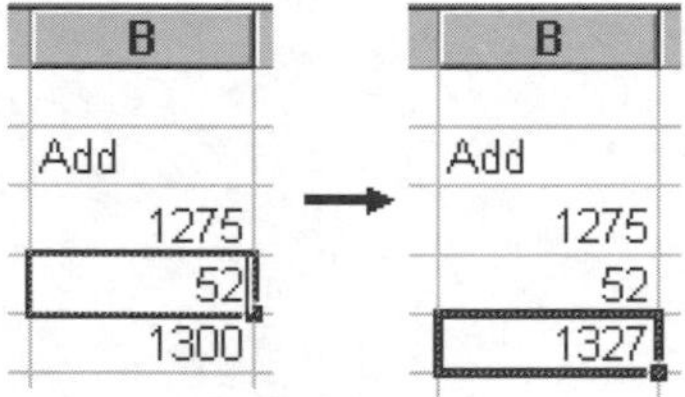

Notice how Excel recalculates B5 (the 'answer cell'), and displays the new result.

Just two numbers are added in this Exercise, but it could as easily have been hundreds or more.

Exercise 4.24: Recalculating a Multiplication

In Exercise 4.22 you entered a sterling-to-dollar exchange rate of 1.64 in cell C46, and a sterling-to-yen rate of 170.94 in cell C47.

1) Click on C46, type 1.68, and press ENTER.
2) Click on C47, type 170.92, and press ENTER.

   Notice how Excel recalculates the foreign currency amounts for all five products, as shown below.

	B	C	D
45			
46	GBP/USD	1.68	
47	GBP/JPY	170.92	
48			
49	Sterling	Dollars	Yen
50	100	168	17092
51	150	252	25638
52	200	336	34184
53	250	420	42730
54	300	504	51276

To gain an appreciation of the power of spreadsheets, imagine Excel recalculating the prices for hundreds of products.

As further practice, revisit Exercise 4.21, change the commission rate (in D35), the tax rate (in D36), and note the effect on the employees' Commission, Gross and Net Income columns.

Error Messages: When Bad Things Happen

If a formula cannot properly calculate a result, Excel displays an error message in the calculated cell indicating the type of error that has taken place. Here are the main error messages that you are likely to meet when following this ECDL Module.

#####
Your cell contains a number or a calculation result that is too wide for the cell to display. This is not really an error: Excel has the correct information, it just can't display it. You will learn about adjusting column width in Section 4.3.

#VALUE!
Your formula contains text (or a cell reference that points to a cell containing text) instead of a number. Edit the formula or cell to fix the problem.

#DIV./0!
You have tried to divide a number by zero, or by a cell reference that points to a cell containing a zero.

You will see the same error message if you try to divide a number by a cell reference that points to an empty cell. Excel interprets a blank cell as containing a zero.

#REF!
Typically, your formula contains a cell reference that points to a cell that has been deleted.

Excel's Zoom Views

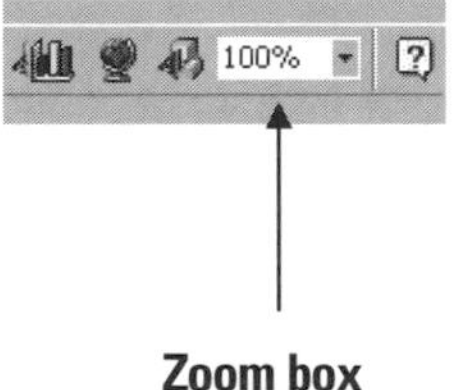

Zoom box

Excel's Zoom feature enables you to magnify or reduce the worksheet display. You can use Zoom in either of two ways:

- Click in the Zoom box on the Standard Toolbar, enter a number between 10 and 400, and press ENTER. (You need not type the percent (%) symbol.)
- Choose the **View | Zoom** command, and select a magnification option from the Zoom dialog box.

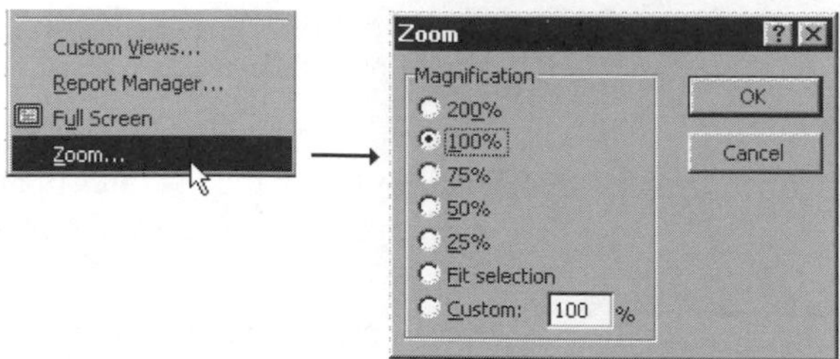

You can choose a preset option (25–200%), or select Custom and enter a number from 10 to 400. Alternatively, select the Fit Selection option. This magnifies the area surrounding the active cell, or a range of selected cells, so that the cell or cells occupy the full screen. (You will learn about ranges of selected cells in Section 4.3.)

To return from an enlarged or reduced view to normal view, select a magnification of 100% or click the Undo button on the Standard Toolbar.

Zoom and Printing

The Zoom feature affects only the way that Excel displays a worksheet on-screen and *not* how Excel prints a worksheet. You will learn how to print a worksheet at a size other than 100% in Section 4.3.

Saving to a Diskette

Have you been saving your workbook as you went along? You should. It is also a good idea to save a copy of your workbook to a diskette. Follow the steps in Exercise 4.25 to learn how.

Exercise 4.25: Saving an Excel Workbook to a Diskette

1) Insert a diskette in the diskette drive of your computer:
   - If it is a new diskette, ensure that it is formatted.
   - If it is a previously used one, ensure that there is sufficient space on it to hold the Excel workbook file. Your workbook should be about 16KB in size.
2) Choose **File | Save As**, locate the A: drive, and click **Save** to save the file. Excel suggests the default file name (in this example, KenBloggs.xls) for you to accept or amend.

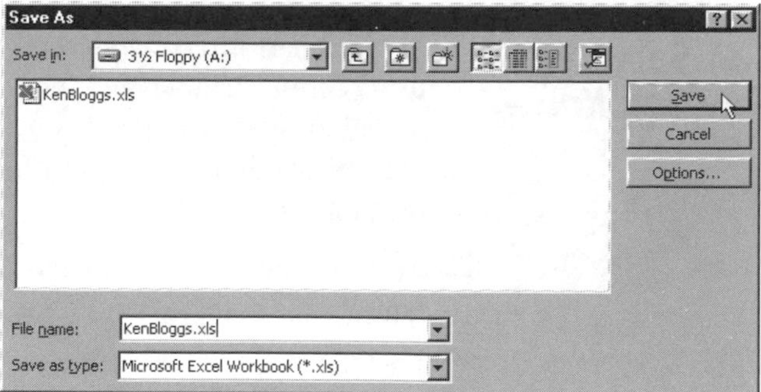

When finished, use **File | Save As** again to resave the workbook to its original location on your computer. (You will be asked if you want to replace the original file: click **OK**.)

If you do not resave your workbook at its original location, saving the file in future (by clicking the Save button on the Standard Toolbar or choosing **File | Save**) will save the workbook to the diskette and not to your computer's hard disk.

You have now completed this Section 4.2 of the ECDL Spreadsheet Module. You can close your workbook and Excel.

Section Summary: So Now You Know

You can perform *calculations* on worksheet cells in two ways: using formulae and using functions. A *formula* begins with an 'equal to' symbol (=) and contains one or more *operators* for example, addition (+), subtraction (-), multiplication (*) or division (/).

The components or *arguments* of a formula can be cell references, numbers or both. A sample formula would be:

=A12+B12+3

A single formula may contain operators of different types: addition and multiplication, for example. Excel follows the rules of arithmetic in calculating formulae: division is carried out first, followed by multiplication, addition and subtraction, in that order. You can use parentheses (brackets) to force Excel to calculate your formula in a particular order. The following two formulae, for example, give different results:

=(A1+A2)*B1

=A1+(A2*B1)

Excel stores the result of a calculation in a *calculated cell*, which contains the formula but displays only the calculation result.

Excel's *Zoom* feature enables you to magnify or reduce the worksheet display. Options range from 10–400% of normal size. Only screen display and not printing is affected by the zooming.

If a formula cannot properly calculate a result, Excel displays an *error message* in the calculated cell indicating the type of error that has taken place.

Section 4.3: Functions, Formatting and Printing

In This Section

Formulae, as you learnt in Section 4.2, enable you to perform calculations on numbers. In this Section you will discover a second type of calculation method, based on functions. You will also meet the very useful AutoSum button.

When you work with numbers, it's important to get the right answers. But it's also important that your answers look good. Excel provides a wide range of formatting, alignment, border and colour features to help you give your worksheets a professional appearance. You will also learn how to change the width of columns and the height of rows.

Other topics in this Section include adjacent and non-adjacent cell ranges, find and replace, headers and footers, and worksheet printing.

New Skills

At the end of this Section you should be able to:

- Use Excel's SUM and AVERAGE functions to perform calculations on cells, and use the AutoSum button on Excel's Standard Toolbar
- Select ranges of adjacent and non-adjacent cells
- Adjust column width and row height
- Change font, font style (bold and italic) and font size
- Align cells horizontally and vertically, and rotate cells
- Apply borders and fills (coloured backgrounds to cells)
- Find, replace and spell-check items on a worksheet
- Change page setup and insert headers and footers
- Print from Excel

New Words

At the end of this Section you should be able to explain the following terms:

- Function
- Adjacent cell range
- Non-adjacent cell range

Excel Functions

You have learnt how Excel's formulae can add, subtract, multiply and divide numbers.

Excel offers a second way to perform calculations: functions.

Function
A predefined formula built in to Excel and used for a specific purpose.

Most Excel functions are of interest only if you are using a spreadsheet for specialised purposes, such as statistical analysis. But two – SUM and AVERAGE – are useful to almost everyone. The SUM and AVERAGE functions are also part of the ECDL syllabus, so you need to know how to use them.

The SUM Function

In Section 4.2, you learnt how to add numbers by using such formulae as:

=B3+B4+B5

You can imagine that addition formulae can become very awkward – and prone to typing errors – when they contain large numbers of arguments. For example, if there were 100 cells to add rather than just three.

Excel's SUM function allows you to calculate the total of a vertical or horizontal list of numbers by entering just three items:

- The name of the function (in this case, SUM)
- The reference of the first cell
- The reference of the last cell

Upper or Lower Case?

As with row and column letters, you can type function names in upper- or lower-case letters. In the same way that Excel accepts A4 or a4, it accepts SUM or sum, AVERAGE or average.

In Excel's online help (and in this book), function names are written in upper-case. When entering functions on a worksheet, however, you will find it quicker to type their names in lower-case, because you need not use the SHIFT key.

The following Exercise shows the SUM function in action.

Exercise 4.26: Using the SUM Function

1) Open the worksheet that you saved in Section 4.2.

2) Click the Sheet2 tab to display the second worksheet of the workbook.

3) In cells B3, B4 and B5, enter the numbers 2356, 4921 and 2903.

4) In cells A3, A4 and A5, enter the text Conway, Murphy and Smith to label the entered numbers.

5) Type the following function in B6 and press ENTER:

=SUM(B3:B5)

	A	B
1		
2		
3	Conway	2356
4	Murphy	4921
5	Smith	2903
6		=sum(b3:b5)
7		

→

	A	B
1		
2		
3	Conway	2356
4	Murphy	4921
5	Smith	2903
6		10180
7		

Well done! You have used Excel's SUM function to add numbers.

The AutoSum Button

Because SUM is such a commonly used function, Microsoft put a button for it on the Standard Toolbar.

Exercise 4.27: Using the AutoSum Button

1) Delete the SUM function, entered in Exercise 4.26, from cell B6.

2) With B6 as the active cell, click the AutoSum button on the Standard Toolbar.

   Excel tries to 'guess' which cells you want to add together. In this example, it assumes (correctly) that the cells start at B3 and end at B5.

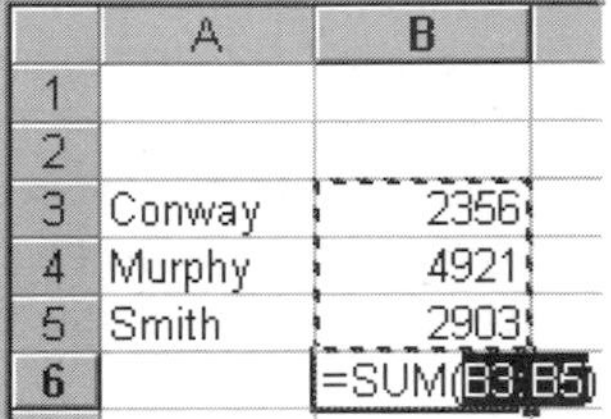

	A	B
1		
2		
3	Conway	2356
4	Murphy	4921
5	Smith	2903
6		=SUM(B3:B5)

3) Press ENTER to confirm that B3, B4 and B5 are the cells for adding.

	A	B
1		
2		
3	Conway	2356
4	Murphy	4921
5	Sullivan	2903
6		10180
7		

SUM Tolerates Text and Spaces

Excel's SUM is a tolerant function. It ignores:

- Cells containing text
- Empty cells

For example, the function =SUM(W12:W16) adds whatever numbers it finds in the cells W12, W13, W14, W15 and W16.

If any cell contains text instead of a number, or is empty, the SUM function does not display an error message. It just ignores the non-numeric cells and continues on adding up the numeric ones.

In the next Exercise you will enter more numbers and text to your worksheet, Sheet2.

Exercise 4.28: Entering More Numbers and Text

1) On Sheet2, enter two further columns of numbers in columns C and D, as shown below. Across the top of columns B, C, D and E, enter a row of labels (text), also as shown below.

   (The month of March is omitted deliberately. You will insert a new column for March in Exercise 4.45 of Section 4.4.)

	A	B	C	D	E
1					
2		January	February	April	Total
3	Conway	2356	3621	4560	
4	Murphy	4921	4055	3542	
5	Smith	2903	3308	3622	

2) Use the AutoSum button to total the numbers in rows 3, 4 and 5. In E3 enter =SUM(B3:D3), in E4 =SUM(B4:D4) and in E5 =SUM(B5:D5).

   When you click on E5 and then click the AutoSum button, Excel will 'guess' which cells you want to total. It assumes (incorrectly) that you want to add the two immediately above it, E3 and E4, as shown on the right.

	E
	Total
60	10537
42	12518
22	=SUM(E3:E4)

When this happens, double-click on E5 (or press F2) to make the cell editable. Next, change the arguments of the SUM function to =SUM(B5:D5).

3) Use the AutoSum button to total, in row 6, the numbers in each of the columns C, D and E. In C6, enter =SUM(C3:C5), in D6 =SUM(D3:D5) and in E6 =SUM(E3:E5).

Your worksheet should now look as shown below.

	A	B	C	D	E
1					
2		January	February	April	Total
3	Conway	2356	3621	4560	10537
4	Murphy	4921	4055	3542	12518
5	Smith	2903	3308	3622	9833
6		10180	10984	11724	32888

The AVERAGE Function

This Excel function – you guessed it – finds the average of a group of numbers.

As with the SUM function, the AVERAGE function begins with the = sign. Then follows the function name, and finally the arguments within parentheses. Exercise 4.29 provides an example of the AVERAGE function in use.

Exercise 4.29: Using the AVERAGE Function

1) Click the Sheet1 tab to display the first worksheet in your workbook.

2) In cell B44 enter the label Average.

3) In cell C44 enter the following formula:

=AVERAGE(C40:C43)

4) C44 now displays the average value of the contents of cells C40, C41, C42 and C43.

5) Repeat step 3) for columns D, E, F G and H to average the cells immediately above them.

Row 44 should now look like that shown below.

44	Average	1450	3350	670	2120	318	1802

Formatting and Aligning Single Cells

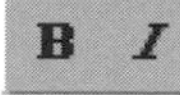

Format buttons

Formatting refers to the *appearance* of numbers and text in cells. It includes such actions as making cell content bolder (heavier) and putting it in italics.

The *position* of numbers and text within cells is called alignment. Three common options are left, centred and right. The quickest way to apply a formatting or alignment option to a cell is to select it and then click the relevant button on Excel's Formatting Toolbar.

You now learn how to format and align cells on a worksheet – in this case, Sheet2 of your workbook.

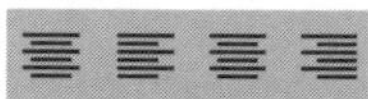

Alignment buttons

Exercise 4.30: Formatting and Aligning Cells

1) On Sheet2 of your worksheet, click on cell B2.
2) Click the Bold button on the Formatting Toolbar. Excel displays the word January in bold.
3) Click the Centre-Align button on the Formatting Toolbar. Excel centre-aligns the word January.
4) Click on cell A3, and then click the Italic button on the Formatting Toolbar. Excel displays the word Conway in italics.

Formatting and Aligning Cell Groups

You can save time and mouse-clicks by formatting or aligning a group of cells in one, single operation. Before you can do so, you must first select the group of cells.

You can select a group of cells by clicking on the top-left cell in the group, and then dragging the mouse across the other cells. Exercise 4.31 shows you how.

Exercise 4.31: Formatting and Aligning a Cell Range

1) Click cell C2.

2		**January**	February	April	Totals
3	*Conway*	2356	3621	4560	10537

2) Drag the mouse across to cell E2.

2		**January**	February	April	Totals
3	*Conway*	2356	3621	4560	10537

3) Click the Bold button on the Formatting Toolbar.
4) Click the Centre Align button on the Formatting Toolbar.
5) Select cell A4.
6) Drag the mouse down to cell A5.

7) Click the Italic button on the Formatting Toolbar.

Sheet2 should now look as shown below.

	A	B	C	D	E
1					
2		**January**	**February**	**April**	**Totals**
3	*Conway*	2356	3621	4560	10537
4	*Murphy*	4921	4055	3542	12518
5	*Smith*	2903	3308	3622	9833
6		10180	10984	11724	32888
7					

Click anywhere on the worksheet outside the selected cells A4 and A5 to deselect the two cells.

Cancelling a Selection

Finished formatting your selected cells? Or selected the wrong cells? To cancel a selection, click anywhere outside the selected cell or range.

Cancelling a selection does not delete the cell or range from the worksheet. It just deselects the selected cells.

Cell Ranges

In Excel, a group of cells in a worksheet is known as a cell range.

Cell Range
A group of cells on a worksheet.

Cell ranges are of two kinds: adjacent and non-adjacent.

Adjacent Cell Range
A group of cells that are directly beside, above or below one another. Adjacent cells are sometimes called contiguous cells.

You identify an adjacent cell range by:

- The cell reference of the top-left cell
- A colon (:)
- The cell reference of the bottom-right cell

For example, the adjacent cell range A1:B2 includes the following four cells: A1, A2, B1 and B2.

Adjacent cell ranges may also include cells in one column only (for example, B2:B5) or in one row only (for example, D9:F9).

Non-Adjacent Cell Range

Can you select cells that are located on different parts of a worksheet as a single range? Yes. This is what Excel calls a non-adjacent cell range.

Non-Adjacent Cell Range
A group of cells that are not directly beside, or above or below, one another. Also called non-contiguous cells.

A non-adjacent cell range can consist of individual cells dotted around the worksheet. Or, as in Exercise 4.32, it can contain a number of smaller, sub-groups of adjacent cells.

You select a non-adjacent cell range by selecting the first cell (or first sub-group of adjacent cells), holding down the CTRL key, and then selecting further cells (or adjacent ranges).

A non-adjacent cell range is written with commas to separate the individual cells (for example, A2, B3, C4) or the smaller, sub-groups of adjacent cells (for example, A2:A6, H4:H8).

Exercise 4.32: Selecting a Non-Adjacent Cell Range

1) Select the first cell or sub-group of adjacent cells. For example, B2:B6 (that is, cells B2, B3, B4, B5 and B6).

	A	B	C	D	E
1					
2		**January**	**February**	**April**	**Totals**
3	*Conway*	2356	3621	4560	10537
4	*Murphy*	4921	4055	3542	12518
5	*Smith*	2903	3308	3622	9833
6		10180	10984	11724	32888

2) Hold down the CTRL key.

3) Select the next cell or next sub-group of adjacent cells. For example, cell range E2:E6.

	A	B	C	D	E
1					
2		**January**	**February**	**April**	**Totals**
3	*Conway*	2356	3621	4560	10537
4	*Murphy*	4921	4055	3542	12518
5	*Smith*	2903	3308	3622	9833
6		10180	10984	11724	32888

You can continue this process until you have selected all the cells in the non-adjacent range that you want to select.

Click anywhere outside the cell range to cancel the selection.

Selected Cells and the Active Cell

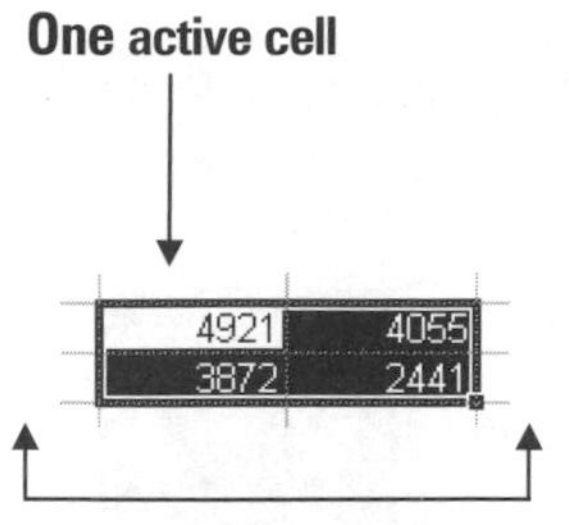

In Section 4.1 you learnt how to select a single cell – by clicking on it with the mouse, moving the cursor to it with the ARROW keys, or entering its cell reference in the Name Box. That cell is then the active cell.

So, for a single cell, the terms 'active cell' and 'selected cell' mean the same thing. And 'Select a cell' is simply another way of saying 'Make a cell the active cell'.

While you can select any number of cells at one time, only one cell can be the active cell. Excel displays selected cells in reverse (white text on black background). The active cell is shown as black text on a white background.

F8: Excel's SELECT Key

In Exercise 4.31 you selected an adjacent cell range by selecting the first cell, and then dragging the mouse across the other cells in the range.

An alternative method is to select the first cell, press F8, and then press the ARROW keys to extend the selected area over the other cells. F8 is Excel's SELECT key. You may find this method faster than using the mouse, but you can use it only for selecting adjacent cell ranges.

Selecting Columns and Rows

Excel offers quick ways of selecting one or more rows or columns. To select an entire row, click on the row heading.

- To select several adjacent rows, click on the top or bottom one, and hold down the mouse button as you drag down or up.
- To select several non-adjacent rows, click on the first, hold down the CTRL key, and click on the others.

To select an entire column, click on the column heading.

- To select several adjacent columns, click on one and then drag with the mouse to the right or left.
- To select several non-adjacent columns, click on the first, hold down the CTRL key, and click on the others.

Deleting Rows and Column Contents

To delete the contents of one or a selection of rows or columns, select the rows or columns, and press the DELETE key.

This operation removes only the row or column cell contents, leaving behind empty rows or columns. It does *not* delete the actual rows or columns. You will learn how to remove rows and columns from worksheets in Section 4.4.

Selecting the Entire Worksheet

To select the whole worksheet, click on the top-left of the worksheet, where the row heading meets the column heading.

A fast way to delete the contents of all cells on a worksheet is to select the entire worksheet, and then press DELETE.

Adjusting Column Width and Row Height

You can change the appearance of your worksheet by adjusting the width of one or more columns, or the height of one or more rows.

- **Column Width:** To change the width of a column, move the mouse to the column heading, and then drag the boundary on the right side of the column heading until the column is the width you want. See Exercise 4.33.
- **Row Height:** To change row height, move the mouse to the row heading, and then drag the boundary below the row heading until the row is the height you want. See Exercise 4.34.

Exercise 4.33: Adjusting Column Width

1) In the column heading of Sheet2, click on the boundary line between columns A and B.

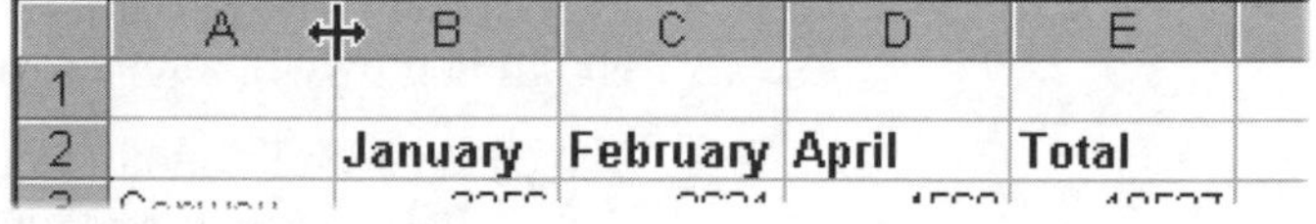

2) Drag the boundary to the left, making column A narrower.

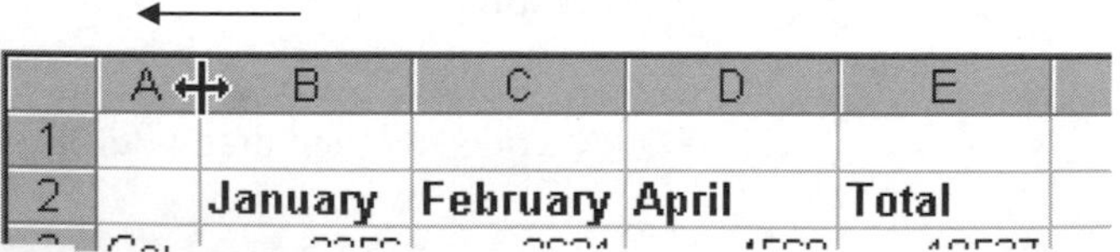

3) Reverse the effect of step 2) by dragging the column A boundary to the right, so restoring column A to its original width.

Exercise 4.34: Adjusting Row Height

1) In the row heading, click on the boundary between rows 2 and 3.

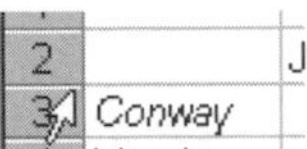

2) Drag the line down about one centimetre until it looks like that shown below.

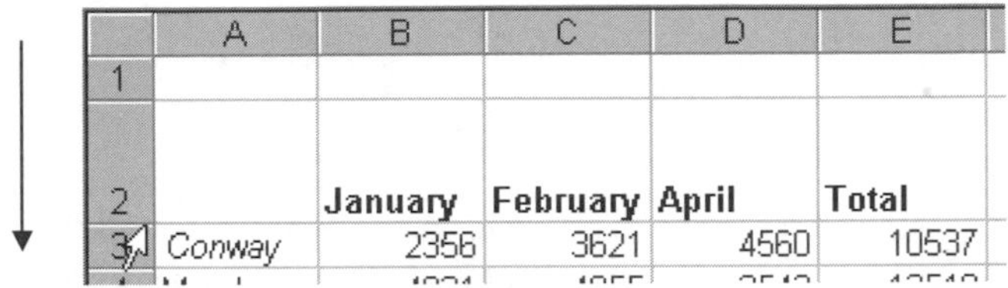

Well done. You have changed the height of a row on your worksheet. Leave the row at its increased height for Exercise 4.35.

Vertical Alignment

The three alignment buttons (left, centre and right) on the Formatting Toolbar enable you to position cell contents horizontally (left-to-right). Excel also allows you to align cell contents vertically (top-to-bottom). Exercise 4.35 provides an example of vertical alignment.

Exercise 4.35: Changing Vertical Alignment

1) Select cell range B2:E2 in row 2, whose height you increased in Exercise 4.34.

2) Choose **Format | Cells**, select the Alignment tab, select the Centre option from the Vertical: list, and click **OK**.

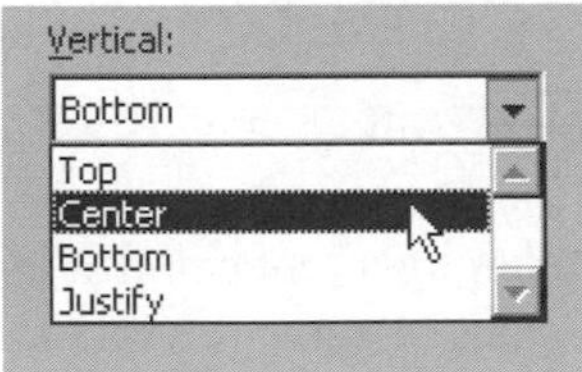

Excel now aligns the cells' content vertically so that it is centred between the top and bottom of the cells' boundaries.

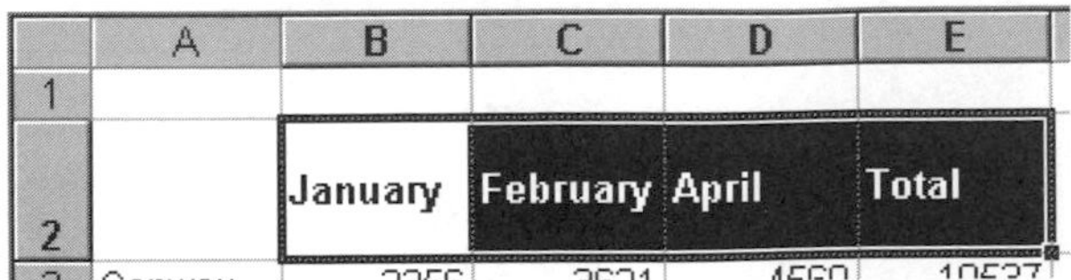

3) Click once on the Undo button on the Standard Toolbar to return the cells to the default vertical alignment of Bottom, and then click a second time to return the row to its original, normal height.

Orientation

Another Excel formatting feature is the ability to rotate or 'orient' the text or numbers at a specified angle within a cell. See Exercise 4.36.

Exercise 4.36: Rotating Cell Content

1) Select cell range B2:E2, choose **Format | Cells**, select the Alignment tab, type 90 in the Degrees box, and click **OK.**

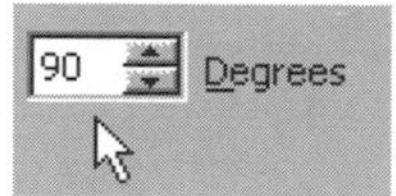

Excel now rotates the cells' content so that it is positioned at ninety degrees to the horizontal, as shown below.

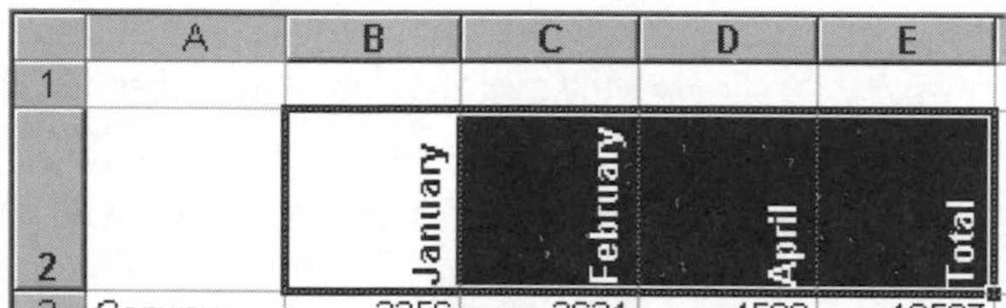

2) Click the Undo button on the Standard Toolbar to return the cells' orientation to the default value of zero degrees.

Entering a positive number in the Degree box rotates the cell content from lower left to upper right. A negative number of degrees rotates the cell content from upper left to lower right.

Fonts

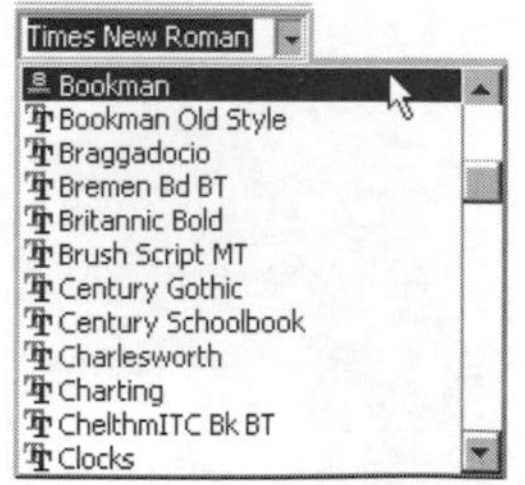

Viewing the fonts on your computer

A font (also called typeface) is a particular style of text. What fonts are installed on your computer? Click the arrow on the drop-down Font box on Excel's Formatting Toolbar to see.

There are really just two kinds (families) of fonts: serif and sans serif. Sans serif just means without serifs. You can recognise which family a font belongs to by asking: Do its characters have serifs (tails or squiggles) at their edges?

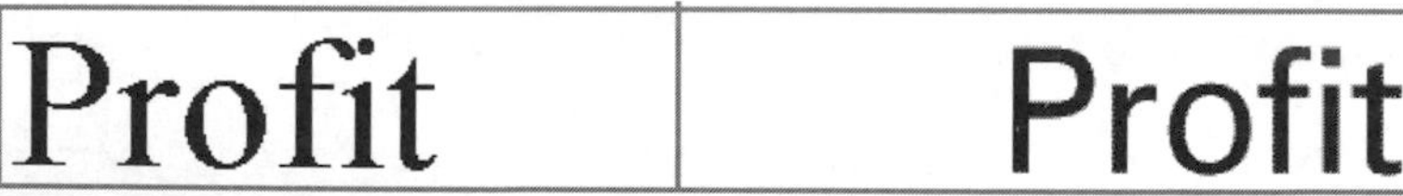

A serif font **A sans serif font**

Excel's default font is Arial, a sans serif font. The most commonly used serif font is named Times New Roman. Arial and other sans serif fonts are usually better for displaying numbers. You may want to apply a serif font to worksheet labels.

Font

A typeface: a particular style of text. The two main font families are serif and sans serif.

You can change the font of any cell or cell range by first selecting the cells and then choosing a new font from the drop-down list on the Formatting Toolbar.

Font Sizes

Font size is measured in a non-metric unit called the point, with approximately 72 points equal to one inch. Excel's default font is 10 point.

You can change the font size of any cell or cell range by first selecting the cells, and then choosing a new font size from the drop-down list on the Formatting Toolbar.

Font Colours

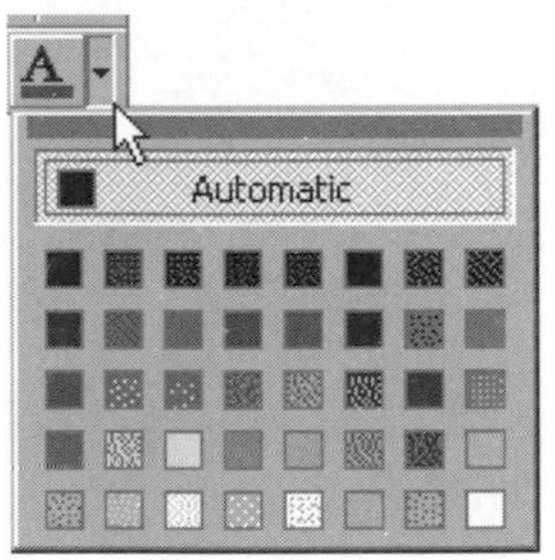

You can change the colour of cell contents from Excel's default of Automatic. What colour is Automatic? Automatic is black, unless the cell background is black or a dark grey, in which case Automatic switches to white.

You can change the colour of the text or number displayed in any cell or cell range by first selecting the cells, clicking the arrow on the right of the Font Colour button on the Formatting Toolbar, and then clicking on a colour.

In the next Exercise you will practise changing the fonts, font sizes and colours of the labels in Sheet1 of your workbook.

Exercise 4.37: Changing Fonts, Font Sizes and Colours

1) Click the Sheet1 tab to display the first worksheet of your workbook.
2) Click cell B2. Hold down the CTRL key and click also on the following cells: D2, F2 and H2.
3) From the Formatting Toolbar, change the font to Times New Roman, the font size to 12 point, and the font colour to dark blue. Next, click on the Bold and Centre Align buttons.

   Your worksheet should now look as shown below. (The headings will be in blue.)

Add		Subtract		Multiply		Divide
1275		1275		1275		1275
52		25		25		25
1327		1250		31875		51

Cell Borders

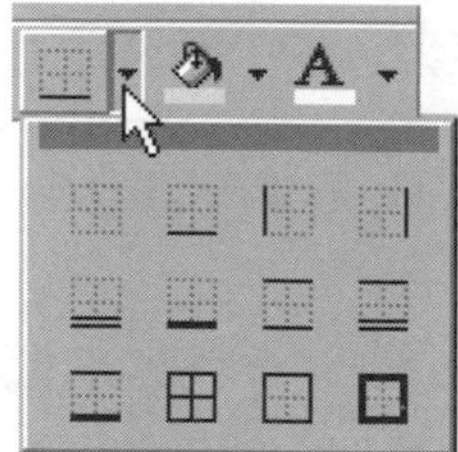

Excel provides a wide choice of borders that you can use to highlight a particular cell or cell range – such as cells containing sub- and final totals on a worksheet. You can access these options by clicking the arrow on the right of the Borders button on the Formatting Toolbar.

The most commonly used cell border options are the single bottom line (the default), the double and heavier bottom lines, and the outline. The last places a border on all four sides of the selected cells. Exercise 4.38 provides an example.

Exercise 4.38: Placing a Bottom Border on Cells

1) Select the non-adjacent cells B4, D4, F4 and H4.

2) Click the arrow on the right of the Borders button, and, from the list of options displayed, click the heavy, single bottom line.

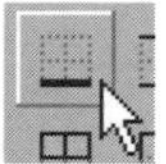

Your worksheet should now look as shown below.

Add		Subtract		Multiply		Divide
1275		1275		1275		1275
52		25		25		25
1327		1250		31875		51

Cell Colour Backgrounds

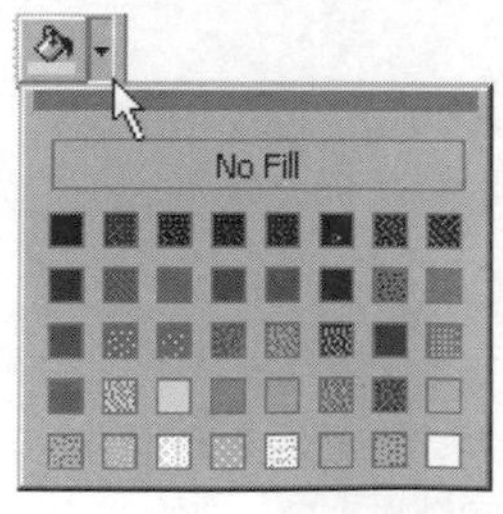

As with cell borders, Excel allows you to change the background colour of a cell – what Excel calls the Fill Colour.

You access this option by clicking the arrow on the right of the Fill Colour button on the Formatting Toolbar.

Exercise 4.39 provides an example.

Exercise 4.39: Changing the Fill Colour

1) Select the adjacent cell range B25:H25.

2) Click the arrow on the right of the Fill Colour button, and click the Yellow button.

Your worksheet should now look as shown. (The headings will be shown against a yellow background.)

Name	Fixed	Variable	Total	Discount	Price	Profit
Product 1	12	2	14	2	21	5
Product 2	34	6	40	8	56	8
Product 3	56	28	84	12	112	16
Product 4	127	92	219	19	290	52

In Exercise 4.40 you will further practise your cell border and fill colour skills.

Exercise 4.40: Further Cell Border and Colour Practice

1) Select the adjacent cell range B25:H29.
2) Click the arrow on the right of the Borders button, and click the outline (all four cell edges) border type.

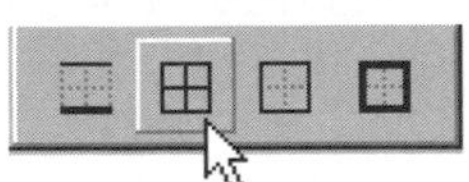

3) Select cell range B35:D36.

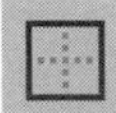

4) Click the arrow on the right of the Borders button, and click the hollow outline (edges only) border type.
5) Select cell range D35:D36.

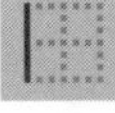

6) Click the arrow on the right of the Borders button, and click the left-edge border type.
7) Select cell range B43:H43.

8) Click the arrow on the right of the Borders button, and click the heavy bottom line border type.
9) Select non-adjacent cell range B46:C47, B49:D54.

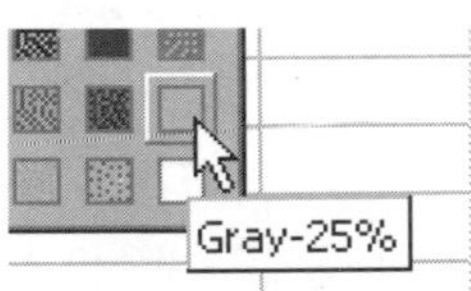

10) Click the arrow on the right of the Borders button, and click the outline (all four cell edges) border type.
11) With the non-adjacent cell range still selected, click the arrow on the right of the Fill Colours button, and click the Grey (25%) option.

Finding Cell Content

You can search a worksheet for label text, numbers that were entered directly, numbers resulting from calculations, and calculation components (function names, cell references, arithmetic operators and constants) as follows:

- Select the range of cells you want to search. (To search the whole worksheet, click any cell.)
- Choose **Edit | Find**.
- In the Find what: box, enter the item you want to find, and select **Find Next**.

You can cancel a Find operation in progress by pressing the ESC key.

Find Options

Excel's Find feature offers the following options:

- **Search:** Select the direction you want to search in: down through columns, or rightwards across rows.
- **Look In:** The type of cells you want to search through.
- **Match Case:** Searches only for characters that match the case of the entered search text. For example, a search for 'smith' does not find 'Smith'.
- **Find Entire Cells Only:** Searches only for complete matches. For example, a search for 'Sm' does not find 'Smith', and 330 does not find 3308.

Replacing Cell Content

Anything that you can search for in a worksheet with **Edit | Find**, you can replace with a specified alternative. For example, you could replace occurrences of cell reference F34 with F36. The procedure is as follows:

- Select the relevant range of cells. (To perform the find-and-replace operation on the whole worksheet, click any cell.)
- Choose **Edit | Replace**.
- In the Find what: box, enter the item you want to replace. In the Replace with: box, enter the replacement item. (You can delete from the selected cells the characters in the Find what: box by leaving the Replace with: box blank.)
- Select **Find Next**. To replace only the highlighted occurrence of the found characters, select **Replace**.
- To replace *all* occurrences of the found characters in the selected cells, click **Replace All**.

Exercise 4.41 provides an example of Excel's find-and-replace feature.

Exercise 4.41: Finding and Replacing Text on a Worksheet

1) Click the Sheet2 tab to display the second worksheet of your workbook.
2) Select the cell range A2:E6.
3) Choose **Edit | Replace**. In the Find what: box, type Smith. In the Replace with: box, type Sullivan.
4) Select the 'Match case' and 'Find entire cells only' options. Select **Replace All**.

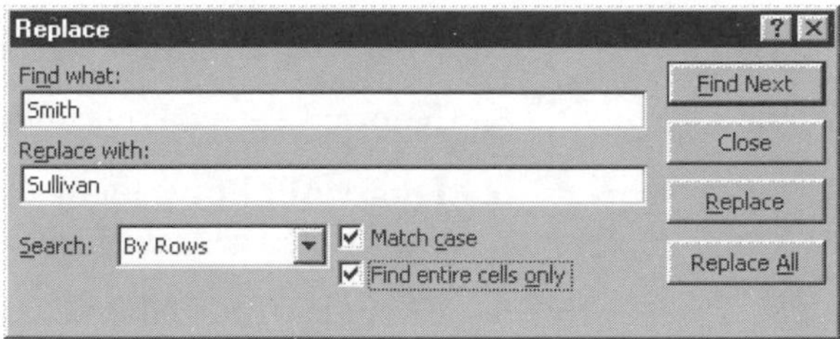

Sheet2 should now look as shown below.

	A	B	C	D	E
1					
2		**January**	**February**	**April**	**Total**
3	*Conway*	2356	3621	4560	10537
4	*Murphy*	4921	4055	3542	12518
5	*Sullivan*	2903	3308	3622	9833
6		10180	10984	11724	32888
7					

Spell-Checking

Spelling button

Excel can check the spelling of text on all or part of a worksheet.

To check your spelling, follow this procedure:

- Select the range of cells whose spelling you want to check. To check the whole worksheet, click any cell.
- Click the Spelling button on Excel's Standard Toolbar.

When Excel meets a word that it does not recognise from its spelling dictionary (the same dictionary used by Microsoft Word), it displays the Spelling dialog box, as shown below.

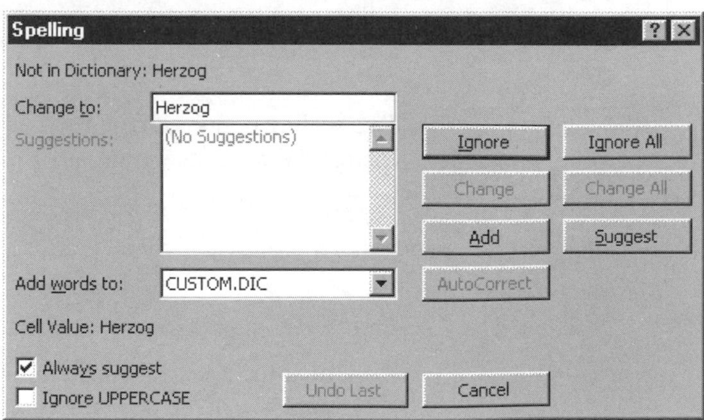

The following are your main options:

- **Ignore:** Leave this occurrence of the word unchanged.
- **Ignore All:** Leave this and all other occurrences of the word in the selected cells unchanged.
- **Change:** Correct this occurrence of the word, but prompt again on further occurrences.
- **Change All:** Correct this occurrence of the word – and all other occurrences without further prompting.
- **Add:** Add the word to the custom (your personal) dictionary. Use this option for the names of people or places, or abbreviations or acronyms, that you type regularly. Excel will recognise such added words during future spell-checks of any worksheet.

Practise by spell-checking Sheet1 and Sheet2 of your workbook.

Page Setup

In the remainder of this Section 4.3 you will learn about Excel's various printing options, beginning with those available on the four tabs of the **File | Page Setup** dialog box: the Page, Margins, Header/Footer, and Sheet tabs.

Paper Size

Located on the Page tab of the **File | Page Setup** dialog box, this option allows you to select the size of the paper you want to print on. The default is A4, the European standard paper size (21 cm wide and 29.7 cm high).

Orientation

Also on the Page tab, orientation is the direction in which the page is printed. Your options are Portrait ('standing up') and Landscape ('on its side').

Scaling

Two scaling options on the Page tab enable you to reduce or enlarge the worksheet printout:

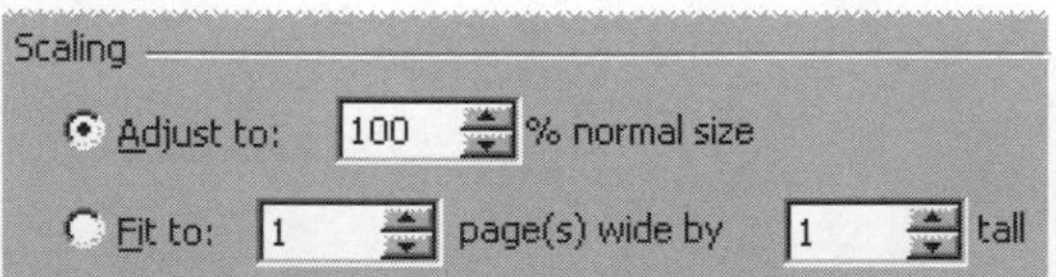

- **Adjust to:** You can enter a number in the range 10–400% of normal size. (You need not type the % symbol.)

- **Fit to:** Reduces the worksheet (or selected cells) so that it fits on the specified number of pages. You can specify the number of pages vertically (tall), horizontally (wide) or both.

Margins

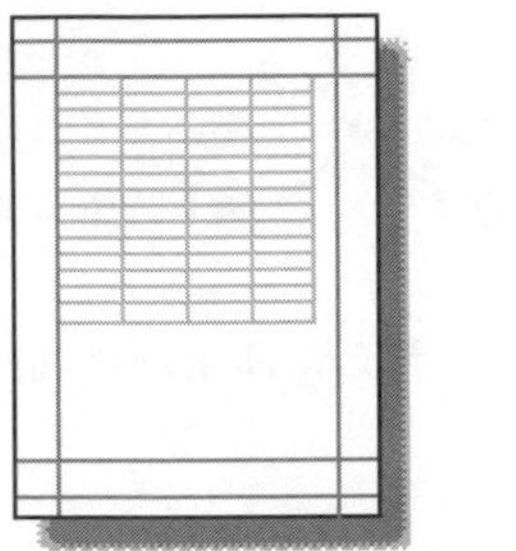

The margins are the distance that the printed worksheet or selected cells are positioned in from the four edges of the printed page. You set this on the Margins tab of the **File | Page Setup** dialog box. You can specify separate margins for headers and footers , which are covered in the next topic.

It is unlikely that you will need to change Excel's default margin values – top and bottom, 2.5 cm, left and right, 1.9 cm.

The Margins tab also allows you to centre your worksheet or selected cells horizontally (positioned evenly between the left and right margins of the printed page), vertically (between the top and bottom margins), or both.

Gridlines and Headings

By default, Excel does not include cell boundary lines or row and column headings on printouts. You can change either or both of these settings on the Sheet tab of the **File | Page Setup** dialog box.

Headers and Footers

These are pieces of text that appear at the top and bottom of every page of a printed worksheet. Typically, they contain such details as file name, author name, date and page number.

With Excel, you need only type in header and/or footer text once, and the program repeats the text on every page. You can apply formatting – font, bold and italics – to text in the headers and footers.

Here are a few facts about headers and footers in Excel:

- You insert them with the Header/Footer tab of the **File | Page Setup** command.
- The Header/Footer tab offers a drop-down list of suggested header and footer texts, from which you can choose the one that best suits your needs.
- You can edit and/or format your chosen header or footer text by clicking the Custom header or Custom footer button on the Header/Footer tab, and then selecting the required options.
- The Custom buttons enable you format the header or footer text, and insert any or all of the following items: page number, total number of pages, date, time, Excel file name and worksheet name.

- When setting header and footer margins on the Margins tab of the **File | Page Setup** dialog box, ensure that the values are less than the top and bottom page margins – otherwise, the header and footer text may overlap the cells on the printout.

Exercise 4.42 provides an example of Excel's header and footer feature in action.

Exercise 4.42: Inserting a Header and Footer

1) With Sheet1 of your workbook selected, choose **File | Page Setup** and select the Header/Footer tab.

2) On the Header drop-down list, select the Excel workbook file name – in this case, KenBloggs.xls.

3) On the Footer drop-down list, select Page 1 of ?.

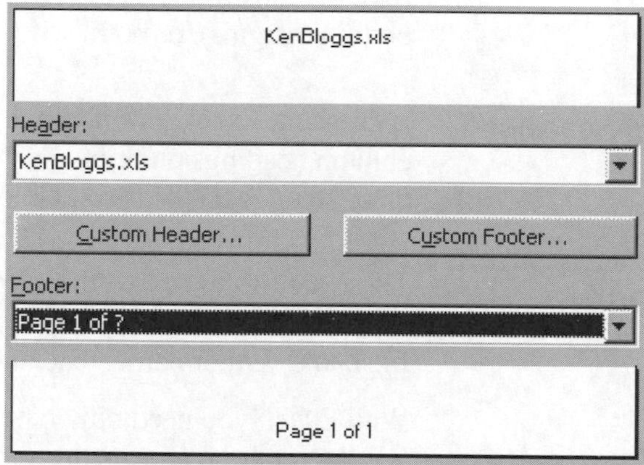

Text Formatting button

4) Click the Custom Header button, select the file name in the Centre section, click the Text Formatting button, and make the file name bold.

5) In the Left section, type My First Worksheet. In the Right section, type ECDL Module 4.

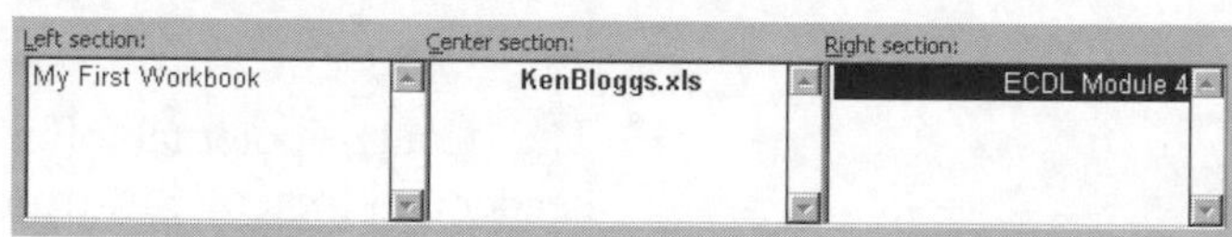

Date button

6) Click **OK** to return to the Header/Footer tab of the Page Setup dialog box.

7) Click the Custom footer button, click in the Left section, and then click the Date button.

8) Click in the Right section, and then click the Time button.

Time button

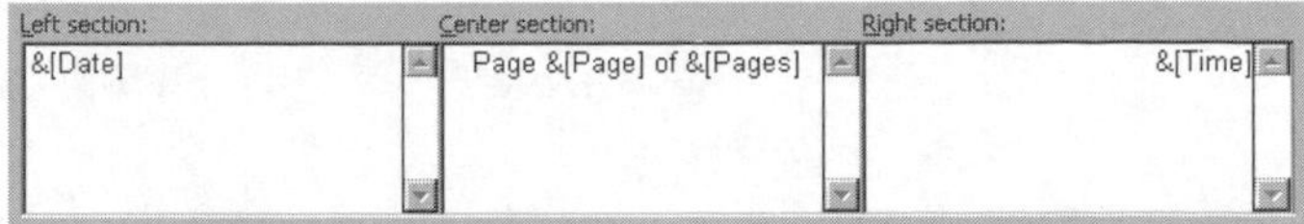

9) Click **OK** to return to the Header/Footer tab of the Page Setup dialog box. Click **OK** again to close the dialog box.

Well done. You have inserted a header and footer in your workbook. You cannot see headers and footers on screen; they appear on printouts only.

Printing Options

Excel offers a wide range of printing options. These include the ability to preview a worksheet on your screen before you print it, and the choice of printing all your worksheet, selected cells or pages, or your entire workbook.

Print Preview

Print Preview button

This displays each page as it will appear when it is printed on paper. To preview your worksheet:

- Choose **File | Print Preview**.

  -or-

- Click the Print Preview button on the Standard Toolbar.

Click **Close** to return to your worksheet.

Print Range Options

When you choose **File | Print**, you have the following options regarding which parts of your workbook you may print:

- **All:** The current worksheet.
- **Pages:** To print one or a range of pages from the current worksheet, enter the page number(s) here.
- **Selection:** Prints only the currently selected cells on the current worksheet.
- **Entire Workbook:** All worksheets that contain data in the workbook.

Other options on the Print dialog box allow you to specify how many copies you want to print, and whether you want the pages collated or not.

Exercise 4.43: Printing a Worksheet

1) Click the Sheet1 tab to select the first worksheet of your workbook.
2) Choose **File | Print**, accept the default options, and click **OK**.

Your printout should look like that shown.

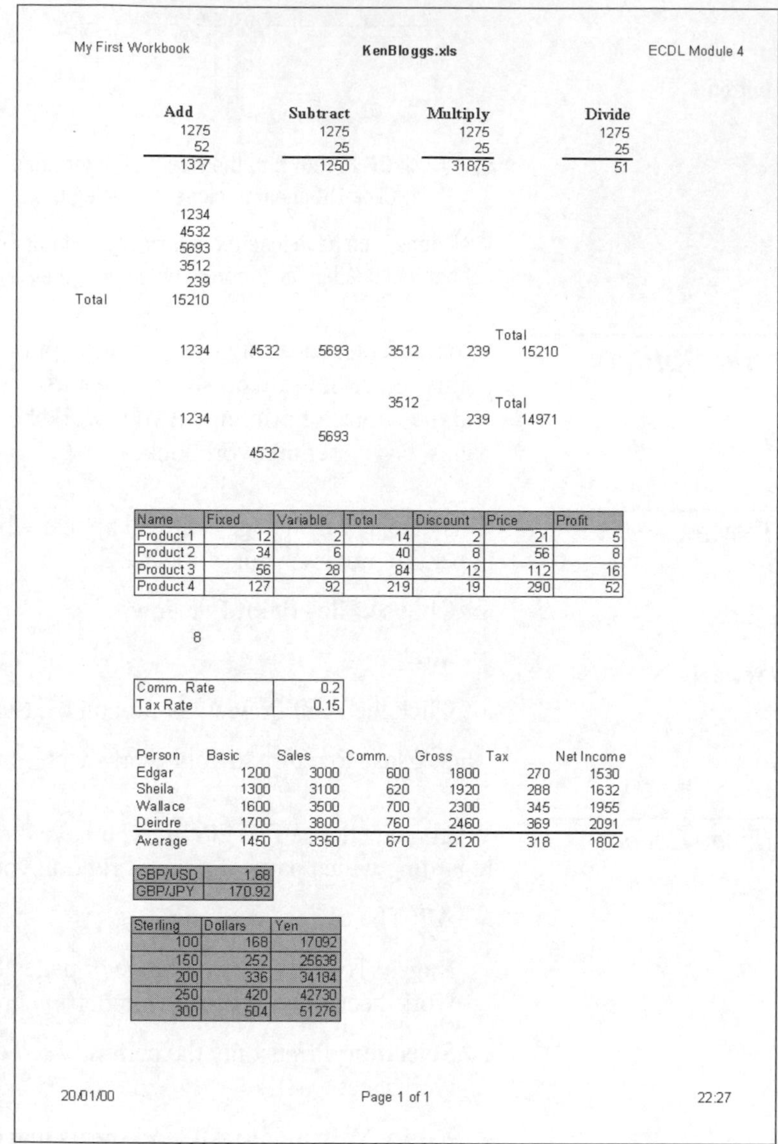

My First Workbook | **KenBloggs.xls** | ECDL Module 4

Add	Subtract	Multiply	Divide
1275	1275	1275	1275
52	25	25	25
1327	1250	31875	51

	1234
	4532
	5693
	3512
	239
Total	15210

					Total
1234	4532	5693	3512	239	15210

			3512		Total
1234				239	14971
		5693			
	4532				

Name	Fixed	Variable	Total	Discount	Price	Profit
Product 1	12	2	14	2	21	5
Product 2	34	6	40	8	56	8
Product 3	56	28	84	12	112	16
Product 4	127	92	219	19	290	52

8

Comm. Rate	0.2
Tax Rate	0.15

Person	Basic	Sales	Comm.	Gross	Tax	Net Income
Edgar	1200	3000	600	1800	270	1530
Sheila	1300	3100	620	1920	288	1632
Wallace	1600	3500	700	2300	345	1955
Deirdre	1700	3800	760	2460	369	2091
Average	1450	3350	670	2120	318	1802

GBP/USD	1.68
GBP/JPY	170.92

Sterling	Dollars	Yen
100	168	17092
150	252	25638
200	336	34184
250	420	42730
300	504	51276

20/01/00 | Page 1 of 1 | 22:27

Save and close your workbook and Excel. You have now completed this Section 4.3 of the ECDL Spreadsheet Module.

Section Summary: So Now You Know

Functions are predefined formulae built in to Excel that allow you to perform specific calculations. As with formulae, functions always begin with an equal to (=) symbol.

With the SUM function, you need enter only two arguments when totalling a vertical or horizontal list of cells: the first and last cell references. An example of a SUM function would be: =SUM(A2:A6)

A fast way to total a vertical or horizontal list of cells is to select them and click the *AutoSum* button. Excel tries to 'guess' which cells you want to add. If Excel has guessed correctly, just press ENTER to confirm the suggested arguments. If not, edit the arguments of the SUM function.

The AVERAGE function, as its name suggests, calculates the average of a vertical or horizontal list of numbers. For example: =AVERAGE(D5:F5)

A *cell range* is a group of cells on a worksheet. You can *select* an *adjacent* cell range by dragging the mouse across it. Select a *non-adjacent* cell range by selecting the first cell (or first sub-group of adjacent cells) and then holding down the CTRL key when selecting further cells (or adjacent ranges).

Selected cells can be *formatted* (bold or italic), *aligned* (horizontally or vertically) and *rotated*. You can also add *borders* and *fills* (coloured backgrounds), and change *fonts* and *sizes*.

You can adjust *column width* and *row height* by dragging the cell boundaries in the row and column headings.

You can *search* all or part of a worksheet for label text, entered numbers, numbers resulting from calculations, and calculation components (function names, cell references, arithmetic operators and constants). And you can *replace* found items with alternatives. You can also *spell-check* all or part of a worksheet.

The standard page size is A4, and pages can be oriented in *portrait* or *landscape*. A *margin* is the distance of the cells from a particular edge of the page.

Headers and *footers* are small text items that occur on every printed page, and typically contain such details as the workbook name, author name and date. Either can also contain the automatically generated *page number*.

Excel's *print options* include a print preview feature and the ability to print selected cells only.

Section 4.4: Inserting, Sorting and Moving Cells

In This Section

Excel users spend only part of their time creating new workbooks and entering and formatting data in the worksheet cells. The remainder is spent reopening existing workbooks and amending previously entered data.

In this Section you will learn how to perform three types of maintenance tasks.

Row and column insertion allow you to position new cells within a worksheet area that already contains cells with data in them. Insertion (or deletion) means that surrounding cells must adjust their position to make way for the new data (or fill the spaces previously occupied by the deleted data).

Copying, cutting and pasting enable you to reproduce or move cells within the same worksheet, between worksheets in the same workbook, or between different workbooks. Copying and cutting of calculations introduce the idea of relative and absolute cell references.

Finally, sorting allows you to rearrange selected cells in a sequence different from that in which they were entered to the worksheet.

New Skills

At the end of this Section you should be able to:

- Insert and delete rows, columns and cells
- Copy, cut and paste the contents of cells
- Explain the difference between relative and absolute cell references, and identify calculations in which absolute cell references are appropriate
- Sort cells according to one or two criteria
- Insert symbols and special characters from Word to Excel.

New Words

At the end of this Section you should be able to explain the following terms:

- Marquee
- Sort
- Relative cell reference
- Sort order
- Absolute cell reference

Inserting and Deleting Rows

Sometimes you need to insert a row or column into your worksheet to hold new data *within* a range of cells that already contain text and numbers.

Exercises 4.44 and 4.45 take you through the steps of inserting new rows and columns.

Exercise 4.44: Inserting a New Row

1) Open the second worksheet of your workbook, Sheet2.

2) Select the heading of the row immediately *below* where you want to insert the new row. For example, to insert a new row below row 4, click on the heading of row 5.

	A	B	C	D	E
1					
2		**January**	**February**	**April**	**Totals**
3	*Conway*	2356	3621	4560	10537
4	*Murphy*	4921	4055	3542	12518
5	*Sullivan*	2903	3308	3622	9833
6		10180	10984	11724	32888

3) Choose **Insert | Rows**. Excel inserts a new row of blank cells.

	A	B	C	D	E
1					
2		**January**	**February**	**April**	**Totals**
3	*Conway*	2356	3621	4560	10537
4	*Murphy*	4921	4055	3542	12518
5					
6	*Sullivan*	2903	3308	3622	9833
7		10180	10984	11724	32888

4) Enter new text and numbers in cells A5, B5, C5 and D5, as shown on the next page. Excel recalculates the totals on row 7 automatically as you add the new numbers.

5) In cell E5, enter the following SUM function to add the cells of row 5:

   =SUM(B5:D5)

   Excel recalculates E7, the total of the Totals column, to include E5, the sum of the numbers that you have entered in row 5. Your worksheet should look as shown on the next page.

	A	B	C	D	E
1					
2		**January**	**February**	**April**	**Totals**
3	*Conway*	2356	3621	4560	10537
4	*Murphy*	4921	4055	3542	12518
5	*Smith*	3872	2441	4949	11262
6	*Sullivan*	2903	3308	3622	9833
7		14052	13425	16673	44150
8					

6) To make your worksheet more readable, insert a blank row above the column totals, as shown.

	A	B	C	D	E
1					
2		**January**	**February**	**April**	**Totals**
3	*Conway*	2356	3621	4560	10537
4	*Murphy*	4921	4055	3542	12518
5	*Smith*	3872	2441	4949	11262
6	*Sullivan*	2903	3308	3622	9833
7					
8		14052	13425	16673	44150

Deleting Rows

To delete a row, select the row heading and choose **Edit | Delete**. The row beneath moves up to fill the space previously occupied by the deleted row.

Inserting and Deleting Columns

Inserting a new column in a worksheet is similar to inserting a new row. Exercise 4.45 shows you how.

Exercise 4.45: Inserting a New Column

1) Select the heading of the column immediately to the right of where you want to insert the new column.

   For example, to insert a new column to the right of column C, click on the heading of column D.

2) Choose **Insert | Columns**. Excel inserts a new column of blank cells.

3) Enter new text and numbers in D2:D6 as shown on the next page.

   Excel recalculates the totals in column F automatically as you add the new numbers in column D.

4) To total the new numbers in column D, enter the following function in cell D8:

   =SUM(D3:D6)

	A	B	C	D	E	F
1						
2		**January**	**February**	**March**	**April**	**Totals**
3	*Conway*	2356	3621	4185	4560	14722
4	*Murphy*	4921	4055	3814	3542	16332
5	*Smith*	3872	2441	2888	4949	14150
6	*Sullivan*	2903	3308	3487	3622	13320
7						
8		14052	13425	14374	16673	58524

5) To make your worksheet more readable, insert a column to the right of the April column.

6) This blank column is wider than it needs to be. In the column heading, click on the boundary between columns F and G, and then drag the boundary to the left.

E	F	G
April		**Totals**
4560		14722

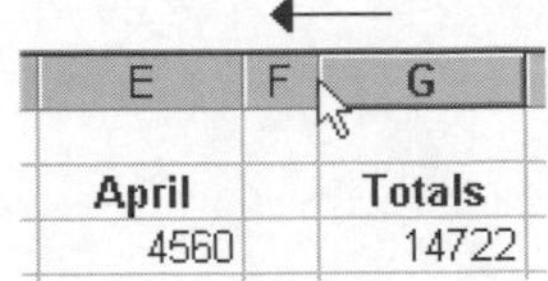

Deleting Columns

To delete a column, select its heading and choose **Edit | Delete**. The column to the right moves left and fills the space previously occupied by the deleted column.

Inserting and Deleting Cells

You can insert individual cells on a worksheet by first selecting a cell immediately below or to the right of where you want to insert the new cell, and then choosing **Insert | Cells**.

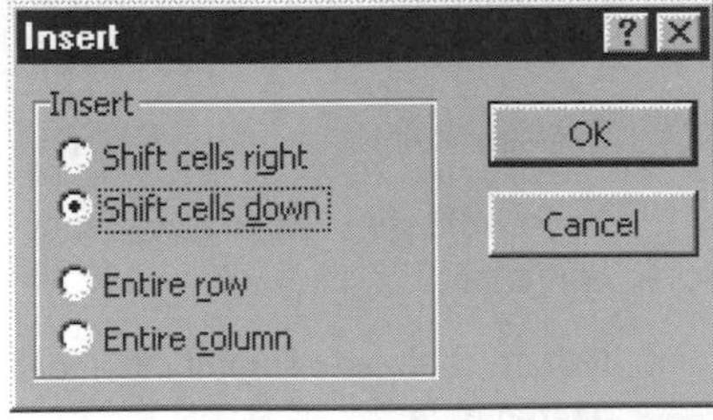

To delete a cell, select it and choose **Edit | Delete**.

Be careful about inserting or deleting a new cell or cell range, because Excel adjusts the position of the surrounding cells accordingly. Excel prompts you to choose whether the surrounding cells should move right or down.

Copying and Pasting Cell Contents

Suppose you have text or a number in one cell, and you want to copy it to another cell. How do you do it? Of the many ways of copying and pasting a cell or cells on a worksheet, here are the two most convenient:

- Drag-and-drop
- Right-clicking

You will learn about each method in Exercises 4.46 and 4.47.

Exercise 4:46: Copy and Paste with Drag-and-Drop

1) Select the cell you want to copy from.
2) For example, click the Sheet1 tab to display your first worksheet. Type 1234 in cell B57 and press ENTER. Next, click B57 to select it.

   See how the cursor is shaped like a plus sign (+).

3) Move the cursor to the bottom edge of the selected cell and hold down the CTRL key. Excel changes the cursor from a plus sign to an arrow with a smaller plus sign.

   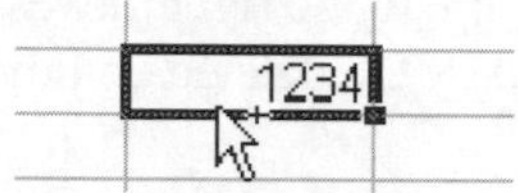

   (You can move the cursor to any edge of the selected cell – it doesn't matter which edge. The cursor still changes shape.)
4) Holding down the CTRL key, drag the cell to the destination cell that you want to paste to – for example, D57.
5) Release the mouse button *first*, and then the CTRL key.

   (If you release CTRL first, Excel cuts rather than copies the cell contents.)

   If there is already something in cell D57, Excel overwrites it with the pasted data.

Well done. You have copied a number from one cell of a worksheet to another – without clicking a toolbar button or choosing a menu command!

Exercise 4:47: Copy and Paste by Right-Clicking

1) Select the cell whose contents you want to copy. As in Exercise 4.46, select B57.
2) Right-click with the mouse.

3) Choose **Copy** from the pop-up menu. Excel places the contents of B57 in the Clipboard.

4) Click cell F57.

5) Right-click with the mouse.

6) Choose **Paste**.

If there is already something in cell F57, Excel overwrites it with the pasted data.

You are not limited to using drag-and-drop and right-clicking with single cells only. You can use both methods with selected ranges of cells.

About the Clipboard

When you copy (or cut) and paste by any means other than drag-and-drop, the copied (or cut) cells are held in a temporary storage area called the Clipboard. Four points you should remember about the Clipboard:

- The Clipboard is temporary. Turn off your computer and the Clipboard contents are deleted.
- The same Clipboard is available to all Windows applications. For example, you can copy from Excel and paste into Word.
- The Clipboard can hold only a single, copied item at a time. If you copy a second item to it, the second overwrites the first.
- An item stays in the Clipboard after you paste from it, so you can paste the same item to as many locations as you need.

The Flashing Marquee

When you copy (or cut) a cell or cell range by any means other than drag-and-drop, Excel surrounds the selected cells with a flashing rectangle called a marquee.

Marquee

A flashing rectangle that Excel uses to surround a cell, or cell range, that you have copied to the Clipboard.

You can remove a marquee at any stage by pressing the ESC key at the top-left of your keyboard.

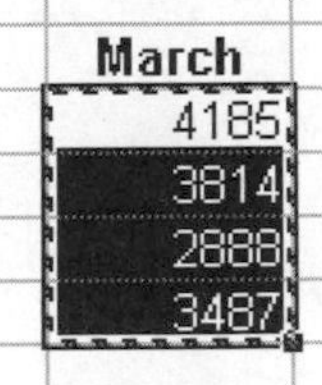

If you remove a marquee, Excel removes the contents of the selected cell or cell range from the Clipboard.

Exercise 4.48: Copy and Paste a Cell Range

In this Exercise you will copy and paste an adjacent cell range. You will use the keyboard shortcuts to perform the copy and paste actions.

1) Type 1234 in cells C57 and E57.
2) Select the cell range B57:F57.
3) Press CTRL+c to copy the cells to the Clipboard.
4) Click cell B59, and press CTRL+v to paste from the Clipboard.

   Excel copies the cells to the new cell range B59:F59, as shown below.

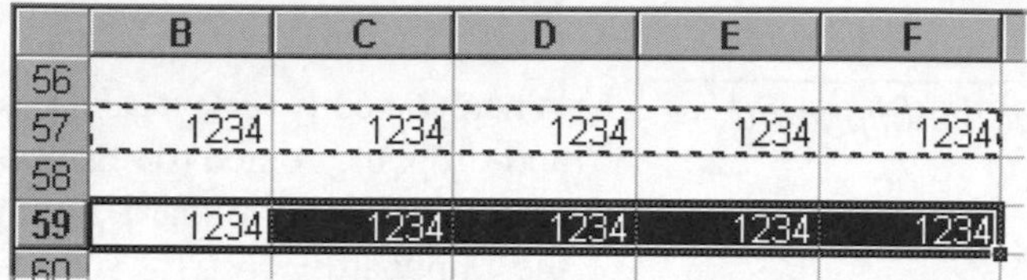

	B	C	D	E	F
56					
57	1234	1234	1234	1234	1234
58					
59	1234	1234	1234	1234	1234
60					

You can paste from the Clipboard to several locations in a single action, as Exercise 4.49 demonstrates.

Exercise 4.49: Copy and Paste to Multiple Locations

1) With cell range B57:F57 still in the Clipboard from Exercise 4.48, select the adjacent cell range B61:F64.
2) Press CTRL+v to paste to the cells. All four adjacent rows of the destination cell range now contain the pasted cells.
3) Select the non-adjacent cell range B66:F66, B68:F68, B70:F70.
4) Press CTRL+v to paste to the cells. The three non-adjacent rows of the destination cell range now contain the pasted cells.

   Your worksheet should look as shown below.

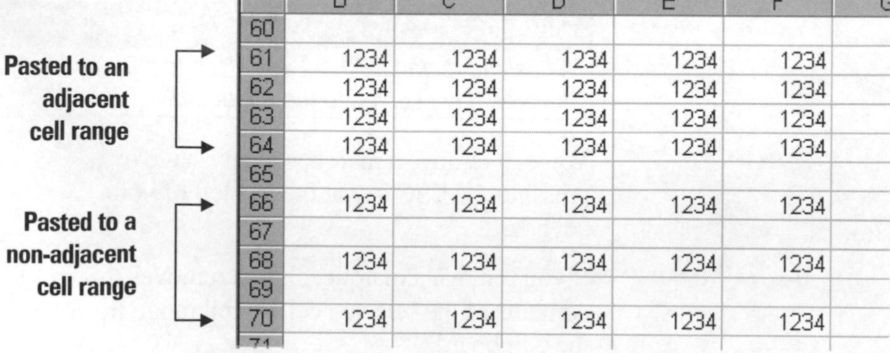

	B	C	D	E	F	G
60						
61	1234	1234	1234	1234	1234	
62	1234	1234	1234	1234	1234	
63	1234	1234	1234	1234	1234	
64	1234	1234	1234	1234	1234	
65						
66	1234	1234	1234	1234	1234	
67						
68	1234	1234	1234	1234	1234	
69						
70	1234	1234	1234	1234	1234	
71						

Cutting and Pasting Cell Contents

Copy button

Cut button

Paste button

Cut and paste differs from copy and paste in that Excel removes the content of the original cell contents, whereas the contents of copied cells remain in their original locations. Cutting does not remove the cells, in the way that the **Edit | Delete** command does. It just removes their contents, leaving behind empty cells.

To cut and paste using drag-and-drop, do not hold down the CTRL key while dragging the cell contents to their new location.

To cut and paste using the pop-up menu, choose **Cut** rather than **Copy**. **Cut**, **Copy** and **Paste** commands are also available on Excel's **Edit** menu. The keyboard shortcut for cutting a cell or cell range is CTRL+x.

Yet another cut or copy and paste method is to use the relevant buttons on Excel's Standard Toolbox.

Copying between Worksheets and Workbooks

You are not limited to copying or cutting and pasting cells within the same worksheet (such as Sheet1). You can also copy or cut and paste between different worksheets of the same workbook (such as Sheet1 and Sheet2 of your workbook), and even between different workbooks.

Exercise 4.50: Copying and Pasting between Workbooks

New button

1) On Sheet2, select cell range A2:G8.
2) Choose **Edit | Copy** to copy the cells to the Clipboard.
3) Click the New button on the Standard Toolbox to open a new workbook. The new workbook opens with Sheet1 displayed.
4) In the Name Box of the new workbook, type A100 and press ENTER. This moves the cursor to cell A100, making it the active cell.
5) Choose **Edit | Paste** to paste the cell range from the Clipboard.

You have completed the Exercise. Close the new workbook without saving it.

Moving Calculations

Numbers and text can be copied or cut and pasted without problems. But what about calculations? Can errors arise when moving formulae or functions?

Yes – but only when fixed-factor calculations are involved. As you learnt in Section 4.2, these are calculations where a common cell reference, indicating the fixed factor, is used in formulae or functions on different rows or columns. Common examples of fixed factors are currency exchange rates, and tax and sales commission rates.

Exercise 4.51 demonstrates the problem that can arise when copying fixed factor calculations.

Exercise 4.51: Copying Fixed Factor Calculations

1) On Sheet1, select the cell range B46:D54, and press CTRL+c to copy it to the Clipboard.

2) Click cell F46, and press CTRL+v. Excel copies the cells to their new location without error.

   If you click on any calculated cell, you can see that Excel has automatically adjusted the formula arguments to reflect the new cell references.

   For example, C50 contains the formula =B50*D46. The corresponding cell in the pasted data, G50, contains the formula =G50*G46.

3) Select the cell range B49:D54, and press CTRL+c to copy it to the Clipboard.

4) Select cell J49, and press CTRL+v to paste from the Clipboard.

   This time the pasting of the cells does produce calculation errors. Excel has changed the cell references of the two fixed factors (the dollar and yen conversion rates) so that the formula cells now 'point to' the new cell locations K46 and K47 – but these cells are empty.

	J	K	L
46			
47			
48			
49	Sterling	Dollars	Yen
50	100	=J50*K46	=J50*K47
51	150	=J51*K46	=J51*K47
52	200	=J52*K46	=J52*K47
53	250	=J53*K46	=J53*K47
54	300	=J54*K46	=J54*K47
55			

   There is a way to remedy this problem. First, select the pasted cell range J49:L54, and delete it with the **Edit | Clear | All** command. This removes *both* the cell content and the cell formatting.

5) Double-click on C50, and change the formula to the following: B50*C46. Similarly, in C51:C54, change all references from C46 to C46.

   Next, in cells D50:D54, change all cell references from C47 to the new format of C47. Your worksheet formulae should now look as shown on the next page.

49	Sterling	Dollars	Yen
50	100	=B50*C46	=B50*C47
51	150	=B51*C46	=B51*C47
52	200	=B52*C46	=B52*C47
53	250	=B53*C46	=B53*C47
54	300	=B54*C46	=B54*C47

6) Select cells B49:D54, and press CTRL+c to copy them.

7) Select cell J49, and press CTRL+v to paste from the Clipboard. No errors! If you click on any of the formula cells, you can see that Excel has not adjusted the cell references that contained the $ symbol. Although pasted to a new location, the calculations continue 'pointing to' the original cell references of the two currency conversion rates.

In this Exercise you have learnt the difference between relative and absolute cell address. The next topic provides further details.

Cell References: The Two Kinds

In Section 4.1 you learnt that each cell on a worksheet has a unique reference, written in the form A1 – column letter first, row number second.

In fact, Excel supports two kinds of cell references: relative (the A1 type you know already) and absolute (the A1 type you met in Exercise 4.51).

Why is one type of cell reference not enough? The answer, as you discovered in Exercise 4.51, lies in the way that Excel copies and pastes calculations that contain cell references.

A cell reference that Excel adjusts automatically when the calculation cell containing it is moved to a new location is called a relative cell reference.

Relative Cell Reference

A reference to a cell or cell range in the format A1. Excel changes a relative cell reference when you copy a formula or function containing such a reference.

An absolute cell reference, however, does not change when the calculation containing it is moved to a new location. Accordingly, you should use absolute cell references when entering fixed factor type calculations. You can make part of a cell reference absolute and part relative. For example, G$13 or $D17.

Absolute Cell Reference

A reference to a cell or cell range in the format A1. Excel does not adjust an absolute cell reference when you copy a calculation containing such a reference.

Exercise 4.52: Working with Absolute Cell References

In this Exercise you will use the Find-and-Replace feature to convert relative cell references to absolute ones, and then copy the related calculations to a new location.

1) On Sheet1, select cell range E40:E43.
2) Choose **Edit | Replace**. Type the values shown below, and select **Replace All.**

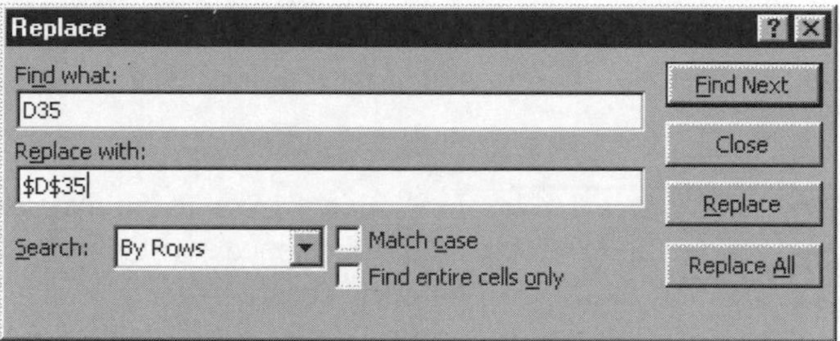

3) Select cell range G40:G43, and repeat step 2). This time, replace all occurrences of D36 with D36.

   You are now ready to copy the cells that 'point to' the two fixed factors, sales commission and taxation rate.
4) Select cell range B39:H44, and press CTRL+c to copy them to the Clipboard.
5) Click cell J39, and press CTRL+v. The calculations copy without error.

Sorting: Reordering Cells by Content

The order in which you typed entries in a worksheet may not be the order in which, later on, you would prefer to display or print that information. Suppose, for example, that you have entered a list of numbers in a column of a worksheet.

By selecting the cell range and choosing the Sort Ascending (or Sort Descending) button, you can rearrange the cells so that Excel displays them in order of increasing (or decreasing) value. The reordered list may now be easier to read than the original, unsorted one.

Sorting
Rearranging columns of cells based on the values in the cells. Sorting does not change the content of cells, only their location.

Excel offers a number of sequencing options, called sort orders.

Sort Order
A particular way of ordering cells based on value. A sort order can be alphabetic or numeric, and can be in ascending (0 to 9, A to Z) or descending (9 to 0, Z to A) sequence.

Exercise 4.53: A Simple Sort

Sort Ascending button

Sort Descending button

1) On Sheet1, click B73 and enter the label Original.
2) In the six cells immediately below B73, type the following vertical list of numbers: 453, 123, 340, 683, 987 and 213.
3) In cells C73 and D73, enter the labels Ascending and Descending.
4) Select the cell range B74:B79, and press CTRL+c.
5) Select the cell range C74:D79, and press CTRL+v.
6) Select the cell range C74:C79, and click the Sort Ascending button on the Standard Toolbar.
7) Select the cell range D74:D79, and click the Sort Descending button on the Standard Toolbar.

   Your worksheet should look as shown below.

	B	C	D
72			
73	Original	Ascending	Decending
74	453	123	987
75	123	213	683
76	340	340	453
77	683	453	340
78	987	683	213
79	213	987	123
80			

The two Sort buttons give you a quick, one-click way of reordering a cell range. As you will discover in Exercise 4.54, Excel's **Data | Sort** menu command provides an additional option: you can sort a cell range based on the values in more than a single column. This is called a 'multiple sort'.

Exercise 4.54: A Complex Sort

The rows of Sheet2 are currently arranged in alphabetic sort order according to surname: Conway first, then Murphy, Smith and, lastly, Sullivan.

	A	B	C	D	E	F	G
1							
2		**January**	**February**	**March**	**April**		**Totals**
3	*Conway*	2356	3621	4185	4560		14722
4	*Murphy*	4921	4055	3814	3542		16332
5	*Smith*	3872	2441	2888	4949		14150
6	*Sullivan*	2903	3308	3487	3622		13320
7							
8		14052	13425	14374	16673		58524

1) Select row 7 by clicking on its row heading, and choose **Insert | Rows**. Next, press CTRL+Y twice. This is the keyboard shortcut for Excel's REPEAT command. Excel inserts three new, blank rows under row 6.

6	*Sullivan*	2903	3308	3487	3622		13320
7							
8							
9							
10							
11		14052	13425	14374	16673		58524

2) Enter in rows 7, 8 and 9 the text and numbers as shown below.

	A	B	C	D	E	F	G
1							
2		**January**	**February**	**March**	**April**		**Totals**
3	*Conway*	2356	3621	4185	4560		14722
4	*Murphy*	4921	4055	3814	3542		16332
5	*Smith*	3872	2441	2888	4949		14150
6	*Sullivan*	2903	3308	3487	3622		13320
7	*Rafferty*	2512	2864	3290	3741		12407
8	*Higgins*	3463	3981	4210	4974		16628
9	*Smith*	5951	6226	6481	6852		25510
10							
11		25978	26496	28355	32240		113069

In row 11, edit the arguments of the SUM functions to include the three new rows. For example, in B11 enter the function =SUM(B3:B9).

Enter new SUM functions in G7, G8 and G9 to calculate the row totals. For example, in G8 enter =SUM(B8:E8).

3) Select column B by clicking on its column heading, and choose the **Insert | Columns** command. In the new column, enter the first names as shown on the next page.

	A	B	C	D	E	F	G	H
1								
2			**January**	**February**	**March**	**April**		**Totals**
3	*Conway*	*John*	2356	3621	4185	4560		14722
4	*Murphy*	*Robert*	4921	4055	3814	3542		16332
5	*Smith*	*Zowie*	3872	2441	2888	4949		14150
6	*Sullivan*	*Andrew*	2903	3308	3487	3622		13320
7	*Rafferty*	*Aidan*	2512	2864	3290	3741		12407
8	*Higgins*	*Tracey*	3463	3981	4210	4974		16628
9	*Smith*	*Catherine*	5951	6226	6481	6852		25510
10								
11			25978	26496	28355	32240		113069

4) Select cell range A3:H9, and choose **Data | Sort**.

By default, Excel shows the first column in the selected range, column A, in the Sort by: drop-down box.

In the Then by: drop-down box, select Column B.

Next, select the sort order of Ascending for both columns A and B, and click **OK**.

Your worksheet should now resemble that below.

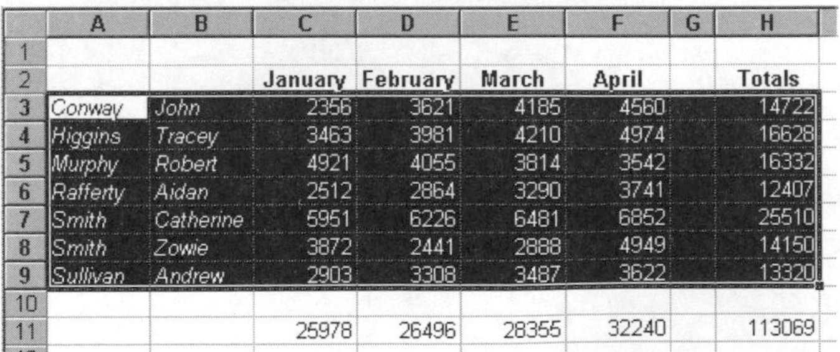

	A	B	C	D	E	F	G	H
1								
2			**January**	**February**	**March**	**April**		**Totals**
3	*Conway*	*John*	2356	3621	4185	4560		14722
4	*Higgins*	*Tracey*	3463	3981	4210	4974		16628
5	*Murphy*	*Robert*	4921	4055	3814	3542		16332
6	*Rafferty*	*Aidan*	2512	2864	3290	3741		12407
7	*Smith*	*Catherine*	5951	6226	6481	6852		25510
8	*Smith*	*Zowie*	3872	2441	2888	4949		14150
9	*Sullivan*	*Andrew*	2903	3308	3487	3622		13320
10								
11			25978	26496	28355	32240		113069

The multiple-column sort is useful where one column has duplicate entries. In this Exercise, cells A5 and A9 both initially contained the same text entry of 'Smith'.

Symbols and Special Characters

If you have completed the ECDL Word-Processing Module, you will know that Microsoft Word allows you to insert symbols and special characters in your documents.

- **Symbols:** Among these are foreign language letters with accents (such as á, é, ä, and ë), fractions, and characters used in science and mathematics.
- **Special Characters:** These include copyright (©), registered (®) and trademark (™), plus typographic characters such as the en (or short) dash, the em (or long) dash, and various types of opening and closing quotes.

Unlike Word, Excel offers no command for inserting symbols or special characters. As Exercise 4.55 shows, however, you can paste symbols and characters from Word to Excel.

Exercise 4.55: Inserting a Special Character and Symbol to a Worksheet

1) On Sheet1 of your workbook, type 100C in B82.
2) Start Microsoft Word. It should open with a new, blank document ready for you to type into.
3) Choose **Insert | Symbol**, select the Symbols tab, and double-click the degree character (°) in the Word document. Click **Close** to close the dialog box.
4) Select the degree character (°) in the Word document, and press CTRL+c. You can now close the Word document and Word itself. You need not save the document.
5) Switch to Excel, double-click cell B82 to make it editable, position the cursor between the 100 and the C, and press CTRL+v. Cell B82 should now look like that shown below.

100°C

Section Summary: So Now You Know

A common maintenance task in Excel is *row and column insertion*. Insertion results in the surrounding cells adjusting their positions to make way for the new data.

Conversely, *row and column deletion* causes the surrounding cells to move up or to the right, to fill the spaces previously occupied by the deleted data. You can also insert and delete individual cells and cell ranges.

You can reproduce (copy) or move (cut) a selected cell or cell range within the same worksheet, between worksheets in the same workbook, or between different workbooks. A wide variety of *copy, cut* and *paste* methods are provided by Excel, including drag-and-drop, commands on the pop-up menu activated by right-clicking, menu-bar commands, keyboard shortcuts, and buttons on the Standard Toolbar.

Excel automatically adjusts the cell references in calculations whenever the calculations are pasted to a new location. To prevent Excel from adjusting a cell reference in this way, specify the cell address as an *absolute cell reference* in the format (A1). Absolute cell references are most commonly used with fixed-factor type calculations.

Sorting allows you to rearrange selected cells on the basis of the values they contain. Sorting changes only the location of cells, and not their content. The *sort order*, the particular way in which cells are arranged by value, can be alphabetic or numeric, and can be in ascending (0–9, A–Z) or descending sequence (9–0, Z–A).

You cannot insert symbols and special characters in Excel directly, but you can insert them in a Word document, and then copy or cut and paste them from Word to Excel.

Section 4.5: More About Numbers, Text and Calculations

In This Section

In Sections 4.1 and 4.2 you learnt the basics of working with numbers, cell references and text. Now it's time to build on what you know.

Here you will discover that there are really four types of number and two types of cell reference, and that Excel treats the different types in different ways.

You will also learn more about entering text, and meet AutoFill, a convenient, time-saving feature for entering data in cells.

New Skills

At the end of this Section you should be able to:

- Choose the appropriate number format for the type of numbers that you want to enter and store in your worksheet
- Enter text across multiple columns
- Enter numbers as text
- Recognise the type of numbers that should be entered in calculations as absolute rather than relative cell references
- Use AutoFill to copy numbers and text, and to increment number series and special entries (dates, days, months and years)
- Use AutoFill to copy calculations that apply to multiple rows or columns

New Words

At the end of this Section you should be able to explain the following terms:

- Number format
- General format
- Comma style
- Currency style
- Percent style
- Relative cell reference
- Absolute cell reference
- Increment
- AutoFill

Numbers: The Different Formats

In Section 4.1 you learnt that a number was one of the four kinds of entries you could type in a worksheet cell – the others were text, cell references, and calculations (formulae and functions).

In fact, Excel recognises many types of numbers, and calls each a number format. Do not confuse this term with the use of the word format for stylistic items such as bold and italic.

Number format affects only the way that a number looks on screen and on printouts – and *not* its value. Consider the following example:

- A cell contains the number 1.2345.
- The same cell has a number format of one decimal place.

The number will display as 1.2. But when its cell is used in calculations, the value used will be 1.2345. This can lead to surprising results on occasion!

In the example on the right, cell A1 is multiplied by B1, and cell A2 by B2. The results are shown in C1 and C2. A1 contains the same value as A2, but is formatted with only one number after the decimal point.

	A	B	C
1	1.2345	2	2.469
2	1.2	2	2.469

Number Format

The way in which Excel displays a number on screen and on printouts. Number format affects only the appearance and not the value of numbers.

The General Format

Excel's default number format is called the General format. Unless you change to a different number format, Excel applies this format to every number you enter.

123.4
345.75
9383.5
45

Here are some things you need to know about the General format.

Zeros after the Decimal Point

The General Format does not display zeros after the decimal point. Enter 123.00, for example, and Excel's General format displays 123.

Trailing Zeros

A zero you enter as the last digit after a decimal point is called a trailing zero.

123.0
456.70
45.450

The General format does not display trailing zeros.

Enter 123.40, for example, and Excel's General format displays 123.4.

Thousands Separators

The General format does not automatically insert the comma symbol (,) to separate thousands.

Enter 2500, for example, and Excel displays it as 2500, not 2,500.

Currency Symbols

If you type a currency symbol (such as £) before a number (such as 123), Excel may treat your entry as text rather than a number. As a result, using the entry of £123 in a calculation may generate Excel's #VALUE! error message.

Unsuitable for Financial Amounts

All the above points make the General format unsuitable for displaying amounts of money on a worksheet.

The Comma Style

Comma Style button

Change to the Comma format for Excel to insert a comma to separate thousands. Excel also displays all numbers to two places of decimals. Exercise 4.56 demonstrates the Comma style.

Exercise 4.56: Changing Number Format to the Comma Style

1) Open Sheet2 of your workbook and select cell range C3:C9.
2) Click on the Comma Style button on the Standard Toolbar.

   Excel inserts commas and two places of decimals in the selected cell range, as shown on the right.

C	→	C
January		January
2356		2,356.00
3463		3,463.00
4921		4,921.00
2512		2,512.00
5951		5,951.00
3872		3,872.00
2903		2,903.00

3) Choose **Edit | Undo Style** (or press CTRL+z) to revert to General Format.

The Currency Style

Currency Style button

Change to the currency format when your numbers represent amounts of money. Exercise 4.57 demonstrates the Currency format.

Exercise 4.57: Changing Number Format to the Currency Style

1) On your worksheet select cell range C3:H11.

2) Click on the Currency Style button on the Standard Toolbar.

Excel inserts the currency symbol (£), the thousands separator (,) and trailing zeros.

	C	D	E	F	G	H
1						
2	**January**	**February**	**March**	**April**		**Total**
3	£ 2,356.00	£ 3,621.00	£ 4,185.00	£ 4,560.00		£ 14,722.00
4	£ 3,463.00	£ 3,981.00	£ 4,210.00	£ 4,974.00		£ 16,628.00
5	£ 4,921.00	£ 4,055.00	£ 3,814.00	£ 3,542.00		£ 16,332.00
6	£ 2,512.00	£ 2,864.00	£ 3,290.00	£ 3,741.00		£ 12,407.00
7	£ 5,951.00	£ 6,226.00	£ 6,481.00	£ 6,852.00		£ 25,510.00
8	£ 3,872.00	£ 2,441.00	£ 2,888.00	£ 4,949.00		£ 14,150.00
9	£ 2,903.00	£ 3,308.00	£ 3,487.00	£ 3,622.00		£ 13,320.00
10						
11	£25,978.00	£26,496.00	£28,355.00	£32,240.00		£113,069.00

The Percent Style

Percent Style button

This number format performs two actions. It:

- Multiplies the selected cell or range by 100.
- Places the percent sign (%) after each selected number.

Use it to display decimal fractions (such as 0.0525) as more readable percentages (such as 5.25%).

In Exercise 4.58 you will generate some decimal fractions suitable for expression as percentages. In Exercise 4.59 you will then change the numbers to the Percent style.

Exercise 4.58: Creating Decimal Fractions

In this Exercise you will add two new items to Sheet2:

- A new column to show each person's total as a proportion of the overall total
- A new row to show each month's total as a proportion of the overall total

1) Enter the percent symbol (%) in cells I2 and B13, and make the symbols bold and centre-align them.

2) In I3 enter the formula =H3/H11 to calculate the percentage of the total contributed by John Conway.

Enter similar formulae for cells I4:I9.

For example, in I5 enter = H5/H11 and in I6 enter =H6/H11.

Column I should look as shown on the right.

I
%
0.130204
0.147061
0.144443
0.109729
0.225614
0.125145
0.117804

3) In C13 enter the formula =C11/H11 to calculate the percentage of the total contributed in January.

Enter similar formulae for cells D13:F13. For example, to D13 enter = D11/H11. Row 13 should look as shown below.

	B	C	D	E	F
12					
13	%	0.22975351	0.23433479	0.25077607	0.28513563

Exercise 4.59: Applying the Percent Style

Now you will display the calculation results from Exercise 4.58 as percentages, using the percent style. You will also apply a fill (coloured background) to the percentage cells.

1) Select range I3:I9 and click the Percent Style button. Also centre-align the cells.

2) With range I3:I9 still selected, click the drop-down arrow to the right of the Fill Colour button on the Formatting Toolbar.

3) From the colour palette, choose Gray 25%. Click **OK**.

4) Select the range C13:F13 and click the Percent Style button.

5) Repeat steps 2) and 3) for C13:F13, filling the cells' background with 25% grey.

6) With C13:F13 still selected, centre-align the cells.

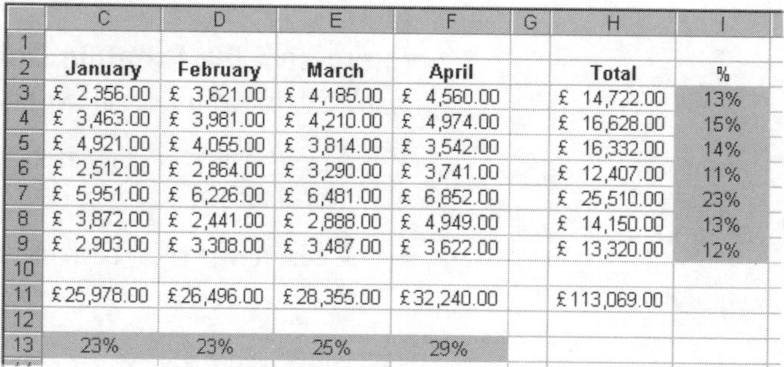

	C	D	E	F	G	H	I
1							
2	January	February	March	April		Total	%
3	£ 2,356.00	£ 3,621.00	£ 4,185.00	£ 4,560.00		£ 14,722.00	13%
4	£ 3,463.00	£ 3,981.00	£ 4,210.00	£ 4,974.00		£ 16,628.00	15%
5	£ 4,921.00	£ 4,055.00	£ 3,814.00	£ 3,542.00		£ 16,332.00	14%
6	£ 2,512.00	£ 2,864.00	£ 3,290.00	£ 3,741.00		£ 12,407.00	11%
7	£ 5,951.00	£ 6,226.00	£ 6,481.00	£ 6,852.00		£ 25,510.00	23%
8	£ 3,872.00	£ 2,441.00	£ 2,888.00	£ 4,949.00		£ 14,150.00	13%
9	£ 2,903.00	£ 3,308.00	£ 3,487.00	£ 3,622.00		£ 13,320.00	12%
10							
11	£25,978.00	£26,496.00	£28,355.00	£32,240.00		£113,069.00	
12							
13	23%	23%	25%	29%			

Well done. You have finished this Exercise. Your worksheet should now look as shown above.

Changing from the General Format

There are two ways that you can change Excel's number format:

- First enter the numbers, and then change the number format.
- Change the number format of the blank cells first, and then enter the numbers.

The second method is better. If you are creating a new worksheet to enter financial amounts, select the whole worksheet and change the number format to Currency style before entering any numbers. The Currency style will affect only the entered numbers and not any text entries.

The Number Format

Spreadsheets are often used to record physical measurements and the results of laboratory experiments. Such numbers do not represent financial amounts, so the Currency style is inappropriate. Moreover, such numbers typically require a number of decimal places greater than two or three. The number format to apply in such situations is called ... Number format. Exercise 4.60 provides an example.

Exercise 4.60: Specifying the Number of Decimal Places

Your task is to record the following numbers to four places of decimals: 3.4512, 5.13, 9.59383 and 4.531.

1) Click the Sheet1 tab to display the first worksheet of your workbook.
2) Select cell range B84:B88 and choose **Format | Cells**.
3) On the Number tab, select the Category of Number, and select 4 for Decimal places.

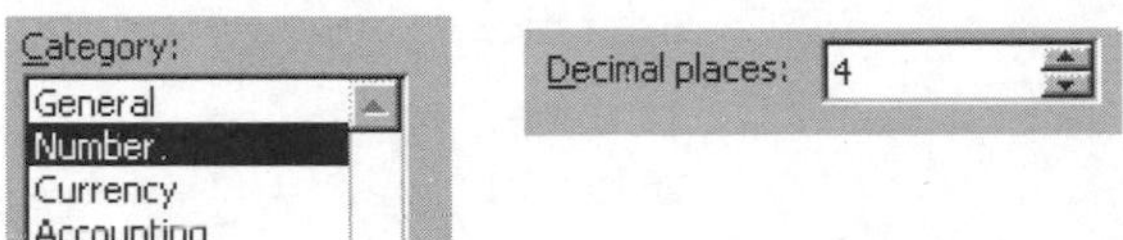

4) Click on B84, and enter the first number. Next, enter the remaining numbers in the other three cells in the range.

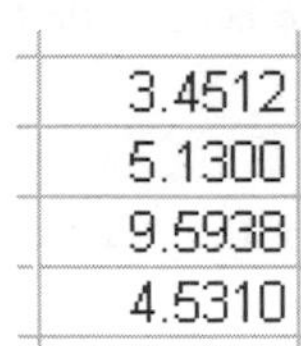

As shown on the left, Excel displays your cell entries to the specified number of decimal places:

- Where an entered number had more than four decimal places, Excel displayed only the first four
- Where the number has less, Excel added trailing zeros

Also available on the Number tab of the **Format | Cells** dialog box is the option to specify the thousands separator (,).

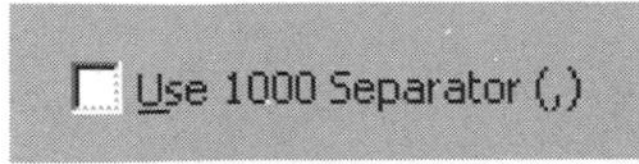

You can select this option whether you specify a fixed number of decimal places or not.

Toolbar Buttons

Two buttons on Excel's Formatting Toolbar offer quick ways of increasing or reducing the number of decimal places displayed in a selected cell or range. Each time you click on a button, the number of decimal places in the selected cells is increased or decreased by one.

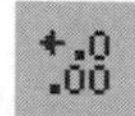

Increase Decimal button

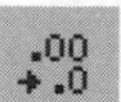

Decrease Decimal button

The buttons work with numbers in the General, Currency and Number formats.

Excel and Dates

Whether entered with financial transactions or results of experiments, dates can be very important in a worksheet. Excel treats dates as numbers, with the serial number one corresponding to the date January 1, 1900. In this way Excel can add and subtract dates, and include them in other calculations.

Entering Dates

Use a slash or a hyphen to separate the parts of a date. For example:

17/10/00
26-Nov-01

If you just type in DD/MM, Excel assumes the current year.

When you type a date that Microsoft Excel recognises, it applies one of its built-in date formats to the cell, and right-aligns it.

If Microsoft Excel cannot recognize the date, the date is recorded as text, and is left-aligned in the cell.

Formatting Dates

The way that Excel displays entered dates depends on the number format applied to the cell containing the dates.

To view a list of possible date options, choose **Format | Cells**, select the Number tab, and select Date in the Category: list. You can then see the date format options in the Type: list.

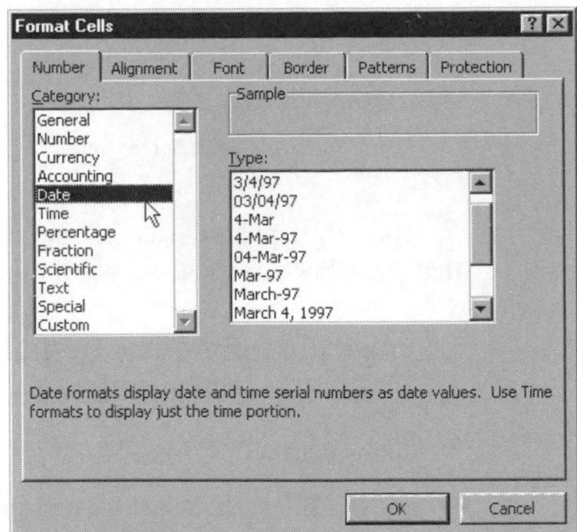

Become familiar with how Excel handles dates by entering a number of dates in different formats in your worksheet. Then, select the cells and apply to your entries some of the formats listed in the **Format | Cells** dialog box.

Regional Settings

Options you select in the Regional Settings of the Windows Control Panel affect both the currency and date conventions applied by Excel to your cell entries:

- **Changing Currency:** To use a different currency on your workbooks, choose **Start | Settings | Control Panel**, and double-click on the Regional Settings icon. On the Regional Settings tab, select the required country. On the Currency tab, accept or amend the currency conventions such as symbol, number of decimal places and digit grouping symbol.
- **Changing Date:** To use the date conventions of another country on your workbooks, select the required country on the Regional Settings tab, and, on the Date tab, accept or amend the calendar conventions.

Excel and Text

Two further items you need to know about Excel and text: you can enter text that displays across several columns of a worksheet, and you can enter numbers as text.

Text across Multiple Columns

Sometimes you may want to enter a line of text that is longer than the width of a single cell. Excel allows you to do this – provided that the text does not run into any cell that has data in it.

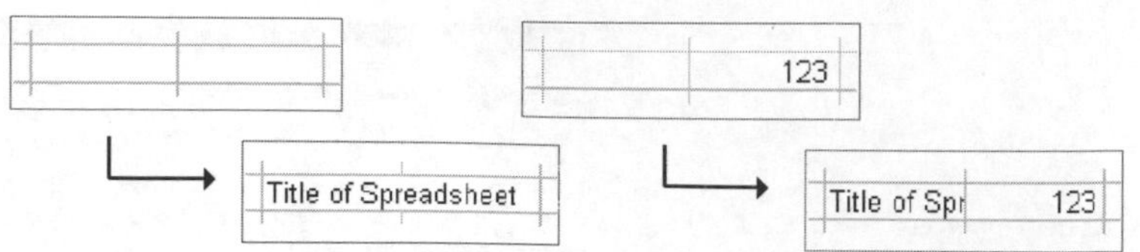

Exercise 4.61 provides an example of entering and displaying text that stretches across several columns.

Exercise 4.61: Entering Text across Multiple Columns

1) Select row 1 of Sheet2 by clicking on the row heading.
2) Choose **Insert | Rows**.
3) Press CTRL+y to repeat the row insertion. You now have two new, blank rows at the top of the worksheet.
4) In C2, enter the following text:

   First Quarter Sales Figures for 2000
5) Select C2, click on the Font Size drop-down box, and select 14 point.

   With C2 still selected, click on the Bold and Italic buttons on the Formatting Toolbar.

   The top rows of Sheet2 should now look as shown.

	A	B	C	D	E	F	G	H
1								
2			***First Quarter Sales Figures for 2000***					

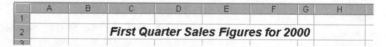

Entering Numbers as Text

Why would you ever want Excel to treat a number as anything other than a number? The answer is when the number is not an amount but an identifier of some kind. Examples include part and model numbers (such as 010-34 or M5339), ID numbers (such as 99-10837), and telephone and fax numbers.

If you find it hard to think of a telephone number as anything other than a number, imagine how ridiculous it would be to add two telephone numbers together!

To enter a number as text, you must first apply the Text format to the empty cells, and then enter the numbers, as shown in Exercise 4.62. If you enter the numbers first, Excel will not apply the Text format to them – you will need to re-enter all the numbers!

Exercise 4.62: Formatting Numbers as Text

1) On Sheet2, select cells B20:B23.
2) Choose **Format | Cells**.

3) On the Number tab, select Text from the Category list, and click **OK.**

4) Enter the numbers in cells B20:B23 as shown below.

010-56
M56-47N
091-10000
W1-S9

Excel treats the numbers as text. You can now delete the four entries from the worksheet.

Excel's AutoFill Feature

Excel provides a very convenient feature called AutoFill for copying or incrementing (increasing in a defined sequence) the entries in a cell or range.

Exercise 4.63: Using AutoFill to Copy and Increment Numbers and Text

1) In Sheet1, enter the following in cell range B19:F19, C20.

19	12	12	Hello	Jan	Mon
20		13			

2) Click on cell B19 and position the cursor over the fill handle – the black square at the bottom-right of the selected cell.

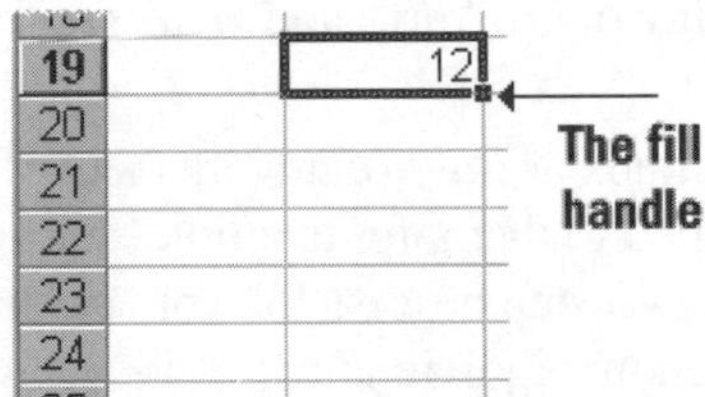

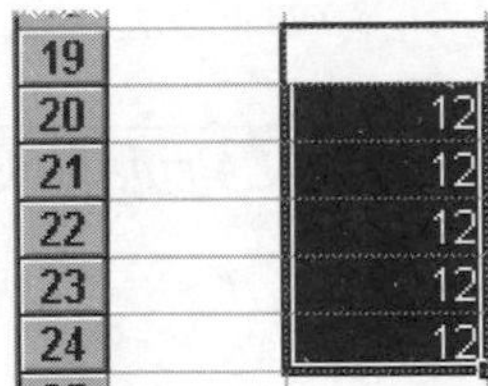

3) Drag the fill handle down to cell B24. Excel copies the contents of cell B19 to the other selected cells.

4) Select cell range C19:C20 and drag the fill handle down to C24.

5) Select D19 and drag the fill handle down to D24.

6) Select E19 and drag the fill handle down to E24.

7) Select F19 and drag the fill handle down to F24.

Your worksheet should now look as shown on the next page.

19	12	12	Hello	Jan	Mon
20	12	13	Hello	Feb	Tue
21	12	14	Hello	Mar	Wed
22	12	15	Hello	Apr	Thu
23	12	16	Hello	May	Fri
24	12	17	Hello	Jun	Sat

AutoFill and Single Numbers and Text

For cell ranges B19:B24 and D19:D24 you began by selecting a single cell containing a number (12) and text item (Hello). As you dragged the fill handle, Excel copied the number and text into the cells that you dragged over.

AutoFill and Number Series

For cell range C19:C24 you began by selecting two cells. Excel recognised that they contained two numbers in an increasing series (12 and 13). As you dragged the fill handle, Excel placed increments of the series (14, 15 and so on) into the cells that you dragged over.

AutoFill and Months, Days, Times and Years

For cell ranges E19:E24 and F19:F24 Excel recognised that the single cell you selected contained the name of a month and a day. As you dragged the fill handle, Excel placed increments of the series (Feb, Mar ... and Tue, Wed ...).

Excel also recognises times (such as 9:00 or 12:30), dates (such as 1-May or 10-April) and years (such as 1996 or 2001).

AutoFill and Calculations

Columns or rows of a worksheet often need the same action applied to them; for example, summing or averaging. Use AutoFill in a two-step process to avoid entering calculations (formulae and functions) individually to sum or average each row or column.

- Enter the calculation for one row or column.
- Use AutoFill to copy the formula or function to the adjacent cells.

AutoFill and Cell References

AutoFill adjusts the cell references as it copies the calculation to the selected cells.

Where a calculation contains a fixed factor – such as a tax, currency conversion or sales commission rate – you will *not* want Excel to adjust the fixed factor's cell reference as it AutoFills the selected cells. In such cases, first change the fixed factor's cell reference to an absolute cell reference. Exercise 4.64 shows AutoFill used with relative and absolute cell references.

Exercise 4.64: Using AutoFill to Copy Calculations

1) On Sheet2, select cell range H6:I11, and press DELETE to delete its contents.

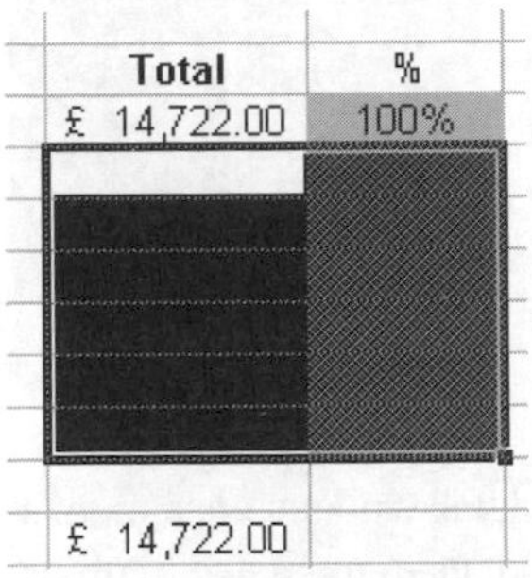

Cell I5 now shows 100%, and the total cell H13 shows £14,722.00.

2) Select cell H5 and drag the fill handle down to cell H11.

AutoFill extends the calculation in H5 to the cells in the range H6:H11.

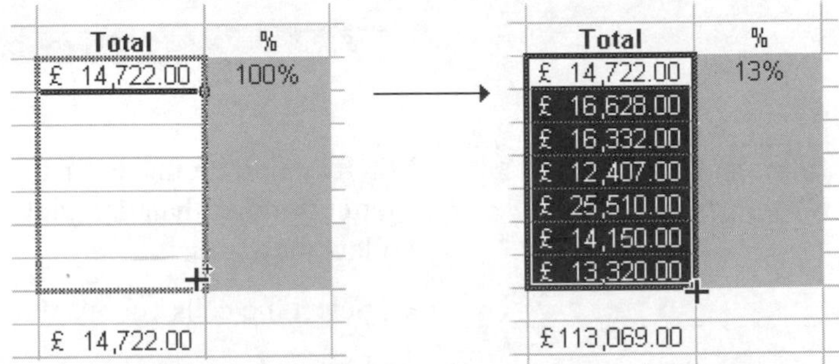

In each case, AutoFill adjusts the cell reference. For example, cell H5 contains the function =SUM(C5:F5) but cell H9 contains the function =SUM(C9:F9).

3) Select cell I5, and edit the function to change relative cell reference H13 to absolute cell reference HI3.

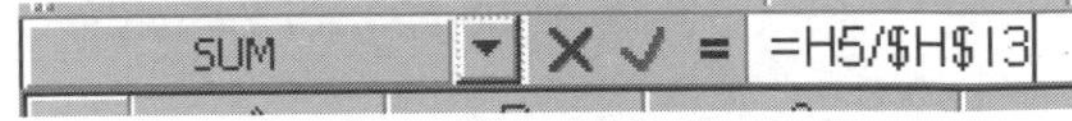

4) With I5 still selected, drag the fill handle down to cell I11.

AutoFill extends the calculation in I5 to the cells in the range I6:I11. As it does so, AutoFill adjusts the relative cell reference H5 but not the absolute cell reference HI3.

Total	%
£ 14,722.00	13%
£ 16,628.00	15%
£ 16,332.00	14%
£ 12,407.00	11%
£ 25,510.00	23%
£ 14,150.00	13%
£ 13,320.00	12%
£113,069.00	

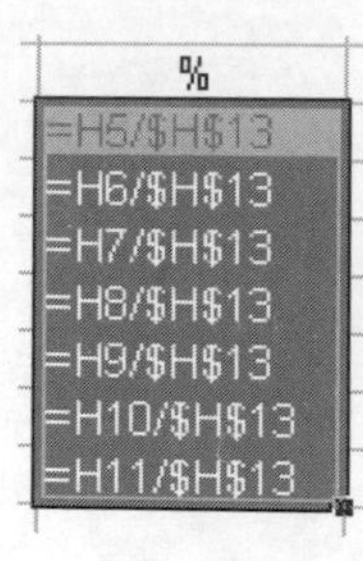

AutoFill works across rows as well as down columns, as you will learn in steps 5) and 6) of this Exercise.

5) Select cell range D13:F13, and press DELETE to delete their contents.

6) Select C13 and drag the fill handle to the right as far as cell F13.

£25,978.00
£26,496.00
£28,355.00
£32,240.00
£113,069.00

AutoFill Keyboard Shortcuts

You may find it quicker to apply AutoFill using the keyboard shortcuts rather than dragging the fill handle with the mouse. Follow these steps:

- Select the cells you want to fill from.
- Drag the mouse down (or right) to select the cells you want to fill.
- Press CTRL+d to fill down or CTRL+r to fill right.

AutoFill

An Excel tool for quickly copying or incrementing (increasing in a defined sequence) the entries in a cell or range.

You have now finished this Section 4.5 of the ECDL Spreadsheet Module. You may save and close your workbook, and close Excel.

Section Summary: So Now You Know

Excel's default number format, the *General format*, does not display trailing zeros, does not automatically insert commas to separate thousands, and is unsuitable for entering financial amounts. The *Comma style* automatically inserts a comma to separate thousands, and displays all numbers to two places of decimals.

The *Currency style* automatically inserts your national currency symbol, and follows your currency's convention for decimal places.

The *Percent style* multiplies numbers by 100, and places the percent sign (%) after each one.

When changing to a non-default number format, it is better to do so *before* you enter your numbers. Only numbers and not text are affected by number formatting.

You can enter *multi-column text* (provided the other, over-typed cells are blank) and format *text as numbers*. This can be useful when the numbers are identifiers (part numbers, phone numbers and so on) rather than amounts.

In calculations, cells can have *relative references* or *absolute references*. Excel changes relative cell references when you copy the calculation to another cell; absolute references are unchanged by copying. Use absolute cell references for cells containing fixed factors such as tax rates.

AutoFill copies the contents of a cell to other, selected cells in the same row or column. AutoFill can also increment a series of numbers, times, dates, days, months, and years.

Section 4.6: Charting with Excel

In This Section

So far you have used Excel to enter, edit, calculate, format and re-position cells on your worksheets.

In this Section you will learn how to present the contents of your worksheet cells in what Excel – an American product – calls a chart. On this side of the Atlantic, we would use the term 'graph' or 'diagram' rather than chart.

New Skills

At the end of this Section you should be able to:

- Use Excel's Chart Wizard to create charts that are based on the numbers, text and calculations in your worksheet
- Choose the appropriate options from the dialog boxes of Excel's Chart Wizard
- Create column, bar and pie charts
- Format chart text and change chart colours
- Add and edit data labels
- Move and resize charts
- Change the scale of chart axes

New Words

At the end of this Section you should be able to explain the following terms:

- Chart
- Chart area
- Plot area
- Data point
- Data series
- Data label

Charting: The Two Steps

You follow two main steps to create a chart in Excel:

- Select the cells whose contents you want to chart.
- Select and run Excel's Chart Wizard.

Excel Chart
A graphic or diagram based on the numbers, text and calculations that are located in the rows and columns of an Excel worksheet

The Four Dialog Boxes to an Excel Chart

When you run the Chart Wizard, Excel presents you with a series of four dialog boxes. These are:

- **Chart Type:** Excel offers lots of different chart types. You decide which is best for your data.
- **Chart Source:** What data do you want to chart – all the cells on your worksheet, or just a selected cell range?
- **Chart Options:** How do you want your chart to look? Excel offers a variety of options.
- **Chart Location:** Where do you want the chart stored – on your current worksheet, on a different worksheet, or in a new workbook? You decide.

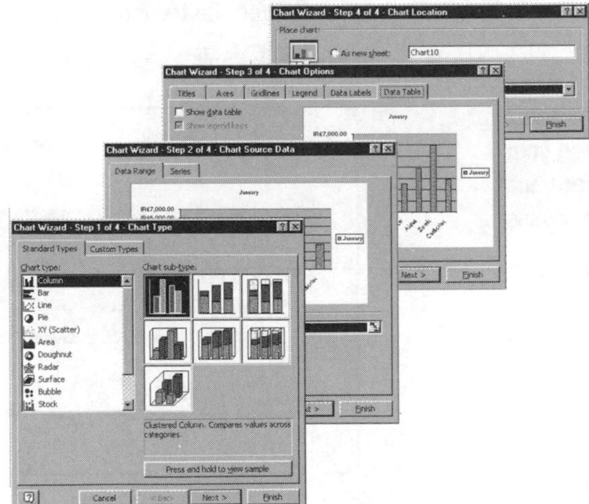

Does this seem like a lot of dialog boxes to learn about? Don't worry. All four dialogs offer a default option that in most cases will create an impressive-looking, ECDL-test-passing chart. So, when in doubt, just click the **Next** button on the first three dialog boxes, and the **Finish** button on the fourth.

Perform Exercise 4.65 to make yourself familiar with charting in Excel.

Exercise 4.65: Creating a Simple Excel Chart

1) Open the workbook that you saved in Section 4.5 and click on Sheet2 to display its second worksheet.

2) Select the non-adjacent cell range A4:A11, C4:C11.

   Do this by clicking in A4, dragging the mouse down to A11, and releasing the mouse button. Next, hold down the CTRL key, click in cell C4 and drag down to C11.

The non-adjacent cell range selected for charting

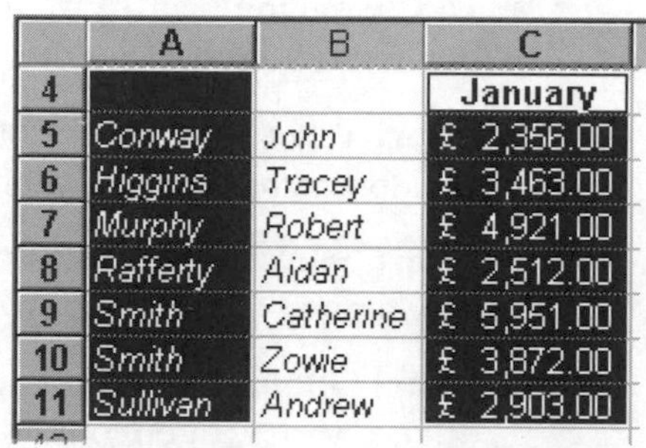

	A	B	C
4			January
5	Conway	John	£ 2,356.00
6	Higgins	Tracey	£ 3,463.00
7	Murphy	Robert	£ 4,921.00
8	Rafferty	Aidan	£ 2,512.00
9	Smith	Catherine	£ 5,951.00
10	Smith	Zowie	£ 3,872.00
11	Sullivan	Andrew	£ 2,903.00

Excel's Chart Wizard button

3) See the button towards the right on the Standard Toolbar? That's Excel's Chart Wizard button. Click on it.

4) Excel displays a series of four dialog boxes. On the first three, click the **Next** button. On the fourth and last, click **Finish**.

   Congratulations. You have drawn your first chart in Excel!

Chart Area: To move your chart to a different position on your worksheet, click here and drag with the mouse

Plot Area: The area of the plotted chart

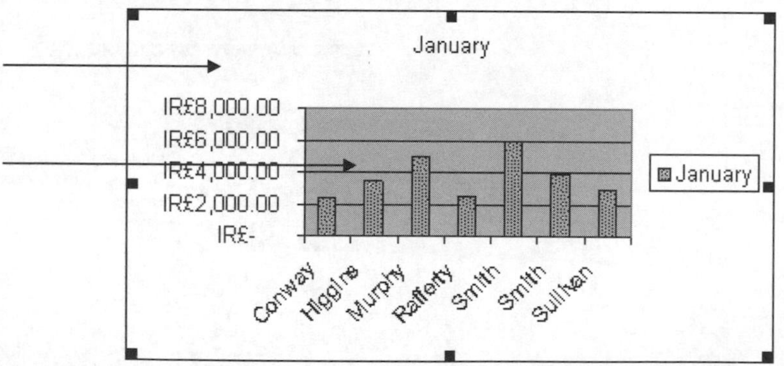

5) Unfortunately, Excel positions your chart on top of your data, so you cannot see both at the same time.

   Move the chart by clicking on any blank part of the chart margin – Excel calls this the Chart Area – and then dragging the chart down until its top-left corner is positioned over the cell B19.

Chart Area

The margin area inside the chart boundaries but outside the actual plotted chart. It typically holds labels identifying the chart axes.

Plot Area

The area containing the actual plot. It is bounded by the two chart axes and is enclosed within the chart area.

Charts: Two Ideas You Need to Know

All charting – in Excel or with pen and paper – is based on two very basic ideas: the *data point* and the *data series*. You will see these two terms a lot on Excel's charting dialog boxes and online help screens. Understand these two ideas and you will be able to exploit fully Excel's charting possibilities.

About Data Points

Data point: the idea is so simple that you will wonder why anyone bothered even to give it a name. Consider the four examples below.

Item	Value
Apples	4
Pears	3
Bananas	6

Item		Value
January	£	1,965.34
February	£	2,451.50
March	£	8,301.49

Item	Value
Mary	15.00%
Catherine	50.00%
Margaret	35.00%

Item	Value
Sales	£4,954,032.00
Costs	£394,823.00
Overheads	£25,068.00

Each example consists of individual items (or people) being measured. They are types of fruit, months of the year, people and amounts of money.

Each item has a number that is its measured value. A *data point* is a single item and its numerical value.

In the first example, the three data points are: Apples and 4, Pears and 3 and Bananas and 6. Other data points from the above examples are February and £2,451.50, Catherine and 50%, and Overheads and £25,068.00

A data point always has two parts: the item and the value. On its own, a number is not a data point, nor is an item. You need both for a data point.

Data Point

An item being measured and its measured value.

About Data Series

A single data point does not tell us very much. A chart is useful only if there is more than one data point. A collection of data points is called a data series.

For instance, you may want to create a chart that shows the company's sales figures for different months. Or a chart that compares one month's sales figures for different departments.

Data Series

A group of related data points. For example, your data series may compare different items measured at the same time, or single items measured at different times.

Single Data Series Charts

We used the word 'simple' to describe the chart that you created in Exercise 4.65. More precisely, it is an example of a single data series chart.

Exercise 4.66: Creating More Single Data Series Charts

1) Practise your charting skills by selecting the four non-adjacent cell ranges below and creating a chart from them.

   Drag the first chart down beneath the chart from Exercise 4.65. And drag the other three down Sheet2 so that each is positioned beneath the previous one.

Data Series: A4:A11, F4:F11

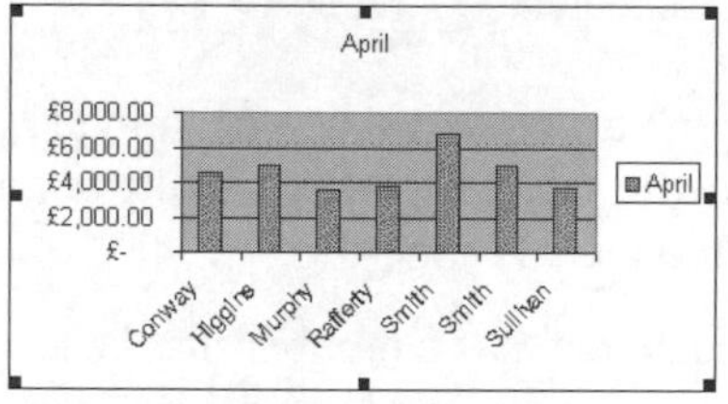

Data Series: A4:A11, I4:I11

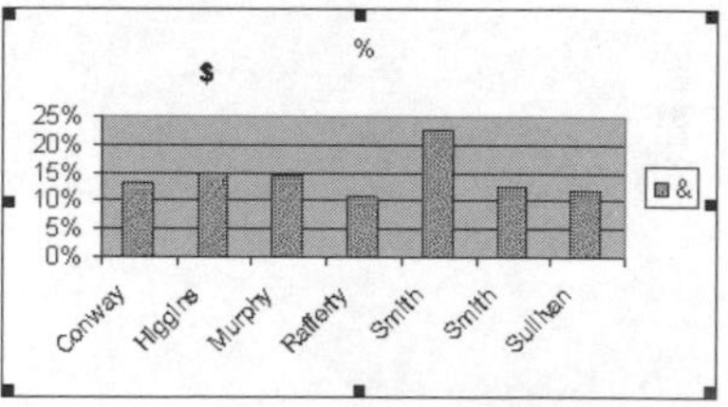

Data Series: C4:F4, C15:F15

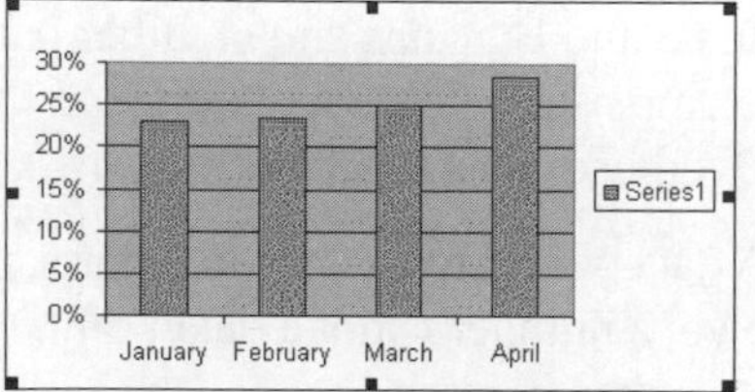

Data Series: B4:B11, H4:H11

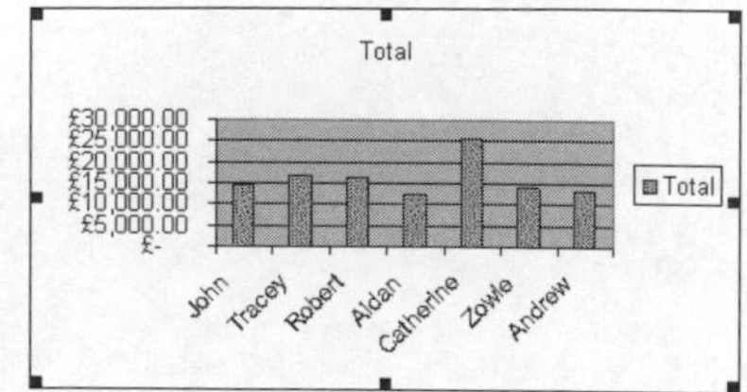

Creating a Multiple Data Series Chart

You can have more than one data series in a collection of related information.

Consider the part of your worksheet shown on the right. How many data series can you see? Answer: two.

	January	February
Conway	IR£ 2,356.00	IR£ 3,621.00
Higgins	IR£ 3,463.00	IR£ 3,981.00
Murphy	IR£ 4,921.00	IR£ 4,055.00
Rafferty	IR£ 2,512.00	IR£ 2,864.00
Smith	IR£ 3,872.00	IR£ 2,441.00
Smith	IR£ 5,951.00	IR£ 6,226.00
Sullivan	IR£ 2,903.00	IR£ 3,308.00

There is one data series for January, and a second for February.

Two data series, one for each of the two months

	January
Conway	IR£ 2,356.00
Higgins	IR£ 3,463.00
Murphy	IR£ 4,921.00
Rafferty	IR£ 2,512.00
Smith	IR£ 3,872.00
Smith	IR£ 5,951.00
Sullivan	IR£ 2,903.00

	February
Conway	IR£ 3,621.00
Higgins	IR£ 3,981.00
Murphy	IR£ 4,055.00
Rafferty	IR£ 2,864.00
Smith	IR£ 2,441.00
Smith	IR£ 6,226.00
Sullivan	IR£ 3,308.00

In Exercise 4.67 and 4.68 you will create a two-data series and a three-data series chart.

Exercise 4.67: Creating a Two-Data Series Chart in Excel

1) Select the cell range A4:A8, C4:D8.
2) Click the Chart Wizard button and accept the default options in the sequence of four dialog boxes. Your chart should look as shown below.

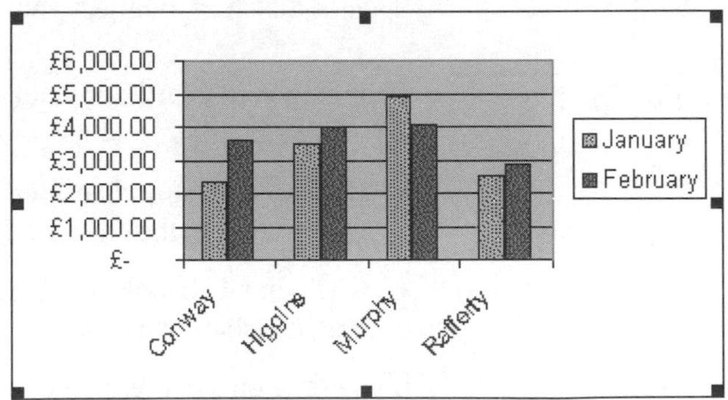

3) Drag your chart down the worksheet to beneath the last of the four charts that you created in Exercise 4.66.

When Excel draws a chart with more than a single data series, it uses a different colour to represent different items.

Exercise 4.68: Creating a Three-Data Series Chart in Excel

1) Select the cell range A4:A8, C4:E8.
2) Click on the Chart Wizard button and accept the default options in the sequence of four dialog boxes. Your chart should look as shown below.

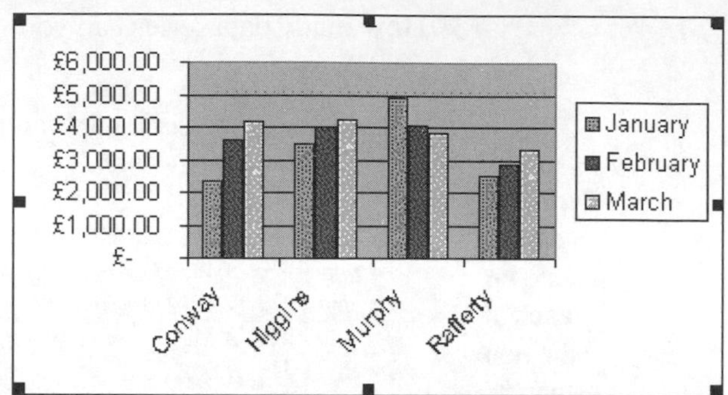

Drag the chart down the worksheet to beneath the chart that you created in Exercise 4.67.

Editing Your Chart

When you create a chart, don't think of it as fixed forever. You can change just about every aspect of a chart.

Changing Chart Data

You can amend the content of worksheet cells on which your chart is based; as soon as you change the cells in your worksheet, Excel updates the chart to reflect your changes.

Resizing the Chart

Changing your chart's size can affect its appearance dramatically. To resize a chart:

- Click once on the chart area. Handles (small black squares) appear around the chart's edges.
- Click on any handle and hold down the mouse button as you drag the chart to a different shape.

If you drag on a corner handle, the chart expands and contracts proportionately to its current size; if you drag on an edge handle, the chart expands or contracts in that direction only. Excel automatically adjusts the font of chart text as you resize.

Changing the Chart Title

To edit the chart title, click anywhere on it, and then click anywhere within the title text. You can now edit the text. To remove the chart title, click on it once, and press DELETE. To reformat the chart title, double-click anywhere on it to display the Format Chart Title dialog box. Select the options you require from the three tabs of the dialog box: Borders and Patterns, Font, and Alignment.

Adding a Chart Title

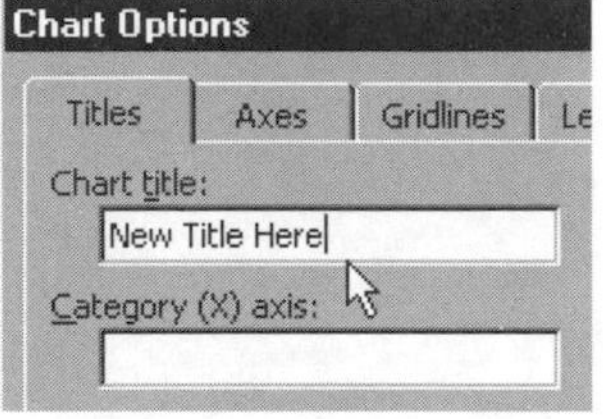

If your chart does not have a title, you can add one as follows:

- Right-click on the chart area.
- From the pop-up menu displayed, choose **Chart Options**, select the Titles tab, type the new title in the Chart title: box, and click **OK.**

Chart Title
Text describing the chart. By default, Excel centres the chart title in the chart area over the plot area.

Adding Data Labels

In an Excel chart a data label is an item showing the name (such as Conway) or value (such as £2,356.00) of a data point in a plotted data series. By default, Excel does not display labels.

You can add two kinds of data labels to a chart:

- **Value Labels**: These indicate the numerical values of the individual data points. See Exercise 4.69.
- **Text Labels**: These display the names of the data points. By default, Excel already displays these names on an axis. See Exercise 4.70.

Exercise 4.69: Adding Data Labels

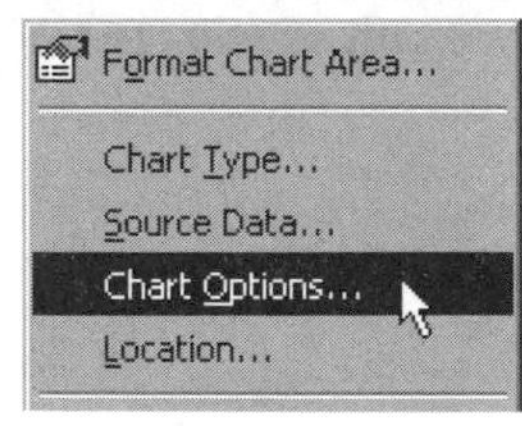

1) On Sheet2, click on the chart area of the first chart you created, the one in Exercise 4.65, and press CTRL+c to copy it to the Clipboard.
2) Click the Sheet3 tab to display the third worksheet of your workbook. Click cell B3 and press CTRL+v to paste the chart from the Clipboard.
3) Right-click on the chart area, choose **Chart Options** from the pop-up menu, and select the Data Labels tab of the dialog box.
4) Select the Show value option, and click **OK**.

   Show value

   Adding data labels to your chart provides more information to the reader, but has the disadvantage of making your chart more cluttered. You can remedy this by stretching the chart horizontally.
5) Click the chart, and then click the middle handle on the right edge of the chart area.

6) Drag with the mouse until the chart's right boundary ends in column K. The axes and plot area of your chart should look as shown below.

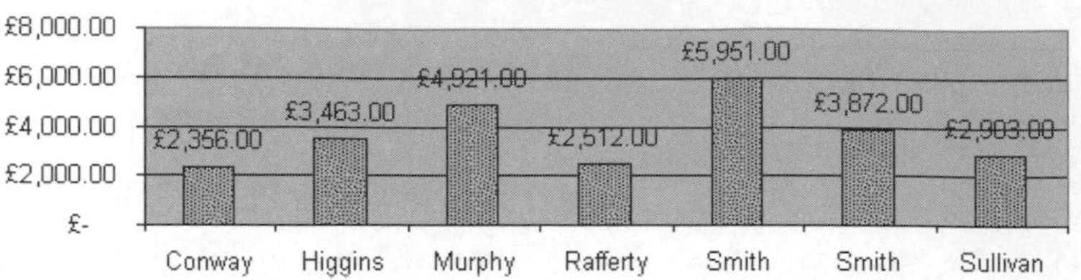

Exercise 4.70: Adding Data Name Labels

1) With the chart from Exercise 4.65 still in the Clipboard, click on a cell beneath the chart pasted in Exercise 4.69, and press CTRL+v. Choose **Chart Options** from the pop-up menu, and select the Data Labels tab of the dialog box.
2) Select the Show label option, and click **OK**.
3) As in Exercise 4.69, drag the chart's right boundary to column K. The axes and plot area of your chart should look as shown below.

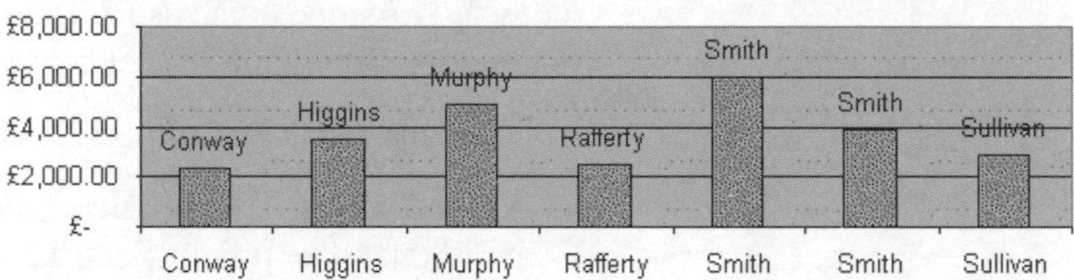

Formatting Data Labels

To format data labels, right-click on a label, choose **Format | Data Labels** from the pop-up menu, and select your required options from the following four dialog box tabs: Patterns, Font, Number, and Alignment.

Data Label

The name or numerical value of a data point in a plotted data series.

Changing the Scale

To change the scale of an axis, double-click anywhere along the axis and choose **Format Axis** from the pop-up menu,

Excel allows you to change the minimum, maximum and increment values displayed for each axis, and the point at which the two axes cross. In Exercise 4.71 you will change the scale of a chart's vertical (or Y) axis.

Exercise 4.71: Changing the Scale of the Vertical Axis

1) Is the first chart you created, the one in Exercise 4.65, still in the Clipboard? If not, copy it to the Clipboard now.

2) Click the Sheet3 tab to display the third worksheet of your workbook. Click on a cell beneath the chart pasted in Exercise 4.70, and press CTRL+v.

3) Click the chart, and then click on the middle handle on its lower edge. Drag down the mouse until the chart is about twice its original height.

4) Double-click anywhere on the chart's vertical axis and, on the Format Axis dialog box, select the Scale tab.

5) Change the Minimum: box from 0 to 2000. And change the value in the Major unit: box from 2000 to 500. Click **OK** to close the dialog box.

6) Double-click again anywhere on the chart's vertical axis, and, on the Format Axis dialog box, reselect the Scale tab.

   Notice that Excel has changed the Category (X) axis Crosses at: box from 0 to 2000. This is because you changed the Minimum: box from 0 to 2000.

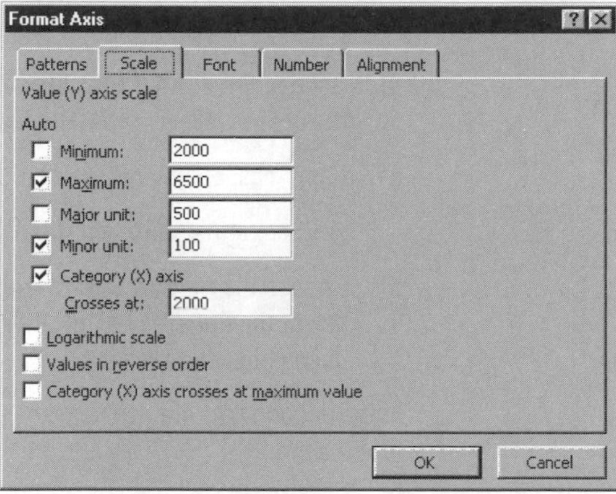

The rescaled and vertically stretched chart should now look as shown.

Rescaled chart: Vertical axis values begin at £2,000 rather than £0

Also, vertical axis is in expressed in units of £500 rather than £2,000

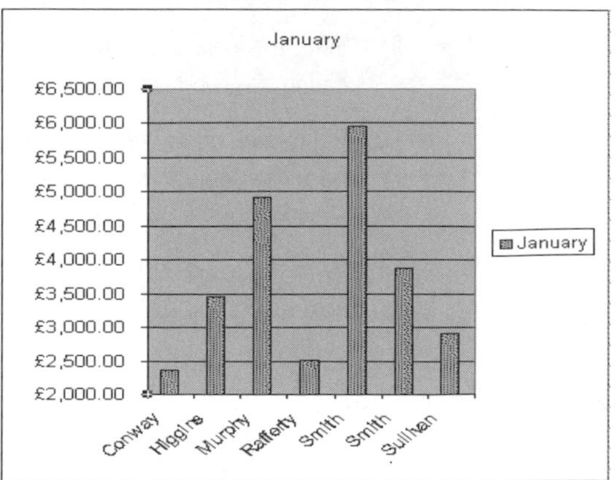

Changing Chart Colours

Excel enables you to change the colours of three parts of a chart: the chart area, the plot area and the data series. In each case, you right-click on the relevant element, choose the **Format** command from the pop-up menu, and select your required fill colour. See Exercise 4.72.

Exercise 4.72: Changing a Chart's Colours

1) Right-click on the chart area of the chart you created in Exercise 4.71.

   (The chart area is the blank margin surrounding the actual plotted chart.)

2) Choose the **Format Chart Area** command from the pop-up menu, select the Patterns tab, click the colour yellow in the Area section of the dialog box, and click **OK.**

3) Right-click on the plot area of the chart.

   (This is the actual plotted chart, bounded by the two chart axes.)

4) Choose the **Format Plot Area** command from the pop-up menu, click the colour yellow in the Area section of the dialog box, and click **OK.**

5) Right-click on any of the chart columns.

   (The columns represent the data series of the chart.)

6) Choose the **Format Data Series** command from the pop-up menu, select the Patterns tab, click the colour red in the Area section of the dialog box, and click **OK.**

In the second part of this Exercise 4.72, you will reformat the text elements of the chart.

7) Double-click the X-axis, select the Font tab, change the font to Bold and the Font Colour to dark blue, and click **OK.**

8) Repeat step 7) for the Y-axis, but do not close the dialog box.

9) With the Y-axis still selected, select the Number tab on the Format Axis dialog box, and set zero as the number of decimal places. Click **OK.**

10) Right-click on the chart title, choose the **Format Chart Title** command from the pop-up menu, select the Font tab, change the Font to Times New Roman, Font Style to Italic and Font Size to 14 point.

11) With the chart title still selected, select the Patterns tab of the dialog box, select the Automatic Border option, and click **OK.**

Well done. You have completed the Exercise. Your chart should now look as shown below.

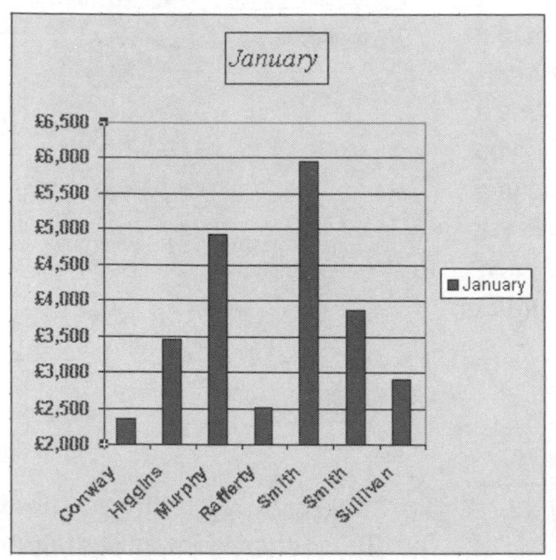

Chart Types

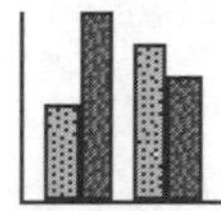

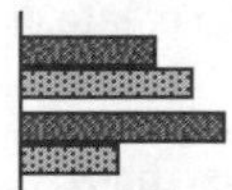

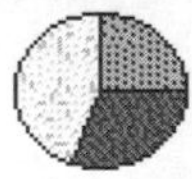

Excel offers over a dozen chart types, but you need only know the following three:

- **Column Chart:** Items are shown horizontally and values vertically. This is Excel's default chart type, and the only one you have used in your charting exercises so far.
- **Bar Chart:** A 'sideways' column chart that shows items horizontally and values vertically.
- **Pie Chart:** Shows the proportion of each item that makes up the total. Unlike column, bar and most other chart types, you can use pie charts for a single data series only.

Setting the Chart Type

When you select a cell range and choose the Chart Wizard, you decide which chart type you want to use in the first of the four dialog boxes displayed by the Wizard, the Chart Type box. As you can see, most chart types offer sub-types or variations.

You can preview how your cell data will look in a particular chart type by selecting a Chart Type option and clicking the Press and Hold to View Sample button

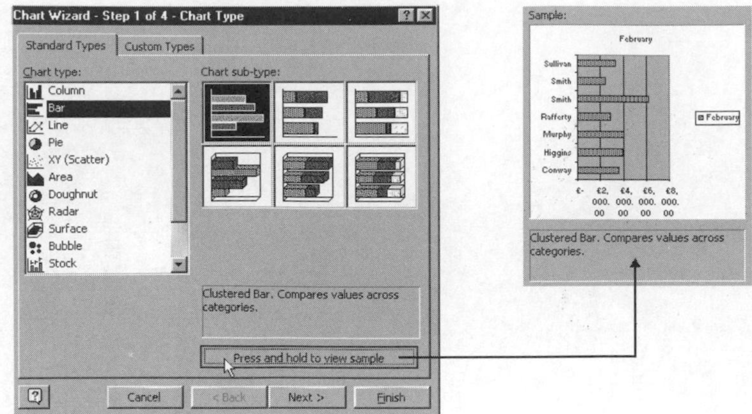

Changing Chart Type

To change the current type of a chart, right-click anywhere within the chart (chart area, plot area or data series – it does not matter), choose the **Chart Type** command from the pop-up menu, and select a different type (or sub-type) from the Chart Type dialog box.

In Exercise 4.73 you will create a new chart of the bar chart type. In Exercise 4.74 you will change a column chart to a bar chart.

Exercise 4.73: Creating a Bar Chart

1) On Sheet3, click on a cell beneath the chart you worked with in Exercise 4.72. This will be the location at which the chart you create in this Exercise will begin.

2) Click the Sheet1 tab to display the first worksheet of your workbook.

3) Select non-adjacent cell range C25:D26, F25:G26, and click the Chart Wizard button.

4) Excel now displays the Standard Types tab of the Chart Wizard – Step 1 of 4 – Chart Type dialog box. Select the Bar chart type and click Next.

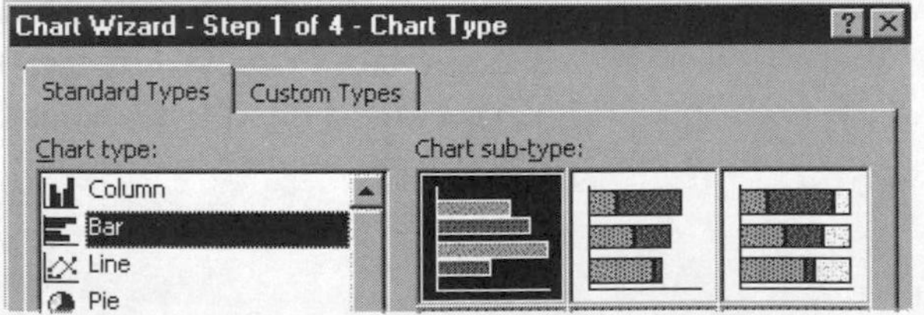

5) Excel now displays the Data Range tab of the Chart Wizard – Step 2 of 4 – Chart Source Data dialog box. Click **Next**.

6) Excel now displays the Data Labels tab of the Chart Wizard – Step 3 of 4 – Chart Options dialog box.

Click the Titles tab, and type a Chart Title of Product 1 and click **Next**.

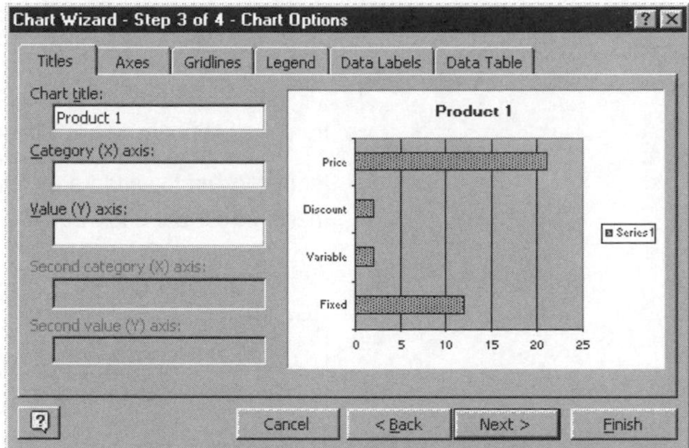

7) Excel now displays the Chart Wizard – Step 4 of 4 – Chart Location dialog box.

Change the As object in: box to Sheet3 and click **Finish**.

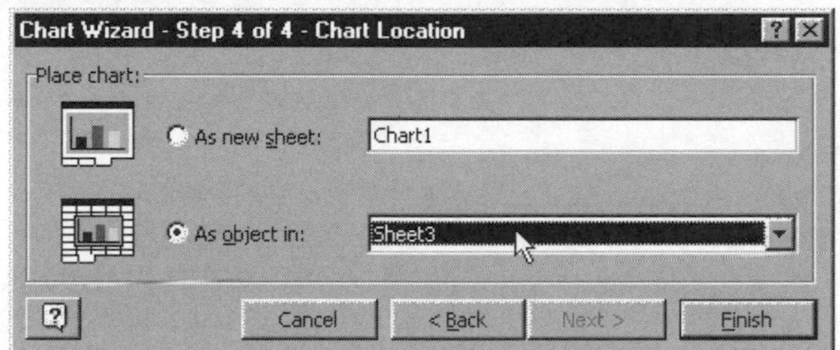

Excel positions the chart on your third worksheet, Sheet3. It positions the chart so that its top-left corner is at the cell you most recently clicked on in that worksheet. Your bar chart should look like that shown.

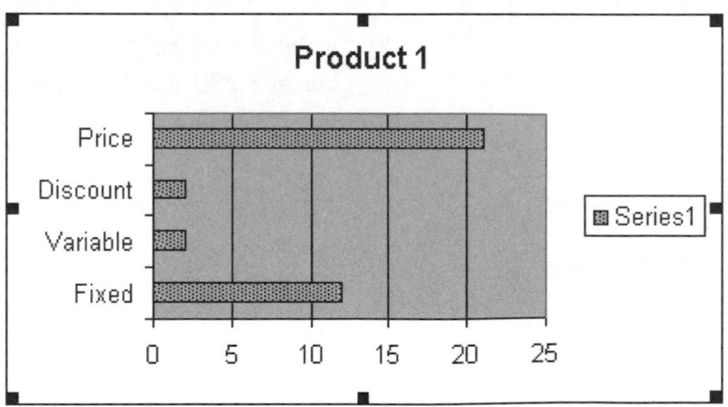

Exercise 4.74: Changing a Column to a Bar Chart

1) On Sheet2, click the third chart you created in Exercise 4.66. It is based on the cell range C4:F4,C15:F15. Copy it to the Clipboard.

2) Click the Sheet3 tab to display your third worksheet. Paste the chart from the Clipboard to a cell beneath the chart from Exercise 4.73.

3) Right-click on the chart area, choose **Chart Type** from the pop-up menu, select Bar chart from the dialog box, and click **OK**.

   Your bar chart should look like that shown.

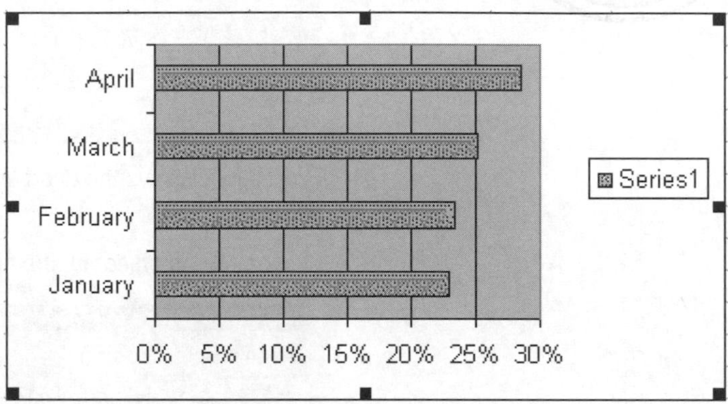

Working with Pie Charts

In Exercise 4.75 you will create a pie chart based on a single data series. You will then format the pie chart, and 'explode' a slice of the pie to draw particular attention to the contribution it represents to the total.

Exercise 4.75: Creating and Formatting a Pie Chart

1) On Sheet2, select the cell range A4:A11, C4:C11.

2) Click the Chart Wizard button.

3) In the Chart Type dialog box, select Pie chart as the Standard Type, and Pie with a 3D visual effect as the Sub-type. Click **Next.**

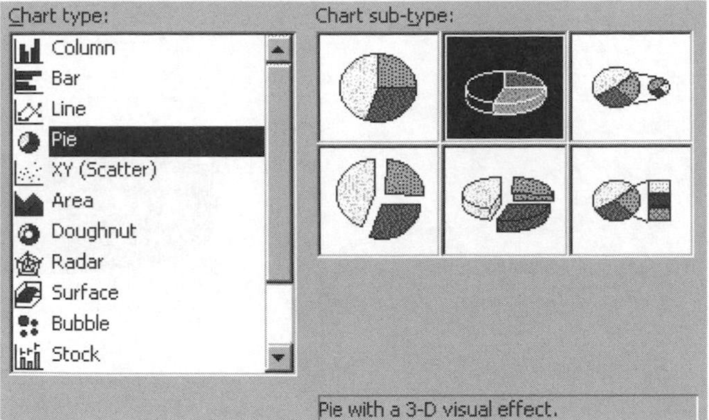

4) On the remaining Chart Wizard dialog boxes, click **Next** and, finally, **Finish.**

   Drag the pie chart down Sheet2 to beneath the chart you created in Exercise 4.68. Your chart should look as shown below.

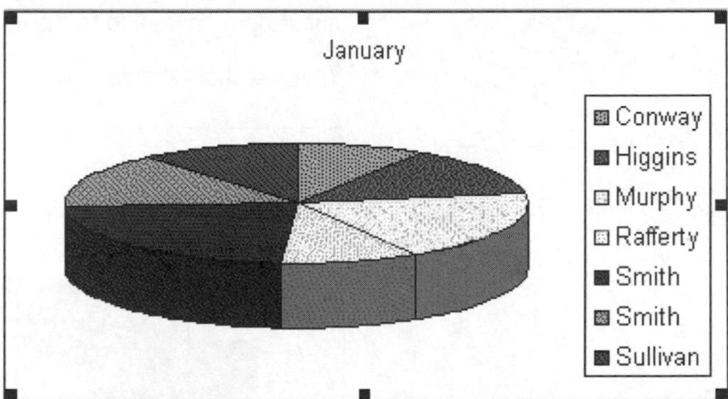

   Because pie charts do not have axes to indicate data point names and values, the various slices are typically accompanied by data labels. You will add these in the next steps of this Exercise.

5) Double-click on the pie chart plot area (and not the surrounding chart area) to display the Format Data Series dialog box.

6) Select the Data Labels tab, select the option Show percent, and click **OK**. Your pie chart should now look as on the next page. Notice how the plot area shrank in size to make room for the percentage data labels.

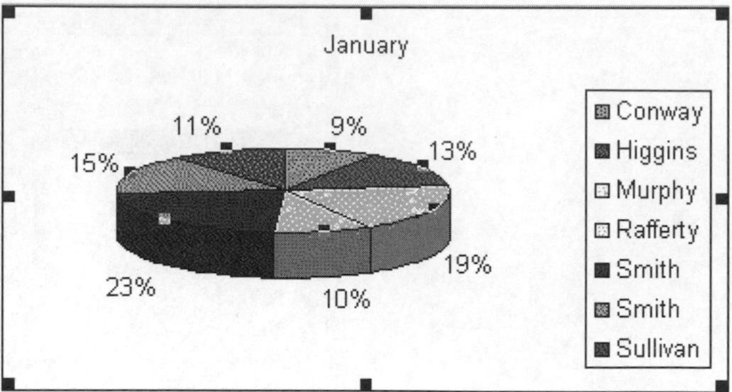

In the final step of this Exercise, you will 'explode' one slice of the pie chart.

7) Click once on the plot area of the pie chart. Next, click on the slice you want to explode and drag it out of the pie.

   For example, click on the largest slice, the one with 23% data label, and drag it down and to the left.

   Your pie chart should now look as shown below.

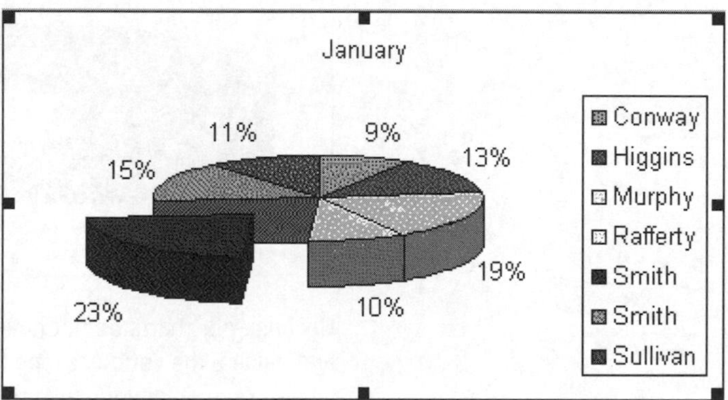

Congratulations. You have now completed this Section 4.6 on charting with Excel. You may close and save your workbook, and close Excel.

Section Summary: So Now You Know

To draw a chart in Excel, first select the cells with the numbers and text that you want to chart, and then run Excel's *Chart Wizard*. The Wizard's default options on its four dialog boxes are acceptable in most cases. If you change any of the data on which a chart is based, Excel updates the chart to reflect the changes.

By default, Excel positions your chart on top of your worksheet data. You can move the chart by clicking on any blank part of the chart margin, and then dragging the chart to a new position.

Charting is based on the ideas of data points and data series. A *data point* is a single item and its related value (for example, the sales figure in January), while a *data series* is a group of related data points (for example, monthly sales figures over a year). You can chart more than one data series at one time.

Excel offers a wide range of *chart types*, with column, bar and pie charts being the most commonly used. You can *format* your chart in a variety of ways by adding data labels, colours and borders.

Section 4.7: File Formats and Data Importing

In This Section

In this Section you will learn how Excel 97, as all other applications, uses a particular file format. You will also discover how to convert your documents into other, non-Excel 97 file formats, so that they can be opened and read by people who work with applications other than Excel 97.

You will also discover how files containing images, graphs and text may be inserted into Excel worksheets.

New Skills

At the end of this Section you should be able to:

- Save Excel 97 files in the following file formats: Excel 97 template, earlier versions of Excel, other spreadsheets, databases, text only and HTML, the file format of the World Wide Web
- Explain the difference between two types of character-delimited text files: tab-delimited and comma-separated
- Explain the difference between character-delimited and column-delimited text files
- Insert image files in an Excel worksheet, and files containing graphs created in applications other than Excel 97
- Import text files using Excel's Text Import Wizard

New Words

At the end of this Section you should be able to explain the following terms:

- File format
- Tab-delimited text file
- Comma-separated values (CSV) text file
- Column-delimited text file

File Formats

In ECDL Module 1 you learnt how all information stored on a computer consists ultimately of just two characters: 1 and 0. This raises two, related questions:

- When you open an Excel workbook file, how are these 1s and 0s translated into the text, numbers and charts you see on your computer screen?
- And, when you save a file, how are the text, numbers and charts converted back to 1s and 0s on your computer?

The answer is that the application developers apply a set of rules that translate between the 1s and 0s and the displayed text, numbers and charts. Such a set of rules is called a file format.

File Format

A set of rules that translates 1s and 0s into text and graphics on computers screens and printouts, and vice versa.

An Excel file, for example, is said to be in Excel file format; an Access file in Access file format, and so on.

Different Applications, Different File Formats

Different software companies, however, use different sets of rules for translating 1s and 0s into the text and graphics on screens and printouts.

Moreover, different versions of the one application often use different file formats. The Microsoft Excel 97 file format, for example, is different from the file formats of previous versions of Excel.

These different file formats, as you can imagine, can create problems:

- In one file format, for example, the characters 10101010 might translate as the number '12' positioned in cell A4.
- In another, the same characters of 10101010 might convert to the label 'Annual Profit' in cell Z54.

File Name Extensions

The format of a file is revealed by its three-letter file name extension, which the software application adds to the file name when the user saves the file.

The file name extension of .xls, for example, indicates an Excel workbook, and .mdb an Access database.

The file format used in pages on the Word Wide Web is HTML, which stands for HyperText Markup Language. HTML file names typically end in .htm.

Excel's File Format Options

Excel 97 offers you the ability to save your documents in a format other than its own. This feature is very useful when you want to provide a file you have created to someone who uses an application other than Excel 97.

To view the file formats in which you can save your Excel 97 documents:

- Open a document.
- Choose **File | Save As**.
- Click on the arrow to the right of the Save as type: box.

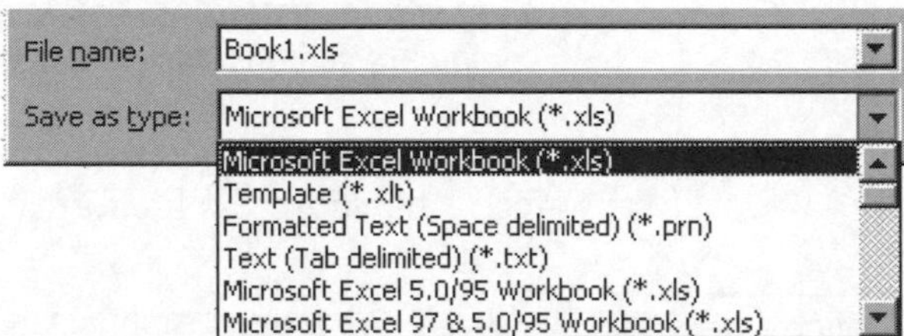

Only some of the listed options are relevant to this ECDL Spreadsheet Module. Note that the features and formatting of a Microsoft Excel 97 workbook might not be available if you save the workbook in the file format of a previous version of Microsoft Excel or of another application.

Excel Template

Excel 97 offers you the ability to save a workbook as a template, and then use the saved template as a basis for quickly creating other, similar workbooks.

For example, you could create a workbook for use as an expense form, enter and format relevant text labels, place borders around certain cells, and enter the function =SUM(C2:C22) in cell C23 so that whatever numbers were typed in the range C2:C22 are totalled and displayed in C23.

By saving such a workbook as a template, you speed up the process of creating further expense forms because the text, formatting and addition calculation need not be re-entered.

To save a workbook as a template, choose **File | Save As** and select the Template (*.xlt) option.

Previous Excel Versions

You can save your Excel 97 workbook in the file formats of previous versions of Microsoft Excel. You have two main options:

- **Microsoft Excel 97 & 5.0/95 Workbook:** This saves a workbook in both Excel 97 and Excel 95 file formats in the same .xls file.
- **Any Earlier Format:** If you save a workbook in such earlier Excel file formats as Excel 4.0 or 3.0, features and formatting unique to Microsoft Excel 97 are lost.

dBASE and Quattro Pro Formats

Select from these options to save your work so that it can be opened and read by users with versions of dBASE, a database application, and Lotus 1-2-3 and Quattro Pro, two other spreadsheet applications.

Only the currently displayed worksheet is converted. To convert other worksheets of a workbook, display and then save each one individually.

Text-Only Format

As its name suggests, this format saves only the text of a file. The word 'text' in this context includes numbers as well as alphabetic characters. All formatting is lost. This format is also called plain-text or ASCII format.

Two of the more commonly used plain-text options are as follows:

- **Text (tab-delimited):** This saves only the currently displayed worksheet. To convert other worksheets of a workbook, switch to each sheet and save it separately. The file name extension added is .txt. In this format, cell entries in different columns but on the same row are separated from each other by the tabs. Different rows are separated by paragraph breaks. As you can see in the example below, text in the tab-delimited format does not necessarily line up vertically in neat columns.

Original data in Excel file

	A	B	C	D	E	F
1						
2		January	February	March	April	May
3		12	45	35	41	56
4		11	42	34	39	47

Excel file saved in tab-delimited format, and viewed in Notepad text editor

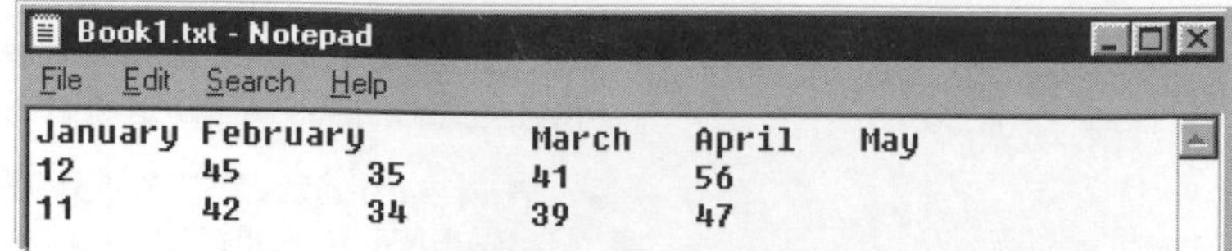

- **CSV (comma-separated):** As tab-delimited above, but with a comma separating cells on the same row. The file name extension added is .csv, meaning comma separated values. As you can see in the example below, text in the comma-separated format does not necessarily line up vertically in neat columns.

Excel file saved in CSV format, and viewed in Notepad text editor

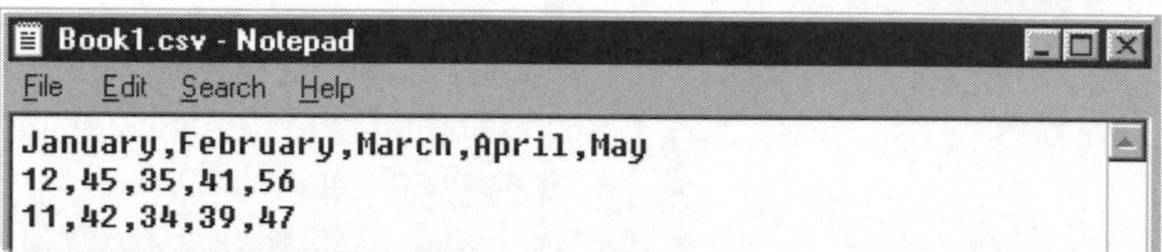

Tab-Delimited Text File

A text format file in which data items are separated horizontally by tabs and vertically by paragraph breaks.

Comma-Separated Values (CSV) Text File

A text format file in which data items are separated horizontally by commas and vertically by paragraph breaks.

HTML (Web) Format

Web pages are created using the HTML file format. The file name extension of this format is .htm (or, sometimes, .html).

You can save an Excel 97 file in HTML format in either of two ways:

- Choose **File | Save As HTML**.

-or-

- Choose **File | Save As**, and select the HTML Document option.

The worksheet cells are converted to table cells in the HTML file. You can display and print HTML format files with a web browser application such as Microsoft Internet Explorer or Netscape Navigator.

Inserting from Other Applications

Microsoft Office applications (and most other Windows applications) allow you to transfer information between them. For this ECDL Spreadsheet Module, you need only know how to insert the following items in Excel:

- Images
- Graphs
- Text

Inserting Images

To insert an image, choose **Insert | Picture**, and then select the relevant option. The range of options available to you depends on whether you have installed the Microsoft Office Clip Art Gallery and whether a scanner is attached to your computer.

- To *reposition* an inserted image, click on it to select it, and then drag the image to a different part of your worksheet.
- To *resize* an inserted image, click on it to select it, then click any handle and drag the image to a different shape.

  If you drag on a corner handle, the image expands and contracts proportionately to its current size; if you drag on an edge handle, the image expands or contracts in that direction only.

Exercise 4.76: Inserting an Image File in Excel

To insert an image in a worksheet, you need an image to work with. If you do not have one to hand, follow steps 1) and 2) of this Exercise to obtain one from the author's website.

1) Connect to the Internet, start Microsoft Internet Explorer (or Netscape Navigator) and visit the author's website at www.munnelly.com.
2) Right-click on the image at the top-left of the first page to display a pop-up menu, choose **Save Picture As** (or, in Netscape, **Save Image As**), and save the image file to your computer as munnelly_com.jpg.
3) Display an Excel worksheet, click on a cell, choose **Insert | Picture | From File**, locate the munnelly_com.jpg image file (or any other image file), and click **Insert.**

Excel inserts the image as shown below.

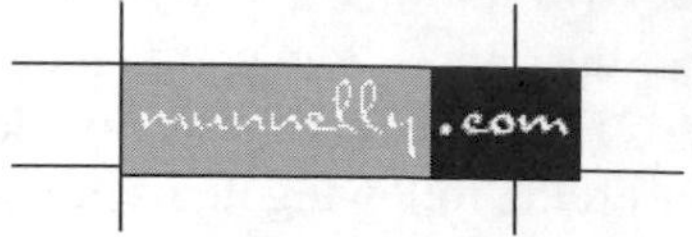

Inserting Graphs

Graphs can be created in applications other than Excel – for example, in PowerPoint or in non-Microsoft applications.

To insert such a graph, select it in the application in which it was created, copy it to the Clipboard, open the Excel worksheet, and choose the **Edit | Paste** command.

Inserting Text

You may want to insert two types of text into an Excel worksheet:

- Small amounts of text, selected from a text file, for use in Excel as worksheet headings, for example, or labels for individual cells. To insert text in a single cell of a worksheet, open the application in which the text was created, copy the text to the Clipboard, switch to Excel, and then use Excel's **Edit | Paste** command to insert it in a selected Excel cell.
- An entire text file, containing numbers as well as text, which you want Excel to 'interpret' and arrange correctly across rows and down columns. To assist you inserting a text file in this way, Excel provides a Text Import Wizard.

Text Import Wizard

Earlier in this Section you learnt about tab-delimited and comma-separated text files in which the tab and comma characters indicate where one column of data ends and the next begins. These are called *character-delimited* files, because a specific character consistently indicates column endings.

In other text files, a column ending may be indicated not by a single occurrence of a specific character but by a series of blank spaces. These are called *column-delimited* files, because the blank spaces cause the data to line up vertically.

In each case, row endings are indicated by paragraph breaks. In Exercise 4.77 you will create a tab-delimited file, and in Exercise 4.78 you will import that file using Excel's Text Import Wizard.

Column-Delimited Text File

A text format file in which data items are separated horizontally by a series of spaces and vertically by paragraph breaks. The blank spaces cause the data to line up vertically.

Exercise 4.77: Creating a Tab-Delimited Text File

1) Using Notepad or other text editor, create a new file.
2) Type the following five words, pressing the TAB key after each word except the last (do not type spaces between the words):
   January February March April May
3) Press ENTER to move the cursor to a new line.
4) Type the following five numbers, pressing the TAB key after each one except the last (do not type spaces between the numbers):
   12 45 35 41 56
5) Press ENTER to move the cursor to a new line.
6) Type the following five numbers, pressing the TAB key after each one except the last (again, do not type spaces between the numbers):
   11 42 34 39 47

   Your file should look as shown below. As you can see, the columns do not line up vertically, as is common in tab-delimited files.

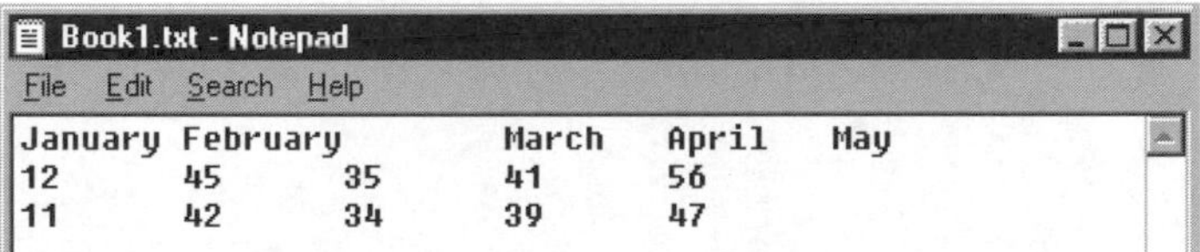

7) Save, name and close the file.

Exercise 4.78: Importing a Tab-Delimited Text File

1) Choose **File | Open**, and select the text file saved in Exercise 4.77.
2) Excel displays the Text Import Wizard dialog box. As you can see, Excel has correctly interpreted it as a tab-delimited file.

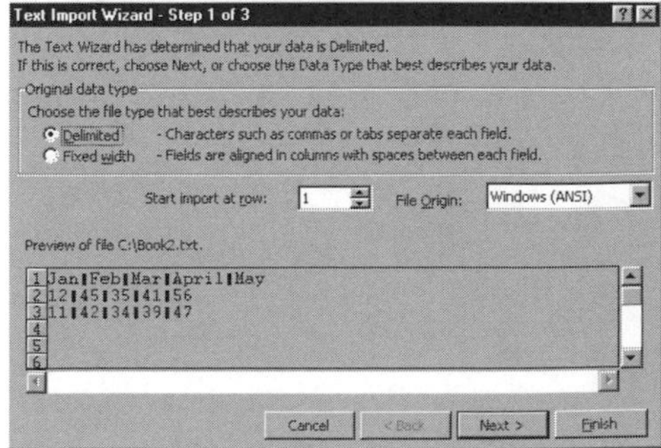

3) Click any **Next** buttons displayed, and finally click **Finish.**

Your worksheet cells should now look as shown below.

	A	B	C	D	E
1	January	February	March	April	May
2	12	45	35	41	56
3	11	42	34	39	47

You can save and close your workbook, and close Excel.

You have now completed the final Section of the ECDL Spreadsheet Module. Congratulations.

Section Summary: So Now You Know

A *file format* is a set of rules that translates between the 1s and 0s used by the computer to store information and the text and graphics displayed on screens and on printouts. Different applications – even different versions of the same application – can use different and incompatible file formats. To help you share your files with others, Excel 97 allows you to save your workbooks in a file format other than its own. The options include: earlier versions of Microsoft Excel, Lotus 1-2-3 and Quattro Pro (other spreadsheets), dBASE (a database) and HTML (the Web page file format).

Another option is to save an Excel 97 workbook as an Excel *template,* and re-use any text, numbers, formatting and calculations in the template as a basis for creating further workbooks.

Excel workbooks can also be saved as *text-only* files, with tabs or commas inserted to separate different columns, and paragraph breaks to separate rows.

You can insert image files into an Excel worksheet, and graphs created in other applications. Excel's Text Import Wizard assists you in opening text files because it can recognise characters that have been inserted in the text files to separate different columns and rows.

Databases

You can never be too rich, too healthy, or too informed. And the best kind of information to have is that which is organised in such a way that you can find the facts you need quickly and easily. It's also important to be able to store new items that you come across.

Databases – structured collections of facts about a particular topic – existed long before computers. Address books, card indexes and telephone directories are all examples of databases. But by storing your facts in a database file on a computer, you gain the power to manage and manipulate that information – even very large amounts of information – in a variety of ways.

You will discover how to view information in your database file from different perspectives, sort and select particular pieces you are interested in, and produce printed reports.

Think of this Module as your chance to file rather than be filed. Good luck with it.

Section 5.1: What Is a Database?

In This Section

A database, as you will learn in this Section, is an organised collection of information relating to the same topic or subject matter. By 'organised' we mean that it should be easy to find a particular item of information in it, and to add new items to the database.

Microsoft Access is an application that enables you to create and work with databases. To give you an idea of what a computer database looks like, this Section will take you on a tour of one of the sample databases provided with Access.

And by considering some examples of practical, everyday databases, you will gain an insight into the kind of decisions that designers need to make before they begin constructing their databases.

New Skills

At the end of this Section you should be able to:

- Explain what a database is
- List some common examples of databases
- State the advantages of computer databases over paper-based ones
- Start and quit Access
- Explore the sample databases provided with Access
- Explain two ways of looking at the information in a computer database
- Decide on a structure for a simple database

New Words

At the end of this Section you should be able to explain the following terms:

- Database
- Database management system
- Table
- Field
- Record
- Datasheet View
- Form View

An Organised Collection of Information

A database is a collection of information relating to the same topic or subject matter. It is usually organised in such a way that you can easily:

- Find the items of information you are interested in, and
- File away the new items that you come across.

Database
A database is an organised collection of related information.

A database does not have to be kept on a computer. For example, address books, card indexes, and telephone directories are all databases (even though very few people would call them that!).

Storing a database on a computer, however, enables you to manipulate the information easily and quickly. For example, using a (paper-based) telephone directory, it is relatively easy to find a person's telephone number, but it is very difficult (but not impossible) to find the person's name if you only have their telephone number.

A computer-based directory enables you to find that information quickly and easily. You could also find the names of everyone who lives on a particular road, or everyone whose first name was Paul. Or you could print a report showing the five most common surnames.

Computer-based databases are flexible: they enable you to deal with information – even very large quantities of information – in a variety of ways. Microsoft Access is an example of a database management system – an application that enables you to create and manage a database on a computer.

Database Management System
An application such as Microsoft Access that enables you to collect information on a computer, organise it in different ways, sort and select pieces of information of interest to you, and produce reports.

Records and Fields

Databases use information broken down into its smallest, most divisible parts. Each part goes into its own named field. For example, if you were entering names and addresses into a database, you would not put all the information into a single field, like this:

James Coogan Sweeney 10744 South Hoyne Chicago Illinois 60643 USA

You would normally enter each piece of information into a separate field, as follows:

FirstName	James
MiddleName:	Coogan
LastName:	Sweeney
FirstAddress:	10744 South Hoyne
SecondAddress:	
City:	Chicago
State:	Illinois
Zipcode:	60643
Country:	USA

Field

A field is a single piece of information about a subject. More precisely, it is the space where that information is held.

In a database, individual pieces of information (such as a telephone number) are called fields, and the set of information relating to one individual is called a record.

Record

A record is one complete set of fields relating to the same subject.

Tables and Databases

A collection of records is called a table. If a database contains just a single table, the table is the database. In this ECDL Module you will be dealing only with single-table databases. All that you need know about multi-table databases is that Access allows you to create them.

When there are thousands or hundreds of thousands of records, a database management system comes into its own. A computer asked to extract and show only records where, for instance, surnames (LastName) begin with 's' and where postcodes (Zipcodes) begin with '60', responds at breathtaking speed, far beyond the capacity of human sorters.

A database management system, however, lacks 'common sense' – it is not able to make judgements. If you did not enter the information in the right field, it will not be retrieved correctly.

Table

A table is a collection of records that contain the same fields.

Two Views: Datasheet and Forms

With Access, and with most database management systems, you can view and manipulate information in two ways: in a datasheet, or in forms. In *Datasheet view*, you can see the information arranged in columns (one for each field) and rows (one for each record); it is similar in appearance to a spreadsheet. See below.

An example of Datasheet view, where you can see several records at once

Number	Bird Name	Colour	Number Seen	Size	Migratory?	Date Seen	Place Seen
1	Great Northern	Black/White	23	69	Yes		
2	Great Crested (	Grey/White/Brown	21	46	No	3/13/99	Dalkey
3	Little Grebe	Black/Brown	14	24	No	4/9/98	Stephen's Green
4	Gannet	White/Black	5	85	No	12/6/98	Ireland's Eye
5	Fulmar	White/Grey	3	45	No		
6	Great Shearwat	White/Brown	7	42	Yes		
7	Manx Shearwat	Black/White	17	30	No		
8	Storm Petrel	Black/White	1	13	No		
9	Cormorant	Black/White	3	83	No	12/6/98	Ireland's Eye
10	Grey Heron	Grey/White	4	90	No		
11	Mute Swan	White	12	144	No	6/14/99	Malahide
12	Brent Goose	Black/White	34	56	Yes	12/12/98	Dollymount
13	Greylag Goose	Grey	22	76	Yes		
14	Shelduck	White/Brown/Black	16	57	No		
15	Goldeneye	White/Black	9	41	Yes		
16	Teal	Grey/Multicolour	14	34	No	9/28/98	Wexford
17	Mallard	Green/White/Brown	16	55	No	9/28/98	Wexford
18	Sparrowhawk	Blue/White	1	28	Yes	7/6/98	
19	Kestrel	Grey/Brown	2	33	No		
20	Pheasant	Green/Gold	6	0	No	9/27/98	Wexford
21	Dodo	Blue/White/Yellow	0	90	No	8/8/81	Mauritius
22	Blue Tit	Blue/Yellow/Black/White	4	6	No	7/6/99	Ballsbridge
utoNumber)			0	0	No		

Datasheet View

A view of a database table where you can see information presented in rows and columns, with several records visible at the same time.

A *Form view* presents all or selected information for a single record at a time. The form can be laid out in a format that is easier to read, perhaps with explanatory text. You can structure the form in such a way that it looks like a paper form, with the fields in the corresponding place on the screen.

An example of Form view, where you can see details from a single record only

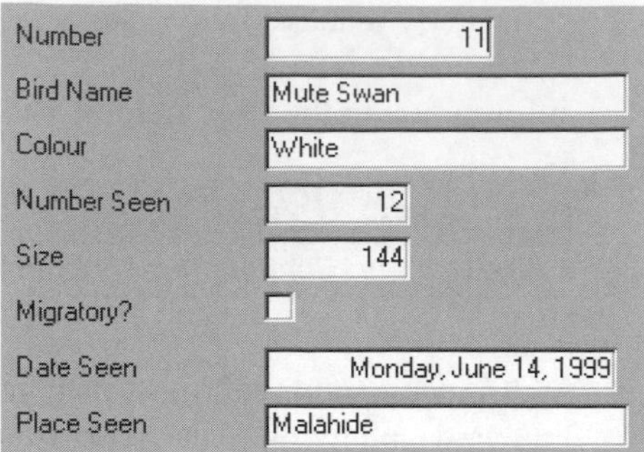

Form View

A view of a database table that presents all or selected information from a single record only.

A good way of learning more about computer databases is by examining some sample ones. Access comes with three sample databases: Northwind, Orders, and Solutions. Exercise 5.1 takes you on a tour of the Northwind database. First, you need to start Access.

Starting Access

To start Access, either:

- Double-click on the Microsoft Access icon.

  -or-

- Choose **Start | Programs | Microsoft Access**.

Access starts and displays a dialog box that gives you the choice of opening an existing database, or of creating a new database.

Now let's take a tour of a database that Microsoft prepared earlier – the Northwind sample database.

Exercise 5.1: Opening the Northwind Database

1) Select the Open an Existing Database option in the opening dialog box.
2) The sample databases may be listed in the dialog box: if they are, select Northwind.mdb.

   If the sample databases are not listed, select the More Files item in the database list. You can then navigate through the folders on your PC to find them. They are most likely to be in the Samples subfolder of your Access folder (C:\Program Files\Microsoft Office\Office\Samples). Use Windows Explorer or My Computer to find them if necessary. When you find Northwind.mdb, select it.

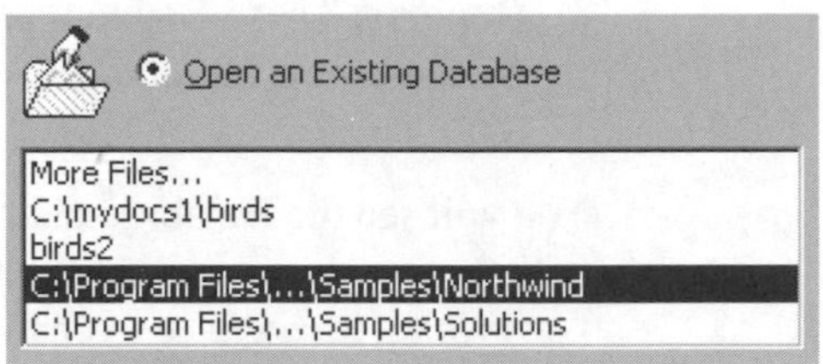

3) Click **OK**.

4) If you are presented with a welcome screen, click **OK** to close it.

Access now displays the Database dialog box.

The Database dialog box – the 'control centre' of Access

From here you can work with the various database objects

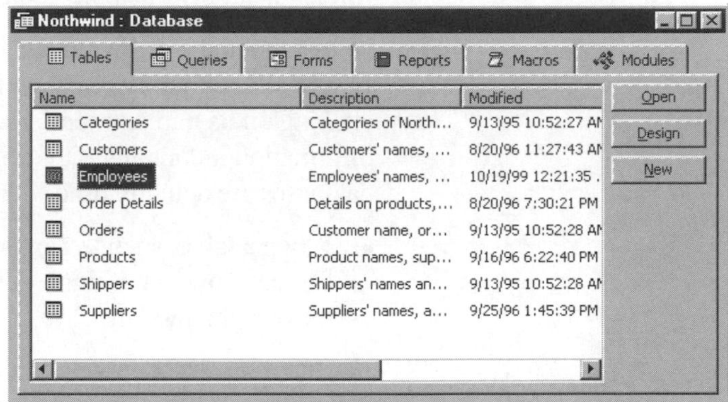

Access File Name Extension

The file names of Access databases end in .mdb (Microsoft database). This helps you to distinguish Access files from other file types such as Excel spreadsheets (.xls) or Word documents (.doc).

The Database Dialog Box

On the Database dialog box you can see six tabs: Tables, Queries, Forms, Reports, Macros, and Modules. They are all sets of items – Access calls them *objects* – that are associated with the database in some way. For ECDL you need learn only about the first four: you don't need to worry about the ones named Macros and Modules.

- **Tables:** You will learn how to create a table in Section 5.2, and modify it in Section 5.3.
- **Queries:** Section 5.4 shows you how to create queries – predefined ways of viewing information from your table on screen.
- **Forms:** Section 5.5 shows you how to create and format the appearance of forms, and how use them to enter and modify records.

- **Reports:** These enable you to extract information from your database as printouts. You will learn about reports in Section 5.6

You will see the Database dialog box a lot when you are working with Access. From here, you can open any of the database objects – to work with them or to change them – and when you are finished with that object, Access returns you to this Database dialog box, from where you can work with any of the other objects easily.

When you first open a database, the Tables tab is normally on top. If it isn't, simply click the Tables tab, and it comes to the top.

Notice that the Northwind database contains several tables. Open Employees, either by selecting it and clicking **Open**, or by double-clicking on its name or icon. Have a look at the type of information it contains. This will give you a good idea of how databases are actually used.

- When a table, such as Employees, contains more fields than can be shown on a single screen, use the horizontal scroll bar to move right and left.

  If you scroll far enough to the right, you will see a Photo column. Double-click any one of these fields to view the employee's photo, then close the photo window.

  Maximise button

  If your horizontal scroll bar is not visible, you will have to click the Maximise button, after which the scroll bar becomes visible.

- When a table contains more records than can be shown on a single screen, use the vertical scroll bar to move up and down the range of records.

Database Design Considerations

In Section 5.2 you will create a database of your very own. But before using Access to build *any* database, take some time to think about the kind of information that you want to put into your database, and how you want to use it.

The following four examples demonstrate the kind of decisions that database designers need to make before they begin constructing their databases.

Example 1: The Wine Buff's Database

Henry is interested in wine. He reads the wine column in the newspapers and notes the recommendations. When he goes to the supermarket, he brings a list with him, so that he can select wine based on the recommendations. When he buys wine, he might have it in the house for some time before he tastes it, and he likes to record his impressions and compare notes with the original review.

Henry might include the following fields in his database:

- Wine Style (Red / White / Rosé / Sparkling / Sweet)
- Name
- Country/Region
- Grower
- Grape Varieties
- Vintage
- Price
- Recommended By
- Review Comments
- Available From (shop)
- Number Bought
- Date Bought
- Date Tasted
- Tasting Notes
- Buy Again?

With such a database, Henry could print out a separate list for each shop, he could list all the red wines, he could list all the white wines that cost less than £10, he could find where the wines by a particular grower were available, he could view the comments on different vintages of the same wine, and so on.

Example 2: The CD Collector's Database

Michelle plays the piano and has a large collection of CDs. When she is learning a new piece, she likes to listen to other people playing it. She has built a database with the following fields:

- CD Title
- Artist
- Track Number
- Name of Tune
- Composer
- Date recorded

By sorting the database on the Name of Tune field, she can quickly identify the particular CDs that include the tune she is working on.

Example 3: The Household Manager's Database

Oscar started his database for insurance purposes: it enabled him to build up a detailed record of his house contents. It included the following fields:

- Room
- Item
- Category
- Date Purchased
- Price Paid

With this database he was able to provide an accurate inventory to the insurance company to support a claim. He could provide the original cost, along with the depreciated value and the replacement value, based on the original cost and the elapsed time since the purchase. He could also quickly give a value for all the paintings in the house, the value of all the clothes in the upstairs rooms, or all the contents of a particular room.

Example 4: The Bird Spotter's Database

Every weekend, Clara goes out with her field glasses and notebook, and spends some time watching birds. When she comes home, she puts details of what she has seen into a database. The database has the following fields:

- Bird Name
- Colour
- Size
- Number Seen
- Migratory?
- Place Seen
- Date Seen

Clara has entered into her database the basic information for the first five fields, based on her reference books, and she records her sightings every week. If she sees a bird that she is unable to identify, she can look up all birds of a certain colour and size. (Obviously this is not enough for identification, but it helps her find the right bird in her reference books.) She can then record the date and place of the sighting. After a while, she will be able to identify the best places and times of the year to spot the different species.

Thinking Hard about Fields

When you are deciding on the fields in the database, think carefully about how they are to be used. If, for example, you want to sort or select wines by country of origin, you should have a column for country: while you might know that Bordeaux is in France, Access doesn't. If you want to find all the albums produced by Nick Lowe, you have to record that information, and preferably in a consistent way (for example, last name followed by first name).

Go back and reread the example of Clara's bird spotting database – this is the database that you will build in Section 5.2.

Closing a Database

To close an Access database, choose **File | Close**, or click the Close button on the Database dialog box.

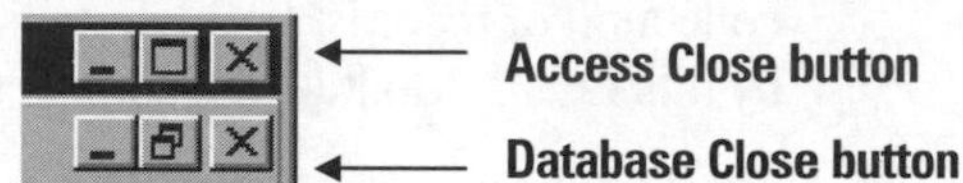

Quitting Access

To leave Access, choose **File | Exit**, or click the Close button on the Access window.

You have now completed this Section 5.1 of the ECDL Database Module.

Section Summary: So Now You Know

A *database* is a collection of information, typically held on a computer, and organised in such a way that you can find what you are looking for quickly and easily, and add new data as you need. Computer-based databases enable their users to manipulate large amounts of information more efficiently that paper-based ones.

Microsoft Access is an example of a *database management system* – an application that stores information on a computer, organises it in different ways, sorts and selects pieces of information of interest to you, and produces reports.

A database holds at least one *table* of information; each table has a number of *records*; and each record has a number of *fields*. A field is a single piece of information about a subject. A record is one complete set of fields relating to the same subject. And a table is a collection of records. In single-table databases of the kind covered by this ECDL Module, the table *is* the database.

The *Database dialog box* is the 'control panel' of Access. Using its tabs, you can open and work with any of the application's *objects* including *Tables*, *Queries*, *Forms* and *Reports*.

Before building any database in Access, consider the information that you want to put into your database, and how you want to use it. Break it down into its smallest (and most useful) divisible parts – each such part should probably be a separate database field.

Section 5.2: Building Your Access Database

In This Section

Get ready to build your first database in Access! This is not as an intimidating a task at it may sound. Access comes with a number of samples that you can use as a basis for just about any new database that you might want to create. So a lot of the work is already done for you!

The decisions you need to make are: which sample table is closest to the one I want? Which of its fields will I use? And what new names will I give to the fields that I select?

Two new concepts you will meet in this Section are keys and indexes. The first is the unique identifier that makes each record in your database different from all the others; the second is a way of speeding up the sorting and retrieval of records. You will also discover another way of looking at your database, called Design View.

One aspect of database creation that Access cannot help you with is data entry: only you can do that.

New Skills

At the end of this Section you should be able to:

- Start the Access Database Wizard
- Select a suitable sample table from the list provided
- Select from the sample table the fields you want in your table
- Rename the fields selected from the sample table to suit your needs
- Select a primary key to identify each of your records uniquely
- Enter data to a table in Datasheet view
- Adjust column width in Datasheet view
- Switch to and from Design view
- Create an index

New Words

At the end of this Section you should be able to explain the following terms:

- Database key
- Design view
- Database index

Overview of Database Creation

In this Section you will create your first Access database. It will be similar to the one that Clara uses to record her bird-watching activities, as outlined in Section 5.1.

Access includes a Database Wizard to simplify the process of creating a database. You will use this automated feature to do some of the work, and you will do some of it the 'hard way', so that you will learn more about how the application works.

Database creation is a nine-step process:

1: Starting the Database Wizard: You begin by starting the Access Database Wizard, and by naming and saving your new database. See Exercise 5.2.

2: Selecting Your Sample Table: Rather than create a new table from scratch, it is easier and faster to base it on one provided by Access. See Exercise 5.3.

3: Selecting Your Fields: You probably won't want every field from the sample table included in your table, so you must specify which ones you need. See Exercise 5.4.

4: Renaming Your Fields: Typically, you will need to rename at least some of the fields that you have selected from the sample table. This is the step at which you also name your table. See Exercise 5.5.

5: Setting Your Primary Key: You need to tell Access which of your fields will act as the key field – the one that uniquely distinguishes each record from all the others. See Exercise 5.6.

6: Entering Your Data: You enter data to your new table in Datasheet view. See Exercise 5.7.

7: Adjusting Column Width: In Datasheet view, some columns may be too narrow; others too wide. You need to know how to change column width. See Exercise 5.8.

8: Switching to Design View: One further step to go, and you can perform it only after you switch from Datasheet view to Design view.

9: Creating Your Index: An index greatly speeds up the sorting and retrieval of data. You create one in Exercise 5.9.

Ready? Let's go build a database.

You begin the creation of your new database by starting the Access Database Wizard.

Step One: Starting the Database Wizard

Exercise 5.2: Starting the Access Database Wizard

1) Start Access, select Database Wizard, and click **OK**.

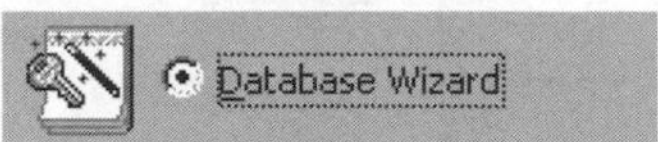

2) In the New dialog box, select the Blank Database icon and click **OK**.
3) In the File New Database dialog, give your new database a name – Birds.mdb – and indicate the folder in which you want to store it.

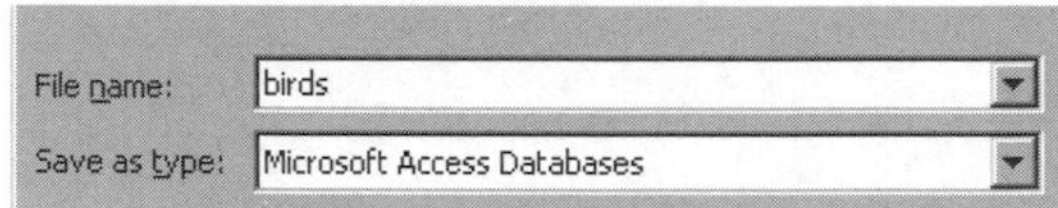

4) Click the **Create** button.

   Access then displays the Database dialog box.
5) Normally, when you create a database, the Tables tab is shown on top in the Database dialog box. If it isn't, click on the Tables tab to bring it to the top.

Notice that, unlike the Northwind sample database, each of the tabs in the database you just created is empty. In this Section 5.2 you will create a table object. In Section 5.4, query and form objects. And in Section 5.6, a report object.

Step Two: Selecting Your Sample Table

It would be impossible for anyone – even Microsoft – to anticipate precisely what you want to do with your database, so the Access Table Wizard offers you a wide range of choices. In the next few Exercises you will pick the options that come closest to matching your needs, and you modify them until they are exactly what you want.

Exercise 5.3: Selecting a Sample Table

1) On the Tables tab of the Database dialog box, click the **New** button at the right. Access displays the New Table dialog box.
2) The New Table dialog box offers five ways to create a new table.

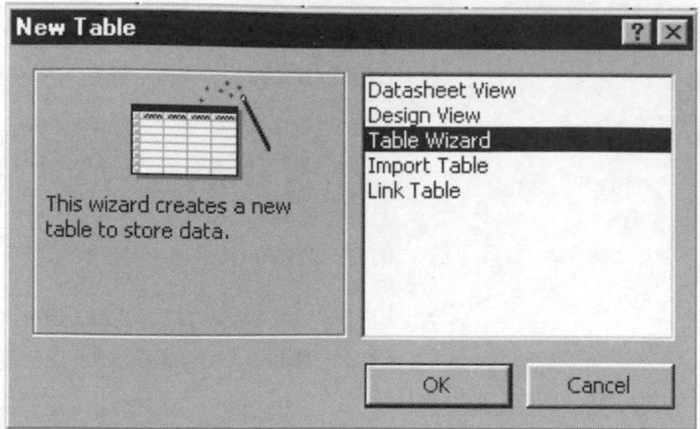

3) Select the Table Wizard option and click **OK**.

4) Look below the Sample Tables list. Can you see two option buttons – Business and Personal? Depending on which of these options you select, Access displays a different list of sample tables.

5) Select Business and browse through the sample tables. For each table in the first list box, scroll through the sample fields in the second list box. None of the tables seems to be particularly appropriate for your needs.

6) Select the Personal option. Again, look through the sample tables. While there is nothing that relates specifically to bird-watching, one of the tables – Plants – could be modified to suit your bird-watching database.

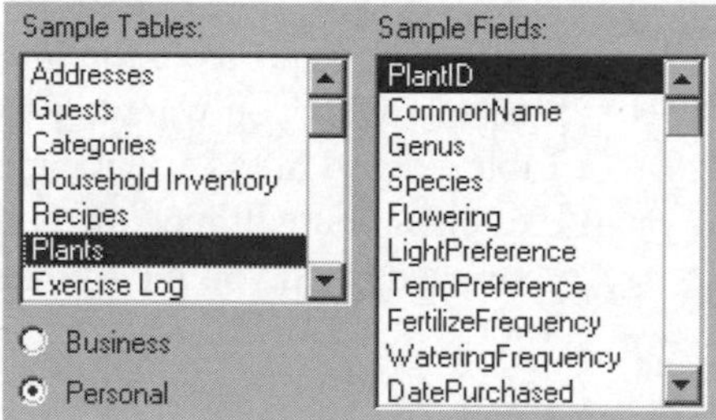

7) Select the Plants table – you will work with it in Exercise 5.4

Step Three: Selecting Your Fields

The first screen of the Table Wizard shows three list boxes. The first displays Access's sample tables. (You selected the Plants table from this list in Exercise 5.3.) The second list shows all the fields supplied with the selected sample table. And the third list shows the fields that you have decided to include in your new table. Initially, the third list is empty.

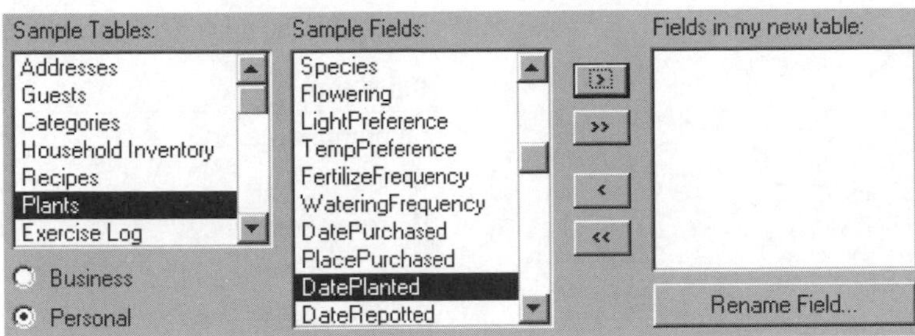

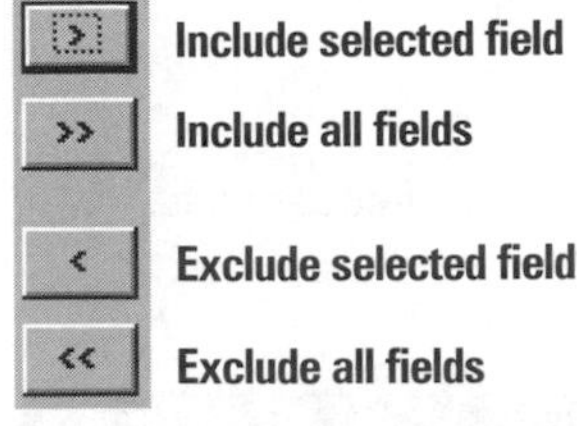

To move a field from the Sample Fields box to the Fields in my new table box, click on it to select it, and then click the > button. If you change your mind about a particular field, select it in the right-hand box and click the < button. You can include all the sample fields by clicking the >> button. Or remove all the fields from the right-hand box by clicking the << button.

Exercise 5.4: Selecting the Fields You Need

1) Move the following fields from the Sample fields list to Fields in my new table list:
   - PlantID
   - CommonName
   - Genus
   - WateringFrequency
   - Flowering
   - DatePurchased
   - PlacePurchased

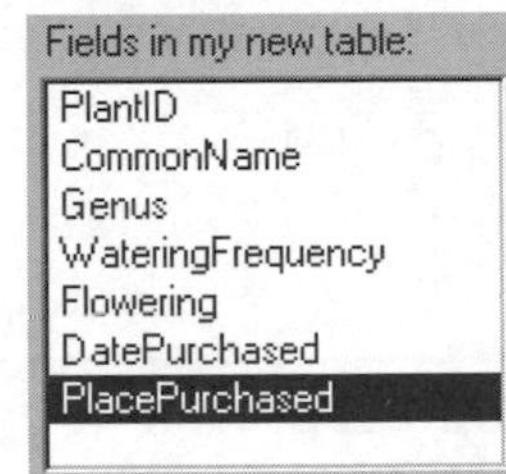

2) When finished, the third list box that shows the fields you selected for your table should look as shown.

Step Four: Renaming Your Fields

Now that you have selected the fields you want to use from the Wizard's sample table, your next task is to give them names suitable for your new table. To rename a field, click on it in the Fields in my new table list and click the **Rename Field** button. You then type the new name for the field in the Rename Field dialog box. Rename your fields as shown in Exercise 5.5.

Exercise 5.5: Renaming Your Fields

1) In the Fields in my new table dialog box, select Plant ID. Click the **Rename Field** button.
2) In the Rename Field dialog box, type the new name for the field: Number. Click **OK**.

3) Repeat for the other fields in your new table, as follows:

Old Name	New Name
CommonName	Bird Name
Genus	Colour
WateringFrequency	Size
Flowering	Migratory?
DatePurchased	Date Seen
PlacePurchased	Place Seen

4) Click the **Next** button.

Congratulations! You have just created your first Access table.

5) Now you have to give it a name.

Apply all your imagination: call your table Birds – the same name as the database that contains it.

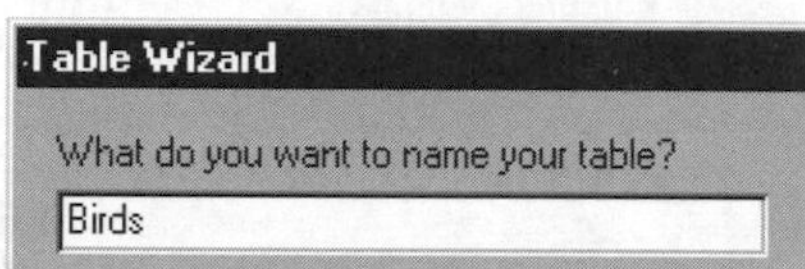

In the same dialog box, Access then asks you whether you want the Wizard to set a primary key, or whether you want to do it yourself. Okay, let's talk about keys.

Step Five: Setting Your Primary Key

In the telephone directory there are many people listed with the surname Murphy; a number of them share the same first name, John. To find the one you want, you need some more information: where do they live? Even that might not be enough – father and son might have the same name, for example – and you might have to ask them some further questions to confirm that you are talking to the right one.

Well, in a computer system, that obviously is not satisfactory. Access needs to know which John Murphy you mean. And you don't want to send a bill, or, worse still, a cheque to the wrong John Murphy. So you give each record an identifier, called a key, which is unique to that record – it is not shared with any other. Exercise 5.6 takes you through the steps.

Database Key

A field (or combination of fields) in a database record that is used to identify that record uniquely.

Exercise 5.6: Setting a Primary Key

1) On the second Table Wizard screen, having specified a name for your new table (in Exercise 5.5), select the option 'No, I'll set the primary key' and click the **Next** button.

2) In answer to the question 'What field will hold data that is unique for each record', select 'Number'.

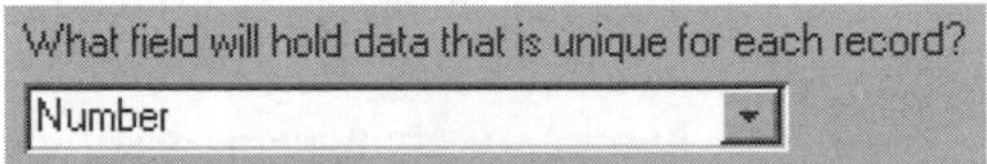

In answer to the question 'What type of data do you want the primary key to contain?', select 'Consecutive Numbers Microsoft Access assigns automatically to new records'.

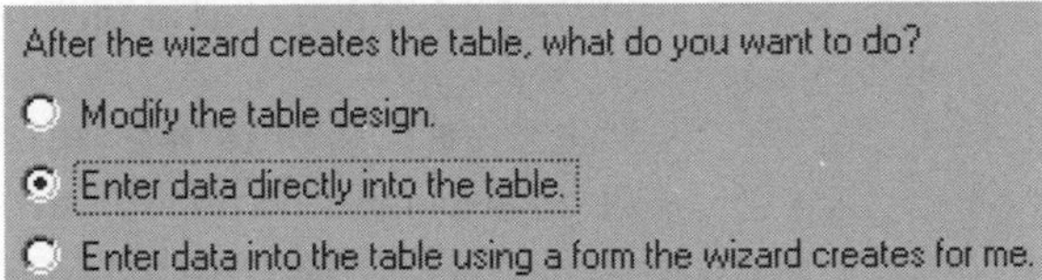

3) Click the **Next** button.

You have now defined your own Primary Key for your table.

4) Access then asks: what do you want to do next – modify the table design, enter data directly into the table, or enter data into a table using a form wizard?

Well, a table with no data is pretty boring, so you probably want to enter data directly into the table without further delay. Choose that option.

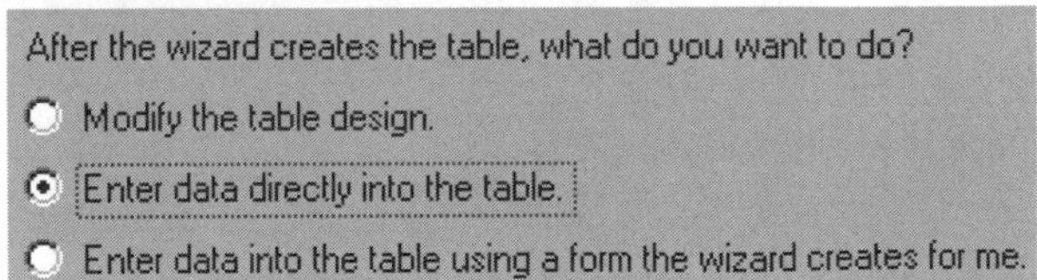

5) Click the **Finish** button.

Step Six: Entering Data in Your Table

When you create a new table, Access displays the table initially in Datasheet view as follows:

- Along the top are column headings that show your field names.
- Underneath the column headings is a single, blank row.

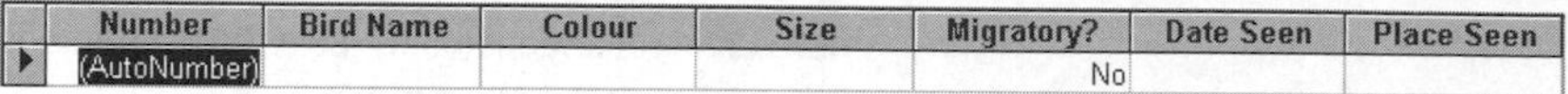

	Number	Bird Name	Colour	Size	Migratory?	Date Seen	Place Seen
▶	(AutoNumber)				No		

Click in any field: you can then enter data in that field. You can move from field to field using the TAB key or the ARROW keys. There is an exception: the Number field (your primary key) is automatically assigned by Access – you cannot enter a new number or change an existing one. You will learn more about this feature in Section 5.3.

As soon as you start entering data for a record, a new line opens up underneath. So, no matter how many records you enter, there is always a blank record at the end where you can enter the next one.

Exercise 5.7: Entering Data to Your Table

1) In the Birds table, fill in the details of a number of birds, as below.

	Number	Bird Name	Colour	Size	Migratory?	Date Seen	Place Seen
▶	1	Great Northern Diver	Black/White	69	Yes		
	2	Great Crested Grebe	Grey/White/Brown	46	No		
	3	Little Grebe	Black/Brown	24	No		
	4	Gannet	White/Black	85	No		
	5	Fulmar	White/Grey	45	No		
	6	Great Shearwater	White/Brown	42	Yes		
	7	Manx Shearwater	Black/White	30	No		
	8	Storm Petrel	Black/White	13	No		
	9	Cormorant	Black/White	83	No		
	10	Grey Heron	Grey/White	90	No		
	11	Mute Swan	White	144	No		
	12	Brent Goose	Black/White	56	Yes		
	13	Greylag Goose	Grey	76	Yes		
	14	Shelduck	White/Brown/Black	57	No		
	15	Goldeneye	White/Black	41	Yes		
	16	Teal	Grey/Multicolour	34	No		
	17	Mallard	Green/White/Brown	55	No		
	18	Sparrowhawk	Blue/White	28	Yes		
	19	Kestrel	Grey/Brown	33	No		
	20	Pheasant	Green/Gold	0	No		
	21	Dodo	Blue/White/Yellow	90	No		
	22	Blue Tit	Blue/Yellow/Black/White	6	No		
*	toNumber)			0	No		

At this stage, some fields may be too small to display all the information you enter: don't worry – you'll learn how to adjust column width in Exercise 5.8.

In the case of Migratory?, if the fields contain check boxes, you indicate that a bird is migratory by clicking on the check box. If the fields contain No instead, you indicate that a bird is migratory by typing Yes in the place of No.

Leave the Place Seen and Date Seen fields blank for the moment.

2) When you have entered the descriptive details of the birds into the datasheet, close it by clicking the lower Close button on the top right of the window. You are then returned to the Database dialog box, this time with one important difference: the new table you created – Birds – is shown on the Tables tab.

That's it. Now you know how to create a table in Access, and how to enter data into it in Datasheet view. (You will learn about entering data in Form view in Section 5.5.)

Step Seven: Changing the Width of Your Columns

This is easy. By now you will have noticed that Access starts off by making all the columns the same width. Some of them are too narrow for their contents to be displayed in full (as, for example, in some of the birds' names).

And some columns are too wide: the datasheet takes up more space than necessary, with the result that some of your data may be pushed off the right of the screen, and you have to use the left-right scroll bar to see it.

To change the width of a column, click on the dividing line (known as the *field delimiter*) between its title and the one to its right.

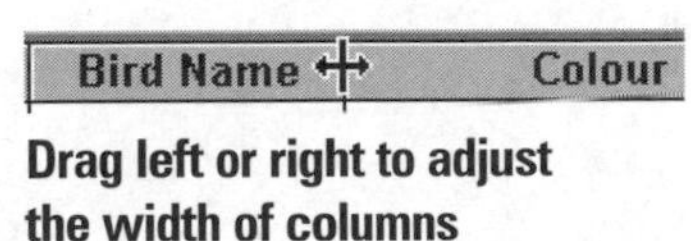

Drag left or right to adjust the width of columns

Notice that the shape of the cursor changes. Then drag the cursor left or right until the column is the right size.

You can make the column width adjust automatically to fit the longest entry in the column by *double-clicking* on the field delimiter.

Exercise 5.8: Adjusting Column Width

1) Change the width of columns in the Birds table to improve the overall appearance of the table.

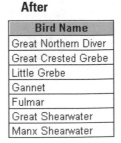

Before

Bird Name
Great Northern
Great Crested (
Little Grebe
Gannet
Fulmar
Great Shearwat
Manx Shearwat

After

Bird Name
Great Northern Diver
Great Crested Grebe
Little Grebe
Gannet
Fulmar
Great Shearwater
Manx Shearwater

Step Eight: Switching to Design View

In Section 5.1 you were introduced to two views of a database: Datasheet view, where you can see several records arranged in rows and columns, and Forms view, where you can see only a single record at a time. In Exercise 5.7 you entered data to your table in Datasheet view.

Now meet a third view: *Design view*. This is the view in which you can change the organisational structure of your table.

Design View button in Datasheet view

Datasheet View button in Design view

- If your table is open in Datasheet view, switch to Design view by choosing **View | Table Design** or by clicking the Design View button on the toolbar.
- If your table is open in Design view, you can return from Design view to Datasheet view by choosing **View | Datasheet** or by clicking the Datasheet View button on the toolbar.

The toolbar buttons enable you to switch quickly between the two views, so that when you make any design changes you can see their effect immediately.

If your table is not open, open it in Design view by selecting it at the Database dialog box, and clicking the Design button.

Design View

A view in which you can change the organisational structure of your table. You create an index in design view.

Step Nine: Creating Your Index

Creating an index from one or more fields can speed up sorting and retrieving records, particularly in large databases. Looking up a name in the index at the back of a book is easier than scanning hundreds of pages of text looking for it; a more sophisticated index might help differentiate between the 57 Smiths, possibly by including first names or addresses in the index.

Access can use table indexes to avoid time-wasting searches through thousands of records. A multiple-field index might, for example, be based on surname, first name and city, since searches are often based on these criteria.

Database Index

A list of keys that a database can use to find and sort records. Indexes make such operations faster, as the database only needs to examine the index fields rather than entire records.

Exercise 5.9 shows you how to build an index for your table.

Exercise 5.9: Creating an Index

1) Open the Birds table in Design view.

Indexes button

2) Choose **View | Indexes** or click the Indexes button on the toolbar. You can see the indexes that are already set, each consisting of just one field.
3) Type a unique name in the Index Name field in an empty row. For example, Where & When.
4) In the Field Name column, select Place Seen from the pop-down list, and, in the row below that, select Date Seen. If you want, you can select a third value – for example, Bird Name – in the row below that again.

You now set up a multiple-field index – the final step in the database creation checklist. You can now save and close your table, and quit Access. You have completed this Section 5.2 of the ECDL Database Module.

Section Summary: So Now You Know

Access offers a *Database Wizard* that simplifies the process of creating a new database by providing a number of *sample tables*. Choose one that resembles the table that you want to create. You can customise your chosen sample table by selecting which of its fields you want to use, and then renaming the selected fields as required.

When you create a new table, Access displays it in Datasheet View, with *column headings* that show your selected field names above a single, blank row. You can type record data into the blank row. As soon as you enter one record, Access opens up a new line underneath, so that there is always a blank record at the end where you can enter the next one.

You can *change column width* manually at any stage, or make column width adjust automatically to the longest entry in the field.

A *key* is a field (or combination of fields) in a database record that uniquely identifies that record. An *index*, which you create in *Design view*, speeds up the sorting and retrieval of records. You must *save* and *name* both the database and the table that the database contains.

Section 5.3: Modifying Your Access Database

In This Section

Now that you have built your first database, you need to learn how to make changes to it. In this Section you will discover how to remove records you no longer need from your database, and reorder existing ones.

Access allows you to add new fields to your records at any time, either at the end of a record or anywhere in the middle. But when you add new fields, you may need to go back and edit all records that you have already entered. So it makes sense to select your fields correctly at database design stage!

As you will also learn in this Section, each field in a table has a particular data type that tells Access how to treat the field, how the data is to be stored, and what kind of data is allowed in it. Ideally, you should select the correct data type for each field before you enter data, because changing a field's data type at a later stage may result in data loss.

Access offers a searchable online help system that you can access in two ways: from the Help menu, and from the question mark button at the top-right of individual dialog boxes.

New Skills

At the end of this Section you should be able to:

- Edit the contents of a field
- Delete a record
- Know when to use the following data types: Text, Memo, Number, Date/Time, Currency, AutoNumber and Yes/No
- Change the data type of a field
- Add a new field
- Reorder fields
- Use Access online help

New Words

At the end of this Section you should be able to explain the following term:

- Data type

Changing and Deleting Database Records

In Section 5.2 you discovered how to create a single-table database in Access. Now it's time to learn how to modify your table in various ways. To change or delete a record in your Birds database, open Access, open the Birds database, and then open the Birds table. By default, your table opens in Datasheet view.

Changing a Field

To change data in a field, begin by clicking on that field.

- If you click on the extreme left of the field, the entire field is selected and anything you type immediately overwrites the whole field.
- If you click anywhere else in the field, you can use the BACKSPACE or DELETE key to delete characters one by one, or you can insert new characters.

Remember that you cannot change the Number field – it is assigned by Access. Change the Migratory? check box by clicking it. If it is already on, clicking it turns it off; if it is off, clicking it turns it on. (If the Migratory? field contains No, you can either leave it alone or change it to Yes; no other input is accepted.)

Deleting a Record

Delete Record button

Indicates a selected record

To delete a record, select it by clicking anywhere in it: it shows an arrowhead at the extreme left. Then choose **Edit | Delete Record**, or click the Delete Record button on the Toolbar. You can then confirm that you want to delete the record, or change your mind and leave it alone.

Exercise 5.10: Changing and Deleting Data

1) Open the Birds table in Datasheet view. Change two fields containing incorrect information in record 20 for the Pheasant.

   The Colour should be Red/Black. The Size should be 53.

2) Delete record 21, concerning the Dodo. It is once more extinct!

3) Type the details in the Date Seen and Place Seen fields.

   Notice that the Date Seen field accepts only valid dates, and forces you to input them in a standard way.

	Date Seen	Place Seen
1		
2	3/13/99	Dalkey
3	4/9/98	Stephen's Green
4	12/6/98	Ireland's Eye
5		
6		
7		
8		
9	12/6/98	Ireland's Eye
10		
11	6/14/99	Malahide
12	12/12/98	Dollymount
13		
14		
15		
16	9/28/98	Wexford
17	9/28/98	Wexford
18	7/6/98	
19		
20	9/27/98	Wexford
21	8/8/81	Mauritius
22	7/6/99	Ballsbridge

4) When you are finished, close the table. You are then returned to the Database dialog box.

If your database records contain an AutoNumber field, and you delete a record, Access does *not* reassign the number of the deleted record to another record. Access ensures that records keep the number initially assigned to them, and it always assigns higher numbers to later additions than to earlier ones.

The Different Data Types

At this stage, if you've followed the Exercises, you're probably thinking that Access is reading your mind. How does it know that the Date Seen column should only contain dates? And how does it know that the Migratory? column is either ticked for Yes, or left blank for No? (Or that input in that field is limited to Yes and No.) Well, the answer is in the table design, and, to be honest, we cheated a bit.

When you set up a table in Access, there are two things you have to do for each field:

- You have to give the field a *name*, and
- You have to give the field a *data type*.

When you used the Wizard to set up the Birds table, the fields you selected from the Plants sample table had the same characteristics as the corresponding fields in the Birds table. You changed the names of the fields to match the bird-watching application. However, because you chose fields carefully, you didn't have to change the data types.

The data type tells Access how to treat the field, how the data is to be stored, and what kind of data is allowed in it.

Data Type

This determines the kind of data that you can store in a field, and tells Access how to handle it.

Access recognises a number of different data types. The most important ones for our purposes are shown as follows:

Data Type	Used For	Examples
Text	Any sort of alphabetic or numeric data. Typically used where there is a limit on the amount of data. No more than 255 characters may be input. (If the data is numeric, it should not be intended for use in calculations.)	Surname, Colour, Zip Code, Telephone Number
Memo	Any sort of alphabetic or numeric data. Typically used for free-form input. Up to 64,000 characters may be input. (Again, if the data is numeric, it should not be intended for use in calculations.)	Description, Where Seen, Notes
Number	Numeric data that may be used in calculations.	Quantity in Stock, Number in Flock, Number Sold
Date/Time	Date or time data.	Date Bought, Arrival Time, Planting Date
Currency	Money values or other numeric data used in calculations where the number of decimal places does not exceed four.	Price, Current Value
AutoNumber	A number assigned to each new record automatically. Access assigns the numbers in sequence, starting with l.	Sequence Number
Yes/No	Fields that can have simple yes/no, true/false, or on/off values only.	Migratory?, Buy Again?, Flowering?

Changing Data Types

It is easy to change the data type of a field, but ideally you should get it right at the design stage. If you try to change the data type after you have input a lot of data, you can confuse Access, and you may lose some of your data.

In Exercise 5.11 you will change some of the data types in the Birds table.

Exercise 5.11: Changing Data Types

1) Open your Birds database.
2) At the Database dialog box, select the Birds table, and click the **Design** button.
3) You then see the Design view of the table: this is divided into two main panes. At the top is the list of field names with their data types.

Field Name	Data Type	
Number	AutoNumber	
Bird Name	Text	
Colour	Text	
Size	Number	
Migratory?	Yes/No	
Date Seen	Date/Time	
Place Seen	Text	

Click on any of the Data Type fields. A drop-down arrow appears beside the data type. Click on this arrow: you see the list of data types described above (along with a few others that we haven't discussed). To change a data type, you simply select the new one from that list.

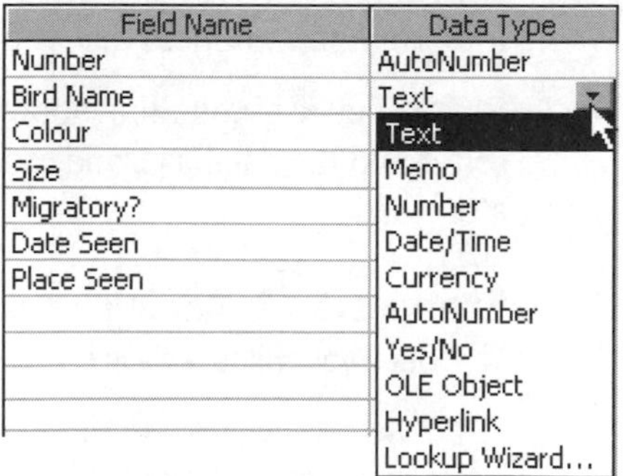

4) Try some experiments.
   - Change the data type of Migratory? from Yes/No to Number. Close the dialog box, and confirm that you want to save the changes. Then open the table. Notice how the data displayed under Migratory? has changed.

- Go back into Design view. (To do this, click the Design View button in the toolbar, or close the table and then click the Design button again.) This time, change the data type of Migratory? to Date/Time.

  Then save the change and have a look at the effect of this change on the data displayed in the datasheet. Notice how changing the data type after you have input data can yield surprising results.

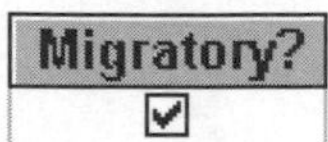

A check box

When you have finished experimenting, change the data type of Migratory? back to Yes/No.

5) If the Migratory? field contains Yes or No, change it to a check box, as follows.
   - Click on the Migratory? field.
   - Then, in the lower pane (Field Properties), choose the Lookup tab, and, in Display Control, choose the option you want: Check Box.
6) In later Exercises you will want to compare the sizes of different birds. To do this, the Size field must be numeric. So change its data type from Text to Number.
7) Finally, save your work.

Adding New Fields to Your Table

Can you add new fields to your database records at any time? Yes. But if you do, you may have to go back and edit all records you have already entered. This applies particularly to numeric fields (where a blank field may be interpreted as 0), and Yes/No fields (where a blank field may be interpreted as No), but it is also important for any field that you use for sorting or filtering data.

So it is better if you think about the fields you want when you are setting up the database, and modify the design as little as possible after that.

Exercise 5.12: Adding New Fields

1) Open your Birds table in Design view.
2) Where do you want to add a new field: at the end of a record or somewhere in the middle?
   - To add a new field at the end of the record, click on the next unused Field Name box. For this Exercise, select this option.
   - To add the new field between two existing fields, click on the title of the field that will end up on the *right* of the new field and choose **Insert | Field**.

3) Enter the title of the new field: Comments.

4) Specify the data type of the new field: Memo.

Field Name	Data Type
Number	AutoNumber
Bird Name	Text
Colour	Text
Size	Number
Migratory?	Yes/No
Date Seen	Date/Time
Place Seen	Text
Comments	Memo
	Text
	Memo
	Number

(A field with Text data type may hold a maximum of 255 characters, whereas a field with Memo data type may hold up to 64,000 characters.)

5) Click the Close button.
-or-
Choose **File | Close**.
-or-
Hold down the CTRL key and type w.
-or-
Click the Datasheet View button.

Access asks you to confirm the change.

You can also insert a new field into a table while you are in Datasheet view: just click on the title of the field that will end up *on the right* of the new field and choose **Insert | Column**. Access assigns this field the Text data type. If that is what you want, fine. If it isn't, you will have to go into Design view to specify the data type you want.

Try this: input a new field Number Seen to the right of the Colour field and make its data type Number. Enter the numbers as shown on the right.

	Number Seen
1	23
2	21
3	14
4	5
5	3
6	7
7	17
8	1
9	3
10	4
11	12
12	34
13	22
14	16
15	9
16	14
17	16
18	1
19	2
20	6
21	0
22	4

Reordering the Fields in a Table

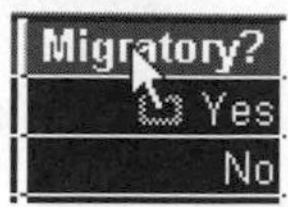

Reordering Fields cursor

To change the order of fields in the table, click on the title of the one you want to move. Then click on it *again*, but this time maintain the click (keep pressure on the left button): note that a box appears on the tail of the cursor.

Now drag it to the new location to the left or right. When you arrive at your chosen destination, note how a bold line has appeared, indicating Access's understanding of where you want to place your moving column: if this is correct, release your finger from the mouse button, and the column moves.

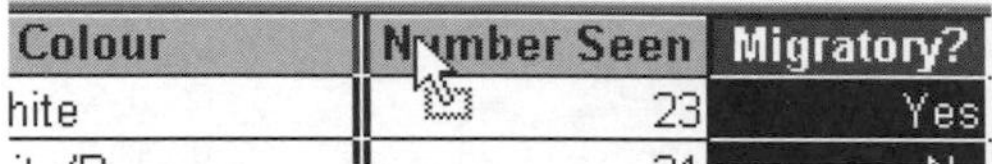

Try this a number of times until you are confident about it.

Saving to a Diskette

Have you been saving your table as you went along? You should. It is also a good idea to save a copy of your database on a diskette. Follow the steps in Exercise 5.13 to learn how to save your database to the A: drive.

Exercise 5.13: Saving Your Access Database to a Diskette

1) Insert a diskette in the diskette drive of your computer:
   - If it is a new diskette, ensure that it is formatted.
   - If it is a previously used one, ensure that there is sufficient space on it to hold your Birds database.
2) With the Birds table open, choose **File | Save As/Export**.
3) Click **OK** to confirm that you want to save the table as an external file.

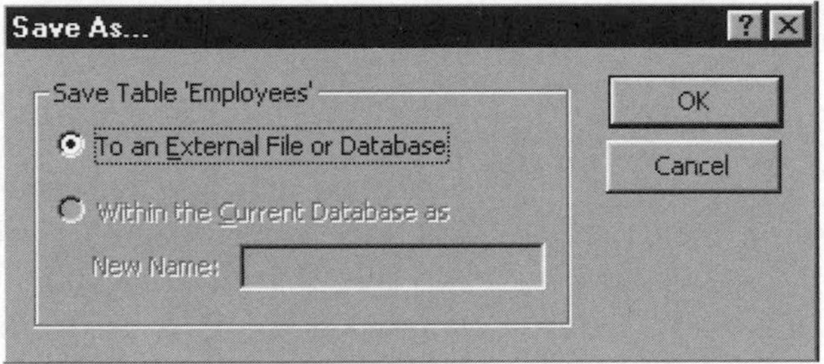

4) Access displays the Save dialog box, with the file name Birds already entered. You can change this file name if you wish.
5) Locate the A: drive, and click **Save** to save your table. You have successfully saved a copy of Birds on the floppy diskette.

Once a database has been saved, Access does not normally thereafter prompt you to Save Changes when you exit – it assumes, unlike most Microsoft applications, that any changes you make are changes you want to keep.

Online Help

Like Excel, PowerPoint and other Microsoft applications, Access offers a searchable online help system. The word 'help' means that the information is there to assist you understand and use the application. The word 'online' means that the material is presented on the computer screen rather than as a traditional printed manual.

You can search through and read online help in two ways: from the **Help** menu, or from dialog boxes.

Using Help Menu Options

Choose **Help | Contents and Index** to display the following three tabs of the Help Topics dialog box.

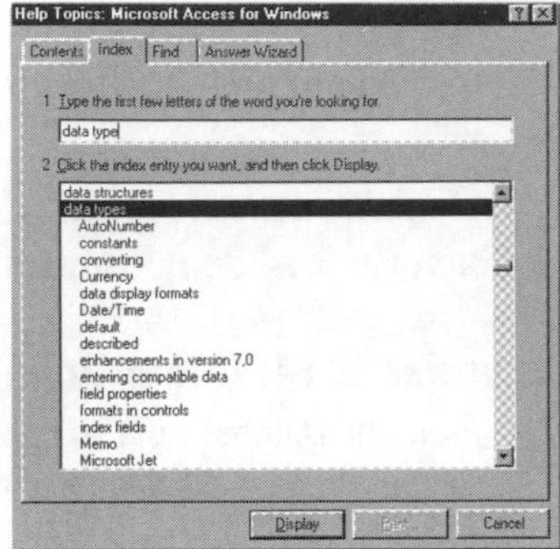

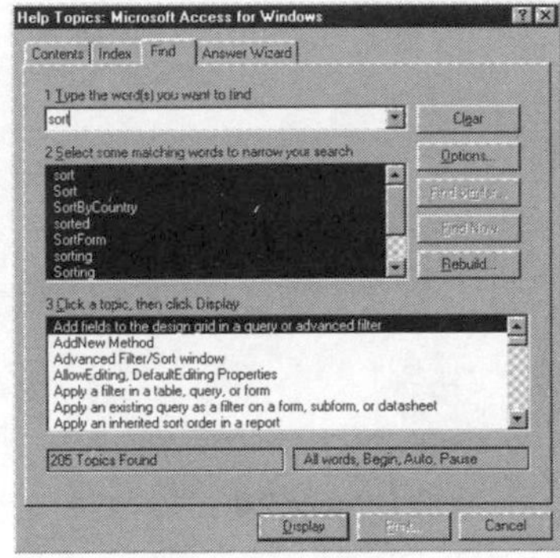

Contents Tab

This offers short descriptions of Access's main features.

Where you see a heading with a book symbol, double-click to view the related sub-headings.

Double-click on a question-mark symbol to read the help text.

Click a Show me arrow for Access to demonstrate how to perform a particular action.

Click a double arrow to view step-by-step instructions.

Index Tab

Reading the material displayed on this tab is like looking through the index of a printed book.

Just type the first letters of the word or phrase you are interested in.

Access responds by displaying all matches from the online help in the lower half of the dialog box.

When you find the index entry that you are looking for, click the **Display** button.

Find Tab

Can't find what you are looking for in the Contents or Index tabs? Try this tab.

When you type a word or phrase, Access performs a deeper search of the online help.

Access also displays some related words to help you narrow your search.

When you find the item you are looking for, double-click on it to display it.

A fourth tab, Answer Wizard, accepts your questions about Access in plain English.

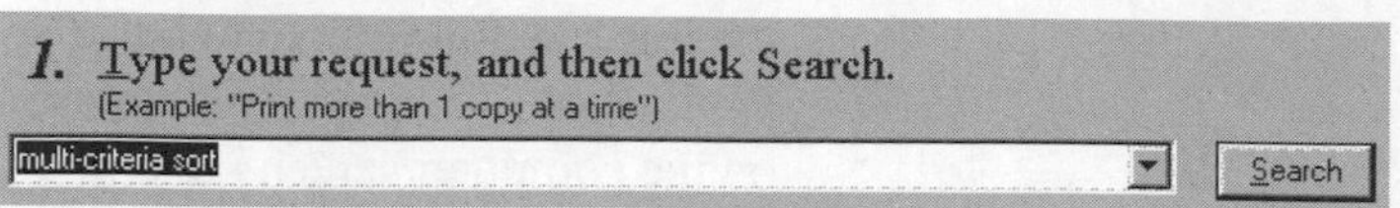
1. Type your request, and then click Search.
(Example: "Print more than 1 copy at a time")
multi-criteria sort
Search

As you search through and read online help topics, you will see the following buttons at the top of the online help window:

- **Help Topics:** Click this to return to the Contents tab.
- **Back:** Click this to return to the previous help topic.
- **Options:** Click this to perform such actions as copying the online help text to a document, or printing it on your printer.

Using Help from the Screen

You can also access online help directly from any Access screen, as Exercise 5.14 demonstrates.

Online Help button

Exercise 5.14: Using Online Help from an Access Screen

1) From the Database dialog box, click the Online Help button on the toolbar. Access displays a question mark to the right of the cursor.
2) Click on the Queries tab label.
3) Access displays online help text telling you about the purpose of selected screen element.

   Queries tab

   Click to display a list of all queries in the current database. Use the buttons to the right of the list to open the selected query, modify the design of the selected query, or create a new query.

4) Click anywhere on the Access screen to remove the online help text.

Practise this Exercise with various screens in Access.

When finished, you can close your database and quit Access.

Access Toolbars

The most frequently used Access functions are available by clicking a single button on the toolbar.

Normally, Access displays the most suitable toolbar – the one containing the buttons for the functions that you are most likely to use.

If you want to hide the toolbar (and choose all your options from the menus), or if you want to display other toolbars, choose **View | Toolbar** and select the toolbars that you want displayed.

Section Summary: So Now You Know

A field's *data type* tells Access how to treat the field, how the data is to be stored, and what kind of data is allowed in it. Commonly used data types are: Text, Memo, Number, Date/Time, Currency, AutoNumber and Yes/No.

Try to select the correct data type for each field before you enter data, because changing a field's data type at a later stage may result in data loss.

You can add new fields to the database at any time, but you may need to go back and edit all records that you have already entered, particularly for numeric fields (where a blank field may be interpreted as 0), and Yes/No fields (where a blank may be interpreted as No).

Access offers a searchable *online help* system that you can access in two ways: from the Help menu, and from the question-mark button at the top-right of individual dialog boxes.

Section 5.4: Making the Database Work for You

In This Section

After Sections 5.2 and 5.3 you might still be asking: why bother? You can use a word processor to keep lists of things, and if you want to put them in neat columns, you can use a spreadsheet. Well, this Section 5.4 should convince you that a database is a very useful tool for managing your information, and for quickly finding the particular items of interest.

For example, the order in which you entered records originally in your table may not be the order in which, later on, you would prefer to display those records. You could reorder – *sort* – a table of customers, for instance, so that the biggest spenders appear at the top of the list. You can even save sorts you use regularly as *queries* so that you can apply them at the click of a button.

Another very useful feature is *filtering* – the ability to reduce the amount of information displayed, either by showing fewer fields in each record, or by showing only those records that match certain criteria.

Finally, as with other Microsoft Office applications, Access includes a *Find* feature that enables you to locate a particular item quickly.

New Skills

At the end of this Section you should be able to:

- Reorder (sort) the database records
- Save a sort as a query and apply it to a database
- Find a particular record or set of records
- Use the Access Find feature

New Words

At the end of this Section you should be able to explain the following terms:

- Sort
- Sort order
- Find
- Filter
- Query

Changing the Order of Records in the Table

Open Access and open your Birds table. Notice that the datasheet shows the records in the order you entered them: the Number field reflects that order – records you added later have higher numbers than ones you added earlier.

However, you can choose to display the records in a different order, by *sorting* them.

Sort

An operation that you carry out on a table to change the order in which the records are displayed. Sorting does not change the content of records, only their location.

Access offers two sequencing options, called sort orders.

Sort Order

A particular way of ordering records based on field values. A sort order can be in alphabetic ascending (A to Z) or descending (Z to A) sequence.

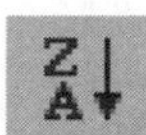

Sort Ascending button

Sort Descending button

Suppose you want the records to be displayed alphabetically by bird name, or in order of size (biggest first, smallest last), how would you go about it? Easy. Click on any bird name. Then click the Sort Ascending button on the toolbar. Done!

Click on any size field. Click the Sort Descending button. Again, done! What could be simpler?

Sorted by name, ascending

Bird Name
Blue Tit
Brent Goose
Cormorant
Dodo
Fulmar
Gannet
Goldeneye
Great Crested Grebe
Great Northern Diver
Great Shearwater
Grey Heron
Greylag Goose
Kestrel
Little Grebe
Mallard
Manx Shearwater
Mute Swan
Pheasant
Shelduck
Sparrowhawk
Storm Petrel
Teal

Sorted by size, descending

Number	Bird Name	Colour	Number Seen	Size
11	Mute Swan	White	12	144
10	Grey Heron	Grey/White	4	90
21	Dodo	Blue/White/Yellow	0	90
4	Gannet	White/Black	5	85
9	Cormorant	Black/White	3	83
13	Greylag Goose	Grey	22	76
1	Great Northern Diver	Black/White	23	69
14	Shelduck	White/Brown/Black	16	57
12	Brent Goose	Black/White	34	56
17	Mallard	Green/White/Brown	16	55
20	Pheasant	Red/Black	6	53
2	Great Crested Grebe	Grey/White/Brown	21	46
5	Fulmar	White/Grey	3	45
6	Great Shearwater	White/Brown	7	42
15	Goldeneye	White/Black	9	41
16	Teal	Grey/Multicolour	14	34
19	Kestrel	Grey/Brown	2	33
7	Manx Shearwater	Black/White	17	30
18	Sparrowhawk	Blue/White	1	28
3	Little Grebe	Black/Brown	14	24
8	Storm Petrel	Black/White	1	13
22	Blue Tit	Blue/Yellow/Black/White	4	6
oNumber)			0	0

These kinds of sorts are called simple, or *single criterion sorts*. Now imagine that you have more complex requirements: you want to sort all the birds by colour, showing the biggest birds of any colour before the smaller ones. These are called *multiple criteria sorts*. Exercise 5.15 shows you how to do them.

Exercise 5.15: Sorting Records Using a Number of Criteria

1) Open the Birds table in Datasheet View. Choose **Records | Filter | Advanced Filter/Sort**.

2) In the lower pane, click on the list button in the first row, first column: a list of all the fields in your table is shown. Select Colour.

3) Click in the second field in the first column. A list button appears. Click on this to choose a sort order. Select Ascending.

4) Click in the first field of the second column: a list button is displayed. Click on it, and choose Size from the list.

5) Click in the field below Size: a list button is displayed. Click on it and choose Descending.

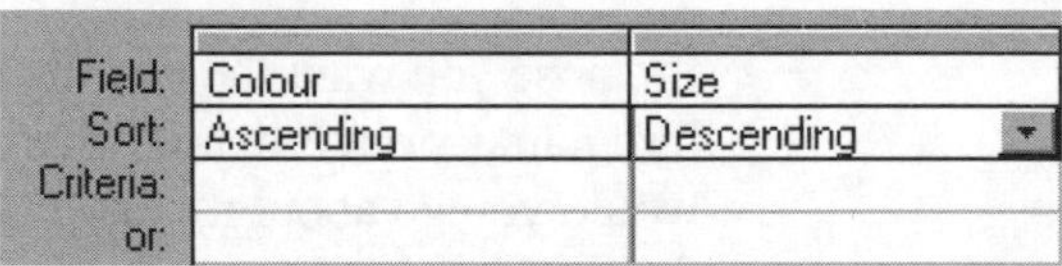

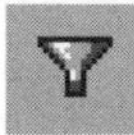
Apply Filter button

6) Then click the Apply Filter button in the toolbar, and the datasheet is shown, this time listing the birds in order of colour, and with the bigger birds of each colour shown before the smaller ones.

Bird Name	Colour	Number Seen	Size
Little Grebe	Black/Brown	14	24
Cormorant	Black/White	3	83
Great Northern Diver	Black/White	23	69
Brent Goose	Black/White	34	56
Manx Shearwater	Black/White	17	30
Storm Petrel	Black/White	1	13
Sparrowhawk	Blue/White	1	28
Dodo	Blue/White/Yellow	0	90
Blue Tit	Blue/Yellow/Black/White	4	6
Mallard	Green/White/Brown	16	55
Greylag Goose	Grey	22	76
Kestrel	Grey/Brown	2	33
Teal	Grey/Multicolour	14	34
Grey Heron	Grey/White	4	90
Great Crested Grebe	Grey/White/Brown	21	46
Pheasant	Red/Black	6	53
Mute Swan	White	12	144
Gannet	White/Black	5	85
Goldeneye	White/Black	9	41
Great Shearwater	White/Brown	7	42
Shelduck	White/Brown/Black	16	57
Fulmar	White/Grey	3	45
		0	0

7) Close your table.

Why is the button called Apply Filter? Well, Access regards this kind of sort as a particular example of a filter. What's a filter? Don't worry about that for now: we'll be looking at filters a little later.

Saving a Query

If you experiment with sorting, you'll see that you can view the information in your table in many different ways. You can, for example, separate the records into migratory and non-migratory birds; you can quickly identify the smallest bird you saw on a particular date; or you can list the birds you have seen in Wexford.

It's quite likely that you will want to repeat some of these sorts regularly. For example, if you have several hundred birds in your database, sorting them by colour and size would help you identify unusual birds. You can enter the sort criteria each time you want to sort the table in this way, or you can make life easy for yourself, by saving the sort criteria as a query.

Query
Queries are used to view database records repeatedly in a particular way defined by you.

Exercise 5.16 shows you how to save your sort criteria as a query.

Exercise 5.16: Saving Sort Criteria as a Query

1) Set up your sort criteria as in steps 1) to 5) of Exercise 5.15.

Save As Query button

2) Choose **File | Save As Query** or click the Save As Query button on the toolbar.

3) Give the query a name: say Colour/Size.

4) Click **OK**, and close the Filter dialog box.

And that's it! Notice that the query shows up on the Query tab on the Database dialog box. From now on, even after you have added more records to the database, or changed the ones that are already there, you simply open this query and the records in the table will be presented in the manner defined by the query.

Note that queries don't make any permanent change to the database; they simply extract information and present it in a certain way.

If you have used a query to view a table in a particular order, you can return to an unsorted view by choosing **Records | Remove Filter/Sort**.

Notice that in this query all of the fields were shown. What if we want to view only selected columns?

Exercise 5.17: Creating a Query for Selected Columns Only

1) From the Database dialog box, click the Queries tab; then click the **New** button on that tab.
2) Select Design View and click **OK**.
3) In the Tables tab, select the Birds table. Click the **Add** button, followed by the **Close** button.
4) Now, as in Exercise 5.15, select Colour in the first Field column and choose Sort Ascending; then select Size in the second Field column, and choose Sort Descending.
5) Click Bird Name in the third Field column, but this time don't specify a Sort order.

Colour	Size	Bird Name
Birds	Birds	Birds
Ascending	Descending	
☑	☑	☑

6) Now, click the Run button in the toolbar.

   This time your Query returns only the referenced columns, and cuts out unnecessary or unwanted information in adjacent columns.

Run button

Colour	Size	Bird Name
Black/Brown	24	Little Grebe
Black/White	13	Storm Petrel
Black/White	30	Manx Shearwater
Black/White	56	Brent Goose
Black/White	69	Great Northern Diver
Black/White	83	Cormorant
Blue/White	28	Sparrowhawk
Blue/White/Yellow	90	Dodo
Blue/Yellow/Black/White	6	Blue Tit
Green/White/Brown	55	Mallard
Grey	76	Greylag Goose
Grey/Brown	33	Kestrel
Grey/Multicolour	34	Teal
Grey/White	90	Grey Heron
Grey/White/Brown	46	Great Crested Grebe
Red/Black	29	Pheasant
White	144	Mute Swan
White/Black	41	Goldeneye
White/Black	85	Gannet
White/Brown	42	Great Shearwater
White/Brown/Black	57	Shelduck
White/Grey	45	Fulmar

7) Close the dialog box. You are prompted to save the query – click the **Yes** button. Give the query a name you will remember, such as '3-Column, Colour/Size/Bird Name'. Click **OK**, and it's saved. You can subsequently view the selected fields of the table in the order you specified, simply by opening the query from the Query tab on the Database dialog box.

Restricting the Information Displayed

Filter by Selection button

You can reduce the amount of information displayed, either by showing fewer fields in each record, or by showing only those records that match certain criteria. This is called filtering.

Filter

A filter restricts the display of your database information to records and fields that match criteria that you specify.

Suppose, for example, you want to concentrate on birds that you have seen in Wexford. Simply find any record that matches your criterion – in this case, one with Wexford in the Place Seen column.

Click on the relevant field – Wexford – and then click on the Filter by Selection button in the toolbar.

The display is immediately restricted to records that match your selection – that is, ones that have Wexford in the Place Seen column.

Number	Bird Name	Colour	Number Seen	Size	Migratory?	Date Seen	Place Seen
16	Teal	Grey/Multicolour	14	34	☐	Monday, September 28, 1998	Wexford
17	Mallard	Green/White/Brown	16	55	☐	Monday, September 28, 1998	Wexford
20	Pheasant	Red/Black	6	29	☐	Sunday, September 27, 1998	Wexford

Remove Filter button

Don't panic: the rest of your records are still in the database. The filter just limits the amount of information in the display. To see all your records again, you remove the filter: click the Remove Filter button in the toolbar.

A word of caution: Recall that you can change the information in the database at any time. And recall that you change a Yes/No check box field by clicking on it: a click turns it on if it was off, and off if it was on. If you are filtering based on a Yes/No check box field, you will change the information when you select it. So in the case of a Yes/No check box field, you will have to click on the field twice before you click on the Filter by Selection button.

For example, suppose you want to study only migratory birds. As before, find one record of a migratory bird. Click on the Migratory? check box: notice what happens – the box changes from checked (Yes, migratory) to unchecked (No, not migratory). Click it again, so that it shows the correct status, and then click the Apply Filter button. The display shows only migratory birds.

Number	Bird Name	Colour	Number Seen	Size	Migratory?	Date Seen
1	Great Northern Diver	Black/White	23	69	☑	
6	Great Shearwater	White/Brown	7	42	☑	
12	Brent Goose	Black/White	34	56	☑	Saturday, December 12, 1998
13	Greylag Goose	Grey	22	76	☑	
15	Goldeneye	White/Black	9	41	☑	
18	Sparrowhawk	Blue/White	1	28	☑	Monday, July 06, 1998

Filtering by Selection

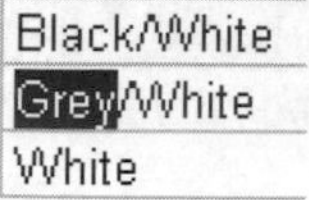

Selecting part of a field for filtering by selection

When you select a field, and then filter based on the contents of that field, the process is known as *filtering by selection*. Note that you don't have to select the whole field: you might be interested in all the Warblers, or all birds that have grey somewhere in their colour. No problem.

As before, find a record that has the characteristic you want – say grey in its colour. Click and drag the mouse over the part of the field that has the word (or part of the word) that you want to match – in this case grey.

Then click the Filter by Selection button. The display shows the birds that have grey anywhere in their colour field.

Number	Bird Name	Colour
2	Great Crested Grebe	Grey/White/Brown
10	Grey Heron	Grey/White
13	Greylag Goose	Grey
16	Teal	Grey/Multicolour
19	Kestrel	Grey/Brown

Filtering by selection includes the ideas 'Beginning with ...' and 'Ending with ...'. If you select the first letter in a field and filter by selection, Access displays all records in which the field *begins with* that letter. Similarly, if you select the last letter in the field, Access displays the records in which the field *ends with* that letter.

So if you want to filter based on the first word or the last word in a field, include the first letter or the last letter only if you want to restrict the display to records that begin with or end with the selection. If you want all records that include the word anywhere in the field, select only *part* of the word – a part in the middle of the word, such as 'hit' for white or 'lac' for black.

Try Filtering by Selection yourself: remove the colour filter, and this time restrict the display to Grebes.

Filtering Filtered Records

If you want to further restrict the records displayed – say to all green-coloured birds spotted in Wexford – you simply repeat the steps above. First, find all the birds spotted in Wexford, then from that list find all the green birds. Alternatively, start by finding all the green birds, then further restrict that list to ones spotted in Wexford.

Bird Name	Colour	Number Seen	Size	Migratory?	Date Seen	Place Seen
Mallard	Green/White/Brown	16	55	☐	Monday, September 28, 1998	Wexford

Find

Find button

Is there a quick way of finding a particular record among hundreds or thousands? Yes. Use the Access Find feature. You can run Find in any of the following ways: choose **Edit | Find**, click the Find button on the toolbar, or use the keyboard shortcut CTRL+f.

Try the following exercise to find a specific record in the Birds table.

Exercise 5.18: Finding a Specific Record

1) Open the Birds table. Click the Find button in the toolbar.

2) In the Find What field, enter 'Goldeneye'.

   Ensure that the Search Only Current Field check box is clear. (Click the check box to remove a checkmark. Click again to insert one.) The Search field should contain 'All', and the Match field 'Whole Field'.

3) Click the **Find First** button and Access should highlight the Goldeneye record.

4) Click the **Find Next** button. Access indicates that there are no further records that match the criterion. Click **OK**.

5) In the Find dialog box, click the **Close** button.

6) Now, on your own, and in separate Find operations, find the following data:

- **Malahide** – This should highlight the Mute Swan record.
- **55** – This should highlight the Mallard record.
- **Grey** – This should highlight the Greylag Goose record – this is the only record for which 'grey' is a whole field.

Now change the Match field to read 'Any Part of Field', and find grey again. This time when you click the **Find Next** button repeatedly, a number of other records should be highlighted – these are records that have 'grey' somewhere in the field.

Section Summary: So Now You Know

A *sort* is an operation that you carry out on a table to change the order in which the records are displayed. Access allows you to perform single criterion and multiple criteria sort operations.

If you perform a particular sort regularly, you can save the sort details as a *query*. You can use queries to view database records repeatedly in a particular way defined by you.

Filtering is the process of reducing the amount of information displayed by Access, either by showing fewer fields in each record, or by showing only those records that match certain criteria. To view all your records again, remove the filter.

You can filter a table by clicking on a particular field, or by dragging the mouse over the word (or part of a word) that you want to match, and then clicking on the Filter by Selection button on the toolbar.

Note that if you are filtering based on a Yes/No field, you need to click on the field twice before you click on the Filter by Selection button. A single click on a Yes/No field will change the information in that field!

You can filter the result of a filter operation to restrict further the information displayed.

Access's *Find* feature provides a quick way of locating a particular record or records based on their field values.

Section 5.5: Working with Forms

In This Section

Until now, you have been looking at your database records in Datasheet View – they have been shown in rows, with a column for each field. Datasheet View can make reading the information difficult, and it's annoying if the fields and records extend beyond the edges of your screen, so that you have to scroll left and right and up and down to see the items of interest.

Forms are better for those times when all you really want is to see information relating to a single record at one time, laid out in an eye-pleasing manner. Forms have the added advantage of being much easier to read, and you can design different, eye-pleasing forms for different purposes.

As you will learn in this Section, everything you can do in a datasheet you can also do in a form. You can input new records and change existing records; you can sort the records into a different order; and you can filter the records so that only ones that match your criteria are displayed.

New Skills

At the end of this Section you should be able to:

- Create a form to display records, in whole or in part, one at a time
- Use a form to create new records
- Use a form to search for and modify a record
- Modify a form that you have previously created
- Import an image or graphic file into a form

Forms: What Are They For?

Remember in Section 5.1 you learnt that Access enables you to view and manipulate information in two ways:

- **Datasheet View:** This shows the information for many records, arranged in columns and rows.
- **Form View:** This presents information for one record at a time.

Creating Your Form with the Form Wizard

Forms are based on tables. You can create a form only *after* you have created a table, such as the Birds table created in Section 5.2. In Exercise 5.19 you will use the Access Form Wizard to create a new form.

Exercise 5.19: Creating a Form

1) Open Access, open your Birds database, and click on the Forms tab.

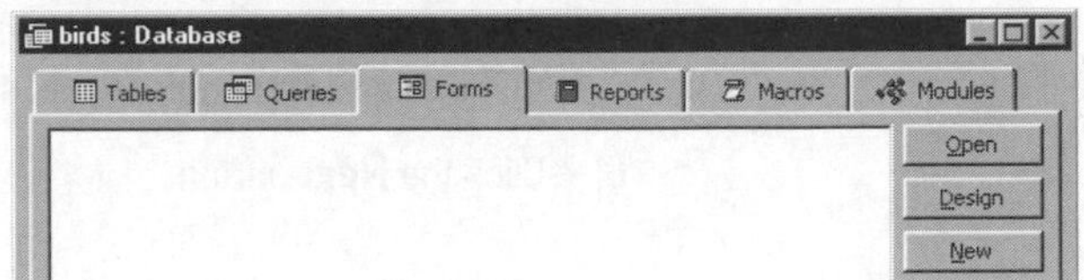

Click the **New** button. As with the Table Wizard,the Form Wizard offers a number of semi-automated options.

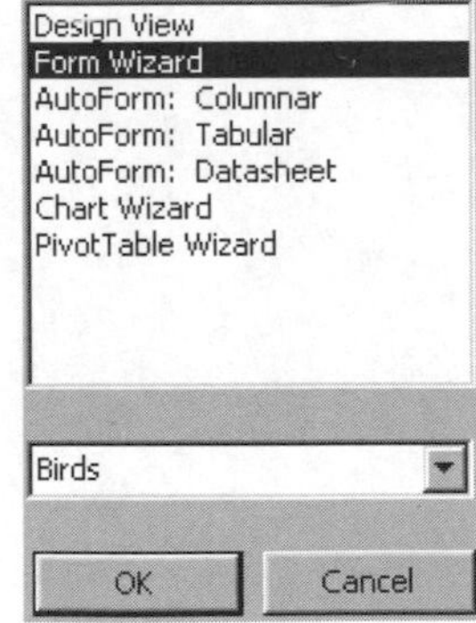

2) Select, for example, the AutoForm: Columnar option, select the Birds table, and have a look at (but don't save) the result.
3) Starting again from the Database dialog box, click the **New** button. This time, choose the Form Wizard.
4) Select the table on which the form is based – Birds.

   Click **OK**. This starts the Form Wizard.
5) You've seen something like this before, when you used the Table Wizard to design your Birds table in Section 5.2. The screen shows two list boxes. In the one on the left you can see all the fields in the table; in the one on the right, the fields that you have chosen to include in the form. Initially, the one on the right is empty.

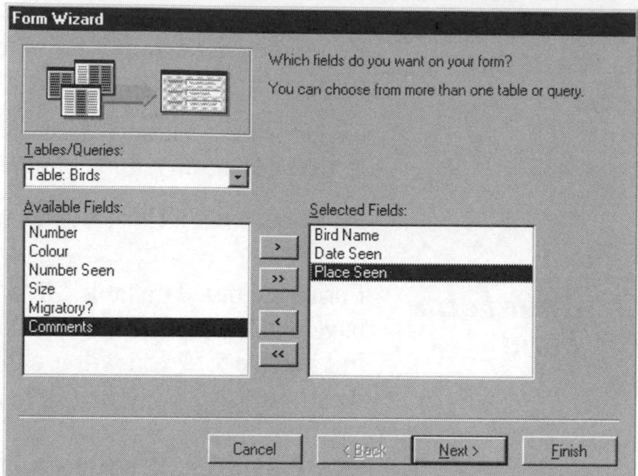

Move the fields you want to use in your form from the Available Fields box to the Selected Fields box by using the arrow buttons. For this Exercise, move the fields shown above.

6) Click the **Next** button.

7) The Form Wizard then presents you with three possible layouts for the form. You can get an idea of what each is like by selecting them in turn. The best for your purposes is Columnar. Select this one, and click the **Next** button.

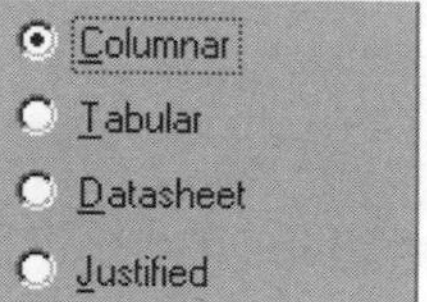

8) The Wizard then offers you a choice of styles for the Form.

   Again, you can preview styles by selecting them in turn.

   For Birds, there can be no contest: the most appropriate style has got to be Clouds.

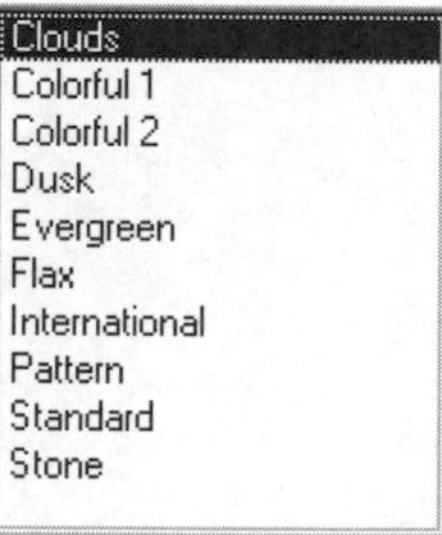

   Select this one and click the **Next** button.

9) Access suggests a name for the Form: change this to 'Birds Spotted' to make it easier to identify later.

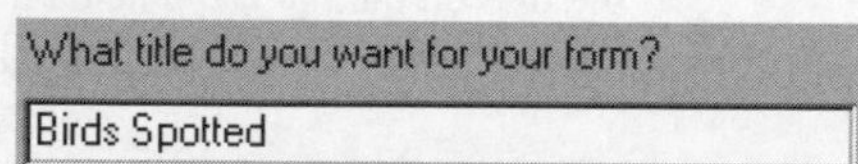

   You can then either use the form immediately, or go back and modify it. Select the option to Open the form.

Do you want to open the form or modify the form's design?

Open the form to view or enter information.

Modify the form's design.

Click the **Finish** button.

You can then use the form to view selected information from the records in your table.

Using Your Form to View Records

When you finish Exercise 5.19 you are immediately presented with a Forms view of the Birds table. At other times, to get to the same point, you start from the Database dialog box, click on the Forms tab, select the form (Birds Spotted), and click the **Open** button.

The form shows the selected fields from the first record in the table.

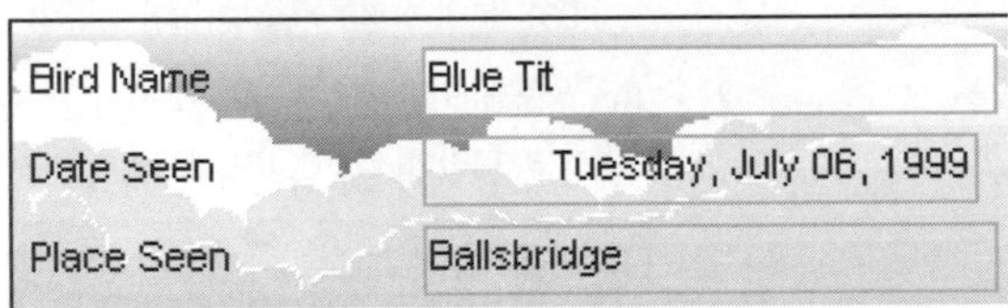

You can step through the different records one at a time by using the navigation buttons shown at the foot of the screen.

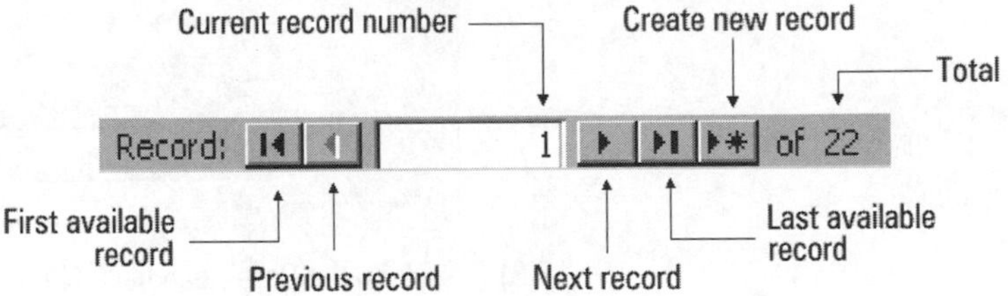

Sorting in Form View

As in Datasheet view, you can sort the records by selection: click on the field that you want to use as the basis for the sort, and click the Sort Ascending or Sort Descending button in the toolbar.

You can also perform a multiple-criteria sort, in exactly the same way as in Datasheet view: choose **Records | Filter | Advanced Filter/Sort**.

Filtering by Selection in Form View

Filter by Selection button

In Form view, you can filter records by selection, exactly as you did in Datasheet view: find a record that meets your criterion, select the relevant field (or the part of it that is of interest) and click the Filter by Selection button in the toolbar. You will see that the number of records shown beside the navigation buttons reflects the smaller number of records that satisfies your criterion.

As in Datasheet view, you can filter these records again to refine further the search for the records that you are interested in.

Filtering by Form

Another option is to Filter by Form. For example, Exercise 5.20 shows you how to restrict the records displayed to those that you have actually spotted.

Filter by Form button

Exercise 5.20: Using a Form to Filter Records

1) Open the Birds Spotted form. Click the Filter by Form button in the toolbar or choose **Records | Filter | Filter by Form.**
2) Access displays a blank form, into which you can enter your filter criteria. In this case, the date is the criterion of interest.

Number	
Bird Name	
Colour	
Number Seen	
Size	
Migratory?	☐
Date Seen	>0
Place Seen	

3) Click on the Date Seen field. Notice that the drop-down list shows all the dates on which you recorded sightings. If you wanted to find all the birds you spotted on a specific date, you'd simply pick the date from the list.
4) What you want, however, is to find the birds you spotted on any date, that is, any record for which the date is not blank (or is greater than zero).

   So enter the following in the Date Seen field: >0.

Apply/Remove Filter button

5) Click the Apply Filter button in the toolbar: the first record with the date filled in is shown, and the record count shows the number of such records in the table.
6) Click the Remove Filter button in the toolbar (as it is now), and all the records in the table are viewable.

Wildcards in Filters and Queries

You don't have to be precise when you are entering your filter criteria: you can use so-called *wildcards* to tell Access 'Give me everyone whose name includes Donnel', and it will get the Donnellys, McDonnells, MacDonnells, O'Donnells, and so on.

The most important wildcards are an asterisk (*) and a question mark (?). When you specify the criteria for a query or a filter, an asterisk (*) means 'anything or nothing', and a question mark (?) means 'any single character'.

Say, for example, you want to find all the birds that have 'Great' in their names. In the Bird Name field in the form, enter the following:

Great

When you apply the filter, only the three records that include 'Great' will be displayed.

Or, if you want to find birds that are coloured black or brown, you construct a filter with the colour specified as b????. When you apply this filter, you will be presented only with records that have the colour specified as five characters beginning with the letter 'b'. You would not, for example, get blue birds (for the obvious reason that 'blue' has only four characters).

Creating an All Fields Form

The easiest way to enter information into your table is to use a form. However, if you are adding new records to the table, the form you created in the previous Exercise is not sufficiently detailed. You need a new form – one that enables you to fill in all the details for each bird (an 'All Fields Form'). Let's make one the quick way.

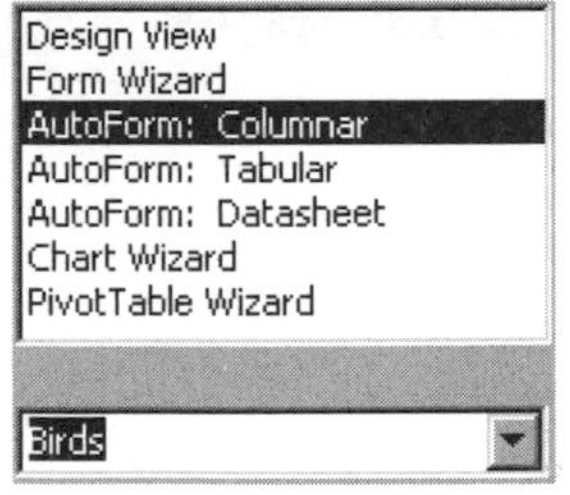

Exercise 5.21: Creating an All Fields Form

1) From the Database dialog box, select the Forms tab. Click the **New** button.

2) Select AutoForm: Columnar, and specify the Birds table.

3) Click **OK**.

   And that's it. Access now presents a new form, ready for use.

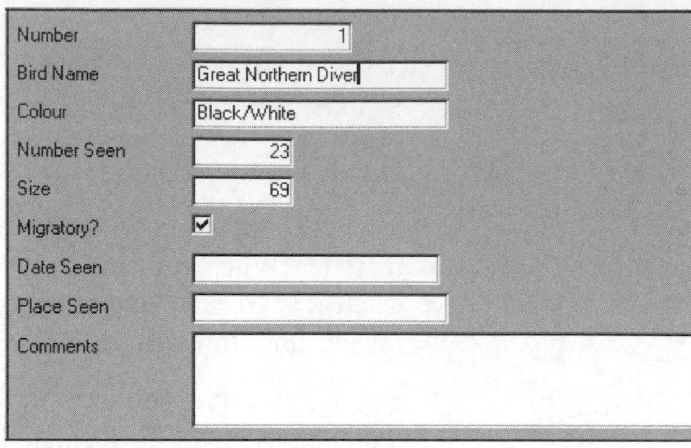

Close your form, and save it with the name Allfields.

You can subsequently access this form at any time from the Forms tab on the Database dialog box, and use it to view the records in your table, to change them, or to create new records.

Using a Form to Create New Records

Create New Record button

To create new records, click on the Create New Record button in the navigation bar at the bottom of the form. Access presents a new, blank form. Fill it in.

You can complete the fields in any order by clicking in the field and entering the information. The easiest way to complete the form, however, is to fill in the first field (Access automatically positions the cursor there when you open the form), and then proceed in order through the fields either by pressing TAB or by pressing ENTER. When you have filled in the last field in the form, press TAB or ENTER to open up a new, blank form.

Exercise 5.22: Using a Form to Enter a New Record

1) Open the Allfields form from the Database dialog box. Click the Create New Record button and enter the details of the Golden Eagle as follows:

Bird Name:	Golden Eagle
Colour:	Golden Brown
Size:	120
Date Seen:	6th September 2000
Place Seen:	Colorado

Using a Form to Modify Existing Records

Any changes you make to the information in a form are immediately reflected in the table. Remember that the Datasheet and the Form views are just two ways of looking at the same information. To use the form to modify the information in your table, locate the record you are interested in (by paging through the records, one at a time, or by sorting or filtering), click on the field you want to change, and delete, overwrite, or add information.

Exercise 5.23: Using a Form to Modify Records

1) Use the Allfields form to complete all the remaining empty fields in all the records in your table. Make up information – for the exercise, it doesn't have to be accurate, or even truthful!

Modifying Form Layout and Content

For the moment, and for most purposes, the Form Wizard does a fine job. However, Access enables you to design forms from scratch, and to redesign ones that have already been designed. To see some of the possibilities (and there is no need to go into this too deeply), try Exercise 5.24.

Exercise 5.24: Changing the Layout and Content of a Form

1) Open the Birds Spotted form in Design view. (To do this, at the Database dialog box, click the Forms tab; then select the Birds Spotted form, and click the Design button.)

2) In Design view you see the different elements in your form set against a grid. Notice how each field has a *title* and a *textbox*.

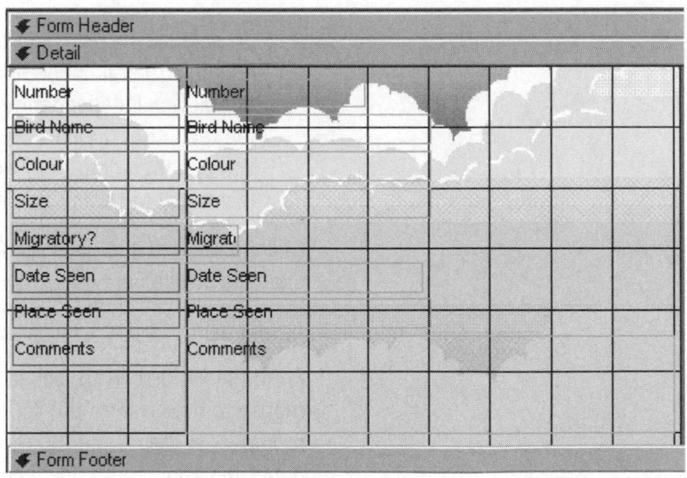

You can change the formatting of both titles and textboxes: select the Bird Name title and click the Bold button in the toolbar. Select the Bird Name text box and click the Italics button in the toolbar.

The toolbar offers a variety of formatting options:

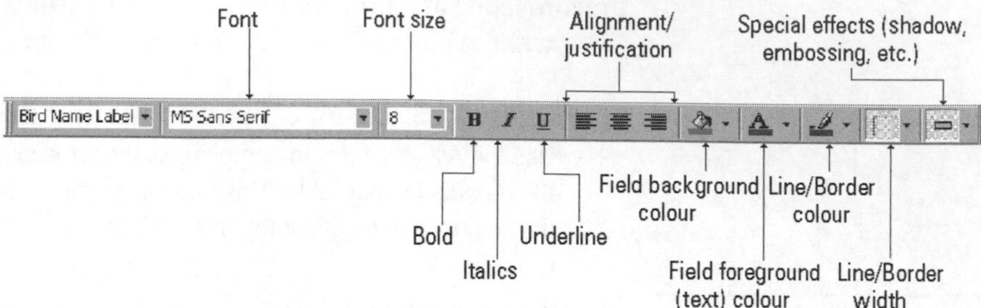

Experiment with these to see the possibilities. Remember, however, that the best forms are simple, are laid out clearly, and use colour and other graphic devices sparingly.

3) You can change the shape and size of a field on the form.

- When you select a field, a number of 'sizing handles' are displayed around it. Click on any of these, and use the mouse to drag the border to the new position.
- You can also change the position of a field: click on the border anywhere *except* on one of the handles. The cursor changes to an 'open hand' shape. You can then drag the field to its new location.
- By default, the label and the text box move together, and maintain their position relative to one another. To move the label or text box independently, click on the larger 'move handle' at the top left of the field. The cursor changes to a 'pointing hand'. You can then drag the field to its new location. You might find this tricky to begin with, but it will become easier with practice.

Change the size and position of the fields and labels as shown in the example on the next page.

4) To add a new field to a cut-down form, choose **View | Field List**.

From the list displayed, select the field you want to add and use the mouse to drag it from the list to the approximate location you want it to appear in the form. (You may have to move the Form Footer Bar out of the way. To do this, click on the top line of the footer until the cursor changes, then drag it and drop it in its new position.)

For example, the following screens show the effect:

Before

Adding the field

After

5) To import an image or graphic file into your form, choose **Insert | Picture**.

   Access displays a dialog box in which you specify the graphic you want to include in the form. You can navigate around the hard disk, diskette, or CD-ROM to find the picture you want. If you don't have one of your own, a variety is available in C:\Program Files\Microsoft Office\Clipart\Popular. Select the file named Dove in that subfolder and then click **OK**.

6) The graphic is now inserted onto your form.

   To change the size of the image, right-click it, and then choose **Properties**; then, on the Format tab, change Size Mode to Zoom.

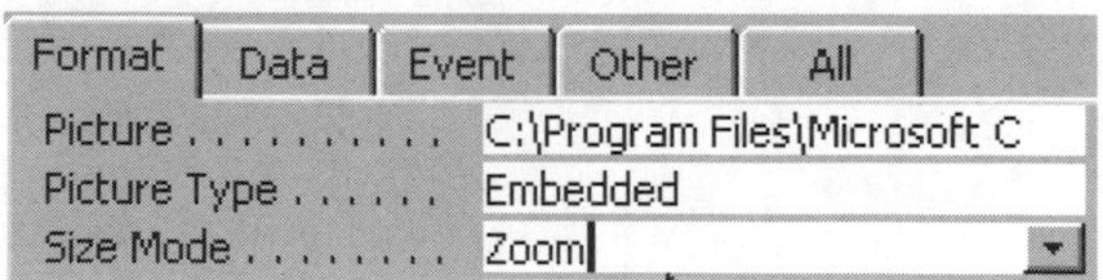

   Close the dialog box; then click on one of the sizing handles at the corners of the picture, and drag it inwards to the required size.

   To move the image to a different location on the form, click on the picture anywhere except on the sizing handles. Hold down the mouse button; the cursor changes to hand. Now drag the picture to the right side of the form and release the mouse button.

Moving a graphic image

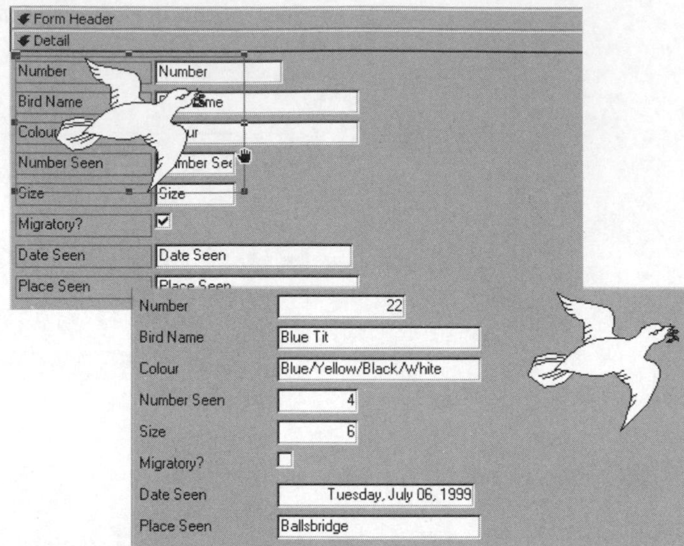

Form View button

Now, click the Form View button on the toolbar and admire your handiwork. Switch back to Design view by clicking the same button again.

7) Click the Close button or choose **File | Close**.

Access prompts you to save your work.

Section Summary: So Now You Know

Forms enable you to view your database records one at a time. As forms are based on tables, you can create a form only *after* you have created a table. Both forms and the datasheet contain the *same information:* any change you make to data in a form is reflected immediately in the datasheet, and any change you make in a datasheet is reflected in the associated forms.

You can create forms quickly and easily with the Access *Form Wizard*. You simply select which fields from the table you want to include on your form, choose from a range of data layouts and decorative styles, and give your form a name.

You can use a form to view existing records in your database. A series of *navigation buttons* along the bottom of the form enable you to step through different records one at a time. Within form view you can sort and filter records, and use *wildcard characters* (* and ?).

An *all fields form* is one that contains every field in your table, and is used typically for entering data. The fastest way to enter data is to fill in the first field and, pressing TAB or ENTER after each one, proceed in order through the fields. When you have filled in the last field in the form, press TAB or ENTER to open up a new, blank form.

To use a form to *modify* the information in your table, locate the record you are interested in (by paging through the records, one at a time, or by sorting or filtering), click on the field you want to change, and delete, overwrite, or add information. You can include graphic images in your forms.

In Design view you can change the formatting of both field titles and text boxes, adjust the shape and size of any field, add new fields, and import, resize and reposition graphic images.

Section 5.6: Working with Reports

In This Section

In the earlier Sections of this Module you learnt how to put information into your database, and how to manipulate it and view it on screen. In this Section you will learn how to get information out, and how to present it in a useful and accessible way.

New Skills

At the end of this Section you should be able to:

- Present information you have extracted from the database on screen
- Print out a report of information from the database
- Create and customise headers and footers

New Words

At the end of this Section you should be able to explain the following terms:

- Report
- Header
- Footer

Your First Report

Generally speaking, a report is a way of presenting information in printed form. However, the word is increasingly used to describe information in a form suitable for printing – even if it is only displayed on screen.

Report
A document (printed or on screen) that presents information in a structured way.

Print button

You have already seen how Access allows you to structure and organise your data, by filtering and sorting records, by using forms to choose the fields you want to display, and so on. You can, of course, print out any of these screens, and this may be quite adequate for your purposes. Simply click the Print button on the toolbar, or choose **File | Print**.

However, Access gives you a great deal of control over how your information is presented. You can lay it out so that important information is highlighted, data can be grouped into categories, and you can give totals and count information for each category, subcategory, and for the entire report. Some of this is beyond the scope of this book, but you will find that Access provides automated solutions that will satisfy most of your requirements, most of the time. The simplest way to produce a report is to use the AutoReports feature of Access.

Exercise 5.25: Using AutoReports to Produce a Report

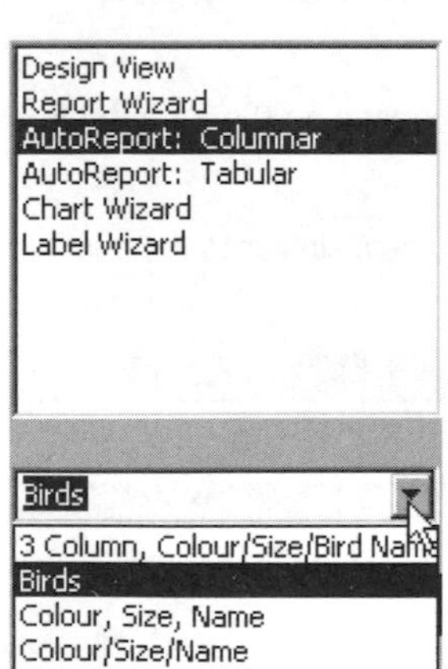

1) From the Database screen, select the Reports tab.
2) Click the **New** button.
3) Choose AutoReport: Columnar
4) In the drop-down list of tables and queries, specify the Birds table.
5) Click **OK** and admire the report on the screen. To view the following pages, click the **Next Page** button at the bottom left of your screen.
6) If you have a printer, click the Print button on the toolbar, or choose **File | Print**. Then hang your finished report on the wall.
7) Close the Report screen, and (if it is displayed) close the Design screen. You will be prompted to save. Save the report as 'My First Report'.

   Now click the Preview button to view it again – then close it. You can store lots of different reports to use and re-use later.

Columnar Format view

Tabular Format view

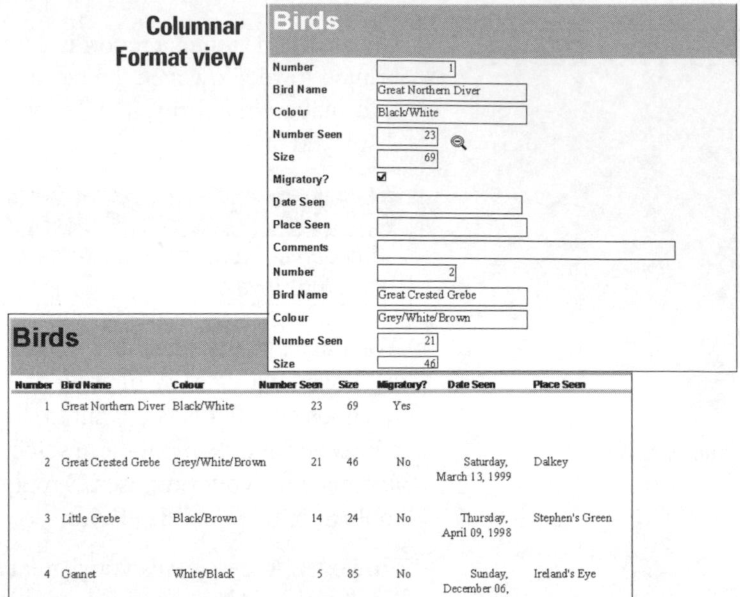
Birds

Number	1
Bird Name	Great Northern Diver
Colour	Black/White
Number Seen	23
Size	69
Migratory?	☑
Date Seen	
Place Seen	
Comments	
Number	2
Bird Name	Great Crested Grebe
Colour	Grey/White/Brown
Number Seen	21
Size	46

Birds

Number	Bird Name	Colour	Number Seen	Size	Migratory?	Date Seen	Place Seen
1	Great Northern Diver	Black/White	23	69	Yes		
2	Great Crested Grebe	Grey/White/Brown	21	46	No	Saturday, March 13, 1999	Dalkey
3	Little Grebe	Black/Brown	14	24	No	Thursday, April 09, 1998	Stephen's Green
4	Gannet	White/Black	5	85	No	Sunday, December 06, 1998	Ireland's Eye
5	Fulmar	White/Grey	3	45	No		

Reports using AutoFormat

While AutoReports make it very easy to produce good-looking reports, you can take full control of the content and layout of your report. But even here Access makes it easy for you: you can use the Wizard.

Exercise 5.26: Using the Report Wizard

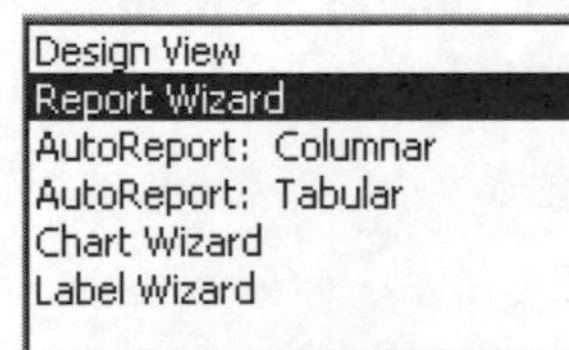

1) From the Database screen, select the Reports tab. Click the **New** button. Select the Report Wizard.

   Specify that you want to produce a report based on the Birds table. Click **OK**.

2) You are presented with a familiar-looking screen, similar to the one used to create tables and forms.

   Available Fields: Number, Colour, Number Seen, Size, Migratory?, Comments

   > >> < <<

   Selected Fields: Bird Name, Date Seen, Place Seen

   Choose the fields you want to include in the report from the list on the left and move them into the list on the right. For this exercise, include the fields shown above.

Click the **Next** button.

3) Specify how you want the records in the report to be grouped. You could, for example, produce a report for each bird, showing when and where you saw it: this would group together all the sightings of a given bird. For this exercise, we'll produce a report by date: this will group together all sightings made on the same date. Select Date Seen and click the > button.

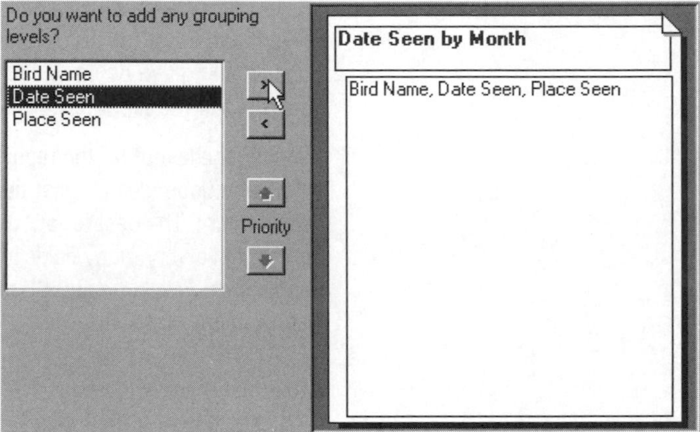

Click the Grouping Options button.

You can group the sightings by year, quarter, month, week, day, etc.

Select Month and click **OK**.

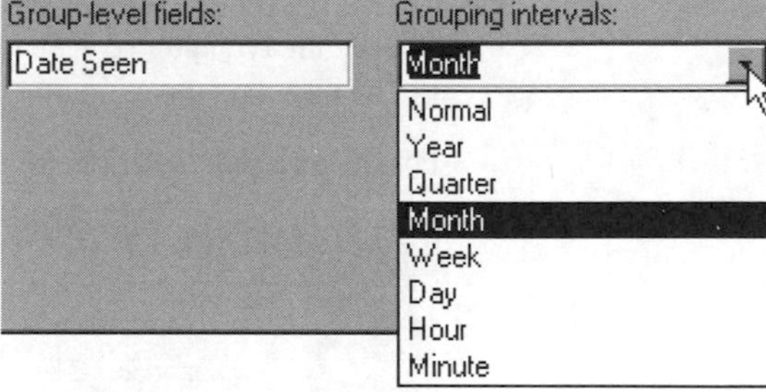

Click the **Next** button.

4) Next specify the order in which you want the records to be shown in the report. Select Date Seen as the first sort criterion. The Sort button is initially set to sort ascending. To change the order, just click the button: each time you click it, it switches between ascending and descending. Make it descending. This means that your report will show the most recent sightings first.

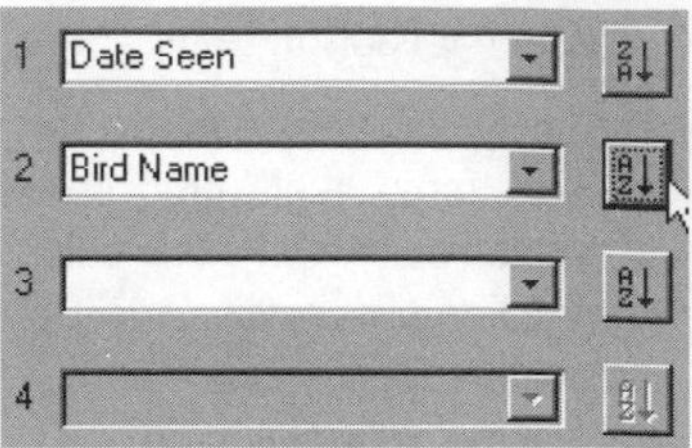

Select Bird Name as the second sort criterion, and make it ascending. This means that the report will show the most recent sightings first, and on any given day it will show the birds sighted in alphabetical order. Click the **Next** button.

5) Specify the layout for the report. As in previous Wizard exercises, you can get a good idea of what the final result will look like by selecting each in turn. The best for our purposes is Outline 2, and, because we do not have very many fields in our report, Portrait. Select these options, and click the **Next** button.

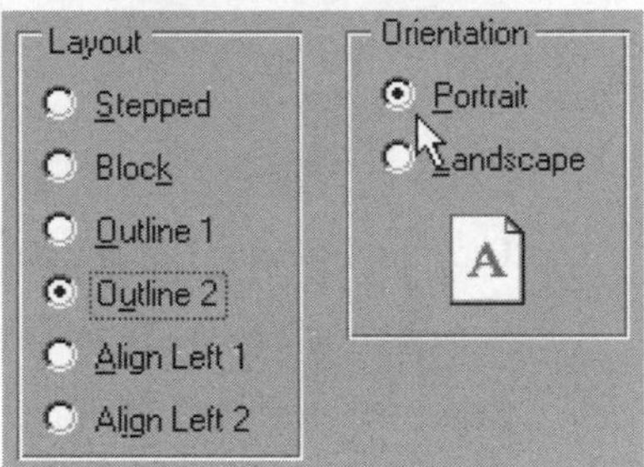

6) Specify the typographic style for the report. Again, see what they look like by selecting them in turn.

For the exercise, select Bold, and click the **Next** button.

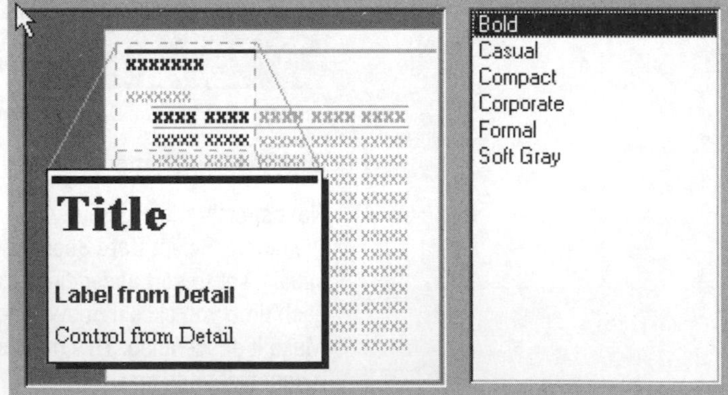

7) Finally, give the report a title: Spotting Record.

What title do you want for your report?

Spotting Record

8) Choose the Preview option.

Do you want to preview the report or modify the report's design?

(•) Preview the report.

( ) Modify the report's design.

Click the **Finish** button.

You then see the report on screen.

If it is exactly what you want, click the Print button on the toolbar, or choose **File | Print**.

Report produced from Report Wizard

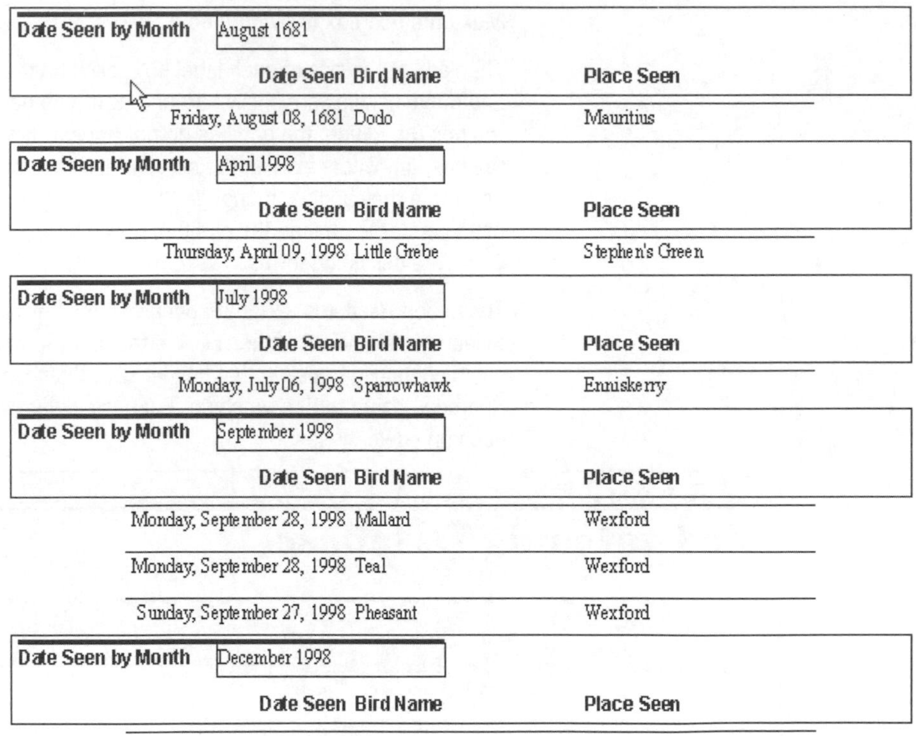

Date Seen by Month August 1681

Date Seen	Bird Name	Place Seen
Friday, August 08, 1681	Dodo	Mauritius

Date Seen by Month April 1998

Date Seen	Bird Name	Place Seen
Thursday, April 09, 1998	Little Grebe	Stephen's Green

Date Seen by Month July 1998

Date Seen	Bird Name	Place Seen
Monday, July 06, 1998	Sparrowhawk	Enniskerry

Date Seen by Month September 1998

Date Seen	Bird Name	Place Seen
Monday, September 28, 1998	Mallard	Wexford
Monday, September 28, 1998	Teal	Wexford
Sunday, September 27, 1998	Pheasant	Wexford

Date Seen by Month December 1998

Date Seen	Bird Name	Place Seen

Modifying the Report Layout

If the report produced by the Report Wizard does not meet your requirements exactly, you may want to fine-tune it. For example, the report you created in Exercise 5.26 needs to be tidied up a little. The range of possibilities in Access is very wide: we'll confine ourselves to a few.

Exercise 5.27: Fine-Tuning Your Report

1) Open in Design View the report you created in Exercise 5.26.

   (To do this, at the Database dialog box, select the Reports tab, then select the Spotting Record report, and click the Design button.)

2) The different elements in your report are shown against a grid. Each field has a title and a text box. You can change the content or formatting of these in the same way as you did when you were designing a form (Exercise 5.24). Double-click in the label boxes listed below, and change them as follows:

Before	After
Date Seen by Month	Month
Date Seen	Date

   Make the text box for Month bold.

   Then adjust the size of each label box: click on the box. The sizing and move handles are shown around it. (If you have already selected the box for editing, the handles do not appear: first click away from the box, anywhere else on the screen, and then click once on the box.) Use the handles to change the shape and size of the box, or the hand pointer to change the position of the box, just like you did when you were designing forms.

3) The Report Header is text that appears at the beginning of your report. Select the text box, and then click in the text (Spotting Record). You can then modify or delete that header text. Change the header text from Spotting Record to Birdwatching Database. Enlarge the text box to accommodate the text.

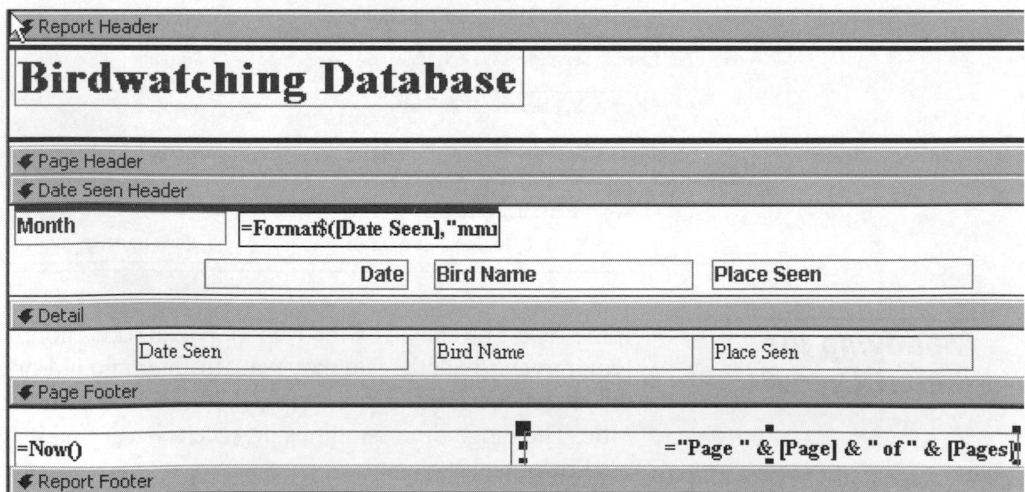

4) The Page Header is text that appears under the Report Header on page 1, and at the top of every page in your report. Move the mouse pointer slowly over the line dividing Page Header and Date Seen Header – it becomes a moving tool.

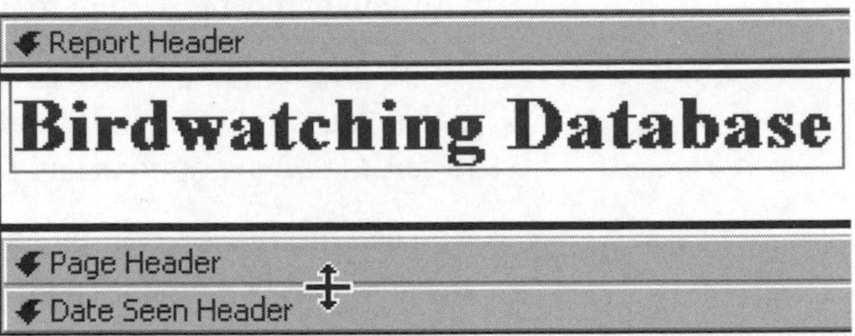

Click, hold and drag the Date Seen Header bar down to make room between it and the Page Header.

Label button

5) Now, click on the Label button of the Toolbox (if the Toolbox is not displayed, choose **View | Toolbox**) and move it over the Page Header field – it is now a text box drawing tool. In the Page Header field, click the mouse where the top-left corner of the text box should be, hold down the mouse button, drag the pointer to where the bottom-right corner should be, and release the mouse button. Type the following text into the newly created text box: Copyright: Your Name.

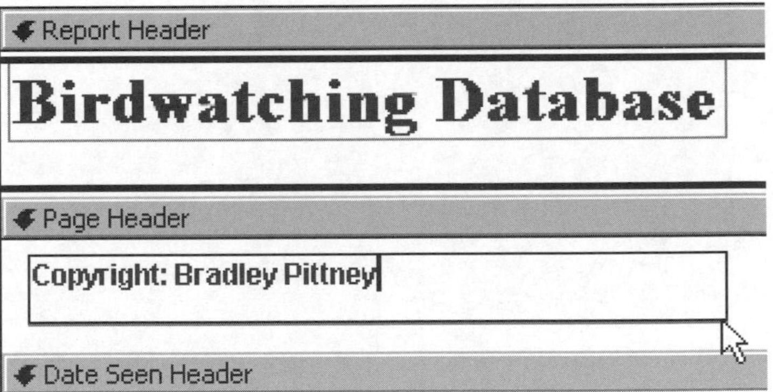

You've now created a Page Header.

6) The Page Footer appears at the end of each page in your report, and the Report Footer appears at the very end of the report. You can create footers in the same way as you created headers. If you do not want a particular header or footer in your report, just reduce the size of the text area to zero (the reverse of what you did in step 4).

7) Close the Report Design dialog box.

   Access prompts you to save your work.

8) From the Database dialog box, click the **Preview** button to open the report again, and critically evaluate the effect of your changes.

Section Summary: So Now You Know

A *database report* is a document (printed or on screen) that presents information in a structured way. Access provides two automated solutions – *AutoReports* and the *Report Wizard* – that will satisfy most reporting requirements.

To use the Report Wizard, choose the relevant table, select the fields you want to include, and specify the *grouping*, the *sort order*, the *layout* options and the typographic *styles*.

You can modify a report by changing the content of each field's title and text box, and by adjusting the size of each field's label.

You can insert or amend *headers* and *footers* to the report as a whole or to each page.

This Module should have given you a glimpse of the power of Access, and enough confidence to explore that power further by yourself. If you want to use more advanced features, the Help features included with Access provide you with plenty of guidance.

Presentations

Tomorrow you have two appointments: a visit to the dentist and a presentation to an audience of strangers and friends.

Which one fills you with greater terror?

Whether it's to a group of potential customers, a national conference of fellow workers, or a local community group, delivering an address can be an intimidating prospect.

Faced with these situations, you'll want to learn about any tools that will help you to feel less pressurised and more organised – tools that will make you more confident and help you make your points more effectively. This is where presentation software comes in.

In this Module you will discover how to create support materials that will reinforce your message, both textually and graphically. You will also find out how to design your materials – both on-screen slides and paper handouts – so as to maximise their audience impact.

Software won't turn a bad presentation into a good one. But it can help a good presentation succeed in its aim: better communication of your bright ideas.

Think of this Module as your chance to speak rather than be spoken to. Good luck with it.

Section 6.1: Presentation Basics

In This Section

This Section deals with the basic concepts of presentation software, introduces you to the terminology you will need, and lets you sample the possibilities on offer.

New Skills

At the end of this Section you should be able to:

- Explain what presentation software is used for
- Start and quit PowerPoint
- Open and close a presentation
- Show a PowerPoint presentation on your computer
- View the presentation in a variety of ways
- Print out a PowerPoint presentation – as OHPs, handouts, or 35mm slides
- Use PowerPoint's online help facilities
- Modify PowerPoint's toolbar display

New Words

At the end of this Section you should be able to explain the following terms:

- Presentation
- Slide
- Slide view
- Outline view
- Slide Sorter view
- Notes Page view
- Slide Show view
- OHP

Presentations and Presentation Software

When you demonstrate a new product, describe the results of your research, or announce a new organisational structure, you typically make a speech. To grab your audience's attention, and reinforce your messages, you show them a variety of visual aids while you are talking. To ensure they retain key information, you give them handouts to take away and study afterwards. That's a presentation.

Presentation software helps you design and produce the visual aids and the handouts. Unfortunately, it doesn't help you with the speech, but it does help you to organise your thoughts, and it helps ensure that questions and comments from the audience don't put you off course. For the ECDL, you have to know how to produce the visual aids and handouts; you don't have to make a speech. Phew!

The visual aids reinforce and complement what you say – they shouldn't *duplicate* it. They should include images wherever possible (pictures, graphs, charts, maps, cartoons, diagrams). Text should be kept to a minimum, using headline style and bullet points.

The visual aids can be printed on paper or on overhead projection foils (OHP), they can be output to 35mm transparencies (slides), they can be displayed directly on the computer screen, or they can be projected from the computer using a directly connected projector. The choice of output depends on the number of people in your audience, the size of the room in which you are making the presentation, and the technology available.

Although 35mm slides are probably the least common form of output, most presentation software packages call the basic element of a presentation a 'slide'.

Slide

A slide is the basic building block of a visual presentation. It is equivalent to a page in a printed document; it can contain both text and graphics.

Starting PowerPoint

Double-click on the PowerPoint icon.

-or-

Choose **Start | Programs | PowerPoint**.

Opening an Existing Presentation

The file names of PowerPoint files end in .ppt, .pps, or .pot. (Each of these is used for different purposes, as you will see later.) This helps you to distinguish them from Word documents (.doc), Excel workbooks (.xls), and other file types.

To open an existing presentation, either:

- Select 'Open an Existing Presentation' on the first dialog box displayed when you start PowerPoint.

  -or-

- (If you have already been working in PowerPoint) Choose **File | Open** (or click the Open button on the Standard Toolbar).

Open button

Then select the file you want from the dialog box.

Exercise 6.1: Opening a Presentation

To experiment in this Section, open Dale Carnegie's presentation on presentations:

1) Choose **File | Open**.

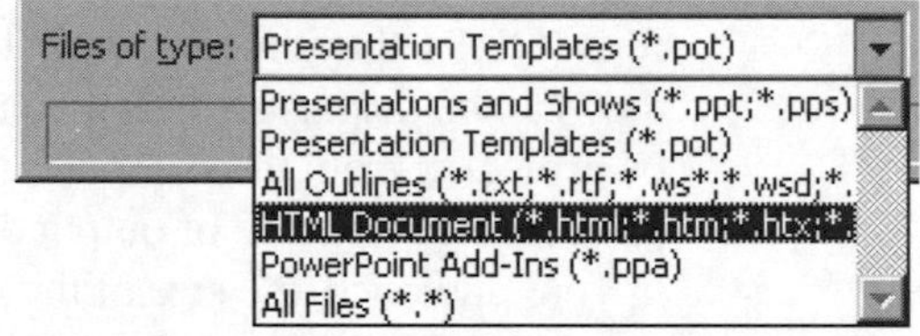

2) From the Files of type drop-down list, choose Presentation Templates. (The example we are going to use is this type of file; however, most PowerPoint files you will be working with are the default Presentations and Shows.)

3) Navigate to the Microsoft Office folder (usually a subfolder in Program Files), and from there to the Templates\Presentations folder. You will see a number of files listed. Scroll down to the Presentation Guidelines file, select it, and click **Open.**

Working with PowerPoint Presentations

PowerPoint enables you to look at the same material in a variety of different formats, to view individual slides, and to print out the presentation.

Different Views

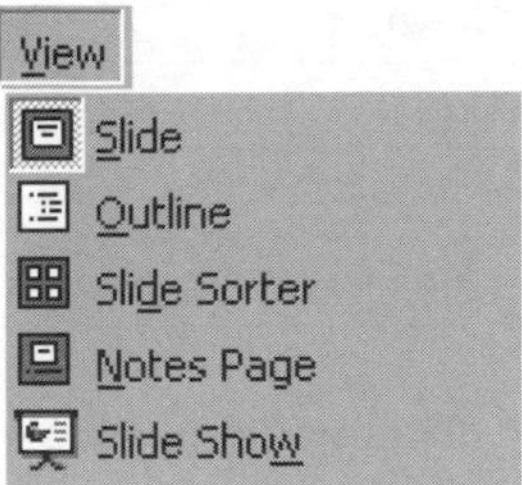

The different viewing options are available from the **View** menu.

- **Slide** lets you see one slide at a time. This is the normal viewing mode when you are creating a presentation: you are able to see what the finished product will look like, and you are able to edit the text, add graphics, and so on.
- **Outline** shows the text of all the slides, without formatting or graphics. It is most useful when you are organising your thoughts, or for checking or changing the overall structure of the presentation.
- **Slide Sorter** shows a miniature version of the entire slide show. You can use this to check the consistency of the layout and colour scheme, and also to check, and if necessary change, the order of the slides.
- **Notes Page** shows the slides one at a time, half-sized, with a space below for speaker's notes.
- **Slide Show** shows the slides full-screen (without any menu bars), exactly as they would appear projected. To exit from Slide Show view, press the ESC key.

At the bottom-left of the screen (except in Slide Show view), there are five icons, representing the five viewing modes – use these to switch quickly from one mode to another.

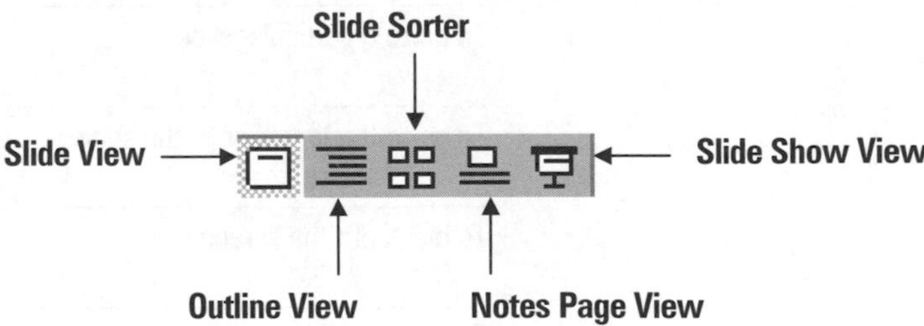

Zoom

The **View** menu also offers a Zoom option: use this to enlarge or reduce the slide shown on the screen.

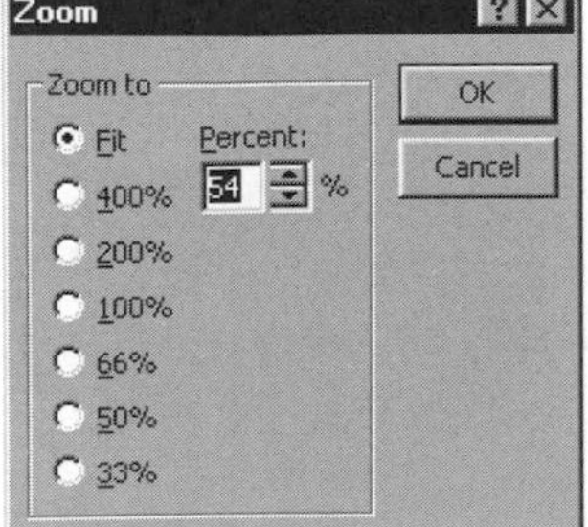

Finding Your Way Around a Presentation

Certain navigation keys can be used in all PowerPoint views:

To advance to the next slide	Press Page Down
To return to the previous slide	Press Page Up
To go to the first slide in the show	Press Home
To go to the last slide	Press End

In all views except Slide Show view, you can also use the scroll bar at the right of the screen to move forwards or backwards.

In Slide Show view, a wider range of options is available:

To advance to the next slide	Left mouse click Spacebar N Right arrow Down arrow ENTER Page Down
To return to the previous slide	BACKSPACE P Left arrow Up arrow Page Up
To go to a particular slide	Type the number of the slide, and press ENTER
To go to the first slide in the show	Hold down both mouse buttons for two seconds
To blank out the screen	B (for black) W (for white)
To return to the presentation	B or W again

If you forget any of these controls, don't worry: press F1 any time during a presentation and the full list of controls is displayed.

Exercise 6.2: Exercises in Navigation

1) In Slide view, go back and forth through the presentation, one slide at a time, using the keyboard.
2) In Slide Show view, go back and forth through the presentation, one slide at a time, using the mouse wherever possible.
3) Go to slide 4. What Tip is given on that slide?

Printing a Presentation

You can print out a PowerPoint presentation in a variety of ways, depending on your requirements and on the hardware at your disposal. Printing in PowerPoint is similar to printing in other applications:

Print button

First, choose **File | Print**, or click the print button in the button bar. Then, in the Print what: drop-down box, you can choose to print slides, outline, speaker notes, or handouts. If you choose handouts, you can choose the number of slides per handout.

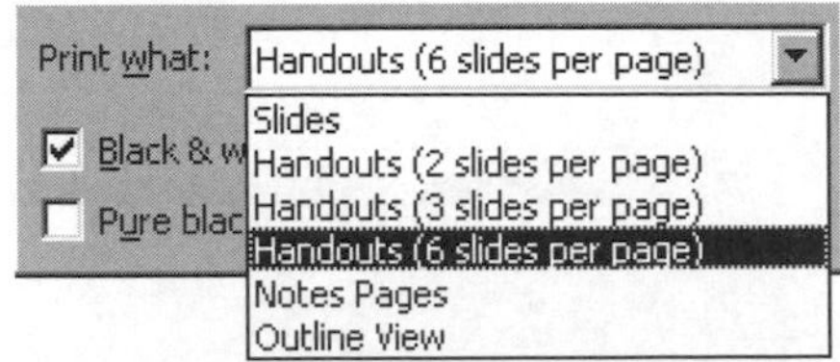

You can then specify, in the Print range area of the dialog box, whether you want to print all slides, the current slide, or a selected range of slides. To print a contiguous range of slides, type the number of the first slide, a hyphen, and the number of the last slide. To print non-contiguous slides, type the individual slide numbers separated by commas.

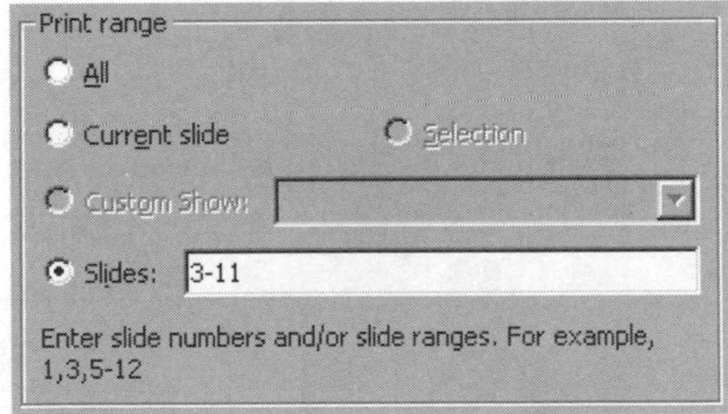

If you wish to produce overhead projection foils (OHPs), you need to load your printer with blank foils before clicking **OK** on the Print dialog.

If you wish to produce 35mm slides, you need to have a special desktop film recorder connected to your computer.

Exercise 6.3: Exercises in Printing

1) Print a set of handouts for the entire presentation with six slides on each page.
2) Print the first three slides of the presentation.
3) Print the first and fourth slide of the presentation.

Using Online Help

The online help built into PowerPoint provides additional information to help you use the various features and to get the most from the software. To use it, click **Help | Contents and Index**, choose the Index tab and type the word you are looking for. A list of topics is then shown: click on the one that most closely matches your interest, then click **Display**.

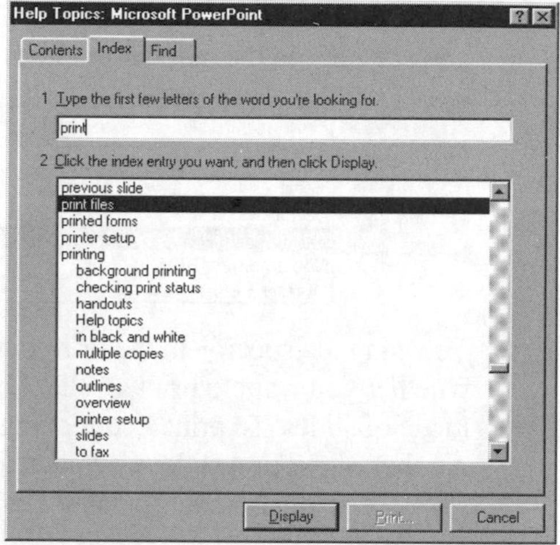

Office Assistant button

You can also get help by clicking the Office Assistant button, or (if PowerPoint is set up this way) by pressing the F1 key.

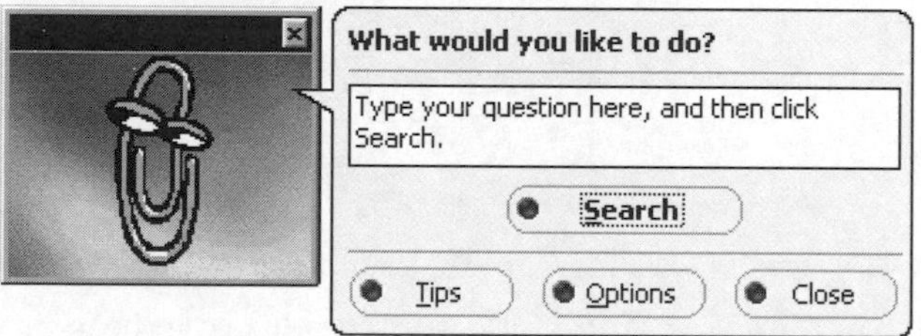

You should familiarise yourself with the online help facility: remember, you can use it while you are doing your ECDL test.

Modifying the Toolbar Display

The options in the menu bar give you access to all of PowerPoint's features. However, it is easier and quicker to select a feature by clicking a single button – and buttons may be displayed in a *button bar* or *toolbar.*

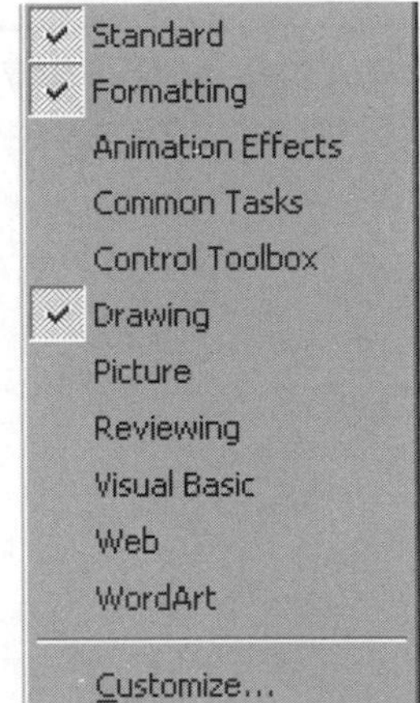

In PowerPoint, you can display a number of different toolbars, each covering a different range of functions. Click **View | Toolbars**. If they are not already displayed, check Standard, Formatting, and Drawing. These will be the most useful for your work in this Module.

Closing a Presentation

To close the presentation, choose **File | Close** or click the Close button on the presentation window.

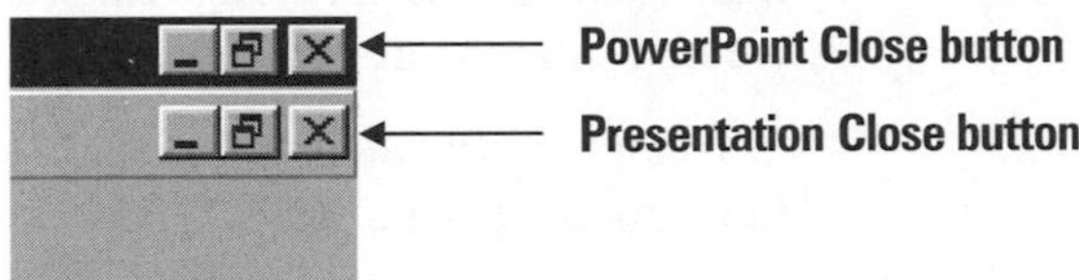

If you have made changes to the presentation since you last saved it, PowerPoint prompts you to save the changes before it closes the file.

Quitting PowerPoint

To leave PowerPoint, choose **File | Exit** or click the Close button on the PowerPoint window.

If you have left open any files containing unsaved work, PowerPoint prompts you to save them. You are then returned to the Windows desktop.

Section Summary: So Now You Know

A *presentation* is an address to an audience, accompanied by visual aids, such as slides or overhead projection foils (OHPs), and possibly handouts for the audience.

Presentation software, such as PowerPoint, helps you prepare all the support materials for a presentation.

The basic building blocks of a presentation are called *slides.*

While you are working with PowerPoint, you can view your slides in five ways – Slide view, Outline view, Slide Sorter view, Notes Page view, and Slide Show view. Slide Show view is what the audience sees when you are making the presentation.

You can move around a presentation using the Page Up and Page Down keys. Other options are available in Slide Show view.

You can print out your presentation materials in a variety of ways.

PowerPoint includes a built-in help facility that contains reference material on all the software's functions, and many helpful tips for creating convincing presentations.

You can modify the toolbar display so that the features you use most often are readily available.

Section 6.2: Creating Your First Slides

In This Section

In this Section you will learn how to use PowerPoint to create simple text-based slides.

New Skills

At the end of this Section you should be able to:

- Create a new, text-based slide
- Enter, edit, and delete text in a slide
- Import text and other objects into a PowerPoint slide
- Delete objects from a slide
- Delete a slide
- Save a presentation to hard disk or diskette

New Words

At the end of this Section you should be able to explain the following terms:

- Placeholder
- AutoLayout
- Portrait
- Landscape

Creating a New Presentation

To create a new presentation:

If you have already been using PowerPoint and it is still open:

- Choose **File | New**, then select the Blank Presentation icon, and click **OK**. Alternatively, click the New button on the Standard Toolbar.

New button

Otherwise:

- Start PowerPoint by double-clicking on the PowerPoint icon or by choosing **Start | Programs | PowerPoint**. Click the Blank presentation button and click **OK.**

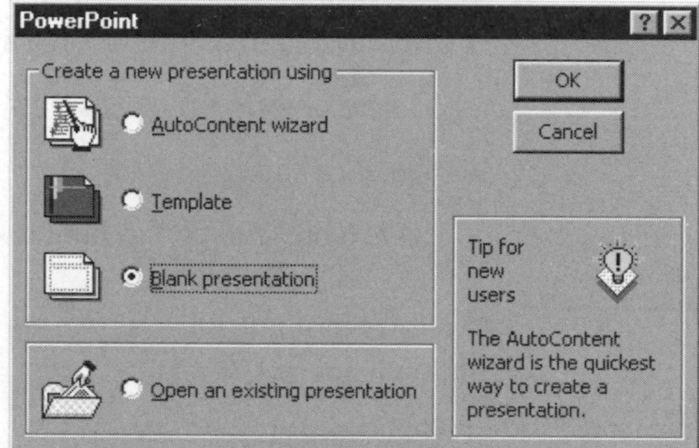

All the exercises in this Section contribute to creating the new presentation.

Exercise 6.4: Using the Placeholders to Enter Text

1) When you create a new presentation, PowerPoint displays a dialog box that offers a choice of ready-made layouts (called AutoLayouts) for your slides. As you click on a layout, PowerPoint shows the name of that layout in an area at the right of the dialog box.

   Select the first layout, which PowerPoint calls Title Slide, and click **OK.**

2) You are now shown a screen that contains two boxes surrounded by dotted lines. PowerPoint calls these boxes *placeholders.*

   Click on the top placeholder.

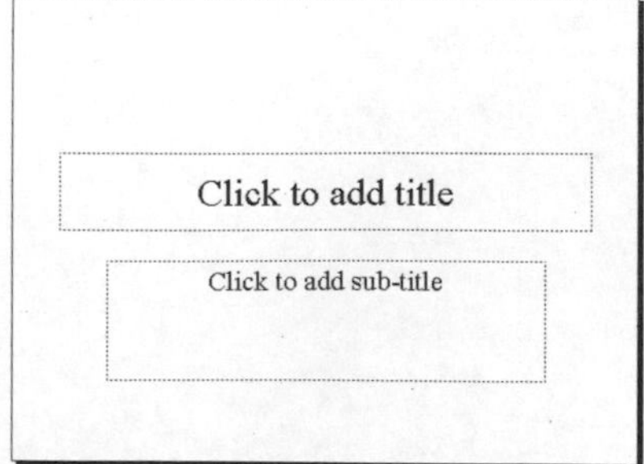

3) The border of the placeholder changes and a blinking text cursor appears inside it. You can now type text in the placeholder.

   Enter the following text in the first placeholder:

   New Product Launch

4) Click on the second placeholder and enter the following text:

   Round Wheels

   Your screen should now look like that shown on the right.

Congratulations! You have created the first slide of your first presentation in PowerPoint.

You can add, edit or delete text to a slide in any PowerPoint view, with the exception of Slide Show. Simply position the cursor where you want to make the changes and edit.

AutoLayout

One of 24 ready-made slide layouts. They typically include placeholders for text and other objects, such as images and charts.

Placeholder

A frame or box within a slide for holding text or graphics.

Remember:

- Click on a placeholder to select it so that you can type or edit text.
- Click outside the placeholder to deselect it.

Landscape or Portrait?

Most cinema screens, television screens and computer screens are wider than they are tall. This format is known as *landscape*; the alternative (taller) is known as *portrait.* Most of your slide presentations will be landscape, but if you ever want to produce a presentation in portrait format, choose **File | Page Setup**, and under Orientation, Slides, click Portrait.

Adding Slides to Your Presentation

New Slide button

After the title slide, you will want to create further slides to hold the main body of your presentation. Do this as follows:

Exercise 6.5: Adding Slides to a Presentation

1) Choose **Insert | New Slide** or click the New Slide button on the Standard Toolbar.
2) Select the slide layout you want to use.

   This time, select the Bulleted List.

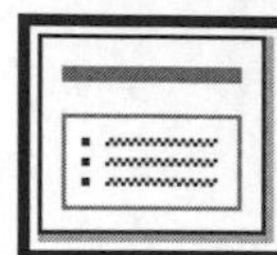

3) Click on the first placeholder and type: Amazing Features
4) Click on the second placeholder and type: Smooth Travelling for Passenger Comfort

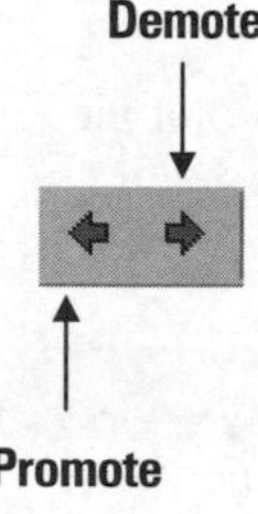

5) Press ENTER. PowerPoint creates a second bullet point on a new line. Type: Reduced Fuel Consumption
6) Press ENTER. Continue to enter the features as shown below. Use the Demote button to create the second level of bullet for the different modes of transport. (Use the Promote button to elevate them to the first level.)

Amazing Features

- Smooth Travelling for Passenger Comfort
- Reduced Fuel Consumption
- Longer Engine Life
- Multiple Uses in Transport Sector
  - Cars
  - Bicycles
  - Trucks

Well done! That's two slides created already.

Using Outline View

Perhaps the best way to organise your ideas is to use Outline view. This enables you to see the text of all your slides, arranged like a table of contents. In Outline view you can add, edit, and delete text. You can also change the order of the slides, and arrange the text so that the more important text is made more prominent.

Outline View

Shows the text of all your slides, so that you can judge how well your ideas and text flow from one slide to the next.

Outline View button

To see your presentation in Outline view, choose **View | Outline**, or click the Outline View button.

You can use the buttons on the Outlining Toolbar to move slides or text, show only slide titles, and change the indent level of titles and text. Try it.

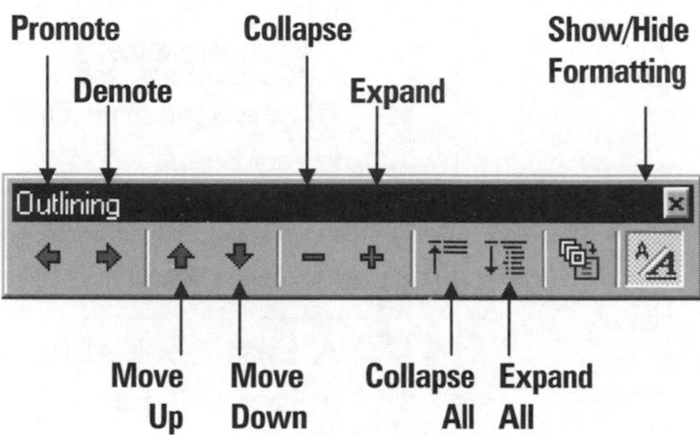

Exercise 6.6: Using Outline View to Add Slides

1) When you open Outline view, you see the text of the slides you have created so far. Click at the end of the text and press ENTER.

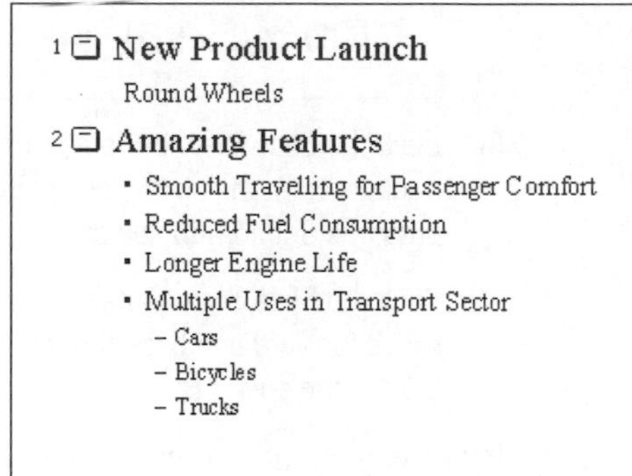

2) Type the headline for the next slide: Advantages and Disadvantages. Notice that the text takes on the attributes of the previous line of text: it appears as a minor bullet on slide number 2.

3) Correct the status of the headline by using the Promote button on the toolbar. Notice that when it reaches the top of the hierarchy (that is, when you have promoted it as far as you can), it is automatically assigned a slide number (3).

4) Add the text of the first advantage: Faster. Press ENTER. Notice once again that the new text takes on the attributes of the previous line of text: it appears as a separate slide. Use the Demote button to establish it as a subordinate point. Then add the remaining advantages and disadvantages, as shown below.

3 Advantages and Disadvantages
- Faster
- Smoother
- Easier to Start
- Harder to Control
- Needs Replacement of Existing Equipment
- Very Boring

5) Add four more slides, with text as shown below. Note that the last three contain only a headline.

4 A First Look at the New Product
- Fantastic Breakthrough in Wheel Technology
- Worldwide Patents Applied For
- Production Commences Q2 2000

5 Sales & Marketing

6 Sales Projections

7 Product Identity Scheme

Slide View button

6) Click the Slide View button, or choose **View | Slide**. Move forward and back through the slides (using any of the methods described in the previous Section) to see the effect of your work.

Slide Show button

7) Click the Slide Show button, or choose **View | Slide Show.** Again, move forward and back through the presentation to see how it would look to the audience.

By now you should realise that you can create an acceptable PowerPoint presentation very quickly.

Notice that PowerPoint assumes that some of the slides will have more text added later, and has created placeholders for that text. (The placeholder text ('Click to add text' etc.) is not displayed in Slide Show view.)

Copying Text within PowerPoint

To copy text from one slide to another, or from one part of a slide to another, select the text by clicking and dragging, then choose **Edit | Copy** (or hold down the CTRL key and press c). Then position your cursor where you want the text to appear and choose **Edit | Paste** (or hold down the CTRL key and press v).

Exercise 6.7: Moving Text within PowerPoint

1) Open slide number 3 (Advantages and Disadvantages) in Slide view.

2) Choose **Format | Slide Layout**, and select the Two Column Text layout.

   Click **Apply**.

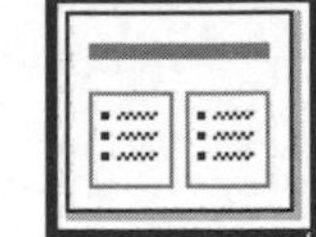

3) Select the last three bulleted points.

4) Choose **Edit | Cut.**

5) Click in the right-hand text placeholder.

6) Choose **Edit | Paste.**

7) The three 'disadvantage' points are moved into position.

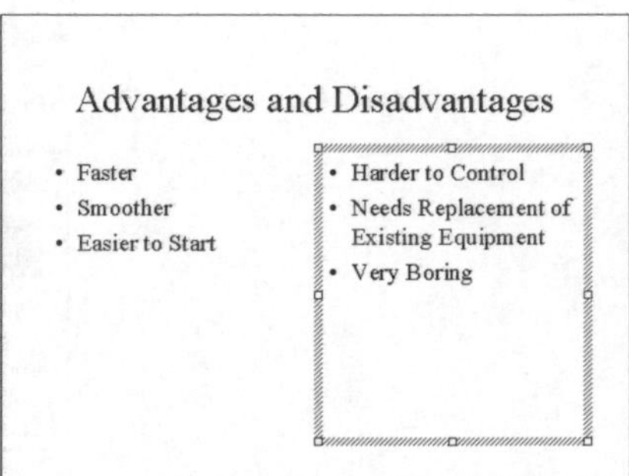

Importing Text from Another Application

If you have text in another application, such as Microsoft Word, you can use that text in PowerPoint without having to retype it. The simplest way is to select the text in the other application, choose **Edit | Copy** (or hold down the CTRL key and press c), and then, in PowerPoint, position your cursor where you want the text to appear and choose **Edit | Paste** (or hold down the CTRL key and press v). You can paste the text in any PowerPoint view except Slide Show.

You can also open a Word file in PowerPoint. Choose **File | Open**, select the file you are interested in, and click **Open.** PowerPoint tries to guess how you want the text treated: if you have not done any formatting in Word, it treats each paragraph as a separate slide. If you have used Word paragraph formats or tabs, PowerPoint interprets these as best it can. In any case, you can rearrange and reformat the text, as shown above.

This exercise shows the copy-and-paste technique.

Exercise 6.8: Copying Text from Another Application

1) Choose **Help | Contents and Index**, choose the Index tab and type the word 'import'. A list of topics is then shown: click on 'Importing data – text'; click **Display.**

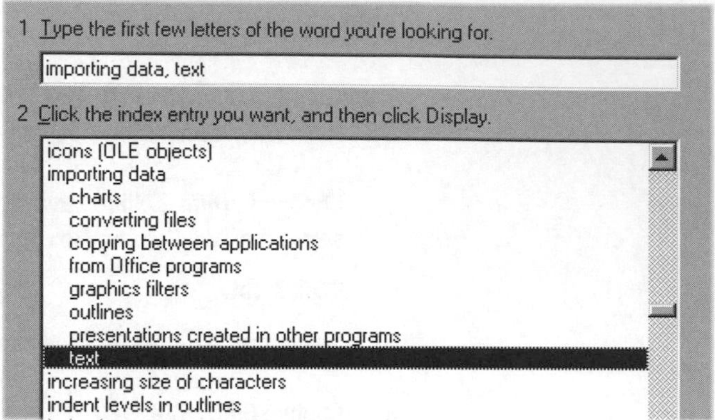

2) Select the first paragraph of text in the help page.

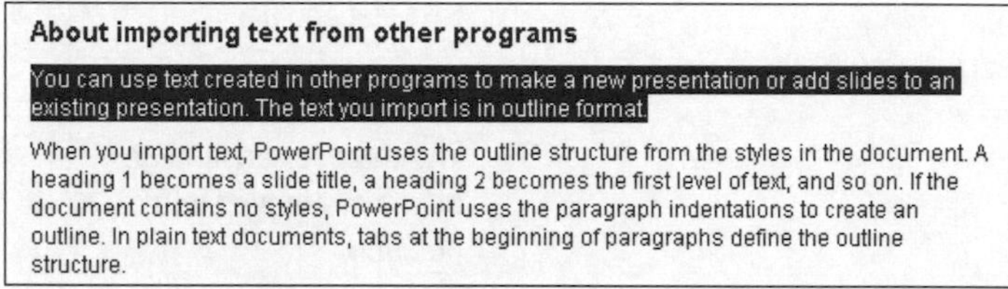

Choose **Edit | Copy.** Close the Help dialog box.

3) In PowerPoint, select Outline view. Position the cursor at the end of slide number 6 (Sales and Marketing).

   Press ENTER (to create a new, blank slide).

4) Choose **Edit | Paste.**

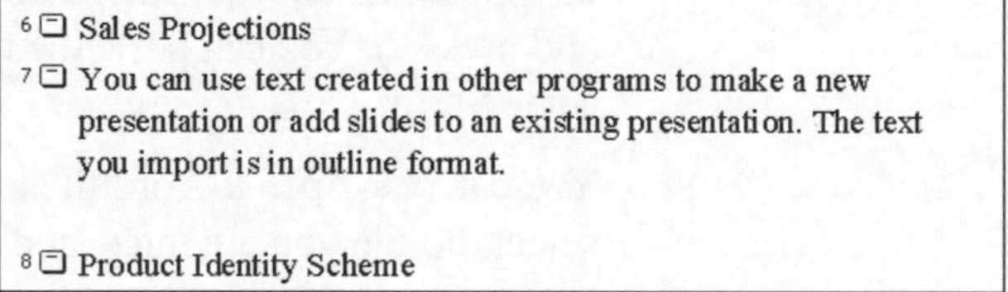

The paragraph from the help text appears as slide number 7.

5) Use the Demote button to make the text part of slide number 6.

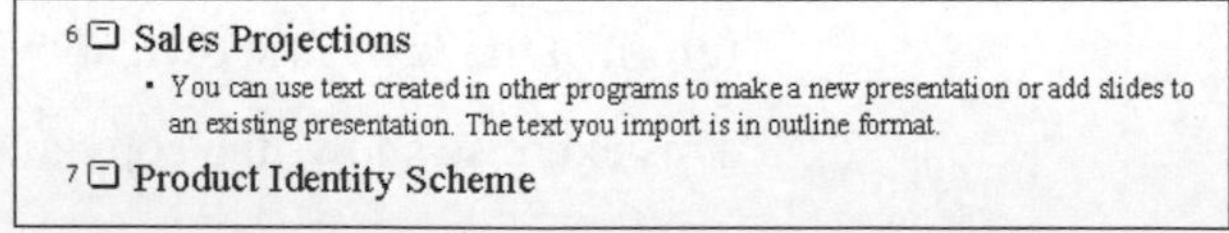

Notice how the final slide is renumbered to take account of the change.

You can use the same technique to copy objects from other applications: for example, you can select a range of cells in an Excel worksheet, copy them (as above), and paste them into a

PowerPoint slide. Or you can copy a chart created in Excel, or a table created in Word, or a graphic file (such as a scanned image) from a graphics program.

Deleting a Slide

To delete a slide, position the cursor anywhere in the slide and choose **Edit | Delete Slide**. You can do this in any view except Slide Show view.

Exercise 6.9: Deleting a Slide

1) Delete slide number 5 (Sales & Marketing) from your presentation.

Hiding a Slide

If you do not want to show a particular slide during a presentation, choose **Slideshow | Hide Slide**.

Undo Feature

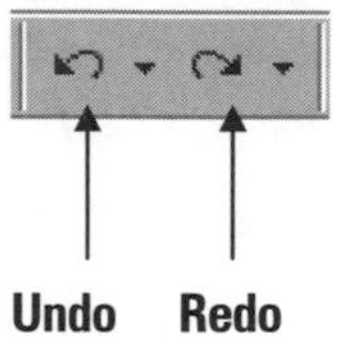

Undo Redo

Enter the wrong text? Press the wrong key? Delete something you didn't mean to? PowerPoint allows you undo your most recent actions if they have produced unwanted results. Choose **Edit | Undo** or click the Undo button on the Standard Toolbar. You can also Redo actions that you have undone: choose **Edit | Redo** or click the Redo button on the Toolbar.

Exercise 6.10: Using Undo

1) Choose **Edit | Undo**. The presentation reverts to the condition it was in before your most recent action.

2) Repeat undoing until the presentation is in the condition it was in before Exercise 6.8.

Saving Your Presentation

Save button

To save your presentation, choose **File | Save** or click the Save button on the Standard Toolbar. As in all programs, you must name your presentation and specify where it is to be saved when you save it for the first time.

Choose **File | Save As** to save a presentation under a different name or in a different location.

Exercise 6.11: Saving Your Presentation to Hard Disk or Diskette

1) Save the presentation that you have created in this Section. Give it a name that you will find easy to remember and recognise. For example, if your initials are KB, call it KBpres1.

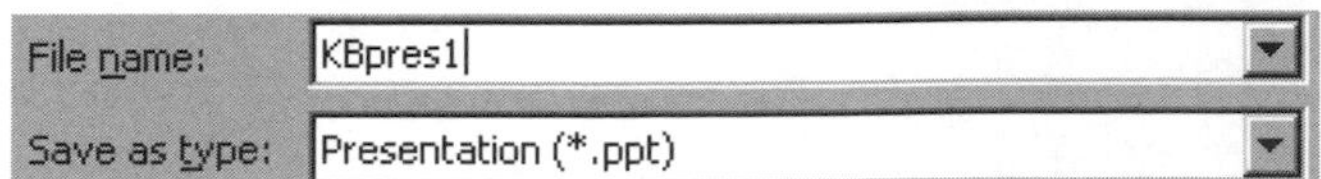

Up One Level button

2) Save the presentation again, this time on diskette. To do this, you will need to click the Up One Level button repeatedly until you are at the My Computer level. Then insert a diskette in the diskette drive, click the icon for the A: drive, and click **Save.**

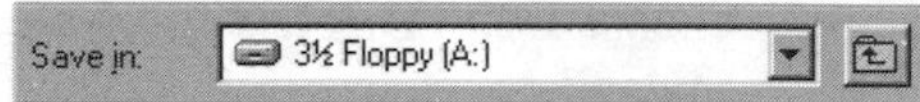

Section Summary: So Now You Know

To create a new slide, you choose an *AutoLayout* that most closely matches your needs.

AutoLayouts contain *placeholders* in which you enter the text.

Alternatively, you can import from another source, such as a word processor.

You can use Outline view to collect and organise your ideas, without worrying too much about formatting and style.

If you make changes that you don't like, you can Undo them. And you can save your presentation to hard disk or diskette.

PowerPoint presentations have the extension .ppt, .pps, or .pot.

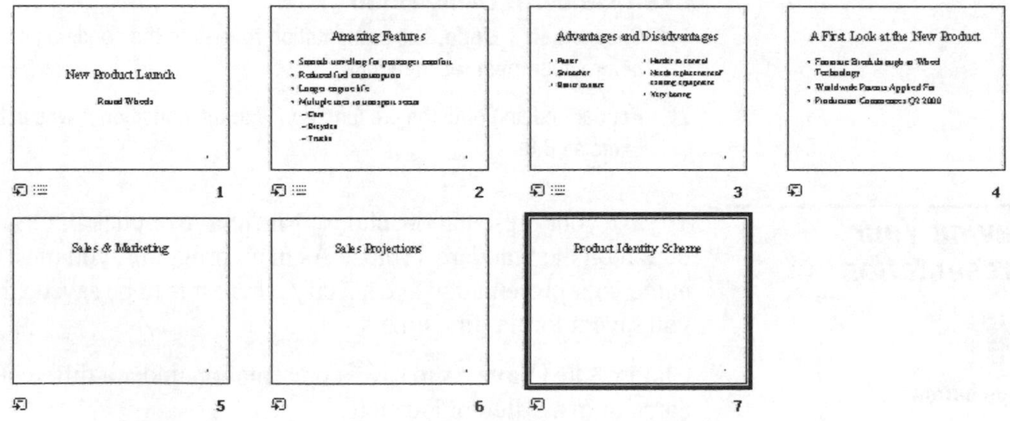

PowerPoint Presentations: The Story So Far

Section 6.3: Adding Graphics and Pictures

In This Section

In this Section you will learn how to include pictures and other graphics in your slides.

New Skills

At the end of this Section, you should be able to:

- Add simple graphic devices (lines, boxes, etc.) to a slide
- Edit and delete graphic devices
- Create and modify organisation charts, bar charts, and pie charts and include them in a presentation
- Import a photograph or clip art image to a slide
- Copy and paste images (within the presentation, between different presentations, and between PowerPoint and another application)
- Move, change the size and shape, rotate, and flip objects in a slide

New Words

At the end of this Section you should be able to explain the following terms:

- AutoShapes
- Organisation chart
- Clip art

The exercises in this Section further develop the presentation created in Section 6.2. Open the presentation before beginning the exercises in this Section.

Using PowerPoint's Drawing Tools

The Drawing Toolbar includes a number of tools for drawing simple objects, including lines, arrows, rectangles, and ellipses.

Line and Arrow Tools

To draw a line, click on the Line button, place the cursor where you want the line to begin, click and drag to where you want the line to end, and release the mouse button.

To draw an arrow, click on the Arrow button and drag it in the same way.

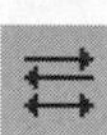

Change the style of arrowhead, or the direction of the arrow, by clicking the Arrow Style button.

Rectangle Tool

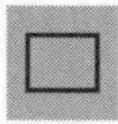

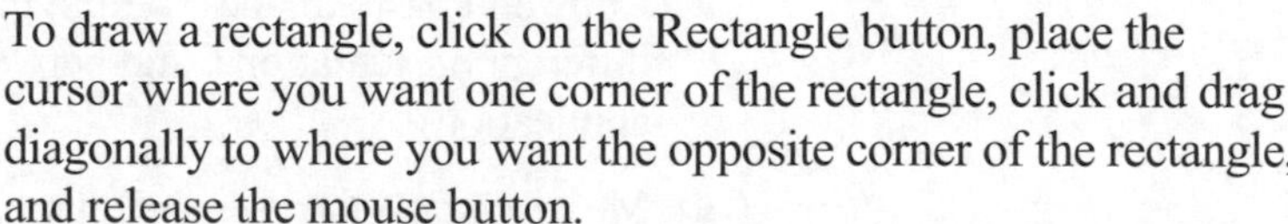

To draw a rectangle, click on the Rectangle button, place the cursor where you want one corner of the rectangle, click and drag diagonally to where you want the opposite corner of the rectangle, and release the mouse button.

To draw a square, hold down the SHIFT key as you drag with the mouse.

Ellipse Tool

To draw an ellipse, click on the Ellipse button, place the cursor where you want the shape to begin, click and drag until the shape is the size you want, and release the mouse button.

To draw a circle, hold down the SHIFT key as you drag with the mouse.

Line Colour and Style

In the case of straight lines, arrows, rectangles, and ellipses, you can specify the colour and thickness of the line. Click on the Line Colour button and select a colour, either before you draw the line, or, with the line selected, after you have drawn it.

Change the thickness of the line by clicking the Line Style button.

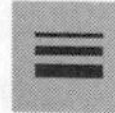

Make the line a dashed line (in a choice of dash styles) by clicking the Dash Style button.

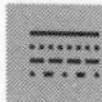

Fill Colour

Use this button to choose the colour with which the inside of the rectangle or ellipse should be filled. Note that the choice of colours pops up when you click the arrow. Again, you can choose the fill colour before you draw the shape, or you can select an existing shape and then choose a fill colour.

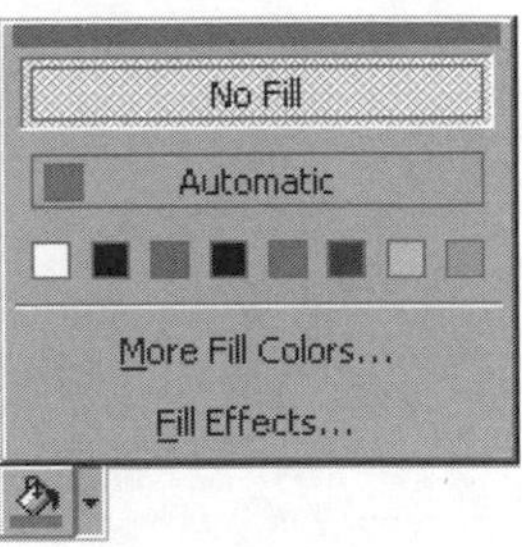

Text Box

A text box is an alternative means of adding text to a slide. Add a text box to a slide in the same way as you add a rectangle. Then type text into it. Change the format of the text by selecting it and then choosing options from the Format menu (in particular, Font, Bullet, and Alignment). Note, however, that text added to a slide using a text box does not appear in Outline view.

Editing Drawn Objects

To change the shape or size of any object created with the drawing tools, click on the object to select it. A number of sizing handles are shown around the object. Click on any of these and drag the handle until the object is the required shape and size.

Text in a Text Box

Repositioning cursor shape

To change the position of any object created with the drawing tools, click on the object to select it. Click on the object anywhere except on a sizing handle. The cursor changes to a cross shape. Drag the object to the desired new location.

To move an object between slides, use the **Cut** and **Paste** commands on the **Edit** menu.

To rotate any object created with the drawing tools by 90° in either direction, click on the object to select it. Click on the **Draw** menu and from the pop-up menu choose **Rotate** or **Flip**. Then choose **Rotate Left** or **Rotate Right**. The object changes its orientation immediately.

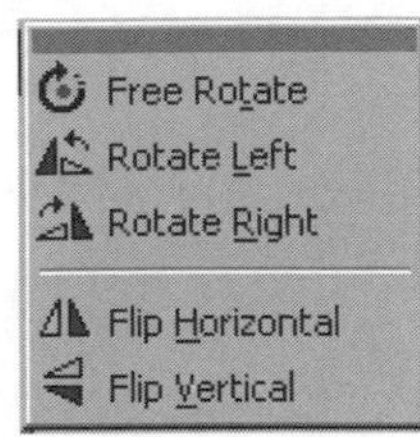

Similarly, to flip any object created with the drawing tools, click on the object to select it, click on the **Draw** menu and from the pop-up menu choose **Rotate** or **Flip**. Then choose **Flip Horizontal** or **Flip Vertical**. The object changes its orientation immediately.

Free Rotating cursor shape

To rotate an object freely, click on the object to select it. Then click on the Free Rotate button. The sizing handles are replaced by rotating handles. Click on any of these (the cursor changes to a shape), and drag the object to its new orientation. You can limit the object's rotation to 15° steps by holding down the SHIFT key as you drag with the mouse.

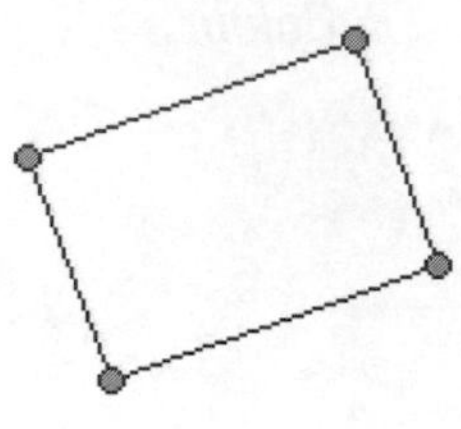

To delete any object created with the drawing tools, click on the object to select it and press DELETE.

Exercise 6.12: Drawing Shapes

1) Open slide number 7 (Product Identity Scheme) in Slide view.

2) We do not want the placeholder: choose **Format | Slide Layout**, and select the Title Only layout. Click **Apply**.

3) Draw three circles, as shown below. The two bigger circles have a line thickness of 6 points; the smallest circle has a line thickness of 3 points. All circles are red, with blue fill.

4) Add a text box to the right of the circles. Add text as shown. Make the text Arial bold, 24 point. Make it bulleted.

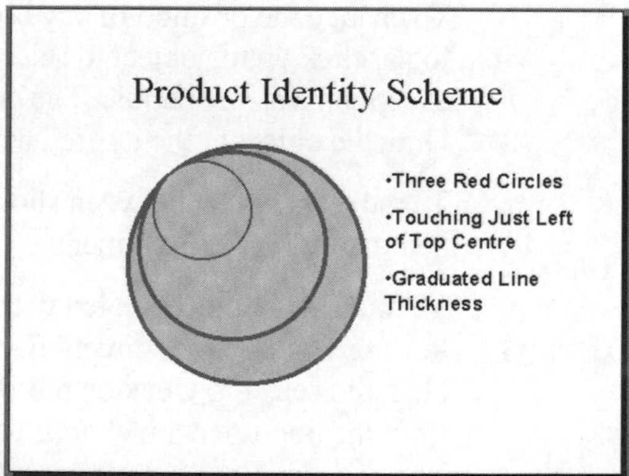

5) Save the presentation.

Grouping and Ungrouping Objects

You can group objects so that you can work with them as if they were a single object. You can format, move, rotate, flip and resize grouped objects in a single operation.

To group objects, hold down SHIFT and click each of the objects in turn. Next, click the Draw button on the Drawing Toolbar and choose the **Group** command.

To ungroup a selected group of objects, click the Draw button on the Drawing Toolbar and choose the **Ungroup** command.

Inserting AutoShapes

AutoShapes are commonly used, ready-made shapes that you can insert in your presentations. They include lines, basic shapes, flowchart elements, stars and banners, and callouts.

When you insert an AutoShape on a slide, you can change its size and colour, and rotate it, as required.

To select an AutoShape, click the AutoShapes button on the Drawing Toolbar and choose from the options offered by the pop-up menu.

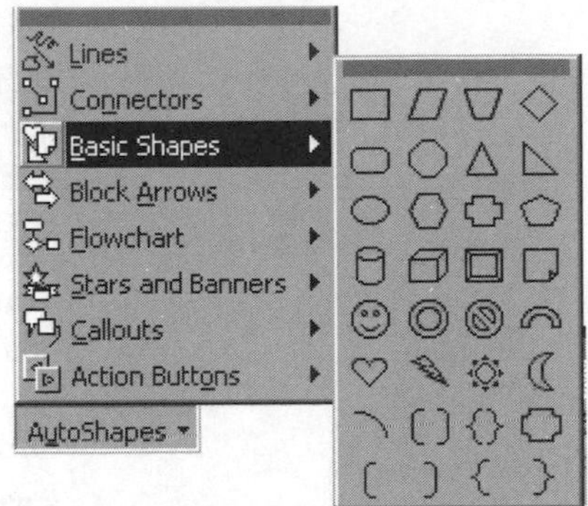

AutoShapes

Ready-made shapes, including lines, geometric shapes and flowchart elements that you can use in your presentations.

Inserting Organisation Charts

Organisation charts are used to illustrate hierarchical organisations or structures. People or units in an organisation are represented by boxes, and their relationships are represented by lines. You could draw them using the drawing tools, but they are used so frequently that PowerPoint provides a tool especially for producing them.

Organisation Chart

A diagram used to illustrate the people or units in an organisation (represented by boxes) and their relationships (represented by lines).

To include an organisation chart in a slide:

- Start with a blank slide, or one with only a title, and choose **Insert | Picture | Organisation Chart**.

  -or-

- Choose **Format | Slide Layout**, and select the Organisation Chart layout. Click **Apply**. Then double-click on the organisation chart icon.

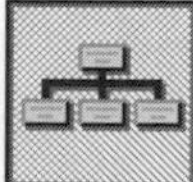

  -or-

- Choose **Insert | New Slide**, and select the Organisation Chart layout. Click **OK**.Then double-click on the organisation chart icon.

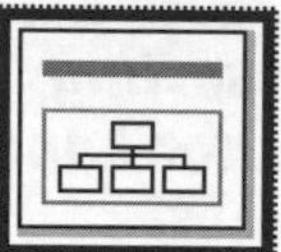

PowerPoint opens a new window that displays an organisation chart template and offers new menus of commands. The **Styles** menu, for example, allows you to choose different chart types, while the **Text, Boxes** and **Lines** menus each allow you to format the respective chart elements.

You can alter the template as you wish. Although the boxes have text labels in them, such as 'Type name here', you can enter any type of information in any box – the labels are for your guidance only.

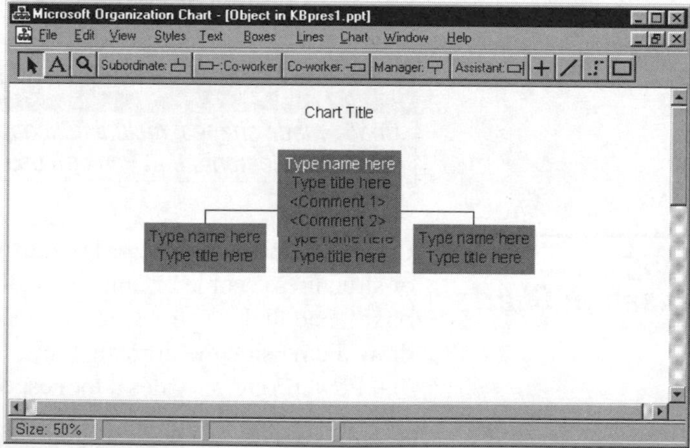

Exercise 6.13: Inserting an Organisation Chart

1) Open slide number 5 (Sales & Marketing) in Slide view.

2) Choose **Format | Slide Layout**, and select the Organisation Chart layout.

   Click **Apply.**

3) Double-click on the organisation chart icon to open the Organisation Chart window.

4) Edit the text in the template as shown below.

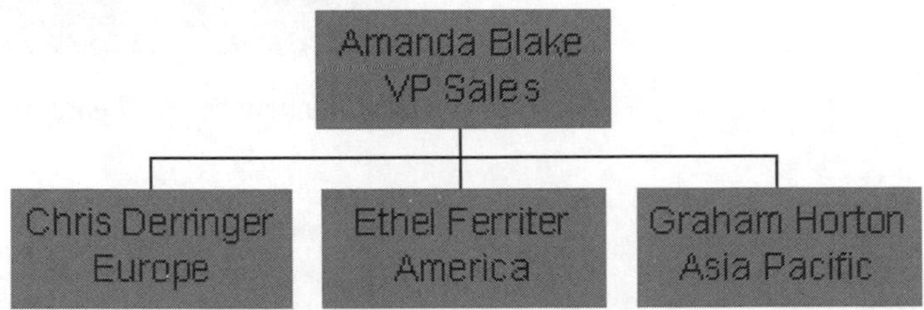

5) When you have finished working in the Organisation Chart window, return to your slide by choosing **File | Exit and Return to,** and then clicking **Yes** on the dialog box displayed.

Within PowerPoint you can move, resize or delete a chart as you would any other object. To make any other changes to the chart, however, you have to double-click on the chart and make your changes in the Organisation Chart window.

Exercise 6.14: Modifying the Structure of an Organisation Chart

1) Open slide number 5 (Sales & Marketing) in Slide view. Double-click on the organisation chart.

2) The chart is opened in the Organisation Chart window. The toolbar provides buttons for adding boxes (Subordinates, Co-workers, Managers, Assistants) and lines.

   Click the second Co-worker button.

   Next, click on the box containing Graham Horton. A new box is created, at the same level in the hierarchy, and the other chart elements are rearranged.

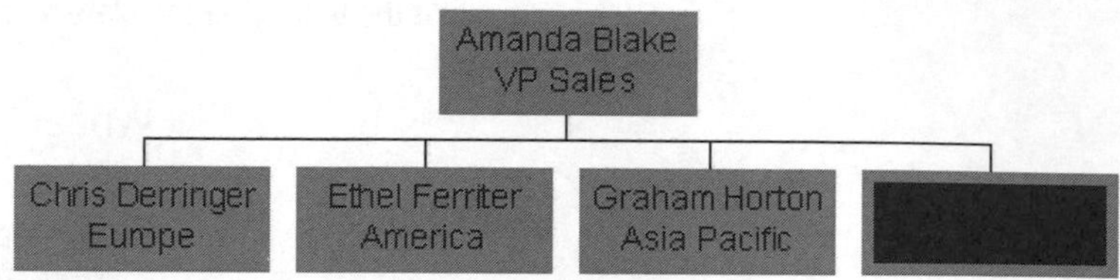

Click the new box, and enter text as shown below.

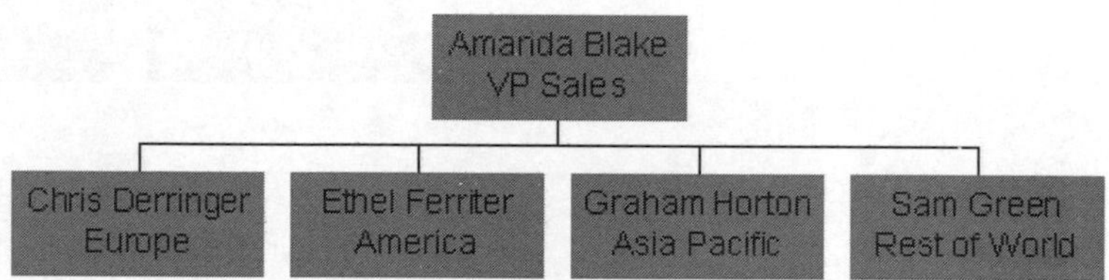

3) Close the Organisation Chart window, and confirm that you want to update the chart in the presentation.

Presenting Quantitative Information

In many circumstances you will need to present quantitative data. This kind of information is often best presented in the form of graphs, or charts. Luckily, PowerPoint provides a facility for including a variety of chart types in your slides.

To include a graph or a chart in a slide:

- Start with a blank slide, or one with only a title, and choose **Insert | Chart**.

  -or-

- Choose **Format | Slide Layout**, and select the Chart layout (or Text & Chart, or Chart & Text). Click **Apply.** Then double-click on the Chart icon.

  -or-

- Choose **Insert | New Slide**, and select the Chart layout. Click **OK.** Then double-click on the Chart button.

PowerPoint inserts a model chart into the slide, and, in a separate window, presents a mini-datasheet showing the numbers and titles upon which the chart is based.

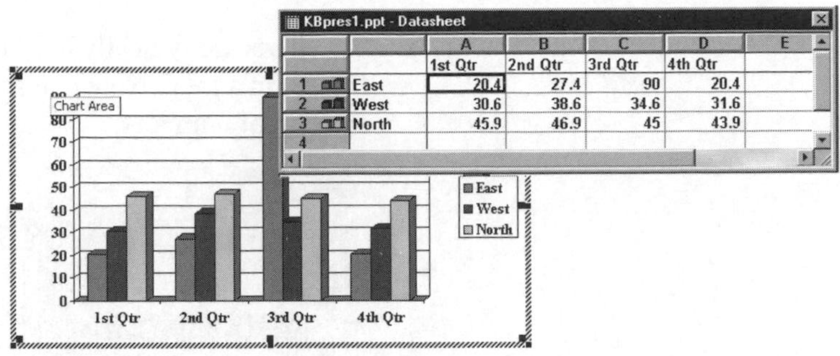

By changing the numbers and titles, you change the underlying chart. You can add new rows and columns by entering data into the datasheet. Delete rows or columns by clicking on the letter at the top of the column or the number at the left of the row (the column/row changes colour) and pressing DELETE. When you are finished, close the datasheet window.

To change the colour or format of any element in the chart, double-click on it: you are presented with options that are relevant to that element.

To change the data:

- Choose **View | Datasheet**.

  -or-

- Right-click on the plot area (that is, in the chart placeholder, but not on any element of the chart), and choose **Datasheet** from the pop-up menu.

The datasheet upon which the chart is based is shown, in which you can make your changes.

To change the chart type:

- Choose **Chart | Chart Type**.

  -or-

- Right-click on the plot area, as above, and choose Chart Type.
- Select the chart type and sub-type from the menu. The most commonly used types are Column, Line, and Pie.
  - Column charts are typically used to show figures that are measured at a particular time
  - Line charts are typically used to illustrate trends over time

- Pie charts are typically used to illustrate the breakdown of figures in a total. Note that a pie chart is based on a single column of numbers.

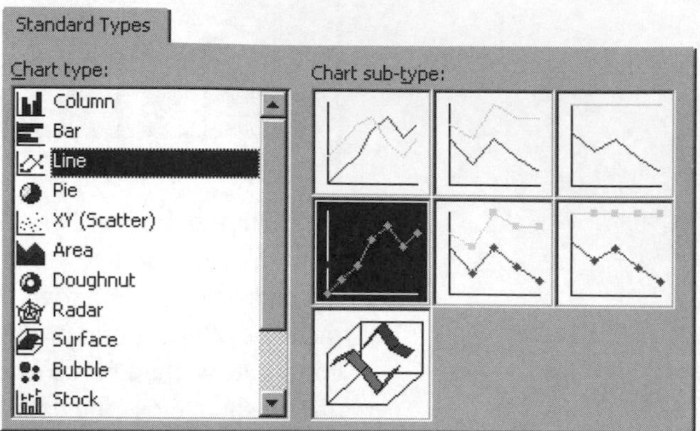

- Click **OK**.

PowerPoint gives you a wide variety of presentation options for charts. Some of them, however, are more decorative than informative: be careful that your message isn't obscured.

Exercise 6.15: Inserting a Chart

1) Open slide number 6 (Sales Projections) in Slide view.
2) Choose **Format | Slide Layout**, and select the Chart layout.
   Click **Apply**.
3) Double-click on the chart icon to open the Datasheet window.
4) Edit the text in the datasheet, as shown below.

		A	B	C	D	E
		1st Qtr	2nd Qtr	3rd Qtr	4th Qtr	
1	Europe	1000	1200	1300	1400	
2	North America	1200	1500	1400	1300	
3	Asia/Pacific	750	500	250	250	
4	Rest of World	750	750	750	750	
5						

5) When you have finished working in the datasheet window, close it and return to your slide.

Within PowerPoint, you can move, resize or delete a chart as you would any other object. To make changes to the data in the chart, however, you have to double-click on the chart and make your changes in the Datasheet window.

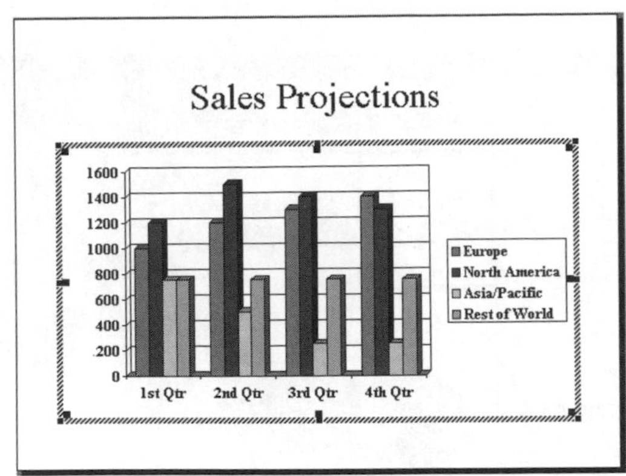

Importing Pictures

You can also illustrate your slides by inserting graphic images – drawings created in other software applications, scanned photographs, or clip art.

PowerPoint includes a gallery of clip art images that you can use in different presentations. They are grouped in categories, ranging from Academic to Food and Travel.

Clip Art
Standard or 'stock' images that can be used and reused in presentations and other documents.

To include a picture in a slide:

- Start with a blank slide, or one with only a title, and choose **Insert | Picture | Clip Art**.

  -or-

- Choose **Format | Slide Layout**, and select the Clip Art & Text (or Text & Clip Art) layout. Click **Apply**. Double-click the clip art icon.

  -or-

- Choose **Insert | New Slide**, and select the Clip Art & Text layout. Click **OK**. Double-click the clip art icon.

You are then presented with a gallery of images. Select the one you want to use, and click **Insert**.

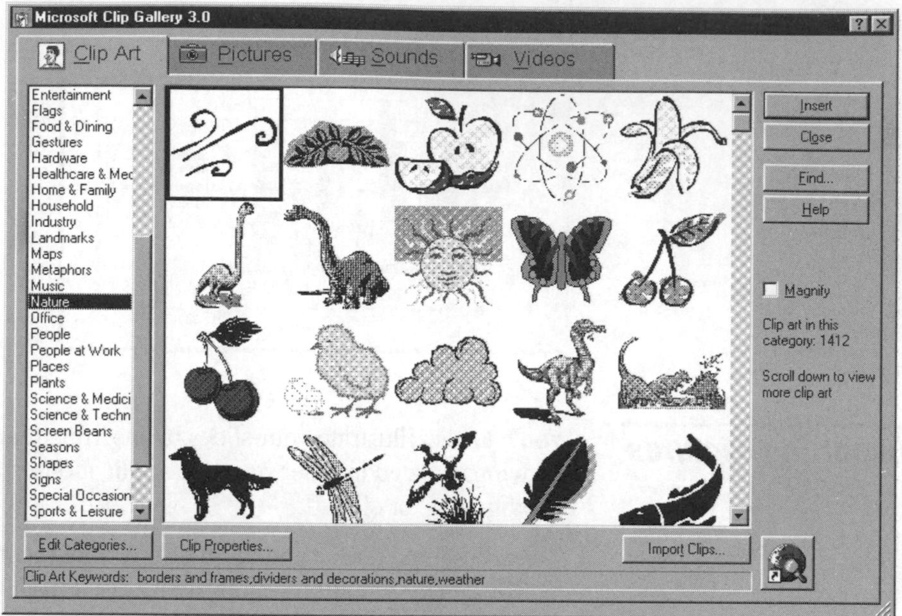

Exercise 6.16: Inserting a Clip Art Image

1) Open slide number 4 (A First Look at the New Product) in Slide view.

2) Choose **Format | Slide Layout**, and select the Clip Art & Text layout. Click **Apply.**

3) Double-click on the clip art icon to open the Gallery.

4) Search the Gallery for a suitable image. (Hint: try the Transportation category, or Shapes. The one in the example is from Sports & Leisure.) Click on the image and click **Insert.**

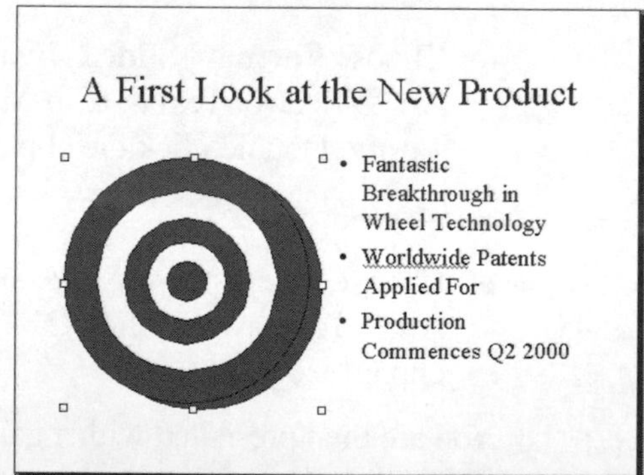

The image is inserted into the slide.

5) Choose **View | Slide Show**, or click the Slide Show button. Move forward and back through the presentation to see how it would look to the audience.

6) Save the presentation.

You can move, resize or delete the image as you would any other object.

To change the colours, brightness, or contrast of the image, you need the Picture Toolbar. Either choose **View | Toolbars | Picture**, or right-click on the image and choose **Show Picture Toolbar** from the pop-up menu.

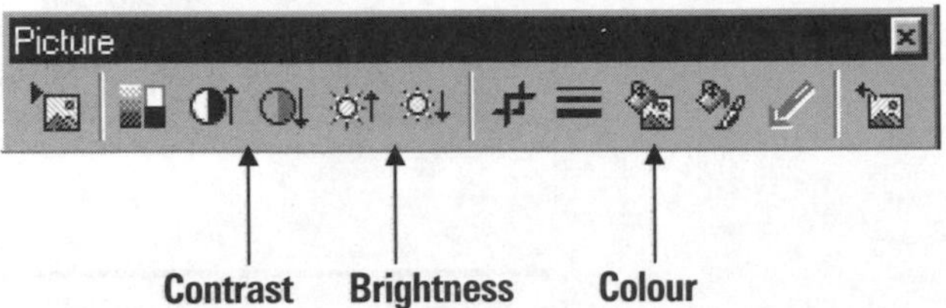

Any changes you make are shown on screen. Click on the Close box at the top-right of the Picture Toolbar when you are finished.

You are not restricted to inserting images on slides whose layout includes a graphic icon. You can insert a clip art image on any slide by choosing **Insert | Picture | Clip Art**.

To insert an image of your own – your company logo, for example – choose **Insert | Picture | From File**, and select the required image file. PowerPoint accepts images in most common image-file formats.

You can also copy images from graphic programs and paste them into PowerPoint slides, as described in the previous Section.

Standing Out from the Crowd

You can make objects in your slides appear to stand out from the background by adding a shadow to them. Select the object, then click the Shadow button on the Drawing Toolbar. You can choose from a variety of shadow styles. Be careful, if you are choosing a colour for the shadow, that you do not interfere with the legibility of your text.

Exercise 6.17: Adding a Shadow to an Object

1) Open slide number 5 (Sales & Marketing) in Slide view.
2) Select the chart by clicking anywhere on it.
3) Click the Shadow button on the Drawing Toolbar. Choose Shadow Style 5.

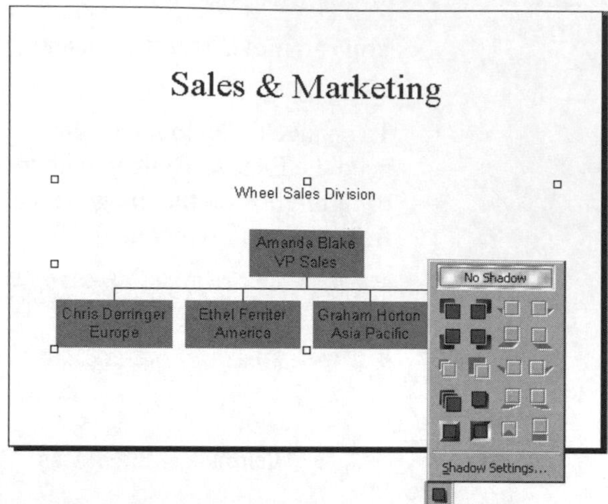

Click the Shadow button again.

4) Click **Shadow Settings**, and in the Shadow Settings button bar, click the Shadow Color button, and pick a mid-blue as the shadow colour.

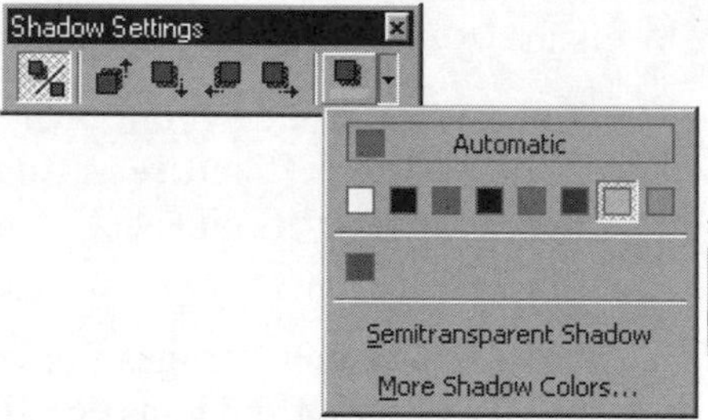

Close the Shadow Settings button bar.

5) Save the presentation.

Section Summary: So Now You Know

You can draw simple shapes (lines, arrows, rectangles, ellipses) within PowerPoint. You can also add more complex shapes (AutoShapes) within PowerPoint.

You can change the shape, size, position, and colour of such shapes, rotate them, flip them, and add shadows behind them.

You can create organisation charts, and a range of graphs and charts to illustrate quantitative data.

You can also import graphics created in other applications – charts, worksheets, tables, diagrams, pictures, photographs, maps, etc.

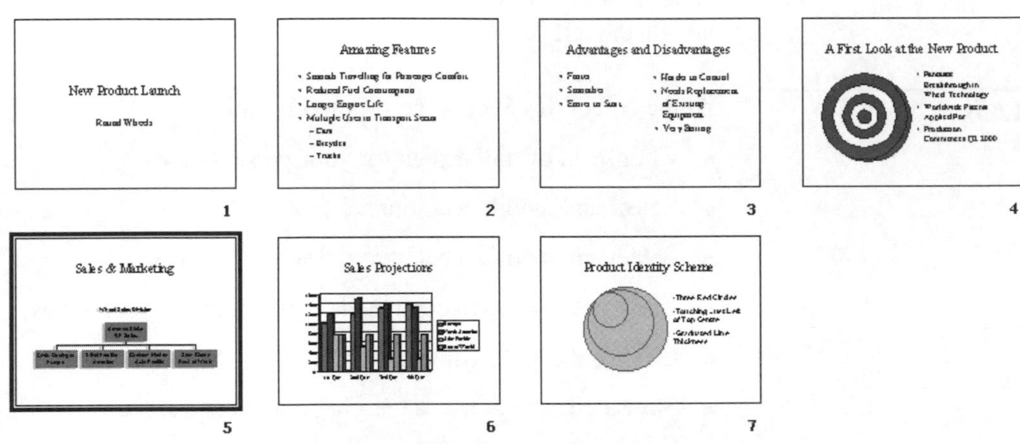

PowerPoint Presentations: The Plot Thickens

Section 6.4: Projecting a Consistent Image

In This Section

In this Section you will learn how to choose an overall style for your presentation, how to pick a colour scheme, and how to establish a coherent typographic style. These are important if your presentation is to convey a strong, confident image. If each of your slides looks entirely different, your message will appear confused and disjointed.

New Skills

At the end of this Section you should be able to:

- Choose an overall design for your presentation
- Select and modify a colour scheme
- Select and modify a background for your slides
- Use master slides to control the consistency of your slides
- Change the text attributes of individual slides
- Save a presentation as a template for subsequent use

New Words

At the end of this Section you should be able to explain the following terms:

- Presentation design
- Colour scheme
- Slide Master
- Presentation template

The exercises in this Section further develop the presentation created in Sections 6.2 and 6.3. Open the presentation before beginning the exercises in this Section.

Using Presentation Designs

PowerPoint is supplied with a variety of presentation designs that you can use in your presentations. You can either use them directly, without any change, or you can adapt them to your particular needs or taste, or to your company identity scheme.

You can either create a new presentation using one of these designs, or you can apply a design to a presentation you have already created.

To create a new presentation using a PowerPoint design, choose **File | New**. Then click the Presentation Designs tab, and select one of the designs: a preview of the design is shown on the right. When you have found one you want to use, click **OK**.

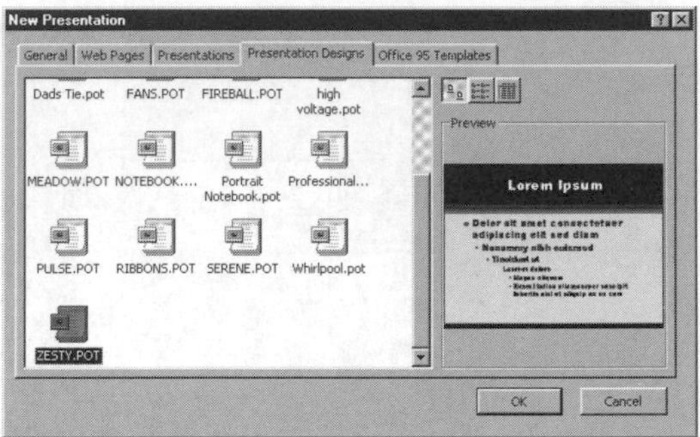

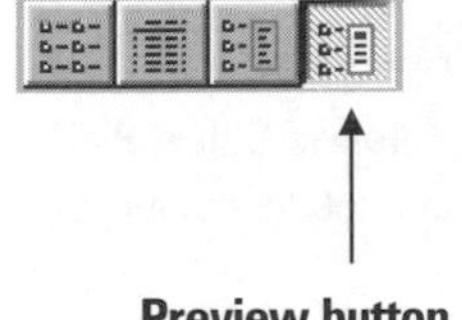

Preview button

To apply a design to an existing presentation, choose **Format | Apply Design**. Locate the designs folder (usually in c:\Program Files\Microsoft Office\Templates\Presentation Designs: the file names end in .pot). Choose the design you want to use. (To see a preview of the design, click the Preview button.) Click **Apply**.

Exercise 6.18: Choosing a Design

1) Apply a new design to the presentation previously created. Use the design called 'Contemporary Portrait'.

2) Save the presentation.

3) Choose **View | Slide Show**, or click the Slide Show button. Move forward and back through the presentation to see how it would look to the audience.

Making the Design Your Own

The design establishes a typographic framework for the presentation, and uses graphic devices (lines, colours, background images) to create an overall image. You can alter these to make the design your own. Rather than changing each slide individually, you can make global changes – this saves effort and it helps make your slides consistent.

Modifying the Colour Scheme

PowerPoint has a number of built-in colour schemes. Each scheme consists of a set of eight co-ordinated colours.

When you select a scheme, PowerPoint applies the different colours of the scheme to specific slide elements, such as title text (the text in the title placeholder), non-title text, background, graphic fills, and so on.

Exercise 6.19: Applying a Colour Scheme

1) Choose **Format | Slide Colour Scheme**. On the Standard tab, select one of the schemes. For this exercise choose the third colour scheme on the second row – the one with the blue background.

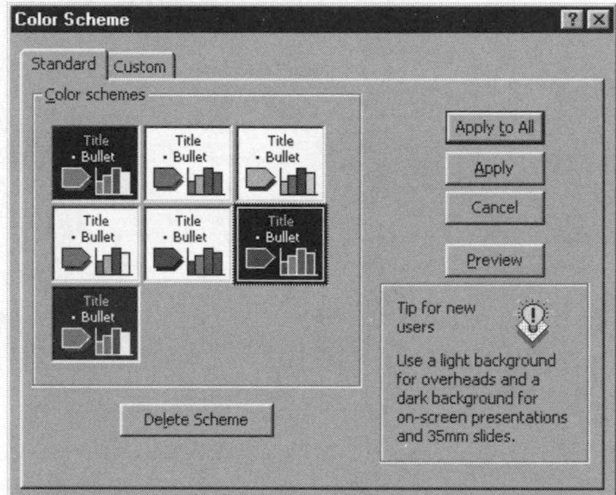

2) On the Custom tab, select Text and lines and click **Change Color**. Pick a bright yellow. Select Accents & Hyperlinks, and change its colour to mid blue. Click **OK**.

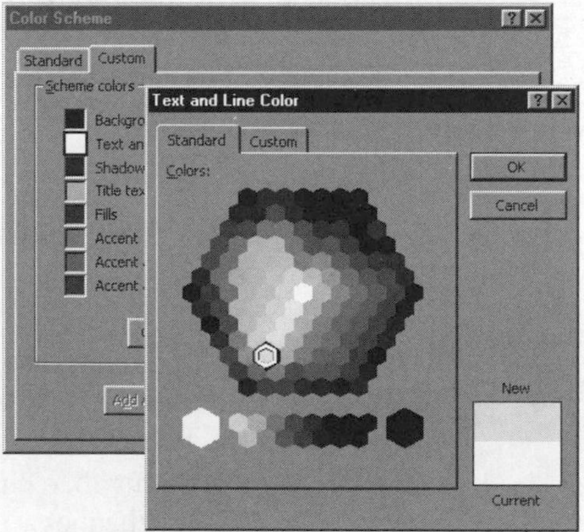

3) Click **Apply to All**. This has the effect of applying the new colour scheme to all the slides in the presentation.

4) Save the presentation.

5) Click the Slide Show button, and move forward and back through the presentation to see how it would look to the audience.

Colour Scheme
A set of eight, preset co-ordinated colours you can use to give your presentation an attractive and consistent appearance.

Modifying the Background

In the colour scheme you can specify only a single background colour. If, instead of a flat colour, you want to specify gradients, textures, patterns, or pictures as the background to your slides, you can do so as shown below. Again, however, a word of caution: these options are intended to make your slides more exciting and dynamic; however, if you do not use them carefully, they can make your slides illegible!

Exercise 6.20: Changing the Background

1) Choose **Format | Background**.

   As in the colour scheme, you can choose a single colour, either from the drop-down palette, or from the More Colors option.

   The more interesting options, however, are found in Fill Effects.

   Click this option.

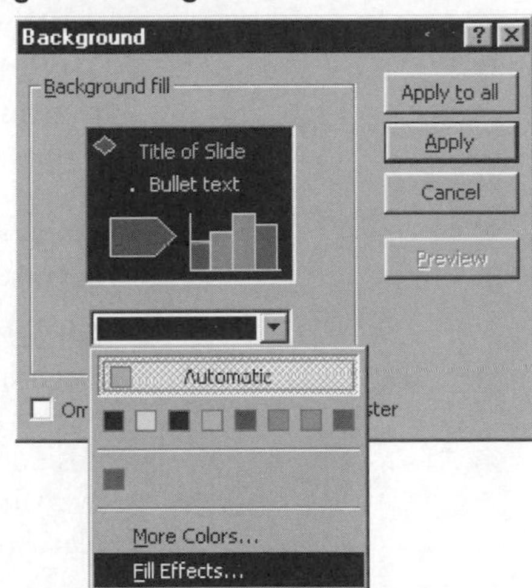

2) The screen shows four tabs – Gradient, Texture, Pattern, and Picture.

   In each, when you select an option, a sample is displayed on the lower right. Explore the options on offer. Then select the Gradient tab.

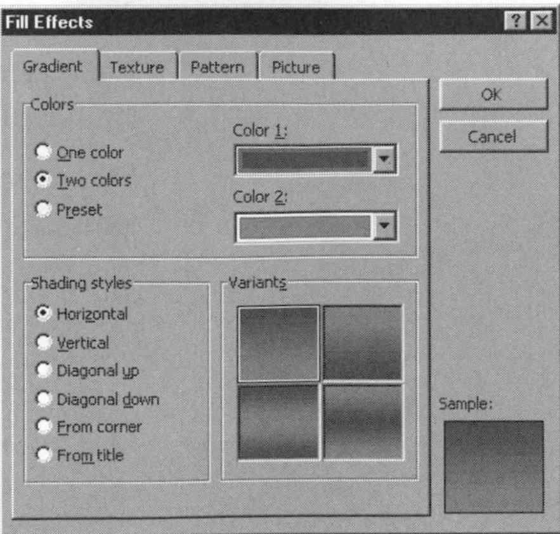

3) Click the Two Colors button. Make Color 1 dark blue, and Color 2 light blue. Click the Horizontal shading style, and the first variant. Click **OK.**

4) Click **Apply to All.** This has the effect of applying the new background to all the slides in the presentation.

5) Save the presentation. Once again, take a look at the whole presentation to see how it would appear to the audience.

The Slide Master

Whether you know it or not, every slide you insert in a PowerPoint presentation is based on the style of the *Slide Master*.

It is from the Slide Master that all slides take their default text formatting and positioning. In addition, anything that you insert on the Slide Master appears automatically on every slide of your presentation. This is useful for company logos or for graphic elements, such as lines and borders.

To view the Slide Master, choose **View | Master | Slide Master**. It consists of two placeholders:

- **Title Placeholder**: Determines the format and positioning of text in every title placeholder in your presentation.
- **Object Placeholder**: Determines the format and positioning of text in every non-title placeholder.

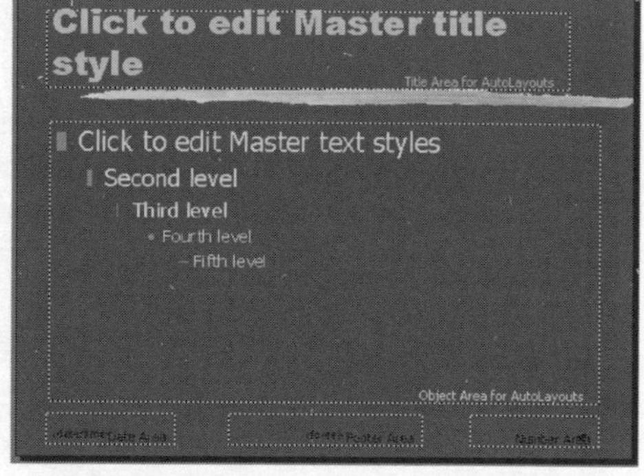

Notice that the Slide Master includes the yellow 'painted' line.

Your audience never sees the Slide Master; they see only its effects on the slides in your presentation.

You can override the defaults supplied by the Slide Master on any individual slide.

Slide Master

The Slide Master stores all the default attributes that you wish to apply to new slides, including text formatting and positioning, background, and standard graphics, such as your company logo.

Exercise 6.21: Reformatting Text in the Slide Master

In this Exercise you change the text format of your presentation by changing the Slide Master.

1) Choose **View | Master | Slide Master** and select all the non-title text in the lower placeholder.

2) Choose **Format | Font**, and change the font of the selected text to Arial Bold.

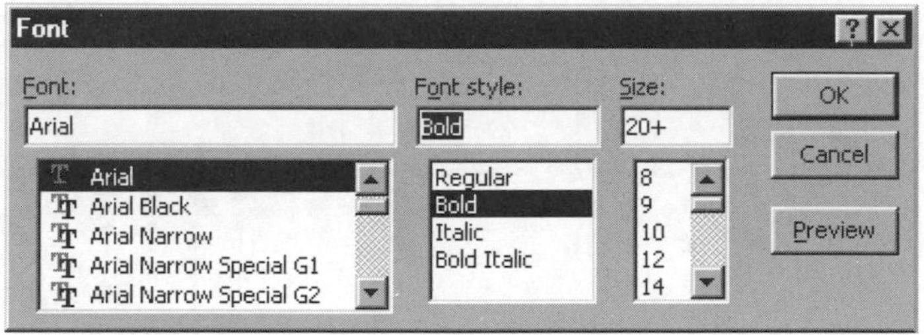

3) Choose **View | Slide**. Notice that the font of the text in all the non-title placeholders of all the slides in your presentation has been changed.

You can use the Slide Master to change other attributes of text in your presentation in exactly the same way: explore the options available in the **Format** menu, and in particular:

- **Bullet**, which allows you to choose the bullet character that applies to each level of text
- **Alignment**, which allows you to specify whether the text is to be ranged left or right, centred, or justified
- **Line Spacing**, which allows you to determine the amount of space between lines in a paragraph and between different paragraphs

Formatting Text on Individual Slides

The design, the colour scheme, and the Slide Master help you to establish rules that apply to all slides in a presentation. You can also, if you wish, break those rules on individual slides – you can make text bigger or smaller, change its font or style, change its alignment, or change the spacing between it and other text.

To do any of these, first select the text you want to change. Then proceed as follows:

- To change the font, size, style (italics, bold, underline, superscript, subscript, etc.), colour, or effects, choose **Format | Font**, or click the relevant button in the Formatting Toolbar.
- To change the alignment of the text, choose **Format | Alignment**, or click the relevant button in the Formatting Toolbar.
- To change the spacing between lines or paragraphs, choose **Format | Line Spacing**, or click the Increase Paragraph Spacing button, or the Decrease Paragraph Spacing button in the Formatting Toolbar.

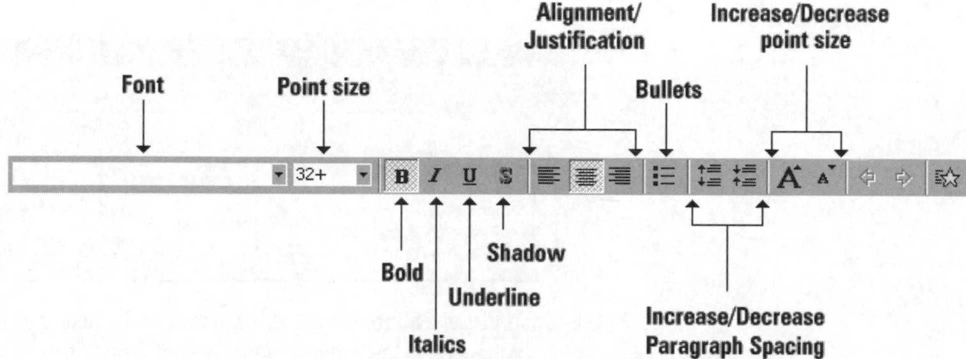

- To change the case of the text (initial capital, all lower-case, all upper-case, initial capitals on all words, or the opposite of the current selection), choose **Format | Change Case**, and select the option that you require.

Exercise 6.22: Formatting Text on a Slide

1) Open slide number 1 (New Product Launch) in Slide View.
2) Click anywhere on the second placeholder to select it. Then drag the mouse across the text to select the text.
3) Choose **Format | Font** and change the font to Arial, 72 point, bold.
4) Enlarge the placeholder so that it is big enough to hold the text on a single line.
5) Select the text again, and click on the Center Alignment button in the Formatting Toolbar. Click the Shadow button in the Formatting Toolbar and choose Shadow Style 5.

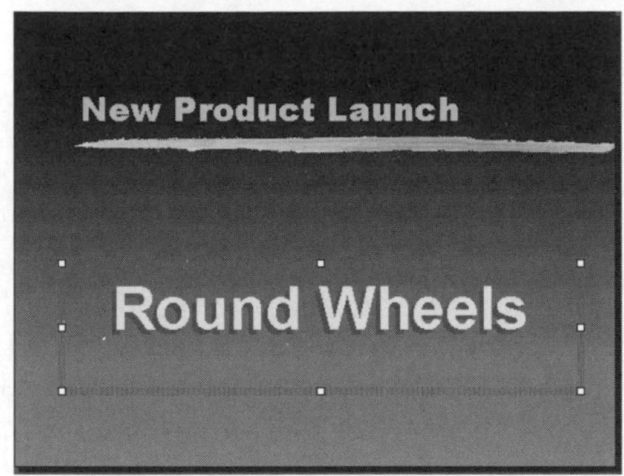

6) Save the presentation, and page through it to see the effect of the changes.

Adding Borders to Objects

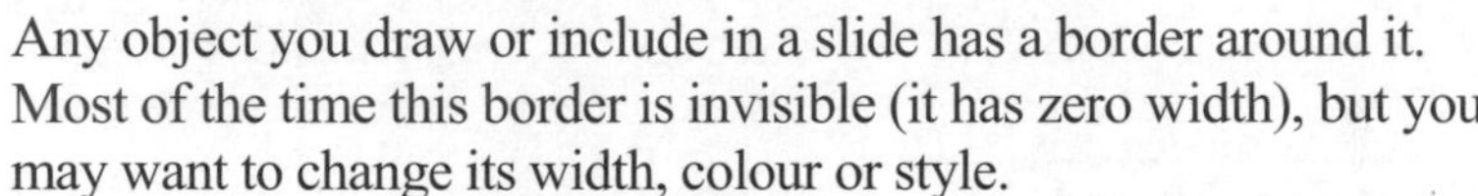

Any object you draw or include in a slide has a border around it. Most of the time this border is invisible (it has zero width), but you may want to change its width, colour or style.

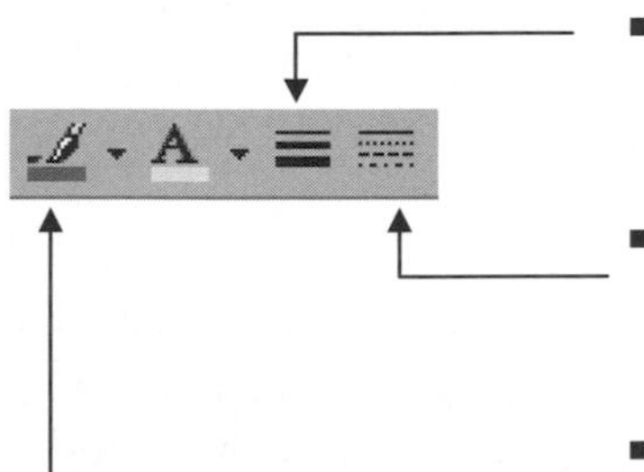

- To change the width of the border around an object, select the object, then click the Line Style button in the Drawing Toolbar and choose from the pop-up menu.
- To change the border around an object to a dashed or dotted line, select the object, then click the Dash Style button in the Drawing Toolbar and choose from the pop-up menu.
- To change the colour of the border around an object, select the object, then click the Line Color button in the Drawing Toolbar, and select from the **Line Color** pop-up menu.
- To delete a border around an object, select **No Line** in the **Line Color** pop-up menu.

Tips for Better Presentations

If you use PowerPoint's built-in designs and colour schemes, your presentation will almost certainly succeed. However, you probably want to personalise it using some of the features described above. But the range of options is so vast that you could end up with a disaster. Here are some guidelines for success.

How Much Should You Put on a Slide?

As little as possible. Write economically, using headlines and bullets. Don't give the audience the opportunity to read ahead: if you do, they won't listen to you, and they won't retain your message. If you are presenting information in bulleted lists, don't have more than eight or nine bullets. If you must have more, divide them into logical groups and split them over several slides.

What Point Size Should You Choose?

It depends on two things: the size of the screen on which the slide will be shown, and the distance from the screen to the back of the audience. Let's say your slides will be viewed on a 4' high screen from a maximum distance of 32' (that is, eight times the height of the screen). Now measure the height of the slide as it appears on your computer screen: if it is 9" high, you can pretend to be in the back row of the audience by looking at it from a distance of 6' (9" multiplied by 8). Choose your minimum point size by looking at your computer from this distance.

The 'eight times' rule is actually a good guideline for most situations: if the room is larger, it is likely that the screen will be bigger. However, if in doubt, choose a bigger size: nobody ever complained that a slide was too legible, but many, many people have complained that slides were illegible.

What Font Should You Choose?

In general for projected images, choose a sans serif font, such as Swiss, Helvetica, Arial, Gill ... (However, for large bodies of *printed* text, a serif font is generally recommended.) Typefaces vary in their legibility, and you might have to choose a bigger point size in certain fonts.

What Colours Should You Choose?

Make sure that the colours you choose for text and background are sharply contrasting. You will find that reversed type (text in a light colour, background in a dark colour) is more legible. (The opposite is true of printed documents.) Remember that viewing conditions are often less than ideal, with lights shining onto the screen. A plain slide that can be read easily is much more valuable (to you and to your audience) than a fancy one that nobody can read.

Using the Same Style Again

If you have created a style that you like, or that reflects your corporate colour scheme, you can save it as a template. Then, the next time you want to create a presentation, you can start with that template and all the slides will take on its characteristics. To do this, choose **File | Save As**. From the Save as type: drop-down list, choose Presentation Template. You can give it a name other than that suggested, if you wish. PowerPoint Template files have the extension .pot.

Section Summary: So Now You Know

PowerPoint contains a variety of *presentation designs*. These determine the overall look of the presentation. You can use them without change, or you can modify them to your requirements.

You can modify the colour scheme used, the background, or the typography.

The attributes of the design are held in the *Slide Master*. Any changes you make to the Slide Master are applied by default to all existing slides in the presentation, and to all new slides you create. You can, however, change text attributes on individual slides.

You can also include graphic devices in the Slide Master: these will then be shown on every slide in the presentation.

When you have tailored a design to your needs, you can save it as a *presentation template*. This enables you to use the same design in subsequent presentations.

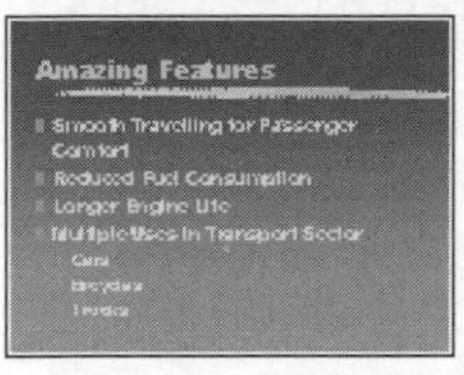

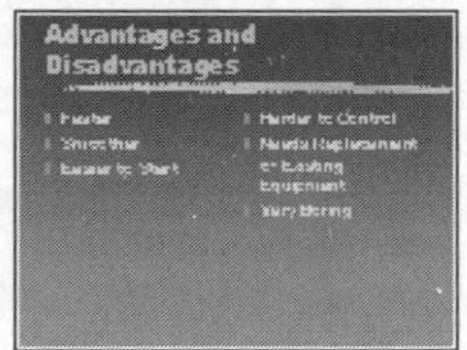

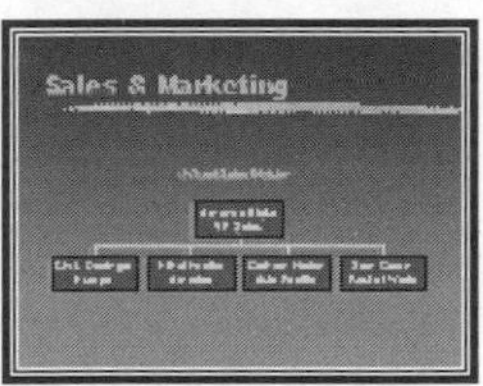

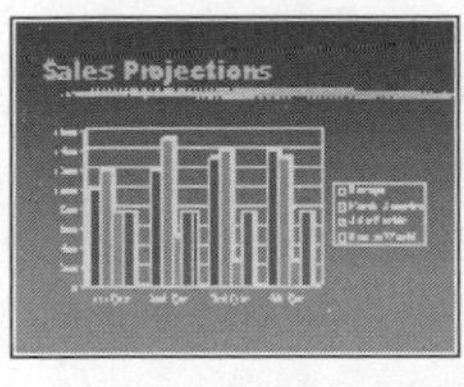

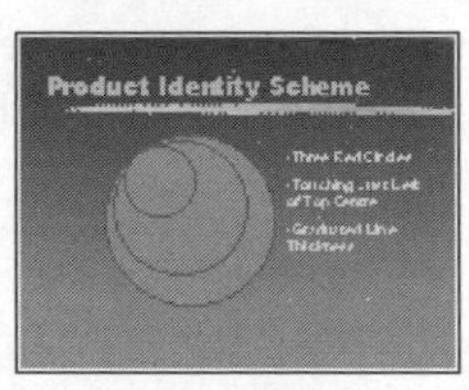

PowerPoint Presentations: Good Enough

Section 6.5: Building a Presentation

In This Section

In the previous Sections, you learnt how to create slides that will impress your audience. In this Section, you will learn how to assemble those slides into a convincing presentation, how to order and reorder your slides, how to insert and delete slides, how to make slides usable in other applications, and how to import slides from other sources.

New Skills

At the end of this Section, you should be able to:

- Reorder slides in a presentation
- Copy slides between presentations
- Delete slides
- Export PowerPoint slides to other applications
- Save presentations for use in other versions of PowerPoint

Once again, the exercises in this Section are based on the presentation created in Sections 6.2, 6.3, and 6.4. Open the presentation before beginning the exercises in this Section.

Using Slide Sorter to Check Your Slides

Use Slide Sorter view to check that your formatting is consistent and that text placeholders are aligned. This is particularly important if you have made changes to the design or formatting of individual slides.

Choose **View | Slide Sorter**. This shows you all the slides in your presentation on a single screen. (If they don't all fit on your screen, use the scroll bar on the right.)

To see or edit a particular slide in Slide view (full size), double-click it.

Changing the Order of Slides

When you have created all your slides, you might decide that you want to present them in a different order, so that the ideas flow better. The easiest way to do this is in Slide Sorter view.

You can reorder your slides in two ways: by dragging them with the mouse (better for small presentations), or using the cut-and-paste commands on the **Edit** menu (better for large presentations).

Reordering by Dragging

In Slide Sorter view, select the slide you want to move, drag it with the mouse so that a vertical line appears to the *right* of where you want to position the slide, and release the mouse button.

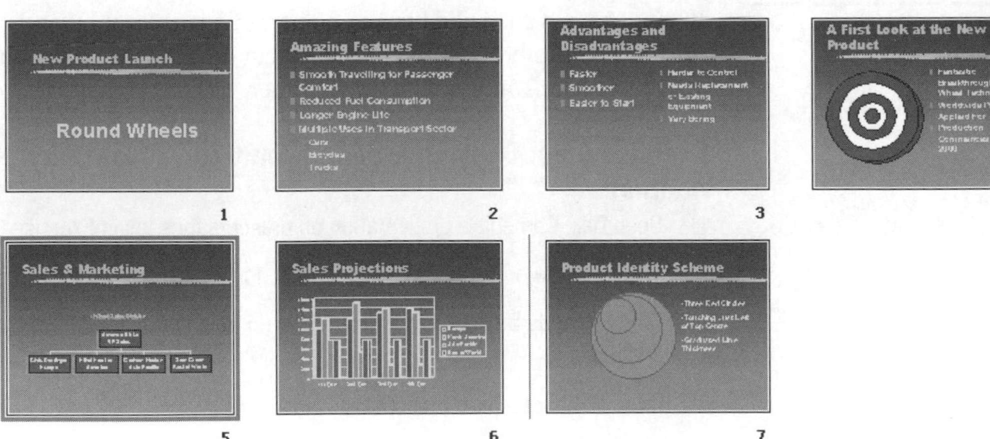

Reordering with Cut and Paste

You can cut, copy, and paste slides in PowerPoint as you would text in a word processor.

In Slide Sorter view, select the slide, choose **Edit | Cut** (or hold down the CTRL key and press x). Click on the slide that will appear *before* the slide you are moving and choose **Edit | Paste** (or hold down the CTRL key and press v).

Exercise 6.23: Re-Ordering Slides

1) In Slide Sorter view, use the dragging technique to reverse the order of slides 5 (Sales & Marketing) and 6 (Sales Projections).

2) Use the cut-and-paste technique to make slide number 7 (Product Identity Scheme) appear after slide number 2 (Amazing Features).

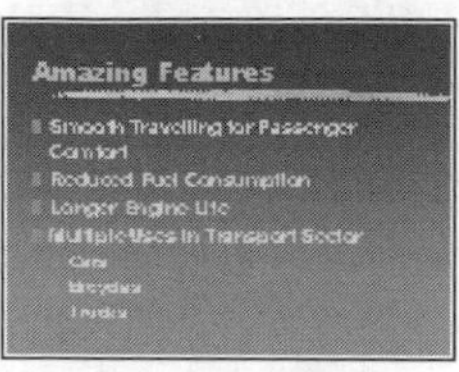

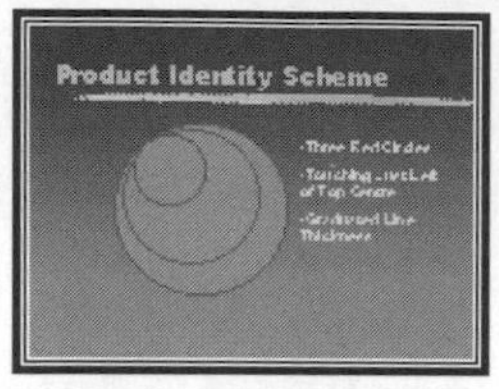

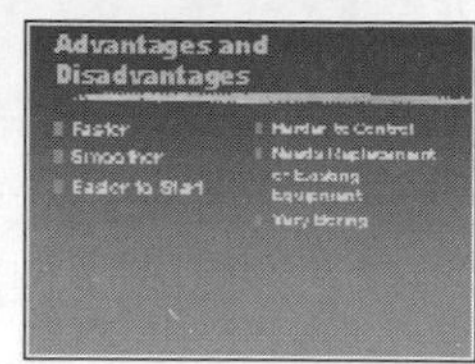

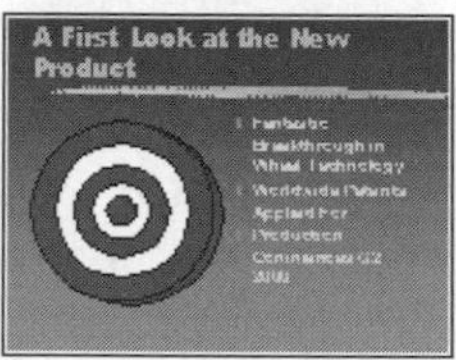

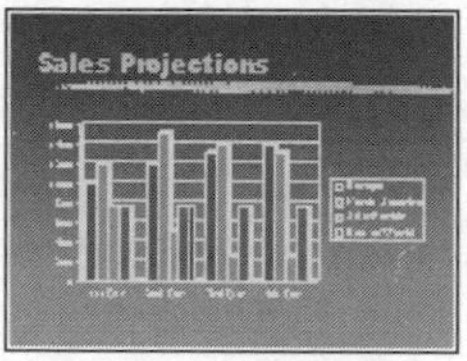

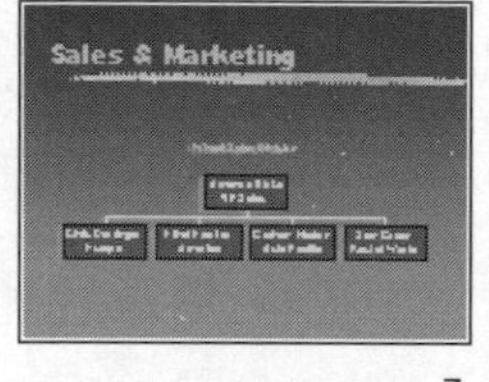

Note that the slides are renumbered to represent their new order: we will refer to them by their new number from now on.

Copying Slides between Presentations

Just as you can cut a slide from one part of a presentation and paste it into another part, you can also cut (or copy) a slide from one presentation and paste it into another. Try it.

Exercise 6.24: Copying a Slide from One Presentation to Another

1) Open Dale Carnegie's presentation on presentations, as in Exercise 6.1.

2) In Slide Sorter view, select slide number 11.

3) Copy the slide by choosing **Edit | Copy** (or hold down the CTRL key and press c).

4) Close Dale Carnegie's presentation.

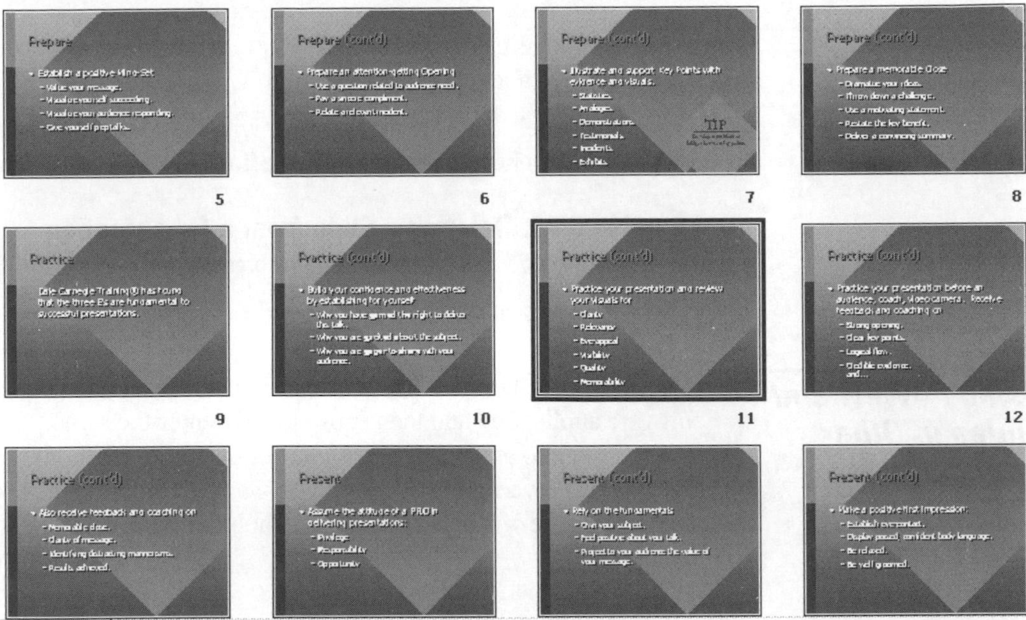

5) Open your own presentation in Slide Sorter view. Select slide number 1 (New Product Launch), and choose **Edit | Paste** (or hold down the CTRL key and press v).

The copied slide appears as slide number 2 in your presentation. Note that, while the content of the slide is exactly the same, the format has changed to agree with the design and layout of your presentation.

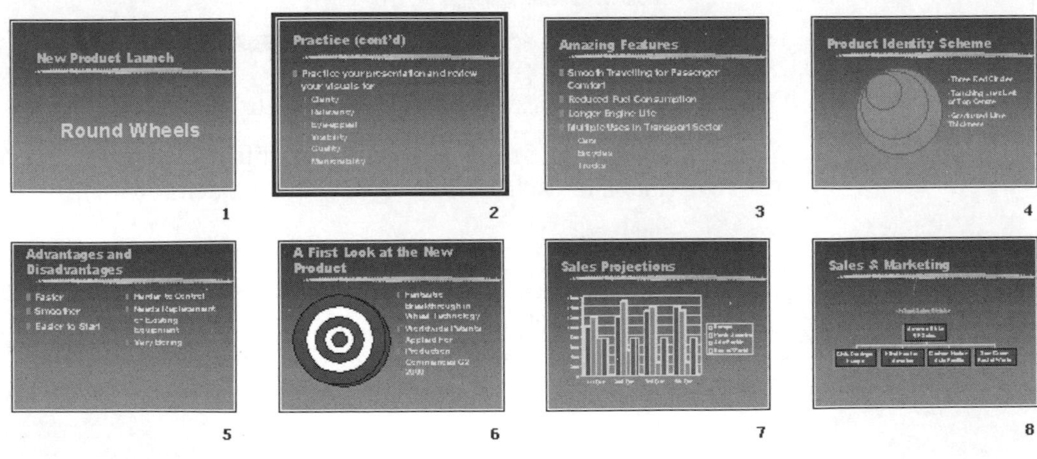

Deleting a Slide

If you want to remove a slide from your presentation, simply cut it, as described above, but don't paste it.

You can also delete a slide in any view, with the exception of Slide Show view, by choosing **Edit | Delete Slide**.

Exercise 6.25: Deleting a Slide from a Presentation

1) Delete the slide that you copied into the presentation in Exercise 6.24.
2) Save the presentation.

Using PowerPoint Slides in Other Applications

In general, you should not have to enter information into one software application and then subsequently enter the same information into another application. For example, when you create your PowerPoint slides and you want to use the same text in a report you are writing in Word, you should not have to type it again.

You don't.

- To use text from a single slide, copy the text in PowerPoint (select it and choose **Edit | Copy**), and paste it in Word (position the cursor and choose **Edit | Paste**).
- To use the text of the whole presentation in Word, choose **File | Save As**. From the Save as type: drop-down list, choose Outline/RTF.

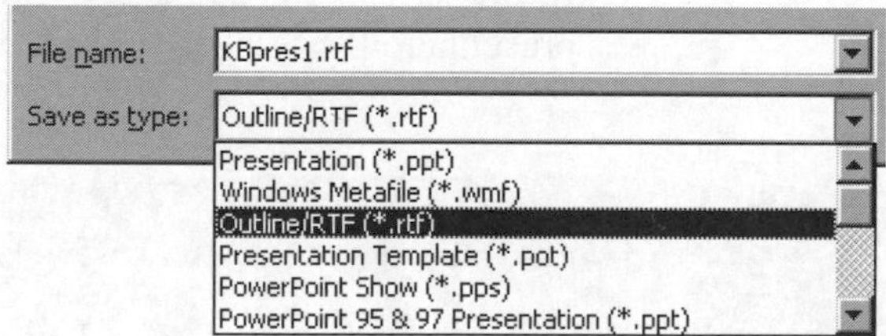

  If you wish, specify a file name other than the one suggested (the same as the presentation, with the extension .rtf).

- Click **Save**.

If you want to use the slides in other graphic programs, or in web pages, you should save them in one of the graphic formats: either JPEG File Interchange Format, or GIF. Try it.

Exercise 6.26: Making Slides Viewable in a Web Browser

1) Choose **File | Save As**. From the Save as type drop-down list, choose GIF. Click **Save**. Note that you can save a single slide or the whole slide show. For this exercise, specify a single slide.
2) Minimise PowerPoint and open the web browser on your computer (typically Microsoft Internet Explorer or Netscape Navigator). There is no need to connect to the Internet: open the program offline.
3) Choose **File | Open** (Microsoft Internet Explorer), or **File | Open Page** (Netscape Navigator). Locate the .gif file you created in step 1 and click **Open**.
4) Check that the slide appears correctly in your browser, and then close the browser.

Working with Earlier Versions of PowerPoint

Each version of the PowerPoint software includes features that were not available in earlier versions. This means that, while you can generally use a later version of the software to open, view, edit, and save a presentation that was created in an earlier version, the reverse is not true.

If, in PowerPoint 97, you save a presentation that was originally created in PowerPoint 95, PowerPoint 4.0, or PowerPoint 3.0, it will be saved in its original format, unless you choose **File | Save As** and specify a different name, a different folder, or a different software version.

If you want a presentation you have created to be viewable with an earlier version of PowerPoint, you must choose **File | Save As** and specify the software version in the Save as Type box. Note that some of the effects that you can specify in PowerPoint 97 will not display properly in earlier versions of the software.

Section Summary: So Now You Know

Once you have created a presentation, you can change the order of slides. The best way to do this is in Slide Sorter view, where you can either drag the slide to its new location, or cut and paste it.

You can copy slides into your presentation from other PowerPoint presentations. When you do, they take on the design and layout of your presentation.

You can use the text of your presentation in another application, such as a word processor, either by cutting and pasting, or by saving the file in .rtf format.

You can save individual slides or the whole presentation in .jpg or .gif format: these formats can be used in graphic programs and in web pages.

And if you want your presentation to be viewable in an earlier version of the software, you have to specify this when you are saving the file.

1

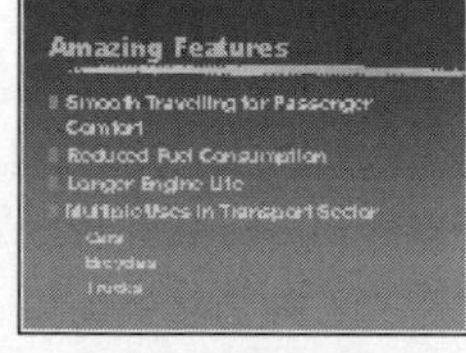

2

3

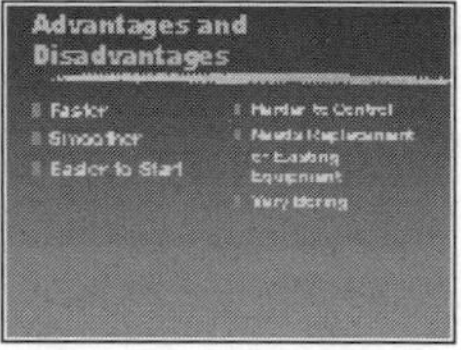

4

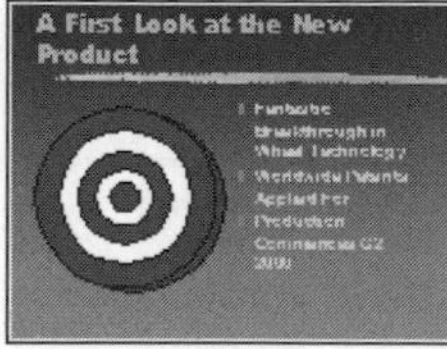

5

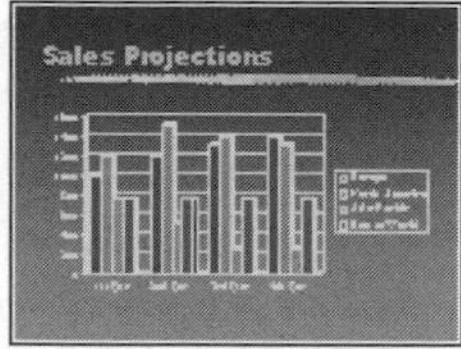

6

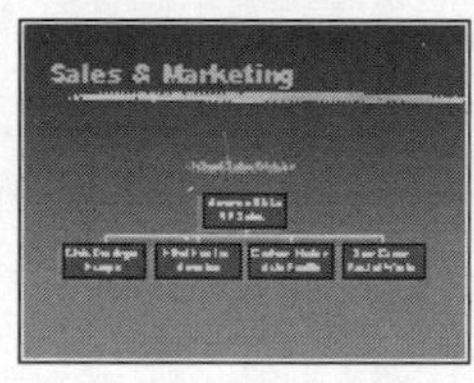

7

PowerPoint Presentations: Getting the Message?

Section 6.6: Wowing the Audience

In This Section

In this Section you will learn how to make your presentation more dynamic, by using animations and transitions. You will learn how to prepare handouts for the audience, and notes for the presenter. And you will learn a few tricks that you can use when delivering your presentation.

New Skills

At the end of this Section you should be able to:

- Specify transition effects
- Create build slides
- Add sound effects to slides
- Prepare handouts for your audience
- Number slides
- Prepare speaker notes
- Check the spellings in your presentation

New Words

At the end of this Section you should be able to explain the following terms:

- Slide transition
- Build slide

The exercises in this Section add professional polish to the presentation created in the earlier Sections of this Coursebook. Open the presentation before beginning the exercises in this Section.

Slide Transitions

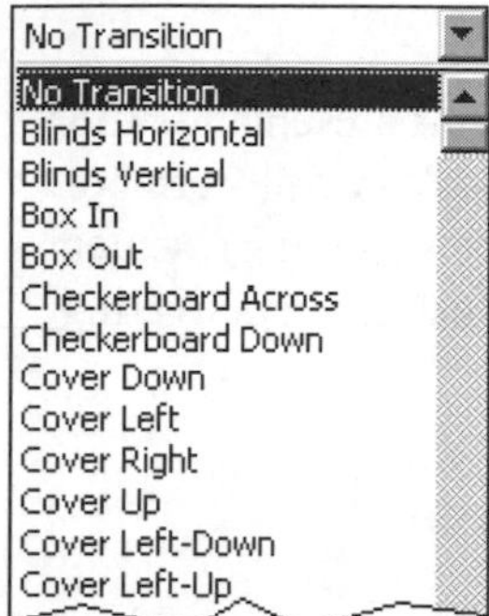

Transition options

A transition is a graphic effect that determines how one slide replaces another – for example, the new slide could appear to drop down from the top of the screen, or the old slide could be made to dissolve, leaving the new slide.

PowerPoint lets you control two aspects of a transition:

- **Effect Type:** The nature of the special effect with which PowerPoint introduces the slide.
- **Effect Timing**: The speed with which PowerPoint runs the visual effect when introducing the slide.

You can also specify that you want a sound to accompany the transition.

Transition

A visual effect, such as a box-out, dissolve, or fade, that determines how one slide in a presentation is replaced by another.

Exercise 6.27: Applying a Transition to Your Presentation

1) With any slide open in Slide view, choose **Slide Show | Slide Transition**.
2) First explore the options on offer:
   - **Effect:** Each time you click an option from the drop-down list, PowerPoint runs the effect in the sample picture. You can rerun the preview by clicking the picture.
   - **Timing:** The options – Slow, Medium or Fast – set the speed at which the transition effect runs. Click an option and PowerPoint runs the effect with that timing in the sample picture.

   For the exercise, select the effect called Dissolve, with Fast Timing.
3) Click **Apply to All**. Note that you have the option of applying a different transition to each slide (by clicking **Apply**), but be careful: this may have the effect of distracting or unsettling your audience.
4) See how the transitions affect the presentation by choosing **View | Slide Show** and paging through the presentation.

Automatic or Manual Advance

You can choose to have your presentation advance from slide to slide:

- On command (as described in Section 6.1)
- Automatically, based on specified timings

- Either, whichever comes first

This is also specified in the Slide Transitions dialog box. The two effects are independent, however: you can automate the running of your slide show without applying a transition, and you can apply a transition without automating your slide show. You should also note that the timings have nothing to do with one another: the effect timing (Slow, Medium, Fast) relates to the speed of the transition from the previous slide; the automated advance time specifies how long the slide is displayed before being replaced.

Automatic advance is often used in presentations that are left running in public areas, such as trade shows, where they are not accompanied by a speaker.

Build Slides

Build slides allow you to reveal the information on a slide gradually. They are typically used for bulleted text: when you first show the slide, the audience sees only the first bullet. You then reveal the remaining bullets, one by one, as you talk to your audience. This has the advantage of keeping your audience engaged with what you are saying, rather than having them read ahead while you are still talking about the first point.

Build Slide

A slide in which different elements are revealed at different times.

With a build slide you can highlight each point in turn, to focus your audience's attention. When you are talking about your second point, you can leave the first one on the screen, but dim it, so that it still serves as a context and reminder, but doesn't distract.

You can also control how each new element arrives on the screen – for example, bullet points can fly in from the right, left, top, or bottom. Let's try it.

Exercise 6.28: Applying a Build to a Slide

1) Display slide number 2 (Amazing Features) in Slide view.
2) Click anywhere in the lower placeholder, where the bulleted text is.
3) Choose **Slide Show | Preset Animation** and select the option called Flying.

4) Choose **View | Slide Show** to see the effect.
5) Choose **Slide Show | Custom Animation**.

Select the following settings:

- In **Timing:** Animate, On mouse click

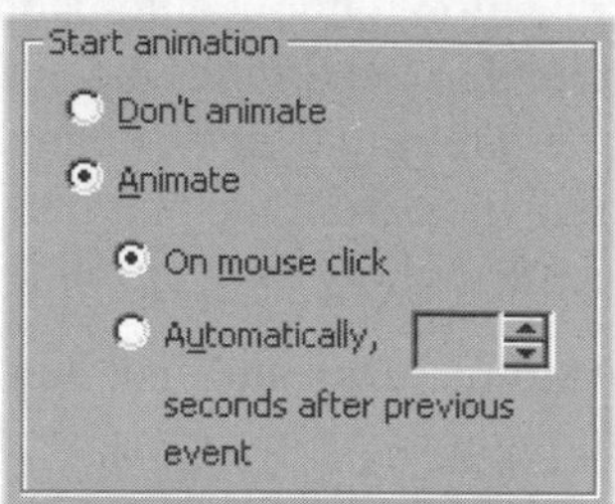

- In **Effects**: Dissolve, No Sound, Light blue, All at once, Grouped by 1st level paragraphs

- Ignore **Chart Effects and Play Settings**.

6) Again, choose **View | Slide Show** to see the effect.

Exercise 6.29: More Complex Builds

1) Display slide number 3 (Product Identity Scheme) in Slide view.

2) Choose **Slide Show | Custom Animation** to display the Custom Animation dialog box.

   In the Timing tab, select in turn each of the three circles (called ovals) and the bulleted text. When you select an object, it is highlighted in the preview screen. For each of these objects, click the Animate and Automatically buttons; specify '1 second after previous event'.

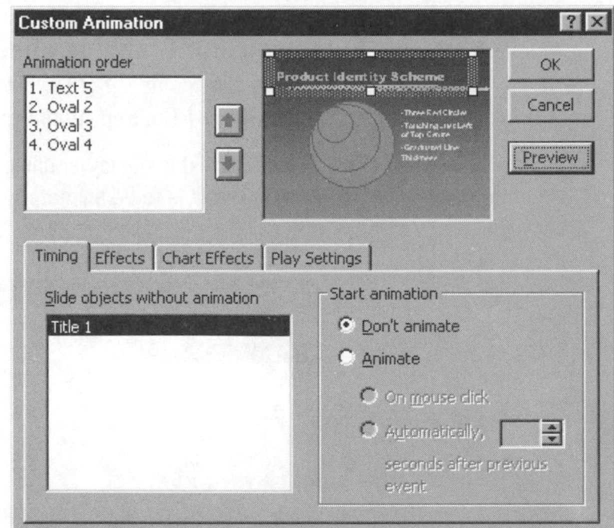

The names of the elements are transferred to the Animation order box.

3) Click **Preview** to see how the slide will be presented.

4) Check that the elements in the Animation order box are in the following order: first the three ovals, biggest first, smallest last, then the text. You can change the order by selecting the name of the object you want to change and using the arrow buttons to move it up or down.

5) Select each of the ovals in turn and, in the Effects tab, specify Fly from Bottom-Right, No Sound, and Don't Dim.

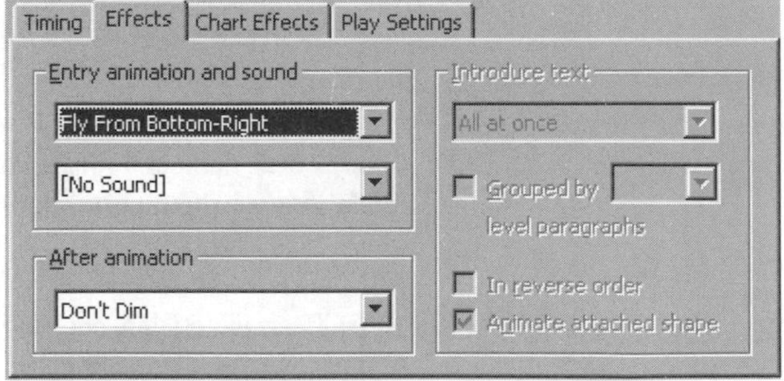

6) Select the text, and in the Effects tab, specify Wipe Down, No Sound, Don't Dim, and All at once.

   Click **Preview** to see the effect.

7) Click **OK** to close the Custom Animation dialog box.

Exercise 6.30: Grabbing Their Attention

1) Display slide number 1 (New Product Launch) in Slide view and choose **Slide Show | Custom Animation**.

2) Select the text in the lower half of the screen (Round Wheels), and specify that it is to be animated, as in the previous exercise.

3) In the Effects tab, specify Spiral, No Sound, Don't Dim, and All at once.

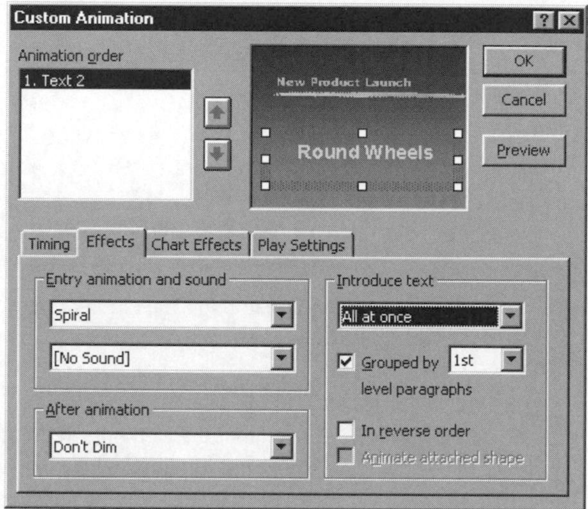

Click **Preview** to see the effect.

Experiment with the alternatives to All at once – By Word and By Letter – and each time click **Preview** to see their effect.

4) Click **OK** to close the Custom Animation dialog box.

Exercise 6.31: Animating a Chart

1) Display slide number 6 (Sales Projections) in Slide view and choose **Slide Show | Custom Animation**

2) In the Timing tab, specify that the chart is to be animated.

3) In the Chart Effects tab, specify By Series, Animate Grid and Legend, Appear, No Sound, and Don't Dim.

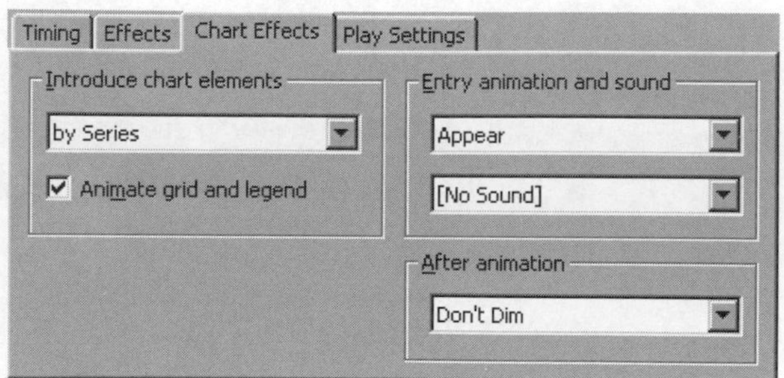

It may be difficult to see the effect of this by using the **Preview** button, so click **OK**, then choose **View | Slide Show** and go through the presentation from the beginning.

Exercise 6.32: On Your Own

1) Animate slide number 4 (Advantages and Disadvantages) so that the advantages appear one at a time, flying in from the left, and the disadvantages appear one at a time, flying in from the right.
2) Animate slide number 5 (A First Look) so that the features appear one at a time, flying in from the right.

Music and Other Noises

If you followed the exercises above, you specified No Sound each time. If you were adventurous, you probably tried out some of the other options. If you didn't, try them now: you can choose a sound to accompany each transition and each animated effect. There is a wide range of sound effects available: the most commonly used are already listed in the Sound drop-down list. You can find others by choosing Other Sounds and selecting any file that has the extension .wav.

Preparing Handouts

You can, if you wish, simply print out your slides and distribute them to your audience. However, this is somewhat inelegant: the size of type that is appropriate for a slide is much too big for normal reading. Instead, PowerPoint gives you the option of producing handouts in which several slides are shown to a page.

To do this, choose **File | Print**, and from the Print what: drop-down list, choose the handout format you want to use.

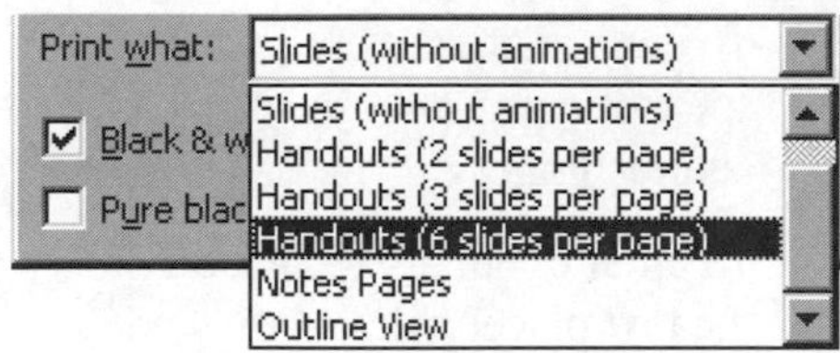

Numbering Your Slides

When people in your audience ask questions, they may want to refer to a specific slide, so it is useful to identify each slide by number.

Exercise 6.33: Adding Slide Numbers

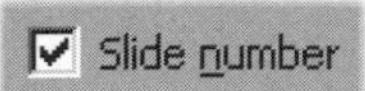

1) Choose **View | Header and Footer.**
2) In the Slide tab, check Slide number. Leave the other options unchecked.

3) Click **Apply to All.**

   Note that this tab also enables you to include the date and time on each slide.

If you choose similar options on the other tab – Notes and Handouts – the page number (or date and time) will be shown only on the handouts and speaker notes, but not on the slides themselves.

Remember that if you want to display a particular slide in Slide Show view, just type the slide number and press ENTER.

Speaker Notes

If you wish to write a script to accompany the slides, or simply make notes to remind you of the key points or additional background information, you can use the speaker notes facility. This enables you to create a document with one page for each slide. The slide is shown in the top half; you enter your notes in the bottom half. (PowerPoint does not display the notes on screen as part of your presentation.)

You can enter text to your speaker notes pages at any stage when creating or editing your presentation.

Speaker Notes
A document that has one page for each slide in the presentation. Each page is divided into two: the slide is shown at the top, and speaker notes are shown at the bottom.

Notes View

To enter, edit, or view speaker notes, choose **View | Notes Page**.

To enter or edit text, click on the text placeholder.

By default, PowerPoint displays a notes page at 40% of its full size. You may wish to increase this to nearer 100% when typing or editing. Do this by choosing **View | Zoom.**

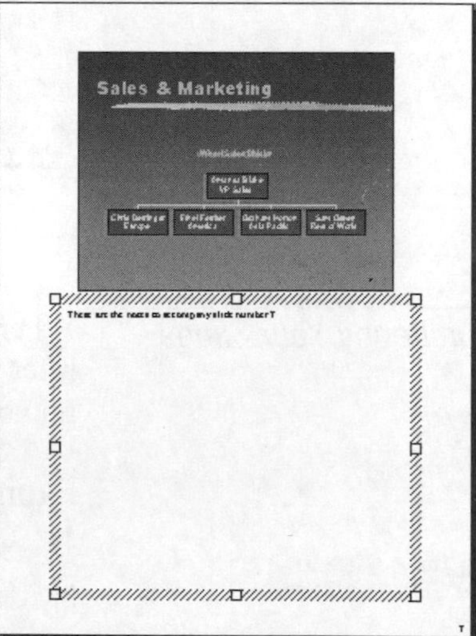

To print out speaker notes, choose **Print**, and from the Print what: drop-down list, choose Notes Page.

Check Your Spelling!

Spelling mistakes really spoil a presentation: they make you look either careless or ignorant – and your effort to impress the audience may be wasted. While it is dangerous to rely totally on a spell-checker, it is also foolish not to use one at all.

To use the spell-checker, choose **Tools | Spelling**, or press F7. Any words that fail the spell check are shown, with suggested alternatives. You can accept one of the suggestions, edit the word yourself, or leave the original unchanged.

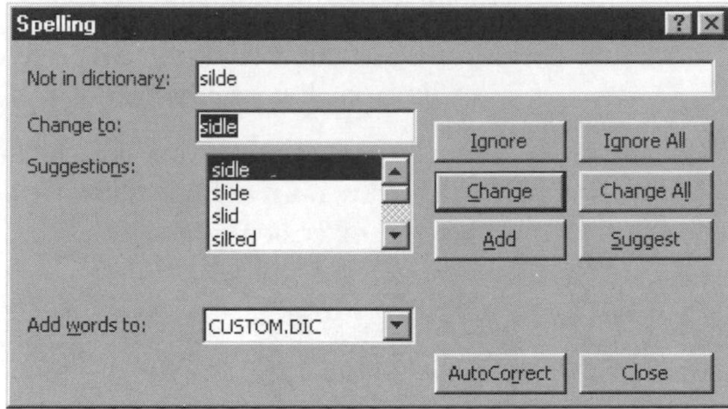

Note that the spell checker will not find incorrect spellings that are themselves valid words (such as 'form' instead of 'from').

Saving Your Presentation as a Slide Show

You already know how to use Slide Show view to start your presentation. Another option is to save the presentation as a slide show, so that it always opens as a slide show, whether you open it within PowerPoint or directly from the desktop. To do this, choose **File | Save As**, and specify PowerPoint Show. The file will be saved with the extension .pps.

Section Summary: So Now You Know

You can control the way a new slide replaces an old one with *transition effects*; these can be as conservative or as dramatic as you like. In addition, you can add sound effects to the transition, so that the new slide arrives with an explosion or a clash of cymbals.

To hold your audience's attention, you can reveal the material on a slide piece by piece, in a *build slide*. Build slides can be animated in a variety of ways.

You can prepare *handouts* for your audience, with several slides to a page, and you can prepare *speaker notes*, with the script that you want to follow, or additional details to support your presentation.

You can number slides for easy reference, and you can check the spelling on all your presentation materials.

Finally, you can save your presentation as a *slide show*, so that it will always open in Slide Show view. If you do this, the file will have the extension .pps.

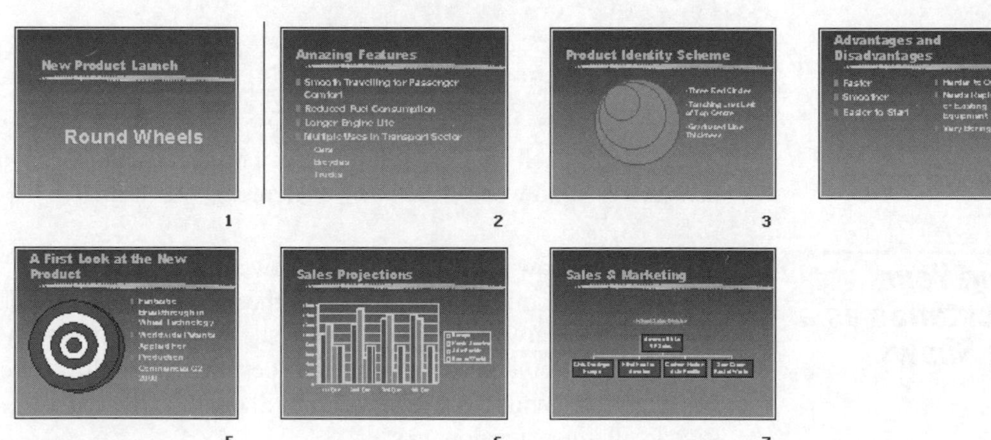

PowerPoint Presentations: Here's One I Prepared Earlier

7 Information and Communication

'The Internet is like a library.' You will hear this kind of statement a lot from people who know little about either.

If the Internet is a library, it's a strange one indeed. For starters, there is no indexing system. At any rate, the books are not arranged on numbered shelves but scattered on the floor. A lot of what is in the books is untrue, even in the non-fiction ones. There is no librarian, and no information desk. Did we mention also that the lights are turned off?

What's more, you can make as much noise as you like when using the Internet, while at the same time collecting facts and figures (and fiction and music and video and sports results and stock prices and weather reports and recipes) from all around the world.

In fact, the principal use of the Internet is for e-mail – a way of sending messages from your computer to someone else's computer, whether they are in the next room or in a different hemisphere.

Think of this Module as your chance to borrow knowledge and skills you won't ever be asked to return, and to become part of an online electronic community. Welcome to the Internet Age!

Section 7.1: Exploring the Web

In This Section

Prepare to take your first steps in exploring the World Wide Web or 'Web' as it is popularly known. In this Section you will visit and explore websites operated by national newspapers based in Australia, France, Germany and Italy, and by a Paris-based art gallery and an American music store.

Also in this Section you will learn the basics of operating Internet Explorer, the Microsoft software application for exploring – otherwise known as browsing or surfing – the Web.

New Skills

At the end of this Section you should be able to:

- Start Internet Explorer and visit a website
- Explore a website by scrolling down pages and clicking on hyperlinks
- Move backwards and forwards through previously visited web pages
- Open several windows at once in Internet Explorer
- Print web pages, and use the main page setup and print options
- Save text, images, and complete pages from the Web
- Access and use Internet Explorer's online help

New Words

At the end of this Section you should be able to explain the following terms:

- Home page
- Address Bar
- Website
- Web server
- Web browser

Starting Internet Explorer

Internet Explorer

Double-click the Internet Explorer icon.
-or-
Choose **Start | Programs | Internet Explorer**.

If your computer has a permanent Internet connection, you are ready to surf the Web with Internet Explorer.

If you have a dial-up connection, you must first dial your Internet Service Provider (ISP). Internet Explorer may be set up to do this automatically. If not, you will need to dial your ISP separately.

Enter your user name and password (if Internet Explorer has not recorded them from the last time that you dialled your ISP), and click **Connect**.

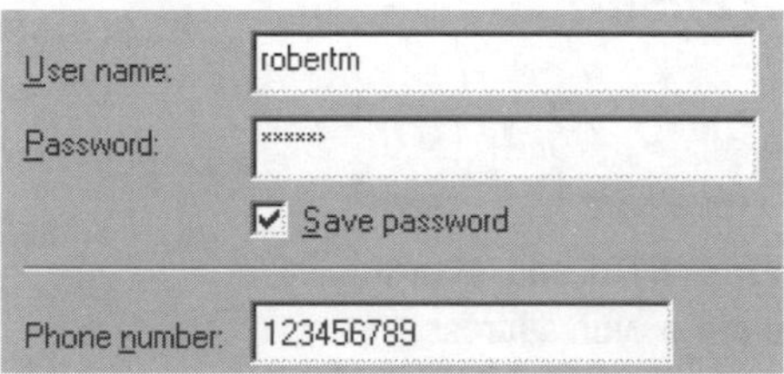

Your Browser's Start Page

Typically, Internet Explorer is set up so that it takes you to a particular web page whenever you start the application.

Home pages of two Internet Service Providers (ISPs)

If you obtained Internet Explorer from your ISP, this start page is probably the front page of the ISP's website. Such a front page is called a home page.

> **Home Page**
>
> *The first or front page of a website. Typically, it presents a series of links that you can follow to view the site's other pages.*

You will learn how to change Internet Explorer's start page in Section 7.4.

Visiting and Exploring a Website

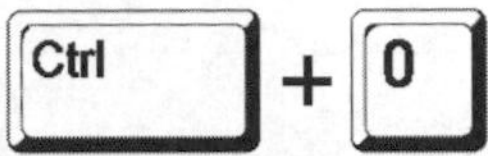

Press CTRL and 'o' to enter a web address

In Exercise 7.1 you visit and explore the website of *The Age*, a newspaper published in Melbourne, Australia.

Exercise 7.1: Visiting and Exploring a Website

1) Choose **File | Open** or press CTRL+o. (That is, hold down the CTRL key and press the letter 'o' key.)
2) In the Open dialog box displayed, type www.theage.com.au, and click **OK**.

Internet Explorer displays the home page of *The Age* website.

Click here

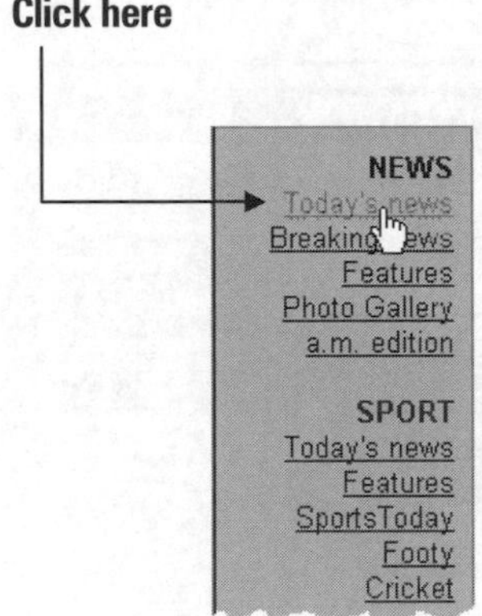

3) Along the left of *The Age*'s home page you can see a list of the newspaper's main sections – Today's News, Breaking News, Photo Gallery, and so on.

   Scroll down the page to view the list in full.

   Each section name is underlined, indicating that it is a hyperlink.

   A hyperlink is an item of text (or a graphic) on a web page that, if clicked, leads to another web page.

   Click the section named Today's News.
4) Internet Explorer now displays a new web page, the Today's News page.

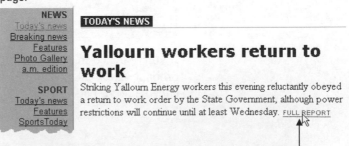

Click here

Here you can see summaries of the day's main news stories. Each summary ends with a hyperlink named Full Report.

5) Click on any Full Report hyperlink to display a web page containing an individual news story.

Leave the news story page open on your screen in preparation for Exercise 7.2.

You are now three pages 'deep' inside *The Age* website.

- First, you visited the front or home page.
- Second, you visited the Today's News page, with its list of news summaries.
- Third, you visited a page containing a particular news story.

Internet Explorer Toolbar

As with Microsoft Office applications such as Word and Excel, Internet Explorer includes a Standard Toolbar that offers fast, one-click access to commonly used actions. Rather than introduce all the Toolbar buttons at once, we will explain each one as it becomes relevant.

Internet Explorer Toolbar

In Exercise 7.2 you will use the Back and Forward buttons on Internet Explorer's Standard Toolbar.

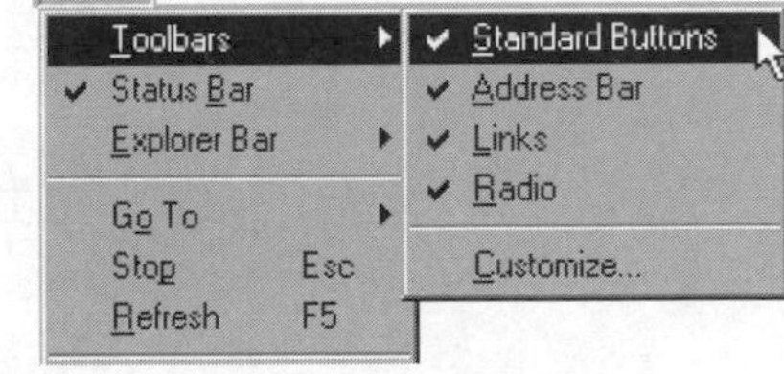

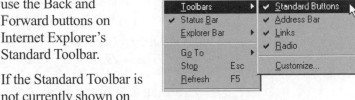

If the Standard Toolbar is not currently shown on your screen, choose **View | Toolbars | Standard Buttons** to display it.

Moving Through a Series of Web Pages

In Exercise 7.2 you learn how to return to web pages that you visited earlier, and then move forward again to the ones you visited most recently.

Exercise 7.2: Moving Backwards and Forwards Through Web Pages

Back button: Returns you to the previously displayed web page

1) With a news story displayed from *The Age* newspaper, click once on the Back button, located on the left of Internet Explorer's Standard Toolbar.

   This returns you to the web page you visited most recently – the Today's News page.

2) With the Today's News page displayed, click a second time on the Back button.

This returns you to the second-last web page that you visited – the website's home page.

3) With *The Age*'s home page displayed, click once on the Forward button. It is located just to the right of the Back button on the Standard Toolbar.

This button moves you forward, one page at a time, retracing your original movement through the website.

Forward button: Reverses the effect of pressing the Back button

4) With the Today's News page displayed, click a second time on the Forward button.

This brings you forward to the web page from which you originally began to move backwards – the individual news story page.

Browsing with the Address Bar

When you visit a web page, notice that its web address is displayed in the area immediately above Internet Explorer's main window. This is called the Address Bar.

You can also use the Address Bar to enter a web address. Although the Address Bar always displays 'http://' before a web address, you need not type 'http://' when entering an address in the Bar.

If the Address Bar is not currently shown on your screen, choose **View | Toolbars | Address Bar** to display it.

Exercise 7.3: Entering an Address in the Address Bar

1) Click anywhere in the Address Bar. This selects the currently displayed web address, which is then shown in reverse (white-on-black).

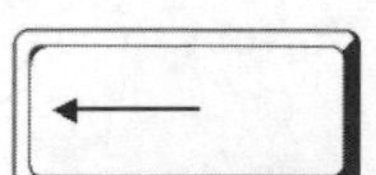

Removes the character to the *left* of the cursor

2) Use the BACKSPACE or DELETE key to remove the currently displayed web address. The Address Bar is now empty.

3) Type the following web address in the Bar, and click **Go** or press ENTER: www.torontostar.ca

Removes the character to the *right* of the cursor

Internet Explorer now displays the front page of Canada's *Toronto Star* newspaper.

Practise your Web browsing skills by clicking on hyperlinks to display pages within the Toronto newspaper, and by scrolling up and down each displayed web page.

Address Bar

An area above the main window that shows the address (preceded by 'http://') of the currently displayed web page. You can also use the Address Bar to enter a web address. (You need not type 'http://'.)

Printing a Web Page

You can print out the currently displayed web page by choosing **File | Print** and then clicking **OK** on the Print dialog box.

Print button

Alternatively, click the Print button on the Internet Explorer Standard Toolbar. Clicking this Print button does *not* display the Print dialog box.

Page Setup Options

Internet Explorer's **File | Page Setup** command enables you to control the following:

- **Paper Size**: A4 is the European paper size standard.
- **Orientation**: Portrait ('standing up') or Landscape ('on its side').
- **Print Range**: Your options are: all pages, a specified range of pages, or the part of the page that you have selected.
- **Number of Copies**: If you select any number greater than one, you can specify whether you want the copies collated or not.
- **Margins**: The distance of the page's printed content (text and graphics) from the edge of the paper. You can set each of the four margins (top, bottom left and right) independently.
- **Header and Footer**: You can include or exclude the following in the header and footer areas of the printed web pages:
  - Page title
  - Web page address
  - Page number in printout
  - Total number of pages in printout
  - Date of printing

Internet Explorer indicates these options by symbols as &P and &d. Do you need to remember all these symbols? No; you can refer to Internet Explorer's online help, even during the ECDL test. You will learn about online help at the end of this Section 7.1.

Saving from the Web

If you see something on the Web that you like – such as an image, some text, or even an entire web page – can you copy it from the website to your computer? Yes. This topic shows you how.

Saving an Image

To save an image from the currently displayed web page, right-click on the image to display a pop-up menu. Next, choose **Save Picture As**, select the location on your computer that you want to save to, accept or change the current name of the image, and click **Save**.

Exercise 7.4 provides an example of image-saving from the Web.

Exercise 7.4: Saving an Image from a Web Page

1) Choose **File | Open** or press CTRL+o and enter the following web address: metalab.unc.edu/wm/paint/auth/monet/

   Internet Explorer displays the Claude Monet page from the Paris-based WebMuseum Project.

2) Click on the following hyperlink: Waterlillies

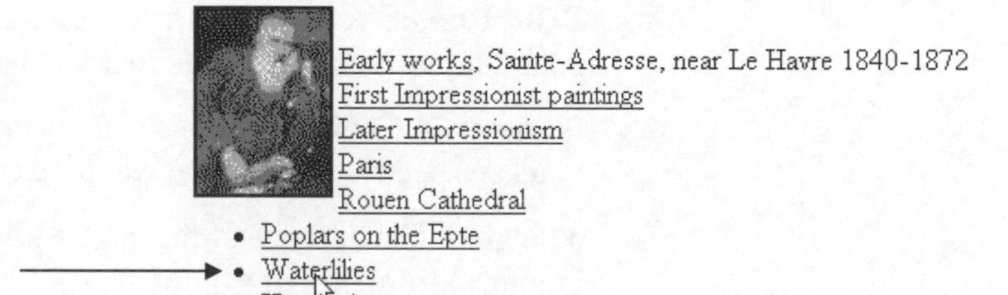

3) On the next web page displayed, click the small picture entitled Water Lillies (The Clouds).

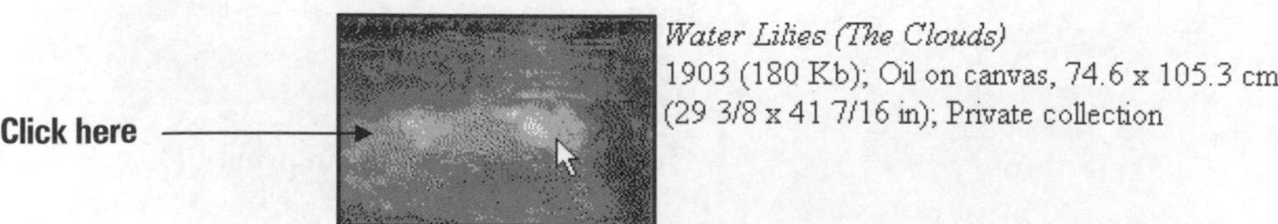

   Internet Explorer now displays a larger version of the image.

4) When it has displayed fully, right-click anywhere on the image, and choose the **Save Picture As** command from the pop-up menu.

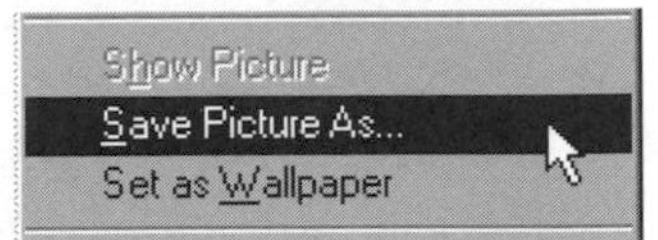

5) In the Save As dialog box then displayed, accept or change the image's file name (monet_wl-clouds.jpg), select the drive and folder you want to save the file to, and click **OK**.

Image File Formats

Most image files on the Web are in either gif (pronounced with a hard 'g', as in gift) or in jpg (pronounced jay-peg) format.

Selecting and Saving Text

You can save and reuse all or a selected part of the text from the currently displayed web page. This is a two-step process:

- **Copy**: You select and then *copy* the text to the Clipboard, a temporary holding area.
- **Paste**: You *paste* the text from the Clipboard into another file such as a Word document or an Excel spreadsheet.

Four points you should remember about the Clipboard:

- The Clipboard is temporary. Turn off your computer and the Clipboard contents are deleted.
- Text stays in the Clipboard after you paste from it, so you can paste the same piece of text into as many different files as you want.
- The Clipboard can hold only a single, copied item at a time. If you copy a second piece of text, the second overwrites the first.
- Text copied from a web page and pasted into Word or other application may lose the formatting that it had on the Web.

Exercise 7.5 takes you through the steps of copying and pasting selected text from a web page.

Exercise 7.5: Saving Text from a Web Page

1) Choose **File | Open** or press CTRL+o, enter the following web address, and press ENTER: www.well.com/user/smalin/miller.html

   Here you will find a copy of George A. Miller's classic essay, *The Magical Number Seven, Plus or Minus Two: Some Limits on Our Capacity for Processing Information*.

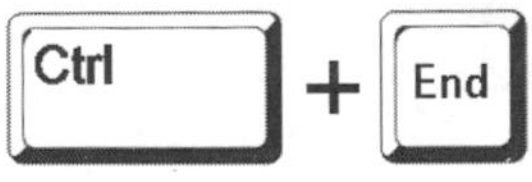

Press CTRL and END to move to the bottom of a web page

2) When the web page has loaded fully, scroll down to the end of the page. (A quick way of moving to the bottom of a page is to press CTRL+END.)

Now, press PAGE UP two or three times until Internet Explorer displays the last paragraph of the essay, which begins with the words 'And finally'.

3) Click at the start of the paragraph and drag the mouse down and right until you have selected the entire paragraph. Your screen should look like that shown.

> And finally, what about the magical number seven? What about the seven wonders of the world, the seven seas, the seven deadly sins, the seven daughters of Atlas in the Pleiades, the seven ages of man, the seven levels of hell, the seven primary colors, the seven notes of the musical scale, and the seven days of the week? What about the seven-point rating scale, the seven categories for absolute judgment, the seven objects in the span of attention, and the seven digits in the span of immediate memory? For the present I propose to withhold judgment. Perhaps there is something deep and profound behind all these sevens, something just calling out for us to discover it. But I suspect that it is only a pernicious, Pythagorean coincidence.

When you select text, Internet Explorer displays that text in reverse (white text on black background), rather like the negative of a photograph.

4) Choose **Edit | Copy** or press CTRL+c to copy the text to the Clipboard.

5) Open Microsoft Word, open a new document, and choose **Edit | Paste** or press CTRL+v to paste the selected text into Word.

When finished, you can close the Word document without saving it, and close Word.

Saving All Text

When you want to save *all* the text from a web page, Internet Explorer offers you two options. You can:

- Choose **Edit | Select All**, and then copy the text to the Clipboard.

-or-

- Choose **File | Save As**, select the Text File (.txt) option, select the location on your computer that you want to save to, accept or change the default file name, and click **Save**.

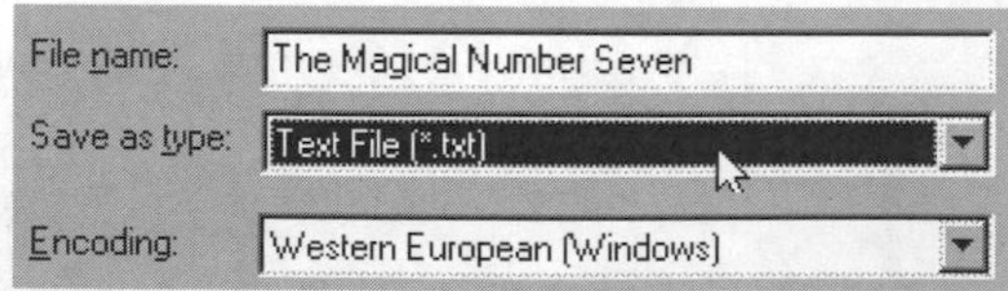

Saving a Web Page

You can save an entire web page – including text, graphics and other components. Exercise 7.6 shows you how.

Exercise 7.6: Saving a Web Page

1) Visit the MP3 music website at www.mp3.com.
2) Choose **File | Save As**, select the Web Page complete option, select the location on your computer to save to, accept or change the default file name, and click **Save**.

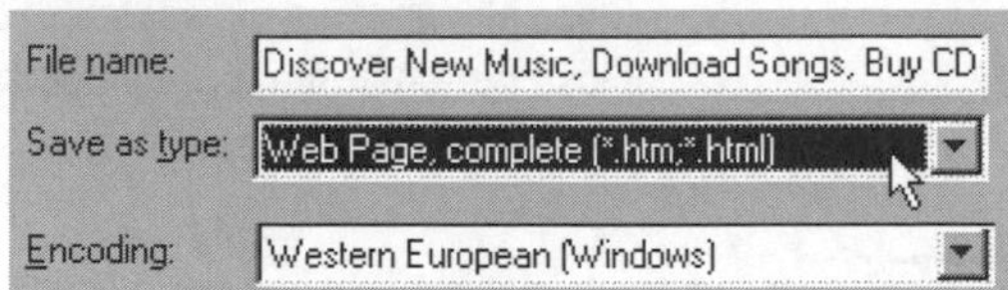

The web page is still on the website. You have saved only a *copy* of that page on your computer.

Copyright

As you have learnt, it's not difficult to copy text and images from the Web to your computer. But it may not always be legal. If you intend reproducing copyright material that you obtained from the Web, ask for permission first.

Opening Multiple Web Pages

Internet Explorer allows you to open several web pages at one time. Follow Exercise 7.7 to discover how.

Exercise 7.7: Opening Multiple Web Pages

1) Visit the following website: www.lemonde.fr

   tout.lemonde.fr

   Internet Explorer now displays the home page of the French newspaper, *Le Monde*.
2) Choose **File | New | Window** or press CTRL+n.

   Internet Explorer opens a new, second window. By default, the new window displays whatever web page is shown in the previous one – in this case, the home page of *Le Monde*.
3) Press CTRL+o and enter www.welt.de, the web address of the German newspaper, *Die Welt*.

4) Open a third window, and enter the following web address: www.lastampa.it. This is the home page of the Italian newspaper, *La Stampa*.

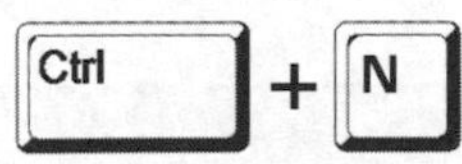

Press CTRL and 'n' to open a new window in Internet Explorer

LA STAMPA *web*

You can continue to open further windows in Internet Explorer – the only limit on the number of simultaneously open windows is the size of your computer's memory.

5) Close all windows except one. You close a window by clicking the Close button at the top-right of the Internet Explorer window or by choosing **File | Close**.

Web Words

In this Section 7.1 we have been using the word 'website'. Let's look at what this and related terms mean.

The Internet or Net is an inter-network – a network of networks. As you may remember from Module 1, a network is a group of computers (and perhaps other devices such as printers and scanners) connected together by some means.

On the Net, the word *site* is used to describe a single network. A Net site becomes a website when it includes a computer that acts as a web server. The Net existed long before web servers, and today not every Net site includes a web server.

Website
An Internet-connected network that is owned and managed by an individual, company or organization, and that includes a web server.

Web Servers and Web Browsers

What's a web server? It's a computer that stores files of a particular format, and makes them available ('serves them up') over the Internet to computer users who have a software application called a web browser.

Web Server
A computer on an Internet-connected network that stores files and delivers them over the Internet in response to requests from web browsers.

What's a web browser? It's a software application that sends requests to a web server for files, and then displays the files on the user's screen. Microsoft Internet Explorer and Netscape Navigator are the two most popular web browser applications.

Web Browser

An application such as Microsoft Internet Explorer that enables a user to request files from a web server over the Internet, and displays the requested files on the user's computer.

The term 'Web' is typically written with an initial capital. When it is used as an adjective, however, a lower-case initial is more common. For example, web server and web browser. The term 'website' is typically written as a single word.

Online Help

Like Excel, Access, PowerPoint and other Microsoft applications, Internet Explorer offers a searchable online help system:

- The 'help' in online help means that the information is there to assist you understand and use the application.
- The 'online' means that the material is presented on the computer screen rather than as a traditional printed manual.

You can search through and read online help in two ways: from dialog boxes, or from the **Help** menu.

Using Help from Dialog Boxes

You can access online help directly from a dialog box, as Exercise 7.8 demonstrates.

Exercise 7.8: Using Online Help in a Dialog Box

1) Choose **File | Page Setup** to display the Page Setup dialog box.
2) Click the question-mark symbol near the top-right of the dialog box. Internet Explorer displays a question mark to the right of the cursor.
3) Drag the mouse down and right, and click anywhere in the Header box.

4) Internet Explorer now displays help text telling you about the various header codes.

Practise Exercise 7.8 with other dialog boxes in Internet Explorer.

Using Help Menu Options

You can also access online help from the **Help** menu. Choose **Help | Contents and Index** to display the three tabs of the Help Topics dialog box.

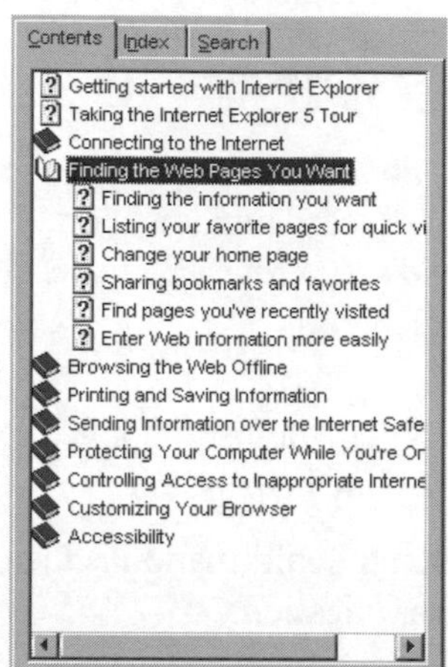

Contents Tab

This offers short descriptions of Internet Explorer's main features.

Where you see a heading with a book symbol, double-click to view the related sub-headings.

Double-click on a question-mark symbol to read the help text.

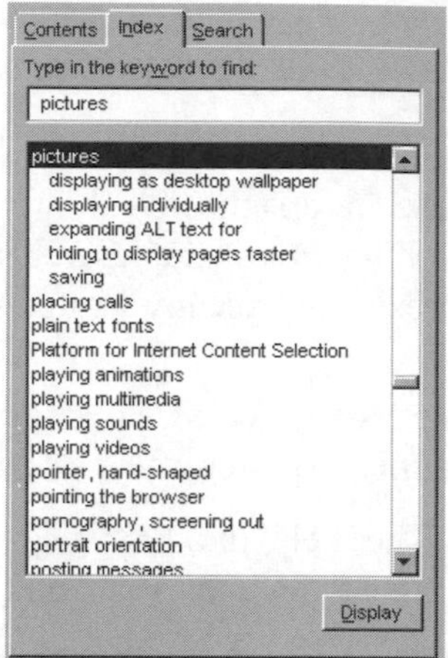

Index Tab

Reading the material displayed on this tab is like looking through the index of a printed book.

Just type the first letters of the word or phrase you are interested in.

Internet Explorer responds by displaying all matches from the online help in the lower half of the dialog box.

When you find the index entry that you are looking for, click the **Display** button.

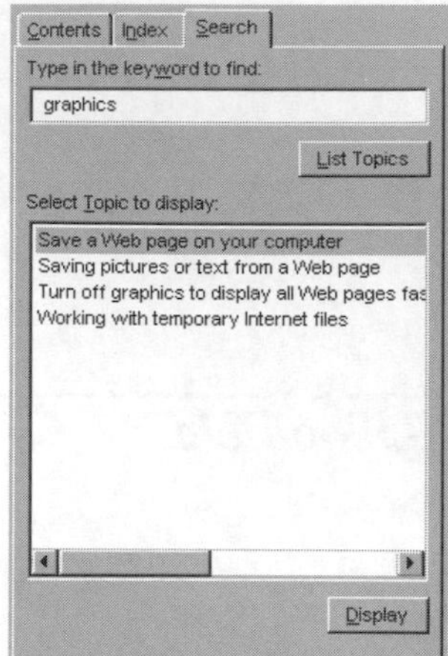

Search Tab

Can't find what you are looking for in the Contents or Index tabs? Try this tab.

When you type a word or phrase and click **List Topics**, Internet Explorer performs a deeper search of the online help.

When you find the item you are looking for, double-click on it to display it.

As you search through and read online help topics, you will see the following buttons at the top of the online help window:

- **Hide/Show:** Hides or displays the left-hand pane of the online help dialog box.
- **Back/Forward**: Moves you backwards and forwards through previously visited help topics.
- **Options:** Offers a number of display choices, and enables you to print the currently displayed online help text.

- **Web Help:** Takes you to Microsoft's Web-based support site for Internet Explorer.

Take a few minutes to look through Internet Explorer's online help system. Remember that you will be free to use online help during an ECDL test.

When finished, you can close Internet Explorer by clicking the Close button or choosing **File | Close**. You have now completed this Section 7.1 of the ECDL Information and Communication Module.

Section Summary: So Now You Know

Internet Explorer is a *web browser* application that enables you request information from *web servers* over the Internet.

Internet Explorer typically takes you to a particular web page – called the *start page* – whenever you start the application. If you obtained Internet Explorer from your ISP, the start page is probably the *home page* of your ISP's website.

A home page is the first or front page of a website. Typically, it presents a series of *hyperlinks* that you can follow to view the site's other pages.

You can enter a web address to Internet Explorer using the **File | Open** command, pressing CTRL+o, or by typing it in the *Address Bar*. The Address Bar, located above the main window, always shows the address of the currently displayed web page.

Along the top of the Internet Explorer window is the *Standard Toolbar* that gives you one-click access to commonly used browsing actions such as moving back and forwards through previously visited web pages.

You can open *multiple windows* in Internet Explorer at one time, and display different web pages in each one. The application also allows you *save* web pages on your computer, or selected images and text from web pages.

Section 7.2: Finding Information within Websites

In This Section

Many websites contain hundreds – even thousands – of pages. The Web-based edition of a daily newspaper, for example, typically consists of a hundred pages or more. If a newspaper offers an online archive of past issues over three years, the total number of pages at its website might exceed ten thousand.

Other examples of very large websites include those run by online retailers that stock tens of thousands of music CDs or several million books. Travel and holiday websites can also contain huge numbers of pages offering timetable and destination information.

How do you find particular items of information on such sites? This Section shows you how.

Also in this Section you learn about web-address standards and how different countries follow slightly different web addressing conventions.

New Skills

At the end of this Section you should be able to:

- Find a word or phrase on a web page
- Use a site index to locate information within a website
- Use a search engine to find information within a website
- Use an interactive form to find information within a website
- Describe the web address standards used in the US, UK, Italy, France, Germany, Australia and South Africa
- Explain how folder and file names are incorporated within web addresses

New Words

At the end of this Section you should be able to explain the following terms:

- Navigation bar
- Keyword
- Website search engine
- Interactive form
- Web address (URL)

Finding Text within a Web Page

To help you find a particular word or phrase on a web page, Internet Explorer provides the **Edit | Find (on this Page)** command. This command searches only:

- The currently *displayed* web page – not the entire website, and not the whole World Wide Web!
- The currently *loaded* part of the web page. So wait until a page is completely loaded (copied from the website to your computer's memory) before using the command.

Status bar indicates when web page has fully loaded

- The *text* of the page. Words that are displayed within images are ignored.

Exercise 7.9 shows you how to use this command on a lengthy, text-intensive web page.

Exercise 7.9: Finding Information within a Web Page

1) Open Internet Explorer and visit the web page containing George A. Miller's essay, *The Magical Number Seven, Plus or Minus Two*. The address is: www.well.com/user/smalin/miller.html
2) Choose **Edit | Find (on this Page)** or press CTRL+f, enter the word 'variance' in the Find dialog box, and click **Find Next**.

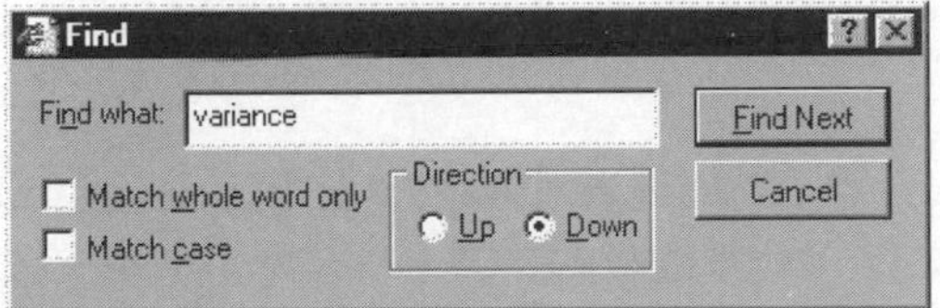

3) Internet Explorer takes you to the first occurrence of the word on the web page. The dialog box stays open on your screen.
4) To find further occurrences, click **Find Next** again. When finished, click **Cancel**.

Finding Information within a Website

Larger websites can contain many hundreds and even thousands of individual web pages. To help you locate particular information, such websites generally offer one or more of the following three features:

- **Site Index**: Sometimes called a site map or site guide, this is a web page that lists the main contents of the website.
- **Search Engine**: A program that searches for occurrences of text (words, numbers or other keyboard characters) that you

enter, and displays a list of all web pages that contain such text, together with a summary description of each listed page.

- **Interactive Forms**: These enable you to request specific information. You will commonly find forms on travel and holiday websites, and on websites that sell highly configurable products (such as computers).

Website Index Pages

Exercises 7.10, 7.11 and 7.12 provide examples of displaying index pages on three websites – an American software developer (Borland), a British airline (British Airways) and a British media organisation (the BBC).

In each Exercise, click on a number of links from the index web page to explore the particular website. And then click the Back button to retrace your steps.

Exercise 7.10: Displaying the Index Page of a Software Developer's Website

Tech Corner
Books
Site Map

1) Visit the website of Borland by entering the following address: www.borland.com
2) Along the left of the home page you will see a number of hyperlinks. Click on the one named Site Map.
3) This brings you to Borland's index page, where you will find a comprehensive listing of the website's contents.

Exercise 7.11: Displaying the Index Page of an Airline Website

1) Visit the British Airways website. The address is: www.britishairways.co.uk

Along the top of the home page you will find a link named Site Index.

2) Click it to display the contents of the airline's website.

Exercise 7.12: Displaying the Index Page of a Media Website

1) Visit the website of the British Broadcasting Corporation at www.bbc.co.uk

Near the top-left of the home page you will find a link named A-Z.

2) Click it to display the contents of the BBC's website.

Some websites display their main links across the top of every front page; others list them down one side of the page. A list of the main website links is called a navigation bar or 'navbar'. A navbar may be made up of text or graphics.

Navigation Bar
A horizontal or vertical list of hyperlinks to the main components of a website, such as Home (the front page), Site Index (or Site Map or Guide), Company Profile, Products, Services and Staff Contacts.

Site Index
Also known as a site map or site guide, this is a web page that lists the main contents of a website.

Website Search Engines

Site indexes can help you to discover the range and depth of information available on a website. To find one or a few specific items, however, search engines are better.

Exercises 7.13, 7.14 and 7.15 provide examples of search engines on three websites – a film information site (Internet Movie Database), a magazine archive (*The Scout Report*), and an online dictionary of computer terminology (PC Webopedia).

Exercise 7.13: Searching a Film Database

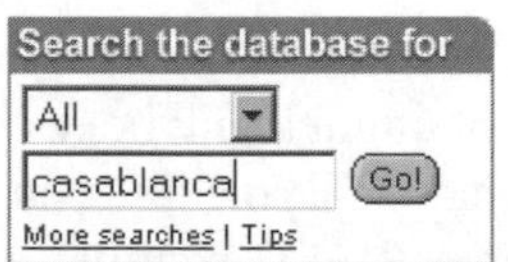

1) Visit the Internet Movie Database by entering the following address: www.imdb.com
2) In the Search box near the top left of the home page, enter a film title – for example, Casablanca – and click the **Go!** button.

The IMDB responds by listing pages from its database that relate to your selected film.

Exercise 7.14: Searching a Magazine Archive

1) Visit *The Scout Report* website. This weekly online publication identifies and reviews Internet resources of interest to researchers and educators. Its address is: www.scout.cs.wisc.edu/report

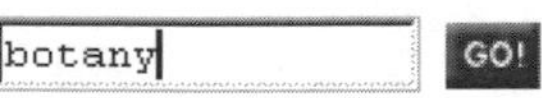

2) In the Search box near the top right of the home page, enter a subject in which you are interested – for example, botany – and click **Go!**

The Scout Report responds by listing articles from its archives that relate to your entered topic.

Exercise 7.15: Searching a Computer Dictionary

1) Visit the PC Webopedia website at www.pcwebopedia.com
2) In the Search box near the top of the home page, enter a term you would like explained – for example, modem – and click **Go!**

PC Webopedia responds by displaying a page containing an explanation of your entered word.

In Section 7.3 you will learn about search engines that enable you to search the Web and not just an individual website. You will also learn how to perform searches with multiple keywords.

Now is a good time to define some of the terms related to searching a website, and to searching the Web as a whole.

Keyword
Text or other keyboard characters entered to a search engine. The engine then displays or 'returns' a list of documents containing the entered text. Typically, the returned list provides links to the individual pages, and displays a summary description of each page.

Website Search Engine
A program that searches a website for keywords entered by the user. It displays or 'returns' a list of web pages on which it found occurrences of the entered word or words.

Interactive Forms

On the Web an interactive form is a page containing blank boxes called fields into which you can enter information. Typically, you use forms to specify the particular type of product (for example, a music CD), service (for example, a legal service) or information (for example, train departure times) that you require.

You can also use forms to submit information to a website. When buying a book from an online book shop, for example, you will be presented with a form into which you enter your name and credit card details.

Interactive Form
A series of fields on a web page that you use to request a specific item of information, or a product or service. You can also use a form to submit information, such as your name and credit card number.

Exercises 7.16 and 7.17 provide two examples of interactive forms on websites. The first enables you to request a train timetable, the

second to specify a PC configuration and view the corresponding price.

Exercise 7.16: Using a Form to Request a Train Timetable

1) Visit the Irish Rail website at www.irishrail.ie
2) On the home page, click the link named Timetables.

3) On the Timetables page now displayed, click the **Let's Go** button alongside the line that says Waterford to Dublin.

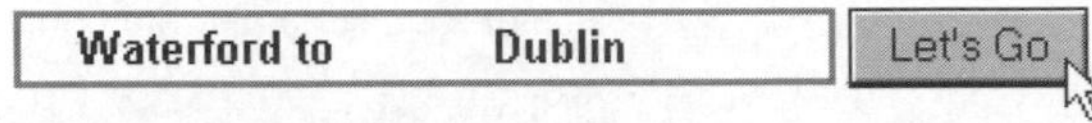

4) On the next web page displayed, make the selections as shown below and click **Let's Go**.

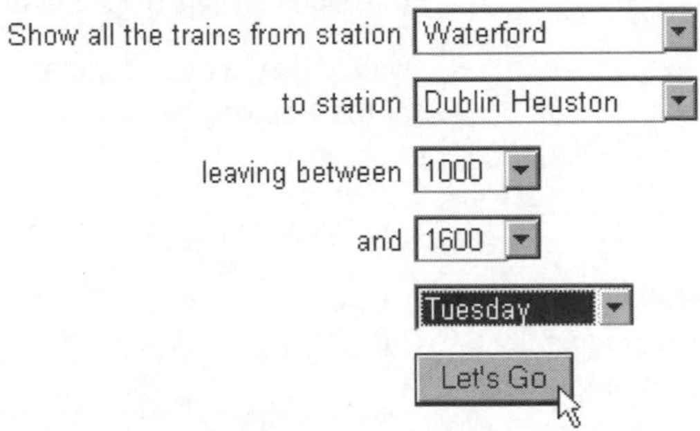

5) The website responds by listing all train services that match your entered requirements.

Timetable from Waterford to Dublin Heuston
For departure times 1000 - 1600
Tuesdays, Wednesdays and Thursdays

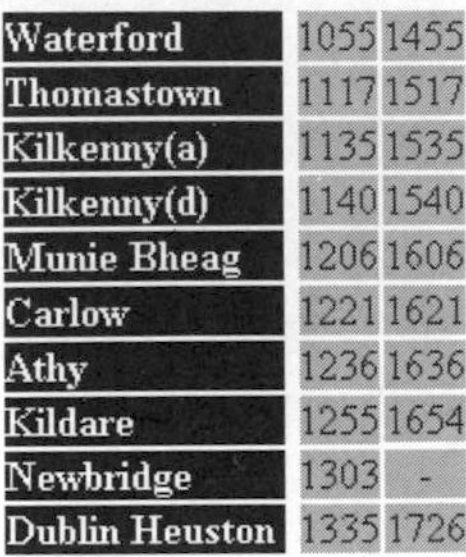

Waterford	1055	1455
Thomastown	1117	1517
Kilkenny(a)	1135	1535
Kilkenny(d)	1140	1540
Munie Bheag	1206	1606
Carlow	1221	1621
Athy	1236	1636
Kildare	1255	1654
Newbridge	1303	-
Dublin Heuston	1335	1726

Cars, sandwiches and personal computers are all examples of highly configurable products whose price varies with the combination of 'ingredients' chosen. In Exercise 7.17 you use a form to specify a PC's configuration and display the resulting price.

Almost all PC manufacturers now sell their products online. Note that the links and link names in the website chosen – Dell UK – may change slightly over time.

Exercise 7.17: Using a Form to Price a Customised PC

1) Visit Dell's British website at www.dell.co.uk

Home & Home Office

2) Click the link named Home & Home Office.

3) Click the link for Desktop. You should now see a new page listing a number of PC models. Click any PC model to see a new page that includes a link named Configure & Buy.

Configure & Buy

4) Click the link named Configure & Buy. You should now see a form that lists several options for such PC components as Memory, Monitor, Hard Drive and so on.

5) Make and change a number of selections.

   Notice that, as you do, the price of the PC, as displayed at the bottom of the web page, changes accordingly.

Example of a form used to specify a PC's configuration

The form recalculates the PC's price according to the cost of the components that you select

Memory

128MB SDRAM (1 x 128Mb)

Monitor

Dell 19" Monitor (17.9" viewable area)

Video Adapter

32Mb Diamond Viper V770D nVidia AGP Video Card

Hard Drive

20.4GB Hard Drive

Speakers

Altec Lansing ACS340 speakers

Network Card

3COM 3C900B Combo (+£40)

Price: £1,639 (excl. VAT)

6) When finished experimenting with the form, click the Back button repeatedly to revisit Dell's home page.

About Web Addresses

In this and the previous Section you have been entering web addresses and visiting the associated web pages. A web page is just another type of computer file. Whereas Word files end in .doc, for example, and Excel files in .xls, web pages end in .htm (or, sometimes, .html or .shtml). Let's look at web addresses in more detail.

To request a web page with Internet Explorer, you need to know two things:

- The name of the *web server* – the Internet-connected computer on which the particular web page is located
- The name of the *web page* (that is, the file) on the web server

Add these two items together and you get what is called a *web address*. Another, more technical, term for a web address is a URL (Uniform Resource Locator).

URL (Web Address)

The unique address of a web page. It contains the name of the web server and includes (or implies) the name of the particular web page.

Sample URLs

The best way to learn about web addresses is to look at a few examples and discover why they are written the way they are. Here are the URLs of three American web sites:

www.latimes.com www.princeton.edu www.cia.gov

In a US web address, the last part of the address – the so-called *suffix* – indicates the type of organisation.

For a commercial business (such as the *Los Angeles Times* newspaper), the suffix is .com; for an educational institution (such as Princeton University), it's .edu; and for a government agency (such as the CIA), it's .gov.

Here are some Italian (.it), French (.fr) and German (.de) URLs:

www.yahoo.it	www.smartweb.fr	www.infoseek.de
www.juventus.it	www.renault.fr	www.bmw.de
www.ferrari.it	www.louvre.fr	www.berlinonline.de

In each case, the suffix indicates only the country. Addresses are not categorised by type.

British web addresses end in .uk, but they also include a component to identify the organisation type: .co for commercial, .ac for the further and higher education sector, and .gov for government. Here are a few examples:

www.cttraining.co.uk	www.mcc.ac.uk
www.landrover.co.uk	www.cam.ac.uk
www.thisislondon.co.uk	www.ox.ac.uk
www.itn.co.uk	www.bcs.org.uk
www.chelseafc.co.uk	www.amnesty.org.uk

A suffix for primary- and second-level schools, .sch.uk, is becoming increasingly popular.

Other countries that use two suffixes – one for organisation type and one for the country itself – are Australia and South Africa. Here are some examples:

www.smh.com.au	www.southafrica.co.za
www.microsoft.com.au	www.icdl.co.za
www.ntu.edu.au	www.unisa.ac.za
www.uwa.edu.au	www.up.ac.za
www.ics.org.au	www.cssa.org.za
www.foe.org.au	www.sarl.org.za
www.deet.gov.au	www.finance.gov.za
www.thesource.gov.au	www.durban.gov.za

Practise your Web surfing skills by visiting some of the URLs listed in this topic.

URLs and Files

A URL specifies *two* things: the name of the web server and the name of a particular web page on that server. So: where is the web page name in this URL?

www.munnelly.com

Answer: when you enter just the web server name, the server displays the default web page. This is the front or main page of the web site, and is usually called index.htm (or index.html).

The web address of www.munnelly.com, therefore, is really:

www.munnelly.com/index.htm

Here are some other URLs with the name of the default web page included as part of the web address:

www.wit.ie/index.html www.ucd.ie/index.html www.ucg.ie/index.html

Notice how a forward slash (/) separates the web page name from the web server name.

When you want to view a web page that is *not* the front or main page, enter a URL that includes the page name. For example:

www.ucg.ie/departments.html	www.refdesk.com/paper.html
www.botany.com/narcissi.html	www.surfnetkids.com/pocahontas.htm

URLs and Folders

On web servers, as on other computers, files are organised into folders. In the four examples above, the web pages are in the main folders of the web servers. But web servers can also store pages in sub-folders or sub-sub-folders. Here are some examples of URLs that include sub-folder names:

www.irlgov.ie/aras/hist.htm
www.lastampa.it/rubriche/ultima/rubriche/lst/cinema/cinemahome.htm
www.fieldandstream.com/bookstore/fishbooks.html
www.ozsports.com.au/cricket/commentary.html

A forward slash (/) separates folder names and page names.

Sometimes a URL contains just the web server and folder name – but not the name of the page within the folder. In such cases, your web browser displays the default web page within *that* folder. Again, this is typically called index.html (or index.htm). For example:

www.tcd.ie/drama/

is really:

www.tcd.ie/drama/index.html

Further practise your web surfing skills by visiting some of the above URLs that contain folder and file names.

When finished, you can close Internet Explorer. You have now completed this Section 7.2 of the ECDL Information and Communication Module.

Section Summary: So Now You Know

Websites typically display a navigation bar or *navbar* – a horizontal or vertical list of hyperlinks to the main components of a website – along the top or down the left of each page.

Larger websites help users to navigate by providing one, two or all three of the following features:

- A *site index*, sometimes known as a site map or site guide, is a web page that lists the main contents of a website. It is similar in purpose to the contents page of a printed book.
- A website *search engine* is a program that searches a website for *keywords* entered by the user. It displays or 'returns' a list of web pages on which it found occurrences of the entered word or words.
- An *interactive form* is a series of fields on a web page that you use to request a specific item of information, or a product or service. You can also use a form to submit information, such as your name and credit card number.

A *URL* is the unique web address that contains the name of the web server and includes (or implies) the name of the particular web page. Where no page is specified in a URL, the browser displays the default page, usually *index.htm* or *index.html*.

URLs have at least two parts, separated by a dot (.). In the US, the first part is the organisation's name; the second indicates its type. Commercial sites end in *.com*, educational sites in *.edu* and government sites in *.gov*.

Italian, German and French sites are not categorised by type. Their domain names consist of just the organisation name and a suffix indicating their nationality (*.it*, *.fr*, and *.de*).

In the UK, commercial sites end in *.co.uk*, academic sites in *.ac.uk* or *sch.uk*, and government sites in *.gov.uk*. Australia and South Africa also categorise web addresses by organisation type.

Section 7.3: Finding Information on the Web

In This Section

A report published in early 2000 revealed that there were over one billion pages on the Web, stored on almost five million websites. Some 85% of the pages were in English, and just over half (55%) of web addresses ended in .com. Faced with such a phenomenal amount of data, how can web surfers hope to locate individual items of information of interest to them?

It's not as difficult as it may sound – once you know how. In this Section you will discover the techniques for searching and finding information on the Web.

New Skills

At the end of this Section you should be able to:

- Locate information on the Web by navigating through the categories of a directory site
- Locate information on the Web by entering a keyword to search engines and meta search engines
- Perform phrase searches using quotation symbols
- Perform multiple keyword searches using the plus (+) and minus (-) logical operators.

New Words

At the end of this Section you should be able to explain the following terms:

- Web directory
- Web search engine
- Web meta search engine
- Logical search

Finding Information on the Web

If you are exploring the Web for information on a particular topic, four types of websites can help you find what you are looking for:

- **Directory Sites:** These are websites that catalogue information on the Web according to subject matter.
- **Search Engines:** These are websites that search the Web for keywords – occurrences of specified words or phrases.
- **Meta Search Engines:** These are websites that submit keywords to several search engines. In effect, they allow you to use multiple search engines at once.
- **Natural Language Search Engines:** These are websites that accept queries in plain English. For example: 'Who is the Prime Minister of New Zealand?'

In this Section you will learn about each type of website and discover how you can best use them to find the information you need.

Web Directory Sites

A directory website organises information in an easy-to-follow, top-down structure. They tend to be selective, so that only the better sources of information are listed. Unfortunately, the Web changes so quickly that directory sites may not be always up-to-date.

The original and biggest directory site is Yahoo!, where you can browse information by category, sub-category, and, more often than not, sub-sub-category. Exercise 7.18 provides an example.

Exercise 7.18: Finding Information on Yahoo!

1) Open Internet Explorer and visit the Yahoo! website at www.yahoo.com
2) Click the link named Astronomy, which is located in the right-hand category column under the Science heading.

   Science
   Animals, Astronomy, Engineering...

3) You are now shown a new web page. It lists astronomy sub-categories in alphabetic order. Click the link named Planetaria.

   - **Pictures** *(86)*
   - **Planetaria** *(63)*
   - **Radio Astronomy** *(77)*

4) You are shown a third web page. This one lists the websites of some fifty planetaria, including Armagh (at www.armagh-planetarium.co.uk). Click on Armagh Planetarium to visit its web page.

- Allentown School District Planetarium
- Armagh Planetarium (United Kingdom)
- Astronaut Memorial Planetarium and Observatory - Brevard Community College

You have now completed the Exercise.

Exercise 7.18 demonstrates both the range and depth of information available on the Web – and the usefulness of directory sites such as Yahoo!

There are country-specific versions of Yahoo! available for a wide range of nations including the UK, Ireland, France, Germany, Italy, Australia and New Zealand. You can link to them from the main site at www.yahoo.com. Other popular web directory sites include About.com and NetGuide.

Web directory sites www.yahoo.com, www.about.com and www.netguide.com

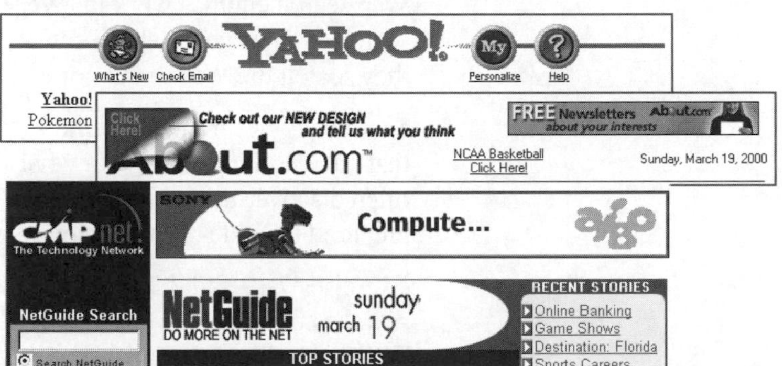

Most directory sites also offer a search-engine facility.

> **Web Directory Site**
>
> *A website that lists and categorises other sites on the Web according to their subject matter. Typically, it offers several hierarchical layers, with a listing of website addresses at the lowest level.*

Web Search Engines

A search engine allows you to enter a word or phrase, searches for instances of it, and then displays ('returns') a list of websites that match your entered word or phrase, with a summary of each. You can then click on the one that seems most appropriate to you.

Search engines *do not* search the entire Web, but their own smaller, regularly updated list of websites, which typically accounts for about 10–15% of the total number of sites on the Web.

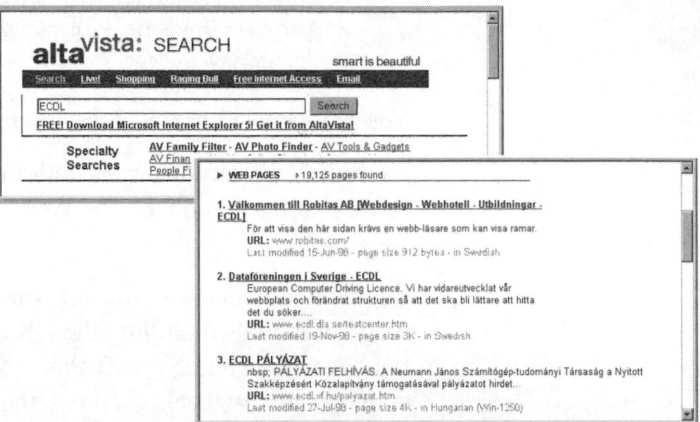

A search for the word 'ECDL' at www.altavista.com returns over 19,000 matching web pages

Web search engines work in a very similar way to the website search engines you met in Section 7.2. The main difference is that they search the Web – and not just an individual website.

Search engines frequently find individual pages from web sites that have nothing to do with what you are looking for. You can often discover unexpected gems of information this way – but be prepared to wade through a lot of irrelevant information too!

Exercises 7.19 and 7.20 provide examples of single keyword searches using search engines. In Exercise 7.19 you use Internet Explorer's default search engine.

Exercise 7.19: Searching with Internet Explorer's Default Search Engine

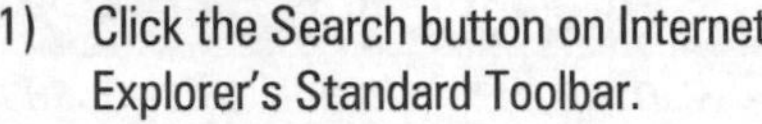

Search button

1) Click the Search button on Internet Explorer's Standard Toolbar.

   This displays the Search bar to the left of the main window.

   (Your Search bar may look slightly different, depending on how Internet Explorer is set up.)

2) With the Search Category at its default setting of Find a Web page, enter the keyword 'ecdl'.

3) Click the **Search** button.

   You should now see a list of web pages that contain the word 'ecdl'.

You can change Internet Explorer's default search engine by clicking **Customize** at the top-right of the Search bar and selecting a different search engine.

The Web offers dozens of search engines. You should explore the various alternatives and choose the one that best suits your needs.

Here are some of the better search engine websites:

www.google.com	www.altavista.com
www.alltheweb.com	www.northernlight.com
www.excite.com	www.hotbot.com
www.webcrawler.com	www.lycos.com
www.go.com	www.snap.com
www.ibound.com	www.mckinley.com

In Exercise 7.20 you visit the Google search engine and use it to find information on ECDL.

Exercise 7.20: Searching the Web with Google

1) Visit the Google search engine at www.google.com
2) Enter the keyword ECDL and click the **Google Search** button.

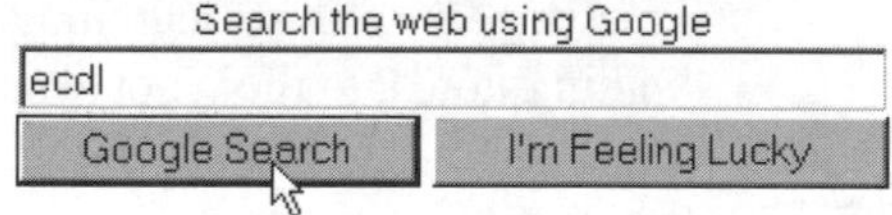

Google responds by displaying a list of web pages that contain your entered keyword.

When your query returns more than a single page of results, search engines provide Next and Previous links at the bottom of each page to allow you to move forwards and backwards through the pages of results.

To print the result of a web search, simply print the results page(s) as you would any other web page.

Web Search Engine Site

A website that enables you to search for material on the Web by entering a word or phrase. The search engine returns a list of sites where the specified words were found.

Phrase Searches

When searching for a phrase – a sequence of words in a particular order – enclose the phrase within double quotes. Phrase searches are commonly used to find information on people and organisations – even song lyrics. Here are some examples:

"Manchester United"
"Edgar Allen Poe"
"Ministry of Defence"
"Candle in the Wind"

Why do you need to enclose phrases inside quotes? The answer is that if you search (say) for Manchester United rather than "Manchester United", your results may include pages that refer to Manchester Council or United Biscuits.

By placing quotes around a query you ensure that you find only pages that:

- Contain *all* the words of your query
- Contain the words in the *order* in which you type them

Phrase Search

A query to a search engine that is placed inside quotes. Only web pages containing all the entered words, in the order entered, are found.

Practise your phrase-searching skills by entering your full name, within quotes, to the Google search engine.

The Plus Operator

Often you want to search for multiple words that are not necessarily adjacent to one another. In such cases, phrase searches are inappropriate. Instead, use the plus (+) operator.

Suppose, for example, you want to find information about the rules of the card game solitaire. You could enter:

solitaire +rules

Only web pages that contain both words should appear in your results. Note three points about the plus operator:

- You don't need to type the plus operator before the first word that you type in your query.
- Don't leave a blank space between the plus operator and the word following it.
- Leave a blank space after each word

Here are some other examples:

Word +97 +templates
Excel +97 +autosum
ECDL +Cyprus
Recipe +Thai
Shakespeare +Hamlet

You can combine the plus operator with phrases inside double quotes, as the following examples show:

algebra +"square roots"
"Excel 97" +"keyboard shortcuts"
Volkswagen +Golf +"metallic blue"
"Manchester United" +"David Beckham"
Shakespeare +"Shall I compare thee"
Bogart +Bacall +"The Big Sleep"

Exercises 7.21, 7.22 and 7.23 provide examples of web queries that contain the plus operator.

Exercise 7.21: Using the Plus Operator on NorthernLight

1) Visit the web search engine www.northernlight.com
2) Type the following terms and click **Search**:
   Bizet +Carmen +Domingo

Your results should include web pages that refer to performances of Bizet's opera Carmen that feature singer Placido Domingo.

Exercise 7.22: Using the Plus Operator on AltaVista

1) Visit the web search engine www.altavista.com
2) Type the following terms and click **Search**:
   "James Bond" +"Sean Connery"

Your results should include web pages about James Bond films that starred actor Sean Connery.

Exercise 7.23: Using the Plus Operator on Excite

1) Visit the web search engine www.excite.com
2) Type the following terms and click **Search**:
   Barcelona +restaurants +vegetarian

Your results should include web pages listing restaurants in Barcelona that cater for vegetarians.

The plus operator is particularly useful when you find yourself overwhelmed with returns from a web search. By adding one or a few terms, each preceded by the plus operator, you can progressively refine your search so that you receive only the information you need.

The Minus Operator

Sometimes, you want a search engine to find pages that contain one word – but do *not* contain another word. You can do this using the minus (-) operator.

Suppose, for example, you want information about the solo career of singer Geri Haliwell, but don't want to be overwhelmed by pages relating to her former group, the Spice Girls. You could enter:

"Geri Haliwell" –"Spice Girls"

Similarly, to find information on the post-Beatles career of John Lennon, you could enter:

"John Lennon" -Beatles

If you are a fan of the original Star Trek series, but don't want pages relating to various follow-up series, you could enter:

"Star Trek" -Voyager –"Deep Space Nine" –"Next Generation"

In Exercise 7.24 you search the Web for information on Windows 98, and exclude pages that mention the other versions of the Microsoft operating system, Windows 3.1, Windows 95, Windows NT, Windows 2000 or Windows CE.

Exercise 7.24: Using the Minus Operator on Go

1) Visit the web search engine www.go.com
2) Type the following and click **Find**:

   Windows -95 -3.1 -NT -2000 -CE

Your search results should provide information on Windows 98 only.

In Exercise 7.25 you will search the Web for references to Dublin that is not Dublin, Ireland.

Exercise 7.25: Using the Minus Operator on Snap

1) Visit the web search engine www.snap.com
2) Type the following and click **Find**:

   Dublin -Ireland

Your search results should list pages that refer to places named Dublin in the USA. Because not every page that refers to the Dublin in Ireland actually contains the word 'Ireland', however, many of your returned pages will relate to Ireland's capital city.

In general, the minus operator helps you to get better results by allowing you to subtract terms that are not of interest. You can combine the plus and minus operators in a single search query.

Logical Searches

A search of the Web – or of a single website – that contains the plus and/or minus operators is called a logical search.

An alternative way of creating a logical search is to use the so-called Boolean operators instead of the plus and minus symbols. Named after their creator, nineteenth-century mathematician George Boole, these operators include the words AND, OR and NOT, and are typically written in upper-case letters.

The following two logical searches, for example, produce the same results:

"James Bond" AND "Sean Connery"
"James Bond" +"Sean Connery"

Boolean searches have been used traditionally for database searches. On the Web, however, the plus and minus operators are supported by more search engines, and are easier to remember and use.

Logical Search

A web search that uses logical operators, such the plus and/or minus symbols, to include and/or exclude specified words or phrases from the results.

Meta Search Engines

A meta search engine is a search engine that searches search engines. Just enter your word or phrase and the meta search engine submits it to a range of individual search engines, and returns the matching results.

Three popular meta search engines are:

www.dogpile.com
www.mamma.com
www.metacrawler.com

Exercise 7.26: Using the Dogpile Metasearch Engine

1) Visit the meta search engine at www.dogpile.com
2) Enter the following and click **Fetch**:
"access 97" +sort

Your results will include web pages, found by a range of individual search engines, that describe sort operations in the Microsoft Access 97 database application.

Natural Language Search Engines

The Ask Jeeves website at www.aj.com is an example of a search engine that accepts questions in plain English. Here are some sample queries that you could enter:

Who is the secretary general of the UN?
Who invented plastic?
Who wrote Catch 22?
What is the currency in Portugal?
What is the temperature in Florence?

A version of the search engine that returns web pages suitable for younger web surfers, Ask Jeeves for Kids, is at www.ajkids.com.

Exercise 7.27: Using the Ask Jeeves Natural Language Search Engine

1) Visit the Ask Jeeves website at www.aj.com
2) Type the following question and click **Ask**: How do I find an email address?

Your results screen should look like that shown below.

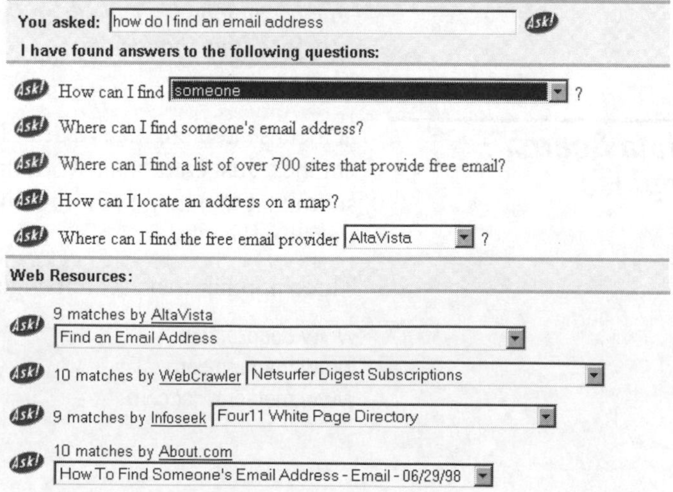

In the top part of the screen Ask Jeeves displays the answers to what it has interpreted as your question. In the lower half it shows the results of entering the words in your question as keywords to various web search engines.

You may now close Internet Explorer. You have completed this Section 7.3 of the ECDL Information and Communication Module.

Section Summary: So Now You Know

Directory websites such as Yahoo! catalogue information on the Web according to subject matter. You can locate information on the Web by navigating through the various category levels.

Web search engines trawl the Web for keywords – occurrences of specified words or phrases, and return a list of websites where the specified words were found.

A *phrase search* is a query to a search engine that is placed inside quotes. Only web pages containing all the entered words, in the order entered, are found. Phrase searches are commonly used to find information on people and organisations.

A *logical search* is a web search that uses logical operators, such the plus and/or minus symbols, to include and/or exclude specified words or phrases from the results.

If you are overwhelmed with irrelevant returns from a web search, add one or a few terms, preceded by the *plus operator*, to refine your search so that you receive only the information you need.

The *minus operator* helps you get better web search results by allowing you subtract terms that are not of interest. You can combine the plus and minus operators in a single search query.

A meta search engine is one that submits keywords to several other search engines, allowing you use multiple search engines at once.

A *natural language search engine* such as Ask Jeeves accepts queries in plain English.

Section 7.4: Taking Control of Internet Explorer

In This Section

In this Section you will discover how to adjust the appearance and operation of Internet Explorer to suit your working needs and personal taste.

You begin by learning how you can explore the Web more quickly by switching off the display of images on web pages. If there is a particular web page that you visit very frequently, you will discover how to make it display automatically each time you start Internet Explorer.

Another convenient feature of Internet Explorer is its ability to save web addresses, and to group saved addresses into folders for easy reference.

Finally, you will learn how to control the display of Internet Explorer's toolbars and various other screen elements, and specify how the application displays web page text.

New Skills

At the end of this Section you should be able to:

- Switch on and off the display of images on web pages
- Save web addresses as favourites
- Organise saved addresses into folders
- Revisit saved web addresses
- Change Internet Explorer's start page
- Display and hide Internet Explorer's Standard Toolbar and Address Bar
- Display and hide Internet Explorer's three Explorer Bars: Search, Favourites and History
- Adjust the text size of displayed web pages

New Words

At the end of this Section you should be able to explain the following term:

- Favourites

Switching Web Page Images Off and On

Internet Explorer icon indicating a non-displayed image on a web page

Web pages with lots of images – or a few large ones – can take an unacceptably long time to display on your computer's screen. Often, these images will be advertisements, company logos and decorative elements that you may regard as inessential – especially if you are the one paying the telephone bill!

Internet Explorer allows you to switch off images, so that you can display web pages more quickly. When you switch off images, Internet Explorer displays only the text of visited web pages, together with a small icon indicating the location of each non-displayed image.

When you arrive at a web page that contains images that you want to display, you can then switch images back on again. Don't be afraid to try this feature – it will save you time and, as Exercise 7.28 shows, it's easy to use.

Exercise 7.28: Switching Off Images

1) Open Internet Explorer and choose **Tools | Internet Options**.
2) Click the Advanced tab, scroll down the list until you come to the Multimedia category, and then deselect Show pictures.

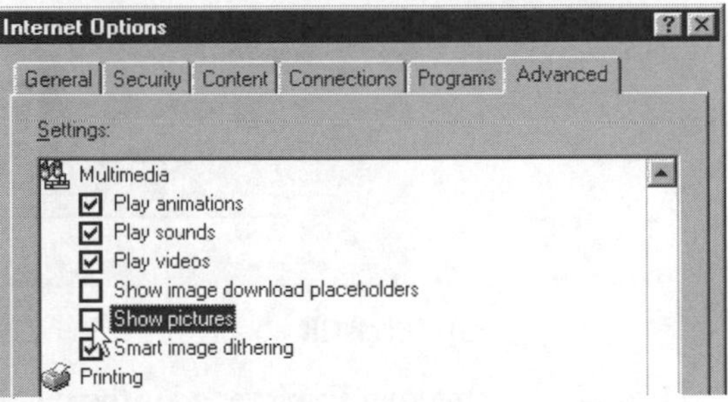

3) Click **OK**.

To display images on all web pages, simply reverse step 2) above.

When images are switched off, you can view an individual image by right-clicking its icon and then choosing **Show Picture**.

Favourites

As you browse the Web, you will discover pages that you would like to return to at a later stage. You can tell Internet Explorer to store a web page's address by using the Favourites feature.

Creating a favourite web page saves you needing to remember (or write down) that page's web address. To revisit such a page, you simply click its name from your list of saved favourites – so much easier than retyping its address each time you want to visit it.

Favourites store just web page addresses on your computer, and *not* the actual pages themselves!

Exercises 7.29 to 7.31 take you through the steps of saving web addresses, organising them into folders, and revisiting them.

Exercise 7.29: Saving a Web Address

Favorites

Favourites button

1) Visit the web page whose web address you want to save. For example: www.yahoo.com
2) Is the Favourites area displayed to the left of Explorer's main window? If not, click the Favourites button on the Standard Toolbar to display it.
3) At the top of the Favourites area, click the **Add** button.

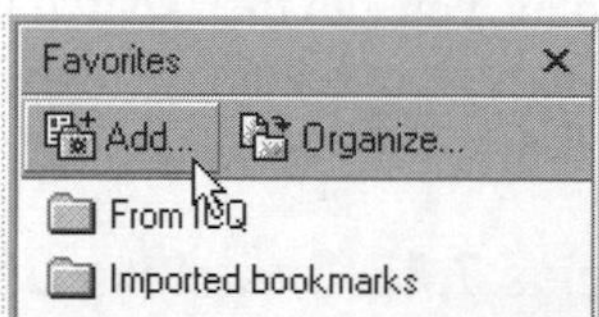

4) You are now shown the Add Favourite dialog box. Accept or change the name of the web page whose address you are saving. (In this case, Yahoo!).

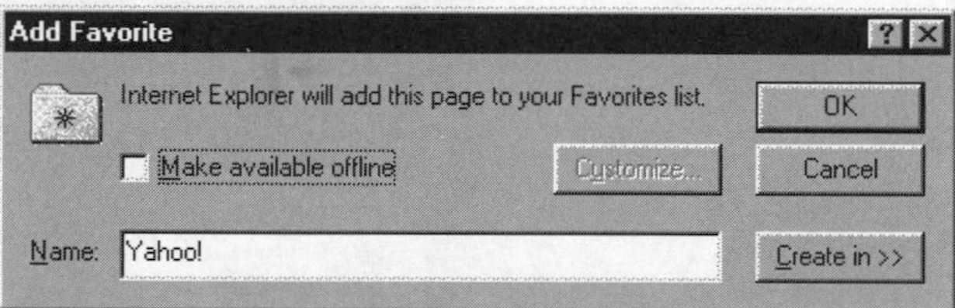

5) Click **OK**.

Internet Explorer adds the name of the currently displayed page as the last item in the Favourites list.

Organising Your Favourites

You can group favourites in folders, so making them easier to find. In Exercise 7.30 you create a folder to store addresses of search engine websites, and then add a number of web addresses to that folder.

Exercise 7.30: Managing Favourites in Folders

1) Is the Favourites area displayed to the left of Internet Explorer's main window? If not, click the Favourites button on the Standard Toolbar to display it.
2) At the top of the Favourites area, click the **Organize** button to display the Organize Favourites dialog box.

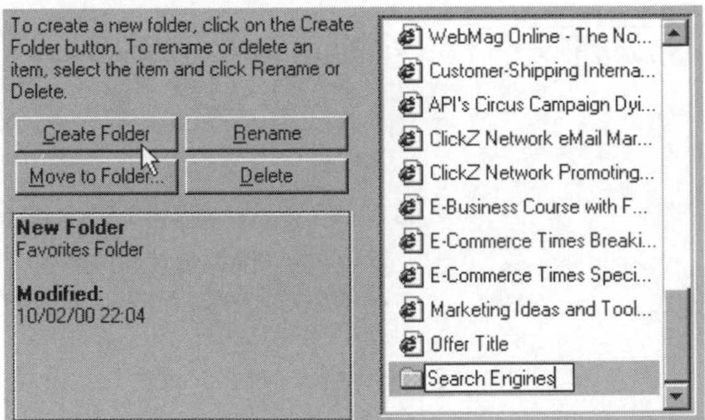

3) Select **Create Folder**, name the new folder Search Engines, and click **Close**.

4) Visit the following website: www.altavista.com

5) At the top of the Favourites area, click the **Add** button.

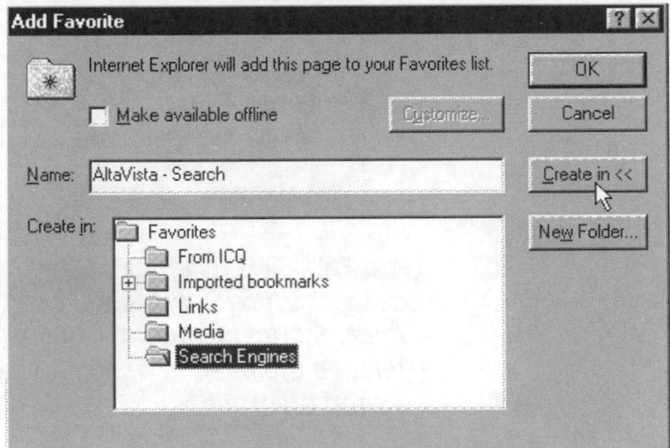

6) In the dialog box displayed, click **Create in <<**, select the Search Engines folder, and click **OK**.

7) Repeat steps 4), 5) and 6) for each of the following other search engine websites:

   www.northernlight.com
   www.alltheweb.com
   www.hotbot.com
   www.google.com
   www.excite.com

Well done. You now have a folder of saved web addresses.

Revisiting a Saved Web Address

Revisiting a saved web address is easy. In Exercise 7.31 you revisit a web address that you added as a favourite in Exercise 7.30.

Exercise 7.31: Revisiting a Saved Web Address

1) Is the Favourites area displayed to the left of Internet Explorer's main window? If not, click the Favourites button on the Standard Toolbar.

2) Scroll down the list of Favourites until you see the Search Engines folder that you created in Exercise 7.30. Click on it.

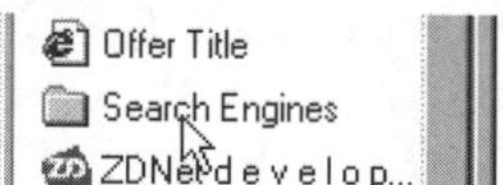

3) Click a saved web address from the Search Engines folder. For example: www.hotbot.com. Internet Explorer displays the associated web page.

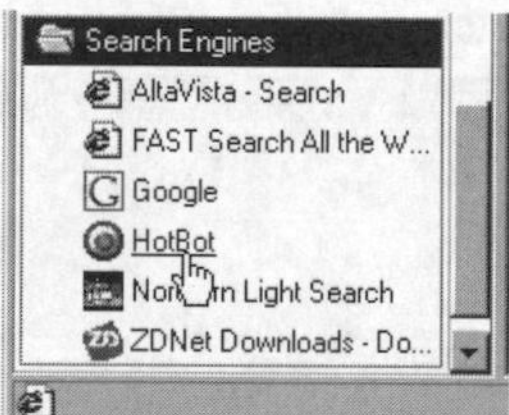

Favourites

A list, stored in Internet Explorer, of website addresses. Favourites remove the need to remember or retype the URLs of frequently visited websites.

Changing Your Start Page

Your start page (which Internet Explorer calls the home page) is the web page that the program visits and displays when you open Internet Explorer.

Exercise 7.32 shows you how to change your start page.

Exercise 7.32: Changing Your Start Page

1) Go to the page you want to display whenever you start Internet Explorer. For example, www.munnelly.com.

2) Choose **Tools | Internet Options** and select the General tab. In the Home page area of the dialog box, select **Use Current** and click **OK**.

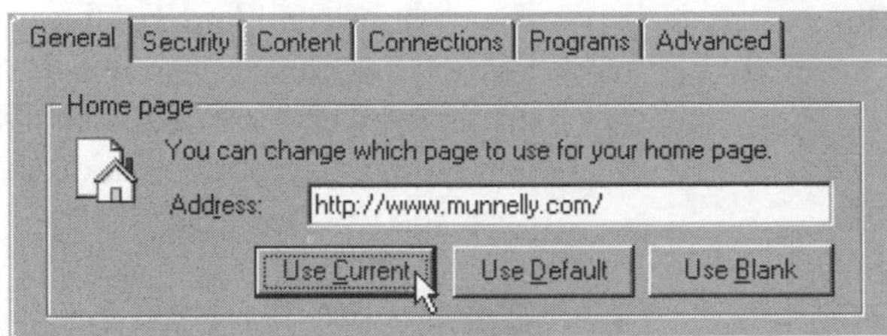

To display your preferred start page at any stage, click the Home button on Internet Explorer's Standard Toolbar.

Home button

You can restore your original start page – the one set up when Internet Explorer was installed – by selecting the **Use Default** option.

To specify a blank start page – that is, no start page – select the **Use Blank** option.

Screen Elements

Internet Explorer's main window is the area in which the application displays the web pages. Surrounding the main window are various screen elements designed to assist you explore and find information on the Web:

- Across the top of the main window are the Standard Toolbar and the Address Bar
- Along the left are the three Explorer Bars: Favourites, History and Search

In this topic you will learn more about these screen elements.

Standard Toolbar

You have already learnt the purpose of the following buttons on Internet Explorer's Standard Toolbar: Back, Forward, Home, Search, Favourites and Print.

Internet Explorer Toolbar

Two other important buttons are Stop and Refresh. Click the Stop button if the web page you are trying to view is taking too long to display. The Refresh button re-requests the current web page from the web site. Click this button if a web page displays incorrectly or incompletely.

To hide the Standard Toolbar, choose **View | Toolbars** and deselect the Standard Buttons option. To redisplay the Toolbar, choose **View | Toolbars** again and reselect Standard Buttons.

Address Bar

Beneath the Standard Toolbar is the Address Bar. As you learnt in Section 7.1, this area shows the web address of the currently displayed web page. You can also use it to enter a web address: you type in the required address and then click the Go button or press the ENTER key.

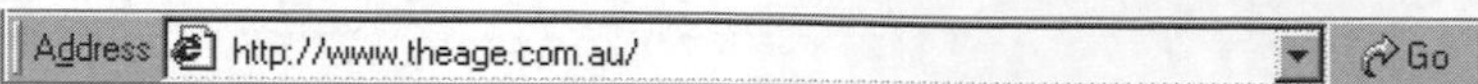

To hide the Address Bar, choose **View | Toolbars** and deselect the Address Bar option. To redisplay the Address Bar, choose **View | Toolbars** again and reselect Address Bar.

Explorer Bars

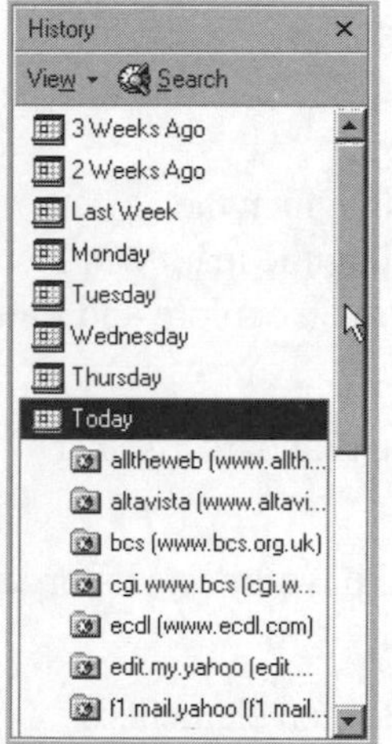

History Internet Explorer Bar

This is the name that Internet Explorer gives to the three screen elements that you can display to the left of the main window. You can display only one at a time:

- To view the Favourites Bar, click the Favourites button on the Standard Toolbar, or choose **View | Explorer Bar** and select the Favourites option. You can then view your list of saved web addresses.
- To view the Search Bar, click the Search button on the Standard Toolbar, or choose **View | Explorer Bar** and select the Search option.
- To view the History Bar, click the History button on the Standard Toolbar, or choose **View | Explorer Bar** and select the History option.

The History Bar shows the web addresses that you visited in previous days and weeks. To revisit a web page in the History bar, click a week or day, click a website folder to display individual pages, and then click the page icon to display the web page.

You can sort or search the History Bar by clicking the relevant arrow next to the View button at the top of the History Bar.

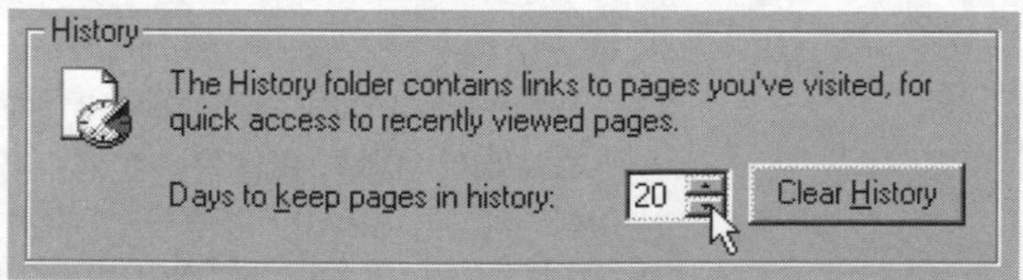

To change the number of days that Internet Explorer keeps track of your visited pages, or to delete the list completely, choose **Tools | Internet Options**, select the General tab, make the required change, and click **OK**.

Text Size Display

You can change the default size in which Internet Explorer displays text – a very useful feature if you have low or limited vision.

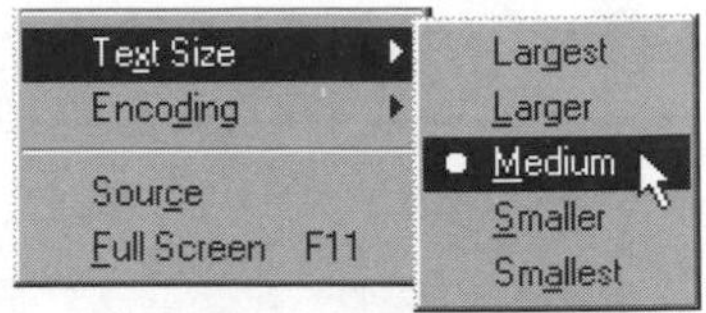

Choose **View | Text Size**, and select the size of text that you want.

You can revert to the default text size of Medium at any stage.

Finally, you can maximise the size of Internet Explorer's main window by choosing **View | Full Screen**.

To revert to normal display, click the Restore button at the top-right of the screen.

Some web pages – such as home pages at www.adobe.com and www.zdnet.com – are designed with fixed-sized fonts, so that using the **View | Text Size** options does not change how they display.

Congratulations. You have now completed the first half of ECDL Module 7, Information and Communication.

Section Summary: So Now You Know

You can adjust the appearance and operation of Internet Explorer to suit your working needs and personal taste.

To display web pages more quickly, switch off the display of images. Internet Explorer displays only the text of visited web pages, together with a small icon indicating the location of each non-displayed image.

You can store web addresses, and organise them into folders for easy reference, using Internet Explorer *Favourites*. If there is a particular web page you visit very frequently, you can make it the default *start page*.

Internet Explorer's *Standard Toolbar* offers quick access to commonly used browsing actions. At the left of the main window you can display any one of the following: the *History Bar*, *Search Bar* or the *Favourites Bar*.

Internet Explorer allows you to adjust the size in which text is displayed on-screen.

Section 7.5: E-Mail with Outlook Express

In This Section

Question: what do most people use the Internet for? Answer: e-mail. It's fast becoming the preferred method of communication in business, and – because it is so inexpensive to use – it is also used by friends and family as a way of staying in contact.

This Section introduces you to Outlook Express, the Microsoft e-mail application. You will explore the application's main screen elements and discover how to arrange them to suit your personal taste.

You will also learn how to address, compose and send an e-mail over the Internet, and how to collect and read incoming e-mails addressed to you.

New Skills

At the end of this Section you should be able to:

- Start and quit Microsoft Outlook Express
- Display the following four screen elements: Folders List, Message List, Preview Pane and Toolbar
- Select an e-mail from a Message List and display it in the Preview Pane
- Select an e-mail from a Message List and display it a separate window
- Compose and send e-mails
- Collect and read incoming e-mails
- Print and delete an e-mail

New Words

At the end of this Section you should be able to explain the following terms:

- Folders List
- Message List
- Preview Pane
- E-mail collection

Starting Outlook Express

Double-click on the Outlook Express icon or choose **Start | Programs | Outlook Express**.

If your computer has a permanent Internet connection, you are ready to send and receive e-mail messages with Outlook Express.

If you have a dial-up connection, you must dial your Internet Service Provider (ISP). Outlook Express may be set up to do this automatically.

If not, you will need to dial your ISP separately.

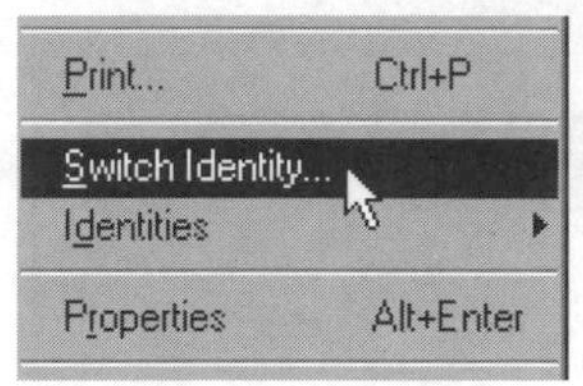

Enter your user name and password (if Outlook Express has not recorded them from the last time that you dialled your ISP), and click **Connect**.

If your computer is used by a number of people, you may have to identify yourself, so that you get your own mail and not someone else's. To do this, choose **File | Switch Identity**, select your name from the list, and click **OK**.

Changing Outlook Layout

You can change the layout of the Outlook Express screen so that the features you use most often are shown, and those you use very seldom are hidden. This means that two people using Outlook Express might have screens that look very different. For the purpose of the exercises in this Module, change the screen layout as directed in Exercise 7.33.

Exercise 7.33: Choosing the Display Elements

1) Choose **View | Layout** for Outlook Express to present a list of layout options, with a check box beside each one.

2) In the upper area of the dialog box, select the Folder List, Status Bar and Toolbar options, and deselect all the others.

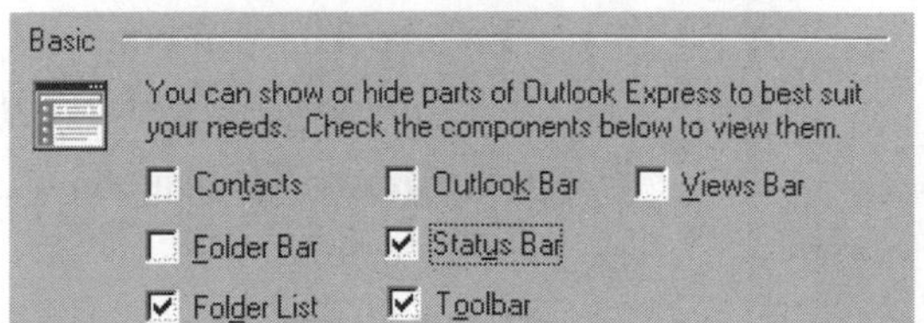

3) In the lower area of the dialog box, select the Show preview pane, Below messages, and Show preview pane header options, and deselect all others.

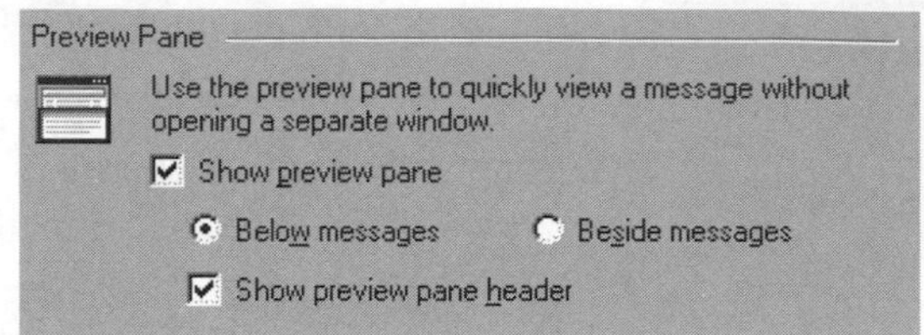

4) Click **OK.**

Your Outlook Express screen should now look like that shown below.

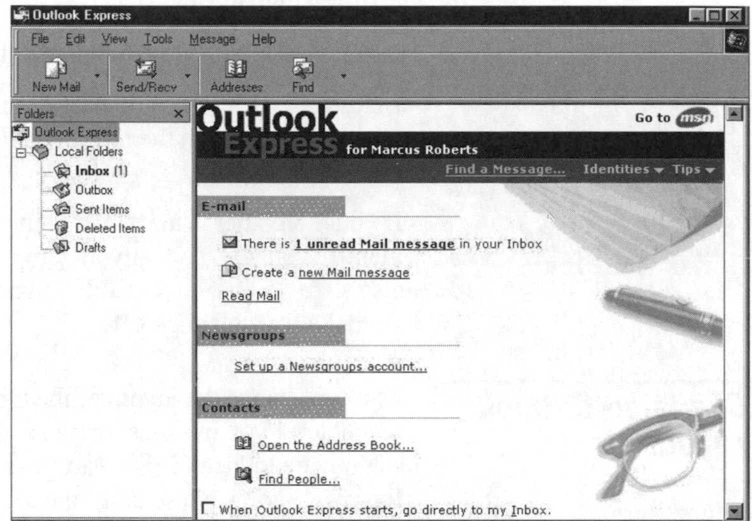

The Four Layout Elements

Let's take a look at the four main screen elements of Outlook Express: Folders List, Message List, Preview Pane and Toolbar.

Folders List

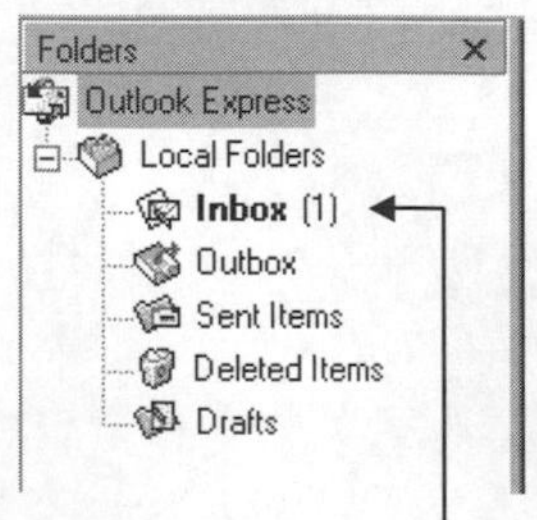

Bold type indicates that a folder contains unread e-mails

The Folders List, on the left, shows five folders:

- **Inbox:** This is where all your incoming e-mails – those sent to you by other people – are held.
- **Outbox**: This can hold all your outgoing e-mails – those you have composed yourself – until you send them.
- **Sent Items**: This can hold copies of all the e-mails you have sent to other people.
- **Deleted Items**: This is where you put all e-mails – both incoming and outgoing – that you no longer want to keep.
- **Drafts**: This is where you store any e-mails that you have not finished composing.

When a folder contains an unread e-mail, Outlook Express displays the folder name in bold, and shows, in brackets, the number of unread e-mails in that folder.

In addition to the five e-mail folders provided with Outlook Express, you can create folders and sub-folders of your own, and move e-mails in and out of them. You will learn how to do this in Section 7.7.

Folders List

The part of Outlook Express where e-mails are stored and grouped according to type: received (Inbox), waiting to be sent (Outbox), already sent (Sent Items), marked for deletion (Deleted Items), and stored for later editing (Drafts). Users can create additional folders and sub-folders for further organising their e-mails.

Message List

When you click any folder in the Folders List, Outlook Express displays the folder's contents in an area on the right of the screen called the Message List. This is called 'opening the folder'.

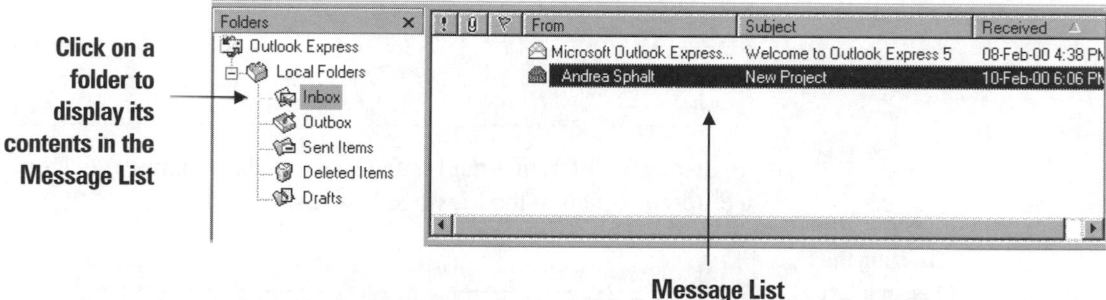

Outlook Express displays some basic details about each e-mail – the sender or recipient, the subject, and the date and time it was sent or received – and uses the following symbols to provide you with more information:

A *read* e-mail, displayed in light type.

An *unread* e-mail, displayed in bold type.

An e-mail, whether read or unread, with one or more *files attached*. (You will learn about e-mail file attachments in Sections 7.6 and 7.7.)

! An e-mail marked as *high-priority*. (You will learn about e-mail priority in Section 7.6.)

Message List

A list of the e-mails contained in the currently selected Outlook Express folder. Outlook Express displays a summary of information about each one.

Preview Pane

When you click on an e-mail in your Message List, Outlook Express displays the e-mail's contents in an area beneath the Message List called the Preview Pane.

Click on an e-mail in the Message List to display its contents in the Preview Pane

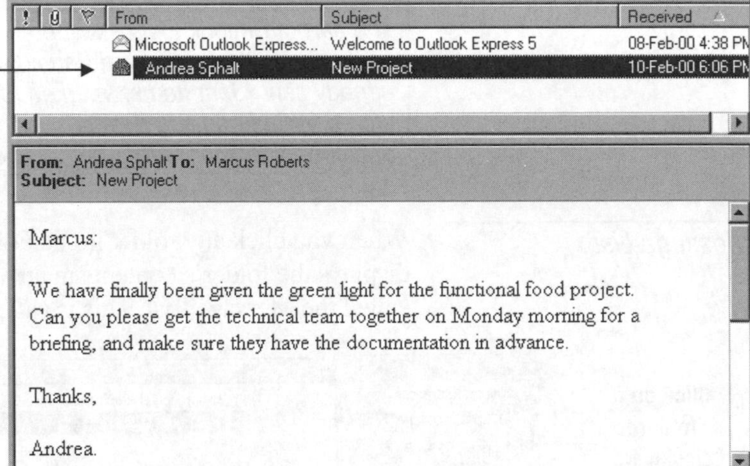

To display a different e-mail in the Preview Pane, simply click on a different e-mail in the Message List.

Resizing the Message List and Preview Pane by dragging with the mouse

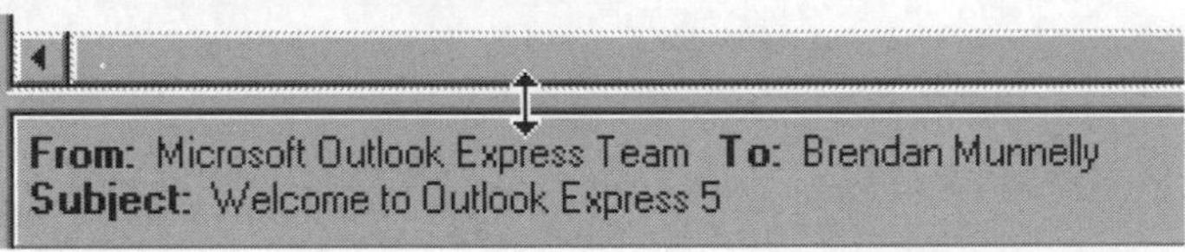

You can resize the Preview Pane and the Message List by clicking on the border between them, holding down the mouse button, and dragging the border up or down.

Preview Pane

An area of the Outlook Express screen that shows the contents of the e-mail that is currently selected in the Message List.

If you receive a long e-mail, you may prefer to read it in a separate window. To do this, double-click the e-mail in the Message List.

Reading an e-mail in a separate window

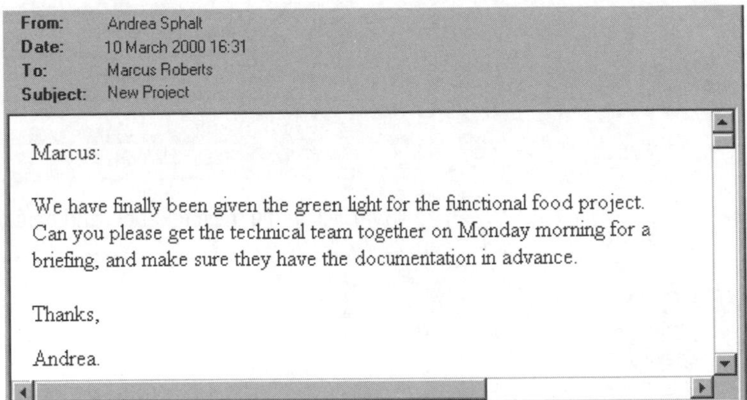
From: Andrea Sphalt
Date: 10 March 2000 16:31
To: Marcus Roberts
Subject: New Project

Marcus:

We have finally been given the green light for the functional food project. Can you please get the technical team together on Monday morning for a briefing, and make sure they have the documentation in advance.

Thanks,

Andrea.

You can then minimise the e-mail's separate window (so that you can come back directly to it at any time), or maximise it (so that it fills the screen). When you are finished with it, close it by clicking the Close button at the top-right of the window. This closes only the e-mail's separate window – and not Outlook Express.

Outlook Express Toolbar

The Outlook Express Toolbar provides buttons that offer one-click access to the e-mail actions you will want to use most frequently. Different buttons are displayed according to which part of the Outlook Express screen you are working in.

Outlook Express Toolbar

Rather than introduce all these buttons at once, we will explain each one as it becomes relevant in this Module.

Composing and Sending an E-Mail

Compose new e-mail button

Exercise 7.34 leads you through the steps of composing and sending an e-mail in Outlook Express.

Exercise 7.34: Composing and Sending an E-mail

1) Choose **File | New | Mail Message** or click the New Mail button on the Toolbar.

   Notice how your e-mail address (for example, marcus@redact.ie) is displayed in the From: box.

2) Click in the To: box, and type the address of the person to whom you are sending the e-mail.

3) Click in the Subject: box, and type a brief description of your e-mail.

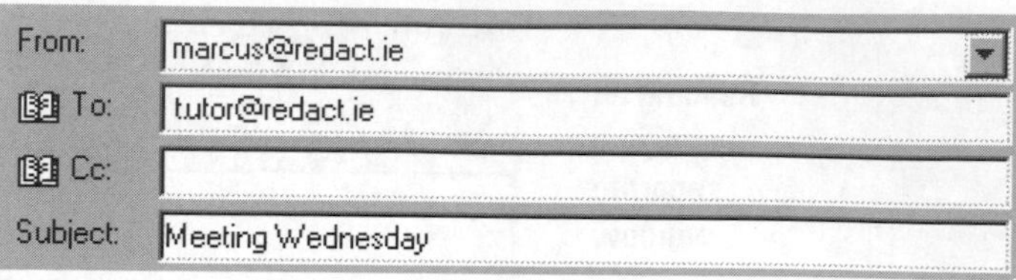

4) Click in the main text box, and type the text of your e-mail.

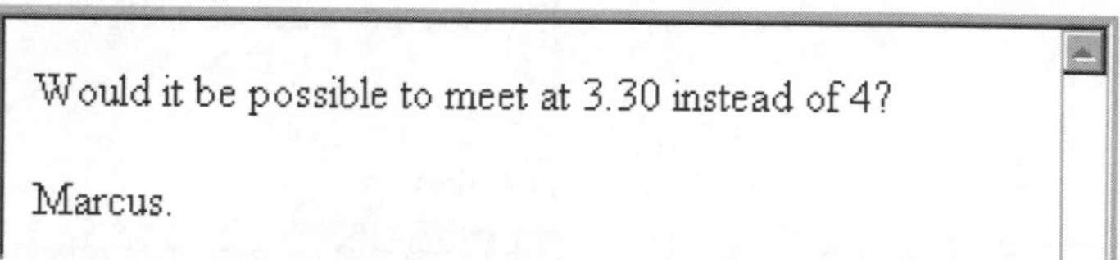

Send e-mail button

5) When finished typing, choose **File | Send Message**, or click the Send button on the New Message Toolbar.

Congratulations! You have now composed and sent your first e-mail.

What happens to your outgoing e-mail? The answer depends on:

- Your type of Internet connection – permanent or dial-up.
- Your selected e-mail sending option – immediate or in a group with other outgoing e-mails.

Outgoing E-mail: Permanent Internet Connection

When you send an e-mail, Outlook Express can transfer it directly to the Internet. To set up this option, choose **Tools | Internet Options**, select the Send tab, select the Send messages immediately option, and click **OK**.

Send and Receive e-mail button

If you do not select this option, your e-mail goes only as far as your Outbox folder. It remains there, along with any other outgoing e-mails, until you choose **Tools | Send and Receive | Send All** or click the Send/Recv button on the Outlook Express Toolbar.

Don't confuse the Send button on the New Message Toolbar with the Send/Recv button on the Outlook Express Toolbar.

- **Send button**: This sends the current e-mail to the Internet or to your Outbox folder, depending on how Outlook Express is set up.
- **Send/Recv button**: This sends all e-mails in your Outbox folder to the Internet.

Outgoing E-mail: Dial-up Connection

As with a permanent Internet connection, you can choose to send each e-mail immediately – or store them in your Outbox for sending later.

You would generally choose to hold all your outgoing messages in your Outbox until you were ready. That way, you can view and type e-mail messages without being connected to the Internet. You need only dial-up your ISP when you are actually sending or receiving the mail, so that you can exchange all your messages (even hundreds of them, to all over the world) in a single local phone call.

Outgoing E-Mail and the Sent Items Folder

Outlook Express can place a copy of all outgoing e-mails in your Sent Items folder, so that you have a copy of them for future reference. To set this option, choose **Tools | Options**, select the Send tab, select 'Save copy of sent messages in the Sent Items folder', and click **OK**.

Collecting and Reading Your E-mail

Just as you can send your outgoing e-mails one at a time or all together, you can collect your incoming e-mail as often as you like, either automatically or manually.

You can collect e-mail from the Internet in two ways:

- Automatically at specified time intervals. Choose **Tools | Options**, select the General tab, select 'Check for new messages every 30 minutes', and click **OK**. You can change the timing to suit your needs.

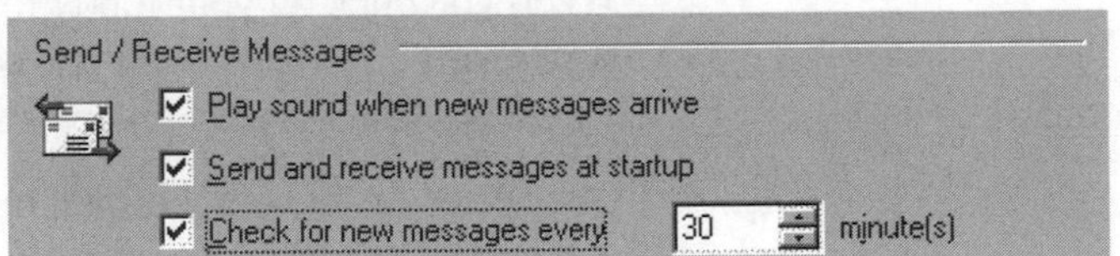

- Manually, by choosing **Tools | Send and Receive | Receive All** or by clicking the Send/Recv button on the Outlook Express Toolbar.

  Even if you have set up automatic, timed e-mail collection, you can click Send/Recv at any stage to check if any new e-mails have been sent to you.

E-mail Collection: Dial-up Connection

If you are using a dial-up connection, you will generally use the same phone call to send your outgoing messages and collect any incoming messages. When you choose **Tools | Send and Receive | Send and Receive All** or click the Send/Recv button, that's what happens.

Don't confuse the action of collecting e-mail with the action of reading it. If you have a dial-up Internet connection, you can read your e-mail whether you are online or not. You need only go online to collect your e-mail from the Internet.

E-mail Collection

The action of transferring e-mails from the Internet to your computer. You must be connected to the Internet to collect e-mail, but you can read your collected messages whether you are online or not.

E-mail Collection at Startup

You can set up Outlook Express so that it automatically collects your e-mails from the Internet when you start the application. To do so, choose **Tools | Options**, select the General tab, select the 'Send and Receive messages at startup' option, and click **OK**.

If you have a dial-up connection to the Internet, you may prefer not to select this option. Otherwise, Outlook Express will attempt to dial-up your ISP every time that you start the application.

Reading an E-mail

Outlook Express places incoming e-mails in your Inbox folder. When you click on your Inbox folder, your Message List shows all your received e-mails, with one e-mail highlighted. The text of that e-mail is shown in the Preview Pane.

Click once on any other e-mail in the Message List to display its text in the Preview Pane. Double-click on any e-mail in the Message List to display its text in a separate window.

The same technique applies irrespective of which folder the message is in: open the folder; select the message; read.

Printing an E-mail

To print an e-mail, choose **File | Print** or click the Print button on the Toolbar.

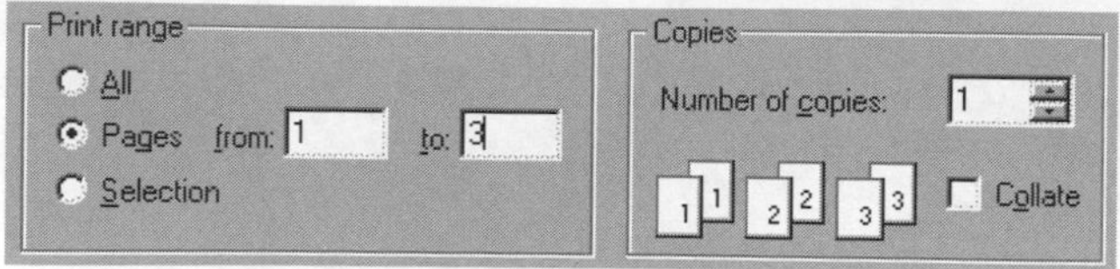

The Print dialog box (which is displayed only if you choose the **File | Print** command and not when you click the Print toolbar button) gives you the options:

- **All**: Prints every page of the e-mail.
- **Selection**: Prints only the currently selected text of the e-mail.
- **Pages**: To print a group of continuous pages, enter the first and last page number of the group.

Other options on the Print dialog box allow you to specify how many copies you want to print of your selected pages, and indicate whether you want the multiple copies collated.

Deleting an E-mail

To delete an e-mail, irrespective of whether it is in your Inbox, Outbox, Sent Items, or Drafts folder, just click on it in the Message List and choose **Edit | Delete** or click the Delete button on the Toolbar.

Is the e-mail really deleted? No. Outlook Express places it in the Deleted Items folder. To retrieve the e-mail:

- Click on the Deleted Items folder in the Folders List. Your Message List now displays all deleted e-mails.
- Click on the e-mail in the Message List, and hold down the mouse button.
- Drag the e-mail from the Message List to the Inbox or other folder in the Folders List.

Manual E-mail Deletion

You can permanently remove all deleted e-mails from Outlook Express by emptying the Deleted Items folder. To do so, select the Deleted Items folder in the Folders List, choose **Edit | Empty Deleted Items Folder**, and click **OK**.

Automatic E-mail Deletion

If you don't want e-mails to be saved in the Deleted Items folder when you quit Outlook Express, choose **Tools | Options**, select the Maintenance tab, select the 'Empty messages from the Deleted Items folder on exit' option, and click **OK**.

Quitting Outlook Express

To leave Outlook Express:

- Choose **File | Exit**, or click the Close button at the top-right of the Outlook Express Window.

Using Online Help

Like Internet Explorer and other Microsoft applications, Outlook Express offers a searchable online help system. You can search through and read online help in two ways: from dialog boxes, or from the **Help** menu.

Using Help from Dialog Boxes

Exercise 7.35 provides an example of accessing online help from a dialog box.

Exercise 7.35: Accessing Online Help from a Dialog Box

1) Choose **Tools | Options**, and click the General tab.

2) Click the question-mark symbol near the top-right of the dialog box. Outlook Express displays a question mark to the right of the cursor.

3) Drag the mouse down to the option named 'Play sound when new messages arrive'.

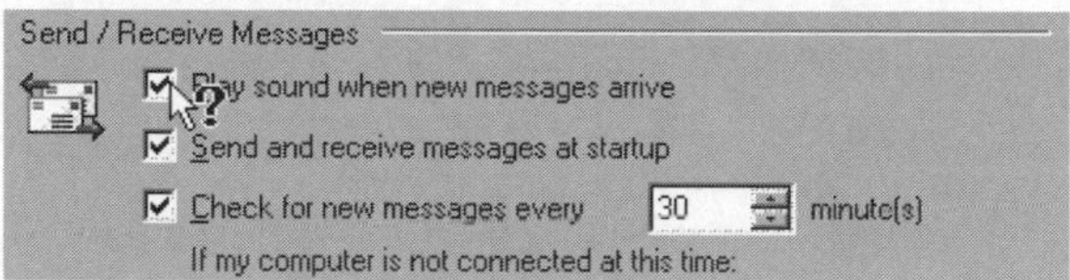

4) Click anywhere on the option check box or name.

Specifies whether your computer plays a sound when new messages arrive. If you clear this check box, you do not hear any sound, but the Outlook Express status bar and message list will indicate that you have unread messages.

Outlook Express now displays help text telling you about the option. Practise Exercise 7.35 with other dialog boxes in Outlook Express.

Using Help Menu Options

You can also access online help from the **Help** menu. Choose **Help | Contents and Index** to display the three tabs of the Help Topics dialog box.

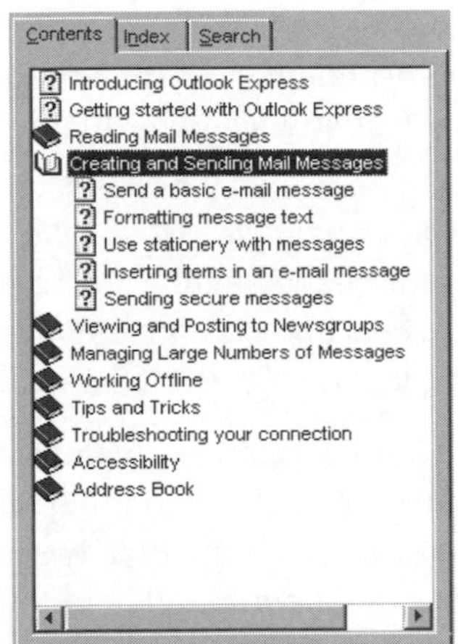

Contents Tab

This offers short descriptions of Outlook Express's main features.

Where you see a heading with a book symbol, double-click to view the related sub-headings.

[?] Double-click on a question-mark symbol to read the help text.

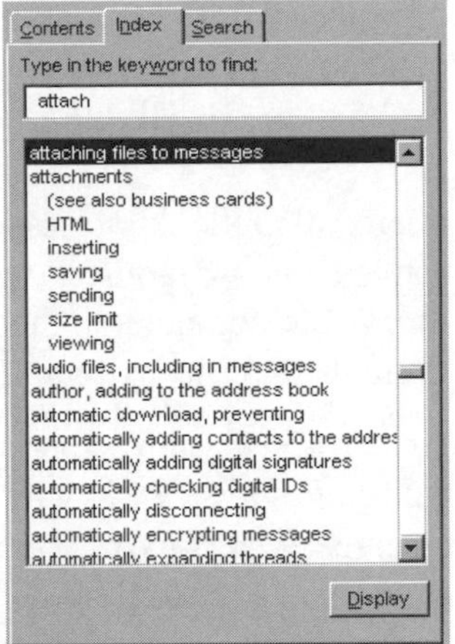

Index Tab

Reading the material displayed on this tab is like looking through the index of a printed book.

Just type the first letters of the word or phrase you are interested in.

Outlook Express responds by displaying all matches from the online help in the lower half of the dialog box.

When you find the index entry that you are looking for, click the **Display** button.

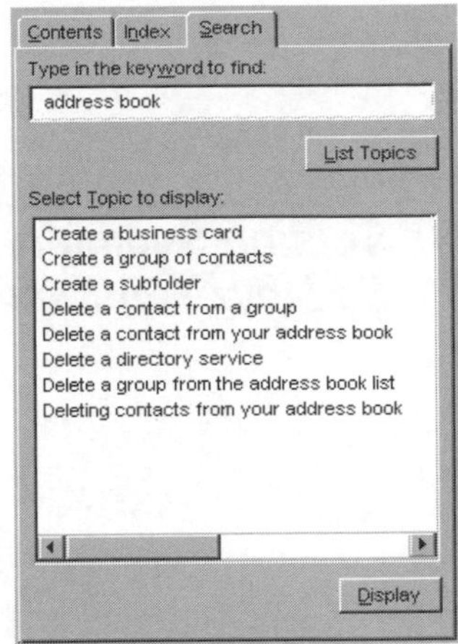

Search Tab

Can't find what you are looking for in the Contents or Index tabs? Try this tab.

When you type a word or phrase and click **List Topics**, Outlook Express performs a deeper search of the online help.

When you find the item you are looking for, double-click on it to display it.

As you search through and read online help topics, you will see the following buttons at the top of the online help window:

- **Hide/Show**: Hides or displays the left-hand pane of the online help dialog box.
- **Back/Forward**: Moves you backwards and forwards through previously visited help topics.
- **Options:** Offers a number of display choices, and enables you to print the currently displayed online help text.
- **Web Help**: Takes you to Microsoft's web-based support site for Outlook Express. Take a few minutes to look through the Outlook Express online help system. Remember that you will be free to use online help during an ECDL test. When finished,

you can close Outlook Express by clicking the Close button or choosing **File | Close**. You have now completed this Section 7.5 of the ECDL Information and Communication Module.

Section Summary: So Now You Know

Microsoft Outlook Express is an *e-mail application* that enables you to *compose* (address, write and edit) new e-mails, *send* e-mails (from your computer to the Internet), *collect* incoming e-mails (from the Internet to your computer), and *read* collected e-mails.

To help you organize your e-mails, Outlook Express contains a built-in *Folders List* in which messages are stored and grouped by type: received (*Inbox*), waiting to be sent (*Outbox*), already sent (*Sent Items*), marked for deletion (*Deleted Items*), and held for later editing (*Drafts*). Users can create additional folders for further organising their e-mails.

You can collect your incoming e-mails *manually* from the Internet, or you can set up Outlook Express to collect them *automatically* each time you start the application and/or at preset time intervals.

You can also tell the application to send each outgoing e-mail as soon as you have finished composing it – or to store outgoing e-mails in your Outbox folder for sending in a group later.

If you have a dial-up Internet connection, you can read and compose your e-mail whether you are online or not. You need only go online to send and collect your e-mail. You can keep copies of all outgoing e-mail in your Sent Items folder.

When you open a folder, Outlook Express displays the e-mails that it contains in a *Message List*, together with a summary of information about each one.

Clicking once on an e-mail in a Message List displays that e-mail's contents in a *Preview Pane* under the Message List. Clicking twice displays the e-mail in a separate window.

When you delete an e-mail, Outlook Express places it in the Deleted Items folder. You can empty the Deleted Items folder manually or set up Outlook Express to empty it automatically each time that you close the application.

Section 7.6: More about Outgoing Mail

In This Section

In this Section you will discover some of the options available for composing and sending e-mails.

You will learn how to copy text into an e-mail from another application, how to check the spelling in your e-mails, how to mark an e-mail as high-priority, and how to send the same e-mail to several people – there are several ways of doing this.

You will also learn how to create a signature and to append it to your outgoing e-mails, and how to attach files to outgoing e-mails – word-processed documents, spreadsheets, or photographs of your dog.

New Skills

At the end of this Section you should be able to:

- Copy text into an e-mail
- Check the spelling in an e-mail
- Send the same e-mail to several recipients
- Send a blind copy of an e-mail
- Set the priority of an outgoing e-mail
- Add a signature to outgoing e-mails
- Attach a file to an outgoing e-mail
- Explain why an e-mail may 'bounce', and know what to do about it
- Manage your outgoing e-mail queue

New Words

At the end of this Section you should be able to explain the following terms:

- Cc (Carbon copy)
- E-mail file attachment
- Message priority
- Drafts folder
- Blind copy (Bcc)
- Signature (sig) file
- Bounced e-mail

Copying Text into E-mails

Typing text directly into Outlook Express is just one way of composing an e-mail. Another is to reuse previously typed text by copying it from another e-mail (whether received or sent), and then pasting it into the new one.

As Exercise 7.36 shows, you can also copy text into an outgoing e-mail from another application such as a Microsoft Word document. (You should be familiar with Microsoft Word and have a Word document ready to use before attempting Exercise 7.36. Otherwise, you'll just have to take our word for it!)

Exercise 7.36: Copying Text from Word to Outlook Express

1) Open Microsoft Word and open the document that contains the text you want to copy into your e-mail.
2) Select the text for copying by clicking at the start and dragging the cursor to the end.

Text selected from Microsoft Word

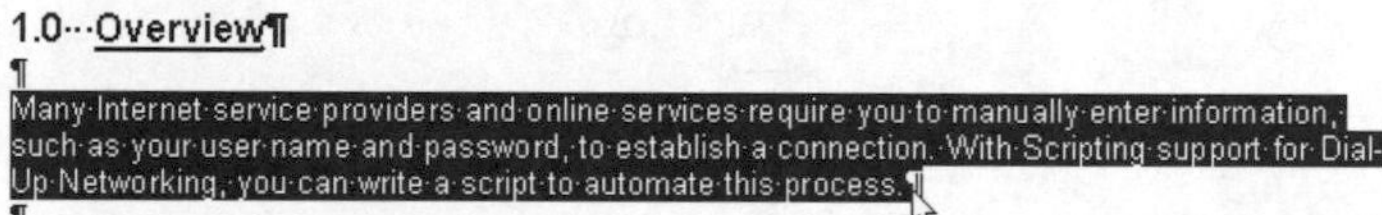

(To select all the text in a Word document, hold down the CTRL key and click anywhere in the left margin.)

3) Choose **Edit | Copy** or press CTRL+c to copy the select text to the Clipboard.
4) Open Outlook Express and either open the e-mail you want to paste the text into, or compose a new e-mail.
5) Position the cursor where you want the copied text to appear in your e-mail, and choose **Edit | Paste** or press CTRL+v.

Text from Word pasted into outgoing e-mail

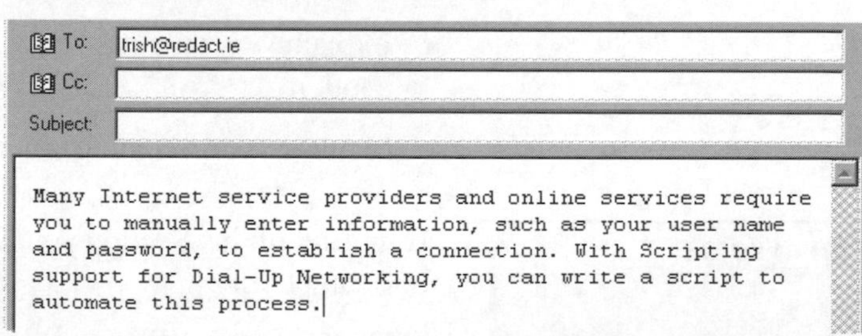

Checking Your Spelling

How's your spelling? Outlook Express can check your spelling and suggest corrections to errors in two ways:

- When you send the e-mail (the automatic option)

Check E-Mail Spelling button

- When you choose the **Tools | Spelling** command or click the Spelling button on the New Message Toolbar (the on-request option).

If automatic spell-checking is switched on, Outlook Express checks your e-mail after you choose **File | Send Message** or click the Send button on the New Message Toolbar.

It uses the same spelling dictionary as Word and other Microsoft Office applications. If you do not have any of these installed on your computer, spell-checking in Outlook Express is not available.

Exercise 7.37: Switching On the Spell Checker

1) Choose **Tools | Options** and click the Spelling tab.
2) Select the following two options, and click **OK:** Always check spelling before sending, and Suggest replacements for misspelled words.

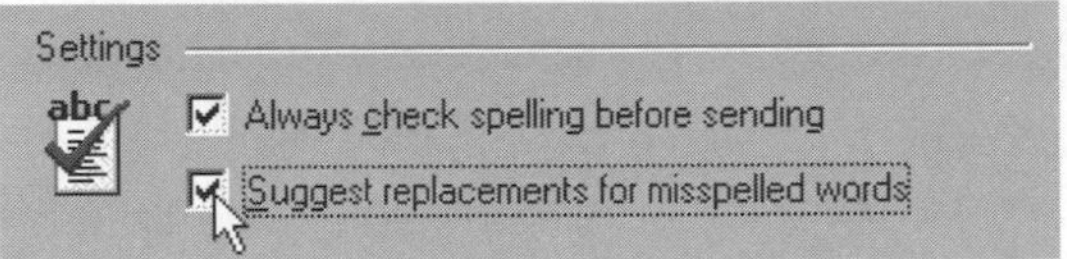

Subsequently, when you send an e-mail, you will be alerted to any word in your e-mail that Outlook Express does not recognise, and offered some alternatives. (Not all unusual spellings are wrong, however, and not all usual spellings are right.)

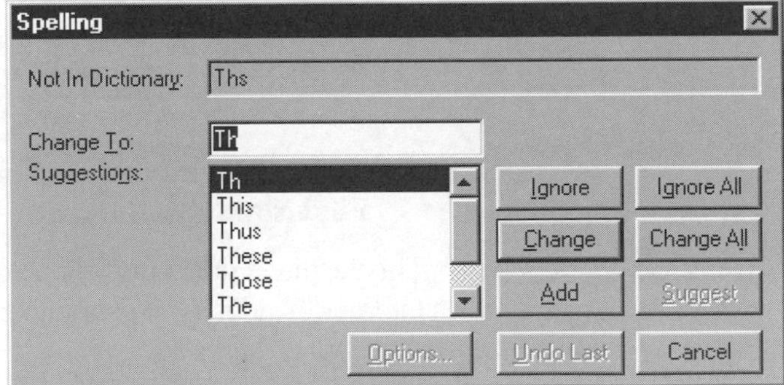

You can **Ignore** the alert, **Change** the problem word to the alternative highlighted, or **Add** the word that caused the problem to the dictionary, so that it does not cause any further alerts.

Finding an E-mail Address

You've seen that sending an e-mail is easy, provided you know the e-mail address of the person you are writing to. Where do you find these addresses? There are five main sources: business cards, incoming e-mails, websites, the Find People option, and the Internet Explorer Address Book:

- **Business cards**: Most people in business today include their e-mail address on the business cards. (Some include *only* their e-mail address – they don't want to be contacted any other way!)
- **Incoming e-mails**: Many of the people you want to send e-mail to have already been in contact with you. Simply go to your Inbox, find an e-mail from the right person, copy their address to the Clipboard and paste it into your e-mail.
- **Websites**: If you know the organisation to which the person belongs, find its website. Many of them (particularly colleges and government agencies) include e-mail directories.
- **Find People option**: Outlook Express provides an option that lets you quickly locate e-mail addresses from web-based directories.
  - Choose **Tools | Address Book** and select the **Edit | Find People** button.
  - From the Look in: drop-down list, select a directory service.

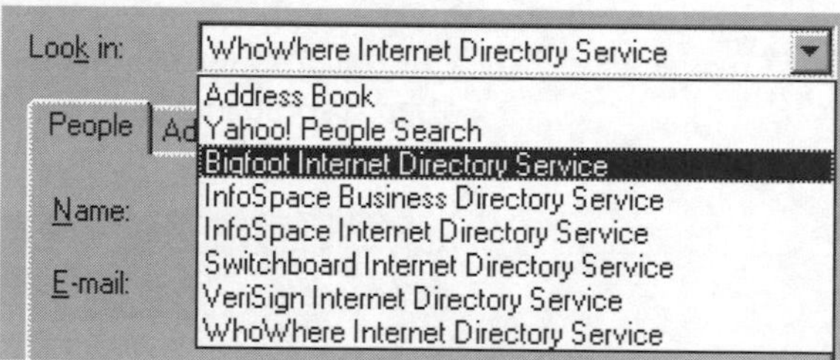

  - Type the name of the person you are looking for, and click **Find Now**.

  This feature works only when you are connected to the Internet. (And it's not guaranteed to find the person you want.)
- **Address Book:** An Outlook Express feature that enables you to record e-mail addresses for easy reference. (You will learn about the address book in Section 7.8.)

E-mailing Multiple Recipients

You can send an e-mail to more than one person. There are three ways of doing this: several equal recipients, one main recipient with copies to others, and blind carbon copy. You use each for different purposes.

Several Equal Recipients

If you want to send the e-mail to several people, enter each of their e-mail addresses in the To: box, separated by a comma or semi-colon. To make a string of multiple addresses easier to read, include a space after each comma or semi-colon.

Multiple to: recipients

To: joe@bloggs.com, wallace@preston.com.au, grommit@sean.co.za

One Main Recipient, with Copy to Another

To send a copy of the e-mail to another person, enter their e-mail address in the Cc: (Carbon copy) box. Generally, you use the Cc: box to enter the e-mail address of other recipients you think should see this e-mail as a matter of courtesy or organisational procedure.

Multiple Cc: recipients

Cc is like that: it conveys those kinds of subtle but powerful messages that make office life exciting. You can enter as many e-mail addresses as you want in the To: box and in the Cc: box.

Cc: (E-mail Carbon Copy)

A field in an e-mail header where you can enter the addresses of people to whom you want to send a copy of the e-mail.

Blind Carbon Copying

With blind copying, you send a copy of the e-mail to the second person, without the main recipient knowing about it. Before doing this, you need to reveal the Bcc: box by choosing **View | All Headers**. The Bcc: box is shown on all e-mail you subsequently compose, until you turn it off (by choosing **View | All Headers** again).

You simply enter in the Bcc: box the e-mail addresses of anyone you want to blind-copy the e-mail to:

- Bcc recipients know the names of the To and Cc recipients.
- The To and Cc recipients do not know the names of the Bcc recipients.
- The Bcc recipients do not know each other's names.

To: and Bcc: recipients

To: trish@redact.ie
Cc:
Bcc: peter@redact.ie

Bcc sends even more subtle messages than Cc. Let's say you send an e-mail to Trish and Bcc Peter. This has the following effects:

- Trish (To recipient) gets the e-mail.
- Peter (Bcc recipient) learns that Trish got the e-mail (and sees what the e-mail was).
- Trish is not aware that Peter knows that she got the e-mail, or what was in it.
- Peter knows that Trish doesn't know that he knows.
- Peter knows that you don't want Trish to know that he knows. Fun, isn't it? Again, you can enter as many e-mail addresses as you wish in the To: box and in the Bcc: box, and you can include both Cc and Bcc recipients in the same e-mail.

Bcc: (E-mail Blind Carbon Copy)

A field in an e-mail header that enables you to copy an e-mail to other recipients. Bcc: recipients can view addresses in the To: and Cc: fields, but not addresses in the Bcc: field. To: and Cc: recipients cannot view any addresses in the Bcc: field.

Mass E-mail and Blind Carbon Copying

A common use (abuse?) of the Bcc: field is for the sending of mass e-mails that advertise products or services.

The sender places *all* the recipients' addresses in the Bcc: field, so that no one recipient knows who else also received the e-mail. Should the e-mail fall into the hands of a competing company, they are unable to view the sender's list of clients and prospects. In the To: field, the sender types his or her own e-mail address.

Every e-mail you send must have at least one address in the To: box; otherwise, it will 'bounce' back to you. (Bounced e-mails are explained later in this Section.)

Attaching Files to E-Mails

Attach File to E-Mail button

E-mails are generally short text messages. But suppose you want to send a family photograph to your uncle, a spreadsheet to your accountant, a PowerPoint presentation to head office, or a beautifully formatted word-processed document to your tutor? Easy. You send it as an *attachment* to your e-mail message.

To learn how to attach a file to an e-mail, follow the steps in Exercise 7.38.

Exercise 7.38: Sending an Attachment

1) Compose your e-mail in the normal way.

2) Choose **Insert | File Attachment** or click the Attach button on the New Message Toolbar.

3) In the Insert Attachment dialog box, locate the file you want to attach to your e-mail, and click **Attach.**

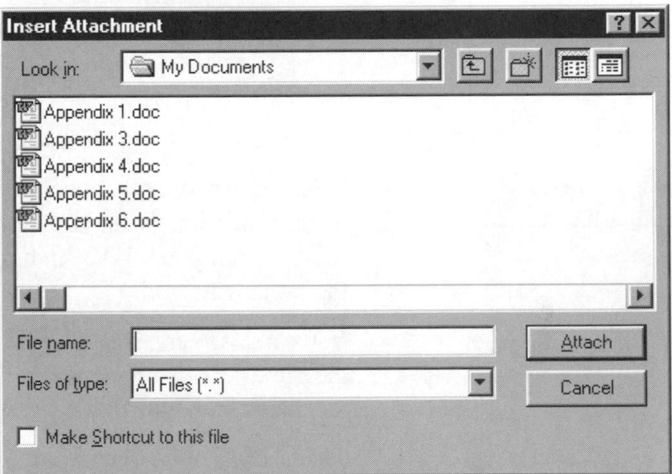

Outlook Express adds a line in the e-mail header to show the attachment file name and file size. To attach multiple files, repeat steps 2) and 3) above.

4) Click **Send** to send the e-mail with its attachment.

Remember that the person who receives your attached file can work with it only if they have the appropriate software application.

E-mail File Attachment

A file, typically a formatted file such as a Word document, that is appended to and sent with an e-mail.

E-mail Priority

All the e-mail you send is important, right? But some of it is more important than others, and you want to make sure that the recipient knows it. Exercise 7.39 shows you how to mark an outgoing e-mail as high-priority.

Exercise 7.39: Sending a High-Priority E-mail

1) Compose the e-mail in the usual way.
2) Choose **Message | Set Priority | High.**

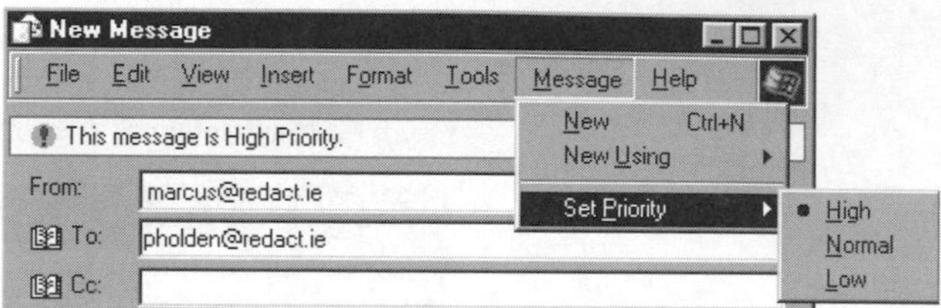

3) Choose **File | Send Message** or click the Send button.

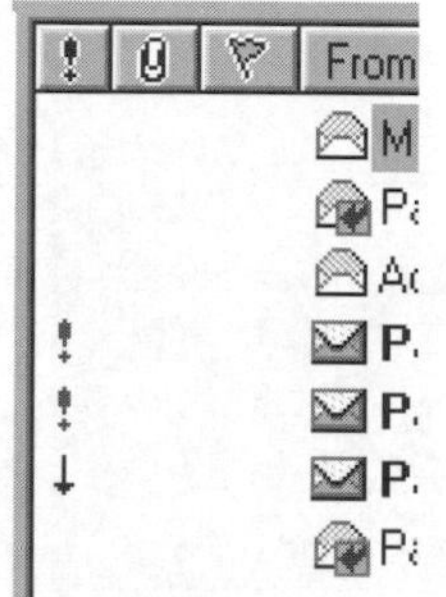

E-mail priority indicators

High-priority e-mails (incoming or outgoing) are identified by a red exclamation mark. Use the high-priority setting sparingly. If every e-mail you send is high priority, they will all be treated in the same way.

You can also send e-mails with a Low Priority setting in exactly the same way. But who wants to do that? (Low priority e-mails are identified by a blue down arrow.)

The priority of an e-mail does *not* affect the speed with which it is transmitted over the Internet or an internal e-mail network.

You can also change the priority of e-mails you have received. This is a useful way of highlighting e-mails that you want to come back to at a later stage.

E-mail Message Priority

An indication to an e-mail recipient of a message's urgency, typically represented by a coloured symbol. The priority of an e-mail has no impact on the speed with which it travels over the Internet or private network.

Bounced Messages

If you send an e-mail to someone and, for whatever reason, it cannot be delivered, you usually receive a message to that effect. Such e-mails are said to 'bounce' – you send them out; they bounce right back.

The most likely reason for an e-mail bouncing is that you have typed an incorrect address: did you spell it right? Did you put in all the right punctuation? Did you put in a hyphen (-) instead of an underscore (_)?

Bounced E-mail

An e-mail that, for whatever reason, fails to reach its recipient, and is returned to its sender with a message to that effect.

Occasionally, your e-mail fails to get through and you don't get any message to that effect. While this is rare, it does happen. Don't assume that because you sent the e-mail, the recipient definitely received it. If it's that important, ask them to acknowledge receipt, either in your e-mail, or automatically. Exercise 7.40 shows you how.

Exercise 7.40: Requesting a Receipt

1) Compose a new e-mail in the normal way.
2) Choose **Tools | Request Read Receipt**.
3) Send the e-mail as normal.

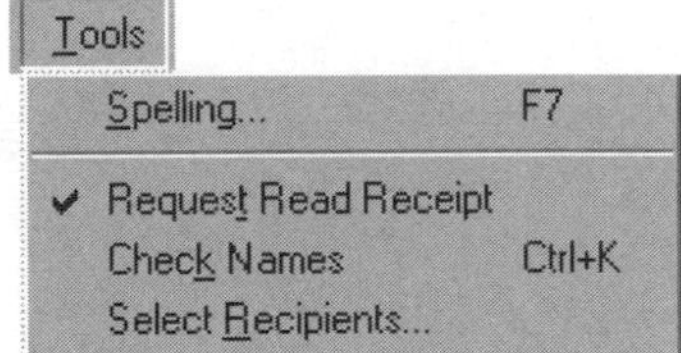

When the e-mail is received and opened by its recipients, they are informed that you have requested confirmation. They can choose to send the confirmation or not, but they don't have to do any work – they just click **Yes**.

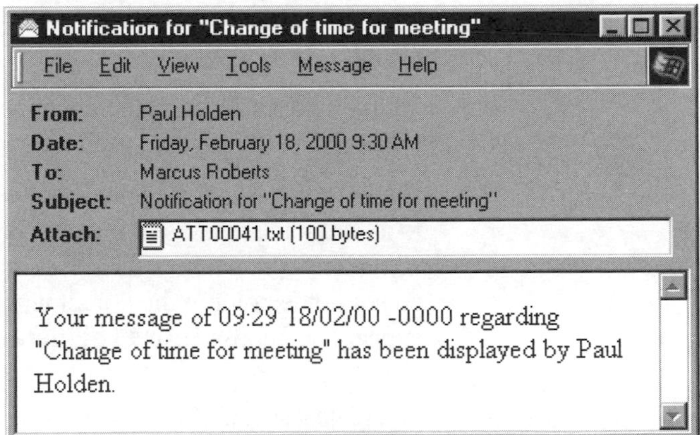

You then get a message like the one above.

Your E-mail Signature

When you compose an e-mail, you may want to finish it off with a small block of text as a signature. The easiest and most efficient way to do this is to create a *signature* (sometimes known as a signature file or a sig file). Outlook Express will append this to your outgoing e-mails – either automatically to all e-mails or only to ones that you select.

Most people include their name and contact details. Some add an advertising slogan, a short message, or a link to their website. You can also create different signature files for different purposes.

Creating a Signature

Follow Exercise 7.41 to learn how to create an e-mail signature file.

Exercise 7.41: Creating Your Signature

1) Choose **Tools | Options**, select the Signatures tab and click **New.**
2) Click the Text button, and in the text box enter your name, address, telephone number and other contact details.

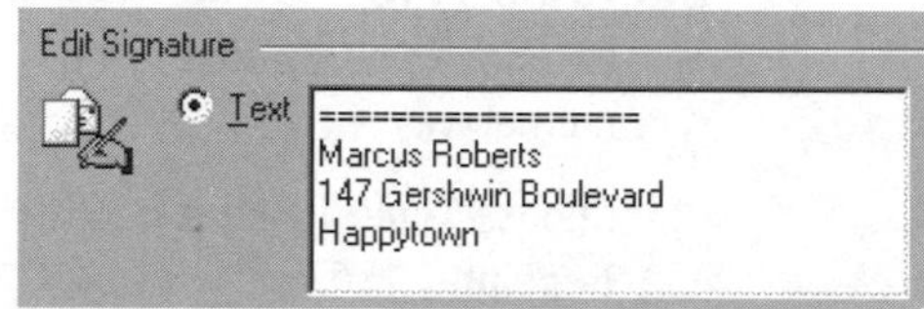

3) Select the 'Add signatures to all outgoing messages' check box, but do not select the 'Don't add signatures to Replies and Forwards' check box.

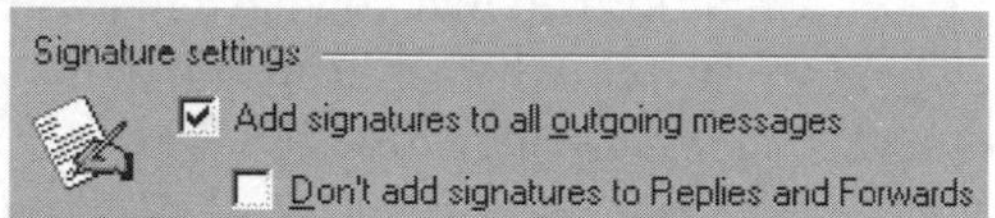

4) Click **OK.**

Outlook Express automatically appends your signature to all subsequent e-mails you compose and send.

If you want to be more selective, do not select the 'Add signatures to all outgoing messages' check box, as in step 2) of Exercise 7.41 above. Instead, when you have composed the e-mail, position the cursor at the point in the e-mail where you want the signature to appear and choose **Insert | Signature**.

Alternative Signature Files

To create a second (or a third ...) signature file, choose **Tools | Options**, and select the Signatures tab. Then click **New**, and proceed exactly as when you created your first signature file.

Choose which of your signatures you want to be the default by clicking it and selecting **Set as Default**. Finally, click **OK**.

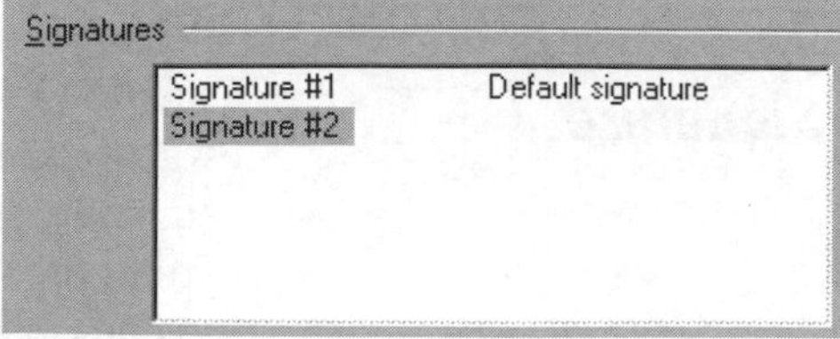

If you have created more than one signature file, and you subsequently choose **Insert | Signature**, you are offered a choice from those available.

Renaming Your Signature File

You can rename your signature files, so that it is easier to identify the right one for the circumstances. You might have a signature file called Business, one called Personal, and one called Family, for example. Or one for your team and another for head office.

To do this, choose **Tools | Options**, and select the Signatures tab. Next, click the signature file you want to rename, and select **Rename**. Then enter the new name for the file. Do the same for the other files you want to rename. When finished, click **OK**.

Editing a Signature File

To edit your signature file, choose **Tools | Options**, and select the Signatures tab.

Your signature files are listed. Select the one you want to change by clicking it. Then make whatever changes you want, by adding, deleting, or overwriting the existing information. When finished, click **OK**.

Signature (Sig) File

An appendage at the end of e-mails. Typical contents include full name, occupation or position, phone and fax numbers, and e-mail and website addresses. Some people also include a favourite quote, company slogan or short personal statement.

The Drafts Folder

If your e-mails are held in your Outbox folder until you click the Send/Recv button, you have the luxury of being able to change your mind.

You can delete an e-mail in the Outbox in the same way as any other e-mail. You select it in the Message List, and do any of the following: click the Delete button on the Toolbar, choose **Edit | Delete**, or press the DELETE key.

Alternatively, you might want to move the e-mail into the Drafts folder while you think about it some more.

Saving E-mail to the Drafts Folder

The Drafts folder is where you keep your half-finished thoughts, your letters of resignation, your job applications, until you are sure that they are right and you want to send them.

To put a new e-mail into the Drafts folder, compose the e-mail as normal and choose **File | Save**. To revisit an e-mail in the Drafts folder, open the folder, select the e-mail in the Message List, and double-click it to open it. You can then make any changes or additions, and either save it again to the Drafts folder, or send it.

You can also move an e-mail directly from the Drafts folder to the Outbox by dragging it from the Message List to the Outbox in the Folders List.

Drafts Folder
An area within Outlook Express where you can store e-mails that you are not yet ready to send. You can open and edit e-mails in the Drafts folder, as required.

Text Size Display

You can change the default size in which Outlook Express displays text – a very useful feature if you have low or limited vision.

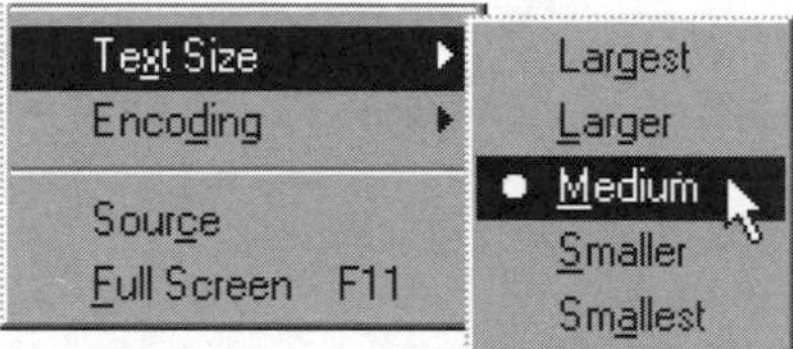

Choose **View | Text Size**, and select the size of text that you want. You can revert to the default text size of Medium at any stage.

When finished, you can close Outlook Express. You have now completed this Section 7.6 of the ECDL Information and Communication Module.

Section Summary: So Now You Know

You can *copy text* from a word processor or other application to an e-mail in Outlook Express, and *spell-check* your e-mail messages as you would a document in Microsoft Word.

You can address an outgoing e-mail to *multiple recipients* – as equal addressees (To:), as *carbon copied* addressees (Cc:), or as *blind carbon copy* addressees (Bcc:). Bcc: recipients can view addresses in the To: and Cc: fields, but not addresses in the Bcc: field. To: and Cc: recipients also cannot view the addresses in the Bcc: field.

When sending an e-mail to several people, separate each e-mail address by a comma or semi-colon. You can optionally include a space after each comma or semi-colon, to make the addresses easier to read.

You can flag your messages as *high* or *low priority*. This indicates the message's urgency to the recipient, but has no impact on the speed with which it is sent over the Internet or private network.

You can append a *signature file* to your outgoing messages, and choose a different signature file for different audiences. Typical signature contents include full name, occupation or position, phone and fax numbers, and e-mail and website addresses. Some people also include a favourite quote, company slogan or short personal statement.

You can *attach formatted files* – such as pictures, spreadsheets and word-processor documents – to your e-mails.

A *bounced e-mail* is an e-mail that, for whatever reason, fails to reach its recipient, and is returned to its sender with a message to that effect.

The *Drafts folder* of Outlook is where you can store messages that you are not yet ready to send.

Section 7.7: More about Incoming Mail

In This Section

In this Section you will explore some of the options available with incoming mail.

You will learn how to forward received e-mails to other people, how to send replies to the sender or to everyone who received the original e-mail, and how to copy text between e-mails or from an e-mail to a word processor or other application.

You will also discover how to open any file attachments that you receive, and how to save or delete them.

Another topic covered is mail folders – how to create new ones of your own, how to sort the e-mails they content in different ways, and how to search through your mail folders for specific e-mails.

New Skills

At the end of this Section you should be able to:

- Forward a received e-mail to another person
- Reply only to the sender of an e-mail
- Reply to all the recipients of the original e-mail
- Copy text between e-mails, and from an e-mail to another application
- Open, save, and delete file attachments
- Create and delete mail folders
- Transfer e-mails between mail folders
- Search in your mail folders for a particular e-mail.

New Words

At the end of this Section you should be able to explain the following terms:

- E-mail forwarding
- E-mail reply to sender only
- E-mail reply all

Actions with Your Incoming Mail

In Section 7.5 you learnt how to display a received e-mail from your Message List by clicking on it once (to view it in the Preview Pane) or twice (to view it in a separate window). In this Section you will discover the various actions that you can perform on a received e-mail. In summary, these are:

- Forward it to someone else
- Reply to the person who sent it only
- Reply to the sender – and to any other people who also received the message
- Copy text from it to an outgoing e-mail, or to Microsoft Word or to another application
- Open, save or delete any files it may have attached to it.

Forwarding an E-mail

If you receive an e-mail that you want to pass on to someone else, the simplest way is to forward it. Follow Exercise 7.42 to discover how.

E-mail Forwarding button

Exercise 7.42: Forwarding an E-mail

1) Select the e-mail you want to forward from your Message List by clicking on it once or twice.

2) Choose **Message | Forward** or click the Forward button on the Toolbar.

   Outlook Express opens a window that looks like a window for creating a new e-mail, with two differences:

   - The Subject: box shows the subject of the original e-mail, preceded by the abbreviation Fw:
   - The original e-mail is shown and identified.

Area for entering your comments with the forwarded e-mail

Text of received e-mail for forwarding

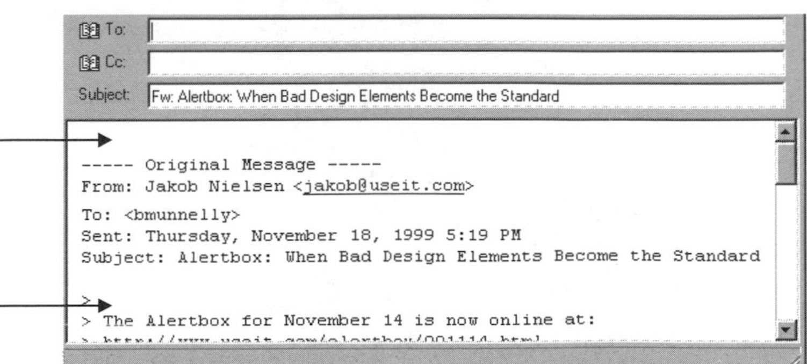

3) In the To: box, type the address of the person to whom you want to forward the e-mail.

4) In the message area, add text of your own. (It is helpful to the recipient if you clearly distinguish your own comments from the original message.)

5) Click **Send.**

E-mail Forwarding
The act of passing to another person an e-mail that you have received. You typically include some comments of your own in the forwarded e-mail.

Replying to Sender Only

When you receive an e-mail message, you can send a reply either to the person who sent it to you (only), or to all the people who received the original e-mail.

Most often, you will want to reply to the person who sent you the e-mail. Exercise 7.43 shows you how.

Exercise 7.43: Replying to the E-mail Sender Only

Reply to E-Mail Sender Only button

1) Select the e-mail you want to reply to from your Message List by clicking on it once or twice.

2) Chose **Message | Reply to Sender** or click the Reply button on the Toolbar. The window that opens up looks like the window for creating a new e-mail, with two differences:

- The To: box and the Subject: box are already completed.
- The original e-mail message is shown and identified.

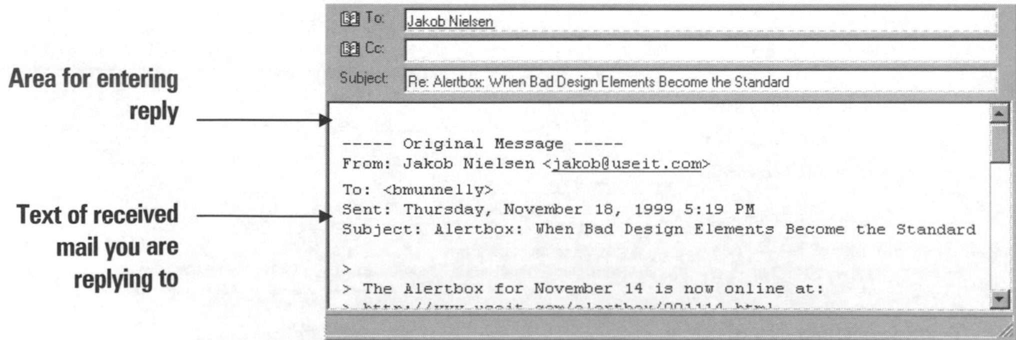

You can edit the Subject: box if you wish. You can also remove all or part of the original e-mail to which you are replying.

3) Enter the text of your reply in the message box, above the words 'Original Message'.

4) Click **Send**.

Remember, it's not very helpful to get a single word reply to an e-mail ('yes', or '4.30'). The person who reads it could have sent hundreds of e-mails, and could be reading your reply several days later. That's why including the original message with your reply is a good idea.

However, if the original message is very long, and your answer is 'yes', it is helpful to cut out those parts of the original message that do not require a response, so that it becomes very obvious what you are agreeing to.

E-mail Reply to Sender Only
The act of replying to a received e-mail. Only the person who sent you the e-mail gets your reply. The reply typically includes the text of the original e-mail.

Replying to All Recipients

Reply To All E-Mail Recipients button

The Reply All option enables you to reply to an e-mail, with your reply going to *everyone* who received the original message. You use it in exactly the same way as the Reply (to sender only) function.

You will find this feature particularly useful when working with a number of people on a project (drawing up a contract, for example), or discussing something that requires unanimous agreement (to schedule a meeting, for example)

To use this option with a received e-mail, choose **Message | Reply to All** or click the Reply All button on the Toolbar.

E-mail Reply All
The act of replying to a received e-mail. Everyone who received the original e-mail also gets your reply. The reply typically includes the text of the original e-mail.

Copying and Moving the Text of a Message

You can reuse the text of one e-mail in another e-mail, or in another application such as Microsoft Word. And you can move text around within the same message. Practise your text-moving skills with Exercises 7.44 and 7.45.

Exercise 7.44: Copying E-mail Text within Outlook Express

1) Open an e-mail, or compose a new one.
2) Select the text you want to copy by clicking at the start of the text and dragging the cursor to the end.
3) Choose **Edit | Copy** or press CTRL+c.
4) Go to where you want to insert the copied text, either within the same e-mail or in another e-mail.
5) Choose **Edit | Paste**, or press CTRL+v.

Exercise 7.45: Copying E-mail Text into Another Application

1) As in Exercise 7.44, select the text you want to copy and press CTRL+c.
2) Open the second application (such as Microsoft Word), position the cursor where you want the copied text to appear, and press CTRL+v.

In each case, you can move the text in question (that is, delete it in its original location and insert it in its new location), by choosing **Edit | Cut** instead of **Edit | Copy**, or pressing CTRL+x instead of CTRL+c.

Deleting Text

To delete text, select the text you want to delete, and do any of the following: choose **Edit | Cut**, press CTRL+x, or press the DELETE key.

Receiving File Attachments

Most e-mails are simple, self-contained text messages. Some, however, come with files attached – spreadsheets, formatted documents, presentations, graphics, or audio files, for example. You can identify an e-mail with a file attachment as follows:

- In the Message List, it is shown with a paper-clip icon.

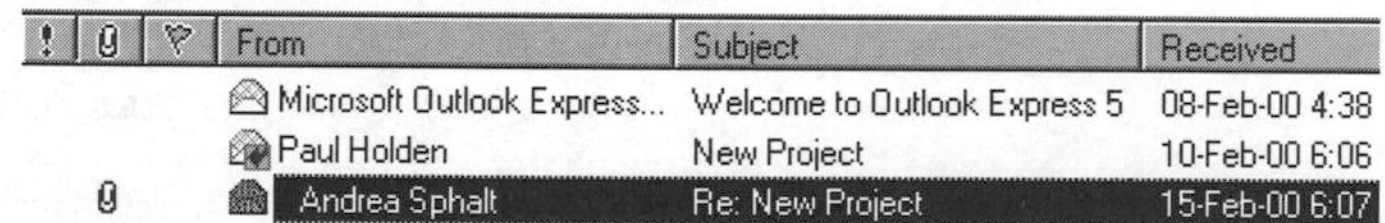

- In the Preview Pane, the e-mail header shows a paper-clip icon.

- If displayed in a separate window, the e-mail header shows an Attach: box, with the name and size of the file.

Opening Attachments

You can open a file attachment only if you have an application that is capable of opening it. If someone sends you an attachment that was created in an application that is not installed on your computer (or even a different version of a program that is installed), you may be unable to open it.

You can open an attached file in either of two ways:

- If viewing the e-mail in the Preview Pane, click the paper-clip icon in the e-mail header to display the file name, and then select the file name from the pop-up menu.

- If viewing the e-mail in a separate window, double-click the file name in the Attach: box.

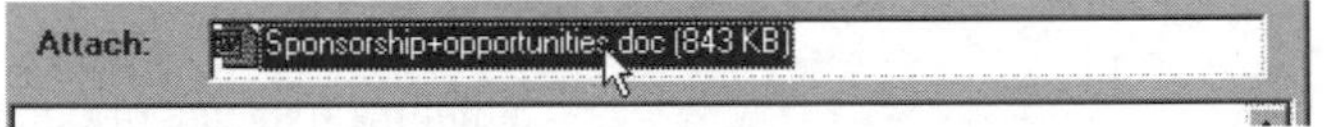

Saving Attachments

You can save an attached file in any of the following ways:

- Choose **File | Save Attachments**. (This command is available whether you are viewing the e-mail in the Preview Pane or in a separate window.)
- In the Preview Pane, click the paper-clip icon in the e-mail header and choose **Save Attachments**.
- In a separate e-mail window, right-click the file name in the Attach: box, and choose **Save As** from the pop-up window.

In each case, you specify where on your computer you want to save the file, accept or change the file name, and click **Save**.

If you open an attachment and do not save it, you can subsequently open it only from within Outlook Express. If you save it, you can subsequently open it from within Outlook Express and from the relevant application.

If you save an attachment and subsequently delete it, you will not be able to open it *either* from within Outlook Express or from within the application. And if you delete the e-mail without first saving the attachment, the attachment is also deleted.

Careful: Attachments Can Be Dangerous

Files attached to e-mail messages are among the most common ways of spreading computer viruses. For this reason, you should install a virus protection application on your computer that scans incoming e-mail attachments.

Using E-mail Folders

Once you start using e-mail, you'll probably get a lot of it. Some of it is important at the time, but has a short shelf-life ('Meet you for lunch' 'OK'). Some of it you need to keep for reference (the minutes of the project meetings). Some of it is simply junk mail. How do you keep it organised so that you can find what you want, when you want it? You create *mail folders*, that's how!

Exercise 7.46: Creating a New Mail Folder

1) Choose **File | New | Folder.**
2) Type the name you want to give the new folder.
3) Click on the name of the folder in which you want your new folder to be located.
   - If you want it to be at the same level as the Inbox, Outbox and other main folders of Outlook Express, click Local Folders.
   - If you want it to be a sub-folder of an existing folder such as your Inbox, click that folder.

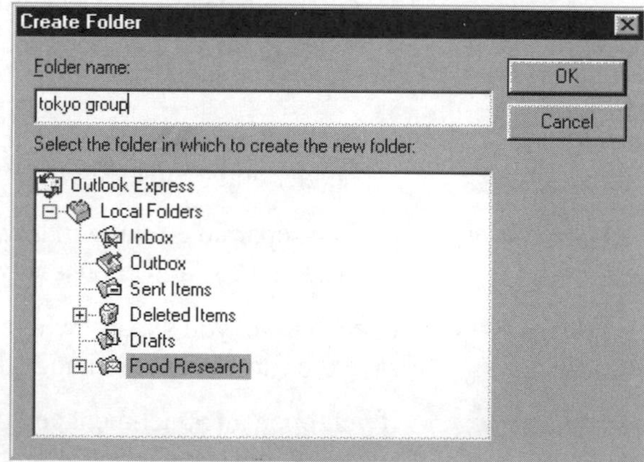

4) Click **OK.**

Transferring E-mails between Folders

As Exercise 7.47 demonstrates, you can transfer an e-mail from one folder to another.

Exercise 7.47: Moving an E-mail from Your Inbox to Another Folder

1) Open your Inbox folder and, in the Message List, select the e-mail you want to move.
2) Choose **Edit | Move to Folder**.
3) Click the folder into which you want to move the message.
4) Click **OK.**

Alternatively, click the e-mail in the Message List, and drag it to the folder in the Folder List on the left of the screen. What folder do you use for the junk mail and last week's invitations to lunch? Deleted Items, of course!

If you choose **Edit | Copy to Folder** in Exercise 7.47 above, the e-mail will be copied to the second folder – it will appear in both folders.

Deleting a Mail Folder

Be careful. It is possible to delete a mail folder, but you can't change your mind. The folder and all its contents will disappear forever. Follow the steps in Exercise 7.48 to discover how.

Exercise 7.48: Deleting a Folder

1) In the Folders List, click to select the folder you want to delete.
2) Choose **File | Folder | Delete** or click the Delete button on the Toolbar.
3) You are asked to confirm that you really do want to delete it.

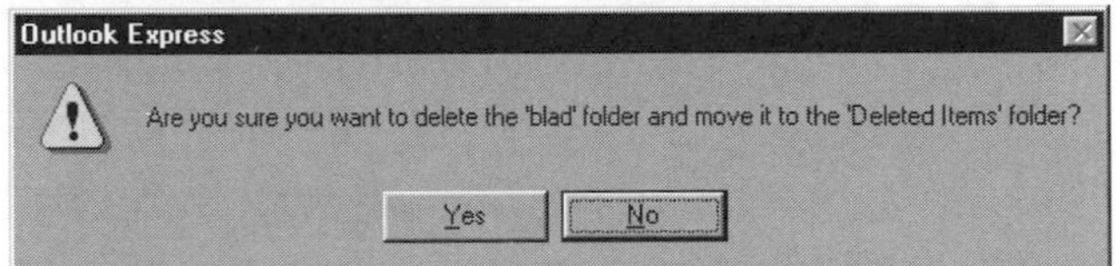

4) Click **Yes.**

Searching for Specific E-mails

You know that someone – you can't remember who – sent you details of the new MP3 music player. Your friend in Australia sent you a message sometime around Christmas. You need to see all the replies you received to your mail on the subject of tomorrow's meeting. How do you find what you want?

The quickest way of finding these needles in your e-mail haystack is to use the Find Message function. Exercise 7.49 provides an example.

Exercise 7.49: Finding a Particular E-mail

1) Choose **Edit | Find | Message** or click the Find button on the Toolbar.
2) If you know which folder the message is in, click **Browse** and select that folder for the Look in: box.

   If you're not sure where it is, choose Local Folders and select the Include subfolders check box.

3) Fill in whatever you know about the message – who it was from (or, if you sent it, who it was to), the subject, or some word or phrase in the text of the message. You don't have to use full words: even a single letter is enough. You can also specify a range of dates.
4) Click **Find Now**. Outlook Express displays a list of messages that satisfy your criteria.

   When you see the one you want, double-click it to open it.

Sorting Messages in a Folder

An alternative way of finding a particular message is to sort the items in the folder. If you sort your Inbox alphabetically by the name of the sender (the From field), you can find all the messages from a particular person, for example. Or you can find your most recently received messages by sorting it on the Received field.

Exercise 7.50: Sorting the Contents of a Mail Folder

1) Click your Inbox in the Folders List.
2) In the Message List, click the word From in the header. Outlook Express sorts your messages alphabetically by the name of the sender.

3) Click on the word From again. Outlook Express re-sorts the messages into reverse alphabetic order.
4) Click the Received field in the header. Outlook Express sorts your messages into the order in which they were received. As before, you can reverse the order by clicking Received again.

When finished, you can close Outlook Exprcss. You havc now completed this Section 7.7 of the ECDL Information and Communication Module.

Section Summary: So Now You Know

Outlook Express allows you to perform various actions on e-mails that you receive from others.

You can *forward* an e-mail to someone else, typically accompanied by some comments of your own which you enter in the text area above the original e-mail. You can *reply to the sender only*, so that just the originator of the e-mail sees your reply. Or you can *reply to all recipients* of the original e-mail.

Another option you have is, by using *copy and paste*, to insert the text of a received e-mail in an outgoing e-mail or in another application such as Microsoft Word.

Outlook Express indicates whether an incoming e-mail has a *file attachment*. You can open, save and delete attachments. File attachments may contain viruses, and you should use a reliable virus protection application to scan them.

You can create *mail folders* to keep your e-mails organised, you can sort the e-mails in any folder, and you can use the *Find* function to search for a particular e-mail by sender, receiver, subject, or date.

Section 7.8: Address Book and Contact Groups

In This Section

By now, you probably noticed that e-mail addresses can be difficult to remember. Some are cryptic (bill@xyz.com); others are complex (bs_p.sales@xy.pqrcorp.co.uk). Even within the one organisation, different people use different conventions (billsmith, bsmith, bill.smith, bill_smith, bsmth ...). How do you remember all these addresses?

You don't – you keep them in your *address book.*

In this Section you will learn how to organise your contacts in your address book, so that you don't have to remember their e-mail addresses and enter them each time you want to send them a message.

You will also discover how to set up contact groups (also called mailing lists), so that you can send the same message to large groups of people in a single operation.

New Skills

At the end of this Section you should be able to:

- Add, change, and delete contacts in your address book
- Create contact groups that can be e-mailed all at once

New Words

At the end of this Section you should be able to explain the following terms:

- E-mail contact
- Address book
- Nickname (alias)
- Mailing list (contact group)

Your Address Book

Outlook Express contains an area called an *address book* where you can keep information about the people you communicate with.

You can record all sorts of details about your contacts – obvious things, like their name, address, and phone number (and e-mail address!), and less obvious things, like their birthday, and the names of their children.

E-mail Contact

A person or organisation whose details (such as name and e-mail address) you have recorded in the address book of your e-mail application.

Address Book button

To explore the variety of information that you can record about your contacts, open Outlook Express, choose **Tools | Address Book** or click the Addresses button on the Outlook Express Toolbar. Next, click the New button on the Address Book Toolbar, and then choose **New Contact**.

Click successively on the seven tabs of the dialog box, view the various fields available, and, when finished, click **Cancel**.

Address Book

A feature of an e-mail application that enables you to record details about your e-mail contacts for easy reference.

Entering Contacts

In Exercise 7.51 you will practise entering a new contact to your Outlook Express address book.

Exercise 7.51: Adding a Contact to Your Address Book

1) Open your Outlook Express address book by choosing **Tools | Address Book.**
2) Click the New button on the Address Book Toolbar, and then select New Contact.
3) In the Name tab, type the First name, Last name and E-mail Address of one of your contacts.
4) In the Nickname field, type a short, easy-to-remember version of their name (even a single letter). Do not enter any spaces within the Nickname.

You can subsequently enter the Nickname in the To: field of an e-mail. (It is often called an alias.)

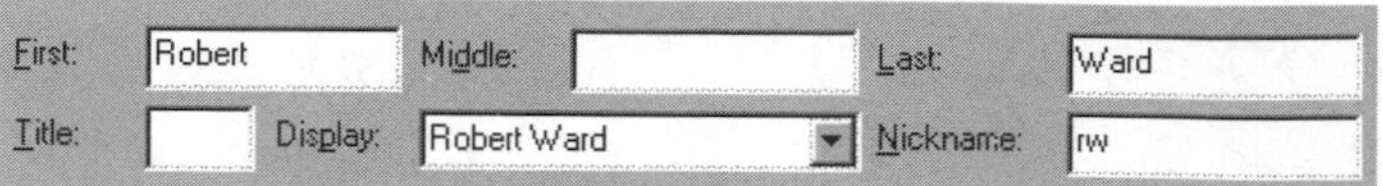

5) Click **OK**.

To create several new contacts in one operation, click **Add** after you type the details of each one. The **Add** button adds new contacts without closing the dialog box. The **OK** button adds the most recently entered contact – and closes the dialog box.

E-mail Nickname (Alias)

A shortened form of an e-mail address that you can enter in the To: field of a message as an alternative to typing the contact's e-mail address in full.

Contacts: The Minimum Details

At a minimum, each contact in your address book must contain a First name, a Last name and a Display name. All other contact details are optional. The first two you enter; the third is supplied, by default, by Outlook Express.

The Display Name is the name that appears in the To: field of e-mails that you send to that contact, and in the From: field of e-mails you receive from that contact.

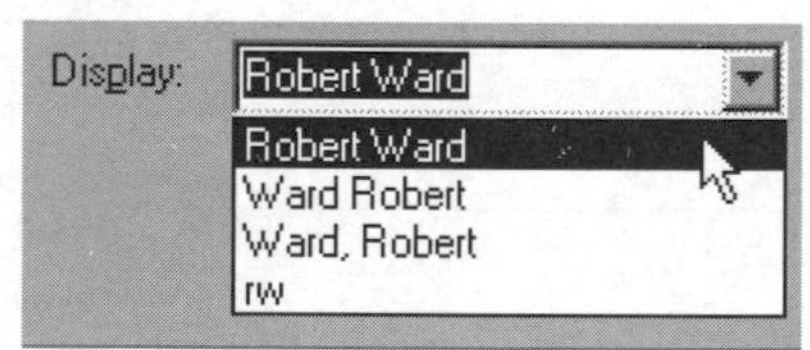

You can change the default Display name by typing in a different name or by selecting an alternative from the drop-down list. The drop-down list contains variations of the First/Middle/Last name, as well as anything you typed in the Nickname box or the Company box of the Business tab.

Editing Contacts

At any time, you can change the details of a contact or add further details, simply by:

- Choosing **Tools | Address Book** to open your address book
- Double-clicking to select the relevant contact

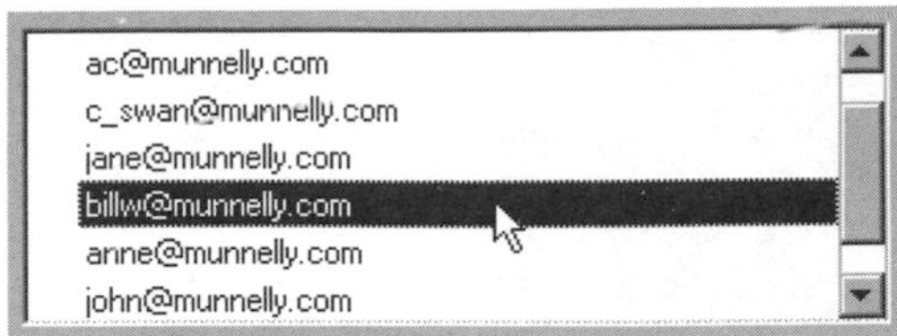

- Overtyping, deleting, or adding the new information

Deleting Contacts

To delete a contact, open your Address Book, select the relevant contact, and do any of the following: click the Delete button, press the DELETE key, or choose **File | Delete**.

Adding Contact Details from E-Mail Messages

In Exercise 7.51 you learnt how to add a new contact by opening your address book, and entering and saving the relevant details. You can add a new contact in two other ways:

- Display the Inbox or Outbox message list, right-click on an e-mail, and choose **Add Sender to Address Book** from the pop-up menu.
- When replying to an e-mail, right-click on the name in the To: field, and choose **Add to Address Book** from the pop-up menu.

You can also get Outlook Express to add all reply recipients to your address book automatically as follows:

- Choose **Tools | Options**.

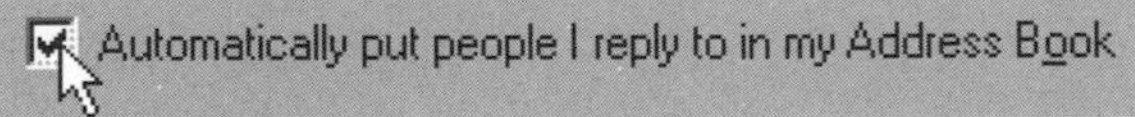

- On the Send tab, select the Automatically put people I reply to in my Address Book option, and click **OK**.

Sorting Your Contacts

You remember her first name but not her last name? You know the telephone number but not the name of the company? With a normal telephone directory, you'd have a problem. With Outlook Express – no problem. Exercise 7.52 and 7.53 take you through the steps.

Exercise 7.52: Sorting by First Name (Method 1)

1) Choose **Tools | Address Book** to open your address book.
2) Choose **View | Sort By.**

3) Select the Name, First Name, and Ascending options.

You may have to repeat step 2) to achieve this.

You can then easily find a person by their first name by scrolling through the list.

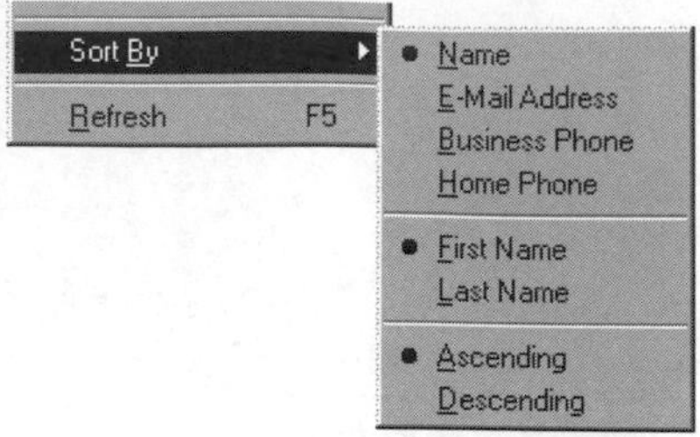

Exercise 7.53: Sorting by Telephone Number (Method 2)

1) If your address book is not open, choose **Tools | Address Book** to open it.

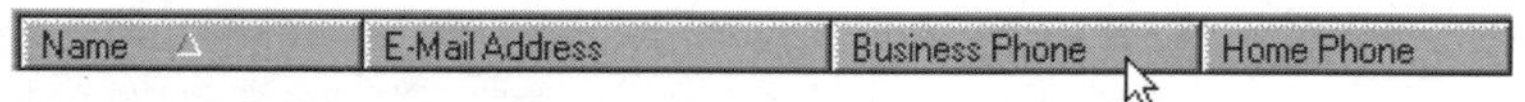

2) Click the words Business Phone in the header row. Click on the same words a second time.

Note that the order changes with each click, from ascending to descending to ascending again. You can now find the name you want by scrolling to the telephone number you recognise.

Mailing Lists (Contact Groups)

If you regularly use e-mail to stay in touch with your football team, your research group, or your extended family, you already know that you can send the same message to them by including all their names in the To: or Cc: box. (Remember to separate them with semi-colons!)

However, after a while, all that typing can get a bit tedious. What do you do? You set up what is generally known as a mailing list but which Outlook Express calls a *contact group*. Exercise 7.54 shows you how to create a contact group and add members to it.

Exercise 7.54: Setting Up a Contact Group

1) If your address book is not open, choose **Tools | Address Book** to open it.

2) Click the **New** button and select New Group.

3) Give the new group a name – preferably a short, easy-to-remember name.

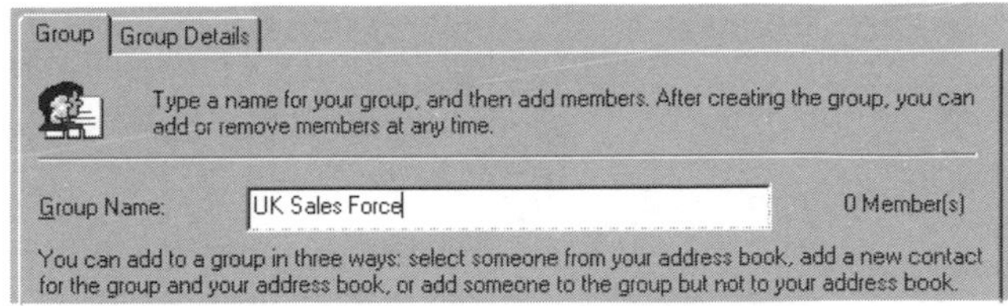

4) Two situations are now possible:

- The people you want to include in your new contact group are in your address book.
- The people you want to include in your new contact group are not in your address book.

If a person is already in your address book, click **Select Members** to view a new dialog box that lists your e-mail contacts. For each contact you want to include, click their name and then click **Select ->**.

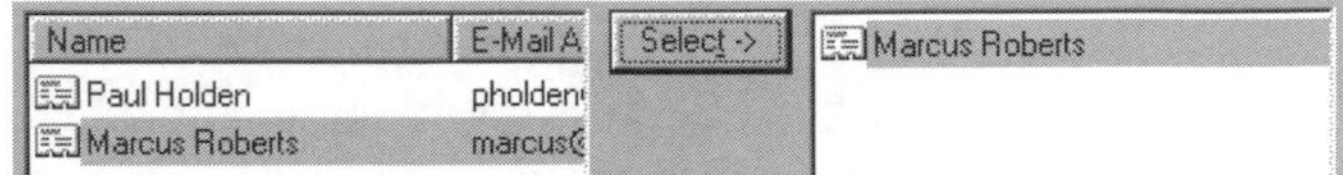

When finished, click **OK** to return to the main contact group dialog box. Now, go to step 5).

If the people you want to include are not in your address book, and you don't want them to be (because you never want to address them as individuals), type their name and e-mail address and click **Add.**

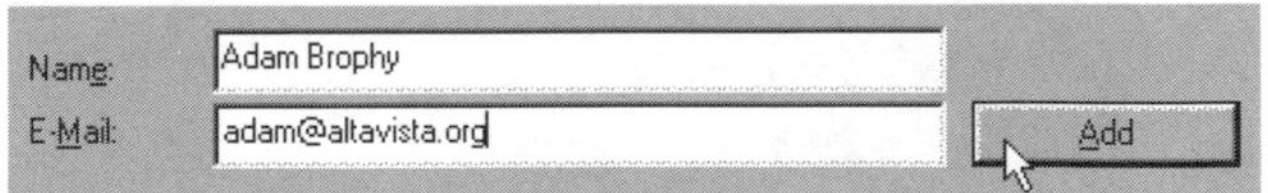

Continue typing names, e-mail addresses and clicking the **Add** button until you have entered the persons who are not in your address book.

5) When you have finished, click **OK**.

Once you have set up the group, you simply insert its name in the To: field of the message. Outlook Express sends the message to everyone in the group.

Mailing List/Contact Group

A list of e-mail addresses to which you can send a message in a single operation by entering the list's name in the To: field of the message.

Groups within Groups

A contact group may contain the names of other contact groups. For example, your Global Sales group might consist of three groups – the Europe Sales group, the US Sales group, and the ROW Sales group.

An individual may be a member of more than one group. At any time you can change the composition of your group by adding new members (exactly as in Exercise 7.54 above) or removing members (as in Exercise 7.55 below).

Exercise 7.55: Removing Members from a Group

1) If your address book is not open, choose **Tools | Address Book** to open it.
2) Double-click on the name of the contact group.
3) Click the name of the person you want to remove, and click **Remove.**
4) Click **OK.**

If you remove a name from a group, they still remain in your address book, and in any other group of which they are a member. However, if you delete (or change) a name in your address book, it is deleted (or changed) in every group of which it is a member. Congratulations!

You have now completed Module 7 of ECDL, Information and Communication.

Section Summary: So Now You Know

An *e-mail contact* is a person or organisation whose details (such as name and e-mail address) you have recorded on e-mail application software. Outlook Express allows you to record a wide variety of information about your contacts, spread over seven tabs of a dialog box.

At a minimum, each contact must contain a first name, a last name and a display name. The first two you enter; the third is supplied, by default, by Outlook Express. An e-mail *nickname* or *alias* is a shortened form of an e-mail address that you can enter in the To: field of a message as an alternative to typing the contact's e-mail address in full.

An *address book* is that part of your e-mail application where your contacts are stored for easy reference. You can type contact information into your address book directly, or you can add contact details to the address book from outgoing or incoming messages.

Outlook Express allows you to edit contact details, and to sort contacts according to such headings as last name and phone number.

A *mailing list* or a *contact group* is a list of e-mail addresses to which you can send a message in a single operation by entering the list's name in the To: field of the message. A contact group may contain the names of other contact groups. You can change the composition of a contact group by adding or removing members. An individual may be a member of more than one group.

Following the Financial News

Financial Markets + Institutions

The Addison-Wesley Series in Finance

Copeland/Weston
Financial Theory and Corporate Policy

Dufey/Giddy
Cases in International Finance

Eakins
Finance: Investments, Institutions, and Management

Eiteman/Stonehill/Moffett
Multinational Business Finance

Gitman
Principles of Managerial Finance

Gitman
Principles of Managerial Finance —Brief Edition

Gitman/Joehnk
Fundamentals of Investing

Gitman/Madura
Introduction to Finance

Hughes/MacDonald
International Banking: Text and Cases

Madura
Personal Finance

McDonald
Derivatives Markets

Megginson
Corporate Finance Theory

Melvin
International Money and Finance

Mishkin/Eakins
Financial Markets and Institutions

Moffett
Cases in International Finance

Moffett/Stonehill/Eiteman
Fundamentals of Multinational Finance

Rejda
Principles of Risk Management and Insurance

Solnik
International Investments

Financial Markets + Institutions

FOURTH EDITION

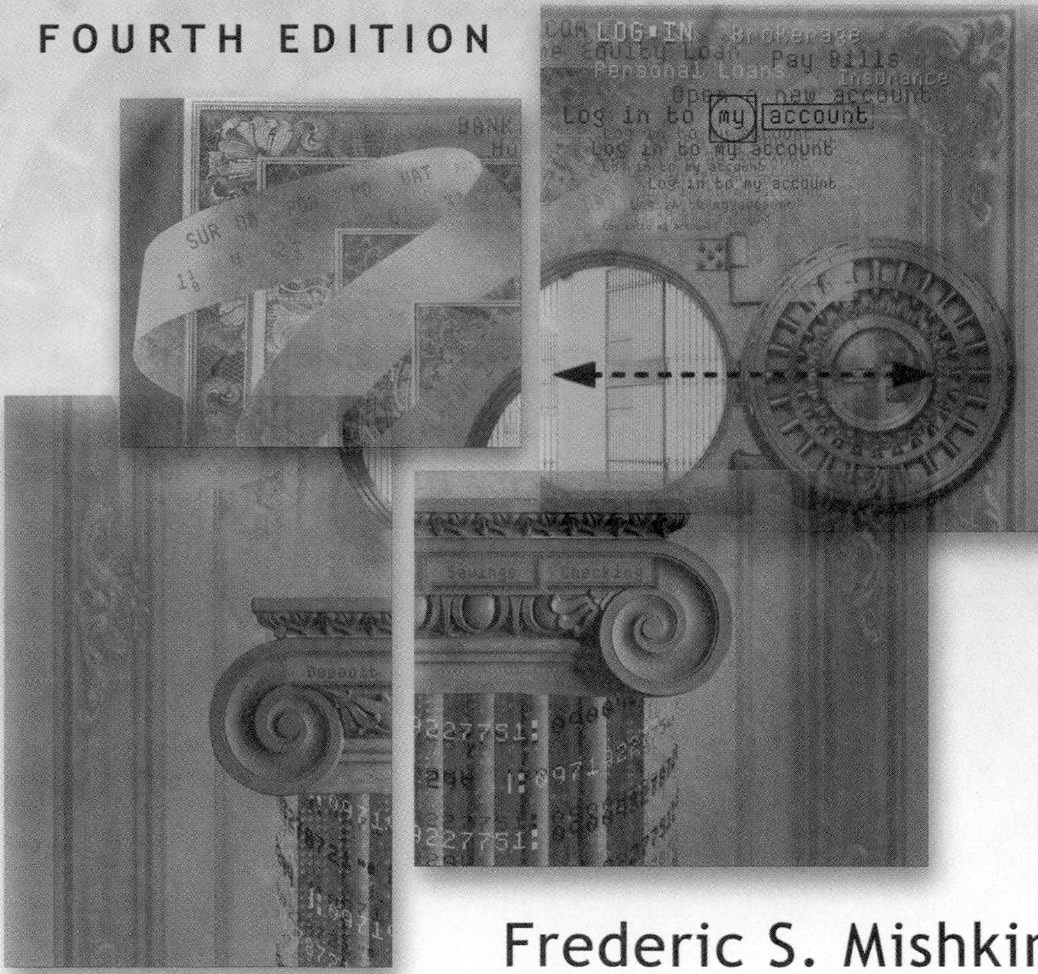

Frederic S. Mishkin
Graduate School of Business, Columbia University

Stanley G. Eakins
East Carolina University

Boston San Francisco New York
London Toronto Sydney Tokyo Singapore Madrid
Mexico City Munich Paris Cape Town Hong Kong Montreal

Editor in Chief: Denise Clinton
Sponsoring Editor: Donna Battista
Development Editor: Rebecca Ferris
Editorial Assistant: Amy Gembala
Production Supervisor: Meredith Gertz
Supplements Editor: Andrea Basso
Marketing Manager: Adrienne D'Ambrosio
Design Manager: Regina Hagen Kolenda
Media Producer: Jennifer Pelland
Project Coordination and Electronic Page Makeup: Electronic Publishing Services Inc., NYC
Cover Designer: Joyce Wells
Cover Image: © 2003 SuperStock, Inc.

Financial Markets and Institutions

ISBN: 0-321-11637-2

WORLD STUDENT SERIES

10 9 8 7 6 5 4 3 2—QWT—06 05 04

To My Dad

— F. S. M.

To My Wife, Laurie

— S. G. E.

Contents in Brief

Contents in Detail

Preface

We have continually strived to improve this textbook with each new edition, and the fourth edition of *Financial Markets and Institutions* is no exception. The book continues to offer features that make it highly distinctive from other textbooks in this field. Other textbooks are almost entirely descriptive and so do not adequately prepare students either for jobs in the financial services industry or for successful interaction with financial institutions, whatever their jobs. In contrast, *Financial Markets and Institutions* provides the following features:

- A unifying analytic framework that uses a few basic principles to organize students' thinking, including:
  - asymmetric information (agency) problems
  - transaction costs
  - supply and demand
  - asset market equilibrium
  - efficient markets
  - measurement and management of risk
- A financial practitioner's approach to financial markets and institutions through emphasis of an applied managerial perspective that includes nearly 20 special applications called "The Practicing Financial Institution Manager"
- A careful step-by-step development of models that enables students to master the material more easily
- A high degree of flexibility that allows professors to teach the course however they want
- Complete integration of an international perspective throughout the text
- Special features called "Following the Financial News" and "Reading the *Wall Street Journal*" to encourage the reading of a financial newspaper
- Numerous applications that increase students' interest by applying theory to real-world data and examples

WHAT'S NEW IN THE FOURTH EDITION

In addition to the expected updating of all data through the end of 2001 whenever possible, there is major new material in every part of the text.

E-Focus

The incredible advances in electronic (computer and telecommunications) technology in recent years have had a major impact on the financial system. The fourth edition of this text reflects these developments by adding many new features with an electronic focus.

Web Enhancement The fourth edition embraces the exploding world of information now available over the World Wide Web. There are few areas where the Internet has been as valuable as in providing financial information. Data that were once difficult and tedious to collect are now readily available. To help students appreciate what they can access on-line we have added a number of new features.

1. **Web Exercises.** This edition of the text adds a new type of end-of-chapter problem called Web Exercises. These require that students collect information from on-line sources or use on-line resources to enhance their learning experience. The Web Exercises are designed to be relatively quick and easy to do, while still accomplishing the goal of familiarizing students with on-line sources of data.

2. **Web Sources.** Much of the data used to create the many tables and charts were collected from sources found on-line. Wherever a URL is available, it is exactly reported as the source. The interested student or instructor can use this URL to see what has happened since the chart or table was created.

3. **Marginal Web References.** In addition to listing the sources of data used to create the charts and graphs, we have also included in the margins URLs to websites that provide information or data that supplement the text material. These references include a brief description of what students will find at the site. The interested student can use these sites to extend their study, and instructors can use these sites to enhance their lecture notes. Because the URLs for web sources and references do sometimes change, the Mishkin-Eakins companion website (located at http://www.aw.com/mishkin_eakins) will provide the new URLs when they are needed.

E-Finance Boxes Since electronic technology is permeating financial markets in more and more ways, we included a new type of special interest box in this edition. The E-Finance boxes relate how changes in technology have affected financial markets or institutions. The placement of these boxes throughout the text helps demonstrate the impact technology has had in a broad range of areas in finance.

Expanded Coverage of the Stock Market

With the wide swings in stock prices in recent years, students of financial markets and institutions have become increasingly interested in what drives the stock market. As a result, we have expanded our discussion of this market by including simple valuation methods. These include using the Gordon Growth Model and the price/earnings ratio to determine stock prices. This material has been merged with the material on efficient capital markets to create a new Chapter 10, "The Stock Market and the Efficient Markets Hypothesis."

Venture Capital

This edition has greatly expanded coverage of venture capital because of its importance to the economy and especially to the technology sector. We discuss the process followed by venture capitalist firms in selecting companies to finance, and follow the life cycle of the typical venture capital deal in Chapter 20, which has been renamed "Venture Capital Firms, Finance Companies, and Financial Conglomerates." We also discuss the role venture capital firms had in fueling the technology bubble and how they are affected by the recession that started in 2001.

Investment Banks and Mutual Funds

In Chapter 21, which has been renamed "Investment Banks, Brokerage Firms, and Mutual Funds," we have extended our discussion of investment banks, which have also grown in importance because they have helped finance the technology sector, to include more details about how new securities are brought to the public. We have also extended our discussion of mutual funds by increasing the amount of detail regarding the various types of funds available and how they may be used by investors.

Other New Material on Financial Institutions

Continuing changes in financial markets and institutions have resulted in the following additional new material.

- Discussion of the rapid collapse of Enron, which resulted in the largest bankruptcy in U.S. history (Chapter 14)
- Discussion of the Gramm-Leach-Bliley Finacial Services Modernization Act of 1999, which has overturned the Glass-Steagall separation of the banking and securities industry (Chapter 16, 18, and 21)
- New material on the Basel Committee on Bank Supervision and where the Basel Accord is heading (Chapter 18)
- Discussion of the spread of deposit insurance throughout the world (Chapter 18)

Increased International Perspective

The growing importance of the global economy continues to encourage us to add new material with an international perspective. A global icon is used to designate text sections and applications, while special-interest boxes with international material are designated as "Global." New material in this edition includes:

- Extensive treatment of the European Monetary Union and the introduction of the euro, including discussion of how it has fared in the currency markets in its first three years (Chapter 12), the birth of the European Monetary Union and the euro (Chapter 13), and whether the euro will challenge the dollar as a reserve currency (Chapter 13)
- New sections on capital controls and the role of the International Monetary Fund in preventing financial crises (Chapter 13)
- Discussion of dollarization and recent developments in Argentina's currency board (Chapter 13)

Streamlined Organization

Helpful comments from reviewers have also encouraged us to improve the flow and streamline the organization of the text. Most important, the material in the previous edition's Chapters 23 and 24 on financial derivatives has been shortened considerably and consolidated into a new Chapter 23 to focus on key issues that should be more relevant to the student.

FLEXIBILITY

There are as many ways to teach financial markets and institutions as there are instructors. Thus, there is a great need to make a textbook flexible in order to satisfy the diverse needs of instructors, and that has been a primary objective in writing this book. This textbook achieves this flexibility in the following ways:

- Core chapters provide the basic analysis used throughout the book, and other chapters or sections of chapters can be assigned or omitted according to instructor preferences. For example, Chapter 2 introduces the financial system and basic concepts such as transaction costs, adverse selection, and moral hazard. After covering Chapter 2, an instructor can decide to teach a more detailed treatment of financial structure in Chapter 14, or can skip this chapter or take any of a number of different paths.
- The approach to internationalizing the text using separate, marked international sections within chapters and separate chapters on the foreign exchange market and the international monetary system is comprehensive yet flexible. Although many instructors will teach all the international material, others will choose not to. Instructors who want less emphasis on international topics can easily skip Chapter 12 (on the foreign exchange market) and Chapter 13 (on the international financial system).
- "The Practicing Financial Institution Manager" applications, as well as Part VI on the management of financial institutions, are self-contained and so can be skipped without loss of continuity. Thus, an instructor wishing to teach a less managerially oriented course, who might want to focus more on public policy issues, will have no trouble doing so. Alternatively, Part VI can be taught earlier in the course, immediately after Chapter 15 on bank management.

The course outlines listed next for a semester teaching schedule illustrate how this book can be used for courses with a different emphasis. More detailed information about how the text can be used flexibly in your course is available in the *Instructor's Resource Manual.*

Financial markets and institutions emphasis: Chapters 1–5, 8–10, 14–16, 18, and six other chapters

Financial markets and institutions with international emphasis: Chapters 1–5, 8–10, 12–16, 18, and four other chapters

Managerial emphasis: Chapters 1–5, 15, 16, 18, 22, 23, and eight other chapters

Public policy emphasis: Chapters 1–7, 14, 15, 18, and eight other chapters

MAKING IT EASIER TO TEACH FINANCIAL MARKETS AND INSTITUTIONS

The demands for good teaching at business schools have increased dramatically in recent years. To meet these demands, we have provided the instructor with supplementary materials, unavailable with any competing text, that should make teaching the course substantially easier.

Along with the usual items in the *Instructor's Resource Manual*—sample course outlines, chapter outlines, overviews, teaching tips, and answers to the end-of-chapter problems that are not included in the text—this manual includes over 300 pages of lecture notes. The lecture notes are comprehensive and outline all the major points covered in the text. They have been class-tested successfully by the authors and should make it much easier for other instructors to prepare their lecture notes as well. The lecture notes are perforated so that they can be easily detached for class use or to make transparency masters.

This edition of the book comes with a powerful teaching tool: an *Instructor's Resource CD-ROM.* Fully compatible with Windows and Macintosh computers, the CD-ROM contains Word files for the entire contents of the *Instructor's Resource Manual* (including the lecture notes), PowerPoint presentations, and Computerized Test Bank files. Using this handy supplement, instructors can prepare student handouts such as solutions to problem sets made up of end-of-chapter problems or the outline of the lecture of the day. We have used handouts of this type in our classes and have found them to be very effective. To facilitate classroom presentation even further, the PowerPoint presentations include all the book's figures and tables in full color, as well as all the lecture notes; all are fully customizable. The Computerized Test Bank software (TestGen-EQ with QuizMaster-EQ for Windows and Macintosh) is a valuable test preparation tool that allows professors to view, edit, and add questions. Instructors have our permission and are encouraged to reproduce all of the materials on the CD-ROM and use them as they see fit in class.

SUPPLEMENTARY MATERIALS

The fourth edition of *Financial Markets and Institutions* includes the most comprehensive program of supplementary materials of any textbook in its field. These items are available to qualified domestic adopters but in some cases may not be available to international adopters. These include the following items:

For the Professor

1. ***Instructor's Resource Manual,*** prepared by the authors, which includes sample course outlines, chapter outlines, overviews, teaching tips, and answers to questions and problems in the text. In addition it has **Lecture Notes**, numbering over 300 in transparency master format, that comprehensively outline the major points covered in the text.
2. ***Instructor's Resource CD-ROM,*** which contains Word files for the *Instructor's Resource Manual,* PowerPoint presentations, and the Computerized Test Bank.
3. **Test Bank**, available in both print and electronic form, which comprises over 2500 multiple-choice, true-false, and essay test items. The Test Bank is computerized so that the instructor can easily produce exams automatically.
4. **Mishkin-Eakins Companion Website** (located at http://www.aw.com/mishkin_eakins), which features mini-case exercises, new managerially focused cases corresponding to the chapters in each of the text's six parts, and links to relevant data sources and Federal Reserve websites. The site also offers multiple-choice quizzes for each chapter. An on-line syllabus builder allows instructors to create a calendar of assignments for each class.

For the Student

1. **Study Guide and Workbook**, which includes chapter synopses and completions, exercises, self-tests, and answers to the exercises and self-tests.
2. **Readings in Financial Markets and Institutions**, edited by James W. Eaton of Bridgewater College and Frederic S. Mishkin. Updated annually, with over half the articles new each year, this valuable resource is available on-line at the text's website (www.aw.com/mishkin_eakins).

PEDAGOGICAL AIDS

A textbook must be a solid motivational tool. To this end, we have incorporated a wide variety of pedagogical features.

1. **Chapter Previews** at the beginning of each chapter tell students where the chapter is heading, why specific topics are important, and how they relate to other topics in the book.
2. **Applications** demonstrate how the analysis in the book can be used to explain many important real-world situations. A special set of applications called "Reading the *Wall Street Journal*" shows students how to read daily columns in this leading financial newspaper.
3. **"The Practicing Financial Institution Manager"** is a set of special applications that introduce students to real-world problems that managers of financial institutions have to solve.
4. **Numerical Examples** guide students through solutions to financial problems using formulas, time lines, and calculator key strokes.
5. **"Following the Financial News" Boxes** introduce students to relevant news articles and data that are reported daily in the press and explain how to read them.
6. **"Inside the Fed" Boxes** give students a feel for what is important in the operation and structure of the Federal Reserve System.
7. **Global Boxes** include interesting material with an international focus.
8. **E-Finance Boxes** relate how changes in technology have affected financial markets and institutions.
9. **Special-Interest Boxes** highlight dramatic historical episodes, interesting ideas, and intriguing facts related to the subject matter.
10. **Study Guides** are highlighted statements scattered throughout the text that provide hints on how to think about or approach a topic as students work their way through it.
11. **Summary Tables** are useful study aids for reviewing material.
12. **Key Statements** are important points that are set in boldface type so that students can easily find them for later reference.
13. **Graphs** with captions, numbering over 60, help students understand the interrelationship of the variables plotted and the principles of analysis.

14. **Summaries** at the end of each chapter list the chapter's main points.
15. **Key Terms** are important words or phrases that appear in boldface type when they are defined for the first time and are listed at the ends of the chapters.
16. **End-of-Chapter Questions and Problems,** numbering 400, help students learn the subject matter by applying economic concepts, and feature a special class of problems that students find particularly relevant, titled "Predicting the Future."
17. **Web Exercises** encourage students to collect information from on-line sources or use on-line resources to enhance their learning experience.
18. **Web Sources** report the URL source of the data used to create the many tables and charts.
19. **Marginal Web References** point the student to websites that provide information or data that supplement the text material.
20. **Glossary** at the back of the book defines all the key terms.
21. **Solutions to Problems** at the back of the book provides the solutions to about half the questions and problems, indicated in the text by an asterisk (*).

ACKNOWLEDGMENTS

As always in so large a project, there are many people to thank. My special gratitude goes to Bruce Kaplan, former economics editor at HarperCollins; Donna Battista, finance editor at Addison-Wesley; and Jane Tufts and Rebecca Ferris, development editors. I also have been assisted by comments from my colleagues at Columbia and from my students.

In addition, I have been guided in this edition and its predecessors by the thoughtful comments of outside reviewers and correspondents. Their feedback has made this a better book. In particular, I thank:

Ibrahim J. Affanen, Indiana University of Pennsylvania
Ronald Anderson, University of Nevada—Las Vegas
Bala G. Arshanapalli, Indiana University Northwest
James C. Baker, Kent State University
Joel Barber, Florida International University
Thomas M. Barnes, Alfred University
Marco Bassetto, Northwestern University
Matej Blusko, University of Georgia
Dallas R. Blevins, University of Montevallo
Paul J. Bolster, Northeastern University
Yea-Mow Chen, San Francisco State University
N.K. Chidambaran, Tulane University
Jeffrey A. Clark, Florida State University
Robert Bruce Cochran, San Jose State University
William Colclough, University of Wisconsin—La Crosse
Elizabeth Cooperman, University of Baltimore
Carl Davison, Mississippi State University
Erik Devos, Binhamton University
Franklin R. Edwards, Columbia University
Marty Eichenbaum, Northwestern University
Elyas Elyasiani, Temple University
Edward C. Erickson, California State University, Stanislaus
E. Bruce Fredrikson, Syracuse University
James Gatti, University of Vermont
Paul Girma, SUNY—New Paltz
Susan Glanz, St. John's University
Beverly L. Hadaway, University of Texas
John A. Halloran, University of Notre Dame
Billie J. Hamilton, East Carolina University

John H. Hand, Auburn University
Don P. Holdren, Marshall University
Adora Holstein, Robert Morris College
Sylvia C. Hudgins, Old Dominion University
Jerry G. Hunt, East Carolina University
Boulis Ibrahim, Heroit-Watt University
William E. Jackson, University of North Carolina—Chapel Hill
Joe James, Sam Houston State University
Melvin H. Jameson, University of Nevada—Las Vegas
Kurt Jessewein, Texas A&M International University
Jack Jordan, Seton Hall University
Taeho Kim, Thunderbird: The American Graduate School of International Management
Taewon Kim, California State University, Los Angeles
Glen A. Larsen Jr., University of Tulsa
James E. Larsen, Wright State University
Rick LeCompte, Wichita State University
Boyden E. Lee, New Mexico State University
John Litvan, Southwest Missouri State
Richard A. Lord, Georgia College
Robert L. Losey, American University
Anthony Loviscek, Seton Hall University
James Lynch, Robert Morris College
Judy E. Maese, New Mexico State University
William Marcum, Wake Forest University
David A. Martin, Albright College
Joseph S. Mascia, Adelphi University
Khalid Metabdin, College of St. Rose
A. H. Moini, University of Wisconsin—Whitewater
Terry Nixon, Indiana University
William E. O'Connell, Jr., The College of William and Mary
Masao Ogaki, Ohio State University
Evren Ors, Southern Illinois University
Coleen C. Pantalone, Northeastern University
Scott Pardee, University of Chicago
James Peters, Fairleigh Dickinson University
Fred Puritz, SUNY—Oneonta
Mahmud Rahman, Eastern Michigan University
Anoop Rai, Hofstra University
Mitchell Ratner, Rider University
David Reps, Pace University—Westchester
Jack Rubens, Bryant College
Charles B. Ruscher, James Madison University
William Sackley, University of Southern Mississippi
Kevin Salyer, University of California—Davis
Siamack Shojai, Manhattan College
Donald Smith, Boston University
Sonya Williams Stanton, Ohio State University
Michael Sullivan, Florida International University
Richard S. Swasey, Jr., Northeastern University
Anjan Thackor, University of Michigan
Janet M. Todd, University of Delaware
James Tripp, Western Illinois University
Carlos Ulibarri, Washington State University
John Wagster, Wayne State University
David A. Whidbee, California State University—Sacramento
Arthur J. Wilson, George Washington University
Shee Q. Wong, University of Minnesota—Duluth
Criss G. Woodruff, Radford University

Finally, I want to thank my wife, Sally; my son, Matthew; and my daughter, Laura, who provide me with a warm and happy environment that enables me to do my work, and my father, Sydney, now deceased, who a long time ago put me on the path that led to this book.

Frederic S. Mishkin

I would like to thank Rick Mishkin for his excellent comments on my contributions. By working with Rick on this text, not only have I gained greater skill as a writer, but I have also gained a friend. I would also like to thank my wife, Laurie, for patiently reading each draft of this manuscript and for helping make this my best work. Through the years, her help and support have made this aspect of my career possible.

Stanley G. Eakins

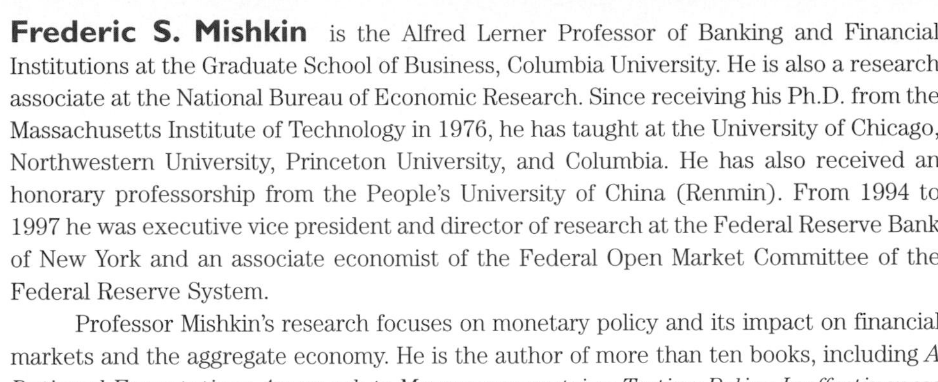

About the Authors

© Peter Murphy

Frederic S. Mishkin is the Alfred Lerner Professor of Banking and Financial Institutions at the Graduate School of Business, Columbia University. He is also a research associate at the National Bureau of Economic Research. Since receiving his Ph.D. from the Massachusetts Institute of Technology in 1976, he has taught at the University of Chicago, Northwestern University, Princeton University, and Columbia. He has also received an honorary professorship from the People's University of China (Renmin). From 1994 to 1997 he was executive vice president and director of research at the Federal Reserve Bank of New York and an associate economist of the Federal Open Market Committee of the Federal Reserve System.

Professor Mishkin's research focuses on monetary policy and its impact on financial markets and the aggregate economy. He is the author of more than ten books, including *A Rational Expectations Approach to Macroeconometrics: Testing Policy Ineffectiveness and Efficient Markets Models* (University of Chicago Press, 1983); *Money, Interest Rates, and Inflation* (Edward Elgar, 1993); *Inflation Targeting: Lessons from the International Experience* (Princeton University Press, 1999); *The Economics of Money, Banking, and Financial Markets*, 6th edition (Addison-Wesley, 2001); and has published over 100 articles in professional journals and books.

Professor Mishkin has served on the editorial board of the *American Economic Review,* has been an associate editor at the *Journal of Business and Economic Statistics* and *Journal of Applied Econometrics,* and was the editor of the Federal Reserve Bank of New York's *Economic Policy Review.* He is currently an associate editor (member of the editorial board) at seven academic journals: the *Journal of Money, Credit and Banking; Macroeconomics and Monetary Economics Abstracts; Journal of International Money and Finance; International Finance; Finance India; Economic Policy Review;* and the *Journal of Economic Perspectives.* He has been a consultant to the Board of Governors of the Federal Reserve System, the World Bank, and the International Monetary Fund, as well as to many central banks throughout the world. He was also a member of the International Advisory Board to the Financial Supervisory Service of South Korea. He is currently an academic consultant to and serves on the Economic Advisory Panel of the Federal Reserve Bank of New York.

Stanley G. Eakins has notable experience as a financial practitioner, serving as vice president and comptroller at the First National Bank of Fairbanks and as a commercial and real estate loan office. A founder of Denali title and escrow agency, a title insurance company in Fairbanks, Alaska, he also ran the operations side of a bank and was the chief finance officer for a multimillion-dollar construction and development company.

Professor Eakins received his Ph.D. from Arizona State University. He is the Chairman of the Finance Department at East Carolina University. His research is focused primarily on the role of institutions in corporate control and how they influence investment practices. He is also interested in integrating multimedia tools into the learning environment and has received grants from East Carolina University in support of this work.

A contributor to journals such as the *Quarterly Journal of Business and Economics,* the *Journal of Financial Research,* and the *International Review of Financial Analysis,* Professor Eakins is also the author of *Finance: Institutions, Investments, and Management* (Addison-Wesley, 2002).

Financial Markets + Institutions

Part 1

Introduction

Chapter 1 Why Study Financial Markets and Institutions?

Preview

On the evening news you have just heard that the bond market has been booming. Does this mean that interest rates will fall so that it is easier for you to finance the purchase of a new computer system for your small retail business? Will the economy improve in the future so that it is a good time to build a new building or add to the one you are in? Should you try to raise funds by issuing stocks or bonds or instead go to the bank for a loan? If you import goods from abroad, should you be concerned that they will become more expensive?

This book provides answers to these questions by examining how financial markets (such as those for bonds, stocks, and foreign exchange) and financial institutions (banks, insurance companies, mutual funds, and other institutions) work. Financial markets and institutions not only affect your everyday life but also involve huge flows of funds—trillions of dollars—throughout our economy, which in turn affect business profits, the production of goods and services, and even the economic well-being of countries other than the United States. What happens to financial markets and institutions is of great concern to our politicians and can even have a major impact on our elections. The study of financial markets and institutions will reward you with an understanding of many exciting issues. In this chapter we provide a road map of the book by outlining these exciting issues and exploring why they are worth studying.

WHY STUDY FINANCIAL MARKETS?

Parts II and III of this book focus on **financial markets,** markets in which funds are transferred from people who have an excess of available funds to people who have a shortage. Financial markets such as the bond and stock markets are important in channeling funds from people who do not have a productive use for them to those who do, resulting in greater economic efficiency. Activities in financial markets also have direct effects on personal wealth, the behavior of businesses and consumers, and the overall performance of the economy.

Debt Markets and Interest Rates

A **security** (also called a *financial instrument*) is a claim on the issuer's future income or **assets** (any financial claim or piece of property that is subject to ownership). A **bond** is a debt security that promises to make payments periodically for a specified period of time.[1] Debt markets, also often referred to generically as the *bond market,* are especially important to economic activity because they enable corporations or governments to borrow to finance their activities and because the bond market is where interest rates are determined. The **interest rate** is the cost of borrowing or the price paid for the rental of funds (usually expressed as a percentage of the rental of $100 per year). There are many interest rates in the economy—mortgage interest rates, car loan rates, and interest rates on many different types of bonds.

Daily, weekly, monthly, quarterly, and annual releases as well as historical data for selected interest rates, foreign exchange rates, etc., are available at

www.federalreserve.gov/releases/

Interest rates are important on a number of levels. On a personal level, high interest rates could deter you from buying a house or a car because the cost of financing it would be high. Conversely, high interest rates could encourage you to save because you can earn more interest income by putting aside some of your earnings as savings. On a more general level, interest rates have an impact on the overall health of the economy because they affect not only consumers' willingness to spend or save but also businesses' investment decisions. High interest rates, for example, may cause a corporation to postpone building a new plant that would ensure more jobs.

The level of interest rates is especially important to financial institutions. A rise in interest rates raises the cost of acquiring funds for financial institutions such as banks and raises the income on assets such as loans. In addition, changes in interest rates affect the prices of securities such as stocks and bonds that are held by financial institutions. Changes in interest rates thus directly affect the profitability and value of financial institutions.

Because changes in interest rates have important effects on individuals, financial institutions, businesses, and the overall economy, it is important to explain fluctuations in interest rates, which have been substantial over the past 30 years. As a matter of fact, in no other 30-year period of United States history have interest-rate fluctuations been as great. For example, the interest rate on long-term U.S. Treasury bonds was about 5% in 1963, rose to close to 15% in 1981, and was at 5.5% at the end of 2001. In the preceding 30-year period, from 1936 to 1966, the rate fluctuated between 2% and 5%.

Because different interest rates have a tendency to move in unison, economists frequently lump interest rates together and refer to "the" interest rate. As Figure 1 shows, however, interest rates on several types of bonds can differ substantially. The interest rate on three-month Treasury bills, for example, fluctuates more than the other interest rates and is lower, on average. The interest rate on Baa (medium-

---

[1]The definition of *bond* used throughout this book is the broad one in common use by academics, which covers short- as well as long-term debt instruments. However, some practitioners in financial markets use the word *bond* only to describe specific long-term debt instruments such as corporate bonds or U.S. Treasury bonds.

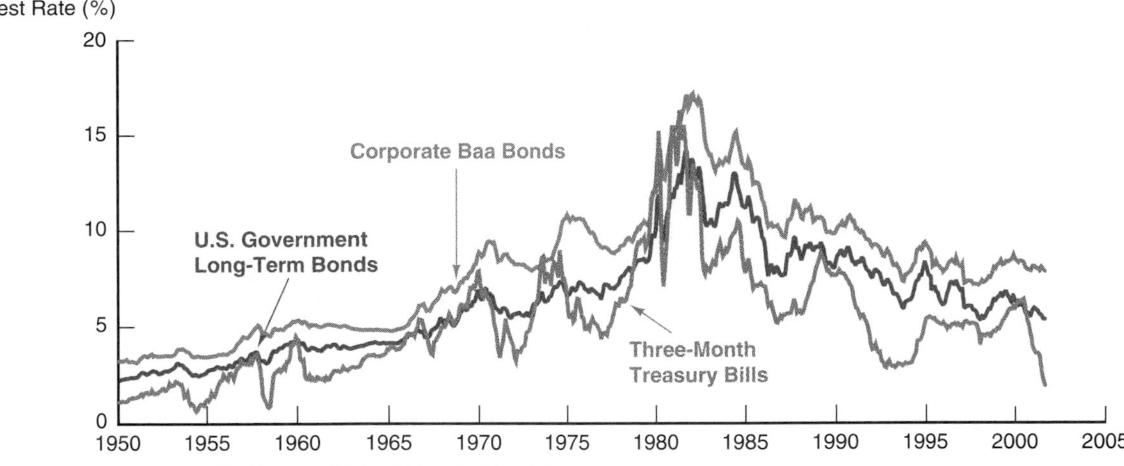

FIGURE 1 Interest Rates on Selected Bonds, 1950–2001

Source: http://www.federalreserve.gov/releases/H15/data.htm

quality) corporate bonds is higher, on average, than the other interest rates, and the spread between it and the other rates became larger in the 1970s.

In Chapters 2, 8, 9 and 11 we study the role of debt markets in the economy, and in Chapters 3 through 5 we examine what an interest rate is, how the common movements in interest rates come about, and why interest rates on different securities vary.

The Stock Market

A **stock** is a security that represents a share of ownership in a corporation. It is a claim on the earnings and assets of the corporation. Issuing stock and selling it to the public is a way for corporations to raise funds to finance their activities. The stock market, in which claims on the earnings of corporations (shares of stock) are traded, is the most widely followed financial market in America (that's why it is often called simply "the market"). A big swing in the prices of shares in the stock market is always a big story on the evening news. People often express their opinion on where the market is heading and will frequently tell you about their latest "big killing" (although you seldom hear about their latest big loss!). The attention that the market receives can probably be best explained by one simple fact: It is a place where people can get rich quickly.

As Figure 2 indicates, stock prices have been extremely volatile. They climbed steadily in the 1950s, reached a peak in 1966, and then fluctuated up and down until 1973, when they fell sharply. Stock prices had recovered substantially by the early 1980s when a major stock market boom began, sending the Dow Jones Industrial Average (DJIA) to a peak of 2722 on August 25, 1987. After a 17% decline over the next month and a half, the stock market experienced the worst one-day drop in its entire history on "Black Monday," October 19, 1987, when the DJIA fell by more than 500 points, a 22% decline. The stock market then recovered, climbing above the 10,000 level in 1998 and fluctuated around that level through the end of 2001. These considerable fluctuations in stock prices affect the size of people's wealth and as a result may affect their willingness to spend.

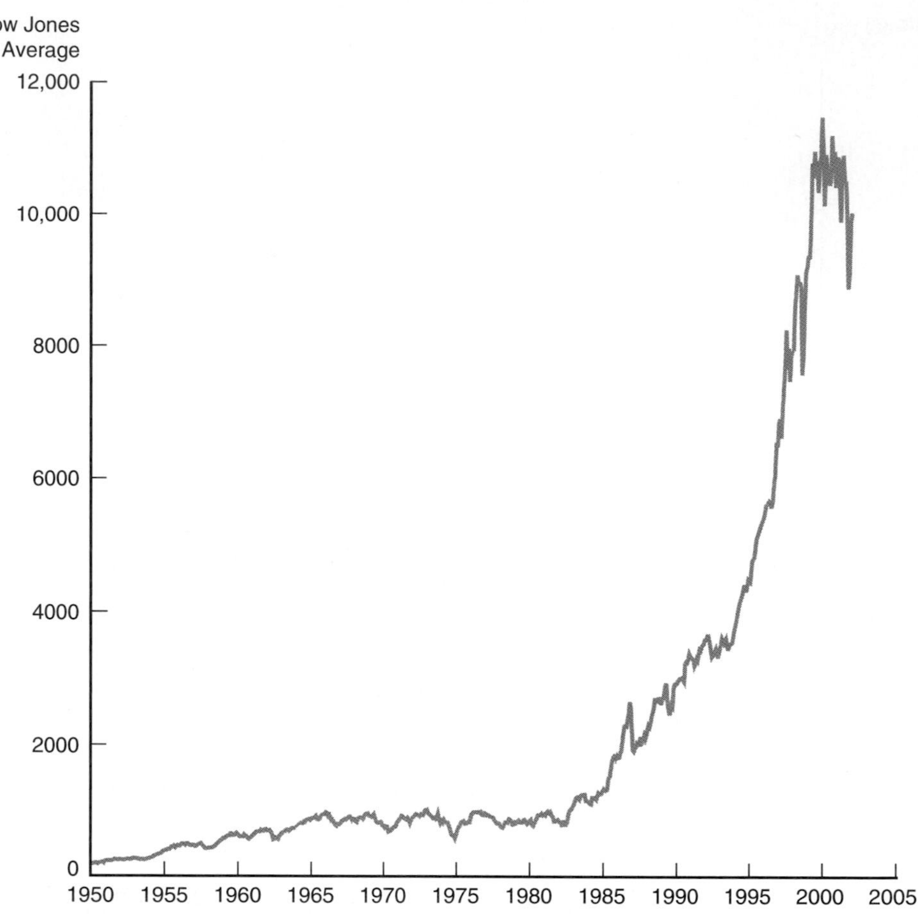

FIGURE 2 Stock Prices as Measured by the Dow Jones Industrial Average, 1950–2001

Source: http://finance.yahoo.com/?u

The stock market is also an important factor in business investment decisions because the price of shares affects the amount of funds that can be raised by selling newly issued stock to finance investment spending. A higher price for a firm's shares means that it can raise a larger amount of funds, which can be used to buy production facilities and equipment.

In Chapter 2 we examine the role that the stock market plays in the financial system, and we return to the issue of how stock prices behave and respond to information in the marketplace in Chapter 10. Stocks are also discussed in Chapter 9.

The Foreign Exchange Market

For funds to be transferred from one country to another, they have to be converted from the currency in the country of origin (say, dollars) into the currency of the country they are going to (say, Euros). The **foreign exchange market** is where this conversion takes place, and so it is instrumental in moving funds between countries. It is also important because it is where the **foreign exchange rate,** the price of one country's currency in terms of another's, is determined.

Figure 3 shows the exchange rate for the U.S. dollar from 1970 to 2002 (measured as the value of the American dollar in terms of a basket of major

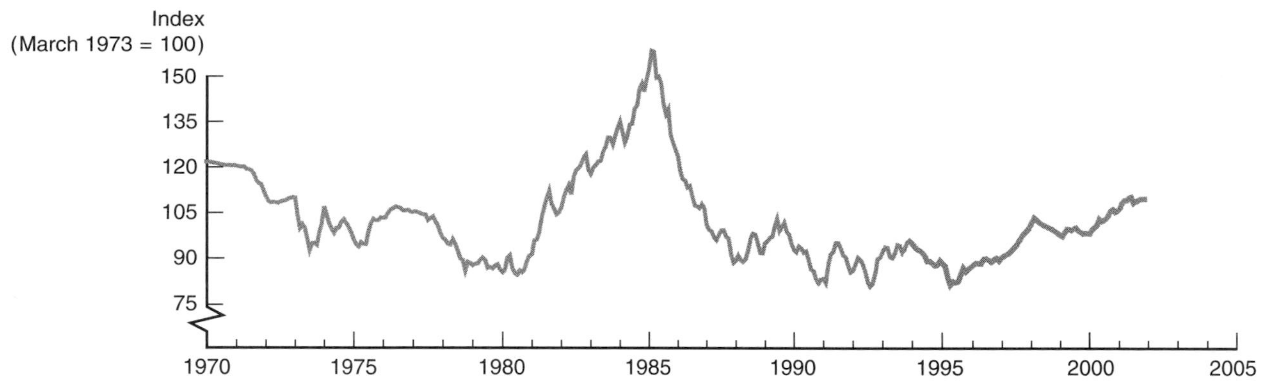

FIGURE 3 Exchange Rate of the U.S. Dollar for a Basket of Foreign Currencies, 1970–2002

Source: Federal Reserve Board at www.federalreserve.gov/releases

foreign currencies). The fluctuations in prices in this market have also been substantial: The dollar weakened considerably from 1971 to 1973, rose slightly in value until 1976, and then reached a low point in the 1978—1980 period. From 1980 to early 1985, the dollar appreciated dramatically in value, but then fell sharply, and appreciated again from 1995 to 2001.

What have these fluctuations in the exchange rate meant to the American public and businesses? A change in the exchange rate has a direct effect on American consumers because it affects the cost of foreign goods. In 1985, when the British currency, the pound sterling, cost approximately $1.30, £100 of British goods (say, Shetland sweaters) would cost $130. When a weaker dollar raised the cost of a pound to $1.60 in 1997, the same £100 of Shetland sweaters cost $160. Thus a weaker dollar leads to more expensive foreign goods, makes vacationing abroad more expensive, and raises the cost of indulging your desire for imported delicacies. When the value of the dollar drops, Americans will decrease their purchases of foreign goods and increase their consumption of domestic goods (such as travel in the United States or American-made sweaters).

Conversely, a strong dollar means that U.S. goods exported abroad will cost more in foreign countries, and hence foreigners will buy fewer of them. Exports of steel, for example, declined sharply when the dollar strengthened between 1980 and 1985. A strong dollar benefited American consumers by making foreign goods cheaper but hurt American businesses and eliminated some jobs by cutting both domestic and foreign sales of their products. The decline in the value of the dollar after 1985 has had the opposite effect: It has made foreign goods more expensive, but it has made American businesses more competitive. Fluctuations in the foreign exchange markets have major consequences for the American economy.

In Chapters 12 and 13 we study how exchange rates are determined in the foreign exchange market in which dollars are bought and sold for foreign currencies.

WHY STUDY FINANCIAL INSTITUTIONS?

The second major focus of this book is financial institutions. Financial institutions are what make financial markets work. Without them, financial markets would not be able to move funds from people who save to people who have productive investment opportunities. They thus also have important effects on the performance of the economy as a whole.

Central Banks and the Conduct of Monetary Policy

The most important financial institution in the financial system is the **central bank,** the government agency responsible for the conduct of monetary policy, which in the United States is the **Federal Reserve System** (also called simply **the Fed**). **Monetary policy** involves the management of interest rates and the quantity of **money,** also referred to as the **money supply** (defined as anything that is generally accepted in payment for goods and services or in the repayment of debt). Because monetary policy affects interest rates, inflation, and business cycles, all of which have a major impact on financial markets and institutions, we study how monetary policy is conducted by central banks in both the United States and abroad in Chapter 6 and 7.

Access general information, monetary policy, banking system, research and economic data from the Federal Reserve at www.federalreserve.gov

Structure of the Financial System

The financial system is complex, comprising many different types of private sector financial institutions, including banks, insurance companies, mutual funds, finance companies, and investment banks, all of which are heavily regulated by the government. If you wanted to make a loan to IBM or General Motors, for example, you would not go directly to the president of the company and offer a loan. Instead, you would lend to such companies indirectly through **financial intermediaries,** institutions such as commercial banks, savings and loan associations, mutual savings banks, credit unions, insurance companies, mutual funds, pension funds, and finance companies that borrow funds from people who have saved and in turn make loans to others.

Why are financial intermediaries so crucial to well-functioning financial markets? Why do they give credit to one party but not to another? Why do they usually write complicated legal documents when they extend loans? Why are they the most heavily regulated businesses in the economy?

We answer these questions by developing a coherent framework for analyzing financial structure both in the United States and in the rest of the world in Chapter 14.

Banks and Other Financial Institutions

Banks are financial institutions that accept deposits and make loans. Included under the term *banks* are firms such as commercial banks, savings and loan associations, mutual savings banks, and credit unions. Banks are the financial intermediaries that the average person interacts with most frequently. A person who needs a loan to buy a house or a car usually obtains it from a local bank. Most Americans keep a large proportion of their financial wealth in banks in the form of checking accounts, savings accounts, or other types of bank deposits. Because banks are the largest financial intermediaries in our economy, they deserve careful study. However, banks are not the only important financial institutions. Indeed, in recent years, other financial institutions such as insurance companies, finance companies, pension funds, mutual funds, and investment banks have been growing at the expense of banks, and so we need to study them as well. We study banks and all these other institutions in Parts 5 and 6.

Financial Innovation

In the good old days, when you took cash out of the bank or wanted to check your account balance, you got to say hello to the friendly teller. Nowadays you are more likely to interact with an automated teller machine when withdrawing cash and can get your account balance from your home computer. To see why these options have been developed, we study why and how financial innovation takes place in Chapters 15, 16, and 18. We also study financial innovation because it shows us how creative thinking on the part of financial institutions can lead to higher profits. By seeing how and why financial institutions have been creative in the past, we obtain a better grasp of how they may be creative in the future. This knowledge provides us with useful clues about how the financial system may change over time and will help keep our knowledge about banks and other financial institutions from becoming obsolete.

Managing Risk in Financial Institutions

In recent years, the economic environment has become an increasingly risky place. Interest rates fluctuate wildly, stock markets have crashed both here and abroad, speculative crises have occurred in the foreign exchange markets, and failures of financial institutions have reached levels unprecedented since the Great Depression. To avoid wild swings in profitability (and even possibly failure) resulting from this environment, financial institutions must be concerned with how to cope with increased risk. We look at techniques that these institutions use when they engage in risk management in Chapter 22. Then in Chapter 23, we look at how these institutions make use of new financial instruments, such as financial futures, options, and swaps, to manage risk.

APPLIED MANAGERIAL PERSPECTIVE

Another reason for studying financial institutions is that they are among the largest employers in the country and frequently pay very high salaries. Hence some of you have a very practical reason for studying financial institutions: It may help you get a good job in the financial sector. Even if your interests lie elsewhere, you should still care about how financial institutions are run because there will be many times in your life, as an individual, an employee, or the owner of a business, when you will interact with these institutions. Knowing how financial institutions are managed may help you get a better deal when you need to borrow from them or if you decide to supply them with funds.

This book emphasizes an applied managerial perspective in teaching you about financial markets and institutions by including special applications headed "The Practicing Financial Institution Manager." These applications introduce you to the real-world problems that managers of financial institutions commonly face and need to solve in their day-to-day jobs. For example, how does the manager of a financial institution come up with a new financial product that will be profitable? How does a financial institution manager manage the risk that the institution faces from fluctuations in interest rates, stock prices, or foreign exchange rates? Should a manager hire an expert on Federal Reserve policymaking, referred to as a "Fed watcher," to help the institution discern where monetary policy might be going in the future?

Not only do the "Practicing Financial Institution Manager" applications, which answer these questions and others like them, provide you with some special analytic tools that you will need if you make your career at a financial institution, but they also give you a feel for what a job as the manager of a financial institution is all about.

HOW WE WILL STUDY FINANCIAL MARKETS AND INSTITUTIONS

Instead of focusing on a mass of dull facts that will soon become obsolete, this textbook stresses a unifying, analytic framework to study financial markets and institutions. This framework uses a few basic concepts to help organize your thinking about the determination of asset prices, the structure of financial markets, bank management, and the role of monetary policy in the economy. The basic concepts are equilibrium, basic supply and demand analysis to explain behavior in financial markets, the search for profits, and an approach to financial structure based on transaction costs and asymmetric information.

The unifying framework used in this book will not only keep your knowledge from becoming obsolete and make the material more interesting but also discourage you from memorizing a mass of facts that will be forgotten soon after the final exam. The framework also provides the tools you need to understand trends in the financial marketplace and in variables such as interest rates and exchange rates. To help you understand and apply the unifying analytic framework, simple models are constructed in which the variables held constant are carefully delineated, each step in the derivation of the model is clearly and carefully laid out, and the models are then used to explain various phenomena by focusing on changes in one variable at a time, holding all other variables constant. To reinforce the models' usefulness, this text also emphasizes the interaction of theoretical analysis and empirical data in order to expose you to real-life events and data. To make the study of financial markets and institutions even more relevant and to help you learn the material, the book contains, besides the "Practicing Financial Institution Manager" applications, numerous additional applications that demonstrate how the analysis in the book can be used to explain many real-world situations.

To function better in the real world outside the classroom, you must have the tools to follow the financial news that appears in leading financial publications such as the *Wall Street Journal*. To help and encourage you to read the financial section of the newspaper, this book contains two special features. The first is a set of special boxed inserts titled "Following the Financial News" that contain actual columns and data from the *Wall Street Journal* that typically appear daily or periodically. These boxes give you the detailed information and definitions you need to evaluate the data being presented. The second feature is a set of special applications titled "Reading the *Wall Street Journal*" that expand on the "Following the Financial News" boxes. These applications show you how the analytic framework in the book can be used directly to make sense of the daily columns in the United States' leading financial newspaper. In addition to these applications, this book also contains nearly 400 end-of-chapter problems that ask you to apply the analytic concepts you have learned to other real-world issues. Particularly relevant is a special class of problems headed "Predicting the Future." So that you can work on many of these problems on your own, answers to half of them are found at the end of the book. These give you an opportunity to review and apply many of the important financial concepts and tools presented throughout the book.

Exploring the Web

The World Wide Web has become an extremely valuable and convenient resource for financial research. We emphasize the importance of this tool in several ways. First, wherever we utilize the Web to find information to build the charts and tables that appear throughout the text, we include the source site's URL. These sites often contain additional information and are updated frequently. Second, in the margin of the text we have included the URLs of pertinent sites. Visit these sites to further explore a topic you find of particular interest. Finally, we have added Web exercises to the end of each chapter. These exercises prompt you to visit sites related to the chapter and to work with real-time data and information.

Website URLs are subject to frequent change. We have selected stable sites, but we realize that even government URLs change. The publisher's website (www.aw.com/mishkin_eakins) will maintain an updated list of current URLs for your reference.

A sample Web exercise has been included in this chapter. This is an especially important example, since it demonstrates how to export data from a website into Excel for further analysis. We suggest you work through this problem on your own so that you will be able to perform this activity when prompted in subsequent Web exercises.

Web Exercise

You have been hired by Risky Ventures, Inc., as a consultant to help them analyze interest rate trends. They are initially interested in determining the historical relationship between long- and short-term interest rates. The biggest task you must immediately undertake is collecting market interest-rate data. You know the best source of this information is the Web.

1. You decide that your best indicator of long-term interest rates is the 30-year U.S. Treasury note. Your first task is to gather historical data. Go to http://www.federalreserve.gov/releases/ and select "H.15 Selected Interest Rates Historical data." The site should look as follows:

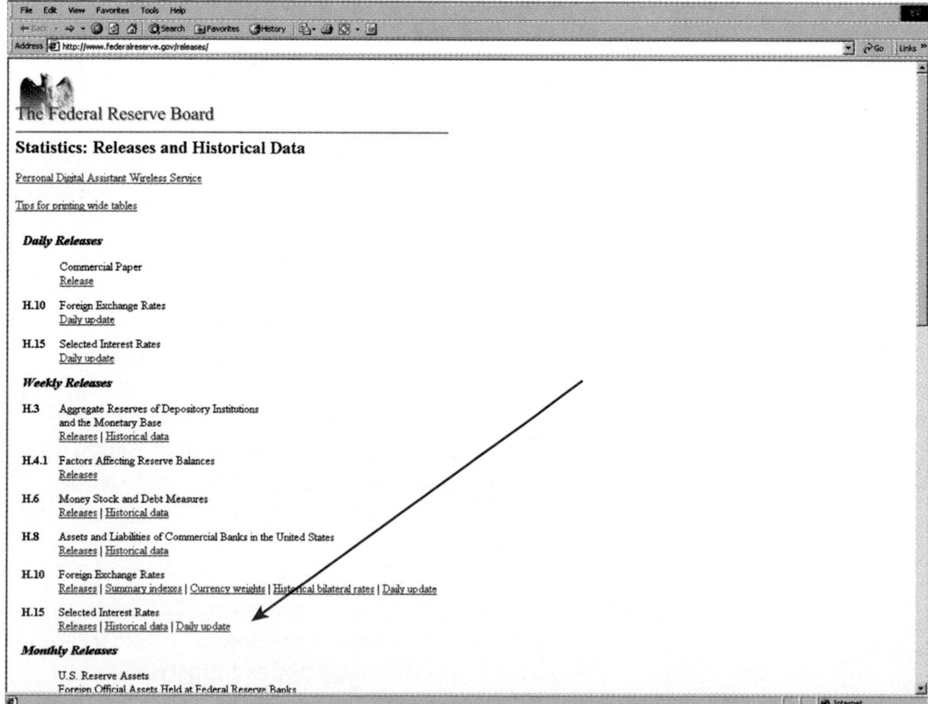

Click on "Historical data." Scroll down to "U.S. Government securities/Treasury constant maturities/30 year." Scroll over to the right and click on "annual."

2. While you have located an accurate source of historical interest rate data, getting it onto a spreadsheet will be very tedious. You recall that Excel (Microsoft® Excel)will let you convert text data into columns. Begin by highlighting the two columns of data (the year and rate). Right click on the mouse and choose COPY. Now open Excel and put the cursor in a cell. Click paste. Now choose DATA from the tool bar and click on TEXT TO COLUMNS. Follow the wizard, checking the fixed-width option. The list of interest rates should now have the year in one column and the interest rate in the next column. Label your columns.

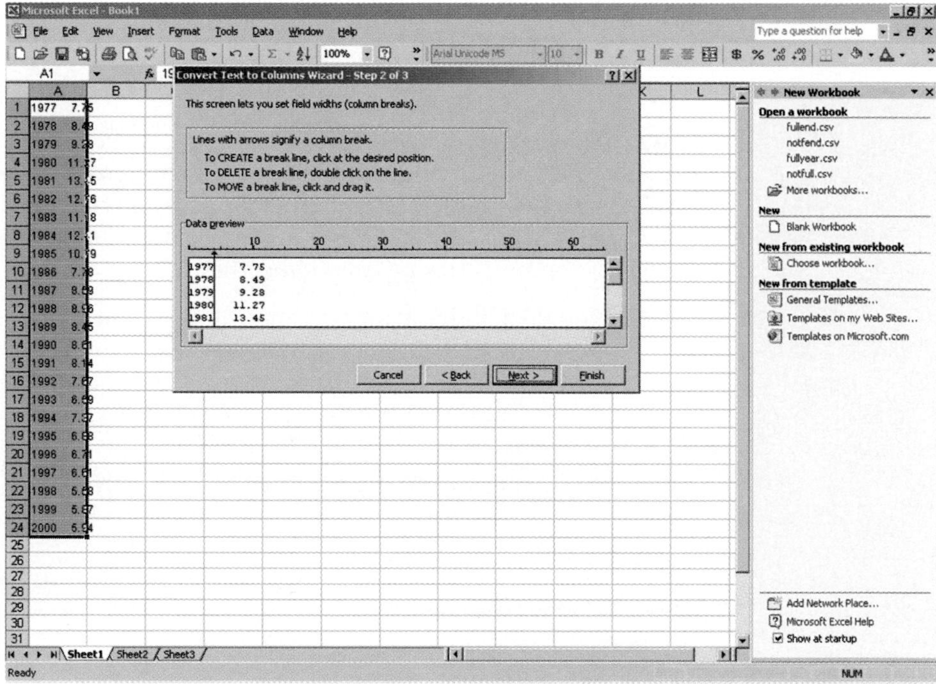

Repeat the above steps to collect the 1-year interest rate series. Put it in the column next to the 30-year series. Be sure to line up the years correctly and delete any years that are not included in both series.

3. You now want to analyze the interest rates by graphing them. Again highlight the two columns of data you just created in Excel. Click on the charts icon on the tool bar (or INSERT/CHART). Select scatter diagram and choose any type of scatter diagram that connects the dots. Let the Excel wizard take you through the steps of completing the graph. (See top of next page.)

4. Now go to http://www.forecasts.org/data/index.htm, click on "stock indices" at the top of the page, and choose "U.S. Stock indices—monthly option." Finally, choose the "Dow Jones Industrial Average" option and again repeat the instructions outlined in steps 2 and 3.

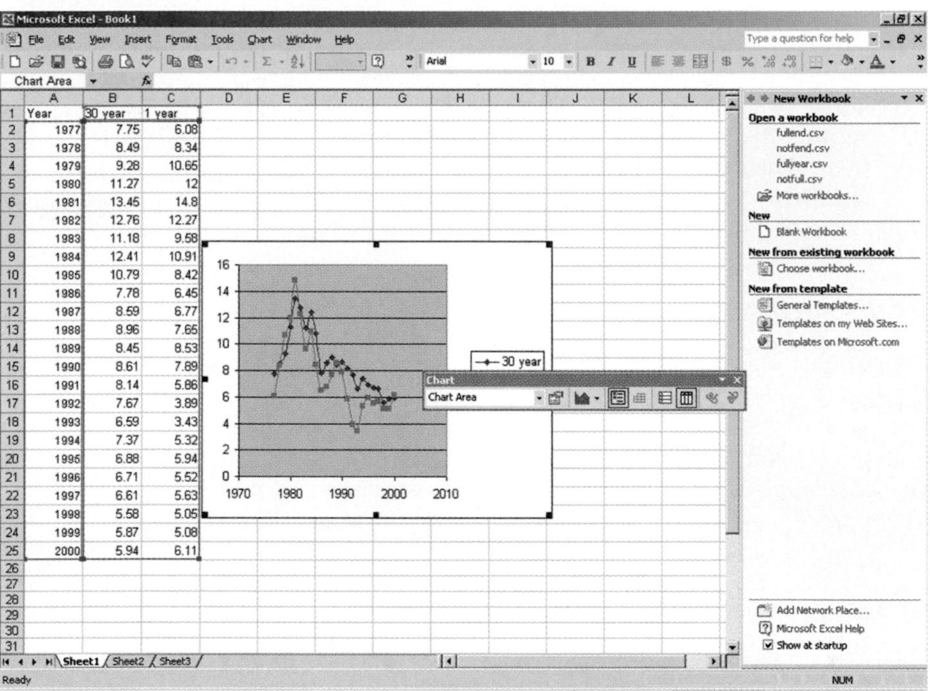

Year	30 year	1 year
1977	7.75	6.08
1978	8.49	8.34
1979	9.28	10.65
1980	11.27	12
1981	13.45	14.8
1982	12.76	12.27
1983	11.18	9.58
1984	12.41	10.91
1985	10.79	8.42
1986	7.78	6.45
1987	8.59	6.77
1988	8.96	7.65
1989	8.45	8.53
1990	8.61	7.89
1991	8.14	5.86
1992	7.67	3.89
1993	6.59	3.43
1994	7.37	5.32
1995	6.88	5.94
1996	6.71	5.52
1997	6.61	5.63
1998	5.58	5.05
1999	5.87	5.08
2000	5.94	6.11

CONCLUDING REMARKS

The field of financial markets and institutions is an exciting one. Not only will you learn material that affects your life directly—for example, gaining skills that would be valuable in your career—but you will also gain a clearer understanding of events in financial markets and institutions you frequently hear about in the news media. Our study of financial markets and institutions will also introduce you to many of the controversies that are currently the subject of hot debate in the political arena.

SUMMARY

1. Activities in financial markets have direct effects on individuals' wealth, the behavior of businesses, and the efficiency of our economy. Three financial markets deserve particular attention: the bond market (debt markets), where interest rates are determined; the stock market, which has a major effect on people's wealth and on firms' investment decisions; and the foreign exchange market, because fluctuations in the foreign exchange rate have major consequences for the American economy.
2. Because monetary policy affects interest rates, inflation, and business cycles, all of which have an important impact on financial markets and institutions, we need to understand how monetary policy is conducted by central banks in the United States and abroad.
3. Banks and other financial institutions channel funds from people who might not put them to productive use to people who can do so and thus play a crucial role in improving the efficiency of the economy.

4. Understanding how financial institutions are managed is important because there will be many times in your life, as an individual, an employee, or the owner of a business, when you will interact with them. The "Practicing Financial Institution Manager" applications provide special analytic tools that are useful if you make your career at a financial institution and also give you a feel for what a job as the manager of a financial institution is all about.
5. This textbook stresses an analytic way of thinking by developing a unifying framework for the study of financial markets and institutions using a few basic principles. This textbook also emphasizes the interaction of theoretical analysis and empirical data.

KEY TERMS

asset, *p. 4*
banks, *p. 8*
bond, *p. 4*
central bank, *p. 8*
Federal Reserve System (the Fed), *p. 8*
financial intermediaries, *p. 8*
financial markets, *p. 3*
foreign exchange market, *p. 6*
foreign exchange rate, *p. 6*
interest rate, *p. 4*
monetary policy, *p. 8*
money (money supply), *p. 8*
security, *p. 4*
stock, *p. 5*

QUESTIONS AND PROBLEMS

1. Why are financial markets important to the health of the economy?

***2**. When interest rates rise, how might businesses and consumers change their economic behavior?

3. How can a change in interest rates affect the profitability of financial institutions?

***4.** Is everybody worse off when interest rates rise?

5. What effect might a fall in stock prices have on business investment?

***6.** What effect might a rise in stock prices have on consumers' decisions to spend?

7. How does a decline in the value of the pound sterling affect British consumers?

***8.** How does an increase in the value of the pound sterling affect American businesses?

9. How can changes in foreign exchange rates affect the profitability of financial institutions?

***10.** Looking at Figure 3, in what years would you have chosen to visit the Grand Canyon in Arizona rather than the Tower of London?

11. What is the basic activity of banks?

***12.** What are the other important financial intermediaries in the economy besides banks?

13. Can you think of any financial innovation in the past ten years that has affected you personally? Has it made you better or worse off? In what way?

***14.** What types of risks do financial institutions face?

15. Why do managers of financial institutions care so much about the activities of the Federal Reserve System?

*Solutions to these problems are provided at the back of the book.

Chapter 2 Overview of the Financial System

Preview

Suppose that you want to start a business that manufactures a recently invented low-cost robot that cleans house (even does windows), mows the lawn, and washes the car, but you have no funds to put this wonderful invention into production. Walter has plenty of savings that he has inherited. If you and Walter could get together so that he could provide you with the funds, your company's robot would see the light of day, and you, Walter, and the economy would all be better off: Walter could earn a high return on his investment, you would get rich from producing the robot, and we would have cleaner houses, shinier cars, and more beautiful lawns.

Financial markets (bond and stock markets) and financial intermediaries (banks, insurance companies, pension funds) have the basic function of getting people such as you and Walter together by moving funds from those who have a surplus of funds (Walter) to those who have a shortage of funds (you). More realistically, when IBM invents a better computer, it may need funds to bring it to market, or a local government may need funds to build a road or a school. Well-functioning financial markets and financial intermediaries are needed to improve our economic well-being and are crucial to our economic health. Indeed, when the financial system breaks down, as it has in Russia and in East Asia recently, severe economic hardship results.

To study the effects of financial markets and financial intermediaries on the economy, we must first acquire an understanding of their general structure and operation. In this chapter we learn about the major financial intermediaries and the instruments that are traded in financial markets.

This chapter offers a preliminary overview of the fascinating study of financial markets and institutions. We will return to a more detailed treatment of the regulation, structure, and evolution of financial markets and institutions in Parts III through V.

FUNCTION OF FINANCIAL MARKETS

Financial markets perform the essential economic function of channeling funds from people who have saved surplus funds by spending less than their income to people who have a shortage of funds because they wish to spend more than their income. This function is shown schematically in Figure 1. Those who have saved and are lending funds, the lender-savers, are at the left, and those who must borrow funds to finance their spending, the borrower-spenders, are at the right. The principal lender-savers are households, but business enterprises and the government (particularly state and local government), as well as foreigners and their governments, sometimes also find themselves with excess funds and so lend them out. The most important borrower-spenders are businesses and the government (particularly the federal government), but households and foreigners also borrow to finance their purchases of cars, furniture, and houses. The arrows show that funds flow from lender-savers to borrower-spenders via two routes.

In *direct finance* (the route at the bottom of Figure 1), borrowers borrow funds directly from lenders in financial markets by selling them *securities* (also called *financial instruments*), which are claims on the borrower's future income or assets. Securities are assets for the person who buys them but **liabilities** (IOUs

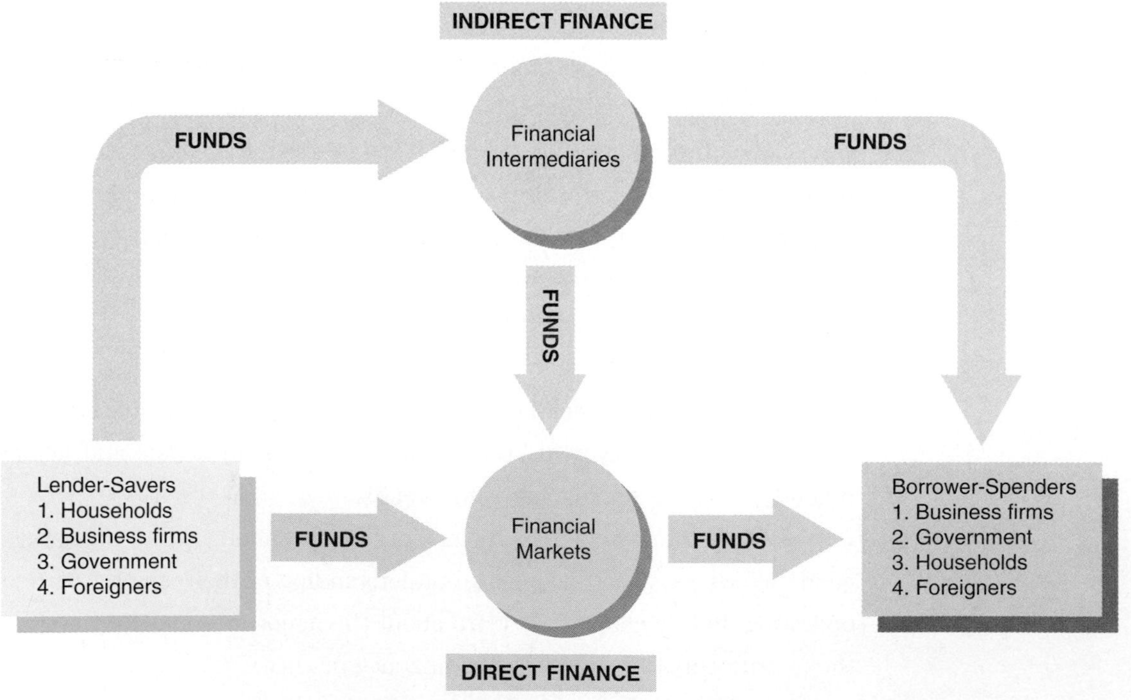

FIGURE 1 Flows of Funds Through the Financial System

or debts) for the individual or firm that sells (issues) them. For example, if General Motors needs to borrow funds to pay for a new factory to manufacture computerized cars, it might borrow the funds from a saver by selling the saver a *bond,* a debt security that promises to make payments periodically for a specified period of time.

Why is this channeling of funds from savers to spenders so important to the economy? The answer is that the people who save are frequently not the same people who have profitable investment opportunities available to them, the entrepreneurs. Let's first think about this on a personal level. Suppose that you have saved $1000 this year, but no borrowing or lending is possible because there are no financial markets. If you do not have an investment opportunity that will permit you to earn income with your savings, you will just hold on to the $1000 and will earn no interest. However, Carl the Carpenter has a productive use for your $1000: He can use it to purchase a new tool that will shorten the time it takes him to build a house, thereby earning an extra $200 per year. If you could get in touch with Carl, you could lend him the $1000 at a rental fee (interest) of $100 per year, and both of you would be better off. You would earn $100 per year on your $1000, instead of the zero amount that you would earn otherwise, while Carl would earn $100 more income per year (the $200 extra earnings per year minus the $100 rental fee for the use of the funds).

In the absence of financial markets, you and Carl the Carpenter might never get together. Without financial markets, it is hard to transfer funds from a person who has no investment opportunities to one who has them; you would both be stuck with the status quo, and both of you would be worse off. Financial markets are thus essential to promoting economic efficiency.

The existence of financial markets is also beneficial even if someone borrows for a purpose other than increasing production in a business. Say that you are recently married, have a good job, and want to buy a house. You earn a good salary, but because you have just started to work, you have not yet saved much. Over time you would have no problem saving enough to buy the house of your dreams, but by then you would be too old to get full enjoyment from it. Without financial markets, you are stuck; you cannot buy the house and will continue to live in your tiny apartment.

If a financial market were set up so that people who had built up savings could lend you the money to buy the house, you would be more than happy to pay them some interest in order to own a home while you are still young enough to enjoy it. Then, when you had saved up enough funds, you would pay back your loan. The overall outcome would be such that you would be better off, as would the persons who made you the loan. They would now earn some interest, whereas they would not if the financial market did not exist.

Now we can see why financial markets have such an important function in the economy. They allow funds to move from people who lack productive investment opportunities to people who have such opportunities. By so doing, financial markets contribute to higher production and efficiency in the overall economy. They also directly improve the well-being of consumers by allowing them to time their purchases better. They provide funds to young people to buy what they need and can eventually afford without forcing them to wait until they have saved up the entire purchase price. Financial markets that are operating efficiently improve the economic welfare of everyone in the society.

STRUCTURE OF FINANCIAL MARKETS

Now that we understand the basic function of financial markets, let's look at their structure. The following descriptions of several categorizations of financial markets illustrate essential features of these markets.

Debt and Equity Markets

A firm or an individual can obtain funds in a financial market in two ways. The most common method is to issue a debt instrument, such as a bond or a mortgage, which is a contractual agreement by the borrower to pay the holder of the instrument fixed dollar amounts at regular intervals (interest and principal payments) until a specified date (the maturity date), when a final payment is made. The **maturity** of a debt instrument is the time (term) to that instrument's expiration date. A debt instrument is **short-term** if its maturity is less than a year and **long-term** if its maturity is ten years or longer. Debt instruments with a maturity between one and ten years are said to be **intermediate-term.**

The second method of raising funds is by issuing **equities,** such as common stock, which are claims to share in the net income (income after expenses and taxes) and the assets of a business. If you own one share of common stock in a company that has issued one million shares, you are entitled to 1 one-millionth of the firm's net income and 1 one-millionth of the firm's assets. Equities usually make periodic payments (**dividends**) to their holders and are considered long-term securities because they have no maturity date. In addition, owning stock means that you own a portion of the firm and thus have the right to vote on issues important to the firm and to elect its directors.

The main disadvantage of owning a corporation's equities rather than its debt is that an equity holder is a *residual claimant;* that is, the corporation must pay all its debt holders before it pays its equity holders. The advantage of holding equities is that equity holders benefit directly from any increases in the corporation's profitability or asset value because equities confer ownership rights on the equity holders. Debt holders do not share in this benefit because their dollar payments are fixed. We examine the pros and cons of debt versus equity instruments in more detail in Chapter 14, which provides an analytical framework for understanding financial structure.

The total value of equities in the United States has typically fluctuated between \$1 and \$20 trillion since the early 1970s, depending on the prices of shares. Although the average person is more aware of the stock market than any other financial market, the size of the debt market greatly exceeds that of the equities market: The value of debt instruments (\$28.8 trillion at the end of 2001) is more than 50% larger than the value of equities (\$13.6 trillion at the end of 2001).

Primary and Secondary Markets

At www.nyse.com, find listed companies, quotes, company historical data, real-time market indices, and more.

A **primary market** is a financial market in which new issues of a security, such as a bond or a stock, are sold to initial buyers by the corporation or government agency borrowing the funds. A **secondary market** is a financial market in which securities that have been previously issued (and are thus secondhand) can be resold.

The primary markets for securities are not well known to the public because the selling of securities to initial buyers often takes place behind closed doors. An important financial institution that assists in the initial sale of securities in the primary market is the **investment bank.** It does this by **underwriting** securities: It guarantees a price for a corporation's securities and then sells them to the public.

The New York and American stock exchanges, in which previously issued stocks are traded, are the best-known examples of secondary markets, although the bond markets, in which previously issued bonds of major corporations and the U.S. government are bought and sold, actually have a larger trading volume. Other examples of secondary markets are foreign exchange markets, futures markets, and options markets. Securities brokers and dealers are crucial to a well-functioning secondary market. **Brokers** are agents of investors who match buyers with sellers of securities; **dealers** link buyers and sellers by buying and selling securities at stated prices.

When an individual buys a security in the secondary market, the person who has sold the security receives money in exchange for the security, but the corporation that issued the security acquires no new funds. A corporation acquires new funds only when its securities are first sold in the primary market. Nonetheless, secondary markets serve two important functions. First, they make it easier to sell these financial instruments to raise cash; that is, they make the financial instruments more **liquid.** The increased liquidity of these instruments then makes them more desirable and thus easier for the issuing firm to sell in the primary market. Second, they determine the price of the security that the issuing firm sells in the primary market. The firms that buy securities in the primary market will pay the issuing corporation no more than the price that they think the secondary market will set for this security. The higher the security's price in the secondary market, the higher will be the price that the issuing firm will receive for a new security in the primary market and hence the greater the amount of capital it can raise. Conditions in the secondary market are therefore the most relevant to corporations issuing securities. It is for this reason that books like this one, which deal with financial markets, focus on the behavior of secondary markets rather than that of primary markets.

Exchanges and Over-the-Counter Markets

Secondary markets can be organized in two ways. One is to organize **exchanges,** where buyers and sellers of securities (or their agents or brokers) meet in one central location to conduct trades. The New York and American stock exchanges for stocks and the Chicago Board of Trade for commodities (wheat, corn, silver, and other raw materials) are examples of organized exchanges.

The other method of organizing a secondary market is to have an **over-the-counter (OTC) market,** in which dealers at different locations have an inventory of securities and stand ready to buy and sell securities "over the counter" to anyone who comes to them and is willing to accept their prices. Because over-the-counter dealers are in computer contact and know the prices set by one another, the OTC market is very competitive and not very different from a market with an organized exchange.

Detailed market and security information for the Nasdaq OTC stock exchange is available at www.nasdaq.com

Many common stocks are traded over-the-counter, although the largest corporations have their shares traded at organized stock exchanges such as the New

York Stock Exchange. The U.S. government bond market, with a larger trading volume than the New York Stock Exchange, is set up as an over-the-counter market. Forty or so dealers establish a "market" in these securities by standing ready to buy and sell U.S. government bonds. Other over-the-counter markets include those that trade other types of financial instruments such as negotiable certificates of deposit, federal funds, banker's acceptances, and foreign exchange.

Money and Capital Markets

Another way of distinguishing between markets is on the basis of the maturity of the securities traded in each market. The **money market** is a financial market in which only short-term debt instruments (original maturity of less than one year) are traded; the **capital market** is the market in which longer-term debt (original maturity of one year or greater) and equity instruments are traded. Money market securities are usually more widely traded than longer-term securities and so tend to be more liquid. In addition, as we will see in Chapter 3, short-term securities have smaller fluctuations in prices than long-term securities, making them safer investments. As a result, corporations and banks actively use this market to earn interest on surplus funds that they expect to have only temporarily. Capital market securities, such as stocks and long-term bonds, are often held by financial intermediaries such as insurance companies and pension funds, which have little uncertainty about the amount of funds they will have available in the future.

INTERNATIONALIZATION OF FINANCIAL MARKETS

The growing internationalization of financial markets has become an important trend. Before the 1980s, U.S. financial markets were much larger than financial markets outside the United States, but in recent years the dominance of U.S. markets has been disappearing. The extraordinary growth of foreign financial markets has been the result of both large increases in the pool of savings in foreign countries such as Japan and the deregulation of foreign financial markets, which has enabled them to expand their activities. American corporations and banks are now more likely to tap international capital markets to raise needed funds, and American investors often seek investment opportunities abroad. Similarly, foreign corporations and banks raise funds from Americans, and foreigners are becoming important investors in the United States. A look at international bond markets and world stock markets will give us a picture of how this globalization of financial markets is taking place.

International Bond Market, Eurobonds, and Eurocurrencies

The traditional instruments in the international bond market are known as **foreign bonds.** Foreign bonds are sold in a foreign country and are denominated in that country's currency. For example, if the German automaker Porsche sells a bond in the United States denominated in U.S. dollars, it is classified as a foreign bond. Foreign bonds have been an important instrument in the international capital market for centuries. In fact, a large percentage of U.S. railroads built in the nineteenth century were financed by sales of foreign bonds in Britain.

A more recent innovation in the international bond market is the **Eurobond,** a bond denominated in a currency other than that of the country in which it is sold—for example, a bond denominated in U.S. dollars sold in London.[1] Currently, over 80% of the new issues in the international bond market are Eurobonds, and the market for these securities has grown very rapidly. As a result, the Eurobond market has passed the U.S. corporate bond market as a source of new funds.

A variant of the Eurobond is **Eurocurrencies,** which are foreign currencies that are deposited in banks outside of the home country. The most important of the Eurocurrencies is **Eurodollars,** which are U.S. dollars deposited in foreign banks outside of the United States or in foreign branches of U.S. banks. These short-term deposits earn interest and so are similar to short-term Eurobonds. American banks borrow Eurodollar deposits from other banks or from their own foreign branches, and Eurodollars are now an important source of funds for American banks (over $100 billion outstanding).

World Stock Markets

Until recently, the U.S. stock market was by far the largest in the world, but foreign stock markets have been growing in importance. Now the United States is not always number one: In the 1980s, the value of stocks traded in Japan at times exceeded the value of stocks traded in the United States. The increased interest in foreign stocks has prompted the development in the United States of mutual funds specializing in trading in foreign stock markets. American investors now pay attention not only to the Dow Jones Industrial Average but also to stock price indexes for foreign stock markets such as the Nikkei 225 Average (Tokyo) and the Financial Times–Stock Exchange 100-Share Index (London).

The internationalization of financial markets is having profound effects on the United States. Foreigners, particularly the Japanese, are not only providing funds to corporations in the United States but are also helping finance a significant fraction of the federal government's huge budget deficit. Without these foreign funds, the U.S. economy would have grown far less rapidly in the last two decades. The internationalization of financial markets is also leading the way to a more integrated world economy in which flows of goods and technology between countries are more commonplace. In later chapters we will encounter many examples of the important roles that international factors play in our economy.

FUNCTION OF FINANCIAL INTERMEDIARIES

As shown in Figure 1, funds can move from lenders to borrowers by a second route, called *indirect finance* because it involves a financial intermediary that stands between the lender-savers and the borrower-spenders and helps transfer funds from one to the other. A financial intermediary does this by borrowing funds from the lender-savers and then using these funds to make loans to borrower-spenders. For example, a bank might acquire funds by issuing a liability to the public in the form of savings deposits. It might then use the funds to acquire an asset by making a loan to General Motors or by buying a GM bond in the financial market. The

[1]Note that the new currency, the euro, can create some confusion about the term *Eurobond.* A Eurobond does not mean a bond denominated in euros. A bond denominated in euros is only called a Eurobond *if it is sold outside the countries that have adopted the euro.*

FOLLOWING THE FINANCIAL NEWS

Foreign Stock Market Indexes

STOCK MARKET INDEXES

Country/Index	12/31/01 Close	Net Chg	Pct Chg	YTD Net Chg	YTD Pct Chg
Argentina Merval Index	a295.39			– 121.38	– 29.12
Australia All Ordinaries	3359.90	– 3.90	– 0.12	+ 205.20	+ 6.50
Belgium Bel-20 Index	a2782.01			– 242.48	– 8.02
Brazil Sao Paulo Bovespa	a13577.57			– 1681.72	– 11.02
Britain London FTSE 100-share	5217.40	– 25.00	– 0.48	– 1005.10	– 16.15
Britain London FTSE 250-share	5939.10	+ 25.40	+ 0.43	– 608.40	– 9.29
Canada Toronto 300 Comp.	7688.41	+ 13.44	+ 0.18	– 1245.27	– 13.94
Chile Santiago IPSA	a109.10			+ 9.10	+ 9.10
China Dow Jones China 88	131.35	+ 0.70	+ 0.54	– 51.41	– 28.13
China Dow Jones Shanghai	192.82	+ 0.70	+ 0.36	– 57.76	– 23.05
China Dow Jones Shenzhen	182.66	+ 0.61	+ 0.34	– 71.80	– 28.22
Europe DJ Stoxx (Euro)	a298.73			– 61.06	– 16.97
Europe DJ Stoxx 50 (Euro)	a3706.93			– 850.20	– 18.66
Euro Zone DJ Euro Stoxx (Euro)	a314.52			– 77.28	– 19.72
Euro Zone DJ Euro Stoxx 50 (Euro)	a3806.13			– 966.26	– 20.25
France Paris CAC 40	a4624.58			– 1301.84	– 21.97
Germany Frankfurt Xetra DAX	a5160.10			– 1273.51	– 19.79
Hong Kong Hang Seng	11397.21	– 34.38	– 0.30	– 3698.32	– 24.50
India Bombay Sensex	3262.33	+ 77.89	+ 2.45	– 709.79	– 17.87
Italy Milan MIBtel	a22855.00			– 7468.00	– 24.63
Japan Tokyo Nikkei 225	a10542.62			– 3243.07	– 23.52
Japan Tokyo Nikkei 300	a205.58			– 57.42	– 21.83
Japan Tokyo Topix Index	a1032.14			– 251.53	– 19.59
Mexico I.P.C. All-Share	6372.28	– 94.81	– 1.47	+ 720.09	+ 12.74
Netherlands Amsterdam AEX	a506.78			– 130.82	– 20.52
Singapore Straits Times	1623.60	– 2.38	– 0.15	– 303.23	– 15.74
South Africa Johannesburg All Share	10441.70	+ 80.40	+ 0.78	+ 2115.50	+ 25.41
South Korea Composite	a693.70			+ 189.08	+ 37.47
Spain IBEX 35	a8397.60			– 712.20	– 7.82
Sweden SX All Share	a239.06			– 47.44	– 16.56
Switzerland Zurich Swiss Market	a6417.80			– 1717.60	– 21.11
Taiwan Weighted Index	5551.24	+ 152.96	+ 2.83	+ 807.30	+ 17.02

NA/Not available, a-Dec 28 trading.

Foreign stock market indexes are published daily in the *Wall Street Journal* next to the "World Markets" column, which reports developments in foreign stock markets.

The first two columns identify the foreign stock exchange and the market index; for example, the colored entry is for the Toronto 300 Composite for the Canada Stock Exchange. The third column, "CLOSE," gives the closing value of the index, which was 7688.41 for the Toronto 300 on 12/31/2001. The "NET CHG" column indicates the change in the index from the previous trading day, +13.44 and the "PCT CHG" column indicates the percentage change in the index, +.18. The final two columns indicate the year-to-date net change and percentage change in the index, -1245.27 and -13.94%.

Source: Wall Street Journal, Jan. 2, 2002, p. C10.

Check out major world stock indices, with charts, news, and components, at http://quote.yahoo.com/m2?u

ultimate result is that funds have been transferred from the public (the lender-savers) to GM (the borrower-spender) with the help of the financial intermediary (the bank).

The process of indirect finance using financial intermediaries, called **financial intermediation,** is the primary route for moving funds from lenders to borrowers. Indeed, although the media focus much of their attention on securities markets, particularly the stock market, financial intermediaries are a far more important source of financing for corporations than securities markets are. This is true not only for the United States but for other industrialized countries as well (see Box 1). Why are financial intermediaries and indirect finance so important in financial markets? To answer this question, we need to understand the role of transaction costs and information costs in financial markets.

Transaction Costs

Transaction costs, the time and money spent in carrying out financial transactions, are a major problem for people who have excess funds to lend. As we have seen, Carl the Carpenter needs $1000 for his new tool, and you know that

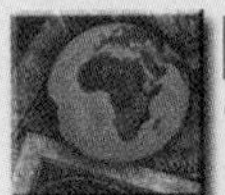

BOX 1: GLOBAL

The Importance of Financial Intermediaries to Securities Markets: An International Comparison

Patterns of financing corporations differ across countries, but one key fact emerges. Studies of the major developed countries, including the United States, Canada, Great Britain, Japan, Italy, Germany, and France, show that when businesses go looking for funds to finance their activities, they usually obtain them indirectly through financial intermediaries and not directly from securities markets. Even in the United States and Canada, which have the most developed securities markets in the world, loans from financial intermediaries are far more important for corporate finance than securities markets are. The countries that have made the least use of securities markets are Germany and Japan; in these two countries, financing from financial intermediaries has been almost ten times greater than that from securities markets. However, with the deregulation of Japanese securities markets in recent years, the share of corporate financing by financial intermediaries has been declining relative to the use of securities markets.

Although the dominance of financial intermediaries over securities markets is clear in all countries, the relative importance of bond versus stock markets differs widely across countries. In the United States, the bond market is far more important as a source of corporate finance: On average, the amount of new financing raised using bonds is ten times the amount using stocks. By contrast, countries such as France and Italy make use of equities markets more than the bond market to raise capital.

*See, for example, Colin Mayer, "Financial Systems, Corporate Finance, and Economic Development," in *Asymmetric Information, Corporate Finance, and Investment*, ed. R. Glenn Hubbard (Chicago: University of Chicago Press, 1990), pp. 307–332.

it is an excellent investment opportunity. You have the cash and would like to lend him the money, but to protect your investment, you have to hire a lawyer to write up the loan contract that specifies how much interest Carl will pay you, when he will make these interest payments, and when he will repay you the $1000. Obtaining the contract will cost you $500. When you figure in this transaction cost for making the loan, you realize that you can't earn enough from the deal (you spend $500 to make perhaps $100) and reluctantly tell Carl that he will have to look elsewhere.

This example illustrates that small savers like you or potential borrowers like Carl might be frozen out of financial markets and thus be unable to benefit from them. Can anyone come to the rescue? Financial intermediaries can.

Financial intermediaries can substantially reduce transaction costs because they have developed expertise in lowering them and because their large size allows them to take advantage of **economies of scale,** the reduction in transaction costs per dollar of transactions as the size (scale) of transactions increases. For example, a bank knows how to find a good lawyer to produce an airtight loan contract, and this contract can be used over and over again in its loan transactions, thus lowering the legal cost per transaction. Instead of a loan contract (which may not be all that well written) costing $500, a bank can hire a topflight lawyer for $5000 to draw up an airtight loan contract that can be used for 2000 loans at a cost of $2.50 per loan. At a cost of $2.50 per loan, it now becomes profitable for the financial intermediary to loan Carl the $1000.

Because financial intermediaries are able to reduce transaction costs substantially, they make it possible for you to provide funds indirectly to people with productive investment opportunities like Carl. In addition, a financial intermediary's low transaction costs mean that it can provide its customers with liquidity services, services that make it easier for customers to conduct transactions. For example, banks provide depositors with checking accounts that enable them to pay their bills easily. In addition, depositors can earn interest on checking and savings accounts and yet still convert them into goods and services whenever necessary.

Asymmetric Information: Adverse Selection and Moral Hazard

The presence of transaction costs in financial markets explains, in part, why financial intermediaries and indirect finance play such an important role in financial markets. An additional reason is that in financial markets, one party often does not know enough about the other party to make accurate decisions. This inequality is called **asymmetric information.** For example, a borrower who takes out a loan usually has better information about the potential returns and risks associated with the investment projects for which the funds are earmarked than the lender does. Lack of information creates problems in the financial system on two fronts: before the transaction is entered into and after.

Adverse selection is the problem created by asymmetric information *before* the transaction occurs. Adverse selection in financial markets occurs when the potential borrowers who are the most likely to produce an undesirable *(adverse)* outcome—the bad credit risks—are the ones who most actively seek out a loan and are thus most likely to be selected. Because adverse selection makes it more likely that loans might be made to bad credit risks, lenders may decide not to make any loans even though there are good credit risks in the marketplace.

To understand why adverse selection occurs, suppose that you have two aunts to whom you might make a loan—Aunt Sheila and Aunt Louise. Aunt Louise is a conservative type who borrows only when she has an investment that she is quite sure will pay off. Aunt Sheila, by contrast, is an inveterate gambler who has just come across a get-rich-quick scheme that will make her a millionaire if she can just borrow \$1000 to invest in it. Unfortunately, as with most get-rich-quick schemes, there is a high probability that the investment won't pay off and that Aunt Sheila will lose the \$1000.

Which of your aunts is more likely to call you to ask for a loan? Aunt Sheila, of course, because she has so much to gain if the investment pays off. You, however, would not want to make a loan to her because there is a high probability that her investment will turn sour and she will be unable to pay you back.

If you knew both your aunts very well—that is, if information was not asymmetric—you wouldn't have a problem because you would know that Aunt Sheila is a bad risk and so you would not lend to her. Suppose, though, that you don't know your aunts well. You are more likely to lend to Aunt Sheila than to Aunt Louise because Aunt Sheila would be hounding you for the loan. Because of the possibility of adverse selection, you might decide not to lend to either of your aunts, even though there are times when Aunt Louise, who is an excellent credit risk, might need a loan for a worthwhile investment.

Moral hazard is the problem created by asymmetric information *after* the transaction occurs. Moral hazard in financial markets is the risk *(hazard)* that the borrower might engage in activities that are undesirable *(immoral)* from the lender's point of view because they make it less likely that the loan will be paid back. Because moral hazard lowers the probability that the loan will be repaid, lenders may decide that they would rather not make a loan.

As an example of moral hazard, suppose that you made a \$1000 loan to another relative, Uncle Melvin, who needs the money to purchase a word processor so that he can set up a business typing students' term papers. Once you have made the loan, however, Uncle Melvin is more likely to slip off to the track and play the horses. If he bets on a 20-to-1 long shot and wins with your money, he is able to pay you back your $1000 and live high off the hog with the remaining $19,000. But if he loses, as is likely, you don't get paid back, and all he has lost is his reputation as a reliable, upstanding uncle. Uncle Melvin therefore has an incentive to go to the track because his gains ($19,000) if he bets correctly may be much greater than the cost to him (his reputation) if he bets incorrectly. If you knew what Uncle Melvin was up to, you would prevent him from going to the track, and he would not be able to increase the moral hazard. However, because it is hard for you to keep informed about his whereabouts—that is, because information is asymmetric—there is a good chance that Uncle Melvin will go to the track and you will not get paid back. The risk of moral hazard might therefore discourage you from making the $1000 loan to Uncle Melvin, even if you were sure that you would be paid back if he used it to set up his business.

Study Guide Because the concepts of adverse selection and moral hazard are extremely useful in understanding the behavior we examine in this and many of the later chapters (and in life in general), you must understand them fully. One way to distinguish between them is to remember that adverse selection is a problem of asymmetric information *before* entering into a transaction, whereas moral hazard is a problem of asymmetric information *after* the transaction has occurred. A helpful way to nail down these concepts is to think of other examples, for financial or other types of transactions, in which adverse selection or moral hazard plays a role. Several problems at the end of the chapter provide additional examples of situations involving adverse selection and moral hazard.

The problems created by adverse selection and moral hazard are an important impediment to well-functioning financial markets. Again, financial intermediaries can alleviate these problems.

With financial intermediaries in the economy, small savers can provide their funds to the financial markets by lending these funds to a trustworthy intermediary, say, the Honest John Bank, which in turn lends the funds out either by making loans or by buying securities such as stocks or bonds. Successful financial intermediaries have higher earnings on their investments because they are better equipped than individuals to screen out good from bad credit risks, thereby reducing losses due to adverse selection. In addition, financial intermediaries have high earnings because they develop expertise in monitoring the parties they lend to, thus reducing losses due to moral hazard. The result is that financial intermediaries can afford to pay lender-savers interest or provide substantial services and still earn a profit.

The success of financial intermediaries is evidenced by the fact that most Americans invest their savings with them and also obtain their loans from them. Financial intermediaries play a key role in improving economic efficiency because they help financial markets channel funds from lender-savers to people with productive investment opportunities. Without a well-functioning set of financial intermediaries, it is very hard for an economy to reach its full potential. We will explore further the role of financial intermediaries in the economy in Part V.

FINANCIAL INTERMEDIARIES

We have seen why financial intermediaries play such an important role in the economy. Now we look at the principal financial intermediaries and how they perform the intermediation function. They fall into three categories: depository institutions (banks), contractual savings institutions, and investment intermediaries. Table 1 provides a guide to the discussion of the financial intermediaries that fit into these three categories by describing their primary liabilities (sources of funds) and assets (uses of funds). The relative size of these intermediaries in the United States is indicated in Table 2, which lists the amount of their assets at the end of 1970, 1980, 1990, and 2001.

Depository Institutions

Depository institutions (which for simplicity we refer to as *banks* throughout this text) are financial intermediaries that accept deposits from individuals and institutions and make loans. These institutions include commercial banks and the so-called **thrift institutions (thrifts):** savings and loan associations, mutual savings banks, and credit unions.

Commercial Banks These financial intermediaries raise funds primarily by issuing checkable deposits (deposits on which checks can be written), savings deposits (deposits that are payable on demand but do not allow their owner to write checks), and time deposits (deposits with fixed terms to maturity). They then use these funds to make commercial, consumer, and mortgage loans and to buy U.S. government securities and municipal bonds. There are approximately 8100 commercial banks in the United States, and as a group, they are the largest financial intermediary and have the most diversified portfolios (collections) of assets.

TABLE 1 Primary Assets and Liabilities of Financial Intermediaries

Type of Intermediary	Primary Liabilities (Sources of Funds)	Primary Assets (Uses of Funds)
Depository Institutions (Banks)		
Commercial banks	Deposits	Business and consumer loans, mortgages, U.S. government securities and municipal bonds
Savings and loan associations	Deposits	Mortgages
Mutual savings banks	Deposits	Mortgages
Credit unions	Deposits	Consumer loans
Contractual Savings Institutions		
Life insurance companies	Premiums from policies	Corporate bonds and mortgages
Fire and casualty insurance companies	Premiums from policies	Municipal bonds, corporate bonds and stock, U.S. government securities
Pension funds, government retirement funds	Employer and employee contributions	Corporate bonds and stock
Investment Intermediaries		
Finance companies	Commercial paper, stocks, bonds	Consumer and business loans
Mutual funds	Shares	Stocks, bonds
Money market mutual funds	Shares	Money market instruments

Source: Federal Reserve Flow of Funds Accounts.

TABLE 2 Principal Financial Intermediaries

Type of Intermediary	Value of Assets ($ billions, end of year) 1970	1980	1990	2001
Depository Institutions (Banks)				
Commercial banks	517	1481	3334	6688
Savings and loan associations and mutual savings banks	250	792	1365	1288
Credit unions	18	67	215	496
Contractual Savings Institutions				
Life insurance companies	201	464	1367	3140
Fire and casualty insurance companies	50	182	533	863
Pension funds (private)	112	504	1629	4039
State and local government retirement funds	60	197	737	2078
Investment Intermediaries				
Finance companies	64	205	610	1137
Mutual funds	47	70	654	3705
Money market mutual funds	0	76	498	2116

Source: http://www.federalreserve.gov/releases/Z1/

Savings and Loan Associations Savings and loan associations (S&Ls) obtain funds primarily through savings deposits (often called shares) and time and checkable deposits. The acquired funds have traditionally been used to make mortgage loans. S&Ls are the second-largest group of financial intermediaries, numbering around 1500. In the 1950s and 1960s, S&Ls grew much more rapidly than commercial banks, but when interest rates climbed sharply from the late 1960s to the early 1980s, S&Ls encountered difficulties that slowed their rapid growth. Because most mortgages are long-term loans, with maturities in excess of 25 years, many were made years earlier when interest rates were substantially lower. When interest rates rose, S&Ls frequently found that the income from their mortgages was well below the cost of acquiring funds. Many of them suffered large losses, and many went out of business.

Until 1980, savings and loans were restricted to making mortgage loans and could not establish checking accounts. Their troubles encouraged Congress to pass legislation in the early 1980s allowing them to offer checking accounts, make consumer loans, and pursue many activities previously restricted to commercial banks. In addition, they are now subject to the same requirements as the commercial banks regarding deposits with the Federal Reserve. The net result of this legislation is that the distinction between savings and loans and commercial banks has blurred, and these intermediaries have become more alike and much more competitive with each other.

Mutual Savings Banks Mutual savings banks are very similar to savings and loans. They raise funds by accepting deposits (often called shares) and use them primarily to make mortgage loans. Their corporate structure is somewhat different from that of S&Ls in that they are always structured as "mutuals," or cooperatives: The depositors own the bank. There are around 500 of these institutions, located primarily in the Northeast. Like savings and loans, until 1980 they were restricted to making mortgage loans, and they suffered similar problems when interest rates rose from the late 1960s to the early 1980s. They were similarly affected by the banking legislation in the 1980s and can now issue checkable deposits and make loans other than mortgages.

Credit Unions These financial institutions, numbering about 10,100, are very small cooperative lending institutions organized around a particular group: union members, employees of a particular firm, and so forth. They acquire funds from deposits called shares and primarily make consumer loans. Thanks to the banking legislation in the 1980s, credit unions are also allowed to issue checkable deposits and can make mortgage loans in addition to consumer loans.

Contractual Savings Institutions

Contractual savings institutions, such as insurance companies and pension funds, are financial intermediaries that acquire funds at periodic intervals on a contractual basis. Because they can predict with reasonable accuracy how much they will have to pay out in benefits in the coming years, they do not have to worry as much as depository institutions about losing funds. As a result, the liquidity of assets is not as important a consideration for them as it is for depository institutions, and they tend to invest their funds primarily in long-term securities such as corporate bonds, stocks, and mortgages.

Life Insurance Companies Life insurance companies insure people against financial hazards following a death and sell annuities (annual income payments upon retirement). They acquire funds from the premiums that people pay to keep their policies in force and use them mainly to buy corporate bonds and mortgages. They also purchase stocks but are restricted in the amount that they can hold. Currently, with $3.1 trillion in assets, they are among the largest of the contractual savings institutions.

Fire and Casualty Insurance Companies These companies insure their policyholders against loss from theft, fire, and accidents. They are very much like life insurance companies, receiving funds through premiums for their policies, but they have a greater possibility of loss of funds if major disasters occur. For this reason, they use their funds to buy more liquid assets than life insurance companies do. Their largest holding of assets is municipal bonds; they also hold corporate bonds and stocks and U.S. government securities.

Pension Funds and Government Retirement Funds Private pension funds and state and local government retirement funds provide retirement income in the form of annuities to employees who are covered by a pension plan. Funds are acquired by contributions from employers or from employees, who either have a contribution automatically deducted from their paychecks or contribute voluntarily. The largest asset holdings of pension funds are corporate bonds and stocks. The establishment of pension funds has been actively encouraged by the federal government both through legislation requiring pension plans and through tax incentives to encourage contributions.

Investment Intermediaries

This category of financial intermediaries includes finance companies, mutual funds, and money market mutual funds.

Finance Companies Finance companies raise funds by selling commercial paper (a short-term debt instrument) and by issuing stocks and bonds. They lend these funds to consumers, who make purchases of such items as furniture, automobiles, and home improvements, and to small businesses. Some finance companies are organized by a parent corporation to help sell its product. For example, Ford Motor Credit Company makes loans to consumers who purchase Ford automobiles.

Mutual Funds These financial intermediaries acquire funds by selling shares to many individuals and use the proceeds to purchase diversified portfolios of stocks and bonds. Mutual funds allow shareholders to pool their resources so that they can take advantage of lower transaction costs when buying large blocks of stocks or bonds. In addition, mutual funds allow shareholders to hold more diversified portfolios than they otherwise would. Shareholders can sell (redeem) shares at any time, but the value of these shares will be determined by the value of the mutual fund's holdings of securities. Because these fluctuate greatly, the value of mutual fund shares will too; therefore, investments in mutual funds can be risky.

Money Market Mutual Funds These relatively new financial institutions have the characteristics of a mutual fund but also function to some extent as a depository institution because they offer deposit-type accounts. Like most mutual funds, they sell shares to acquire funds that are then used to buy money market instruments that are both safe and very liquid. The interest on these assets is then paid out to the shareholders.

A key feature of these funds is that shareholders can write checks against the value of their shareholdings. There are generally restrictions on the use of the check-writing privilege, however; checks frequently cannot be written for amounts less than a set minimum, such as $500, and a substantial amount of money is required initially to open an account. In effect, shares in a money market mutual fund function like checking account deposits that pay interest, but with some restrictions on the check-writing privilege. Money market mutual funds have experienced extraordinary growth since 1971, when they first appeared. By 2001, their assets had climbed to over $2.1 trillion.

REGULATION OF THE FINANCIAL SYSTEM

The financial system is among the most heavily regulated sectors of the American economy. The government regulates financial markets for three main reasons: to increase the information available to investors, to ensure the soundness of the financial system, and to improve control of monetary policy. We will examine how these three reasons have led to the present regulatory environment. As a study aid, the principal regulatory agencies of the U.S. financial system are listed in Table 3.

The United States Securities and Exchange Commission home page, www.sec.gov, contains vast SEC resources, laws and regulations, investor information, and litigation updates.

Increasing Information Available to Investors

Asymmetric information in financial markets means that investors may be subject to adverse selection and moral hazard problems that may hinder the efficient operation of financial markets. Risky firms or outright crooks may be the most eager to sell securities to unwary investors, and the resulting adverse selection problem may keep investors out of financial markets. Furthermore, once an investor has bought a security, thereby lending money to a firm, the borrower may

TABLE 3 Principal Regulatory Agencies of the U.S. Financial System

Regulatory Agency	Subject of Regulation	Nature of Regulations
Securities and Exchange Commission (SEC)	Organized exchanges and financial markets	Requires disclosure of information, restricts insider trading
Commodities Futures Trading Commission (CFTC)	Futures market exchanges	Regulates procedures for trading in futures markets
Office of the Comptroller of the Currency	Federally chartered commercial banks	Charters and examines the books of federally chartered commercial banks and imposes restrictions on assets they can hold
National Credit Union Administration (NCUA)	Federally chartered credit unions	Charters and examines the books of federally chartered credit unions and imposes restrictions on assets they can hold
State banking and insurance commissions	State-chartered depository institutions	Charter and examine the books of state-chartered banks and insurance companies, impose restrictions on assets they can hold, and impose restrictions on branching
Federal Deposit Insurance Corporation (FDIC)	Commercial banks, mutual savings banks, savings and loan associations	Provides insurance of up to $100,000 for each depositor at a bank, examines the books of insured banks, and imposes restrictions on assets they can hold
Federal Reserve System	All depository institutions	Examines the books of commercial banks that are members of the system, sets reserve requirements for all banks
Office of Thrift Supervision	Savings and loan associations	Examines the books of savings and loan associations, imposes restrictions on assets they can hold

have incentives to engage in risky activities or to commit outright fraud. The presence of this moral hazard problem may also keep investors away from financial markets. Government regulation can reduce adverse selection and moral hazard problems in financial markets and increase their efficiency by increasing the amount of information available to investors.

As a result of the stock market crash in 1929 and revelations of widespread fraud in the aftermath, political demands for regulation culminated in the Securities Act of 1933 and the establishment of the Securities and Exchange Commission (SEC). The SEC requires corporations issuing securities to disclose certain information about their sales, assets, and earnings to the public and restricts trading by the largest stockholders (known as insiders) in the corporation. By requiring disclosure of this information and by discouraging insider trading, which could be used to manipulate security prices, the SEC hopes that investors will be better informed and be protected from some of the abuses in financial markets that occurred before 1933. Indeed, in recent years, the SEC has been particularly active in prosecuting people involved in insider trading.

Ensuring the Soundness of Financial Intermediaries

Asymmetric information can also lead to widespread collapse of financial intermediaries, referred to as a **financial panic.** Because providers of funds to financial intermediaries may not be able to assess whether the institutions holding their funds are sound or not, if they have doubts about the overall health of financial intermediaries, they may want to pull their funds out of both sound and unsound institutions. The possible outcome is a financial panic that produces large losses for the public and causes serious damage to the economy. To protect the public and the economy from financial panics, the government has implemented six types of regulations.

Restrictions on Entry State banking and insurance commissions, as well as the Office of the Comptroller of the Currency (an agency of the federal government), have created very tight regulations as to who is allowed to set up a financial intermediary. Individuals or groups that want to establish a financial intermediary, such as a bank or an insurance company, must obtain a charter from the state or the federal government. Only if they are upstanding citizens with impeccable credentials and a large amount of initial funds will they be given a charter.

Disclosure There are stringent reporting requirements for financial intermediaries. Their bookkeeping must follow certain strict principles, their books are subject to periodic inspection, and they must make certain information available to the public.

Restrictions on Assets and Activities There are restrictions on what financial intermediaries are allowed to do and what assets they can hold. Before you put your funds into a bank or some other such institution, you would want to know that your funds are safe and that the bank or other financial intermediary will be able to meet its obligations to you. One way of doing this is to restrict the financial intermediary from engaging in certain risky activities. Legislation passed in 1933 separates commercial banking from the securities industry so that banks do not engage in risky ventures associated with this industry. Another way is to restrict financial intermediaries from holding certain risky assets, or at least from holding a greater quantity of these risky assets than is prudent. For example, commercial banks and other depository institutions are not allowed to hold common stock because stock prices experience substantial fluctuations. Insurance companies are allowed to hold common stock, but their holdings cannot exceed a certain fraction of their total assets.

Deposit Insurance The government can insure people providing funds to a financial intermediary from any financial loss if the financial intermediary should fail. The most important government agency that provides this type of insurance is the Federal Deposit Insurance Corporation (FDIC), which insures each depositor at a commercial bank or mutual savings bank up to a loss of $100,000 per account. All commercial and mutual savings banks, with a few minor exceptions, make contributions into the FDIC's Bank Insurance Fund, which are used to pay off depositors in the case of a bank's failure. The FDIC was created in 1934 after the massive bank failures of 1930–1933 in which the savings of many depositors at commercial banks were wiped out. Similar government agencies exist for other depository institutions: The Savings Association Insurance Fund (part of the FDIC) provides deposit insurance for savings and loan associations, and the National Credit Union Share Insurance Fund (NCUSIF) does the same for credit unions.

Limits on Competition Politicians have often declared that unbridled competition among financial intermediaries promotes failures that will harm the public. Although the evidence that competition does this is extremely weak, it has not stopped the state and federal governments from imposing many restrictive regulations. These regulations have taken two forms. First are the restrictions on the opening of additional locations (branches). In the past, banks were not allowed to open up branches in other states, and in some states banks were restricted from opening additional locations.

Restrictions on Interest Rates Competition has also been inhibited by regulations that impose restrictions on interest rates that can be paid on deposits. For decades after 1933, banks were prohibited from paying interest on checking accounts. In addition, until 1986, the Federal Reserve System had the power under **Regulation Q** to set maximum interest rates that banks could pay on savings deposits. These regulations were instituted because of the widespread belief that unrestricted interest-rate competition helped encourage bank failures during the Great Depression. Later evidence does not seem to support this view, and restrictions like Regulation Q have been abolished.

Improving Control of Monetary Policy

Because banks play a very important role in determining the supply of money (which in turn affects many aspects of the economy), much regulation of these financial intermediaries is intended to improve control over the money supply. One such regulation is **reserve requirements,** which make it obligatory for all depository institutions to keep a certain fraction of their deposits in accounts with the Federal Reserve System (the Fed), the central bank in the United States. Reserve requirements help the Fed exercise more precise control over the money supply. Deposit insurance regulation can also be rationalized along these lines: The FDIC gives depositors confidence in the banking system and eliminates widespread bank failures, which can in turn cause large, uncontrollable fluctuations in the quantity of money.

In later chapters, we will look more closely at government regulation of financial markets and will see whether it has improved the functioning of financial markets.

Financial Regulation Abroad

Not surprisingly, given the similarity of the economic system here and in Japan, Canada, and the nations of Western Europe, financial regulation in these countries is similar to financial regulation in the United States. The provision of information is improved by requiring corporations issuing securities to report details about assets and liabilities, earnings, and sales of stock and by prohibiting insider trading. The soundness of intermediaries is ensured by licensing, periodic inspection of financial intermediaries' books, and the provision of deposit insurance (although its coverage is smaller and its existence is often intentionally not advertised).

The major differences between financial regulation in the United States and abroad relate to bank regulation. In the past, the United States was the only industrialized country to subject banks to restrictions on branching, which limited banks' size and restricted them to certain geographic regions. U.S. banks are also the most restricted in the range of financial services they may provide and the assets they may hold. Banks abroad frequently hold shares in commercial firms; in Japan and Germany, those stakes can be sizable.

SUMMARY

1. The basic function of financial markets is to channel funds from savers who have an excess of funds to spenders who have a shortage of funds. Financial markets can do this either through direct finance, in which borrowers borrow funds directly from lenders by selling them securities, or through indirect finance, which involves a financial intermediary who stands between the lender-savers and the borrower-spenders and helps transfer funds from one to the other. This channeling of funds improves the economic welfare of everyone in the society because it allows funds to move from people who have no productive investment opportunities to those who have such opportunities, thereby contributing to increased efficiency in the economy. In addition, it directly benefits consumers by allowing them to make purchases when they need them most.
2. Financial markets can be classified as debt and equity markets, primary and secondary markets, exchanges and over-the-counter markets, and money and capital markets.
3. An important trend in recent years is the growing internationalization of financial markets. Eurobonds, which are denominated in a currency other than that of the country in which they are sold, are now the dominant security in the international bond market and have surpassed U.S. corporate bonds as a source of new funds. Eurodollars, which are U.S. dollars deposited in foreign banks, are an important source of funds for American banks.
4. Financial intermediaries are financial institutions that acquire funds by issuing liabilities and in turn use those funds to acquire assets by purchasing securities or making loans. Financial intermediaries play such an important role in the financial system because they reduce transaction costs and solve problems created by adverse selection and moral hazard. As a result, financial intermediaries allow small savers and borrowers to benefit from the existence of financial markets, thereby increasing the efficiency of the economy.
5. The principal financial intermediaries fall into three categories: (a) banks—commercial banks, savings and loan associations, mutual savings banks, and credit unions; (b) contractual savings institutions—life insurance companies, fire and casualty insurance companies, and pension funds; and (c) investment intermediaries—finance companies, mutual funds, and money market mutual funds.
6. The government regulates financial markets and financial intermediaries for three main reasons: to increase the information available to investors, to ensure the soundness of the financial system, and to improve control of monetary policy. Regulations include requiring disclosure of information to the public, restrictions on who can set up a financial intermediary, restrictions on what assets financial intermediaries can hold, the provision of deposit insurance, reserve requirements, and the setting of maximum interest rates that can be paid on checking accounts and savings deposits.

KEY TERMS

adverse selection, *p. 24*
asymmetric information, *p. 24*
brokers, *p. 19*
capital market, *p. 20*
dealers, *p. 19*
dividends, *p. 18*
economies of scale, *p. 23*
equities, *p. 18*
Eurobonds, *p. 21*
Eurocurrencies, *p. 21*
Eurodollars, *p. 21*
exchanges, *p. 19*
financial intermediation, *p. 22*
financial panic, *p. 30*
foreign bonds, *p. 20*
intermediate-term, *p. 18*
investment banks, *p. 19*
liabilities, *p. 16*
liquid, *p. 19*
long-term, *p. 18*
maturity, *p. 18*
money market, *p. 20*
moral hazard, *p. 24*
over-the-counter (OTC) market, *p. 19*
primary market, *p. 18*
Regulation Q, *p. 32*
reserve requirements, *p. 32*
secondary market, *p. 18*
short-term, *p. 18*
thrift institutions (thrifts), *p. 26*
transaction costs, *p. 22*
underwriting, *p. 19*

QUESTIONS AND PROBLEMS

*1. Why is a share of IBM common stock an asset for its owner and a liability for IBM?

2. If I can buy a car today for $5000 and it is worth $10,000 next year in extra income to me because it enables me to get a job as a traveling anvil seller, should I take out a loan from Larry the Loan Shark at a 90% interest rate if no one else will give me a loan? Will I be better or worse off as a result of taking out this loan? Can you make a case for legalizing loan-sharking?

*3. Some economists suspect that one of the reasons that economies in developing countries grow so slowly is that they do not have well-developed financial markets. Does this argument make sense?

4. In the nineteenth century the U.S. economy borrowed heavily from the British to build a railroad system. What was the principal debt instrument used? Why did this make both countries better off?

*5. "Because corporations do not actually raise any funds in secondary markets, they are less important to the economy than primary markets." Comment.

6. If you suspect that a company will go bankrupt next year, which would you rather hold—bonds issued by the company or equities issued by the company? Why?

*7. How can the adverse selection problem explain why you are more likely to make a loan to a family member than to a stranger?

8. Think of one example in which you have had to deal with the adverse selection problem.

*9. Why do loan sharks worry less about moral hazard in connection with their borrowers than some other lenders do?

10. If you are an employer, what kinds of moral hazard problems might you worry about with your employees?

*11. If there were no asymmetry in the information that a borrower and a lender had, could there still be a moral hazard problem?

12. "In a world without information and transaction costs, financial intermediaries would not exist." Is this statement true, false, or uncertain? Explain your answer.

*13. Why might you be willing to make a loan to your neighbor by putting funds in a savings account earning a 5% interest rate at the bank and having the bank loan her the funds at a 10% interest rate, rather than loan her the funds yourself?

14. In two lists, rank the following money market instruments in terms of their liquidity and their safety:
   a. U.S. Treasury bills
   b. Negotiable CDs
   c. Repurchase agreements
   d. Commercial paper

*15. Discuss some of the manifestations of the globalization of world capital markets.

WEB EXERCISES

Overview of the Financial System

1. One of the single best sources of information about financial institutions is the "U.S. Flow of Funds Report" produced by the Federal Reserve. This document contains data on most financial intermediaries. To access this report, go to http://www.federalreserve.gov/releases/Z1/. Click on the most current release. (You may have to load Acrobat Reader if your computer does not already have it. The site has a link for a free patch.) Go to the "Level Tables" and answer the following questions.
   a. What is the date of the most current release?
   b. What percent of assets do commercial banks hold in loans? What percent of assets are held in mortgage loans?
   c. What percent of assets do savings and loans hold in mortgage loans?
   d. What percent of assets do credit unions hold in mortgage loans and in consumer loans?

2. The most famous financial market in the world is the New York Stock Exchange. Check out their website at http://www.nyse.com and answer the following questions.
   a. What is the mission of the NYSE?
   b. Firms must pay a fee to list their shares for sale on the NYSE. What would be the fee for a firm with 5 million shares common outstanding?

Part 2

Fundamentals of Interest Rates

Chapter 3 Understanding Interest Rates

Preview

At www.bloomberg.com/markets/ under the "Rates & Bonds" heading, you can access information on key interest rates, U.S. Treasuries, government bonds, and municipal bonds.

Interest rates are among the most closely watched variables in the economy. Their movements are reported almost daily by the news media because they directly affect our everyday lives and have important consequences for the health of the economy. They affect personal decisions such as whether to consume or save, whether to buy a house, and whether to purchase bonds or put funds into a savings account. Interest rates also affect the economic decisions of businesses and households, such as whether to use their funds to invest in new equipment for factories or to save their money in a bank.

Before we can go on with the study of financial markets, we must understand exactly what the phrase *interest rates* means. In this chapter we see that a concept known as the *yield to maturity* is the most accurate measure of interest rates; the yield to maturity is what financial economists mean when they use the term *interest rate.* We discuss how the yield to maturity is measured on credit market instruments and examine alternative (but less accurate) ways in which interest rates are quoted. We also see that a bond's interest rate does not necessarily indicate how good an investment the bond is because what it earns (its rate of return) can differ from its interest rate. Finally, we explore the distinction between real interest rates, which are adjusted for changes in the price level, and nominal interest rates, which are not.

Although learning definitions is not always the most exciting of pursuits, it is important to read carefully and understand the concepts presented in this chapter. Not only are they continually used throughout the remainder of this text, but a firm grasp of these terms will give you a clearer understanding of the role that interest rates play in your life as well as in the general economy.

MEASURING INTEREST RATES

Debt market instruments fall into four types:

1. A **simple loan** provides the borrower with an amount of funds (principal) that must be repaid to the lender at the maturity date along with an additional amount known as an *interest* payment. For example, if a bank made you a simple loan of $100 for one year, you would have to repay the principal of $100 in one year's time along with an additional interest payment of, say, $10. Commercial loans to businesses are often of this type.
2. A **fixed-payment loan** provides a borrower with an amount of funds that is to be repaid by making the same payment every month, consisting of part of the principal and interest for a set number of years. For example, if you borrowed $1000, a fixed-payment loan might require you to pay $126 every year for 25 years. Installment loans (such as auto loans) and mortgages are frequently of the fixed-payment type.
3. A **coupon bond** pays the owner of the bond a fixed interest payment (coupon payment) every year until the maturity date, when a specified final amount **(face value** or **par value)** is repaid. The coupon payment is so named because the bondholder used to obtain payment by clipping a coupon off the bond and sending it to the bond issuer, who then sent the payment to the holder. Nowadays, for most coupon bonds it is no longer necessary to send in coupons to receive these payments. A coupon bond with $1000 face value, for example, might pay you a coupon payment of $100 per year for ten years and at the maturity date repay you the face value amount of $1000. (The face value of a bond is usually in $1000 increments.)

   A coupon bond is identified by three pieces of information. First is the corporation or government agency that issues the bond. Second is the maturity date of the bond. Third is the bond's **coupon rate,** the dollar amount of the yearly coupon payment expressed as a percentage of the face value of the bond. In our example, the coupon bond has a yearly coupon payment of $100 and a face value of $1000. The coupon rate is then $100/$1000 = 0.10, or 10%. Treasury bonds and notes and corporate bonds are examples of coupon bonds.
4. A **discount bond** (also called a **zero-coupon bond**) is bought at a price below its face value (at a discount), and the face value is repaid at the maturity date. Unlike a coupon bond, a discount bond does not make any interest payments; it just pays off the face value. For example, a discount bond with a face value of $1000 might be bought for $900 and in a year's time the owner would be repaid the face value of $1000. U.S. Treasury bills, U.S. savings bonds, and long-term zero-coupon bonds are examples of discount bonds.

These four types of instruments require payments at different times: Simple loans and discount bonds make payment only at their maturity dates, whereas fixed-payment loans and coupon bonds have payments periodically until maturity. How would you decide which of these instruments provides you with more income? They all seem so different because they make payments at different times. To solve this problem, we use the concept of *present value* to provide us with a procedure for measuring interest rates on these different types of instruments.

Present Value

The concept of **present value** is based on the commonsense notion that a dollar paid to you one year from now is less valuable to you than a dollar paid to you today; this notion is true because you can deposit the dollar in a savings account that earns interest and have more than a dollar in one year. We will now define this concept more formally.

In the case of a simple loan, the interest payment divided by the amount of the loan is a natural and sensible way to measure the cost of borrowing funds: The measure of the cost is the *simple interest rate*. In the example we used to describe the simple loan, a loan of \$100 today requires the borrower to repay the \$100 a year from now and to make an additional interest payment of \$10. Hence, using the definition just given, the simple interest rate i is

$$i = \frac{\$10}{\$100} = 0.10 = 10\%$$

If you make this \$100 loan, at the end of the year you would receive \$110, which can be rewritten as

$$\$100 \times (1 + 0.10) = \$110$$

If you then loaned out the \$110, at the end of the second year you would receive

$$\$110 \times (1 + 0.10) = \$121$$

or, equivalently,

$$\$100 \times (1 + 0.10) \times (1 + 0.10) = \$100 \times (1 + 0.10)^2 = \$121$$

Continuing with the loan again, you would receive at the end of the third year

$$\$121 \times (1 + 0.10) = \$100 \times (1 + 0.10)^3 = \$133$$

The amounts you would have at the end of each year can be seen in the following time line:

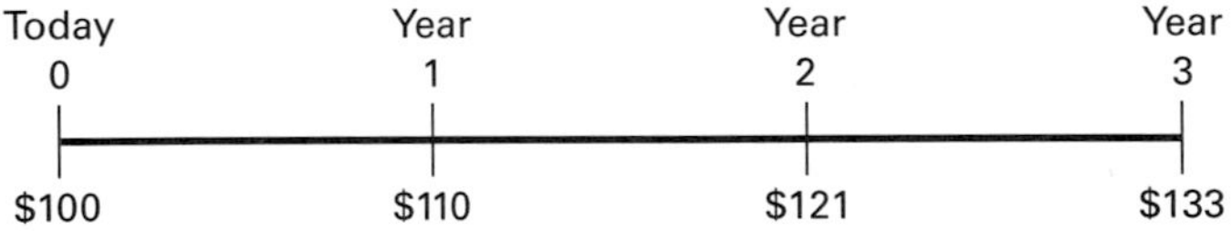

These calculations of the proceeds from a simple loan can be generalized as follows: If the simple interest rate i is expressed as a decimal fraction (such as 0.10 for the 10% interest rate in our example), then after making these loans for n years, you will receive a total payment of

$$\$100 \times (1 + i)^n$$

We can also work these calculations backward. Because \$100 today will turn into \$110 next year when the simple interest rate is 10%, we could say that \$110 next year is worth only \$100 today. Or we could say that no one would pay more than \$100 today to get \$110 next year. Similarly, we could say that \$121 two years from now or \$133 three years from now is worth \$100 today. This process of calculating what dollars received in the future are worth today is called *discounting the future.* We have been implicitly solving our forward-looking equations for today's value of a future dollar amount. For example, in the case of the \$133 received three years from now, when $i = 0.10$,

Today	Future
\$100	$\$100 \times (1 + i)^3 = \$133$

so that

$$\$100 = \frac{\$133}{(1 + i)^3}$$

More generally, we can solve this equation to tell us the present value *(PV)*, or **present discounted value,** of the future dollar amount—that is, the value *today* of a future payment *(FV)* received n years from now when the simple interest rate is i:

$$PV = \frac{FV}{(1 + i)^n} \quad (1)$$

Intuitively, what Equation 1 tells us is that if you are promised \$1 for certain ten years from now, this dollar would not be as valuable to you as \$1 is today because if you had the \$1 today, you could invest it and end up with more than \$1 in ten years.

EXAMPLE 1: Simple Present Value

What is the present value of \$250 to be paid in two years if the interest rate is 15%?

Solution

The present value would be \$189.04. Using Equation 1:

$$PV = \frac{FV}{(1 + i)^n}$$

where

FV = amount in two years = \$250

i = annual interest rate = 0.15

n = number of years = 2

Thus

$$PV = \frac{\$250}{(1 + 0.15)^2} = \frac{\$250}{1.3225} = \$189.04$$

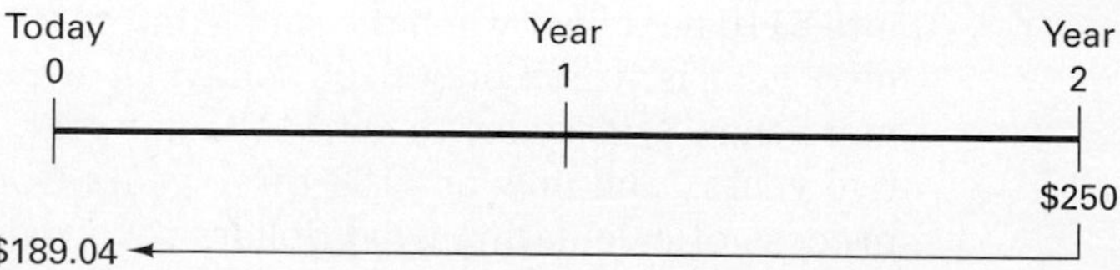

The concept of present value is extremely useful because it allows us to figure out today's value of a credit market instrument at a given simple interest rate i by just adding up the present value of all the future payments received. The present value concept allows us to compare the value of two instruments with very different timing of their payments, such as a discount bond and a coupon bond. As we will see, this concept also allows us to obtain an equivalent measure of the interest rate on all four types of credit market instruments discussed here.

Application **Cost of the S&L Bailout: Was It Really $500 Billion?**

The government bailout of the savings and loan industry in 1989 was one of the major news stories of the past decade. Statements frequently appeared in the press that the cost of the bailout to taxpayers would exceed $500 billion—more than $2000 for every man, woman, and child in the United States. The $500 billion–plus figure made for wonderful political rhetoric, but was the cost really this high?

The answer is no, and the concept of present value tells us why. The $500 billion figure includes bond payments over the next 40 years. The present value concept tells us that to figure out the cost of these payments in today's dollars, we have to discount them back to the present. When we do this, the present value of these payments is on the order of $150 billion, not $500 billion. It is still true that a present value of the bailout of $150 billion is nothing to sneeze at, but it is not quite as scary as a figure more than three times that size. (Chapter 17 contains an extensive discussion of the S&L crisis and bailout.)

Yield to Maturity

Of the several common ways of calculating interest rates, the most important is the **yield to maturity,** the interest rate that equates the present value of payments received from a debt instrument with its value today. Because the concept behind the calculation of the yield to maturity makes good economic sense, financial economists consider it the most accurate measure of interest rates.

To understand the yield to maturity better, we now look at how it is calculated for the four types of credit market instruments.

Simple Loan Using the concept of present value, the yield to maturity on a simple loan is easy to calculate. For the one-year loan we discussed, today's value is $100, and the payments in one year's time would be $110 (the repayment of $100 plus the interest payment of $10). We can use this information to solve for the yield to maturity i by recognizing that the present value of the future payments must equal today's value of a loan.

EXAMPLE 2: Simple Loan

If Pete borrows $100 from his sister and next year she wants $110 back from him, what is the yield to maturity on this loan?

Solution

The yield to maturity on the loan is 10%.

$$PV = \frac{FV}{(1+i)^n}$$

where

PV = amount borrowed = \$100

FV = amount in one year = \$110

n = number of years = 1

Thus

$$\$100 = \frac{\$110}{(1+i)}$$

$$(1+i)\$100 = \$110$$

$$(1+i) = \frac{\$110}{\$100}$$

$$i = 1.10 - 1 = 0.10 = 10\%$$

Today 0 — Year 1

\$100 — \$110

→ i = 10% ←

This calculation of the yield to maturity should look familiar because it equals the interest payment of \$10 divided by the loan amount of \$100; that is, it equals the simple interest rate on the loan. An important point to recognize is that ***for simple loans, the simple interest rate equals the yield to maturity.*** Hence the same term i is used to denote both the yield to maturity and the simple interest rate.

Study Guide The key to understanding the calculation of the yield to maturity is equating today's value of the debt instrument with the present value of all of its future payments. The best way to learn this principle is to apply it to other specific examples of the four types of credit market instruments in addition to those we discuss here. See if you can develop the equations that would allow you to solve for the yield to maturity in each case.

Fixed-Payment Loan Recall that this type of loan has the same payment every year throughout the life of the loan. On a fixed-rate mortgage, for example, the borrower makes the same payment to the bank every month until the maturity date, when the loan will be completely paid off. To calculate the yield to maturity for a fixed-payment loan, we follow the same strategy we used for the simple loan—we equate today's value of the loan with its present value. Because the fixed-payment loan involves more than one payment, the present value of the fixed-payment loan is calculated as the sum of the present values of all payments (using Equation 1).

In the case of our earlier example, the loan is $1000, and the yearly payment is $85.81 for the next 25 years. The present value is calculated as follows: At the end of one year, there is a $85.81 payment with a *PV* of $85.81/(1 + i); at the end of two years, there is another $85.81 payment with a *PV* of $85.81/$(1 + i)^2$; and so on until at the end of the twenty-fifth year, the last payment of $85.81 with a *PV* of $85.81/$(1 + i)^{25}$ is made. Making today's value of the loan ($1000) equal to the sum of the present values of all the yearly payments gives us

$$\$1000 = \frac{\$85.81}{1+i} + \frac{\$85.81}{(1+i)^2} + \frac{\$85.81}{(1+i)^3} + \cdots + \frac{\$85.81}{(1+i)^{25}}$$

More generally, for any fixed-payment loan,

$$LV = \frac{FP}{1+i} + \frac{FP}{(1+i)^2} + \frac{FP}{(1+i)^3} + \ldots + \frac{FP}{(1+i)^n} \qquad (2)$$

where

LV = loan value
FP = fixed yearly payment
n = number of years until maturity

For a fixed-payment loan amount, the fixed yearly payment and the number of years until maturity are known quantities, and only the yield to maturity is not. So we can solve this equation for the yield to maturity i. Because this calculation is not easy, tables have been created that allow you to find i given the loan's numbers for *LV*, *FP*, and n. For example, in the case of the 25-year loan with yearly payments of $85.81, the yield to maturity from the table that solves Equation 2 is 7%. Real estate brokers always have such a table handy (or a pocket calculator that can solve such equations) so that they can immediately tell the prospective house buyer exactly what the yearly (or monthly) payments will be if the house purchase is financed by taking out a mortgage (see Figure 1).

EXAMPLE 3: Fixed-Payment Loan

You decide to purchase a new home and need a $100,000 mortgage. You take out a loan from the bank that has an interest rate of 7%. What is the yearly payment to the bank to pay off the loan in 20 years?

Solution

The yearly payment to the bank is $9,439.29.

$$LV = \frac{FP}{1+i} + \frac{FP}{(1+i)^2} + \frac{FP}{(1+i)^3} + \ldots + \frac{FP}{(1+i)^n}$$

where

LV = loan value amount = $100,000
i = annual interest rate = 0.07
n = number of years = 20

Thus

$$\$100{,}000 = \frac{FP}{1+0.07} + \frac{FP}{(1+0.07)^2} + \frac{FP}{(1+0.07)^3} + \ldots + \frac{FP}{(1+0.07)^{20}}$$

7% — Monthly Payment Necessary to Amortize a Loan

	Term (years)						
Amount($)	5	10	15	17	20	25	30
25	.50	.29	.22	.21	.19	.18	.17
50	.99	.58	.45	.42	.39	.35	.33
75	1.49	.87	.67	.63	.58	.53	.50
100	1.98	1.16	.90	.84	.78	.71	.67
200	3.96	2.32	1.80	1.68	1.55	1.41	1.33
300	5.94	3.48	2.70	2.52	2.33	2.12	2.00
400	7.92	4.64	3.60	3.36	3.10	2.83	2.66
500	9.90	5.81	4.49	4.20	3.88	3.53	3.33
600	11.88	6.97	5.39	5.04	4.65	4.24	3.99
700	13.86	8.13	6.29	5.88	5.43	4.95	4.66
800	15.84	9.29	7.19	6.72	6.20	5.65	5.32
900	17.82	10.45	8.09	7.56	6.98	6.36	5.99
1000	19.80	11.61	8.99	8.40	7.75	7.07	6.65
2000	39.60	23.22	17.98	16.79	15.51	14.14	13.31
3000	59.40	34.83	26.96	25.19	23.26	21.20	19.96
4000	79.20	46.44	35.95	33.59	31.01	28.27	26.61
5000	99.01	58.05	44.94	41.98	38.76	35.34	33.27

FIGURE 1 A Mortgage Payment Table

This table is for loans with a 7% interest rate. To find the monthly payment for the loan, pick out the amount of the loan in the first column and then follow that row across to the entry in the column with the number of years to maturity of the loan. For a $1000, 25-year fixed-payment loan with a 7% interest rate, following this procedure indicates that the monthly payment is $7.07 ($84.84 per year).

To find the monthly payment for the loan using the mortgage payment table in Figure 1, pick out the loan in the first column and then follow across to the entry in the column with the number of years to maturity of the loan. For a $100,000, 20-year fixed-payment loan with a 7% interest rate, the yearly payment is $9,300 (7.75 × $100 × 12). The monthly payment computed using the table is an approximation.

To solve using a financial calculator:

n = number of years = 20

PV = amount of the loan (LV) = −100,000

FV = amount of the loan after 20 years = 0

i = annual interest rate = .07

Then push the *PMT* button = fixed yearly payment (*FP*) = $9,439.29.

Coupon Bond To calculate the yield to maturity for a coupon bond, follow the same strategy used for the fixed-payment loan: Equate today's value of the bond with its present value. Because coupon bonds also have more than one payment, the present value of the bond is calculated as the sum of the present values of all the coupon payments plus the present value of the final payment of the face value of the bond.

The present value of a $1000 face value bond with ten years to maturity and yearly coupon payments of $100 (a 10% coupon rate) can be calculated as follows: At the end of one year, there is a $100 coupon payment with a *PV* of $\$100/(1 + i)$;

10.00%	Bond Values per $100 of Face Value									
	Years to Maturity									
Yield (%)	1	2	3	4	5	6	7	8	9	10
10.00	100.00	100.00	100.00	100.00	100.00	100.00	100.00	100.00	100.00	100.00
10.25	99.77	99.57	99.38	99.21	99.06	98.92	98.79	98.68	98.57	98.48
10.50	99.55	99.14	98.77	98.43	98.13	97.85	97.61	97.38	97.18	96.99
10.75	99.32	98.71	98.16	97.66	97.21	96.80	96.44	96.11	95.81	95.54
11.00	99.10	98.29	97.56	96.90	96.30	95.77	95.29	94.85	94.46	94.11
11.25	98.88	97.87	96.96	96.14	95.41	94.75	94.16	93.62	93.15	92.71
11.50	98.65	97.45	96.37	95.40	94.53	93.74	93.04	92.42	91.85	91.35
11.75	98.43	96.03	95.78	94.66	93.65	92.75	91.95	91.23	90.59	90.01
12.00	98.21	96.62	95.20	93.93	92.79	91.78	90.87	90.06	89.34	88.70
12.25	98.00	96.21	94.62	93.20	91.94	90.81	89.81	88.92	88.12	87.42
12.50	97.78	95.80	94.05	92.49	91.10	89.87	88.77	87.79	86.93	86.16
12.75	97.56	95.40	93.48	91.78	90.27	88.93	87.74	86.69	85.76	84.93

FIGURE 2 A Bond Table

This table is for bonds with a 10% coupon rate. To find the price of the bond, pick out its yield to maturity in the first column and then follow that row across to the entry in the column with the number of years to maturity for the bond. For an eight-year, 10% coupon rate bond with a yield to maturity of 12.25%, following this procedure indicates that the price of the bond is $88.92 per $100 of face value (which means that a $1000 face value bond sells for $889.20).

at the end of the second year, there is another $100 coupon payment with a *PV* of $\$100/(1 + i)^2$; and so on until at maturity, there is a $100 coupon payment with a *PV* of $\$100/(1 + i)^{10}$ plus the repayment of the $1000 face value with a *PV* of $\$1000/(1 + i)^{10}$. Setting today's value of the bond (its current price, denoted by *P*) equal to the sum of the present values of all the payments for this bond gives

$$P = \frac{\$100}{1 + i} + \frac{\$100}{(1 + i)^2} + \frac{\$100}{(1 + i)^3} + \cdots + \frac{\$100}{(1 + i)^{10}} + \frac{\$1000}{(1 + i)^{10}}$$

More generally, for any coupon bond,[1]

$$P = \frac{C}{1 + i} + \frac{C}{(1 + i)^2} + \frac{C}{(1 + i)^3} + \ldots + \frac{C}{(1 + i)^n} + \frac{F}{(1 + i)^n} \quad (3)$$

where
P = price of coupon bond
C = yearly coupon payment
F = face value of the bond
n = years to maturity date

In Equation 3, the coupon payment, the face value, the years to maturity, and the price of the bond are known quantities, and only the yield to maturity is not. Hence we can solve this equation for the yield to maturity i.[2] Just as in the case of the fixed-payment loan, this calculation is not easy, so bond tables (see Figure 2) have been created that allow you to read off the yield to maturity for a

[1]Most coupon bonds actually make coupon payments on a semiannual basis rather than once a year as assumed here. The effect on the calculations is only very slight and will be ignored here.

[2]In other contexts, it is also called the *internal rate of return.*

bond given its coupon rate, its years to maturity, and its price. Some business-oriented pocket calculators have built-in programs that solve this equation for you.

EXAMPLE 4: Coupon Bond

Find the price of a 10% coupon bond with a face value of $1,000, a 12.25% yield to maturity, and eight years to maturity.

Solution

The price of the bond is $889.20. Using Figure 2, pick out its yield to maturity in the left-hand column, then follow the row across to the entry in the column with the number of years to maturity for the bond. Figure 2 indicates that the price of the bond is $88.92 per $100 of face value. Since the face value of the bond in the example is $1000, the bond price is $889.20 ($88.92 × 10).

To solve using a financial calculator:

n = years to maturity = 8

FV = face value of the bond = −1000

i = annual interest rate = 12.25%

PMT = yearly coupon payments = 100

Then push the *PV* button = price of the bond = $889.20.

Table 1 shows the yields to maturity calculated for several bond prices. Three interesting facts emerge:

1. When the coupon bond is priced at its face value, the yield to maturity equals the coupon rate.
2. The price of a coupon bond and the yield to maturity are negatively related; that is, as the yield to maturity rises, the price of the bond falls. If the yield to maturity falls, the price of the bond rises.
3. The yield to maturity is greater than the coupon rate when the bond price is below its face value.

These three facts are true for any coupon bond and are really not surprising if you think about the reasoning behind the calculation of the yield to maturity. When you put $1000 in a bank account with an interest rate of 10%, you can take out $100 every year and you will be left with the $1000 at the end of ten years. This is similar to buying the $1000 bond with a 10% coupon rate analyzed in Table 1, which pays a $100 coupon payment every year and then repays $1000

TABLE 1 Yields to Maturity on a 10% Coupon Rate Bond Maturing in Ten Years (Face Value = $1000)

Price of Bond ($)	Yield to Maturity (%)
1200	7.13
1100	8.48
1000	10.00
900	11.75
800	13.81

at the end of ten years. If the bond is purchased at the par value of \$1000, its yield to maturity must equal the interest rate of 10%, which is also equal to the coupon rate of 10%. The same reasoning applied to any coupon bond demonstrates that if the coupon bond is purchased at its par value, the yield to maturity and the coupon rate must be equal.

It is straightforward to show that the bond price and the yield to maturity are negatively related. As i, the yield to maturity, rises, all denominators in the bond price formula must necessarily rise. Hence a rise in the interest rate as measured by the yield to maturity means that the price of the bond must fall. Another way to explain why the bond price falls when the interest rises is that a higher interest rate implies that the future coupon payments and final payment are worth less when discounted back to the present; hence the price of the bond must be lower.

Check out a review of the key financial concepts: time value of money, annuities, perpetuities at www.teachmefinance.com

There is one special case of a coupon bond that is worth discussing because its yield to maturity is particularly easy to calculate. This bond is called a **perpetuity;** it is a perpetual bond with no maturity date and no repayment of principal that makes fixed coupon payments of $\$C$ forever. The formula in Equation 3 for the price of a perpetuity, P, simplifies to the following:[3]

$$P = \frac{C}{i} \tag{4}$$

where P = price of the perpetuity
C = yearly payment

One nice feature of perpetuities is that you can immediately see that as i goes up, the price of the bond falls. For example, if a perpetuity pays \$100 per year forever and the interest rate is 10%, its price will be \$1000 = \$100/0.10. If the interest rate rises to 20%, its price will fall to \$500 = \$100/0.20. We can also rewrite this formula as

$$i = \frac{C}{P} \tag{5}$$

EXAMPLE 5: Perpetuity

What is the yield to maturity on a bond that has a price of \$2000 and pays \$100 annually forever?

[3]The bond price formula for a perpetuity is

$$P = \frac{C}{1+i} + \frac{C}{(1+i)^2} + \frac{C}{(1+i)^3} + \cdots$$

which can be written as

$$P = C(x + x^2 + x^3 + \ldots)$$

in which $x = 1/(1 + i)$. From your high school algebra you might remember the formula for an infinite sum:

$$1 + x + x^2 + x^3 + \ldots = \frac{1}{1-x} \quad \text{for} \quad x < 1$$

and so

$$P = C\left(\frac{1}{1-x} - 1\right) = C\left[\frac{1}{1 - 1/(1+i)} - 1\right]$$

which by suitable algebraic manipulation becomes

$$P = C\left(\frac{1+i}{i} - \frac{i}{i}\right) = \frac{C}{i}$$

Solution

The yield to maturity would be 5%.

$$i = \frac{C}{P}$$

where

C = yearly payment = \$100

P = price of bond = \$2000

Thus

$$i = \frac{\$100}{\$2000}$$

$$i = 0.05 = 5\%$$

Discount Bond The yield-to-maturity calculation for a discount bond is similar to that for the simple loan. Let us consider a discount bond such as a one-year U.S. Treasury bill, which pays a face value of \$1000 in one year's time. If the current purchase price of this bill is \$900, then equating this price to the present value of the \$1000 received in one year, using Equation 1, gives

$$\$900 = \frac{\$1000}{1 + i}$$

and solving for i,

$$(1 + i) \times \$900 = \$1000$$

$$\$900 + \$900i = \$1000$$

$$\$900i = \$1000 - \$900$$

$$i = \frac{\$1000 - \$900}{\$900} = 0.111 = 11.1\%$$

More generally, for any one-year discount bond, the yield to maturity can be written as

$$i = \frac{F - P}{P} \tag{6}$$

where F = face value of the discount bond

P = current price of the discount bond

In other words, the yield to maturity equals the increase in price over the year $F - P$ divided by the initial price P. In normal circumstances, investors earn positive returns from holding these securities and so they sell at a discount, meaning that the current price of the bond is below the face value. Therefore, $F - P$ should be positive, and the yield to maturity should be positive as well. However, this is not always the case, as recent extraordinary events in Japan indicate (see Box 1).

BOX 1: GLOBAL

Negative T-Bill Rates? Japan Shows the Way

We normally assume that interest rates must always be positive. Negative interest rates would imply that you are willing to pay more for a bond today than you will receive for it in the future (as our formula for yield to maturity on a discount bond demonstrates). Negative interest rates therefore seem like an impossibility because you would do better by holding cash that has the same value in the future as it does today.

The Japanese have demonstrated that this reasoning is not quite correct. In November 1998, interest rates on Japanese six-month Treasury bills became negative, yielding an interest rate of –0.004%, with investors paying more for the bills than their face value. This is an extremely unusual event because no other country in the world has seen negative interest rates during the past 50 years. How could this happen?

As we will see in Chapter 4, the weakness of the Japanese economy and a negative inflation rate have driven Japanese interest rates to low levels, but they can't explain the negative rates. The answer is that large investors find it more convenient to hold these six-month bills as a store of value rather than holding cash because the bills are denominated in larger amounts and can be stored electronically. These advantages of the Japanese T-bills result in some investors being willing to hold them, given their negative rates, even though in monetary terms the investors would be better off holding cash. Clearly, the convenience of T-bills only goes so far, and thus their interest rates can go only a little bit below zero.

An important feature of this equation is that it indicates that for a discount bond, the yield to maturity is negatively related to the current bond price. This is the same conclusion that we reached for a coupon bond. For example, Equation 6 shows that a rise in the bond price from \$900 to \$950 means that the bond will have a smaller increase in its price over its lifetime, and the yield to maturity falls from 11.1% to 5.3%. Similarly, a fall in the yield to maturity means that the price of the discount bond has risen.

Summary The concept of present value tells you that a dollar in the future is not as valuable to you as a dollar today because you can earn interest on this dollar. Specifically, a dollar received n years from now is worth only $\$1/(1 + i)^n$ today. The present value of a set of future payments on a debt instrument equals the sum of the present values of each of the future payments. The yield to maturity for an instrument is the interest rate that equates the present value of the future payments on that instrument to its value today. Because the procedure for calculating the yield to maturity is based on sound economic principles, this is the measure that financial economists think most accurately describes the interest rate.

Our calculations of the yield to maturity for a variety of bonds reveal the important fact that ***current bond prices and interest rates are negatively related: When the interest rate rises, the price of the bond falls, and vice versa.***

OTHER MEASURES OF INTEREST RATES

The yield to maturity is the most accurate measure of interest rates and is what financial economists mean when they use the term *interest rate.* Unless otherwise specified, the terms *interest rate* and *yield to maturity* are used synonymously in this book. However, because the yield to maturity is sometimes difficult to calculate, other, less accurate measures of interest rates have come into common use in bond markets. You will frequently encounter two of these measures, the *current yield* and the *yield on a discount basis,* when reading the newspaper, and it is important for you to understand what they mean and how they differ from the more accurate measure of interest rates, the yield to maturity.

Current Yield

The **current yield** is an approximation of the yield to maturity on coupon bonds that is often reported because in contrast to the yield to maturity, it is easily calculated. It is defined as the yearly coupon payment divided by the price of the security,

$$i_c = \frac{C}{P} \tag{7}$$

where i_c = current yield
P = price of the coupon bond
C = yearly coupon payment

This formula is identical to the formula in Equation 5, which describes the calculation of the yield to maturity for a perpetuity. Hence for a perpetuity, the current yield is an exact measure of the yield to maturity. When a coupon bond has a long term to maturity (say, 20 years or more), it is very much like a perpetuity, which pays coupon payments forever. Thus you would expect the current yield to be a rather close approximation of the yield to maturity for a long-term coupon bond, and you can safely use the current yield calculation instead of looking up the yield to maturity in a bond table. However, as the time to maturity of the coupon bond shortens (say, it becomes less than five years), it behaves less and less like a perpetuity and so the approximation afforded by the current yield becomes worse and worse.

We have also seen that when the bond price equals the par value of the bond, the yield to maturity is equal to the coupon rate (the coupon payment divided by the par value of the bond). Because the current yield equals the coupon payment divided by the bond price, the current yield is also equal to the coupon rate when the bond price is at par. This logic leads us to the conclusion that when the bond price is at par, the current yield equals the yield to maturity. This means that the nearer the bond price is to the bond's par value, the better the current yield will approximate the yield to maturity.

The current yield is negatively related to the price of the bond. In the case of our 10% coupon rate bond, when the price rises from $1000 to $1100, the current yield falls from 10% (= $100/$1000) to 9.09% (= $100/$1100). As Table 1 indicates, the yield to maturity is also negatively related to the price of the bond; when the price rises from $1000 to $1100, the yield to maturity falls from 10% to 8.48%. In this we see an important fact: The current yield and the yield to maturity always move together; a rise in the current yield always signals that the yield to maturity has also risen.

EXAMPLE 6: Current Yield

What is the current yield for a bond that has a par value of $1000 and a coupon interest rate of 10.95%? The current market price for the bond is $921.01.

Solution

The current yield is 11.89%.

$$i_c = \frac{C}{P}$$

where

C = yearly payment $= 0.1095 \times \$1000 = \$109.50$

P = price of the bond $= \$921.01$

Thus

$$i_c = \frac{\$109.50}{\$921.01} = 0.1189 = 11.89\%$$

The general characteristics of the current yield (the yearly coupon payment divided by the bond price) can be summarized as follows: The current yield better approximates the yield to maturity when the bond's price is nearer to the bond's par value and the maturity of the bond is longer. It becomes a worse approximation when the bond's price is further from the bond's par value and the bond's maturity is shorter. Regardless of whether the current yield is a good approximation of the yield to maturity, a change in the current yield *always* signals a change in the same direction of the yield to maturity.

Yield on a Discount Basis

Before the advent of calculators and computers, dealers in U.S. Treasury bills found it difficult to calculate interest rates as a yield to maturity. Instead, they quoted the interest rate on bills as a **yield on a discount basis** (or **discount yield**), and they still do so today. Formally, the yield on a discount basis is defined by the following formula:

$$i_{db} = \frac{F - P}{F} \times \frac{360}{\text{days to maturity}} \tag{8}$$

where i_{db} = yield on a discount basis
F = face value of the discount bond
P = purchase price of the discount bond

This method for calculating interest rates has two peculiarities. First, it uses the percentage gain on the face value of the bill $(F - P)/F$ rather than the percentage gain on the purchase price of the bill $(F - P)/P$ used in calculating the yield to maturity. Second, it puts the yield on an annual basis by taking the year to be 360 days long rather than 365 days.

Because of these peculiarities, the discount yield understates the interest rate on bills as measured by the yield to maturity. On our one-year bill, which is selling for \$900 and has a face value of \$1000, the yield on a discount basis would be as follows:

$$i_{db} = \frac{\$1000 - \$900}{\$1000} \times \frac{360}{365} = 0.099 = 9.9\%$$

whereas the yield to maturity for this bill, which we calculated before, is 11.1%. The discount yield understates the yield to maturity by a factor of over 10%. A little more than 1% can be attributed to the understatement of the length of the year: When the bill has one year to maturity, the second term on the right-hand side of the formula is 360/365 = 0.986 rather than 1.0, as it should be.

The more serious source of the understatement, however, is the use of the percentage gain on the face value rather than on the purchase price. Because, by definition, the purchase price of a discount bond is always less than the face value, the percentage gain on the face value is necessarily smaller than the percentage gain on the purchase price. The greater the difference between the purchase price and the face value of the discount bond, the more the discount yield understates the yield to maturity. Because the difference between the purchase price and the face value gets larger as maturity gets longer, we can draw the following conclusion about the relationship of the yield on a discount basis to the yield to maturity: The yield on a discount basis always understates the yield to maturity, and this understatement becomes more severe the longer the maturity of the discount bond.

Another important feature of the discount yield is that, like the yield to maturity, it is negatively related to the price of the bond. For example, when the price of the bond rises from $900 to $950, the formula indicates that the yield on a discount basis declines from 9.9% to 4.9%. At the same time, the yield to maturity declines from 11.1% to 5.3%. Here we see another important factor about the relationship of yield on a discount basis to yield to maturity: They always move together; that is, a rise in the discount yield always means that the yield to maturity has risen, and a decline in the discount yield means that the yield to maturity has declined as well.

EXAMPLE 7: Yield on a Discount Basis

What is the discount yield (or yield on a discount basis) for a one-year bond that was purchased for $875 and has a face value of $1000?

Solution

The discount yield (or yield on a discount basis) is 12.33%.

$$i_{db} = \frac{F - P}{F} \times \frac{360}{\text{days to maturity}}$$

where

F = face value of the bond = \$1000

P = purchase price of the bond = \$875

days to maturity = one year = 365 days

Thus

$$i_{db} = \frac{\$1000 - \$875}{\$1000} \times \frac{360}{365}$$

$$i_{db} = 0.1250 \times 0.9863 = 0.1233 = 12.33\%$$

The characteristics of the yield on a discount basis can be summarized as follows: Yield on a discount basis understates the more accurate measure of the interest rate, the yield to maturity; and the longer the maturity of the discount bond, the greater this understatement becomes. Even though the discount yield is a somewhat misleading measure of the interest rates, however, a change in the discount yield always indicates a change in the same direction for the yield to maturity.

Application The Bond Page

READING THE *WALL STREET JOURNAL*

Now that we understand the different interest-rate definitions, let's apply our knowledge and take a look at what kind of information appears on the bond page of a typical newspaper, in this case the *Wall Street Journal*. The "Following the Financial News" boxes contain the *Journal*'s listings for three different types of bonds on Wednesday, January 2, 2002. The first box contains the information on U.S. Treasury bonds and notes. Both are coupon bonds, the only difference being their time to maturity from when they were originally issued: Notes have a time to maturity of less than ten years; bonds have a time to maturity of more than ten years.

The information found in the "Rate" and "Maturity" columns identifies the bond by coupon rate and maturity date. For example, T-bond 1 has a coupon rate of $6\frac{1}{4}\%$, indicating that it pays out \$62.50 per year on a \$1000 face value bond and matures in January 2002. In bond market parlance, it is referred to as the Treasury's $6\frac{1}{4}$s of 2002. The next three columns tell us about the bond's price. By convention, all prices in the bond market are quoted per \$100 of face value. Furthermore, the numbers after the colon represent thirty-seconds. In the case of T-bond 1, the first price of 100:11 represents $100\frac{11}{32} = 100.343$, or an actual price of \$1003.43 for a \$1000 face value bond. The bid price tells you what price you will receive if you sell the bond, and the asked price tells you what you must pay for the bond. (You might want to think of the bid price as the "wholesale" price and the asked price as the "retail" price.) The "Chg." column indicates how much the bid price has changed in 32nds (in this case, $-\frac{1}{32}$) from the previous trading day.

Notice that for all the bonds and notes, the asked price is more than the bid price. Can you guess why this is so? The difference between the two (the *spread*) provides the bond dealer who trades these securities with a profit. For T-bond 1, the dealer who buys it at 100:11 and sells it for 100:12 makes a profit of $\frac{1}{32}$. This profit is what enables the dealer to make a living and provide the service of allowing you to buy and sell bonds at will.

The "Ask Yld." column provides the yield to maturity, which is 1.45% for T-bond 1. It is calculated with the method described earlier in this chapter using the asked price as the price of the bond. The asked price is used in the calculation because the yield to maturity is most relevant to a person who is going to buy and hold the security and thus earn the yield. The person selling the security is not going to be holding it and hence is less concerned with the yield.

The figure for the current yield is not usually included in the newspaper's quotations for Treasury securities, but it has been added in the box to give you some real-world examples of how well the current yield approximates the yield to maturity. Our previous discussion provided us with some rules for deciding when the current yield is likely to be a good approximation and when it is not.

T-bonds 3 and 4 mature in more than 20 years, meaning that their characteristics are like those of a perpetuity. The current yields should then be a good

FOLLOWING THE FINANCIAL NEWS
Treasury Bonds and Notes

Bond prices and interest rates are published daily. In the *Wall Street Journal,* the prices and yields on Treasury bonds and notes can be found in the "Treas./Govt. Issues" section of the paper, under the general heading of "Treasury Bonds, Notes & Bills."

GOVT. BOND & NOTES

	Rate	Maturity Mo/Yr	Bid	Asked	Chg.	Ask Yld.	
T-bond 1	$6\frac{1}{4}$	Jan 02n	100:11	100:12	— 1	1.45	Current Yield = 6.23%
	$6\frac{3}{8}$	Jan 02n	100:11	100:12	— 1	1.57	
	$14\frac{1}{4}$	Feb 02	101:15	101:16	— 2	1.47	
T-bond 2	$6\frac{1}{4}$	Feb 02n	100:22	100:23	— 1	1.54	Current Yield = 6.21%
T-bond 3	8	Nov 21	126:17	126:18	+ 35	5.74	Current Yield = 6.32%
	$7\frac{1}{4}$	Aug 22	117:23	117:24	+ 33	5.77	
	$7\frac{5}{8}$	Nov 22	122:14	122:15	+ 34	5.76	
T-bond 4	$7\frac{1}{8}$	Feb 23	116:14	116:15	+ 34	5.77	Current Yield = 6.12%

Monday, Dec. 31, 2001

Representative Over-the-Counter quotation based on transactions of $1 million or more.

Treasury bond, note and bill quotes are as of mid-afternoon. Colons in bid-and-asked quotes represent 32nds; 101:01 means 101 1/32. Net changes in 32nds. n-Treasury note. i-inflation-indexed issue. Treasury bill quotes in hundredths, quoted in terms of a rate of discount. Days to maturity calculated from settlement date. All yields are to maturity and based on the asked quote. Latest 13-week and 26-week bills are boldfaced. For bonds callable prior to maturity, yields are computed to the earliest call date for issues quoted above par and to the maturity date for issues quoted below par.

Source:eSpeed/Cantor Fitzgerald. *-when issued.

U.S. Treasury strips as of 2 p.m. Eastern time, also based on transactions of $1 million or more. Colons in bid-and-asked quotes represent 32nds; 99:01 means 99 1/32. Net changes in 32nds. Yields calculated on the asked quotation. ci-stripped coupon interest. bp-Treasury bond, stripped principal. np-Treasury note, stripped principal. For bonds callable prior to maturity, yields are computed to the earliest call date for issues quoted above par and to the maturity date for issues below par.

Source: Bear, Stearns & Co. via Street Software Technology Inc.

Source: Wall Street Journal, January 2, 2002, p. C13. Republished by permission of Dow Jones, Inc. via Copyright Clearance Center, Inc.

approximation of the yields to maturity, and they are: The current yields are within six-tenths of a percentage point of the values for the yields to maturity. This approximation is reasonable even for T-bond 3, which has a price over 25% above its face value.

Now let's take a look at T-bonds 1 and 2, which have a much shorter time to maturity. The prices of T-bond 1 and T-bond 2 differ by less than 1% from the par value, and look how poor an approximation the current yield is for the yield to maturity; it overstates the yield to maturity by almost 5 percentage points. This bears out what we learned earlier about the current yield: It can be a very misleading guide to the value of the yield to maturity for a short-term bond if the bond price is not extremely close to par.

Two other categories of bonds are reported much like the Treasury bonds and notes in the newspaper. Government agency and miscellaneous securities include securities issued by U.S. government agencies such as Ginnie Mae, which makes loans to savings and loan institutions, and international agencies such as the World Bank. Tax-exempt bonds are the other category reported in a manner similar to Treasury bonds and notes, except that yield-to-maturity calcula-

FOLLOWING THE FINANCIAL NEWS

Treasury Bills

In the *Wall Street Journal,* the yields on Treasury bills can also be found in the "Treas./Govt. Issues" section of the paper, under the general heading of "Treasury Bonds, Notes & Bills."

TREASURY BILLS

Maturity	Days to Mat.	Bid	Asked	Chg.	Ask Yld.
Jan 03 '02	1	1.68	1.67	–0.01	1.69
Jan 10 '02	8	1.67	1.66	–0.01	1.68
Jan 17 '02	15	1.67	1.66	....	1.68
Jan 24 '02	22	1.69	1.68	–0.01	1.71
Jan 31 '02	29	1.63	1.62	+0.01	1.64
Feb 07 '02	36	1.67	1.66	+0.01	1.69
Feb 14 '02	43	1.70	1.69	+0.01	1.72
Feb 21 '02	50	1.70	1.69	+0.01	1.72
Feb 28 '02	57	1.70	1.69	+0.01	1.72
Mar 07 '02	64	1.71	1.70	....	1.73
Mar 14 '02	71	1.70	1.69	....	1.72
Mar 21 '02	78	1.69	1.68	....	1.71
Mar 28 '02	**85**	**1.69**	**1.68**	**....**	**1.71**

Maturity	Days to Mat.	Bid	Asked	Chg.	Ask Yld.
Apr 04 '02	92	1.70	1.69	+0.01	1.72
Apr 11 '02	99	1.70	1.69	+0.01	1.72
Apr 18 '02	106	1.70	1.69	....	1.72
Apr 25 '02	113	1.70	1.69	+0.01	1.72
May 02 '02	120	1.71	1.70	....	1.73
May 09 '02	127	1.73	1.72	+0.01	1.75
May 16 '02	134	1.74	1.73	....	1.77
May 23 '02	141	1.75	1.74	....	1.78
May 30 '02	148	1.76	1.75	+0.01	1.79
Jun 13 '02	162	1.79	1.78	+0.01	1.82
Jun 13 '02	162	1.79	1.78	+0.01	1.82
Jun 20 '02	169	1.79	1.78	+0.01	1.82
Jun 27 '02	**176**	**1.79**	**1.78**	**+0.01**	**1.82**

Source: Wall Street Journal, January 2, 2002, p. C13. Republished by permission of Dow Jones, Inc. via Copyright Clearance Center, Inc.

tions are not usually provided. Tax-exempt bonds include bonds issued by local government and public authorities whose interest payments are exempt from federal income taxes.

The second "Following the Financial News" box quotes yields on U.S. Treasury bills, which, as we have seen, are discount bonds. Since there is no coupon, these securities are identified solely by their maturity dates, which you can see in the first column. The next column, "Days to Mat.," provides the number of days to maturity of the bill. Dealers in these markets always refer to prices by quoting the yield on a discount basis. The "Bid" column gives the discount yield for people selling the bills to dealers, and the "Asked" column gives the discount yield for people buying the bills from dealers. As with bonds and notes, the dealers' profits are made by the asked price being higher than the bid price, leading to the asked discount yield being lower than the bid discount yield.

The "Chg." column indicates how much the asked discount yield changed from the previous day. When financial analysts talk about changes in the yield, they frequently describe the changes in terms of **basis points,** which are hundredths of a percentage point. For example, a financial analyst would describe the –0.01 change in the asked discount yield for the January 3, 2002, T-bill by saying that it had fallen by 1 basis point.

As we learned earlier, the yield on a discount basis understates the yield to maturity, which is reported in the column headed "Ask Yld." This is evident from a comparison of the "Ask Yld." and "Asked" columns. As we would also expect from our discussion of the calculation of yields on a discount basis, the understatement grows as the maturity of the bill lengthens.

FOLLOWING THE FINANCIAL NEWS
Corporate Bonds

In the *Wall Street Journal,* the prices and yields on corporate bonds are found in the "NYSE\AMEX Bonds" section of the paper.

CORPORATION BONDS

Volume, $1,932,000

	Bonds	Cur Yld	Vol	Close	Net Chg.	
Bond 1	ATT 7 3/4 07	7.4	10	104 1/4	– 3/4	Yield to Maturity = 6.72%
	ATT 6s 09	6.3	46	95 1/2	– 1/8	
	ATT 8 1/8 22	8.1	15	100 1/8	....	
	ATT 6 1/2 29	7.6	10	85 3/4	– 1 1/4	
Bond 2	ATT 8 5/8 31	8.5	20	102	– 5/8	Yield to Maturity = 8.44%

Source: Wall Street Journal, December 26, 2001, p. C16. Republished by permission of Dow Jones, Inc. via Copyright Clearance Center, Inc.

The third "Following the Financial News" box has quotations for corporate bonds traded on the New York Stock Exchange. Corporate bonds traded on the American Stock Exchange are reported in like manner. The first column identifies the bond by indicating the corporation that issued it. The bonds we are looking at have all been issued by American Telephone and Telegraph (AT&T). The next column tells the coupon rate and the maturity date ($7\frac{3}{4}$ and 2007 for Bond 1). The "Cur. Yld." column reports the current yield (7.4), and "Vol." gives the volume of trading in that bond (10 bonds of $1000 face value traded that day). The "Close" price is the last traded price that day per $100 of face value. The price of $104\frac{1}{4}$ represents $1042.50 for a $1000 face value bond. The "Net Chg." is the change in the closing price from the previous trading day.

The yield to maturity is also given for two bonds. This information is not usually provided in the newspaper, but it is included here because it shows how misleading the current yield can be for a bond with a short maturity such as the $7\frac{3}{4}$s of 2007. The current yield of 7.4% is a misleading measure of the interest rate because the yield to maturity is actually 6.72%. By contrast, for the $8\frac{5}{8}$s of 2031, with over 30 years to maturity, the current yield and the yield to maturity are almost exactly equal.

THE DISTINCTION BETWEEN REAL AND NOMINAL INTEREST RATES

At www.martincapital.com/charts.htm, click on "Interest Rates and Yields" and then "Nominal versus Real Market Rates" to view 30 years of nominal interest rates compared to real rates for the 30-year T-Bond and 90-day T-Bill.

So far in our discussion of interest rates, we have ignored the effects of inflation on the cost of borrowing. What we have up to now been calling the interest rate makes no allowance for inflation, and it is more precisely referred to as the **nominal interest rate,** which is to distinguish it from the **real interest rate,** the interest rate that is adjusted by subtracting expected changes in the price level so that it more accurately reflects the true cost of borrowing.[4] The real interest rate is more accurately defined by the *Fisher equation,* named for Irving Fisher, one of the great monetary economists of the twentieth century. The Fisher equa-

[4]The real interest rate defined in the text is more precisely referred to as the *ex ante real interest rate* because it is adjusted for *expected* changes in the price level. This is the real interest rate that is most important to economic decisions, and typically it is what financial economists mean when they make reference to the "real" interest rate. The interest rate that is adjusted for *actual* changes in the price level is called the *ex post real interest rate.* It describes how well a lender has done in real terms *after the fact.*

tion states that the nominal interest rate i equals the real interest rate i_r plus the expected rate of inflation π^e.[5]

$$i = i_r + \pi^e \tag{9}$$

Rearranging terms, we find that the real interest rate equals the nominal interest rate minus the expected inflation rate:

$$i_r = i - \pi^e \tag{10}$$

To see why this definition makes sense, let us first consider a situation in which you have made a one-year simple loan with a 5% interest rate (i = 5%) and you expect the price level to rise by 3% over the course of the year (π^e = 3%). As a result of making the loan, at the end of the year you will have 2% more in **real terms,** that is, in terms of real goods and services you can buy.

In this case, the interest rate you have earned in terms of real goods and services is 2%; that is,

$$i_r = 5\% - 3\% = 2\%$$

as indicated by the Fisher definition.

EXAMPLE 8: Real and Nominal Interest Rates

What is the real interest rate if the nominal interest rate is 8% and the expected inflation rate is 10% over the course of a year?

Solution

The real interest rate is –2%. Although you will be receiving 8% more dollars at the end of the year, you will be paying 10% more for goods. The result is that you will be able to buy 2% fewer goods at the end of the year, and you are 2% worse off in real terms.

$$i_r = i - \pi^e$$

where

i = nominal interest rate = 0.08

π^e = expected inflation rate = 0.10

Thus

$$i_r = 0.08 - 0.10 = -0.02 = -2\%$$

As a lender, you are clearly less eager to make a loan in Example 8 because in terms of real goods and services you have actually earned a negative interest

[5]A more precise formulation of the Fisher equation is

$$i = i_r + \pi^e + (i_r \times \pi^e)$$

because

$$1 + i = (1 + i_r)(1 + \pi^e) = 1 + i_r + \pi^e + (i_r \times \pi^e)$$

and subtracting 1 from both sides gives us the first equation. For small values of i_r and π^e, the term $i_r \times \pi^e$ is so small that we ignore it, as in the text.

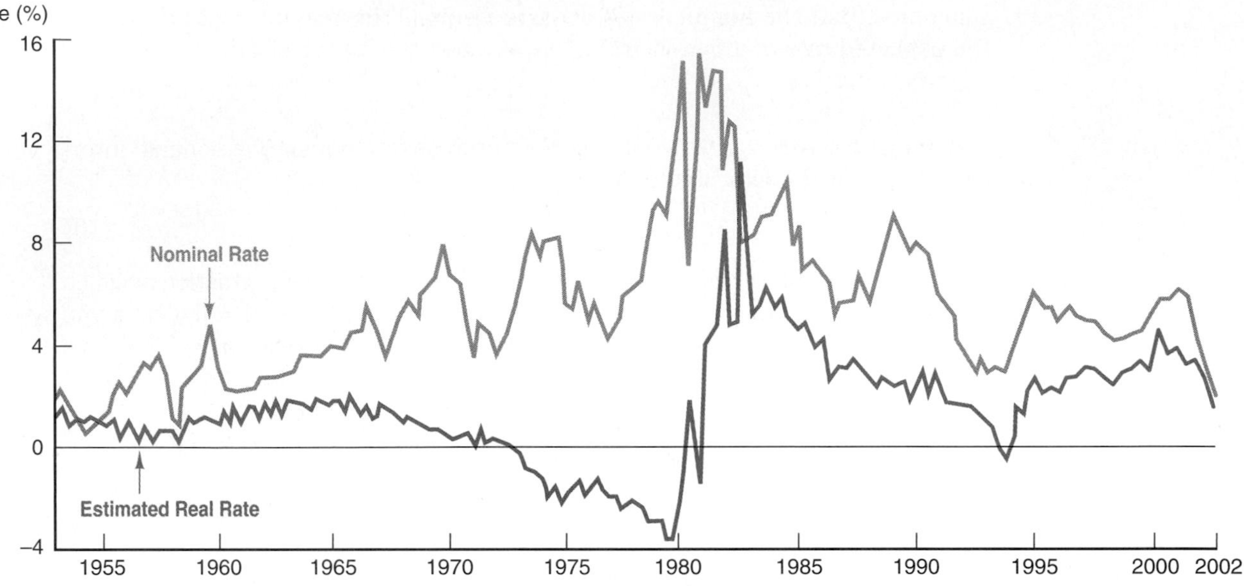

FIGURE 3 Real and Nominal Interest Rates (Three-Month Treasury Bill), 1953–2001

Sources: Nominal rates from the Citibase databank. The real rate is constructed using the procedure outlined in Frederic S. Mishkin, "The Real Interest Rate: An Empirical Investigation," *Carnegie–Rochester Conference Series on Public Policy* 15 (1981): 151–200. This involves estimating expected inflation as a function of past interest rates, inflation, and time trends and then subtracting the expected inflation measure from the nominal interest rate.

rate of 2%. By contrast, as the borrower, you fare quite well because at the end of the year, the amounts you will have to pay back will be worth 2% less in terms of goods and services—you as the borrower will be ahead by 2% in real terms. ***When the real interest rate is low, there are greater incentives to borrow and fewer incentives to lend.***

The distinction between real and nominal interest rates is important because the real interest rate, which reflects the real cost of borrowing, is likely to be a better indicator of the incentives to borrow and lend. It appears to be a better guide to how people will be affected by what is happening in credit markets. Figure 3, which presents estimates from 1953 to 2001 of the real and nominal interest rates on three-month U.S. Treasury bills, shows us that nominal and real rates often do not move together. (This is also true for nominal and real interest rates in the rest of the world.) In particular, when nominal rates in the United States were high in the 1970s, real rates were actually extremely low, often negative. By the standard of nominal interest rates, you would have thought that credit market conditions were tight in this period because it was expensive to borrow. However, the estimates of the real rates indicate that you would have been mistaken. In real terms, the cost of borrowing was actually quite low.[6]

Until recently, real interest rates in the United States were not observable, because only nominal rates were reported. This all changed in January 1997, when

[6]Because most interest income in the United States is subject to federal income taxes, the true earnings in real terms from holding a debt instrument are not reflected by the real interest rate defined by the Fisher equation but rather by the *after-tax real interest rate,* which equals the nominal interest rate *after income tax payments have been subtracted,* minus the expected inflation rate. For a person facing a 30% tax rate, the after-tax interest rate earned on a bond yielding 10% is only 7% because 30% of the interest income must be paid to the Internal Revenue Service. Thus the after-tax real interest rate on this bond when expected inflation is 20% equals –13% (= 7% – 20%). More generally, the after-tax real interest rate can be expressed as

$$i(1 - \tau) - \pi^e$$

BOX 2

With TIPS, Real Interest Rates Have Become Observable in the United States

When the U.S. Treasury decided to issue TIPS (Treasury Inflation Protection Securities), a version of indexed coupon bonds, it was somewhat late in the game. Other countries such as the United Kingdom, Canada, Australia, and Sweden had already beaten the United States to the punch. (In September 1998, the U.S. Treasury also began issuing the Series I savings bond, which provides inflation protection for small investors.)

These indexed securities have successfully acquired a niche in the bond market, enabling governments to raise more funds. In addition, because their interest and principal payments are adjusted for changes in the price level, the interest rate on these bonds provides a direct measure of a real interest rate. These indexed bonds are very useful to policymakers, especially monetary policymakers, because by subtracting their interest rate from a nominal interest rate, they generate more insight into expected inflation, a valuable piece of information. For example, on January 26, 1999, the interest rate on the ten-year Treasury bond was 5.1%, while that on the ten-year TIPS was 3.8%. Thus the implied expected inflation rate for the next ten years, derived from the difference between these two rates, was 1.3%. The private sector finds the information provided by TIPS very useful: Many commercial and investment banks routinely publish the expected U.S. inflation rates derived from these bonds.

the U.S. Treasury began to issue **indexed bonds,** bonds whose interest and principal payments are adjusted for changes in the price level (see Box 2).

THE DISTINCTION BETWEEN INTEREST RATES AND RETURNS

Many people think that the interest rate on a bond tells them all they need to know about how well off they are as a result of owning it. If Irving the Investor thinks he is better off when he owns a long-term bond yielding a 10% interest rate and the interest rate rises to 20%, he will have a rude awakening: As we will shortly see, Irving has lost his shirt! How well a person does by holding a bond or any other security over a particular time period is accurately measured by the **return** or, in more precise terminology, the **rate of return.** For any security, the rate of return is defined as the payments to the owner plus the change in its value, expressed as a fraction of its purchase price. To make this definition clearer, let us see what the return would look like for a \$1000-face-value coupon bond with a coupon rate of 10% that is bought for \$1000, held for one year, and then sold for \$1200. The payments to the owner are the yearly coupon payments of \$100, and the change in its value is \$1200 − \$1000 = \$200. Adding these together and expressing them as a fraction of the purchase price of \$1000 gives us the one-year holding-period return for this bond:

$$\frac{\$100 + \$200}{\$1000} = \frac{\$300}{\$1000} = 0.30 = 30\%$$

where τ = the income tax rate.

This formula for the after-tax real interest rate also provides a better measure of the effective cost of borrowing for many corporations and individuals in the United States because in calculating income taxes, they can deduct interest payments on loans from their income. Thus if you face a 30% tax rate and take out a mortgage loan with a 10% interest rate, you are able to deduct the 10% interest payment and thus lower your taxes by 30% of this amount. Your after-tax nominal cost of borrowing is then 7% (10% minus 30% of the 10% interest payment), and when the expected inflation rate is 20%, the effective cost of borrowing in real terms is again −13% (= 7% − 20%).

As the example (and the formula) indicates, after-tax real interest rates are always below the real interest rate defined by the Fisher equation. For a further discussion of measures of after-tax real interest rates, see Frederic S. Mishkin, "The Real Interest Rate: An Empirical Investigation," *Carnegie-Rochester Conference Series on Public Policy* 15 (1981): 151–200.

You may have noticed something quite surprising about the return that we have just calculated: It equals 30%, yet as Table 1 indicates, initially the yield to maturity was only 10%. This demonstrates that ***the return on a bond will not necessarily equal the interest rate on that bond.*** We now see that the distinction between interest rate and return can be important, although for many securities the two may be closely related.

Study Guide The concept of return discussed here is extremely important because it is used continually throughout the book. Make sure that you understand how a return is calculated and why it can differ from the interest rate. This understanding will make the material presented later in the book easier to follow.

More generally, the return on a bond held from time t to time $t + 1$ can be written as

$$R = \frac{C + P_{t+1} - P_t}{P_t} \tag{11}$$

where
R = return from holding the bond from time t to time $t + 1$
P_t = price of the bond at time t
P_{t+1} = price of the bond at time $t + 1$
C = coupon payment

EXAMPLE 9: Rate of Return

What would the rate of return be on a bond bought for $1000 and sold one year later for $800? The bond has a face value of $1000, and a coupon rate of 8%.

Solution

The rate of return on the bond for holding if one year is –12%.

$$R = \frac{C + P_{t+1} - P_t}{P_t}$$

where

C = coupon payment = $\$1000 \times 0.08$ = \$80
P_{t+1} = price of the bond one year later = \$800
P_t = price of the bond today = \$1000

Thus

$$R = \frac{\$80 + (\$800 - \$1000)}{\$1000} = \frac{-120}{1000} = -0.12 = -12\%$$

A convenient way to rewrite the return formula in Equation 11 is to recognize that it can be split into two separate terms:

$$R = \frac{C}{P_t} + \frac{P_{t+1} - P_t}{P_t}$$

The first term is the current yield i_c (the coupon payment over the purchase price):

$$\frac{C}{P_t} = i_c$$

The second term is the **rate of capital gain,** or the change in the bond's price relative to the initial purchase price:

$$\frac{P_{t+1} - P_t}{P_t} = g$$

where g = rate of capital gain. Equation 11 can then be rewritten as

$$R = i_c + g \tag{12}$$

which shows that the return on a bond is the current yield i_c plus the rate of capital gain g. This rewritten formula illustrates the point we just discovered. Even for a bond for which the current yield i_c is an accurate measure of the yield to maturity, the return can differ substantially from the interest rate. Returns will differ from the interest rate especially if there are sizable fluctuations in the price of the bond that produce substantial capital gains or losses.

To explore this point even further, let's look at what happens to the returns on bonds of different maturities when interest rates rise. Table 2 calculates the one-year return on several 10% coupon rate bonds all purchased at par when interest rates on all these bonds rise from 10% to 20%. Several key findings in this table are generally true of all bonds:

- The only bond whose return equals the initial yield to maturity is one whose time to maturity is the same as the holding period (see the last bond in Table 2).
- A rise in interest rates is associated with a fall in bond prices, resulting in capital losses on bonds whose terms to maturity are longer than the holding period.
- The more distant a bond's maturity, the greater the size of the price change associated with an interest-rate change.
- The more distant a bond's maturity, the lower the rate of return that occurs as a result of the increase in the interest rate.

TABLE 2 One-Year Returns on Different-Maturity 10% Coupon Rate Bonds When Interest Rates Rise from 10% to 20%

(1)	(2)	(3)	(4)	(5)	(6)
Years to Maturity When Bond Is Purchased	Initial Current Yield (%)	Initial Price ($)	Price Next Year* ($)	Rate of Capital Gain (%)	Rate of Return (2 + 5) (%)
30	10	1000	503	−49.7	−39.7
20	10	1000	516	−48.4	−38.4
10	10	1000	597	−40.3	−30.3
5	10	1000	741	−25.9	−15.9
2	10	1000	917	− 8.3	+ 1.7
1	10	1000	1000	0.0	+10.0

*Calculated using Equation 3.

- Even though a bond has a substantial initial interest rate, its return can turn out to be negative if interest rates rise.

At first it frequently puzzles students that a rise in interest rates can mean that a bond has been a poor investment (as it puzzles poor Irving the Investor). The trick to understanding this is to recognize that a rise in the interest rate means that the price of a bond has fallen. A rise in interest rates therefore means that a capital loss has occurred, and if this loss is large enough, the bond can be a poor investment indeed. For example, we see in Table 2 that the bond that has 30 years to maturity when purchased has a capital loss of 49.7% when the interest rate rises from 10% to 20%. This loss is so large that it exceeds the current yield of 10%, resulting in a negative return (loss) of –39.7%. If Irving does not sell the bond, the capital loss is often referred to as a "paper loss." This is a loss nonetheless because if he had not bought this bond and had instead put his money in the bank, he would now be able to buy more bonds at their lower price than he presently owns.

Maturity and the Volatility of Bond Returns: Interest-Rate Risk

The finding that the prices of longer-maturity bonds respond more dramatically to changes in interest rates helps explain an important fact about the behavior of bond markets: ***Prices and returns for long-term bonds are more volatile than those for shorter-term bonds.*** Price changes of +20% and –20% within a year, with corresponding variations in returns, are common for bonds more than 20 years away from maturity.

We now see that changes in interest rates make investments in long-term bonds quite risky. Indeed, the riskiness of an asset's return that results from interest-rate changes is so important that it has been given a special name, **interest-rate risk.** Dealing with interest-rate risk is a major concern of managers of financial institutions, as we will see in later chapters (see also Box 3).

Although long-term debt instruments have substantial interest-rate risk, short-term debt instruments do not. Indeed, bonds with a maturity that is as short as the holding period have no interest-rate risk.[7] We see this for the coupon bond at the bottom of Table 2, which has no uncertainty about the rate of return because it equals the yield to maturity, which is known at the time the bond is purchased. The key to understanding why there is no interest-rate risk for *any* bond whose time to maturity matches the holding period is to recognize that (in this case) the price at the end of the holding period is already fixed at the face value. The change in interest rates can then have no effect on the price at the end of the holding period for these bonds, and the return will therefore be equal to the yield to maturity known at the time the bond is purchased.

---

[7]The statement that there is no interest-rate risk for any bond whose time to maturity matches the holding period is literally true only for discount bonds and zero-coupon bonds that make no intermediate cash payments before the holding period is over. A coupon bond that makes an intermediate cash payment before the holding period is over requires that this payment be reinvested at some future date. Because the interest rate at which this payment can be reinvested is uncertain, there is some uncertainty about the return on this coupon bond even when the time to maturity equals the holding period. However, the riskiness of the return on a coupon bond from reinvesting the coupon payments is typically quite small, and so the basic point that a coupon bond with a time to maturity equaling the holding period has very little risk still holds true.

BOX 3

Helping Investors Select Desired Interest-Rate Risk

Because many investors want to know how much interest-rate risk they are exposed to, some mutual fund companies try to educate investors about the perils of interest-rate risk, as well as to offer investment alternatives that match their investors' preferences.

Vanguard Group, for example, offers eight separate high-grade bond mutual funds. In its prospectus, Vanguard separates the funds by the average maturity of the bonds they hold and demonstrates the effect of interest-rate changes by computing the percentage change in bond value resulting from a 1% increase and decrease in interest rates. Three of the funds invest in bonds with average maturities of one to three years, which Vanguard rates as having the lowest interest-rate risk. Three other funds hold bonds with average maturities of five and ten years, which Vanguard rates as having medium interest-rate risk. Two funds hold long-term bonds with maturities of 15 to 30 years, which Vanguard rates as having high interest-rate risk.

By providing this information, Vanguard hopes to increase its market share in the sales of bond funds. Not surprisingly, Vanguard is one of the most successful mutual fund companies in the business.

Reinvestment Risk

Up to now, we have been assuming that all holding periods are short and equal to the maturity on short-term bonds and are thus not subject to interest-rate risk. However, if an investor's holding period is longer than the term to maturity of the bond, the investor is exposed to a type of interest-rate risk called **reinvestment risk.** Reinvestment risk occurs because the proceeds from the short-term bond need to be reinvested at a future interest rate that is uncertain.

To understand reinvestment risk, suppose that Irving the Investor has a holding period of two years and decides to purchase a $1000 one-year bond at face value and will then purchase another one at the end of the first year. If the initial interest rate is 10%, Irving will have $1100 at the end of the year. If the interest rate on one-year bonds rises to 20% at the end of the year, as in Table 2, Irving will find that buying $1100 worth of another one-year bond will leave him at the end of the second year with $1100 × (1 + 0.20) = $1320. Thus Irving's two-year return will be ($1320 − $1000)/$1000 = 0.32 = 32%, which equals 14.9% at an annual rate. In this case, Irving has earned more by buying the one-year bonds than if he had initially purchased the two-year bond with an interest rate of 10%. Thus when Irving has a holding period that is longer than the term to maturity of the bonds he purchases, he benefits from a rise in interest rates. Conversely, if interest rates on one-year bonds fall to 5% at the end of the year, Irving will have only $1155 at the end of two years: $1100 × (1 + 0.05). Thus his two-year return will be ($1155 − $1000)/$1000 = 0.155 = 15.5%, which is 7.2% at an annual rate. With a holding period greater than the term to maturity of the bond, Irving now loses from a fall in interest rates.

We have thus seen that when the holding period is longer than the term to maturity of a bond, the return is uncertain because the future interest rate when reinvestment occurs is also uncertain—in short, there is reinvestment risk. We also see that if the holding period is longer than the term to maturity of the bond, the investor benefits from a rise in interest rates and is hurt by a fall in interest rates.

Summary

The return on a bond, which tells you how good an investment it has been over the holding period, is equal to the yield to maturity in only one special case: when the holding period and the maturity of the bond are identical. Bonds whose term to maturity is longer than the holding period are subject to interest-rate risk: Changes in interest rates lead to capital gains and losses that produce substantial differences between the return and the yield to maturity known at the time the bond is purchased. Interest-rate risk is especially important for long-term bonds, where the capital gains and losses can be substantial. This is why long-term bonds are not considered to be safe assets with a sure return over short holding periods. Bonds whose term to maturity is shorter than the holding period are also subject to reinvestment risk. Reinvestment risk occurs because the proceeds from the short-term bond need to be reinvested at a future interest rate that is uncertain.

Application

Should Retirees Invest in "Gilt-Edged" Long-Term Bonds?

A common bit of conventional wisdom is that retirees should invest their money in "gilt-edged" securities like long-term U.S Treasury bonds because this will provide them with a safe return. Is this good advice given today's financial markets?

The concept of interest-rate risk indicates that the answer is no because long-term bonds have very volatile returns. To see this, let's examine the returns on a long-term Treasury bond such as the Treasury $11\frac{1}{4}$s of 2015 (a coupon bond with a coupon rate of $11\frac{1}{4}\%$, maturing in 2015). Table 3 provides the prices and one-year returns for this bond from 1990 to 2001. (To make sure you understand the concepts of a return and a coupon bond, you might try to calculate these returns yourself using the formula in Equation 11.)

As you can see, there have been big swings in the returns on this supposedly safe investment, with low returns and even losses occurring in some years. If retirees at times need to sell bonds to pay bills so that they might hold bonds for periods only as short as a year, they may find themselves in financial difficulties when the bonds decline in value. Conclusion: True safety lies only in short-term bonds. Retirees beware!

TABLE 3 Prices and One-Year Returns on U.S. Treasury $11^1/_4$ s of 2015, 1990–2001

Year	Price at End of Year	Return (%)
1990	$129\ ^{24}/_{32}$	+ 5.4
1991	$141\ ^{27}/_{32}$	+ 18.0
1992	$141\ ^{14}/_{32}$	+ 7.6
1993	$154\ ^{6}/_{32}$	+ 17.0
1994	$132\ ^{3}/_{32}$	− 7.0
1995	160	+ 29.6
1996	$149\ ^{12}/_{32}$	+ 0.4
1997	$156\ ^{4}/_{32}$	+ 12.1
1998	$156\ ^{8}/_{32}$	+ 7.3
1999	$141\ ^{4}/_{32}$	− 2.5
2000	$156\ ^{14}/_{32}$	+ 18.8
2001	$153\ ^{3}/_{32}$	+ 5.1

THE PRACTICING FINANCIAL INSTITUTION MANAGER

Calculating Duration to Measure Interest-Rate Risk

Earlier in our discussion of interest-rate risk, we saw that when interest rates change, a bond with a longer term to maturity has a larger change in its price and hence more interest-rate risk than a bond with a shorter term to maturity. Although this is a useful general fact, in order to measure interest-rate risk, the manager of a financial institution needs more precise information on the actual capital gain or loss that occurs when the interest rate changes by a certain amount. To do this, the manager needs to make use of the concept of **duration,** the average lifetime of a debt security's stream of payments.

The fact that two bonds have the same term to maturity does not mean that they have the same interest-rate risk. A long-term discount bond with ten years to maturity, a so-called zero-coupon bond, makes all of its payments at the end of the ten years, whereas a 10% coupon bond with ten years to maturity makes substantial cash payments before the maturity date. Since the coupon bond makes payments earlier than the zero-coupon bond, we might intuitively guess that the coupon bond's *effective maturity*, the term to maturity that accurately measures interest-rate risk, is shorter than it is for the zero-coupon discount bond.

Indeed, this is exactly what we find in example 10.

EXAMPLE 10: Rate of Capital Gain

Calculate the rate of capital gain or loss on a ten-year zero-coupon bond for which the interest rate has increased from 10% to 20%. The bond has a face value of $1000.

Solution

The rate of capital gain or loss is –49.7%.

$$g = \frac{P_{t+1} - P_t}{P_t}$$

where

$$P_{t+1} = \text{price of the bond one year from now} = \frac{\$1000}{(1 + 0.20)^9} = \$193.81$$

$$P_t = \text{price of the bond today} = \frac{\$1000}{(1 + 0.10)^{10}} = \$385.54$$

Thus

$$g = \frac{\$193.81 - \$385.54}{\$385.54}$$

$$g = -0.497 = -49.7\%$$

But as we have already calculated in Table 2, the capital gain on the 10% ten-year coupon bond is –40.3%. We see that interest-rate risk for the ten-year coupon bond is less than for the ten-year zero-coupon bond, so the effective maturity on the coupon bond (which measures interest-rate risk) is, as expected, shorter than the effective maturity on the zero-coupon bond.

Calculating Duration

To calculate the duration or effective maturity on any debt security, Frederick Macaulay, a researcher at the National Bureau of Economic Research, invented the concept of duration more than half a century ago. Because a zero-coupon bond makes no cash payments before the bond matures, it makes sense to define its effective maturity as equal to its actual term to maturity. Macaulay then realized that he could measure the effective maturity of a coupon bond by recognizing that a coupon bond is equivalent to a set of zero-coupon discount bonds. A ten-year 10% coupon bond with \$1000 face value has cash payments identical to the following set of zero-coupon bonds: a \$100 one-year zero-coupon bond (which pays the equivalent of the \$100 coupon payment made by the \$1000 ten-year 10% coupon bond at the end of one year), a \$100 two-year zero-coupon bond (which pays the equivalent of the \$100 coupon payment at the end of two years),..., a \$100 ten-year zero-coupon bond (which pays the equivalent of the \$100 coupon payment at the end of ten years), and a \$1000 ten-year zero-coupon bond (which pays back the equivalent of the coupon bond's \$1000 face value). This set of coupon bonds is shown in the following time line:

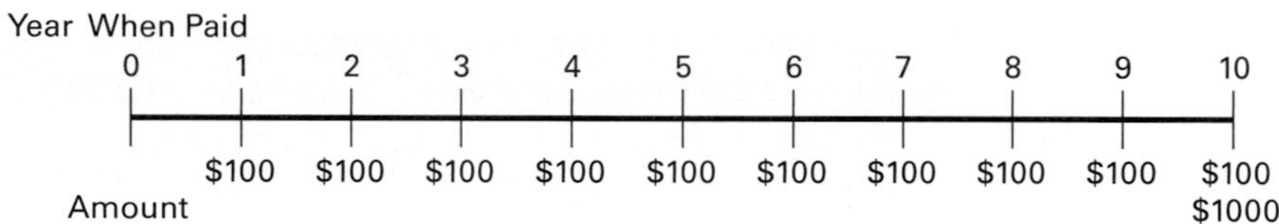

This same set of coupon bonds is listed in column (2) of Table 4, which calculates the duration on the ten-year coupon bond when its interest rate is 10%.

TABLE 4 Calculating Duration on a \$1000 Ten-Year 10% Coupon Bond When Its Interest Rate Is 10%

(1)	(2)	(3)	(4)	(5)
Year	Cash Payments (Zero-Coupon Bonds) (\$)	Present Value (*PV*) of Cash Payments (i = 10%) (\$)	Weights (% of total *PV* = *PV*/\$1000) (%)	Weighted Maturity (1 × 4)/100 (years)
1	100	90.91	9.091	0.09091
2	100	82.64	8.264	0.16528
3	100	75.13	7.513	0.22539
4	100	68.30	6.830	0.27320
5	100	62.09	6.209	0.31045
6	100	56.44	5.644	0.33864
7	100	51.32	5.132	0.35924
8	100	46.65	4.665	0.37320
9	100	42.41	4.241	0.38169
10	100	38.55	3.855	0.38550
10	1000	385.54	38.554	3.85500
Total		1000.00	100.000	6.75850

To get the effective maturity of this set of zero-coupon bonds, we would want to sum up the effective maturity of each zero-coupon bond, weighting it by the percentage of the total value of all the bonds that it represents. In other words, the duration of this set of zero-coupon bonds is the weighted average of the effective maturities of the individual zero-coupon bonds, with the weights equaling the proportion of the total value represented by each zero-coupon bond. We do this in several steps in Table 4. First we calculate the present value of each of the zero-coupon bonds when the interest rate is 10% in column (3). Then in column (4) we divide each of these present values by \$1000, the total present value of the set of zero-coupon bonds, to get the percentage of the total value of all the bonds that each bond represents. Note that the sum of the weights in column (4) must total 100%, as shown at the bottom of the column.

To get the effective maturity of the set of zero-coupon bonds, we add up the weighted maturities in column (5) and obtain the figure of 6.76 years. This figure for the effective maturity of the set of zero-coupon bonds is the duration of the 10% ten-year coupon bond because the bond is equivalent to this set of zero-coupon bonds. In short, we see that ***duration is a weighted average of the maturities of the cash payments.***

The duration calculation done in Table 4 can be written as follows:

$$DUR = \sum_{t=1}^{n} t\frac{CP_t}{(1+i)^t} \Bigg/ \sum_{t=1}^{n} \frac{CP_t}{(1+i)^t} \qquad (13)$$

where DUR = duration
t = years until cash payment is made
CP_t = cash payment (interest plus principal) at time t
i = interest rate
n = years to maturity of the security

This formula is not as intuitive as the calculation done in Table 4, but it does have the advantage that it can easily be programmed into a calculator or computer, making duration calculations very easy.

If we calculate the duration for an 11-year 10% coupon bond when the interest rate is again 10%, we find that it equals 7.14 years, which is greater than the 6.76 years for the ten-year bond. Thus we have reached the expected conclusion: ***All else being equal, the longer the term to maturity of a bond, the longer its duration.***

You might think that knowing the maturity of a coupon bond is enough to tell you what its duration is. However, that is not the case. To see this and to give you more practice in calculating duration, in Table 5 we again calculate the duration for the ten-year 10% coupon bond, but when the current interest rate is 20% rather than 10% as in Table 4. The calculation in Table 5 reveals that the duration of the coupon bond at this higher interest rate has fallen from 6.76 years to 5.72 years. The explanation is fairly straightforward. When the interest rate is higher, the cash payments in the future are discounted more heavily and become less important in present-value terms relative to the total present value of all the payments. The relative weight for these cash payments drops as we see in Table 5, and so the effective maturity of the bond falls. We have come to an important conclusion: ***All else being equal, when interest rates rise, the duration of a coupon bond falls.***

The duration of a coupon bond is also affected by its coupon rate. For example, consider a ten-year 20% coupon bond when the interest rate is 10%. Using the

TABLE 5 Calculating Duration on a $1000 Ten-Year 10% Coupon Bond When Its Interest Rate Is 20%

(1)	(2)	(3)	(4)	(5)
Year	Cash Payments (Zero-Coupon Bonds) ($)	Present Value (*PV*) of Cash Payments (i = 20%) ($)	Weights (% of total *PV* = *PV*/$580.76) (%)	Weighted Maturity (1 × 4)/100 (years)
1	100	83.33	14.348	0.14348
2	100	69.44	11.957	0.23914
3	100	57.87	9.965	0.29895
4	100	48.23	8.305	0.33220
5	100	40.19	6.920	0.34600
6	100	33.49	5.767	0.34602
7	100	27.91	4.806	0.33642
8	100	23.26	4.005	0.32040
9	100	19.38	3.337	0.30033
10	100	16.15	2.781	0.27810
10	$1000	161.51	27.808	2.78100
Total		580.76	100.000	5.72204

same procedure, we find that its duration at the higher 20% coupon rate is 5.98 years versus 6.76 years when the coupon rate is 10%. The explanation is that a higher coupon rate means that a relatively greater amount of the cash payments are made earlier in the life of the bond, and so the effective maturity of the bond must fall. We have thus established a third fact about duration: ***All else being equal, the higher the coupon rate on the bond, the shorter the bond's duration.***

Study Guide To make certain that you understand how to calculate duration, practice doing the calculations in Tables 4 and 5. Try to produce the tables for calculating duration in the case of an 11-year 10% coupon bond and also for the ten-year 20% coupon bond mentioned in the text when the current interest rate is 10%. Make sure your calculations produce the same results found in the text. You can get more practice by doing some of the problems involving duration calculations at the end of the chapter.

One additional fact about duration makes this concept useful when applied to a portfolio of securities. Our examples have shown that duration is equal to the weighted average of the durations of the cash payments (the effective maturities of the corresponding zero-coupon bonds). So if we calculate the duration for two different securities, it should be easy to see that the duration of a portfolio of the two securities is just the weighted average of the durations of the two securities, with the weights reflecting the proportion of the portfolio invested in each.

EXAMPLE 11: Duration

A manager of a financial institution is holding 25% of a portfolio in a bond with a five-year duration and 75% in a bond with a ten-year duration. What is the duration of the portfolio?

Solution

The duration of the portfolio is 8.75 years.

$$(0.25 \times 5) + (0.75 \times 10) = 1.25 + 7.5 = 8.75 \text{ years}$$

We now see that ***the duration of a portfolio of securities is the weighted average of the durations of the individual securities, with the weights reflecting the proportion of the portfolio invested in each.*** This fact about duration is often referred to as the *additive property of duration,* and it is extremely useful because it means that the duration of a portfolio of securities is easy to calculate from the durations of the individual securities.

To summarize, our calculations of duration for coupon bonds have revealed four facts:

1. The longer the term to maturity of a bond, everything else being equal, the greater its duration.
2. When interest rates rise, everything else being equal, the duration of a coupon bond falls.
3. The higher the coupon rate on the bond, everything else being equal, the shorter the bond's duration.
4. Duration is additive: The duration of a portfolio of securities is the weighted average of the durations of the individual securities, with the weights reflecting the proportion of the portfolio invested in each.

Duration and Interest-Rate Risk

Now that we understand how duration is calculated, we want to see how it can be used by the practicing financial institution manager to measure interest-rate risk. Duration is a particularly useful concept because it provides a good approximation, particularly when interest-rate changes are small, for how much the security price changes for a given change in interest rates, as the following formula indicates:

$$\%\Delta P \approx -DUR \times \frac{\Delta i}{1 + i} \tag{14}$$

where $\%\Delta P = (P_{t+1} - P_t)/P_t$ = percent change in the price of the security from t to $t + 1$ = rate of capital gain
DUR = duration
i = interest rate

EXAMPLE 12: Duration and Interest-Rate Risk

A pension fund manager is holding a ten-year 10% coupon bond in the fund's portfolio and the interest rate is currently 10%. What loss would the fund be exposed to if the interest rate rises to 11% tomorrow?

Solution

The approximate percentage change in the price of the bond is –6.15%.

As the calulation in Table 4 shows, the duration of a ten-year 10% coupon bond is 6.76 years.

$$\%\Delta P \approx -DUR \times \frac{\Delta i}{1+i}$$

where

DUR = duration = 6.76

Δi = change in interest rate = 0.11 – 0.10 = 0.01

i = current interest rate = 0.10

Thus

$$\%\Delta P \approx -6.76 \times \frac{0.01}{1+0.10}$$

$$\%\Delta P \approx -0.0615 = -6.15\%$$

EXAMPLE 13: Duration and Interest-Rate Risk

Now the pension manager has the option to hold a ten-year coupon bond with a coupon rate of 20% instead of 10%. As mentioned earlier, the duration for this 20% coupon bond is 5.98 years when the interest rate is 10%. Find the approximate change in the bond price when the interest rate increases from 10% to 11%.

Solution

This time the approximate change in bond price is –5.4%. This change in bond price is much smaller than for the higher-duration coupon bond.

$$\%\Delta P \approx -DUR \times \frac{\Delta i}{1+i}$$

where

DUR = duration = 5.98

Δi = change in interest rate = 0.11 – 0.10 = 0.01

i = current interest rate = 0.10

Thus

$$\%\Delta P \approx -5.98 \times \frac{0.01}{1+0.10}$$

$$\%\Delta P \approx -0.054 = -5.4\%$$

The pension fund manager realizes that the interest-rate risk on the 20% coupon bond is less than on the 10% coupon, so he switches the fund out of the 10% coupon bond and into the 20% coupon bond.

Examples 12 and 13 have led the pension fund manager to an important conclusion about the relationship of duration and interest-rate risk: ***The greater the duration of a security, the greater the percentage change in the market value of the security for a given change in interest rates. Therefore, the greater the duration of a security, the greater its interest-rate risk.***

This reasoning applies equally to a portfolio of securities. So by calculating the duration of the fund's portfolio of securities using the methods outlined here, a pension fund manager can easily ascertain the amount of interest-rate risk the entire fund is exposed to. As we will see in Chapter 22, duration is a highly useful concept for the management of interest-rate risk that is widely used by managers of banks and other financial institutions.

SUMMARY

1. The yield to maturity, which is the measure that most accurately reflects the interest rate, is the interest rate that equates the present value of future payments of a debt instrument with its value today. Application of this principle reveals that bond prices and interest rates are negatively related: When the interest rate rises, the price of the bond must fall, and vice versa.
2. Two less accurate measures of interest rates are commonly used to quote interest rates on coupon and discount bonds. The current yield, which equals the coupon payment divided by the price of a coupon bond, is a less accurate measure of the yield to maturity the shorter the maturity of the bond and the greater the gap between the price and the par value. The yield on a discount basis (also called the discount yield) understates the yield to maturity on a discount bond, and the understatement worsens the more distant the maturity of the discount security. Even though these measures are misleading guides to the size of the interest rate, a change in them always signals a change in the same direction for the yield to maturity.
3. The real interest rate is defined as the nominal interest rate minus the expected rate of inflation. It is a better measure of the incentives to borrow and lend than the nominal interest rate, and it is a more accurate indicator of the tightness of credit market conditions than the nominal interest rate.
4. The return on a security, which tells you how well you have done by holding this security over a stated period of time, can differ substantially from the interest rate as measured by the yield to maturity. Long-term bond prices have substantial fluctuations when interest rates change and thus bear interest-rate risk. The resulting capital gains and losses can be large, which is why long-term bonds are not considered to be safe assets with a sure return. Bonds whose maturity is shorter than the holding period are also subject to reinvestment risk, which occurs because the proceeds from the short-term bond need to be reinvested at a future interest rate that is uncertain.
5. Duration, the average lifetime of a debt security's stream of payments, is a measure of effective maturity, the term to maturity that accurately measures interest-rate risk. Everything else being equal, the duration of a bond is greater the longer the maturity of a bond, when interest rates fall, or when the coupon rate of a coupon bond falls. Duration is additive: The duration of a portfolio of securities is the weighted average of the durations of the individual securities, with the weights reflecting the proportion of the portfolio invested in each. The greater the duration of a security, the greater the percentage change in the market value of the security for a given change in interest rates. Therefore, the greater the duration of a security, the greater its interest-rate risk.

KEY TERMS

basis point, *p. 55*
coupon bond, *p. 38*
coupon rate, *p. 38*
current yield, *p. 50*
discount bond (zero-coupon bond), *p. 38*
duration, *p. 65*
face value (par value), *p. 38*
fixed-payment loan, *p. 38*
indexed bond, *p. 59*
interest-rate risk, *p. 62*
nominal interest rate, *p. 56*
perpetuity, *p. 47*
present value (present discounted value), *p. 39*
rate of capital gain, *p. 61*
real interest rate, *p. 56*
real terms, *p. 57*
reinvestment risk, *p. 63*
return (rate of return), *p. 59*
simple loan, *p. 38*
yield on a discount basis (discount yield), *p. 51*
yield to maturity, *p. 41*

QUESTIONS AND PROBLEMS

***1.** Would a dollar tomorrow be worth more to you today when the interest rate is 20% or when it is 10%?

2. You have just won $20 million in the state lottery, which promises to pay you $1 million (tax free) every year for the next 20 years. Have you really won $20 million?

***3.** If the interest rate is 10%, what is the present value of a security that pays you $1100 next year, $1210 the year after, and $1331 the year after that?

4. If the security in Problem 3 sold for $3500, is the yield to maturity greater or less than 10%? Why?

***5.** Write down the formula that is used to calculate the yield to maturity on a 20-year 10% coupon bond with $1000 face value that sells for $2000.

6. What is the yield to maturity on a $1000-face-value discount bond maturing in one year that sells for $800?

***7.** What is the yield to maturity on a simple loan for $1 million that requires a repayment of $2 million in five years' time?

8. To pay for college, you have just taken out a $1000 government loan that makes you pay $126 per year for 25 years. However, you don't have to start making these payments until you graduate from college two years from now. Why is the yield to maturity necessarily less than 12%, the yield to maturity on a normal $1000 fixed-payment loan in which you pay $126 per year for 25 years?

***9.** Which $1000 bond has the higher yield to maturity, a 20-year bond selling for $800 with a current yield of 15% or a one-year bond selling for $800 with a current yield of 5%?

10. Pick five U.S. Treasury bonds from the bond page of the newspaper, and calculate the current yield. Note when the current yield is a good approximation of the yield to maturity.

***11.** You are offered two bonds, a one-year U.S. Treasury bond with a yield to maturity of 9% and a one-year U.S. Treasury bill with a yield on a discount basis of 8.9%. Which would you rather own?

12. If there is a decline in interest rates, which would you rather be holding, long-term bonds or short-term bonds? Why? Which type of bond has the greater interest-rate risk?

***13.** A financial adviser has just given you the following advice: "Long-term bonds are a great investment because their interest rate is over 20%." Is the financial adviser necessarily right?

14. If mortgage rates rise from 5% to 10% but the expected rate of increase in housing prices rises from 2% to 9%, are people more or less likely to buy houses?

***15.** Interest rates were lower in the mid-1980s than they were in the late 1970s, yet many observers have commented that real interest rates were actually much higher in the mid-1980s than in the late 1970s. Does this make sense? Do you think that these observers are right?

16. When interest rates rise, would you rather be holding a ten-year coupon bond with a 5% coupon rate or one with a 10% coupon rate?

***17.** Calculate the duration on a five-year 8% coupon bond when the interest rate is 3%.

18. Calculate the duration on a five-year 5% coupon bond when the interest rate is 3%. Compare your answer to the answer to Problem 17 given at the back of the book. What is the rationale behind the difference in the answers?

***19.** If a bond has a duration of eight years and interest rates rise from 7% to 8%, what will be the approximate percentage change in the price of the bond?

20. Calculate the approximate price change of two bonds, one with a three-year duration and the other with a five-year duration, when interest rates rise from 4% to 5%. Which of the bonds would you rather hold? Does this accord with your intuition?

WEB EXERCISES

Understanding Interest Rates

1. Investigate the data available from the Federal Reserve at http://www.federalreserve.gov/releases/. Then answer the following questions.
   a. What is the difference in the interest rates on commercial paper for financial firms versus non-financial firms?
   b. What was the interest rate on the one month eurodollar at the end of 1971?
   c. What is the most recent interest rate report for the 30-year Treasury note?
2. Figure 3 in the chapter shows the estimated real and nominal rates for three-month treasury bills. Go to http://www.martincapital.com/charts.htm. Click on "interest rates and yields" then on "Nominal versus Real Market Rates."
   a. Compare the three-month real rate to the long-term real rate. Which is greater?
   b. Compare the short-term nominal rate to the long-term nominal rate. Which appears most volatile?
3. In this chapter we have discussed bonds as if there were only one type: long-term interest-paying corporate bonds. In fact, there are also discount bonds. A discount bond is sold at a low price, and the whole return comes in the form of a price appreciation. You can easily compute the current price of a discount bond using the financial calculator at http://app.ny.frb.org/sbr/.

   To compute the redemption values for savings bonds, fill in the information at the site and click on the "Compute Values" button. A maximum of five years of data will be displayed for each computation.

Chapter 4

The Behavior of Interest Rates

Preview

In the early 1950s, nominal interest rates on three-month Treasury bills were about 1% at an annual rate; by 1981, they had reached over 15%, then fell to 3% in 1993, and rose above 5% by the mid–1990s. What explains these substantial fluctuations in interest rates? One reason we study financial markets and institutions is to provide some answers to this question.

In this chapter we examine how the overall level of *nominal* interest rates (which we refer to simply as "interest rates") is determined and the factors that influence their behavior. We learned in Chapter 3 that interest rates are negatively related to the price of bonds, so if we can explain why bond prices change, we can also explain why interest rates fluctuate. Here we will apply supply and demand analysis to examine how bond prices and interest rates change.

DETERMINANTS OF ASSET DEMAND

An **asset** is a piece of property that is a store of value. Items such as money, bonds, stocks, art, land, houses, farm equipment, and manufacturing machinery are all assets. Facing the question of whether to buy and hold an asset or whether to buy one asset rather than another, an individual must consider the following factors:

1. **Wealth,** the total resources owned by the individual, including all assets
2. **Expected return** (the return expected over the next period) on one asset relative to alternative assets
3. **Risk** (the degree of uncertainty associated with the return) on one asset relative to alternative assets
4. **Liquidity** (the ease and speed with which an asset can be turned into cash) relative to alternative assets

Study Guide As we discuss each factor that influences asset demand, remember that we are always holding all the other factors constant. Also, think of additional examples of how changes in each factor would influence your decision to purchase a particular asset, say, a house or a share of common stock. This intuitive approach will help you understand how the theory works in practice.

Wealth

When we find that our wealth has increased, we have more resources available with which to purchase assets and so, not surprisingly, the quantity of assets we demand increases.[1] Therefore, the effect of changes in wealth on the quantity demanded of an asset can be summarized as follows: ***Holding everything else constant, an increase in wealth raises the quantity demanded of an asset.***

Expected Returns

In Chapter 3 we saw that the return on an asset (such as a bond) measures how much we gain from holding that asset. When we make a decision to buy an asset, we are influenced by what we expect the return on that asset to be. If a Mobil Oil Corporation bond, for example, has a return of 15% half of the time and 5% the other half of the time, its expected return (which you can think of as the average return) is 10%. More formally, the expected return on an asset is the weighted average of all possible returns, where the weights are the probabilities of occurrence of that return:

$$R^e = p_1R_1 + p_2R_2 + \ldots + p_nR_n \tag{1}$$

where
R^e = expected return
n = number of possible outcomes (states of nature)
R_i = return in the ith state of nature
p_i = probability of occurrence of the return R_i

EXAMPLE 1: Expected Return

What is the expected return on the Mobil Oil bond if the return is 12% two-thirds of the time and 8% one-third of the time?

Solution

The expected return is 10.68%.

$$R^e = p_1R_1 + p_2R_2$$

where

p_1 = probability of occurrence of return 1 $= \frac{2}{3} = .67$
R_1 = return in state 1 $= 12\% = 0.12$

[1]Although it is possible that some assets (called *inferior assets*) might have the property that the quantity demanded does not increase as wealth increases, such assets are rare. Hence we will always assume that demand for an asset increases as wealth increases.

p_2 = probability of occurrence return 2 $= \frac{1}{3} = .33$

R_2 = return in state 2 $= 8\% = 0.08$

Thus

$$R^e = (.67)(0.12) + (.33)(0.08) = 0.1068 = 10.68\%$$

If the expected return on the Mobil Oil bond rises relative to expected returns on alternative assets, holding everything else constant, then it becomes more desirable to purchase it, and the quantity demanded increases. This can occur in either of two ways: (1) when the expected return on the Mobil Oil bond rises while the return on an alternative asset—say, stock in IBM—remains unchanged or (2) when the return on the alternative asset, the IBM stock, falls while the return on the Mobil Oil bond remains unchanged. To summarize, ***an increase in an asset's expected return relative to that of an alternative asset, holding everything else unchanged, raises the quantity demanded of the asset.***

Risk

The degree of risk or uncertainty of an asset's returns also affects the demand for the asset. Consider two assets, stock in Fly-by-Night Airlines and stock in Feet-on-the-Ground Bus Company. Suppose that Fly-by-Night stock has a return of 15% half of the time and 5% the other half of the time, making its expected return 10%, while stock in Feet-on-the-Ground has a fixed return of 10%. Fly-by-Night stock has uncertainty associated with its returns and so has greater risk than stock in Feet-on-the-Ground, whose return is a sure thing.

To see this more formally, we can use a measure of risk called the **standard deviation.** The standard deviation of returns on an asset is calculated as follows. First you need to calculate the expected return, R^e; then you subtract the expected return from each return to get a deviation; then you square each deviation and multiply it by the probability of occurrence of that outcome; finally, you add up all these weighted squared deviations and take the square root. The formula for the standard deviation, σ, is thus:

$$\sigma = \sqrt{p_1(R_1 - R^e)^2 + p_2(R_2 - R^e)^2 + \ldots + p_n(R_n - R^e)^2} \quad (2)$$

The higher the standard deviation, σ, the greater the risk of an asset.

EXAMPLE 2: Standard Deviation

What is the standard deviation of the returns on the Fly-by-Night Airlines stock and Feet-on-the Ground Bus Company, with the same return outcomes and probabilities described above? Of these two stocks, which is riskier?

Solution

Fly-by-Night Airlines has a standard deviation of returns of 5%.

$$\sigma = \sqrt{p_1(R_1 - R^e)^2 + p_2(R_2 - R^e)^2}$$

$$R^e = p_1R_1 + p_2R_2$$

where

p_1 = probability of occurrence of return 1 $= \frac{1}{2}$ $= .50$

R_1 = return in state 1 $= 15\%$ $= 0.15$

p_2 = probability of occurrence of return 2 $= \frac{1}{2}$ $= .50$

R_2 = return in state 2 $= 5\%$ $= 0.05$

R^e = expected return $= (.50)(0.15) + (.50)(0.05)$ $= 0.10$

Thus

$$\sigma = \sqrt{(.50)(0.15 - 0.10)^2 + (.50)(0.05 - 0.10)^2}$$
$$\sigma = \sqrt{(.50)(0.0025) + (.50)(0.0025)} = \sqrt{0.0025} = 0.05 = 5\%$$

Feet-on-the-Ground Bus Company has a standard deviation of returns of 0%.

$$\sigma = \sqrt{p_1(R_1 - R^e)^2}$$
$$R^e = p_1 R_1$$

where

p_1 = probability of occurrence of return 1 $= 1.0$

R_1 = return in state 1 $= 10\% = 0.10$

R^e = expected return $= (1.0)(0.10) = 0.10$

Thus

$$\sigma = \sqrt{(1.0)(0.10 - 0.10)^2}$$
$$= \sqrt{0} = 0 = 0\%$$

Clearly, Fly-by-Night Airlines is a riskier stock because its standard deviation of returns of 5% is higher than the zero standard deviation of returns for Feet-on-the-Ground Bus Company, which has a certain return.

A *risk-averse* person prefers stock in the Feet-on-the-Ground (the sure thing) to Fly-by-Night stock (the riskier asset), even though the stocks have the same expected return, 10%. By contrast, a person who prefers risk is a *risk preferrer* or *risk lover.* Most people are risk-averse: Everything else being equal, they prefer to hold the less risky asset. Hence, ***holding everything else constant, if an asset's risk rises relative to that of alternative assets, its quantity demanded will fall.***

Liquidity

Another factor that affects the demand for an asset is how quickly it can be converted into cash without incurring large costs—its liquidity. An asset is liquid if the market in which it is traded has depth and breadth, that is, if the market has many buyers and sellers. A house is not a very liquid asset because it may be hard to find a buyer quickly; if a house must be sold to pay off bills, it might have to be sold for a much lower price. And the transaction costs in selling a house (broker's commissions, lawyer's fees, and so on) are substantial. A U.S. Treasury bill, by contrast,

TABLE 1 SUMMARY Response of the Quantity of an Asset Demanded to Changes in Income or Wealth, Expected Returns, Risk, and Liquidity

Variable	Change in Variable	Change in Quantity Demanded
Income or wealth	↑	↑
Expected return relative to other assets	↑	↑
Risk relative to other assets	↑	↓
Liquidity relative to other assets	↑	↑

Note: Only increases (↑) in the variables are shown. The effect of decreases in the variables on the change in demand would be the opposite of those indicated in the rightmost column.

is a highly liquid asset. It can be sold in a well-organized market where there are many buyers, so it can be sold quickly at low cost. ***The more liquid an asset is relative to alternative assets, holding everything else unchanged, the more desirable it is, and the greater will be the quantity demanded.***

Summary

All the determining factors we have just discussed can be summarized by stating that, holding all of the other factors constant:

1. The quantity demanded of an asset is usually positively related to wealth, with the response being greater if the asset is a luxury than if it is a necessity.
2. The quantity demanded of an asset is positively related to its expected return relative to alternative assets.
3. The quantity demanded of an asset is negatively related to the risk of its returns relative to alternative assets.
4. The quantity demanded of an asset is positively related to its liquidity relative to alternative assets.

These results are summarized in Table 1.

BENEFITS OF DIVERSIFICATION

Our discussion of the determinants of asset demand indicates that most people like to avoid risk; that is, they are risk-averse. Why, then, do many investors hold many risky assets rather than just one? Doesn't holding many risky assets expose the investor to more risk?

The old warning about not putting all your eggs in one basket holds the key to the answer: Because holding a variety of risky assets (called **diversification**) reduces the overall risk an investor faces, diversification is beneficial. To see why this is so, let's look at some specific examples of how an investor fares when holding two risky securities.

Consider two assets, common stock of Frivolous Luxuries, Inc., and common stock of Bad Times Products, Unlimited. When the economy is strong, which we'll assume is half of the time, Frivolous Luxuries has high sales and the return on the stock is 15%; when the economy is weak, the other half of the time, sales are low and the return on the stock is 5%. In contrast, suppose that Bad Times Products thrives when the economy is weak so that its stock has a return of 15%, but it earns less when the economy is strong and has a return on the stock of 5%. Both stocks have a return of 15% half of the time and 5% the other half of the time, and both have an expected return of 10%. However, both stocks carry a fair amount of risk because there is uncertainty about their actual returns.

Suppose now that instead of buying one stock or the other, Irving the Investor puts half his savings in Frivolous Luxuries stock and the other half in Bad Times Products stock. When the economy is strong, Frivolous Luxuries stock has a return of 15% and Bad Times Products has a return of 5%. The result is that Irving earns a return of 10% (the average of 5% and 15%) on his holdings of the two stocks. When the economy is weak, Frivolous Luxuries has a return of only 5% and Bad Times Products has a return of 15%, so Irving still earns a return of 10%. If Irving diversifies by buying both stocks, he earns a return of 10% regardless of whether the economy is strong or weak. Irving is better off from this strategy of diversification because his expected return is 10%, the same as from holding either Frivolous Luxuries or Bad Times Products alone, yet he is not exposed to *any* risk.

Although the case we have described demonstrates the benefits of diversification, it is somewhat unrealistic. It is hard to find two securities with the characteristic that when the return of one is low, the return of the other is always high.[2] In the real world, we are more likely to find at best returns on securities that are independent of each other; that is, when one is low, the other is just as likely to be high as to be low.

Suppose that both securities have an expected return of 10%, with a return of 5% half of the time and 15% the other half of the time. Sometimes both securities will earn the higher return, and sometimes both will earn the lower return. In this case, if Irving holds equal amounts of each security, he will on average earn the same return as if he had just put all his savings into one of the securities. However, because the returns on these two securities are independent, it is just as likely that when one earns the high 15% return, the other earns the low 5% return, and vice versa, giving Irving a return of 10% (equal to the expected return). Because Irving is more likely to earn what he expected to earn when he holds both securities instead of just one, we can see that Irving has again reduced his risk through diversification.

The one case in which Irving will not benefit from diversifying occurs when the returns on the two securities move perfectly together. In this case, when the first security has a return of 15%, the other also has a return of 15%, and holding both securities results in a return of 15%. When the first security has a return of 5%, the other has a return of 5%, and holding both results in a return of 5%. The result of diversifying by holding both securities is a return of 15% half of the time and 5% the other half of the time, which is exactly the same returns that are earned by holding only one of the securities. Consequently, diversification in this case does not lead to any reduction of risk.

The examples we have just examined illustrate the following important points about diversification:

1. Diversification is almost always beneficial to the risk-averse investor because it reduces risk except in the extremely rare case where returns on securities move perfectly together.

2. The less the returns on two securities move together, the more benefit (risk reduction) there is from diversification.

---

[2]Such a case is described by saying that the returns on the two securities are perfectly *negatively* correlated.

LOANABLE FUNDS FRAMEWORK: SUPPLY AND DEMAND IN THE BOND MARKET

We first approach the analysis of interest-rate determination by studying the supply of and demand for bonds. Because interest rates on different securities tend to move together, in this chapter we will act as if there is only one type of security and a single interest rate in the entire economy. In Chapter 5, we will expand our analysis to look at why interest rates on different securities differ.

The first step is to use the analysis of the determinants of asset demand to obtain a **demand curve,** which shows the relationship between the quantity demanded and the price when all other economic variables are held constant (that is, values of other variables are taken as given). You may recall from previous finance and economics courses that the assumption that all other economic variables are held constant is called *ceteris paribus,* which means "other things being equal" in Latin.

Demand Curve

To clarify our analysis, let us consider the demand for one-year discount bonds, which make no coupon payments but pay the owner the $1000 face value in a year. If the holding period is one year, then as we have seen in Chapter 3, the return on the bonds is known absolutely and is equal to the interest rate as measured by the yield to maturity. This means that the expected return on this bond is equal to the interest rate i, which, using Equation 6 in Chapter 3, is

$$i = R^e = \frac{F - P}{P}$$

where
i = interest rate = yield to maturity
R^e = expected return
F = face value of the discount bond
P = initial purchase price of the discount bond

This formula shows that a particular value of the interest rate corresponds to each bond price. If the bond sells for $950, the interest rate and expected return is

$$\frac{(\$1000 - \$950)}{\$950} = 0.053 = 5.3\%$$

At this 5.3% interest rate and expected return corresponding to a bond price of $950, let us assume that the quantity of bonds demanded is $100 billion, which is plotted as point A in Figure 1. To display both the bond price and the corresponding interest rate, Figure 1 has two vertical axes. The left vertical axis shows the bond price, with the price of bonds increasing from $750 near the bottom of the axis toward $1000 at the top. The right vertical axis shows the interest rate, which increases in the *opposite* direction from 0% at the top of the axis to 33% near the bottom. The right and left vertical axes run in opposite directions because, as we learned in Chapter 3, bond price and interest rate are always negatively related: As the price of the bond rises, the interest rate on the bond necessarily falls.

At a price of $900, the interest rate and expected return equals

$$\frac{(\$1000 - \$900)}{\$900} = 0.111 = 11.1\%$$

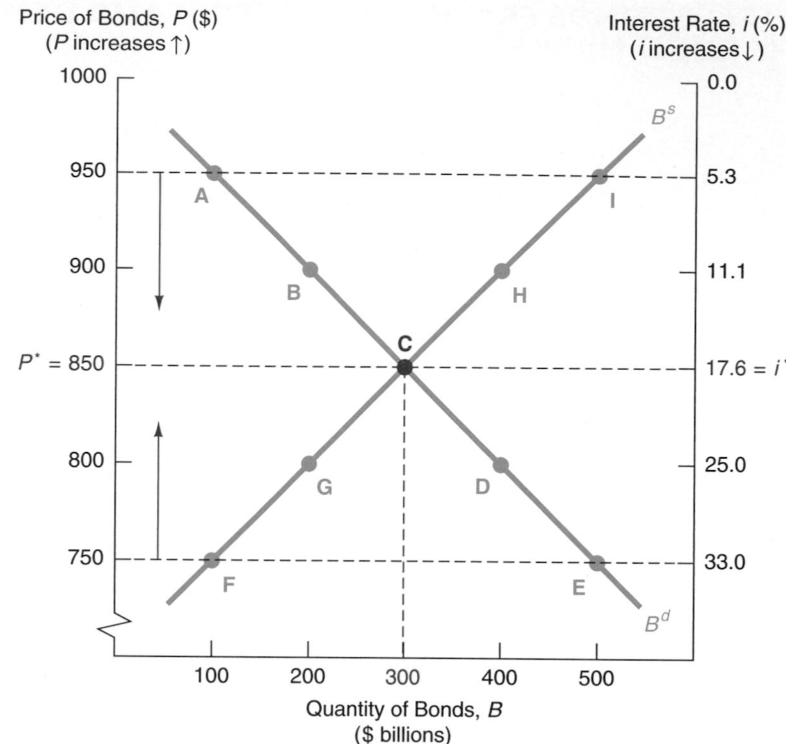

FIGURE 1 Supply and Demand for Bonds

Equilibrium in the bond market occurs at point C, the intersection of the bond demand curve B^d and the bond supply curve B^s. The equilibrium price is $P^* = \$850$, and the equilibrium interest rate is $i^* = 17.6\%$. (*Note*: P and i increase in opposite directions. P on the left vertical axis increases as we go up the axis from $750 near the bottom to $1000 at the top, while i on the right vertical axis increases as we go down the axis from 0% at the top to 33% near the bottom.)

Because the expected return on these bonds is higher, with all other economic variables (such as income, expected returns on other assets, risk, and liquidity) held constant, the quantity demanded of bonds will be higher as predicted by our analysis of the determinants of asset demand. Point B in Figure 1 shows that the quantity of bonds demanded at the price of $900 has risen to $200 billion. Continuing with this reasoning, if the bond price is $850 (interest rate and expected return = 17.6%), the quantity of bonds demanded (point C) will be greater than at point B. Similarly, at the lower prices of $800 (interest rate = 25%) and $750 (interest rate = 33.3%), the quantity of bonds demanded will be even higher (points D and E). The curve B^d, which connects these points, is the demand curve for bonds. It has the usual downward slope, indicating that at lower prices of the bond (everything else being equal), the quantity demanded is higher.[3]

[3]Note that although our analysis indicates that the demand curve is downward-sloping, it does not imply that the curve is a straight line. For ease of exposition, however, we will draw demand curves and supply curves as straight lines.

Supply Curve

An important assumption behind the demand curve for bonds in Figure 1 is that all other economic variables besides the bond's price and interest rate are held constant. We use the same assumption in deriving a **supply curve,** which shows the relationship between the quantity supplied and the price when all other economic variables are held constant.

When the price of the bonds is \$750 (interest rate = 33.3%), point F shows that the quantity of bonds supplied is \$100 billion for the example we are considering. If the price is \$800, the interest rate is the lower rate of 25%. Because at this interest rate it is now less costly to borrow by issuing bonds, firms will be willing to borrow more through bond issues, and the quantity of bonds supplied is at the higher level of \$200 billion (point G). An even higher price of \$850, corresponding to a lower interest rate of 17.6%, results in a larger quantity of bonds supplied of \$300 billion (point C). Higher prices of \$900 and \$950 result in even greater quantities of bonds supplied (points H and I). The B^s curve, which connects these points, is the supply curve for bonds. It has the usual upward slope found in supply curves, indicating that as the price increases (everything else being equal), the quantity supplied increases.

Market Equilibrium

In finance and economics, **market equilibrium** occurs when the amount that people are willing to buy (*demand*) equals the amount that people are willing to sell (*supply*) at a given price. In the bond market, this is achieved when the quantity of bonds demanded equals the quantity of bonds supplied:

$$B^d = B^s \tag{3}$$

In Figure 1, equilibrium occurs at point C, where the demand and supply curves intersect at a bond price of \$850 (interest rate of 17.6%) and a quantity of bonds of \$300 billion. The price of $P^* = 850$, where the quantity demanded equals the quantity supplied, is called the *equilibrium* or *market-clearing* price. Similarly, the interest rate of $i^* = 17.6\%$ that corresponds to this price is called the equilibrium or market-clearing interest rate.

The concepts of market equilibrium and equilibrium price or interest rate are useful because there is a tendency for the market to head toward them. We can see that it does in Figure 1 by first looking at what happens when we have a bond price that is above the equilibrium price. When the price of bonds is set too high, at, say, \$950, the quantity of bonds supplied at point I is greater than the quantity of bonds demanded at point A. A situation like this, in which the quantity of bonds supplied exceeds the quantity of bonds demanded, is called a condition of **excess supply.** Because people want to sell more bonds than others want to buy, the price of the bonds will fall, and this is why the downward arrow is drawn in the figure at the bond price of \$950. As long as the bond price remains above the equilibrium price, there will continue to be an excess supply of bonds, and the price will continue to fall. This will stop only when the price has reached the equilibrium price of \$850, where the excess supply of bonds has been eliminated.

Now let's look at what happens when the price of bonds is below the equilibrium price. If the price of the bonds is set too low, at, say, \$750, the quantity demanded at point E is greater than the quantity supplied at point F. This is called a condition of **excess demand.** People now want to buy more bonds than others are willing to sell, and so the price of bonds will be driven up. This is illustrated by the upward arrow drawn in the figure at the bond price of $750. Only when the excess demand for bonds is eliminated by the price rising to the equilibrium level of $850 is there no further tendency for the price to rise.

We can see that the concept of equilibrium price is a useful one because it indicates where the market will settle. Because each price on the left vertical axis of Figure 1 corresponds to a value of the interest rate on the right vertical axis, the same diagram also shows that the interest rate will head toward the equilibrium interest rate of 17.6%. When the interest rate is below the equilibrium interest rate, as it is when it is at 5.3%, the price of the bond is above the equilibrium price, and there will be an excess supply of bonds. The price of the bond then falls, leading to a rise in the interest rate toward the equilibrium level. Similarly, when the interest rate is above the equilibrium level, as it is when it is at 33.3%, there is excess demand for bonds, and the bond price will rise, driving the interest rate back down to the equilibrium level of 17.6%.

Supply and Demand Analysis

Our Figure 1 is a conventional supply and demand diagram with price on the left vertical axis and quantity on the horizontal axis. Because the interest rate that corresponds to each bond price is also marked on the right vertical axis, this diagram allows us to read the equilibrium interest rate, giving us a model that describes the determination of interest rates. It is important to recognize that a supply and demand diagram like Figure 1 can be drawn for *any* type of bond because the interest rate and price of a bond are *always* negatively related for any type of bond, be it a discount bond or a coupon bond.

One disadvantage of the diagram in Figure 1 is that interest rates run in an unusual direction on the right vertical axis: As we go up the right axis, interest rates fall. Because financial economists are typically more concerned with the value of interest rates rather than the price of bonds, we could plot the supply of and demand for bonds on a diagram that has only a left vertical axis that provides the values of the interest rates running in the usual direction, rising as we go up the axis. Figure 2 is such a diagram, in which points A through I match the corresponding points in Figure 1.

However, making interest rates run the "usual" direction on the vertical axis presents us with a problem. Our demand curve for bonds, points A through E, now looks peculiar because it has an upward slope. This upward slope is, however, completely consistent with our usual demand analysis, which produces a negative relationship between price and quantity. The inverse relationship between bond prices and interest rates means that in moving from point A to point B to point C, bond prices are falling and, consistent with usual demand analysis, the quantity demanded is rising. Similarly, our supply curve for bonds, points F through I, has an unusual-looking downward slope but is completely consistent with the usual view that price and the quantity supplied are positively related.

One way to give the demand curve the usual downward slope and the supply curve the usual upward slope is to rename the horizontal axis and the demand and supply curves. Because a firm supplying bonds is in fact taking out a loan from a person buying a bond, "supplying a bond" is equivalent to "demanding a loan." Thus the supply curve for bonds can be reinterpreted as indicating the *quantity of loans demanded* for each value of the interest rate. If we rename the horizontal axis **loanable funds,** defined as the quantity of loans, the supply of bonds can

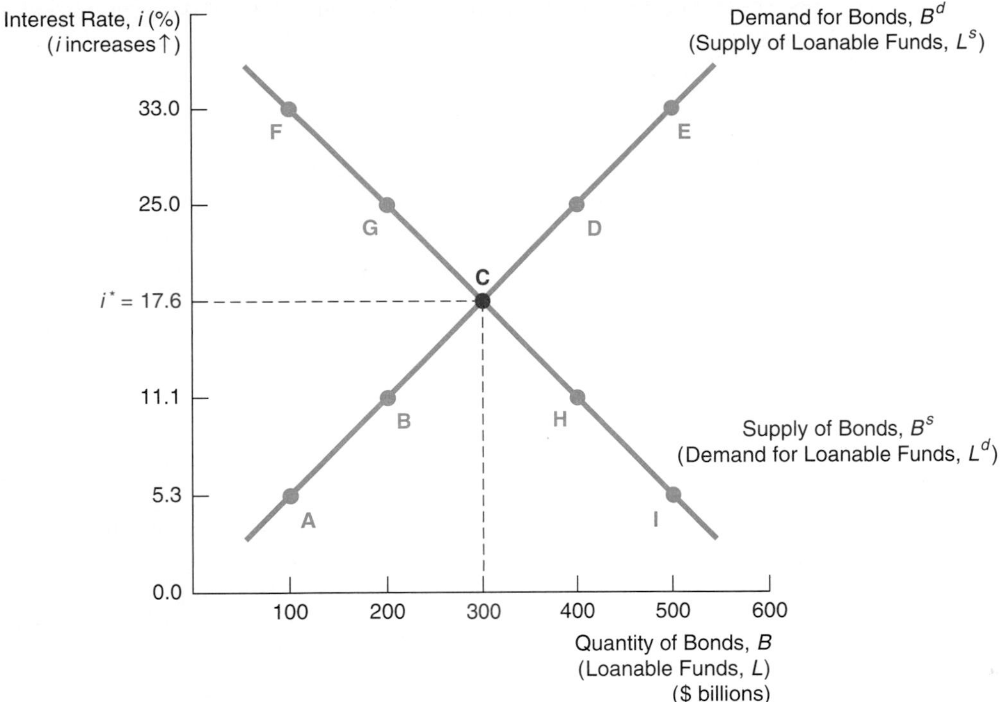

FIGURE 2 A Comparison of Terminology: Loanable Funds and Supply and Demand for Bonds

The demand for bonds is equivalent to the supply of loanable funds, and the supply of bonds is equivalent to the demand for loanable funds. (*Note*: *i* increases as we go up the vertical axis, in contrast to Figure 1, in which the opposite occurs.)

be reinterpreted as the *demand for loanable funds.* Similarly, the demand curve for bonds can be reidentified as the *supply of loanable funds* because buying (demanding) a bond is equivalent to supplying a loan. Figure 2 relabels the curves and the horizontal axis using the loanable funds terminology in parentheses, and now the renamed loanable funds demand curve has the usual downward slope and the renamed loanable funds supply curve the usual upward slope.

Because supply and demand diagrams that explain how interest rates are determined in the bond market most commonly use the loanable funds terminology, this analysis is frequently referred to as the **loanable funds framework.** However, because in later chapters describing the conduct of monetary policy we focus on how the demand for and supply of bonds is affected, we will continue to conduct supply and demand analysis in terms of bonds, as in Figure 1, rather than loanable funds. Whether the analysis is done in terms of loanable funds or in terms of the demand for and supply of bonds, the results are the same; the two ways of analyzing the determination of interest rates are equivalent.

An important feature of the analysis here is that supply and demand are always in terms of *stocks* (amounts at a given point in time) of assets, not in terms of *flows.* This approach is somewhat different from certain loanable funds analyses, which are conducted in terms of flows (loans per year). The **asset market approach** for understanding behavior in financial markets—which emphasizes stocks of assets rather than flows in determining asset prices—is now the dominant methodology used by financial economists because correctly conducting analyses in terms of flows is very tricky, especially when we encounter inflation.

(See the appendix to this chapter for an application of the asset market approach to another market.)

CHANGES IN EQUILIBRIUM INTEREST RATES

We will now use the supply and demand framework for bonds to analyze why interest rates change. To avoid confusion, it is important to make the distinction between *movements along* a demand (or supply) curve and *shifts in* a demand (or supply) curve. When quantity demanded (or supplied) changes as a result of a change in the price of the bond (or, equivalently, a change in the interest rate), we have a *movement along* the demand (or supply) curve. The change in the quantity demanded when we move from point A to B to C in Figure 1 or Figure 2, for example, is a movement along a demand curve. A *shift in* the demand (or supply) curve, by contrast, occurs when the quantity demanded (or supplied) changes *at each given price (or interest rate)* of the bond in response to a change in some other factor besides the bond's price or interest rate. When one of these factors changes, causing a shift in the demand or supply curve, there will be a new equilibrium value for the interest rate.

In the following pages we will look at how the supply and demand curves shift in response to changes in variables, such as expected inflation and wealth, and what effects these changes have on the equilibrium value of interest rates.

Shifts in the Demand for Bonds

Our analysis of the determinants of asset demand at the beginning of the chapter provides a framework for deciding what factors cause the demand curve for bonds to shift. These factors include changes in four parameters:

1. Wealth
2. Expected returns on bonds relative to alternative assets
3. Risk of bonds relative to alternative assets
4. Liquidity of bonds relative to alternative assets

To see how a change in each of these factors (holding all other factors constant) can shift the demand curve, let us look at some examples. (As a study aid, Table 2 summarizes the effects of changes in these factors on the bond demand curve.)

Wealth When the economy is growing rapidly in a business cycle expansion and wealth is increasing, the quantity of bonds demanded at each bond price (or interest rate) increases as shown in Figure 3. To see how this works, consider point B on the initial demand curve for bonds B^d_1. It tells us that at a bond price of \$900 and an interest rate of 11.1%, the quantity of bonds demanded is \$200 billion. With higher wealth, the quantity of bonds demanded at the same interest rate must rise, say, to \$400 billion (point B′). Similarly, the higher wealth causes the quantity demanded at a bond price of \$800 and an interest rate of 25% to rise from \$400 billion to \$600 billion (point D to D′). Continuing with this reasoning for every point on the initial demand curve B^d_1, we can see that the demand curve shifts to the right from B^d_1 to B^d_2 as is indicated by the arrows.

The conclusion we have reached is that ***in a business cycle expansion with growing wealth, the demand for bonds rises and the demand curve for bonds shifts to the right.*** Using the same reasoning, ***in a recession, when***

TABLE 2 SUMMARY Factors That Shift the Demand Curve for Bonds

Variable	Change in Variable	Change in Quantity Demanded	Shift in Demand Curve
Wealth	↑	↑	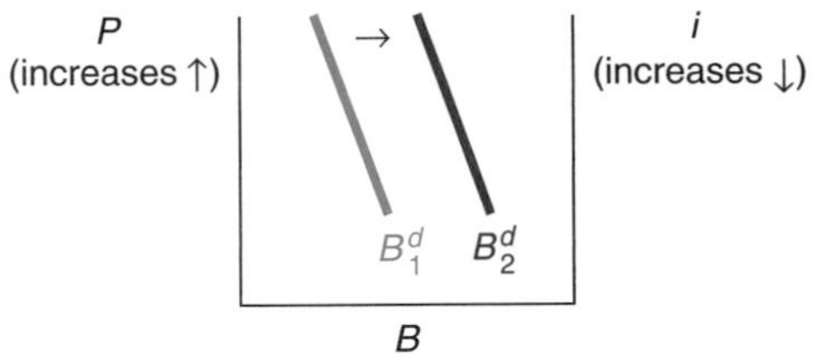 P (increases ↑), i (increases ↓); curve shifts right → from B^d_1 to B^d_2; horizontal axis B
Expected interest rate	↑	↓	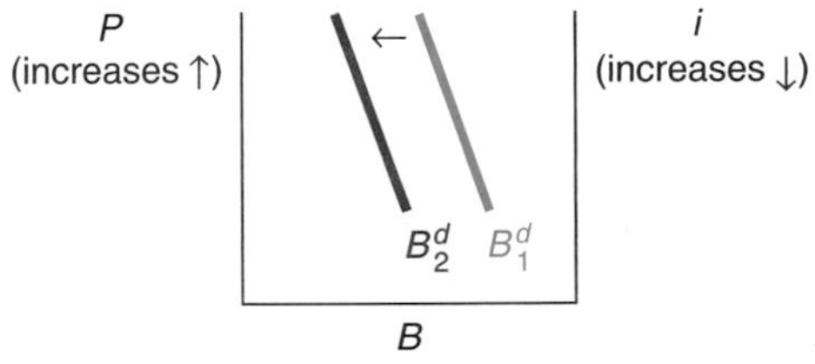 P (increases ↑), i (increases ↓); curve shifts left ← from B^d_1 to B^d_2; horizontal axis B
Expected inflation	↑	↓	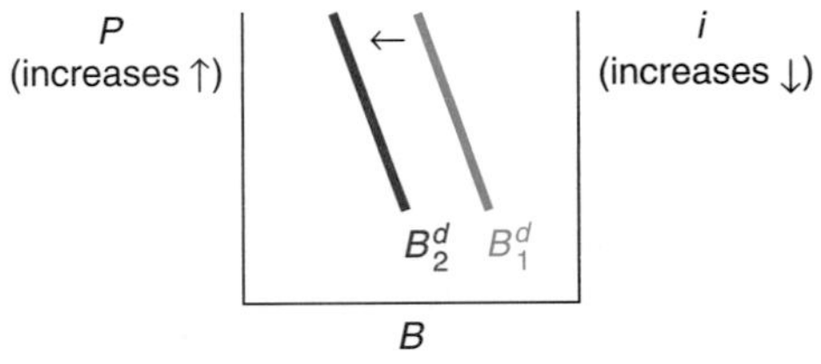 P (increases ↑), i (increases ↓); curve shifts left ← from B^d_1 to B^d_2; horizontal axis B
Riskiness of bonds relative to other assets	↑	↓	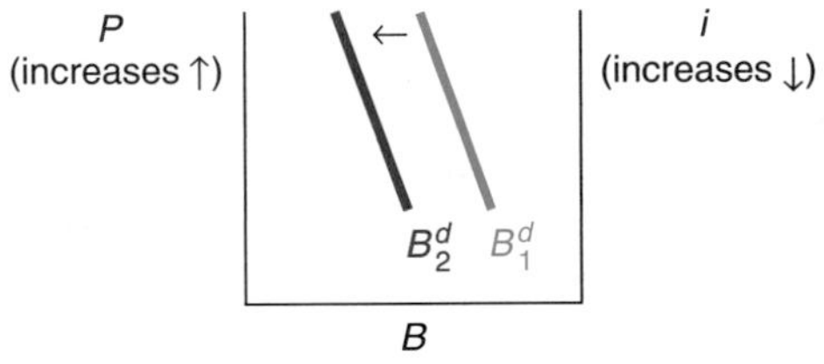 P (increases ↑), i (increases ↓); curve shifts left ← from B^d_1 to B^d_2; horizontal axis B
Liquidity of bonds relative to other assets	↑	↑	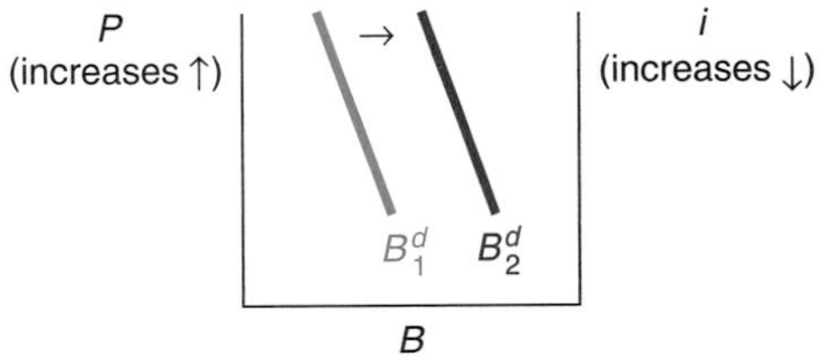 P (increases ↑), i (increases ↓); curve shifts right → from B^d_1 to B^d_2; horizontal axis B

Note: Only increases (↑) in the variables are shown. The effect of decreases in the variables on the change in demand would be the opposite of those indicated in the remaining columns.

income and wealth are falling, the demand for bonds falls, and the demand curve shifts to the left.

Another factor that affects wealth is the public's propensity to save. If households save more, wealth increases and, as we have seen, the demand for bonds rises and the demand curve for bonds shifts to the right. Conversely, if people save less, wealth and the demand for bonds will fall and the demand curve shifts to the left.

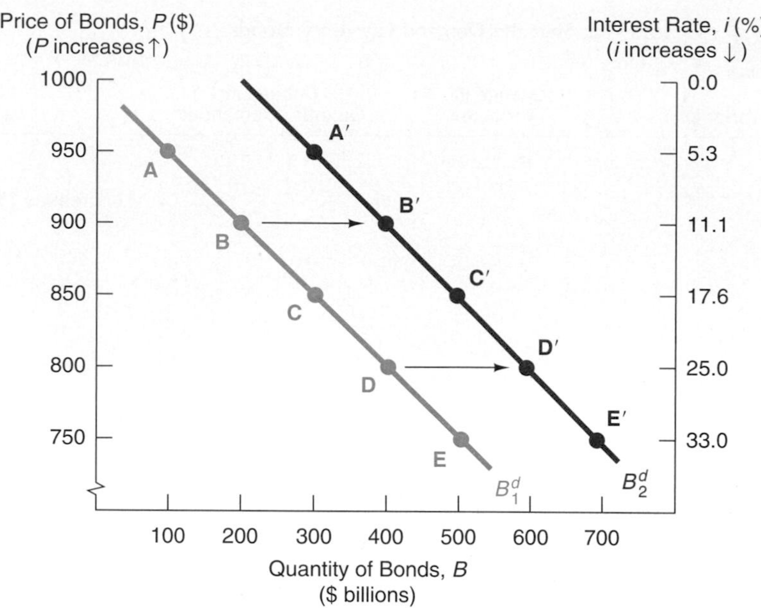

FIGURE 3 Shift in the Demand Curve for Bonds

When the demand for bonds increases, the demand curve shifts to the right as shown. (*Note*: P and i increase in opposite directions. P on the left vertical axis increases as we go up the axis, while i on the right vertical axis increases as we go down the axis.)

Expected Returns For a one-year discount bond and a one-year holding period, the expected return and the interest rate are identical. No component of the expected return is unrelated to the bond price or the interest rate.

For bonds with maturities of greater than one year, the expected return may differ from the interest rate. For example, we saw in Chapter 3, Table 2, that a rise in the interest rate on a long-term bond from 10% to 20% would lead to a sharp decline in price and a very negative return. Hence if people begin to think that interest rates will be higher next year than they had originally anticipated, the expected return today on long-term bonds would fall, and the quantity demanded would fall at each interest rate. ***Higher expected interest rates in the future decrease the demand for long-term bonds and shift the demand curve to the left.***

By contrast, a revision downward of expectations of future interest rates would mean that long-term bond prices would be expected to rise more than originally anticipated, and the resulting higher expected return today would raise the quantity demanded at each bond price and interest rate. ***Lower expected interest rates in the future increase the demand for long-term bonds and shift the demand curve to the right*** (as in Figure 3).

Changes in expected returns on other assets can also shift the demand curve for bonds. If people suddenly became more optimistic about the stock market and began to expect higher stock prices in the future, both expected capital gains and expected returns on stocks would rise. With the expected return on bonds held constant, the expected return on bonds today relative to stocks would fall, lowering the demand for bonds and shifting the demand curve to the left.

A change in expected inflation is likely to alter expected returns on physical assets (also called *real assets*) such as automobiles and houses, which affect the demand for bonds. An increase in expected inflation, say, from 5% to 10%, will lead to higher prices on cars and houses in the future and hence higher nominal capital gains. The resulting rise in the expected returns today on these real assets will lead to a fall in the expected return on bonds relative to the expected return on real assets today and thus cause the demand for bonds to fall. Alternatively, we can think of the rise in expected inflation as lowering the real interest rate on bonds, and the resulting decline in the relative expected return on bonds causes the demand for bonds to fall. ***An increase in the expected rate of inflation will cause the demand for bonds to decline and the demand curve to shift to the left.***

Risk If prices in the bond market become more volatile, the risk associated with bonds increases, and bonds become a less attractive asset. ***An increase in the riskiness of bonds causes the demand for bonds to fall and the demand curve to shift to the left.***

Conversely, an increase in the volatility of prices in another asset market, such as the stock market, would make bonds more attractive. ***An increase in the riskiness of alternative assets causes the demand for bonds to rise and the demand curve to shift to the right*** (as in Figure 3).

Liquidity If more people started trading in the bond market and as a result it became easier to sell bonds quickly, the increase in their liquidity would cause the quantity of bonds demanded at each interest rate to rise. ***Increased liquidity of bonds results in an increased demand for bonds, and the demand curve shifts to the right*** (see Figure 3). ***Similarly, increased liquidity of alternative assets lowers the demand for bonds and shifts the demand curve to the left.*** The reduction of brokerage commissions for trading common stocks that occurred when the fixed-rate commission structure was abolished in 1975, for example, increased the liquidity of stocks relative to bonds, and the resulting lower demand for bonds shifted the demand curve to the left.

Shifts in the Supply of Bonds

Certain factors can cause the supply curve for bonds to shift, among them these:

1. Expected profitability of investment opportunities
2. Expected inflation
3. Government activities

We will look at how the supply curve shifts when each of these factors changes (when all others remain constant). (As a study aid, Table 3 summarizes the effects of changes in these factors on the bond supply curve.)

Expected Profitability of Investment Opportunities The more profitable investments that a firm expects it can make, the more willing it will be to borrow and increase the amount of its outstanding debt in order to finance these investments. When the economy is growing rapidly, as in a business cycle expansion, investment opportunities that are expected to be profitable abound, and the quantity of bonds supplied at any given bond price and interest rate will increase (see Figure 4). Therefore, ***in a business cycle expansion, the supply of bonds increases, and the supply curve shifts to the right. Likewise, in a recession, when there are far fewer expected profitable investment opportunities, the supply of bonds falls, and the supply curve shifts to the left.***

TABLE 3 SUMMARY Factors That Shift the Supply of Bonds

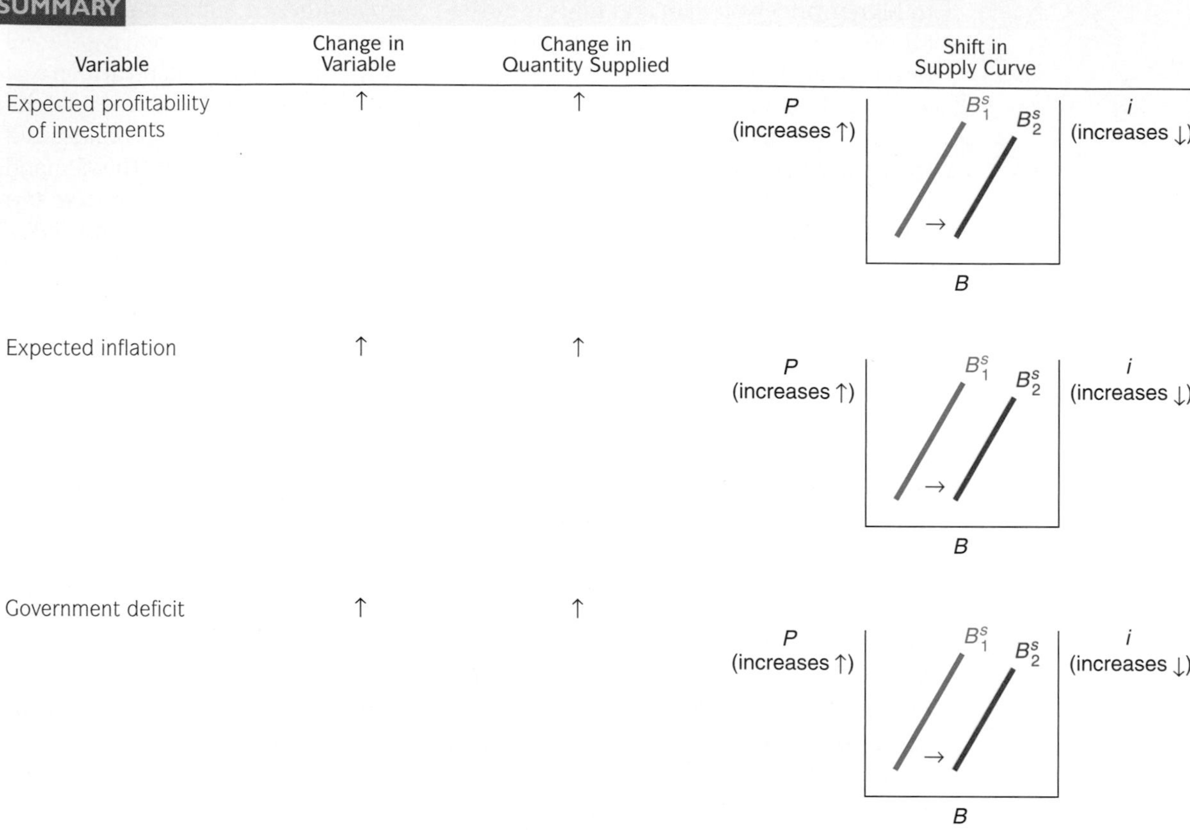

Variable	Change in Variable	Change in Quantity Supplied	Shift in Supply Curve
Expected profitability of investments	↑	↑	P (increases ↑), i (increases ↓); B^s_1 → B^s_2; B
Expected inflation	↑	↑	P (increases ↑), i (increases ↓); B^s_1 → B^s_2; B
Government deficit	↑	↑	P (increases ↑), i (increases ↓); B^s_1 → B^s_2; B

Note: Only increases (↑) in the variables are shown. The effect of decreases in the variables on the change in supply would be the opposite of those indicated in the remaining columns.

Weekly updates on domestic and global economic, monetary, and policy trends influencing inflation are available at www.forecasts.org/inflationwatch/index.htm For information on expected inflation, go to www.forecasts.org/inflationwatch/monthly/inflation.htm

Expected Inflation As we saw in Chapter 3, the real cost of borrowing is more accurately measured by the real interest rate, which equals the (nominal) interest rate minus the expected inflation rate. For a given interest rate, when expected inflation increases, the real cost of borrowing falls; hence the quantity of bonds supplied increases at any given bond price and interest rate. ***An increase in expected inflation causes the supply of bonds to increase and the supply curve to shift to the right*** (see Figure 4).

Government Activities The activities of the government can influence the supply of bonds in several ways. The U.S. Treasury issues bonds to finance government deficits, the gap between the government's expenditures and its revenues. When these deficits are large, as they have been recently, the Treasury sells more bonds, and the quantity of bonds supplied at each bond price and interest rate increases. ***Higher government deficits increase the supply of bonds and shift the supply curve to the right*** (see Figure 4). ***On the other hand, government surpluses, as occurred in the late 1990s and early 2000s, decrease the supply of bonds and shift the supply curve to the left.***

State and local governments and other government agencies also issue bonds to finance their expenditures, and this can also affect the supply of bonds. We will see in later chapters that the conduct of monetary policy involves the purchase and sale of bonds, which in turn influences the supply of bonds.

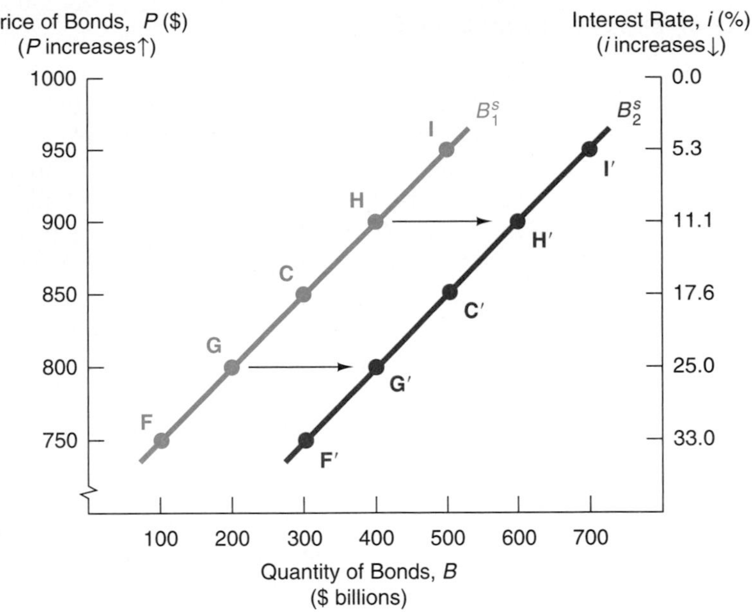

FIGURE 4 Shift in the Supply Curve for Bonds

When the supply of bonds increases, the supply curve shifts to the right. (*Note*: *P* and *i* increase in opposite directions. *P* on the left vertical axis increases as we go up the axis, while *i* on the right vertical axis increases as we go down the axis.)

Application Changes in the Equilibrium Interest Rate Due to Expected Inflation or Business Cycle Expansions

We can now use our knowledge of how supply and demand curves shift to analyze how the equilibrium interest rate can change. The best way to do this is to pursue several applications that are particularly relevant to our understanding of how monetary policy affects interest rates.

Study Guide Supply and demand analysis for the bond market is best learned by practicing applications. When there is an application in the text and we look at how the interest rate changes because some economic variable increases, see if you can draw the appropriate shifts in the supply and demand curves when this same economic variable decreases. While you are practicing applications, keep two things in mind:

1. When you examine the effect of a variable change, remember that we are assuming that all other variables are unchanged; that is, we are making use of the *ceteris paribus* assumption.
2. Remember that the interest rate is negatively related to the bond price, so when the equilibrium bond price rises, the equilibrium interest rate falls. Conversely, if the equilibrium bond price moves downward, the equilibrium interest rate rises.

Changes in Expected Inflation: The Fisher Effect

We have already done most of the work to evaluate how a change in expected inflation affects the nominal interest rate in that we have already analyzed how a change in expected inflation shifts the supply and demand curves. Figure 5 shows the effect on the equilibrium interest rate of an increase in expected inflation.

Suppose that expected inflation is initially 5% and the initial supply and demand curves B_1^s and B_1^d intersect at point 1, where the equilibrium bond price is P_1 and the equilibrium interest rate is i_1. If expected inflation rises to 10%, the expected return on bonds relative to real assets falls for any given bond price and interest rate. As a result, the demand for bonds falls, and the demand curve shifts to the left from B_1^d to B_2^d. The rise in expected inflation also shifts the supply curve. At any given bond price and interest rate, the real cost of borrowing has declined, causing the quantity of bonds supplied to increase, and the supply curve shifts to the right from B_1^s to B_2^s.

When the demand and supply curves shift in response to the change in expected inflation, the equilibrium moves from point 1 to point 2, which is the intersection of B_2^d and B_2^s. The equilibrium bond price has fallen from P_1 to P_2, and because the bond price is negatively related to the interest rate (as is indicated by the interest rate rising as we go down the right vertical axis), this means that the interest rate has risen from i_1 to i_2. Note that Figure 5 has been drawn so that the equilibrium quantity of bonds remains the same for both point 1 and point 2. However, depending on the size of the shifts in the supply and demand curves, the equilibrium quantity of bonds could either rise or fall when expected inflation rises.

Our supply and demand analysis has led us to an important observation: ***When expected inflation rises, interest rates will rise.*** This result has been named

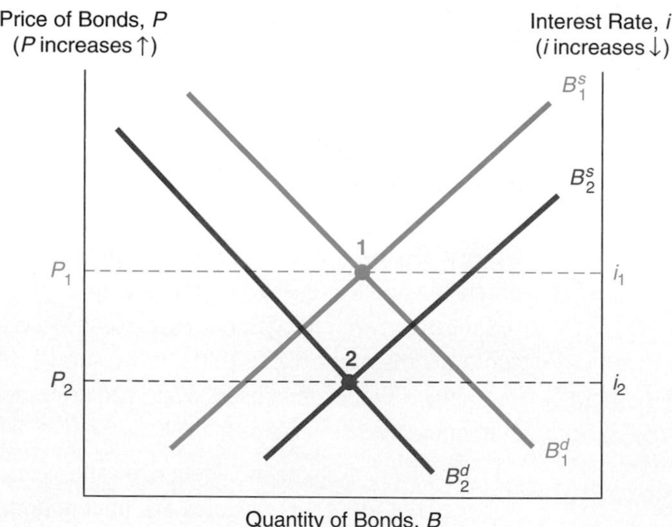

FIGURE 5 Response to a Change in Expected Inflation

When expected inflation rises, the supply curve shifts from B_1^s to B_2^s, and the demand curve shifts from B_1^d to B_2^d. The equilibrium moves from point 1 to point 2, with the result that the equilibrium bond price (left axis) falls from P_1 to P_2 and the equilibrium interest rate (right axis) rises from i_1 to i_2. (*Note*: *P* and *i* increase in opposite directions. *P* on the left vertical axis increases as we go up the axis, while *i* on the right vertical axis increases as we go down the axis.)

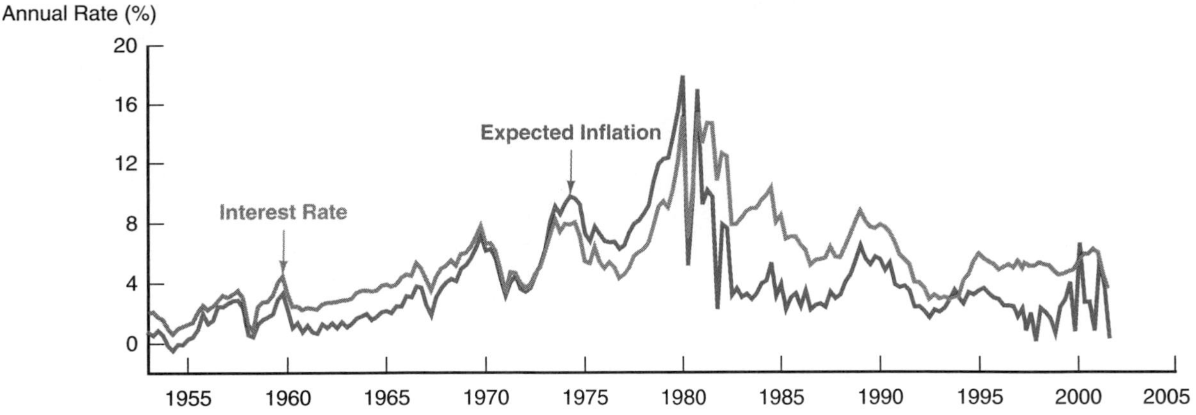

FIGURE 6 Expected Inflation and Interest Rates (Three-Month Treasury Bills), 1953–2001

Source: Expected inflation calculated using procedures outlined in Frederic S. Mishkin, "The Real Interest Rate: An Empirical Investigation," *Carnegie-Rochester Conference Series on Public Policy* 15 (1981): 151–200. This involves estimating expected inflation as a function of past interest rates, inflation, and time trends.

the **Fisher effect,** after Irving Fisher, the economist who first pointed out the relationship of expected inflation to interest rates. The accuracy of this prediction is shown in Figure 6. The interest rate on three-month Treasury bills has usually moved along with the expected inflation rate. Consequently, it is understandable that many economists recommend that the fight against inflation must be won if we want to lower interest rates.

Business Cycle Expansion

Figure 7 analyzes the effects of a business cycle expansion on interest rates. In a business cycle expansion, the amount of goods and services being produced in the economy rises, so national income increases. When this occurs, businesses will be more willing to borrow because they are likely to have many profitable investment opportunities for which they need financing. Hence at a given bond price and interest rate, the quantity of bonds that firms want to sell (that is, the supply of bonds) will increase. This means that in a business cycle expansion, the supply curve for bonds shifts to the right (see Figure 7) from B_1^s to B_2^s.

The expanding economy will also affect the demand for bonds. Our discussion of the determinants of asset demand tells us that as the economy expands and wealth increases, the demand for bonds will rise as well. We see this in Figure 7, where the demand curve has shifted to the right from B_1^d to B_2^d.

Given that both the supply and demand curves have shifted to the right, we know that the new equilibrium reached at the intersection of B_2^d and B_2^s must also move to the right. However, depending on whether the supply curve shifts more than the demand curve or vice versa, the new equilibrium interest rate can either rise or fall.

The supply and demand analysis used here gives us an ambiguous answer to the question of what will happen to interest rates in a business cycle expansion. The figure has been drawn so that the shift in the supply curve is greater than the shift in the demand curve, causing the equilibrium bond price to fall to P_2, leading to a rise in the equilibrium interest rate to i_2. The reason the figure has been drawn so that a business cycle expansion and a rise in income lead to a higher

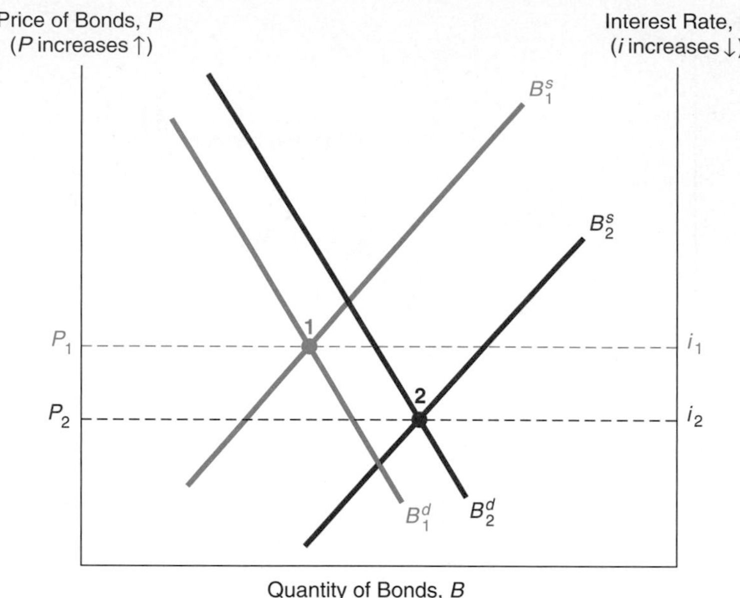

FIGURE 7 Response to a Business Cycle Expansion

In a business cycle expansion, when income and wealth are rising, the demand curve shifts rightward from B_1^d to B_2^d, and the supply curve shifts rightward from B_1^s to B_2^s. If the supply curve shifts to the right more than the demand curve, as in this figure, the equilibrium bond price (left axis) moves down from P_1 to P_2, and the equilibrium interest rate (right axis) rises from i_1 to i_2. (*Note*: P and i increase in opposite directions. P on the left vertical axis increases as we go up the axis, while i on the right vertical axis increases as we go down the axis.)

interest rate is that this is the outcome we actually see in the data. Figure 8 plots the movement of the interest rate on three-month U.S. Treasury bills from 1951 to 2001 and indicates when the business cycle is undergoing recessions (shaded areas). As you can see, the interest rate rises during business cycle expansions and falls during recessions, which is what the supply and demand diagram indicates.

Application

Explaining Low Japanese Interest Rates

In the 1990s and early 2000s, Japanese interest rates became the lowest in the world. Indeed, in November 1998, an extraordinary event occurred: Interest rates on Japanese six-month Treasury bills turned slightly negative (see Chapter 3). Why did Japanese rates drop to such low levels?

In the late 1990s, Japan had been experiencing a prolonged recession, accompanied by a negative inflation rate. Using these facts, analysis similar to that used in the preceding application explains the low Japanese interest rates.

Negative inflation causes the demand for bonds to rise because the expected return on real assets falls, thereby raising the relative expected return on bonds and in turn causing the demand curve to shift to the right. The negative inflation also raises the real interest rate and therefore the real cost of borrowing for any given nominal rate, thereby causing the supply of bonds to contract and the supply curve to shift to the left. The outcome is then exactly the opposite of that graphed in Figure 5: The rightward shift of the demand curve and leftward shift of the supply curve lead to a rise in the bond price and a fall in interest rates.

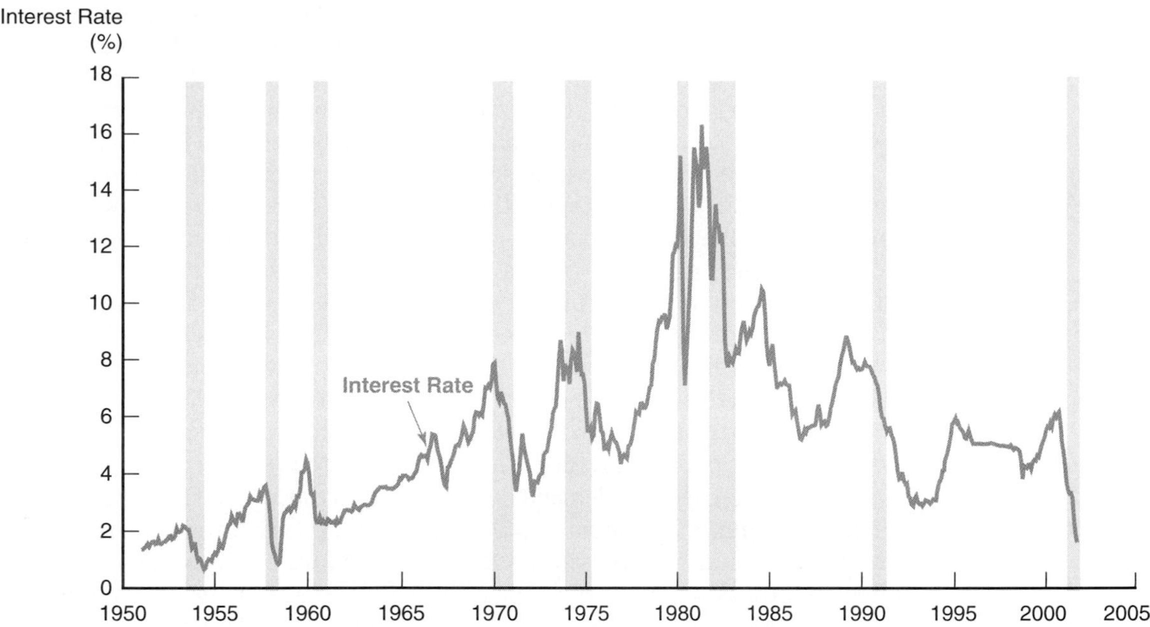

FIGURE 8 Business Cycle and Interest Rates (Three-Month Treasury Bills), 1951–2001

Shaded areas indicate periods of recession. The figure shows that interest rates rise during business cycle expansions and fall during contractions, which is what Figure 7 suggests would happen.

Source: Federal Reserve Board at www.federalreserve.gov/releases

The business cycle contraction in Japan also leads to lower interest rates because the resulting lack of investment opportunities decreases the supply of bonds, shifting the supply curve to the left. Although the demand curve also shifts to the left because wealth decreases during the business cycle contraction, we have seen in the preceding application that the demand curve shifts less than the supply curve, so that we get exactly the opposite outcome as that in Figure 7: The bond price rises, and the interest rates fall.

Usually we think that low interest rates are a good thing because they make it cheap to borrow. But the Japanese example shows that just as there is a fallacy in the adage "You can never be too rich or too thin"—maybe you can't be too rich, but you certainly can be too thin and do damage to your health—there is a fallacy in always thinking that lower interest rates are better. In Japan, the low and even negative interest rates are a sign that the Japanese economy is in real trouble, with falling prices and a contracting economy. Only when the Japanese economy returns to health will interest rates rise back to more normal levels.

Application The "Credit Markets" Column

READING THE *WALL STREET JOURNAL*

Now that we have an understanding of how supply and demand determines prices and interest rates in the bond market, we can use our analysis to understand discussions about bond prices and interest rates appearing in the financial press. Every day, the *Wall Street Journal* reports on developments in the bond market on the previous business day in its "Credit Markets" column, an example of which is found in the "Following the Financial News" box. Let's see how statements in the "Credit Markets" column can be explained using our supply and demand framework.

The column featured in the "Following the Financial News" box begins by stating that Treasury prices fell sharply as the economy showed improvement. This is exactly what our supply and demand analysis predicts would happen.

A stronger economy rises the supply of bonds because of increased investment opportunities and thus shifts the supply curve out to the right, while it also increases the demand for bonds and shift the demand curve out to the right because a stronger economy raises wealth and income. However, as illustrated in Figure 7, because the supply curve generally shifts by more than the demand curve when the economy get stronger, the price of bonds falls rather than rises.

The column also points out that prospects of a stronger economy raise the fear that the Federal Reserve will raise interest rates in the future. Higher future interest rates imply that the price of long-term bonds will be lower in the future, thus decreasing their expected return. The lower expected return causes the demand for bonds to decrease, the demand curve to shift to the left and the price of bonds to fall. The column also mentions that the outlook (expected return) for non-government bonds is improving as the economy improves, so that the relative expected returns for Treasury bonds falls, thus also causing the demand for Treasury's to fall and the demand curve to shift to the left. This provides an additional reason for weakness in the Treasury bond market.

Application

Have Negative Savings Rates in the United States Led to Higher Interest Rates?

Since 1980, the United States has experienced a sharp drop in personal savings rates, falling from 8% of personal income to negative levels in recent years. Many commentators, including high officials of the Federal Reserve System, have blamed the profligate behavior of the American public for high interest rates. Are they right?

Our supply and demand analysis of the bond market indicates that they could be. The decline in savings means that the wealth of American households is lower than would otherwise be the case. This smaller amount of wealth decreases the demand for bonds and shifts the demand curve to the left from B_1^d to B_2^d in Figure 9. The result is that the equilibrium bond price drops from P_1 to P_2 and the interest rate rises from i_1 to i_2. Low savings can thus raise interest rates, and the higher rates may retard investment in capital goods. The low savings rate of Americans may therefore lead to a less productive economy and is of serious concern to both economists and policymakers. Suggested remedies for the problem range from changing the tax code to encourage saving to forcing Americans to save more by mandating increased contributions into retirement plans.

LIQUIDITY PREFERENCE FRAMEWORK: SUPPLY AND DEMAND IN THE MARKET FOR MONEY

Whereas the loanable funds framework determines the equilibrium interest rate using the supply of and demand for bonds, an alternative model developed by John Maynard Keynes, known as the **liquidity preference framework,** determines the equilibrium interest rate in terms of the supply of and demand for money. Although the two frameworks look different, the liquidity preference analysis of

FOLLOWING THE FINANCIAL NEWS

The "Credit Markets" Column

The "Credit Markets" column appears daily in the *Wall Street Journal;* an example is presented here. It is found in the third section, "Money and Investing."

CREDIT MARKETS

Treasurys Drop on Signs Economy Is Improving As Funds Are Moved to Bonds With Higher Yields

BY STEVEN VAMES
Dow Jones Newswires

NEW YORK—Treasurys prices fell sharply in the first trading session of 2002, as the economy showed improvement and money managers shifted funds into higher-yielding bonds.

Declines came across the spectrum, but were especially heavy in short-dated securities. That reflected a belief that short-dated issues had become less attractive because of their relatively lower yields and a risk that their prices will fall further as the market continues to grapple with economic data that suggest the economy is improving.

Selling in longer-dated securities was said to be related to pending issuance of corporate bonds.

Trading was halted Tuesday for the New Year's holiday.

Compared with levels Monday, the benchmark 10-year Treasury note at 4 p.m. yesterday was down 1 1/32 points, or $10.3125 per $1,000 face value, at 98 26/32. Its yield rose to 5/157% from 5.020% Monday, as yields move inversely to prices.

The 30-year Treasury bond's price was down 1 12/32 points at 97 11/32 to yield 5.560%, up from 5.463% Monday.

People in the market said much of the weakness in Treasurys was driven by repositioning by funds managers into bonds that offer higher returns than Treasurys.

"Municipal bonds and corporate bonds are holding their ground," said Zane Brown, director of fixed income at Lord, Abbett in New York. "Investors see great value in (nongovernment bonds) because they are historically cheap relative to Treasurys, and they will continue to improve as the economy improves," he added.

Bond underwriters were also said to be selling Treasurys as they hedged coming bond offerings, using transactions known as rate locks to protect against interest rate moves. The transactions involve selling Treasurys or Treasury futures. When corporate deals are done, underwriters make offsetting purchases of Treasurys.

"When we see a major seller of bond futures like we did today, we can presume there is a rate-lock activity going on," said Gerald Lucas, senior government bond strategist at Merrill Lynch in New York.

Coming offerings include a $1.25 billion, 10-year deal from Goldman Sachs Group and a $3 billion three-year deal from the Federal Home Loan Bank, though it was unclear whether the rate-locks activity seen was related to those deals.

Many fund managers still entrenched in heavy positions in short-dated Treasurys may be fleeing because of what they see as a growing risk that the economy will recover sooner than many had expected. If coming date continue to suggest a quick start to economic recovery, that could spark fear that the Federal Reserve will start raising interest rates, which would likely result in more selling in Treasurys.

Signs of recovery came yesterday in a report indicating that conditions improved for the nation's manufacturers in December.

The Institute of Supply Management, formerly known as the National Association of Purchasing Management, said its index of manufacturing activity rose to 48.2 in December from 44.5 in November and 39.8 in October.

Readings above 50 indicate expansion of activity, while readings under 50 denote contraction. December's was the 17th straight month of contraction in manufacturing. Economists had expected the index to move to 46.0, but gains in orders for new goods helped push it higher.

"The data are positive for the economy and reinforce the notion for investors that the economy is bottoming out and is poised for a recovery some time this year," said Kevin Flanagan, fixed-income strategist at Morgan Stanley.

The next major economic signpost is today's Labor Department release of weekly initial claims for unemployment benefits. Economists expect to se a rise of about 6,000, according to a Dow Jones Newswires/CNBC survey.

Tomorrow, the Labor Department will release its December employment report. That report, which is widely watched, is seen by many economists as a make-or-break factor for expectations about whether Fed policymakers will continue to cut rates when they meet in late January.

Source: Wall Street Journal, January 3, 2002, p. C12. Republished by permission of Dow Jones, Inc. via Copyright Clearance Center, Inc.

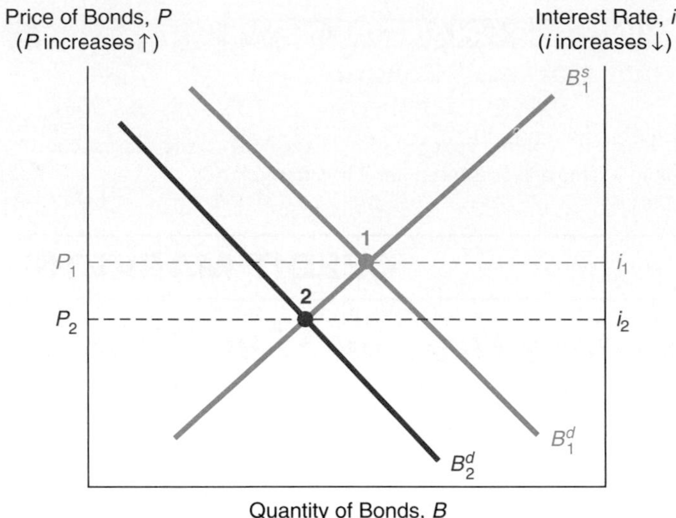

FIGURE 9 Response to a Lower Savings Rate

With a lower savings rate, wealth decreases, and the demand curve shifts in from B_1^d to B_2^d. The equilibrium moves from point 1 to point 2, with the result that the equilibrium bond price (left axis) drops from P_1 to P_2 and the equilibrium interest rate (right axis) rises from i_1 to i_2. (*Note*: P and i increase in opposite directions. P on the left vertical axis increases as we go up the axis, while i on the right vertical axis increases as we go down the axis.)

the market for money is closely related to the loanable funds framework of the bond market.[4]

The starting point of Keynes's analysis is his assumption that there are two main categories of assets that people use to store their wealth: money and bonds. Therefore, total wealth in the economy must equal the total quantity of bonds plus money in the economy, which equals the quantity of bonds supplied B^s plus the quantity of money supplied M^s. The quantity of bonds B^d and money M^d that people want to hold and thus demand must also equal the total amount of wealth because people cannot purchase more assets than their available resources allow. The conclusion is that the quantity of bonds and money supplied must equal the quantity of bonds and money demanded:

$$B^s + M^s = B^d + M^d \tag{4}$$

Collecting the bond terms on one side of the equation and the money terms on the other, this equation can be rewritten as

$$B^s - B^d = M^d - M^s \tag{5}$$

The rewritten equation tells us that if the market for money is in equilibrium ($M^s = M^d$), the right-hand side of Equation 5 equals zero, implying that $B^s = B^d$, meaning that the bond market is also in equilibrium.

Thus it is the same to think about determining the equilibrium interest rate by equating the supply and demand for bonds or by equating the supply and

[4]Note that the term *market for money* refers to the market for the medium of exchange, money. This market differs from the *money market* referred to by finance practitioners, which is the financial market in which short-term debt instruments are traded.

demand for money. In this sense, the liquidity preference framework, which analyzes the market for money, is equivalent to the loanable funds framework, which analyzes the bond market. In practice, the approaches differ because by assuming that there are only two kinds of assets, money and bonds, the liquidity preference approach implicitly ignores any effects on interest rates that arise from changes in the expected returns on real assets such as automobiles and houses. In most instances, both frameworks yield the same predictions.

The reason that we approach the determination of interest rates with both frameworks is that the loanable funds framework is easier to use when analyzing the effects from changes in expected inflation, whereas the liquidity preference framework provides a simpler analysis of the effects from changes in income, the price level, and the supply of money.

Because the definition of money that Keynes used includes currency (which earns no interest) and checking account deposits (which in his time typically earned little or no interest), he assumed that money has a zero rate of return. Bonds, the only alternative asset to money in Keynes's framework, have an expected return equal to the interest rate i.[5] As this interest rate rises (holding everything else unchanged), the expected return on money falls relative to the expected return on bonds, and this causes the demand for money to fall.

We can also see that the demand for money and the interest rate should be negatively related by using the concept of **opportunity cost,** the amount of interest (expected return) sacrificed by not holding the alternative asset—in this case, a bond. As the interest rate on bonds i rises, the opportunity cost of holding money rises, and so money is less desirable and the quantity of money demanded must fall.

Figure 10 shows the quantity of money demanded at a number of interest rates, with all other economic variables, such as income and the price level, held constant. At an interest rate of 25%, point A shows that the quantity of money demanded is $100 billion. If the interest rate is at the lower rate of 20%, the opportunity cost of money is lower, and the quantity of money demanded rises to $200 billion, as indicated by the move from point A to point B. If the interest rate is even lower, the quantity of money demanded is even higher, as is indicated by points C, D, and E. The curve M^d connecting these points is the demand curve for money, and it slopes downward.

At this point in our analysis, we will assume that a central bank controls the amount of money supplied at a fixed quantity of $300 billion, so the supply curve for money M^s in the figure is a vertical line at $300 billion. The equilibrium where the quantity of money demanded equals the quantity of money supplied occurs at the intersection of the supply and demand curves at point C, where

$$M^d = M^s \tag{6}$$

The resulting equilibrium interest rate is at $i^* = 15\%$.

We can again see that there is a tendency to approach this equilibrium by first looking at the relationship of money demand and supply when the interest rate is above the equilibrium interest rate. When the interest rate is 25%, the quantity of money demanded at point A is $100 billion, yet the quantity of money supplied is $300 billion. The excess supply of money means that people are holding more money than they desire, so they will try to get rid of their excess money balances by trying to buy bonds. Accordingly, they will bid up the price of bonds,

[5]Keynes did not actually assume that the expected returns on bonds equaled the interest rate but rather argued that they were closely related. This distinction makes no appreciable difference in our analysis.

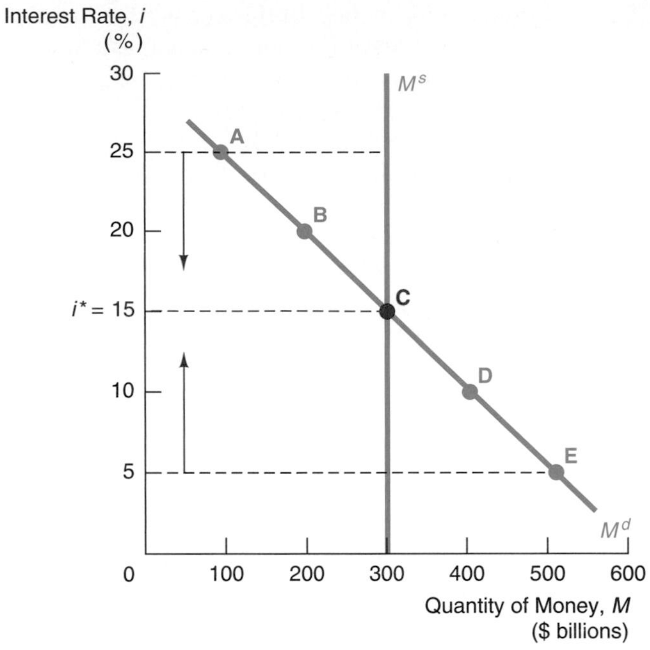

FIGURE 10 Equilibrium in the Market for Money

and as the bond price rises, the interest rate will fall toward the equilibrium interest rate of 15%. This tendency is shown by the downward arrow drawn at the interest rate of 25%.

Likewise, if the interest rate is 5%, the quantity of money demanded at point E is \$500 billion, but the quantity of money supplied is only \$300 billion. There is now an excess demand for money because people want to hold more money than they currently have. To try to get the money, they will sell their only other asset—bonds—and the price will fall. As the price of bonds falls, the interest rate will rise toward the equilibrium rate of 15%. Only when the interest rate is at its equilibrium value will there be no tendency for it to move further, and the interest rate will settle to its equilibrium value.

CHANGES IN EQUILIBRIUM INTEREST RATES

Analyzing how the equilibrium interest rate changes using the liquidity preference framework requires that we understand what causes the demand and supply curves for money to shift.

> **Study Guide** Learning the liquidity preference framework also requires practicing applications. When there is an application in the text to examine how the interest rate changes because some economic variable increases, see if you can draw the appropriate shifts in the supply and demand curves when this same economic variable decreases. And remember to use the *ceteris paribus* assumption: When examining the effect of a change in one variable, hold all other variables constant.

Shifts in the Demand for Money

In Keynes's liquidity preference analysis, two factors cause the demand curve for money to shift: income and the price level.

Income Effect In Keynes's view, there were two reasons why income would affect the demand for money. First, as an economy expands and income rises, wealth increases and people will want to hold more money as a store of value. Second, as the economy expands and income rises, people will want to carry out more transactions using money, with the result that they will also want to hold more money. The conclusion is that ***a higher level of income causes the demand for money to increase and the demand curve to shift to the right.***

Price-Level Effect Keynes took the view that people care about the amount of money they hold in real terms, that is, in terms of the goods and services that it can buy. When the price level rises, the same nominal quantity of money is no longer as valuable; it cannot be used to purchase as many real goods or services. To restore their holdings of money in real terms to its former level, people will want to hold a greater nominal quantity of money, so ***a rise in the price level causes the demand for money to increase and the demand curve to shift to the right.***

Shifts in the Supply of Money

We will assume that the supply of money is completely controlled by the central bank, which in the United States is the Federal Reserve. (Actually, the process that determines the money supply is substantially more complicated and involves banks, depositors, and borrowers from banks. We will study it in more detail later in the book.) For now, all we need to know is that ***an increase in the money supply engineered by the Federal Reserve will shift the supply curve for money to the right.***

Application Changes in the Equilibrium Interest Rate Due to Changes in Income, the Price Level, or the Money Supply

To see how the liquidity preference framework can be used to analyze the movement of interest rates, we will again look at several applications that will be useful in evaluating the effect of monetary policy on interest rates. (As a study aid, Table 4 summarizes the shifts in the demand and supply curves for money.)

Changes in Income

When income is rising during a business cycle expansion, we have seen that the demand for money will rise. It is shown in Figure 11 by the shift rightward in the demand curve from M_1^d to M_2^d The new equilibrium is reached at point 2 at the intersection of the M_2^d curve with the money supply curve M^s. As you can see, the equilibrium interest rate rises from i_1 to i_2. The liquidity preference framework thus generates the conclusion that ***when income is rising during a business cycle expansion (holding other economic variables constant), interest rates will rise.*** This conclusion is unambiguous when contrasted to the

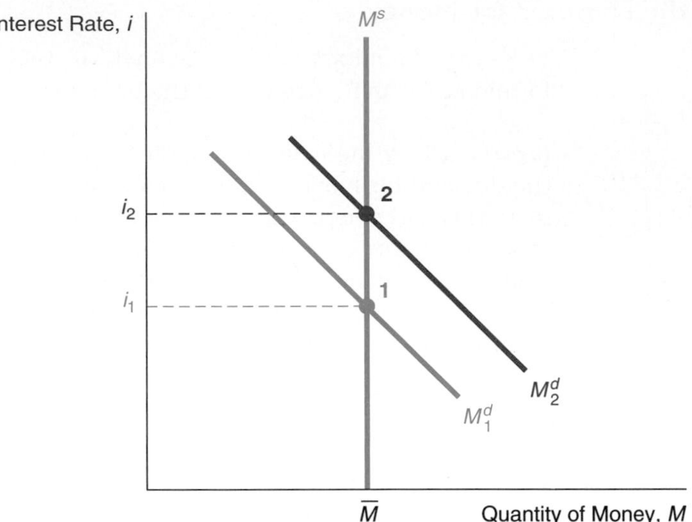

FIGURE 11 Response to a Change in Income

In a business cycle expansion, when income is rising, the demand curve shifts from M_1^d to M_2^d. The supply curve is fixed at $M^s = \overline{M}$. The equilibrium interest rate rises from i_1 to i_2.

conclusion reached about the effects of a change in income on interest rates using the loanable funds framework.

Changes in the Price Level

When the price level rises, the value of money in terms of what it can purchase is lower. To restore their purchasing power in real terms to its former level, people will want to hold a greater nominal quantity of money. A higher price level shifts the demand curve for money to the right from M_1^d to M_2^d (see Figure 12 on page 104). The equilibrium moves from point 1 to point 2, where the equilibrium interest rate has risen from i_1 to i_2, illustrating that ***when the price level increases, with the supply of money and other economic variables held constant, interest rates will rise.***

Money supply data, which the Federal Reserve reports at 4:30 p.m. every Thursday, are available online at www.federalreserve.gov/releases/H6/Current

Changes in the Money Supply

An increase in the money supply due to expansionary monetary policy by the Federal Reserve implies that the supply curve for money shifts to the right. As is shown in Figure 13 (page 104) by the movement of the supply curve from M_1^s to M_2^s, the equilibrium moves from point 1 down to point 2, where the M_2^s supply curve intersects with the demand curve M^d and the equilibrium interest rate has fallen from i_1 to i_2. ***When the money supply increases (everything else remaining equal), interest rates will decline.***[6]

[6]This same result can be generated using the loanable funds framework. The primary way that a central bank produces an increase in the money supply is by buying bonds and thereby decreasing the supply of bonds to the public. The resulting shift to the left of the supply curve for bonds will lead to a decline in the equilibrium interest rate.

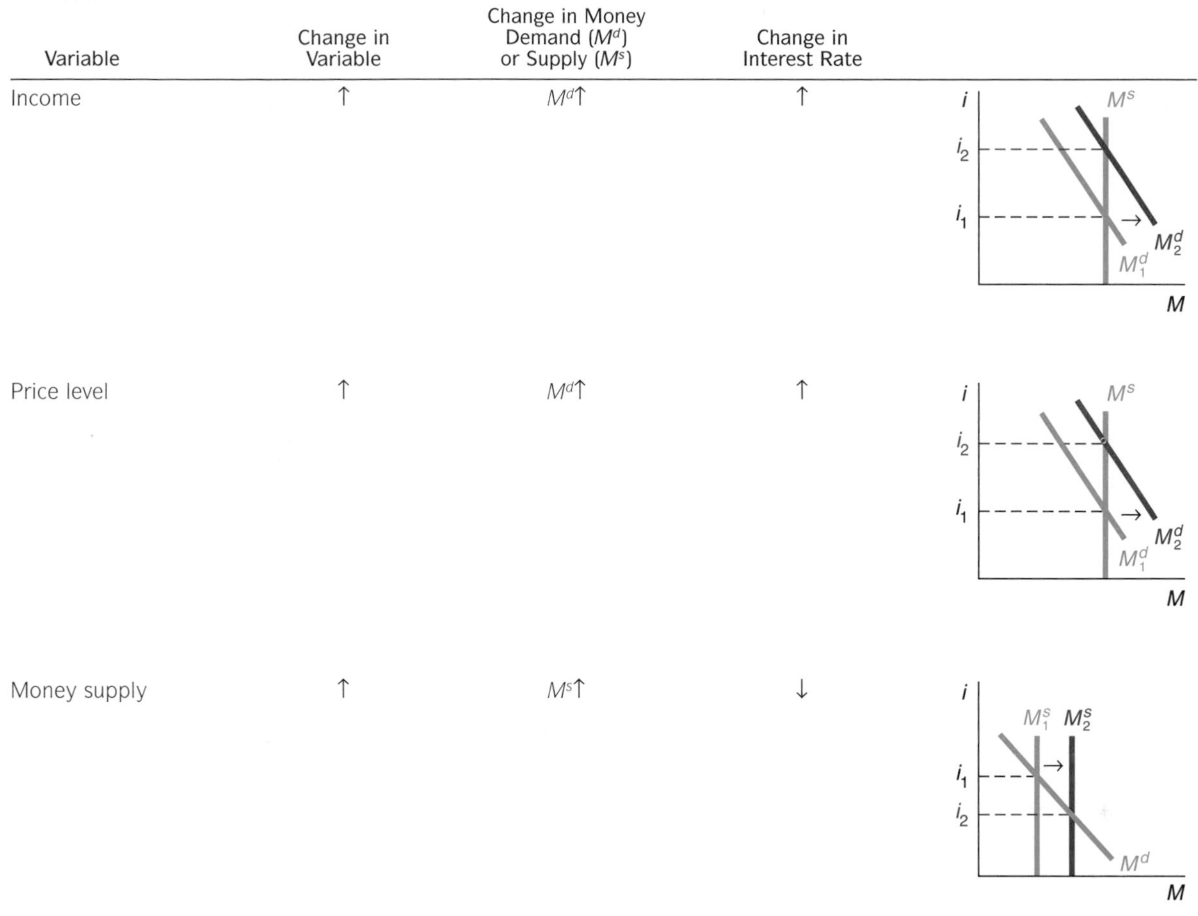

TABLE 4 SUMMARY Factors That Shift the Demand for and Supply of Money

Variable	Change in Variable	Change in Money Demand (M^d) or Supply (M^s)	Change in Interest Rate
Income	↑	M^d↑	↑
Price level	↑	M^d↑	↑
Money supply	↑	M^s↑	↓

Note: Only increases (↑) in the variables are shown. The effect of decreases in the variables on the change in demand or supply would be the opposite of those indicated in the remaining columns.

Application Money and Interest Rates

The liquidity preference analysis in Figure 13 seems to lead to the conclusion that an increase in the money supply will lower interest rates. This conclusion has important policy implications because it has frequently caused politicians to call for a more rapid growth of the money supply in order to drive down interest rates.

But is this conclusion that money and interest rates should be negatively related correct? Might there be other important factors left out of the liquidity preference analysis in Figure 13 that would reverse this conclusion? We will provide answers to these questions by applying the supply and demand analysis we have learned in this chapter to obtain a deeper understanding of the relationship between money and interest rates.

An important criticism of the conclusion that a rise in the money supply lowers interest rates has been raised by Milton Friedman, a Nobel laureate in economics. He acknowledges that the liquidity preference analysis is correct and calls

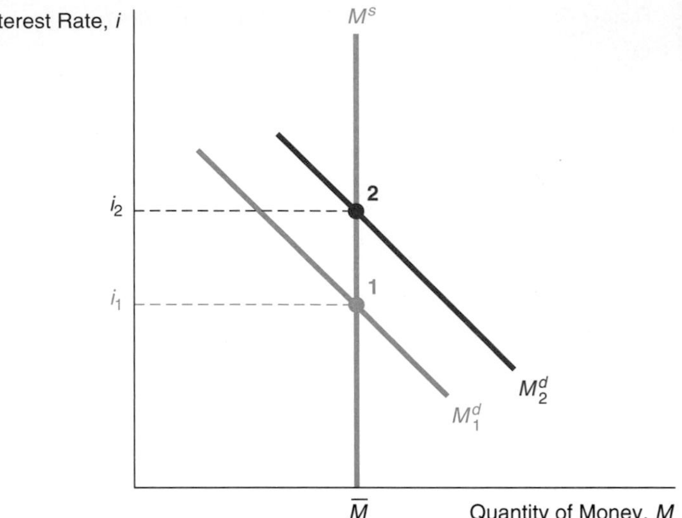

FIGURE 12 Response to a Change in the Price Level

An increase in price level shifts the money demand curve from M_1^d to M_2^d, and the equilibrium interest rate rises from i_1 to i_2.

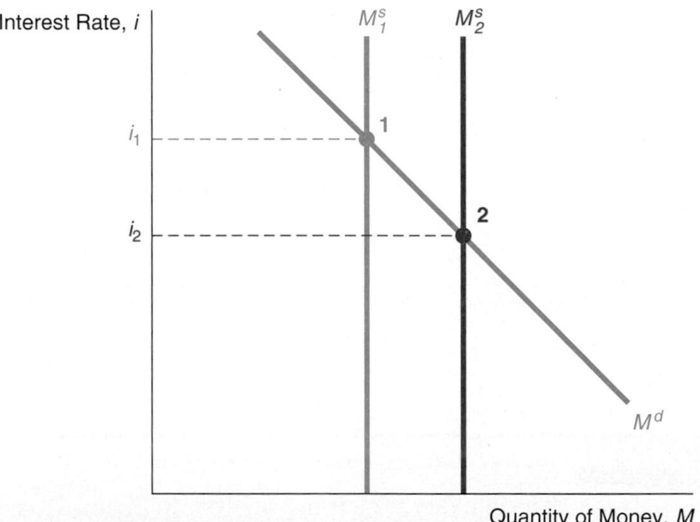

FIGURE 13 Response to a Change in the Money Supply

When the money supply increases, the supply curve shifts from M_1^s to M_2^s, and the equilibrium interest rate falls from i_1 to i_2.

the result—that an increase in the money supply (*everything else remaining equal*) lowers interest rates—the *liquidity effect.* However, he views the liquidity effect as merely part of the story: An increase in the money supply might not leave "everything else equal" and will have other effects on the economy that may make interest rates rise. If these effects are substantial, it is entirely possible that when the money supply rises, interest rates too may rise.

We have already laid the groundwork to discuss these other effects because we have shown how changes in income, the price level, and expected inflation affect the equilibrium interest rate.

Study Guide To get further practice with the loanable funds and liquidity preference frameworks, show how the effects discussed here work by drawing the supply and demand diagrams that explain each effect. This exercise will also improve your understanding of the effect of money on interest rates.

1. *Income Effect.* Because an increasing money supply is an expansionary influence on the economy, it should raise national income and wealth. Both the liquidity preference and loanable funds frameworks indicate that interest rates will then rise (see Figures 7 and 11). Thus ***the income effect of an increase in the money supply is a rise in interest rates in response to the higher level of income.***

2. *Price-Level Effect.* An increase in the money supply can also cause the overall price level in the economy to rise. The liquidity preference framework predicts that this will lead to a rise in interest rates. So ***the price-level effect from an increase in the money supply is a rise in interest rates in response to the rise in the price level.***

3. *Expected-Inflation Effect.* The rising price level (the higher inflation rate) that results from an increase in the money supply also affects interest rates by affecting the expected inflation rate. Specifically, an increase in the money supply may lead people to expect a higher price level in the future—hence the expected inflation rate will be higher. The loanable funds framework has shown us that this increase in expected inflation will lead to a higher level of interest rates. Therefore, ***the expected-inflation effect of an increase in the money supply is a rise in interest rates in response to the rise in the expected inflation rate.***

At first glance it might appear that the price-level effect and the expected-inflation effect are the same thing. They both indicate that increases in the price level induced by an increase in the money supply will raise interest rates. However, there is a subtle difference between the two, and this is why they are discussed as two separate effects.

Suppose that there is a onetime increase in the money supply today that leads to a rise in prices to a permanently higher level by next year. As the price level rises over the course of this year, the interest rate will rise via the price-level effect. Only at the end of the year, when the price level has risen to its peak, will the price-level effect be at a maximum.

The rising price level will also raise interest rates via the expected-inflation effect because people will expect that inflation will be higher over the course of the year. However, when the price level stops rising next year, inflation and the expected inflation rate will fall back down to zero. Any rise in interest rates as a result of the earlier rise in expected inflation will then be reversed. We thus see that in contrast to the price-level effect, which reaches its greatest impact next year, the expected-inflation effect will have its smallest impact (zero impact) next year. The basic difference between the two effects, then, is that the price-level effect remains even after prices have stopped rising, whereas the expected-inflation effect disappears.

An important point is that the expected-inflation effect will persist only as long as the price level continues to rise. A onetime increase in the money supply will not produce a continually rising price level; only a higher rate of money supply growth will. Thus a higher rate of money supply growth is needed if the expected-inflation effect is to persist.

Does a Higher Rate of Growth of the Money Supply Lower Interest Rates?

We can now put together all the effects we have discussed to help us decide whether our analysis supports the politicians who advocate a greater rate of growth of the money supply when they feel that interest rates are too high. Of all the effects, only the liquidity effect indicates that a higher rate of money growth will cause a decline in interest rates. In contrast, the income, price-level, and expected-inflation effects indicate that interest rates will rise when money growth is higher. Which of these effects are largest, and how quickly do they take effect? The answers are critical in determining whether interest rates will rise or fall when money supply growth is increased.

Generally, the liquidity effect from the greater money growth takes effect immediately because the rising money supply leads to an immediate decline in the equilibrium interest rate. The income and price-level effects take time to work because the increasing money supply takes time to raise the price level and income, which in turn raise interest rates. The expected-inflation effect, which also raises interest rates, can be slow or fast, depending on whether people adjust their expectations of inflation slowly or quickly when the money growth rate is increased.

Three possibilities are outlined in Figure 14; each shows how interest rates respond over time to an increased rate of money supply growth starting at time T. Panel (a) shows a case in which the liquidity effect dominates the other effects so that the interest rate falls from i_1 at time T to a final level of i_2. The liquidity effect operates quickly to lower the interest rate, but as time goes by, the other effects start to reverse some of the decline. Because the liquidity effect is larger than the others, however, the interest rate never rises back to its initial level.

Panel (b) has a lesser liquidity effect than the other effects, with the expected-inflation effect operating slowly because expectations of inflation are slow to adjust upward. Initially, the liquidity effect drives down the interest rate. Then the income, price-level, and expected-inflation effects begin to raise it. Because these effects are dominant, the interest rate eventually rises above its initial level to i_2. In the short run, lower interest rates result from increased money growth, but eventually they end up climbing above the initial level.

Panel (c) has the expected-inflation effect dominating as well as operating rapidly because people quickly raise their expectation of inflation when the rate of money growth increases. The expected-inflation effect begins immediately to overpower the liquidity effect, and the interest rate immediately starts to climb. Over time, as the income and price-level effects start to take hold, the interest rate rises even higher, and the eventual outcome is an interest rate that is substantially above the initial interest rate. The result shows clearly that increasing money supply growth is not the answer to reducing interest rates but rather that money growth should be reduced in order to lower interest rates!

An important issue for economic policymakers is which of these three scenarios is closest to reality. If a decline in interest rates is desired, then an increase in money supply growth is called for when the liquidity effect dominates the other effects, as in panel (a). A decrease in money growth is appropriate if the other

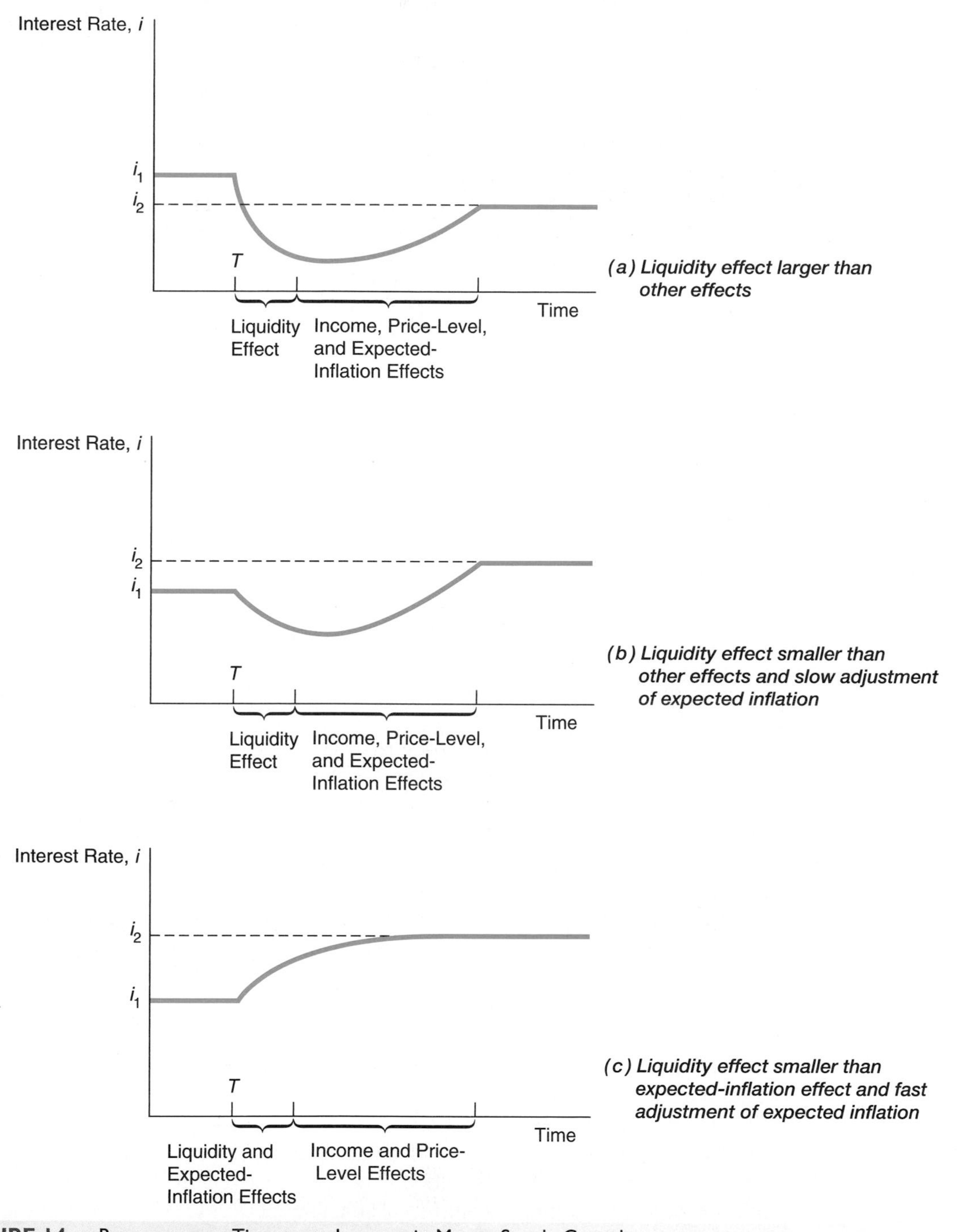

FIGURE 14 Response over Time to an Increase in Money Supply Growth

effects dominate the liquidity effect and expectations of inflation adjust rapidly, as in panel (c). If the other effects dominate the liquidity effect but expectations of inflation adjust only slowly, as in panel (b), then whether you want to increase or decrease money growth depends on whether you care more about what happens in the short run or the long run.

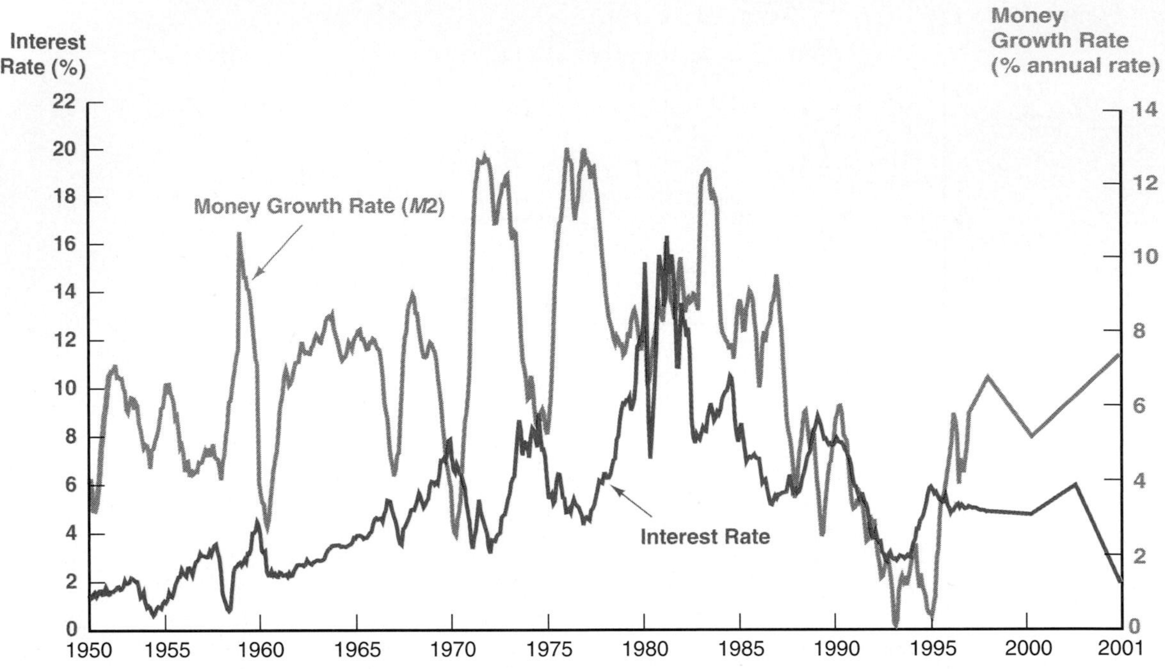

FIGURE 15 Money Growth (M2, Annual Rate) and Interest Rates (Three-Month Treasury Bills), 1950–2001

Sources: Federal Reserve *Bulletin*, various years. Tables 1.1 line 6 and http://www.federalreserve.gov/releases/H15/data.htm

Which scenario is supported by the evidence? The relationship of interest rates and money growth from 1950 to 2001 is plotted in Figure 15. When the rate of money supply growth began to climb in the mid–1960s, interest rates rose, indicating that the liquidity effect was dominated by the price-level, income, and expected-inflation effects. By the 1970s, interest rates reached levels unprecedented in the period after World War II, as did the rate of money supply growth.

The scenario depicted in panel (a) of Figure 14 seems doubtful, and the case for lowering interest rates by raising the rate of money growth is much weakened. Looking back at Figure 6, which shows the relationship between interest rates and expected inflation, you should not find this too surprising. The rise in the rate of money supply growth in the 1960s and 1970s is matched by a large rise in expected inflation, which would lead us to predict that the expected-inflation effect would be dominant. It is the most plausible explanation for why interest rates rose in the face of higher money growth. However, Figure 15 does not really tell us which one of the two scenarios, panel (b) or panel (c) of Figure 14, is more accurate. It depends critically on how fast people's expectations about inflation adjust. However, recent research using more sophisticated methods than just looking at a graph like Figure 15 does indicate that increased money growth temporarily lowers short-term interest rates.[7]

[7]See Lawrence J. Christiano and Martin Eichenbaum, "Identification and the Liquidity Effect of a Monetary Policy Shock," in *Business Cycles, Growth, and Political Economy,* ed. Alex Cukierman, Zvi Hercowitz, and Leonardo Leiderman (Cambridge, Mass.: MIT Press, 1992), pp. 335–370; Eric M. Leeper and David B. Gordon, "In Search of the Liquidity Effect," *Journal of Monetary Economics* 29 (1992): 341–370; Steven Strongin, "The Identification of Monetary Policy Disturbances: Explaining the Liquidity Puzzle," *Journal of Monetary Economics* 35 (1995): 463–497; and Adrian Pagan and John C. Robertson, "Resolving the Liquidity Effect," *Federal Reserve Bank of St. Louis Review* 77 (May–June 1995): 33–54.

THE PRACTICING FINANCIAL INSTITUTION MANAGER

Profiting from Interest-Rate Forecasts

Given the importance of interest rates, the media frequently report interest-rate forecasts, as the "Following the Financial News" box indicates. Because changes in interest rates have a major impact on the profitability of financial institutions, financial managers care a great deal about the path of future interest rates. Managers of financial institutions obtain interest-rate forecasts either by hiring their own staff economists to generate forecasts or by purchasing forecasts from other financial institutions or economic forecasting firms.

Several methods are used to produce interest-rate forecasts. One of the most popular is based on the loanable funds framework described earlier in the chapter, and it is used by financial institutions such as Salomon Smith Barney, Morgan Guaranty Trust Company, and the Prudential Insurance Company. Using the loanable funds framework, analysts predict what will happen to the factors that affect the supply of and demand for bonds—factors such as the strength of the economy, the profitability of investment opportunities, the expected inflation rate, and the size of government deficits and borrowing. They then use the supply and demand analysis outlined in the chapter to come up with their interest-rate forecasts. A variation of this approach makes use of the *Flow of Funds Accounts* produced by the Federal Reserve. These data show the sources and uses of funds by different sectors of the American economy. By looking at how well the supply of credit and the demand for credit by different sectors match up, forecasters attempt to predict future changes in interest rates.

Forecasting done with the loanable funds framework often does not make use of formal economic models but rather depends on the judgment or "feel" of the forecaster. An alternative method of forecasting interest rates makes use of **econometric models,** models whose equations are estimated with statistical procedures using past data. These models involve interlocking equations that, once input variables such as the behavior of government spending and monetary policy are plugged in, produce simultaneous forecasts of many variables including interest rates. The basic assumption of these forecasting models is that the estimated relationships between variables will continue to hold up in the future. Given this assumption, the forecaster makes predictions of the expected path of the input variables and then lets the model generate forecasts of variables such as interest rates.

Many of these econometric models are quite large, involving hundreds and sometimes over a thousand equations, and consequently require computers to produce their forecasts. In addition, many of these models rely heavily on the liquidity preference framework to produce their interest-rate forecasts and so are particularly concerned with developments in the market for money along lines we have discussed in the text. Prominent examples of these large-scale econometric models used by the private sector include those developed by Wharton Econometric Forecasting Associates, Chase Econometric Associates, and Data Resources, Inc. To generate its interest-rate forecasts, the Board of Governors of the Federal Reserve System makes use of its own large-scale econometric model, although it makes use of judgmental forecasts as well.

Managers of financial institutions rely on these forecasts to make decisions about which assets they should hold. A manager who believes that the forecast that long-term interest rates will fall in the future is reliable would seek to purchase long-term bonds for the asset account because, as we have seen in Chapter 3, the drop in interest rates will produce large capital gains. Conversely, if forecasts say that interest rates are likely to rise in the future, the manager will

FOLLOWING THE FINANCIAL NEWS

Forecasting Interest Rates

Forecasting interest rates is a time-honored profession. Financial economists are hired (sometimes at very high salaries) to forecast interest rates because businesses need to know what the rates will be in order to plan their future spending, and banks and investors require interest-rate forecasts in order to decide which assets to buy. Interest-rate forecasters predict what will happen to the factors that affect the supply and demand for bonds and for money—factors such as the strength of the economy, the profitability of investment opportunities, the expected inflation rate, and the size of government budget deficits and borrowing. They then use the supply and demand analysis we have outlined in this chapter to come up with their interest-rate forecasts.

The *Wall Street Journal* reports interest-rate forecasts by leading prognosticators twice a year (early January and July) in its "Economy" column or in its "Credit Markets" column, which surveys developments in the bond market daily. Forecasting interest rates is a perilous business. To their embarrassment, even the top experts are frequently far off in their forecasts.

THE WALL STREET JOURNAL FORECASTING SURVEY FOR 2002

In percent except for dollar vs. yen and dollar vs. euro

	JULY 2001 SURVEY						NEW FORECASTS FOR 2002									
	3-MO. TREASURY BILLS-a Dec.	30-YR. TREASURY BONDS Dec.	GDP-b 1ST–3RD QTR. 2001	CPI-c Nov.	DLR. VS. YEN Dec.	UNEMPL. Nov.	3-MO. TREASURY BILLS-a June	30-YR. TREASURY BONDS June	GDP-b 1ST QTR. 2002	GDP-b 2ND QTR. 2002	GDP-b 3RD QTR. 2002	GDP-b 4TH QTR. 2002	CPI-c May	DLR VS. YEN June	DLR VS. EURO June	UNEMPL. May
James F. Smith, Univ. of North Carolina	5.35	4.96	1.1	4.4	133	5.3	1.95	3.75	**5.4**	4.2	6.8	3.5	1.6	133	0.84	5.5
Ram Bhagavatula, Royal Bank of Scotland	3.50	5.40	2.9	3.3	120	5.0	2.25	5.00	**4.0**	3.5	3.0	3.0	1.4	132	0.89	5.7
John Mueller, LBMC	4.00	6.00	3.2	2.5	113	5.0	2.00	6.00	**4.0**	5.5	5.4	5.4	0.6	135	0.83	5.7
Henry Willmore, Barclays Capital	3.40	5.50	N.A.	3.2	130	5.2	2.10	5.00	**3.5**	4.0	4.0	3.0	1.2	135	0.83	6.2
Lawrence Kudlow, Kudlow & Co., LLC	3.50	5.25	0.7	2.3	130	5.3	2.10	5.25	**3.1**	3.8	3.5	4.5	1.5	150	0.83	5.7
David L. Littmann, Comerica Bank	3.44	5.18	2.3	2.7	127	4.8	1.80	5.20	**3.0**	3.3	3.7	4.5	0.8	135	0.89	5.9
Susan M. Sterne, Economic Analysis Assoc.	4.00	5.20	1.6	3.0	124	5.3	2.50	5.00	**3.0**	1.4	3.2	3.1	2.2	125	1.00	5.8
Robert Fry, DuPont	N.A.	N.A.	N.A.	N.A.	N.A.	N.A.	1.80	4.75	**3.0**	2.8	4.0	3.0	1.0	125	0.89	6.5
Richard D. Rippe, Prudential Securities	3.45	5.60	2.1	3.2	125	5.0	1.80	5.20	**2.6**	3.5	4.3	4.5	1.5	130	0.90	6.3
Daniel Laufenberg, American Express	3.60	5.30	3.8	3.2	125	4.6	1.75	5.10	**2.5**	3.2	3.3	3.2	1.3	125	0.92	5.9
N. Lazar/E. Hyman, ISI Group	3.20	4.75	1.5	2.8	130	5.0	1.50	5.50	**2.5**	3.5	3.5	3.5	0.7	130	0.90	6.5
Richard Yamarone, Argus Research	3.50	5.65	2.6	3.0	130	4.9	2.30	5.85	**2.5**	4.4	4.0	4.1	2.9	130	0.88	5.7
Ian Shepherdson, High Frequency Econ.	3.00	5.60	1.8	3.0	130	4.9	2.50	5.50	**2.5**	3.5	3.0	4.5	1.1	140	0.85	6.8
Gail Fosler, Conference Board	3.00	5.70	4.1	3.8	117	4.4	1.75	5.15	**2.3**	2.0	3.6	3.2	2.3	119	0.88	6.4
David Resler, Nomura Securities Int'l.	3.10	5.25	2.4	2.6	128	5.0	1.85	5.25	**2.3**	3.7	3.3	3.2	1.3	128	0.91	6.1
Paul A. McCulley, PIMCO	3.40	5.10	1.3	3.2	130	5.0	1.80	5.40	**1.5**	3.5	2.5	2.0	1.4	135	0.92	6.8
Thomas W. Synnott III, U.S. Trust Co. of NY	2.70	5.00	2.5	2.8	125	5.5	1.60	5.20	**1.4**	2.3	3.4	4.3	1.6	130	0.91	6.2
Neal Soss, Credit Suisse First Boston	3.50	4.75	2.5	3.6	134	4.9	1.35	3.75	**1.3**	2.0	3.2	3.4	0.7	130	0.92	6.2
Gary Thayer, A.G. Edwards	3.50	5.50	2.7	2.7	130	4.7	2.10	5.50	**1.0**	2.5	2.0	3.5	1.8	140	0.85	6.1
David Wyss, Standard & Poor's	3.20	5.70	N.A.	3.3	125	4.8	1.70	5.10	**1.0**	2.6	3.3	4.6	1.4	130	0.91	6.6
Mickey Levy, Bank of America	3.83	5.50	2.1	3.2	129	4.9	2.30	5.38	**1.0**	3.9	4.6	3.9	1.3	137	0.84	6.0
Robert V. DiClemente, Citigroup/Salomon	2.75	5.25	2.0	2.3	130	5.1	1.55	5.20	**1.0**	3.0	5.6	5.0	1.2	132	0.93	6.0
Michael Cosgrove, Econoclast	3.00	5.20	1.7	3.0	130	5.0	2.50	5.50	**1.0**	2.8	4.0	4.0	1.8	135	0.95	6.2
Saul Hymans, RSQE Univ. of Michigan	3.40	4.80	2.1	3.2	124	5.3	1.70	4.70	**1.0**	1.3	3.3	3.3	1.3	121	0.95	6.5
Tracy Herrick, Jeffries & Co.	2.70	5.05	–0.3	2.9	120	5.0	1.40	4.25	**1.0**	2.0	2.5	3.0	1.2	140	0.95	6.7
Maria F. Ramirez, MFR	3.85	5.25	1.6	3.2	128	4.9	2.00	5.25	**0.9**	1.4	2.7	3.7	1.4	135	0.93	6.2
William B. Hummer, Wayne Hummer Inv.	3.61	5.32	2.4	3.4	118	4.5	2.00	5.24	**0.9**	2.6	3.4	3.9	1.8	121	0.92	6.1
Richard DeKaser, National City	3.75	5.68	3.1	3.0	114	4.8	2.08	5.42	**0.8**	3.2	3.5	3.1	1.1	140	0.92	6.1
David W. Berson, Fannie Mae	3.50	5.30	2.2	3.0	124	4.8	2.00	5.15	**0.8**	2.5	4.1	4.0	1.8	135	0.85	5.9
Stephen Gallagher, Societe Generale	3.60	5.75	2.8	2.9	130	4.9	1.75	5.50	**0.7**	2.4	4.3	4.1	1.5	145	0.85	6.1
William T. Wilson, Ernst & Young	2.75	4.50	1.0	1.8	135	5.3	1.35	4.00	**0.7**	1.8	2.7	2.2	0.9	140	0.88	6.2
John Lonski, Moody's Investors Service	3.70	5.80	2.7	2.8	123	4.9	2.35	5.40	**0.6**	3.5	4.2	4.2	1.4	135	0.90	5.9
Kathleen Camilli, Camilli Economics	3.00	4.80	–0.1	3.0	116	5.0	2.00	5.00	**0.5**	2.0	3.0	3.5	1.7	130	0.86	6.0
Peter Hooper, Deutsche Bank Alex. Brown	3.50	5.25	1.3	2.8	135	5.0	2.00	5.00	**0.5**	3.3	4.5	4.7	1.5	130	0.98	6.4
Sung Won Sohn, Wells Fargo & Co.	3.50	5.60	2.3	2.0	130	5.0	2.50	6.00	**0.2**	2.1	3.2	3.8	2.0	135	0.85	6.5
Diane C. Swonk, Bank One	3.60	6.00	3.2	3.0	129	4.5	1.70	5.10	**0.1**	3.8	5.0	4.8	1.9	117	0.99	6.2
Michael K. Evans, Evans, Carroll & Assoc.	N.A.	N.A.	N.A.	N.A.	N.A.	N.A.	1.50	5.50	**0.0**	1.0	3.0	3.5	2.5	132	0.90	6.4
R. Berner/D. Greenlaw, Morgan Stanley	3.90	5.35	0.7	2.4	115	5.0	2.50	5.35	**–0.2**	1.9	4.8	4.4	0.4	125	0.97	6.5
Andrew Hodge, DRI-WEFA	N.A.	N.A.	N.A.	N.A.	N.A.	N.A.	1.97	5.40	**–0.2**	1.7	3.0	4.3	1.8	137	1.06	6.3
D. Malpass/J. Ryding, Bear Stearns-e	3.30	5.00	1.2	2.8	128	5.0	1.50	4.50	**–0.3**	1.7	2.9	3.8	0.8	140	0.90	6.4
Brian S. Wesbury, Griffin, Kubik	3.45	4.75	0.0	2.8	135	5.0	1.90	5.00	**–0.3**	1.1	2.7	3.8	0.9	145	0.92	6.1
Bruce Steinberg, Merrill Lynch	3.40	5.50	23	2.4	135	5.0	1.70	5.00	**–0.5**	3.0	5.0	5.0	1.0	135	0.92	6.7
Mark Zandi, Economy.com	3.65	5.25	2.3	3.0	115	4.8	2.10	5.30	**–0.5**	1.3	3.0	4.5	1.5	125	0.92	6.3
J. Dewey Daane, Vanderbilt University	3.06	5.50	1.5	4.0	125	5.2	2.00	5.50	**–0.5**	0.9	1.5	2.5	2.3	128	0.90	6.2
Allen Sinai, Decision Economics	3.18	5.05	1.7	2.7	131	5.1	1.90	4.92	**–0.8**	1.0	2.8	3.3	0.9	155	0.81	6.1
Maureen Allyn, Zurich Scudder Investments	3.00	4.90	2.4	3.2	130	5.0	1.80	4.10	**–0.9**	1.1	2.1	2.8	1.0	135	0.92	6.2

Maury Harris, UBS Warburg	3.65	5.50	1.8	2.8	140	5.0	1.70	4.70	**–1.0**	3.0	3.2	4.0	1.2	130	0.90	6.2
David Orr, Wachovia	3.35	5.35	2.2	2.9	130	4.9	1.60	5.00	**–1.0**	1.5	2.5	3.0	1.5	132	0.92	6.5
William Dudley, Goldman, Sachs	3.25	5.10	1.6	2.9	125	4.8	1.75	4.80	**–1.0**	3.0	2.5	2.5	1.1	128	1.01	6.3
Jim Coons, Huntington National Bank	3.50	5.55	1.7	3.0	115	5.0	2.00	4.60	**–1.0**	1.5	2.8	3.6	1.2	125	0.90	6.0
Kurt Karl, Swiss Re	2.90	5.80	3.1	2.8	126	4.6	1.50	5.30	**–1.2**	–0.4	2.7	4.5	1.3	130	0.93	6.2
Stuart G. Hoffman, PNC Financial Services	3.10	5.10	2.0	3.3	127	4.9	1.75	4.80	**–1.2**	2.0	3.5	4.0	1.6	133	0.91	6.3
Nicholas S. Perna, Perna Associates	3.28	5.61	1.6	3.0	120	4.9	2.39	5.59	**–1.4**	2.5	4.4	4.1	1.3	127	0.93	6.6
Van Jolissaint, DaimlerChrysler	3.25	5.10	1.9	2.6	127	5.1	1.52	4.40	**–2.0**	1.4	4.3	3.1	0.8	130	0.85	6.6
A. Gary Shilling, Shilling & Co.	3.00	4.40	–2.7	2.0	135	5.3	1.25	4.00	**–2.8**	–2.5	–2.3	1.0	–0.5	145	0.85	6.7
AVERAGE-d	3.39	5.30	1.9	2.9	126	5.0	1.89	5.06	**0.9**	2.4	3.4	3.7	1.4	133	0.90	6.2
ACTUAL NUMBERS as of Dec. 31, 2001	**1.70**	**5.02**	**0.1**	**1.9**	**131**	**5.7**										

N.A. Not Available; a-Treasury bill rates are on a bond-equivalent basis; b-Real gross domestic product, average annualized rate for first three quarters, based on January and July surveys; c-Year-to-Year change in the consumer price index; d-Averages are for analysts polled at time of survey; e-David Malpass and John Ryding replace Wayne Angell at Bear Stearns.

Source: Wall Street Journal, January 4, 2002, p. A2. Republished by permission of Dow Jones, Inc. via Copyright Clearance Center, Inc.

prefer to hold short-term bonds or loans in the portfolio in order to avoid potential capital losses on long-term securities.

Forecasts of interest rates also help managers decide whether to borrow long-term or short-term. If interest rates are forecast to rise in the future, the financial institution manager will want to lock in the low interest rates by borrowing long-term; if the forecasts say that interest rates will fall, the manager will seek to borrow short-term in order to take advantage of low interest-rate costs in the future.

Clearly, good forecasts of future interest rates are extremely valuable to the financial institution manager, who, not surprisingly, would be willing to pay a lot for accurate forecasts. Unfortunately, interest-rate forecasting is a perilous business, and even the top forecasters, to their embarrassment, are frequently far off in their forecasts.

SUMMARY

1. The quantity demanded of an asset is (a) positively related to wealth, (b) positively related to the expected return on the asset relative to alternative assets, (c) negatively related to the riskiness of the asset relative to alternative assets, and (d) positively related to the liquidity of the asset relative to alternative assets.
2. Diversification (the holding of more than one asset) benefits investors because it reduces the risk they face, and the benefits are greater the less returns on securities move together.
3. The supply and demand analysis for bonds, known as the loanable funds framework, provides one theory of how interest rates are determined. It predicts that interest rates will change when there is a change in demand because of changes in income (or wealth), expected returns, risk, or liquidity, or when there is a change in supply because of changes in the attractiveness of investment opportunities, the real cost of borrowing, or government activities.
4. An alternative theory of how interest rates are determined is provided by the liquidity preference framework, which analyzes the supply of and demand for money. It shows that interest rates will change when there is a change in the demand for money because of changes in income or the price level or when there is a change in the supply of money.
5. There are four possible effects of an increase in the money supply on interest rates: the liquidity effect, the income effect, the price-level effect, and the expected-inflation effect. The liquidity effect indicates that a rise in money supply growth will lead to a decline in interest rates; the other effects work in the opposite direction. The evidence seems to indicate that the income, price-level, and expected-inflation effects dominate the liquidity effect such that an increase in money supply growth leads to higher rather than lower interest rates.

KEY TERMS

asset, *p 75*
asset market approach, *p. 84*
demand curve, *p. 81*
diversification, *p. 79*
econometric model, *p. 109*
excess demand, *p. 83*
excess supply, *p. 83*
expected return, *p. 75*
Fisher effect, *p. 93*
liquidity, *p. 75*
liquidity preference framework, *p. 96*
loanable funds, *p. 84*
loanable funds framework, *p. 84*
market equilibrium, *p. 83*
opportunity cost, *p. 99*
risk, *p. 75*
standard deviation, *p. 77*
supply curve, *p. 83*
wealth, *p. 75*

QUESTIONS AND PROBLEMS

1. Explain why you would be more or less willing to buy a share of Polaroid stock in the following situations:
   a. Your wealth falls.
   b. You expect it to appreciate in value.
   c. The bond market becomes more liquid.
   d. You expect gold to appreciate in value.
   e. Prices in the bond market become more volatile.

***2.** Explain why you would be more or less willing to buy a house under the following circumstances:
   a. You just inherited $100,000.
   b. Real estate commissions fall from 6% of the sales price to 4% of the sales price.
   c. You expect Polaroid stock to double in value next year.
   d. Prices in the stock market become more volatile.
   e. You expect housing prices to fall.

3. "The more risk-averse people are, the more likely they are to diversify." Is this statement true, false, or uncertain? Explain your answer.

***4.** I own a professional football team, and I plan to diversify by purchasing shares in either a company that owns a pro basketball team or a pharmaceutical company. Which of these two investments is more likely to reduce the overall risk I face? Why?

5. "No one who is risk-averse will ever buy a security that has a lower expected return, more risk, and less liquidity than another security." Is this statement true, false, or uncertain? Explain your answer.

For items 6–15, answer each question by drawing the appropriate supply and demand diagrams.

***6.** An important way in which the Federal Reserve decreases the money supply is by selling bonds to the public. Using the loanable funds framework, show what effect this action has on interest rates. Is your answer consistent with what you would expect to find with the liquidity preference framework?

7. Using both the liquidity preference and loanable funds frameworks, show why interest rates are procyclical (rising when the economy is expanding and falling during recessions).

***8.** Why should a rise in the price level (but not in expected inflation) cause interest rates to rise when the nominal money supply is fixed?

9. Find the "Credit Markets" column in the *Wall Street Journal.* Underline the statements in the column that explain bond price movements, and draw the appropriate supply and demand diagrams that support these statements.

10. What effect will a sudden increase in the volatility of gold prices have on interest rates?

***11.** How might a sudden increase in people's expectations of future real estate prices affect interest rates?

12. Explain what effect a large federal deficit might have on interest rates.

***13.** Using both the loanable funds and liquidity preference frameworks, show what the effect is on interest rates when the riskiness of bonds rises. Are the results the same in the two frameworks?

14. If the price level falls next year, remaining fixed thereafter, and the money supply is fixed, what is likely to happen to interest rates over the next two years? (Hint: Take account of both the price-level effect and the expected-inflation effect.)

***15.** Will there be an effect on interest rates if brokerage commissions on stocks fall? Explain your answer.

Predicting the Future

16. The president of the United States announces in a press conference that he will fight the higher inflation rate with a new anti-inflation program. Predict what will happen to interest rates if the public believes him.

***17.** The chairman of the Fed announces that interest rates will rise sharply next year, and the market believes him. What will happen to today's interest rate on AT&T bonds, such as the $8\frac{1}{8}$s of 2022?

18. Predict what will happen to interest rates if the public suddenly expects a large increase in stock prices.

***19.** Predict what will happen to interest rates if prices in the bond market become more volatile.

20. If the next chair of the Federal Reserve Board has a reputation for advocating an even slower rate of money growth than the current chair, what will happen to interest rates? Discuss the possible resulting situations.

WEB EXERCISES

The Behavior of Interest Rates

1. One of the largest single influences on the level of interest rates is inflation. There are a number of sites that report inflation over time. Go to ftp://ftp.bls.gov/pub/special.requests/cpi/cpiai.txt and review the data available. Note that the last columns report various averages. Move these data into an Excel spreadsheet using the method in Chapter 1. What has the average rate of inflation been since 1950, 1960, 1970, 1980, and 1990? What year had the lowest level of inflation? What year had the highest level of inflation?

2. Increasing prices erode the purchasing power of the dollar. It is interesting to compute what goods would have cost at some point in the past after adjusting for inflation. Go to www.interest.com/hugh/calc/cpi.cgi. What would a car that cost $22,000 today have cost during the year that you were born?

3. One of the points made in this chapter is that inflation erodes investment returns. Go to http://www.src-net.com/InvestmentMultiplier/iminflation.htm and review how changes in inflation alter your real return. What happens to the difference between the adjusted value of an investment compared to its inflation-adjusted value as:

a. Inflation increases?

b. The investment horizon lengthens?

c. Expected return increases?

Chapter 4

Appendix: Applying the Asset Market Approach to a Commodity Market: The Case of Gold

Both models of interest-rate determination in Chapter 4 make use of an asset market approach in which supply and demand are always considered in terms of stocks of assets (amounts at a given point in time). The asset market approach is useful in understanding not only why interest rates fluctuate but also how any asset's price is determined.

One asset that has fascinated people for thousands of years is gold. It has been a driving force in history: The conquest of the Americas by Europeans was to a great extent the result of the quest for gold, to cite just one example. The fascination with gold continues to the present day, and developments in the gold market are followed closely by financial analysts and the media. This appendix shows how the asset market approach can be applied to understanding the behavior of commodity markets, in particular the gold market. (The analysis in this appendix can also be used to understand behavior in many other asset markets.)

SUPPLY AND DEMAND IN THE GOLD MARKET

The analysis of a commodity market, such as the gold market, proceeds in a similar fashion to the analysis of the bond market by examining the supply of and demand for the commodity. We again use our analysis of the determinants of asset demand to obtain a demand curve for gold, which shows the relationship between the quantity of gold demanded and the price when all other economic variables are held constant.

Demand Curve

To derive the relationship between the quantity of gold demanded and its price, we again recognize that an important determinant of the quantity demanded is its expected return:

$$R^e = \frac{P^e_{t+1} - P_t}{P_t} = g^e$$

where
R^e = expected return
P_t = price of gold today
P^e_{t+1} = expected price of gold next year
g^e = expected capital gain

In deriving the demand curve, we hold all other variables constant, particularly the expected price of gold next year P^e_{t+1}. With a given value of the expected price of gold next year P^e_{t+1}, a lower price of gold today P_t means that there will be a greater appreciation in the price of gold over the coming year. The result is that a lower price of gold today implies a higher expected capital gain over the coming year and hence a higher expected return: $R^e = (P^e_{t+1} - P_t)/P_t$. Thus becausethe price of gold today (which for simplicity we will denote as P) is lower, the expected return on gold is higher, and the quantity demanded is higher. Consequently, the demand curve G^d_1 slopes downward in Figure A1.

Supply Curve

To derive the supply curve, expressing the relationship between the quantity supplied and the price, we again assume that all other economic variables are held constant. A higher price of gold will induce producers to mine for extra gold and also possibly induce governments to sell some of their gold stocks to the public, thus increasing the quantity supplied. Hence the supply curve G^s_1 in Figure A1 slopes upward. Notice that the supply curve in the figure is drawn to be very steep. The reason for this is that the actual amount of gold produced in any year is only a tiny fraction of the outstanding stock of gold that has been accumulated over hundreds of years. Thus the increase in the quantity of the gold supplied in response to a higher price is only a small fraction of the stock of gold, resulting in a very steep supply curve.

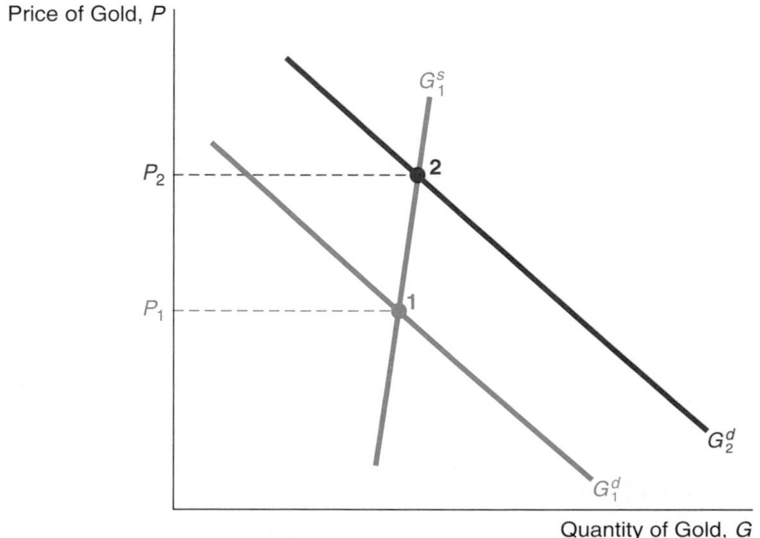

FIGURE A1 A Change in the Equilibrium Price of Gold

When the demand curve shifts rightward from G^d_1 to G^d_2, say, because expected inflation rises, equilibrium moves from point 1 to point 2, and the equilibrium price of gold rises from P_1 to P_2.

Market Equilibrium

Market equilibrium in the gold market occurs when the quantity of gold demanded equals the quantity of gold supplied:

$$G^d = G^s$$

With the initial demand and supply curves of G_1^d and G_1^s, equilibrium occurs at point 1, where these curves intersect at a gold price of P_1. At a price above this equilibrium, the amount of gold supplied exceeds the amount demanded, and this condition of excess supply leads to a decline in the gold price until it reaches P_1, the equilibrium price. Similarly, if the price is below P_1, there is excess demand for gold, which drives the price upward until it settles at the equilibrium price P_1.

CHANGES IN THE EQUILIBRIUM PRICE OF GOLD

Changes in the equilibrium price of gold occur when there is a shift in either the supply curve or the demand curve, that is, when the quantity demanded or supplied changes at each given price of gold in response to a change in some factor other than today's gold price.

Shift in the Demand Curve for Gold

Our analysis of the determinants of asset demand in the chapter provides the factors that shift the demand curve for gold: wealth, expected return on gold relative to alternative assets, riskiness of gold relative to alternative assets, and liquidity of gold relative to alternative assets. The analysis of how changes in each of these factors shift the demand curve for gold is the same as that found in the chapter.

When wealth rises, at a given price of gold, the quantity demanded increases, and the demand curve shifts to the right, as in Figure A1. When the expected return on gold relative to other assets rises—either because speculators think that the future price of gold will be higher or because the expected return on other assets declines—gold becomes more desirable; the quantity demanded therefore increases at any given price of gold, and the demand curve shifts to the right, as in Figure A1. When the relative riskiness of gold declines, either because gold prices become less volatile or because returns on other assets become more volatile, gold becomes more desirable, the quantity demanded at every given price rises, and the demand curve again shifts to the right. When the gold market becomes relatively more liquid and gold therefore becomes more desirable, the quantity demanded at any given price rises, and the demand curve also shifts to the right, as in Figure A1.

Shifts in the Supply Curve for Gold

The supply curve for gold shifts when there are changes in technology that make gold mining more efficient or when governments at any given price of gold decide to increase sales of their holdings of gold. In these cases, the quantity of gold supplied at any given price increases, and the supply curve shifts to the right.

Application Changes in the Equilibrium Price of Gold Due to a Rise in Expected Inflation

To illustrate how changes in the equilibrium price of gold occur when supply and demand curves shift, let's look at what happens when there is a change in expected inflation.

Suppose that expected inflation is 5% and the initial supply and demand curves are at G_1^s and G_1^d so that the equilibrium price of gold is at P_1 in Figure A1. If expected inflation now rises to 10%, prices of goods and commodities next year will be expected to be higher than they otherwise would have been, and the price of gold next year P_{t+1}^e will also be expected to be higher than otherwise. Now at any given price of gold today, gold is expected to have a greater rate of appreciation over the coming year and hence a higher expected capital gain and return. The greater expected return means that the quantity of gold demanded increases at any given price, thus shifting the demand curve from G_1^d to G_2^d. Equilibrium therefore moves from point 1 to point 2, and the price of gold rises from P_1 to P_2.

By using a supply and demand diagram like that in Figure A1, you should be able to see that if the expected rate of inflation falls, the price of gold today will also fall. We thus reach the following conclusion: ***The price of gold should be positively related to the expected inflation rate.***

Because the gold market responds immediately to any changes in expected inflation, it is considered a good barometer of the trend of inflation in the future. Indeed, Alan Greenspan, the chairman of the Board of Governors of the Federal Reserve System, has advocated using the price of gold as an indicator of inflationary pressures in the economy. Not surprisingly, then, the gold market is followed closely by financial analysts and monetary policymakers.

Study Guide To give yourself practice with supply and demand analysis in the gold market, see if you can analyze what happens to the price of gold for the following situations, remembering that all other things are held constant: (1) Interest rates rise, (2) the gold market becomes more liquid, (3) the volatility of gold prices increases, (4) the stock market is expected to turn bullish in the near future, (5) investors suddenly become fearful that there will be a collapse in real estate prices, and (6) Russia sells a lot of gold in the open market to raise hard currency to feed its people.

The analysis in this appendix can also be applied to many other asset markets. See if you can apply the analysis here to understand fluctuations in the prices of classic comic books, old baseball cards, oil, Rembrandt paintings, or other commodities mentioned in the following application.

Application The "Commodities" Column

READING THE *WALL STREET JOURNAL*

The supply and demand analysis in this appendix can help you evaluate events in commodity markets that are reported in the media. Every day, the *Wall Street Journal* reports on developments in the commodities markets on the previous business day in its "Commodities" column, an example of which is found in the "Following the Financial News" box.

The column points out that soybean prices fell to new contract lows with fears of a bumper crop of soybeans in South America. Our supply and demand analysis explains why these fears would cause soybean prices to fall.

FOLLOWING THE FINANCIAL NEWS

The "Commodities" Column

The "Commodities" column appears daily in the *Wall Street Journal;* an example is presented here. It is typically found in the third section, "Money and Investing."

FUTURES PRICES

Soybean Prices Drop on Fears of a Bumper Crop

COMMODITIES

By Dyanna DeCola
Dow Jones Newswires

CHICAGO—Chicago Board of Trade soybean prices tumbled yesterday within four cents of making new contract lows as speculators sold aggressively and fears circulated about a huge South American soybean crop.

Tuesday's monthly report from the U.S. Department of Agriculture included a raised estimate for Argentine production, while analysts also pointed to favorable weather for the Brazilian and Argentine crops.

The January contract fell five cents to $4.3250 per bushel.

Traders said the selloff was mostly technical in nature, with sell stops—preplaced sales orders—triggered as the market fell through what were seen as key levels on price charts.

Many traders said the price performance yesterday suggested more losses are ahead. Some believe that by week's end, January soybeans could test and possibly break the contract low of $4.2625.

"We could get there this week if we keep doing this," said Victor Lespinasse, a grain trader with A.G. Edwards, Chicago. "We were going down in fairly good volume today."

Market watchers said ideal planting and growing conditions in the Southern Hemisphere continue to weigh on the market. "Favorable South American weather has hung over the soy complex for most of the past month," said Dan Basse, executive vice president of consulting firm AgResource Co. in Chicago.

Another Hill of Beans?

Soybean-futures prices fell on talk of a possible bumper crop in Argentina; settle price in dollars per bushel

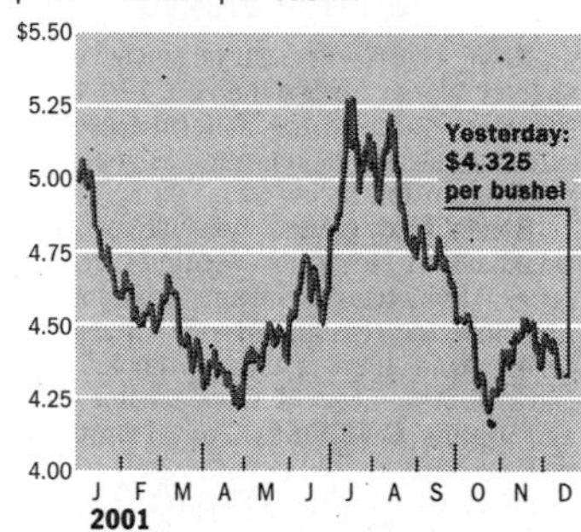

Source: Chicago Board of Trade via Thomson Financial/Datastream

COMMODITY INDEXES

Wednesday, December 12, 2001

	CLOSE	NET CHG.	YR. AGO
Dow Jones-AIG Futures..	87.557	– 0.331	111.417
Dow Jones Spot...........	95.82	– 0.69	113.81
Reuter U.K....................	1177.74	+ 1.55	1404.50
C R B Bridge Futures...	188.15	– 0.76	227.32

The U.S. is the world's largest producer of soybeans. Brazil and Argentina trail the U.S.

Brazilian farmers are in the final stages of the planting season, and Argentina is roughly two-thirds finished with planting.

"We're just now entering the real critical stage for yields in South America," said Jim Bower of Bower Trading, a brokerage firm in Lafayette, Ind. "As we enter this stage, it's important the trade focuses on the weather down there over the next five to six weeks."

On Tuesday, the Agriculture Department pegged Argentina's crop at 28.8 million metric tons, up 800,000 metric tons from its November estimate.

"Evidence of higher Argentine bean production has bolstered talk of impending competition and kept buying interests limited," said Professional Farmers of America, an agricultural-consulting firm in Ceder Falls, Iowa.

Brazil's 2001-02 soybean crop is projected by the Agriculture Department at 41.5 million metric tons, unchanged from the previous month's estimate and above the 38.8 million tons projected for 2000-01.

Also in the background, talk of economic woes in Argentina remains a bearish factor in the marketplace, some brokers said.

In other commodity markets:

CRUDE OIL: Prices gained moderately at the New York Mercantile Exchange on inventory data from the Department of Energy. The January contract rose 28 cents to $18.36 a barrel. The department said inventories shrank by 2.4 million barrels to 309.1 million barrels in the week ended Dec. 7, as imports dropped.

COPPER: Prices fell on the Comex division of the New York Mercantile Exchange as speculative funds sold and after another large rise in warehouse stocks overnight. The March contract dropped a penny to 67.90 cents a pound.

The column discusses why the soybean crop is likely to be so good in the near future. The resulting expanded supply will cause the supply curve for soybeans to shift out to the right, thus causing soybean prices to fall in the future. This will cause soybean prices in today's market to fall because the lower future prices means that the expected return on soybeans has declined, thus shifting the demand curve for soybeans today to the left.

Chapter 5 The Risk and Term Structure of Interest Rates

Preview

In our supply and demand analysis of interest-rate behavior in Chapter 4, we examined the determination of just one interest rate. Yet we saw earlier that there are enormous numbers of bonds on which the interest rates can and do differ. In this chapter we complete the interest-rate picture by examining the relationship of the various interest rates to one another. Understanding why they differ from bond to bond can help businesses, banks, insurance companies, and private investors decide which bonds to purchase as investments or which ones to sell.

We first look at why bonds with the same term to maturity have different interest rates. The relationship among these interest rates is called the **risk structure of interest rates,** although risk, liquidity, and income tax rules all play a role in determining the risk structure. A bond's term to maturity also affects its interest rate, and the relationship among interest rates on bonds with different terms to maturity is called the **term structure of interest rates.** In this chapter we examine the sources and causes of fluctuations in interest rates relative to one another and look at a number of theories that explain these fluctuations.

RISK STRUCTURE OF INTEREST RATES

Figure 1 shows the yields to maturity for several categories of long-term bonds from 1919 to 2001. It shows us two important features of interest-rate behavior for bonds of the same maturity: Interest rates on different categories of bonds differ from one another in any given year, and the spread (or difference) between the interest rates varies over time. The interest rates on municipal bonds, for example, are above those on U.S. government (Treasury) bonds in the late 1930s but lower thereafter. In addition, the spread between the interest rates on Baa corporate bonds (riskier than Aaa corporate bonds) and U.S. government bonds is

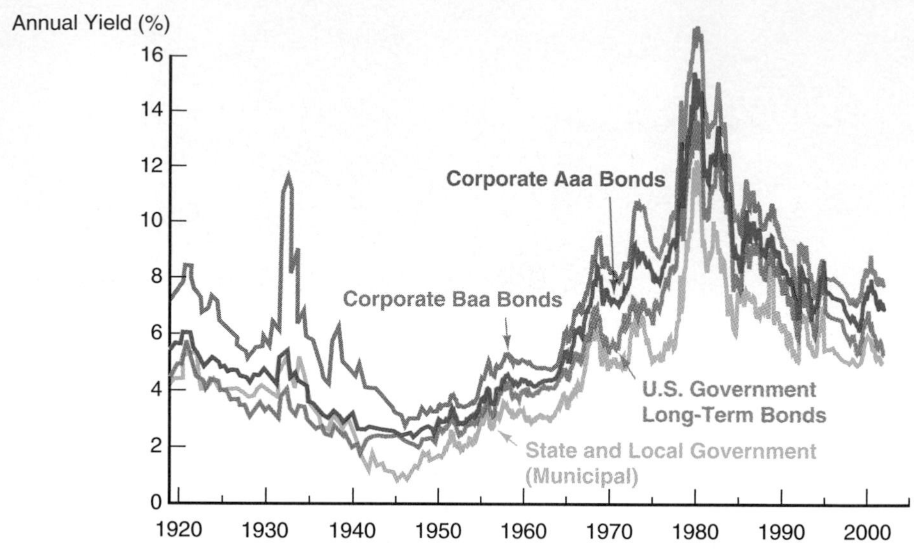

FIGURE 1 Long-Term Bond Yields, 1919–2001

Source: http://www.federalreserve.gov/releases/H15/data.htm

very large during the Great Depression years 1930–1933, is smaller during the 1940s–1960s, and then widens again afterwards. What factors are responsible for these phenomena?

Default Risk

One attribute of a bond that influences its interest rate is its **default risk,** the chance that the issuer of the bond will **default,** that is, be unable to make interest payments or pay off the face value when the bond matures. A corporation suffering big losses, such as Chrysler Corporation did in the 1970s, might be more likely to suspend interest payments on its bonds.[1] The default risk on its bonds would therefore be quite high. By contrast, U.S. Treasury bonds have usually been considered to have no default risk because the federal government can always increase taxes or even print money to pay off its obligations. Bonds like these with no default risk are called **default-free bonds.** (However, during the budget negotiations in Congress in 1995 and 1996, the Republicans threatened to let Treasury bonds default, and this had an impact on the bond market, as the application following this section indicates.) The spread between the interest rates on bonds with default risk and default-free bonds, called the **risk premium,** indicates how much additional interest people must earn in order to be willing to hold a risky bond. Our supply and demand analysis of the bond market in Chapter 4 can be used to explain why a bond with default risk always has a positive risk premium and why the higher the default risk is, the larger the risk premium will be.

[1]Chrysler did not default on its loans in this period, but it would have were it not for a government bailout plan intended to preserve jobs that in effect provided Chrysler with funds that were used to pay off creditors.

Study Guide Two exercises will help you gain a better understanding of the risk structure:

1. Put yourself in the shoes of an investor—see how your purchase decision would be affected by changes in risk and liquidity.
2. Practice drawing the appropriate shifts in the supply and demand curves when risk and liquidity change. For example, see if you can draw the appropriate shifts in the supply and demand curves when, in contrast to the examples in the text, a corporate bond has a decline in default risk or an improvement in its liquidity.

To examine the effect of default risk on interest rates, let us look at the supply and demand diagrams for the default-free (U.S. Treasury) and corporate long-term bond markets in Figure 2. To make the diagrams somewhat easier to read, let's assume that initially there is no possibility of default on the corporate bonds, so they are default-free like U.S. Treasury bonds. In this case, these two bonds have the same attributes (identical risk and maturity); their equilibrium prices and interest rates will initially be equal ($P_1^c = P_1^T$ and $i_1^c = i_1^T$), and the risk premium on corporate bonds ($i_1^c - i_1^T$) will be zero.

If the possibility of a default increases because a corporation begins to suffer large losses, the default risk on corporate bonds will increase, and the expected return on these bonds will decrease. In addition, the corporate bond's return will be more uncertain as well. Our analysis of the determinants of asset demand predicts that because the expected return on the corporate bond falls relative to the expected return on the default-free Treasury bond while its relative riskiness rises,

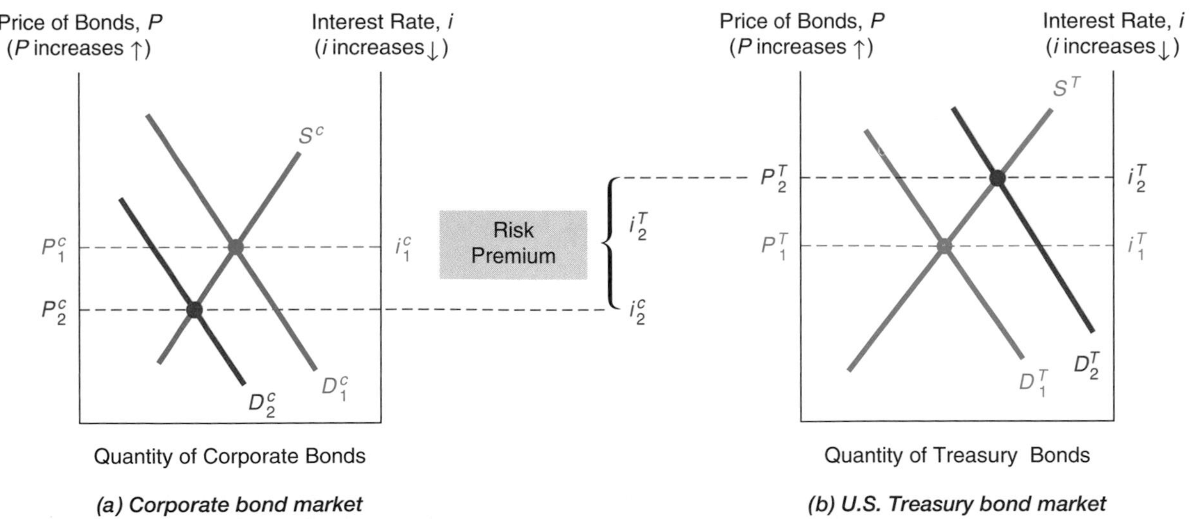

FIGURE 2 Response to an Increase in Default Risk on Corporate Bonds

An increase in default risk on corporate bonds shifts the demand curve from D_1^c to D_2^c. Simultaneously, it shifts the demand curve for Treasury bonds from D_1^T to D_2^T. The equilibrium price for corporate bonds (left axis) falls from P_1^c to P_2^c, and the equilibrium interest rate on corporate bonds (right axis) rises from i_1^c to i_2^c. In the Treasury market, the equilibrium bond price rises from P_1^T to P_2^T, and the equilibrium interest rate falls from i_1^T to i_2^T. The brace indicates the difference between i_2^c and i_2^T, the risk premium on corporate bonds. (*Note: P* and *i* increase in opposite directions. *P* on the left vertical axis increases as we go up the axis, while *i* on the right vertical axis increases as we go down the axis.)

the corporate bond is less desirable (holding everything else equal), and demand for it will fall. The demand curve for corporate bonds in panel (a) of Figure 2 then shifts to the left from D_1^c to D_2^c.

At the same time, the expected return on default-free Treasury bonds increases relative to the expected return on corporate bonds while their relative riskiness declines. The Treasury bonds thus become more desirable, and demand rises, as shown in panel (b) by the rightward shift in the demand curve for these bonds from D_1^T to D_2^T.

As we can see in Figure 2, the equilibrium price for corporate bonds (left axis) falls from P_1^c to P_2^c, and since the bond price is negatively related to the interest rate, the equilibrium interest rate on corporate bonds (right axis) rises from i_1^c to i_2^c. At the same time, however, the equilibrium price for the Treasury bonds rises from P_1^T to P_2^T, and the equilibrium interest rate falls from i_1^T to i_2^T. The spread between the interest rates on corporate and default-free bonds—that is, the risk premium on corporate bonds—has risen from zero to $i_2^c - i_2^T$. We can now conclude that ***a bond with default risk will always have a positive risk premium, and an increase in its default risk will raise the risk premium.***

Because default risk is so important to the size of the risk premium, purchasers of bonds need to know whether a corporation is likely to default on its bonds. Two major investment advisory firms, Moody's Investors Service and Standard and Poor's Corporation, provide default risk information by rating the quality of corporate and municipal bonds in terms of the probability of default. The ratings and their description are contained in Table 1. Bonds with relatively low risk of default are called *investment-grade* securities and have a rating of Baa (or BBB) and above. Bonds with ratings below Baa (or BBB) have higher default risk and have been aptly dubbed speculative-grade or **junk bonds.**

Next let's look back at Figure 1 and see if we can explain the relationship between interest rates on corporate and U.S. Treasury bonds. Corporate bonds

Access ratings of various bonds and institutions at www.standardandpoors.com/RatingsActions/index.html

TABLE 1 Bond Ratings by Moody's and Standard and Poor's

Rating			
Moody's	Standard and Poor's	Description	Examples of Corporations with Bonds Outstanding in 2002
Aaa	AAA	Highest quality (lowest default risk)	General Electric, Pfizer Inc., Road Management Services Inc.
Aa	AA	High quality	Hewlett-Packard, Mobil Oil, Upjohn Inc., Wal-Mart
A	A	Upper medium grade	Anheuser-Busch, McDonalds Inc., Motorola Inc.
Baa	BBB	Medium grade	Albertson's, Ford Motor, Marriott
Ba	BB	Lower medium grade	Rite Aid Corp., Rayo Vac, Six Flags Theme Park
B	B	Speculative	Revlon, Mary Kay Inc., U.S. Can Inc.
Caa	CCC, CC	Poor (high default risk)	U.S. Airways Inc.,
Ca	C	Highly speculative	Metrocall,
C	D	Lowest grade	KMart, Carmike Cinemas, Enron

always have higher interest rates than U.S. Treasury bonds because they always have some risk of default, whereas U.S. Treasury bonds do not. Because Baa-rated corporate bonds have a greater default risk than the higher-rated Aaa bonds, their risk premium is greater, and the Baa rate therefore always exceeds the Aaa rate.

We can use the same analysis to explain the huge jump in the risk premium on Baa corporate bond rates during the Great Depression years 1930–1933 and the rise in the risk premium in the last 30 years (see Figure 1). The depression period saw a very high rate of business failures and defaults. As we would expect, these factors led to a substantial increase in default risk for bonds issued by vulnerable corporations, and the risk premium for Baa bonds reached unprecedentedly high levels. The 1970s and following decades again saw higher levels of business failures and defaults, although they were still well below Great Depression levels. Again, as expected, default risks and risk premiums for corporate bonds rose, widening the spread between interest rates on corporate bonds and Treasury bonds.

Application The Stock Market Crash of 1987 and the Junk Bond–Treasury Spread

The stock market crash on "Black Monday," October 19, 1987, when the Dow Jones Industrial Average fell more than 500 points, had a major impact not only on prices of stocks but on the bond market as well. Let's see how our supply and demand analysis explains the behavior of the spread between interest rates on junk bonds and Treasury securities in the aftermath of the crash using Figure 2.

As a consequence of the Black Monday crash, many investors began to doubt the financial health of corporations with lower credit ratings that had issued junk bonds. The increase in default risk for junk bonds made them less desirable at any given interest rate, decreased the quantity demanded, and shifted the demand curve for junk bonds to the left. As shown in panel (a) of Figure 2, the interest rate on junk bonds should have risen, which is indeed what happened: Interest rates on junk bonds shot up by about one percentage point. But the increase in the perceived default risk for junk bonds after the crash made default-free U.S. Treasury bonds relatively more attractive and shifted the demand curve for these securities to the right—an outcome described by some analysts as a "flight to quality." Just as our analysis predicts in Figure 2, interest rates on Treasury securities fell by about one percentage point. The overall outcome was that the spread between interest rates on junk bonds and government bonds rose by two percentage points, from 4% before the crash to 6% immediately after.

Application What if Treasury Securities were no Longer Default-Free?

Throughout our history, the U.S. Treasury has never defaulted on its securities. However, in late 1995 and early 1996, a budget battle between congressional Republicans and President Clinton almost led to an unprecedented default. In an attempt to get their way in the budget negotiations, the Republicans threatened to refuse to raise the federal government debt ceiling. If the threat had been carried out, the Treasury would have missed interest payments on its debt because it would not have been able to issue new debt to cover its interest outlays and other expenditures when the debt ceiling was reached. Default was averted when a budget compromise was finally reached and the debt ceiling was raised after several shutdowns of the federal government in which "nonessential" government workers were sent home. What would have been the impact of a Treasury default?

Our analysis in Figure 2 provides the answer. Default on Treasury bonds would mean that they would no longer be considered default-free and would now have the attributes of corporate bonds in panel (a) of Figure 2. The increase in default risk would decrease the quantity of Treasury bonds demanded at any given interest rate and would thus cause their demand curve to shift to the left. As we see in panel (a), this would result in a fall in their bond price and a rise in their interest rate. Indeed, just as our analysis predicts, when budget talks stalled on December 18, 1995, and fear of a possible government default rose, the Treasury bond market slumped: Bond prices fell, and the interest rate on 30-year Treasury bonds rose by 11/100s of a percentage point, the largest one-day rise in more than six months.

Liquidity

Another attribute of a bond that influences its interest rate is its liquidity. As we learned in Chapter 4, a liquid asset is one that can be quickly and cheaply converted into cash if the need arises. The more liquid an asset is, the more desirable it is (holding everything else constant). U.S. Treasury bonds are the most liquid of all long-term bonds because they are so widely traded that they are the easiest to sell quickly and the cost of selling them is low. Corporate bonds are not as liquid because fewer bonds for any one corporation are traded; thus it can be costly to sell these bonds in an emergency because it may be hard to find buyers quickly.

How does the reduced liquidity of the corporate bonds affect their interest rates relative to the interest rate on Treasury bonds? We can use supply and demand analysis to show that the lower liquidity of corporate bonds relative to Treasury bonds increases the spread between the interest rates on these two bonds. Let us start the analysis by assuming that initially corporate and Treasury bonds are equally liquid and all their other attributes are the same. As shown in Figure 3, their equilibrium prices and interest rates will initially be equal: $P_1^c = P_1^T$ and $i_1^c = i_1^T$. If the corporate bond becomes less liquid than the Treasury bond because it is less widely traded, then as our analysis of the determinants of asset demand indicates, its demand will fall, shifting its demand curve from D_1^c to D_2^c as in panel (a). The Treasury bond now becomes relatively more liquid in comparison with the corporate bond, so its demand curve shifts rightward from D_1^T to D_2^T as in panel (b). The shifts in the curves in Figure 3 show that the price of the less liquid corporate bond falls and its interest rate rises, while the price of the more liquid Treasury bond rises and its interest rate falls.

The result is that the spread between the interest rates on the two bond types has risen. Therefore, the differences between interest rates on corporate bonds and Treasury bonds (that is, the risk premiums) reflect not only the corporate bond's default risk but its liquidity too. This is why a risk premium is sometimes called a *liquidity premium.* Most accurately, it should be called a "risk and liquidity premium," but convention dictates that it be called a *risk premium.*

Income Tax Considerations

Returning to Figure 1, we are still left with one puzzle—the behavior of municipal bond rates. Municipal bonds are certainly not default-free: State and local

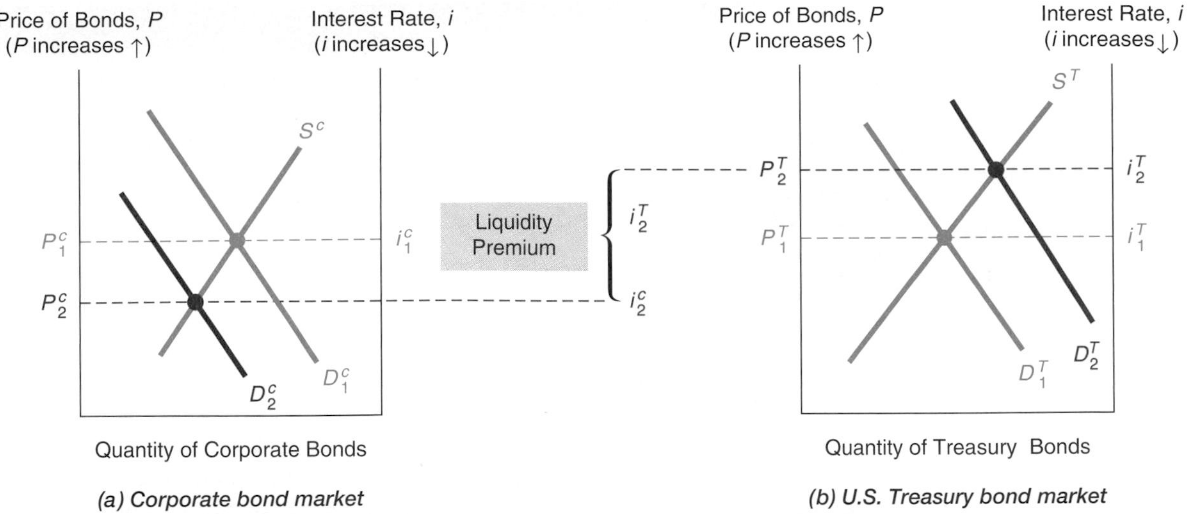

(a) Corporate bond market

(b) U.S. Treasury bond market

FIGURE 3 Response to a Decrease in the Liquidity of Corporate Bonds

A decrease in the liquidity of corporate bonds shifts the demand curve from D^c_1 to D^c_2. Simultaneously, it shifts the demand curve for Treasury bonds from D^T_1 to D^T_2. The equilibrium price for corporate bonds (left axis) falls from P^c_1 to P^c_2, and the equilibrium interest rate on corporate bonds (right axis) rises from i^c_1 to i^c_2. In the Treasury market, the equilibrium bond price rises from P^T_1 to P^T_2, and the equilibrium interest rate falls from i^T_1 to i^T_2. The brace indicates the difference between i^c_2 and i^T_2, the liquidity premium on corporate bonds. (*Note: P* and *i* increase in opposite directions. *P* on the left vertical axis increases as we go up the axis, while *i* on the right vertical axis increases as we go down the axis.)

governments have defaulted on the municipal bonds they have issued in the past, particularly during the Great Depression and even more recently in the case of Orange County, California, in 1994 (more on this in Chapter 18). Also, municipal bonds are not as liquid as U.S. Treasury bonds.

Why is it, then, that these bonds have had lower interest rates than U.S. Treasury bonds for at least 40 years, as indicated in Figure 1? The explanation lies in the fact that interest payments on municipal bonds are exempt from federal income taxes, a factor that has the same effect on the demand for municipal bonds as an increase in their expected return.

Let us imagine that you have a high enough income to put you in the 40% income tax bracket, where for every extra dollar of income you have to pay 40 cents to the government. If you own a $1000 face value U.S. Treasury bond that sells for $1000 and has a coupon payment of $100, you get to keep only $60 of the payment after taxes. Although the bond has a 10% interest rate, you actually earn only 6% after taxes.

Suppose, however, that you put your savings into a $1000 face value municipal bond that sells for $1000 and pays only $80 in coupon payments. Its interest rate is only 8%, but because it is a tax-exempt security, you pay no taxes on the $80 coupon payment, so you earn 8% after taxes. Clearly, you earn more on the municipal bond after taxes, so you are willing to hold the riskier and less liquid municipal bond even though it has a lower interest rate than the U.S. Treasury bond. (This was not true before World War II, when the tax-exempt status of municipal bonds did not convey much of an advantage because income tax rates were extremely low.)

EXAMPLE 1: Income Tax Considerations

Suppose you had the opportunity to buy either a municipal bond or a corporate bond, both of which have a face value and purchase price of $1000. The municipal bond has coupon payments of $60 and a coupon rate of 6%. The corporate bond has coupon payments of $80 and an interest rate of 8%. Which bond would you choose to purchase, assuming a 40% tax rate?

Solution

You would choose to purchase the municipal bond because it will earn you $60 in coupon payments and an interest rate after taxes of 6%. Since municipal bonds are tax-exempt, you pay no taxes on the $60 coupon payments and earn 6% after taxes. However, you have to pay taxes on corporate bonds. You will keep only 60% of the $80 coupon payment because the other 40% goes to taxes. Therefore, you receive $48 of the coupon payment and have an interest rate of 4.8% after taxes. Buying the municipal bond would yield you higher earnings.

Another way of understanding why municipal bonds have lower interest rates than Treasury bonds is to use the supply and demand analysis displayed in Figure 4. To begin with, we assume that municipal and Treasury bonds have identical attributes and so have the same bond prices and interest rates as drawn in the figure: $P^m_1 = P^T_1$ and $i^m_1 = i^T_1$. Once the municipal bonds are given a tax

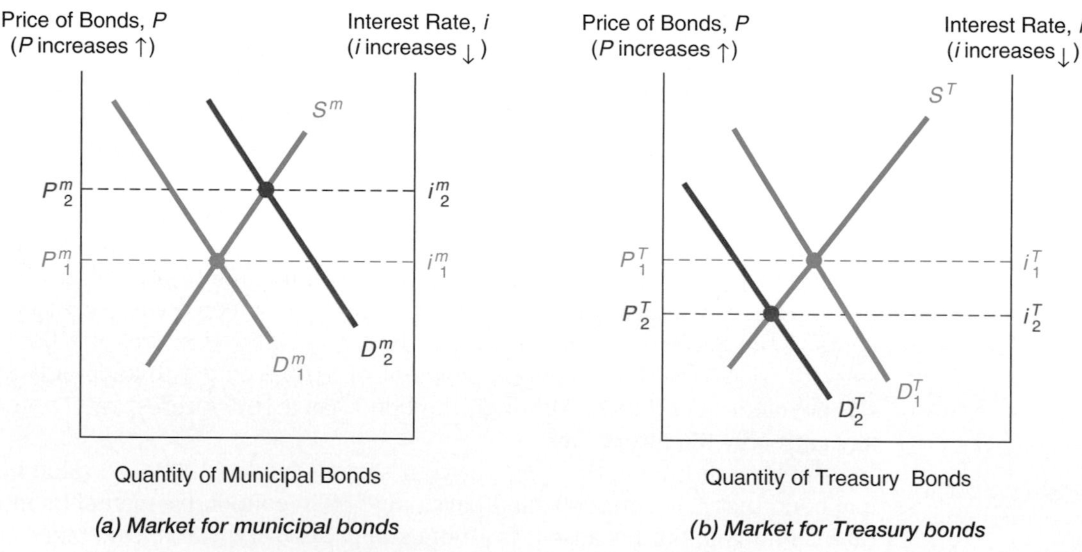

FIGURE 4 Interest Rates on Municipal and Treasury Bonds

When the municipal bond is given tax-free status, demand for the municipal bond shifts rightward from D^m_1 to D^m_2 and demand for the Treasury bond shifts leftward from D^T_1 to D^T_2. The equilibrium price of the municipal bond (left axis) rises from P^m_1 to P^m_2, so its interest rate (right axis) falls from i^m_1 to i^m_2 while the equilibrium price of the Treasury bond falls from P^T_1 to P^T_2 and its interest rate rises from i^T_1 to i^T_2. The result is that municipal bonds end up with lower interest rates than those on Treasury bonds. (*Note: P* and *i* increase in opposite directions. *P* on the left vertical axis increases as we go up the axis, while *i* on the right vertical axis increases as we go down the axis.)

advantage that raises their after-tax expected return relative to Treasury bonds and makes them more desirable, demand for them rises, and their demand curve shifts to the right from D^m_1 to D^m_2. The result is that their equilibrium bond price rises from P^m_1 to P^m_2, and their equilibrium interest rate falls from i^m_1 to i^m_2. By contrast, Treasury bonds have now become less desirable relative to municipal bonds, demand for Treasury bonds decreases, and D^T_1 shifts to D^T_2. The Treasury bond price falls from P^T_1 to P^T_2, and the interest rate rises from i^T_1 to i^T_2. The resulting lower interest rates for municipal bonds and higher interest rates for Treasury bonds explains why municipal bonds can have interest rates below those of Treasury bonds.[2]

Summary

The risk structure of interest rates (the relationship among interest rates on bonds with the same maturity) is explained by three factors: default risk, liquidity, and the income tax treatment of the bond's interest payments. As a bond's default risk increases, the risk premium on that bond (the spread between its interest rate and the interest rate on a default-free Treasury bond) rises. The greater liquidity of Treasury bonds also explains why their interest rates are lower than interest rates on less liquid bonds. If a bond has a favorable tax treatment, as do municipal bonds, whose interest payments are exempt from federal income taxes, its interest rate will be lower.

Application Effects of the Bush Tax Cut on Bond Interest Rates

The Bush tax cut passed in 2001 schedules a reduction of the top income tax bracket from 39% to 35%. What is the effect of this income tax decrease on interest rates in the municipal bond market relative to those in the Treasury bond market?

The supply and demand analysis in Figure 4 provides the answer. A decreased income tax rate for rich people means that the after-tax expected return on tax-free municipal bonds relative to that on Treasury bonds is lower because the interest on Treasury bonds is now taxed at a lower rate. Because municipal bonds now become less desirable, their demand decreases, shifting the demand curve to the left, which lowers their price and raises their interest rate. Conversely, the lower income tax rate makes Treasury bonds more desirable; that shifts their demand curve to the right, raises their price, and lowers their interest rates.

Our analysis thus shows that the Bush tax cut raises the interest rates on municipal bonds relative to interest rates on Treasury bonds.

TERM STRUCTURE OF INTEREST RATES

We have seen how risk, liquidity, and tax considerations (collectively embedded in the risk structure) can influence interest rates. Another factor that influences the interest rate on a bond is its term to maturity: Bonds with identical risk, liquidity, and tax characteristics may have different interest rates because the time remaining to maturity is different. A plot of the yields on bonds with differing terms

---

[2]In contrast to corporate bonds, Treasury bonds are exempt from state and local income taxes. Using the analysis in the text, you should be able to show that this feature of Treasury bonds provides an additional reason why interest rates on corporate bonds are higher than those on Treasury bonds.

to maturity but the same risk, liquidity, and tax considerations is called a **yield curve,** and it describes the term structure of interest rates for particular types of bonds, such as government bonds. The "Following the Financial News" box shows several yield curves for Treasury securities that were published in the *Wall Street Journal.* Yield curves can be classified as upward-sloping, flat, and downward-sloping (the last sort is often referred to as an **inverted yield curve**). When yield curves slope upward, as in the "Following the Financial News" box, the long-term interest rates are above the short-term interest rates; when yield curves are flat, short- and long-term interest rates are the same; and when yield curves are inverted, long-term interest rates are below short-term interest rates. Yield curves can also have more complicated shapes in which they first slope up and then down, or vice versa. Why do we usually see upward slopes of the yield curve as in the "Following the Financial News" box but sometimes other shapes?

Besides explaining why yield curves take on different shapes at different times, a good theory of the term structure of interest rates must explain the following three important empirical facts:

1. As we see in Figure 5, interest rates on bonds of different maturities move together over time.
2. When short-term interest rates are low, yield curves are more likely to have an upward slope; when short-term interest rates are high, yield curves are more likely to slope downward and be inverted.
3. Yield curves almost always slope upward, as in the "Following the Financial News" box.

Three theories have been put forward to explain the term structure of interest rates, that is, the relationship among interest rates on bonds of different

Check out today's Treasury yield curve at www.ratecurve.com/yc2.html

FOLLOWING THE FINANCIAL NEWS

Yield Curves

The *Wall Street Journal* publishes a daily plot of the yield curves for Treasury securities, an example of which is presented here. It is typically found next to the "Credit Markets" column.

The numbers on the vertical axis indicate the interest rate for the Treasury security, with the maturity given by the numbers on the horizontal axis. For example, the yield curve marked "Monday" indicates that the interest rate on the three-month Treasury bill was 1.7%, while the two-year bill had an interest rate of 3.1% and the ten-year bond had an interest rate of 5.1%. As you can see, the yield curves in the plot has a steep upward slope.

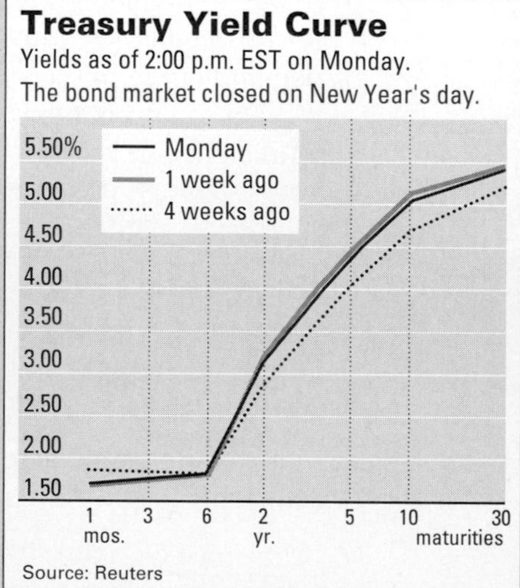

Source: *Wall Street Journal,* January 2, 2002, p. C13. Republished by permission of Dow Jones, Inc. via Copyright Clearance Center, Inc.

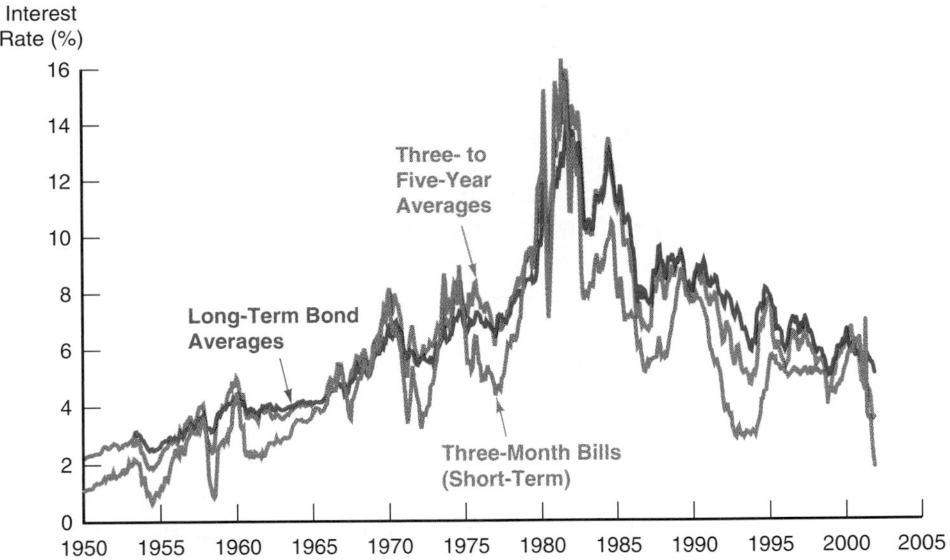

FIGURE 5 Movements over Time of Interest Rates on U.S. Government Bonds with Different Maturities

Sources: http://www.federalreserve.gov/releases/H15/data/m/tcm3y.txt, http://www.federalreserve.gov/releases/H15/data/m/tcm5y.txt, http://www.federalreserve.gov/releases/H15/data/m/tcm30y.txt

maturities reflected in yield curve patterns: (1) pure expectations theory, (2) market segmentation theory, and (3) liquidity premium theory. The pure expectations theory does a good job of explaining the first two facts on our list but not the third. The market segmentation theory can explain fact 3 but not the other two facts, which are well explained by the pure expectations theory. Because each theory explains facts that the other cannot, a natural way to seek a better understanding of the term structure is to combine features of both theories, which leads us to the liquidity premium theory, which can explain all three facts.

If the liquidity premium theory does a better job of explaining the facts and is consequently widely accepted, why do we spend time discussing the other two theories? There are two reasons. First, the ideas in these two theories provide the groundwork for the liquidity premium theory. Second, it is important to see how financial economists modify theories to improve them when they find that the predicted results are inconsistent with the empirical evidence.

Pure Expectations Theory

The **pure expectations theory** of the term structure states the following commonsense proposition: The interest rate on a long-term bond will equal an average of short-term interest rates that people expect to occur over the life of the long-term bond. For example, if people expect that short-term interest rates will be 10% on average over the coming five years, the expectations hypothesis predicts that the interest rate on bonds with five years to maturity will be 10% too. If short-term interest rates were expected to rise even higher after this five-year period so that the average short-term interest rate over the coming 20 years is 11%, then the interest rate on 20-year bonds would equal 11% and would be higher than the interest rate on five-year bonds. We can see that the explanation provided by the pure expectations theory for why interest rates on bonds of different maturities differ is that short-term interest rates are expected to have different values at future dates.

The key assumption behind this theory is that buyers of bonds do not prefer bonds of one maturity over another, so they will not hold any quantity of a bond if its expected return is less than that of another bond with a different maturity. Bonds that have this characteristic are said to be *perfect substitutes.* What this means in practice is that if bonds with different maturities are perfect substitutes, the expected return on these bonds must be equal.

To see how the assumption that bonds with different maturities are perfect substitutes leads to the pure expectations theory, let us consider the following two investment strategies:

1. Purchase a one-year bond, and when it matures in one year, purchase another one-year bond.
2. Purchase a two-year bond and hold it until maturity.

Because both strategies must have the same expected return if people are holding both one- and two-year bonds, the interest rate on the two-year bond must equal the average of the two one-year interest rates.

EXAMPLE 2: Pure Expectations Theory

The current interest rate on a one-year bond is 9%, and you expect the interest rate on the one-year bond next year to be 11%. What is the expected return over the two years? What interest rate must a two-year bond have to equal the two one-year bonds?

Solution

The expected return over the two years will average 10% per year ([9% + 11%]/2 = 10%). The bondholder will be willing to hold both the one- and two-year bonds only if the expected return per year of the two-year bond equals 10%. Therefore, the interest rate on the two-year bond must equal 10%, the average interest rate on the two one-year bonds. Graphically, we have:

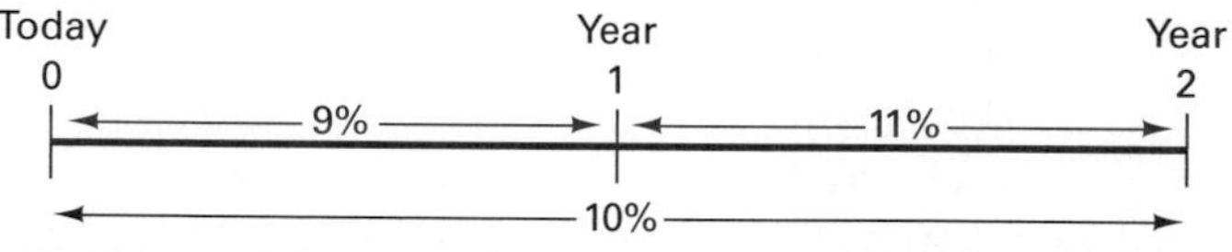

We can make this argument more general. For an investment of $1, consider the choice of holding, for two periods, a two-period bond or two one-period bonds. Using the definitions

i_t = today's (time t) interest rate on a one-period bond
i^e_{t+1} = interest rate on a one-period bond expected for next period (time $t + 1$)
i_{2t} = today's (time t) interest rate on the two-period bond

the expected return over the two periods from investing $1 in the two-period bond and holding it for the two periods can be calculated as

$$(1 + i_{2t})(1 + i_{2t}) - 1 = 1 + 2i_{2t} + (i_{2t})^2 - 1$$

This calculation is derived by recognizing that after the second period, the $1 investment is worth $(1 + i_{2t})\,(1 + i_{2t})$. Then subtracting the $1 initial investment from this amount and dividing by the initial $1 investment gives the rate of return calculated in the previous equation. Because $(i_{2t})^2$ is extremely small—if $i_{2t} = 10\% = 0.10$, then $(i_{2t})^2 = 0.01$—we can simplify the expected return for holding the two-period bond for the two periods to

$$2i_{2t}$$

With the other strategy, in which one-period bonds are bought, the expected return on the $1 investment over the two periods is

$$(1 + i_t)(1 + i^e_{t+1}) - 1$$
$$= 1 + i_t + i^e_{t+1} + i_t(i^e_{t+1}) - 1$$

After the first period, the $1 investment becomes $1 + i_t$, and this is reinvested in the one-period bond for the next period, yielding an amount $(1 + i_t)(1 + i^e_{t+1})$. Subtracting the $1 initial investment from this amount and dividing by the initial investment of $1 gives the expected return for the strategy of holding one-period bonds for the two periods. Because $i_t(i^e_{t+1})$ is also extremely small—if $i_t = i^e_{t+1} = 0.10$, then $i_t(i^e_{t+1}) = 0.01$—we can simplify this to

$$i_t + i^e_{t+1}$$

Both bonds will be held only if these expected returns are equal, that is, when

$$2i_{2t} = i_t + i^e_{t+1}$$

Solving for i_{2t} in terms of the one-period rates, we have

$$i_{2t} = \frac{i_t + i^e_{t+1}}{2} \tag{1}$$

which tells us that the two-period rate must equal the average of the two one-period rates. Graphically, we have

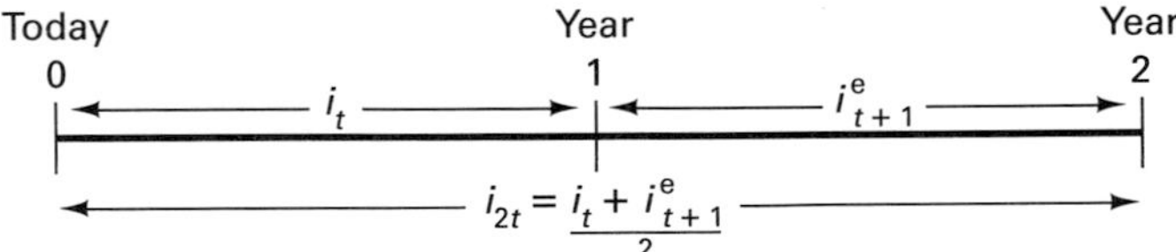

We can conduct the same steps for bonds with a longer maturity so that we can examine the whole term structure of interest rates. Doing so, we will find that the interest rate of i_{nt} on an n-period bond must equal

$$i_{nt} = \frac{i_t + i^e_{t+1} + i^e_{t+2} + \cdots + i^e_{t+(n-1)}}{n} \tag{2}$$

Equation 2 states that the n-period interest rate equals the average of the one-period interest rates expected to occur over the n-period life of the bond. This is a restatement of the pure expectations theory in more precise terms.[3]

[3]The analysis here has been conducted for discount bonds. Formulas for interest rates on coupon bonds would differ slightly from those used here but would convey the same principle.

EXAMPLE 3: Pure Expectations Theory

The one-year interest rate over the next five years is expected to be 5%, 6%, 7%, 8%, and 9%. Given this information, what are the interest rates on a two-year bond and a five-year bond? Explain what is happening to the yield curve.

Solution

The interest rate on the two-year bond would be 5.5%.

$$i_{nt} = \frac{i_t + i^e_{t+1} + i^e_{t+2} + \ldots + i^e_{t+(n-1)}}{n}$$

where

$$\begin{aligned} i_t &= \text{year 1 interest rate} = 5\% \\ i^e_{t+1} &= \text{year 2 interest rate} = 6\% \\ n &= \text{number of years} = 2 \end{aligned}$$

Thus

$$i_{2t} = \frac{5\% + 6\%}{2} = 5.5\%$$

The interest rate on the five-year bond would be 7%.

$$i_{nt} = \frac{i_t + i^e_{t+1} + i^e_{t+2} + \ldots + i^e_{t+(n-1)}}{n}$$

where

$$\begin{aligned} i_t &= \text{year 1 interest rate} = 5\% \\ i^e_{t+1} &= \text{year 2 interest rate} = 6\% \\ i^e_{t+2} &= \text{year 3 interest rate} = 7\% \\ i^e_{t+3} &= \text{year 4 interest rate} = 8\% \\ i^e_{t+4} &= \text{year 5 interest rate} = 9\% \\ n &= \text{number of years} = 5 \end{aligned}$$

Thus

$$i_{5t} = \frac{5\% + 6\% + 7\% + 8\% + 9\%}{5} = 7.0\%$$

Using the same equation for the one-, three-, and four-year interest rates, you will be able to verify the one-year to five-year rates as 5.0%, 5.5%, 6.0%, 6.5%, and 7.0% respectively. The rising trend in short-term interest rates produces an upward-sloping yield curve along which interest rates rise as maturity lengthens.

The pure expectations theory provides an elegant explanation of why the term structure of interest rates (as represented by yield curves) changes at different times. When the yield curve is upward-sloping, the pure expectations theory suggests that short-term interest rates are expected to rise in the future, as we have seen in our numerical example. In this situation, in which the long-term rate is currently above the short-term rate, the average of future short-term rates is expected to be higher than the current short-term rate, which can occur only if short-term interest rates are expected to rise. This is what we see in our numerical example. When the yield curve slopes downward and is inverted, the average of future short-term interest rates is expected to be below the current short-term rate, implying that short-term interest rates are expected to fall, on average, in the future. Only when the yield curve is flat does the pure expectations theory suggest that short-term interest rates are not expected to change, on average, in the future.

The pure expectations theory also explains fact 1—that interest rates on bonds with different maturities move together over time. Historically, short-term interest rates have had the characteristic that if they increase today, they will tend to be higher in the future. Hence a rise in short-term rates will raise people's expectations of future short-term rates. Because long-term rates are related to the average of expected future short-term rates, a rise in short-term rates will also raise long-term rates, causing short- and long-term rates to move together.

The pure expectations theory also explains fact 2—that yield curves tend to have an upward slope when short-term interest rates are low and are inverted when short-term rates are high. When short-term rates are low, people generally expect them to rise to some normal level in the future, and the average of future expected short-term rates is high relative to the current short-term rate. Therefore, long-term interest rates will be substantially above current short-term rates, and the yield curve would then have an upward slope. Conversely, if short-term rates are high, people usually expect them to come back down. Long-term rates would then drop below short-term rates because the average of expected future short-term rates would be below current short-term rates and the yield curve would slope downward and become inverted.[4]

The pure expectations theory is an attractive theory because it provides a simple explanation of the behavior of the term structure, but unfortunately it has a major shortcoming: It cannot explain fact 3—that yield curves usually slope upward. The typical upward slope of yield curves implies that short-term interest rates are usually expected to rise in the future. In practice, short-term interest rates are just as likely to fall as they are to rise, and so the pure expectations theory suggests that the typical yield curve should be flat rather than upward-sloping.

Market Segmentation Theory

As the name suggests, the **market segmentation theory** of the term structure sees markets for different-maturity bonds as completely separate and segmented. The interest rate for each bond with a different maturity is then determined by

[4]The pure expectations theory explains another important fact about the relationship between short-term and long-term interest rates. As you can see looking back at Figure 5, short-term interest rates are more volatile than long-term rates. If interest rates are mean-reverting—that is, if they tend to head back down after they are at unusually high levels or go back up when they are at unusually low levels—then an average of these short-term rates must necessarily have lower volatility than the short-term rates themselves. Because the pure expectations theory suggests that the long-term rate will be an average of future short-term rates, it implies that the long-term rate will have lower volatility than short-term rates.

the supply of and demand for that bond with no effects from expected returns on other bonds with other maturities.

The key assumption in market segmentation theory is that bonds of different maturities are not substitutes at all, so the expected return from holding a bond of one maturity has no effect on the demand for a bond of another maturity. This theory of the term structure is at the opposite extreme to the pure expectations theory, which assumes that bonds of different maturities are perfect substitutes.

The argument for why bonds of different maturities are not substitutes is that investors have strong preferences for bonds of one maturity but not for another, so they will be concerned with the expected returns only for bonds of the maturity they prefer. This might occur because they have a particular holding period in mind, and if they match the maturity of the bond to the desired holding period, they can obtain a certain return with no risk at all.[5] (We have seen in Chapter 3 that if the term to maturity equals the holding period, the return is known for certain because it equals the yield exactly, and there is no interest-rate risk.) For example, people who have a short holding period would prefer to hold short-term bonds. Conversely, if you were putting funds away for your young child to go to college, your desired holding period might be much longer, and you would want to hold longer-term bonds.

In market segmentation theory, differing yield curve patterns are accounted for by supply and demand differences associated with bonds of different maturities. If, as seems sensible, investors generally prefer bonds with shorter maturities that have less interest-rate risk, market segmentation theory can explain fact 3, that yield curves typically slope upward. Because the demand for long-term bonds is relatively lower than that for short-term bonds in the typical situation, long-term bonds will have lower prices and higher interest rates, and hence the yield curve will typically slope upward.

Although market segmentation theory can explain why yield curves usually tend to slope upward, it has a major flaw in that it cannot explain facts 1 and 2. Because it views the market for bonds of different maturities as completely segmented, there is no reason for a rise in interest rates on a bond of one maturity to affect the interest rate on a bond of another maturity. Therefore, it cannot explain why interest rates on bonds of different maturities tend to move together (fact 1). Second, because it is not clear how demand and supply for short- versus long-term bonds changes with the level of short-term interest rates, the theory cannot explain why yield curves tend to slope upward when short-term interest rates are low and to be inverted when short-term interest rates are high (fact 2).

Because each of our two theories explains empirical facts that the other cannot, a logical step is to combine the theories, which leads us to the liquidity premium theory.

---

[5]The statement that there is no uncertainty about the return if the term to maturity equals the holding period is literally true only for a discount bond. For a coupon bond with a long holding period, there is some risk because coupon payments must be reinvested before the bond matures. Our analysis here is thus being conducted for discount bonds. However, the gist of the analysis remains the same for coupon bonds because the amount of this risk from reinvestment is small when coupon bonds have the same term to maturity as the holding period.

Liquidity Premium Theory

The **liquidity premium theory** of term structure states that the interest rate on a long-term bond will equal an average of short-term interest rates expected to occur over the life of the long-term bond plus a liquidity premium that responds to supply and demand conditions for that bond.

The liquidity premium theory's key assumption is that bonds of different maturities are substitutes, which means that the expected return on one bond *does* influence the expected return on a bond of a different maturity, but it allows investors to prefer one bond maturity over another. In other words, bonds of different maturities are assumed to be substitutes but not perfect substitutes. Investors tend to prefer shorter-term bonds because these bonds bear less interest-rate risk. For this reason, investors must be offered a positive liquidity premium to induce them to hold longer-term bonds. Such an outcome would modify the pure expectations theory by adding a positive liquidity premium to the equation that describes the relationship between long- and short-term interest rates. The liquidity premium theory is thus written

$$i_{nt} = \frac{i_t + i^e_{t+1} + i^e_{t+2} + \ldots + i^e_{t+(n-1)}}{n} + \ell_{nt} \tag{3}$$

where ℓ_{nt} = the liquidity premium for the n-period bond at time t, which is always positive and rises with the term to maturity of the bond, n.

The relationship between the pure expectations theory and the liquidity premium theory is shown in Figure 6. There we see that because the liquidity premium is always positive and grows as the term to maturity increases, the yield curve implied by the liquidity premium theory is always above the yield curve implied by the pure expectations theory and has a steeper slope.

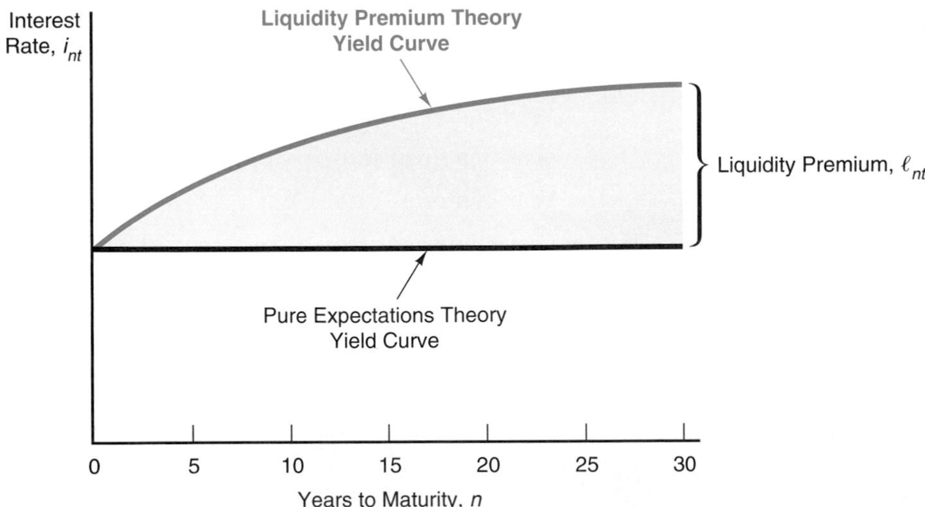

FIGURE 6 The Relationship Between the Liquidity Premium and Pure Expectations Theories

Because the liquidity premium is always positive and grows as the term to maturity increases, the yield curve implied by the liquidity premium theory is always above the yield curve implied by the pure expectations theory and has a steeper slope.

EXAMPLE 4: Liquidity Premium Theory

As in Example 3, let's suppose that the one-year interest rate over the next five years is expected to be 5%, 6%, 7%, 8%, and 9%. Investors' preferences for holding short-term bonds have the liquidity premiums for one-year to five-year bonds as 0%, 0.25%, 0.5%, 0.75%, and 1.0%, respectively. What is the interest rate on a two-year bond and a five-year bond? Compare these findings with the answer from Example 3 dealing with the pure expectations theory.

Solution

The interest rate on the two-year bond would be 5.75%.

$$i_{nt} = \frac{i_t + i^e_{t+1} + i^e_{t+2} + \ldots + i^e_{t+(n-1)}}{n} + \ell_{nt}$$

where

$$\begin{aligned} i_t &= \text{year 1 interest rate} = 5\% \\ i^e_{t+1} &= \text{year 2 interest rate} = 6\% \\ \ell_{nt} &= \text{liquidity premium} = 0.25\% \\ n &= \text{number of years} = 2 \end{aligned}$$

Thus

$$i_{2t} = \frac{5\% + 6\%}{2} + 0.25\% = 5.75\%$$

The interest rate on the five-year bond would be 8%.

$$i_{nt} = \frac{i_t + i^e_{t+1} + i^e_{t+2} + \ldots + i^e_{t+(n-1)}}{n} + \ell_{nt}$$

where

$$\begin{aligned} i_t &= \text{year 1 interest rate} = 5\% \\ i^e_{t+1} &= \text{year 2 interest rate} = 6\% \\ i^e_{t+2} &= \text{year 3 interest rate} = 7\% \\ i^e_{t+3} &= \text{year 4 interest rate} = 8\% \\ i^e_{t+4} &= \text{year 5 interest rate} = 9\% \\ \ell_{2t} &= \text{liquidity premium} = 1\% \\ n &= \text{number of years} = 5 \end{aligned}$$

Thus

$$i_{5t} = \frac{5\% + 6\% + 7\% + 8\% + 9\%}{5} + 1\% = 8.0\%$$

If you did similar calculations for the one-, three-, and four-year interest rates, the one-year to five-year interest rates would be as follows: 5.0%, 5.75%, 6.5%, 7.25%, and 8.0%, respectively. Comparing these findings with those for the pure expectations theory, we can see that the liquidity preference theory produces yield curves that slope more steeply upward because of investors' preferences for short-term bonds.

Let's see if the liquidity premium theory is consistent with all three empirical facts we have discussed. It explains fact 1 that interest rates on different-maturity bonds move together over time: A rise in short-term interest rates indicates that short-term interest rates will, on average, be higher in the future, and the first term in Equation 3 then implies that long-term interest rates will rise along with them.

It also explains why yield curves tend to have an especially steep upward slope when short-term interest rates are low and to be inverted when short-term rates are high (fact 2). Because investors generally expect short-term interest rates to rise to some normal level when they are low, the average of future expected short-term rates will be high relative to the current short-term rate. With the additional boost of a positive liquidity premium, long-term interest rates will be substantially above current short-term rates, and the yield curve would then have a steep upward slope. Conversely, if short-term rates are high, people usually expect them to come back down. Long-term rates would then drop below short-term rates because the average of expected future short-term rates would be so far below current short-term rates that despite positive liquidity premiums, the yield curve would slope downward.

The liquidity premium theory explains fact 3 that yield curves typically slope upward by recognizing that the liquidity premium rises with a bond's maturity because of investors' preferences for short-term bonds. Even if short-term interest rates are expected to stay the same on average in the future, long-term interest rates will be above short-term interest rates, and yield curves will typically slope upward.

How can the liquidity premium theory explain the occasional appearance of inverted yield curves if the liquidity premium is positive? It must be that at times short-term interest rates are expected to fall so much in the future that the average of the expected short-term rates is well below the current short-term rate. Even when the positive liquidity premium is added to this average, the resulting long-term rate will still be below the current short-term interest rate.

As our discussion indicates, a particularly attractive feature of the liquidity premium theory is that it tells you what the market is predicting about future short-term interest rates just by looking at the slope of the yield curve. A steeply rising yield curve, as in panel (a) of Figure 7, indicates that short-term interest rates are expected to rise in the future. A moderately steep yield curve, as in panel (b), indicates that short-term interest rates are not expected to rise or fall much in the future. A flat yield curve, as in panel (c), indicates that short-term rates are expected to fall moderately in the future. Finally, an inverted yield curve, as in panel (d), indicates that short-term interest rates are expected to fall sharply in the future.

Evidence on the Term Structure

In the 1980s, researchers examining the term structure of interest rates questioned whether the slope of the yield curve provides information about movements of future short-term interest rates.[6] They found that the spread between long- and

[6]Robert J. Shiller, John Y. Campbell, and Kermit L. Schoenholtz, "Forward Rates and Future Policy: Interpreting the Term Structure of Interest Rates," *Brookings Papers on Economic Activity* 1 (1983): 173–217; N. Gregory Mankiw and Lawrence H. Summers, "Do Long-Term Interest Rates Overreact to Short-Term Interest Rates?" *Brookings Papers on Economic Activity* 1 (1984): 243–247.

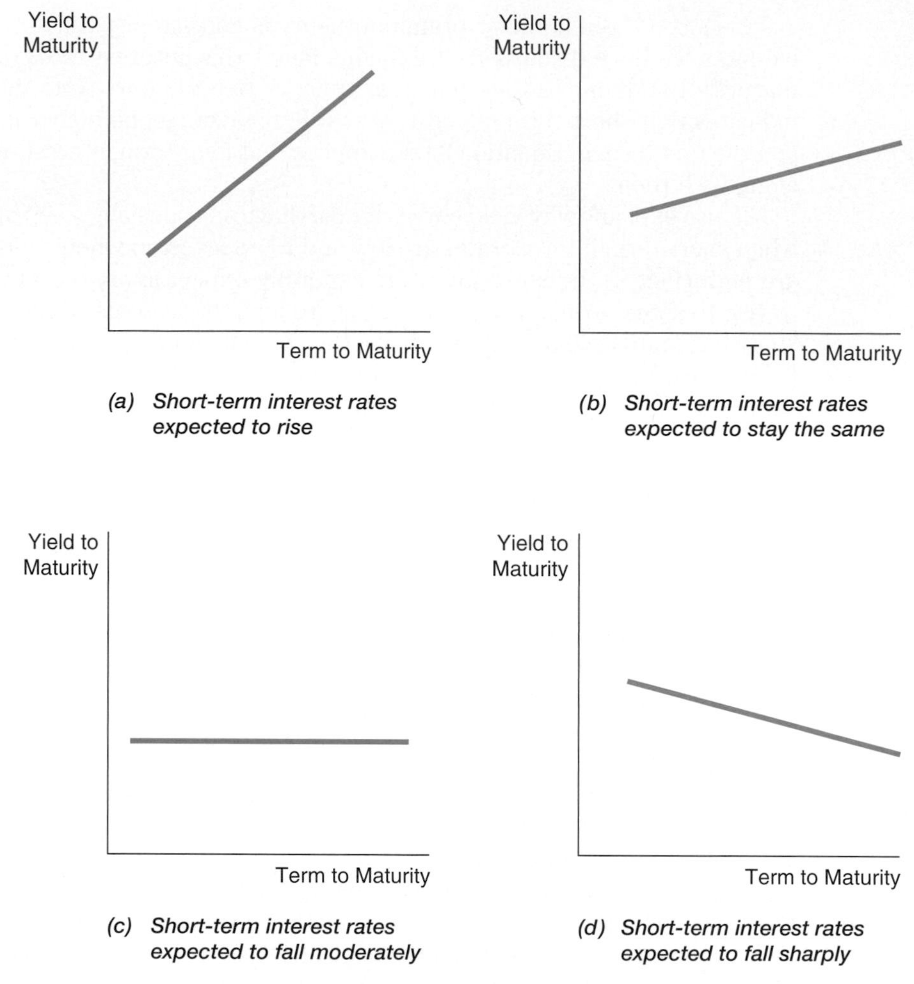

FIGURE 7 Yield Curves and the Market's Expectations of Future Short-Term Interest Rates

short-term interest rates does not always help predict future short-term interest rates, a finding that may stem from substantial fluctuations in the liquidity premium for long-term bonds. More recent research using more discriminating tests now favors a different view. It shows that the term structure contains quite a bit of information for the very short run, over the next several months, and the long run, over several years, but is unreliable at predicting movements in interest rates over the intermediate term, the time in between.[7]

[7]Eugene Fama, "The Information in the Term Structure," *Journal of Financial Economics* 13 (1984): 509–528; Eugene Fama and Robert Bliss, "The Information in Long-Maturity Forward Rates," *American Economic Review* 77 (1987): 680–692; John Y. Campbell and Robert J. Shiller, "Cointegration and Tests of the Present Value Models," *Journal of Political Economy* 95 (1987): 1062–1088; John Y. Campbell and Robert J. Shiller, "Yield Spreads and Interest Rate Movements: A Bird's Eye View," *Review of Economic Studies* 58 (1991): 495–514.

Summary

The liquidity premium theory is the most widely accepted theory of the term structure of interest rates because it explains the major empirical facts about the term structure so well. It combines the features of both the pure expectations theory and market segmentation theory by asserting that a long-term interest rate will be the sum of a liquidity premium and the average of the short-term interest rates that are expected to occur over the life of the bond.

The liquidity premium theory explains the following facts: (1) Interest rates on bonds of different maturities tend to move together over time, (2) yield curves usually slope upward, and (3) when short-term interest rates are low, yield curves are more likely to have a steep upward slope, whereas when short-term interest rates are high, yield curves are more likely to be inverted.

The theory also helps us predict the movement of short-term interest rates in the future. A steep upward slope of the yield curve means that short-term rates are expected to rise, a mild upward slope means that short-term rates are expected to remain the same, a flat slope means that short-term rates are expected to fall moderately, and an inverted yield curve means that short-term rates are expected to fall sharply.

Application Interpreting Yield Curves, 1980–2002

Figure 8 illustrates several yield curves that have appeared for U.S. government bonds in recent years. What do these yield curves tell us about the public's expectations of future movements of short-term interest rates?

Study Guide Try to answer the question before reading further in the text. If you have trouble answering it with the liquidity premium theory, first try answering it with the pure expectations theory (which is simpler because you don't have to worry about the liquidity premium). When you understand what the expectations of future interest rates are in this case, modify your analysis by taking the liquidity premium into account.

The steep inverted yield curve that occurred on January 15, 1981, indicated that short-term interest rates were expected to decline sharply in the future. In order for longer-term interest rates with their positive liquidity premium to be well below the short-term interest rate, short-term interest rates must be expected to decline so sharply that their average is far below the current short-term rate. Indeed, the public's expectations of sharply lower short-term interest rates evident in the yield curve were realized soon after January 15; by March, three-month Treasury bill rates had declined from the 16% level to 13%.

The steep upward-sloping yield curves on March 28, 1985, and especially January 2, 2002 indicated that short-term interest rates would climb in the future. The long-term interest rate is above the short-term interest rate when short-term interest rates are expected to rise because their average plus the liquidity premium will be above the current short-term rate. The moderately upward-sloping yield curves on May 16, 1980, and March 3, 1997, indicated that short-term interest rates were expected neither to rise nor to fall in the near future. In this case, their average remains the same as the current short-term rate, and the positive liquidity premium for longer-term bonds explains the moderate upward slope of the yield curve.

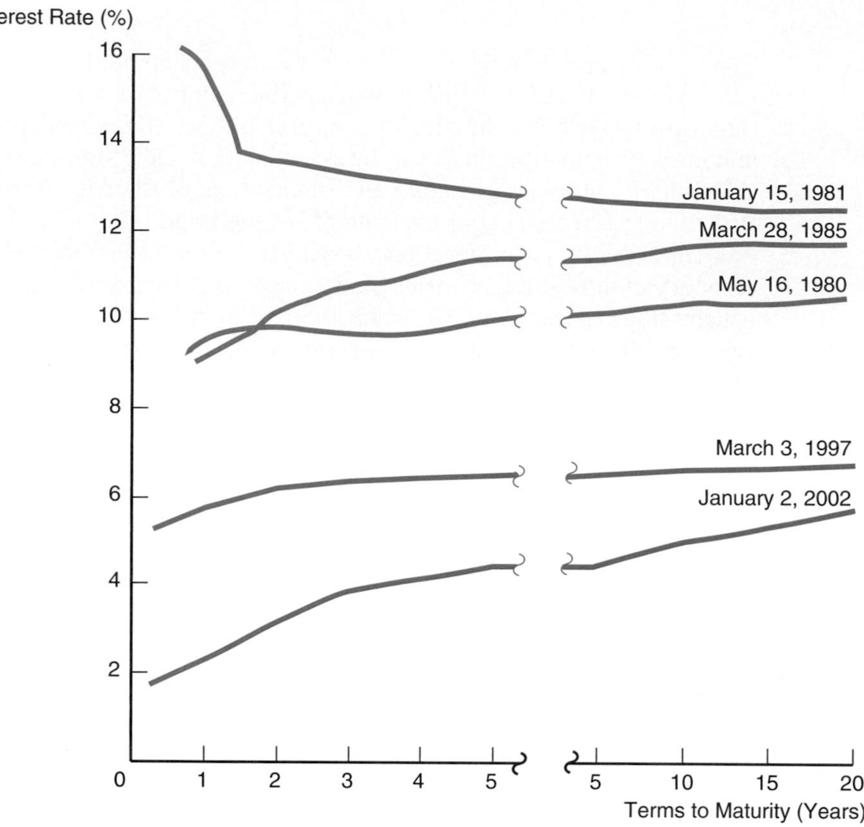

FIGURE 8 Yield Curves for U.S. Government Bonds

Sources: Federal Reserve Bank of St. Louis; *U.S. Financial Data,* various issues; *Wall Street Journal,* various dates.

THE PRACTICING FINANCIAL INSTITUTION MANAGER

Using the Term Structure to Forecast Interest Rates

As was discussed in Chapter 4, interest-rate forecasts are extremely important to managers of financial institutions because future changes in interest rates have a significant impact on the profitability of their institutions. Furthermore, interest-rate forecasts are needed when managers of financial institutions have to set interest rates on loans that are promised to customers in the future. Our discussion of the term structure of interest rates has indicated that the slope of the yield curve provides general information about the market's prediction of the future path of interest rates. For example, a steeply upward-sloping yield curve indicates that short-term interest rates are predicted to rise in the future, and a downward-sloping yield curve indicates that short-term interest rates are predicted to fall. However, a financial institution manager needs much more specific information on interest-rate forecasts than this. Here we show how the manager of a financial institution can generate specific forecasts of interest rates using the term structure.

To see how this is done, let's start the analysis using the approach we took in developing the pure expectations theory. Recall that because bonds of different maturities are perfect substitutes, we assumed that the expected return over two periods from investing \$1 in a two-period bond, which is $(1 + i_{2t})(1 + i_{2t}) - 1$, must equal the expected return from investing \$1 in one-period bonds, which is $(1 + i_t)(1 + i^e_{t+1}) - 1$. This is shown graphically as follows:

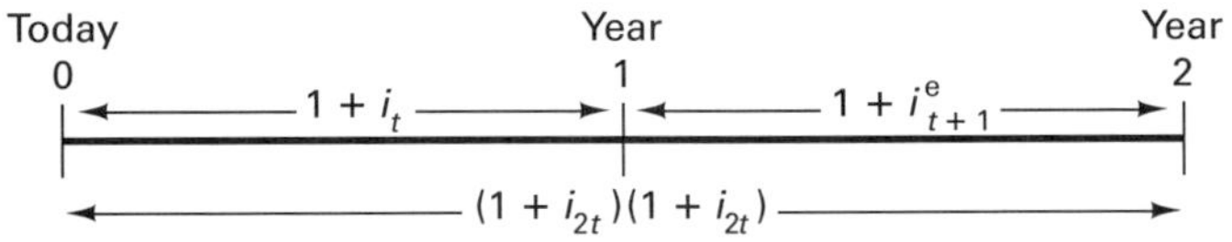

Today 0 — Year 1 — Year 2

$1 + i_t$ (from 0 to 1) $\quad$ $1 + i^e_{t+1}$ (from 1 to 2)

$(1 + i_{2t})(1 + i_{2t})$ (from 0 to 2)

In other words,

$$(1 + i_t)(1 + i^e_{t+1}) - 1 = (1 + i_{2t})(1 + i_{2t}) - 1$$

Through some tedious algebra we can solve for i^e_{t+1}:

$$i^e_{t+1} = \frac{(1 + i_{2t})^2}{1 + i_t} - 1 \tag{4}$$

This measure of i^e_{t+1} is called the **forward rate** because it is the one-period interest rate that the pure expectations theory of the term structure indicates is expected to prevail one period in the future. To differentiate forward rates derived from the term structure from actual interest rates that are observed at time t, we call these observed interest rates **spot rates.**

Going back to Example 3, which we used to discuss the pure expectations theory earlier in this chapter, at time t the one-year interest rate is 5% and the two-year rate is 5.5%. Plugging these numbers into Equation 4 yields the following estimate of the forward rate one period in the future:

$$i^e_{t+1} = \frac{(1 + 0.055)^2}{1 + 0.05} - 1 = 0.06 = 6\%$$

Not surprisingly, this 6% forward rate is identical to the expected one-year interest rate one year in the future that we used in Example 3. This is exactly what we should find, as our calculation here is just another way of looking at the pure expectations theory.

We can also compare holding the three-year bond against holding a sequence of one-year bonds, which reveals the following relationship:

$$(1 + i_t)(1 + i^e_{t+1})(1 + i^e_{t+2}) - 1 = (1 + i_{3t})(1 + i_{3t})(1 + i_{3t}) - 1$$

and plugging in the estimate for i^e_{t+1} derived in Equation 4, we can solve for i^e_{t+2}:

$$i^e_{t+2} = \frac{(1 + i_{3t})^3}{(1 + i_{2t})^2} - 1$$

Continuing with these calculations, we obtain the general solution for the forward rate n periods into the future:

$$i^e_{t+n} = \frac{(1 + i_{n+1t})^{n+1}}{(1 + i_{nt})^n} - 1 \tag{5}$$

Our discussion indicated that the pure expectations theory is not entirely satisfactory because investors must be compensated with liquidity premiums to induce them to hold longer-term bonds. Hence we need to modify our analysis, as we did when discussing the liquidity premium theory, by allowing for these liquidity premiums in estimating predictions of future interest rates.

Recall from the discussion of those theories that because investors prefer to hold short-term rather than long-term bonds, the n-period interest rate differs from that indicated by the pure expectations theory by a liquidity premium of ℓ_{nt}. So to allow for liquidity premiums, we need merely subtract ℓ_{nt} from i_{nt} in our formula to derive i^e_{t+n}:

$$i^e_{t+n} = \frac{(1 + i_{n+1t} - \ell_{n+1t})^{n+1}}{(1 + i_{nt} - \ell_{nt})^n} - 1 \tag{6}$$

This measure of i^e_{t+n} is referred to, naturally enough, as the *adjusted forward-rate forecast*.

In the case of i^e_{t+1}, Equation 6 produces the following estimate:

$$i^e_{t+1} = \frac{(1 + i_{2t} - \ell_{2t})^2}{1 + i_t} - 1$$

Using Example 4 in our discussion of the liquidity premium theory, at time t the ℓ_{2t} liquidity premium is 0.25%, $\ell_{1t} = 0$, the one-year interest rate is 5%, and the two-year interest rate is 5.75%. Plugging these numbers into our equation yields the following adjusted forward-rate forecast for one period in the future:

$$i^e_{t+1} = \frac{(1 + 0.0575 - 0.0025)^2}{1 + 0.05} - 1 = 0.06 = 6\%$$

which is the same as the expected interest rate used in Example 3, as it should be.

Our analysis of the term structure thus provides managers of financial institutions with a fairly straightforward procedure for producing interest-rate forecasts. First they need to estimate ℓ_{nt}, the values of the liquidity premiums for various n. Then they need merely apply the formula in Equation 6 to derive the market's forecasts of future interest rates.

EXAMPLE 5: Forward Rate

A customer asks a bank if it would be willing to commit to making the customer a one-year loan at an interest rate of 8% one year from now. To compensate for the costs of making the loan, the bank needs to charge one percentage point more than the expected interest rate on a Treasury bond with the same maturity if it is to make a profit. If the bank manager estimates the liquidity premium to be 0.4%, and the one-year Treasury bond rate is 6% and the two-year bond rate is 7%, should the manager be willing to make the commitment?

Solution

The bank manager is unable to make the loan because at an interest rate of 8%, the loan is likely to be unprofitable to the bank.

$$i^e_{t+n} = \frac{(1 + i_{n+1t} - \ell_{n+1t})^{n+1}}{(1 + i_{nt} - \ell_{nt})^n} - 1$$

where

i_{n+1t} = two-year bond rate = 0.07
ℓ_{n+1t} = liquidity premium = 0.004
i_{nt} = one-year bond rate = 0.06
ℓ_{1t} = liquidity premium = 0
n = number of years = 1

Thus

$$i^e_{t+1} = \frac{(1 + 0.07 - 0.004)^2}{1 + 0.06} - 1 = 0.072 = 7.2\%$$

The market's forecast of the one-year Treasury bond rate one year in the future is therefore 7.2%. Adding the 1% necessary to make a profit on the one-year loan means that the loan is expected to be profitable only if it has an interest rate of 8.2% or higher.

As we will see in Chapter 10, the bond market's forecasts of interest rates may be the most accurate ones possible. If this is the case, the estimates of the market's forecasts of future interest rates using the simple procedure outlined here may be the best interest-rate forecasts that a financial institution manager can obtain.

Study Guide To make sure you understand how to generate interest-rate forecasts from the term structure, calculate the forecasts of the one-year interest rates using Equation 6 for two, three, and four years in the future using the liquidity premiums and one-year through five-year interest rates in Example 4. The resulting forecasts should equal the expected future interest rates found in the example. Problems 14 and 15 at the end of the chapter will give you more practice in generating interest-rate forecasts from the term structure.

SUMMARY

1. Bonds with the same maturity will have different interest rates because of three factors: default risk, liquidity, and tax considerations. The greater a bond's default risk, the higher its interest rate relative to other bonds; the greater a bond's liquidity, the lower its interest rate; and bonds with tax-exempt status will have lower interest rates than they otherwise would. The relationship among interest rates on bonds with the same maturity that arise because of these three factors is known as the risk structure of interest rates.
2. Several theories of the term structure provide explanations of how interest rates on bonds with different terms to maturity are related. The pure expectations theory views long-term interest rates as equaling the average of future short-term interest rates expected to occur over the life of the bond; by contrast, market segmentation theory treats the determination of interest rates for each bond's maturity as the outcome of supply and demand in that market only. Neither of these theories by itself can explain both the fact that interest rates on bonds of different maturities move together over time and the fact that yield curves usually slope upward.
3. The liquidity premium theory combines the features of the other two theories and by so doing is able to explain the facts just mentioned. It views long-term interest rates as equaling the average of future short-term interest rates expected to occur

over the life of the bond plus a liquidity premium that reflects the supply of and demand for bonds of different maturities.

4. These theories allow us to infer the market's expectations about the movement of future short-term interest rates from the yield curve. A steeply upward-sloping curve indicates that future short-term rates are expected to rise, a mildly upward-sloping curve indicates that short-term rates are expected to stay the same, a flat curve indicates that short-term rates are expected to decline slightly, and an inverted yield curve indicates that a substantial decline in short-term rates is expected in the future.

KEY TERMS

default, *p. 120*
default-free bonds, *p. 120*
default risk, *p. 120*
forward rate, *p. 141*
inverted yield curve, *p. 128*
junk bonds, *p. 122*
liquidity premium theory, *p. 135*
market segmentation theory, *p. 133*
pure expectations theory, *p. 129*
risk premium, *p. 120*
risk structure of interest rates, *p. 119*
spot rate, *p. 141*
term structure of interest rates, *p. 119*
yield curve, *p. 128*

QUESTIONS AND PROBLEMS

1. Which should have the higher risk premium on its interest rates, a corporate bond with a Moody's Baa rating or a corporate bond with a C rating? Why?

***2.** Why do U.S. Treasury bills have lower interest rates than large-denomination negotiable bank CDs?

3. Risk premiums on corporate bonds are usually anticyclical; that is, they decrease during business cycle expansions and increase during recessions. Why is this so?

***4.** "If bonds of different maturities are close substitutes, their interest rates are more likely to move together." Is this statement true, false, or uncertain? Explain your answer.

5. If yield curves, on average, were flat, what would this say about the liquidity premiums in the term structure? Would you be more or less willing to accept the pure expectations theory?

***6.** Assuming that the pure expectations theory is the correct theory of the term structure, calculate the interest rates in the term structure for maturities of one to five years, and plot the resulting yield curves for the following series of one-year interest rates over the next five years:
a. 5%, 7%, 7%, 7%, 7%
b. 5%, 4%, 4%, 4%, 4%

How would your yield curves change if people preferred shorter-term bonds over longer-term bonds?

7. Assuming that the pure expectations theory is the correct theory of the term structure, calculate the interest rates in the term structure for maturities of one to five years, and plot the resulting yield curves for the following path of one-year interest rates over the next five years:
a. 5%, 6%, 7%, 6%, 5%
b. 5%, 4%, 3%, 4%, 5%

How would your yield curves change if people preferred shorter-term bonds over longer-term bonds?

***8.** If a yield curve looks like the one shown below, what is the market predicting about the movement of future short-term interest rates? What might the yield curve indicate about the market's predictions about the inflation rate in the future?

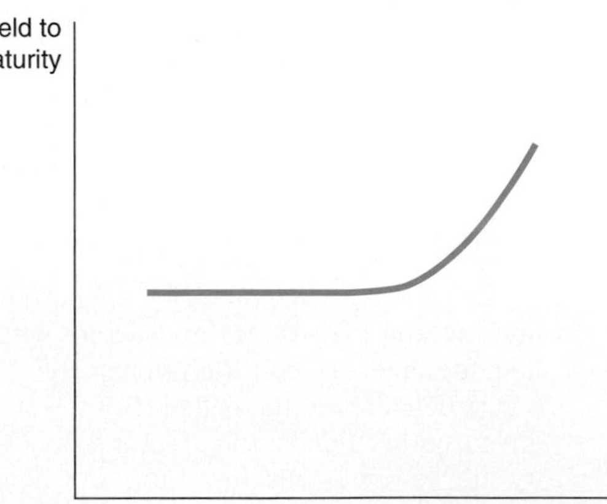

9. If a yield curve looks like the one shown at the top of the next column, what is the market predicting about the movement of future short-term interest rates? What might the yield curve indicate about the market's predictions about the inflation rate in the future?

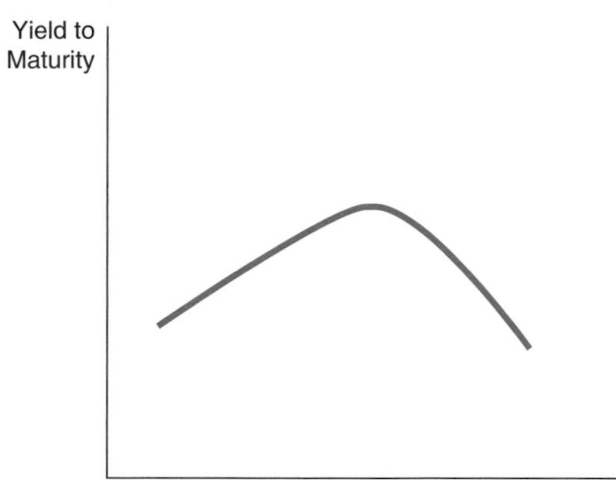

***10.** What effect would reducing income tax rates have on the interest rates of municipal bonds? Would interest rates of Treasury securities be affected and, if so, how?

Predicting the Future

11. Predict what will happen to interest rates on a corporation's bonds if the federal government guarantees today that it will pay creditors if the corporation goes bankrupt in the future. What will happen to the interest rates on Treasury securities?

***12.** Predict what would happen to the risk premiums on corporate bonds if brokerage commissions were lowered in the corporate bond market.

13. If the income tax exemption on municipal bonds were abolished, what would happen to the interest rates on these bonds? What effect would it have on interest rates on U.S. Treasury securities?

***14.** If the interest rates on one- to five-year bonds are currently 4%, 5%, 6%, 7%, and 8% and the term premiums for one- to five-year bonds are 0%, 0.25%, 0.35%, 0.40%, and 0.50%, predict what the one-year interest rate will be two years from now.

15. If the interest rates on one- to five-year bonds are currently 7%, 6%, 5%, 6%, and 7% and the term premiums for one- to five-year bonds are 0%, 0.15%, 0.25%, 0.30%, and 0.60%, predict what the one-year interest rate will be four years from now.

WEB EXERCISES

The Risk and Term Structure of Interest Rates

1. The amount of additional interest investors receive due to the various premiums changes over time. Sometimes the risk premiums are much larger than at other times. For example, the default risk premium was very small in the late 1990s, when the economy was healthy and business failures were rare. It follows that this risk premium increases during recessions.

   Go to http://www.federalreserve.gov/releases/release/H.15 (historical data) and find the interest rate listings for AAA and Baa-rated bonds at three points in time: the most recent, June 1, 1995, and June 1, 1992. Prepare a graph that shows these three time periods (see Figure 1 in this chapter for an example). Are the risk premiums stable, or do they change over time?

2. Figure 8 in this chapter shows a number of yield curves at various points in time. Go to http://www.bloomberg.com and click on "Markets" at the top of the page. Find the Treasury yield curve. Does the current yield curve fall above or below the most recent one listed in Figure 8? Is the current yield curve flatter or steeper than the most recent one reported in Figure 8?

3. Investment companies attempt to explain to investors the nature of the risk the investor incurs when buying shares in their mutual funds. For example, Vanguard carefully explains interest-rate risk and offers alternative funds with different interest-rate risks. Go to http://majestic.vanguard.com/FP/DA.
   - **a.** Select the bond fund you would recommend to an investor who has very low tolerance for risk and a short investment horizon. Justify your answer.
   - **b.** Select the bond fund you would recommend to an investor who has very high tolerance for risk and a long investment horizon. Justify your answer.

Part 3

Central Banking and the Conduct of Monetary Policy

Chapter 6

Structure of Central Banks and the Federal Reserve System

Preview

The most important players in financial markets throughout the world are central banks, the government authorities in charge of monetary policy. Central banks' actions affect interest rates, the amount of credit, and the money supply, all of which have direct impacts not only on financial markets but also on aggregate output and inflation. To understand the role that central banks play in financial markets and the overall economy, we need to understand how these organizations work. Who controls central banks and determines their actions? What motivates their behavior? Who holds the reins of power?

In this chapter we look at the institutional structure of major central banks and particularly focus on the Federal Reserve System, the most important central bank in the world. We start by focusing on the formal institutional structure of the Fed and then examine the more relevant informal structure that determines where the true power within the Federal Reserve System lies. By understanding who makes the decisions, we will have a better idea of how they are made. We then look at several other major central banks and see how they are organized. With this information, we will be more able to comprehend the actual conduct of monetary policy described in the following chapters.

ORIGINS OF THE FEDERAL RESERVE SYSTEM

Of all the central banks in the world, the Federal Reserve System probably has the most unusual structure. To understand why this structure arose, we must go back before 1913, when the Federal Reserve System was created.

Before the twentieth century, a major characteristic of American politics was the fear of centralized power, as seen in the checks and balances of the Constitution and the preservation of states' rights. This fear of centralized power was one source of the American resistance to the establishment of a central bank (see

Chapter 16). Another source was the traditional American distrust of moneyed interests, the most prominent symbol of which was a central bank. The open hostility of the American public to the existence of a central bank resulted in the demise of the first two experiments in central banking, whose function was to police the banking system: The First Bank of the United States was disbanded in 1811, and the national charter of the Second Bank of the United States expired in 1836 after its renewal was vetoed in 1832 by President Andrew Jackson.

The termination of the Second Bank's national charter in 1836 created a severe problem for American financial markets because there was no lender of last resort who could provide reserves to the banking system to avert a bank panic. Hence in the nineteenth and early twentieth centuries, nationwide bank panics became a regular event, occurring every 20 years or so, culminating in the panic of 1907. The 1907 panic resulted in such widespread bank failures and such substantial losses to depositors that the public was finally convinced that a central bank was needed to prevent future panics.

The hostility of the American public to banks and centralized authority created great opposition to the establishment of a single central bank like the Bank of England. Fear was rampant that the moneyed interests on Wall Street (including the largest corporations and banks) would be able to manipulate such an institution to gain control over the economy and that federal operation of the central bank might result in too much government intervention in the affairs of private banks. Serious disagreements existed over whether the central bank should be a private bank or a government institution. Because of the heated debates on these issues, a compromise was struck. In the great American tradition, Congress wrote an elaborate system of checks and balances into the Federal Reserve Act of 1913, which created the Federal Reserve System with its 12 regional Federal Reserve banks (see Box 1).

FORMAL STRUCTURE OF THE FEDERAL RESERVE SYSTEM

Check out information on the structure of the Federal Reserve System at www.federalreserve.gov/pubs/frseries/frseri.htm

The formal structure of the Federal Reserve System was intended by writers of the Federal Reserve Act to diffuse power along regional lines, between the private sector and the government, and among bankers, businesspeople, and the public.

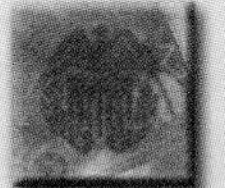

BOX 1: INSIDE THE FED

The Political Genius of the Founders of the Federal Reserve System

The history of the United States has been one of public hostility to banks and especially to a central bank. How were the politicians who founded the Federal Reserve able to design a system that has become one of the most prestigious institutions in the United States?

The answer is that the founders recognized that if power was too concentrated in either Washington or New York, cities that Americans love to hate, an American central bank might not have enough public support to operate effectively. They thus decided to set up a decentralized system with 12 Federal Reserve banks spread throughout the country to make sure that all regions of the country were represented in monetary policy deliberations. In addition, they made the Federal Reserve banks quasi-private institutions overseen by directors from the private sector living in that district who represent views from that region and are in close contact with the president of the Federal Reserve bank. The unusual structure of the Federal Reserve System has promoted a concern in the Fed with regional issues as is evident in Federal Reserve bank publications. Without this unusual structure, the Federal Reserve System might have been far less popular with the public, making the institution far less effective.

This initial diffusion of power has resulted in the evolution of the Federal Reserve System to include the following entities: the **Federal Reserve banks,** the **Board of Governors of the Federal Reserve System,** the **Federal Open Market Committee (FOMC),** the Federal Advisory Council, and around 3600 member commercial banks. Figure 1 outlines the relationships of these entities to one another and to the three policy tools of the Fed (open market operations, the discount rate, and reserve requirements) discussed in Chapter 7.

Federal Reserve Banks

Each of the 12 Federal Reserve districts has one main Federal Reserve bank, which may have branches in other cities in the district. The locations of these districts, the Federal Reserve banks, and their branches are shown in Figure 2. The three largest Federal Reserve banks in terms of assets are those of New York, Chicago, and San Francisco—combined they hold over 50% of the assets (discount loans, securities, and other holdings) of the Federal Reserve System. The New York bank,

Find addresses and phone numbers of Federal Reserve banks, branches, and RCPCs as well as links to the main pages of the 12 reserve banks and Board of Governors at www.federalreserve.gov/otherfrb.htm

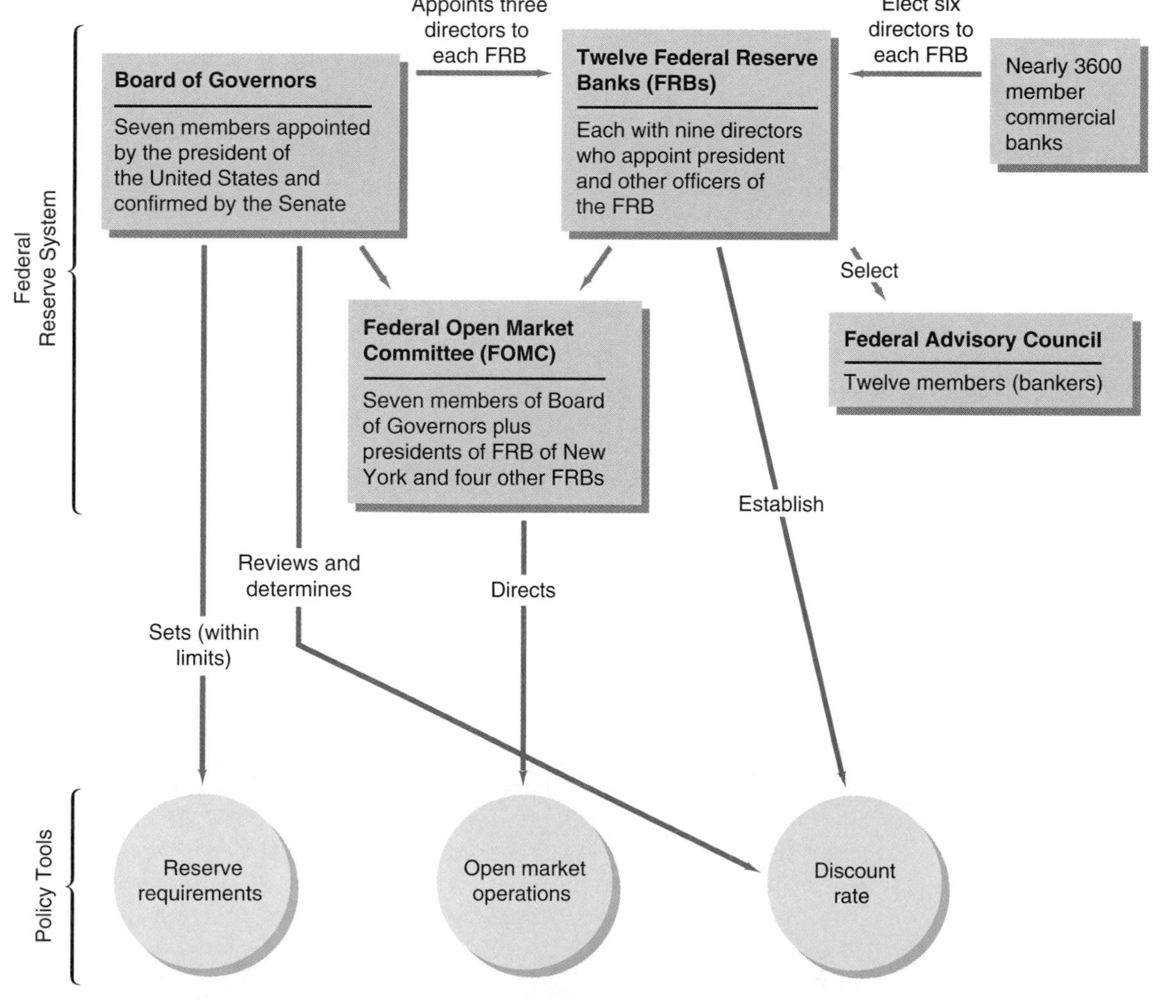

FIGURE 1 Formal Structure and Allocation of Policy Tools in the Federal Reserve

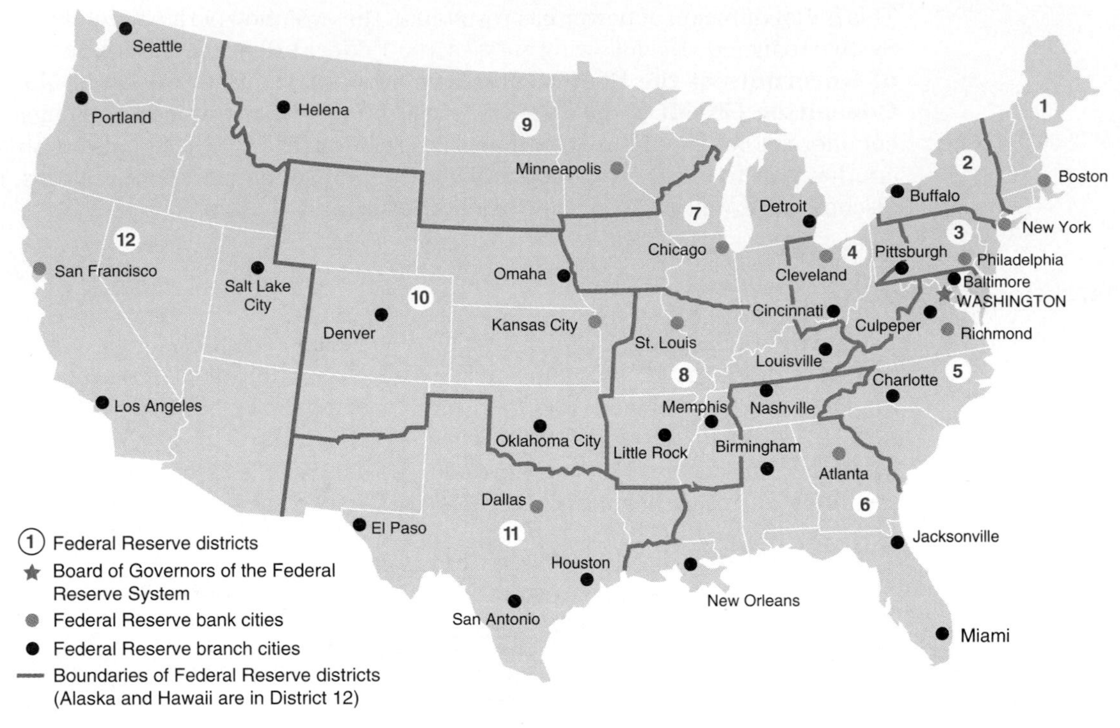

FIGURE 2 Federal Reserve System

Source: Federal Reserve *Bulletin.*

with around one-quarter of the assets, is the most important of the Federal Reserve banks (see Box 2).

Each of the Federal Reserve banks is a quasi-public (part private, part government) institution owned by the private commercial banks in the district who are members of the Federal Reserve System. These member banks have purchased stock in their district Federal Reserve bank (a requirement of membership), and the dividends paid by that stock are limited by law to 6% annually. The member banks elect six directors for each district bank; three more are appointed by the Board of Governors. Together, these nine directors appoint the president of the bank (subject to the approval of the Board of Governors).

The directors of a district bank are classified into three categories, A, B, and C: The three A directors (elected by the member banks) are professional bankers, and the three B directors (also elected by the member banks) are prominent leaders from industry, labor, agriculture, or the consumer sector. The three C directors, who are appointed by the Board of Governors to represent the public interest, are not allowed to be officers, employees, or stockholders of banks. This design for choosing directors was intended by the framers of the Federal Reserve Act to ensure that the directors of each Federal Reserve bank would reflect all constituencies of the American public.

The 12 Federal Reserve banks perform the following functions:

- Clear checks.
- Issue new currency.
- Withdraw damaged currency from circulation.

- Evaluate proposed mergers and applications for banks to expand their activities.
- Administer and make discount loans to banks in their districts.
- Act as liaisons between the business community and the Federal Reserve System.
- Examine bank holding companies and state-chartered member banks.
- Collect data on local business conditions.
- Use their staffs of professional economists to research topics related to the conduct of monetary policy.

The 12 Federal Reserve banks are involved in monetary policy in several ways:

- Their directors "establish" the discount rate (although the discount rate in each district is reviewed and determined by the Board of Governors).
- They decide which banks, member and nonmember alike, can obtain discount loans from the Federal Reserve bank.
- Their directors select one commercial banker from each bank's district to serve on the Federal Advisory Council, which consults with the

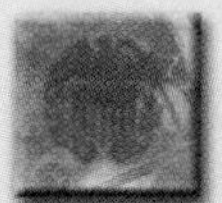

BOX 2: INSIDE THE FED

Special Role of the Federal Reserve Bank of New York

The Federal Reserve Bank of New York plays a special role in the Federal Reserve System for several reasons. First, its district contains many of the largest commercial banks in the United States, the safety and soundness of which are paramount to the health of the U.S. financial system. The Federal Reserve Bank of New York conducts examinations of bank holding companies and state-chartered banks in its district, making it the supervisor of some of the most important financial institutions in our financial system. Not surprisingly, given this responsibility, the Bank Supervision group is one of the largest units of the New York Fed and is by far the largest bank supervision group in the Federal Reserve System.

The second reason for the New York Fed's special role is its active involvement in the bond and foreign exchange markets. The New York Fed houses the open market desk, which conducts open market operations—the purchase and sale of bonds—that determine the amount of reserves in the banking system. Because of this involvement in the Treasury securities market, as well as its walking-distance location near the New York and American Stock Exchanges, the officials at the Federal Reserve Bank of New York are in constant contact with the major domestic financial markets in the United States. In addition, the Federal Reserve Bank of New York also houses the foreign exchange desk, which conducts foreign exchange interventions on behalf of the Federal Reserve System and the U.S. Treasury. Its involvement in these financial markets means that the New York Fed is an important source of information on what is happening in domestic and foreign financial markets, particularly during crisis periods, as well as a liaison between officials in the Federal Reserve System and private participants in the markets.

The third reason for the Federal Reserve Bank of New York's prominence is that it is the only Federal Reserve bank to be a member of the Bank for International Settlements (BIS). Thus the president of the New York Fed, along with the chairman of the Board of Governors, represent the Federal Reserve System in its regular monthly meetings with other major central bankers at the BIS. This close contact with foreign central bankers and interaction with foreign exchange markets means that the New York Fed has a special role in international relations, both with other central bankers and with private market participants. Adding to its prominence in international circles is that the New York Fed is the repository for over $100 billion of the world's gold, an amount greater than the gold at Fort Knox.

Finally, the president of the Federal Reserve Bank of New York, currently William McDonough, is the only permanent member of the FOMC among the Federal Reserve bank presidents, serving as the vice chairman of the committee. Thus he, the chairman, and the vice chairman of the Board of Governors are the three most important officials in the Federal Reserve System.

Board of Governors and provides information that helps in the conduct of monetary policy.

- Five of the 12 bank presidents each have a vote in the Federal Open Market Committee, which directs **open market operations** (the purchase and sale of government securities that affect both interest rates and the amount of reserves in the banking system). As explained in Box 2, the president of the New York Fed always has a vote in the FOMC, making it the most important of the banks; the other four votes allocated to the district banks rotate annually among the remaining 11 presidents.

Member Banks

All *national banks* (commercial banks chartered by the Office of the Comptroller of the Currency) are required to be members of the Federal Reserve System. Commercial banks chartered by the states are not required to be members, but they can choose to join. Currently, around one-third of the commercial banks in the United States are members of the Federal Reserve System, having declined from a peak figure of 49% in 1947.

Before 1980, only member banks were required to keep reserves as deposits at the Federal Reserve banks. Nonmember banks were subject to reserve requirements determined by their states, which typically allowed them to hold much of their reserves in interest-bearing securities. Because no interest is paid on reserves deposited at the Federal Reserve banks, it was costly to be a member of the system, and as interest rates rose, the relative cost of membership rose, and more and more banks left the system.

This decline in Fed membership was a major concern of the Board of Governors (one reason was that it lessened the Fed's control over the money supply, making it more difficult for the Fed to conduct monetary policy). The chairman of the Board of Governors repeatedly called for new legislation that required all commercial banks to be members of the Federal Reserve System. One result of the Fed's pressure on Congress was a provision in the Depository Institutions Deregulation and Monetary Control Act of 1980: All depository institutions became subject (by 1987) to the same requirements to keep deposits at the Fed, so member and nonmember banks would be on an equal footing in terms of reserve requirements. In addition, all depository institutions were given access to the Federal Reserve facilities, such as the discount window (discussed in Chapter 7) and Fed check clearing, on an equal basis. These provisions ended the decline in Fed membership and reduced the distinction between member and nonmember banks.

Board of Governors of the Federal Reserve System

At the head of the Federal Reserve System is the seven-member Board of Governors, headquartered in Washington, D.C. Each governor is appointed by the president of the United States and confirmed by the Senate. To limit the president's control over the Fed and insulate the Fed from other political pressures, the governors serve one nonrenewable 14-year term, with one governor's term expiring every other January.[1] The governors (many are professional economists) are

[1]Although technically the governor's term is nonrenewable, a governor can resign just before the term expires and then be reappointed by the president. This explains how one governor, William McChesney Martin Jr., served for 28 years. Since Martin, the chairman from 1951 to 1970, retired from the board in 1970, the practice of extending a governor's term beyond 14 years has become a rarity.

required to come from different Federal Reserve districts to prevent the interests of one region of the country from being overrepresented. The chairman of the Board of Governors is chosen from among the seven governors and serves a four-year term. It is expected that once a new chairman is chosen, the old chairman resigns from the Board of Governors, even if there are many years left to his or her term as a governor.

The Board of Governors is actively involved in decisions concerning the conduct of monetary policy. All seven governors are members of the FOMC and vote on the conduct of open market operations. Because there are only 12 voting members on this committee (seven governors and five presidents of the district banks), the board has the majority of the votes. The board also sets reserve requirements (within limits imposed by legislation) and effectively controls the discount rate by the "review and determination" process, whereby it approves or disapproves the discount rate "established" by the Federal Reserve banks. The chairman of the board advises the president of the United States on economic policy, testifies in Congress, and speaks for the Federal Reserve System to the media. The chairman and other governors may also represent the United States in negotiations with foreign governments on economic matters. The board has a staff of professional economists (larger than those of individual Federal Reserve banks), which provides economic analysis that the board uses in making its decisions. (Box 3 discusses the role of the research staff.)

Through legislation, the Board of Governors has often been given duties not directly related to the conduct of monetary policy. In the past, for example, the board set the maximum interest rates payable on certain types of time deposits under Regulation Q. (Since Regulation Q was eliminated in 1986, the board no longer has this authority.) Under the Credit Control Act of 1969 (which expired in 1982), the board had the ability to regulate and control credit once the president of the United States approved. The Board of Governors also sets margin requirements, the fraction of the purchase price of the securities that has to be paid for with cash rather than borrowed funds. It also sets the salary of the president and all officers of each Federal Reserve bank and reviews each bank's budget. Finally, the board has substantial bank regulatory functions: It approves bank mergers and applications for new activities, specifies the permissible activities of bank holding companies, and supervises the activities of foreign banks in the United States.

Federal Open Market Committee (FOMC)

Find general information on the FOMC, including its schedule of meetings, statements, minutes, and transcripts, information on its members, and the beige book at www.federalreserve.gov/fomc

The FOMC usually meets eight times a year (about every six weeks) and makes decisions regarding the conduct of open market operations, which influence the monetary base. The committee consists of the seven members of the Board of Governors, the president of the Federal Reserve Bank of New York, and presidents of four other Federal Reserve banks. The chairman of the Board of Governors also presides as the chairman of the FOMC. Even though only presidents of five of the Federal Reserve banks are voting members of the FOMC, the other seven presidents of the district banks attend FOMC meetings and participate in discussions. Hence they have some input into the committee's decisions.

Because open market operations are the most important policy tool that the Fed has for controlling the money supply, the FOMC is necessarily the focal point for policymaking in the Federal Reserve System. Although reserve requirements and the discount rate are not actually set by the FOMC, decisions in regard to

BOX 3: INSIDE THE FED

Role of the Research Staff

The Federal Reserve System is the largest employer of economists not just in the United States but in the world. The system's research staff has around 1000 people, half of whom are economists. Of these 500 economists, 250 are at the Board of Governors, 100 are at the Federal Reserve Bank of New York, and the remainder are at the other Federal Reserve banks. What do all these economists do?

The most important task of the Fed's economists is to follow the incoming data from government agencies and private sector organizations on the economy and provide guidance to the policymakers on where the economy may be heading and what the impact of monetary policy actions on the economy might be. Before each FOMC meeting, the research staff at each Federal Reserve bank briefs its president and the senior management of the bank on its forecast for the U.S. economy and the issues that are likely to be discussed at the meeting. The research staff also provides briefing materials or a formal briefing on the economic outlook for the bank's region, something that each president discusses at the FOMC meeting. Meanwhile, at the Board of Governors, economists maintain a large econometric model (a model whose equations are estimated with statistical procedures) that helps them produce their forecasts of the national economy, and they too brief the governors on the national economic outlook.

The research staffers at the banks and the board also provide support for the bank supervisory staff, tracking developments in the banking sector and other financial markets and institutions and providing bank examiners with technical advice that they might need in the course of their examinations. Because the Board of Governors has to decide on whether to approve bank mergers, the research staff at both the board and the bank in whose district the merger is to take place prepare information on what effect the proposed merger might have on the competitive environment. To assure compliance with the Community Reinvestment Act, economists also analyze a bank's performance in its lending activities in different communities.

Because of the increased influence of developments in foreign countries on the U.S. economy, the research staff, particularly at the New York Fed and the board, produce reports on the major foreign economies. They also conduct research on developments in the foreign exchange market because of its growing importance in the monetary policy process and to support the activities of the foreign exchange desk. Economists also help support the operation of the open market desk by projecting reserve growth and the growth of the monetary aggregates.

Staff economists also engage in basic research on the effects of monetary policy on output and inflation, developments in the labor markets, international trade, international capital markets, banking and other financial institutions, financial markets, and the regional economy, among other topics. This research is published widely in academic journals and in Reserve bank publications. (Federal Reserve bank reviews are a good source of supplemental material for finance students.)

Another important activity of the research staff primarily at the Reserve banks is in the public education area. Staff economists are called on frequently to make presentations to the board of directors at their banks or to make public speeches in their district.

these policy tools are effectively made there. The FOMC does not actually carry out securities purchases or sales. Rather it issues directives to the trading desk at the Federal Reserve Bank of New York, where the manager for domestic open market operations supervises a roomful of people who execute the purchases and sales of the government or agency securities. The manager communicates daily with the FOMC members and their staffs concerning the activities of the trading desk.

The FOMC Meeting

The FOMC meeting takes place in the boardroom on the second floor of the main building of the Board of Governors in Washington. The seven governors and the 12 Reserve Bank presidents, along with the secretary of the FOMC, the board's director of the Research and Statistics Division and his deputy, and the directors of the Monetary Affairs and International Finance Divisions, sit around a massive conference table. Although only five of the Reserve Bank presidents have voting rights on the FOMC at any given time, all actively participate in the deliberations. Seated around the sides of the room are the directors of research at each of the Reserve banks and other senior board and Reserve Bank officials, who, by tradition, do not speak at the meeting.

Except for the meetings before the February and July testimony by the chairman of the Board of Governors before Congress, the meeting starts on Tuesdays at 9:00 A.M. sharp with a quick approval of the minutes of the previous meeting of the FOMC. The first substantive agenda item is the reports by the manager of system open market operations on foreign currency and domestic open market operations and other issues related to these topics. After the governors and Reserve Bank presidents finish asking questions and discussing these reports, a vote is taken to ratify them.

The next stage in the meeting is a presentation of the board staff's national economic forecast, which is referred to as the "green book" forecast (see Box 4), by the director of the Research and Statistics Division at the board. After the governors and Reserve Bank presidents have queried the division director about the forecast, the so-called *go-round* occurs: Each bank president presents an overview of economic conditions in his or her district and the bank's assessment of the national outlook, and each governor, except for the chairman, gives a view of the national outlook. By tradition, remarks avoid the topic of monetary policy at this time.

After a coffee break, everyone returns to the boardroom and the agenda turns to current monetary policy and the domestic policy directive. The board's director of the Monetary Affairs Division then leads off the discussion by outlining the different scenarios for monetary policy actions outlined in the blue book (see Box 4) and may describe an issue relating to how monetary policy should be conducted. After a question-and-answer period, the chairman (currently Alan Greenspan) sets the stage for the following discussion by presenting his views on the state of the economy and then typically makes a recommendation for what monetary policy action should be taken. Then each of the FOMC members as well as the nonvoting bank presidents expresses his or her views on monetary policy, and the chairman summarizes the discussion and proposes specific wording

BOX 4: INSIDE THE FED

Green, Blue, and Beige: What Do These Colors Mean at the Fed?

Three research documents play an important role in the monetary policy process and at Federal Open Market Committee meetings. The national forecast for the next two years, generated by the Federal Reserve Board of Governors' Research and Statistics Division, is placed between green covers and is thus known as the "green book." It is provided to all who attend the FOMC meeting. The "blue book," in blue covers, is also provided to all participants at the FOMC meeting. It contains the projections for the monetary aggregates prepared by the Monetary Affairs Division at the Board of Governors and contains typically three alternative scenarios for monetary policy (labeled A, B, and C). The "beige book," with beige covers, is produced by the Reserve banks and details evidence gleaned either from surveys or from talks with key businesses and financial institutions on the state of the economy in each of the Federal Reserve districts. This is the only one of the three books that is distributed publicly, and it often receives a lot of attention in the press.

for the statement to the open market desk. The secretary of the FOMC formally reads the proposed statement, and the members of the FOMC vote.[2]

Then there is an informal buffet lunch, and while eating, the participants hear a presentation on the latest developments in Congress on banking legislation and other legislation relevant to the Federal Reserve. Around 2:15 P.M. the meeting breaks up and the public announcement is made about the outcome of the meeting: whether the federal funds rate and discount rate have been raised, lowered, or left unchanged, and an assessment of the "balance of risks"[3] in the future, whether toward higher inflation or toward a weaker economy. The postmeeting announcement is an innovation initiated in 1994. Before then, no such announcement was made, and the markets had to guess what policy action was taken. The decision to announce this information was a step in the direction of greater openness by the Fed.

INFORMAL STRUCTURE OF THE FEDERAL RESERVE SYSTEM

The Federal Reserve Act and other legislation give us some idea of the formal structure of the Federal Reserve System and who makes decisions at the Fed. What is written in black and white, however, does not necessarily reflect the reality of the power and decision-making structure.

As envisioned in 1913, the Federal Reserve System was to be a highly decentralized system designed to function as 12 separate, cooperating central banks. In the original plan, the Fed was not responsible for the health of the economy through its control of the money supply and its ability to affect interest rates. Over time, it has acquired the responsibility for promoting a stable economy, and this responsibility has caused the Federal Reserve System to evolve slowly into a more unified central bank.

The framers of the Federal Reserve Act of 1913 intended the Fed to have only one basic tool of monetary policy, the control of discount loans to member banks. The use of open market operations as a tool for monetary control was not yet well understood, and reserve requirements were fixed by the Federal Reserve Act. The discount tool was to be controlled by the joint decision of the Federal Reserve banks and the Federal Reserve Board (which later became the Board of Governors), so that both would share equally in the determination of monetary policy. However, the board's ability to "review and determine" the discount rate effectively allowed it to dominate the district banks in setting this policy.

Banking legislation during the Great Depression years centralized power within the newly created Board of Governors by giving it effective control over the remaining two tools of monetary policy, open market operations and changes in reserve requirements. The Banking Act of 1933 granted the FOMC authority to determine open market operations, and the Banking Act of 1935 gave the board the majority of votes in the FOMC. The Banking Act of 1935 also gave the board authority to change reserve requirements.

---

[2]The decisions expressed in the directive may not be unanimous, and the dissenting views are made public. However, except in rare cases, the chairman's vote is always on the winning side.

[3]The meetings before the February and July chairman's testimony before Congress, in which the *Monetary Report to Congress* is presented, have a somewhat different format. Rather than start Tuesday morning at 9 A.M. like the other meetings, they start in the afternoon on Tuesday and go over to Wednesday, with the usual announcement around 2:15 P.M. These longer meetings consider the longer-term economic outlook as well as the current conduct of open market operations.

Since the 1930s, then, the Board of Governors has acquired the reins of control over the tools for conducting monetary policy. In recent years, the power of the board has become even greater. Although the directors of a Federal Reserve bank choose its president with the approval of the board, the board sometimes suggests a choice (often a professional economist) for president of a Federal Reserve bank to the directors of the bank, who then often follow the board's suggestions. Since the board sets the salary of the bank's president and reviews the budget of each Federal Reserve bank, it has further influence over the district banks' activities.

If the Board of Governors has so much power, what power do the Federal Advisory Council and the "owners" of the Federal Reserve banks—the member banks—actually have within the Federal Reserve System? The answer is almost none. Although member banks own stock in the Federal Reserve banks, they have none of the usual benefits of ownership. First, they have no claim on the earnings of the Fed and get paid only a 6% annual dividend, regardless of how much the Fed earns. Second, they have no say over how their property is used by the Federal Reserve System, in contrast to stockholders of private corporations. Third, there is usually only a single candidate for each of the six A and B directorships "elected" by the member banks, and this candidate is frequently suggested by the president of the Federal Reserve bank (who, in turn, is approved by the Board of Governors). The net result is that member banks are essentially frozen out of the political process at the Fed and have little effective power. Fourth, as its name implies, the Federal Advisory Council has only an advisory capacity and has no authority over Federal Reserve policymaking. Although the member bank "owners" do not have the usual power associated with being a stockholder, they do play an important but subtle role in the Federal Reserve System (see Box 5).

A fair characterization of the Federal Reserve System as it has evolved is that it functions as a central bank, headquartered in Washington, D.C., with branches in 12 cities. Because all aspects of the Federal Reserve System are essentially controlled by the Board of Governors, who controls the board? Although the chairman of the Board of Governors does not have legal authority to exercise control

BOX 5: INSIDE THE FED

Role of Member Banks in the Federal Reserve System

Although the member bank stockholders in each Federal Reserve bank have little direct power in the Federal Reserve System, they do play an important role. Their six representatives on the board of directors of each bank have a major oversight function. Along with the three public interest directors, they oversee the audit process for the Federal Reserve bank, making sure it is being run properly, and also share their management expertise with the senior management of the bank. Because they vote on recommendations by each bank to raise, lower, or maintain the discount rate at its current level, they engage in discussions about monetary policy and transmit their private sector views to the president and senior management of the bank. They also get to understand the inner workings of the Federal Reserve banks and the system so that they can help explain the position of the Federal Reserve to their contacts in the private and political sectors. Advisory councils like the Federal Advisory Council and others that are often set up by the district banks—for example, the Small Business and Agriculture Advisory Council and the Thrift Advisory Council at the New York Fed—are a conduit for the private sector to express views on both the economy and the state of the banking system.

So even though the owners of the Reserve banks do not have the usual voting rights, they are important to the Federal Reserve System because they make sure it does not get out of touch with the needs and opinions of the private sector.

over this body, he effectively does so through his ability to act as spokesperson for the Fed and negotiate with Congress and the president of the United States. He also exercises control by setting the agenda of board and FOMC meetings. For example, the fact that the agenda at the FOMC has the chairman speak first about monetary policy enables him to have greater influence over what the policy action will be. The chairman also influences the board through the force of stature and personality. Chairmen of the Board of Governors (including Marriner S. Eccles, William McChesney Martin Jr., Arthur Burns, Paul A. Volcker, and Alan Greenspan) have typically had strong personalities and have wielded great power.

The chairman also exercises power by supervising the board's staff of professional economists and advisers. Because the staff gathers information for the board and conducts the analyses that the board uses in its decisions, it also has some influence over monetary policy. In addition, in the past, several appointments to the board itself have come from within the ranks of its professional staff, making the chairman's influence even farther-reaching and longer-lasting than a four-year term.

The informal power structure of the Fed, in which power is centralized in the chairman of the Board of Governors, is summarized in Figure 3.

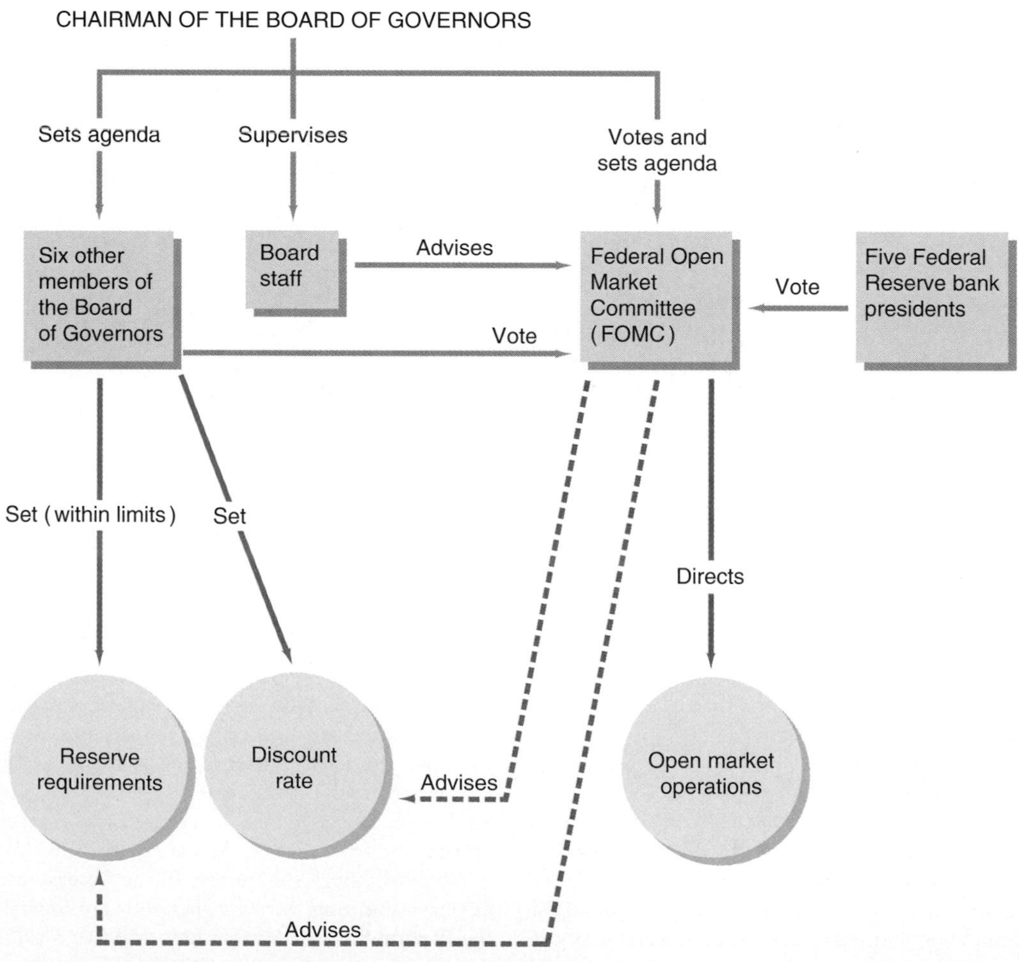

FIGURE 3 Informal Power Structure of the Federal Reserve System

HOW INDEPENDENT IS THE FED?

When we look, in the next chapter, at how the Federal Reserve conducts monetary policy, we will want to know why it decides to take certain policy actions but not others. To understand its actions, we must understand the incentives that motivate the Fed's behavior. How free is the Fed from presidential and congressional pressures? Do economic, bureaucratic, or political considerations guide it? Is the Fed truly independent of outside pressures?

The Federal Reserve appears to be remarkably free of the political pressures that influence other government agencies. Not only are the members of the Board of Governors appointed for a 14-year term (and so cannot be ousted from office), but also the term is technically not renewable, eliminating some of the incentive for the governors to curry favor with the president and Congress.

Probably even more important to its independence from the whims of Congress is the Fed's independent and substantial source of revenue from its holdings of securities and, to a lesser extent, from its loans to banks. In recent years, for example, the Fed has had net earnings after expenses of around $20 billion per year—not a bad living if you can find it! Because it returns the bulk of these earnings to the Treasury, it does not get rich from its activities, but this income gives the Fed an important advantage over other government agencies: It is not subject to the appropriations process usually controlled by Congress. Indeed, the General Accounting Office, the auditing agency of the federal government, cannot audit the monetary policy or foreign exchange market functions of the Federal Reserve. Because the power to control the purse strings is usually synonymous with the power of overall control, this feature of the Federal Reserve System contributes to its independence more than any other factor.

Yet the Federal Reserve is still subject to the influence of Congress because the legislation that structures it is written by Congress and is subject to change at any time. When legislators are upset with the Fed's conduct of monetary policy, they frequently threaten to take control of the Fed's finances and force it to submit a budget request like other government agencies. A recent example is the call by Senators Dorgan and Reid in 1996 for Congress to have budgetary authority over the nonmonetary activities of the Federal Reserve. This is a powerful club to wave, and it certainly has some effect in keeping the Fed from straying too far from congressional wishes.

Congress has also passed legislation to make the Federal Reserve more accountable for its actions. In 1975, Congress passed House Concurrent Resolution 133, which requires the Fed to announce its objectives for the growth rates of the monetary aggregates. In the Full Employment and Balanced Growth Act of 1978 (the Humphrey-Hawkins Act), the Fed is required to explain how these objectives are consistent with the economic plans of the president of the United States. In recent years, Representative Henry Gonzalez, the former chairman of the House Banking Committee, has pressured the Fed to be less secretive in its deliberations about monetary policy—with some success, as the Fed's move to a post-FOMC announcement testifies.

The president can also influence the Federal Reserve. Because congressional legislation can affect the Fed directly or affect its ability to conduct monetary policy, the president can be a powerful ally through his influence on Congress. Second, although ostensibly a president might be able to appoint only one or two members to the Board of Governors during each presidential term, in actual practice the president appoints members far more often. One reason is that most governors do not serve out a full 14-year term. (Governors' salaries are substantially below what they can earn in the private sector, thus providing an incentive for them to take private sector jobs before their term expires.) In addition, the president is able to appoint a new chairman of the Board of Governors every four years, and a chairman who is not reappointed is expected to resign from the board so that a new member can be appointed.

The power that the president enjoys through his appointments to the Board of Governors is limited, however. Because the term of the chairman is not necessarily concurrent with that of the president, a president may have to deal with a chairman of the Board of Governors appointed by a previous administration. Alan Greenspan, for example, was appointed chairman in 1987 by President Ronald Reagan and was reappointed to another term by another Republican president, George Bush. When Bill Clinton, a Democrat, became president in 1993, Greenspan had several years left to his term. Clinton was put under tremendous pressure to reappoint Greenspan when his term expired and did so in 1996, even though Greenspan is a Republican.[4]

You can see that the Federal Reserve has extraordinary independence for a government agency and is one of the most independent central banks in the world. Nonetheless, the Fed is not free from political pressures. Indeed, to understand the Fed's behavior, we must recognize that public support for the actions of the Federal Reserve plays a very important role.

STRUCTURE AND INDEPENDENCE OF FOREIGN CENTRAL BANKS

In contrast to the Federal Reserve System, which is decentralized into 12 district banks, which are privately owned, central banks in other industrialized countries consist of one centralized unit that is owned by the government. Here we examine the structure and degree of independence of four of the most important foreign central banks: the Bank of Canada, the Bank of England, the Bank of Japan, and the European Central Bank.

Bank of Canada

Canada was late in establishing a central bank: The Bank of Canada was founded in 1934. Its directors are appointed by the government to three-year terms, and they appoint the governor, who has a seven-year term. A governing council, consisting of the four deputy governors and the governor, is the policymaking body comparable to the FOMC that makes decisions about monetary policy.

The Bank Act was amended in 1967 to give the ultimate responsibility for monetary policy to the government. So on paper, the Bank of Canada is not as independent as the Federal Reserve. In practice, however, the Bank of Canada does essentially control monetary policy. In the event of a disagreement between the bank and the government, the minister of finance can issue a directive that the bank must follow. However, because the directive must be in writing and specific

[4]Similary, William McChesney Martin Jr., the chairman from 1951 to 1970, was appointed by President Truman (Dem.) but was reappointed by Presidents Eisenhower (Rep.), Kennedy (Dem.), and Nixon (Rep.). Also Paul Volcker, the chairman from 1979 to 1987, was appointed by President Carter (Dem.) but was reappointed by President Reagan (Rep.).

and applicable for a specified period, it is unlikely that such a directive would be issued, and none has been to date.

Bank of England

Founded in 1694, the Bank of England is one of the oldest central banks. The Bank Act of 1946 gave the government statutory authority over the Bank of England. The Court (equivalent to a board of directors) of the Bank of England is made up of the governor and two deputy governors, who are appointed for five-year terms, and 16 nonexecutive directors, who are appointed for three-year terms.

Until 1997, the Bank of England was the least independent of the central banks examined in this chapter because the decision to raise or lower interest rates resided not within the Bank of England but with the chancellor of the Exchequer (the equivalent of the U.S. secretary of the Treasury). All of this changed when the new Labour government came to power in May 1997. At this time, the new chancellor of the Exchequer, Gordon Brown, made a surprise announcement that the Bank of England would henceforth have the power to set interest rates. However, the Bank was not granted total independence: The governement can overrule the Bank and set rates "in extreme economic circumstances" and "for a limited period." Nonetheless, as in Canada, because overruling the Bank would be so public and is supposed to occur only in highly unusual circumstances and for a limited time, it is unlikely that the government will ever overrule the Bank.

The decision to set interest rates resides in the Monetary Policy Committee, made up of the governor, four other central bank officials (two deputy governors and two other central bank officials chosen by the governor), plus four outside economic experts appointed by the chancellor. (Surprisingly, two of the four outside experts initially appointed to this committee were not British citizens—one was Dutch and the other American, although both were residents of the United Kingdom.)

Bank of Japan

The Bank of Japan (Nippon Ginko) was founded in 1882 during the Meiji Restoration. Monetary policy is determined by the Policy Board, which is composed of the governor, two vice governors, and six outside members appointed by the cabinet and approved by the parliament, all of whom serve for five-year terms.

Until recently, the Bank of Japan was not formally independent of the government, with ultimate power residing with the Ministry of Finance. However, the new Bank of Japan Law, which took effect in April 1998—the first major change in the powers of the Bank of Japan in 55 years—has changed this. In addition to stipulating that the objective of monetary policy is to attain price stability, the law granted greater independence to the Bank of Japan. Before this, the government had two voting members on the Policy Board, one from the Ministry of Finance and the other from the Economic Planning Agency. Now the government may send two representatives from these agencies to board meetings, but they no longer have voting rights, although they do have the ability to request delays in monetary policy decisions. In addition, the Ministry of Finance lost its authority to oversee many of the operations of the Bank of Japan, particularly the right to dismiss senior officials. However, the Ministry of Finance continues to have control over the part of the Bank's budget that is unrelated to monetary policy. Some critics of the new law argue that giving the ministry veto power over most of the Bank's budget may substantially limit the independence of the Bank of Japan.

European Central Bank

Gather general information about the organizational structure of ECB, its history and goals, its monetary policy strategy and operational framework by clicking on "About the ECB" at www.ecb.int

The Maasricht Treaty established the European Central Bank (ECB) and the European System of Central Banks (ESCB), which began operation in January 1999. The structure of the central bank is patterned after the U.S. Federal Reserve System in that central banks for each country have a role similar to that of the Federal Reserve banks. The executive board of the ECB is made up of the president, a vice president, and four other members, who are appointed for eight-year terms. The monetary policymaking body of the bank includes the five members of the executive board and the central-bank governors from the 11 euro countries, all of whom must have five-year terms at a minimum.

The European Central Bank will be the most independent in the world, even more independent than the German central bank, the Bundesbank, which, before the establishment of the ECB, was considered the world's most independent central bank, along with the Swiss National Bank. The ECB is independent of both the European Union and the national governments and has complete control over monetary policy. In addition, the ECB's mandated mission is the pursuit of price stability. The ECB is far more independent than any other central bank in the world because its charter cannot be changed by legislation: It can be changed only by revision of the Maasricht Treaty, a difficult process because all signatories to the treaty would have to agree.

The Trend Toward Greater Independence

As our survey of the structure and independence of the major central banks indicates, in recent years we have been seeing a remarkable trend toward increasing independence. It used to be that the Federal Reserve was substantially more independent than almost all other central banks, with the exception of those in Germany and Switzerland. Now the newly established European Central Bank is far more independent than the Fed, and greater independence has been granted to central banks like the Bank of England and the Bank of Japan, putting them more on a par with the Fed, as well as to central banks in such diverse countries as New Zealand, Sweden, and the euro nations. Both theory and experience suggest that more independent central banks produce better monetary policy, thus providing an impetus for this trend.

EXPLAINING CENTRAL BANK BEHAVIOR

One view of government bureaucratic behavior is that bureaucracies serve the public interest (this is the *public interest view*). Yet some economists have developed a theory of bureaucratic behavior that suggests other factors that influence how bureaucracies operate. The *theory of bureaucratic behavior* suggests that the objective of a bureaucracy is to maximize its own welfare, just as a consumer's behavior is motivated by the maximization of personal welfare and a firm's behavior is motivated by the maximization of profits. The welfare of a bureaucracy is related to its power and prestige. Thus this theory suggests that an important factor affecting a central bank's behavior is its attempt to increase its power and prestige.

What predictions does this view of a central bank like the Fed suggest? One is that the Federal Reserve will fight vigorously to preserve its autonomy, a prediction verified time and time again as the Fed has continually counterattacked congressional attempts to control its budget. In fact, it is extraordinary how effectively the Fed has been able to mobilize a lobby of bankers and businesspeople to preserve its independence when threatened.

Another prediction is that the Federal Reserve will try to avoid conflict with powerful groups that may threaten to curtail its power and reduce its autonomy. The Fed's behavior may take several forms. One possible factor explaining why the Fed is sometimes slow to increase interest rates and so smooths out their fluctuations is that it wishes to avoid a conflict with the president and Congress over increases in interest rates. The desire to avoid conflict with Congress and the president may also explain why in the past the Fed (particularly the chairman of the Board of Governors) devised clever stratagems to avoid blame for its past mistakes (see Box 6).

The desire of the Fed to hold as much power as possible also explains why it vigorously pursued a campaign to gain control over more banks. The campaign culminated in legislation that expanded jurisdiction of the Fed's reserve requirements to *all* banks (not just the member commercial banks) by 1987.

The theory of bureaucratic behavior seems applicable to the Federal Reserve's actions, but we must recognize that this view of the Fed as being solely concerned with its own self-interest is too extreme. Maximizing one's welfare does not rule out altruism. (You might give generously to a charity because it makes you feel good about yourself, but in the process you are helping a worthy cause.) The

BOX 6: INSIDE THE FED

Games the Fed Plays

As the theory of bureaucratic behavior predicts, the Fed may play games to obscure its actions in order to avoid congressional interference in its activities. In 1975, Congress passed House Concurrent Resolution 133, which instructed the Fed to report quarterly to the banking committees of the House and the Senate its target ranges for the growth in the monetary aggregates over the next 12 months and how successful it had been in achieving its previous targets. One game that the Fed played was to report on several monetary aggregates (such as M1, M2, and M3) rather than on one: When the Fed testified to Congress on its success in achieving its past targets, it would focus on the particular monetary aggregate whose growth rate was closest to the target range.

In addition to this clever tactic, the Fed devised a procedure for setting its target for monetary aggregates (called *base drift*) that made it more likely that it would hit its targets, thereby avoiding conflict with Congress. Every quarter, the Fed would revise the target values for monetary aggregates by applying target growth rates to the amount at which the aggregate had ended up (a new base). When the Fed overshot its targets, as frequently occurred after 1975, it revised future target values upward, making it less likely that the monetary aggregates would exceed target ranges in the future. Similarly, if the Fed undershot its targets, it revised future target values downward, making it less likely that the monetary aggregates would fall below the target ranges in the future. Subsequent legislation now restricts the Fed to changing the base for its target ranges only once a year, reducing the extent of base drift.

Another indication that the Fed actively wanted to obscure its actions was its desire for secrecy, as reflected in the active defense of its delay in releasing FOMC directives to Congress or to the public. A former Fed official has stated that "a lot of staffers would concede that [secrecy] is designed to shield the Fed from political oversight." However, this official also stated that this was not a bad thing because "most politicians have a shorter time horizon than is optimal for monetary policy."* However, as discussed earlier, the Fed has provided more information about its monetary policy decisions in recent years.

*Quoted in "Monetary Zeal: How Federal Reserve Under Volcker Finally Slowed Down Inflation," *Wall Street Journal*, December 7, 1984, p. 23.

Fed is surely concerned that it conduct monetary policy in the public interest. However, much uncertainty and disagreement exist over what monetary policy should be. When it is unclear what is in the public interest, other motives may influence the Fed's behavior. In these situations, the theory of bureaucratic behavior may be a useful guide to predicting what motivates the Fed.

SHOULD THE FED BE INDEPENDENT?

As we have seen, the Federal Reserve is probably the most independent government agency in the United States. Every few years, the question arises in Congress as to whether the independence of the Fed should be curtailed. Politicians who strongly oppose a Fed policy often want to bring it under their supervision in order to impose a policy more to their liking. Should the Fed be independent, or would we be better off with a central bank under the control of the president or Congress?

The Case for Independence

The strongest argument for an independent Federal Reserve rests on the view that subjecting the Fed to more political pressures would impart an inflationary bias to monetary policy. In the view of many observers, politicians in a democratic society are shortsighted because they are driven by the need to win their next election. With this as the primary goal, they are unlikely to focus on long-run objectives, such as promoting a stable price level. Instead, they will seek short-run solutions to problems, like high unemployment and high interest rates, even if the short-run solutions have undesirable long-run consequences. For example, we saw in Chapter 4 that high money growth might lead initially to a drop in interest rates but might cause an increase later as inflation heats up. Would a Federal Reserve under the control of Congress or the president be more likely to pursue a policy of excessive money growth when interest rates are high, even though it would eventually lead to inflation and even higher interest rates in the future? The advocates of an independent Federal Reserve say yes. They believe that a politically insulated Fed is more likely to be concerned with long-run objectives and thus be a defender of a sound dollar and a stable price level.

A variation on the preceding argument is that the political process in America leads to the so-called **political business cycle,** in which just before an election, expansionary policies are pursued to lower unemployment and interest rates. After the election, the bad effects of these policies—high inflation and high interest rates—come home to roost, requiring contractionary policies that politicians hope the public will forget before the next election. There is some evidence that such a political business cycle exists in the United States, and a Federal Reserve under the control of Congress or the president might make the cycle even more pronounced.

Putting the Fed under the control of the president (making it more subject to influence by the Treasury) is also considered dangerous because the Fed can be used to facilitate Treasury financing of large budget deficits by its purchases of Treasury bonds.[5] Treasury pressure on the Fed to "help out" might lead to a more inflationary bias in the economy. An independent Fed is better able to resist this pressure from the Treasury.

[5]The Federal Reserve Act prohibited the Fed from buying Treasury bonds directly from the Treasury (except to roll over maturing securities); instead the Fed buys Treasury bonds on the open market. One possible reason for this prohibition is consistent with the foregoing argument: The Fed would find it harder to facilitate Treasury financing of large budget deficits.

Another argument for Fed independence is that control of monetary policy is too important to leave to politicians, a group that has repeatedly demonstrated a lack of expertise at making hard decisions on issues of great economic importance, such as reducing the budget deficit or reforming the banking system. Another way to state this argument is in terms of the principal-agent problem discussed in Chapters 14 and 17. Both the Federal Reserve and politicians are agents of the public (the principals), and as we have seen, both politicians and the Fed have incentives to act in their own interest rather than in the interest of the public. The argument supporting Federal Reserve independence is that the principal-agent problem is worse for politicians than for the Fed because politicians have fewer incentives to act in the public interest.

Indeed, some politicians may prefer to have an independent Fed, which can be used as a public "whipping boy" to take some of the heat off their shoulders. It is possible that a politician who in private opposes an inflationary monetary policy will be forced to support such a policy in public for fear of not being reelected. An independent Fed can pursue policies that are politically unpopular yet in the public interest.

The Case Against Independence

Proponents of a Fed under the control of the president or Congress argue that it is undemocratic to have monetary policy (which affects almost everyone in the economy) controlled by an elite group responsible to no one. The current lack of accountability of the Federal Reserve has serious consequences: If the Fed performs badly, there is no provision for replacing members (as there is with politicians). True, the Fed needs to pursue long-run objectives, but elected officials of Congress vote on long-run issues also (foreign policy, for example). If we push the argument further that policy is always performed better by elite groups like the Fed, we end up with such conclusions as the Joint Chiefs of Staff should determine military budgets or the IRS should set tax policies with no oversight from the president or Congress. Would you advocate this degree of independence for the Joint Chiefs or the IRS?

The public holds the president and Congress responsible for the economic well-being of the country, yet they lack control over the government agency that may well be the most important factor in determining the health of the economy. In addition, to achieve a cohesive program that will promote economic stability, monetary policy must be coordinated with fiscal policy (management of government spending and taxation). Only by placing monetary policy under the control of the politicians who also control fiscal policy can these two policies be prevented from working at cross-purposes.

Another argument against Federal Reserve independence is that an independent Fed has not always used its freedom successfully. The Fed failed miserably in its stated role as lender of last resort during the Great Depression, and its independence certainly didn't prevent it from pursuing an overly expansionary monetary policy in the 1960s and 1970s that contributed to rapid inflation in this period.

Our earlier discussion also suggests that the Federal Reserve is not immune from political pressures.[6] Its independence may encourage it to pursue a course of narrow self-interest rather than the public interest.

[6]For evidence on this issue, see Robert E. Weintraub, "Congressional Supervision of Monetary Policy," *Journal of Monetary Economics* 4 (1978): 341–362. Some economics suggest that lessening the independence of the Fed might even reduce the incentive for politically motivated monetary policy; see Milton Friedman, "Monetary Policy: Theory and Practice," *Journal of Money, Credit and Banking* 14 (1982): 98–118.

There is yet no consensus on whether Federal Reserve independence is a good thing, although public support for independence of the central bank seems to have been growing in both the United States and abroad. As you might expect, people who like the Fed's policies are more likely to support its independence, while those who dislike its policies advocate a less independent Fed.

CENTRAL BANK INDEPENDENCE AND MACROECONOMIC PERFORMANCE IN SEVENTEEN COUNTRIES

We have seen that advocates of an independent central bank believe that macroeconomic performance will be improved by making the central bank more independent. Recent research seems to support this conjecture: When central banks are ranked from 1 (least independent) to 4 (most independent), inflation performance is found to be the best for countries with the most independent central banks.[7] As you can see in Figure 4, Germany and Switzerland, with the two most independent central banks, were also the countries with the lowest inflation rates in the 1973—1988 period. By contrast, the countries with the highest inflation in those years—Spain, New Zealand, Australia, and Italy—were also the

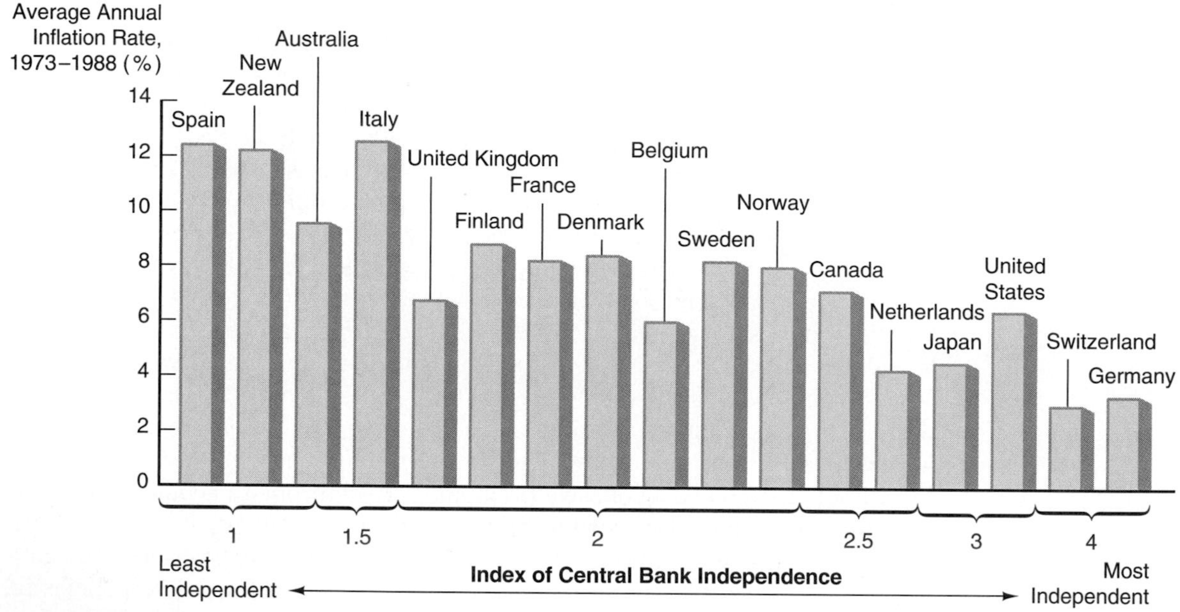

FIGURE 4 Central Bank Independence and Macroeconomic Performance in Seventeen Countries

On the horizontal axis, the 17 central banks are rated from least independent, 1, to most independent, 4. More independent banks have generally produced lower inflation than less independent central banks.

Source: Alberto Alesina and Lawrence H. Summers, "Central Bank Independence and Macroeconomic Performance: Some Comparative Evidence," *Journal of Money, Credit and Banking* 25 (1993): 151–162.

[7] Alberto Alesina and Lawrence H. Summers, "Central Bank Independence and Macroeconomic Performance: Some Comparative Evidence," *Journal of Money, Credit and Banking* 25 (1993): 151–162. However, Adam Posen, "Central Bank Independence and Disinflationary Credibility: A Missing Link," Federal Reserve Bank of New York Staff Report No. 1, May 1995, has cast some doubt on whether the casuality runs from central bank independence to improved inflation perfomance.

countries with the least independent central banks. (The Spanish and New Zealand central banks have since gained greater independence.) Although a more independent central bank appears to lead to a lower inflation rate, this is not achieved at the expense of poorer real economic performance. Countries with independent central banks are no more likely to have high unemployment or greater output fluctuations than countries with less independent central banks.

SUMMARY

1. The Federal Reserve System was created in 1913 to lessen the frequency of bank panics. Because of public hostility to central banks and the centralization of power, the Federal Reserve System was created with many checks and balances to diffuse power.
2. The formal structure of the Federal Reserve System consists of 12 regional Federal Reserve banks, around 4000 member commercial banks, the Board of Governors of the Federal Reserve System, the Federal Open Market Committee, and the Federal Advisory Council.
3. Although on paper the Federal Reserve System appears to be decentralized, in practice it has come to function as a unified central bank controlled by the Board of Governors, especially the board's chairman.
4. The Federal Reserve is more independent than most agencies of the U.S. government, but it is still subject to political pressures because the legislation that structures the Fed is written by Congress and can be changed at any time. The theory of bureaucratic behavior indicates that one factor driving the Fed's behavior is its attempt to increase its power and prestige. This view explains many of the Fed's actions, although the agency may also try to act in the public interest.
5. The case for an independent Federal Reserve rests on the view that curtailing the Fed's independence and subjecting it to more political pressures would impart an inflationary bias to monetary policy. An independent Fed can afford to take the long view and not respond to short-run problems that will result in expansionary monetary policy and a political business cycle. The case against an independent Fed holds that it is undemocratic to have monetary policy (so important to the public) controlled by an elite that is not accountable to the public. An independent Fed also makes the coordination of monetary and fiscal policy difficult.

KEY TERMS

Board of Governors of the Federal Reserve System, *p. 151*

Federal Open Market Committee (FOMC), *p. 151*

Federal Reserve banks, *p. 151*

open market operations, *p. 154*

political business cycle, *p. 166*

QUESTIONS AND PROBLEMS

*1. Why was the Federal Reserve System set up with 12 regional Federal Reserve banks rather than one central bank, as in other countries?

2. What political realities might explain why the Federal Reserve Act of 1913 placed two Federal Reserve banks in Missouri?

*3. "The Federal Reserve System resembles the U.S. Constitution in that it was designed with many checks and balances." Discuss.

4. In what ways can the regional Federal Reserve banks influence the conduct of monetary policy?

*5. Which entities in the Federal Reserve System control the discount rate? Reserve requirements? Open market operations?

6. Do you think that the 14-year nonrenewable terms for governors effectively insulate the Board of Governors from political pressure?

*7. Over time, which entities have gained power in the Federal Reserve System and which have lost power? Why do you think this has happened?

8. The Fed is the most independent of all U.S. government agencies. What is the main difference

between it and other government agencies that explains its greater independence?

*9. What is the primary tool that Congress uses to exercise some control over the Fed?

10. In the 1960s and 1970s, the Federal Reserve System lost member banks at a rapid rate. How can the theory of bureaucratic behavior explain the Fed's campaign for legislation to require all commercial banks to become members? Was the Fed successful in this campaign?

*11. "The theory of bureaucratic behavior indicates that the Fed never operates in the public interest." Is this statement true, false, or uncertain? Explain your answer.

12. Why might eliminating the Fed's independence lead to a more pronounced political business cycle?

*13. "The independence of the Fed leaves it completely unaccountable for its actions." Is this statement true, false, or uncertain? Explain your answer.

14. "The independence of the Fed has meant that it takes the long view and not the short view." Is this statement true, false, or uncertain? Explain your answer.

*15. The Fed promotes secrecy by not releasing FOMC minutes to Congress or the public immediately. Discuss the pros and cons of this policy.

WEB EXERCISES

Structure of Central Banks and the Federal Reserve System

1. Go to http://www.federalreserve.gov/general.htm and click on the link for general information. Choose "Structure of the Federal Reserve." According to the Federal Reserve, what is the most important responsibility of the Board of Governors?

2. Go to the previously mentioned site and click on "Monetary Policy" to find the beige book. According to the summary of the most recently published book, is the economy weakening or recovering?

Chapter 7

Conduct of Monetary Policy: Tools, Goals, and Targets

Preview

Understanding the conduct of monetary policy is important because it affects not only the money supply and interest rates but also the level of economic activity and hence our well-being. To explore this subject, we look first at the Federal Reserve's balance sheet and how the tools of monetary policy affect the money supply and interest rates. Then we examine in more detail how the Fed uses these tools and what goals the Fed and other countries' central banks establish for monetary policy. After examining strategies for conducting monetary policy, we can evaluate central banks' conduct of monetary policy in the past, with the hope that it will give us some clues to where monetary policy may head in the future.

THE FEDERAL RESERVE'S BALANCE SHEET

The conduct of monetary policy by the Federal Reserve involves actions that affect its balance sheet (holdings of assets and liabilities). Here we discuss the following simplified balance sheet:

Federal Reserve System

Assets	Liabilities
Government securities	Currency in circulation
Discount loans	Reserves

Liabilities

The two liabilities on the balance sheet, currency in circulation and reserves, are often referred to as the *monetary liabilities* of the Fed. They are an important part of the money supply story because increases in either or both will lead to an increase in the money supply (everything else being constant). The sum of

Historic and current data on the aggregate reserves of depository institutions and the monetary base is available at http://www.federalreserve.gov/releases/H3

the Fed's monetary liabilities (currency in circulation and reserves) and the U.S. Treasury's monetary liabilities (Treasury currency in circulation, primarily coins) is called the **monetary base.** When discussing the monetary base, we will focus only on the monetary liabilities of the Fed because the monetary liabilities of the Treasury account for less than 10% of the base.[1]

1. *Currency in circulation.* The Fed issues currency (those green-and-gray pieces of paper in your wallet that say "Federal Reserve Note" at the top). Currency in circulation is the amount of currency in the hands of the public (outside of banks)—an important component of the money supply. (Currency held by depository institutions is also a liability of the Fed but is counted as part of reserves.)

Federal Reserve notes are IOUs from the Fed to the bearer and are also liabilities, but unlike most, they promise to pay back the bearer solely with Federal Reserve notes; that is, they pay off IOUs with other IOUs. Accordingly, if you bring a $100 bill to the Federal Reserve and demand payment, you will receive two $50s, five $20s, ten $10s, or one hundred $1 bills.

People are more willing to accept IOUs from the Fed than from you or me because Federal Reserve notes are a recognized medium of exchange; that is, they are accepted as a means of payment and so function as money. Unfortunately, neither you nor I can convince people that our own IOUs are worth anything more than the paper they are written on.[2]

2. *Reserves.* All banks have an account at the Fed in which they hold deposits. **Reserves** consist of deposits at the Fed plus currency that is physically held by banks (called vault cash because it is stored in bank vaults). Reserves are assets for the banks but liabilities for the Fed because the banks can demand payment on them at any time and the Fed is obliged to satisfy its obligation by paying Federal Reserve notes. As you will see, an increase in reserves leads to an increase in the level of deposits and hence in the money supply.

Total reserves can be divided into two categories: reserves that the Fed requires banks to hold (**required reserves**) and any additional reserves the banks choose to hold (**excess reserves**). For example, the Fed might require that for every dollar of deposits at a depository institution, a certain fraction (say, 10 cents) must be held as reserves. This fraction (10%) is called the **required reserve ratio**. Currently, the Fed pays no interest on reserves.

Assets

The two assets on the Fed's balance sheet are important for two reasons. First, changes in the asset items leads to changes in reserves and consequently to changes

[1]It is also safe to ignore the Treasury's monetary liabilities when discussing the monetary base because the Treasury cannot actively supply its monetary liabilities to the economy due to legal restrictions.

[2]The currency item on the Fed's balance sheet refers only to currency in circulation, that is, the amount in the hands of the public. Currency that has been printed by the U.S. Bureau of Engraving and Printing is not automatically a liability of the Fed. For example, consider the importance of having $1 million of your own IOUs printed up. You give out $100 worth to other people and keep the other $999,900 in your pocket. The $999,900 of IOUs does not make you richer or poorer and does not affect your indebtedness. You care only about the $100 of liabilities from the $100 of circulated IOUs. The same reasoning applies for the Fed in regard to its Federal Reserve notes.

For similar reasons, the currency component of the money supply, no matter how it is defined, includes only currency in circulation. It does not include any additional currency that is not yet in the hands of the public. The fact that currency has been printed but is not circulating means that it is not anyone's asset or liability and thus cannot affect anyone's behavior. Therefore, it makes sense not to include it in the money supply.

in the money supply. Second, because these assets (government securities and discount loans) earn interest while the liabilities (currency in circulation and reserves) do not, the Fed makes billions of dollars every year—its assets earn income, and its liabilities cost nothing. Although it returns most of its earnings to the federal government, the Fed does spend some of it on "worthy causes," such as supporting economic research.

1. *Government securities.* This category of assets covers the Fed's holdings of securities issued by the U.S. Treasury. As you will see, the Fed provides reserves to the banking system by purchasing securities, thereby increasing its holdings of these assets. An increase in government securities held by the Fed leads to an increase in the money supply.

2. *Discount loans.* The Fed can provide reserves to the banking system by making discount loans to banks. An increase in discount loans can also be the source of an increase in the money supply. The interest rate charged banks for these loans is called the **discount rate.**

Open Market Operations

Open market operations, the central bank's purchase or sale of bonds in the open market, are the most important monetary policy tool because they are the primary determinant of changes in reserves in the banking system and interest rates. To see how they work, let's use T-accounts to examine what happens when the Fed conducts an open market purchase in which $100 of bonds are bought from the public.

When the person or corporation that sells the $100 of bonds to the Fed deposits the Fed's check in the local bank, the nonbank public's T-account after this transaction is

Nonbank Public

Assets		Liabilities	
Securities	−$100		
Checkable deposits	+$100		

When the bank receives the check, it credits the depositor's account with the $100 and then deposits the check in its account with the Fed, thereby adding to its reserves. The banking system's T-account becomes

Banking System

Assets		Liabilities	
Reserves	+$100	Checkable deposits	+$100

The effect on the Fed's balance sheet is that it has gained $100 of securities in its assets column, while reserves have increased by $100, as shown in its liabilities column:

Federal Reserve System

Assets		Liabilities	
Securities	+$100	Reserves	+$100

As you can see, the result of the Fed's open market purchase is an expansion of reserves and deposits in the banking system. Another way of seeing this is to recognize that open market purchases of bonds expand reserves because the central bank pays for the bonds with reserves. Because the monetary base equals currency plus reserves, we have shown that an open market purchase increases the monetary base by an equal amount. Also because deposits are an important component of the money supply, another result of the open market purchase is an increase in the money supply. This leads to the following important conclusion: ***An open market purchase leads to an expansion of reserves and deposits in the banking system and hence to an expansion of the monetary base and the money supply.***

Similar reasoning indicates that when a central bank conducts an open market sale, the public pays for the bonds by writing a check that causes deposits and reserves in the banking system to fall. Thus ***an open market sale leads to a contraction of reserves and deposits in the banking system and hence to a decline in the monetary base and the money supply.***

Discount Lending

Open market operations are not the only way the Federal Reserve can affect the amount of reserves. Reserves are also changed when the Fed makes a discount loan to a bank. For example, suppose that the Fed makes a $100 discount loan to the First National Bank. The Fed then credits $100 to the bank's reserve account. The effects on the balance sheets of the banking system and the Fed are illustrated by the following T-accounts:

Banking System		Federal Reserve System	
Assets	Liabilities	Assets	Liabilities
Reserves +$100	Discount loans +$100	Discount loans +$100	Reserves +$100

We thus see that ***a discount loan leads to an expansion of reserves, which can be lent out as deposits, thereby leading to an expansion of the monetary base and the money supply.*** Similar reasoning indicates that ***when a bank repays its discount loan and so reduces the total amount of discount lending, the amount of reserves decreases along with the monetary base and the money supply.***

THE MARKET FOR RESERVES AND THE FEDERAL FUNDS RATE

We have just seen how open market operations and discount lending affect the balance sheet of the Fed and the amount of reserves. Now we will analyze the market for reserves to see how the resulting changes in reserves affect the **federal funds rate,** the interest rate on overnight loans of reserves from one bank to another. The federal funds rate is particularly important in the conduct of monetary policy because it is the interest rate that the Fed tries to influence directly. Thus it is indicative of the Fed's stance of monetary policy.

Open market operations and discount policy are the principal tools that the Fed uses to influence the federal funds rate. In addition, there is a third tool, **reserve requirements,** the regulations making it obligatory for depository institutions to keep a certain fraction of their deposits as reserves with the Fed. We will also analyze how reserve requirements affect the market for reserves and thereby affect the federal funds rate.

Supply and Demand in the Market for Reserves

The analysis of the market for reserves proceeds in a fashion similar to the analysis of the bond market we conducted in Chapter 4. We derive a demand and supply curve for reserves, and the market equilibrium in which the quantity of reserves demanded equals the quantity supplied then determines the federal funds rate, the interest rate charged on the loans of these reserves.

Demand Curve To derive the demand curve for reserves, we need to ask what happens to the quantity of reserves demanded, holding everything else constant, as the federal funds rate changes. Recall from the preceding section that the amount of reserves can be split up into two components: (1) required reserves, which equals the required reserve ratio times the amount of deposits on which reserves are required, and (2) excess reserves, the additional reserves banks choose to hold. Therefore, the quantity of reserves demanded equals required reserves plus the quantity of excess reserves demanded. Excess reserves are insurance against deposit outflows, and the cost of holding these excess reserves is their opportunity cost, the interest rate that could have been earned on loaning these reserves out, which is equivalent to the federal funds rate. Thus as the federal funds rate decreases, the opportunity cost of holding excess reserves falls and, holding everything else constant, including the quantity of required reserves, the quantity of reserves demanded rises. Consequently, the demand curve for reserves, R^d, slopes downward in Figure 1.

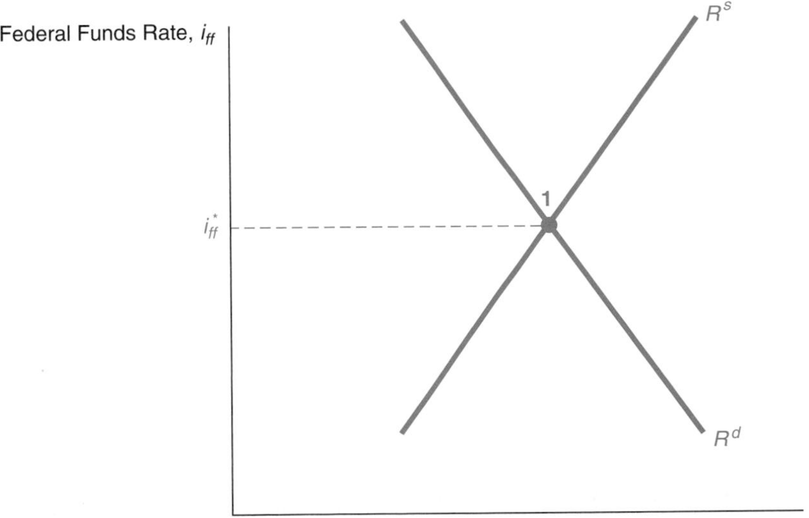

FIGURE 1 Equilibrium in the Market for Reserves

Equilibrium occurs at the intersection of the supply curve, R^s, and the demand curve, R^d, at point 1 and an interest rate of i^*_{ff}

Supply Curve As we saw in the preceding section, when discount lending increases, the quantity of reserves supplied to the banking system also increases. When banks borrow from the Fed, their principal benefit is the earnings from lending these funds out at the federal funds rate. Thus holding everything else constant, when the federal funds rate increases, banks will borrow more from the Fed, and the resulting rise in discount lending means that the quantity of reserves supplied rises. For this reason, the supply curve for reserves, R^s, slopes upward, as shown in Figure 1.

Market Equilibrium Market equilibrium occurs where the quantity of reserves demanded equals the quantity supplied, $R^d = R^s$. Equilibrium therefore occurs at the intersection of the demand curve, R^d, and the supply curve, R^s, at point 1, with an equilibrium federal funds rate of i^*_{ff}.

How Changes in the Tools of Monetary Policy Affect the Federal Funds Rate

Now that we understand how the federal funds rate is determined, we can examine how changes in the three tools of monetary policy—open market operations, discount lending, and reserve requirements—affect the equilibrium federal funds rate.

Open Market Operations We have already seen that an open market purchase leads to a greater quantity of reserves supplied; this is true at any given federal funds rate. An open market purchase therefore shifts the supply curve to the right from R^s_1 to R^s_2 in Figure 2 and moves the equilibrium from point 1 to point 2, low-

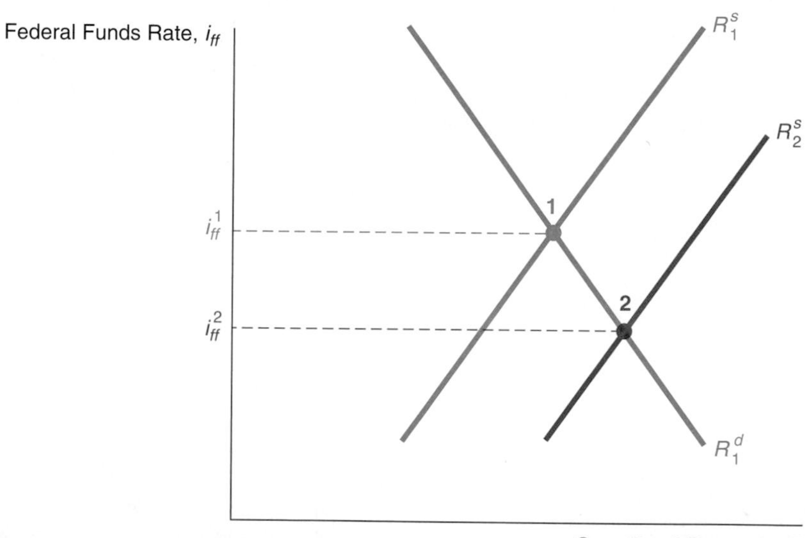

FIGURE 2 Response to an Open Market Operation or a Change in the Discount Rate

An open market purchase increases reserves supplied, shifts the supply curve from R^s_1 to R^s_2, and moves the equilibrium from point 1 to point 2, lowering the federal funds rate from i^1_{ff} to i^2_{ff}. Likewise, a fall in the discount rate causes discount lending and reserves supplied to increase, shifts the supply curve from R^s_1 to R^s_2, and moves the equilibrium from point 1 to point 2, lowering the federal funds rate from i^1_{ff} to i^2_{ff}.

ering the federal funds rate from i^1_{ff} to i^2_{ff}.[3] The same reasoning implies that an open market sale decreases the quantity of reserves supplied, shifts the supply curve to the left, and causes the federal funds rate to rise.

The result is that ***an open market purchase causes the federal funds rate to fall, and an open market sale causes the federal funds rate to rise.***

Discount Lending We have also seen that increases in discount lending raise the quantity of reserves supplied. The primary cost of borrowing discount loans from the Fed is the interest rate the Fed charges on these loans, the discount rate. A lower discount rate, with the federal funds rate held constant, leads to a greater quantity of reserves supplied and shifts the supply curve to the right from R^s_1 to R^s_2 in Figure 2. The result is that the equilibrium moves from point 1 to point 2, lowering the federal funds rate from i^1_{ff} to i^2_{ff}.

The conclusion is that ***when the Fed lowers the discount rate, the federal funds rate falls.***[4]

Similar reasoning implies that when the discount rate is raised, discount lending falls, the supply curve for reserves shifts to the left, and the federal funds rate rises. Therefore, ***when the Fed raises the discount rate, it leads to a rise in the federal funds rate.***

Reserve Requirements When the required reserve ratio increases, required reserves increase and hence the quantity of reserves demanded increases for any given interest rate. Thus a rise in the required reserves ratio shifts the demand curve to the right from R^d_1 to R^d_2 in Figure 3, moves the equilibrium from point 1 to point 2, and in turn raises the federal funds rate from i^1_{ff} to i^2_{ff}.

The result is that ***when the Fed raises reserve requirements, the federal funds rate rises.***[5]

Similarly, a decline in the required reserves ratio lowers the quantity of reserves demanded, shifts the demand curve to the left, and causes the federal funds rate to fall. ***When the Fed decreases reserve requirements, it leads to a fall in the federal funds rate.***

TOOLS OF MONETARY POLICY

Now that we understand how the three tools of monetary policy—open market operations, discount lending, and reserve requirements—can be used by the Fed to manipulate the money supply and interest rates, we will examine each of them in turn to see how the Fed wields them in practice and how relatively useful each tool is.

---

[3]We come to the same conclusion by realizing that an open market purchase raises reserves and the money supply, and then from the liquidity preference framework in Chapter 4, we can show that interest rates fall.

[4]We can obtain the same conclusion by recognizing that a decline in the discount rate raises discount lending, which increases reserves and the money supply. Then using the liquidity preference framework, we can show that the interest rate falls.

[5]Because an increase in the required reserve ratio means that the same amount of reserves is able to support a smaller amount of deposits, a rise in the required reserve ratio leads to a decline in the money supply. Using the liquidity preference framework, the fall in the money supply results in a rise in interest rates, yielding the same conclusion in the text that raising reserve requirements leads to higher interest rates.

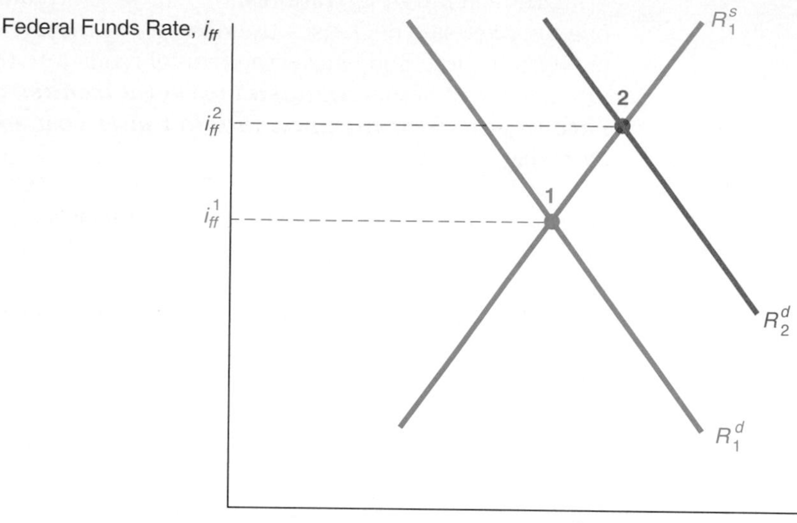

FIGURE 3 Response to a Change in Required Reserves

When the Fed raises reserve requirements, required reserves increase, which increases the demand for reserves. The demand curve shifts from R_1^d to R_2^d, moves the equilibrium from point 1 to point 2, and raises the federal funds rate from i_{ff}^1 to i_{ff}^2.

Open Market Operations

There are two types of open market operations: **Dynamic open market operations** are intended to change the level of reserves, and **defensive open market operations** are intended to offset movements in other factors that affect reserves, such as changes in Treasury deposits with the Fed. The Fed conducts open market operations in U.S. Treasury and government agency securities, especially U.S. Treasury bills.[6] The Fed conducts most of its open market operations in Treasury securities because the market for these securities is the most liquid and has the largest trading volume. It has the capacity to absorb the Fed's substantial volume of transactions without experiencing excessive price fluctuations that would disrupt the market.

As we saw in Chapter 6, the decision-making authority for open market operations is the Federal Open Market Committee (FOMC). The actual execution of these operations, however, is conducted by the trading desk at the Federal Reserve Bank of New York. The best way to see how these transactions are executed is to look at a typical day at the trading desk, located in a newly built trading room on the ninth floor of the Federal Reserve Bank of New York.

A Day at the Trading Desk

The head of domestic open market operations, currently Sandy Krieger, supervises the analysts and traders who execute the purchases and sales of securities. To

[6]To avoid conflicts of interest, the Fed does not conduct open market operations in privately issued securities. (For example, think of the conflict if the Federal Reserve purchased bonds issued by a company owned by the chairman's brother-in-law.)

get a grip on what might happen in the federal funds market that day, her workday and her staff's begins with a review of developments in the federal funds market the previous day and with an update on the actual amount of reserves in the banking system the day before. Later in the morning, Sandy's staff issues updated reports that contain detailed forecasts of what will be happening to some of the short-term factors affecting the supply and demand of reserves.

This information will help Sandy and her staff decide how large a change in reserves is needed to obtain a desired level of the federal funds rate. If the amount of reserves in the banking system is too large, many banks will have excess reserves to lend that other banks may have little desire to borrow, and the federal funds rate will probably fall. If the level of reserves is too low, banks seeking to borrow reserves from the few banks that have excess reserves to lend may push the funds rate higher than the desired level. Also during the morning, the staff will monitor the behavior of the federal funds rate and contact some of the major participants in the funds market, which may provide independent information about whether a change in reserves is needed to achieve the desired level of the federal funds rate.

Early in the morning, members of Sandy's staff contact several representatives of the so-called **primary dealers,** government securities dealers (who operate out of private firms or commercial banks) that the open market desk trades with. Her staff finds out how the dealers view market conditions to get a feel for what may happen to the prices of the securities they trade in over the course of the day. They also call the Treasury to get updated information on the expected level of Treasury balances at the Fed in order to refine their estimates of the supply of reserves.

Afterward, members of the Monetary Affairs Division at the Board of Governors are contacted, and the New York Fed's forecasts of reserve supply and demand are compared with the Board's. On the basis of these projections and the observed behavior of the federal funds market, the desk will formulate and propose a course of action to be taken that day, which may involve plans to add reserves to or drain reserves from the banking system through open market operations. If an operation is contemplated, the type, size, and maturity will be discussed.

The whole process is currently completed by midmorning, at which time a daily conference call is arranged linking the desk with the Office of the Director of Monetary Affairs at the Board and with one of the four voting Reserve Bank presidents outside of New York. During the call, a member of Sandy's unit will outline the desk's proposed reserve management strategy for the day. After the plan is approved, the desk is instructed to execute immediately any temporary open-market operations that were planned for that day. (Outright operations, to be described shortly, may be conducted at other times of the day.)

The desk is linked electronically with its domestic open market trading counterparties by a computer system called TRAPS (Trading Room Automated Processing System), and all open market operations are now performed over this system. A message will be electronically transmitted simultaneously to all the primary dealers over TRAPS indicating the type and maturity of the operation being arranged. The dealers are given several minutes to respond via TRAPS with their propositions. The propositions are then assembled and displayed on a computer screen for evaluation. The desk will select all propositions, beginning with the most attractively priced, up to the point where the desired amount is purchased or sold, and it will then notify each dealer via TRAPS which of its propositions have been chosen. The entire selection process is typically completed in a matter of minutes.

These temporary transactions are of two basic types. In a **repurchase agreement** (often called a **repo**), the Fed purchases securities with an agreement that the seller will repurchase them in a short period of time, anywhere from 1 to 15 days from the original date of purchase. Because the effects on reserves of a repo are reversed on the day the agreement matures, a repo is actually a temporary open market purchase and is an especially desirable way of conducting a defensive open market purchase that will be reversed shortly. When the Fed wants to conduct a temporary open market sale, it engages in a **matched sale-purchase transaction** (sometimes called a **reverse repo**) in which the Fed sells securities and the buyer agrees to sell them back to the Fed in the near future.

At times, the desk may see the need to address a persistent reserve shortage or surplus and wish to arrange an operation that will have a permanent impact on the supply of reserves. Outright transactions, which involve a purchase or sale of securities that is not self-reversing, are also conducted over TRAPS. These operations are traditionally executed at times of day when temporary operations are not being conducted.

Discount Policy

For information on the operation of the discount window and data on current and historical interest rates, go to www.frbdiscountwindow.org/

Recall from Chapter 6 that discount loans are loans from the central bank to depository institutions and that the discount rate is the interest rate charged on these loans. Discount policy, which primarily involves changes in the discount rate, affects reserves in the banking system because when a discount loan is extended, the central bank increases a bank's reserves by an equal amount. The Federal Reserve facility at which discount loans are made to banks is called the **discount window.** It is easiest to understand how the Fed affects the volume of discount loans by looking at how the discount window operates.

Operation of the Discount Window

The Fed can affect the volume of discount loans in two ways: by affecting the *price* of the loans (the discount rate) or by affecting the *quantity* of the loans through its administration of the discount window.[7]

The mechanism through which the Fed's discount rate affects the volume of discount loans is straightforward: A higher discount rate raises the cost of borrowing from the Fed, so banks will take out fewer discount loans; a lower discount rate makes discount loans more attractive to banks, and loan volume will increase.

To examine how the Fed affects the quantity of discount loans through its administration of the discount window, we have to examine more closely how these loans are made.

The Fed's discount loans to the banks are of three types: adjustment credit, seasonal credit, and extended credit. *Adjustment credit loans* are the discount loans that play the most important role in monetary policy. They are intended to be used by banks to help them with short-term liquidity problems that may result from a temporary deposit outflow, and the rate charged on them is the basic discount rate established by the Federal Reserve banks and approved by the Board of Governors. Adjustment credit, which can be obtained with a phone call, is

[7]Each Federal Reserve bank administers its own discount window facility. In our discussion here of discount policy, when we discuss the Fed's administration of the discount window, we are actually referring to the district banks' administration of their discount window facilities.

expected to be repaid fairly quickly—by the end of the next business day for the larger banks. In the 1990s, adjustment credit has shrunk to very low levels, with the result that discount lending has been playing a less important role in monetary policy (see Box 1).

Seasonal credit is given to meet the needs of a limited number of banks in vacation and agricultural areas that have a seasonal pattern. Since 1992, the interest rate charged on seasonal credit is tied to the monthly average federal funds and certificate of deposit rates, with the basic discount rate as a floor. *Extended credit*, given to banks that have experienced severe liquidity problems because of deposit outflows, is not expected to be repaid quickly. The interest rate on these loans is set at one-half of a percentage point above the interest rate charged on seasonal credit. Banks obtaining extended credit have to submit a proposal outlining the need for extended credit and a plan for restoring the liquidity of the bank. The most important example of extended credit to a bank was the Fed's loans to Continental Illinois in 1984, which exceeded $5 billion.

A bank faces three costs when it borrows from the discount window: the interest cost represented by the discount rate, the cost of concerns that might be raised about the health of the bank if the market guesses that the bank has gone to the discount window, and the cost of being more likely to be turned down for a discount loan in the future because of too frequent trips to the discount window. The Fed's setting of rules for use of the discount window is frequently referred to as *moral suasion*.

Lender of Last Resort

In addition to its use as a tool to influence reserves in the banking system and the money supply, discounting is important in preventing financial panics. When the Federal Reserve System was created, its most important role was intended to be as the **lender of last resort;** it was to provide reserves to banks when no one else would in order to prevent bank failures from spinning out of control, thereby preventing bank and financial panics. Discounting is a particularly effective way to provide reserves to the banking system during a banking crisis because reserves are immediately channeled to the banks that need them most.

BOX 1: INSIDE THE FED

Why Has Adjustment Credit Borrowing Shrunk to Such Low Levels?

In recent years, adjustment credit borrowing has declined to very low levels, averaging below $100 million, making discount lending less important to the monetary policy process. Why has this occurred?

The Federal Reserve has not changed its rules on this kind of lending or discouraged its use, so the answer must lie with choices made by the borrowing banks. The problems in the banking industry in the late 1980s and early 1990s described in Chapter 18 provide a likely explanation for the decline in adjustment credit borrowing. Banks became reluctant to go to the discount window to borrow because often market participants are able to guess who had done so. In an environment of concern about the health of banks, some banks fear that if they are perceived as seeking increased liquidity from the discount window, market participants will become concerned that the bank is in trouble and may begin pulling funds out of the bank. Consequently, even though perfectly healthy banks may need short-term liquidity, they have been reluctant to come to the discount window. With the return to health of the banking industry in recent years, these fears may diminish, and adjustment credit lending may increase again.

Using the discount tool to avoid financial panics by performing the role of lender of last resort is an extremely important requirement of successful monetary policymaking. Financial panics can also severely damage the economy because they interfere with the ability of these markets to move funds to people with productive investment opportunities (see Chapter 14).

Unfortunately, the discount tool has not always been used by the Fed to prevent financial panics, as the massive failures during the Great Depression attest. The Fed learned from its mistakes of that period and has performed admirably in its role of lender of last resort in the post–World War II period. Two examples of the use of the Fed's discount weapon to avoid bank panics are the provisions of huge loans to Franklin National Bank in 1974 and to Continental Illinois ten years later (see Box 2).

At first glance, it might appear as though the presence of the FDIC, which insures depositors from losses due to a bank's failure up to a limit of $100,000 per account, would make the lender-of-last-resort function of the Fed superfluous. (The FDIC is described in detail in Chapter 18.) There are two reasons why this is not the case. First, it is important to recognize that the FDIC's insurance fund amounts to around 1% of the amount of these deposits outstanding. If a large number of bank failures occurred, the FDIC would not be able to cover all the depositors' losses. Indeed, the large number of bank failures in the 1980s and early 1990s, described in Chapter 18, led to large losses and a shrinkage in the FDIC's insurance fund, which reduced the FDIC's ability to cover depositors' losses. This fact has not weakened the confidence of small depositors in the banking system because the Fed has been ready to stand behind the banks to provide whatever reserves are needed to prevent bank panics. Second, the nearly $500 billion of large-denomination deposits in the banking system are not guaranteed by the FDIC because they exceed the $100,000 limit. A loss of confidence in the banking system could still lead to runs on banks from the large-denomination depositors,

BOX 2: INSIDE THE FED

Discounting to Troubled Banks: Franklin National and Continental Illinois

In May 1974, the public learned that Franklin National Bank, the twentieth-largest bank in the United States, with deposits close to $3 billion, had suffered large losses in foreign exchange trading and had made many bad loans. Large depositors, whose accounts exceeded the $100,000 limit insured by the FDIC, began to withdraw their deposits, and the failure of the bank was imminent. Because the immediate failure of Franklin National would have had repercussions on other vulnerable banks, possibly leading to more bank failures, the Fed announced that discount loans would be made available to Franklin National so that depositors, including the largest, would not suffer any losses. By the time Franklin National was merged into the European-American Bank in October 1974, the Fed had lent Franklin National the sum of $1.75 billion, nearly 5% of the total amount of reserves in the banking system. The quick Fed action was completely successful in preventing any other bank failures, and a possible bank panic was avoided.

A 1984 episode involved Continental Illinois National Bank and the Fed in a similar action. Continental Illinois had made many bad loans (primarily to businesses in the energy industry and to foreign countries), and rumors of financial trouble in early May 1984 caused large depositors to withdraw over $10 billion of deposits from the bank. The FDIC arranged a rescue effort in July 1984 that culminated in a $4.5 billion commitment of funds to save the bank; still, the Fed had to lend Continental Illinois over $5 billion—making its $1.75 billion loan to Franklin National look like small potatoes! The Fed's action prevented further bank failures, and again a potential bank panic was averted.

and bank panics could still occur despite the existence of the FDIC. The importance of the Federal Reserve's role as lender of last resort is, if anything, more important today because of the high number of bank failures experienced in the 1980s and early 1990s.

Not only can the Fed be a lender of last resort to banks, but it can also play the same role for the financial system as a whole. The existence of the Fed's discount window can help prevent financial panics that are not triggered by bank failures, as was the case during the Black Monday stock market crash of October 1987 and the terrorist destruction of The World Trade Center in September 2001 (see Box 3).

Although the Fed's role as the lender of last resort has the benefit of preventing bank and financial panics, it does have a cost. If a bank expects that the Fed will provide it with discount loans when it gets into trouble, as occurred with Continental Illinois, it will be willing to take on more risk knowing that the Fed will come to the rescue. The Fed's lender-of-last-resort role has thus created a moral hazard problem similar to the one created by deposit insurance (discussed in Chapter 18): Banks take on more risk, thus exposing the deposit insurance agency, and hence taxpayers, to greater losses. The moral hazard problem is most severe for large banks, which may believe that the Fed and the FDIC view them as "too big to fail"; that is, they will always receive Fed loans when they are in trouble because their failure would be likely to precipitate a bank panic.

Similarly, Federal Reserve actions to prevent financial panic, as occurred after the October 1987 stock market crash, may encourage financial institutions other than banks to take on greater risk. They, too, expect the Fed to ensure that they could get loans if a financial panic seemed imminent. When the Fed considers using the discount weapon to prevent panics, it therefore needs to consider the trade-off between the moral hazard cost of its role as lender of last resort and the benefit of preventing financial panics. This trade-off explains why the Fed must be careful not to perform its role as lender of last resort too frequently.

Announcement Effect

Discount policy serves another function for the Federal Reserve: It can be used to signal the Fed's intentions about future monetary policy. Hence if the Fed decides to slow the expansion of the economy by increasing the federal funds rate, it can amplify the announcement that it makes after the FOMC meeting by also raising the discount rate. This signal alone may rein in economic expansion because the public will expect monetary policy to be less expansionary in the future.

The problem with the announcement effect is that it is subject to misinterpretation. If the federal funds rate is rising relative to the discount rate, the volume of discount loans will rise because banks will find it advantageous to borrow more with discount loans and then lend the proceeds out in the federal funds market. In such a situation, the Fed may have no intention of amplifying the announcement of a federal funds rate increase, but to keep the amount of discounting from becoming excessive, it may raise the discount rate to keep it more in line with market interest rates. When the discount rate rises, the market may interpret this as a signal that the Fed is moving to a more contractionary policy, even if that is not the case. The announcement effect may be a hindrance rather than a help. Another approach is for the Fed to communicate directly with the public by announcing its intentions about monetary policy outright and then carrying them out. Fed announcements would be believed, and the market would respond accordingly.

BOX 3: INSIDE THE FED

Discounting to Prevent a Financial Panic: The Black Monday Stock Market Crash of October 1987 and the Terrorist Destruction of the World Trade Center in September 2001

Although October 19, 1987, dubbed "Black Monday," will go down in the history books as the largest one-day percentage decline in stock prices to date (the Dow Jones Industrial Average declined by more than 20%), it was on Tuesday, October 20, 1987, that financial markets almost stopped functioning. Felix Rohatyn, one of the most prominent men on Wall Street, stated flatly: "Tuesday was the most dangerous day we had in 50 years."* Much of the credit for prevention of a market meltdown after Black Monday must be given to the Federal Reserve System and the chairman of the Board of Governors, Alan Greenspan.

The stress of keeping markets functioning during the sharp decline in stock prices on Monday, October 19, meant that many brokerage houses and specialists (dealer-brokers who maintain orderly trading on the stock exchanges) were severely in need of additional funds to finance their activities. However, understandably enough, New York banks, as well as foreign and regional U.S. banks, growing very nervous about the financial health of securities firms, began to cut back credit to the securities industry at the very time when it was most needed. Panic was in the air. One chairman of a large specialist firm commented that on Monday, "from 2 P.M. on, there was total despair. The entire investment community fled the market. We were left alone on the field." It was time for the Fed, like the cavalry, to come to the rescue.

Upon learning of the plight of the securities industry, Alan Greenspan and E. Gerald Corrigan, then president of the Federal Reserve Bank of New York and the Fed official most closely in touch with Wall Street, became fearful of a spreading collapse of securities firms. To prevent this from occurring, Greenspan announced before the market opened on Tuesday, October 20, the Federal Reserve System's "readiness to serve as a source of liquidity to support the economic and financial system." In addition to this extraordinary announcement, the Fed made it clear that it would provide discount loans to any bank that would make loans to the securities industry, although this did not prove to be necessary. As one New York banker said, the Fed's message was, "We're here. Whatever you need, we'll give you."

The outcome of the Fed's timely action was that a financial panic was averted. The markets kept functioning on Tuesday, and a market rally ensued that day, with the Dow Jones Industrial Average climbing over 100 points.

A similar lender-of-last resort operation was carried out in the aftermath of the destruction of the World Trade Center on Tuesday, September 11, 2001, in the worst terrorist incident in U.S. history. Because of the disruption of the most important financial center in the world, the liquidity needs of the financial system skyrocketed. To satisfy this need and so keep the financial system from seizing up, within a few hours of the incident, the Fed made a similar announcement to that made after the crash of 1987, stating, "The Federal Reserve System is open and operating. The discount window is available to meet liquidity needs."** The Fed then proceeded to provide $45 billion to banks through the discount window, a 200-fold increase over the previous week. As a result of this action, along with as much of $80 billion of reserves injected into the banking system through open market operations, the financial system kept functioning. When the stock market reopened on Monday, September 17, trading was orderly, although the Dow Jones average did decline 7%.

The terrorists were able to bring down the twin towers of the World Trade Center with over 3000 dead. However, they were unable to bring down the U.S. financial system because of the timely actions of the Federal Reserve.

*"Terrible Tuesday: How the Stock Market Almost Disintegrated a Day After the Crash," *Wall Street Journal*, November 20, 1987, p. 1. This article provides a fascinating and more detailed view of the events described here and is the source of all the quotations cited.

**"Economic Front: How Policy Makers Regrouped to Defend the Financial System," *Wall Street Journal*, Tuesday, September 18, 2001, p. A1, provides more detail on this episode.

Reserve Requirements

Changes in reserve requirements affect the demand for reserves: A rise in reserve requirements means that banks must hold more reserves, and a reduction means that they are required to hold less. The Depository Institutions Deregulation and Monetary Control Act of 1980 provided a simple scheme for setting reserve requirements. All depository institutions, including commercial banks, savings and loan associations, mutual savings banks, and credit unions, are now subject to the same reserve requirements, as follows: Required reserves on all checkable deposits—including non-interest-bearing checking accounts, NOW accounts, super-NOW accounts, and ATS (automatic transfer savings) accounts—are equal to 3% of the bank's first $49.3 million of checkable deposits[8] and 10% of the checkable deposits over $49.3 million, and the percentage set initially at 10% can be varied between 8% and 14% at the Fed's discretion. In extraordinary circumstances, the percentage can be raised as high as 18%.

Reserve requirements have been rarely used as a monetary policy tool because raising them can cause immediate liquidity problems for banks with low excess reserves. When the Fed has raised these requirements in the past, it has usually softened the blow by conducting open market purchases or by making the discount window more available, thus providing reserves to banks that needed them. Continually fluctuating reserve requirements would also create more uncertainty for banks and make their liquidity management more difficult.

Advantages of Open Market Operations Over the Other Tools

Of the three tools of monetary policy available to the Fed, the primary tool used is open market operations. This is because open market operations have several advantages over the other tools of monetary policy.

First, open market operations occur at the initiative of the Fed, which has complete control over their volume. This control is not found, for example, in discount operations, in which the Fed can encourage or discourage banks to take out discount loans by altering the discount rate but cannot directly control the volume of discount loans.

Second, open market operations are flexible and precise; they can be used to any extent. No matter how small a change in reserves is desired, open market operations can achieve it with a small purchase or sale of securities. Conversely, if the desired change in reserves or the monetary base is very large, the open market operations tool is strong enough to do the job through a very large purchase or sale of securities.

Third, open market operations are easily reversed. If a mistake is made in conducting an open market operation, the Fed can immediately reverse it. If the Fed decides that the federal funds rate is too low because it has made too many open market purchases, it can immediately make a correction by conducting open market sales.

Fourth, open market operations can be implemented quickly; they involve no administrative delays. When the Fed decides that it wants to change reserves, it just places orders with securities dealers, and the trades are executed immediately.

GOALS OF MONETARY POLICY

Six basic goals are continually mentioned by personnel at the Federal Reserve and other central banks when they discuss the objectives of monetary policy: (1) high employment, (2) economic growth, (3) price stability, (4) interest-rate stability, (5) stability of financial markets, and (6) stability in foreign exchange markets.

[8]The $49.3 million figure is as of the beginning of 1999. Each year, the figure is adjusted upward by 80% of the percentage increase in checkable deposits in the United States.

High Employment

The site http://stats.bls.gov/ contains statistics on employment level, summary of employment situation, and other useful information related to employment issues.

The Employment Act of 1946 and the Full Employment and Balanced Growth Act of 1978 (more commonly called the Humphrey-Hawkins Act) commit the U.S. government to promoting high employment consistent with a stable price level. High employment is a worthy goal for two main reasons: (1) the alternative situation, high unemployment, causes much human misery, with families suffering financial distress, loss of personal self-respect, and increase in crime (though this last conclusion is highly controversial), and (2) when unemployment is high, the economy has not only idle workers but also idle resources (closed factories and unused equipment), resulting in a loss of output (lower GDP).

Although it is clear that high employment is desirable, how high should it be? At what point can we say that the economy is at full employment? At first, it might seem that full employment is the point at which no worker is out of a job, that is, when unemployment is zero. But this definition ignores the fact that some unemployment, called *frictional unemployment*, which involves searches by workers and firms to find suitable matchups, is beneficial to the economy. For example, a worker who decides to look for a better job might be unemployed for a while during the job search. Workers often decide to leave work temporarily to pursue other activities (raising a family, travel, returning to school), and when they decide to reenter the job market, it may take some time for them to find the right job. The benefit of having some unemployment is similar to the benefit of having a nonzero vacancy rate in the market for rental apartments. As many of you who have looked for an apartment have discovered, when the vacancy rate in the rental market is too low, you will have a difficult time finding the right apartment.

Another reason that unemployment is not zero when the economy is at full employment is due to what is called *structural unemployment*, a mismatch between job requirements and the skills or availability of local workers. Clearly, this kind of unemployment is undesirable. Nonetheless, it is something that monetary policy can do little about.

The goal for high employment should therefore not seek an unemployment level of zero but rather a level above zero consistent with full employment at which the demand for labor equals the supply of labor. This level is called the **natural rate of unemployment.**

Although this definition sounds neat and authoritative, it isn't, because it leaves a troublesome question unanswered: What unemployment rate is consistent with full employment? On the one hand, in some cases, it is obvious that the unemployment rate is too high: The unemployment rate in excess of 20% during the Great Depression, for example, was clearly far too high. In the early 1960s, on the other hand, policymakers thought that a reasonable goal was 4%, a level that was probably too low because it led to accelerating inflation. Current estimates of the natural rate of unemployment place it between 5% and 6%, but even this estimate is subject to a great deal of uncertainty and disagreement. In addition, it is possible that appropriate government policy, such as the provision of better information about job vacancies or job training programs, might decrease the natural rate of unemployment.

Economic Growth

The goal of steady economic growth is closely related to the high-employment goal because businesses are more likely to invest in capital equipment to increase productivity and economic growth when unemployment is low. Conversely, if unemployment is high and factories are idle, it does not pay for a firm to invest in additional plants and equipment. Although the two goals are closely related, policies can be specifically aimed at promoting economic growth by directly encouraging firms to invest or by encouraging people to save, which provides more funds for firms to invest. In fact, this is the stated purpose of so-called supply-side economics policies, which are intended to spur economic growth by providing tax incentives for businesses to invest in factories and equipment and for taxpayers to save more. There is also an active debate over what growth role monetary policy can play in boosting growth.

Price Stability

Over the past few decades, policymakers in the United States have become more aware of the social and economic costs of inflation and more concerned with a stable price level as a goal of economic policy. (The growing commitment to price stability is also evident in Europe—see Box 4.) Price stability is desirable because a rising price level (inflation) creates uncertainty in the economy, and that may hamper economic growth. For example, the information conveyed by the prices of goods and services is harder to interpret when the overall level of prices is changing, which complicates decision making for consumers, businesses, and government. Not only do public opinion surveys indicate that the public is very hostile to inflation, but also a growing body of evidence suggests that inflation leads to lower economic growth.[9] The most extreme example of unstable prices is *hyperinflation*, such as Argentina, Brazil, and Russia have experienced in the recent past. Many economists attribute the slower growth that these countries have experienced to their problems with hyperinflation.

Inflation also makes it hard to plan for the future. For example, it is more difficult to decide how much funds should be put aside to provide for a child's

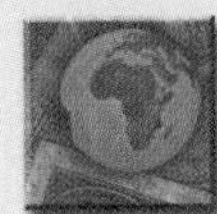

BOX 4: GLOBAL
The Growing European Commitment to Price Stability

Not surprisingly, given Germany's experience with hyperinflation in the 1920s, its central bank has the strongest commitment to price stability. In contrast to statutes for the German central bank, the statutes of other central banks in Europe set various objectives for policy, including all the goals outlined here in the text. However, European policymakers have been coming around to the view that the primary objective for a central bank should be price stability. The increased importance of this goal is reflected in the December 1991 Treaty of European Union, known as the Maastricht Treaty, which proposed the creation of the European System of Central Banks, which would function very much like the Federal Reserve System. The statute of the European System of Central Banks sets price stability as the primary objective of this system and indicates that the general economic policies of the European Union are to be supported only if they are not in conflict with price stability.

[9]For example, see Stanley Fischer, "The Role of Macroeconomic Factors in Growth," *Journal of Monetary Economics* 32 (1993): 485–512.

college education in an inflationary environment. Further, inflation may strain a country's social fabric: Conflict may result because each group in the society may compete with other groups to make sure that its income keeps up with the rising level of prices.

Interest-Rate Stability

Interest-rate stability is desirable because fluctuations in interest rates can create uncertainty in the economy and make it harder to plan for the future. Fluctuations in interest rates that affect consumers' willingness to buy houses, for example, make it more difficult for consumers to decide when to purchase a house and for construction firms to plan how many houses to build. A central bank may also want to reduce upward movements in interest rates for the reasons we discussed in Chapter 6: Upward movements in interest rates generate hostility toward central banks like the Fed and lead to demands that their power be curtailed.

Stability of Financial Markets

As our analysis in Chapter 14 will show, financial crises can interfere with the ability of financial markets to channel funds to people with productive investment opportunities, thereby leading to a sharp contraction in economic activity. The promotion of a more stable financial system in which financial crises are avoided is thus an important goal for a central bank. Indeed, as discussed in Chapter 6, the Federal Reserve System was created in response to the bank panic of 1907 to promote financial stability.

The stability of financial markets is also fostered by interest-rate stability because fluctuations in interest rates create great uncertainty for financial institutions. An increase in interest rates produces large capital losses on long-term bonds and mortgages, losses that can cause the failure of the financial institutions holding them. In recent years, more pronounced interest-rate fluctuations have been a particularly severe problem for savings and loan associations and mutual savings banks, many of which got into serious financial trouble in the 1980s and early 1990s.

Stability in Foreign Exchange Markets

With the increasing importance of international trade to the U.S. economy, the value of the dollar relative to other currencies has become a major consideration for the Fed. As we will see in Chapter 12, a rise in the value of the dollar makes American industries less competitive with those abroad, and declines in the value of the dollar stimulate inflation in the United States. In addition, preventing large changes in the value of the dollar makes it easier for firms and individuals purchasing or selling goods abroad to plan ahead. Stabilizing extreme movements in the value of the dollar in foreign exchange markets is thus viewed as a worthy goal of monetary policy. In other countries, which are even more dependent on foreign trade, stability in foreign exchange markets takes on even greater importance.

Conflict Among Goals

Although many of the goals mentioned are consistent with each other—high employment with economic growth, interest-rate stability with financial market stability—this is not always the case. The goal of price stability often conflicts with the goals of interest-rate stability and high employment in the short run (but probably not in the long run). For example, when the economy is expanding and unemployment is falling, both inflation and interest rates may start to rise. If the central bank tries to prevent a rise in interest rates, this may cause the economy to overheat and stimulate inflation. But if a central bank raises interest rates to prevent inflation, in the short run unemployment may rise. The conflict among goals may thus present central banks like the Federal Reserve with some hard choices.

CENTRAL BANK STRATEGY: USE OF TARGETS

The central bank's problem is that it wishes to achieve certain goals, such as price stability with high employment, but it does not directly influence the goals. It has a set of tools to employ (open market operations, changes in the discount rate, and changes in reserve requirements) that can affect the goals indirectly after a period of time (typically more than a year). If the central bank waits to see what the price level and employment will be one year later, it will be too late to make any corrections to its policy—mistakes will be irreversible.

All central banks consequently pursue a different strategy for conducting monetary policy by aiming at variables that lie between its tools and the achievement of its goals. The strategy is as follows: After deciding on its goals for employment and the price level, the central bank chooses a set of variables to aim for, called **intermediate targets,** such as the monetary aggregates (various measures of the money supply denoted by M1, M2, or M3) or interest rates (short- or long-term), which have a direct effect on employment and the price level. However, even these intermediate targets are not directly affected by the central bank's policy tools. Therefore, it chooses another set of variables to aim for, called **operating targets,** or alternatively called *instruments*, such as reserve aggregates (reserves, nonborrowed reserves, monetary base, or nonborrowed base) or interest rates (federal funds rate or Treasury bill rate), which are more responsive to its policy tools. (Nonborrowed reserves are total reserves minus borrowed reserves, which are the amount of discount loans; the monetary base is the sum of currency plus reserves in the banking system; the nonborrowed base is the monetary base minus borrowed reserves; and the federal funds rate is the interest rate on funds loaned overnight between banks.)[10]

The central bank pursues this strategy because it is easier to hit a goal by aiming at targets than by aiming at the goal directly. Specifically, by using intermediate and operating targets, it can more quickly judge whether its policies are on the right track, rather than waiting until it sees the final outcome of its policies on employment and the price level.[11] By analogy, NASA employs the strategy of using targets when it is trying to send a spaceship to the moon. It will check to see whether the spaceship is positioned correctly as it leaves the atmosphere (we can think of this as NASA's "operating target"). If the spaceship is off course

[10]There is some ambiguity as to whether to call a particular variable an operating target or an intermediate target. The monetary base and the Treasury bill rate are often viewed as possible intermediate targets, even though they may function as operating targets as well. In addition, if the Fed wants to pursue a goal of interest-rate stability, an interest rate can be both a goal and a target.

[11]This reasoning for the use of monetary targets has come under attack because information on employment and the price level can be useful in evaluating policy. See Benjamin M. Friedman, "The Inefficiency of Short-Run Monetary Targets for Monetary Policy," *Brookings Papers on Economic Activity* 2 (1977): 292–346.

at this stage, NASA engineers will adjust its thrust (a policy tool) to get it back on target. NASA may check the position of the spaceship again when it is halfway to the moon (NASA's "intermediate target") and can make further midcourse corrections if necessary.

The central bank's strategy works in a similar way. Suppose that the central bank's employment and price-level goals are consistent with a nominal GDP growth rate of 5%. If the central bank feels that the 5% nominal GDP growth rate will be achieved by a 4% growth rate for M2 (its intermediate target), which will in turn be achieved by a growth rate of $3\frac{1}{2}$% for the monetary base (its operating target), it will carry out open market operations (its tool) to achieve the $3\frac{1}{2}$% growth in the monetary base. After implementing this policy, the central bank may find that the monetary base is growing too slowly, say, at a 2% rate; then it can correct this too slow growth by increasing the amount of its open market purchases. Somewhat later, the central bank will begin to see how its policy is affecting the growth rate of the money supply. If M2 is growing too fast, say, at a 7% rate, the central bank may decide to reduce its open market purchases or make open market sales to reduce the M2 growth rate.

One way of thinking about this strategy (illustrated in Figure 4) is that the central bank is using its operating and intermediate targets to direct monetary policy (the spaceship) toward the achievement of its goals. After the initial setting of the policy tools (the liftoff), an operating target such as the monetary base, which the central bank can control fairly directly, is used to reset the tools so that monetary policy is channeled toward achieving the intermediate target of a certain rate of money supply growth. Midcourse corrections in the policy tools can be made again when the central bank sees what is happening to its intermediate target, thus directing monetary policy so that it will achieve its goals of high employment and price stability (the spaceship reaches the moon).

CHOOSING THE TARGETS

As we see in Figure 4, there are two different types of target variables: interest rates and aggregates (monetary aggregates and reserve aggregates). In our example, the central bank chose a 4% growth rate for M2 to achieve a 5% rate of growth for nominal GDP. It could have chosen to lower the interest rate on the three-

Tools of the Central Bank

Open market operations
Discount policy
Reserve requirements

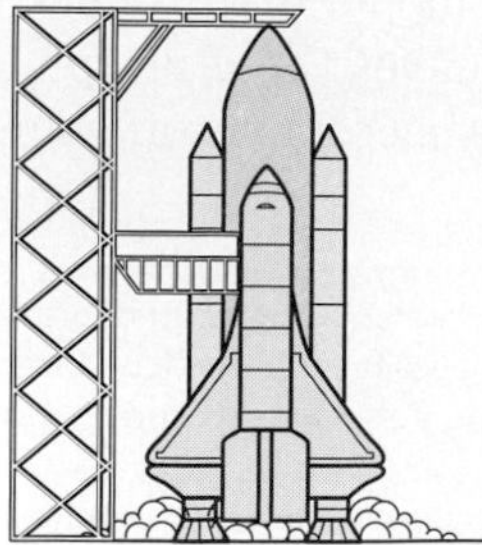

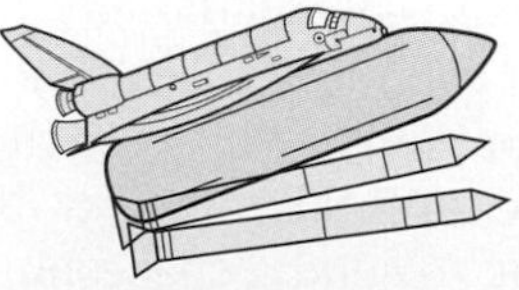

Operating Targets

Reserve aggregates (reserves, nonborrowed reserves, monetary base, nonborrowed base)
Interest rates (short-term such as federal funds rate)

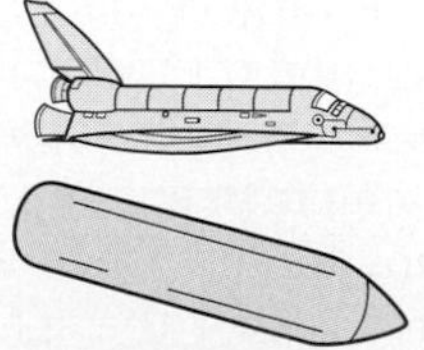

Intermediate Targets

Monetary aggregates (M1, M2, M3)
Interest rates (short- and long-term)

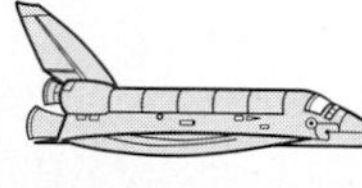

Goals

High employment, price stability, financial market stability, and so on

FIGURE 4 Central Bank Strategy

month Treasury bills to, say, 3% to achieve the same goal. Can the central bank choose to pursue both of these targets at the same time? The answer is no. The application of the supply and demand analysis of the market for money that we covered in Chapter 4 explains why a central bank must choose one or the other.

Let's first see why a monetary aggregate target involves losing control of the interest rate. Figure 5 contains a supply and demand diagram for the market for money. Although the central bank expects the demand curve for money to be at M^{d*}, it fluctuates between $M^{d'}$ and $M^{d''}$ because of unexpected increases or decreases in output or changes in the price level. The money demand curve might also shift unexpectedly because the public's preferences about holding bonds versus money may change. If the central bank's monetary aggregate target of a 4% growth rate in M2 results in a money supply of M^*, it expects that the interest rate will be i^*. However, as the figure indicates, the fluctuations in the money demand curve between $M^{d'}$ and $M^{d''}$ will result in an interest rate fluctuating between i' and i''. Pursuing a monetary aggregate target implies that interest rates will fluctuate.

The supply and demand diagram in Figure 6 shows the consequences of an interest-rate target set at i^*. Again, the central bank expects the money demand curve to be at M^{d*}, but it fluctuates between $M^{d'}$ and $M^{d''}$ due to unexpected changes in output, the price level, or the public's preferences toward holding money. If the demand curve rises to $M^{d''}$, the interest rate will begin to rise above i^*, and the price of bonds will fall. With an interest-rate target, the central bank will prevent the interest rate from rising by buying bonds to drive their price back up and the interest rate back down to its former level. The central bank open market purchase of bonds will mean that reserves and deposits in the banking system will rise because the central bank pays for these bonds with reserves, thus

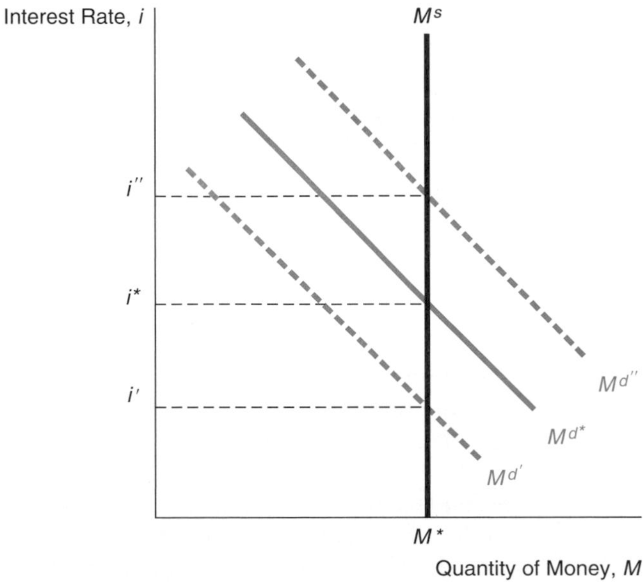

FIGURE 5 Result of Targeting on the Money Supply

Targeting on the money supply at M^* will lead to fluctuations in the interest rate between i' and i'' because of fluctuations in the money demand curve between $M^{d'}$ and $M^{d''}$.

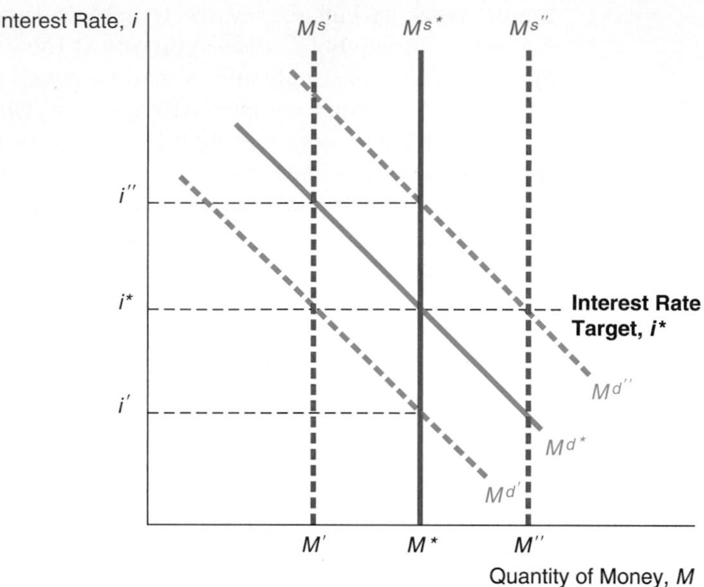

FIGURE 6 Result of Targeting on the Interest Rate

Targeting the interest rate at i^* will lead to fluctuations of the money supply between M' and M'' because of fluctuations in the money demand curve between $M^{d\prime}$ and $M^{d\prime\prime}$.

raising the money supply. The central bank will continue to make open market purchases until the money supply rises to $M^{s\prime}$, at which point the equilibrium interest rate is again i^*. Conversely, if the demand curve falls to $M^{d\prime\prime}$ and lowers the interest rate, the central bank would keep interest rates from falling by selling bonds to keep their prices from rising. The central bank will make open market sales until the money supply falls to $M^{s\prime}$ and the equilibrium interest rate is i^*. The central bank's adherence to the interest-rate target thus leads to a fluctuating money supply as well as fluctuations in reserve aggregates.

The conclusion from the supply and demand analysis is that interest-rate and monetary aggregate targets are incompatible: A central bank can hit one or the other but not both. Because a choice between them has to be made, we need to examine what criteria should be used to decide on the target variable.

Criteria for Choosing Intermediate Targets

The rationale behind a central bank's strategy of using targets suggests three criteria for choosing an intermediate target: It must be measurable, it must be controllable by the central bank, and it must have a predictable effect on the goal.

Measurability Quick and accurate measurement of an intermediate-target variable is necessary because the intermediate target will be useful only if it signals when policy is off track more rapidly than the goal. What good does it do for the central bank to plan to hit a 4% growth rate for M2 if it has no way of quickly and accurately measuring M2? Data on the monetary aggregates are obtained after a two-week delay, and interest-rate data are available almost immediately. Data on a variable like GDP that serves as a goal, by contrast, are compiled quarterly and are made available with a month's delay. In addition, the GDP data are less accurate than data on the monetary aggregates or interest rates. On these grounds alone, focusing on interest rates and monetary aggregates as intermediate targets rather than on a goal like GDP can provide clearer signals about the status of the central bank's policy.

At first glance, interest rates seem to be more measurable than monetary aggregates and hence more useful as intermediate targets. Not only are the data on interest rates available more quickly than on monetary aggregates, but they are also measured more precisely and are rarely revised, in contrast to the monetary aggregates, which are subject to a fair amount of revision. However, as we learned in Chapter 3, the interest rate that is quickly and accurately measured, the nominal interest rate, is typically a poor measure of the real cost of borrowing, which indicates with more certainty what will happen to GDP. This real cost of borrowing is more accurately measured by the real interest rate—the interest rate adjusted for expected inflation ($i_r = i - \pi^e$). Unfortunately, the real interest rate is extremely hard to measure because we have no direct way to measure expected inflation. Since both interest rate and monetary aggregates have measurability problems, it is not clear whether one should be preferred to the other as an intermediate target.

Controllability A central bank must be able to exercise effective control over a variable if it is to function as a useful target. If the central bank cannot control an intermediate target, knowing that it is off track does little good because the bank has no way of getting back on track. Some economists have suggested that nominal GDP should be used as an intermediate target, but since the central bank has little direct control over nominal GDP, it will not provide much guidance on how the Fed should set its policy tools. A central bank does, however, have a good deal of control over the monetary aggregates and interest rates.

Our discussion of the money supply process and the central bank's policy tools indicates that a central bank does have the ability to exercise a powerful effect on the money supply, although its control is not perfect. We have also seen that open market operations can be used to set interest rates by directly affecting the price of bonds. Because a central bank can set interest rates directly whereas it cannot completely control the money supply, it might appear that interest rates dominate the monetary aggregates on the controllability criterion. However, a central bank cannot set real interest rates because it does not have control over expectations of inflation. So again, a clear-cut case cannot be made that interest rates are preferable to monetary aggregates as an intermediate target or vice versa.

Predictable Effect on Goals The most important characteristic a variable must have to be useful as an intermediate target is that it must have a predictable impact on a goal. If a central bank can accurately and quickly measure the price of tea in China and can completely control its price, what good will it do? The central bank cannot use the price of tea in China to affect unemployment or the price level in its country. Because the ability to affect goals is so critical to the usefulness of an intermediate-target variable, the linkage of the money supply and interest rates with the goals—output, employment, and the price level—is a matter of much debate.

Criteria for Choosing Operating Targets

The choice of an operating target can be based on the same criteria used to evaluate intermediate targets. Both the federal funds rate and reserve aggregates are measured accurately and are available daily with almost no delay; both are easily controllable using the policy tools that we discussed earlier in the chapter. When we look at the third criterion, however, we can think of the intermediate target as the goal for the operating target. An operating target that has a more predictable impact on the most desirable intermediate target is preferred. If the desired intermediate target is an interest rate, the preferred operating target will be an interest-rate variable like the federal funds rate because interest rates are closely tied to each other (as we saw in Chapter 5). However, if the desired intermediate target is a monetary aggregate, a reserve aggregate operating target such as the monetary base will be preferred. Because there does not seem to be much reason to choose an interest rate over a reserve aggregate on the basis of measurability or controllability, the choice of which operating target is better rests on the choice of the intermediate target (the goal of the operating target).

FED POLICY PROCEDURES: HISTORICAL PERSPECTIVE

The well-known adage "The road to hell is paved with good intentions" applies as much to the Federal Reserve as it does to human beings. Understanding a central bank's goals and the strategies it can use to pursue them cannot tell us how monetary policy is actually conducted. To understand the practical results of the theoretical underpinnings, we have to look at how central banks have actually conducted policy in the past. First we will look at the Federal Reserve's past policy procedures: its choice of goals, policy tools, operating targets, and intermediate targets. This historical perspective will not only show us how our central bank carries out its duties but will also help us interpret the Fed's activities and see where U.S. monetary policy may be heading in the future. Once we are done studying the Fed, we will then examine central banks' experiences in other countries.

The Early Years: Discount Policy as the Primary Tool

When the Fed was created, changing the discount rate was the primary tool of monetary policy—the Fed had not yet discovered that open market operations were a more powerful tool for influencing the money supply, and the Federal Reserve Act made no provisions for changes in reserve requirements. The guiding principle for the conduct of monetary policy was that as long as loans were being made for "productive" purposes—that is, to support the production of goods and services—providing reserves to the banking system to make these loans would not be inflationary.[12] This theory, now thoroughly discredited, became known as the **real bills doctrine.** In practice, it meant that the Fed would make loans to member commercial banks when they showed up at the discount window with *eligible paper*, loans to facilitate the production and sale of goods and services. (Note that since the 1920s, the Fed has not conducted discount operations in this way.) The Fed's act of making loans to member banks was initially called *rediscounting*

[12]Another guiding principle was the maintenance of the gold standard, which we will discuss in Chapter 13.

because the original bank loans to businesses were made by discounting (loaning less than) the face value of the loan, and the Fed would be discounting them again. (Over time, when the Fed's emphasis on eligible paper diminished, the Fed's loans to banks became known as *discounts*, and the interest rate on these loans the *discount rate*, which is the terminology we use today.)

By the end of World War I, the Fed's policy of rediscounting eligible paper and keeping interest rates low to help the Treasury finance the war had led to a raging inflation; in 1919 and 1920, the inflation rate averaged 14%. The Fed decided that it could no longer follow the passive policy prescribed by the real bills doctrine because it was inconsistent with the goal of price stability, and for the first time the Fed accepted the responsibility of playing an active role in influencing the economy. In January 1920, the Fed raised the discount rate from $4\frac{3}{4}$% to 6%, the largest jump in its history, and eventually raised it further to 7% in June 1920, where it remained for nearly a year. The result of this policy was a sharp decline in the money supply and an especially sharp recession in 1920–1921. Although the blame for this severe recession can clearly be laid at the Fed's doorstep, in one sense the Fed's policy was very successful: After an initial decline in the price level, the inflation rate went to zero, paving the way for the prosperous Roaring Twenties.

Discovery of Open Market Operations

In the early 1920s, a particularly important event occurred: The Fed accidentally discovered open market operations. When the Fed was created, its revenue came exclusively from the interest it received on the discount loans that it made to member banks. After the 1920–1921 recession, the volume of discount loans shrank dramatically, and the Fed was pressed for income. It solved this problem by purchasing income-earning securities. In doing so, the Fed noticed that reserves in the banking system grew and interest rates fell. A new monetary policy tool was born, and by the end of the 1920s, it was the most important weapon in the Fed's arsenal.

The Great Depression

The stock market boom in 1928 and 1929 created a dilemma for the Fed. It wanted to temper the boom by raising the discount rate, but it was reluctant to do so because that would mean raising interest rates to businesses and individuals who had legitimate needs for credit. Finally, in August 1929, the Fed raised the discount rate, but by then it was too late; the speculative excesses of the market boom had already occurred, and the Fed's action only hastened the stock market crash and pushed the economy into recession.

The weakness of the economy, particularly in the agricultural sector, led to a "contagion of fear" that triggered substantial withdrawals from banks, building to a full-fledged bank panic in November and December 1930. For the next two years, the Fed sat idly by while one bank panic after another occurred, culminating in the final panic in March 1933, at which point the new president, Franklin Delano Roosevelt, declared a bank holiday. (Why the Fed failed to engage in its lender-of-last-resort role during this period is discussed in Box 5.) The spate of bank panics from 1930 to 1933 were the most severe in U.S. history, and Roosevelt aptly summed up the problem in his statement, "The only thing we have to fear is fear itself." By the time the panics were over in March 1933, more than one-third of the commercial banks in the United States had failed.

BOX 5: INSIDE THE FED

Bank Panics of 1930–1933: Why Did the Fed Let Them Happen?

The Federal Reserve System was totally passive during the bank panics of the Great Depression period and did not perform its intended role of lender of last resort to prevent them. In retrospect, the Fed's behavior seems quite extraordinary, but hindsight is always clearer than foresight.

The primary reason for the Fed's inaction was that Federal Reserve officials did not understand the negative impact bank failures could have on the money supply and economic activity. Friedman and Schwartz report that the Federal Reserve officials "tended to regard bank failures as regrettable consequences of bank management or bad banking practices, or as inevitable reactions to prior speculative excesses, or as a consequence but hardly a cause of the financial and economic collapse in process." In addition, bank failures in the early stages of the bank panics "were concentrated among smaller banks and, since the most influential figures in the system were big-city bankers who deplored the existence of smaller banks, their disappearance may have been viewed with complacency."*

Friedman and Schwartz also point out that political infighting may have played an important role in the passivity of the Fed during this period. The Federal Reserve Bank of New York, which until 1928 was the dominant force in the Federal Reserve System, strongly advocated an active program of open market purchases to provide reserves to the banking system during the bank panics. However, other powerful figures in the Federal Reserve System opposed the New York bank's position, and the bank was outvoted. (Friedman and Schwartz's discussion of the politics of the Federal Reserve System during this period makes for fascinating reading, and you might enjoy their highly readable book.)

*Milton Friedman and Anna Jacobson Schwartz, *A Monetary History of the United States, 1867–1960* (Princeton, N.J.: Princeton University Press, 1963), p. 358.

War Finance and the Pegging of Interest Rates: 1942–1951

With the entrance of the United States into World War II in late 1941, government spending skyrocketed, and to finance it, the Treasury issued huge amounts of bonds. The Fed agreed to help the Treasury finance the war cheaply by pegging interest rates at the low levels that had prevailed before the war: $\frac{3}{8}$% on Treasury bills and $2\frac{1}{2}$% on long-term Treasury bonds. Whenever interest rates would rise above these levels and the price of bonds would begin to fall, the Fed would make open market purchases, thereby bidding up bond prices and driving interest rates down again. The result was a rapid growth in the monetary base and the money supply. The Fed had thus in effect relinquished its control of monetary policy to meet the financing needs of the government.

When the war ended, the Fed continued to peg interest rates, and because there was little pressure on them to rise, this policy did not result in an explosive growth in the money supply. When the Korean War broke out in 1950, however, interest rates began to climb, and the Fed found that it was again forced to expand the money supply at a rapid rate. Because inflation began to heat up (the consumer price index rose 8% between 1950 and 1951), the Fed decided that it was time to reassert its control over monetary policy by abandoning the interest-rate peg. An often bitter debate ensued between the Fed and the Treasury, which wanted to keep its interest costs down and so favored a continued pegging of interest rates at low levels. In March 1951, the Fed and the Treasury came to an agreement known as the Accord, in which pegging was abandoned but the Fed promised that it would not allow interest rates to rise precipitously. After Eisenhower's election as president in 1952, the Fed was given complete freedom to pursue its monetary policy objectives.

Targeting Money Market Conditions: The 1950s and 1960s

With its freedom restored, the Federal Reserve, then under the chairmanship of William McChesney Martin Jr., took the view that monetary policy should be grounded in intuitive judgment based on a feel for the money market. The policy procedure that resulted can be described as one in which the Fed targeted on money market conditions, a vague collection of variables that were supposed to describe supply and demand conditions in the money market. Included among these variables were short-term interest rates and **free reserves,** equal to excess reserves in the banking system minus the volume of discount loans.

The Fed considered free reserves a particularly good indicator of money market conditions because it thought that they represented the amount of slack in the banking system. The Fed viewed banks as having a first priority in using their excess reserves to repay their discount loans, so only the excess reserves not borrowed from the Fed represented the *free* reserves that could be used to make loans and create deposits. The Fed interpreted an increase in free reserves as an easing of money market conditions and used open market sales to withdraw reserves from the banking system. A fall in free reserves meant a tightening of money market conditions, and the Fed made open market purchases.

By the late 1960s, the rising chorus of criticism from monetarists who advocated an increased focus on monetary aggregates in the conduct of monetary policy and concerns about inflation finally led the Fed to abandon its focus on money market conditions.

Targeting Monetary Aggregates: The 1970s

In 1970, Arthur Burns was appointed chairman of the Board of Governors, and soon thereafter the Fed stated that it was committing itself to the use of monetary aggregates as intermediate targets.

Every six weeks, the Federal Open Market Committee would set target ranges for the growth rate of various monetary aggregates and would determine what federal funds rate (the interest rate on funds loaned overnight between banks) it thought consistent with these aims. The target ranges for the growth in monetary aggregates were fairly broad—a typical range for the growth of M1 (a monetary aggregate that consists primarily of currency and checkable deposits) might be 3% to 6%; for M2 (a monetary aggregate that adds to M1 money market mutual funds and deposit accounts, small-denomination time deposits, saving deposits, and overnight repurchase agreements and eurodollars), 4% to 7%—while the range for the federal funds rate was a narrow band, say, from $7\frac{1}{2}\%$ to $8\frac{1}{4}\%$. The trading desk at the Federal Reserve Bank of New York was then instructed to meet both sets of targets, but as we saw earlier, interest-rate targets and monetary aggregate targets might not be compatible. If the two targets were incompatible—say, the federal funds rate began to climb higher than the top of its target band when M1 was growing too rapidly—the trading desk was instructed to give precedence to the federal funds rate target. In the situation just described, this would mean that although M1 growth was too high, the trading desk would make open market purchases to keep the federal funds rate within its target range.

The Fed was actually using the federal funds rate as its operating target. During the six-week period between FOMC meetings, an unexpected rise in income (which would cause the federal funds rate to hit the top of its target band) would then induce open market purchases and a too rapid growth of the money supply. When the FOMC met again, it would try to bring money supply growth back on track by raising the target range on the federal funds rate. However, if income continued to rise unexpectedly, money growth would overshoot again. This is exactly what occurred from June 1972 to June 1973, when the economy boomed unexpectedly: M1 growth greatly exceeded its target, increasing at approximately an 8% rate, while the federal funds rate climbed from $4\frac{1}{2}\%$ to $8\frac{1}{2}\%$. The economy soon became overheated, and inflationary pressures began to mount.

The opposite chain of events occurred at the end of 1974, when the economic contraction was far more severe than anyone had predicted. The federal funds rate fell dramatically from over 12% to 5% and persistently bumped against the bottom of its target range. The trading desk conducted open market sales to keep the federal funds rate from falling, and money growth dropped precipitously, actually turning negative by the beginning of 1975. Clearly, this sharp drop in money growth when the United States was experiencing one of the worst economic contractions of the postwar era was a serious mistake.

Using the federal funds rate as an operating target promoted a procyclical monetary policy despite the Fed's lip service to monetary aggregate targets. If the Federal Reserve really intended to pursue monetary aggregate targets, it seems peculiar that it would have chosen an interest rate for an operating target rather than a reserve aggregate. (However, as the discussion of the conduct of Japanese monetary policy later in this chapter makes clear, more effective monetary control can be achieved even when an interest rate is used as an operating target.) The explanation for why the Fed chose an interest rate as an operating target is that it was still very concerned with achieving interest-rate stability and was reluctant to relinquish control over interest-rate movements. The incompatibility of the Fed's policy procedure with its stated intent of targeting on the monetary aggregates had become very clear by October 1979, when the Fed's policy procedures underwent drastic revision.

New Fed Operating Procedures: October 1979–October 1982

In October 1979, two months after Paul Volcker became chairman of the Board of Governors, the Fed finally deemphasized the federal funds rate as an operating target by widening its target range more than fivefold: A typical range might be from 10% to 15%. The primary operating target became nonborrowed reserves that the Fed would set after estimating the volume of discount loans the banks would borrow. Figure 7 shows what happened to the federal funds rate and the growth rate of the M1 money supply both before and after October 1979. Not surprisingly, the federal funds rate underwent much greater fluctuations after it was deemphasized as an operating target. What is surprising, however, is that the deemphasis of the federal funds target did not result in improved monetary control: After October 1979, the fluctuations in the rate of money supply growth *increased* rather than decreased as would have been expected. In addition, the Fed missed its M1 growth target ranges in all three years of the 1979–1982 period.[13] What went wrong?

[13]The M1 target ranges and actual growth rates for 1980–1982 were as follows:

Year	Target Range (%)	Actual Growth (%)
1980	4.5–7.0	7.5
1981	6.0–8.5	5.1
1982	2.5–5.5	8.8

Source: Board of Governors of the Federal Reserve System, *Monetary Policy Objectives, 1981–1983.*

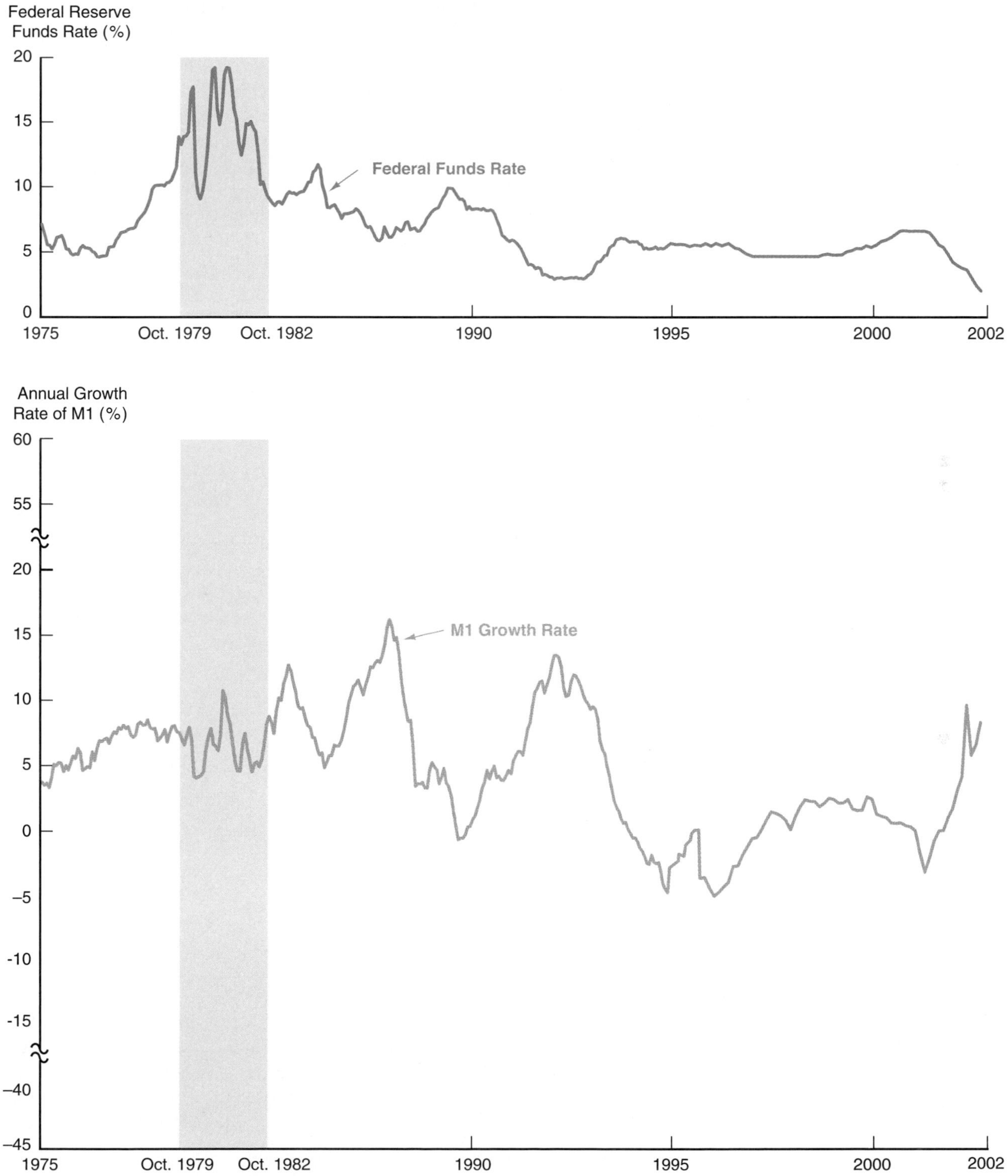

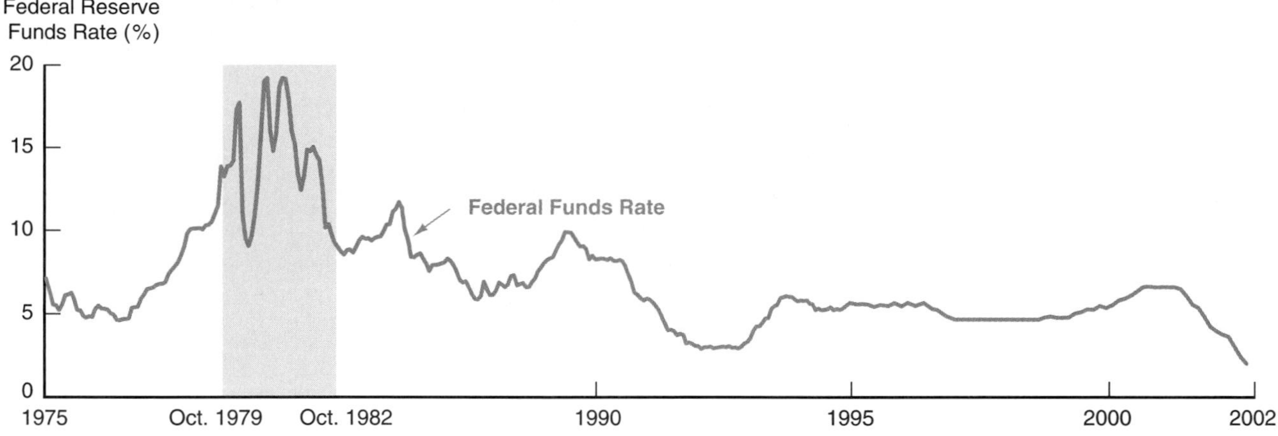

FIGURE 7 Federal Funds Rate and Growth Rate of the Money Supply: Before and After October 1979

Source: http://www.federalreserve.gov/releases/H6/hist/h6hist1.txt

There are several possible answers to this question. The first is that the economy was exposed to several shocks during this period that made monetary control more difficult: the acceleration of financial innovation and deregulation, which added new categories of deposits such as NOW accounts to the measures of monetary aggregates; the imposition by the Fed of credit controls from March to July 1980, which restricted the growth of consumer and business loans; and the back-to-back recessions of 1980 and 1981–1982.[14]

A more persuasive explanation for poor monetary control, however, is that controlling the money supply was never really the intent of Volcker's policy shift. Despite Volcker's statements about the need to target monetary aggregates, he was not committed to these targets. Rather, he was far more concerned with using interest-rate movements to wring inflation out of the economy. Volcker's primary reason for changing the Fed's operating procedure was to free his hand to manipulate interest rates in order to fight inflation. It was necessary to abandon interest-rate targets if Volcker were to be able to raise interest rates sharply when a slowdown in the economy was required to dampen inflation. This view of Volcker's strategy suggests that the Fed's announced attachment to monetary aggregate targets may have been a smokescreen to keep the Fed from being blamed for the high interest rates that would result from the new policy.

The interest-rate movements in Figure 7 support this interpretation of Fed strategy. After the October 1979 announcement, short-term interest rates were driven up by nearly 5%, until in March 1980 they exceeded 15%. With the imposition of credit controls in March 1980 and the rapid decline in real GDP in the second quarter of 1980, the Fed eased up on its policy and allowed interest rates to decline sharply. When recovery began in July 1980, inflation remained persistent, still exceeding 10%. Because the inflation fight was not yet won, the Fed tightened the screws again, sending short-term rates above the 15% level for a second time. The 1981–1982 recession and its large decline in output and high unemployment began to bring inflation down. The inflationary psychology apparently broken, interest rates were allowed to fall.

The Fed's anti-inflation strategy during the October 1979–October 1982 period was neither intended nor likely to produce smooth growth in the monetary aggregates. Indeed, the large fluctuations in interest rates and the business cycle, along with financial innovation, helped generate volatile money growth.

Deemphasis of Monetary Aggregates: October 1982–Early 1990s

In October 1982, with inflation in check, the Fed returned, in effect, to a policy of smoothing interest rates. It did this by placing less emphasis on monetary aggregate targets and shifting to borrowed reserves (discount loan borrowings) as an operating target. To see how a borrowed reserves target produces interest-rate smoothing, let's consider what happens when the economy expands so that interest rates are driven up. The rise in interest rates increases the incentives for banks to borrow more from the Fed, so borrowed reserves rise. To prevent the resulting rise in borrowed reserves from exceeding the target level, the Fed must lower

[14]Another explanation focuses on the technical difficulties of monetary control when using a nonborrowed reserves operating target under a system of lagged reserve requirements, in which required reserves for a given week are calculated on the basis of the level of deposits two weeks earlier. See David Lindsey, "Nonborrowed Reserve Targeting and Monetary Control," in *Improving Money Stock Control*, ed. Laurence Meyer (Boston: Kluwer-Nijhoff, 1983), pp. 3–41.

interest rates by bidding up the price of bonds through open market purchases. The outcome of targeting on borrowed reserves, then, is that the Fed prevents a rise in interest rates.

The deemphasis of monetary aggregates and the change to a borrowed reserves target are visible in Figure 7, where we see much smaller fluctuations in the federal funds rate after October 1982 but continue to have large fluctuations in money supply growth. Finally, in February 1987, the Fed announced that it would no longer even set M1 targets. The abandonment of M1 targets was defended on two grounds. The first was that the rapid pace of financial innovation and deregulation had made the definition and measurement of money very difficult. The second is that there had been a breakdown in the stable relationship between M1 and economic activity. These two arguments suggested that a monetary aggregate such as M1 might no longer be a reliable guide for monetary policy. As a result, the Fed switched its focus to the broader monetary aggregate M2, which it felt had a more stable relationship with economic activity. However, in the early 1990s, this relationship also broke down, and in July 1993, Board of Governors Chairman Alan Greenspan testified before Congress that the Fed would no longer use any monetary targets, including M2, as a guide for conducting monetary policy. Finally, legislation in 2000 amending the Federal Reserve Act dropped the requirement that the Fed report target ranges for monetary aggregates to Congress.

Federal Funds Targeting Again: Early 1990s and Beyond

Having abandoned monetary aggregates as a guide for monetary policy, the Federal Reserve returned to using a federal funds target in the early 1990s. Indeed, from late 1992 until February 1994, a period of a year and a half, the Fed kept the federal funds rate targeted at the constant rate of 3%, a low level last seen in the 1960s. The explanation for this unusual period of keeping the federal funds rate pegged so low for such a long period of time was fear on the part of the Federal Reserve that the credit crunch (described in Chapter 15) was putting a drag on the economy (the "headwinds" referred to by Greenspan) that was producing a sluggish recovery from the 1990–1991 recession. Starting in February 1994, after the economy returned to rapid growth, the Fed began a preemptive strike to head off any future inflationary pressures by raising the federal funds rate in steps to 6% by early 1995. The Fed not only has engaged in preemptive strikes against a rise in inflation but has acted preemptively against negative shocks to demand. It lowered the federal funds rate in early 1996 to deal with a possible slowing in the economy, and took the dramatic step of reducing the federal funds rate by three-quarters of a percentage point when the collapse of Long Term Capital Management in the fall of 1998 (discussed in Chapter 12) led to concerns about the health of the financial system. With the strong growth of the economy in 1999 and heightened concerns about inflation, the Fed reversed course and began to raise the federal funds rate again. The Fed's timely actions kept the economy on track, helping to produce the longest business cycle expansion in U.S. history. With a weakening economy, in January 2001, the Fed reversed course again, and began to sharply reduce the federal funds rate from its height of 6.5% to below the 2% level.

In February 1994, with the first change in the federal funds rate in a year and half, the Fed adopted a new policy procedure. Instead of keeping the federal funds target secret, as it had done previously, the Fed now announced any federal funds rate target change. As mentioned in Chapter 6, at around 2:15 P.M., after every FOMC meeting, the Fed now announces whether the federal funds rate target has been raised, lowered, or kept the same. This move to greater transparency of Fed policy was followed by another such move when in February 1999, the Fed indicated that in the future it would announce the direction of bias to where the federal funds rate will head in the future. However, dissatisfaction with the confusion that the bias announcement created for market participants led the Fed to revise its policy, and starting in February 2000, the Fed switched to an announcement of a statement outlining the "balance of risks" in the future, whether toward higher inflation or toward a weaker economy. As a result of these announcements, the outcome of the FOMC meeting is now big news, and the media devotes much more attention to FOMC meetings because announced changes in the federal funds rate feed into changes in other interest rates that affect consumers and businesses.

INTERNATIONAL CONSIDERATIONS

The increasing importance of international trade to the American economy has brought international considerations to the forefront of Federal Reserve policymaking in recent years. By 1985, the strength of the dollar had contributed to a deterioration in American competitiveness with foreign businesses. In public pronouncements, Chairman Volcker and other Fed officials made it clear that the dollar was at too high a value and needed to come down. Because, as we will see in Chapter 12, expansionary monetary policy is one way to lower the value of the dollar, it is no surprise that the Fed engineered an acceleration in the growth rates of the monetary aggregates in 1985 and 1986 and that the value of the dollar declined. By 1987, policymakers at the Fed agreed that the dollar had fallen sufficiently, and sure enough, monetary growth in the United States slowed. These monetary policy actions by the Fed were encouraged by the process of **international policy coordination** (agreements among countries to enact policies cooperatively) that led to the Plaza Agreement in 1985 and the Louvre Accord in 1987 (see Box 6). International considerations, although not the primary focus of the Federal Reserve, are likely to be a major factor in the conduct of American monetary policy in the future.

MONETARY TARGETING IN OTHER COUNTRIES

To understand more about how monetary policy is conducted, we must compare our experiences with those of other nations. Here we examine how central banks in other countries have conducted monetary policy. Note that many of their experiences parallel those in the United States.

As we noted in our study of the conduct of U.S. monetary policy, the Federal Reserve has flirted with monetary targeting as its basic monetary policy strategy. And the Fed was not alone in adopting a monetary targeting framework in the 1970s; many other central banks did as well. Why did monetary targeting become so popular in the 1970s?[15]

The primary reason was the rise in inflation throughout the industrialized world. Central banks realized that using nominal interest rates as a target vari-

[15]The discussion here is based on Ben Bernanke and Frederic S. Mishkin, "Central Bank Behavior and the Strategy of Monetary Policy: Observations from Six Industrialized Countries," in *NBER Macroeconomics Annual, 1992,* ed. Oliver Blanchard and Stanley Fischer (Cambridge, Mass.: MIT Press, 1992), pp. 183–228.

BOX 6: GLOBAL

International Policy Coordination: The Plaza Agreement and the Louvre Accord

By 1985, the decrease in the competitiveness of American corporations as a result of the strong dollar was raising strong sentiment in Congress for restricting imports. This protectionist threat to the international trading system stimulated finance ministers and the heads of central banks from the Group of Five (G–5) industrial countries—the United States, the United Kingdom, France, West Germany, and Japan—to reach an agreement at New York's Plaza Hotel in September 1985 to bring down the value of the dollar. From September 1985 until the beginning of 1987, the value of the dollar did indeed undergo a substantial decline, falling by 35% on average relative to foreign currencies. At this point, there was growing controversy over the decline in the dollar, and another meeting of policymakers from the G–5 countries plus Canada took place in February 1987 at the Louvre Museum in Paris. There the policymakers agreed that exchange rates should be stabilized around the levels currently prevailing. Although the value of the dollar did continue to fluctuate relative to foreign currencies after the Louvre Accord, its downward trend had been checked as intended.

Because subsequent exchange rate movements were pretty much in line with the Plaza Agreement and the Louvre Accord, these attempts at international policy coordination have been considered successful. However, other aspects of the agreements were not adhered to by all signatories. For example, West German and Japanese policymakers agreed that their countries should pursue more expansionary policies by increasing government spending and cutting taxes, and the United States agreed to try to bring down its budget deficit. At that time, the United States was not particularly successful in lowering its deficit, and the Germans were reluctant to pursue expansionary policies because of their concerns about inflation.

able could lead to rising inflationary pressures. They believed that monetary aggregates could serve as a guidepost, or *nominal anchor,* that could promote a less inflationary monetary policy. Of probably even more importance, central banks believed that monetary targets could help send almost immediate signals to both the public and markets about the stance of monetary policy and the intentions of the policymakers to keep inflation in check. These signals might then help fix inflation expectations and help produce lower wage and price increases and thus less actual inflation.

We examine the experiences of four foreign countries—the United Kingdom, Canada, Germany, and Japan—to evaluate the extent to which monetary targeting has been a successful strategy for monetary policy.

United Kingdom

As in the United States, the British introduced monetary targeting in late 1973 in response to mounting concerns about inflation. The Bank of England targeted M3, a broader monetary target than the Fed used, but did not pursue it seriously: Announced targets were consistently overshot, and the Bank of England frequently revised its targets midstream or abandoned them entirely. The outcome was greater volatility of British monetary aggregates compared to American ones. After inflation accelerated in the late 1970s, Prime Minister Margaret Thatcher in 1980 introduced the Medium-Term Financial Strategy, which proposed a gradual deceleration of M3 growth. Unfortunately, the M3 targets ran into problems similar to those of the M1 targets in the United States: They were not reliable indicators of the tightness of monetary policy. After 1983, arguing that financial innovation was wreaking havoc with the relationship between M3 and national income, the Bank of England began to deemphasize M3 in favor of a narrower monetary aggregate, M0 (the monetary base). The target for M3 was temporarily suspended in October 1985 and was completely dropped in 1987, and monetary targets were abandoned altogether when the nation tied its exchange rate to the deutsche mark and became part of the European Monetary System (EMS) in October 1990.

Canada

The Canadian experience with monetary policy closely parallels that of the United States. This is not surprising given the strong ties between the two economies and the fact that the value of the Canadian dollar has been closely linked to the U.S dollar.

In response to rising inflation in the early 1970s, the Bank of Canada introduced a program of "monetary gradualism" under which M1 growth would be controlled within a gradually falling target range. Monetary gradualism was no more successful in Canada than the initial attempts at monetary targeting in the United States and the United Kingdom. By 1978, only three years after monetary targeting had begun, the Bank of Canada began to distance itself from this strategy out of concern for the exchange rate. Because of the conflict with exchange rate goals, as well as the uncertainty about M1 as a reliable guide to monetary policy, the M1 targets were abandoned in November 1982. From November 1982 to January 1988, the Bank of Canada pursued a monetary policy strategy without an explicit nominal anchor, but in January 1988, John Crow, the governor (head) of the Bank of Canada, announced that the bank would subsequently pursue an objective of price stability.

Germany

Germany's central bank, the Bundesbank, also responded to rising inflation in the early 1970s by adopting monetary targets in 1975. The monetary aggregate chosen was a narrow one known as *central bank money*, the sum of currency in circulation and bank deposits weighted by the 1974 required reserve ratios. The Bundesbank has allowed growth outside of its target ranges for periods of two to three years, and overshoots of its targets have subsequently been reversed. The primary reason for allowing deviations from its targets has been exchange rate considerations, which have been important to international agreements such as the European Monetary System, the Plaza Agreement, and the Louvre Accord. In 1988, the Bundesbank switched targets from central bank money to M3. German monetary policy using monetary targeting has been quite successful in maintaining a low and stable inflation rate.

The reunification of Germany in 1990 created some difficult problems for monetary policy. The Bundesbank was torn between trying to restrain the inflationary pressures created by reunification and keeping its exchange rate in line with those in other European countries. These strains contributed to an exchange rate crisis in Europe in September 1992, which will be discussed further in Chapter 13. The Bundesbank continued to subscribe to monetary targeting until it became part of The European System of Central Banks in January 1999, but recent research suggests that its commitment may have been weaker than its rhetoric suggested.[16]

---

[16]See Richard Clarida and Mark Gertler, "How the Bundesbank Conducts Monetary Policy," National Bureau of Economic Research Working Paper No. 5581, May 1996.

Japan

The increase in oil prices in late 1973 was a major shock for Japan, which experienced a huge jump in the inflation rate to greater than 20% in 1974—a surge facilitated by money growth in 1973 in excess of 20%. The Bank of Japan, like the other central banks discussed here, began to pay more attention to money growth rates. In 1978, the Bank of Japan began to announce "forecasts" at the beginning of each quarter for M2 + CDs. Although the Bank of Japan was not officially committed to monetary targeting, monetary policy appeared to be more money-focused after 1978. For example, after the second oil price shock in 1979, the Bank of Japan quickly reduced M2 + CDs growth, rather than allowing it to shoot up as occurred after the first oil shock. The Bank of Japan conducted monetary policy with operating procedures that are similar in many ways to those that the Federal Reserve has used in the United States. The Bank of Japan uses the interest rate in the Japanese interbank market (which has a function similar to that of the federal funds market in the United States) as its daily operating target, just as the Fed has done.

The Bank of Japan's monetary policy performance during the 1978–1987 period was much better than the Fed's. Money growth in Japan slowed gradually, beginning in the mid–1970s, and was much less variable than in the United States. The outcome was a more rapid braking of inflation and an average inflation rate that was lower in Japan. In addition, these excellent results on inflation were achieved with lower variability in real output in Japan than in the United States. The success of Japanese monetary policy in the 1978–1987 period using an interest rate as an operating target, in contrast to the lack of success in the 1970–1979 period in the United States when the Fed used a similar operating procedure, suggests that using an interest rate as an operating target is not necessarily a barrier to successful monetary policy. More important might be a commitment to a low inflation rate, something that was true for the Bank of Japan in this period.

In parallel with the United States, financial innovation and deregulation in Japan began to reduce the usefulness of the M2 + CDs monetary aggregate as an indicator of monetary policy. Because of concerns about the appreciation of the yen, the Bank of Japan significantly increased the rate of money growth from 1987 to 1989. Many observers blame speculation in Japanese land and stock prices (the so-called bubble economy) on the increase in money growth, and to reduce this speculation, in 1989 the Bank of Japan switched to a tighter monetary policy aimed at slower money growth. The aftermath has been a substantial decline in land and stock prices and the collapse of the bubble economy.

Lessons from Monetary Targeting Experiences

There are several lessons to be drawn from the experience with monetary targeting in the four countries and the United States. First, successful use of monetary targeting seems to require that the central bank pursue its targeting strategy seriously. Countries like the United States, Canada, and especially the United Kingdom were unable to use monetary targeting to bring inflation under control because the procedures they used to implement the targets did not imply a strong commitment to the strategy and they consistently overshot their monetary targets. Germany and Japan, by contrast, were more successful in using monetary aggregates to keep inflation in check. This did not mean that the Bundesbank and the Bank of Japan always met their targets; more critical to their success was that they subsequently reversed overshoots of the targets. A further lesson from the Japanese experience is that the success of monetary targeting can be achieved with operating procedures that focus on interest rates as the operating target. The final lesson is that the breakdown in the relationship between monetary aggregates and the goal variables, nominal GDP and inflation, in many countries made the monetary targeting strategy untenable. As the former governor of the Bank of Canada, John Crow, is said to have stated, "We didn't abandon monetary aggregates; they abandoned us."

THE NEW INTERNATIONAL TREND IN MONETARY POLICY STRATEGY: INFLATION TARGETING

Although central banks have abandoned monetary targeting, the reasons they adopted it in the first place remain. Central banks still see the need to have a nominal anchor that will promote price stability. Another nominal anchor for monetary policy can be the foreign exchange rate. As we will see in Chapter 13, some countries have achieved low inflation by tying the value of their currency to the currency of a country with a good inflation record. However, the problem with this strategy is that, as shown in Chapter 13, with a fixed exchange rate, a country no longer exercises control over its own monetary policy and so cannot use monetary policy to respond to domestic shocks.

The search for a nominal anchor has led many countries to pursue inflation targeting as their basic monetary strategy. To understand what inflation targeting is all about, we look at the experience in three countries: New Zealand, which was the first to adopt this strategy; Canada; and the United Kingdom.[17]

New Zealand

As part of a general reform of the government's role in the economy, the New Zealand parliament in 1989 passed the Reserve Bank of New Zealand Act, which became effective on February 1, 1990. Besides increasing the independence of the central bank, the Reserve Bank of New Zealand, transforming it from one of the least independent to one of the most independent among the developed countries, the act also committed the Reserve Bank to the sole objective of price stability. The act stipulated that the minister of finance and the governor of the Reserve Bank should negotiate and make public a "policy targets agreement" that sets out the targets against which monetary policy performance will be evaluated. These agreements have specified numerical target ranges for inflation and the dates by which they were to be reached. An unusual feature of the New Zealand legislation is that the governor of the Reserve Bank is held personally accountable for the success of monetary policy. If the goals set forth in the policy targets agreement are not met, the governor is subject to dismissal.

The first policy targets agreement, signed by the minister of finance and the governor of the Reserve Bank on March 2, 1990, directed the Reserve Bank to

[17]The discussion here is based on Frederic S. Mishkin and Adam S. Posen, "Inflation Targeting: Lessons from Four Countries," Federal Reserve Bank of New York, *Economic Policy Review* 3 (1997): 9–110, and Ben S. Bernanke, Thomas Laubach, Frederic S. Mishkin, and Adam S. Posen, *Inflation Targeting: Lessons from the International Experience* (Princeton, N.J.: Princeton University Press, 1999).

achieve an annual inflation rate within the 0% to 2% range, and subsequent agreements stuck with this range until November 1996, when the upper limit was increased to 3%. As a result of tight monetary policy, the inflation rate was brought down from above 5% to below 2% by the end of 1992, but at the cost of a deep recession and a sharp rise in unemployment. Through 1998, inflation typically remained within the 0% to 2% range, with the exception of a brief period in 1995, when it exceeded the upper limit by a few tenths of a percentage point. (Under the Reserve Bank Act, the governor, Don Brash, could have been dismissed, but after parliamentary debate, he was retained in his job.) Since 1992, New Zealand's growth rate has on average been strong, with some years exceeding 5%, and unemployment has come down significantly.

Canada

On February 26, 1991, a joint announcement by the minister of finance and the governor of the Bank of Canada established formal inflation targets. The target ranges were 2% to 4% by the end of 1992, 1.5% to 3.5% by June 1994, and 1% to 3% by December 1996. After the new government took office in late 1993, the target range was set at 1% to 3% starting December 1995 and has been kept there by subsequent governments. Canadian inflation has also fallen dramatically since the adoption of inflation targets, from above the 5% level in 1991 to within the target range of 1% to 3% since 1995. However, as in New Zealand, this decline was not without cost: Unemployment soared beyond the 10% level from 1991 until 1994 but has since fallen.

United Kingdom

When the United Kingdom left the European Monetary System after the speculative attack on the pound in September 1992 (more on this in Chapter 13), the British decided to turn to inflation targets to replace the exchange rate as the nominal anchor. As you may recall from Chapter 6, the central bank in the United Kingdom, the Bank of England, at that time did not have statutory authority over monetary policy; it could only make recommendations. Thus it was the chancellor of the Exchequer (the equivalent of the U.S. Treasury secretary) who announced an inflation target for the nation on October 8, 1992. Three weeks later, he "invited" the governor of the Bank of England to issue on a quarterly basis a report on the progress being made in achieving the target—an invitation that the governor accepted. The inflation target range was set at 1% to 4% until the next election (May 1997), with the intent that the inflation rate should settle down to the lower half of the range (below 2.5%). In 1997, the range was changed to a point target of 2.5%. Along with this inflation target, the government implemented the institutional changes mentioned in Chapter 6, which, along with the governor's report, gave the Bank of England a more independent voice on monetary policy, culminating in the granting of the power to set interest rates to the Bank in May 1997.

Before the adoption of inflation targets, inflation had already been falling in the United Kingdom, from a peak of 9% at the beginning of 1991 to 4% at the time of adoption. After a small upward movement in early 1993, inflation continued to fall until by the third quarter of 1994, it was at 2.2%, within the intended range articulated by the chancellor. Subsequently inflation rose, climbing above the 2.5% level by 1996, but has remained close to 2.5% since then. Meanwhile, growth of the U.K. economy has been strong, causing a reduction in the unemployment rate.

Lessons from Inflation Targeting Experiences

Several lessons can be drawn from the inflation targeting experiences in these three countries. First, as the New Zealand and Canadian experience indicates, inflation targets have not been able to produce a decline in inflation without a substantial decline in output and a rise in unemployment. Hopes that inflation targets would lead to disinflation at a lower cost have not been realized. Second, inflation targets have so far worked well in keeping inflation at moderate levels. One important advantage of inflation targets is that they keep the goal of price stability in the public's eye, thus making the central bank more accountable for keeping inflation low, which can also help reduce political pressures on the central bank to pursue inflationary monetary policy.

How successful will inflation targeting be at keeping inflation low in the countries examined here? It is still too early to tell. Nonetheless, many other countries have followed New Zealand, Canada, and the United Kingdom in adopting inflation targets, including Australia, Israel, Sweden, Switzerland, Brazil, Chile, South Africa, Poland, and Thailand. The growing popularity of inflation targeting indicates that it might become the wave of the future for central bank strategy.

THE PRACTICING FINANCIAL INSTITUTION MANAGER

Using a Fed Watcher

As we have seen, the most important player in the determination of the U.S. money supply and interest rates is the Federal Reserve. When the Fed wants to inject reserves into the system, it conducts open market purchases of bonds, which cause their prices to increase and their interest rates to fall, at least in the short term. If the Fed withdraws reserves from the system, it sells bonds, thereby depressing their price and raising their interest rates. From a longer-run perspective, if the Fed pursues an expansionary monetary policy with high money growth, inflation will rise and, as we saw in Chapter 4, interest rates will rise as well. Contractionary monetary policy is likely to lower inflation in the long run and lead to lower interest rates.

Knowing what actions the Fed might be taking can thus help financial institution managers predict the future course of interest rates with greater accuracy. Because, as we have seen, changes in interest rates have a major impact on a financial institution's profitability, the managers of these institutions are particularly interested in scrutinizing the Fed's behavior. To help in this task, managers hire so-called Fed watchers, experts on Federal Reserve behavior who may have worked in the Federal Reserve System and so have an insider's view of Federal Reserve operations.

Divining what the Fed is up to is by no means easy. Box 6 in Chapter 6 suggests that the Fed has a penchant for secrecy. The Fed does not disclose the content of the minutes of FOMC meetings at which it decides the course of monetary policy until six weeks after each meeting. In addition, the Fed does not provide information on the amount of certain transactions and frequently tries to obscure from the market whether it is injecting reserves into the banking system by making open market purchases and sales simultaneously.

Fed watchers, with their specialized knowledge of the ins and outs of the Fed, scrutinize the public pronouncements of Federal Reserve officials to get a feel for where monetary policy is heading. They also carefully study the data on past Federal Reserve actions and current events in the bond markets to determine what the Fed is up to.

If a Fed watcher tells a financial institution manager that Federal Reserve concerns about inflation are high and the Fed will pursue a tight monetary policy and raise short-term interest rates in the near future, the manager may decide immediately to acquire funds at the currently low interest rates in order to keep the cost of funds from rising. If the financial institution trades foreign exchange, the rise in interest rates and the attempt by the Fed to keep inflation down might lead the manager to instruct traders to purchase dollars in the foreign exchange market. As we will see in Chapter 12, these actions by the Fed would be likely to cause the value of the dollar to appreciate, so the purchase of dollars by the financial institution should lead to substantial profits.

If, conversely, the Fed watcher thinks that the Fed is worried about a weak economy and will thus pursue an expansionary policy and lower interest rates, the financial institution manager will take very different actions. Now the manager might instruct loan officers to make as many loans as possible so as to lock in the higher interest rates that the financial institution can earn currently. Or the manager might buy bonds, anticipating that interest rates will fall and their prices will rise, giving the institution a nice profit. The more expansionary policy is also likely to lower the value of the dollar in the foreign exchange market, so the financial institution manager might tell foreign exchange traders to buy foreign currencies and sell dollars in order to make a profit when the dollar falls in the future.

A Fed watcher who is right is a very valuable commodity to a financial institution. Successful Fed watchers are actively sought out by financial institutions and often earn high salaries, well into the six-figure range.

SUMMARY

1. The conduct of monetary policy involves actions that affect the Federal Reserve's balance sheet. Open market purchases lead to an expansion of reserves and deposits in the banking system and hence to an expansion of the monetary base and the money supply. An increase in discount loans leads to an expansion of reserves, thereby causing an expansion of the monetary base and the money supply.
2. A supply and demand analysis of the market for reserves yields the following results: (a) When the Fed makes an open market purchase, lowers the discount rate, or lowers reserve requirements, the federal funds rate declines; (b) when the Fed makes an open market sale, raises the discount rate, or raises reserve requirements, the federal funds rate rises.
3. The three basic tools of monetary policy are open market operations, discount policy, and reserve requirements. Open market operations are the primary tool used by the Fed to control the money supply because they occur at the initiative of the Fed, are flexible, are easily reversed, and can be implemented quickly.
4. The six basic goals of monetary policy are high employment, economic growth, price stability, interest-rate stability, stability of financial markets, and stability in foreign exchange markets.
5. By using intermediate and operating targets, a central bank like the Fed can more quickly judge whether its policies are on the right track and make midcourse corrections, rather than waiting to see the final outcome of its policies on such goals as employment and the price level. The Fed's policy tools directly affect its operating targets, which in turn affect the intermediate targets, which in turn affect the goals.
6. Because interest-rate and monetary aggregate targets are incompatible, a central bank must choose

between them on the basis of three criteria: measurability, controllability, and the ability to affect goal variables predictably. Unfortunately, these criteria do not establish an overwhelming case for one set of targets over another.

7. The historical record of the Fed's conduct of monetary policy reveals that the Fed has switched its operating targets many times, returning to a federal funds rate target in recent years.

8. In response to the rise in inflation in the early 1970s, central banks around the world also began to target monetary aggregates. Monetary targeting seems to have been most effective when it has been pursued seriously, which does not mean that targets are always met; more critical to success was a reversal of overshoots of the targets. Unfortunately, the breakdown in many countries of the relationship between monetary aggregates and the goal variables, nominal GDP and inflation, made the monetary targeting strategy untenable.

9. After disappointments with monetary targeting, the search for a nominal anchor has lead several countries to pursue inflation targeting as their basic monetary strategy. Although inflation targeting so far has been successful in keeping inflation rates low in countries that have adopted it, hopes that inflation targets would lead to disinflation at a lower cost have not been realized.

10. Because predicting the Federal Reserve's actions can help managers of financial institutions predict the course of future interest rates, which has a major impact on the financial institutions' profitability, such managers value the services of Fed watchers, experts on Federal Reserve behavior.

KEY TERMS

defensive open market operations, *p. 178*
discount rate, *p. 173*
discount window, *p. 180*
dynamic open market operations, *p. 178*
excess reserves, *p. 172*
federal funds rate, *p. 174*
free reserves, *p. 197*
intermediate target, *p. 189*
international policy coordination, *p. 202*
lender of last resort, *p. 181*
matched sale-purchase transaction (reverse repo), *p. 180*
monetary base, *p. 172*
natural rate of unemployment, *p. 186*
open market operations, *p. 173*
operating target, *p. 189*
primary dealer, *p. 179*
real bills doctrine, *p. 194*
repurchase agreement (repo), *p. 180*
required reserve ratio, *p. 172*
required reserves, *p. 172*
reserve requirements, *p. 174*
reserves, *p. 172*

QUESTIONS AND PROBLEMS

*1. "Unemployment is a bad thing, and the government should make every effort to eliminate it." Do you agree or disagree? Explain your answer.

2. Which goals of the Fed frequently conflict?

*3. "If the demand for money did not fluctuate, the Fed could pursue both a money supply target and an interest-rate target at the same time." Is this statement true, false, or uncertain? Explain your answer.

4. Classify each of the following as either an operating target or an intermediate target, and explain why.
   a. The three-month Treasury bill rate
   b. The monetary base
   c. M2

*5. What procedures can the Fed use to control the three-month Treasury bill rate? Why does control of this interest rate imply that the Fed will lose control of the money supply?

6. If the Fed has an interest-rate target, why will an increase in money demand lead to a rise in the money supply?

*7. "Interest rates can be measured more accurately and more quickly than the money supply. Hence an interest rate is preferred over the money supply as an intermediate target." Do you agree or disagree? Explain your answer.

8. Compare the monetary base to M2 on the grounds of controllability and measurability. Which do you prefer as an intermediate target? Why?

*9. "Discounting is no longer needed because the presence of the FDIC eliminates the possibility of bank panics." Is this statement true, false, or uncertain? Explain your answer.

10. The benefits of using Fed discount operations to prevent bank panics are straightforward. What are the costs?

***11.** Explain why the rise in the discount rate in 1920 led to a sharp decline in the money supply.

12. Excess reserves are frequently called idle reserves, suggesting that they are not useful. Does the episode of the rise in reserve requirements in 1936–1937 bear out this view?

***13.** How did the Fed's failure to perform its role as the lender of last resort contribute to the decline of the money supply in the 1930–1933 period?

14. Why is pegging the nominal interest rate problematic for a central bank?

***15.** How have the Federal Reserve's concerns about the value of the U.S. exchange rate affected monetary policy?

16. "The failure of the Fed to control the money supply in the 1970s and 1980s suggests that the Fed is not able to control the money supply." Do you agree or disagree? Explain your answer.

***17.** "When the economy enters a recession, either a free reserve target or an interest-rate target will lead to a slower rate of growth for the money supply." Explain why this statement is true. What does it say about the use of free reserves or interest rates as targets?

18. How can bank behavior and the Fed's behavior cause money supply growth to be procyclical (rising in booms and falling in recessions)?

***19.** Which is more likely to produce smaller fluctuations in the federal funds rate, a nonborrowed reserves target or a borrowed reserves target? Why?

20. Why might the Fed say that it wants to control the money supply but in reality not be serious about doing so?

WEB EXERCISES

Conduct of Monetary Policy: Tools Goals, and Targets

1. The Federal Open Market Committee (FOMC) meets about every six weeks to assess the state of the economy and to determine what actions the central bank should take. The minutes of these meetings are released after the next scheduled meeting. However, a brief press release is made available immediately. Find the schedule of minutes and press releases at http://www.federalreserve.gov/fomc/.

a. When was the last scheduled meeting of the FOMC? When is the next meeting?

b. Review the press release from the last meeting. What did the committee decide to do about short-term interest rates?

c. Review the most recently published meeting minutes. What areas of the economy seemed to be of most concern to the committee members?

2. It is possible to access other central bank websites to learn about their structure. One example is the European Central Bank (ECB). Go to http://www.ecb.int/. On the ECB home page, locate the link to the current exchange rate between the euro and the dollar. When the euro debuted in January 1999 it was valued at $1.18. What is it at now?

Part 4

Financial Markets

Chapter 8 The Money Markets

Preview

In January 2002, an interest-bearing checking account at Wachovia Bank paid less than 1% per year. This same money invested in a three-month Treasury bill would have paid 3.5%. It is no wonder that individuals, as well as businesses, have aggressively pursued alternatives to low-interest-rate bank accounts. One such alternative is provided by the money markets, which we first introduced in Chapter 2. Recall that money market securities are short-term, low-risk, and very liquid. Because of the high degree of safety and liquidity these securities exhibit, they are close to being money, hence their name.

The money markets have been active since the early 1800s but have become much more important since 1970, when interest rates rose above historic levels. In fact, the rise in short-term rates, coupled with a regulated ceiling on the rate that banks could pay for deposits, resulted in a rapid outflow of funds from financial institutions in the late 1970s and early 1980s. This outflow in turn caused many banks and savings and loans to fail. The industry regained its health only after massive changes were made to bank regulations with regard to money market interest rates.

This chapter carefully reviews the money markets and the securities that are traded there. In addition, we discuss why the money markets are important to our financial system.

THE MONEY MARKETS DEFINED

The term *money market* is actually a misnomer. Money—currency—is not traded in the money markets. Because the securities that do trade there are short-term and highly liquid, however, they are close to being money. Money market securities, which are discussed in detail later in this chapter, have three basic characteristics in common:

- They are usually sold in large denominations.
- They have low default risk.
- They mature in one year or less *from their original issue date.* Most money market instruments mature in less than 120 days.

Money market transactions do not take place in any one particular location or building. Instead, traders usually arrange purchases and sales between participants over the phone and complete them electronically. Because of this characteristic, money market securities usually have an active *secondary market.* This means that after the security has been sold initially, it is relatively easy to find buyers who will purchase it in the future. An active secondary market makes money market securities very flexible instruments to use to fill short-term financial needs.

Another characteristic of the money markets is that they are **wholesale markets.** This means that most transactions are very large, usually in excess of $1 million. The size of these transactions prevents most individual investors from participating directly in the money markets. Instead, dealers and brokers, operating in the trading rooms of large banks and brokerage houses, bring customers together. These traders will buy or sell $50 or $100 million in mere seconds—certainly not a job for the faint of heart!

As you may recall from Chapter 2, flexibility and innovation are two important characteristics of any financial market, and the money markets are no exception. Despite the wholesale nature of the money market, innovative securities and trading methods have been developed to give small investors access to money market securities. We will discuss these securities and their characteristics later in the chapter.

Why Do We Need the Money Markets?

In theory, the money markets should not be needed. The banking industry exists primarily to provide short-term loans and to accept short-term deposits. Banks should have an efficiency advantage in gathering information, an advantage that should eliminate the need for the money markets. Thanks to continuing relationships with customers, banks should be able to offer loans more cheaply than diversified markets, which must evaluate each borrower every time a new security is offered. Furthermore, short-term securities offered for sale in the money markets are neither as liquid nor as safe as deposits placed in banks and thrifts. Given the advantages that banks have, why do the money markets exist at all?

The banking industry exists primarily to mediate the asymmetric information problem between saver-lenders and borrower-spenders, and banks can earn profits by capturing economies of scale while providing this service. However, the banking industry is subject to more regulations and governmental costs than the money markets are. In situations where the asymmetric information problem is not severe, the money markets have a distinct cost advantage over banks in providing short-term funds.

Cost Advantages

Banks must put aside a portion of their deposits in the form of reserves that are held without interest at the Federal Reserve. Thus, for every dollar deposited, the bank can invest only between 90 to 97 cents.[1] This means that it must pay a lower interest rate to the depositor than if the full deposit could be reinvested.

Interest-rate regulations were a second competitive obstacle for banks. One of the principal purposes of the banking regulations of the 1930s was to reduce competition among banks. Without competition, regulators felt, banks were less likely to fail. The cost to consumers of the greater profits banks earned because of the lack of free market competition was justified by the greater economic stability that a healthy banking system would provide.

One way that banking profits were assured was by regulations that set a ceiling on the rate of interest that banks could pay for funds. The Glass-Steagall Act of 1933 prohibited payment of interest on checking accounts and limited the interest that could be paid on time deposits. The limits on interest rates were not particularly relevant until the late 1950s. The limits became especially troublesome to banks in the late 1970s and early 1980s when inflation pushed short-term interest rates above the level that banks could pay. Investors pulled their money out of banks and put it into money market security accounts offered by many brokerage firms. These new investors caused the money markets to grow rapidly.

Banks continue to provide valuable intermediation, as we will see in several later chapters. In some situations, however, the cost structure of the banking industry makes it unable to compete effectively in the market for short-term funds against the less restricted money markets.

THE PURPOSE OF THE MONEY MARKETS

The well-developed secondary market for money market instruments makes the money market an ideal place for a firm or financial institution to "warehouse" surplus funds for short periods of time until they are needed. Similarly, the money markets provide a low-cost source of funds to firms, the government, and intermediaries that need a short-term infusion of funds.

Most investors in the money market who are temporarily warehousing funds are ordinarily not trying to earn unusually high returns on their money market funds. Rather, they use the money market as an interim investment that provides a higher return than holding cash or money in banks. They may feel that market conditions are not right to warrant the purchase of additional stock, or they may expect interest rates to rise and hence not want to purchase bonds. It is important to keep in mind that holding idle surplus cash is expensive for an investor because cash balances earn no income for the owner. Idle cash represents an *opportunity cost* in terms of lost interest income. Recall from Chapter 4 that an asset's opportunity cost is the amount of interest sacrificed by not holding an alternative asset. The money markets provide a means to invest idle funds and to reduce this opportunity cost.

---

[1]The reserve requirement on nonpersonal time deposits with an original maturity of less than $1\frac{1}{2}$ years was reduced from 3% to 0% in December 1990.

Investment advisers often hold some funds in the money market so that they will be able to act quickly to take advantage of investment opportunities they identify. Most investment funds and financial intermediaries also hold money market securities to meet investment or deposit outflows.

The sellers of money market securities find that the money market provides a low-cost source of temporary funds. Table 1 shows the interest rates available on a variety of money market instruments sold by a variety of firms and institutions. For example, banks may issue federal funds (we will define the money market securities later in this chapter) to obtain funds in the money market to meet short-term reserve requirement shortages. The government funds a large portion of the U.S. debt with Treasury bills. Finance companies like GMAC (General Motors Acceptance Company, the financing division of General Motors) may enter the money market to raise the funds that it uses to make car loans.

Why do corporations and the U.S. government sometimes need to get their hands on funds quickly? The primary reason is that cash inflows and outflows are rarely synchronized. Government tax revenues, for example, usually come only at certain times of the year, but expenses are incurred all year long. The government can borrow short-term funds that it will pay back when it receives tax revenues. Businesses also face problems caused by revenues and expenses occurring at different times. The money markets provide an efficient, low-cost way of solving these problems.

WHO PARTICIPATES IN THE MONEY MARKETS?

An obvious way to discuss the players in the money market would be to list those who borrow and those who lend. The problem with this approach is that most money market participants operate on both sides of the market. For example, any large bank will borrow aggressively in the money market by selling large commercial CDs. At the same time, it will lend short-term funds to businesses through its commercial lending departments. Nevertheless, we can identify the primary money market players—the U.S. Treasury, the Federal Reserve System, commercial banks, businesses, investments and securities firms, and individuals—and discuss their roles (summarized in Table 2).

U.S. Treasury Department

The U.S. Treasury Department is unique because it is always a demander of money market funds and never a supplier. The U.S. Treasury is the largest of all money market borrowers worldwide. It issues Treasury bills (often called T-bills) and other securities that are popular with other money market participants. Short-term issues enable the government to raise funds until tax revenues are received. The Treasury also issues T-bills to replace maturing issues.

Federal Reserve System

The Federal Reserve is the Treasury's agent for the distribution of all government securities. The Fed holds vast quantities of Treasury securities that it sells if it believes that the money supply should be reduced. Similarly, the Fed will purchase Treasury securities if it believes that the money supply should be expanded. The Fed's responsibility for the money supply makes it the single most influential participant in the U.S. money market. The Federal Reserve's role in con-

TABLE 1 Sample Money Market Rates, January 2, 2002

Instrument	Interest Rate (%)
Prime rate	4.75
Federal funds	2.5
Commercial paper	1.75
Certificate of deposit	1.8
Banker's acceptance	1.91
London interbank offer rate	1.87
Foreign prime rates	
Canada	4.0
Germany	3.25
Japan	1.375
Treasury bills	1.71
Merrill Lynch Ready Assets Trust	1.94

Source: Wall Street Journal, January 2, 2002, p. C14.

trolling the economy through open market operations was discussed further in Chapters 6 and 7.

Commercial Banks

Commercial banks hold a larger percentage of U.S. government securities than any other group of financial institutions, approximately 12%. This is partly because of regulations that limit the investment opportunities available to banks. Specifically, banks are prohibited from owning risky securities, such as stocks or corporate bonds. There are no restrictions against holding Treasury securities because of their low risk and liquidity.

Banks are also the major issuer of negotiable certificates of deposit (CDs), banker's acceptances, federal funds, and repurchase agreements (we will discuss these securities in the next section). In addition to using money market securities to help manage their own liquidity, many banks trade on behalf of their customers.

Not all commercial banks deal for their customers in the secondary money market. The ones that do are among the largest in the country and are often referred to as *money center banks.* The biggest money center banks include Citibank, Bank of America, Chemical Bank, Morgan Guaranty, and Chase Manhattan.

Businesses

Many businesses buy and sell securities in the money markets. Such activity is usually limited to major corporations because of the large dollar amounts involved. As discussed earlier, the money markets are used extensively by businesses both to warehouse surplus funds and to raise short-term funds. We will discuss the specific money market securities that businesses issue later in this chapter.

Investment and Securities Firms

The other financial institutions that participate in the money markets are listed in Table 2.

Investment Companies Large diversified brokerage firms are active in the money markets. The largest of these include Bear Stearns, Salomon Smith Barney,

TABLE 2 Money Market Participants

Participant	Role
U.S. Treasury Department	Sells U.S. Treasury securities to fund the national debt
Federal Reserve System	Buys and sells U.S. Treasury securities as its primary method of controlling the money supply
Businesses	Buy and sell various short-term securities as a regular part of their cash management
Commercial banks	Buy U.S. Treasury securities; sell certificates of deposit and make short-term loans; offer individual investors accounts that invest in money market securities
Investment companies (brokerage firms)	Trade on behalf of commercial accounts
Finance companies (commercial leasing companies)	Lend funds to individuals
Insurance companies (property and casualty insurance companies)	Maintain liquidity needed to meet unexpected demands
Pension funds	Maintain funds in money market instruments in readiness for investment in stocks and bonds
Individuals	Buy money market mutual funds
Money market mutual funds	Allow small investors to participate in the money market by aggregating their funds to invest in large-denomination money market securities

Merrill Lynch, PaineWebber, and Morgan Stanley. The primary function of these dealers is to "make a market" for money market securities by maintaining an inventory from which to buy or sell. These firms are very important to the liquidity of the money market because they ensure that both buyers and sellers can readily market their securities. We discuss investment companies in Chapter 21.

Finance Companies Finance companies raise funds in the money markets primarily by selling commercial paper. They then lend the funds to consumers for the purchase of durable goods such as cars, boats, or home improvements. Finance companies and related firms are discussed in Chapter 20.

Insurance Companies Property and casualty insurance companies must maintain liquidity because of their unpredictable need for funds. When hurricane Fran hit North Carolina in 1996, for example, insurance companies paid out billions of dollars in benefits to policyholders. To meet this demand for funds, the insurance companies sold some of their money market securities to raise cash. Insurance companies are discussed in Chapter 19.

Pension Funds Pension funds invest a portion of their cash in the money markets so that they can take advantage of investment opportunities that they may identify in the stock or bond markets. Like insurance companies, pension funds must have sufficient liquidity to meet their obligations. However, because their obligations are reasonably predictable, large money market security holdings are unnecessary. Pension funds are discussed in Chapter 19.

Individuals

When inflation rose in the late 1970s, the interest rates that banks were offering on deposits became unattractive to individual investors. At this same time, brokerage houses began promoting money market mutual funds, which paid much higher rates.

Banks could not stop large amounts of cash from moving out to mutual funds because regulations capped the rate they could pay on deposits. To combat this flight of money from banks, the authorities revised the regulations. Banks quickly raised rates in an attempt to recapture individual investors' dollars. This halted the rapid movement of funds, but money market mutual funds remain a popular individual investment option. The advantage of mutual funds is that they give investors with relatively small amounts of cash to invest access to large-denomination securities. We will discuss money market mutual funds in more depth later in this chapter.

MONEY MARKET INSTRUMENTS

A variety of money market instruments are available to meet the diverse needs of market participants. One security will be perfect for one investor; a different security may be best for another. Here we gain a greater understanding of money market security characteristics and how money market participants use them to manage their cash.

Treasury Bills

To finance the national debt, the U.S. Treasury Department issues a variety of debt securities. The most widely held liquid security is the Treasury bill. Treasury bills have 91-day, 182-day, or 12-month maturities. The Treasury bill had a minimum denomination of $10,000 until 1998, at which time new $1000 T-bills became available. The Fed has set up a direct purchase option that individuals may use to purchase Treasury bills over the Internet. First available in September 1998, this method of buying securities represented an effort to make Treasury securities more widely available.

The government does not actually pay interest on Treasury bills. Instead they are issued at a discount from par (their value at maturity). The investor's yield comes from the increase in the value of the security between the time it was purchased and the time it matures.

Application Discounting the Price of Treasury Securities to Pay the Interest

Most money market securities do not pay interest. Instead, the investor pays less for the security than it will be worth when it matures, and the increase in price provides a return. This is called **discounting** and is common to short-term securities because they often mature before the issuer can mail out interest checks. (We discussed discounting in Chapter 3.)

The yield on an investment is found by computing the increase in value in the security during its holding period and dividing by the amount paid for the security. This yield is converted into an annual yield by multiplying by 365 divided by the number of days until maturity. This gives the following equation:

$$i_{yt} = \frac{F - P}{P} \times \frac{365}{n} \tag{1}$$

where

i_{yt} = annualized yield on the investment
F = face value (amount paid to the investor at maturity)
P = purchase price
n = number of days until maturity

EXAMPLE 1: Discounting

You decide to purchase a 91-day Treasury bill for $9850. When it matures, the bill will be worth $10,000. What is the bill's annualized yield?

Solution

You would earn 6.11% on the 91-day investment in the Treasury bill.

$$i_{yt} = \frac{F - P}{P} \times \frac{365}{n}$$

where

$F =$ face value (amount paid to investor at maturity) $= \$10{,}000$

$P =$ purchase price $= \$9850$

$n =$ number of days until maturity $= 91$

Thus

$$i_{yt} = \frac{\$10{,}000 - \$9850}{\$9850} \times \frac{365}{91} = 0.0611 = 6.11\%$$

EXAMPLE 2: Discounting

Now suppose that you decide to sell the Treasury bill 31 days before it matures. By selling before it matures, you will receive $9948. What is the bill's annualized yield?

Solution

On this 60-day investment in the Treasury bill, you would earn 6.05%.

$$i_{yt} = \frac{F - P}{P} \times \frac{365}{n}$$

where

$F =$ face value (in this case amount paid to investor before maturity) $= \$9948$

$P =$ purchase price $= \$9850$

$n =$ number of days security held $= 91 - 31$ $= 60$

Thus

$$i_{yt} = \frac{\$9948 - \$9850}{\$9850} \times \frac{365}{60} = 0.0605 = 6.05\%$$

Risk Treasury bills have virtually zero default risk because even if the government ran out of money, it could simply print more to pay them off when they mature. The risk of unexpected changes in inflation is also low because of the short term to maturity. The market for Treasury bills is extremely deep and liquid. A **deep market** is one with many different buyers and sellers. A **liquid market** is one in which securities can be bought and sold quickly and with low transaction costs. Investors in markets that are deep and liquid have little risk that they will not be able to sell their securities when they want to.

The budget debates in early 1996 almost caused the government to default on its debt, despite the long-held belief that such a thing could not happen. Congress attempted to force President Clinton to sign a budget bill by refusing to approve a temporary spending package. If the stalemate had lasted much longer, we would have witnessed the first-ever U.S. government security default. We can only speculate what the long-term effect on interest rates might have been if the market decided to add a default risk premium to all government securities.

Find information about upcoming auctions, results, debt buyback operations, and historical information at www.publicdebt.treas.gov/of/ofaucrt.htm

Treasury Bill Auctions Every Thursday, the Treasury announces how many 91-day (13-week) and 182-day (26-week) Treasury bills it will offer for sale. Buyers must submit bids by the following Monday, and awards are made the following morning. The 52-week Treasury bills are offered similarly, but only once a month. The Treasury accepts the bids offering the highest price. The highest bidder is satisfied first. Subsequent bidders are satisfied in the order of their bid amount until the total amount of securities is distributed. Note that this implies that not everyone at the auction pays the same price for the securities.

As an alternative to the **competitive bidding** procedure just outlined, the Treasury also permits **noncompetitive bidding.** When competitive bids are offered, investors state both the amount of securities desired and the price they are willing to pay. By contrast, noncompetitive bids include only the amount of securities the investor wants. The price is set as the weighted average of the competitive bids accepted. For example, if 30% of the issue was sold for \$98 per \$100 of par value, 50% for \$97, and the remaining 20% for \$96, the weighted average would be

$$\text{Weighted average price} = 0.30(\$98) + 0.50(\$97) + 0.20(\$96) = \$97.10$$

Bidders submitting noncompetitive bids would pay \$97.10 per \$100 of Treasury bills purchased.

Table 3 presents the results of a typical Treasury auction as reported in the *Wall Street Journal.* About 90% of the bids submitted to the Fed for 4-week securities were accepted at the low price. A relatively small number of bids were submitted noncompetitively.

In 1976, the Treasury switched the entire marketable portion of the federal debt over to **book entry** securities, replacing engraved pieces of paper. In a book entry system, ownership of Treasury securities is documented only in the Fed's computer: Essentially, a ledger entry replaces the actual security. This procedure reduces the cost of issuing Treasury securities as well as the cost of transferring them as they are bought and sold in the secondary market.

The Treasury auction of securities is supposed to be highly competitive and fair. To ensure proper levels of competition, no one dealer is allowed to purchase more than 35% of any one issue. About 40 primary dealers regularly participate

TABLE 3 Treasury Bill Auction Results, December 19, 2001

	4-Week
Applications	\$30,119,736,000
Accepted bids	\$12,000,276,000
Accepted at low price	90.31%
Accepted noncompetitively	\$24,736,000
Auction price	99.868 (1.70%)

Source: Wall Street Journal, December 19, 2001, p. C16.

in the auction. Salomon Smith Barney was caught violating the limits on the percentage of one issue a dealer may purchase, with serious consequences. (See Box 1 on the Salomon Smith Barney scandal.)

Treasury Bill Interest Rates Treasury bills are very close to being risk-free. As expected for a risk-free security, the interest rate earned on Treasury bill securities is among the lowest in the economy. Investors in Treasury bills have found that in some years, their earnings did not even compensate them for changes in purchasing power due to inflation. Figure 1 shows the interest rate on Treasury bills and the inflation rate over the period 1973–2002. As discussed in Chapter 3, the *real rate* of interest has occasionally been less than zero. For example, in 1973–1977 and again in 1990–1991, the inflation rate matched or exceeded the earnings on T-bills. Clearly, the T-bill is not an investment to be used for anything but temporary storage of excess funds, because it barely keeps up with inflation.

Federal Funds

Federal funds are short-term funds transferred (loaned or borrowed) between financial institutions, usually for a period of one day. The term *federal funds* (or *fed funds*) is misleading. Fed funds really have nothing to do with the federal government. The term is a holdover from when the fed funds market began in the 1920s and banks with excess reserves loaned them to banks that needed them. The interest rate for borrowing these funds was close to the rate that the Federal Reserve charged on discount loans.

Purpose of Fed Funds The Federal Reserve has set minimum reserve requirements that all banks must maintain to ensure that they have adequate liquidity. To meet these reserve requirements, banks must maintain a certain percentage of their total deposits with the Federal Reserve. The main purpose for fed funds is to provide banks with an immediate infusion of reserves should they be short. Banks can borrow directly from the Federal Reserve, but many prefer to borrow from

BOX 1

Treasury Bill Auctions Go Haywire

Every Thursday, the Treasury announces how many 91-day and 182-day Treasury bills it will offer for sale. Buyers must submit bids by the following Monday, and awards are made the next morning. Fifty-two-week Treasury bills are offered similarly once a month. The Treasury accepts the bids offering the highest price.

The Treasury auction of securities is supposed to be highly competitive and fair. To ensure proper levels of competition, no one dealer is allowed to purchase more than 35% of any one issue. About 40 primary dealers regularly participate in the auction.

In 1991, the disclosure that Salomon Smith Barney had broken the rules to corner the market cast the fairness of the auction in doubt. Salomon Smith Barney purchased 35% of the Treasury securities in its own name by submitting a relatively high bid. It then bought additional securities in the names of its customers, often without their knowledge or consent. Salomon then bought the securities from the customers. As a result of these transactions, Salomon cornered the market and was able to charge a monopolylike premium. The investigation of Salomon Smith Barney revealed that during one auction in May 1991, the brokerage managed to gain control of 94% of an $11 billion issue. During the scandal that followed this disclosure, John Gutfreund, the firm's chairman, and several other top executives with Salomon retired. The Treasury has instituted new rules since then to ensure that the market remains competitive.

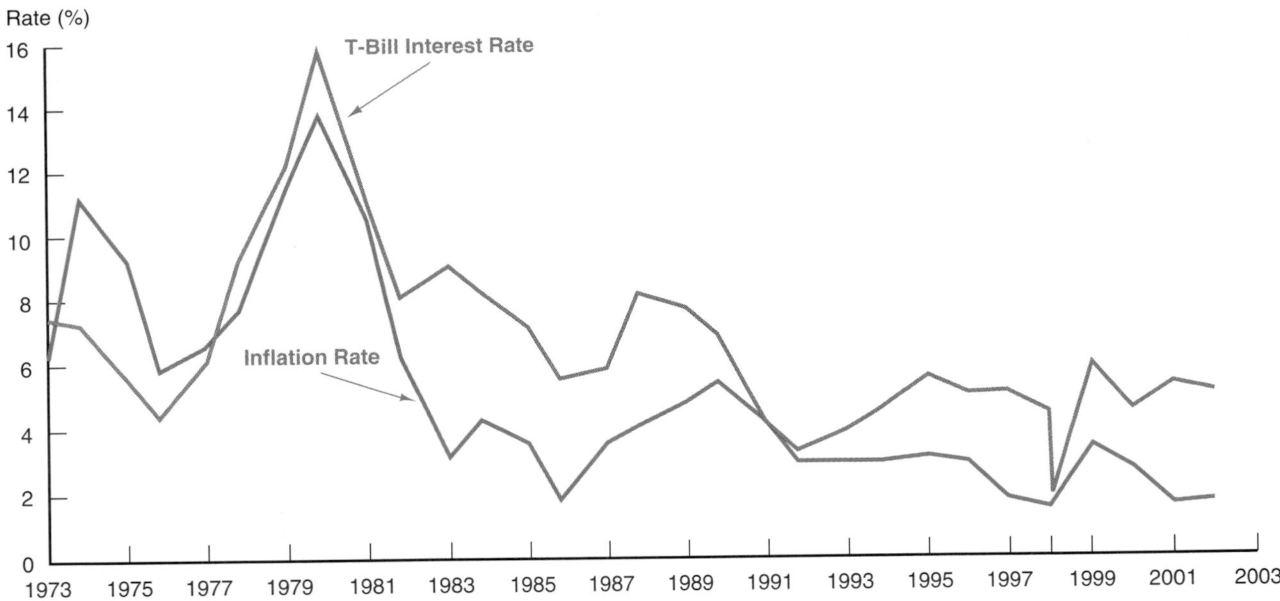

FIGURE 1 Treasury Bill Interest Rate and the Inflation Rate, January 1973–January 2002

Source: ftp://ftp.bls.gov/special.requests/cpi/cpiai.txt

other banks so that they do not alert the Fed to any liquidity problems. The reason that banks like to lend in the fed funds market is that money held at the Federal Reserve in excess of what is required does not earn any interest. So even though the interest rate on fed funds is low, it beats the alternative. One indication of the popularity of fed funds is that on a typical day a quarter of a trillion dollars in fed funds will change hands. The calculation of reserve requirements is discussed in "The Practicing Financial Institutional Manager" in Chapter 18.

Terms for Fed Funds Fed funds are usually overnight investments. Banks analyze their reserve position on a daily basis and either borrow or invest in fed funds, depending on whether they have excess or deficit reserves. Suppose that a bank finds that it has $50 million in excess reserves. It will call its correspondent banks (banks that have reciprocal accounts) to see if they need reserves that day. The bank will sell its excess funds to the bank that offers the highest rate. Once an agreement has been reached, the bank with excess funds will wire the funds to the borrowing bank. This involves telecommunicating to the Federal Reserve bank instructions to take funds out of the seller's account at the Fed and deposit the funds in the borrower's account. The next day, the funds are transferred back, and the process begins again.

Most fed funds borrowings are unsecured. Typically, the entire agreement is supported only by oral communication between buyer and seller.

Federal Funds Interest Rates The forces of supply and demand set the fed funds interest rate. This is a competitive market that analysts watch closely for indications of what is happening to short-term rates. The fed funds rate reported by the press is known as the *effective rate,* which is defined in the *Federal Reserve Bulletin* as the weighted average of rates on trades through New York brokers.

The Federal Reserve cannot directly control fed funds rates. It can and does indirectly influence them by adjusting the level of reserves available to banks in the system. The Fed can increase the amount of money in the financial system by buying securities, as was demonstrated in Chapter 7. When investors sell securities to the Fed, the proceeds are deposited in their banks' accounts at the Federal Reserve. These deposits increase the supply of reserves in the financial system and lower interest rates. If the Fed removes reserves by selling securities, fed funds rates will increase. The Fed will often announce its intention to raise or lower the fed funds rate in advance. Though these rates directly affect few businesses or consumers, analysts consider them an important indicator of the direction in which the Federal Reserve wants the economy to move. Figure 2 compares the fed funds rate with the T-bill rate. Clearly, the two track together.

Repurchase Agreements

Repurchase agreements (repos) work much the same as fed funds except that nonbanks can participate. A firm can sell Treasury securities in a repurchase agreement whereby the firm agrees to buy back the securities at a specified future date. Most repos have a very short term, the most common being for 3 to 14 days. There is a market, however, for one- to three-month repos.

The Use of Repurchase Agreements Government securities dealers frequently engage in repos. The dealer may sell the securities to a bank with the promise to buy the securities back the next day. This makes the repo essentially a short-

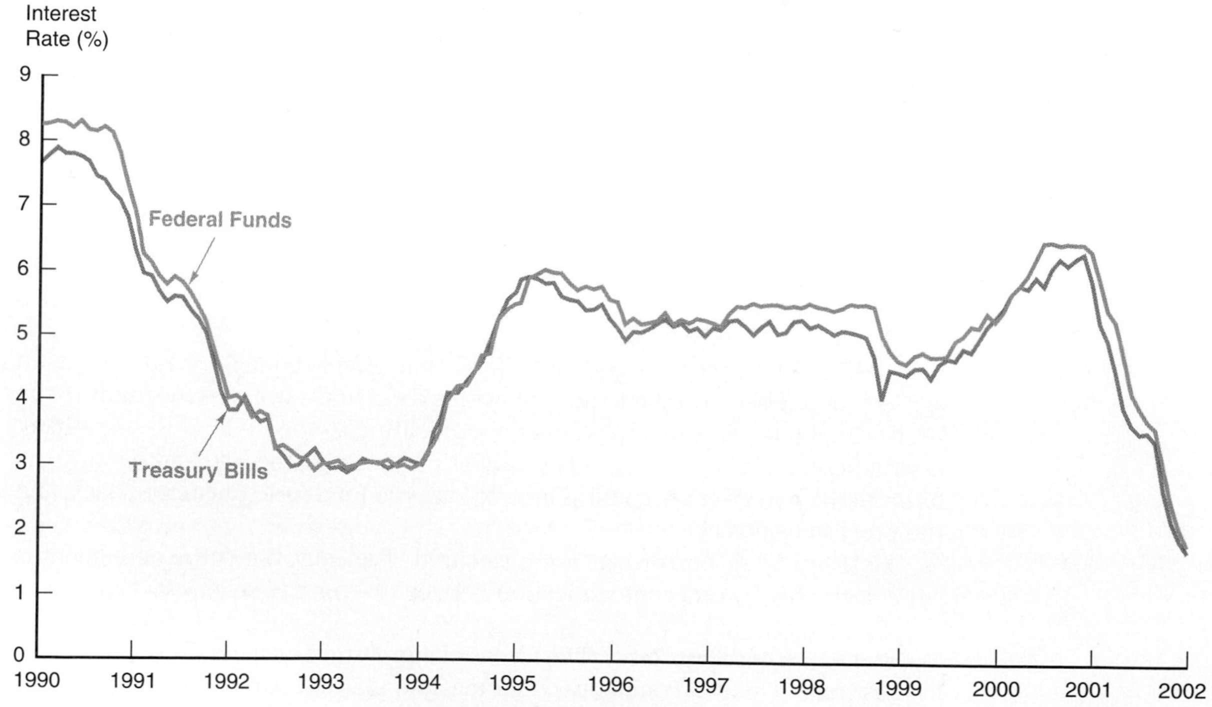

FIGURE 2 Federal Funds and Treasury Bill Interest Rates, January 1990–January 2002

Source: http://www.federalreserve.gov/releases

term collateralized loan. Securities dealers use the repo to manage their liquidity and to take advantage of anticipated changes in interest rates.

The Federal Reserve also uses repos in conducting monetary policy. We presented the details of monetary policy in Chapter 7. Recall that the conduct of monetary policy typically requires that the Fed adjust bank reserves on a temporary basis. To accomplish this adjustment, the Fed will buy or sell Treasury securities in the repo market. The maturities of Federal Reserve repos never exceed 15 days.

Interest Rate on Repos Because repos are collateralized with Treasury securities, they are usually low-risk investments and therefore have low interest rates. Though rare, losses have occurred in these markets. For example, in 1985, ESM Government Securities and Bevill, Bresler, and Schulman declared bankruptcy. These firms had used the same securities as collateral for more than one loan. The resulting losses to municipalities that had purchased the repos exceeded $500 million. Such losses also caused the failure of the state-insured thrift insurance system in Ohio.

Negotiable Certificates of Deposit

A negotiable certificate of deposit is a bank-issued security that documents a deposit and specifies the interest rate and the maturity date. Because a maturity date is specified, a CD is a **term security** as opposed to a **demand deposit:** Term securities have a specified maturity date; demand deposits can be withdrawn at any time. A negotiable CD is also called a **bearer instrument.** This means that whoever holds the instrument at maturity receives the principal and interest. The CD can be bought and sold until maturity.

Terms of Negotiable Certificates of Deposit The denominations of negotiable certificates of deposit range from $100,000 to $10 million. Few negotiable CDs are denominated less than $1 million. The reason that these instruments are so large is that dealers have established the round lot size to be $1 million. A round lot is the minimum quantity that can be traded without incurring higher than normal brokerage fees.

Negotiable CDs typically have a maturity of one to four months. Some have six-month maturities, but there is little demand for ones with longer maturities.

History of the CD Citibank issued the first large certificates of deposit in 1961. The bank offered the CD to counter the long-term trend of declining demand deposits at large banks. Corporate treasurers were minimizing their cash balances and investing their excess funds in safe, income-generating money market instruments such as T-bills. The attraction of the CD was that it paid a market interest rate. There was a problem, however. The rate of interest that banks could pay on CDs was restricted by Regulation Q. As long as interest rates on most securities were low, this regulation did not affect demand. But when interest rates rose above the level permitted by Regulation Q, the market for these certificates of deposit evaporated. In response, banks began offering the certificates overseas, where they were exempt from Regulation Q limits. In 1970, Congress amended Regulation Q to exempt certificates of deposit over $100,000. By 1972, the CD represented approximately 40 percent of all bank deposits. The certificate of deposit is now the second most popular money market instrument, behind only the T-bill.

Interest Rate on CDs Figure 3 plots the interest rate on negotiable CDs along with that on T-bills. The rates paid on negotiable CDs are negotiated between the bank and the customer. They are similar to the rate paid on other money market instruments because the level of risk is relatively low. Large money center banks can offer rates a little lower than other banks because many investors in the market believe that the government would never allow one of the nation's largest banks to fail. This belief makes these banks' obligations less risky. CD rates tend to be slightly above the T-bill rate because of the slightly greater chance of default.

Commercial Paper

Find detailed information on commercial paper, including criteria used for calculating commercial paper interest rates and historical discount rates at www.federalreserve.gov/releases/CP/

Commercial paper securities are unsecured promissory notes, issued by corporations, that mature in no more than 270 days. Because these securities are unsecured, only the largest and most creditworthy corporations issue commercial paper. The interest rate the corporation is charged reflects the firm's level of risk.

Terms and Issuance Commercial paper always has an original maturity of less than 270 days. This is to avoid the need to register the security issue with the Securities and Exchange Commission. (To be exempt from SEC registration, the issue must have an original maturity of less than 270 days and be intended for current transactions.) Most commercial paper actually matures in 20 to 45 days. Like T-bills, most commercial paper is issued on a discounted basis.

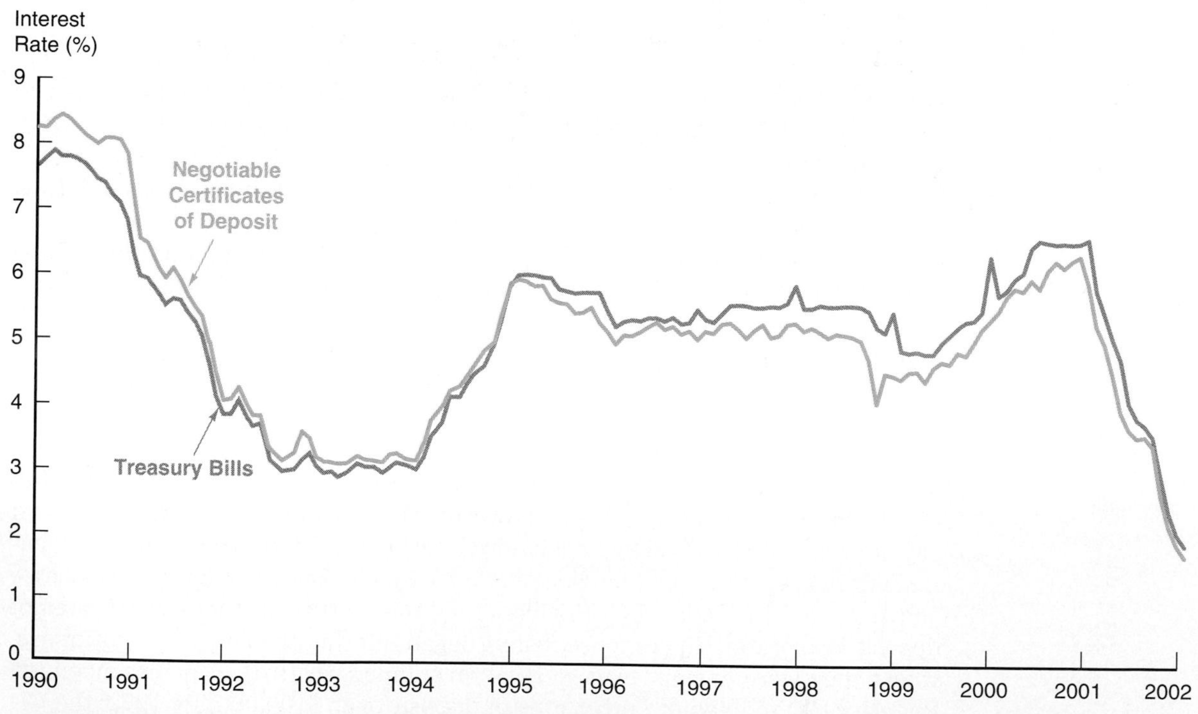

FIGURE 3 Interest Rates on Negotiable Certificates of Deposit and on Treasury Bills, January 1990–January 2002

Source: http://www.federalreserve.gov/releases

About 60% of commercial paper is sold directly by the issuer to the buyer. The balance is sold by dealers in the commercial paper market. A strong secondary market for commercial paper does not exist. A dealer will redeem commercial paper if a purchaser has a dire need for cash, though this is generally not necessary.

History of Commercial Paper Commercial paper has been used in various forms since the 1920s. In 1969, a tight-money environment caused bank holding companies to issue commercial paper to finance new loans. In response, to keep control over the money supply, the Federal Reserve imposed reserve requirements on bank-issued commercial paper in 1970. These reserve requirements removed the major advantage to banks of using commercial paper. Bank holding companies still use commercial paper to fund leasing and consumer finance.

The use of commercial paper increased substantially in the early 1980s because of the rising cost of bank loans. Figure 4 graphs the interest rate on commercial paper against the bank prime rate for the period January 1990–January 2002. Commercial paper has become an important alternative to bank loans primarily because of its lower cost.

Market for Commercial Paper Nonbank corporations use commercial paper extensively to finance the loans that they extend to their customers. For example, General Motors Acceptance Corporation (GMAC) borrows money by issuing commercial paper and uses the money to make loans to consumers buying General Motors cars. Similarly, Household Finance and Chrysler Credit use commercial paper to fund loans made to consumers. The total number of firms issuing commercial

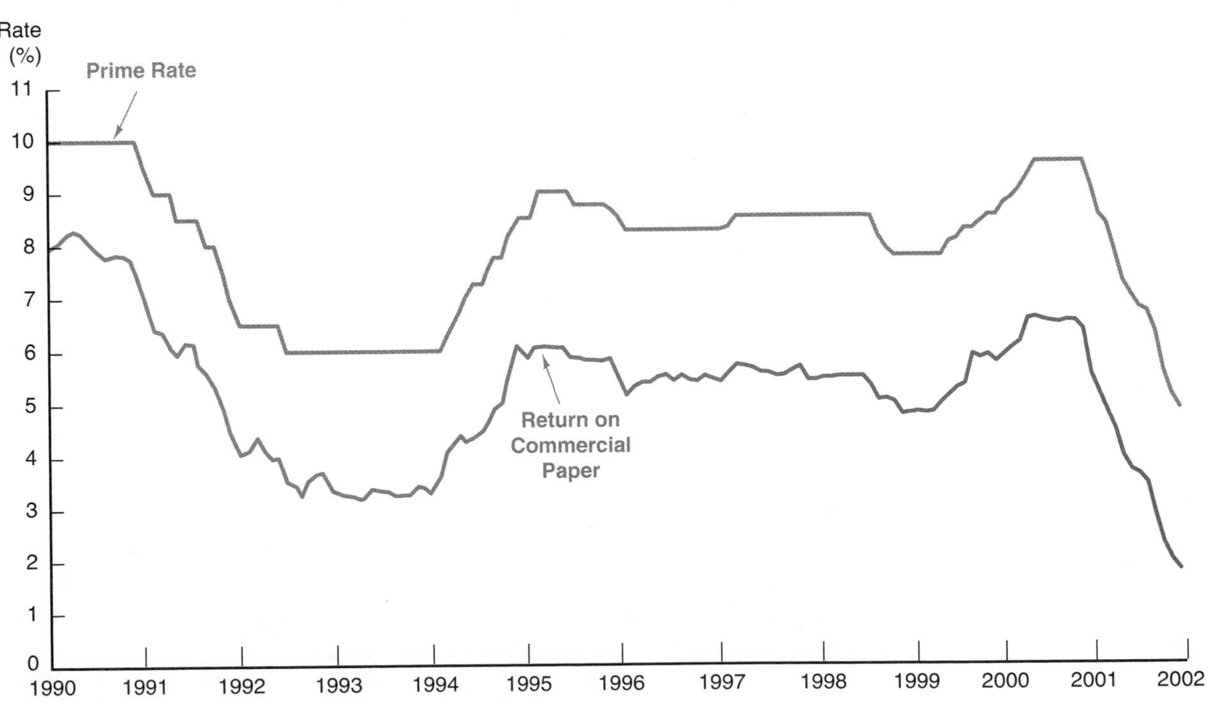

FIGURE 4 Return on Commercial Paper and the Prime Rate, January 1990–January 2002

Source: http://www.federalreserve.gov/releases

paper varies between 600 to 800, depending on the level of interest rates. Most of these firms use one of about 30 commercial paper dealers who match up buyers and sellers. The large New York City money center banks are very active in this market. Some of the larger issuers of commercial paper choose to distribute their securities with **direct placements.** In a direct placement, the issuer bypasses the dealer and sells directly to the end investor. The advantage of this method is that the issuer saves the 0.125% commission that the dealer charges.

Most issuers of commercial paper back up their paper with a line of credit at a bank. This means that in the event the issuer cannot pay off or roll over the maturing paper, the bank will lend the firm funds for this purpose. The line of credit reduces the risk to the purchasers of the paper and so lowers the interest rate. The bank that provides the backup line of credit agrees in advance to make a loan to the issuer if needed to pay off the outstanding paper. The bank charges a fee of 0.5% to 1% for this commitment. Issuers pay this fee because they are able to save more than this in lowered interest costs by having the line.

Commercial banks were the original purchasers of commercial paper. Today the market has greatly expanded to include large insurance companies, nonfinancial businesses, bank trust departments, and government pension funds. These firms are attracted by the relatively low default risk, short maturity, and high yields these securities offer. Currently, about $1.5 trillion in commercial paper is outstanding (see Figure 5).

Banker's Acceptances

A banker's acceptance is an order to pay a specified amount of money to the bearer on a given date. Banker's acceptances have been in use since the twelfth century. However, they were not major money market securities until the volume of international trade ballooned in the 1960s. They are used to finance goods that

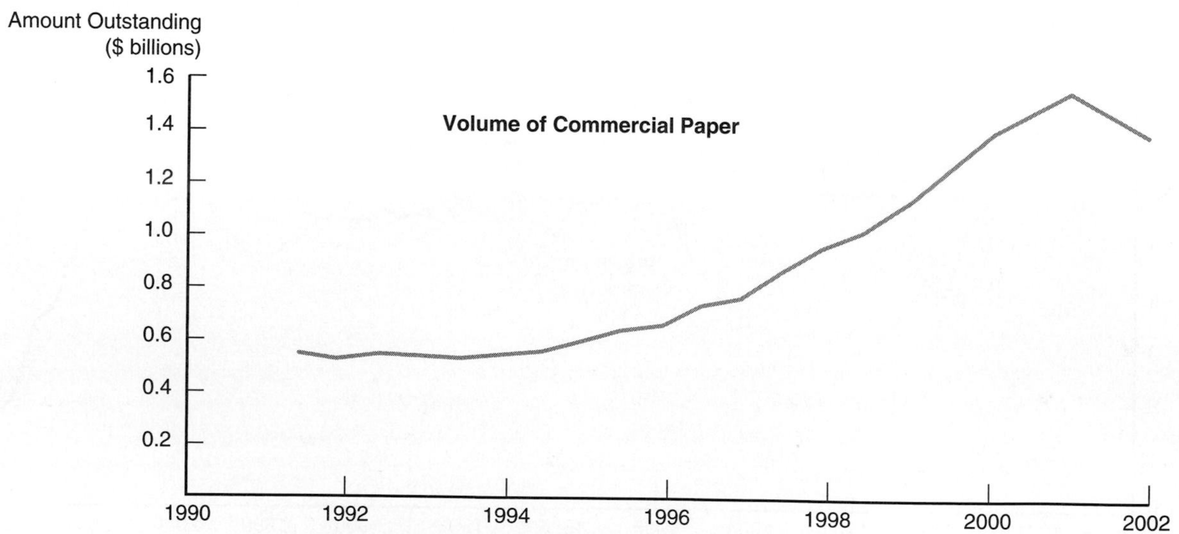

FIGURE 5 Volume of Commercial Paper Outstanding

Source: http:www.federalreserve.gov/releases/cp/table1.htm

have not yet been transferred from the seller to the buyer. For example, suppose that Builtwell Construction Company wants to buy a bulldozer from Komatsu in Japan. Komatsu does not want to ship the bulldozer without being paid because Komatsu has never heard of Builtwell and realizes that it would be difficult to collect if payment were not forthcoming. Similarly, Builtwell is reluctant to send money to Japan before receiving the equipment. A bank can intervene in this standoff by issuing a banker's acceptance.

Using a Banker's Acceptance The transaction would begin with Builtwell obtaining a letter of credit from its bank. A letter of credit simply says that if Builtwell has not paid its obligation by a certain time, the bank will make payment. This particular letter of credit will also authorize the exporter (Komatsu or its bank) to draw a time draft for the amount of the sale. A time draft is like a postdated check: It can be cashed only after a certain date. Builtwell sends the order for the bulldozer, along with the letter of credit, to Komatsu.

When Komatsu receives these documents, it is willing to ship the equipment because the bank's credit standing has been substituted for that of the actual buyer. Once the equipment has been shipped, Komatsu will present the letter of credit and the shipping documents to its own bank in Japan. This bank will create the time draft authorized by the letter of credit and send it to Builtwell's bank. When Builtwell's bank receives the time draft and the shipping documents, it will stamp the time draft "accepted" and return it to Komatsu's bank.

This accepted time draft is now a banker's acceptance. Because it is backed by the credit of a bank, it can be traded on the secondary market. Typically, the exporter's bank will sell it so that the exporter can receive funds before the maturity date. It will be sold at a discount so that the buyer can earn a fair return for holding it until its maturity date.

The transaction is completed when Builtwell deposits the funds in its bank to cover the amount of the time draft (now a banker's acceptance). When the banker's acceptance finally matures and is presented for payment, the issuing bank withdraws funds from Builtwell's account to make payment. Of course, if for some reason Builtwell was unable to make the required deposit, its bank would pay the acceptance anyway and attempt to collect from Builtwell later.

Let us summarize the steps for using banker's acceptances.

1. The importer requests its bank to send an irrevocable letter of credit to the exporter.
2. The exporter receives the letter, ships the goods, and is paid by presenting to its bank the letter along with proof that the merchandise was shipped.
3. The exporter's bank creates a time draft based on the letter of credit and sends it along with proof of shipment to the importer's bank.
4. The importer's bank stamps the time draft "accepted" and sends the banker's acceptance back to the exporter's bank so that the exporter's bank can sell it on the secondary market to collect payment.
5. The importer deposits funds at its bank sufficient to cover the banker's acceptance when it matures.

Advantages of Banker's Acceptances As the bulldozer example demonstrates, banker's acceptances are crucial to international trade. Without them, many transactions simply would not occur because the parties would not feel properly protected from losses. There are other advantages as well:

- The exporter is paid immediately. This is important when delivery times are long after shipment.
- The exporter is shielded from foreign exchange risk because the local bank pays in domestic funds.
- The exporter does not have to assess the creditworthiness of the importer because the importer's bank guarantees payment.

Secondary Market for Banker's Acceptances Because banker's acceptances are payable to the bearer, they can be bought and sold until they mature. They are sold on a discounted basis like commercial paper and T-bills. Dealers in this market match up firms that want to discount a banker's acceptance (sell it for immediate payment) with companies wishing to invest in banker's acceptances.

Interest rates on banker's acceptances are low because the risk of default is very low. For example, no investor in banker's acceptances in the United States has suffered a loss of principal in more than 60 years. The reason is that only large money center banks are involved in this market.

Eurodollars

Many contracts around the world call for payment in U.S. dollars due to the dollar's stability. For this reason, many companies and governments choose to hold dollars. Prior to World War II, most of these deposits were held in New York money center banks. However, as a result of the Cold War that followed, there was fear that deposits held on U.S. soil could be expropriated. Some large London banks responded to this opportunity by offering to hold dollar-denominated deposits in British banks. These deposits were dubbed Eurodollars (see Box 2).

The Eurodollar market has continued to grow rapidly. The primary reason is that depositors receive a higher rate of return on a dollar deposit in the Eurodollar market than in the domestic market. At the same time, the borrower is able to receive a more favorable rate in the Eurodollar market than in the domestic market. This is because multinational banks are not subject to the same regulations restricting U.S. banks and because they are willing and able to accept narrower spreads between the interest paid on deposits and the interest earned on loans.

BOX 2: GLOBAL
Ironic Birth of the Eurodollar Market

One of capitalism's great ironies is that the Eurodollar market, one of the most important financial markets used by capitalists, was fathered by the Soviet Union. In the early 1950s, during the height of the Cold War, the Soviets had accumulated a substantial amount of dollar balances held by banks in the United States. Because the Russians feared that the U.S. government might freeze these assets in the United States, they wanted to move the deposits to Europe, where they would be safe from expropriation. (This fear was not unjustified—consider the U.S. freeze on Iranian assets in 1979 and Iraqi assets in 1990.) However, they also wanted to keep the deposits in dollars so that they could be used in their international transactions. The solution was to transfer the deposits to European banks but to keep the deposits denominated in dollars. When the Soviets did this, the Eurodollar was born.

London Interbank Market Some large London banks act as brokers in the interbank Eurodollar market. Recall that fed funds are used by banks to make up temporary shortfalls in their reserves. Eurodollars are an alternative to fed funds. Banks from around the world buy and sell overnight funds in this market. The rate paid by banks buying funds is the **London interbank bid rate (LIBID).** Funds are offered for sale in this market at the **London interbank offer rate (LIBOR).** Because many banks participate in this market, it is extremely competitive. The spread between the bid and the offer rate seldom exceeds 0.125%. Eurodollar deposits are time deposits, which means that they cannot be withdrawn for a specified period of time. Although the most common time period is overnight, different maturities are available. Each maturity has a different rate.

The overnight LIBOR and the fed funds rate tend to be very close to each other. This is because they are near-perfect substitutes. Suppose that the fed funds rate exceeded the overnight LIBOR. Banks that need to borrow funds will borrow overnight Eurodollars, thus tending to raise rates, and banks with funds to lend will lend fed funds, thus tending to lower rates. The demand and supply pressure will cause a rapid adjustment that will drive the two rates together.

At one time, most short-term loans with adjustable interest rates were tied to the Treasury bill rate. However, the market for Eurodollars is so broad and deep that it has recently become the standard rate against which others are compared. For example, the U.S. commercial paper market now quotes rates as a spread over LIBOR, rather than over the T-bill rate.

The Eurodollar market is not limited to London banks anymore. The primary brokers in this market maintain offices in all of the major financial centers worldwide.

Eurodollar Certificates of Deposit Because Eurodollars are time deposits with fixed maturities, they are to a certain extent illiquid. As usual, the financial markets created new types of securities to combat this problem. These new securities were transferable negotiable certificates of deposit (negotiable CDs). Because most Eurodollar deposits have a relatively short term to begin with, the market for Eurodollar negotiable CDs is relatively limited, comprising less than 10% of the amount of regular Eurodollar deposits. The market for the negotiable CDs is still thin.

Other Eurocurrencies The Eurodollar market is by far the largest short-term security market in the world. This is due to the international popularity of the U.S. dollar for trade. However, the market is not limited to dollars. It is possible to have an account denominated in Japanese yen held in a London or New York bank. Such an account would be termed a Euroyen account. Similarly, you may also have Euromark or Europeso accounts denominated in marks and pesos, respectively, and held in various banks around the world. Keep in mind that if market participants have a need for a particular security and are willing to pay for it, the financial markets stand ready and willing to create it.

COMPARING MONEY MARKET SECURITIES

Although money market securities share many characteristics, such as liquidity, safety, and short maturities, they all differ in some aspects.

Interest Rates

Figure 6 compares the interest rates on many of the money market instruments we have discussed. The most notable feature of this graph is that all of the money market instruments appear to move very closely together over time. This is because all have a very low risk and a short term. They all have deep markets and so are priced competitively. In addition, because these instruments have so many of the same risk and term characteristics, they are close substitutes. Consequently, if one rate should temporarily depart from the others, market supply and demand forces would soon cause a correction.

The *Wall Street Journal* reports money market rates in a table called "Money Rates," which appears daily in the third section. This table contains a brief description of each security and the most recent available interest rate. The "Following the Financial News" box shows a "Money Rates" table from the *Wall Street Journal.*

Liquidity

As we discussed in Chapter 3, the *liquidity* of a security refers to how quickly, easily, and cheaply it can be converted into cash. Typically, the depth of the secondary market where the security can be resold determines its liquidity. For example, the secondary market for Treasury bills is extensive and well developed. As a result, Treasury bills can be converted into cash quickly and with little cost. By contrast, there is no well-developed secondary market for commercial paper. Most holders of commercial paper hold the securities until maturity. In the event

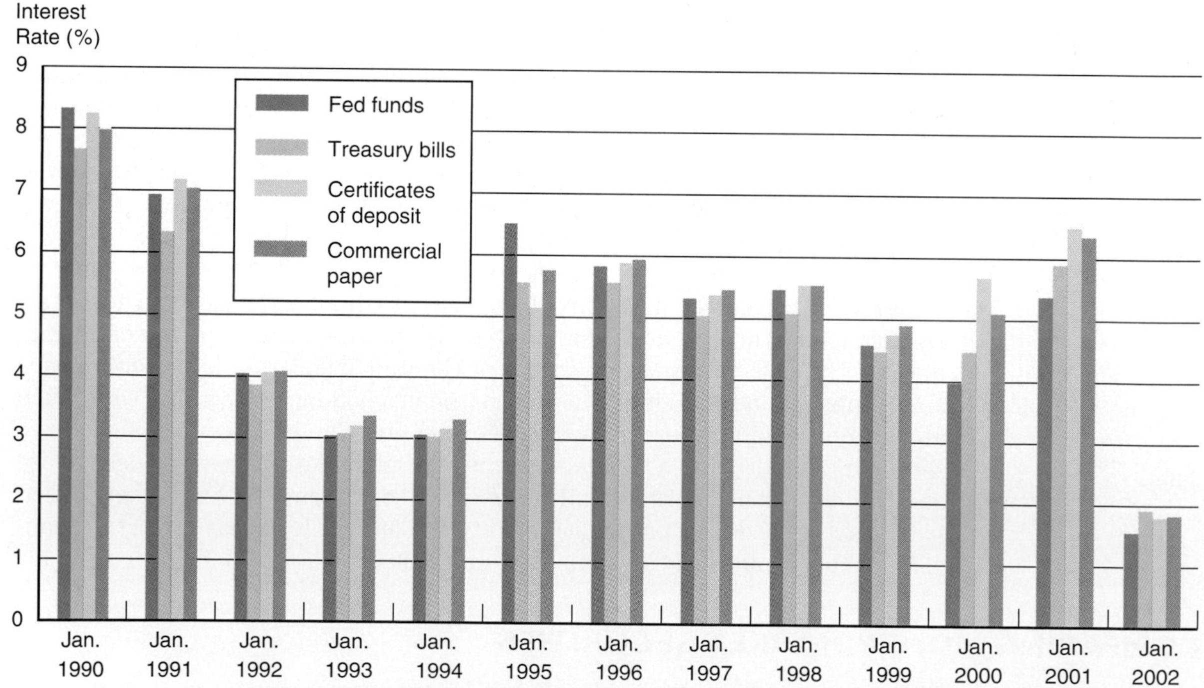

FIGURE 6 Interest Rates on Money Market Securities, 1990–2002

Source: http://www.federalreserve.gov/releases

that a commercial paper investor needed to sell the securities to raise cash, it is likely that brokers would charge relatively high fees.

In some ways, the depth of the secondary market is not as critical for money market securities as it is for long-term securities such as stocks and bonds. This is because money market securities are short-term to start with. Nevertheless, many investors desire *liquidity intervention:* They seek an intermediary to provide liquidity where it did not previously exist. This is one function of money market mutual funds (discussed in the next section).

Table 4 summarizes the money market securities and the depth of the secondary market.

MONEY MARKET MUTUAL FUNDS

Earlier in this chapter we pointed out that the money markets are wholesale markets where most securities trade in large denominations. This characteristic effectively blocks most individuals from investing directly in these securities. However, the markets usually find a way to correct for such deficiencies, especially when potential customers are available. Money market mutual funds represent one such correction.

Money market mutual funds (MMMFs) are funds that aggregate money from a group of small investors and invest it in money market instruments. They have grown enormously popular since their inception in the early 1970s because they provide a means for small investors to take advantage of the returns offered on money market securities. These securities would be out of reach to most small investors because of their large minimum denominations.

History of Money Market Mutual Funds

Money market mutual funds have existed since the early 1970s; however, the low market interest rates before 1977 (which were either below or just slightly above Regulation Q ceilings of 5.25% to 5.5%) kept them from being particularly advantageous relative to bank deposits. In 1978, Merrill Lynch recognized that it could provide better service to its customers if it offered an account that customers could use to warehouse money. Prior to the introduction of MMMFs as a small-investor

TABLE 4 Money Market Securities and Their Markets

Money Market Security	Issuer	Buyer	Usual Maturity	Secondary Market
Treasury bills	U.S. government	Consumers and companies	13 weeks, 26 weeks, 1 year	Excellent
Federal funds	Banks	Banks	1 to 7 days	None
Repurchase agreements	Businesses and banks	Businesses and banks	1 to 15 days	Good
Negotiable certificates of deposit	Large money center banks	Businesses	14 to 120 days	Good
Commercial paper	Finance companies and businesses	Businesses	1 to 270 days	Poor
Banker's acceptance	Banks	Businesses	30 to 180 days	Good
Eurodollar deposits	Non-U.S. banks	Businesses, governments, and banks	1 day to 1 year	Poor

FOLLOWING THE FINANCIAL NEWS

Money Market Rates

The *Wall Street Journal* publishes daily a listing of interest rates on many different financial instruments in its "Money Rates" column. (See "Today's Contents" on page 1 of the *Journal* for the location.)

The four interest rates in the "Money Rates" column that are discussed most frequently in the media are these:

Prime rate: The base interest rate on corporate bank loans, an indicator of the cost of business borrowing from banks

Federal funds rate: The interest rate charged on overnight loans in the federal funds market, a sensitive indicator of the cost to banks of borrowing funds from other banks and the stance of monetary policy

Treasury bill rate: The interest rate on U.S. Treasury bills, an indicator of general interest-rate movements

Federal Home Loan Mortgage Corporation rates: Interest rates on "Freddie Mac"—guaranteed mortgages, an indicator of the cost of financing residential housing purchases

Source: *Wall Street Journal.* January 2, 2002, p. C14. Republished by permission of Dow Jones, Inc. via Copyright Clearance Center, Inc.

MONEY RATES

Monday, December 31, 2001

The key U.S. and foreign interest rates below are a guide to general levels but don't always represent actual transactions.

PRIME RATE: 4.75% (effective 12/12/01). The base rate on corporate loans posted by at least 75% of the nation's 30 largest banks.

DISCOUNT RATE: 1.25% (effective 12/11/01). The charge on loans to depository institutions by the Federal Reserve Banks.

FEDERAL FUNDS: 2 1/2% high, 1/2% low, 1 1/2% near closing bid, 2% offered. Reserves traded among commercial banks for overnight use in amounts of $1 million or more. Source: Prebon Yamane (U.S.A.) Inc. FOMC fed funds target rate 1.75% effective 12/11/01.

CALL MONEY: 3.50% (effective 12/12/01). The charge on loans to brokers on stock exchange collateral. Source: Reuters.

COMMERCIAL PAPER: Placed directly by General Electric Capital Corp.: 1.75% 30 to 43 days; 1.74% 44 to 63 days; 1.76% 64 to 89 days; 1.78% 90 to 179 days; 1.84% 180 to 239 days; 1.97% 240 to 270 days.

EURO COMMERCIAL PAPER: Market Closed.

DEALER COMMERCIAL PAPER: High-grade unsecured notes sold through dealers by major corporations: 1.78% 30 days; 1.75% 60 days; 1.75% 90 days.

CERTIFICATES OF DEPOSIT: Typical rates in the secondary market: 1.80% one month; 1.77% three months; 1.88% six months.

BANKERS ACCEPTANCES: 1.91% 30 days; 1.87% 60 days; 1.83% 90 days; 1.88% 120 days; 1.90% 150 days; 1.94% 180 days. Offered rates of negotiable, bank-backed business credit instruments typically financing an import order. Source: Reuters.

LONDON LATE EURODOLLARS: 1.94% - 1.81% one month; 1.94% - 1.81% two months; 1.88% - 1.75% three months; 1.94% - 1.81% four months; 1.94% - 1.81% five months; 2.00% - 1.88% six months.

LONDON INTERBANK OFFERED RATES (LIBOR): 1.87375% one month; 1.88125% three months; 1.98125% six months; 2.4425% one year. British Bankers' Association average of interbank offered rates for dollar deposits in the London market based on quotations at 16 major banks. Effective rate for contracts entered into two days from date appearing at top of this column.

EURO LIBOR: 3.33000% one month; 3.30000% three months; 3.25438% six months; 3.33750% one year. British Bankers' Association average of interbank offered rates for euro deposits in the London market based on quotations at 16 major banks. Effective rate for contracts entered into two days from date appearing at top of this column.

EURO INTERBANK OFFERED RATES (EURIBOR): Market Closed.

FOREIGN PRIME RATES: Canada 4.00%; Germany 3.25%; Japan 1.375%; Switzerland 3.75%; Britain 4.00%. These rate indications aren't directly comparable; lending practices vary widely by location.

TREASURY BILLS: Results of the Monday, December 31, 2001, auction of short-term U.S. government bills, sold at a discount from face value in units of $1,000 to $1 million: 1.710% 13 weeks; 1.800% 26 weeks. Wednesday, December 26, 2001 auction; 1.750% 4 weeks.

OVERNIGHT REPURCHASE RATE: 1.80%. Dealer financing rate for overnight sale and repurchase of Treasury securities. Source: Reuters.

FREDDIE MAC: Posted yields on 30-year mortgage commitments. Delivery within 30 days 6.81%, 60 days 6.94%, standard conventional fixed-rate mortgages; 3.875%, 2% rate capped one-year adjustable rate mortgages. Source: Reuters.

FANNIE MAE: Posted yields on 30 year mortgage commitments (priced at par) for delivery within 30 days 6.94%, 60 days 7.07%, standard conventional fixed rate-mortgages; 3.75%, 6/2 rate capped one-year adjustable rate mortgages. Source: Reuters.

MERRILL LYNCH READY ASSETS TRUST: 1.94%. Annualized average rate of return after expenses for the past 30 days; not a forecast of future returns.

CONSUMER PRICE INDEX: November 177.4, up 1.9% from a year ago. Bureau of Labor Statistics.

account, customers had to bring checks to the brokerage house when they wanted to invest and had to pick up checks when they sold securities. Customers who had MMMF accounts, however, could simply direct the broker to take funds out of this account to buy stocks or to deposit funds in this account when they sold securities. Initially, Merrill Lynch did not look on the MMMF as a major source of income.

In the early 1980s, inflation and interest rates skyrocketed. Regulation Q restricted banks from paying more than 5.25% in interest on savings accounts. With interest rates in the money market exceeding 15%, investors flocked to

MMMFs. Figure 7 shows the growth in money market mutual funds between 1975 and 2000.

The loss of deposits from banks and thrifts to these MMMFs caused serious liquidity and profitability problems in both the banking and thrift industries. These problems are discussed further in Chapter 15.

Description of Money Market Mutual Funds

MMMFs are open-end investment funds that invest only in money market securities. An *open-ended fund* is one that invests in securities and sells direct claims on the securities to investors. Most funds do not charge investors any fee for purchasing or redeeming shares. The funds usually have a minimum initial investment

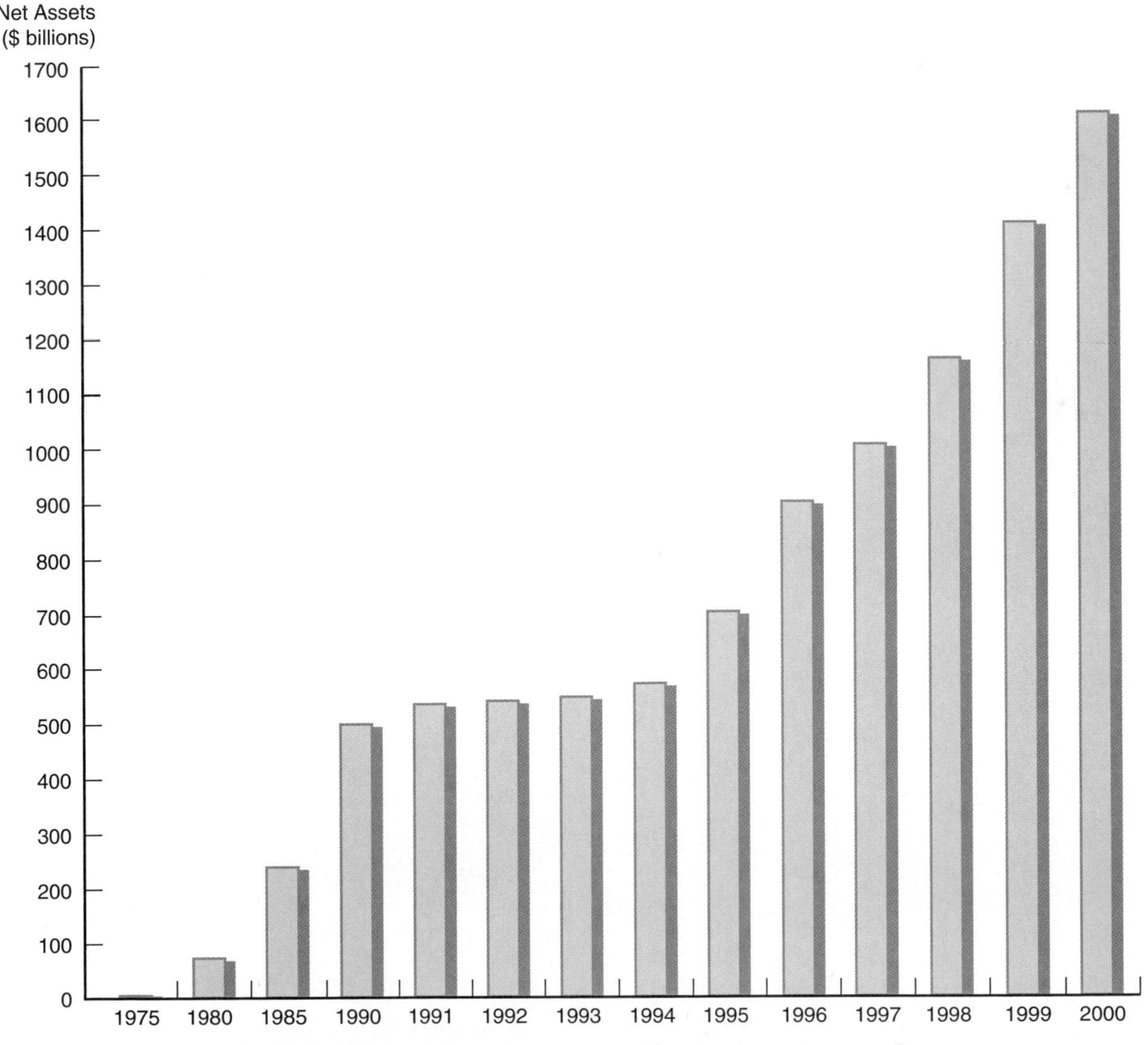

FIGURE 7 Net Assets of Money Market Mutual Funds, 1975–2000

Source: Investment Company Institute, *Mutual Fund Fact Book,* 2001, p. 64.

The most recent statistics on the net assets of money market mutual funds can be found at www.ici.org/newsroom/stats_trends.html by clicking on "Money Market Mutual Fund Assets."

of \$500 to \$20,000. The funds yields depends entirely on the performance of the securities purchased.

An important feature of MMMFs is that many have check-writing privileges. They often do not charge a fee for writing checks or have any minimum check amount as long as the balance in the account is above a stated level. This convenience, along with market interest rates, makes the accounts very popular with small investors.

Brokerage houses do not have the computer facilities needed to handle the volume of transactions generated by MMMF accounts. Instead of incurring the cost of developing these facilities, most brokerage firms contract with banks to provide the processing. For example, Merrill Lynch set up a joint venture with BancOne Corporation of Columbus, Ohio, to service its tremendously popular Cash Management Account. Customers using MMMFs had to learn to bank by mail and over the telephone because brokerage houses did not have extensive branch systems. Once the customers became accustomed to this way of banking, many found it convenient and well worth the trouble for the extra income earned on these accounts.

MMMF Risk

Investors took their money out of federally *insured* banks and thrifts and put it into *uninsured* MMMFs. An important question is why they were willing to take this extra level of risk. The reason is that the extra risk was really very small. The money invested in MMMFs was in turn invested in money market instruments. Commercial paper is by far the largest component of these funds, followed by certificates of deposit and repurchase agreements and then by banker's acceptances. Figure 8 shows the average distribution of money market fund assets. Because the

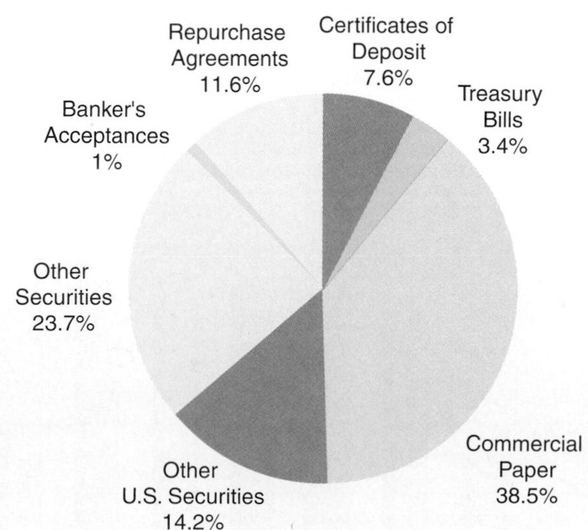

FIGURE 8 Average Distribution of Money Market Fund Assets, 2001

Source: Investment Company Institute, *Mutual Fund Fact Book*, 2001, p. 93.

risk of default on these securities is very low, the risk of MMMFs is very low. Investors recognized this and so were willing to abandon the safety of their banks and thrifts.

Because money market mutual funds exhibit very low risk, the SEC permits these funds to maintain a fixed investment price per share of $1. The daily yield is based on the asset yield.

The SEC severely limits money market mutual funds to investments in short-term, low-risk securities. Low-quality investments cannot exceed 5% of assets, and no more than 1% of fund assets may be invested in one issue.

Current Trends in MMMFs

Legislation in 1980 and 1982 removed most of the restrictions on bank interest-rate ceilings. These changes were aimed at reducing the flow of funds out of banks into brokerage houses. And by the mid–1980s, interest rates had begun to fall. The combined effect was to reduce the growth rate of MMMFs. Currently, investors can still earn a 0.5% to 1% higher return by investing in MMMFs rather than placing their money in a bank. For this reason, MMMFs remain popular.

SUMMARY

1. Money market securities are short-term instruments with an original maturity of less than one year. These securities trade in the money markets. They include Treasury bills, commercial paper, federal funds, repurchase agreements, negotiable certificates of deposit, banker's acceptances, and Eurodollars.
2. Money market securities are used to "warehouse" funds until needed. The returns earned on these investments are low due to their low risk and high liquidity.
3. Many participants in the money markets both buy and sell money market securities. The U.S. Treasury, commercial banks, businesses, and individuals all benefit by having access to low-risk short-term investments.
4. Interest rates on all money market securities tend to follow one another closely over time. Treasury bill returns are the lowest because they are virtually devoid of default risk. Banker's acceptances and negotiable certificates of deposit are next lowest because they are backed by the creditworthiness of large money center banks.
5. Money market mutual funds aggregate the funds of many small investors and purchase money market instruments. The returns on these instruments are passed on to the investors. Money market mutual funds have grown rapidly since 1978. Higher market interest rates occurred at a time when banks were limited as to the maximum rate they could pay to retain deposits. This made the returns to money market mutual funds very attractive.

KEY TERMS

bearer instrument, *p. 227*
book entry, *p. 223*
competitive bidding, *p. 223*
deep market, *p. 222*
demand deposit, *p. 227*
direct placement, *p. 230*
discounting, *p. 221*
liquid market, *p. 222*
London interbank bid rate, (LIBID), *p. 233*
London interbank offer rate, (LIBOR), *p. 233*
noncompetitive bidding, *p. 223*
term security, *p. 227*
wholesale market, *p. 216*

QUESTIONS AND PROBLEMS

***1.** What characteristics define the money markets?

2. Is a Treasury bond issued 29 years ago with six months remaining before it matures a money market instrument?

***3.** Why do banks not eliminate the need for money markets?

4. Distinguish between a term security and a demand security.

***5.** What was the purpose motivating regulators to impose interest ceilings on bank savings accounts? What impact did this eventually have on the money markets?

6. Why does the U.S. government use the money markets?

***7.** Why do businesses use the money markets?

8. What purpose initially motivated Merrill Lynch to offer money market mutual funds to its customers?

***9.** Why are more funds from property and casualty insurance companies than funds from life insurance companies invested in the money markets?

10. Which of the money market securities is the most liquid and considered the most risk-free? Why?

***11.** Distinguish between competitive bidding and noncompetitive bidding for Treasury securities.

12. Who issues federal funds, and what is the usual purpose of these funds?

***13.** Does the Federal Reserve *directly* set the federal funds interest rate?

14. Who issues commercial paper and for what purpose?

***15.** Why are banker's acceptances so popular for international transactions?

WEB EXERCISES

The Money Markets

1. Up-to-date interest rates are available from the Federal Reserve at http://www.federalreserve.gov/releases. Locate the current rate on the following securities:

a. Prime rate
b. Federal funds
c. Commercial paper (financial)
d. Certificates of deposit
e. Discount rate
f. one-month Eurodollar deposits

Compare these rates on a–d to those reported in Table 1. Have short-term rates generally increased or decreased?

2. The Treasury conducts auctions of money market treasury securities at regular intervals. Go to http://www.publicdebt.treas/gov/of/ofaucrt.htm and locate the schedule of auctions. When is the next auction of 4-week bills? When is the next auction of 13- and 26-week bills? How often are these securities auctioned?

Chapter 9

The Capital Markets

Preview

In 1996, Netscape emerged as the leading software used for browsing the Internet. The firm needed additional cash to fund its explosive growth and to fight off efforts by Microsoft to capture the market. The managers of Netscape did not want to use short-term funds like those available in the money markets. Instead, they required long-term capital that could be used to fund long-term growth. Netscape 's managers could have raised the funds using any of a number of long-term securities, but they decided to do it by offering stock for sale to the public in one of the decade's most closely watched stock offerings. The founders of Netscape became instant billionaires as a result.

This chapter discusses securities that have an original maturity that is *greater* than one year, such as the stock issued by Netscape. These securities trade in the capital markets. The best-known capital market securities are stocks and bonds. Mortgages, which also trade in the capital markets, are discussed in Chapter 11.

PURPOSE OF THE CAPITAL MARKET

Firms that issue capital market securities and the investors who buy them have very different motivations than they have when they operate in the money markets. Firms and individuals use the money markets primarily to warehouse funds for short periods of time until a more important need or a more productive use for the funds arises. By contrast, firms and individuals use the capital markets for long-term investments. The capital markets provide an alternative to investment in assets such as real estate or gold.

Suppose that after a careful financial analysis, your firm determines that it needs a new plant to meet the increased demand for its products. This analysis will be made using interest rates that reflect the *current* long-term cost of funds to the firm. Now suppose that your firm chooses to finance this plant by issuing money market securities, such as commercial paper. As long as interest rates do not rise, all is well: When these short-term securities mature, they can be reissued at the same interest rate. However, if interest rates rise, as they did in 1980, the firm may find that it does not have the cash flows or income to support the plant because when the short-term securities mature, the firm will have to reissue them at a higher interest rate. If long-term securities, such as bonds or stock, had been used, the increased interest rates would not have been as critical. The primary reason that individuals and firms choose to borrow long-term is to reduce the risk that interest rates will rise before they pay off their debt. This reduction in risk comes at a cost, however. As you may recall from Chapter 5, most long-term interest rates are higher than short-term rates due to risk premiums. Despite the need to pay higher interest rates to borrow in the capital markets, these markets remain very active.

CAPITAL MARKET PARTICIPANTS

The primary issuers of capital market securities are federal and local governments and corporations. The federal government issues long-term notes and bonds to fund the national debt. State and municipal governments also issue long-term notes and bonds to finance capital projects, such as school and prison construction. Governments never issue stock because they cannot sell ownership claims.

Corporations issue both bonds and stock. One of the most difficult decisions a firm faces can be whether it should finance its growth with debt or equity. The distribution of a firm's capital between debt and equity is its capital structure. (The factors that influence the capital structure decision are discussed in Chapter 14.) Corporations may enter the capital markets because they do not have sufficient capital to fund their investment opportunities. Alternatively, firms may choose to enter the capital markets because they want to preserve their capital to protect against unexpected needs. In either case, the availability of efficiently functioning capital markets is crucial to the continued health of the business sector.

The largest purchasers of capital market securities are households. Frequently, individuals and households deposit funds in financial institutions, such as mutual funds and pension funds, that use the funds to purchase capital market instruments such as bonds or stock.

CAPITAL MARKET TRADING

Initial public offering news and information, including advanced search tools for IPO offerings, venture capital research reports, etc., is available at www.ipo.com

Capital market trading occurs in either the *primary market* or the *secondary market.* The primary market is where new issues of stocks and bonds are introduced. Investment funds, corporations, and individual investors can all purchase securities offered in the primary market. You can think of a primary market transaction as one where the issuer of the security actually receives the proceeds of the sale. When firms sell securities for the very first time, the issue is an **initial public offering (IPO).** Subsequent sales of a firm's new stocks or bonds to the public are simply primary market transactions (as opposed to an initial one).

The capital markets have well-developed secondary markets. A secondary market is where the sale of previously issued securities takes place, and it is important because most investors plan to sell long-term bonds before they reach maturity and eventually to sell their holdings of stock as well. There are two types of exchanges in the secondary market for capital securities: *organized exchanges* and *over-the-counter exchanges.* Whereas most money market transactions originate over the phone, most capital market transactions, measured by volume, occur in organized exchanges.

Organized Securities Exchanges

An organized exchange has a building where securities (including stocks, bonds, options, and futures) trade. Exchange rules govern trading to ensure the efficient and legal operation of the exchange, and the exchange's board constantly reviews these rules to ensure that they result in competitive trading.

Organized exchanges account for over 72% of the total dollar volume of domestic stock shares traded. Organized exchanges also support trading in bonds. The largest of the organized stock exchanges in the United States is the New York Stock Exchange (NYSE). The NYSE occupies a building in downtown New York City, and only traders who are members of the exchange may engage in trading. To become a member, an individual or firm must buy a "seat." There are 1366 seats on the NYSE, most of them owned by brokerage houses. Today seats on the New York Stock Exchange can sell for as much as $1.2 million (see Box 1), depending on the market's perception of the profit potential in being a trader. Average daily volume on the NYSE in 1998 was 712.7 million shares of stocks with a total of about 100 billion shares traded during the year. By contrast, a total of about 10 million bonds were traded on organized exchanges during 1998.

Find listed companies, member information, real-time market indices, and current stock quotes at www.nyse.com

There are also major organized stock exchanges around the world. The most active exchange in the world is the Nikkei in Tokyo. Other major exchanges include the London Stock Exchange in England, the DAX in Germany, and the Toronto Stock Exchange in Canada.

To have a stock listed for trading on one of the organized exchanges, a firm must file an application and meet certain criteria set by the exchange designed to enhance trading. For example, the NYSE encourages only the largest firms to list so that transaction volume will be high. To list on the NYSE, a firm must meet the following minimum requirements:

- At least 2000 stockholders, each owning 100 shares or more
- A minimum of 1.1 million shares traded publicly
- Pretax earnings of $2.5 million at the time of listing plus at least $2 million in pretax earnings in each of the prior two years
- Market value of public shares of $100 million or more

BOX 1

The Most Expensive Seat in Town

In October 2001 a seat on the NYSE sold for $2.2 million, a $100,000 decrease from the last sale that took place two weeks earlier. Owning one of the 1,366 NYSE seats is the admission ticket to trading on the world's largest stock exchange. Membership gives the holders the right to trade stocks and vote at exchange meetings. The highest price ever paid for a Big Board seat was $2.65 million on August 23, 1999. As expensive as a seat on the exchange is, consider this: It doesn't even include a chair. If you want to sit down, you have to bring your own stool.

Source: www.NYSE.com/glossary/NT00011442.html

About 3000 companies around the world list their shares on the New York Stock Exchange. More than 70% of NYSE-listed companies have joined the exchange since 1986. The average new firm on the exchange had a market value of $540.6 million. On October 28, 1998, the NYSE volume topped 1 billion shares for the first time,[1] and in 2000, there were 148 days with volume over 1 billion shares.

The NYSE switched to a decimal system of reporting stock prices on January 29, 2001. Prior to this change, prices were quoted in eighths. This change was prompted by the SEC in the hope that it would reduce bid-ask spreads.

The second-largest organized stock exchange in the United States is the American Stock Exchange. About 700 firms trade on it. The American Stock Exchange has less restrictive listing requirements. Regional exchanges, such as the Philadelphia and Pacific Stock Exchanges, are even easier to list on. Some firms choose to list on more than one exchange, believing that more exposure will increase the demand for their stock and hence its price. Many firms also believe that there is a certain amount of prestige in being listed on one of the major exchanges. They may even include this fact in their advertising. There is little conclusive research to support this belief, however. Microsoft, for example, is not listed on any organized exchange, yet its stock had a total market value of over $320 billion in late 2001.

Over-the-Counter Markets

If Microsoft's stock is not traded on any of the organized stock exchanges, where does it sell its stock? Securities not listed on one of the exchanges trade in the over-the-counter market. This market is not organized in the sense of having a building where trading takes place. Instead, trading occurs over a sophisticated telecommunications network, called the **National Association of Securities Dealers Automated Quotation System (NASDAQ).** This system, introduced in 1971, provides current bid and ask prices on about 4000 actively traded securities. Dealers "make a market" in these stocks by buying for inventory when investors want to sell and selling from inventory when investors want to buy. These dealers provide small stocks with the liquidity that is essential to their acceptance in the market. Total volume on the NASDAQ is usually slightly lower than on the NYSE; however, NASDAQ volume has been growing and occasionally exceeds NYSE volume. Figure 1 reports the number of firms listed on the NASDAQ, NYSE, and Amex.

Not all publicly traded stocks list on one of the organized exchanges or on NASDAQ. Securities that trade very infrequently or trade primarily in one region of the country are usually handled by the regional offices of various brokerage houses. These offices often maintain small inventories of regionally popular securities. Dealers that make a market for stocks that trade in low volume are very important to the success of the over-the-counter market. Without these dealers standing ready to buy or sell shares, investors would be reluctant to buy shares of stock in regional or unknown firms, and it would be very difficult for start-up firms to raise needed capital. Recall from Chapter 4 that the more liquid an asset is, the greater the quantity demanded. By providing liquidity intervention, dealers increase demand for thinly traded securities.

[1]*NYSE Fact Book,* 2000 data, May 2000.

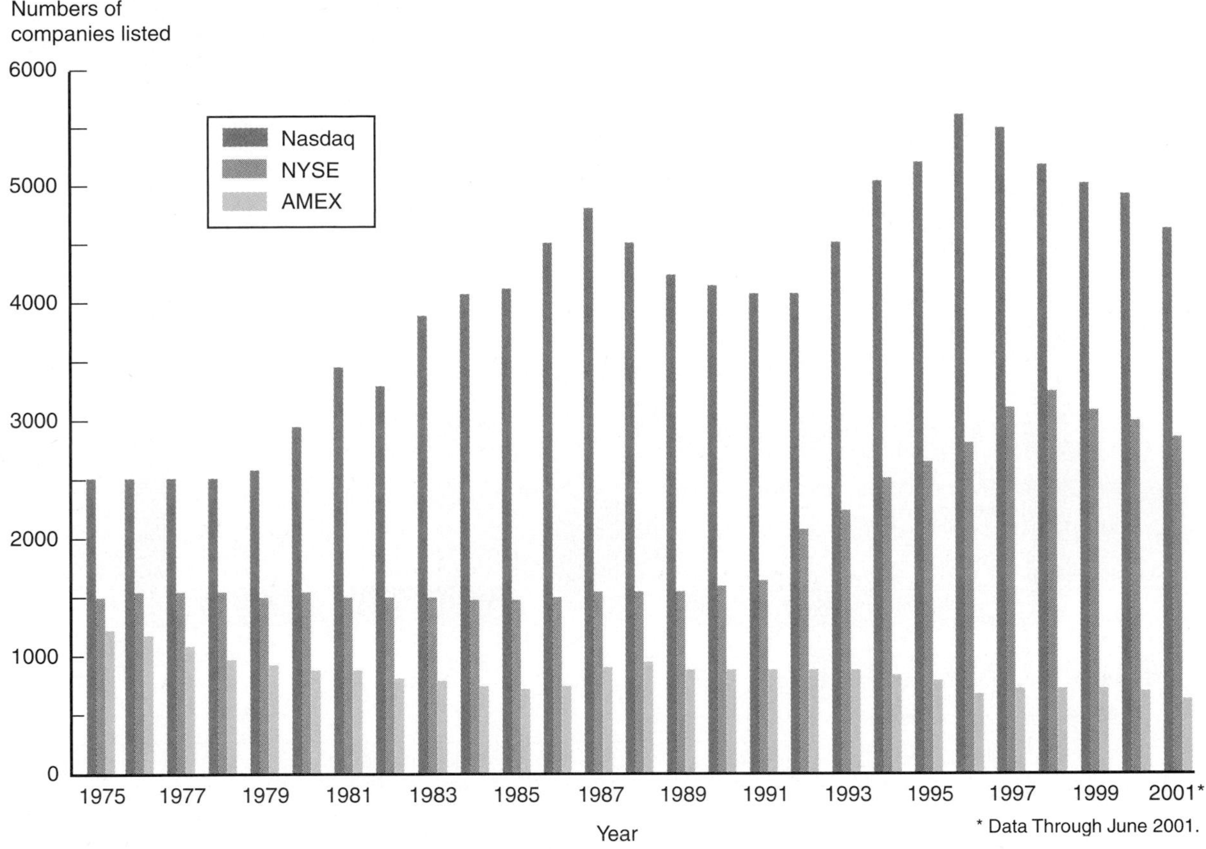

FIGURE 1 Number of Listed Companies Yearly Comparison with NYSE, AMEX, and Nasdaq

Data through June 2001, http://www.marketdata.nasdaq.com/asp/Sec1ComComp.asp

CAPITAL MARKET SECURITIES: BONDS

The capital markets are where securities with original maturities of greater than one year trade. Capital market securities fall into three categories: bonds, stocks, and mortgages. In this section, we look at bonds.

Bonds are securities that represent a debt owed by the issuer to the investor. Bonds obligate the issuer to pay a specified amount at a given date, generally with periodic interest payments. The par, face, or maturity value of the bond is the amount that the issuer must pay at maturity. The coupon rate is the rate of interest that the issuer must pay. This rate is usually fixed for the duration of the bond and does not fluctuate with market interest rates. If the repayment terms of a bond are not met, the holder of a bond has a claim on the assets of the issuer. Look at Figure 2. The face value of the bond is given in the top right corner. The interest rate of $8\frac{5}{8}\%$, along with the maturity date, is reported several times on the face of the bond.

Long-term bonds traded in the capital market include long-term government notes and bonds, municipal bonds, and corporate bonds.

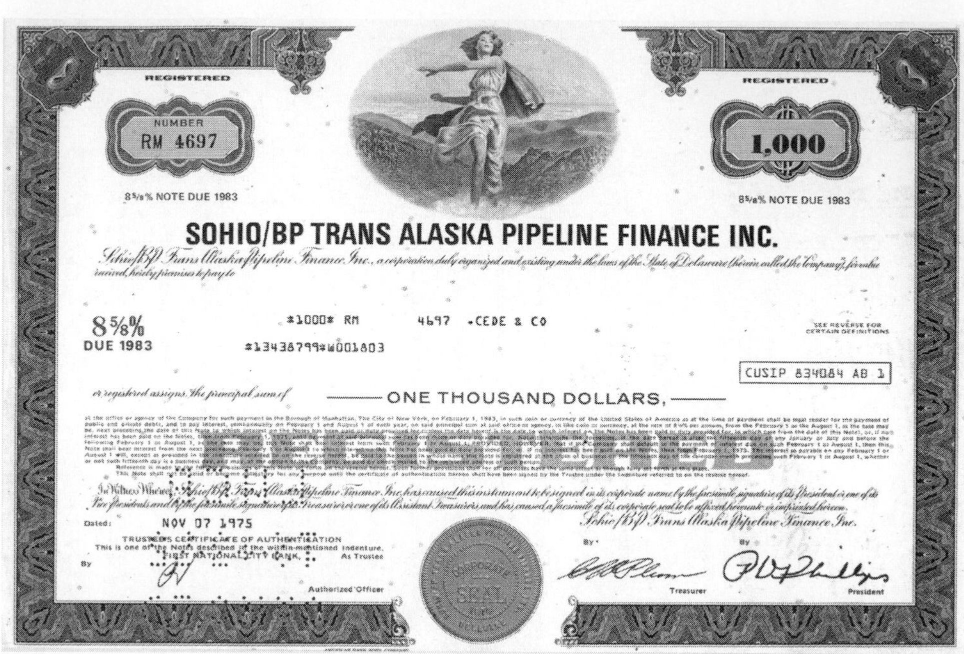

FIGURE 2 Sohio/BP Corporate Bond

Source: Eakins, *Finance: Investments, Institutions, & Management*, p. 39.

TREASURY BONDS

The U.S. Treasury issues notes and bonds to finance the national debt. The difference between a note and a bond is that notes have an original maturity of 1 to 10 years while bonds have an original maturity of 10 to 20 years. (Recall from Chapter 8 that Treasury *bills* mature in less than one year.) Table 1 summarizes the maturity differences among Treasury securities. The prices of Treasury notes, bonds, and bills are quoted as a percentage of $100 face value. (Chapter 3 explains how newspaper bond quotes can be converted into market prices.)

On November 1, 2001 the Treasury announced that it would no longer issue 30-year Treasury securities. The motivation for this change was to reduce the interest cost on the government debt by using shorter-term securities that usually carry a lower interest rate. The announcement caused an immediate increase in 30-year bond prices as investors snapped up those that were available.

TABLE 1 Treasury Securities

Type	Maturity
Treasury bill	Less than 1 year
Treasury note	1 to 10 years
Treasury bond	10 to 20 years

Federal government notes and bonds are free of default risk because the government can always print money to pay off the debt if necessary.[2] This does *not* mean that these securities are risk-free. There is still the possibility that market interest rates will rise, making the bonds fall in value.

Application **Interest-Rate Risk in Bond Investment**

The risk that the value of a bond will fall when market interest rates rise is called *interest-rate risk* (discussed in Chapter 3). Suppose that you wanted to sell a bond that pays 4.5% for $1000 when new ones that pay 5.5% are available. To sell an old bond when rates have risen, the holder will have to discount the bond until the yield to the buyer is the same as the market rate. In this example, if there were 20 years until the bond matured, the seller would have to drop the asking price to $879.61 to give the buyer a 5.5% yield. We did not discuss interest-rate risk in Chapter 8 because securities in the money market have short maturities and interest rates do not usually change greatly in the short run. When they do, the change does not influence the price of the security as much as when the security has a long time until maturity.

Treasury Bond Interest Rates

Treasury bonds have very low interest rates because they have no default risk. Although investors in Treasury bonds have found themselves earning less than the rate of inflation in some years (see Figure 3), most of the time, the interest rate

[2]We noted in Chapter 8 that Treasury bills were also considered default-risk-free except that a budget stalemate in 1996 almost caused default. The same small chance of default applies to Treasury bonds.

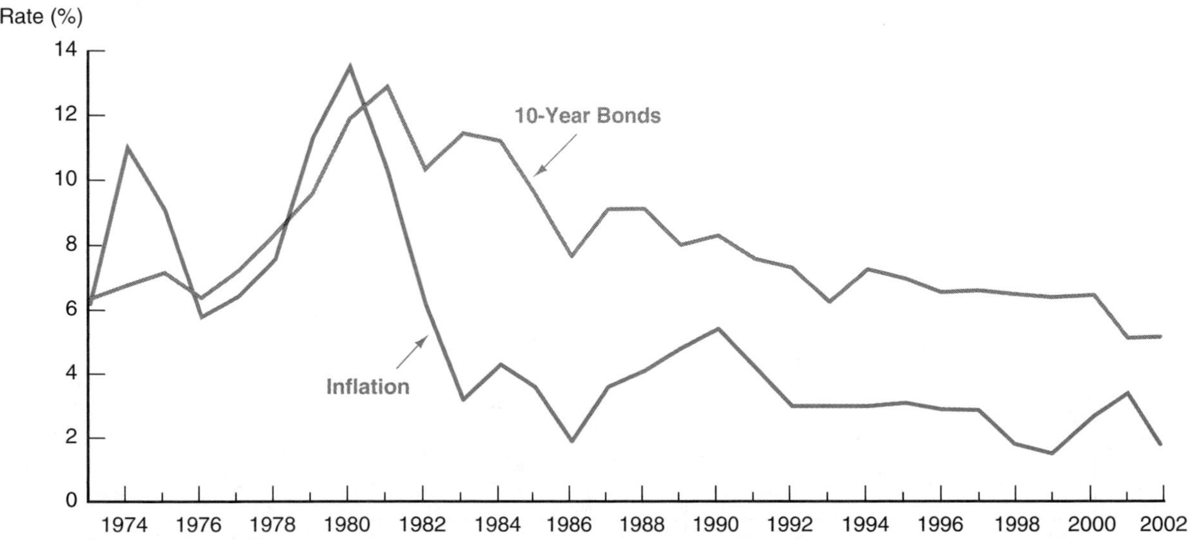

FIGURE 3 Interest Rate on Treasury Bonds and the Inflation Rate, 1973–2002

Sources: http://www.federalreserve.gov/releases and ftp://ftp.bls.gov/pub/special.requests/cpi/cpiai.txt

on Treasury notes and bonds is above that on money market securities because of interest-rate risk.

Figure 4 plots the yield on 20-year Treasury bonds against the yield on 90-day Treasury bills. Two things are noteworthy in this graph. First, in most years, the rate of return on the short-term bill is below that on the 20-year bond. Second, short-term rates are more volatile than long-term rates. Short-term rates are more influenced by the current rate of inflation. Investors in long-term securities expect extremely high or low inflation rates to return to more normal levels, so long-term rates do not typically change as much as short-term rates.

Treasury Inflation-Indexed Securities

In 1997, the Treasury Department began offering an innovative bond designed to remove inflation risk from holding treasuries. The new inflation-indexed bonds have an interest rate that does not change throughout the term of the security. However, the principal amount used to compute the interest payment does change based on the consumer price index. At maturity, the securities are redeemed at the greater of their inflation-adjusted principal or par amount at original issue.

The advantage of inflation-indexed securities is that they give both individual and institutional investors a chance to buy a security whose value won't be eroded by inflation. These securities can be used by retirees who want to hold a very low-risk portfolio.

Treasury STRIPS

In addition to bonds, notes, and bills, in 1985 the Treasury began issuing to depository institutions bonds in book entry form called **Separate Trading of**

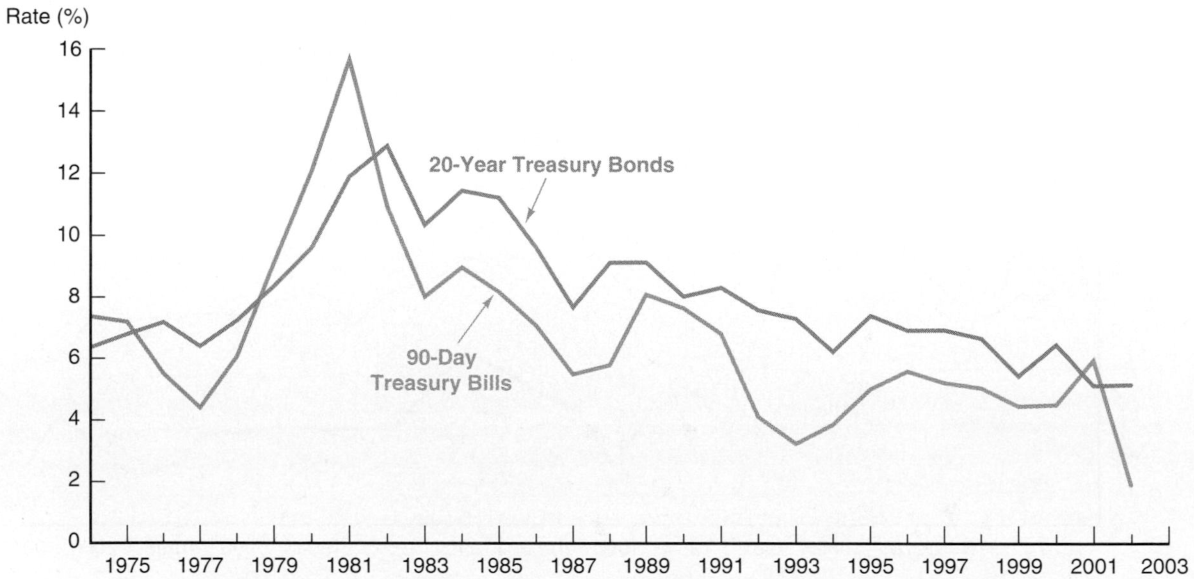

FIGURE 4 Interest Rate on Treasury Bills and Treasury Bonds, 1973–2002 (January of each year)

Source: http://www.federalreserve.gov/releases

Registered Interest and Principal Securities, more commonly called **STRIPS.** Recall from Chapter 8 that to be sold in book entry form means that no physical document exists; instead, the security is issued and accounted for electronically. A STRIP separates the periodic interest payments from the final principal repayment. When a Treasury fixed-principal or inflation-indexed note or bond is stripped, each interest payment and the principal payment becomes a separate zero-coupon security. Each component has its own identifying number and can be held or traded separately. For example, a Treasury note with five years remaining to maturity consists of a single principal payment at maturity and ten interest payments, one every six months for five years. When this note is stripped, each of the ten interest payments and the principal payment becomes a separate security. Thus, the single Treasury note becomes 11 separate securities that can be traded individually. STRIPS are also called **zero-coupon securities** because the only time an investor receives a payment during the life of a STRIP is when it matures.

Before the government introduced these securities, the private sector had created them indirectly. In the early 1980s, Merrill Lynch created the Treasury Investment Growth Fund (TIGRs, pronounced "tigers"), in which it purchased Treasury securities and then stripped them to create principal-only securities and interest-only securities. Currently, more than $50 billion in stripped Treasury securities are outstanding.

Agency Bonds

Congress has authorized a number of U.S. agencies to issue bonds. The government does not explicitly guarantee agency bonds, though most investors feel that the government would not allow the agencies to default. Issuers of agency bonds include the Government National Mortgage Association, the Farmers Home Administration, the Federal Housing Administration, the Veterans Administrations, the Federal National Mortgage Association (Fannie Mae), the Federal Land Banks, the Federal Home Loan Mortgage Corporation, and the Student Loan Marketing Association. These agencies issue bonds to raise funds that are used for purposes that Congress has deemed to be in the national interest. For example, the Government National Mortgage Association (Ginnie Mae) issues bonds to raise funds that are used to finance home loans. Similarly, the Student Loan Marketing Association (Sallie Mae) issues bonds to fund student loans.

The risk on agency bonds is actually very low. They are usually secured by the loans that are made with the funds raised by the bond sales. In addition, the federal agencies may use their lines of credit with the Treasury Department should they have trouble meeting their obligations. Finally, it is unlikely that the federal government would permit its agencies to default on their obligations.

Despite this low level of risk, these securities offer interest rates that are significantly higher than those available on Treasury securities. For example, on August 17, 2001, 30-year Fannie Mae bonds yielded 6.88%, while 30-year Treasury bonds yielded 5.5%. A portion of the higher yield available on agencies may be due to their lower liquidity: Though a secondary market in agency securities exists, it is not as well developed or as deep as the market for government securities. (Chapter 5 discusses the effect liquidity has on interest rates.) Many investors feel that agency bonds represent an attractive alternative to low-interest-rate Treasuries.

MUNICIPAL BONDS

www.bloomberg.com/markets/munibondyield.html supplies the latest municipal bond events, experts' insights and analyses, and a municipal bond yields table.

Municipal bonds are securities issued by local, county, and state governments. The proceeds from these bonds are used to finance public interest projects such as schools, utilities, and transportation systems. Municipal bonds that are issued to pay for essential public projects are exempt from federal taxation. As we saw in Chapter 5, this allows the municipality to borrow at a lower cost because investors will be satisfied with lower interest rates on tax-exempt bonds. You can use the following equation to determine what tax-free rate of interest is equivalent to a taxable rate:

$$\text{Equivalent tax-free rate} = \text{taxable interest rate} \times (1 - \text{marginal tax rate})$$

EXAMPLE 1: Municipal Bonds

Suppose that the interest rate on a taxable corporate bond is 9% and that the marginal tax is 28%. Suppose a tax-free municipal bond with a rate of 6.75% were available. Which security would you choose?

Solution

The tax-free municipal interest rate is 6.48%.

$$\text{Equivalent tax-free rate} = \text{taxable interest rate} \times (1 - \text{marginal tax rate})$$

where

$$\text{Taxable interest rate} = 0.09$$

$$\text{Marginal tax rate} = 0.28$$

Thus

$$\text{Equivalent tax-free rate} = 0.09 \times (1 - 0.28) = 0.0648 = 6.48\%$$

Since the tax-free municipal bond rate is higher than the equivalent tax-free rate, choose the municipal bond.

There are two types of municipal bonds: general obligation bonds and revenue bonds. **General obligation bonds** do not have specific assets pledged as security or a specific source of revenue allocated for their repayment. Instead, they are backed by the "full faith and credit" of the issuer. This phrase means that the issuer promises to use every resource available to repay the bond as promised. Most general obligation bond issues must be approved by the taxpayers because the taxing authority of the government is pledged for their repayment.

Revenue bonds, by contrast, are backed by the cash flow of a particular revenue-generating project. For example, revenue bonds may be issued to build a toll bridge, with the tolls being pledged as repayment. If the revenues are not sufficient to repay the bonds, they may go into default, and investors may suffer losses. This occurred on a large scale in 1983 when the Washington Public Power

Supply System (since called "WHOOPS") used revenue bonds to finance the construction of two nuclear power plants. As a result of falling energy costs and tremendous cost overruns, the plants never became operational, and buyers of these bonds lost their investments. Revenue bonds tend to be issued more frequently than general obligation bonds (see Figure 5). Figure 6 shows how tax-exempt funds are used.

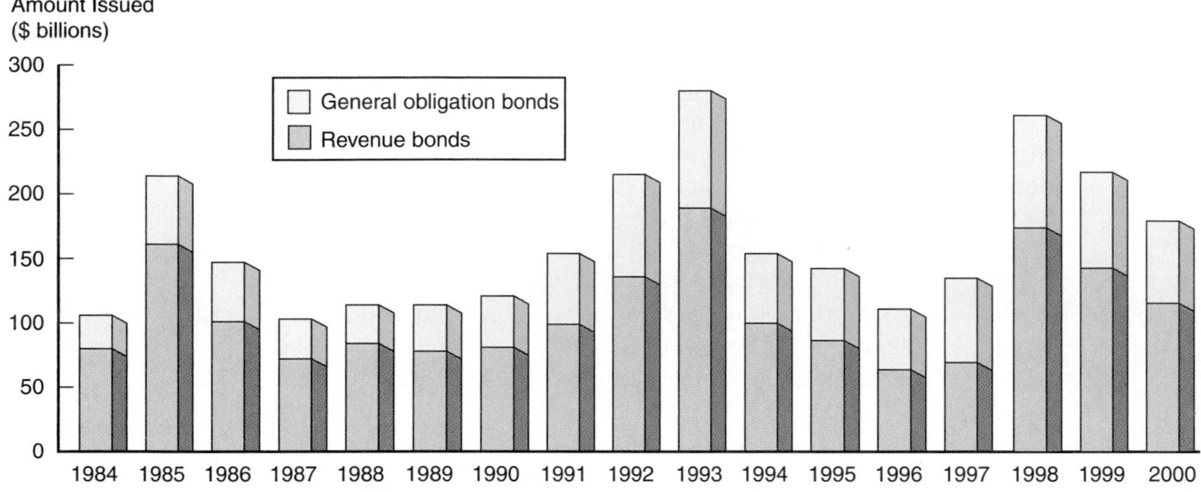

FIGURE 5 Issuance of Revenue and General Obligation Bonds, 1984–2000 (End of year)

Source: Federal Reserve Bulletin, various issues, Table 1.45.

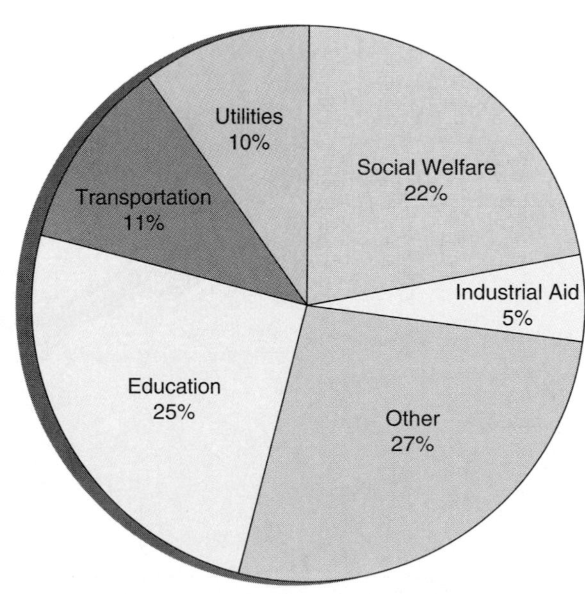

FIGURE 6 Use of Tax-Exempt State and Local Government Bonds

Risk in the Municipal Bond Market

Municipal bonds are not default-free. For example, defaults on municipal bonds amounted to $1.4 billion in 1990. This was primarily attributed to the weaker economy in 1990; however, it points out that governments are not exempt from financial distress. Unlike the federal government, local governments cannot print money, and there are real limits on how high they can raise taxes without driving the population away.[3]

CORPORATE BONDS

When large corporations need to borrow funds for long periods of time, they may issue bonds. Most corporate bonds have a face value of $1000 and pay interest semiannually (twice per year). Most are also callable, meaning that the issuer may redeem the bonds after a specified date.

The **bond indenture** is a contract that states the lender's rights and privileges and the borrower's obligations. Any collateral offered as security to the bondholders will also be described in the indenture.

The degree of risk varies widely among issues because the risk of default depends on the company's health, which can be affected by a number of variables. The interest rate on corporate bonds varies with the level of risk, as we discussed in Chapter 5. As Figure 7 shows, bonds with lower risk and a higher rating (AAA

[3]Review Chapter 4 for a complete discussion on the determinants of interest rates for securities.

At http://bonds.yahoo.com, access information on 10-year Treasury yield, composite bond rates for U.S. Treasury bonds, municipal bonds, and corporate bonds.

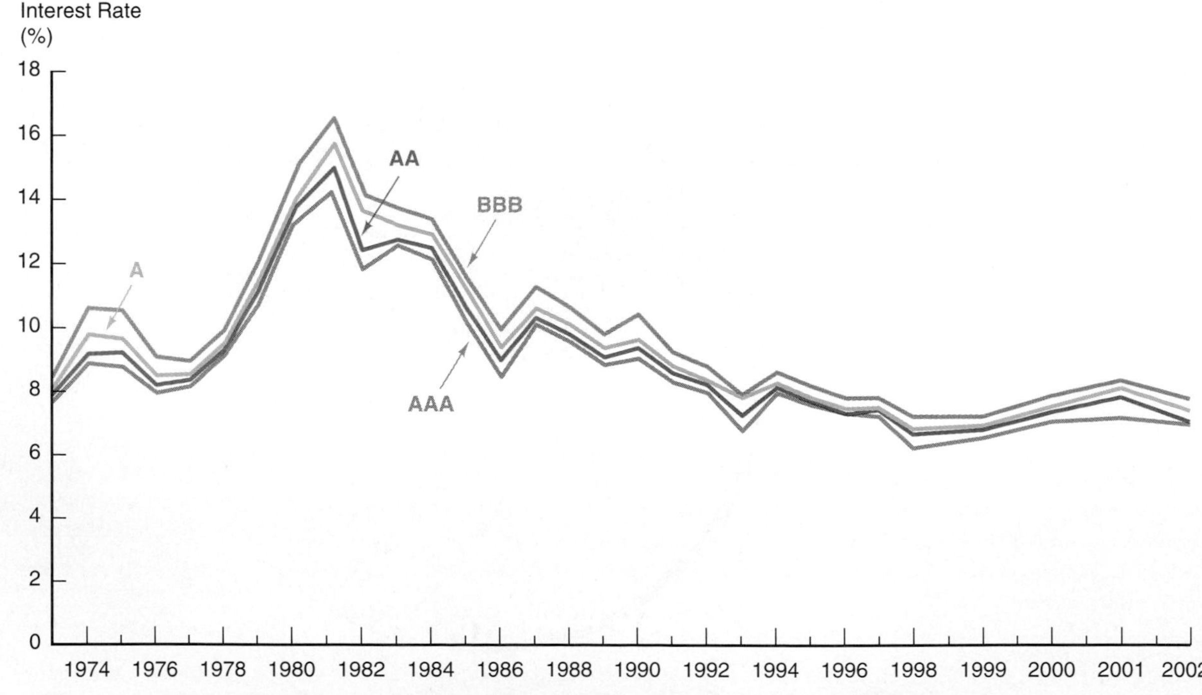

FIGURE 7 Corporate Bond Interest Rates, 1973–2002 (End of year)

Source: Federal Reserve Bulletin, various issues.

being the highest) have lower interest rates than more risky bonds (BBB). A bond's interest rate will depend on its features and characteristics, which are described in the following sections.

Characteristics of Corporate Bonds

At one time bonds were sold with attached coupons that the owner of the bond clipped and mailed to the firm to receive interest payments. These were called *bearer bonds* because payments were made to whoever had physical possession of the bonds. The Internal Revenue Service did not care for this method of payment, however, because it made tracking interest income difficult. Bearer bonds have now been largely replaced by **registered bonds,** which do not have coupons. Instead, the owner must register with the firm to receive interest payments. The firms are required to report to the IRS the name of the person who receives interest income. Despite the fact that bearer bonds with attached coupons have been phased out, the interest paid on bonds is still called the "coupon interest payment," and the interest rate on bonds is the coupon interest rate.

Restrictive Covenants A corporation's financial managers are hired, fired, and compensated at the direction of the board of directors, which represents the corporation's *stockholders.* This arrangement implies that the managers will be more interested in protecting stockholders than they are in protecting bondholders. You should recognize this as an example of the moral hazard problem introduced in Chapter 2 and discussed further in Chapter 14. Managers may not use the funds provided by the bonds as the bondholders might prefer. Since bondholders cannot look to managers for protection when the firm gets into trouble, they must include rules and restrictions on managers designed to protect the bondholders' interests. These are known as **restrictive covenants.** They usually limit the amount of dividends the firm can pay and the ability of the firm to issue additional debt. Other financial policies, such as the firm's involvement in mergers, may also be restricted. Restrictive covenants are included in the bond indenture. Typically, the interest rate will be lower the more restrictions are placed on management through restrictive covenants because the bonds will be considered safer by buyers.

Call Provisions Most corporate indentures include a **call provision,** which states that the issuer has the right to force the holder to sell the bond back. The call provision usually requires a waiting period between the time the bond is initially issued and the time when it can be called. The price bondholders are paid for the bond is usually set at the bond's par price or slightly higher (usually by one year's interest cost). For example, a 10% coupon rate $1000 bond may have a call price of $1100.

If interest rates fall, the price of the bond will rise. If rates fall enough, the price will rise above the call price, and the firm will call the bond. Because call provisions put a limit on the amount that bondholders can earn from the appreciation of a bond's price, investors do not like call provisions.

A second reason that issuers of bonds include call provisions is to make it possible for them to buy back their bonds according to the terms of the **sinking fund.** A sinking fund is a requirement in the bond indenture that the firm pay off a portion of the bond issue each year. This provision is attractive to bondholders because it reduces the probability of default when the issue matures. Because a sinking fund provision makes the issue more attractive, the firm can reduce the bond's interest rate.

A third reason firms usually issue only callable bonds is that firms may have to retire a bond issue if the covenants of the issue restrict the firm from some activity that it feels is in the best interest of stockholders. Suppose that a firm needed to borrow additional funds to expand its storage facilities. If the firm's bonds carried a restriction against adding debt, the firm would have to retire its existing bonds before issuing new bonds or taking out a loan to build the new warehouse.

Finally, a firm may choose to call bonds if it wishes to alter its capital structure. A maturing firm with excess cash flow may wish to reduce its debt load if few attractive investment opportunities are available.

Because bondholders do not generally like call provisions, callable bonds must have a higher yield than comparable noncallable bonds. Despite the higher cost, firms still typically issue callable bonds because of the flexibility this feature provides the firm.

Conversion Some bonds can be converted into shares of common stock. This feature permits bondholders to share in the firm's good fortunes if the stock price rises. Most convertible bonds will state that the bond can be converted into a certain number of common shares at the discretion of the bondholder. The conversion ratio will be such that the price of the stock must rise substantially before conversion is likely to occur.

Issuing convertible bonds is one way firms avoid sending a negative signal to the market. If a firm chooses to issue stock, the market usually interprets this action as indicating that the stock price is relatively high or that it is going to fall in the future. The market makes this interpretation because it believes that managers are most concerned with looking out for the interests of existing stockholders and will not issue stock when it is undervalued. If managers believe that the firm will perform well in the future, they can, instead, issue convertible bonds. If the managers are correct and the stock price rises, the bondholders will convert to stock at a relatively high price that managers believe is fair. Alternatively, bondholders have the option not to convert if managers turn out to be wrong about the company's future.

Bondholders like a conversion feature. It is very similar to buying just a bond but receiving both a bond and a stock option (stock options are discussed fully in Chapter 23). The price of the bond will reflect the value of this option and so will be higher than the price of comparable nonconvertible bonds. The higher price received for the bond by the firm implies a lower interest rate.

Types of Corporate Bonds

A variety of corporate bonds is available. They are usually distinguished by the type of collateral that secures the bond and by the order in which the bond is paid off if the firm defaults.

Secured Bonds Secured bonds are ones with collateral attached. *Mortgage bonds* are used to finance a specific project. For example, a building may be the collateral for bonds issued for its construction. In the event that the firm fails to make payments as promised, mortgage bondholders have the right to liquidate the property in order to be paid. Because these bonds have specific property pledged as collateral, they are less risky than comparable unsecured bonds. As a result, they will have a lower interest rate.

Equipment trust certificates are bonds secured by tangible non-real estate property, such as heavy equipment or airplanes. Typically, the collateral backing these bonds is more easily marketed than the real property backing mortgage bonds. As with mortgage bonds, the presence of collateral reduces the risk of the bonds and so lowers their interest rates.

Unsecured Bonds *Debentures* are long-term unsecured bonds that are backed only by the general creditworthiness of the issuer. No specific collateral is pledged to repay the debt. In the event of default, the bondholders must go to court to seize assets. Collateral that has been pledged to other debtors is not available to the holders of debentures. *Debentures* usually have attached to them a contract that spells out the terms of the bond and the responsibilities of management. The contract attached to the debenture is called an *indenture* (Be careful not to confuse the terms *debenture* and *indenture.*) Debentures have lower priority than secured bonds if the firm defaults. As a result, they will have a higher interest rate than otherwise comparable secured bonds.

Subordinated debentures are similar to debentures except that they have a lower priority claim. This means that in the event of a default, subordinated debenture holders are paid only after nonsubordinated bondholders have been paid in full. As a result, subordinated debenture holders are at greater risk of loss.

Variable-rate bonds (which may be secured or unsecured) are a financial innovation spurred by increased interest-rate variability in the 1980s and 1990s. The interest rate on these securities is tied to another market interest rate, such as the rate on Treasury bonds, and is adjusted periodically. The interest rate on the bonds will change over time as market rates change.

Junk Bonds Recall from Chapter 5 that all bonds are rated by various companies according to their default risk. These companies study the issuer's financial characteristics and make a judgment about the issuer's possibility of default. A bond with a rating of AAA has the highest grade possible. Bonds *above* Moody's Baa or Standard and Poor's BBB rating are considered of investment grade. Those rated *below* this level are usually considered speculative (see Table 2). Speculative-grade bonds are often called **junk bonds.** Before the late 1970s, primary issues of speculative-grade securities were very rare; almost all new bond issues consisted of investment-grade bonds. However, when companies ran into financial difficulties, their bond ratings would fall. Holders of these downgraded bonds found that they were difficult to sell because no well-developed secondary market existed. It is easy to understand why investors would be leery of these securities, as they were usually unsecured.

In 1977, Michael Milken, at the investment banking firm of Drexel Burnham Lambert, recognized that there were many investors who would be willing to take on greater risk if they were compensated with greater returns. First, however, Milken had to address two problems that hindered the market for low-grade bonds. The first was that they suffered from poor liquidity. Whereas underwriters of investment-grade bonds continued to make a market after the bonds were issued, no such market maker existed for junk bonds. Drexel agreed to assume

TABLE 2 Debt Ratings

Standard and Poor's	Moody's	Average Interest Rate* (%)	Definition
AAA	Aaa	7.27	Best quality and highest rating. Capacity to pay interest and repay principal is extremely strong. Smallest degree of investment risk.
AA	Aa	7.38	High quality. Very strong capacity to pay interest and repay principal and differs from AAA/Aaa in a small degree.
A	A	7.79	Strong capacity to pay interest and repay principal. Possess many favorable investment attributes and are considered upper-medium-grade obligations. Somewhat more susceptible to the adverse effects of changes in circumstances and economic conditions.
BBB	Baa	8.12	Medium-grade obligations. Neither highly protected nor poorly secured. Adequate capacity to pay interest and repay principal. May lack long-term reliability and protective elements to secure interest and principal payments.
BB	Ba		Moderate ability to pay interest and repay principal. Have speculative elements and future cannot be considered well assured. Adverse business, economic, and financial conditions could lead to inability to meet financial obligations.
B	B		Lack characteristics of desirable investment. Assurance of interest and principal payments over long period of time may be small. Adverse conditions likely to impair ability to meet financial obligations.
CCC	Caa		Poor standing. Identifiable vulnerability to default and dependent on favorable business, economic, and financial conditions to meet timely payment of interest and repayment of principal.
CC	Ca		Represent obligations that are speculative to a high degree. Issues often default and have other marked shortcomings.
C	C		Lowest-rated class of bonds. Have extremely poor prospects of attaining any real investment standard. May be used to cover a situation where bankruptcy petition has been filed, but debt service payments are continued.
CI			Reserved for income bonds on which no interest is being paid.
D			Payment default.
NR			No public rating has been requested.
(+) or (−)			Ratings from AA to CCC may be modified by the addition of a plus or minus sign to show relative standing within the major rating categories.

*Average interest rates are reported in the *Bulletin* only for the top four risk categories.

Source: Federal Reserve Bulletin, Table 1.35, Lines 40–43, December 2001.

this role as market maker for junk bonds. That assured that a secondary market existed, an important consideration for investors, who seldom want to hold the bonds to maturity.

The second problem with the junk bond market was that there was a very real chance that the issuing firms would default on their bond payments. By comparison, the default risk on investment-grade securities was negligible. To reduce the probability of losses, Milken acted much as a commercial bank for junk bond issuers. He would renegotiate the firm's debt or advance additional funds if needed to prevent the firm from defaulting. Milken's efforts substantially reduced the default risk, and the demand for junk bonds soared.

During the early and mid–1980s, many firms took advantage of junk bonds to finance the takeover of other firms. When a firm greatly increases its debt level (by issuing junk bonds) to finance the purchase of another firm's stock, the increase in leverage makes the bonds high-risk. Frequently, part of the acquired firm is eventually sold to pay down the debt incurred by issuing the junk bonds. Some 1800 firms accessed the junk bond market during the 1980s.

Milken and his brokerage firm were very well compensated for their efforts. Milken earned a fee of 2% to 3% of each junk bond issue, which made Drexel the most profitable firm on Wall Street in 1987. Milken's personal income between 1983 and 1987 was in excess of $1 billion.

Unfortunately for holders of junk bonds, both Milken and Drexel were caught and convicted of insider trading. With Drexel unable to support the junk bond market, 250 companies defaulted between 1989 and 1991. Drexel itself filed bankruptcy in 1990 due to losses on its own holdings of junk bonds. Milken was sentenced to three years in prison for his part in the scandal. *Fortune* magazine reported that Milken's personal fortune still exceeded $400 million.[4]

The junk bond market has recovered since its low in 1990 and now continues to permit medium-size firms to obtain financing that might otherwise be unavailable to them because of the relatively high risk.

FINANCIAL GUARANTEES FOR BONDS

Financially weaker security issuers frequently purchase **financial guarantees** to lower the risk of their bonds. A financial guarantee ensures that the lender (bond purchaser) will be paid both principal and interest in the event the issuer defaults. Large, well-known insurance companies write what are actually insurance policies to back bond issues. With such a financial guarantee, bond buyers no longer have to be concerned with the financial health of the bond issuer. Instead, they are interested only in the strength of the insurer. Essentially, the credit rating of the insurer is substituted for the credit rating of the issuer. The resulting reduction in risk lowers the interest rate demanded by bond buyers. Of course, issuers must pay a fee to the insurance company for the guarantee. Financial guarantees make sense only when the cost of the insurance is less than the interest savings that result.

Financial guarantees were developed in the early 1970s to insure municipal bonds. More recently, their use has been expanded to cover a variety of corporate bonds as well.

TRENDS IN THE BOND MARKET

During the first half of the 1980s, interest rates were very high, and firms were reluctant to borrow in the long-term market. In the second half of the 1980s, declining interest rates and a healthy economy combined to encourage bond issuance. Issuance again fell in 1990 when the economy entered a recession, and interest rates rose. Falling interest rates and a rebounding economy contributed toward record-breaking volumes in the bond markets in the late 1990s. Figure 8 shows the volume of new bonds issued by all entities between 1983 and 2000 in comparison with the volume of new stocks issued in the same period.

[4]A complete history of Milken was reported in *Fortune,* September 30, 1996, pp. 80–105.

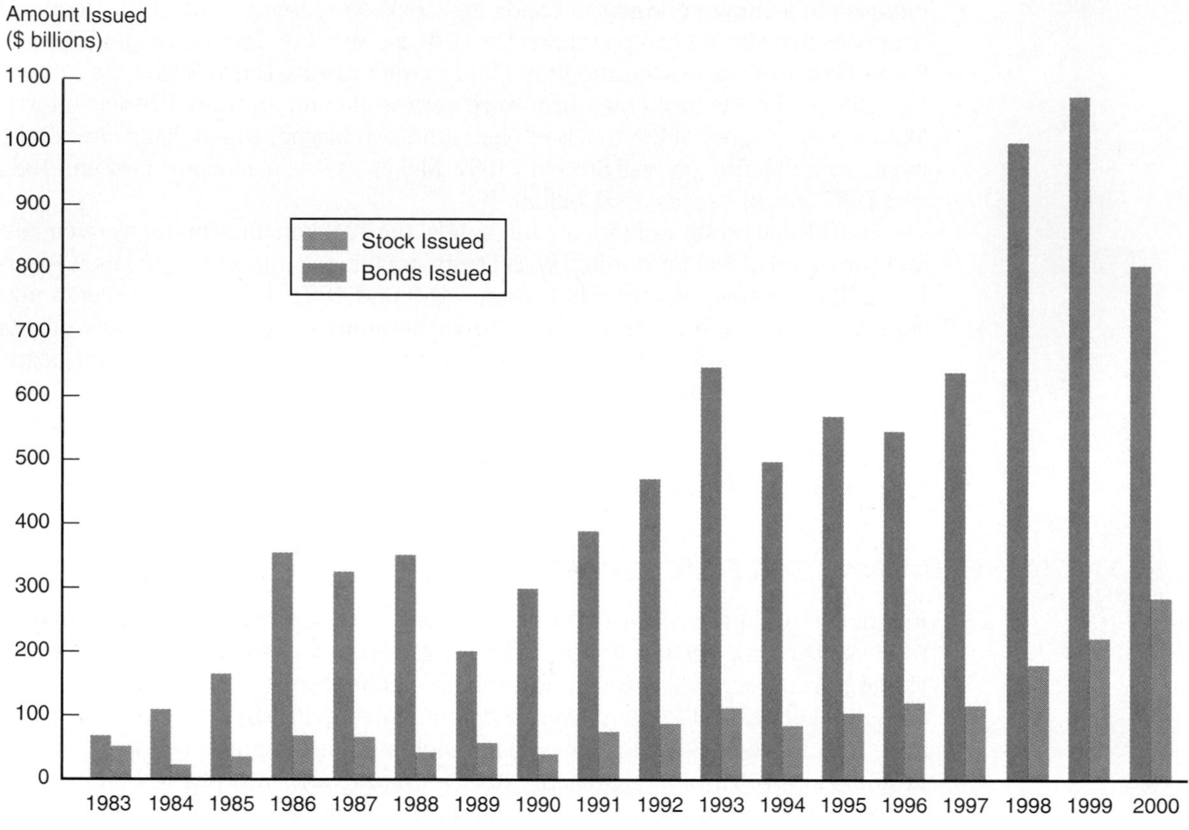

FIGURE 8 Bonds and Stocks Issued, 1983–2000

Source: Federal Reserve Bulletin, various issues. Table 1.46.

CAPITAL MARKET SECURITIES: STOCK

A share of stock in a firm represents ownership. A stockholder owns a percentage interest in a firm, consistent with the percentage of outstanding stock held. This ownership is in contrast to a bondholder, who holds no ownership interest but is rather a creditor of the firm.

Investors can earn a return from stock in one of two ways. Either the price of the stock rises over time, or the firm pays the stockholder dividends. Frequently, investors earn a return from both sources. Stock is riskier than bonds because stockholders have a lower priority than bondholders when the firm is in trouble, the returns to investors are less assured because dividends can be easily changed, and stock price increases are not guaranteed. Despite these risks, it is possible to make a great deal of money by investing in stock, whereas that is very unlikely by investing in bonds. Another distinction between stock and bonds is that stock does not mature.

Ownership of stock gives the stockholder certain rights regarding the firm. One is the right of a *residual claimant:* Stockholders have a claim on all assets and income left over after all other claimants have been satisfied. If nothing is left over, they get nothing. As noted, however, it is possible to get rich as a stockholder if the firm does well.

Most stockholders have the *right to vote* for directors and on certain issues, such as amendments to the corporate charter and whether new shares should be issued.

Notice that the stock certificate shown in Figure 9 does not list a maturity date, face value or an interest rate, which were indicated on the bond.

Common Stock Versus Preferred Stock

There are two types of stock, common and preferred. A share of **common stock** in a firm represents an ownership interest in that firm. Common stockholders vote, receive dividends, and hope that the price of their stock will rise. There are various classes of common stock, usually denoted as type A, type B, and so on. Unfortunately, the type does not have any meaning that is standard across all companies. The differences among the types usually involve either the distribution of dividends or voting rights. It is important for an investor in stocks to know exactly what rights go along with the shares of stock being contemplated.

Preferred stock is a form of equity from a legal and tax standpoint. However, it differs from common stock in several important ways. First, because preferred stockholders receive a fixed dividend that never changes, a share of preferred stock is as much like a bond as it is like common stock. Second, because the dividend does not change, the price of preferred stock is relatively stable. Third, preferred stockholders do not usually vote unless the firm has failed to pay the promised dividend. Finally, preferred stockholders hold a claim on assets that has priority over the claims of common shareholders but after that of creditors such as bondholders.

Less than 25 percent of new equity issues are preferred stock, and only about 5 percent of all capital is raised using preferred stock. This may be because

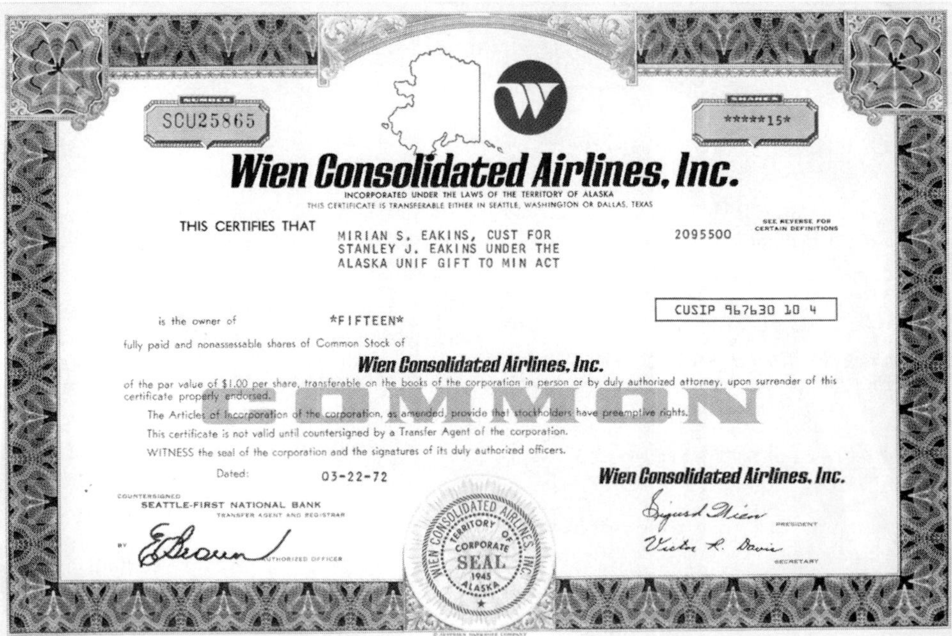

SCU25865

*****15*

Wien Consolidated Airlines, Inc.

INCORPORATED UNDER THE LAWS OF THE TERRITORY OF ALASKA

THIS CERTIFICATE IS TRANSFERABLE EITHER IN SEATTLE, WASHINGTON OR DALLAS, TEXAS

THIS CERTIFIES THAT MIRIAN S. EAKINS, CUST FOR STANLEY J. EAKINS UNDER THE ALASKA UNIF GIFT TO MIN ACT

2095500

SEE REVERSE FOR CERTAIN DEFINITIONS

CUSIP 967630 10 4

is the owner of *FIFTEEN*

fully paid and nonassessable shares of Common Stock of

Wien Consolidated Airlines, Inc.

of the par value of $1.00 per share, transferable on the books of the corporation in person or by duly authorized attorney, upon surrender of this certificate properly endorsed.

COMMON

The Articles of Incorporation of the corporation, as amended, provide that stockholders have preemptive rights.

This certificate is not valid until countersigned by a Transfer Agent of the corporation.

WITNESS the seal of the corporation and the signatures of its duly authorized officers.

Dated: 03-22-72

COUNTERSIGNED SEATTLE-FIRST NATIONAL BANK TRANSFER AGENT AND REGISTRAR

BY AUTHORIZED OFFICER

WIEN CONSOLIDATED AIRLINES, INC. TERRITORY OF ALASKA CORPORATE SEAL 1945

Wien Consolidated Airlines, Inc.

PRESIDENT

SECRETARY

FIGURE 9 Wien Consolidated Airlines Stock

Source: Eakins, *Finance Investments, Institutions, & Management*, p. 43.

preferred dividends are not tax-deductible to the firm but bond interest payments are. Consequently, issuing preferred stock usually costs the firm more than issuing debt, even though it shares many of the characteristics of a bond.

Stock Value

The price of a share of stock is the present value of expected future cash flows, which consist of dividends plus a final selling price. (The "Following the Financial News" box shows how stock market prices are reported each day.) Investors are willing to pay a price for stock that reflects the sum of all of the future cash flows the security will generate, after adjusting for the time value of money. The problem, of course, is predicting the future cash flows of the firm. If a firm does well, the residual cash flows available for dividends can be large, and a high share price is justified. If a firm does poorly, there may not be any cash flows available to pay any dividend at all.

FOLLOWING THE FINANCIAL NEWS
Stock Prices

Stock prices are published daily, and in the *Wall Street Journal* they are reported in the sections "NYSE—Composite Transactions," "Amex—Composite Transactions," and "Over-the-Counter Markets." The New York Stock Exchange (NYSE) and American Stock Exchange (Amex) stocks' prices are quoted in the following format:

YTD %CHG	52 WEEKS HI	52 WEEKS LO	STOCK (SYM)	DIV	YLD %	PE	VOL 100S	LAST	NET CHG
+ 31.1	26.68	17.85	IntAlum **IAL**	1.20	5.0	25	32	24	−0.10
+ 42.3	124.70	82.13	IBM **IBM**	.56	.5	27	34159	120.96	−1.94
+ 46.3	31.69	18.88	IntFlavor **IFF**	.60	2.0	33	2115	29.71	−0.15
+ 42.3	71.95	35.70	IntGameTch **IGT**	.12	.2	24	19261	68.30	−1.70
+ 17.7	24.67	15.89	IntMultfood **IMC**	.80	3.3	28	394	23.90	....

Source: *Wall Street Journal*, January 3, 2002.

Get detailed stock quotes, charts, and historical stock data at http://stocks.tradingcharts.com

The following information is included in each column. International Business Machines (IBM) common stock is used as an example.

Ytd % Chg: Year-to-date percentage change in price. Since this listing is for close of business December 31, 2001, the +42.3 reflects the increase in price over the entire year.

52 Weeks Hi: Highest price of a share in the past 52 weeks: $124.70 for IBM stock

52 Weeks Lo: Lowest price of a share in the past 52 weeks: 82.13 for IBM stock

Stock: Company name: IBM for International Business Machines

Sym: Symbol that identifies company: IBM

Div: Annual dividends per share: $0.56 for IBM

Yld %: Yield for stock expressed as annual dividends divided by today's closing price: 0.5% (= 0.56 ÷ 120.96) for IBM stock

PE: Price-earnings ratio; the stock price divided by the annual earnings per share: 27.

Vol 100s: Number of shares (in hundreds) traded that day: 3,415,900 shares for IBM

Last: Closing price (last price) that day: $120.96.

Net Chg: Change in the closing price from the previous day: −$1.94

Prices quoted for shares traded over-the-counter (through dealers rather than on an organized exchange) are sometimes quoted with the same information, but in many cases only the bid price (the price the dealer is willing to pay for the stock) and the asked price (the price the dealer is willing to sell the stock for) are quoted.

We discuss the theory and mechanics of stock valuation further in the next chapter.

Stock Market Indexes

A stock market index is used to monitor the behavior of a group of stocks. By reviewing the average behavior of a group of stocks, investors are able to gain some insight as to how a broad group of stocks may have performed. Various stock market indexes are reported to give investors an indication of the performance of different groups of stocks. The most commonly quoted index is the Dow Jones Industrial Average, an index based on the performance of the stocks of 30 large companies. Box 2 provides more background on this famous index. Table 3 lists the 30 stocks that made up the index in August 2001.

Other indexes, such as Standard and Poor's 500 Index, the NASDAQ composite, and the NYSE composite, may be more useful for following the performance

TABLE 3 The Thirty Companies That Make Up the Dow Jones Industrial Average

Alcoa Inc.	General Electric Co.	McDonald's Corp.
American Express Co.	General Motors Corp.	Merck & Co. Inc.
AT&T Corp.	Hewlett-Packard Co.	Microsoft Corp.
Boeing Co.	Home Depot Inc.	Minnesota Mining & Manufacturing Co.
Caterpillar Inc.	Honeywell International Inc.	Philip Morris Cos.
Citigroup Inc.	Intel Corp.	Procter & Gamble Co.
Coca-Cola Co.	International Business Machines Corp.	SBC Communications Inc.
E.I. DuPont de Nemours & Co.	International Paper Co.	United Technologies Corp.
Eastman Kodak Co.	J. P. Morgan Chase & Co.	Wal-Mart Stores Inc.
Exxon Mobil Corp.	Johnson & Johnson	Walt Disney Co.

BOX 2

History of the Dow Jones Industrial Average

The Dow Jones Industrial Average (DJIA) is an index composed of 30 "blue chip" industrial firms. On May 26, 1896, Charles H. Dow added up the prices of 12 of the best-known stocks and created an average by dividing by the number of stocks. In 1916, eight more stocks were added, and in 1928, the 30-stock average made its debut.

Today the editors of the *Wall Street Journal* select the firms that make up the DJIA. They take a broad view of the type of firm that is considered "industrial": In essence, it is almost any company that is not in the transportation or utility business (because there are also Dow Jones averages for those kinds of stocks). In choosing a new company for the DJIA, they look among substantial industrial companies with a history of successful growth and wide interest among investors. The components of the DJIA are changed periodically. For example, in 1997, Bethlehem Steel, Texaco, Westinghouse, and Woolworth were replaced with Hewlett-Packard, Johnson & Johnson, Travelers Group, and Wal-Mart. In 1999, Home Depot, Intel, Microsoft, and SBC Communications joined the average, replacing Union Carbide, Goodyear Tire & Rubber, Sears, and Chevron.

Most market watchers agree that the DJIA is not the best indicator of the market's overall day-to-day performance. Indeed, it varies substantially from broader-based stock indexes in the short run. It continues to be followed so closely primarily because it is the oldest index and was the first to be quoted by other publications. But it tracks the performance of the market reasonably well over the long run.

Table 4 shows the greatest one-day gains and losses since the initiation of the DJIA.

of different groups of stocks. The *Wall Street Journal* reports on 23 different indexes in its "Stock Market Daily Data Bank." Figure 10 shows the DJIA since 1980.

Buying Foreign Stocks

In Chapter 4 we learned that diversification of a portfolio reduces risk. In recent years, investors have come to realize that some risk can also be eliminated by diversifying across different countries. When one country is suffering from a recession, others may be booming. If inflationary concerns in the United States cause stock prices to drop, falling inflation in Japan may cause Japanese stocks to rise.

TABLE 4 Greatest One-Day Changes in the Dow Jones Industrial Average

Rank	Date	Percent Gain	Date	Percent Loss
1	October 6, 1931	14.87	October 19, 1987	−22.61
2	October 30, 1929	12.34	October 28, 1929	−12.82
3	September 21, 1932	11.36	October 29, 1929	−11.73
4	October 21, 1987	10.15	November 6, 1929	−9.92
5	August 3, 1932	9.52	December 18, 1899	−8.72
6	February 11, 1932	9.47	August 12, 1932	−8.40
7	November 14, 1929	9.36	March 14, 1907	−8.29
8	December 18, 1931	9.35	October 26, 1987	−8.04
9	February 13, 1932	9.19	July 21, 1933	−7.84
10	May 6, 1932	9.08	October 18, 1937	−7.75

Source: Dow Jones Corp., www.djindexes.com provides a wealth of information about the current DJIA and its history.

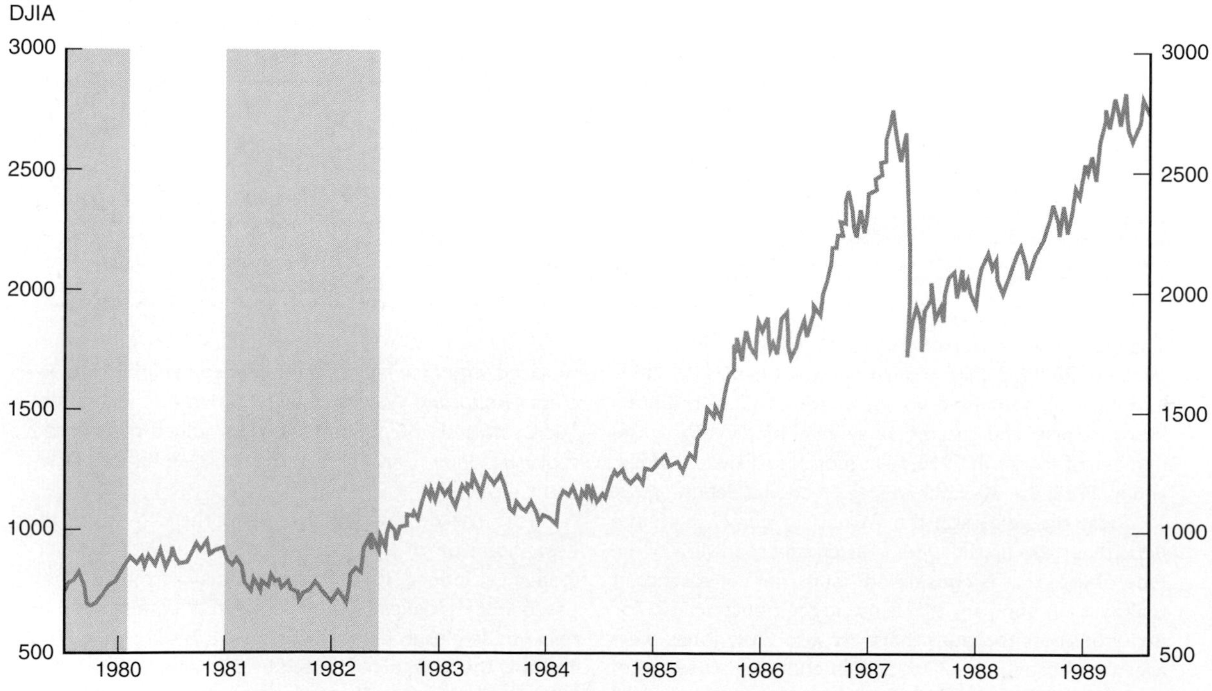

FIGURE 10 Dow Jones Industrial Averages, 1980–2002

Shaded areas indicate periods of recession.

Source: http://finance.yahoo.com/?u

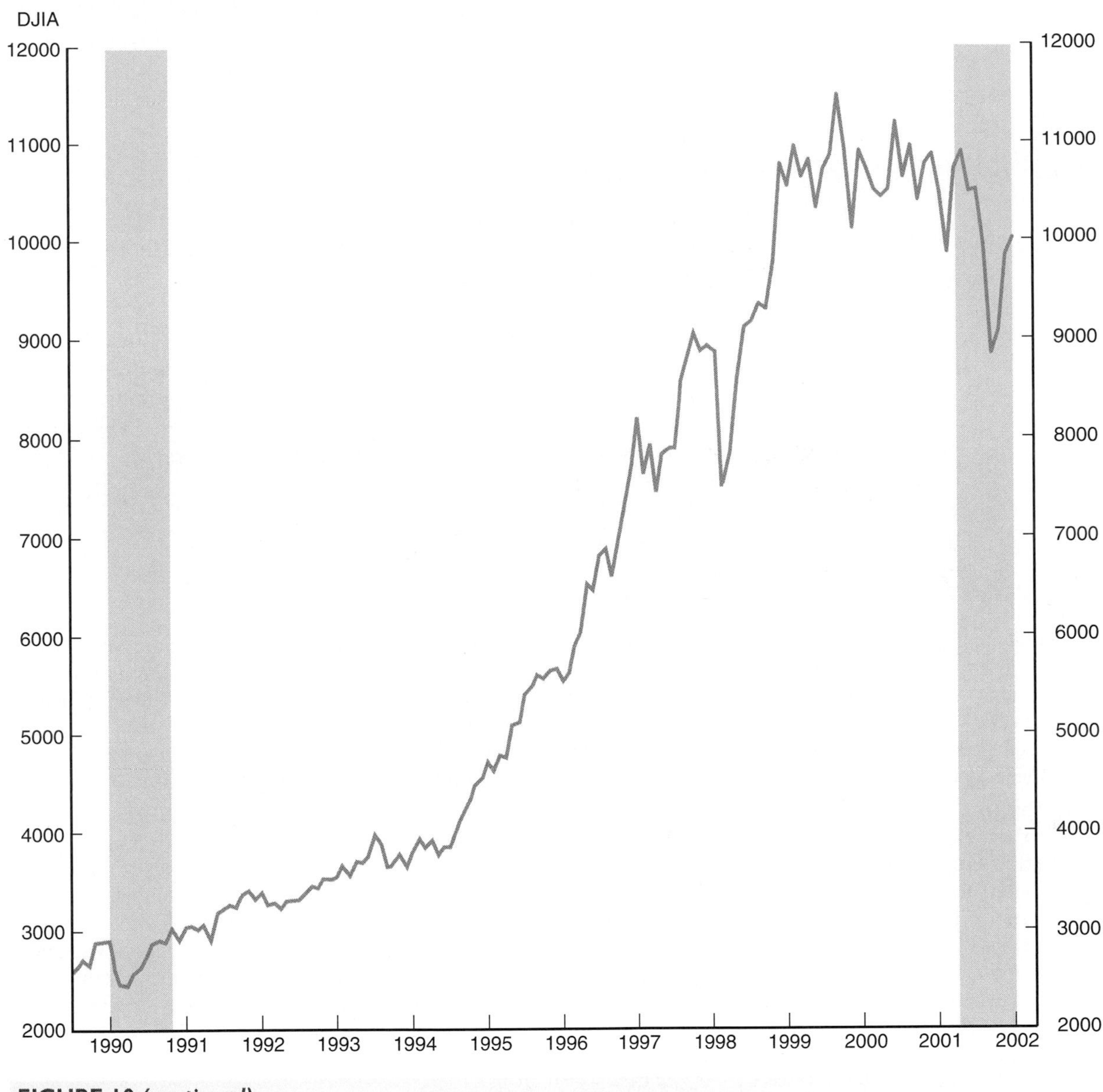

FIGURE 10 ***(continued)***

The problem with buying foreign stocks is that most foreign companies are not listed on any of the U.S. stock exchanges, so the purchase of shares is difficult. Intermediaries have found a way to solve this problem by selling **American depository receipts (ADRs).** A U.S. bank buys the shares of a foreign company and places them in its vault. The bank then issues receipts against these shares, and these receipts can be traded domestically, usually on the NASDAQ. Trade in ADRs is conducted entirely in U.S. dollars, and the bank converts stock dividends into U.S. currency. One advantage of the ADR is that it allows foreign firms to trade in the United States without the firms having to meet the disclosure rules required by the SEC.

Foreign stock trading has been growing rapidly. Since 1979, cross-border trade in equities has grown at a rate of 28% a year and now exceeds $2 trillion annually. Interest is particularly keen in the stocks of firms in emerging economies such as Mexico, Brazil, and South Korea.

PUBLIC ISSUES OF STOCKS AND BONDS

Once a firm determines that it should issue stocks or bonds, it must somehow get them into the public's hands at the highest price possible. The more the public pays for either the stocks or the bonds of a firm, the lower the cost of capital to that firm, all other things being equal.

There are two principal ways for a firm to sell securities to the public: through a public sale organized by investment bankers who are underwriting the issue or through a private placement. **Underwriting** means that the investment bankers handle the details of placing the securities in the public's hands. The role of investment bankers in security distribution is discussed in Chapter 21.

SUMMARY

1. The capital markets exist to provide financing for long-term capital assets. Households, often through investments in pension and mutual funds, are net investors in the capital markets. Corporations and the federal and state governments are net users of these funds.
2. The three main capital market instruments are bonds, stocks, and mortgages. Bonds represent borrowing by the issuing firm. Stock represents ownership in the issuing firm. Mortgages are long-term loans secured by real property. Only corporations can issue stock. Corporations and governments can issue bonds. In any given year, far more funds are raised with bonds than with stock.
3. There are both organized and over-the-counter exchanges. Organized exchanges are distinguished by a physical building where trading takes place. The over-the-counter market operates primarily over phone lines and computer links. Typically, larger firms trade on organized exchanges and smaller firms in the over-the-counter market, though there are exceptions to this rule.
4. Firm managers are hired by stockholders to protect and increase their wealth. Bondholders must rely on a contract called an indenture to protect their interests. Bond indentures contain covenants that restrict the firm from activities that increase risk and hence the chance of default on the bonds. Bond indentures also contain many provisions that make them more or less attractive to investors, such as a call option, convertibility, or a sinking fund.

KEY TERMS

American depository receipts (ADRs), *p.* 263
bond indenture, *p.* 252
call provision, *p.* 253
common stock, *p.* 259
financial guarantee, *p.* 257
general obligation bonds, *p.* 250
junk bond, *p.* 255
National Association of Securities Dealers Automated Quotation System (NASDAQ), *p.* 244
preferred stock, *p.* 259
registered bonds, *p.* 253
restrictive covenants, *p.* 253
revenue bonds, *p.* 250
Separate Trading of Registered Interest and Principal Securities (STRIPS), *p.* 248
sinking fund, *p.* 253

QUESTIONS AND PROBLEMS

*1. Contrast investors' use of capital markets with their use of money markets.

2. What are the primary capital market securities, and who are the primary purchasers of these securities?

*3. Distinguish between the primary market and the secondary market for securities.

4. Discuss the features that differentiate organized exchanges from the over-the-counter market.

*5. What is the National Association of Securities Dealers Automated Quotation System (NASDAQ)?

6. A bond provides information about its par value, coupon interest rate, and maturity date. Define each of these.

*7. The U.S. Treasury issues bills, notes, and bonds. How do these three securities differ?

8. As interest rates in the market change over time, the market price of bonds rises and falls. The change in the value of bonds due to changes in interest rates is a risk incurred by bond investors. What is this risk called?

*9. In addition to Treasury securities, some agencies of the government issue bonds. List three such agencies, and state what the funds raised by the bond issues are used for.

10. A call provision on a bond allows the issuer to redeem the bond at will. Investors do not like call provisions and so require higher interest on callable bonds. Why do issuers continue to issue callable bonds anyway?

*11. What is a sinking fund? Do investors like bonds that contain this feature?

12. What is the document called that lists the terms of a bond?

*13. What distinguishes stocks from bonds?

14. Describe the two ways whereby capital market securities pass from the issuer to the public.

*15. Review the list of firms now included in the Dow Jones Industrial Average listed in Table 3. How many firms appear to be technology related? Discuss what this means in terms of the risk of the index.

WEB EXERCISES

The Capital Markets

1. Stocks tend to get more publicity than bonds, but many investors, especially those nearing or in retirement, find that bonds are more consistent with their risk preferences. One site that will help an investor choose among bonds can be found at http://bonds.yahoo.com. Click on the calculators tab and choose the calculator titled, "Which bond is better." Look at the example provided. Do the results change if you assume a 28% tax bracket and that you will sell the bond in two years?

2. There are a number of indexes that track the performance of the stock market. It is interesting to review how well they track along with each other. Go to http://bloomberg.com. Click on the "Charts" tab at the top of the screen. Put checks in the boxes to display the DJIA, S&P 500, NASDAQ, and the Russell 2000. Set the time frame to five years. Click on "Get Chart." You may want to add one index to the chart at a time to keep track of which color corresponds to each index.
   a. Which index has been most volatile over the last five years?
   b. Which index has posted the greatest gains over the last five years?
   c. Now adjust the time frame to intraday. Which index has performed the best today? Which has been most volatile?

3. The capital markets are where individuals go to invest for their long-term retirement needs. These markets provide a variety of securities to meet different risk tolerances with different expected rates of return. An excellent site for computing your retirement needs and showing a possible distribution of investment assets can be found at http://www.quicken.com/retirement/planner/js/notemplates/intronn.dcg?partner=cnnfn. After responding to the questions posed on this site, discuss how you will save for your retirement.

Chapter 10

The Stock Market and the Efficient Market Hypothesis

Preview

The market for stocks is undoubtedly the financial market that receives the most attention and scrutiny. Great fortunes are made and lost as investors attempt to anticipate the market's ups and downs. We have witnessed an unprecedented period of volatility over the last decade. Stock indexes hit record highs in the late 1990s, largely led by technology companies, and then fell precipitously in 2000. In this chapter we begin looking at how this important market works.

We begin by discussing the fundamental theories that underlie the valuation of stocks. These theories are critical to an understanding of the forces that cause the value of stocks to rise and fall minute by minute and day by day. We will learn that determining a value for a common stock is very difficult and that it is this difficulty that leads to so much volatility in the stock markets.

Once we have learned the methods required for stock valuation, we will explore how good a job the markets do in establishing fair prices for securities. The idea that markets do a good job so that security prices fully reflect all available information is referred to as the ***efficient market hypothesis.*** We will examine whether the evidence supports this hypothesis.

COMPUTING THE PRICE OF COMMON STOCK

Common stock is the principal way that corporations raise equity capital. Holders of common stock own an interest in the corporation consistent with the

At http://stocks.tradingcharts.com, access detailed stock quotes, charts, and historical stock data.

percentage of outstanding shares owned. This ownership interest gives **stockholders**—those who hold stock in a corporation—a bundle of rights. The most important are the right to vote and to be the **residual claimant** of all funds flowing into the firm (known as **cash flows**), meaning that the stockholder receives whatever remains after all other claims against the firm's assets have been satisfied. Stockholders are paid dividends from the net earnings of the corporation. **Dividends** are payments made periodically, usually every quarter, to stockholders. The board of directors of the firm sets the level of the dividend, usually upon the recommendation of management. In addition, the stockholder has the right to sell the stock.

One basic principle of finance is that the value of any investment is found by computing the value today of all cash flows the investment will generate over its life. For example, a commercial building will sell for a price that reflects the net cash flows (rents − expenses) it is projected to have over its useful life. Similarly, we value common stock as the value in today's dollars of all future cash flows. As noted above, the cash flows a stockholder may earn from stock are dividends, the sales price, or both.

To develop the theory of stock valuation, we begin with the simplest possible scenario. This assumes that you buy the stock, hold it for one period to get a dividend, then sell the stock. We call this the *one-period valuation model.*

The One-Period Valuation Model

Suppose that you have some extra money to invest for one year. After a year you will need to sell your investment to pay tuition. After watching *Wall Street Week* on TV you decide that you want to buy Intel Corp. stock. You call your broker and find that Intel is currently selling for $50 per share and pays $0.16 per year in dividends. The analyst on *Wall Street Week* predicts that the stock will be selling for $60 in one year. Should you buy this stock?

To answer this question you need to determine whether the current price accurately reflects the analyst's forecast. To value the stock today, you need to find the present discounted value of the expected cash flows (future payments) using the formula in Equation 1 of Chapter 3 in which the discount factor used to discount the cash flows is the required return on investments in equity rather than the interest rate. The cash flows consist of one dividend payment plus a final sales price, which, when discounted back to the present, leads to the following equation which computes the current price of the stock.

$$P_0 = \frac{Div_1}{(1 + k_e)} + \frac{P_1}{(1 + k_e)} \tag{1}$$

where

P_0 = the current price of the stock. The zero subscript refers to time period zero, or the present.

Div_1 = the dividend paid at the end of year 1.

k_e = the required return on investments in equity.

P_1 = the price at the end of the first period. This is the assumed sales price of the stock.

EXAMPLE 1: Stock Valuation

Find the price of the Intel stock given the figures reported above. You will need to know the required return on equity to find the present value of the cash flows. Since a stock is more risky than a bond, you will require a higher return than that offered in the bond market. Assume that after careful consideration you decide that you would be satisfied to earn 12% on the investment.

Solution

Putting the numbers into Equation 1 yields the following:

$$P_0 = \frac{.16}{1 + 0.12} + \frac{\$60}{1 + 0.12} = \$.14 + \$53.57 = \$53.71$$

Based on your analysis you find that the stock is worth $53.71. Since the stock is currently available for $50 per share, you would choose to buy it. Why is the stock selling for less than $53.71? It may be because other investors place a different risk on the cash flows or estimate the cash flows to be less than you do.

The Generalized Dividend Valuation Model

The one-period dividend valuation model can be extended to any number of periods. The concept remains the same. The value of stock is the present value of all future cash flows. The only cash flows that an investor will receive are dividends and a final sales price when the stock is ultimately sold. The generalized formula for stock can be written as in Equation 2.

$$P_0 = \frac{D_1}{(1 + k_e)^1} + \frac{D_2}{(1 + k_e)^2} + \dots + \frac{D_n}{(1 + k_e)^n} + \frac{P_n}{(1 + k_e)^n} \tag{2}$$

If you were to attempt to use Equation 2 to find the value of a share of stock, you would soon realize that you must first estimate the value the stock will have at some point in the future before you can estimate its value today. In other words, you must find P_n in order to find P_0. However, if P_n is far in the future, it will not affect P_0. For example, the present value of a share of stock that sells for $50 seventy-five years from now using a 12% discount rate is just one cent [$\$50/(1.12^{75}) = \$0.01$]. This means that the current value of a share of stock can be found as simply the present value of the future dividend stream. The **generalized dividend model** is rewritten in Equation 3 without the final sales price.

$$P_0 = \sum_{t=1}^{\infty} \frac{D_t}{(1 + k_e)^t} \tag{3}$$

Consider the implications of Equation 3 for a moment. The generalized dividend model says that the price of stock is determined only by the present value of the dividends and that nothing else matters. Many stocks do not pay dividends, so how is it that these stocks have value? *Buyers of the stock expect that the firm will pay dividends someday.* Most of the time a firm institutes dividends as soon as it has completed the rapid growth phase of its life cycle. The stock price increases as the time approaches for the dividend stream to begin.

The generalized dividend valuation model requires that we compute the present value of an infinite stream of dividends, a process that could be difficult, to say the least. Therefore, simplified models have been developed to make the calculations easier. One such model is the **Gordon growth model** that assumes constant dividend growth.

The Gordon Growth Model

Many firms strive to increase their dividends at a constant rate each year. Equation 4 rewrites Equation 3 to reflect this constant growth in dividends.

$$P_0 = \frac{D_0 \times (1+g)^1}{(1+k_e)^1} + \frac{D_0 \times (1+g)^2}{(1+k_e)^2} + \dots + \frac{D_0 \times (1+g)^\infty}{(1+k_e)^\infty} \quad (4)$$

where D_0 = the most recent dividend paid
g = the expected constant growth rate in dividends
k_e = the required return on an investment in equity

Equation 4 has been simplified using algebra to obtain Equation 5.[1]

$$P_0 = \frac{D_0 \times (1+g)}{(k_e - g)} = \frac{D_1}{(k_e - g)} \quad (5)$$

This model is useful for finding the value of stock, given a few assumptions:

1. *Dividends are assumed to continue growing at a constant rate forever.* Actually, as long as they are expected to grow at a constant rate for an extended period of time, the model should yield reasonable results. This is because errors about distant cash flows become small when discounted to the present.
2. *The growth rate is assumed to be less than the required return on equity, k_e.* Myron Gordon, in his development of the model, demonstrated that this is a reasonable assumption. In theory, if the growth rate were faster than the rate demanded by holders of the firm's equity, in the long run the firm would grow impossibly large.

[1]To generate Equation 5 from Equation 4, first multiply both sides of Equation 4 by $(1 + k_e)/(1 + g)$ and subtract Equation 4 from the result. This yields

$$\frac{P_0 \times (1+k_e)}{(1+g)} - P_0 = D_0 - \frac{D_0 \times (1+g)^\infty}{(1+k_e)^\infty}$$

Assuming that k_e is greater than g, the term on the far right will approach zero and can be dropped. Thus, after factoring P_0 out of the left hand side

$$P_0 \times \left[\frac{1+k_e}{1+g} - 1\right] = D_0$$

Next simplify by combining terms to

$$P_0 \times \frac{(1+k_e) - (1+g)}{1+g} = D_0$$

$$P_0 = \frac{D_0 \times (1+g)}{k_e - g} = \frac{D_1}{k_e - g}$$

EXAMPLE 2: Stock Valuation, Constant Growth

Find the current market price of Coca-Cola stock assuming dividends grow at a constant rate of 10.95%, D_0 = $1.00, and the required return is 13%.

Solution

$$P_0 = \frac{D_0 \times (1 + g)}{k_e - g}$$

$$P_0 = \frac{\$1.00 \times (1.1095)}{.13 - .1095}$$

$$P_0 = \frac{\$1.1095}{0.0205} = \$54.12$$

Coca Cola stock should sell for $54.12 if the assumptions regarding the constant growth rate and required return are correct.

Price Earnings Valuation Method

Theoretically, the best method of stock valuation is the dividend valuation approach. Sometimes, however, it is difficult to apply. If a firm is not paying dividends or has a very erratic growth rate, the results may not be satisfactory. Other approaches to stock valuation are sometimes applied. Among the more popular is the price/earnings multiple.

The **price earnings ratio (PE)** is a widely watched measure of how much the market is willing to pay for $1 of earnings from a firm. A high PE has two interpretations.

1. A higher than average PE may mean that the market expects earnings to rise in the future. This would return the PE to a more normal level.
2. A high PE may alternatively indicate that the market feels the firm's earnings are very low risk and is therefore willing to pay a premium for them.

The PE ratio can be used to estimate the value of a firm's stock. Note that algebraically the product of the PE ratio times expected earnings is the firm's stock price.

$$\frac{P}{E} \times E = P \qquad (6)$$

Firms in the same industry are expected to have similar PE ratios in the long run. The value of a firm's stock can be found by multiplying the average industry PE times the expected earnings per share.

EXAMPLE 3: Stock Valuation, PE Ratio Approach

The average industry PE ratio for restaurants similar to Applebee's, a pub restaurant chain, is 23. What is the current price of Applebee's if earnings per share are projected to be $1.13?

Solution

Using Equation 6 and the data given we find:

$$P_0 = P/E \times E$$

$$P_0 = 23 \times \$1.13 = \$26$$

The PE ratio approach is especially useful for valuing privately held firms and firms that do not pay dividends. The weakness of the PE approach to valuation is that by using an industry average PE ratio, firm-specific factors that might contribute to a long-term PE ratio above or below the average are ignored in the analysis. A skilled analyst will adjust the PE ratio up or down to reflect unique characteristics of a firm when estimating its stock price.

HOW THE MARKET SETS SECURITY PRICES

Suppose you went to an auto auction. The cars are available for inspection before the auction begins, and you find a little Mazda Miata that you like. You test-drive it in the parking lot and notice that it makes a few strange noises, but you decide that you would still like the car. You decide \$5000 would be a fair price that would allow you to pay some repair bills should the noises turn out to be serious. You see that the auction is ready to begin, so you go in and wait for the Miata to enter.

Suppose there is another buyer who also spots the Miata. He test-drives the car and recognizes that the noises are simply the result of worn brake pads that he can fix himself at a nominal cost. He decides that the car is worth \$7000. He also goes in and waits for the Miata to enter.

Who will buy the car and for how much? Suppose only the two of you are interested in the Miata. You begin the bidding at \$4000. He ups your bid to \$4500. You bid your top price of \$5000. He counters with \$5100. The price is now higher than you are willing to pay, so you stop bidding. The car is sold to the more informed buyer for \$5100.

This simple example raises a number of points. First, the price is set by the buyer willing to pay the highest price. The price is not necessarily the highest price the asset could fetch, but it is incrementally greater than what any other buyer is willing to pay.

Second, the market price will be set by the buyer who can take best advantage of the asset. The buyer who purchased the car knew that he could fix the noise easily and cheaply. Because of this he was willing to pay more for the car than you were. The same concept holds for other assets. For example, a piece of property or a building will sell to the buyer who can put the asset to the most productive use. Consider why one company often pays a substantial premium over current market prices to acquire ownership of another (target) company. The acquiring firm may believe that it can put the target firm's assets to work better than they are currently and that this justifies the premium price.

Finally, the example shows the role played by information in asset pricing. Superior information about an asset can increase its value by reducing its risk. When you consider buying a stock, there are many unknowns about the future cash flows. The buyer who has the best information about these cash flows will discount them at a lower interest rate than will a buyer who is very uncertain.

Now let us apply these ideas to stock valuation. Suppose that you are considering the purchase of stock expected to pay dividends of $2 next year. The firm is expected to grow at 3% indefinitely. You are quite *uncertain* about both the constancy of the dividend stream and the accuracy of the estimated growth rate. To compensate yourself for this risk, you require a return of 15%.

Now suppose Jennifer, another investor, has spoken with industry insiders and feels more confident about the projected cash flows. Jennifer only requires a 12% return because her perceived risk is lower than yours. Bud, on the other hand, is dating the CEO of the company. He knows with near certainty what the future of the firm actually is. He thinks that both the estimated growth rate and the estimated cash flows are lower than what they will *actually* be in the future. Because he sees almost no risk in this investment, he only requires a 7% return.

What are the values each investor will give to the stock? Applying the Gordon growth model yields the following stock prices.

Investor	Discount Rate	Stock Price
You	15%	$16.67
Jennifer	12%	$22.22
Bud	7%	$50.00

You are willing to pay $16.67 for the stock. Jennifer would pay up to $22.22, and Bud would pay $50. The investor with the lowest perceived risk is willing to pay the most for the stock. If there were no other traders, the market price would be just above $22.22. If you already held the stock, you would sell it to Bud.

The point of this section is that the players in the market, bidding against each other, establish the market price. When new information is released about a firm, expectations change and with them, prices change. New information can cause changes in expectations about the level of future dividends or the risk of those dividends. Since market participants are constantly receiving new information and constantly revising their expectations, it is reasonable that stock prices are constantly changing as well.

ERRORS IN VALUATION

In this chapter, we learned about several asset valuation models. An interesting exercise is to apply these models to real firms. Students who do this find that computed stock prices do not match market prices much of the time. Students often question whether the models are wrong or incomplete or whether they are simply being used incorrectly. There are many opportunities for errors in applying the models. These include problems estimating growth, estimating risk, and forecasting dividends.

Problems with Estimating Growth

The constant growth model requires the analyst to estimate the constant rate of growth the firm will experience. You may estimate future growth by computing the historical growth rate in dividends, sales, or net profits. This approach fails to consider any changes in the firm or economy that may affect the growth rate. Robert Haugen, a professor of finance at the University of California, writes in his book, *The*

New Finance, that competition will prevent high-growth firms from being able to maintain their historical growth rate. He demonstrates that, despite this, the stock prices of historically high-growth firms tend to reflect a continuation of the high growth rate. The result is that investors in these firms receive lower returns than they would by investing in mature firms. This just points out that even the experts have trouble estimating future growth rates. Table 1 shows the stock price for a firm with a 15% required return, a $2 dividend, and a range of different growth rates. The stock price varies from $14.43 at 1% growth to $228 at 14% growth rate. Estimating growth at 13% instead of 12% results in a $38.33 price difference.

Problems with Estimating Risk

The dividend valuation model requires the analyst to estimate the required return for the firm's equity. Table 2 shows how the price of a share of stock offering a $2 dividend and a 5% growth rate changes with different estimates of the required return. Clearly, stock price is highly dependent on the required return, despite our uncertainty regarding how it is found.

Problems with Forecasting Dividends

Even if we are able to accurately estimate a firm's growth rate and its required return, we are still faced with the problem of determining how much of the firm's earnings will be paid as dividends. Clearly, many factors can influence the dividend payout ratio. These will include the firm's future growth opportunities and management's concern over future cash flows.

Putting all of these concerns together, we see that stock analysts are seldom very certain that their stock price projections are accurate. This is why stock prices

TABLE 1 Stock Prices for a Security with $D_0 = \$2.00$, $k_e = 15\%$, and Constant Growth Rates as Listed

Growth (%)	Price
1	$ 14.43
3	17.17
5	21.00
10	44.00
11	55.50
12	74.67
13	113.00
14	228.00

TABLE 2 Stock Prices for a Security with $D_0 = \$2.00$, $g = 5\%$, and Required Returns as Listed

Required Return (%)	Price
10	$42.00
11	35.00
12	30.00
13	26.25
14	23.33
15	21.00

fluctuate so widely on news reports. For example, information that the economy is slowing can cause analysts to revise their growth expectations. When this happens across a broad spectrum of stocks, major market indexes can change.

Does all this mean that you should not invest in the market? No, it only means that short-term fluctuations in stock prices are expected and natural. Over the long term, the stock price will adjust to reflect the true earnings of the firm. If high-quality firms are chosen for your portfolio, they should provide fair returns over time. We investigate this issue further in the next section.

THE EFFICIENT MARKET HYPOTHESIS

To learn more about the efficient market hypothesis, go to www.investorhome.com/emh.htm

To more fully understand what determines stock prices, we need to look at how information in the market affects these prices. To do this we examine the **efficient market hypothesis** (also referred to as the **theory of efficient capital markets**), which states that prices of securities in financial markets fully reflect all available information. But what does this mean?

You may recall from Chapter 3 that the rate of return from holding a security equals the sum of the capital gain on the security (the change in the price) plus any cash payments, divided by the initial purchase price of the security:

$$R = \frac{P_{t+1} - P_t + C}{P_t} \tag{7}$$

where R = rate of return on the security held from time t to time $t + 1$ (say, the end of 2002 to the end of 2003)

P_{t+1} = price of the security at time $t + 1$, the end of the holding period

P_t = the price of the security at time t, the beginning of the holding period

C = cash payment (coupon or dividend payments) made in the period t to $t + 1$

Let's look at the expectation of this return at time t, the beginning of the holding period. Because the current price and the cash payment C are known at the beginning, the only variable in the definition of the return that is uncertain is the price next period P_{t+1}.[2] Denoting the expectation of the security's price at the end of the holding period as P^e_{t+1}, the expected return R^e is

$$R^e = \frac{P^e_{t+1} - P_t + C}{P_t}$$

The efficient market hypothesis views expectations as equal to optimal forecasts using all available information. What exactly does this mean? An optimal forecast is the best guess of the future using all available information. This does not mean that the forecast is perfectly accurate, but only that it is the *best possible* given the available information. This can be written more formally as:

$$P^e_{t+1} = P^{of}_{t+1}$$

[2]There are cases where C might not be known at the beginning of the period, but that does not make a substantial difference to the analysis. We would in that case assume that not only price expectations but also the expectations of C are optimal forecasts using all available information.

which in turn implies that the expected return on the security will equal the optimal forecast of the return:

$$R^e = R^{of} \tag{8}$$

Unfortunately, we cannot observe either R^e or P^e_{t+1}, so the equations above by themselves do not tell us much about how the financial market behaves. However, if we can devise some way to measure the value of R^e, these equations will have important implications for how prices of securities change in financial markets.

The supply and demand analysis of the bond market developed in Chapter 4 shows us that the expected return on a security (the interest rate in the case of the bond examined) will have a tendency to head toward the equilibrium return that equates the quantity demanded to the quantity supplied. Supply and demand analysis enables us to determine the expected return on a security with the following equilibrium condition: The expected return on a security R^e equals the equilibrium return R^*, which equates the quantity of the security demanded to the quantity supplied; that is,

$$R^e = R^* \tag{9}$$

The academic field of finance explores the factors (risk and liquidity, for example) that influence the equilibrium returns on securities. For our purposes, it is sufficient to know that we can determine the equilibrium return and thus determine the expected return with the equilibrium condition.

We can derive an equation to describe pricing behavior in an efficient market by using the equilibrium condition to replace R^e with R^* in Equation 8. In this way we obtain

$$R^{of} = R^* \tag{10}$$

This equation tells us that ***current prices in a financial market will be set so that the optimal forecast of a security's return using all available information equals the security's equilibrium return.*** Financial economists state it more simply: A security's price fully reflects all available information in an efficient market.

EXAMPLE 4: The Efficient Market Hypothesis

Suppose that a share of Microsoft had a closing price yesterday of \$90, but new information was announced after the market closed that caused a revision in the forecast of price next year to go to \$120. If the annual equilibrium return on Microsoft is 15%, what does the efficient market hypothesis indicate the price will go to today when the market opens? (Assume that Microsoft pays no dividends.)

Solution

The price would rise to \$104.35 after the opening.

$$R^{of} = \frac{P^{of}_{t+1} - P_t + C}{P_t} = R^*$$

where

R^{of} = optimal forecast of the return = 15% = 0.15

R^* = equilibrium return = 15% = 0.15

P^{of}_{t+1} = optimal forecast of price next year = \$120

P_t = price today after opening

C = cash (dividend) payment = 0

Thus

$$0.15 = \frac{\$120 - P_t}{P_t}$$

$$P_t \times 0.15 = \$120 - P_t$$

$$P_t(1.15) = \$120$$

$$P_t = \$104.35$$

Rationale Behind the Hypothesis

Let's see what the efficient market condition means in practice and why it is a sensible characterization of pricing behavior. Suppose that the equilibrium return on a security, say, Exxon common stock, is 10% at an annual rate, and its current price P_t is lower than the optimal forecast of tomorrow's price P^{of}_{t+1} so that the optimal forecast of the return at an annual rate is 50%, which is greater than the equilibrium return of 10%. We are now able to predict that, on average, Exxon's return would be abnormally high. This situation is called an **unexploited profit opportunity** because, on average, people would be earning more than they should, given the characteristics of that security. Knowing that, on average, you can earn such an abnormally high rate of return on Exxon because $R^{of} > R^*$, you would buy more, which would in turn drive up its current price relative to the expected future price P^{of}_{t+1}, thereby lowering R^{of}. When the current price had risen sufficiently so that R^{of} equals R^* and the efficient market condition (Equation 10) is satisfied, the buying of Exxon will stop, and the unexploited profit opportunity will have disappeared.

Similarly, a security for which the optimal forecast of the return is – 5% while the equilibrium return is 10% ($R^{of} < R^*$) would be a poor investment because, on average, it earns less than the equilibrium return. In such a case, you would sell the security and drive down its current price relative to the expected future price until R^{of} rose to the level of R^* and the efficient market condition is again satisfied. What we have shown can be summarized as follows:

$$\left.\begin{array}{l} R^{of} > R^* \rightarrow P_t\uparrow \rightarrow R^{of}\downarrow \\ R^{of} < R^* \rightarrow P_t\downarrow \rightarrow R^{of}\uparrow \end{array}\right\} \quad \text{until} \quad R^{of} = R^*$$

Another way to state the efficient market condition is this: ***In an efficient market, all unexploited profit opportunities will be eliminated.***

An extremely important factor in this reasoning is that ***not everyone in a financial market must be well informed about a security or have rational expectations for its price to be driven to the point at which the efficient market condition holds.*** Financial markets are structured so that many participants can play. As long as a few keep their eyes open for unexploited profit opportunities, they will eliminate the profit opportunities that appear because in so doing, they make a profit. The efficient market hypothesis makes sense because it does not require everyone in a market to be cognizant of what is happening to every security.

Stronger Version of the Efficient Market Hypothesis

Many financial economists take the efficient market hypothesis one step further in their analysis of financial markets. Not only do they define an efficient market as one in which expectations are optimal forecasts using all available information, but they also add the condition that an efficient market is one in which prices reflect the true fundamental (intrinsic) value of the securities. Thus in an efficient market, all prices are always correct and reflect **market fundamentals** (items that have a direct impact on future income streams of the securities). This stronger view of market efficiency has several important implications in the academic field of finance. First, it implies that in an efficient capital market, one investment is as good as any other because the securities' prices are correct. Second, it implies that a security's price reflects all available information about the intrinsic value of the security. Third, it implies that security prices can be used by managers of both financial and nonfinancial firms to assess their cost of capital (cost of financing their investments) accurately and hence that security prices can be used to help them make the correct decisions about whether a specific investment is worth making or not. The stronger version of market efficiency is a basic tenet of much analysis in the finance field.

EVIDENCE ON THE EFFICIENT MARKET HYPOTHESIS

Early evidence on the efficient market hypothesis was quite favorable to it, but in recent years, deeper analysis of the evidence suggests that the hypothesis may not always be entirely correct. Let's first look at the earlier evidence in favor of the hypothesis and then examine some of the more recent evidence that casts some doubt on it.

Evidence in Favor of Market Efficiency

Evidence in favor of market efficiency has examined the performance of investment analysts and mutual funds, whether stock prices reflect publicly available information, the random-walk behavior of stock prices, and the success of so-called technical analysis.

Performance of Investment Analysts and Mutual Funds We have seen that one implication of the efficient market hypothesis is that when purchasing a security, you cannot expect to earn an abnormally high return, a return greater than the equilibrium return. This implies that it is impossible to beat the market. Many studies shed light on whether investment advisers and mutual funds (some of which charge steep sales commissions to people who purchase them) beat the market. One common test that has been performed is to take buy and sell recommendations from a group of advisers or mutual funds and compare the performance of the resulting selection of stocks with the market as a whole. Sometimes the advisers' choices have even been compared to a group of stocks chosen by putting a copy of the financial page of the newspaper on a dartboard and throwing darts. The *Wall Street Journal,* for example, has a regular feature called "Investment Dartboard" that compares how well stocks picked by investment advisers do relative to stocks picked by throwing darts. Do the advisers win? To their embarrassment, the dartboard beats them as often as they beat the dartboard. Furthermore, even when the comparison includes only advisers who have been successful in the past in predicting the stock market, the advisers still don't regularly beat the dartboard.

Consistent with the efficient market hypothesis, mutual funds are also not found to beat the market. Mutual funds not only do not outperform the market on average, but when they are separated into groups according to whether they had the highest or lowest profits in a chosen period, the mutual funds that did well in the first period do not beat the market in the second period.[3]

The conclusion from the study of investment advisers and mutual fund performance is this: ***Having performed well in the past does not indicate that an investment adviser or a mutual fund will perform well in the future.*** This is not pleasing news to investment advisers, but it is exactly what the efficient market hypothesis predicts. It says that some advisers will be lucky and some will be unlucky. Being lucky does not mean that a forecaster actually has the ability to beat the market. (An exception that proves the rule is discussed in Box 1.)

Do Stock Prices Reflect Publicly Available Information? The efficient market hypothesis predicts that stock prices will reflect all publicly available information.

[3]An early study that found that mutual funds do not outperform the market is Michael C. Jensen, "The Performance of Mutual Funds in the Period 1945–64," *Journal of Finance* 23 (1968): 389–416. More recent studies on mutual fund performance are Mark Grimblatt and Sheridan Titman, "Mutual Fund Performance: An Analysis of Quarterly Portfolio Holdings," *Journal of Business* 62 (1989): 393–416, R. A. Ippolito, "Efficiency with Costly Information: A Study of Mutual Fund Performance, 1965–84," *Quarterly Journal of Economics* 104 (1989): 1–23, J. Lakonishok, A. Shleifer, and R. Vishny, "The Structure and Performance of the Money Management Industry," *Brookings Papers on Economic Activity, Microeconomics* (1992), B. Malkiel, "Returns from Investing in Equity Mutual Funds, 1971–1991," *Journal of Finance* 50: 549–72.

BOX 1

An Exception That Proves the Rule: Ivan Boesky

The efficient market hypothesis indicates that investment advisers should not have the ability to beat the market. Yet that is exactly what Ivan Boesky was able to do until 1986, when he was charged by the Securities and Exchange Commission with making unfair profits (rumored to be in the hundreds of millions of dollars) by trading on inside information. In an out-of-court settlement, Boesky was banned from the securities business, fined $100 million, and sentenced to three years in jail. (After serving his sentence, Boesky was released from jail in 1990.) If the stock market is efficient, can the SEC legitimately claim that Boesky was able to beat the market? The answer is yes.

Ivan Boesky was the most successful of the so-called *arbs* (short for *arbitrageurs*) who made hundreds of millions in profits for himself and his clients by investing in the stocks of firms that were about to be taken over by other firms at an above-market price. Boesky's continuing success was assured by an arrangement whereby he paid cash (sometimes in a suitcase) to Dennis Levine, an investment banker who had inside information about when a takeover was to take place because his firm was arranging the financing of the deal. When Levine found out that a firm was planning a takeover, he would inform Boesky, who would then buy the stock of the company being taken over and sell it after the stock had risen.

Boesky's ability to make millions year after year in the 1980s is an exception that proves the rule that financial analysts cannot continually outperform the market; yet it supports the efficient markets claim that only information *unavailable to the market* enables an investor to do so. Boesky profited from knowing about takeovers before the rest of the market; this information was known to him but unavailable to the market.

Thus if information is already publicly available, a positive announcement about a company will not, on average, raise the price of its stock because this information is already reflected in the stock price. Early empirical evidence also confirmed this conjecture from the efficient market hypothesis: Favorable earnings announcements or announcements of stock splits (a division of a share of stock into multiple shares, which is usually followed by higher earnings) do not, on average, cause stock prices to rise.[4]

Random-Walk Behavior of Stock Prices The term **random walk** describes the movements of a variable whose future changes cannot be predicted (are random) because, given today's value, the variable is just as likely to fall as to rise. An important implication of the efficient market hypothesis is that stock prices should approximately follow a random walk; that is, ***future changes in stock prices should, for all practical purposes, be unpredictable.*** The random-walk implication of the efficient market hypothesis is the one most commonly mentioned in the press because it is the most readily comprehensible to the public. In fact, when people mention the "random-walk theory of stock prices," they are in reality referring to the efficient market hypothesis.

The case for random-walk stock prices can be demonstrated. Suppose that people could predict that the price of Happy Feet Corporation (HFC) stock would rise 1% in the coming week. The predicted rate of capital gains and rate of return on HFC stock would then be over 50% at an annual rate. Since this is very likely to be far higher than the equilibrium rate of return on HFC stock ($R^{of} > R^*$), the efficient market hypothesis indicates that people would immediately buy this stock and bid up its current price. The action would stop only when the predictable change in the price dropped to near zero so that $R^{of} = R^*$.

Similarly, if people could predict that the price of HFC stock would fall by 1%, the predicted rate of return would be negative ($R^{of} < R^*$), and people would immediately sell. The current price would fall until the predictable change in the price rose back to near zero, where the efficient market condition again holds. The efficient market hypothesis suggests that the predictable change in stock prices will be near zero, leading to the conclusion that stock prices will generally follow a random walk.[5]

Financial economists have used two types of tests to explore the hypothesis that stock prices follow a random walk. In the first, they examine stock market records to see if changes in stock prices are systematically related to past changes and hence could have been predicted on that basis. The second type of test examines the data to see if publicly available information other than past stock prices could have been used to predict changes. These tests are somewhat more stringent because additional information (money supply growth, government spending, interest rates, corporate profits) might be used to help forecast stock returns.

---

[4]Ray Ball and Philip Brown, "An Empirical Evaluation of Accounting Income Numbers," *Journal of Accounting Research* 6 (1968): 159–178; Eugene F. Fama, Lawrence Fisher, Michael C. Jensen, and Richard Roll, "The Adjustment of Stock Prices to New Information," *International Economic Review* 10 (1969): 1–21.

[5]Note that the random-walk behavior of stock prices is only an *approximation* derived from the efficient market hypothesis. It would hold exactly only for a stock for which an unchanged price leads to its having the equilibrium return. Then, when the predictable change in the stock price is exactly zero, $R^{of} = R^*$.

Early results from both types of tests generally confirmed the efficient market view that stock prices are not predictable and follow a random walk.[6]

Technical Analysis A popular technique used to predict stock prices, called *technical analysis,* is to study past stock price data and search for patterns such as trends and regular cycles. Rules for when to buy and sell stocks are then established on the basis of the patterns that emerge. The efficient market hypothesis suggests that technical analysis is a waste of time. The simplest way to understand why is to use the random-walk result derived from the efficient market hypothesis that holds that past stock price data cannot help predict changes. Therefore, technical analysis, which relies on such data to produce its forecasts, cannot successfully predict changes in stock prices.

Two types of tests bear directly on the value of technical analysis. The first performs the empirical analysis described earlier to evaluate the performance of any financial analyst, technical or otherwise. The results are exactly what the efficient market hypothesis predicts: Technical analysts fare no better than other financial analysts; on average, they do not outperform the market, and successful past forecasting does not imply that their forecasts will outperform the market in the future. The second type of test (first performed by Sidney Alexander) takes the rules developed in technical analysis for when to buy and sell stocks and applies them to new data.[7] The performance of these rules is then evaluated by the profits that would have been made using them. These tests also discredit technical analysis: It does not outperform the overall market.

Application

Should Foreign Exchange Rates Follow A Random Walk?

Although the efficient market hypothesis is usually applied to the stock market, it can also be used to show that foreign exchange rates, like stock prices, should generally follow a random walk. To see why this is the case, consider what would happen if people could predict that a currency would appreciate by 1% in the coming week. By buying this currency, they could earn a greater than 50% return at

[6]The first type of test, using only stock market data, is referred to as a test of *weak-form efficiency* because the information that can be used to predict stock prices is restricted solely to past price data. The second type of test is referred to as a test of *semistrong-form efficiency* because the information set is expanded to include all publicly available information, not just past stock prices. A third type of test is called a test of *strong-form efficiency* because the information set includes insider information, known only to the owners of the corporation, as when they plan to declare a high dividend. Strong-form tests do sometimes indicate that insider information can be used to predict changes in stock prices. This finding does not contradict efficient markets theory because the information is not available to the market and hence cannot be reflected in market prices. In fact, there are strict laws against using insider information to trade in financial markets. For an early survey on the three forms of tests, see Eugene F. Fama, "Efficient Capital Markets: A Review of Theory and Empirical Work," *Journal of Finance* 25 (1970): 383–416.

[7]Sidney Alexander, "Price Movements in Speculative Markets: Trends or Random Walks?" *Industrial Management Review,* May 1961, pp. 7–26; and Sidney Alexander, "Price Movements in Speculative Markets: Trends or Random Walks? No. 2" in *The Random Character of Stock Prices,* ed. Paul Cootner (Cambridge, Mass.: MIT Press, 1964), pp. 338–372 More recent evidence also seems to discredit technical analysis, for example, F. Allen and R. Karjalainen, "Using Genetic Algorithms to Find Technical Trading Rules," *Journal of Financial Economics* (1999) 51: 245–71. However, some other research is more favorable to technical analysis, e.g., R. Sullivan, A. Timmerman, and H. White, "Data-Snooping, Technical Trading Rule Performance and the Bootstrap," Centre for Economic Policy Research Discussion Paper No. 1976, 1998.

an annual rate, which is likely to be far above the equilibrium return for holding a currency. As a result, people would immediately buy the currency and bid up its current price, thereby reducing the expected return. The process would stop only when the predictable change in the exchange rate dropped to near zero so that the optimal forecast of the return no longer differed from the equilibrium return. Likewise, if people could predict that the currency would depreciate by 1% in the coming week, they would sell it until the predictable change in the exchange rate was again near zero. The efficient market hypothesis therefore implies that future changes in exchange rates should, for all practical purposes, be unpredictable; in other words, exchange rates should follow random walks. This is exactly what empirical evidence finds.[8]

Evidence Against Market Efficiency

All the early evidence supporting the efficient market hypothesis appeared to be overwhelming, causing Eugene Fama, a prominent financial economist, to state in his famous 1970 survey of the empirical evidence on the efficient market hypothesis, "The evidence in support of the efficient markets model is extensive, and (somewhat uniquely in economics) contradictory evidence is sparse."[9] However, in recent years, the theory has begun to show a few cracks, referred to as *anomalies,* and empirical evidence indicates that the efficient market hypothesis may not always be generally applicable.

Small-Firm Effect One of the earliest reported anomalies in which the stock market did not appear to be efficient is called the *small-firm effect.* Many empirical studies have shown that small firms have earned abnormally high returns over long periods of time, even when the greater risk for these firms has been taken into account.[10] The small-firm effect seems to have diminished in recent years but is still a challenge to the theory of efficient markets. Various theories have been developed to explain the small-firm effect, suggesting that it may be due to rebalancing of portfolios by institutional investors, tax issues, low liquidity of small-firm stocks, large information costs in evaluating small firms, or an inappropriate measurement of risk for small-firm stocks.

January Effect Over long periods of time, stock prices have tended to experience an abnormal price rise from December to January that is predictable and hence inconsistent with random-walk behavior. This so-called **January effect** seems to have diminished in recent years for shares of large companies but still occurs for shares of small companies.[11] Some financial economists argue that the

---

[8]See Richard A. Meese and Kenneth Rogoff, "Empirical Exchange Rate Models of the Seventies: Do They Fit out of Sample?" *Journal of International Economics* 14 (1983): 3–24.

[9]Eugene F. Fama, "Efficient Capital Markets: A Review of Theory and Empirical Work," *Journal of Finance* 25 (1970): 383–416.

[10]For example, see Marc R. Reinganum, "The Anomalous Stock Market Behavior of Small Firms in January: Empirical Tests of Tax Loss Selling Effects," *Journal of Financial Economics* 12 (1983): 89–104; Jay R. Ritter, "The Buying and Selling Behavior of Individual Investors at the Turn of the Year," *Journal of Finance* 43 (1988): 701–717; and Richard Roll, "Vas Ist Das? The Turn-of-the-Year Effect: Anomaly or Risk Mismeasurement?" *Journal of Portfolio Management* 9 (1988): 18–28.

[11]For example, see Donald B. Keim, "The CAPM and Equity Return Regularities," *Financial Analysts Journal* 42 (May–June 1986): 19–34.

January effect is due to tax issues. Investors have an incentive to sell stocks before the end of the year in December because they can then take capital losses on their tax return and reduce their tax liability. Then when the new year starts in January, they can repurchase the stocks, driving up their prices and producing abnormally high returns. Although this explanation seems sensible, it does not explain why institutional investors such as private pension funds, which are not subject to income taxes, do not take advantage of the abnormal returns in January and buy stocks in December, thus bidding up their price and eliminating the abnormal returns.[12]

Market Overreaction Recent research suggests that stock prices may overreact to news announcements and that the pricing errors are corrected only slowly.[13] When corporations announce a major change in earnings, say, a large decline, the stock price may overshoot, and after an initial large decline, it may rise back to more normal levels over a period of several weeks. This violates the efficient market hypothesis because an investor could earn abnormally high returns, on average, by buying a stock immediately after a poor earnings announcement and then selling it after a couple of weeks when it has risen back to normal levels.

Excessive Volatility A closely related phenomenon to market overreaction is that the stock market appears to display excessive volatility; that is, fluctuations in stock prices may be much greater than is warranted by fluctuations in their fundamental value. In an important paper, Robert Shiller of Yale University found that fluctuations in the S&P 500 stock index could not be justified by the subsequent fluctuations in the dividends of the stocks making up this index. There has been much subsequent technical work criticizing these results, but Shiller's work, along with research that finds that there are smaller fluctuations in stock prices when stock markets are closed, has produced a consensus that stock market prices appear to be driven by factors other than fundamentals.[14]

Mean Reversion Some researchers have also found that stock returns display **mean reversion:** Stocks with low returns today tend to have high returns in the future, and vice versa. Hence stocks that have done poorly in the past are more likely to do well in the future because mean reversion indicates that there will be a predictable positive change in the future price, suggesting that stock prices are not a random walk. Other researchers have found that mean reversion is not nearly as strong in data after World War II and so have raised doubts

---

[12]Another anomaly that makes the stock market seem less than efficient is the fact that the *Value Line Survey,* one of the most prominent investment advice newsletters, has produced stock recommendations that have yielded abnormally high returns on average. See Fischer Black, "Yes, Virginia, There Is Hope: Tests of the Value Line Ranking System," *Financial Analysts Journal* 29 (September–October 1973): 10–14, and Gur Huberman and Shmuel Kandel, "Market Efficiency and Value Line's Record," *Journal of Business* 63 (1990): 187–216. Whether the excellent performance of the *Value Line Survey* will continue in the future is, of course, a question mark.

[13]Werner F. M. De Bondt and Richard Thaler, "Further Evidence on Investor Overreaction and Stock Market Seasonality," *Journal of Finance* 62 (1987): 557–580.

[14]Robert Shiller, "Do Stock Prices Move Too Much to Be Justified by Subsequent Changes in Dividends?" *American Economic Review* 71 (1981): 421–436, and Kenneth R. French and Richard Roll, "Stock Return Variances: The Arrival of Information and the Reaction of Traders," *Journal of Financial Economics* 17 (1986): 5–26.

about whether it is currently an important phenomenon. The evidence on mean reversion remains controversial.[15]

New Information Is Not Always Immediately Incorporated into Stock Prices Although it is generally found that stock prices adjust rapidly to new information, as is suggested by the efficient market hypothesis, recent evidence suggests that, inconsistent with the efficient market hypothesis, stock prices do not instantaneously adjust to profit announcements. Instead, on average stock prices continue to rise for some time after the announcement of unexpectedly high profits, and they continue to fall after surprisingly low profit announcments.[16]

Overview of the Evidence on the Efficient Market Hypothesis

As you can see, the debate on the efficient market hypothesis is far from over. The evidence seems to suggest that the efficient market hypothesis may be a reasonable starting point for evaluating behavior in financial markets. However, there do seem to be important violations of market efficiency that suggest that the efficient market hypothesis may not be the whole story and so may not be generalizable to all behavior in financial markets.

THE PRACTICING FINANCIAL INSTITUTION MANAGER

Practical Guide to Investing in the Stock Market

The efficient market hypothesis has numerous applications to the real world. It is especially valuable because it can be applied directly to an issue that concerns managers of financial institutions (and the general public as well): how to make profits in the stock market. A practical guide to investing in the stock market, which we develop here, provides a better understanding of the use and implications of the efficient market hypothesis.

HOW VALUABLE ARE PUBLISHED REPORTS BY INVESTMENT ADVISERS?

Suppose that you have just read in the "Heard on the Street" column of the *Wall Street Journal* that investment advisers are predicting a boom in oil stocks

---

[15]Evidence for mean reversion has been reported by James M. Poterba and Lawrence H. Summers, "Mean Reversion in Stock Prices: Evidence and Implications," *Journal of Financial Economics* 22 (1988): 27–59; Eugene F. Fama and Kenneth R. French, "Permanent and Temporary Components of Stock Prices," *Journal of Political Economy* 96 (1988): 246–273; and Andrew W. Lo and A. Craig MacKinlay, "Stock Market Prices Do Not Follow Random Walks: Evidence from a Simple Specification Test," *Review of Financial Studies* 1 (1988): 41–66. However, Myung Jig Kim, Charles R. Nelson, and Richard Startz, "Mean Reversion in Stock Prices? A Reappraisal of the Evidence," *Review of Economic Studies* 58 (1991): 515–528, question whether some of these findings are valid. For an excellent summary of this evidence, see Charles Engel and Charles S. Morris, "Challenges to Stock Market Efficiency: Evidence from Mean Reversion Studies," Federal Reserve Bank of Kansas City *Economic Review,* September–October 1991, pp. 21–35. See also N. Jegadeesh and Sheridan Titman, "Returns to Buying Winners and Selling Losers: Implications for Stock Market Efficiency," *Journal of Finance* 48 (1993): 65–92, which shows that mean reversion also occurs for individual stocks.

[16]For example, see R. Ball and P. Brown, "An Empirical Evaluation of Accounting Income Numbers," *Journal of Accounting Research* (1968) 6: 159–78, L. Chan, N. Jegadeesh, and J. Lakonishok, "Momentum Strategies," *Journal of Finance* (1996) 51: 1681–1713, and Eugene Fama, "Market Efficiency, Long-Term Returns and Behavioral Finance," *Journal of Financial Economics* (1998) 49: 283–306.

because an oil shortage is developing. Should you proceed to withdraw all your hard-earned savings from the bank and invest it in oil stocks?

The efficient market hypothesis tells us that when purchasing a security, we cannot expect to earn an abnormally high return, a return greater than the equilibrium return. Information in newspapers and in the published reports of investment advisers is readily available to many market participants and is already reflected in market prices. So acting on this information will not yield abnormally high returns, on average. As we have seen, the empirical evidence for the most part confirms that recommendations from investment advisers cannot help us outperform the general market. Indeed, as Box 2 suggests, human investment advisers in San Francisco do not on average even outperform an orangutan!

Probably no other conclusion is met with more skepticism by students than this one when they first hear it. We all know or have heard of somebody who has been successful in the stock market for a period of many years. We wonder, how could someone be so consistently successful if he or she did not really know how to predict when returns would be abnormally high? The following story, reported in the press, illustrates why such anecdotal evidence is not reliable.

A get-rich-quick artist invented a clever scam. Every week, he wrote two letters. In letter A, he would pick team A to win a particular football game, and in letter B, he would pick the opponent, team B. A mailing list would then be separated into two groups, and he would send letter A to the people in one group and letter B to the people in the other. The following week he would do the same thing but would send these letters only to the group who had received the first letter with the correct prediction. After doing this for ten games, he had a small cluster of people who had received letters predicting the correct winning team for every game. He then mailed a final letter to them, declaring that since he was obviously an expert predictor of the outcome of football games (he had picked winners ten weeks in a row) and since his predictions were profitable for the recipients who bet on the games, he would continue to send his predictions only if he were paid a substantial amount of money. When one of his clients figured out what he was up to, the con man was prosecuted and thrown in jail!

What is the lesson of the story? Even if no forecaster is an accurate predictor of the market, there will always be a group of consistent winners. A person who has done well regularly in the past cannot guarantee that he or she will do well in the future. Note that there will also be a group of persistent losers, but you rarely hear about them because no one brags about a poor forecasting record.

BOX 2

Should You Hire an Ape as Your Investment Adviser?

The *San Francisco Chronicle* came up with an amusing way of evaluating how successful investment advisers are at picking stocks. They asked eight analysts to pick five stocks at the beginning of the year and then compared the performance of their stock picks to those chosen by Jolyn, an orangutan living at Marine World/Africa USA in Vallejo, California. Consistent with the results found in the "Investment Dartboard" feature of the *Wall Street Journal*, Jolyn beat the investment advisers as often as they beat her. Given this result, you might be just as well off hiring an orangutan as your investment adviser as you would hiring a human being!

SHOULD YOU BE SKEPTICAL OF HOT TIPS?

Suppose that your broker phones you with a hot tip to buy stock in the Happy Feet Corporation (HFC) because it has just developed a product that is completely effective in curing athlete's foot. The stock price is sure to go up. Should you follow this advice and buy HFC stock?

The efficient market hypothesis indicates that you should be skeptical of such news. If the stock market is efficient, it has already priced HFC stock so that its expected return will equal the equilibrium return. The hot tip is not particularly valuable and will not enable you to earn an abnormally high return.

You might wonder, though, if the hot tip is based on new information and would give you an edge on the rest of the market. If other market participants have gotten this information before you, the answer is no. As soon as the information hits the street, the unexploited profit opportunity it creates will be quickly eliminated. The stock's price will already reflect the information, and you should expect to realize only the equilibrium return. But if you are one of the first to know the new information (as Ivan Boesky was—see Box 1), it can do you some good. Only then can you be one of the lucky ones who, on average, will earn an abnormally high return by helping eliminate the profit opportunity by buying HFC stock.

DO STOCK PRICES ALWAYS RISE WHEN THERE IS GOOD NEWS?

If you follow the stock market, you might have noticed a puzzling phenomenon: When good news about a stock, such as a particularly favorable earnings report, is announced, the price of the stock frequently does not rise. The efficient market hypothesis and the random-walk behavior of stock prices explain this phenomenon.

Because changes in stock prices are unpredictable, when information is announced that has already been expected by the market, the stock price will remain unchanged. The announcement does not contain any new information that should lead to a change in stock prices. If this were not the case and the announcement led to a change in stock prices, it would mean that the change was predictable. Because that is ruled out in an efficient market, ***stock prices will respond to announcements only when the information being announced is new and unexpected.*** If the news is expected, there will be no stock price response. This is exactly what the evidence that we described earlier suggests will occur—that stock prices reflect publicly available information.

Sometimes a stock price declines when good news is announced. Although this seems somewhat peculiar, it is completely consistent with the workings of an efficient market. Suppose that although the announced news is good, it is not as good as expected. HFC's earnings may have risen 15%, but if the market expected earnings to rise by 20%, the new information is actually unfavorable, and the stock price declines.

EFFICIENT MARKETS PRESCRIPTION FOR THE INVESTOR

What does the efficient market hypothesis recommend for investing in the stock market? It tells us that hot tips, investment advisers' published recommendations, and technical analysis—all of which make use of publicly available information—cannot help an investor outperform the market. Indeed, it indicates that anyone without better information than other market participants cannot expect to beat the market. So what is an investor to do?

The efficient market hypothesis leads to the conclusion that such an investor (and almost all of us fit into this category) should not try to outguess the market by constantly buying and selling securities. This process does nothing but boost the income of brokers, who earn commissions on each trade.[17] Instead, the investor should pursue a "buy and hold" strategy—purchase stocks and hold them for long periods of time. This will lead to the same returns, on average, but the investor's net profits will be higher because fewer brokerage commissions will have to be paid.[18]

It is frequently a sensible strategy for a small investor, whose costs of managing a portfolio may be high relative to its size, to buy into a mutual fund rather than individual stocks. Because the efficient market hypothesis indicates that no mutual fund can consistently outperform the market, an investor should not buy into one that has high management fees or that pays sales commissions to brokers but rather should purchase a no-load (commission-free) mutual fund that has low management fees.

As we have seen, the evidence indicates that it will not be easy to beat the prescription suggested here, although some of the anomalies to the efficient market hypothesis suggest that an extremely clever investor (which rules out most of us) may be able to outperform a buy-and-hold strategy.

Application What Does the Stock Market Crash of 1987 Tell Us About the Efficient Market Hypothesis?

Some observers have suggested that the October 19, 1987, stock market crash should make us question the validity of the efficient market hypothesis. They do not believe that an efficient market could have produced such a massive swing in share prices. To what degree should the stock market crash make us doubt the validity of the efficient market hypothesis?

Nothing in the efficient market hypothesis rules out large one-day changes in stock prices. A large change in stock prices can result from new information that produces a dramatic change in optimal forecasts of the future valuation of firms. Some financial economists have pointed out that there are many possible explanations for why optimal forecasts of the future value of firms might have dropped dramatically on October 19, 1987: moves in Congress to restrict corporate takeovers, the disappointing performance of the trade deficit, congressional failure to reduce the budget deficit substantially, increased fears of inflation, the decline of the dollar, and increased fears of financial distress in the banking industry. Other financial economists doubt whether these explanations are enough to explain the stock market drop because none of these market fundamentals seems important enough.

One lesson from the Black Monday stock market crash appears to be that factors other than market fundamentals may have had an effect on stock prices. The crash of 1987 has therefore convinced many financial economists that the stronger version of the efficient market hypothesis, which states that asset prices reflect the true fundamental (intrinsic) value of securities, is incorrect. They attrib-

[17]The investor may also have to pay Uncle Sam capital gains taxes on any profits that are realized when a security is sold—an additional reason why continual buying and selling does not make sense.

[18]As we saw in Chapter 4, the investor can also minimize risk by holding a diversified portfolio. The investor will be better off by pursuing a buy-and-hold strategy with a diversified portfolio or with a mutual fund that has a diversified portfolio.

ute a large role in the determination of stock prices to market psychology and to the institutional structure of the marketplace. However, nothing in this view contradicts the basic reasoning behind the weaker version of the efficient market hypothesis—that market participants eliminate unexploited profit opportunities. Even though stock market prices may not always solely reflect market fundamentals, as long as the stock market crash was unpredictable, many of the basic lessons of the efficient market hypothesis hold.

Some financial economists have come up with theories of what they call *rational bubbles* to explain events such as the stock market crash. A **bubble** is a situation in which the price of an asset differs from its fundamental market value. In a rational bubble, investors can have expectations that a bubble is occurring because the asset price is above its fundamental value but continue to hold the asset anyway. They might do this because they believe that someone else will buy the asset for a higher price in the future. In a rational bubble, asset prices can therefore deviate from their fundamental value for a long time because the bursting of the bubble cannot be predicted and so there are no unexploited profit opportunities.

However, other financial economists believe that the stock market crash of 1987 suggests that there may be unexploited profit opportunities and that even the weaker version of the efficient market hypothesis may be fundamentally flawed. The controversy over whether capital markets are efficient continues.

SUMMARY

1. Stocks are valued as the present value of the dividends. Unfortunately, we do not know very precisely what these dividends will be. This introduces a great deal of error to the valuation process. The Gordon growth model is a simplified method of computing stock value that depends on the assumption that the dividends are growing at a constant rate forever. Given our uncertainty regarding future dividends, this assumption is often the best we can do.
2. An alternative method for estimating stock price is to multiply the firm's earnings per share times the industry price earnings ratio. This ratio can be adjusted up or down to reflect specific characteristics of the firm.
3. The interaction among traders in the market is what actually sets prices on a day-to-day basis. The trader that values the security the most either because of less uncertainty about the cash flows or because of greater estimated cash flows will be willing to pay the most. As new information is released, investors will revise their estimates of the true value of the security and will either buy or sell it depending upon how the market price compares to their estimated valuation. Because small changes in estimated growth rates or required return result in large changes in price, it is not surprising that the markets are often volatile.
4. The efficient market hypothesis states that current security prices will fully reflect all available information because in an efficient market, all unexploited profit opportunities are eliminated. The elimination of unexploited profit opportunities necessary for a financial market to be efficient does not require that all market participants be well informed.
5. The evidence on the efficient market hypothesis is quite mixed. Early evidence on the performance of investment analysts and mutual funds, whether stock prices reflect publicly available information, the random-walk behavior of stock prices, and the success of so-called technical analysis was quite favorable to the efficient market hypothesis. However, in recent years, evidence on the small-firm effect, the January effect, market overreaction, excessive volatility, mean reversion and new information is not always incorporated into stock prices, suggesting that the hypothesis may not always be entirely correct. The evidence seems to suggest that the efficient market hypothesis may be a reasonable starting point for evaluating behavior in financial markets but may not be generalizable to all behavior in financial markets.

6. The efficient market hypothesis indicates that hot tips, investment advisers' published recommendations, and technical analysis cannot help an investor out-perform the market. The prescription for investors is to pursue a buy-and-hold strategy—purchase stocks and hold them for long periods of time. Empirical evidence generally supports these implications of the efficient market hypothesis in the stock market.
7. The stock market crash of 1987 has convinced many financial economists that the stronger version of the efficient market hypothesis, which states that asset prices reflect the true fundamental (intrinsic) value of securities, is not correct. It is less clear that the stock market crash shows that the weaker version of the efficient market hypothesis is wrong. Even if the stock market was driven by factors other than fundamentals, the crash does not clearly demonstrate that many of the basic lessons of the efficient market hypothesis are no longer valid as long as the crash could not have been predicted.

KEY TERMS

bubble, *p.* 288
cash flows, *p.* 268
dividends, *p.* 268
efficient market hypothesis, *p.* 267
generalized dividend model, *p.* 269
Gordon growth model, *p.* 270
January effect, *p.* 282
market fundamentals, *p.* 278
mean reversion, *p.* 283
price earnings ratio (PE), *p.* 271
random walk, *p.* 280
residual claimant, *p.* 268
stockholders, *p.* 268
theory of efficient capital markets, *p.* 275
unexploited profit opportunity, *p.* 277

QUESTIONS AND PROBLEMS

1. What basic principle of finance can be applied to the valuation of any investment asset?

*2. Identify the cash flows available to an investor in stock. How reliably can these cash flows be estimated? Compare the problem of estimating stock cash flows to estimating bond cash flows. Which security would you predict to be more volatile?

3. Compute the price of a share of stock that pays a $1 per year dividend and that you expect to be able to sell in one year for $20, assuming you require a 15% return.

*4. After careful analysis, you have determined that a firm's dividends should grow at 7% on average in the foreseeable future. Its last dividend was $3. Compute the current price of this stock, assuming the required return is 18%.

5. The projected earnings per share for Risky Ventures, Inc., is $3.50. The average PE ratio for the industry composed of Risky Ventures' closest competitors is 21. After careful analysis, you decide that Risky Ventures is a little more risky than average, so decide a PE ratio of 23 better reflects the market's perception of the firm. Estimate the current price of the firm's stock.

*6. "Forecasters' predictions of inflation are notoriously inaccurate, so their expectations of inflation cannot be rational." Is this statement true, false, or uncertain? Explain your answer.

7. "Whenever it is snowing when Joe Commuter gets up in the morning, he misjudges how long it will take him to drive to work. Otherwise, his expectations of the driving time are perfectly accurate. Considering that it snows only once every ten years where Joe lives, Joe's expectations are almost always perfectly accurate." Are Joe's expectations rational? Why or why not?

*8. If a forecaster spends hours every day studying data to forecast interest rates but his expectations are not as accurate as predicting that tomorrow's interest rates will be identical to today's interest rate, are his expectations rational?

9. "If stock prices did not follow a random walk, there would be unexploited profit opportunities in the market." Is this statement true, false, or uncertain? Explain your answer.

*10. Suppose that increases in the money supply lead to a rise in stock prices. Does this mean that when you see that the money supply has had a sharp rise in the past week, you should go out and buy stocks? Why or why not?

11. If the public expects a corporation to lose $5 a share this quarter and it actually loses $4, which is still the

largest loss in the history of the company, what does the efficient market hypothesis say will happen to the price of the stock when the $4 loss is announced?

*12. If I read in the *Wall Street Journal* that the "smart money" on Wall Street expects stock prices to fall, should I follow that lead and sell all my stocks?

13. If my broker has been right in her five previous buy and sell recommendations, should I continue listening to her advice?

*14. Can a person with rational expectations expect the price of IBM to rise by 10% in the next month?

15. "If most participants in the stock market do not follow what is happening to the monetary aggregates, prices of common stocks will not fully reflect information about them." Is this statement true, false, or uncertain? Explain your answer.

*16. "An efficient market is one in which no one ever profits from having better information than the rest." Is this statement true, false, or uncertain? Explain your answer.

17. If higher money growth is associated with higher future inflation and if announced money growth turns out to be extremely high but is still less than the market expected, what do you think would happen to long-term bond prices?

*18. "Foreign exchange rates, like stock prices, should follow a random walk." Is this statement true, false, or uncertain? Explain your answer.

19. Can we expect the value of the dollar to rise by 2% next week if our expectations are rational?

*20. "Human fear is the source of stock market crashes, so these crashes indicate that expectations in the stock market cannot be rational." Is this statement true, false, or uncertain? Explain your answer.

WEB EXERCISES

The Stock Market and the Efficient Market Hypothesis

1. Visit http://www.forecasts.org/data/index.htm. Click on "Stock Index" at the very top of the page. Now choose "U.S. Stock Indices-monthly." Review the indices for the DJIA, the S&P 500, and the NASDAQ composite. Which index appears most volatile? In which index would you have rather invested in 1985 if the investment had been allowed to compound until now?

2. The Internet is a great source of information on stock prices and stock price movements. There are many sites that provide up-to-the minute data on stock market indices. One of the best is found at http://finance.lycos.com/home/livecharts. This site provides free real-time streaming of stock market data. Click on the $indu to have the chart display the Dow Jones Industrial Average. Look at the stock trend over various intervals by adjusting the update frequency (click on INT at the top of the chart). Have stock prices been going up or down over the last day, week, month, and year?

Chapter 11 The Mortgage Markets

Preview

Part of the classic American dream is to own your own home. With the price of the average house now over $140,000, few of us could hope to do this until late in life if we were not able to borrow the bulk of the purchase price. Similarly, businesses rely on borrowed capital far more than on equity investment to finance their growth. Many small firms do not have access to the bond market and must find alternative sources of funds. Consider the state of the mortgage loan markets 100 years ago. They were organized mostly to accommodate the needs of businesses and the very wealthy. Much has changed since then. The purpose of this chapter is to discuss these changes.

Chapter 8 discussed the *money markets,* the markets for short-term funds. Chapter 9 discussed the *capital markets,* the markets for long-term funds. This chapter discusses the *mortgage markets,* where borrowers—individuals, businesses, and governments—can obtain long-term collateralized loans. From one perspective, the mortgage markets form a subcategory of the capital markets because mortgages involve long-term funds. But the mortgage markets differ from the stock and bond markets in important ways. First, the usual borrowers in the capital markets are government entities and businesses, whereas the usual borrowers in the mortgage markets are individuals. Second, mortgage loans are made for varying amounts and maturities, depending on the borrowers' needs, features that cause problems for developing a secondary market.

In this chapter we will identify the characteristics of typical residential mortgages, discuss the usual term and types of mortgages available, and review who provides and services these loans. We will also discuss the growth of the mortgage-backed security market.

WHAT ARE MORTGAGES?

A **mortgage** is a long-term loan secured by real estate. A developer may obtain a mortgage loan to finance the construction of an office building, or a family may obtain a mortgage loan to finance the purchase of a home. In either case, the loan is **amortized:** The borrower pays it off over time in some combination of principal and interest payments that result in full payment of the debt by maturity. Table 1 shows the distribution of mortgage loan borrowers. Because over 82% of mortgage loans finance residential home purchases, that will be the primary focus of this chapter.

One way to understand the modern mortgage is to review its history. Originally, many states had laws that prevented banks from funding mortgages so that banks would not tie up their funds in long-term loans. The National Banking Act of 1863 further restricted mortgage lending. As a result, most mortgage contracts in the past were arranged between individuals, usually with the help of a lawyer who brought the parties together and drew up the papers. Such loans were generally available only to the wealthy and socially connected. As the demand for long-term funds increased, however, more mortgage brokers surfaced. They often originated loans in the rapidly developing western part of the country and sold them to savings banks and insurance companies in the East.

By 1880, mortgage bankers had learned to streamline their operations by selling bonds to raise the long-term funds they lent. They would gather a port-folio of mortgage contracts and use them as security for an issue of bonds that were sold publicly. Many of these loans were used to finance agricultural expansion in the Midwest. Unfortunately, an agricultural recession in the 1890s resulted in many defaults. Land prices fell, and a large number of the mortgage bankers went bankrupt.

Thereafter, it was very difficult to obtain long-term loans until after World War I, when national banks were authorized to make mortgage loans. This regulatory change caused a tremendous real estate boom, and mortgage lending expanded rapidly.

The mortgage market was again devastated by the Great Depression in the 1930s. Millions of borrowers were without work and were unable to make their loan payments. This led to foreclosures and land sales that caused property values to collapse. Mortgage-lending institutions were again hit hard, and many failed.

One reason that so many borrowers defaulted on their loans was the type of mortgage loan they had. Most mortgages in this period were **balloon loans:** The borrower paid only interest for three to five years, at which time the entire loan amount became due. The lender was usually willing to renew the debt with some reduction in principal. However, if the borrower were unemployed, the lender would not renew, and the borrower would default.

As part of the recovery program from the depression, the federal government stepped in and restructured the mortgage market. The government took over delinquent balloon loans and allowed borrowers to repay them over long periods

TABLE 1 Mortgage Loan Borrowing, 2001

Type of Property	Mortgage Loans Issued ($ billions)	Proportion of Total (%)
One- to four-family dwelling	5,285	75.33
Multifamily dwelling	419	5.97
Commercial building	1,203	17.15
Farm	110	1.55

Source: Federal Reserve Bulletin, 2001, Table 1.54.

of time. It is no surprise that these new types of loans were very popular. The surviving savings and loans began offering home buyers similar loans, and the high demand contributed to restoring the health of the mortgage industry.

CHARACTERISTICS OF THE RESIDENTIAL MORTGAGE

The modern mortgage lender has continued to refine the long-term loan to make it more desirable to borrowers. Even in the past 20 years, both the nature of the lenders and the instruments have undergone substantial changes. One of the biggest changes is the development of an active secondary market for mortgage contracts. We will examine the nature of mortgage loan contracts and then look at their secondary market.

The mortgage market has become very competitive in recent years. Twenty years ago, savings and loan institutions and the mortgage departments of large banks originated most mortgage loans. Currently, there are many loan production offices that compete in real estate financing. Some of these offices are subsidiaries of banks, and others are independently owned. As a result of the competition for mortgage loans, borrowers can choose from a variety of terms and options.

Mortgage Interest Rates

Track mortgage rates and shop for mortgage rates in different geographic areas at www.interest.com

The interest rate borrowers pay on their mortgages is probably the most important factor in their decision of how much and from whom to borrow. The interest rate on the loan is determined by three factors: current long-term market rates, the life (term) of the mortgage, and the number of discount points paid.

1. *Market rates.* Long-term market rates are determined by the supply of and demand for long-term funds, which are in turn influenced by a number of global, national, and regional factors. As Figure 1 shows, mortgage rates

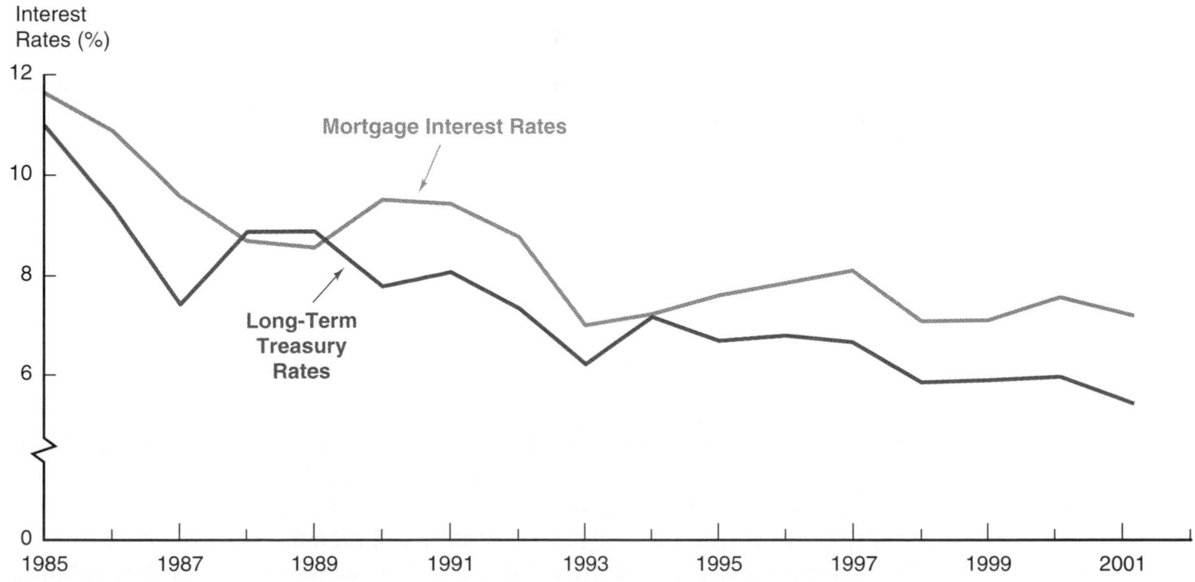

FIGURE 1 Mortgage Rates and Long-Term Treasury Interest Rates, 1985–2002

Source: Federal Reserve Bulletin, various issues, Table 1.53 Line 7 and Table 1.35 Line 35.

tend to stay above the less risky Treasury bonds most of the time but tend to track along with them.

2. *Term.* Longer-term mortgages have higher interest rates than shorter-term mortgages. The usual mortgage lifetime is either 15 or 30 years. Lenders also offer 20-year loans, though they are not as popular. Because interest-rate risk falls as the term to maturity decreases, the interest rate on the 15-year loan will be substantially less than on the 30-year loan. For example, in August, 2001, the average 30-year mortgage rate was 6.73%, and the 15-year rate was 6.25%.

3. *Discount points.* **Discount points** (or simply *points*) are interest payments made at the beginning of a loan. A loan with one discount point means that the borrower pays 1% of the loan amount at *closing,* the moment when the borrower signs the loan paper and receives the proceeds of the loan. In exchange for the points, the lender reduces the interest rate on the loan. In considering whether to pay points, borrowers must determine whether the reduced interest rate over the life of the loan fully compensates for the increased up-front expense. To make this determination, borrowers must take into account how long they will hold on to the loan.

Application — The Discount Point Decision

Suppose that you are offered two loan alternatives. In the first, you pay no discount points and the interest rate is 12%. In the second, you pay 2 discount points but receive a lower interest rate of 11.5%. Which alternative do you choose?

To answer this question you must first compute the effective annual rate without discount points. Since the loan is compounded monthly, you pay 1% per month. Because of the compounding, the effective annual rate is greater than the simple annual rate. To compute the effective rate, raise 1 plus the monthly rate to the twelfth power and subtract 1. The effective annual rate on the no-point loan is thus

$$\text{Effective annual rate} = (1.01)^{12} - 1 = 0.1268 = 12.68\%$$

Because of monthly compounding, a 12% annual percentage rate has an effective annual rate of 12.68%. On a 30-year, $100,000 house loan, your payment will be $1028.61 as found on a financial calculator.

Now compute the effective annual rate if you pay 2 discount points. Let's assume that the amount of the loan is still $100,000. If you pay 2 points, instead of receiving $100,000, you will receive only $98,000 ($100,000 – $2000). Your payment is computed on the $100,000, but at the lower interest rate. Using a financial calculator, we find that the monthly payment is $990.29 and your monthly rate is 0.9804%.[1] The effective annual rate after compounding is

$$\text{Effective annual rate} = (1.009804)^{12} - 1 = 0.1242 = 12.42\%$$

As a result of paying the 2 discount points, the effective annual rate has dropped from 12.68% to 12.42%. On the surface, it would seem like a good idea to pay the points. The problem is that these calculations were made assuming the loan would be held for 30 years. What happens if you sell the house before the loan matures?

If the loan is paid off early, the borrower will benefit from the lower interest rate for a shorter length of time, and the discount points are spread over a shorter

[1]The application on page 297 discusses how mortgage loan payments are computed.

TABLE 2 Effective Rate of Interest on a Loan at 12% with 2 Discount Points

Year of Prepayment	Effective Rate of Interest (%)	Year of Prepayment	Effective Rate of Interest (%)
1	14.54	6	12.65
2	13.40	7	12.60
3	13.02	10	12.52
4	12.84	15	12.45
5	12.73	30	12.42

period of time. The result of these two factors is that the effective interest rate rises the shorter the time the loan is held before being paid. This relationship is demonstrated in Table 2. If the 2-point loan is held for 15 years, the effective rate is 12.45%. At 10 years, the effective rate is up to 12.52%. Even at six years, when the effective rate is 12.65%, paying the discount points has saved the borrower money. However, if the loan is paid off at 5 years, the effective rate is 12.73%, which is higher than the 12.68% effective rate if no points were paid.[2]

Loan Terms

Mortgage loan contracts contain many legal and financial terms, most of which protect the lender from financial loss.

Collateral One characteristic common to mortgage loans is the requirement that collateral, usually the real estate being financed, be pledged as security. The lending institution will place a **lien** against the property, and this remains in effect until the loan is paid off. A lien is a public record that attaches to the title of the property, advising that the property is security for a loan, and it gives the lender the right to sell the property if the underlying loan defaults.

No one can buy the property and obtain clear title to it without paying off this lien. For example, if you purchased a piece of property with a loan secured by a lien, the lender would file notice of this lien at the public recorder's office. The lien gives notice to the world that if there is a default on the loan, the lender has the right to seize the property. If you try to sell the property without paying off the loan, the lien would remain attached to the title or deed to the property. Since the lender can take the property away from whoever owns it, no one would buy it unless you paid off the loan. The existence of liens against real estate explains why a title search is an important part of any mortgage loan transaction. During the title search, a lawyer or title company searches the public record for any liens. Title insurance is then sold that guarantees the buyer that the property is free of *encumbrances,* any questions about the state of the title to the property, including the existence of liens.

Down Payments To obtain a mortgage loan, the lender also requires the borrower to make a **down payment** on the property, that is, to pay a portion of the purchase

[2]For example, to compute the effective rate if the loan is prepaid after 2 years, find the FV if I = 11.5%, PV = 100,000, N = 360, and PMT = 990.29. Now set PV equal to 98,000 and compute I. Divide this I by 12, add 1, and raise the result to the twelfth power.

price. The balance of the purchase price is paid by the *loan proceeds.* Down payments (like liens) are intended to make the borrower less likely to default on the loan. A borrower who does not make a down payment could walk away from the house and the loan and lose nothing. Furthermore, if real estate prices drop even a small amount, the balance due on the loan will exceed the value of the collateral. As we discussed in Chapter 2, the down payment reduces *moral hazard* for the borrower. The amount of the down payment depends on the type of mortgage loan. Many lenders require that the borrower pay 5% of the purchase price; in other situations, up to 20% may be required.

Private Mortgage Insurance Another way that lenders protect themselves against default is by requiring the borrower to purchase **private mortgage insurance (PMI)**. PMI is an insurance policy that guarantees to make up any discrepancy between the value of the property and the loan amount, should a default occur. For example, if the balance on your loan was $120,000 at the time of default and the property was worth only $100,000, PMI would pay the lending institution $20,000. The default still appears on the credit record of the borrower, but the lender avoids sustaining the loss. PMI is usually required on loans that have less than a 20% down payment. If the loan-to-value ratio falls because of payments being made or because the value of the property increases, the borrower can request that the PMI requirement be dropped. PMI usually costs between $20 and $30 per month for a $100,000 loan.

Borrower Qualification Before granting a mortgage loan, the lender will determine whether the borrower qualifies for it. Qualifying for a mortgage loan is different from qualifying for a bank loan because most lenders sell their mortgage loans to one of a few federal agencies in the secondary mortgage market. These agencies establish very precise guidelines that must be followed before they will accept the loan. If the lender gives a mortgage loan to a borrower who does not fit these guidelines, the lender may not be able to resell the loan. That ties up the lender's funds. Banks can be more flexible with loans that will be kept on the bank's own books.

The rules for qualifying a borrower are complex and constantly changing, but a rule of thumb is that the loan payment, including taxes and insurance, should not exceed 25% of gross monthly income. Furthermore, the sum of the monthly payments on all loans to the borrower, including car loans and credit cards, cannot exceed 33% of gross monthly income. A borrower who fails this income test can pay off some of the outstanding debt, increase the down payment, or find a less expensive house to buy.

Mortgage Loan Amortization

Mortgage loan borrowers agree to pay a monthly amount of principal and interest that will fully amortize the loan by its maturity. "Fully amortize" means that the payments will pay off the outstanding indebtedness by the time the loan matures. During the early years of the loan, the lender applies most of the payment to the interest on the loan and a small amount to the outstanding principal balance. Many borrowers are surprised to find that after years of making payments, their loan balance has not dropped appreciably.

Table 3 shows the distribution of principal and interest for a 30-year, $130,000 loan at 8.5% interest. Only $78.75 of the first payment is applied to reduce the loan

TABLE 3 Amortization of a 30-Year, $130,000 Loan at 8.5%

Payment Number	Beginning Balance of Loan	Monthly Payment	Amount Applied to Interest	Amount Applied to Principal	Ending Balance of Loan
1	130,000.00	999.59	920.83	78.75	129,921.24
24	128,040.25	999.59	906.95	92.66	127,947.62
60	124,256.74	999.59	880.15	119.43	124,137.31
120	115,365.63	999.59	817.17	182.41	115,183.22
180	101,786.23	999.59	720.99	278.60	101,507.63
240	81,046.41	999.59	574.08	425.51	80,620.90
360	991.77	999.59	7.82	991.77	0

balance. At the end of two years, the balance due is $127,947, and at the end of five years, the balance due is $124,137. Put another way, of $59,975.40 in loan payments made during the first five years, only $5862.69 is applied to the principal. Over the life of the $130,000 loan, a total of $229,850 in interest will be paid.

If the loan in Table 3 had been financed for 15 years instead of for 30, the payment would have increased by about $280 per month to $1279.59, but the interest savings over the life of the loan would be nearly $130,000. It is no wonder why so many borrowers prefer the shorter-term loans.

Application

Computing the Payment on Mortgage Loans

We can apply the techniques for computing loan payments introduced in Chapter 3 to computing the payment on mortgage loans. Suppose that you have graduated and want to buy a condominium instead of renting an apartment. The condo costs $100,000, and a 5% down payment is required by your mortgage lender. How much will your monthly loan payment be?

To compute fixed-amount loan payments, we recognize that the lender must equate the present value of the stream of payments you will pay to the amount of the loan. In equation form,

$$\text{Loan amount} = \frac{P}{1+i} + \frac{P}{(1+i)^2} + \frac{P}{(1+i)^3} + \cdots + \frac{P}{(1+i)^n} \quad (1)$$

where

P = fixed payment
i = interest rate on the loan
n = term of the loan

An alternative form for Equation 1, which takes advantage of present value tables included at the end of most introductory finance texts, is

$$\text{Loan amount} = P\,(PVIFA_{i,n}) \quad (2)$$

where $PVIFA$ is the present value interest factor with an interest rate of i for n periods. P can then be found by looking up the factor for the term and interest rate on the loan you are interested in and dividing this factor into the loan amount. Most factor tables include only 50 or 60 periods, so we cannot use this method to compute the payment on 30-year loans with monthly payments ($30 \times 12 = 360$ periods). Instead, a close approximation of the monthly payment can be found by computing the annual payment and dividing by 12.

EXAMPLE 1: Mortgage Loans

You obtain a 30-year loan at 8% on the $95,000 you need to finance your new condo. The price of the condo is $100,000 minus a $5000 down payment. Use Table 4 and Equation 2 to calculate the fixed payment on the loan.

Solution

The fixed payment on the loan would be $703 per month.

$$\text{Loan amount} = P\ (PVIFA_{i,n})$$

where

$$\begin{aligned} \text{Loan amount} &= \text{amount loaned by the bank} = \$95{,}000 \\ i &= \text{interest rate on the loan} = 0.08 \\ n &= \text{term of the loan} = 30 \end{aligned}$$

Thus

$$\$95{,}000 = P_{ann}(PVIFA_{8\%,30})$$

$$\$95{,}000 = P_{ann}(11.2578)$$

$$P_{ann} = \frac{\$95{,}000}{11.2578}$$

$$P_{ann} = \$8{,}439$$

$$P_{mo} = \frac{\$8{,}439}{12 \text{ months}} = \$703 \text{ per month}$$

To find the present value interest factor in Table 4, pick out the payment period in the left-hand column and then move across the row to the entry in the column for the interest rate on the loan. For a 30-year loan at 8%, the present value interest factor is 11.2578.

To solve using a financial calculator:

$$\begin{aligned} \text{N} &= \text{number of periods} = 30 \text{ years} \times 12 \text{ months} = 360 \\ \text{PV} &= \text{amount of the loan (LV)} = -95{,}000 \\ \text{FV} &= \text{amount of the loan after 30 years} = 0 \\ \text{I} &= \text{monthly interest rate} = 8/12 \text{ months} = 0.6667 \end{aligned}$$

Then push the PMT button = fixed monthly payment (P) = $697

(Note: small differences between the table solution and the calculator solution are due to rounding.)

TABLE 4 Present Value Interest Factor at Various Rates of Interest

	Interest Rate					
Payment Periods	5%	6%	7%	8%	9%	10%
15	10.3797	9.7122	9.1079	8.5595	8.0607	7.6061
20	12.4622	11.4699	10.5940	9.8181	9.1285	8.5136
25	14.0939	12.7834	11.6536	10.6748	9.8226	9.0770
30	15.3725	13.7648	12.4090	11.2578	9.8226	9.0770

TYPES OF MORTGAGE LOANS

A number of types of mortgage loans are available in the market. Different borrowers may qualify for different ones. A skilled mortgage banker can help find the best type of mortgage loan for each particular situation.

Insured and Conventional Mortgages

Mortgages are classified as either *insured* or *conventional.* **Insured mortgages** are originated by banks or other mortgage lenders but are guaranteed by either the Federal Housing Administration (FHA) or the Veterans Administration (VA). Applicants for FHA and VA loans must meet certain qualifications, such as having served in the military or having income below a given level, and can borrow only up to a certain amount. The FHA or VA then guarantees the bank making the loans against any losses—that is, the agency guarantees that it will pay off the mortgage loan if the borrower defaults. One important advantage to a borrower who qualifies for an FHA or VA loan is that only a very low or zero down payment is required.

Conventional mortgages are originated by the same sources as insured loans but are not guaranteed. Private mortgage companies now insure many conventional loans against default. As we noted, most lenders require the borrower to obtain private mortgage insurance on all loans with a loan-to-value ratio exceeding 80%.

Fixed- and Adjustable-Rate Mortgages

In standard mortgage contracts, borrowers agree to make regular payments on the principal and interest they owe to lenders. As we saw earlier, the interest rate significantly affects the size of this monthly payment. In *fixed-rate mortgages,* the interest rate and the monthly payment do not vary over the life of the mortgage.

The interest rate on *adjustable-rate mortgages (ARMs)* is tied to some market interest rate and therefore changes over time. ARMs usually have limits, called *caps,* on how high (or low) the interest rate can move in one year and during the term of the loan. A typical ARM might tie the interest rate to the average Treasury bill rate plus 2%, with caps of 2% per year and 6% over the lifetime of the mortgage. Caps make ARMs more palatable to borrowers.

Borrowers tend to prefer fixed-rate loans to ARMs because ARMs may cause financial hardship if interest rates rise. However, fixed-rate borrowers do not benefit if rates fall unless they are willing to refinance their mortgage (pay it off by obtaining a new mortgage at a lower interest rate). The fact that individuals are risk-averse means that fear of hardship most often overwhelms anticipation of savings.

Lenders, by contrast, prefer ARMs because ARMs lessen interest-rate risk. Recall from Chapter 3 that interest-rate risk is the risk that rising interest rates will cause the value of debt instruments to fall. The effect on the value of the debt is greatest when the debt has a long term to maturity. Since mortgages are usually long-term, their value is very sensitive to interest-rate movements. Lending institutions can reduce the sensitivity of their portfolios by making ARMs instead of standard fixed-rate loans.

Seeing that lenders prefer ARMs and borrowers prefer fixed-rate mortgages, lenders must entice borrowers by offering lower initial interest rates on ARMs than on fixed-rate loans. For example, in August 2001, the reported interest rate for 30-year fixed-rate mortgage loans was 6.75%. The rate at that time for adjustable-rate mortgages was 6.0%. The rate on the ARM would have to rise .75% before the borrower of the ARM would be in a worse position than the fixed-rate borrower.

Other Types of Mortgages

As the market for mortgage loans becomes more competitive, lenders are offering more innovative mortgage contracts in an effort to attract borrowers. We discuss some of these mortgages here.

Graduated-Payment Mortgages (GPMs) Graduated-payment mortgages are useful for home buyers who expect their incomes to rise. The GPM has lower payments in the first few years; then the payments rise. The early payments may not even be sufficient to cover the interest due, in which case the principal balance increases. As time passes, the borrower expects income to increase so that the higher payment will not be a burden.

The advantage of the GPM is that borrowers will qualify for a larger loan than if they requested a conventional mortgage. This may help buyers purchase adequate housing now and avoid the need to move to more expensive homes as their family size increases. The disadvantage is that the payments escalate whether the borrower's income does or not.

Growing-Equity Mortgages (GEMs) Lenders designed the growing-equity mortgage loan to help the borrower pay off the loan in a shorter period of time. With a GEM, the payments will initially be the same as on a conventional mortgage. However, over time the payment will increase. This increase will reduce the principal more quickly than the conventional payment stream would. For example, a typical contract may call for level payments for the first two years. The payments may increase by 5% per year for the next five years, then remain the same until maturity. The result is to reduce the life of the loan from 30 years to about 17.

GEMs are popular among borrowers who expect their incomes to rise in the future. It gives them the benefit of a small payment at the beginning while still retiring the debt early. Although the increase in payments is *required* in GEMs, most mortgage loans have no prepayment penalty. This means that a borrower with a 30-year loan could create a GEM by simply increasing the monthly payments beyond what is required and designating that the excess be applied entirely to the principal.

The GEM is similar to the graduated-payment mortgage; the difference is that the goal of the GPM is to help the borrower qualify by reducing the first few years' payments. The loan still pays off in 30 years. The goal of the GEM is to let the borrower pay off early.

Shared-Appreciation Mortgages (SAMs) When interest rates are high, the monthly payments on mortgage loans are also high. That prevents many borrowers from qualifying for loans. To help borrowers qualify and to keep loan volume high, lenders created the shared-appreciation mortgage. In a SAM, the lender lowers the interest rate on the mortgage in exchange for a share of any appreciation in the real estate (if the property sells for more than a stated amount, the lender is entitled to a portion of the gain). As interest rates and inflation fell in the late 1980s and into the 1990s, the popularity of these loans also diminished.

Equity Participation Mortgages In a shared-appreciation mortgage, the lender shares in the appreciation of the property. In an equity participation mortgage, an outside investor rather than the lender shares in the appreciation of the property. This investor will either provide a portion of the purchase price of the property or supplement the monthly payments. In return, the investor receives a portion of any appreciation in the property. As with the SAM, the borrower benefits by being able to qualify for a larger loan than without such help.

Second Mortgages Second mortgages are loans that are secured by the same real estate that is used to secure the first mortgage. The second mortgage is junior to the original loan. This means that should a default occur, the second mortgage holder will be paid only after the original loan has been paid off, if sufficient funds remain.

Second mortgages have two purposes. The first is to give borrowers a way to use the equity they have in their homes as security for another loan. An alternative to the second mortgage would be to refinance the home at a higher loan amount than is currently owed. The cost of obtaining a second mortgage is often much lower than refinancing.

Another purpose of the second mortgage is to take advantage of one of the few remaining tax deductions available to the middle class. The interest on loans secured by residential real estate is tax-deductible (the tax laws allow borrowers to deduct the interest on the primary residence and one vacation home). No other kind of consumer loan has this tax deduction. Many banks now offer lines of credit secured by second mortgages. In most cases, the value of the security is not of great interest to the bank. Consumers prefer that the line of credit be secured so that they can deduct the interest on the loan from their taxes.

Reverse Annuity Mortgages (RAMs) The reverse annuity mortgage is an innovative method for retired people to live on the equity they have in their homes. The contract for a RAM has the bank advancing funds on a monthly schedule. This increasing-balance loan is secured by the real estate. The borrower does not make any payments against the loan. When the borrower dies, the borrower's estate sells the property to retire the debt.

The advantage of the RAM is that it allows retired people to use the equity in their homes without the necessity of selling it. For retirees in need of supplemental funds to meet living expenses, the RAM can be a desirable option.

The various mortgage types are summarized in Table 5.

TABLE 5 Summary of Mortgage Types

Conventional mortgage	Loan is not guaranteed; usually requires private mortgage insurance; 5% to 20% down payment
Insured mortgage	Loan is guaranteed by FHA or VA; low or zero down payment
Adjustable-rate mortgage (ARM)	Interest rate is tied to some other security and is adjusted periodically; size of adjustment is subject to annual limits
Graduated-payment mortgage (GPM)	Initial low payment increases each year; loan amortizes in 30 years
Growing-equity mortgage (GEM)	Initial payment increases each year; loan amortizes in less than 30 years
Shared-appreciation mortgage (SAM)	In exchange for providing a low interest rate, the lender shares in any appreciation of the real estate
Equity participation mortgage	In exchange for paying a portion of the down payment or for supplementing the monthly payments, an outside investor shares in any appreciation of the real estate
Second mortgage	Loan is secured by a second lien against the real estate; often used for lines of credit or home improvement loans
Reverse annuity mortgage	Lender disburses a monthly payment to the borrower on an increasing-balance loan; loan comes due when the real estate is sold

MORTGAGE-LENDING INSTITUTIONS

Originally, the thrift industry was established with the mandate from Congress to provide mortgage loans to families. Congress gave these institutions the ability to attract depositors by allowing S&Ls to pay slightly higher interest rates on deposits. For many years, the thrift industry did its job well. Thrifts raised short-term funds by attracting deposits and used these funds to make long-term mortgage loans. The growth of the housing industry owes much of its success to these institutions. (The thrift industry is discussed further in Chapter 17.)

Until the 1970s, interest rates remained relatively stable, and when fluctuations did occur, they tended to be small and short-lived. But in the 1970s, interest rates rose rapidly, along with inflation, and thrifts became the victims of interest-rate risk. As market interest rates rose, the value of their fixed-rate mortgage loan portfolios fell. Because of the losses the thrifts suffered, they stopped being the primary source of mortgage loans.

Another serious problem with the early mortgage market was that thrift institutions were restricted from nationwide branching by federal and state laws and were forbidden to lend outside of their normal lending territory, about 100 miles from their offices. So even if an institution appeared very diversified, with thousands of different loans, all of the loans were from the same region. When that region had economic problems, many of the loans would default at the same time. For example, Texas and Oklahoma experienced a recession in the mid–1980s due to falling oil prices. Many mortgage loans defaulted because real estate values fell at the same time as the region's unemployment rate rose. That other areas of the country remained healthy was of no help to local lenders.

Figure 2 shows the share of the total mortgage market held by the major mortgage-lending institutions in the United States. (Mortgage pools and trusts are discussed later in this chapter.)

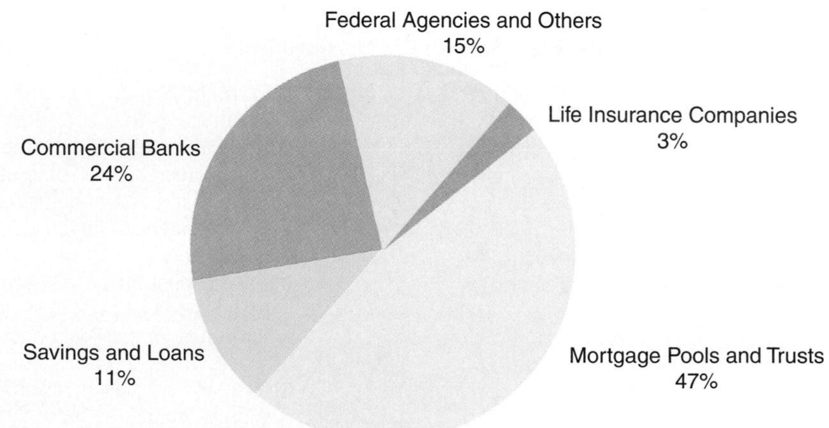

FIGURE 2 Share of the Mortgage Market Held by Major Mortgage-Lending Institutions

Source: Federal Reserve Bulletin, 2001, Table 1.54.

LOAN SERVICING

Many of the institutions making mortgage loans do not want to hold large portfolios of long-term securities. Commercial banks, for example, obtain their funds from short-term sources. Investing in long-term loans would subject them to unacceptably high interest-rate risk. Commercial banks, thrifts, and most other loan originators do, however, make money through the fees that they earn for packaging loans for other investors to hold. Loan origination fees are typically 1% of the loan amount, though this varies with the market.

Once a loan has been made, many lenders immediately sell the loan to another investor. The borrower may not even be aware that the original lender transferred the loan. By selling the loan, the originator frees up funds that can be lent to another borrower, thereby generating additional fee income.

Some of the originators also provide servicing of the loan. The loan-servicing agent collects payments from the borrower, passes the principal and interest on to the investor, keeps required records of the transaction, and maintains **reserve accounts.** Reserve accounts are established for most mortgage loans to permit the lender to make tax and insurance payments for the borrower. Lenders prefer to make these payments because they protect the security of the loan. Loan-servicing agents usually earn 0.5% per year of the total loan amount for their efforts.

In summary, there are three distinct elements to most mortgage loans:

1. The originator packages the loan for an investor.
2. The investor holds the loan.
3. The servicing agent handles the paperwork.

One, two, or three different intermediaries may provide these functions.

Mortgage loans are increasingly obtained from the Web. E-Finance Box 1 discusses this new source of mortgage loans.

BOX 1: E-FINANCE
Borrowers Shop the Web for Mortgages

One business area that has been significantly affected by the Web is mortgage banking. Historically, borrowers went to local banks, savings and loans, and mortgage banking companies to obtain mortgage loans. These offices packaged the loans and resold them. In recent years, hundreds of new Web-based mortgage banking companies have emerged.

The mortgage market is well suited to providing on-line service for several reasons. First, it is information-based and no products have to be shipped or inventoried. Second, the product (a loan) is homogeneous across providers. A borrower does not really care who provides the money as long as it is provided efficiently. Third, because home buyers tend not to obtain mortgage loans very often, they have little loyalty to any local lender. Finally, on-line lenders can often offer loans at lower cost because they can operate with lower overhead than firms that must greet the public.

The on-line mortgage market makes it much easier for borrowers to shop interest rates and terms. By filling out one application, Web service companies will provide a number of alternative loan options. Borrowers can then select the option that best suits their requirements.

On-line mortgage firms, such as Lending Tree, have made mortgage lending more competitive. This may lead to lower rates and better service. It has also led lenders to offer an often confusing array of loan alternatives that most borrowers have difficulty interpreting. This makes comparison shopping more difficult than simply comparing interest rates.

SECONDARY MORTGAGE MARKET

The federal government founded the secondary market for mortgages. As we noted earlier, the mortgage market had all but collapsed during the Great Depression. To help spur the nation's economic activity, the government established several agencies to buy mortgages. The Federal National Mortgage Association (Fannie Mae) was set up to buy mortgages from thrifts so that these institutions could make more mortgage loans. This agency would fund these purchases by selling bonds to the public.

At about the same time, the Federal Housing Administration was established to insure certain mortgage contracts. This made it easier to sell the mortgages because the buyer did not have to be concerned with the borrower's credit history or the value of the collateral. A similar insurance program was set up through the Veterans Administration to insure loans to veterans after World War II.

One advantage of the insured loans was that they were required to be written on a standard loan contract. This standardization was an important factor in the growth of the secondary market for mortgages.

As the secondary market for mortgage contracts took shape, a new intermediary, the mortgage bank, emerged. Because this firm did not accept deposits, it was able to open offices across the country. The mortgage bank originated the loans, funding them initially with its own capital. After a group of similar loans were made, they would be bundled and sold, either to one of the federal agencies or to an insurance or pension fund. There were several advantages to the mortgage banks. Because of their size, they were able to capture economies of scale in loan origination and servicing. They were also able to bundle loans from different regions together, which helped reduce their risk. The increased competition for loans among these intermediaries led to lower rates for borrowers.

SECURITIZATION OF MORTGAGES

Intermediaries still faced several problems when trying to sell mortgages. The first was that mortgages are usually too small to be wholesale instruments. The average mortgage loan is now about $130,000. This is far below the $5 million round lot established for commercial paper, for example. Many institutional investors do not want to deal in such small denominations.

The second problem with selling mortgages in the secondary market was that they were not standardized. They have different times to maturity, interest rates, and contract terms. That makes it difficult to bundle a large number of mortgages together.

Third, mortgage loans are relatively costly to service. Compare the servicing a mortgage loan requires to that of a corporate bond. The lender must collect monthly payments, often pay property taxes and insurance premiums, and service reserve accounts. None of this is required if a bond is purchased.

Finally, mortgages have unknown default risk. Investors in mortgages do not want to spend a lot of time evaluating the credit of borrowers. These problems inspired the creation of the **mortgage-backed security.**

What Is a Mortgage-Backed Security?

By the late 1960s, the secondary market for mortgages was declining, mostly because fewer veterans were obtaining guaranteed loans. The government reorganized Fannie Mae and also created two new agencies: the Government National Mortgage Association (GNMA, or Ginnie Mae) and the Federal Home Loan Mortgage Corporation (FHLMC, or Freddie Mac). These three agencies were now able to offer new securities backed by both insured and, for the first time, uninsured mortgages.

An alternative to selling mortgages directly to investors is to create a new security backed by (secured by) a large number of mortgages assembled into what is called a *mortgage pool.* A trustee, such as a bank or a government agency, holds the mortgage pool, which serves as collateral for the new security. This process is called securitization. The most common type of mortgage-backed security is the **mortgage pass-through,** a security that has the borrower's mortgage payments pass through the trustee before being disbursed to the investors in the mortgage pass-through. If borrowers prepay their loans, investors receive more principal than expected. For example, investors may buy mortgage-backed securities on which the average interest rate is 9%. If interest rates fall and borrowers refinance at lower rates, the securities will pay off early. The possibility that mortgages will prepay and force investors to seek alternative investments, usually with lower returns, is called *prepayment risk.*

As is evident in Figure 3, the dollar volume of outstanding mortgage pools increased steadily since 1984. The reason that mortgage pools have become so popular is that they permit the creation of new securities (like mortgage pass-throughs) that make investing in mortgage loans much more efficient. For example, an institutional investor can invest in one large mortgage pass-through secured by a mortgage pool rather than investing in many small and dissimilar mortgage contracts.

Types of Pass-Through Securities

There are several types of mortgage pass-through securities: GNMA pass-throughs, FHLMC pass-throughs, and private pass-throughs.

Government National Mortgage Association (GNMA) Pass-Throughs Ginnie Mae began guaranteeing pass-through securities in 1968. Since then, the popularity of these instruments has increased dramatically.

A variety of financial intermediaries, including commercial banks and mortgage companies, originate Ginnie Mae mortgages. Ginnie Mae aggregates these mortgages into a pool and issues pass-through securities that are collateralized by the interest and principal payments from the mortgages. Ginnie Mae also guarantees the pass-through securities against default. The usual minimum denomination for pass-throughs is $25,000. The minimum pool size is $1 million. One pool may back up many pass-through securities.

Federal Home Loan Mortgage Corporation (FHLMC) Pass-Throughs Freddie Mac was created to assist savings and loan associations, which are not eligible to originate Ginnie Mae–guaranteed loans. Freddie Mac purchases mortgages for its own account and also issues pass-through securities similar to those issued by Ginnie Mae. Pass-through securities issued by Freddie Mac are called *participation certificates (PCs).* Freddie Mac pools are distinct from Ginnie Mae pools in that they contain conventional (nonguaranteed) mortgages, are not federally insured, contain mortgages with different rates, are larger (ranging up to several hundred million dollars), and have a minimum denomination of $100,000.

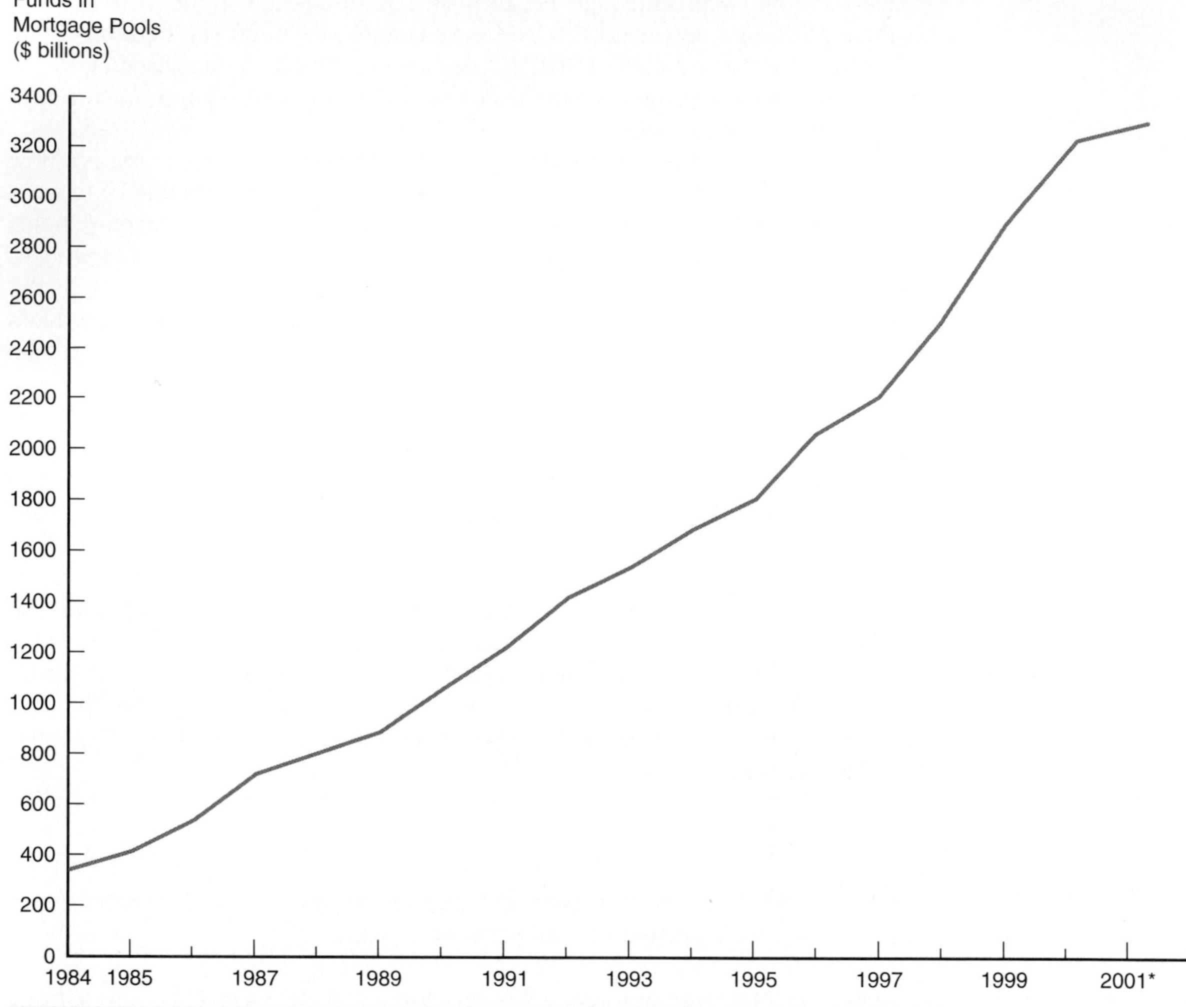

FIGURE 3 Value of Mortgage Principal Held in Mortgage Pools, 1984–2001

*First quarter.

Source: Federal Reserve Bulletin, various issues, Table 1.54

A relatively recent innovation in the FHLMC pass-through market has been the **collateralized mortgage obligation (CMO).** CMOs are securities classified by when prepayment is likely to occur and are issued by Freddie Mac. These differ from traditional mortgage-backed securities in that they are offered in different maturity groups. These securities help reduce prepayment risk, which is a problem with other types of pass-through securities.

CMOs backed by a particular mortgage pool are divided into classes. When principal is repaid, the investors in the first class are paid first, then those in the second class, and so on. Investors choose a class that matches their maturity requirements. For example, if they will need cash from their investment in a few years, they purchase class 1 or 2 CMOs. If they want the investment to be long-term, they can purchase CMOs from the last class.

Even when an investor purchases a CMO, there are no guarantees about how long the investment will last. If interest rates fall significantly, many borrowers will pay off their mortages early by refinancing at lower rates.

Real estate mortgage investment conduits (REMICs) were authorized by the 1986 Tax Reform Act to allow originators to pass through all interest payments tax-free. Only their legal and tax consequences distinguish REMICs from CMOs.

Private Pass-Throughs (PIPs) In addition to the agency pass-throughs, intermediaries in the private sector have offered privately issued pass-through securities. The first of these PIPs was offered by BankAmerica in 1977.

One mortgage market opportunity available to private institutions is for mortgages larger than the maximum size set by the government. These so-called *jumbo mortgages* are often bundled into pools to back private pass-throughs. The *Wall Street Journal* reports prices and yields on various mortgage-backed securities and CMOs daily (see "Following the Financial News").

Mortgage-Backed Securities Clearing Corporation

The homepage of the MBSCC, www.mbscc.com, gives information on this provider of automated post-trade comparison, netting, risk management, and pool-notification services to the mortgage-backed securities market.

The Mortgage Backed Securities Clearing Corporation (MBSCC) was formed by the Midwest Stock Exchange in 1979 to automate the trading of mortgage-backed securities. Both parties to an exchange of mortgage-backed securities submit information to the MBSCC. The computer system checks that the information is in agreement and then confirms the trade.

Mortgage-Backed Mutual Funds Mortgage-backed mutual funds offer individual investors an opportunity to invest in mortgage-backed securities despite their

FOLLOWING THE FINANCIAL NEWS

Mortgage-Backed Securities

Indicative, not guaranteed; from Bear Stearns Cos./Street Software Technology Inc.

		PRICE (Jan) (PtS-32ds)	PRICE CHANGE (32ds)	AVG LIFE (years)	SPRD TO AVG LIFE (8ps)	SPREAD CHANGE	PSA (Prepay speed)	YIELD TO MAT.*
30-YEAR								
FMAC GOLD	6.5%	100-03	+ 17	7.9	174	+ 6	185	6.52
FMAC GOLD	7.0%	101-29	+ 14	4.9	220	+ 8	324	6.51
FMAC GOLD	7.5%	103-04	+ 10	2.8	276	+ 4	541	6.17
FNMA	6.5%	100-00	+ 16	7.8	174	+ 7	192	6.50
FNMA	7.0%	101-28	+ 12	4.5	228	+ 17	364	6.43
FNMA	7.5%	103-06	+ 10	2.8	266	+ 4	541	6.08
GNMA	6.5%	100-11	+ 17	8.1	167	+ 4	178	6.48
GNMA	7.0%	102-04	+ 12	5.2	211	+ 2	295	6.48
GNMA	7.5%	103-13	+ 09	4.9	228	+ 3	305	6.60
15-YEAR								
FMAC GOLD	6.5%	102-01	+ 13	4.0	194	unch	300	5.90
FNMA	6.5%	101-30	+ 12	4.1	190	unch	300	5.87
GNMA	6.5%	102-17	+ 12	4.0	179	unch	300	5.74

*Extrapolated from benchmarks based on projections from Bear Stearns prepayment model, assuming interest rates remain unchanged.

COLLATERALIZED MORTGAGE OBLIGATIONS

Spread of CMO yields above U.S. Treasury securities of comparable maturity. In basis points (100 basis points = 1 percentage point of interest)

MAT	SPREAD	CHG FROM PREV DAY
SEQUENTIALS		
2-year	210	unch
5-year	215	unch
7-year	215	unch
10-year	167	unch
20-year	145	unch
PACS		
2-year	150	unch
5-year	165	unch
7-year	160	unch
10-year	160	unch
20-year	132	unch

Source: Wall Street Journal, January 2, 2002, p. C13. Republished by permission of Dow Jones, Inc. via Copyright Clearance Center, Inc.

large denomination. Since mortgage-backed securities offer a higher return than Treasury bonds but are considered only slightly riskier, investors find them attractive. A typical mortgage-backed mutual fund will hold a combination of pass-throughs, CMOs, and Treasury bonds. Investors in these funds must be aware that when interest rates fall, many of the loans will pay off and be replaced with lower-interest mortgages. As a result, the fund's return will fall.

THE IMPACT OF SECURITIZED MORTGAGES ON THE MORTGAGE MARKET

Mortgage-backed securities (also called **securitized mortgages**) have been a very important development in the financial markets in recent years. These new debt instruments compete for funds with government bonds, corporate bonds, and stocks. Securitized mortgages are low-risk securities that have higher yields than comparable government bonds and attract funds from around the world.

One benefit of the securitized mortgage is that it reduces the problems caused by regional lending institutions' sensitivity to local economic fluctuations. Because the loans are sold nationally and internationally, regional variations are no longer as great a source of risk to lenders.

A second benefit of the securitized mortgage is that borrowers now have access to a national capital market. In the early twentieth century, borrowers could choose among mortgages offered by only a few local lenders. The new securitized mortgages function much more like the rest of the capital markets. As a result, rates in the mortgage market follow other capital market rates much more closely.

Another benefit of the securitized mortgages is that an investor can enjoy the low-risk and long-term nature of investing in mortgages without having to service the loan.

A side effect of the development of securitized mortgages has been that mortgage rates are now more open to national and international influences. As a result, mortgage rates are more volatile than they were in the past.

SUMMARY

1. Mortgages are long-term loans secured by real estate. Both individuals and businesses obtain mortgage loans to finance real estate purchases.
2. Mortgage interest rates are relatively low due to competition among various institutions that want to make mortgage loans. In addition to keeping interest rates low, the competition has resulted in a variety of terms and options for mortgage loans. For example, borrowers may choose to obtain a 30-year fixed-rate loan or an adjustable-rate loan that has its interest rate tied to the Treasury bill rate.
3. Several features of mortgage loans are designed to reduce the likelihood that the borrower will default. For example, a down payment is usually required so that the borrower will suffer a loss if the lender repossesses the property. Most lenders also require that the borrower purchase private mortgage insurance unless the loan-to-value ratio drops below 80%.
4. A variety of mortgages is available to meet the needs of most borrowers. The graduated-payment mortgage has low initial payments that increase over time. The growing-equity mortgage has increasing payments that cause the loan to be paid off in a shorter period than a level-payment loan. Shared-appreciation loans were used when interest rates and inflation were high. The lender shared in the increase in the real estate's value in exchange for lower interest rates.
5. Securitized mortgages have been growing in popularity in recent years as institutional investors look for attractive investment opportunities. Securitized mortgages are securities collateralized by a pool of mortgages. The payments on the pool are passed through to the investors. Ginnie Mae, Freddie Mac, and private banks issue pass-through securities.

KEY TERMS

QUESTIONS AND PROBLEMS

***1.** What distinguishes the mortgage markets from other capital markets?

2. Most mortgage loans once had balloon payments; now most current mortgage loans fully amortize. What is the difference between a balloon loan and an amortizing loan?

***3.** What features contribute to keeping long-term mortgage interest rates low?

4. What are discount points, and why do some mortgage borrowers choose to pay them?

***5.** What is a lien, and when is it used in mortgage lending?

6. What is the purpose of requiring that a borrower make a down payment before receiving a loan?

***7.** What kind of insurance do lenders usually require of borrowers who have less than an 80% loan-to-value ratio?

8. Lenders tend not to be as flexible about the qualifications required of mortgage customers as they can be for other types of bank loans. Why is this so?

***9.** Distinguish between conventional mortgage loans and insured mortgage loans.

10. Interpret what is meant when a lender quotes the terms on a loan as "floating with the T-bill plus 2 with caps of 2 and 6"?

***11.** The monthly payments on both graduated-payment loans and growing-equity loans increase over time. Despite this similarity, the two types of loans have different purposes. What is the motivation behind each type of loan?

12. Many banks offer lines of credit that are secured by a second mortgage (or lien) on real property. These loans have been very popular among bank customers. Why are homeowners so willing to pledge their homes as security for these lines of credit?

***13.** The reverse annuity mortgage (RAM) allows retired people to live off the equity they have in their homes without having to sell the home. Explain how a RAM works.

14. What is a securitized mortgage?

***15.** Describe how a mortgage pass-through works.

WEB EXERCISES

The Mortgage Market

1. You may be looking into acquiring a home in the near future. One common question you may have is how large a mortgage loan you can afford. Go to http://interest.com and click on "Mortgage Calculators." Choose the calculator labeled "How much mortgage loan you can afford to borrow." Input your expected future salary data. How large a mortgage can you afford according to the calculator? Increase your debt to see the impact on the amount of mortgage loan you will qualify for.

2. One of the more difficult decisions faced by homeowners is whether it pays to refinance a mortgage loan when rates have dropped. Go to http://interest.com and click on "Mortgage Calculators". Choose the calculator that computes how long it will take to recoup the costs of refinancing your mortgage loan. Assume you obtained a 30-year $130,000 loan four years ago at 7%. Now rates have dropped and your income is higher. Determine how much you will save if you get a new loan for 15 years at 6.25%.

Chapter 12

The Foreign Exchange Market

Preview

In the 1980s, American businesses became less competitive with their foreign counterparts; in the 1990s, their competitiveness had increased. Was this swing in competitiveness primarily the result of American management falling down on the job in the 1980s, then getting its act together in the 1990s? Not really. American businesses became less competitive in the 1980s because American dollars became worth more in terms of foreign currencies, making American goods more expensive relative to foreign goods. By the 1990s, the value of the U.S. dollar had fallen appreciably from its highs in the mid-1980s, making American goods cheaper and enabling American businesses to be more competitive.

The price of one currency in terms of another is called the **exchange rate.** It affects the economy because when the U.S. dollar becomes more valuable relative to foreign currencies, American goods become more expensive for foreigners and foreign goods become cheaper for Americans. When the U.S. dollar falls in value, American goods become cheaper for foreigners and foreign goods become more expensive for Americans. In addition, changes in the exchange rate have a major impact on financial institutions because many of their assets are denominated in foreign currencies; when the value of foreign currencies changes, the market value of financial institutions changes as well. To understand why exchange rates change, we need to examine the market in which they are determined, the **foreign exchange market.**

As you can see in Figure 1, exchange rates have been highly volatile, with the dollar generally increasing in value relative to foreign currencies from 1980 to 1985, falling in value until 1998, and then appreciating since then. What factors explain the dollar's former strength and later weakness that have caused major

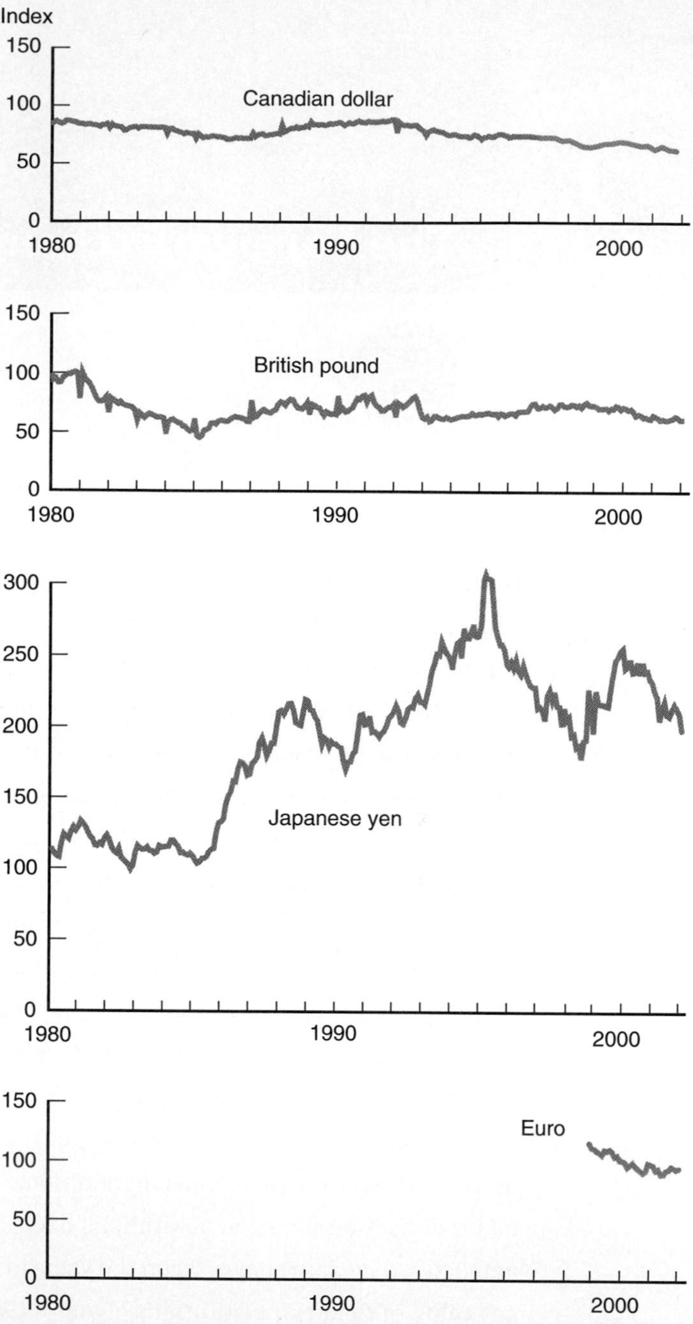

FIGURE 1 Exchange Rates, 1980–2001

Dollar prices of selected foreign currencies (monthly averages; index: March 1973 = 100 for all currencies except the euro; January 1999 = 100 for the euro). Note that a decline in these plots means a strengthening of the dollar, and an increase indicates a weakening of the dollar.

Sources: International Monetary Fund, *International Financial Statistics,* Citibase databank; www.federalreserve.gov/releases/H10/hist/

swings in the competitiveness of American businesses? Why are exchange rates so volatile from day to day?

To answer these questions, we develop a modern view of exchange rate determination that explains recent behavior in the foreign exchange market.

FOREIGN EXCHANGE MARKET

Most countries of the world have their own currencies: The United States has its dollar; France, the euro; Brazil, its real; and India, its rupee. Trade between countries involves the mutual exchange of different currencies (or, more usually, bank deposits denominated in different currencies). When an American firm buys foreign goods, services, or financial assets, for example, U.S. dollars (typically, bank deposits denominated in U.S. dollars) must be exchanged for foreign currency (bank deposits denominated in the foreign currency).

At www.ny.frb.org/fxc/ you can obtain various reports and documents concerning the foreign exchange market.

The trading of currency and bank deposits denominated in particular currencies takes place in the foreign exchange market. The volume of these transactions worldwide averages over $1 trillion daily. Transactions conducted in the foreign exchange market determine the rates at which currencies are exchanged, which in turn determine the cost of purchasing foreign goods and financial assets.

What Are Foreign Exchange Rates?

There are two kinds of exchange rate transactions. The predominant ones, called **spot transactions,** involve the immediate (two-day) exchange of bank deposits. **Forward transactions** involve the exchange of bank deposits at some specified future date. The **spot exchange rate** is the exchange rate for the spot transaction, and the **forward exchange rate** is the exchange rate for the forward transaction.

When a currency increases in value, it experiences **appreciation;** when it falls in value and is worth fewer U.S. dollars, it undergoes **depreciation.** At the beginning of 1999, for example, the euro was valued at $1.18, and, as indicated in the "Following the Financial News" box, on December 31, 2001, it was valued at 89.15 cents. The euro *depreciated* by 25%: (.8915 − 1.18)/1.18 = −0.25 = −25%. Conversely, we could say that the U.S. dollar, which went from a value of .85 euros per dollar in 1999 to a value of 1.12 euros per dollar by January 2002, *appreciated* by 32%: (1.12 − 0.85)/0.85 = 0.32 = 32%.

Why Are Exchange Rates Important?

Exchange rates are important because they affect the relative price of domestic and foreign goods. The dollar price of French goods to an American is determined by the interaction of two factors: the price of French goods in euros and the euro/dollar exchange rate.

Suppose that Wanda the Winetaster, an American, decides to buy a bottle of 1961 (a very good year) Château Lafite Rothschild to complete her wine cellar. If the price of the wine in France is 1000 euros and the exchange rate is $0.8915 to the euro, the wine will cost Wanda $892 (= 1000 euros × $0.8915/euro). Now suppose that Wanda delays her purchase by two months, at which time the euro

At http://quotes.ino.com/chart/, click on "Foreign Exchange" to get market rates and time charts for U.S. dollar to major world currencies.

FOLLOWING THE FINANCIAL NEWS

Foreign Exchange Rates

Foreign exchange rates are published daily and appear in the "Currency Trading" column of the *Wall Street Journal.* The entries from one such column, shown here, are explained in the text.

The first entry for the euro lists the exchange rate for the spot transaction (the spot exchange rate) on December 31, 2001, and is quoted in two ways: $0.8915 per euro and 1.1217 euros per dollar. Americans generally regard the exchange rate with the euro as $0.8915 per euro, while the Europeans think of it as 1.1217 euros per dollar. The three entries immediately below some spot exchange rates give the rates for forward transactions (the forward exchange rates) that will take place 1 month, 3 months, and 6 months in the future.

CURRENCY TRADING

EXCHANGE RATES

Monday, December 31, 2001

The New York foreign exchange mid-range rates below apply to trading among banks in amounts of $1 million and more, as quoted at 4 p.m. Eastern time by Reuters and other sources. Retail transactions provide fewer units of foreign currency per dollar. Rates for the 12 Euro currency countries are derived from the latest dollar-euro rate using the exchange ratios set 1/1/99.

	U.S. $ equiv.		Currency Per U.S. $	
Country	**Mon**	**Fri**	**Mon**	**Fri**
Argentina (Peso)	1.0009	1.0009	.9991	.9991
Australia (Dollar)	.5104	.5116	1.9591	1.9547
Austria (Schilling)	.06479	.06423	15.435	15.570
Bahrain (Dinar)	2.6525	2.6525	.3770	.3770
Belgium (Franc)	.0221	.0219	45.2495	45.6437
Brazil (Real)	.4327	.4326	2.3110	2.3115
Britain (Pound)	1.4560	1.4501	.6868	.6896
1-month forward	1.4533	1.4473	.6881	.6909
3-months forward	1.4484	1.4425	.6904	.6932
6-months forward	1.4411	1.4352	.6939	.6968
Canada (Dollar)	.6282	.6292	1.5919	1.5893
1-month forward	.6280	.6291	1.5923	1.5896
3-months forward	.6278	.6289	1.5928	1.5901
6-months forward	.6279	.6290	1.5925	1.5898
Chile (Peso)	.001513	.001513	661.15	661.15
China (Renminbi)	.1208	.1208	8.2766	8.2768
Colombia (Peso)	.0004391	.0004391	2277.50	2277.50
Czech. Rep. (Koruna)				
Commercial rate	.02811	.02783	35.569	35.929
Denmark (Krone)	.1198	.1188	8.3475	8.4180
Ecuador (US Dollar)-e	1.0000	1.0000	1.0000	1.0000
Finland (Markka)	.1499	.1486	6.6694	6.7275
France (Franc)	.1359	.1347	7.3579	7.4220
1-month forward	.1357	.1346	7.3673	7.4315
3-months forward	.1354	.1343	7.3835	7.4479
6-months forward	.1351	.1339	7.4036	7.4679
Germany (Mark)	.4558	.4519	2.1939	2.2130
1-month forward	.4552	.4513	2.1966	2.2158
3-months forward	.4542	.4503	2.2015	2.2207
6-months forward	.4530	.4491	2.2075	2.2266
Greece (Drachma)	.002616	.002594	382.23	385.55
Hong Kong (Dollar)	.1282	.1282	7.7985	7.7975
Hungary (Forint)	.003644	.003613	274.43	276.80
India (Rupee)	.02074	.02073	48.220	48.240
Indonesia (Rupiah)	.0000962	.0000955	10400	10475
Ireland (Punt)	1.1320	1.1222	.8834	.8911
Israel (Shekel)	.2267	.2273	4.4120	4.3990
Italy (Lira)	.0004604	.0004564	2171.92	2190.85
Japan (Yen)	.007595	.007628	131.67	131.10
1-month forward	.007607	.007640	131.47	130.89
3-months forward	.007629	.007662	131.08	130.51
6-months forward	.007667	.007702	130.44	129.84
Jordan (Dinar)	1.4108	1.4108	.7088	.7088
Kuwait (Dinar)	3.2563	3.2563	.3071	.3071
Lebanon (Pound)	.0006606	.0006606	1513.75	1513.75
Malaysia (Ringgit)-b	.2632	.2632	3.8001	3.8001
Malta (Lira)	2.2282	2.2158	.4488	.4513
Mexico (Peso)				
Floating rate	.1094	.1089	9.1370	9.1800
Netherlands (Guilder)	.4045	.4011	2.4719	2.4934
New Zealand (Dollar)	.4173	.4157	2.3964	2.4056
Norway (Krone)	.1118	.1111	8.9451	9.0005
Pakistan (Rupee)	.01669	.01646	59.900	60.750
Peru (new Sol)	.2908	.2906	3.4385	3.4414
Philippines (Peso)	.01940	.01939	51.550	51.580
Poland (Zloty)-d	.2524	.2514	3.9625	3.9770
Portugal (Escudo)	.004447	.004408	224.88	226.84
Russia (Ruble) -a	.03279	.03279	30.495	30.495
Saudi Arabia (Riyal)	.2666	.2666	3.7509	3.7505
Singapore (Dollar)	.5416	.5411	1.8465	1.8480
Slovak Rep. (Koruna)	.02084	.02065	47.981	48.420
South Africa (Rand)	.0834	.0835	11.9850	11.9800
South Korea (Won)	.0007613	.0007587	1313.50	1318.00
Spain (Peseta)	.005358	.005312	186.64	188.26
Sweden (Krona)	.0958	.0950	10.4425	10.5257
Switzerland (Franc)	.6031	.5969	1.6582	1.6754
1-month forward	.6031	.5969	1.6580	1.6752
3-months forward	.6031	.5969	1.6581	1.6753
6-months forward	.6034	.5971	1.6574	1.6747
Taiwan (Dollar)	.02858	.02855	34.985	35.030
Thailand (Baht)	.02261	.02262	44.235	44.200
Turkey (Lira)-f	.00000069	.00000069	1450000	1448500
United Arab (Dirham)	.2723	.2723	3.6728	3.6730
Uruguay (New Peso)				
Financial	.07168	.07168	13.950	13.950
Venezuela (Bolivar)	.001320	.001305	757.50	766.50
SDR	1.2557	1.2557	.7964	.7964
Euro	.8915	.8838	1.1217	1.1315

Special Drawing Rights (SDR) are based on exchange rates for the U.S., German, British, French, and Japanese currencies.
Source: International Monetary Fund.
a-Russian Central Bank rate.
b-Government rate. d-Floating rate; trading band suspended on 4/11/00. e-Adopted U.S. dollar as of 9/11/00. f-Floating rate, eff. Feb.22

Source: Wall Street Journal, Jan. 2, 2002, C11. Republished by permission of Dow Jones, Inc. via Copyright Clearance Center, Inc.

has appreciated to $1 per euro. If the domestic price of the bottle of Lafite Rothschild remains 1000 euros, its dollar cost will have risen from $892 to $1000.

The same currency appreciation, however, makes the price of foreign goods in France less expensive. At an exchange rate of $0.8915 per euro, a Dell computer priced at $2000 costs Claude the Programmer 2,243 euros; if the exchange rate increases to $1 per euro, the computer will cost only 2,000 euros.

A depreciation of the euro lowers the cost of French goods in America but raises the cost of American goods in France. If the euro drops in value to $0.50, Wanda's bottle of Lafite Rothschild will cost her only $500 instead of $892, and the Dell computer will cost Claude 4000 euros rather than 2,243.

Such reasoning leads to the following conclusion: ***When a country's currency appreciates (rises in value relative to other currencies), the country's goods abroad become more expensive and foreign goods in that country become cheaper (holding domestic prices constant in the two countries). Conversely, when a country's currency depreciates, its goods abroad become cheaper and foreign goods in that country become more expensive.***

Appreciation of a currency can make it harder for domestic manufacturers to sell their goods abroad and can increase competition at home from foreign goods because they cost less. From 1980 to early 1985, the appreciating dollar hurt U.S. industries. For instance, the U.S. steel industry was hurt not just because sales of the more expensive American steel declined abroad but also because sales of relatively cheap foreign steel in the United States increased. Although appreciation of the U.S. dollar hurt some domestic businesses, American consumers benefited because foreign goods were less expensive. Japanese videocassette recorders and cameras and the cost of vacationing in Europe fell in price as a result of the strong dollar.

How Is Foreign Exchange Traded?

You cannot go to a centralized location to watch exchange rates being determined; currencies are not traded on exchanges such as the New York Stock Exchange. Instead, the foreign exchange market is organized as an over-the-counter market in which several hundred dealers (mostly banks) stand ready to buy and sell deposits denominated in foreign currencies. Because these dealers are in constant telephone and computer contact, the market is very competitive; in effect, it functions no differently from a centralized market.

An important point to note is that while banks, companies, and governments talk about buying and selling currencies in foreign exchange markets, they do not take a fistful of dollar bills and sell them for British pound notes. Rather, most trades involve the buying and selling of bank deposits denominated in different currencies. So when we say that a bank is buying dollars in the foreign exchange market, what we actually mean is that the bank is buying deposits *denominated in dollars*.

Trades in the foreign exchange market consist of transactions in excess of $1 million. The market that determines the exchange rates in the "Following the Financial News" box is not where one would buy foreign currency for a trip abroad. Instead, we buy foreign currency in the retail market from dealers such as American Express or from banks. Because retail prices are higher than wholesale, when we buy foreign exchange, we obtain fewer units of foreign currency per dollar than exchange rates in the box indicate.

EXCHANGE RATES IN THE LONG RUN

Like the price of any good or asset in a free market, exchange rates are determined by the interaction of supply and demand. To simplify our analysis of exchange rates in a free market, we divide it into two parts. First, we examine how exchange rates are determined in the long run; then we use our knowledge of the long-run determinants of the exchange rate to help us understand how they are determined in the short run.

Law of One Price

The starting point for understanding how exchange rates are determined is a simple idea called the **law of one price:** If two countries produce an identical good, the price of the good should be the same throughout the world no matter which country produces it. Suppose that American steel costs $100 per ton and identical Japanese steel costs 10,000 yen per ton. The law of one price suggests that the exchange rate between the yen and the dollar must be 100 yen per dollar ($0.01 per yen) in order for one ton of American steel to sell for 10,000 yen in Japan (the price of Japanese steel) and one ton of Japanese steel to sell for $100 in the United States (the price of U.S. steel). If the exchange rate were 200 yen to the dollar, Japanese steel would sell for $50 per ton in the United States, or half the price of American steel, and American steel would sell for 20,000 yen per ton in Japan, twice the price of the Japanese steel. Because American steel would be more expensive than Japanese steel in both countries and is identical to Japanese steel, the demand for American steel would go to zero. Given a fixed dollar price for American steel, the resulting excess supply of American steel will be eliminated only if the exchange rate falls to 100 yen per dollar, making the price of American steel and Japanese steel the same in both countries.

EXAMPLE 1: Law of One Price

Recently, the yen price of Japanese steel has increased by 10% (to 11,000 yen) relative to the dollar price of American steel (unchanged at $100). By what amount must the dollar increase or decrease in value for the law of one price to hold true?

Solution

For the law of one price to hold, the exchange rate must rise to 110 yen per dollar, which is a 10% appreciation of the dollar.

The exchange rate rises to 110 yen so that the price of Japanese steel in dollars remains unchanged at $100 (= 11,000 yen/110 yen per dollar). In other words, the 10% depreciation of the yen (10% appreciation of the dollar) just offsets the 10% increase in the yen price of the Japanese steel.

The purchasing power parities home, www.oecd.org/std/ppp/pps.htm, includes a PPP program overview, statistics, research, publications, and OECD meetings on PPP.

Theory of Purchasing Power Parity

One of the most prominent theories of how exchange rates are determined is the **theory of purchasing power parity (PPP).** It states that exchange rates between any two currencies will adjust to reflect changes in the price levels of the two countries. The theory of PPP is simply an application of the law of one price to national price levels.

As Example 1 illustrates, if the law of one price holds, a 10% rise in the yen price of Japanese steel results in a 10% appreciation of the dollar. Applying the law of one price to the price levels in the two countries produces the theory of purchasing power parity, which maintains that if the Japanese price level rises 10% relative to the U.S. price level, the dollar will appreciate by 10%. As our U.S./Japanese example illustrates, ***the theory of PPP suggests that if one country's price level rises relative to another's, its currency should depreciate (the other country's currency should appreciate).***

As you can see in Figure 2, this prediction of the theory of PPP is borne out in the long run. From 1973 to 2001, the British price level rose 99% relative to the U.S. price level, and as the theory of PPP predicts, the dollar appreciated against sterling, though by 73%, an amount smaller than the 99% increase predicted by PPP.

Yet, as the same figure indicates, PPP theory often has little predictive power in the short run. From early 1985 to the end of 1987, for example, the British price level rose relative to that of the United States. Instead of appreciating, as PPP theory predicts, the U.S. dollar actually depreciated by 40%. So even though PPP theory provides some guidance to the long-run movement of exchange rates, it is not perfect and in the short run is a particularly poor predictor. What explains PPP theory's failure to predict well?

Why the Theory of Purchasing Power Parity Cannot Fully Explain Exchange Rates

The PPP conclusion that exchange rates are determined solely by changes in relative price levels rests on the assumption that all goods are identical in both countries. When this assumption is true, the law of one price states that the relative

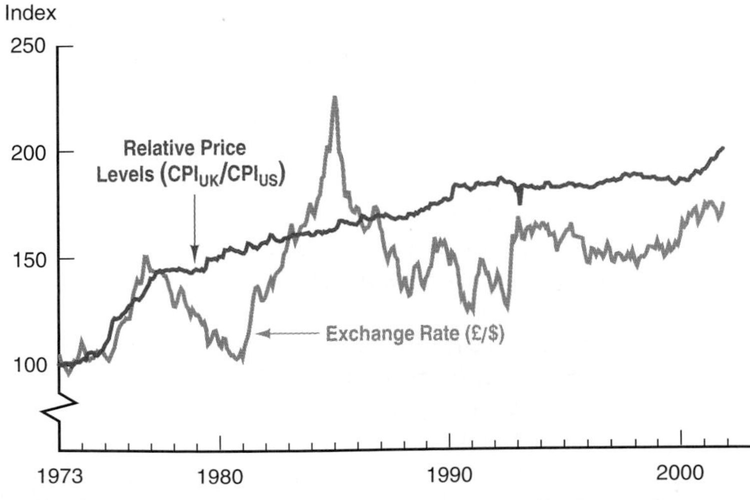

FIGURE 2 Purchasing Power Parity, United States/United Kingdom, 1973–2001 (Index: March 1973 = 100)

Source: http://www.statistics.gov.uk/statbase/

prices of all these goods (that is, the relative price level between the two countries) will determine the exchange rate. The assumption that goods are identical may not be too unreasonable for American and Japanese steel, but is it a reasonable assumption for American and Japanese cars? Is a Toyota the equivalent of a Chevrolet?

Because Toyotas and Chevys are obviously not identical, their prices do not have to be equal. Toyotas can be more expensive relative to Chevys and both Americans and Japanese will still purchase Toyotas. Because the law of one price does not hold for all goods, a rise in the price of Toyotas relative to Chevys will not necessarily mean that the yen must depreciate by the amount of the relative price increase of Toyotas over Chevys.

PPP theory furthermore does not take into account that many goods and services (whose prices are included in a measure of a country's price level) are not traded across borders. Housing, land, and services such as restaurant meals, haircuts, and golf lessons are not traded goods. So even though the prices of these items might rise and lead to a higher price level relative to another country's, there would be little direct effect on the exchange rate.

Factors That Affect Exchange Rates in the Long Run

Our analysis indicates that relative price levels and additional factors affect the exchange rate. In the long run, there are four major factors: relative price levels, tariffs and quotas, preferences for domestic versus foreign goods, and productivity. We examine how each of these factors affects the exchange rate while holding the others constant.

The basic reasoning proceeds along the following lines: Anything that increases the demand for domestic goods relative to foreign goods tends to appreciate the domestic currency because domestic goods will continue to sell well even when the value of the domestic currency is higher. Similarly, anything that increases the demand for foreign goods relative to domestic goods tends to depreciate the domestic currency because domestic goods will continue to sell well only if the value of the domestic currency is lower.

Relative Price Levels In line with PPP theory, when prices of American goods rise (holding prices of foreign goods constant), the demand for American goods falls and the dollar tends to depreciate so that American goods can still sell well. By contrast, if prices of Japanese goods rise so that the relative prices of American goods fall, the demand for American goods increases, and the dollar tends to appreciate because American goods will continue to sell well even with a higher value of the domestic currency. ***In the long run, a rise in a country's price level (relative to the foreign price level) causes its currency to depreciate, and a fall in the country's relative price level causes its currency to appreciate.***

Trade Barriers Barriers to free trade such as **tariffs** (taxes on imported goods) and **quotas** (restrictions on the quantity of foreign goods that can be imported) can affect the exchange rate. Suppose that the United States imposes a tariff or a quota on Japanese steel. These trade barriers increase the demand for American steel, and the dollar tends to appreciate because American steel will still sell well even with a higher value of the dollar. ***Increasing trade barriers causes a country's currency to appreciate in the long run.***

Preferences for Domestic Versus Foreign Goods If the Japanese develop an appetite for American goods—say, for Florida oranges and American movies—the increased demand for American goods (exports) tends to appreciate the dollar because the American goods will continue to sell well even at a higher value for the dollar. Likewise, if Americans decide that they prefer Japanese cars to American cars, the increased demand for Japanese goods (imports) tends to depreciate the dollar. ***Increased demand for a country's exports causes its currency to appreciate in the long run; conversely, increased demand for imports causes the domestic currency to depreciate.***

Productivity If one country becomes more productive than other countries, businesses in that country can lower the prices of domestic goods relative to foreign goods and still earn a profit. As a result, the demand for domestic goods rises, and the domestic currency tends to appreciate. If, however, its productivity lags behind that of other countries, its goods become relatively more expensive, and the currency tends to depreciate. ***In the long run, as a country becomes more productive relative to other countries, its currency appreciates.***[1]

Study Guide The trick to figuring out what long-run effect a factor has on the exchange rate is to remember the following: ***If a factor increases the demand for domestic goods relative to foreign goods, the domestic currency will appreciate, and if a factor decreases the relative demand for domestic goods, the domestic currency will depreciate.*** See how this works by explaining what happens to the exchange rate when any of the factors in Table 1 declines rather than increases.

Our long-run theory of exchange rate behavior is summarized in Table 1. We use the convention that the exchange rate E is quoted so that an appreciation of the currency corresponds to a rise in the exchange rate. In the case of the United

TABLE 1 SUMMARY Factors That Affect Exchange Rates in the Long Run

Factor	Change in Factor	Response of the Exchange Rate, E^*
Domestic price level†	↑	↓
Trade barriers†	↑	↑
Import demand	↑	↓
Export demand	↑	↑
Productivity†	↑	↑

*Units of foreign currency per dollar: ↑ indicates currency appreciation; ↓ , depreciation.

†Relative to other countries.

Note: Only increases (↑) in the factors are shown; the effects of decreases in the variables on the exchange rate are the opposite of those indicated in the "Response" column.

[1]A country might be so small that a change in productivity or the preferences for domestic or foreign goods would have no effect on prices of these goods relative to foreign goods. In this case, changes in productivity or changes in preferences for domestic or foreign goods affect the country's income but will not necessarily affect the value of the currency. In our analysis, we are assuming that these factors can affect relative prices and consequently the exchange rate.

States, this means that we are quoting the exchange rate as units of foreign currency per dollar (say, yen per dollar).[2]

EXCHANGE RATES IN THE SHORT RUN

We have developed a theory of the long-run behavior of exchange rates. However, if we are to understand why exchange rates exhibit such large changes (sometimes several percent) from day to day, we must develop a theory of how current exchange rates (spot exchange rates) are determined in the short run.

The key to understanding the short-run behavior of exchange rates is to recognize that an exchange rate is the price of domestic bank deposits (those denominated in the domestic currency) in terms of foreign bank deposits (those denominated in the foreign currency). Because the exchange rate is the price of one asset in terms of another, the natural way to investigate the short-run determination of exchange rates is through an asset market approach that relies heavily on our analysis of the determinants of asset demand developed in Chapter 4. As you will see, however, the long-run determinants of the exchange rate we have just outlined also play an important role in the short-run asset market approach.[3]

Earlier approaches to exchange rate determination emphasized the role of import and export demand. The more modern asset market approach used here does not emphasize the flows of purchases of exports and imports over short periods because these transactions are quite small relative to the amount of domestic and foreign bank deposits at any given time. For example, foreign exchange transactions in the United States each year are well over 25 times greater than the amount of U.S. exports and imports. Thus over short periods such as a year, decisions to hold domestic or foreign assets play a much greater role in exchange rate determination than the demand for exports and imports does.

Comparing Expected Returns on Domestic and Foreign Deposits

In this analysis, we treat the United States as the home country, so domestic bank deposits are denominated in dollars. For simplicity, we use euros to stand for any foreign country's currency, so foreign bank deposits are denominated in euros. Our analysis of the determinants of asset demand suggests that the most important factor affecting the demand for domestic (dollar) deposits and foreign (euro) deposits is the expected return on these assets relative to each other. When Americans or foreigners expect the return on dollar deposits to be high relative to the return on foreign deposits, there is a higher demand for dollar deposits and a correspondingly lower demand for euro deposits. To understand how the demands for dollar and foreign deposits change, we need to compare the expected returns on dollar deposits and foreign deposits.

---

[2]In professional writing, many economists quote exchange rates as units of domestic currency per foreign currency so that an appreciation of the domestic currency is portrayed as a fall in the exchange rate. The opposite convention is used in the text here because it is more intuitive to think of an appreciation of the domestic currency as a rise in the exchange rate.

[3]For a further description of the modern asset market approach to exchange rate determination that we use here, see Paul Krugman and Maurice Obstfeld, *International Economics,* 4th ed. (Reading, Mass.: Addison Wesley Longman, 1997).

To illustrate further, suppose that dollar deposits have an interest rate (expected return payable in dollars) of i^D, and foreign bank deposits have an interest rate (expected return payable in the foreign currency, euros) of i^F. To compare the expected returns on dollar deposits and foreign deposits, investors must convert the returns into the currency unit they use.

First let us examine how François the Foreigner compares the returns on dollar deposits and foreign deposits denominated in his currency, the euro. When he considers the expected return on dollar deposits in terms of euros, he recognizes that it does not equal i^D; instead, the expected return must be adjusted for any expected appreciation or depreciation of the dollar. If the dollar were expected to appreciate by 7%, for example, the expected return on dollar deposits in terms of euros would be 7% higher because the dollar has become worth 7% more in terms of euros. Thus if the interest rate on dollar deposits is 10%, with an expected appreciation of the dollar of 7%, the expected return on dollar deposits in terms of euros is 17%: the 10% interest rate plus the 7% expected appreciation of the dollar. Conversely, if the dollar were expected to depreciate by 7% over the year, the expected return on dollar deposits in terms of euros would be only 3%: the 10% interest rate minus the 7% expected depreciation of the dollar.

Writing the currency exchange rate (the spot exchange rate) as E_t and the expected exchange rate for the next period as E^e_{t+1}, we can write the expected rate of appreciation of the dollar as $(E^e_{t+1} - E_t)/E_t$. Our reasoning indicates that the expected return on dollar deposits R^D in terms of foreign currency can be written as the sum of the interest rate on dollar deposits plus the expected appreciation of the dollar:[4]

$$R^D \text{ in terms of euros} = i^D + \frac{E^e_{t+1} - E_t}{E_t}$$

However, François's expected return on foreign deposits R^F in terms of euros is just i^F. Thus in terms of euros, the relative expected return on dollar deposits (that is, the difference between the expected return on dollar deposits and euro deposits) is calculated by subtracting i^F from the expression just given to yield

$$\text{Relative } R^D = i^D - i^F + \frac{E^e_{t+1} - E_t}{E_t} \qquad (1)$$

As the relative expected return on dollar deposits increases, foreigners will want to hold more dollar deposits and fewer foreign deposits.

[4]This expression is actually an approximation of the expected return in terms of euros, which can be more precisely calculated by thinking how a foreigner invests in the dollar deposit. Suppose that François decides to put one euro into dollar deposits. First he buys $1/E_t$ of U.S. dollar deposits (recall that E_t, the exchange rate between dollar and euro deposits, is quoted in euros per dollar), and at the end of the period he is paid $(1 + i^D)(1/E_t)$ in dollars. To convert this amount into the number of euros he expects to receive at the end of the period, he multiplies this quantity by E^e_{t+1}. François's expected return on his initial investment of one euro can thus be written as $(1 + i^D)E^e_{t+1}/E_t)$ minus his initial investment of one euro:

$$(1 + i^D)\left(\frac{E^e_{t+1}}{E_t}\right) - 1$$

which can be rewritten as

$$i^D\left(\frac{E^e_{t+1}}{E_t}\right) + \frac{E^e_{t+1} - E_t}{E_t}$$

which is approximately equal to the expression in the text because E^e_{t+1}/E_t is typically close to 1.

Next let us look at the decision to hold dollar deposits versus euro deposits from Al the American's point of view. Following the same reasoning we used to evaluate the decision for François, we know that the expected return on foreign deposits R^F in terms of dollars is the interest rate on foreign deposits i^F plus the expected appreciation of the foreign currency, equal to minus the expected appreciation of the dollar, $-(E^e_{t+1} - E_t)/E_t$, that is,

$$R^F \text{ in terms of dollars} = i^F - \frac{E^e_{t+1} - E_t}{E_t}$$

If the interest rate on euro deposits is 5%, for example, and the dollar is expected to appreciate by 4%, then the expected return on euro deposits in terms of dollars is 1%. Al earns the 5% interest rate, but he expects to lose 4% because he expects the euro to be worth 4% less in terms of dollars as a result of the dollar's appreciation.

Al's expected return on the dollar deposits R^D in terms of dollars is just i^D. Hence in terms of dollars, the relative expected return on dollar deposits is calculated by subtracting the expression just given from i^D to obtain

$$\text{Relative } R^D = i^D - \left(i^F - \frac{E^e_{t+1} - E_t}{E_t}\right) = i^D - i^F + \frac{E^e_{t+1} - E_t}{E_t}$$

This equation is the same as the one describing François's relative expected return on dollar deposits (calculated in terms of euros). The key point here is that the relative expected return on dollar deposits is the same whether it is calculated by François in terms of euros or by Al in terms of dollars. Thus as the relative expected return on dollar deposits increases, both foreigners and domestic residents respond in exactly the same way—both will want to hold more dollar deposits and fewer foreign deposits.

Interest Parity Condition

We currently live in a world in which there is **capital mobility:** Foreigners can easily purchase American assets such as dollar deposits, and Americans can easily purchase foreign assets such as euro deposits. Because foreign bank deposits and American bank deposits have similar risk and liquidity and because there are few impediments to capital mobility, it is reasonable to assume that the deposits are perfect substitutes (that is, equally desirable). When capital is mobile and when bank deposits are perfect substitutes, if the expected return on dollar deposits is above that on foreign deposits, both foreigners and Americans will want to hold only dollar deposits and will be unwilling to hold foreign deposits. Conversely, if the expected return on foreign deposits is higher than on dollar deposits, both foreigners and Americans will not want to hold any dollar deposits and will want to hold only foreign deposits. For existing supplies of both dollar deposits and foreign deposits to be held, it must therefore be true that there is no difference in their expected returns; that is, the relative expected return in Equation 1 must equal zero. This condition can be rewritten as

$$i^D = i^F - \frac{E^e_{t+1} - E_t}{E_t} \qquad (2)$$

This equation is called the **interest parity condition,** and it states that the domestic interest rate equals the foreign interest rate minus the expected appreciation of the domestic currency. Equivalently, this condition can be stated in a more intuitive way: The domestic interest rate equals the foreign interest rate plus the expected appreciation of the foreign currency. If the domestic interest rate is above the foreign interest rate, this means that there is a positive expected appreciation of the foreign currency, which compensates for the lower foreign interest rate.

EXAMPLE 2: Interest Parity Condition

If interest rates in the United States and Japan are 6% and 3%, respectively, what is the expected rate of appreciation of the foreign (Japanese) currency?

Solution

The expected appreciation of the foreign currency is 3%.

$$i^D = i^F - \frac{E^e_{t+1} - E_t}{E_t}$$

where

i^D = interest rate on dollars = 6%

i^F = interest rate on foreign currency = 3%

Thus

$$6\% = 3\% - \frac{E^e_{t+1} - E_t}{E_t}$$

$$-\frac{E^e_{t+1} - E_t}{E_t} = \text{rate of appreciation of the foreign currency} = 6\% - 3\% = 3\%$$

There are several ways to look at the interest parity condition. First, we should recognize that interest parity means simply that the expected returns are the same on both dollar deposits and foreign deposits. To see this, note that the left side of the interest parity condition (Equation 2) is the expected return on dollar deposits, while the right side is the expected return on foreign deposits, both calculated in terms of a single currency, the U.S. dollar. Given our assumption that domestic and foreign bank deposits are perfect substitutes (equally desirable), the interest parity condition is an equilibrium condition for the foreign exchange market. Only when the exchange rate is such that expected returns on domestic and foreign deposits are equal—that is, when interest parity holds—will the outstanding domestic and foreign deposits be willingly held.

Equilibrium in the Foreign Exchange Market

To see how the interest parity equilibrium condition works in determining the exchange rate, our first step is to examine how the expected returns on euro and dollar deposits change as the current exchange rate changes.

Expected Return on Euro Deposits As we demonstrated earlier, the expected return in terms of dollars on foreign deposits R^F is the foreign interest rate minus the expected appreciation of the domestic currency: $i^F - (E^e_{t+1} - E_t)/E_t$. Suppose that the foreign interest rate i^F is 10% and that the expected exchange rate next period E^e_{t+1} is 1 euro per dollar. When the current exchange rate E_t is 0.95 euros per dollar, the expected appreciation of the dollar is $(1 - 0.95)/0.95 = 0.052 = 5.2\%$, so the expected return on euro deposits R^F in terms of dollars is 4.8% (equal to the 10% foreign interest rate minus the 5.2% dollar appreciation). This expected return when $E_t = 0.95$ euros per dollar is plotted as point A in Figure 3. At a higher current exchange rate of $E_t = 1$ euro per dollar, the expected appreciation of the dollar is zero because E^e_{t+1} also equals 1 euro per dollar. Hence R^F, the expected dollar return on euro deposits, is now just $i^F = 10\%$. This expected return on euro deposits when $E_t = 1$ euro per dollar is plotted as point B. At an even higher exchange rate of $E_t = 1.05$ euros per dollar, the expected change in the value of the dollar is now -4.8% [$= (1 - 1.05)/1.05 = -0.048$], so the expected dollar return on foreign deposits R^F has now risen to 14.8% [$= 10\% - (-4.8\%)$]. This combination of exchange rate and expected return on euro deposits is plotted as point C.

The curve connecting these points is the schedule for the expected return on euro deposits in Figure 3, labeled R^F, and as you can see, it slopes upward; that is, as the exchange rate E_t rises, the expected return on euro deposits rises. The intuition for this upward slope is that because the expected next-period exchange rate is held constant as the current exchange rate rises, there is less expected appreciation of the dollar. Hence a higher current exchange rate means

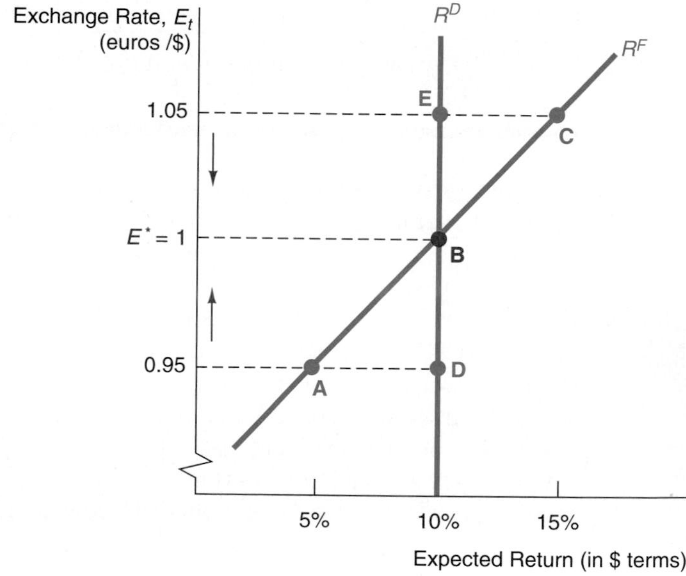

FIGURE 3 Equilibrium in the Foreign Exchange Market

Equilibrium in the foreign exchange market occurs at the intersection of the schedules for the expected return on euro deposits R^F and the expected return on dollar deposits R^D at point B. The equilibrium exchange rate is $E^* = 1$ euro per dollar.

a greater expected appreciation of the foreign currency in the future, which increases the expected return on foreign deposits in terms of dollars.

Expected Return on Dollar Deposits The expected return on dollar deposits in terms of dollars R^D is always the interest rate on dollar deposits i^D no matter what the exchange rate is. Suppose that the interest rate on dollar deposits is 10%. The expected return on dollar deposits whether at an exchange rate of 0.95, 1, or 1.05 euros per dollar, is always 10% (points D, B, and E). The line connecting these points is the schedule for the expected return on dollar deposits, labeled R^D in Figure 3.

Equilibrium The intersection of the schedules for the expected return on dollar deposits R^D and the expected return on euro deposits R^F is where equilibrium occurs in the foreign exchange market; in other words,

$$R^D = R^F$$

At the equilibrium point B where the exchange rate E^* is 1 euro per dollar, the interest parity condition is satisfied because the expected returns on dollar deposits and on euro deposits are equal.

To see that the exchange rate actually heads toward the equilibrium exchange rate E^*, let's see what happens if the exchange rate is 1.05 euros per dollar, a value above the equilibrium exchange rate. As we can see in Figure 3, the expected return on euro deposits at point C is greater than the expected return on dollar deposits at point E. Since dollar and euro deposits are perfect substitutes, people will not want to hold any dollar deposits, and holders of dollar deposits will try to sell them for euro deposits in the foreign exchange market (which is referred to as "selling dollars" and "buying euros"). However, because the expected return on these dollar deposits is below that on euro deposits, no one holding euros will be willing to exchange them for dollar deposits. The resulting excess supply of dollar deposits means that the price of the dollar deposits relative to euro deposits must fall; that is, the exchange rate (amount of euros per dollar) falls as is illustrated by the downward arrow drawn in the figure at the exchange rate of 1.05 euros per dollar. The decline in the exchange rate will continue until point B is reached at the equilibrium exchange rate of 1 euro per dollar, where the expected return on dollar and euro deposits is now equalized.

Now let us look at what happens when the exchange rate is 0.95 euros per dollar, a value below the equilibrium level. Here the expected return on dollar deposits is greater than that on euro deposits. No one will want to hold euro deposits, and everyone will try to sell them to buy dollar deposits ("sell euros" and "buy dollars"), thus driving up the exchange rate as illustrated by the upward arrow. As the exchange rate rises, there is a smaller expected appreciation of the dollar and so a higher expected appreciation of the euro, thereby increasing the expected return on euro deposits. Finally, when the exchange rate has risen to $E^* = 1$ euro per dollar, the expected return on euro deposits has risen enough so that it again equals the expected return on dollar deposits.

EXPLAINING CHANGES IN EXCHANGE RATES

To explain how an exchange rate changes over time, we have to understand the factors that shift the expected-return schedules for domestic (dollar) deposits and foreign (euro) deposits.

Shifts in the Expected-Return Schedule for Foreign Deposits

As we have seen, the expected return on foreign (euro) deposits depends on the foreign interest rate i^F minus the expected appreciation of the dollar $(E^e_{t+1} - E_t)/E_t$. Because a change in the current exchange rate E_t results in a movement along the expected-return schedule for euro deposits, factors that shift this schedule must work through the foreign interest rate i^F and the expected future exchange rate E^e_{t+1}. We examine the effect of changes in these factors on the expected-return schedule for euro deposits R^F, holding everything else constant.

Study Guide To grasp how the expected-return schedule for euro deposits shifts, just think of yourself as an investor who is considering putting funds into foreign deposits. When a variable changes (i^F for example), decide whether at a given level of the current exchange rate, holding all other variables constant, you would earn a higher or lower expected return on euro deposits.

Changes in the Foreign Interest Rate If the interest rate on foreign deposits i^F increases, holding everything else constant, the expected return on these deposits must also increase. Hence at a given exchange rate, the increase in i^F leads to a rightward shift in the expected-return schedule for euro deposits from R^F_1 to R^F_2 in Figure 4. As you can see in the figure, the outcome is a depreciation of the dollar from E_1 to E_2. An alternative way to see this is to recognize that the increase in the expected return on euro deposits at the original equilibrium exchange rate resulting from the rise in i^F means that people will want to buy euros and sell dol-

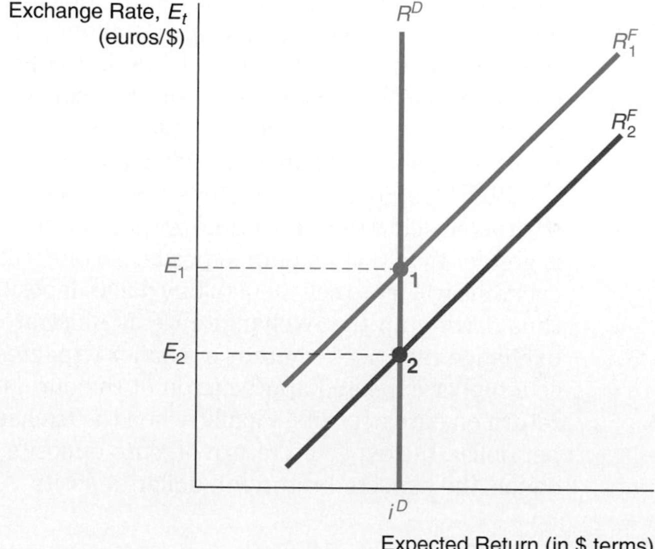

FIGURE 4 Shifts in the Schedule for the Expected Return on Foreign Deposits R^F

An increase in the expected return on foreign deposits, which occurs when either the foreign interest rate rises or the expected future exchange rate falls, shifts the schedule for the expected return on foreign deposits from R^F_1 to R^F_2, and the exchange rate falls from E_1 to E_2.

lars, so the value of the dollar must fall. Our analysis thus generates the following conclusion: ***An increase in the foreign interest rate i^F shifts the R^F schedule to the right and causes the domestic currency to depreciate ($E\downarrow$).***

Conversely, if i^F falls, the expected return on euro deposits falls, the R^F schedule shifts to the left, and the exchange rate rises. This yields the following conclusion: ***A decrease in i^F shifts the R^F schedule to the left and causes the domestic currency to appreciate ($E\uparrow$).***

Changes in the Expected Future Exchange Rate Any factor that causes the expected future exchange rate E^e_{t+1} to fall decreases the expected appreciation of the dollar and hence raises the expected appreciation of the euro. The result is a higher expected return on euro deposits, which shifts the schedule for the expected return on euro deposits to the right and leads to a decline in the exchange rate as in Figure 4. Conversely, a rise in E^e_{t+1} raises the expected appreciation of the dollar, lowers the expected return on foreign deposits, shifts the R^F schedule to the left, and raises the exchange rate. To summarize, ***a rise in the expected future exchange rate shifts the R^F schedule to the left and causes an appreciation of the domestic currency; a fall in the expected future exchange rate shifts the R^F schedule to the right and causes a depreciation of the domestic currency.***

Summary Our analysis of the long-run determinants of the exchange rate indicates the factors that influence the expected future exchange rate: the relative price level, relative trade barriers, import demand, export demand, and relative productivity (refer to Table 1). The theory of purchasing power parity suggests that if a higher American price level relative to the foreign price level is expected to persist, the dollar will depreciate in the long run. A higher expected relative American price level should thus have a tendency to raise the expected return on euro deposits, shift the R^F schedule to the right, and lower the current exchange rate.

Similarly, the other long-run determinants of the exchange rate we discussed earlier can also influence the expected return on euro deposits and the current exchange rate. Briefly, the following changes will increase the expected return on euro deposits, shift the R^F schedule to the right, and cause a depreciation of the domestic currency, the dollar: (1) expectations of a rise in the American price level relative to the foreign price level, (2) expectations of lower American trade barriers relative to foreign trade barriers, (3) expectations of higher American import demand, (4) expectations of lower foreign demand for American exports, and (5) expectations of lower American productivity relative to foreign productivity.

Shifts in the Expected-Return Schedule for Domestic Deposits

Since the expected return on domestic (dollar) deposits is just the interest rate on these deposits i^D, this interest rate is the only factor that shifts the schedule for the expected return on dollar deposits.

Changes in the Domestic Interest Rate A rise in i^D raises the expected return on dollar deposits, shifts the R^D schedule to the right, and leads to a rise in the exchange rate, as is shown in Figure 5. Another way of seeing this is to recognize that a rise in i^D, which raises the expected return on dollar deposits, creates an excess demand for dollar deposits at the original equilibrium exchange rate, and the resulting purchases of dollar deposits cause an appreciation of the dollar. ***A rise***

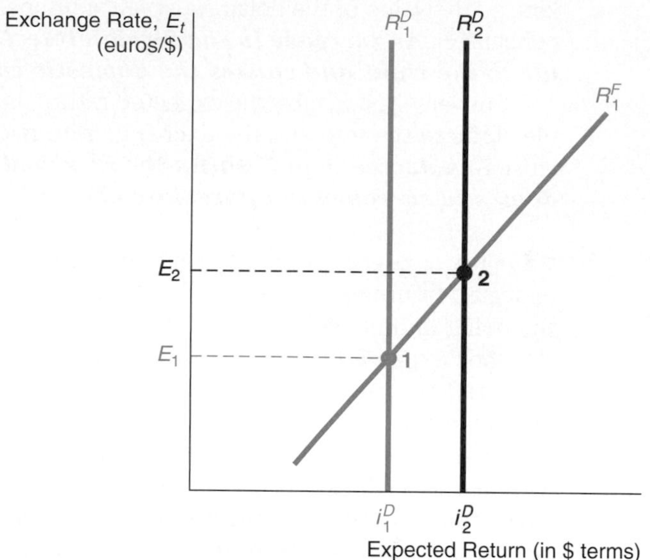

FIGURE 5 Shifts in the Schedule for the Expected Return on Domestic Deposits R^D

An increase in the expected return on dollar deposits i^D shifts the expected return on domestic (dollar) deposits from R^D_1 to R^D_2 and the exchange rate rises from E_1 to E_2.

in the domestic interest rate i^D shifts the R^D schedule to the right and causes an appreciation of the domestic currency; a fall in i^D shifts the R^D schedule to the left and causes a depreciation of the domestic currency.

Study Guide As a study aid, the factors that shift the R^F and R^D schedules and lead to changes in the current exchange rate E_t are listed in Table 2. The table shows what happens to the exchange rate when there is an increase in each of these variables, holding everything else constant. To give yourself practice, see if you can work out what happens to the R^F and R^D schedules and to the exchange rate if each of these factors falls rather than rises. Check your answers by seeing if you get the opposite change in the exchange rate to those indicated in Table 2.

Application

Changes in the Equilibrium Exchange Rate: Two Examples

Our analysis has revealed the factors that affect the value of the equilibrium exchange rate. Now we use this analysis to take a close look at the response of the exchange rate to changes in interest rates and money growth.

Changes in Domestic Interest Rates

Changes in domestic interest rates i^D are often cited as a major factor affecting exchange rates. For example, we see headlines in the financial press like this one: "Dollar Recovers As Interest Rates Edge Upward." But is the view presented in this headline always correct?

TABLE 2 SUMMARY **Factors That Shift the R^F and R^D Schedules and Affect the Exchange Rate**

Factor	Change in Factor	Response of the Exchange Rate, E_t	
Domestic interest rate, i^D	↑	↑	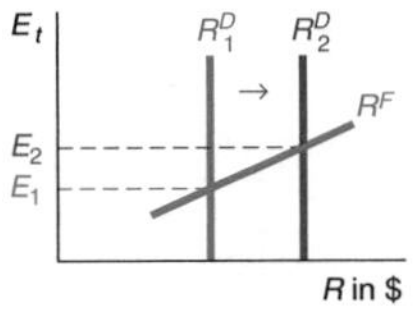
Foreign interest rate, i^F	↑	↓	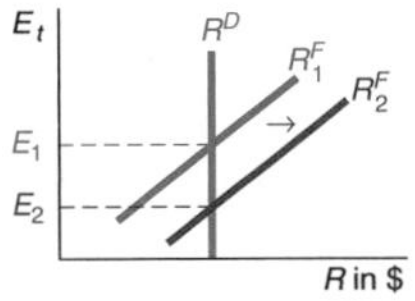
Expected domestic price level*	↑	↓	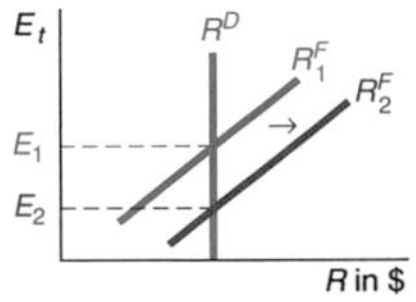
Expected trade barriers*	↑	↑	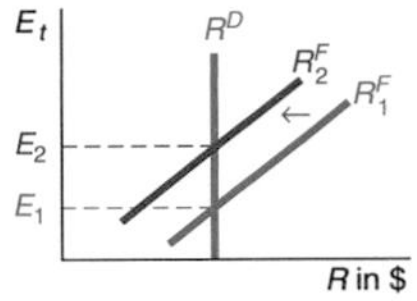
Expected import demand	↑	↓	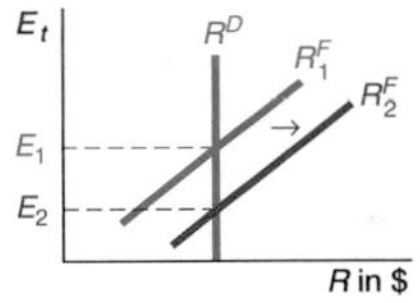
Expected export demand	↑	↑	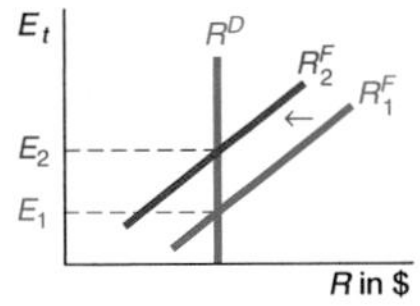
Productivity*	↑	↑	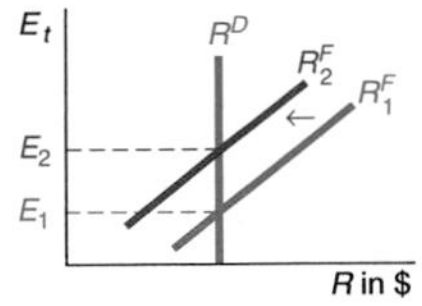

*Relative to other countries.

Note: Only increases (↑) in the factors are shown; the effects of decreases in the variables on the exchange rate are the opposite of those indicated in the "Response" column.

Not necessarily, because to analyze the effects of interest rate changes, we must carefully distinguish the sources of the changes. The Fisher equation (Chapter 3) states that a (nominal) interest rate equals the *real* interest rate plus expected inflation: $i = i_r + \pi^e$. The Fisher equation indicates that an interest rate i can change for two reasons: Either the real interest rate i_r changes or the expected inflation rate π^e changes. The effect on the exchange rate is quite different, depending on which of these two factors is the source of the change in the nominal interest rate.

Suppose that the domestic real interest rate increases so that the nominal interest rate i^D rises while expected inflation remains unchanged. In this case, it is reasonable to assume that the expected appreciation of the dollar will be unchanged because expected inflation is unchanged, and so the expected return on foreign deposits will remain unchanged for any given exchange rate. The result is that the R^F schedule stays put and the R^D schedule shifts to the right, and we end up with the situation depicted in Figure 5, which analyzes an increase in i^D, holding everything else constant. Our model of the foreign exchange market produces the following result: ***When domestic real interest rates rise, the domestic currency appreciates.***

When the nominal interest rate rises because of an increase in expected inflation, we get a different result from the one shown in Figure 5. The rise in expected domestic inflation leads to a decline in the expected appreciation of the dollar (a higher appreciation of the euro), which is typically thought to be larger than the increase in the domestic interest rate i^D.[5] As a result, at any given exchange rate, the expected return on foreign deposits rises more than the expected return on dollar deposits. Thus, as we see in Figure 6, the R^F schedule shifts to the right more than the R^D schedule, and the exchange rate falls. Our analysis leads to

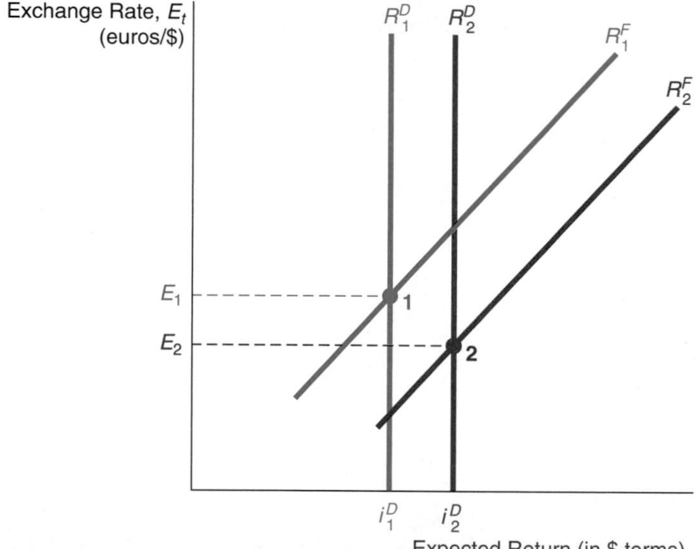

FIGURE 6 Effect of a Rise in the Domestic Nominal Interest Rate as a Result of an Increase in Expected Inflation

Because a rise in domestic expected inflation leads to a decline in expected dollar appreciation that is larger than the resulting increase in the domestic interest rate, the expected return on foreign deposits rises by more than the expected return on domestic (dollar) deposits. R^F shifts to the right more than R^D, and the equilibrium exchange rate falls from E_1 to E_2.

[5]This conclusion is standard in asset market models of exchange rate determination; see Rudiger Dornbusch, "Expectations and Exchange Rate Dynamics," *Journal of Political Economy* 84 (1976): 1061–1076. It is also consistent with empirical evidence that suggests that nominal interest rates do not rise one-for-one with increases in expected inflation. See Frederic S. Mishkin, "The Real Interest Rate: An Empirical Investigation," *Carnegie-Rochester Conference Series on Public Policy* 15 (1981): 151–200; and Lawrence Summers, "The Nonadjustment of Nominal Interest Rates: A Study of the Fisher Effect," in *Macroeconomics, Prices and Quantities,* ed. James Tobin (Washington, D.C.: Brookings Institution, 1983), pp. 201–240.

this conclusion: ***When domestic interest rates rise due to an expected increase in inflation, the domestic currency depreciates.***

Because this conclusion is completely different from the one reached when the rise in the domestic interest rate is associated with a higher real interest rate, we must always distinguish between *real* and *nominal* measures when analyzing the effects of interest rates on exchange rates.

Changes in the Money Supply

Suppose that the Federal Reserve decides to increase the level of the money supply in order to reduce unemployment, which it believes to be excessive. The higher money supply will lead to a higher American price level in the long run and hence to a lower expected future exchange rate. The resulting decline in the expected appreciation of the dollar increases the expected return on foreign deposits at any given current exchange rate and so shifts the R^F schedule rightward from R^F_1 to R^F_2 in Figure 7. In addition, the higher money supply will lead to a higher real money supply M/P because the price level does not immediately increase in the short run. As suggested in Chapter 4, the resulting rise in the real money supply causes the domestic interest rate to fall from i^D_1 to i^D_2, which lowers the expected return on domestic (dollar) deposits, shifting the R^D schedule in from R^D_1 to R^D_2. As we can see in Figure 7, the result is a decline in the exchange rate from E_1 to E_2. The conclusion is this: ***A higher domestic money supply causes the domestic currency to depreciate.***

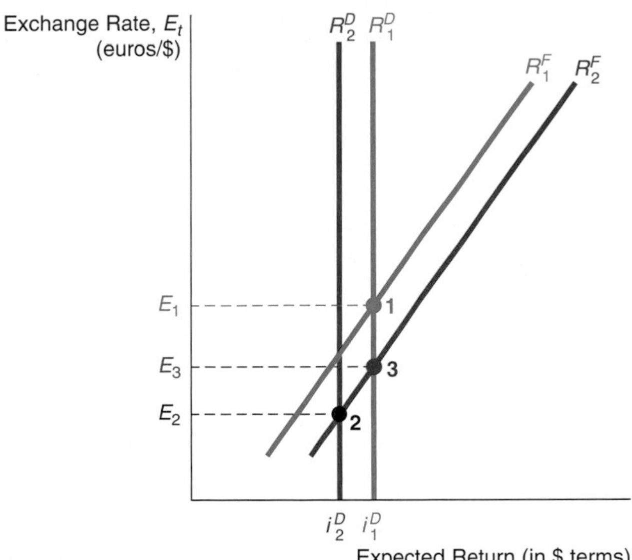

FIGURE 7 Effect of a Rise in the Money Supply

A rise in the money supply leads to a higher domestic price level in the long run, which in turn leads to a lower expected future exchange rate. The resulting decline in the expected appreciation of the dollar raises the expected return on foreign deposits, shifting the R^F schedule rightward from R^F_1 to R^F_2. In the short run, the domestic interest rate i^D falls, shifting R^D from R^D_1 to R^D_2. The short-run outcome is that the exchange rate falls from E_1 to E_2. In the long run, however, the interest rate returns to i^D_1 and R^D returns to R^D_1. The exchange rate thus rises from E_2 to E_3 in the long run.

Exchange Rate Overshooting

Our analysis of the effect of a money supply increase on the exchange rate is not yet over—we still need to look at what happens to the exchange rate in the long run. A basic proposition in monetary theory, called **monetary neutrality,** states that in the long run, a onetime percentage rise in the money supply is matched by the same onetime percentage rise in the price level, leaving unchanged the real money supply and all other economic variables such as interest rates. An intuitive way to understand this proposition is to think of what would happen if our government announced overnight that an old dollar would now be worth 100 new dollars. The money supply in new dollars would be 100 times its old value and the price level would also be 100 times higher, but nothing in the economy would really have changed; interest rates and the real money supply would remain the same. Monetary neutrality tells us that in the long run, the rise in the money supply would not lead to a change in the domestic interest rate and so it would return to i_1^D in the long run, and the schedule for the expected return on domestic deposits would return to R_1^D. As we can see in Figure 7, this means that the exchange rate would rise from E_2 to E_3 in the long run.

The phenomenon we have described here in which the exchange rate falls by more in the short run than it does in the long run when the money supply increases is called **exchange rate overshooting.** It is important because, as we will see in the following application, it can help explain why exchange rates exhibit so much volatility.

Another way of thinking about why exchange rate overshooting occurs is to recognize that when the domestic interest rate falls in the short run, equilibrium in the foreign exchange market means that the expected return on foreign deposits must be lower. With the foreign interest rate given, this lower expected return on foreign deposits means that there must be an expected appreciation of the dollar (depreciation of the euro) in order for the expected return on foreign deposits to decline when the domestic interest rate falls. This can occur only if the current exchange rate falls below its long-run value.

Application Why Are Exchange Rates So Volatile?

The high volatility of foreign exchange rates surprises many people. Thirty or so years ago, economists generally believed that allowing exchange rates to be determined in the free market would not lead to large fluctuations in their values. Recent experience has proved them wrong. If we return to Figure 1, we see that exchange rates over the 1980–2001 period have been very volatile.

The asset market approach to exchange rate determination that we have outlined in this chapter gives a straightforward explanation of volatile exchange rates. Because expected appreciation of the domestic currency affects the expected return on foreign deposits, expectations about the price level, inflation, trade barriers, productivity, import demand, export demand, and the money supply play important roles in determining the exchange rate. When expectations about any of these variables change, our model indicates that there will be an immediate effect on the expected return on foreign deposits and therefore on the exchange rate. Since expectations on all these variables change with just about every bit of news that appears, it is not surprising that the exchange rate is volatile. In addition, we have seen that our exchange rate analysis produces exchange rate overshooting when the money supply increases. Exchange rate overshooting is an additional reason for the high volatility of exchange rates.

Because earlier models of exchange rate behavior focused on goods markets rather than asset markets, they did not emphasize changing expectations as a source of exchange rate movements, and so these earlier models could not predict substantial fluctuations in exchange rates. The failure of earlier models to explain volatility is one reason why they are no longer so popular. The more modern approach developed here emphasizes that the foreign exchange market is like any other asset market in which expectations of the future matter. The foreign exchange market, like other asset markets such as the stock market, displays substantial price volatility, and foreign exchange rates are notoriously hard to forecast.

Application Explaining the Rise and Fall of the Dollar in the 1980s

In the chapter preview we mentioned that the dollar was weak in the late 1970s, rose substantially from 1980 to 1985, and declined thereafter. We can use our analysis of the foreign exchange market to understand exchange rate movements and help explain the dollar's rise and fall in the 1980s.

Some important information for tracing the dollar's changing value is presented in Figure 8, which plots measures of real and nominal interest rates and the value of the dollar in terms of a basket of foreign currencies (called an **effective exchange rate index**). We can see that the value of the dollar and the measure of real interest rates rise and fall together. In the late 1970s, real interest rates were at low levels, and so was the value of the dollar. Beginning in 1980, however, real interest rates in the United States began to climb sharply, and at the same time so did the dollar. After 1984, the real interest rate declined substantially, as did the dollar.

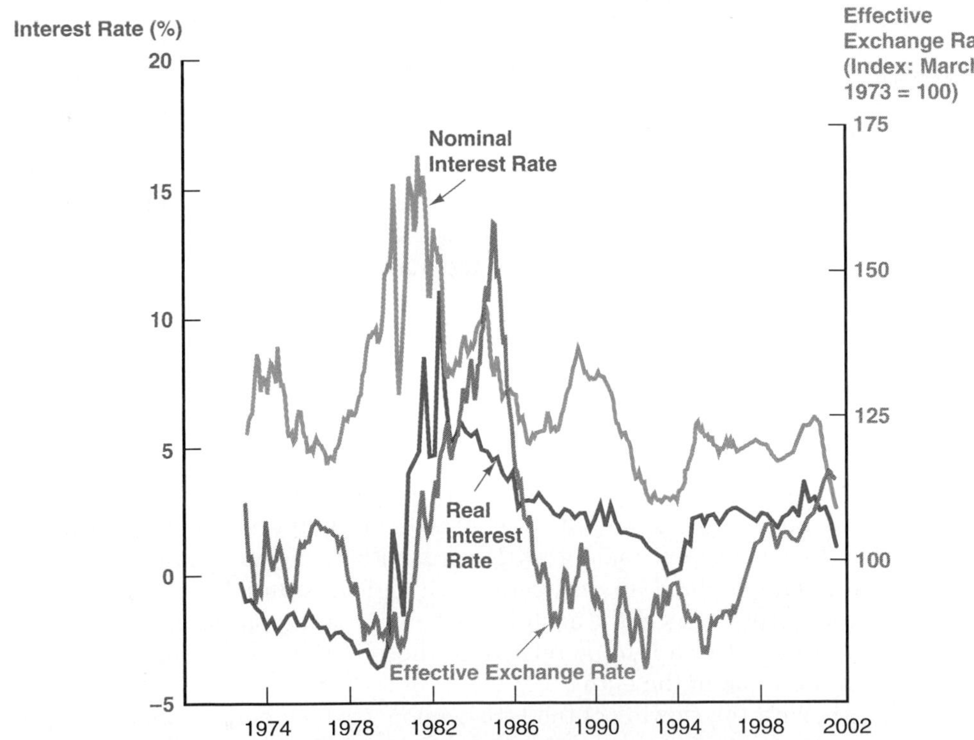

FIGURE 8 Value of the Dollar and Interest Rates, 1973–2001

Source: http://www.federalreserve.gov/releases/H10/summary/indexbc_m.txt

Our model of exchange rate determination helps explain the rise and fall in the dollar in the 1980s. As Figure 5 indicates, a rise in the U.S. real interest rate raises the expected return on dollar deposits while leaving the expected return on foreign deposits unchanged. The resulting increased demand for dollar deposits then leads to purchases of dollar deposits (and sales of foreign deposits), which raise the exchange rate. This is exactly what occurred in the 1980–1984 period. The subsequent fall in U.S. real interest rates then lowered the expected return on dollar deposits relative to foreign deposits, and the resulting sales of dollar deposits (and purchases of foreign deposits) lowered the exchange rate.

The plot of *nominal* interest rates in Figure 8 also demonstrates that the correspondence between nominal interest rates and exchange rate movements is not nearly as close as that between *real* interest rates and exchange rate movements. This is also exactly what our analysis predicts. The rise in nominal interest rates in the late 1970s was not reflected in a corresponding rise in the value of the dollar; indeed, the dollar actually fell in the late 1970s. Figure 8 explains why the rise in nominal rates in the late 1970s did not produce a rise in the dollar. As a comparison of the real and nominal interest rates in the late 1970s indicates, the rise in nominal interest rates reflected an increase in expected inflation and not an increase in real interest rates. As our analysis in Figure 6 demonstrates, the rise in nominal interest rates stemming from a rise in expected inflation should lead to a decline in the dollar, and that is exactly what transpired.

If there is a moral to the story, it is that a failure to distinguish between real and nominal interest rates can lead to poor predictions of exchange rate movements: The weakness of the dollar in the late 1970s and the strength of the dollar in the early 1980s can be explained by movements in *real* interest rates but not by movements in *nominal* interest rates.

Application — The Euro's First Three Years

READING THE *WALL STREET JOURNAL*

With much fanfare, the euro debuted on January 1, 1999, at an exchange rate of 1.18 dollars per euro. Despite initial hopes that the euro would be a strong currency, it has actually proved to be weak, declining 30% to a low of 83 cents per euro in October 2000, only to recover slightly to 89 cents by the beginning of 2002. What explains the weakness of the euro in its first two years, and the meager recovery in its third year?

The previous application has shown how changes in real interest rates are an important factor determining the exchange rate. When the domestic real interest rate falls relative to the foreign real interest rate, then the domestic currency declines in value. Indeed, this is exactly what has happened to the euro. While the euro was coming into existence, European economies were experiencing only a slow recovery from recession, thus causing both real and nominal interest rates to fall. In contrast, in 1999 and 2000, the United States experienced very rapid growth, substantially higher than Europe, which kept real and nominal interest rates high and substantially above their European counterparts. As in the analysis of the previous application, the falling, low real interest rates in Europe relative to those in the United States led to a decline in the value of the euro.

With the slowing of the U.S. economy, which entered into recession in the spring of 2001, the process above reversed. The U.S. growth rate fell slightly behind Europe's, lowering its relative real and nominal interest rates, setting the stage for a limited recovery in the euro.

Application The "Foreign Exchange" Column

READING THE *WALL STREET JOURNAL*

Now that we have an understanding of how exchange rates are determined, we can use our analysis to understand discussions about developments in the foreign exchange market reported in the financial press.

Every day, the *Wall Street Journal* reports on developments in the foreign exchange market on the previous business day in its "Foreign Exchange" column, an example of which is presented in the "Following the Financial News" box.

The column indicates that the introduction of the euro notes and coins with the new year of 2002 has started well (and is the euro's second honeymoon given its initial introduction as a unit of account in January 1999). Our analysis of the foreign exchange market explains why this development has led to an appreciation of the euro against both the dollar and the yen.

The successful introduction of euro notes and coins has led to "euphoria" which brightens the prospects for the euro's value in the future. The higher expected value of the euro means that the yen and the dollar are expected to have a lower value in the future. In an analysis with the euro as the domestic currency, the R^F curve will shift to the left because the lower future value of the dollar and the yen imply a lower expected return on deposits denominated in these currencies. The improved prospects for the euro thus lead to the sharp appreciation of the euro. However, the column does caution that a similar phenomenon occurred when the euro was introduced in 1999, and so euphoria about the euro could fade.

The column also points out that another factor that may have caused the euro to appreciate was the U.S. Congress's failure to approve a fiscal stimulus program that could have stimulated the U.S. economy. A possibly weaker U.S. economy would mean lower U.S. interest rates in the future. These lower rates would then lower the expected return for dollar denominated deposits, also shifting the R^F curve to the left and lead to an appreciation of the euro.

THE PRACTICING FINANCIAL INSTITUTION MANAGER

Profiting from Foreign Exchange Forecasts

Managers of financial institutions care a great deal about what foreign exchange rates will be in the future because these rates affect the value of assets on their balance sheet that are denominated in foreign currencies. In addition, financial institutions often engage in trading foreign exchange, both for their own account and for their customers. Forecasts of future foreign exchange rates can thus have a big impact on the profits that financial institutions make on their foreign exchange trading operations.

Managers of financial institutions obtain foreign exchange forecasts either by hiring their own staff economists to generate them or by purchasing forecasts from other financial institutions or economic forecasting firms. In predicting exchange rate movements, forecasters look at the factors mentioned in this chapter. For example, if they expect domestic real interest rates to rise, they will predict, in line with our analysis, that the domestic currency will appreciate; conversely, if they expect domestic inflation to increase, they will predict that the domestic currency will depreciate.

Managers of financial institutions, particularly those engaged in international banking, rely on foreign exchange forecasts to make decisions about which assets denominated in foreign currencies they should hold. For example, if a financial

FOLLOWING THE FINANCIAL NEWS

The "Foreign Exchange" Column

The "Foreign Exchange" column appears daily in the *Wall Street Journal;* an example is presented here. It is found in the third section, "Money and Investing."

Euro's Second Honeymoon Starts Well, But Traders Warn Euphoria Could Fade

FOREIGN EXCHANGE

By MICHAEL R. SESIT
Staff Reporter of THE WALL STREET JOURNAL

LONDON—The euro's second honeymoon began swimmingly, but traders cautioned that the euphoria could quickly fade as it did following the currency's creation three years ago.

The euro rose sharply against the dollar and yen on the first trading day since the smooth introduction of euro notes and coins, bringing relief to officials throughout the 12-nation euro zone.

"I think it was very important that the first day would be a good day, which is the case," European Central Bank governing-council member and Bank of France Governor Jean-Claude Trichet said in an interview on CNN. "It's extraordinary to see what I would call enthusiasm, which has not been foreseen."

With a rally that began in Asian trading, accelerated during European trading and picked up even more steam as New York opened, Europe's common currency at its peak yesterday stood at a two-week high against the dollar and a 28-month high against the yen. Traders attributed the currency's climb to the relatively trouble-free issue of euro-denominated bank notes and coins, coupled with signs of recovery in euro-zone manufacturing and continued disenchantment with Japan's economic prospects.

In late London trading, the euro stood at 90.30 U.S. cents and 119.24 yen, compared with 89.15 cents and 117.38 yen late in New York on Dec. 31. At one point in intraday activity, the common currency rose to a 16-day high of 90.69 cents and 119.91 yen, its highest level since Aug. 18, 1999. Late yesterday in New York, the euro was at 90.36 cents, up from 89.15 cents late Monday. The dollar was at 132.14 yen, up from 131.67 yen on Monday. The dollar was at 1.6444 Swiss francs, down from 1.6582 francs. Sterling was at $1.4461, down from $1.4560.

"The reason [the euro] is up really is a reflection of a psychological boost on the back of a successful notes and coins introduction on Jan. 1," said Shahab Jalinoos, a currency strategist at UBS Warburg, adding that the euro could climb to back toward 92 cents in the current environment.

That said, Mr. Jalinoos advised not to read too much into the initial trading enthusiasm. "We would caution that we saw a similar euro rally on the back of its introduction in January 1999, which broke down in spectacular fashion as the inadequacies of the euro-zone economy became apparent," he said.

What's more, UBS Warburg strategists don't discount this happening again. "At the moment, people are focused on the sheer fact that European policy makers have brought the [euro] project to a conclusion without a crisis," said Mr. Jalinoos. "But the cold reality of a weak European economy could come back to haunt euro bulls."

Besides the introduction of notes and coins, another factor that may have boosted the euro yesterday was the U.S. Congress's recent failure to approve a fiscal stimulus program that many had been counting on to ignite a U.S. economic recovery. Although somewhat old news, Paul Meggyesi, director of foreign-exchange strategy at Deutsche Bank, said that the holidays may have kept many investors from focusing on its impact.

Flowing from the congressional inaction, Deutsche Bank's economists have cut their forecast of U.S. growth for the second half of this year by a full percentage point to 3.5% from 4.5%. The absence of additional government spending has also prompted them to reduce their projections of Federal Reserve interest-rate increases.

In Sweden, which isn't part of the common currency, talk of possible participation helped to drive the Swedish currency to a 20-week high of 9.2 kronor to the euro, before it retreated on profit taking. "Public opinion has swung in Sweden, and is now euro-supportive," which should strengthen the krona against the euro, BNP Paribas strategists told clients in a memorandum.

Source: Wall Street Journal, January 3, 2002, p. C15. Republished by permission of Dow Jones, Inc. via Copyright Clearance Center, Inc.

institution manager has a reliable forecast that the euro will appreciate in the future but the yen will depreciate, the manager will want to sell off assets denominated in yen and instead purchase assets denominated in euros. Alternatively, the manager might instruct loan officers to make more loans denominated in euros and fewer loans denominated in yen. Likewise, if the yen is forecast to appreciate and the euro to depreciate, the manager would want to switch out of euro-denominated assets into yen-denominated assets and would want to make more loans in yen and fewer in euros.

If the financial institution has a foreign exchange trading operation, a forecast of an appreciation of the yen means that the financial institution manager should tell foreign exchange traders to buy yen. If the forecast turns out to be correct, the higher value of the yen means that the trader can sell the yen in the future and pocket a tidy profit. If the euro is forecast to depreciate, the trader can sell euros and buy them back in the future at a lower price if the forecast turns out to be correct, and again the financial institution will make a profit.

Accurate foreign exchange rate forecasts can thus help a financial institution manager generate substantial profits for the institution. Unfortunately, exchange rate forecasters are no more or less accurate than other economic forecasters, and they often make large errors. Reports on foreign exchange rate forecasts and how well forecasters are doing appear from time to time in the *Wall Street Journal* and in the trade magazine *Euromoney.*

SUMMARY

1. Foreign exchange rates (the price of one country's currency in terms of another's) are important because they affect the price of domestically produced goods sold abroad and the cost of foreign goods bought domestically.
2. The theory of purchasing power parity suggests that long-run changes in the exchange rate between two countries are determined by changes in the relative price levels of the two countries. Other factors that affect exchange rates in the long run are tariffs and quotas, import demand, export demand, and productivity.
3. Exchange rates are determined in the short run by the interest parity condition, which states that the expected return on domestic deposits is equal to the expected return on foreign deposits.
4. Any factor that changes the expected returns on domestic or foreign deposits will lead to changes in the exchange rate. Such factors include changes in the interest rates on domestic and foreign deposits as well as changes in any of the factors that affect the long-run exchange rate and hence the expected future exchange rate. Changes in the money supply lead to exchange rate overshooting, causing the exchange rate to change by more in the short run than in the long run.
5. The asset market approach to exchange rate determination can explain both the volatility of exchange rates and the rise of the dollar in the 1980–1984 period and its subsequent fall.
6. Forecasts of foreign exchange rates are very valuable to managers of financial institutions because these rates influence decisions about which assets denominated in foreign currencies the institutions should hold and what kinds of trades should be made by their traders in the foreign exchange market.

KEY TERMS

appreciation, *p. 313*
capital mobility, *p. 322*
depreciation, *p. 313*
effective exchange rate index, *p. 333*
exchange rate, *p. 311*
exchange rate overshooting, *p. 332*
foreign exchange market, *p. 311*
forward exchange rate, *p.313*
forward transaction, *p. 313*
interest parity condition, *p. 323*
law of one price, *p. 316*
monetary neutrality, *p. 332*

quotas, *p. 318*
spot exchange rate, *p. 313*
spot transaction, *p. 313*
tariffs, *p. 318*
theory of purchasing power parity (PPP), *p. 316*

QUESTIONS AND PROBLEMS

1. When the euro appreciates, are you more likely to drink California or French wine?

*2. "A country is always worse off when its currency is weak (falls in value)." Is this statement true, false, or uncertain? Explain your answer.

3. Check in a newspaper the exchange rates for the foreign currencies listed in the "Following the Financial News" box on page 336. Which of these currencies have appreciated and which have depreciated since December 31, 2001?

*4. If the European price level rises by 5% relative to the price level in the United States, what does the theory of purchasing power parity predict will happen to the value of the euro in terms of dollars?

5. If the demand for a country's exports falls at the same time that tariffs on imports are raised, will the country's currency tend to appreciate or depreciate in the long run?

*6. In the mid- to late 1970s, the yen appreciated relative to the dollar even though Japan's inflation rate was higher than America's. How can this be explained by an improvement in the productivity of Japanese industry relative to American industry?

Predicting the Future

Answer the remaining problems by drawing the appropriate exchange market diagrams.

7. The president of the United States announces that he will reduce inflation with a new anti-inflation program. If the public believes him, predict what will happen to the U.S. exchange rate.

*8. If the British central bank prints money to reduce unemployment, what will happen to the value of the pound in the short run and the long run?

9. If the European government unexpectedly announces that it will be imposing higher tariffs on foreign goods one year from now, what will happen to the value of the euro today?

*10. If nominal interest rates in America rise but real interest rates fall, predict what will happen to the U.S. exchange rate.

11. If American auto companies make a breakthrough in automobile technology and are able to produce a car that gets 60 miles to the gallon, what will happen to the U.S. exchange rate?

*12. If Americans go on a spending spree and buy twice as much French perfume, Japanese TVs, English sweaters, Swiss watches, and Italian wine, what will happen to the value of the U.S. dollar?

13. If expected inflation drops in Europe so that interest rates fall there, predict what will happen to the U.S. exchange rate.

*14. If the European central bank decides to contract the money supply in order to fight inflation, what will happen to the value of the U.S. dollar?

15. If there is a strike in France, making it harder to buy French goods, what will happen to the value of the euro?

WEB EXERCISES

The Foreign Exchange Market

1. The Federal Reserve maintains a website that lists the exchange rate between the United States and many other currencies. Go to http://www.federalreserve.gov/releases/H10/hist/. Go to the historical data from 1990 on and find the euro. What has the percentage change in the euro-dollar exchange rate been between introduction and now? What has been the annual percentage change in the euro-dollar exchange rate for each year since the euro's introduction?

2. International travelers and businesspeople frequently need to accurately convert from one currency to another. It is often easy to find the rate needed to convert the U.S. dollar into another currency. It can more difficult to find cross-conversion rates. Go to http://www.oanda.com/convert/classic. This site lets you convert from any currency into any other currency. How many Lithuanian litas can you currently buy with one Chilean peso?

Chapter 13

The International Financial System

Preview

Thanks to the growing interdependence between the U.S. economy and the economies of the rest of the world, the international financial system now plays a more prominent role in economic events in the United States. In this chapter we examine the evolution of the international financial system during the past half century and where it may be heading in the future. In addition, we see how international financial transactions and the structure of the international financial system affect monetary policy in the United States and provide substantial profit opportunities for financial institutions.

INTERVENTION IN THE FOREIGN EXCHANGE MARKET

In Chapter 12 we analyzed the foreign exchange market as if it were a completely free market that responds to all market pressures. However, the foreign exchange market, like many others, is not free of government intervention; central banks regularly engage in international financial transactions called **foreign exchange interventions** in order to influence exchange rates. In our current international financial arrangement, called a **managed float regime** (or a dirty float), exchange rates fluctuate from day to day, but central banks attempt to influence their countries' exchange rates by buying and selling currencies. The exchange rate analysis we developed in Chapter 12 is used here to explain the impact that central bank intervention has on the foreign exchange market.

Foreign Exchange Intervention and the Money Supply

The first step in understanding how central bank intervention in the foreign exchange market affects exchange rates is to see the impact on the monetary base and the money supply from a central bank sale in the foreign exchange market of some of its holdings of assets denominated in a foreign currency (called **international reserves**). Suppose that the Fed decides to sell $1 billion of its foreign assets in exchange for $1 billion of U.S. currency. (This transaction is done at the foreign exchange desk at the Federal Reserve Bank of New York—see Box 1.) The Fed's purchase of dollars has two effects. First, it reduces the Fed's holding of international reserves by $1 billion. Second, because its purchase of currency removes it from the hands of the public, currency in circulation falls by $1 billion. To see this we make use of a simplified balance sheet called a **T-account,** with lines in the form of a T, that lists only the changes that occur in balance sheet items starting from an initial balance sheet position. The T-account for the Federal Reserve illustrating this transaction is as follows:

Federal Reserve System

Assets		Liabilities	
Foreign assets (international reserves)	−$1 billion	Currency in circulation	−$1 billion

Because the monetary base is made up of currency in circulation plus reserves, this decline in currency implies that the monetary base has fallen by $1 billion.

If instead of paying for the foreign assets sold by the Fed with currency, the persons buying the foreign assets pay for them by checks written on accounts at domestic banks, then the Fed deducts the $1 billion from the deposit accounts

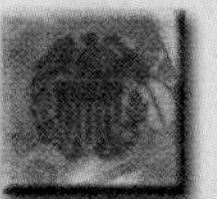

BOX 1: INSIDE THE FED

A Day at the Federal Reserve Bank of New York's Foreign Exchange Desk

Although the U.S. Treasury is primarily responsible for foreign exchange policy, decisions to intervene in the foreign exchange market are made jointly by the U.S. Treasury and the Federal Reserve as represented by the FOMC (Federal Open Market Committee). The actual conduct of foreign exchange intervention is the responsibility of the foreign exchange desk at the Federal Reserve Bank of New York, which is right next to the open market desk.

Dino Kos, the head of the markets group at the New York Fed, supervises the traders and analysts who follow developments in the foreign exchange market. Every morning at 7:30, a trader on Kos's staff who has arrived at the New York Fed in the predawn hours speaks on the telephone with counterparts at the U.S. Treasury and provides an update on overnight activity in overseas financial and foreign exchange markets. Later in the morning, at 9:30, Kos and his staff hold a conference call with senior staff at the Board of Governors of the Federal Reserve in Washington. In the afternoon, at 2:30, they have a second conference call, which is a joint briefing of officials at the board and the Treasury. Although by statute the Treasury has the lead role in setting foreign exchange policy, it strives to reach a consensus among all three parties—the Treasury, the Board of Governors, and the Federal Reserve Bank of New York. If they decide that a foreign exchange intervention is necessary that day—an unusual occurrence, as a year may go by without a U.S. foreign exchange intervention—Kos instructs his traders to carry out the agreed-on purchase or sale of foreign currencies. Because funds for exchange rate intervention are held separately by the Treasury (in its Exchange Stabilization Fund) and the Federal Reserve, Kos and his staff are not trading the funds of the Federal Reserve Bank of New York; rather they act as an agent for the Treasury and the FOMC in conducting these transactions.

As part of their duties, before every FOMC meeting, Kos and his staff help prepare a lengthy document full of data for the FOMC members, other Reserve Bank presidents, and Treasury officials that describes developments in the domestic and foreign markets over the previous five or six weeks, a task that keeps them especially busy right before the FOMC meeting.

these banks have with the Fed. The result is that deposits with the Fed (reserves) decline by $1 billion, as shown in the following T-account:

Federal Reserve System			
Assets		Liabilities	
Foreign assets (international reserves)	−$1 billion	Deposits with the Fed (reserves)	−$1 billion

In this case, the outcome of the Fed sale of foreign assets and the purchase of dollar deposits is a $1 billion decline in reserves and a $1 billion decline in the monetary base because reserves are also a component of the monetary base.

We now see that the outcome for the monetary base is exactly the same when a central bank sells foreign assets to purchase domestic bank deposits or domestic currency. This is why when we say that a central bank has purchased its domestic currency, we do not have to distinguish whether it actually purchased currency or bank deposits denominated in the domestic currency. We have thus reached an important conclusion: ***A central bank's purchase of domestic currency and corresponding sale of foreign assets in the foreign exchange market leads to an equal decline in its international reserves and the monetary base.***

We could have reached the same conclusion by a more direct route. A central bank sale of a foreign asset is no different from an open market sale of a government bond. We learned in Chapter 7 that an open market sale leads to an equal decline in the monetary base; therefore, a sale of foreign assets also leads to an equal decline in the monetary base. By similar reasoning, a central bank purchase of foreign assets paid for by selling domestic currency, like an open market purchase, leads to an equal rise in the monetary base. Thus we reach the following conclusion: ***A central bank's sale of domestic currency to purchase foreign assets in the foreign exchange market results in an equal rise in its international reserves and the monetary base.***

The intervention we have just described, in which a central bank allows the purchase or sale of domestic currency to have an effect on the monetary base and hence on the money supply, is called an **unsterilized foreign exchange intervention.** But what if the central bank does not want the purchase or sale of domestic currency to affect the monetary base and the money supply? All it has to do is to counter the effect of the foreign exchange intervention by conducting an offsetting open market operation in the government bond market. For example, in the case of a $1 billion purchase of dollars by the Fed and a corresponding $1 billion sale of foreign assets, which we have seen would decrease the monetary base by $1 billion, the Fed can conduct an open market purchase of $1 billion of government bonds, which would increase the monetary base by $1 billion. The resulting T-account for the foreign exchange intervention and the offsetting open market operation leaves the monetary base unchanged:

Federal Reserve System			
Assets		Liabilities	
Foreign assets (international reserves)	−$1 billion	Monetary base (currency in circulation plus reserves)	0
Government bonds	+$1 billion		

A foreign exchange intervention with an offsetting open market operation that leaves the monetary base unchanged is called a **sterilized foreign exchange intervention.**

Now that we understand that there are two types of foreign exchange interventions, unsterilized and sterilized, let's look at how each affects the exchange rate.

Unsterilized Intervention

Your intuition might lead you to suspect that if a central bank wants to lower the value of the domestic currency, it should sell its currency in the foreign exchange market and purchase foreign assets. Indeed, this intuition is correct for the case of an unsterilized intervention.

Recall that in an unsterilized intervention, if the Federal Reserve decides to sell dollars in order to buy foreign assets in the foreign exchange market, this works just like an open market purchase of bonds that increases the monetary base and the money supply. Hence we find ourselves analyzing exactly the situation described in Figure 7 of Chapter 12, which is reproduced here as Figure 1. The higher money supply leads to a higher U.S. price level in the long run and so to a lower expected future exchange rate. The resulting decline in the expected appreciation of the dollar increases the expected return on foreign deposits and shifts the R^F schedule to the right. In addition, the increase in the money supply will lead to a higher real money supply in the short run, which causes the interest rate on dollar deposits to fall. The resulting lower expected return on dollar

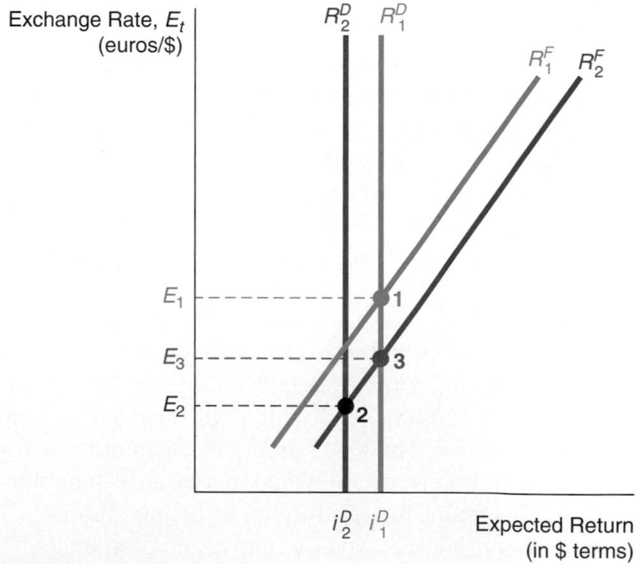

FIGURE 1 Effect of a Sale of Dollars and a Purchase of Foreign Assets

A sale of dollars and the consequent open market purchase of foreign assets increase the monetary base. The resulting rise in the money supply leads to a higher domestic price level in the long run, which leads to a lower expected future exchange rate. The resulting decline in the expected appreciation of the dollar raises the expected return on foreign deposits, shifting the R^F schedule rightward from R^F_1 to R^F_2. In the short run, the domestic interest rate i^D falls, shifting R^D from R^D_1 to R^D_2. The short-run outcome is that the exchange rate falls from E_1 to E_2. In the long run, however, the interest rate returns to i^D_1, and R^D returns to R^D_1. The exchange rate therefore rises from E_2 to E_3 in the long run.

deposits translates as a leftward shift in the R^D schedule. The fall in the expected return on dollar deposits and the increase in the expected return on foreign deposits means that foreign assets have a higher expected return than dollar deposits at the old equilibrium exchange rate. Hence people will try to sell their dollar deposits, and the exchange rate will fall. Indeed, as we saw in Chapter 12, the increase in the money supply will lead to exchange rate overshooting, whereby the exchange rate falls by more in the short run than it does in the long run.

Our analysis leads us to the following conclusion about unsterilized interventions in the foreign exchange market: ***An unsterilized intervention in which domestic currency is sold to purchase foreign assets leads to a gain in international reserves, an increase in the money supply, and a depreciation of the domestic currency.***

The reverse result is found for an unsterilized intervention in which domestic currency is purchased by selling foreign assets. The purchase of domestic currency by selling foreign assets (reducing international reserves) works like an open market sale to reduce the monetary base and the money supply. The decrease in the money supply raises the interest rate on dollar deposits and shifts R^D rightward while causing R^F to shift leftward because it leads to a lower U.S. price level in the long run and thus to a higher expected appreciation of the dollar and hence a lower expected return on foreign deposits. The increase in the expected return on dollar deposits relative to foreign deposits will mean that people will want to buy more dollar deposits, and the exchange rate will rise. ***An unsterilized intervention in which domestic currency is purchased by selling foreign assets leads to a drop in international reserves, a decrease in the money supply, and an appreciation of the domestic currency.***

Sterilized Intervention

The key point to remember about a sterilized intervention is that the central bank engages in offsetting open market operations so that there is no impact on the monetary base and the money supply. In the context of the model of exchange rate determination we have developed here, it is straightforward to show that a sterilized intervention has *no effect* on the exchange rate. Remember that in our model, foreign and domestic deposits are perfect substitutes, so equilibrium in the foreign exchange market occurs when the expected returns on foreign and domestic deposits are equal. A sterilized intervention leaves the money supply unchanged and so has no way of directly affecting interest rates or the expected future exchange rate.[1] Because the expected returns on dollar and foreign deposits are unaffected, the expected return schedules remain at R^D_1 and R^F_1 in Figure 1, and the exchange rate remains unchanged at E_1.

At first it might seem puzzling that a central bank purchase or sale of domestic currency that is sterilized does not lead to a change in the exchange rate. A

[1]Note that a sterilized intervention could indicate what central banks want to happen to the future exchange rate and so might provide a signal about the course of future monetary policy. In this way, a sterilized intervention could lead to shifts in the R^F schedule, but in reality it is the future change in monetary policy, not the sterilized intervention, that is the ultimate source of exchange rate effects. For a discussion of the signaling effect, see Maurice Obstfeld, "The Effectiveness of Foreign Exchange Intervention: Recent Experience, 1985–1988," in *International Policy Coordination and Exchange Rate Fluctuations,* ed. William H. Branson, Jacob A. Frenkel, and Morris Goldstein (Chicago: University of Chicago Press, 1990), pp. 197–237.

central bank purchase of domestic currency cannot raise the exchange rate because with no effect on the domestic money supply or interest rates, any resulting rise in the exchange rate would mean that the expected return on foreign deposits would be greater than the expected return on domestic deposits. Given our assumption that foreign and domestic deposits are perfect substitutes (equally desirable), this would mean that no one would want to hold domestic deposits.[2] So the exchange rate would have to fall back to its previous level, where the expected returns on domestic and foreign deposits were equal.

BALANCE OF PAYMENTS

The site www.stls.frb.org/fred/data/exchange.html contains exchange rates, balance of payments, and trade data.

Because international financial transactions such as foreign exchange interventions have considerable effect on monetary policy, it is worth knowing how these transactions are measured. The **balance of payments** is a bookkeeping system for recording all payments that have a direct bearing on the movement of funds between a nation (private sector and government) and foreign countries.

The balance-of-payments account in the accompanying "Following the Financial News" box uses a standard double-entry bookkeeping system much like one that you or I might use to keep a record of payments and receipts. All transactions involving payments from foreigners to Americans are entered in the "Receipts" column with a plus sign (+) to reflect that they are credits; that is, they result in a flow of funds to Americans. Receipts include foreign purchases of American products such as computers and wheat (exports), purchases from foreign tourists (services), income earned from American investment abroad (investment income), foreign gifts and pensions paid to Americans (unilateral transfers), and foreign payments for American assets (capital inflows).

All payments to foreigners are entered in the "Payments" column with a minus sign (−) to reflect that they are debits because they result in flows of funds to other countries. Payments include American purchases of foreign products such as French wine and Japanese cars (imports), American travel abroad (services), income earned by foreigners from investments in the United States (investment income), foreign aid and gifts and pensions paid to foreigners (unilateral transfers), and American payments for foreign assets (capital outflows).

Current Account

The **current account** shows international transactions that involve currently produced goods and services. The difference between merchandise exports (line 1) and imports (line 2) is called the **trade balance.** When merchandise imports are greater than exports (here by −$450 billion), we have a trade balance deficit; if exports are greater than imports, we have a trade balance surplus.

The next three items in the current account are the net payments or receipts that arise from investment income, the purchase and sale of services, and unilateral transfers (gifts, pensions, and foreign aid). In 2000, for example, net invest-

[2]If domestic and foreign deposits are not perfect substitutes, a sterilized intervention can affect the exchange rate. However, most studies find little evidence to support the position that sterilized intervention has a significant impact on foreign exchange rates. For a further discussion of the effects of sterilized versus unsterilized intervention, see Paul Krugman and Maurice Obstfeld, *International Economics,* 5th ed. (Reading, Mass.: Addison Wesley Longman, 2000).

FOLLOWING THE FINANCIAL NEWS

The Balance of Payments

Newspapers periodically report information on the balance of payments. Balance-of-trade figures (merchandise exports minus imports) are reported monthly in the last week of the month. The complete set of items in the balance of payments is published on a quarterly basis, with the previous quarter's figures published between the eighteenth and twentieth day of the last month of the following quarter. An example of the balance-of-payments accounts for the United States appears here.

U.S. Balance of Payments, 2000 ($ billions)

	Receipts (+)	Payments (−)	Balance
Current Account			
(1) Merchandise exports	+773		
(2) Merchandise imports		−1,223	
Trade balance			−450
(3) Net investment income		−14	
(4) Net services	+81		
(5) Net unilateral transfers		−53	
Current account balance: (1) + (2) + (3) + (4) + (5)			−436
Capital Account			
(6) Capital outflows		−553	
(7) Capital inflows	+952		
(8) Statistical discrepancy	+35		
Official reserve transactions balance: (1) + (2) + (3) + (4) + (5) + (6) + (7) + (8)			−2
Method of Financing			
(9) Increase in U.S. official reserve assets		−33	
(10) Increase in foreign official reserve assets	+35		
Total financing of surplus: (9) + (10)			+2
Balance of Payments			
Sum: (1) through (10)			0

Source: Survey of Current Business, April 2001.

ment income was minus $14 billion (in line 3) for the United States because Americans received less investment income from abroad than they paid out. Americans bought less in services from foreigners than foreigners bought from Americans, so net services generated $81 billion in receipts (line 4). Since Americans made more unilateral transfers to foreign countries (especially foreign aid) than foreigners made to the United States, a $53 billion payment is shown in line 5.

The sum of the items in lines 1 through 5 is the current account balance, which in 2000 showed a deficit of $436 billion. The current account balance is an important balance-of-payments concept for several reasons. As we can see from the balance-of-payments account, any surplus or deficit in the current account must be balanced either by capital account transactions (lending or borrowing abroad) or by changes in government reserve asset items:

$$\text{Current account} + \text{capital account} = \text{change in government reserve assets}$$

The current account balance tells us whether the United States (private sector and government combined) is increasing or decreasing its claims on foreign wealth. A surplus indicates that America is increasing its claims on foreign wealth, and a deficit, as in 2000, indicates that the country is reducing its claims on foreign wealth.[3]

Financial analysts follow the current account balance closely because they believe that it can provide information on the future movement of exchange rates. The current account balance provides some indication of what is happening to the demand for imports and exports, which, as we saw in Chapter 12, can affect the exchange rate. In addition, the current account balance provides information about what will be happening to U.S. claims on foreign wealth in the long run. Because a movement of foreign wealth to American residents can affect the demand for dollar assets, changes in U.S. claims on foreign wealth, reflected in the current account balance, can affect the exchange rate over time.[4]

Capital Account

The **capital account** describes the flow of capital between the United States and other countries. Capital outflows are American purchases of foreign assets (a "Payments" item), and capital inflows are foreign purchases of American assets (a "Receipts" item). The capital outflows (line 6) are less than the capital inflows (line 7), resulting in a net flow of $399 billion in funds from foreigners in exchange for claims against American individuals and corporations.

The statistical discrepancy (line 8) represents errors due to unrecorded transactions involving smuggling and other capital flows. The statistical discrepancy, which keeps the balance-of-payments account in balance, is +$35 billion, which suggests that some of the other items in the balance of payments may not be measured very accurately. Many experts believe that the statistical discrepancy is primarily the result of large hidden capital flows, and so the item has been placed in the capital account part of the balance of payments.

Official Reserve Transactions Balance

The sum of lines 1 through 8, called the **official reserve transactions balance,** equals the current account balance plus the items in the capital account. When we refer to a surplus or a deficit in the balance of payments, we actually mean a surplus or deficit in the official reserve transactions balance. Because the balance-of-payments account must balance, the official reserve transactions balance tells us the net amount of international reserves that must move between central banks to finance international transactions. One reason we are particularly interested in the movements of international reserves is that, as we saw earlier in the chapter, these movements can have an important impact on the money supply and exchange rates.

---

[3]The current account balance can also be viewed as showing by how much total saving exceeds private sector and government investment in the United States. We can see this by noting that total U.S. saving equals the increase in total wealth held by the U.S. private sector and government. Total investment equals the increase in the U.S. capital stock (wealth physically in the United States). The difference between them is the increase in U.S. claims on foreign wealth.

[4]If American residents have a greater preference for dollar assets than foreigners do, a movement of foreign wealth to American residents when there is a balance-of-payments surplus will increase the demand for dollar assets over time and will cause the dollar to appreciate.

Methods of Financing the Balance of Payments

Because most countries' currencies are not held by other countries as international reserves, these countries must finance an excess of payments over receipts (a deficit in the balance of payments) by providing international reserves to foreign governments and central banks. A balance-of-payments deficit is associated with a loss of international reserves; likewise, a balance-of-payments surplus is associated with a gain.

In contrast to other countries' currencies, the U.S. dollar and dollar-denominated assets are the major component of international reserves held by other countries. Thus a U.S. balance-of-payments deficit can be financed by a decrease in U.S. international reserves, an increase in foreign central banks' holdings of international reserves (dollar assets), or both. Conversely, a U.S. balance-of-payments surplus can be financed by an increase in U.S. international reserves, a decrease in foreign central banks' international reserves, or both.

For the United States in 2000, the official reserve transactions deficit of –$2 billion was financed by a $33 billion increase in U.S. international reserves (–33 in the "Payments" column of line 9) and an $35 billion increase of foreign holdings of dollars (in the "Receipts" column of line 10).[5] On net, the United States' indebtedness to foreign governments (central banks) increased by $2 billion (the $35 billion foreign increase in holdings of U.S. dollars minus the $33 billion increase in U.S. holdings of international reserves). This $2 billion increase in net U.S. government indebtedness just matches the $2 billion official reserve transactions deficit, so the sum of lines 1 through 10 is zero, and the account balances.

EVOLUTION OF THE INTERNATIONAL FINANCIAL SYSTEM

Before examining the impact of international financial transactions on monetary policy, we need to understand the past and current structure of the international financial system.

Gold Standard

Before World War I, the world economy operated under the **gold standard,** meaning that the currency of most countries was convertible directly into gold. American dollar bills, for example, could be turned in to the U.S. Treasury and exchanged for approximately $\frac{1}{20}$ ounce of gold. Likewise, the British Treasury would exchange $\frac{1}{4}$ ounce of gold for £1 sterling. Because an American could convert $20 into 1 ounce of gold, which could be used to buy £4, the exchange rate between the pound and the dollar was effectively fixed at $5 to the pound. Tying currencies to gold resulted in an international financial system with fixed exchange rates between currencies. The fixed exchange rates under the gold standard had the important advantage of encouraging world trade by eliminating the uncertainty that occurs when exchange rates fluctuate.

To see how the gold standard operated in practice, let us see what occurs if, under the gold standard, the British pound begins to appreciate above the $5 par value. If an American importer of £100 of English tweed tries to pay for the tweed

[5]At first it may seem strange that when the United States gains $1 billion of international reserves, it is entered in the balance of payments as a payment with a negative sign. Recall, however, that when a central bank gains international reserves, it has purchased foreign assets. Thus an increase in international reserves is just like an outflow of capital in the capital account and appears as a payment with a negative sign.

with dollars, it costs more than the $500 it cost before. Nevertheless, the importer has another option involving the purchase of gold that can reduce the cost of the tweed. Instead of using dollars to pay for the tweed, the American importer can exchange the $500 for gold, ship the gold to Britain, and convert it into £100. The shipment of gold to Britain is cheaper as long as the British pound is above the $5 par value (plus a small amount to pay for the cost of shipping the gold).

The appreciation of the pound leads to a British gain of international reserves (gold) and an equal U.S. loss. Because a change in a country's holdings of international reserves (gold) leads to an equal change in its monetary base, the movement of gold from the United States to Britain causes the British monetary base to rise and the American monetary base to fall. The resulting rise in the British money supply raises the British price level, while the fall in the U.S. money supply lowers the U.S. price level. The resulting increase in the British price level relative to the United States then causes the pound to depreciate. This process will continue until the value of the pound falls back down to its $5 par value.

A depreciation of the pound below the $5 par value, on the contrary, stimulates gold shipments from Britain to the United States. These shipments raise the American money supply and lower the British money supply, causing the pound to appreciate back toward the $5 par value. We thus see that under the gold standard, a rise or fall in the exchange rate sets in motion forces that return it to the par value.

As long as countries abided by the rules under the gold standard and kept their currencies backed by and convertible into gold, exchange rates remained fixed. However, adherence to the gold standard meant that a country had no control over its monetary policy because its money supply was determined by gold flows between countries. Furthermore, monetary policy throughout the world was greatly influenced by the production of gold and gold discoveries. When gold production was low in the 1870s and 1880s, the money supply throughout the world grew slowly and did not keep pace with the growth of the world economy. The result was deflation (falling price levels). Gold discoveries in Alaska and South Africa in the 1890s then greatly expanded gold production, which caused money supplies to increase rapidly and price levels to rise (inflation) until World War I.

Bretton Woods System and the IMF

World War I caused massive trade disruptions. Countries could no longer convert their currencies into gold, and the gold standard collapsed. Despite attempts to revive it in the interwar period, the worldwide depression, beginning in 1929, led to its permanent demise. As the Allied victory in World War II was becoming certain in 1944, the Allies met in Bretton Woods, New Hampshire, to develop a new international monetary system to promote world trade and prosperity after the war. In the agreement worked out among the Allies, central banks bought and sold their own currencies to keep their exchange rates fixed at a certain level (called a **fixed exchange rate regime**). The agreement lasted from 1945 to 1971 and was known as the **Bretton Woods system.**

The Bretton Woods agreement created the **International Monetary Fund (IMF),** headquartered in Washington, D.C., which had 30 original member countries in 1945 and currently has over 150. The IMF was given the task of promoting the growth of world trade by setting rules for the maintenance of fixed exchange rates and by making loans to countries that were experiencing balance-of-payments difficulties.[6] As part of its role of monitoring the compliance of member countries with its rules, the IMF also took on the job of collecting and standardizing international economic data.

The Bretton Woods agreement also set up the International Bank for Reconstruction and Development, commonly referred to as the **World Bank,** also headquartered in Washington, which provides long-term loans to help developing countries build dams, roads, and other physical capital that would contribute to their economic development. The funds for these loans are obtained primarily by issuing World Bank bonds, which are sold in the capital markets of the developed countries.[7]

Because the United States emerged from World War II as the world's largest economic power, with over half of the world's manufacturing capacity and the greater part of the world's gold, the Bretton Woods system of fixed exchange rates was based on the convertibility of U.S. dollars into gold (for foreign governments and central banks only) at $35 per ounce. The fixed exchange rates were to be maintained by intervention in the foreign exchange market by central banks in countries besides the United States who bought and sold dollar assets, which they held as international reserves. The U.S. dollar, which was used by other countries to denominate the assets that they held as international reserves, was called the **reserve currency.** Thus an important feature of the Bretton Woods system was the establishment of the United States as the reserve currency country. Even after the breakup of the Bretton Woods system, the U.S. dollar has kept its position as the reserve currency in which most international financial transactions are conducted. However, with the creation of the euro in 1999, the U.S. dollar may be subject to a serious challenge to its supremacy (see Box 2).

[6]Rules for the conduct of trade between countries (the setting of tariffs and quotas) were given to the General Agreement on Tariffs and Trade (GATT), headquartered in Geneva. For a discussion of how this agency operates, see John Williamson, *The Open Economy and the World Economy* (New York: Basic Books, 1983).

[7]In 1960, the World Bank established an affiliate, the International Development Association (IDA), which provides particularly attractive loans to third-world countries (with 50-year maturities and zero interest rates, for example). Funds for these loans are obtained by direct contributions of member countries.

BOX 2: GLOBAL

The Euro's Challenge to the Dollar

With the adoption of the euro by countries in the European Monetary System, in the future the U.S. dollar may face a challenge to its position as the key reserve currency in international financial transactions. Adoption of the euro has increased integration of Europe's financial markets, which could help them rival those in the United States. The resulting increase in the use of euros in financial markets is making it more likely that international transactions are carried out in the euro. The economic clout of the European Union rivals that of the United States: Both have a similar share of world GDP (around 20%) and world exports (around 15%). If the European Central Bank can make sure that inflation remains low so that the euro becomes a sound currency, this should bode well for the euro.

However, for the euro to eat significantly into the dollar's position as a reserve currency, the European Union must function as a cohesive political entity that is able to exert its influence on the world stage. There are serious doubts on this score, and most analysts think that it will be a long time before the euro beats out the dollar in international financial transactions.

How a Fixed Exchange Rate Regime Works The most important feature of the Bretton Woods system was that it set up a fixed exchange rate regime. Figure 2 shows how a fixed exchange rate regime works in practice using the model of exchange rate determination we learned in Chapter 12. Panel (a) describes a situation in which the domestic currency is initially overvalued: The schedule for the expected return on foreign deposits R_1^F intersects the schedule for the expected return on domestic deposits R_1^D at exchange rate E_1, which is lower than the par (fixed) value of the exchange rate E_{par}. To keep the exchange rate at E_{par}, the central bank must intervene in the foreign exchange market to purchase domestic currency by selling foreign assets, and this action, like an open market sale, means that the monetary base and the money supply decline. Because the exchange rate will continue to be fixed at E_{par}, the expected future exchange rate remains unchanged, and so the schedule for the expected return on foreign deposits remains at R_1^F. However, the purchase of domestic currency, which leads to a fall in the money supply, also causes the interest rate on domestic deposits i^D to rise. This increase in turn shifts the expected return on domestic deposits R^D to the right. The central bank will continue purchasing domestic currency and selling foreign assets until the R^D curve reaches R_2^D and the equilibrium exchange rate is at E_{par} at point 2 in panel (a).

We have thus come to the conclusion that ***when the domestic currency is overvalued, the central bank must purchase domestic currency to keep the exchange rate fixed, but as a result it loses international reserves.***

Panel (b) in Figure 2 shows how a central bank intervention keeps the exchange rate fixed at E_{par} when the exchange rate is initially undervalued, that

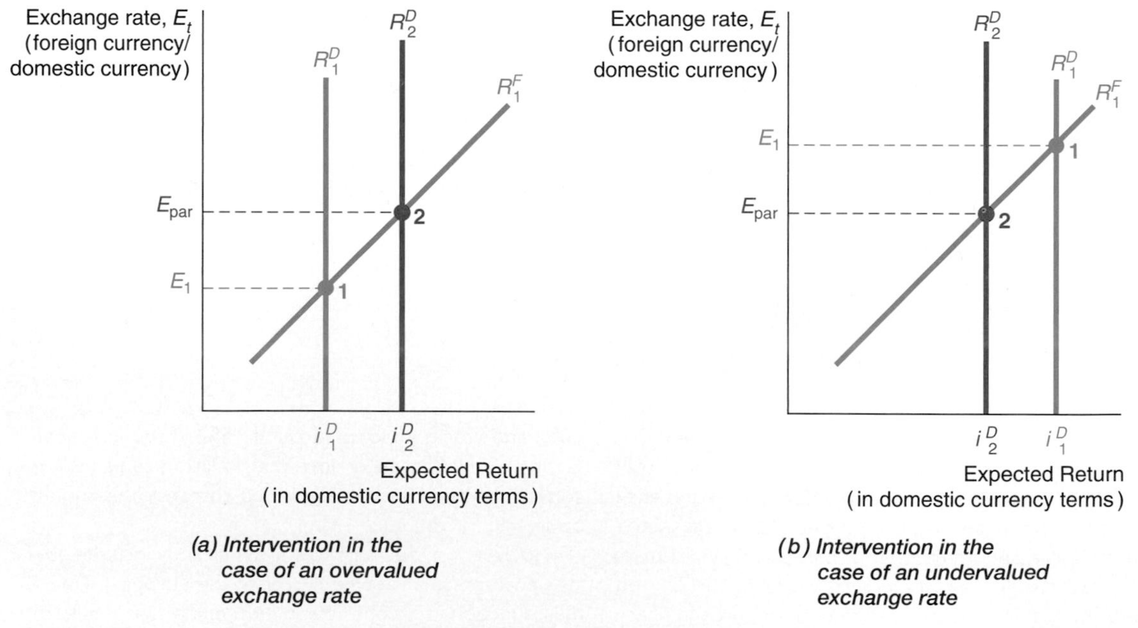

FIGURE 2 Intervention in the Foreign Exchange Market under a Fixed Exchange Rate Regime

In panel (a), the exchange rate at E_{par} is overvalued. To keep the exchange rate at E_{par} (point 2), the central bank must purchase domestic currency to shift the schedule for the expected return on domestic deposits to R_2^D. In panel (b), the exchange rate at E_{par} is undervalued, so a central bank sale of domestic currency is needed to shift R^D to R_2^D to keep the exchange rate at E_{par} (point 2).

is, when R_1^F and the initial R_1^D intersect at exchange rate E_1, which is above E_{par}. Here the central bank must sell domestic currency and purchase foreign assets, and this works like an open market purchase to raise the money supply and to lower the interest rate on domestic deposits i^D. The central bank keeps selling domestic currency and lowers i^D until R^D shifts all the way to R_2^D, where the equilibrium exchange rate is at E_{par} – point 2 in panel (b). Our analysis thus leads us to the following result: ***When the domestic currency is undervalued, the central bank must sell domestic currency to keep the exchange rate fixed, but as a result it gains international reserves.***

As we have seen, if a country's currency has an overvalued exchange rate, its central bank's attempts to keep the currency from depreciating will result in a loss of international reserves. If the country's central bank eventually runs out of international reserves, it cannot keep its currency from depreciating, and a **devaluation** must occur, meaning that the par exchange rate is reset at a lower level.

If, by contrast, a country's currency has an undervalued exchange rate, its central bank's intervention to keep the currency from appreciating leads to a gain of international reserves. Because, as we will see shortly, the central bank might not want to acquire these international reserves, it might want to reset the par value of its exchange rate at a higher level (a **revaluation**).

Note that if domestic and foreign deposits are perfect substitutes, as is assumed in the model of exchange rate determination used here, a sterilized exchange rate intervention would not be able to keep the exchange rate at E_{par} because, as we have seen in Chapter 12, neither R^F nor R^D will shift. For example, if the exchange rate is overvalued, a sterilized purchase of domestic currency will still leave the expected return on domestic deposits below the expected return on foreign deposits at the par exchange rate—so pressure for a depreciation of the domestic currency is not removed. If the central bank keeps on purchasing its domestic currency but continues to sterilize, it will just keep on losing international reserves until it finally runs out of them and is forced to let the value of the currency seek a lower level.

One implication of the foregoing analysis is that a country that ties its exchange rate to a larger country's currency loses control of its monetary policy. If the larger country pursues a more contractionary monetary policy and decreases its money supply, this would lead to lower expected inflation in the larger country, thus causing an appreciation of the larger country's currency and a depreciation of the smaller country's currency. The smaller country, having locked its exchange rate, will now find its currency overvalued and will therefore have to sell the larger country's currency and buy its own to keep its currency from depreciating. The result of this foreign exchange intervention will then be a decline in the smaller country's international reserves, a contraction of the monetary base, and thus a decline in its money supply. Sterilization of this foreign exchange intervention is not an option because this would just lead to a continuing loss of international reserves until the smaller country was forced to devalue. The smaller country no longer controls its monetary policy because movements in its money supply are completely determined by movements in the larger country's money supply.

Smaller countries are often willing to tie their exchange rate to that of a larger country in order to inherit the more disciplined monetary policy of their bigger neighbor, thus ensuring a lower inflation rate. An extreme example of such a strategy is the currency board, which has been used by Hong Kong and has recently been adopted by countries such as Argentina (see Box 3), Latvia, and Estonia. An even more extreme strategy is **dollarization,** in which a country abandons its currency altogether and adopts that of another country, typically the U.S. dollar (see Box 4).

Bretton Woods System of Fixed Exchange Rates Under the Bretton Woods system, exchange rates were supposed to change only when a country was experiencing a "fundamental disequilibrium," that is, large persistent deficits or surpluses in its balance of payments. To maintain fixed exchange rates when countries had balance-of-payments deficits and were losing international reserves, the IMF would loan deficit countries international reserves contributed by other members. As a result of its power to dictate loan terms to borrowing countries, the IMF could encourage deficit countries to pursue contractionary monetary policies that would strengthen their currency or eliminate their balance-of-payment deficits. If the IMF loans were not sufficient to prevent depreciation of a currency, the country was allowed to devalue its currency by setting a new, lower exchange rate.

BOX 3: GLOBAL

Argentina's Currency Board

Argentina has a long history of monetary instability, with inflation rates fluctuating dramatically and sometimes surging beyond 1000% a year. To end this cycle of inflationary surges, Argentina decided to adopt a currency board in April 1991. A *currency board system* is one in which the domestic currency has 100% backing in foreign reserves and in which the note-issuing authority, whether the central bank or the government, adopts a fixed exchange rate against a particular foreign currency and then stands ready to exchange domestic currency for foreign currency at that rate whenever the public requests it.

The Argentine currency board worked as follows. Under Argentina's convertibility law, the peso/dollar exchange rate was fixed at one to one, and a member of the public could go to the Argentine central bank and exchange a peso for a dollar, or vice versa, at any time. A currency board is just a variant of a fixed exchange rate regime in which the commitment to the fixed exchange rate is especially strong because the conduct of monetary policy is in effect put on autopilot and is completely taken out of the hands of the central bank and the government. The money supply could expand only when dollars were exchanged for pesos at the central bank, meaning that the increased amount of pesos was matched by an equal increase in foreign exchange reserves. The central bank therefore no longer had the ability to print money and thereby cause inflation.

The early years of Argentina's currency board looked stunningly successful. Inflation, which had been running at an 800% rate in 1990, fell below 5% by the end of 1994, and economic growth was rapid, averaging almost 8% annually from 1991 to 1994. However, a currency board is not without problems. In the aftermath of the Mexican peso crisis, concern about the health of the Argentine economy resulted in the public's pulling money out of the banks (deposits fell by 18%) and exchanging pesos for dollars, thus causing a contraction of the Argentine money supply. The result was a sharp decline in Argentine economic activity, with real GDP down more than 5% in 1995 and the unemployment rate jumping above 15%. Only in 1996 did the economy begin to recover.

However, in 1998 Argentina entered another recession which has been both severe and very long lasting. By the end of 2001, unemployment had reached nearly 20%, a level comparable to that experienced in the United States during the Great Depression of the 1930s. The result had been civil unrest and the fall of the elected government, as well as a major banking crisis and a default on government debt. Because the Central Bank of Argentina had no control over monetary policy under the currency board system, it was unable to use monetary policy to expand the economy and get out of its recession. Furthermore, because the currency board did not allow the central bank to create pesos and lend them to banks, it had very little capability to act as a lender of last resort. Finally, in January 2002, Argentina abandoned its currency board.

BOX 4: GLOBAL
Dollarization

Dollarization, which involves the adoption of another country's currency, usually the U.S. dollar (but other sound currencies like the euro or the yen are also possibilities), is a more extreme version of fixed exchange rate than is a currency board. A currency board can be abandoned, allowing a change in the value of the currency, but a change of value is impossible with dollarization: A dollar bill is always worth one dollar whether it is held in the United States or outside of it. Panama has been dollarized since the inception of the country in the early twentieth century, while El Salvador and Ecuador have recently adopted dollarization.

Dollarization, like a currency board, prevents a central bank from creating inflation. Another key advantage is that it completely avoids the possibility of a speculative attack on the domestic currency (because there is none) that is still a danger even under a currency board arrangement. However, like a currency board, dollarization does not allow a country to pursue its own monetary policy or have a lender of last resort. Dollarization has one additional disadvantage not characteristic of a currency board: Because a country adopting dollarization no longer has its own currency, it loses the revenue that a government receives by issuing money, which is called *seigniorage*. Because governments (or their central banks) do not have to pay interest on their currency, they earn revenue (seigniorage) by using this currency to purchase income-earning assets such as bonds. In the case of the Federal Reserve in the United States, this revenue is on the order of $20 billion dollars per year. If an emerging-market country dollarizes and give up its currency, it needs to make up this loss of revenue somewhere, which is not always easy for a poor country.

A notable weakness of the Bretton Woods system was that although deficit countries losing international reserves could be pressured into devaluing their currency or pursuing contractionary policies, the IMF had no way to force surplus countries to revise their exchange rates upward or pursue more expansionary policies. Particularly troublesome in this regard was the fact that the reserve currency country, the United States, could not devalue its currency under the Bretton Woods system even if the dollar was overvalued. When the United States attempted to reduce domestic unemployment in the 1960s by pursuing an inflationary monetary policy, a fundamental disequilibrium of an overvalued dollar developed. Because surplus countries were not willing to revise their exchange rates upward, adjustment in the Bretton Woods system did not take place, and the system collapsed in 1971. Attempts to patch up the Bretton Woods system with the Smithsonian Agreement in December 1971 proved unsuccessful, and by 1973, America and its trading partners had agreed to allow exchange rates to float.

Managed Float

Although exchange rates are currently allowed to change daily in response to market forces, central banks have not been willing to give up their option of intervening in the foreign exchange market. Preventing large changes in exchange rates makes it easier for firms and individuals purchasing or selling goods abroad to plan into the future. Furthermore, countries with surpluses in their balance of payments frequently do not want to see their currencies appreciate because it makes their goods more expensive abroad and foreign goods cheaper in their country. Because an appreciation might hurt sales for domestic businesses and increase unemployment, surplus countries have often sold their currency in the foreign exchange market and acquired international reserves.

Countries with balance-of-payments deficits do not want to see their currency lose value because it makes foreign goods more expensive for domestic consumers and can stimulate inflation. To keep the value of the domestic currency high, deficit countries have often bought their own currency in the foreign exchange market and given up international reserves.

The current international financial system is a hybrid of a fixed and a flexible exchange rate system. Rates fluctuate in response to market forces but are not determined solely by them. Furthermore, many countries continue to keep the value of their currency fixed against other currencies, as in the European Monetary System (to be described shortly).

The IMF continues to function as a data collector and international lender but does not attempt to encourage fixed exchange rates. The IMF's role of international lender has also become important recently because of situations like the third-world debt crisis of the 1980s and the more recent Mexican peso crisis (discussed later in the chapter). The IMF has been directly involved in helping developing countries with difficulties in repaying their loans and provided large loans to Mexico and other countries in the aftermath of the Mexican peso crisis.

At www.imf.org/external/np/exr/facts/sdr.htm, check out a special drawing rights fact sheet with information on allocation, valuation, and an SDR user's guide.

Another important feature of the current system is the continuing de-emphasis of gold in international financial transactions. Not only has the United States suspended convertibility of dollars into gold for foreign central banks, but since 1970 the IMF has been issuing a paper substitute for gold, called **special drawing rights (SDRs).** Like gold in the Bretton Woods system, SDRs function as international reserves. Unlike gold, whose quantity is determined by gold discoveries and the rate of production, SDRs can be created by the IMF whenever it decides that there is a need for additional international reserves to promote world trade and economic growth.

The use of gold in international transactions was further deemphasized by the IMF's elimination of the official gold price in 1975 and by the sale of gold by the U.S. Treasury and the IMF to private interests in order to demonetize it. Currently, the price of gold is determined in a free market. Investors who want to speculate in it are able to purchase and sell at will, as are jewelers and dentists who use gold in their businesses.

European Monetary System (EMS)

In March 1979, eight members of the European Economic Community (Germany, France, Italy, the Netherlands, Belgium, Luxembourg, Denmark, and Ireland) set up the European Monetary System (EMS), in which they agreed to fix their exchange rates vis-à-vis one another and to float jointly against the U.S. dollar. Spain joined the EMS in June 1989, the United Kingdom in October 1990, and Portugal in April 1992.

The exchange rate mechanism (ERM) of the European Monetary System worked as follows. The exchange rate between every pair of currencies of the participating countries was not allowed to fluctuate outside narrow limits around a fixed exchange rate. (The limits were typically $\pm$ 2.25% but were raised to $\pm$ 15% in July 1993.) When the exchange rate between two countries' currencies moved outside of these limits, the central banks of both countries were supposed to intervene in the foreign exchange market. If, for example, the French franc depreciated below its lower limit against the German mark, the Bank of France was required to buy francs and sell marks, thereby giving up international reserves. Similarly, the German central bank also was required to intervene to buy marks and sell francs and consequently increase its international reserves. The EMS thus required that intervention be symmetric when a currency fell outside the limits, with the central bank with the weak currency giving up international reserves and the one with the strong currency gaining them. Central bank intervention was also very common even when the exchange rate was within the limits, but in this case, if one central bank intervened, no others were required to intervene as well.

A serious shortcoming of fixed exchange rate systems such as the Bretton Woods system or the European Monetary System is that they can lead to foreign exchange crises involving a "speculative attack" on a currency—massive sales of a weak currency or purchases of a strong currency to cause a sharp change in the exchange rate. In the following application, we use our model of exchange rate determination to understand how the September 1992 exchange rate crisis that rocked the European Monetary System came about.

Application The Foreign Exchange Crisis of September 1992

In the aftermath of German reunification in October 1990, the German central bank, the Bundesbank, faced rising inflationary pressures, with inflation having accelerated from below 3% in 1990 to near 5% by 1992. To get monetary growth under control and to dampen inflation, the Bundesbank raised German interest rates to near double-digit levels. Figure 3 shows the consequences of these actions by the Bundesbank in the foreign exchange market for sterling. Note that in the diagram, the pound sterling is the domestic currency and R^D is the expected return on sterling deposits, while the foreign currency is the German mark (deutsche mark, DM), so R^F is the expected return on mark deposits.

The increase in German interest rates i^F shifted the R^F schedule rightward to R_2^F in Figure 3, so that the intersection of the R_1^D and the R_2^F schedules at point 1′

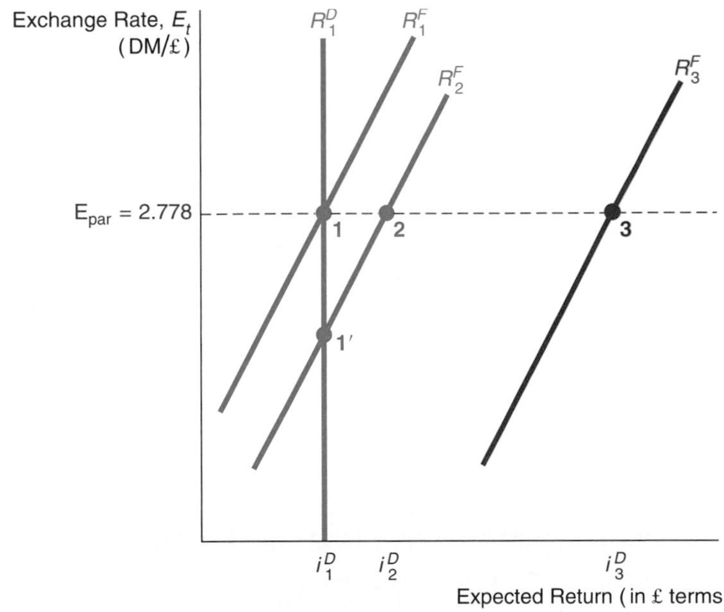

FIGURE 3 Foreign Exchange Market for British Pounds in 1992

The realization by speculators that the United Kingdom would soon devalue the pound increased the expected return on foreign (German mark, DM) deposits and shifted R_2^F rightward to R_3^F. The result was the need for a much greater purchase of pounds by the British central bank to raise the interest rate to i_3^D to keep the exchange rate at DM 2.778 per pound.

was below the lower exchange rate limit (2.778 marks per pound, denoted E_{par}) under the exchange rate mechanism. To lower the value of the mark relative to the pound and restore the pound/mark exchange rate to within the ERM limits, either the Bank of England had to pursue a contractionary monetary policy, thereby raising British interest rates to i_2^D and shifting the R_1^D schedule to the right to point 2, or the Bundesbank could pursue an expansionary monetary policy, thereby lowering German interest rates, which would shift the R^F schedule to the left to move back to point 1. (The shifts in R^D to point 2 or R^F to point 1 are not shown in the figure.)

The catch was that the Bundesbank, whose primary goal is fighting inflation, was unwilling to pursue an expansionary monetary policy, while the British, who were facing their worst recession in the postwar period, were unwilling to pursue a contractionary monetary policy to prop up the pound. This impasse became clear when in response to great pressure from other members of the EMS, the Bundesbank was willing to lower its lending rates by only a token amount on September 14 after a speculative attack was mounted on the currencies of the Scandinavian countries. So at some point in the near future, the value of the pound would have to decline to point 1′. Speculators now knew that the appreciation of the mark was imminent and hence that the value of foreign (mark) deposits would rise in value relative to the pound. As a result, the expected return on mark deposits increased sharply, shifting the R^F schedule to R_3^F in Figure 3.

The huge potential losses on pound deposits and potential gains on mark deposits caused a massive sell-off of pounds (and purchases of marks) by speculators. The need for the British central bank to intervene to raise the value of the pound now became much greater and required a huge rise in British interest rates all the way to i_3^D. After a major intervention effort on the part of the Bank of England, which included a rise in its lending rate from 10% to 15% that still wasn't enough, the British were finally forced to give up on September 16: They pulled out of the ERM indefinitely, allowing the pound to depreciate by 10% against the mark.

Speculative attacks on other currencies forced devaluation of the Spanish peseta by 5% and the Italian lira by 15%. To defend its currency, the Swedish central bank was forced to raise its daily lending rate to the astronomical level of 500%! By the time the crisis was over, the British, French, Italian, Spanish, and Swedish central banks had intervened to the tune of $100 billion; the Bundesbank alone had laid out $50 billion for foreign exchange intervention. Because foreign exchange crises lead to large changes in central banks' holdings of international reserves and thus affect the official reserve asset items in the balance of payments, these crises are also referred to as **balance-of-payments crises.**

The attempt to prop up the European Monetary System was not cheap for these central banks. It is estimated that they lost $4 to $6 billion as a result of exchange rate intervention during the crisis.

THE PRACTICING FINANCIAL INSTITUTION MANAGER

Profiting from a Foreign Exchange Crisis

Large banks and other financial institutions often conduct foreign exchange trading operations that generate substantial profits for their parent institution. When a foreign exchange crisis like the one that occurred in September 1992 comes along, foreign exchange traders and speculators are presented with a golden opportunity. The foregoing analysis of this crisis helps explain why.

As we saw in Figure 3, the high German interest rates resulted in a situation in which the British pound was overvalued, in that the equilibrium exchange rate in the absence of intervention by the British and German central banks was below the lower exchange rate limit of 2.778 German marks per British pound. Once foreign exchange traders realized that the central banks would not be willing to intervene sufficiently or alter their policies to keep the value of the pound above the 2.778-mark-per-pound lower limit, the traders were presented with a "heads I win, tails you lose" bet. They knew that there was only one direction in which the exchange rate could go—down—and so they were almost sure to make money by buying marks and selling pounds. Our analysis of Figure 3 reflects this state of affairs; another way of looking at this one-sided bet is to recognize that it implies that the expected return on mark-denominated deposits increased sharply, shifting the R^F schedule to R^F_3 in Figure 3.

Savvy foreign exchange traders, who read the writing on the wall early in September 1992, sold pounds and bought marks. When the pound depreciated 10% against the mark after September 16, they made huge profits because the marks they had bought could now be sold at a price 10% higher. Foreign exchange traders at Citibank are reported to have made $200 million in the week of the September 1992 exchange rate crisis—not bad for a week's work! But these profits pale in comparison to those made by George Soros, an investment fund manager whose funds are reported to have run up profits of $1 billion during the crisis. (However, Soros gave some of these profits back in 1994 when he acknowledged that he had suffered a $600 million loss from trades on the yen.) Clearly, foreign exchange trading can be a highly profitable enterprise for financial institutions, particularly during foreign exchange rate crises.

Application The Mexican Peso Crisis of December 1994

As part of a reform plan initiated in 1987 to stabilize the Mexican economy, the Mexican government decided to put limits on the movements of the peso against the dollar. When the ruling party's presidential candidate was assassinated in March 1994, investors became concerned that the government might devalue the currency despite promises not to do so. The result was a speculative attack on the peso that not only brought down the peso but also threatened to bring down the currencies of other developing countries, particularly those in Latin America. Figure 3 can be used to understand the sequence of events during the Mexican peso crisis. We just need to recognize that R^D is now the expected return on peso deposits and, since the foreign currency is the dollar, R^F is the expected return on dollar deposits, with both denominated in the domestic currency, the peso.

Because of investors' concerns that the peso might be devalued after the March assassination, the expected return on dollar deposits rose, thus moving the R^F schedule from R^F_1 to R^F_2 in Figure 3. The result was that the intersection of R^D_1 and R^F_2 was below the lower exchange limit E_{par} of around 30 cents per peso. To keep the peso from falling through this limit, the Mexican authorities needed to buy pesos and sell dollars, to raise interest rates to i^D_2 by shifting the R^D curve to the right. This is exactly what they did, raising interest rates from around 10% to over 20% and losing close to half of their $30 billion in international reserves in the process. For the time being, the peso held, but more bad luck was to hit the Mexicans. An uprising in the southern state of Chiapas, the assassination of another high official in the ruling party, and concerns about the large current account deficit and particularly about the health of the banking system led to further rumors of devaluation. Now the R^F curve shifted even farther to the right, say, to R^F_3, and the Mexican authorities intervened further, doubling interest rates again and almost completely exhausting the nation's foreign exchange reserves. Once speculators guessed that the Mexicans were running out of reserves, the game was up. With near certainty that the new Mexican government installed on December 1 would be forced to devalue, the expected return on dollar deposits increased sharply, shifting R^F even farther to the right, making a devaluation inevitable. On December 20, Mexico's government had to devalue the peso; it had lost more than half its value by early 1995.

Application The East Asian Currency Crisis of 1997

The East Asian currency crisis in 1997 started in Thailand. We use Figure 3 to demonstrate what happened during this crisis, again assuming that dollars are the foreign currency so that R^D is the expected return on deposits denominated in the Thai currency, the baht, and R^F is the expected return on dollar deposits. By May 1997, concerns about the large current account deficit in Thailand and the weakness in the Thai financial system made foreign creditors nervous and caused speculators to suspect that Thailand might be forced to devalue its currency. The result was a rise in the expected return on dollar deposits, which shifted the R^F schedule from R^F_1 to R^F_2, so that the intersection of the R^D_1 and R^F_2 curves was below the pegged value E_{par} of around 4 cents per baht. Intervention by the Thai central bank to purchase baht, which raised interest rates to i^D_2, was successful in containing this speculative attack. However, the failure of a major finance company, Finance One, imposed losses on creditors, causing foreign creditors to begin pulling out of the market in earnest and speculators to become even more confident that the Thais could not continue defending the baht. Thus the expected return on dollar deposits shot up further, and R^F moved much farther to the right, to R^F_3. Given the weakness in the financial sector and the loss of reserves, the Thai monetary authorities could not continue to intervene and were forced to give up and let the baht depreciate on July 2.

Concerns that similar problems might be present in other East Asian countries generated speculative attacks against other currencies as well, leading to a scenario akin to that depicted in Figure 3. The result was that one by one, Indonesia, Malaysia, South Korea, and the Philippines were forced to devalue. The outcome was severe depreciations of all these currencies against the dollar: over 30% for the Thai baht, the Malaysian ringgit, the South Korean won, and the Philippine peso, and over 75% for the Indonesian rupiah. Even Hong Kong, Singapore, and Taiwan were subjected to speculative attacks, but because the financial systems in these countries were healthy, the attacks were successfully averted.

As we will see in Chapter 14, the sharp depreciation in Mexico and East Asia led to full-scale financial crises that severely damaged these countries' economies. The foreign exchange crisis that shocked the European Monetary System in September 1992 cost central banks a lot of money, but the public in European countries were not seriously affected. By contrast, the public in Mexico and the crisis countries of East Asia were not so lucky: The speculative attacks that triggered the collapse of those currencies produced severe depressions that caused hardship and political unrest.

European Monetary Union (EMU)

As part of the December 1991 Maastricht Treaty on European Union, the European Economic Commission outlined a plan to achieve the creation of a single European currency starting in 1999. Despite concerns that the plan might blow up, the European Monetary Union with its new common currency, the euro, came into existence right on schedule in January 1999, with eleven of the fifteen European Union countries participating in the monetary union: Austria, Belgium, Finland, France, Germany, Italy, Ireland, Luxembourg, the Netherlands, Portugal and Spain. Denmark, Sweden and the United Kingdom choose not to participate initially, while Greece took some time to meet the economic criteria specified by the Maastricht Treaty (such as having a budget deficit less than 3% of GDP and total government debt less than 60% of GDP) and joined the European Monetary Union in January, 2001.

Starting January 1, 1999 the exchange rates of countries entering the monetary union were fixed permanently to the euro (which became a unit of account), the European Central Bank took over monetary policy from the individual national central banks, and the governments of the member countries began to issue debt in euros. In January 2002 euro notes and coins began to circulate, and by June 2002 the old national currencies were phased out completely and only euros are used in the member countries.

Advocates of monetary union point out the advantages that the single currency has in eliminating the transactions costs incurred in exchanging one currency for another. In addition, the use of a single currency may promote further integration of the European economies and enhance competition. Skeptics who think that monetary union may be bad for Europe suggest that, because labor will not be very mobile across national boundaries and because fiscal transfers (i.e., tax income from one region being spent on another) from better performing regions to worse performing regions will not take place as occurs in the United States, a single currency may lead to some regions of Europe being depressed for substantial periods of time while other regions are booming.

Whether the euro will be good for the economies of Europe and increase their GDP is an open question. However, the motive behind monetary union may be more political than economic. European monetary union may encourage political union, producing a unified Europe that can play a stronger economic and political role on the world stage.

CAPITAL CONTROLS

Because capital flows have been an important element in the currency crises in Mexico and East Asia, politicians and some economists have advocated that capital mobility in emerging market countries should be restricted with capital controls in order to avoid financial instability. Are capital controls a good idea?

Controls on Capital Outflows

Capital outflows can promote financial instability in emerging market countries because when domestic residents and foreigners pull their capital out of a country, the resulting capital outflow forces a country to devalue its currency. This is why recently some politicians in emerging market countries have found capital controls particularly attractive. For example, Prime Minister Mahathir of Malaysia instituted capital controls in 1998 to restrict outflows in the aftermath of the East Asian crisis.

Although these controls sound like a good idea, they suffer from several disadvantages. First, empirical evidence indicates that controls on capital outflows are seldom effective during a crisis because the private sector finds ingenious ways to evade them and has little difficulty moving funds out of the country.[8] Second, the evidence suggests that capital flight may even increase after controls are put into place because confidence in the government is weakened. Third, controls on capital outflows often lead to corruption, as government officials get paid off to look the other way when domestic residents are trying to move funds abroad. Fourth, controls on capital outflows may lull governments into thinking they do not have to take the steps to reform their financial systems to deal with the crisis, with the result that opportunities are lost to improve the functioning of the economy.

Controls on Capital Inflows

Although most economists find the arguments against controls on capital outflows persuasive, controls on capital inflows receive more support. Supporters reason that if speculative capital cannot come in, then it cannot go out suddenly and create a crisis. Our analysis of the financial crises in East Asia in Chapter 7 provides support for this view by suggesting that capital inflows can lead to a lending boom and excessive risk taking on the part of banks, which then helps trigger a financial crisis.

However, controls on capital inflows have the undesirable feature that they may block from entering a country funds that would be used for productive investment opportunities. Although such controls may limit the fuel supplied to lending booms through capital flows, over time they produce substantial distortions and misallocation of resources as households and businesses try to get around them. Indeed, just as with controls on capital outflows, controls on capital inflows can lead to corruption. There are serious doubts whether capital controls can be effective in today's environment, in which trade is open and where there are many financial instruments that make it easier to get around these controls.

On the other hand, there is a strong case for improving bank regulation and supervision so that capital inflows are less likely to produce a lending boom and encourage excessive risk taking by banking institutions. For example, restricting banks in how fast their borrowing could grow might have the impact of substantially limiting capital inflows. Supervisory controls of this type, focusing on the sources of financial fragility rather than the symptoms, can enhance the efficiency of the financial system rather than hampering it.

THE ROLE OF THE IMF

The International Monetary Fund was originally set up under the Bretton Woods system to help countries deal with balance-of-payments problems and stay with the fixed exchange rate by lending to deficit countries. With the collapse of the

[8]See Sebastian Edwards, "How Effective are Capital Controls?" *Journal of Economic Perspectives*, Winter 2000; vol. 13, no. 4, pp. 65–84.

Bretton Woods system of fixed exchange rates in 1971, the IMF has taken on new roles.

The IMF continues to function as a data collector and provides technical assistance to its member countries. Although the IMF no longer attempts to encourage fixed exchange rates, its role as an international lender has become more important recently. This role first came to the fore in the 1980s during the third-world debt crisis, in which the IMF assisted developing countries in repaying their loans. The financial crises in Mexico in 1994–95 and in East Asia in 1997–98 led to huge loans by the IMF to these and other affected countries to help them recover from their financial crises and to prevent the spread of these crises to other countries. This role, in which the IMF acts like an international lender of last resort to cope with financial instability, is indeed highly controversial.

Should the IMF Be an International Lender of Last Resort?

As we saw in Chapter 7, in industrialized countries when a financial crisis occurs and the financial system threatens to seize up, domestic central banks can address matters with a lender-of-last-resort operation to limit the degree of instability in the banking system. In emerging markets, however, where the credibility of the central bank as an inflation-fighter may be in doubt and debt contracts are typically short-term and in foreign currencies, a lender-of-last-resort operation becomes a two-edged sword—as likely to exacerbate the financial crisis as to alleviate it. For example, when the U.S. Federal Reserve engaged in a lender-of-last-resort operation during the 1987 stock market crash (Chapter 7), there was almost no sentiment in the markets that there would be substantially higher inflation. However, for a central bank having less inflation-fighting credibility than the Fed, central bank lending to the financial system in the wake of a financial crisis—even under the lender-of-last-resort rhetoric—may well arouse fears of inflation spiraling out of control, causing an even greater currency depreciation and still greater deterioration of balance sheets. The resulting increase in moral hazard and adverse selection problems in financial markets, along the lines discussed in Chapter 14, would only make the financial crisis worse.

Central banks in emerging market countries therefore have only a very limited ability to successfully engage in a lender-of-last-resort operation. However, liquidity provided by an international lender of last resort does not have these undesirable consequences, and in helping to stabilize the value of the domestic currency it strengthens domestic balance sheets. Moreover, an international lender of last resort may be able to prevent contagion, the situation in which a successful speculative attack on one emerging market currency leads to attacks on other emerging market currencies, spreading financial and economic disruption as it goes. Since a lender of last resort for emerging market countries is needed at times, and since it cannot be provided domestically, there is a strong rationale for an international institution to fill this role. Indeed, since Mexico's financial crisis in 1994, the International Monetary Fund and other international agencies have stepped into the lender-of-last-resort role and provided emergency lending to countries threatened by financial instability.

However, support from an international lender of last resort brings risks of its own, especially the risk that the perception it is standing ready to bail out irresponsible financial institutions may lead to excessive risk taking of the sort that makes financial crises more likely. In the Mexican and East Asian crises, governments in the crisis countries have used IMF support to protect depositors and other creditors of banking institutions from losses. This safety net creates a well-known moral hazard problem because the depositors and other creditors have less incentive to monitor these banking institutions and withdraw their deposits if the institutions are taking on too much risk. The result is that these institutions are encouraged to take on excessive risks. Indeed, critics of the IMF, most prominently the Congressional Commission headed by Professor Alan Meltzer of Carnegie-Mellon University, contend that its lending in the Mexican crisis, which was used to bail out foreign lenders, set the stage for the East Asian crisis because these lenders expected to be bailed out if things went wrong and thus provided funds that were used to fuel excessive risk taking.[9]

An international lender of last resort must find ways to limit this moral hazard problem, or it can actually make the situation worse. The international lender of last resort can make it clear that it will extend liquidity to governments that put the proper measures in place to prevent excessive risk taking. In addition, it can reduce the incentives for risk taking by restricting the ability of governments to bail out stockholders and large uninsured creditors of domestic financial institutions.

One problem that arises for international organizations like the IMF engaged in lender-of-last-resort operations is that they know that if they don't come to the rescue, the emerging market country will suffer extreme hardship and possible political instability. Politicians in the crisis country may exploit these concerns and engage in a game of chicken with the international lender of last resort: they resist necessary reforms, hoping that the IMF will cave in. Elements of this game were present in the Mexico crisis of 1995 and were also a particularly important feature of the negotiations between the IMF and Indonesia during the Asian crisis.

The IMF would produce better outcomes if it makes it clear that it will not play this game. Just as giving in to ill-behaved children may be the easy way out in the short run, but supports a pattern of poor behavior in the long run, some critics worry that the IMF may not be tough enough when confronted by short-run humanitarian concerns. For example, these critics have been particularly critical of the IMF's lending to the Russian government, which has resisted adopting appropriate reforms to stabilize its financial system.

The IMF has also been criticized for imposing on the East Asian countries so-called austerity programs that focus on tight macroeconomic policies rather than on microeconomic policies to fix the crisis-causing problems in the financial sector. Such programs are likely to increase resistance to IMF recommendations, particularly in emerging market countries. Austerity programs allow these politicians to label institutions such as the IMF as being anti-growth, rhetoric that helps the politicians to mobilize the public against the IMF and avoid doing what they really need to do to reform the financial system in their country. IMF programs focused instead on microeconomic policies related to the financial sector would increase the likelihood that the IMF will be seen as a helping hand in the creation of a more efficient financial system.

An important historical feature of successful lender-of-last-resort operations is that the faster the lending is done, the lower is the amount that actually has to be lent. An excellent example occurred in the aftermath of the stock market crash on October 19, 1987 (Chapter 7). At the end of that day, in order to service their customers' accounts, securities firms needed to borrow several billion dol-

[9]See International Financial Institution Advisory Commission, *Report* (IFIAC: Washington, D.C., 2000).

lars to maintain orderly trading. However, given the unprecedented developments, banks were very nervous about extending further loans to these firms. Upon learning this, the Federal Reserve engaged in an immediate lender-of-last-resort operation, with the Fed making it clear that it would provide liquidity to banks making loans to the securities industry. Indeed, what is striking about this episode is that the extremely quick intervention of the Fed resulted not only in a negligible impact of the stock market crash on the economy, but also meant that the amount of liquidity that the Fed needed to supply to the economy was not very large.

The ability of the Fed to engage in a lender-of-last-resort operation within a day of a substantial shock to the financial system is in sharp contrast to the amount of time it has taken the IMF to supply liquidity during the recent crises in Mexico and Asian countries, which exceeded $50 billion. Because IMF lending facilities were originally designed to provide funds after a country was experiencing a balance of payments crisis and because the conditions for the loan had to be negotiated, it took several months before the IMF made funds available. By this time, the crisis had gotten much worse—and much larger sums of funds were needed to cope with the crisis, often stretching the resources of the IMF. One reason that central banks can lend so much more quickly than the IMF is that they have set up procedures in advance to provide loans, with the terms and conditions for this lending agreed upon beforehand. The need for quick provision of liquidity to keep the loan amount manageable argues for similar credit facilities at the international lender of last resort so that funds can be provided quickly as long as the borrower meets conditions such as properly supervising its banks or keeping budget deficits low. A step in this direction was made in 1999 when the IMF set up a new lending facility, the Contingent Credit Line, so it can provide liquidity faster during a crisis.

The debate on whether the world will be better off with the IMF operating as an international lender of last resort is currently a hot one. Much attention is being focused on making the IMF more effective in performing this role, and redesign of the IMF is at the center of proposals for a new international financial architecture to help reduce international financial instability.

INTERNATIONAL CONSIDERATIONS AND MONETARY POLICY

Our analysis in this chapter so far has suggested several ways in which monetary policy can be affected by international events. And these occurrences can have significant implications for the way monetary policy is conducted.

Direct Effects of the Foreign Exchange Market on the Money Supply

When central banks intervene in the foreign exchange market, they acquire or sell off international reserves, and their monetary base is affected. When a central bank intervenes in the foreign exchange market, it gives up some control of its money supply. For example, in the early 1970s, the German central bank faced a dilemma. In attempting to keep the German mark from appreciating too much against the U.S. dollar, the Germans acquired huge quantities of international reserves, leading to a rapid rate of money growth that the German central bank considered inflationary.

The Bundesbank could have tried to halt the growth of the money supply by stopping its intervention in the foreign exchange market and reasserting control over its own money supply. Such a strategy has a major drawback when the central bank is under pressure not to allow its currency to appreciate: The lower price of imports and higher price of exports as a result of an appreciation in its currency will hurt domestic producers and increase unemployment.

Because the U.S. dollar has been a reserve currency, the U.S. monetary base and money supply have been less affected by developments in the foreign exchange market. As long as foreign central banks, rather than the Fed, intervene to keep the value of the dollar from changing, American holdings of international reserves are unaffected. The ability to conduct monetary policy is typically easier when a country's currency is a reserve currency.[10]

Balance-of-Payments Considerations

Under the Bretton Woods system, balance-of-payments considerations were more important than they are under the current managed float regime. When a nonreserve currency country is running balance-of-payments deficits, it necessarily gives up international reserves. To keep from running out of these reserves, under the Bretton Woods system it had to implement contractionary monetary policy to strengthen its currency. Exactly that occurred in the United Kingdom before its devaluation of the pound in 1967. When policy became expansionary, the balance of payments deteriorated, and the British were forced to "slam on the brakes" by implementing a contractionary policy. Once the balance of payments improved, policy became more expansionary until the deteriorating balance of payments again forced the British to pursue a contractionary policy. Such on-again, off-again actions became known as a "stop-go" policy, and the domestic instability it created was criticized severely.

Because the United States is a major reserve currency country, it can run large balance-of-payments deficits without losing huge amounts of international reserves. This does not mean, however, that the Federal Reserve is never influenced by developments in the U.S. balance of payments. Current account deficits in the United States suggest that American businesses may be losing some of their ability to compete because the value of the dollar is too high. In addition, large U.S. balance-of-payments deficits lead to balance-of-payments surpluses in other countries, which can in turn lead to large increases in their holdings of international reserves (that was especially true under the Bretton Woods system). Because such increases put a strain on the international financial system and may stimulate world inflation, the Fed worries about U.S. balance-of-payments and current account deficits. To help shrink these deficits, the Fed might pursue a more contractionary monetary policy.

Exchange Rate Considerations

Unlike balance-of-payments considerations, which have become less important under the current managed float system, exchange rate considerations now play a greater role in the conduct of monetary policy. If a central bank does not want to see its currency fall in value, it may pursue a more contractionary monetary policy of reducing the money supply to raise the domestic interest rate, thereby strengthening its currency. Similarly, if a country experiences an appreciation in

[10]However, the central bank of a reserve currency country must worry about a shift away from the use of its currency for international reserves.

its currency, domestic industry may suffer from increased foreign competition and may pressure the central bank to pursue a higher rate of money growth in order to lower the exchange rate.

The pressure to manipulate exchange rates seems to be greater for central banks in countries other than the United States, but even the Federal Reserve is not completely immune. The growing tide of protectionism stemming from the inability of American firms to compete with foreign firms because of the strengthening dollar from 1980 to early 1985 stimulated congressional critics of the Fed to call for a more expansionary monetary policy to lower the value of the dollar. As we saw in Chapter 7, the Fed then did let money growth surge to very high levels. A policy to bring the dollar down was confirmed in the Plaza Agreement of September 1985, in which the finance ministers from the five most important industrial nations in the free world (the United States, Japan, West Germany, the United Kingdom, and France) agreed to intervene in foreign exchange markets to achieve a decline in the dollar. The dollar continued to fall rapidly after the Plaza Agreement, and the Fed played an important role in this decline by continuing to expand the money supply at a rapid rate.

SUMMARY

1. An unsterilized central bank intervention in which the domestic currency is sold to purchase foreign assets leads to a gain in international reserves, an increase in the money supply, and a depreciation of the domestic currency. Available evidence suggests, however, that sterilized central bank interventions have little long-term effect on the exchange rate.

2. The balance of payments is a bookkeeping system for recording all payments between a country and foreign countries that have a direct bearing on the movement of funds between them. The official reserve transactions balance is the sum of the current account balance plus the items in the capital account. It indicates the amount of international reserves that must be moved between countries to finance international transactions.

3. Before World War I, the gold standard was predominant. Currencies were convertible into gold, thus fixing exchange rates between countries. After World War II, the Bretton Woods system and the IMF were established to promote a fixed exchange rate system in which the U.S. dollar was convertible into gold. The Bretton Woods system collapsed in 1971. We now have an international financial system that has elements of a managed float and a fixed exchange rate system. Some exchange rates fluctuate from day to day, although central banks intervene in the foreign exchange market, while other exchange rates are fixed, as in the European Monetary System.

4. Controls on capital outflows receive support because they might prevent domestic residents and foreigners from pulling capital out of a country during a crisis and make devaluation less likely. Controls on capital inflows make sense under the theory that if speculative capital cannot flow in, then it cannot go out suddenly and create a crisis. However, capital controls suffer from several disadvantages: They are seldom effective, they lead to corruption, and they may allow governments to avoid taking the steps to reform their financial systems to deal with the crisis.

5. The IMF has recently taken on the role of an international lender of last resort. Because central banks in emerging market countries are unlikely to be able to perform a lender-of-last-resort operation successfully, an international lender of last resort like the IMF is needed to prevent financial instability. However, the IMF's role as an international lender of last resort creates a serious moral hazard problem that can encourage excessive risk taking and make a financial crisis more likely. The IMF thus needs to limit the moral hazard created by its lender-of-last-resort role, but it may find this politically hard to do. In addition, it needs to be able to provide liquidity quickly during a crisis in order to keep manageable the amount of funds lent.

6. Three international considerations affect the conduct of monetary policy: direct effects of the foreign exchange market on the money supply, balance-of-payments considerations, and exchange rate considerations. Inasmuch as the United States has been a reserve currency country in the post-World War II period, U.S. monetary policy has been less affected by developments in the foreign exchange market and its balance of payments than is true for other countries. However, in recent years, exchange rate considerations have been playing a more prominent role in influencing U.S. monetary policy.

KEY TERMS

balance of payments, *p. 344*
balance-of-payments crisis, *p. 356*
Bretton Woods system, *p. 348*
capital account, *p. 346*
current account, *p. 344*
devaluation, *p. 351*
dollarization, *p. 352*
fixed exchange rate regime, *p. 348*
foreign exchange intervention, *p. 339*
gold standard, *p. 347*
International Monetary Fund (IMF), *p. 348*
international reserves, *p. 339*
managed float regime (dirty float), *p. 339*
official reserve transactions balance, *p. 346*
reserve currency, *p. 349*
revaluation, *p. 351*
special drawing rights (SDRs), *p. 354*
sterilized foreign exchange intervention, *p. 342*
T-account, *p. 340*
trade balance, *p. 344*
unsterilized foreign exchange intervention, *p. 341*
World Bank, *p. 349*

QUESTIONS AND PROBLEMS

1. If the Federal Reserve buys dollars in the foreign exchange market but conducts an offsetting open market operation to sterilize the intervention, what will be the impact on international reserves, the money supply, and the exchange rate?

***2.** If the Federal Reserve buys dollars in the foreign exchange market but does not sterilize the intervention, what will be the impact on international reserves, the money supply, and the exchange rate?

3. For each of the following, identify in which part of the balance-of-payments account it appears (current account, capital account, or method of financing) and whether it is a receipt or a payment.

a. A British subject's purchase of a share of Johnson & Johnson stock

b. An American's purchase of an airline ticket from Air France

c. The Swiss government's purchase of U.S. Treasury bills

d. A Japanese's purchase of California oranges

e. $50 million of foreign aid to Honduras

f. A loan by an American bank to Mexico

g. An American bank's borrowing of Eurodollars

***4.** Why does a balance-of-payments deficit for the United States have a different effect on its international reserves than a balance-of-payments deficit for the Netherlands?

5. Under the gold standard, if Britain became more productive relative to the United States, what would happen to the money supply in the two countries? Why would the changes in the money supply help preserve a fixed exchange rate between the United States and Britain?

***6.** What is the exchange rate between dollars and euros if one dollar is convertible into $\frac{1}{20}$ ounce of gold and one euro is convertible into $\frac{1}{40}$ ounce of gold?

7. If a country's par exchange rate was undervalued during the Bretton Woods fixed exchange rate regime, what kind of intervention would that country's central bank be forced to undertake, and what effect would it have on its international reserves and the money supply?

***8.** How can a large balance-of-payments surplus contribute to the country's inflation rate?

9. "If a country wants to keep its exchange rate from changing, it must give up some control over its money supply." Is this statement true, false, or uncertain? Explain your answer.

***10.** Why can balance-of-payments deficits force some countries to implement a contractionary monetary policy?

11. "Balance-of-payments deficits always cause a country to lose international reserves." Is this statement true, false, or uncertain? Explain your answer.

***12.** How can persistent U.S. balance-of-payments deficits stimulate world inflation?

13. "Inflation is not possible under the gold standard." Is this statement true, false, or uncertain? Explain your answer.

***14.** Why is it that in a pure flexible exchange rate system, the foreign exchange market has no direct effects on the money supply? Does this mean that the foreign exchange market has no effect on monetary policy?

15. "The abandonment of fixed exchange rates after 1973 has meant that countries have pursued more independent monetary policies." Is this statement true, false, or uncertain? Explain your answer.

***16.** Are capital controls on capital outflows a good idea? Why or why not?

17. Discuss the pros and cons of capital controls on capital inflows.

***18.** Why might central banks in emerging-market countries find that engaging in a lender-of-last resort operation might be counterproductive? Does this provide a rationale for having an international lender of last resort like the IMF?

19. Has the IMF done a good job in performing the role of the international lender of last resort?

***20.** What steps should an international lender of last resort take to limit moral hazard?

WEB EXERCISES

The International Financial System and Monetary Policy

1. The Federal Reserve publishes information on-line that explains the workings of the foreign exchange market. One such publication can be found at http://www.ny.frb.org/pihome/addpub/usfxm/. Review the table of contents and open Chapter 10, "The Evolution of the International Monetary System." Read this chapter and write a one-page summary that discusses why each monetary standard was dropped in favor of the succeeding one.

2. The International Monetary Fund stands ready to help nations facing monetary crises. Go to http://www.imf.org. Click on the tab labeled "About IMF." What is the stated purpose of the IMF? How many nations participate, and when was it established?

Part 5

The Financial Institutions Industry

Chapter 14 Theory of Financial Structure

Preview

A healthy and vibrant economy requires a financial system that moves funds from people who save to people who have productive investment opportunities. But how does the financial system make sure that your hard-earned savings get channeled to those with productive investment opportunities?

This chapter answers that question by providing a theory for understanding how our financial structure is designed to promote economic efficiency. The theoretical analysis focuses on a few simple but powerful economic concepts that enable us to explain features of our financial markets such as why financial contracts are written as they are, why financial intermediaries are more important than securities markets for getting funds to borrowers, and why financial crises occur and have such severe consequences for the health of the economy.

BASIC FACTS ABOUT FINANCIAL STRUCTURE THROUGHOUT THE WORLD

The financial system is complex in structure and function throughout the world. There are many different types of institutions: banks, insurance companies, mutual funds, stock and bond markets, and so on—all of which are regulated by government. The financial system channels billions of dollars per year from savers to people with productive investment opportunities. If we take a close look at financial structure all over the world, we need to explain eight basic (and sometimes surprising) facts in order to understand how the financial system works.

The pie chart in Figure 1 indicates how American businesses financed their activities using external funds (those obtained from outside the business itself) in the period 1970–1996. The *Bank loans* category is made up primarily of bank loans; *Nonbank loans* is made up primarily of loans by other financial intermediaries. The *bonds* category includes marketable debt securities such as corporate

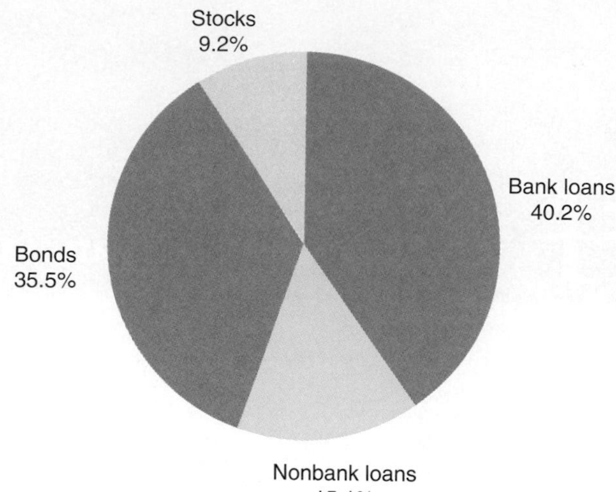

FIGURE 1 Sources of External Funds for Nonfinancial Businesses in the United States

The categories of external funds are as follows: *Bank loans,* which is made up primarily of bank loans; *nonbank loans,* which includes loans from other financial intermediaries; *bonds,* which includes marketable debt securities such as corporate bonds and commercial paper; and *stock,* which consists of issues of new equity (stock market shares). The data are for the period 1970–1996 and are gross flows as percentage of the total, not including trade and other credit data, which are not available.

Source: Reinhard H. Schmidt, "Differences Between Financial Systems in European Countries: Consequences for EMU," in Deutsche Bundesbank, ed., *The Monetary Transmission Process: Recent Developments and Lessons for Europe* (Hampshire: Palgrave Publishers, 2001), p. 222.

bonds and commercial paper. *Stock* consists of issues of new equity (stock market shares). Figure 2 uses the same classifications as Figure 1, and compares the U.S. data to those of Germany and Japan.

Now let us explore the eight basic facts.

1. ***Stocks are not the most important source of external financing for businesses.*** Because so much attention in the media is focused on the stock market, many people have the impression that stocks are the most important sources of financing for American corporations. However, as we can see from the pie chart in Figure 1, the stock market accounted for only a small fraction of the external financing of American businesses in the 1970—1996 period, 9.2%.[1] Similarly small figures apply in the other countries presented in Figure 2 as well. Why is the stock market less important than other sources of financing in the United States and other countries?

[1]The 9.2% figure for the percentage of external financing provided by stocks is based on the flows of external funds to corporations. However, this flow figure is somewhat misleading because when a share of stock is issued, it raises funds permanently, whereas when a bond is issued, it raises funds only temporarily until they are paid back at maturity. To see this, suppose that a firm raises $1000 by selling a share of stock and another $1000 by selling a $1000 one-year bond. In the case of the stock issue, the firm can hold on to the $1000 it raised this way, but to hold on to the $1000 it raised through debt, it has to issue a new $1000 bond every year. If we look at the flow of funds to corporations over a 26-year period, as in Figure 1, the firm will have raised $1000 with a stock issue only once in the 26-year period, while it will have raised $1000 with debt 26 times, once in each of the 26 years. Thus it will look like debt is 26 times more important than stocks in raising funds, even though our example indicates that they are actually equally important for the firm.

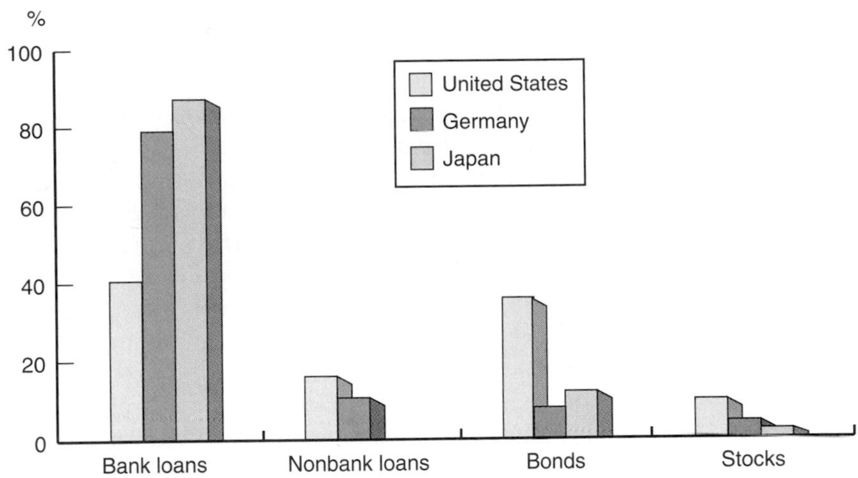

FIGURE 2 Sources of External Funds for Nonfinancial Businesses: A Comparison of the United States with Germany and Japan

The categories of external funds are the same as in Figure 1 and the data are for the period 1970–1996.

Source: Reinhard H. Schmidt, "Differences Between Financial Systems in European Countries: Consequences for EMU," in Deutsche Bundesbank, ed., *The Monetary Transmission Process: Recent Developments and Lessons for Europe* (Hampshire: Palgrave Publishers, 2001), p. 222.

2. *Issuing marketable debt and equity securities is not the primary way in which businesses finance their operations.* Figure 1 shows that bonds are a far more important source of financing than stocks in the United States (35.5% versus 9.2%). However, stocks and bonds combined (44.7%), which make up the total share of marketable securities, still supply less than one-half of the external funds corporations need to finance their activities. The fact that issuing marketable securities is not the most important source of financing is true elsewhere in the world as well. Indeed, as we see in Figure 2, most countries have a much smaller share of external financing supplied by marketable securities than the United States. Why don't businesses use marketable securities more extensively to finance their activities?

3. *Indirect finance, which involves the activities of financial intermediaries, is many times more important than direct finance, in which businesses raise funds directly from lenders in financial markets.* Direct finance involves the sale to households of marketable securities such as stocks and bonds. The 44.7% share of stocks and bonds as a source of external financing for American businesses actually greatly overstates the importance of direct finance in our financial system. Since 1970, less than 5% of newly issued corporate bonds and commercial paper and around 50% of stocks have been sold directly to American households. The rest of these securities have been bought primarily by financial intermediaries such as insurance companies, pension funds, and mutual funds. These figures indicate that direct finance is used in less than 5% of the external funding of American business. Because in most countries marketable securities are an even less important source of finance than in the United States, direct finance is also far less important than indirect finance in the rest of the world. Why have financial intermediaries and indirect finance been so important in financial markets? In recent years, indirect finance has been declining in importance. Why is this happening?

4. *Banks are the most important source of external funds used to finance businesses.* As we can see in Figures 1 and 2, the primary sources of external funds for businesses throughout the world are loans (55.3% in the United States). Most of these loans are bank loans, so the data suggest that banks have the most important role in financing business activities. An extraordinary fact that surprises most people is that in an average year in the United States, over 4 times more funds are raised with bank loans than with stocks. Banks are even more important in countries such as Germany and Japan than they are in the United States, and in developing countries banks play an even more important role in the financial system than they do in the industrialized countries. What makes banks so important to the workings of the financial system? Although banks are very important, their share of external funds for businesses has been declining in recent years. What is driving this decline?

5. *The financial system is among the most heavily regulated sectors of the economy.* You learned in Chapter 2 that the financial system is heavily regulated, not only in the United States but in all other developed countries as well. Governments regulate financial markets primarily to promote the provision of information in part to protect consumers, and to ensure the soundness (stability) of the financial system. Why are financial markets so extensively regulated throughout the world?

6. *Only large, well-established corporations have easy access to securities markets to finance their activities.* Individuals and smaller businesses that are not well established are less likely to raise funds by issuing marketable securities. Instead, they most often obtain their financing from banks. Why do only large, well-known corporations find it easier to raise funds in securities markets?

7. *Collateral is a prevalent feature of debt contracts for both households and businesses.* **Collateral** is property that is pledged to the lender to guarantee payment in the event that the borrower should be unable to make debt payments. Collateralized debt (which is also known as **secured debt** to contrast it with **unsecured debt,** such as credit card debt, which is not collateralized) is the predominant form of household debt and is widely used in business borrowing as well. The majority of household debt in the United States consists of collateralized loans: Your automobile is collateral for your auto loan, and your house is collateral for your mortgage. Commercial and farm mortgages, for which property is pledged as collateral, make up one-quarter of borrowing by nonfinancial businesses; corporate bonds and other bank loans also often involve pledges of collateral. Why is collateral such an important feature of debt contracts?

8. *Debt contracts are typically extremely complicated legal documents that place substantial restrictions on the behavior of the borrower.* Many students think about a debt contract as a simple IOU that can be written on a single piece of paper. The reality of debt contracts is far different, however. In all countries, bond or loan contracts are typically long legal documents with provisions (called **restrictive covenants**) that restrict and specify certain activities that the borrower can engage in. Restrictive covenants are not just a feature of debt contracts for businesses; for example, personal automobile loan and home mortgage contracts have restrictive covenants that require the borrower to maintain sufficient insurance on the automobile or house purchased with the loan. Why are debt contracts so complex and restrictive?

As you may recall from Chapter 2, an important feature of financial markets is that they have substantial transaction and information costs. A theoretical analysis of how these costs affect financial markets provides us with solutions to the eight basic facts, which in turn provide us with a much deeper understanding of how our financial system works. In the next section we examine the impact of transaction costs on the structure of our financial system. Then we turn to how information costs affect financial structure.

TRANSACTION COSTS

Transaction costs are a major problem in financial markets. An example will make this clear.

How Transaction Costs Influence Financial Structure

Say you have $5000 you would like to invest, and you think about investing in the stock market. Because you have only $5000, you can buy only a small number of shares. The stockbroker tells you that your purchase is so small that the brokerage commission for buying the stock you picked will be a large percentage of the purchase price of the shares. If instead you decide to buy a bond, the problem is even worse because the smallest denomination for some bonds you might want to buy is as much as $10,000 and you do not have that much to invest. Indeed, the broker may not even be interested in your business at all because the small size of your account doesn't make spending time on it worthwhile. You are disappointed and realize that you will not be able to use financial markets to earn a return on your hard-earned savings. You can take some consolation, however, in the fact that you are not alone in being stymied by high transaction costs. This is a fact of life for most of us: Most American households never own any securities.

You also face another problem because of transaction costs. Because you have only a small amount of funds available, you can make only a restricted number of investments. That is, you have to put all your eggs in one basket, and your inability to diversify will subject you to a lot of risk.

How Financial Intermediaries Reduce Transaction Costs

This example of the problems posed by transaction costs and the example outlined in Chapter 2 when legal costs kept you from making a loan to Carl the Carpenter illustrate that small savers like you are frozen out of financial markets and are unable to benefit from them. Fortunately, financial intermediaries, an important part of the financial structure, have evolved to reduce transaction costs and allow small savers and borrowers to benefit from the existence of financial markets.

Economies of Scale One solution to the problem of high transaction costs is to bundle the funds of many investors together so that they can take advantage of *economies of scale,* the reduction in transaction costs per dollar of investment as the size (scale) of transactions increases. By bundling investors' funds together, transaction costs for each individual investor are far smaller. Economies of scale exist because the total cost of carrying out a transaction in financial markets increases only a little as the size of the transaction grows. For example, the cost of arranging a purchase of 10,000 shares of stock is not much greater than the cost of arranging a purchase of 50 shares of stock.

The presence of economies of scale in financial markets helps explain why financial intermediaries developed and are such an important part of our financial structure. The clearest example of a financial intermediary that arose because of economies of scale is a mutual fund. A *mutual fund* is a financial intermediary that sells shares to individuals and then invests the proceeds in bonds or stocks. Because it buys large blocks of stocks or bonds, a mutual fund can take advantage of lower transaction costs. These cost savings are then passed on to individual investors after the mutual fund has taken its cut in the form of management fees for administering their accounts. An additional benefit for individual investors is that a mutual fund is large enough to purchase a widely diversified portfolio of securities. The increased diversification for individual investors reduces their risk, thus making them better off.

Economies of scale are also important in lowering the costs of things, such as computer technology, that financial institutions need to accomplish their tasks. Once a large mutual fund has invested a lot of money in setting up a telecommunications system, for example, it can be used for a huge number of transactions at a low cost per transaction.

Expertise Financial intermediaries also arise because they are better able to develop expertise to lower transaction costs. Mutual funds, banks, and other financial intermediaries develop expertise in computer technology so that they can cheaply provide convenient services such as toll-free numbers that allow you to check on how well your investments are doing or the ability to write checks on your account.

An important outcome of a financial intermediary's low transaction costs is that they allow a financial intermediary to provide its customers with *liquidity services,* services that make it easier for customers to conduct transactions. Money market mutual funds, for example, allow shareholders to write checks that enable them to pay their bills easily while at the same time paying them high interest rates.

ASYMMETRIC INFORMATION: ADVERSE SELECTION AND MORAL HAZARD

The presence of transaction costs in financial markets explains in part why financial intermediaries and indirect finance play such an important role in financial markets (fact 3). To understand financial structure more fully, however, we turn to the role of information in financial markets.[2]

Asymmetric information—one party having insufficient knowledge about the other party involved in a transaction to make accurate decisions—is an important aspect of financial markets. For example, managers of a corporation know

[2]An excellent survey of the literature on information and financial structure that expands on the topics discussed in the rest of this chapter is contained in Mark Gertler, "Financial Structure and Aggregate Economic Activity: An Overview," *Journal of Money, Credit and Banking* 20 (1988): 559–588.

whether they are honest or have better information about how well their business is doing than the stockholders do. The presence of asymmetric information leads to adverse selection and moral hazard problems, which were introduced in Chapter 2.

Adverse selection is an asymmetric information problem that occurs *before* the transaction occurs: Potential bad credit risks are the ones who most actively seek out loans. Thus the parties who are the most likely to produce an undesirable outcome are most likely to want to engage in the transaction. For example, big risk takers or outright crooks might be the most eager to take out a loan because they know that they are unlikely to pay it back. Because adverse selection increases the chances that a loan might be made to a bad credit risk, lenders may decide not to make any loans even though there are good credit risks in the marketplace.

Moral hazard arises *after* the transaction occurs: The lender runs the risk that the borrower will engage in activities that are undesirable from the lender's point of view because they make it less likely that the loan will be paid back. For example, once borrowers have obtained a loan, they may take on big risks (which have possible high returns but also run a greater risk of default) because they are playing with someone else's money. Because moral hazard lowers the probability that the loan will be repaid, lenders may decide that they would rather not make a loan.

THE LEMONS PROBLEM: HOW ADVERSE SELECTION INFLUENCES FINANCIAL STRUCTURE

A particular characterization of the adverse selection problem and how it interferes with the efficient functioning of a market was outlined in a famous article by George Akerlof, a Nobel prize-winner. It is referred to as the "lemons problem" because it resembles the problem created by lemons in the used-car market.[3] Potential buyers of used cars are frequently unable to assess the quality of the car; that is, they can't tell whether a particular used car is a good car that will run well or a lemon that will continually give them grief. The price that a buyer pays must therefore reflect the *average* quality of the cars in the market, somewhere between the low value of a lemon and the high value of a good car.

The owner of a used car, by contrast, is more likely to know whether the car is a peach or a lemon. If the car is a lemon, the owner is more than happy to sell it at the price the buyer is willing to pay, which, being somewhere between the value of a lemon and a good car, is greater than the lemon's value. However, if the car is a peach, the owner knows that the car is undervalued by the price the buyer is willing to pay, and so the owner may not want to sell it. As a result of this adverse selection, very few good used cars will come to the market. Because the average quality of a used car available in the market will be low and because very few people want to buy a lemon, there will be few sales. The used-car market will then function poorly, if at all.

---

[3]George Akerlof, "The Market for 'Lemons': Quality, Uncertainty and the Market Mechanism," *Quarterly Journal of Economics* 84 (1970): 488–500. Two important papers that have applied the lemons problem analysis to financial markets are Stewart Myers and N. S. Majluf, "Corporate Financing and Investment Decisions When Firms Have Information That Investors Do Not Have," *Journal of Financial Economics* 13 (1984): 187–221, and Bruce Greenwald, Joseph E. Stiglitz, and Andrew Weiss, "Information Imperfections in the Capital Market and Macroeconomic Fluctuations," *American Economic Review* 74 (1984): 194–199.

Lemons in the Stock and Bond Markets

A similar lemons problem arises in securities markets, that is, the debt (bond) and equity (stock) markets. Suppose that our friend Irving the Investor, a potential buyer of securities such as common stock, can't distinguish between good firms with high expected profits and low risk and bad firms with low expected profits and high risk. In this situation, Irving will be willing to pay only a price that reflects the *average* quality of firms issuing securities—a price that lies between the value of securities from bad firms and the value of those from good firms. If the owners or managers of a good firm have better information than Irving and *know* that they are a good firm, they know that their securities are undervalued and will not want to sell them to Irving at the price he is willing to pay. The only firms willing to sell Irving securities will be bad firms (because the price is higher than the securities are worth). Our friend Irving is not stupid; he does not want to hold securities in bad firms, and hence he will decide not to purchase securities in the market. In an outcome similar to that in the used-car market, this securities market will not work very well because few firms will sell securities in it to raise capital.

The analysis is similar if Irving considers purchasing a corporate debt instrument in the bond market rather than an equity share. Irving will buy a bond only if its interest rate is high enough to compensate him for the average default risk of the good and bad firms trying to sell the debt. The knowledgeable owners of a good firm realize that they will be paying a higher interest rate than they should, and so they are unlikely to want to borrow in this market. Only the bad firms will be willing to borrow, and because investors like Irving are not eager to buy bonds issued by bad firms, they will probably not buy any bonds at all. Few bonds are likely to sell in this market, and so it will not be a good source of financing.

The analysis we have just conducted explains fact 2—why marketable securities are not the primary source of financing for businesses in any country in the world. It also partly explains fact 1—why stocks are not the most important source of financing for American businesses. The presence of the lemons problem keeps securities markets such as the stock and bond markets from being effective in channeling funds from savers to borrowers.

Tools to Help Solve Adverse Selection Problems

In the absence of asymmetric information, the lemons problem goes away. If buyers know as much about the quality of used cars as sellers so that all involved can tell a good car from a bad one, buyers will be willing to pay full value for good used cars. Because the owners of good used cars can now get a fair price, they will be willing to sell them in the market. The market will have many transactions and will do its intended job of channeling good cars to people who want them.

Similarly, if purchasers of securities can distinguish good firms from bad, they will pay the full value of securities issued by good firms, and good firms will sell their securities in the market. The securities market will then be able to move funds to the good firms that have the most productive investment opportunities.

Private Production and Sale of Information The solution to the adverse selection problem in financial markets is to eliminate asymmetric information by furnishing people supplying funds with full details about the individuals or firms seeking to finance their investment activities. One way to get this material to saver-lenders is to have private companies collect and produce information that distinguishes good from bad firms and then sell it to purchasers of securities. In the United States, companies such as Standard and Poor's, Moody's, and Value Line gather information on firms' balance sheet positions and investment activities, publish these data, and sell them to subscribers (individuals, libraries, and financial intermediaries involved in purchasing securities).

The system of private production and sale of information does not completely solve the adverse selection problem in securities markets, however, because of the so-called **free-rider problem.** The free-rider problem occurs when people who do not pay for information take advantage of the information that other people have paid for. The free-rider problem suggests that the private sale of information will be only a partial solution to the lemons problem. To see why, suppose that you have just purchased information that tells you which firms are good and which are bad. You believe that this purchase is worthwhile because you can make up the cost of acquiring this information, and then some, by purchasing the securities of good firms that are undervalued. However, when our savvy (free-riding) investor Irving sees you buying certain securities, he buys right along with you, even though he has not paid for any information. If many other investors act as Irving does, the increased demand for the undervalued good securities will cause their low price to be bid up immediately to reflect the securities' true value. As a result of all these free riders, you can no longer buy the securities for less than their true value. Now because you will not gain any profits from purchasing the information, you realize that you never should have paid for this information in the first place. If other investors come to the same realization, private firms and individuals may not be able to sell enough of this information to make it worth their while to gather and produce it. The weakened ability of private firms to profit from selling information will mean that less information is produced in the marketplace, and so adverse selection (the lemons problem) will still interfere with the efficient functioning of securities markets.

Government Regulation The free-rider problem prevents the private market from producing enough information to eliminate all the asymmetric information that leads to adverse selection. Could financial markets benefit from government intervention? The government could, for instance, produce information to help investors distinguish good from bad firms and provide it to the public free of charge. This solution, however, would involve the government in releasing negative information about firms, a practice that might be politically difficult. A second possibility (and one followed by the United States and most governments throughout the world) is for the government to regulate securities markets in a way that encourages firms to reveal honest information about themselves so that investors can determine how good or bad the firms are. In the United States, the Securities and Exchange Commission (SEC) is the government agency that requires firms selling their securities in public markets to adhere to standard accounting principles and to disclose information about their sales, assets, and earnings. Similar regulations are found in other countries. However, disclosure requirements do not work well, as the recent collapse of Enron suggests (Box 1).

The asymmetric information problem of adverse selection in financial markets helps explain why financial markets are among the most heavily regulated sectors in the economy (fact 5). Government regulation to increase information for investors is needed to reduce the adverse selection problem, which interferes with the efficient functioning of securities (stock and bond) markets.

BOX 1

The Enron Implosion

Until 2001, Enron Corporation, a firm that specialized in trading in the energy market, appeared to be spectacularly successful. It had a quarter of the energy-trading market and was valued as high as $77 billion in August 2000, just a little over a year before its collapse, making it the seventh largest corporations in the United States at that time. However, toward the end of 2001, Enron came crashing down. In October 2001 Enron announced a big third-quarter loss of $618 million and disclosed accounting "mistakes." The SEC then engaged in a formal investigation of Enron's financial dealings with partnerships led by its former finance chief. It then became clear that Enron was engaged in a complex set of transactions that enabled it to keep substantial amounts of debt and financial contracts off of its balance sheet, thus enabling it to hide its financial difficulties. Despite securing as much as $1.5 billion of new financing from J.P. Morgan Chase and Citigroup in December, the company was forced to declare bankruptcy, making it the largest in U.S. history.

Enron's incredibly rapid collapse has raised concerns that disclosure and accounting regulations may be inadequate for firms that are involved in complicated financial transactions. Congressional hearings will probably result in new regulations that should make future Enrons less likely. The Enron collapse also illustrates that although government regulation lessens asymmetric information problems, it cannot eliminate them. When a firm is in trouble, its management has tremendous incentives to hide its problems, making it hard for investors to know the true value of the firm.

Although government regulation lessens the adverse selection problem, it does not eliminate it. Even when firms provide information to the public about their sales, assets, or earnings, they still have more information than investors: There is a lot more to knowing the quality of a firm than statistics can provide. Furthermore, bad firms have an incentive to make themselves look like good firms because this would enable them to fetch a higher price for their securities. Bad firms will slant the information they are required to transmit to the public, thus making it harder for investors to sort out the good firms from the bad.

Financial Intermediation So far we have seen that private production of information and government regulation to encourage provision of information lessen but do not eliminate the adverse selection problem in financial markets. How, then, can the financial structure help promote the flow of funds to people with productive investment opportunities when there is asymmetric information? A clue is provided by the structure of the used-car market.

An important feature of the used-car market is that most used cars are not sold directly by one individual to another. An individual considering buying a used car might pay for privately produced information by subscribing to a magazine like *Consumer Reports* to find out if a particular make of car has a good repair record. Nevertheless, reading *Consumer Reports* does not solve the adverse selection problem because even if a particular make of car has a good reputation, the specific car someone is trying to sell could be a lemon. The prospective buyer might also bring the used car to a mechanic for a once-over. But what if the prospective buyer doesn't know a mechanic who can be trusted or if the mechanic would charge a high fee to evaluate the car?

Because these roadblocks make it hard for individuals to acquire enough information about used cars, most used cars are not sold directly by one individual to another. Instead, they are sold by an intermediary, a used-car dealer who purchases used cars from individuals and resells them to other individuals. Used-car dealers produce information in the market by becoming experts in determining whether a car is a peach or a lemon. Once they know that a car is good, they can sell it with some form of a guarantee: either a guarantee that is explicit, such as a warranty, or an implicit guarantee in which they stand by their reputation for honesty. People are more likely to purchase a used car because of a dealer's guarantee, and the dealer is able to make a profit on the production of information about automobile quality by being able to sell the used car at a higher price than the dealer paid for it. If dealers purchase and then resell cars on which they have produced information, they avoid the problem of other people free-riding on the information they produced.

Just as used-car dealers help solve adverse selection problems in the automobile market, financial intermediaries play a similar role in financial markets. A financial intermediary such as a bank becomes an expert in the production of information about firms so that it can sort out good credit risks from bad ones. Then it can acquire funds from depositors and lend them to the good firms. Because the bank is able to lend mostly to good firms, it is able to earn a higher return on its loans than the interest it has to pay to its depositors. As a result, the bank earns a profit, which allows it to engage in this information production activity.

An important element in the ability of the bank to profit from the information it produces is that it avoids the free-rider problem by primarily making private loans rather than by purchasing securities that are traded in the open market. Because a private loan is not traded, other investors cannot watch what the bank is doing and bid up the loan's price to the point that the bank receives no compensation for the information it has produced. The bank's role as an intermediary that holds mostly nontraded loans is the key to its success in reducing asymmetric information in financial markets.

Our theoretical analysis of adverse selection indicates that financial intermediaries in general, and banks in particular because they hold a large fraction of nontraded loans, should play a greater role in moving funds to corporations than securities markets do. Our analysis thus explains facts 3 and 4: why indirect finance is so much more important than direct finance and why banks are the most important source of external funds for financing businesses.

Another important fact that is explained by the analysis here is the greater importance of banks in the financial systems of developing countries. As we have seen, when the quality of information about firms is better, asymmetric information problems will be less severe, and it will be easier for firms to issue securities. Information about private firms is even harder to collect in developing countries than in industrialized countries; therefore, the smaller role played by securities markets leaves a greater role for financial intermediaries such as banks. A corollary of this analysis is that as information about firms becomes easier to acquire, the role of banks should decline. A major development in the past 20 years in the United States has been huge improvements in information technology. Thus the analysis here suggests that the lending role of financial institutions such as banks in the United States should have declined, and this is exactly what has occurred (see Chapter 16).

Our analysis of adverse selection also explains which firms are more likely to obtain funds from banks and financial intermediaries, an indirect route, rather than directly from the securities markets. The better known a corporation is, the more information about its activities is available in the marketplace. Thus it is easier for investors to evaluate the quality of the corporation and determine whether it is a good firm or a bad one. Because investors have fewer worries about adverse selection with well-known corporations, they will be willing to invest directly in their securities. Hence we have an explanation for fact 6: The larger and more mature a corporation is, the more information investors have about it, and the more likely it is that the corporation can raise funds in securities markets.

Collateral and Net Worth Adverse selection interferes with the functioning of financial markets only if a lender suffers a loss when a borrower is unable to make loan payments and thereby defaults. Collateral, property promised to the lender if the borrower defaults, reduces the consequences of adverse selection because it reduces the lender's losses in the event of a default. If a borrower defaults on a loan, the lender can sell the collateral and use the proceeds to make up for the losses on the loan. For example, if you fail to make your mortgage payments, the lender can take title to your house, auction it off, and use the receipts to pay off the loan. Lenders are thus more willing to make loans secured by collateral, and borrowers are willing to supply collateral because the reduced risk for the lender makes it more likely they will get the loan in the first place and perhaps at a better loan rate. The presence of adverse selection in credit markets thus provides an explanation for why collateral is an important feature of debt contracts (fact 7).

Net worth (also called **equity capital**), the difference between a firm's assets (what it owns or is owed) and its liabilities (what it owes), can perform a similar role to collateral. If a firm has a high net worth, then even if it engages in investments that cause it to have negative profits and so defaults on its debt payments, the lender can take title to the firm's net worth, sell it off, and use the proceeds to recoup some of the losses from the loan. In addition, the more net worth a firm has in the first place, the less likely it is to default because the firm has a cushion of assets that it can use to pay off its loans. Hence when firms seeking credit have high net worth, the consequences of adverse selection are less important and lenders are more willing to make loans. This analysis lies behind the often-heard lament, "Only the people who don't need money can borrow it!"

Summary So far we have used the concept of adverse selection to explain seven of the eight basic facts about financial structure introduced earlier: The first four emphasize the importance of financial intermediaries and the relative unimportance of securities markets for the financing of corporations; the fifth, that financial markets are among the most heavily regulated sectors of the economy; the sixth, that only large, well-established corporations have access to securities markets; and the seventh, that collateral is an important feature of debt contracts. In the next section we will see that the other asymmetric information concept of moral hazard provides additional reasons for the importance of financial intermediaries and the relative unimportance of securities markets for the financing of corporations, the prevalence of government regulation, and the importance of collateral in debt contracts. In addition, the concept of moral hazard can be used to explain our final basic fact (fact 8) of why debt contracts are complicated legal documents that place substantial restrictions on the behavior of the borrower.

HOW MORAL HAZARD AFFECTS THE CHOICE BETWEEN DEBT AND EQUITY CONTRACTS

Moral hazard is the asymmetric information problem that occurs after the financial transaction takes place, when the seller of a security may have incentives to hide information and engage in activities that are undesirable for the purchaser of the security. Moral hazard has important consequences for whether a firm finds it easier to raise funds with debt rather than with equity contracts.

Moral Hazard in Equity Contracts: The Principal-Agent Problem

Equity contracts, such as common stock, are claims to a share in the profits and assets of a business. Equity contracts are subject to a particular type of moral hazard called the **principal-agent problem.** When managers own only a small fraction of the firm they work for, the stockholders who own most of the firm's equity (called the *principals*) are not the same people as the managers of the firm, who are the *agents* of the owners. This separation of ownership and control involves moral hazard in that the managers in control (the agents) may act in their own interest rather than in the interest of the stockholder-owners (the principals) because the managers have less incentive to maximize profits than the stockholder-owners do.

To understand the principal-agent problem more fully, suppose that your friend Steve asks you to become a silent partner in his ice-cream store. The store requires an investment of $10,000 to set up, but Steve has only $1000. So you purchase an equity stake (stock shares) for $9000, which entitles you to 90% of the ownership of the firm, while Steve owns only 10%. If Steve works hard to make tasty ice cream, keeps the store clean, smiles at all the customers, and hustles to wait on tables quickly, after all expenses (including Steve's salary), the store will have $50,000 in profits per year, of which Steve receives 10% ($5000) and you receive 90% ($45,000).

But if Steve doesn't provide quick and friendly service to his customers, uses the $50,000 in income to buy artwork for his office, and even sneaks off to the beach while he should be at the store, the store will not earn any profit. Steve can only earn the additional $5000 (his 10% share of the profits) over his salary if he works hard and forgoes unproductive investments (such as art for his office). Steve might decide that the extra $5000 just isn't enough to make him want to expend the effort to be a good manager; he might decide that it would be worth his while only if he earned an extra $10,000. If Steve feels this way, he does not have enough incentive to be a good manager and will end up with a beautiful office, a good tan, and a store that doesn't show any profits. Because the store won't show any profits, Steve's decision not to act in your interest will cost you $45,000 (your 90% of the profits if he had chosen to be a good manager instead).

The moral hazard arising from the principal-agent problem might be even worse if Steve were not totally honest. Because his ice-cream store is a cash business, Steve has the incentive to pocket $50,000 in cash and tell you that the profits were zero. He now gets a return of $50,000, but you get nothing. The moral hazard incentive to underreport profits is illustrated by the experience with accounting practices in the movie industry described in Box 2.

Further indications that the principal-agent problem created by equity contracts can be severe are provided by examples of managers who build luxurious offices for themselves or drive high-priced corporate automobiles. Besides pursuing personal benefits, managers might also pursue corporate strategies (such as the acquisition of other firms) that enhance their personal power but do not increase the corporation's profitability.

The principal-agent problem would not arise if the owners of a firm had complete information about what the managers were up to and could prevent wasteful expenditures or fraud. The principal-agent problem, which is an example of moral hazard, arises only because a manager, like Steve, has more information about his activities than the stockholder does—that is, there is asymmetric information. The principal-agent problem would also not arise if Steve alone owned the store and there was no separation of ownership and control. If this were the case,

BOX 2

"Hollywood Accounting": Was *Forrest Gump* a Money Loser?

Accounting practices in the movie industry are notorious, giving the phrase "Hollywood accounting" a dubious reputation. A standard practice at movie studios is to keep two sets of books, a practice that might not be tolerated in other businesses but is in the movie business, where standards of morality are not always the highest. One set is maintained according to the generally accepted accounting principles in other industries; that set is used to report profits to management and to shareholders. The second set of books, referred to as "contractual accounting," is used when a studio commits to paying out percentages of a movie's "net profits" among actors, directors, writers, and other parties as part of contractual arrangements. Given that the movie studios have a moral hazard incentive to minimize these "net profits," not surprisingly they are rarely positive. For example, *Forrest Gump*, which took in over $600 million at the box office, did not show any profits according to Paramount, the filmmaker. The same has also been the case for other blockbusters such as the first *Batman* movie, *J.F.K.*, and *Coming to America.* Can we really believe that *Forrest Gump*, one of the most successful movies of all time, was a money loser, or is this just an example of the principal-agent problem at work?

The dubious accounting practices of the movie industry have been coming under attack as a result of numerous lawsuits. In addition, the squeaky-clean Walt Disney Company is trying to change industry practices by going on record that it will not use contractual accounting and a second set of books when it compensates movie actors, directors, and writers.

Steve's hard work and avoidance of unproductive investments would yield him a profit (and extra income) of $50,000, an amount that would make it worth his while to be a good manager.

Tools to Help Solve the Principal-Agent Problem

Production of Information: Monitoring You have seen that the principal-agent problem arises because managers have more information about their activities and actual profits than stockholders do. One way for stockholders to reduce this moral hazard problem is for them to engage in a particular type of information production, the monitoring of the firm's activities: auditing the firm frequently and checking on what the management is doing. The problem is that the monitoring process can be expensive in terms of time and money, as reflected in the name financial economists give it, **costly state verification.** Costly state verification makes the equity contract less desirable, and it explains, in part, why equity is not a more important element in our financial structure.

As with adverse selection, the free-rider problem decreases the amount of information production that would reduce the moral hazard (principal-agent) problem. In this example, the free-rider problem decreases monitoring. If you know that other stockholders are paying to monitor the activities of the company you hold shares in, you can take a free ride on their activities. Then you can use the money you save by not engaging in monitoring to vacation on a Caribbean island. If you can do this, though, so can other stockholders. Perhaps all the stockholders will go to the islands, and no one will spend any resources on monitoring the firm. The moral hazard problem for shares of common stock will then be severe, making it hard for firms to issue them to raise capital.

Government Regulation to Increase Information As with adverse selection, the government has an incentive to try to reduce the moral hazard problem created by asymmetric information. Governments everywhere have laws to force firms to adhere to standard accounting principles that make profit verification easier. They also pass laws to impose stiff criminal penalties on people who commit the fraud of hiding and stealing profits. However, these measures can only be partly effective. Catching this kind of fraud is not easy; fraudulent managers have the incentive to make it very hard for government agencies to find or prove fraud.

Financial Intermediation Financial intermediaries have the ability to avoid the free-rider problem in the face of moral hazard. One financial intermediary that helps reduce the moral hazard arising from the principal-agent problem is the **venture capital firm.** Venture capital firms pool the resources of their partners and use the funds to help budding entrepreneurs start new businesses. In exchange for the use of the venture capital, the firm receives an equity share in the new business. Because verification of earnings and profits is so important in eliminating moral hazard, venture capital firms usually insist on having several of their own people participate as members of the managing body of the firm, the board of directors, so that they can keep a close watch on the firm's activities. When a venture capital firm supplies start-up funds, the equity in the firm is not marketable to anyone *but* the venture capital firm. Thus other investors are unable to take a free ride on the venture capital firm's verification activities. As a result of this arrangement, the venture capital firm is able to garner the full benefits of its verification activities and is given the appropriate incentives to reduce the moral hazard problem.

Debt Contracts Moral hazard arises with an equity contract, which is a claim on profits in all situations, whether the firm is making or losing money. If a contract could be structured so that moral hazard would exist only in certain situations, there would be a reduced need to monitor managers, and the contract would be more attractive than the equity contract. The debt contract has exactly these attributes because it is a contractual agreement by the borrower to pay the lender *fixed* dollar amounts at periodic intervals. When the firm has high profits, the lender receives the contractual payments and does not need to know the exact profits of the firm. If the managers are hiding profits or are pursuing activities that are personally beneficial but don't increase profitability, the lender doesn't care as long as these activities do not interfere with the ability of the firm to make its debt payments on time. Only when the firm cannot meet its debt payments, thereby being in a state of default, is there a need for the lender to verify the state of the firm's profits. Only in this situation do lenders involved in debt contracts need to act more like equity holders; now they need to know how much income the firm has in order to get their fair share.

The advantage of a less frequent need to monitor the firm, and thus a lower cost of state verification, helps explain why debt contracts are used more frequently than equity contracts to raise capital. The concept of moral hazard thus helps explain fact 1, why stocks are not the most important source of financing for businesses.[4]

[4]Another factor that encourages the use of debt contracts rather than equity contracts in the United States is our tax code. Debt interest payments are a deductible expense for American firms, whereas dividend payments to equity shareholders are not.

HOW MORAL HAZARD INFLUENCES FINANCIAL STRUCTURE IN DEBT MARKETS

Even with the advantages just described, debt contracts are still subject to moral hazard. Because a debt contract requires the borrowers to pay out a fixed amount and lets them keep any profits above this amount, the borrowers have an incentive to take on investment projects that are riskier than the lenders would like.

For example, suppose that because you are concerned about the problem of verifying the profits of Steve's ice-cream store, you decide not to become an equity partner. Instead, you lend Steve the $9000 he needs to set up his business and have a debt contract that pays you an interest rate of 10%. As far as you are concerned, this is a surefire investment because there is a strong and steady demand for ice cream in your neighborhood. However, once you give Steve the funds, he might use them for purposes other than you intended. Instead of opening up the ice-cream store, Steve might use your $9000 loan to invest in chemical research equipment because he thinks he has a 1-in-10 chance of inventing a diet ice cream that tastes every bit as good as the premium brands but has no fat or calories.

Obviously, this is a very risky investment, but if Steve is successful, he will become a multimillionaire. He has a strong incentive to undertake the riskier investment with your money because the gains to him would be so large if he succeeded. You would clearly be very unhappy if Steve used your loan for the riskier investment because if he were unsuccessful, which is highly likely, you would lose most, if not all, of the money you gave him. And if he were successful, you wouldn't share in his success—you would still get only a 10% return on the loan because the principal and interest payments are fixed. Because of the potential moral hazard (Steve might use your money to finance a very risky venture), you would probably not make the loan to Steve, even though an ice-cream store in the neighborhood is a good investment that would provide benefits for everyone.

Tools to Help Solve Moral Hazard in Debt Contracts

Net Worth When borrowers have more at stake because their *net worth* (the difference between their assets and their liabilities) is high, the risk of moral hazard—the temptation to act in a manner that lenders find objectionable—will be greatly reduced because the borrowers themselves have a lot to lose. Let's return to Steve and his ice-cream business. Suppose that the cost of setting up either the ice-cream store or the research equipment is $100,000 instead of $10,000. So Steve needs to put $91,000 of his own money into the business (instead of $1000) in addition to the $9000 supplied by your loan. Now if Steve is unsuccessful in inventing the no-calorie nonfat ice cream, he has a lot to lose, the $91,000 of net worth ($100,000 in assets minus the $9000 loan from you). He will think twice about undertaking the riskier investment and is more likely to invest in the ice-cream store, which is more of a sure thing. Hence when Steve has more of his own money (net worth) in the business, you are more likely to make him the loan.

One way of describing the solution that high net worth provides to the moral hazard problem is to say that it makes the debt contract **incentive-compatible;** that is, it aligns the incentives of the borrower with those of the lender. The greater the borrower's net worth, the greater the borrower's incentive to behave in the way that the lender expects and desires, the smaller the moral hazard problem in the debt contract is, and the easier it is for the firm to borrow. Conversely, when the borrower's net worth is lower, the moral hazard problem is greater, and it is harder for the firm to borrow.

Monitoring and Enforcement of Restrictive Covenants As the example of Steve and his ice-cream store shows, if you could make sure that Steve doesn't invest in anything riskier than the ice-cream store, it would be worth your while to make him the loan. You can ensure that Steve uses your money for the purpose *you* want it to be used for by writing provisions (restrictive covenants) into the debt contract that restrict his firm's activities. By monitoring Steve's activities to see whether he is complying with the restrictive covenants and enforcing the covenants if he is not, you can make sure that he will not take on risks at your expense.

Restrictive covenants are directed at reducing moral hazard either by ruling out undesirable behavior or by encouraging desirable behavior. There are four types of restrictive covenants that achieve this objective:

1. *Covenants to Discourage Undesirable Behavior.* Covenants can be designed to lower moral hazard by keeping the borrower from engaging in the undesirable behavior of undertaking risky investment projects. Some such covenants mandate that a loan can be used only to finance specific activities, such as the purchase of particular equipment or inventories. Others restrict the borrowing firm from engaging in certain risky business activities, such as purchasing other businesses.

2. *Covenant to Encourage Desirable Behavior.* Restrictive covenants can encourage the borrower to engage in desirable activities that make it more likely that the loan will be paid off. One restrictive covenant of this type requires the breadwinner in a household to carry life insurance that pays off the mortgage upon that person's death. Restrictive covenants of this type for businesses focus on encouraging the borrowing firm to keep its net worth high because higher borrower net worth reduces moral hazard and makes it less likely that the lender will suffer losses. These restrictive covenants typically specify that the firm must maintain minimum holdings of certain assets relative to the firm's size.

3. *Covenants to Keep Collateral Valuable.* Because collateral is an important protection for the lender, restrictive covenants can encourage the borrower to keep the collateral in good condition and make sure that it stays in the possession of the borrower. This is the type of covenant ordinary people encounter most often. Automobile loan contracts, for example, require the car owner to maintain a minimum amount of collision and theft insurance and prevent the sale of the car unless the loan is paid off. Similarly, the recipient of a home mortgage must have adequate insurance on the home and must pay off the mortgage when the property is sold.

4. *Covenants to Provide Information.* Restrictive covenants also require a borrowing firm to provide information about its activities periodically in the form of quarterly accounting and income reports, thereby making it easier for the lender to monitor the firm and reduce moral hazard. This type of covenant may also stipulate that the lender has the right to audit and inspect the firm's books at any time.

We now see why debt contracts are often complicated legal documents with numerous restrictions on the borrower's behavior (fact 8): Debt contracts require complicated restrictive covenants to lower moral hazard.

Financial Intermediation Although restrictive covenants help reduce the moral hazard problem, they do not eliminate it completely. It is almost impossible to write covenants that rule out *every* risky activity. Furthermore, borrowers may be clever enough to find loopholes in restrictive covenants that make them ineffective.

Another problem with restrictive covenants is that they must be monitored and enforced. A restrictive covenant is meaningless if the borrower can violate it knowing that the lender won't check up or is unwilling to pay for legal recourse. Because monitoring and enforcement of restrictive covenants are costly, the free-rider problem arises in the debt securities (bond) market just as it does in the stock market. If you know that other bondholders are monitoring and enforcing the restrictive covenants, you can free-ride on their monitoring and enforcement. But other bondholders can do the same thing, so the likely outcome is that not enough resources are devoted to monitoring and enforcing the restrictive covenants. Moral hazard therefore continues to be a severe problem for marketable debt.

As we have seen before, financial intermediaries, particularly banks, have the ability to avoid the free-rider problem as long as they primarily make private loans. Private loans are not traded, so no one else can free-ride on the intermediary's monitoring and enforcement of the restrictive covenants. The intermediary making private loans thus receives the benefits of monitoring and enforcement and will work to shrink the moral hazard problem inherent in debt contracts. The concept of moral hazard has provided us with additional reasons why financial intermediaries play a more important role in channeling funds from savers to borrowers than marketable securities do, as described in facts 1 through 4.

Summary

The presence of asymmetric information in financial markets leads to adverse selection and moral hazard problems that interfere with the efficient functioning of those markets. Tools to help solve these problems involve the private production and sale of information, government regulation to increase information in financial markets, the importance of collateral and net worth to debt contracts, and the use of monitoring and restrictive covenants. A key finding from our theoretical analysis is that the existence of the free-rider problem for traded securities such as stocks and bonds indicates that financial intermediaries, particularly banks, should play a greater role than securities markets in financing the activities of businesses. Theoretical analysis of the consequences of adverse selection and moral hazard has helped elucidate the basic features of our financial system and has provided explanations for the eight basic facts about our financial structure outlined at the beginning of this chapter.

Application Financial Development and Economic Growth

Recent research has found that an important reason why many developing countries or ex-communist countries like Russia experience very low rates of growth is that their financial systems are underdeveloped (a situation referred to as *financial repression*).[5] The theoretical analysis of financial structure helps explain how an underdeveloped financial system leads to a low state of economic development and economic growth.

[5]World Bank, *Finance for Growth: Policy Choices in a Volatile World* (World Bank and Oxford University Press: Oxford 2001) for a survey of this literature and a list of further references.

The financial systems in developing and ex-communist countries face several difficulties that keep them from operating efficiently. As we have seen, two important tools used to help solve adverse selection and moral hazard problems in credit markets are collateral and restrictive covenants. In many developing countries, the legal system functions poorly, making it hard to make effective use of these two tools. In these countries, bankruptcy procedures are often extremely slow and cumbersome. For example, in many countries, **creditors** (holders of debt) must first sue the defaulting debtor for payment, which can take several years, and then once a favorable judgment has been obtained, the creditor has to sue again to obtain title to the collateral. The process can take in excess of five years, and by the time the lender acquires the collateral, it well may have been neglected and thus have little value. In addition, governments often block lenders from foreclosing on borrowers in politically powerful sectors such as agriculture. Where the market is unable to use collateral effectively, the adverse selection problem will be worse because the lender will need even more information about the quality of the borrower in order to screen out a good loan from a bad one. The result is that it will be harder for lenders to channel funds to borrowers with the most productive investment opportunities, thereby leading to less productive investment and hence a slower-growing economy. Similarly, a poorly developed legal system may make it extremely difficult for borrowers to enforce restrictive covenants. Thus they may have a much more limited ability to reduce moral hazard on the part of borrowers and so will be less willing to lend. Again the outcome will be less productive investment and a lower growth rate for the economy.

Governments in developing and ex-communist countries have also often decided to use their financial systems to direct credit to themselves or to favored sectors of the economy by setting interest rates at artificially low levels for certain types of loans, by creating so-called development finance institutions to make specific types of loans, or by directing existing institutions to lend to certain entities. As we have seen, private institutions have an incentive to solve adverse selection and moral hazard problems and lend to borrowers with the most productive investment opportunities. Governments have less incentive to do so because they are not driven by the profit motive and so their directed credit programs may not channel funds to sectors that will produce high growth for the economy. The outcome is again likely to result in less efficient investment and slower growth.

In addition, banks in many developing and ex-communist countries have been nationalized by their governments. Again because of the absence of the profit motive, these nationalized banks have little incentive to allocate their capital to the most productive uses. Indeed, the primary loan customer of these nationalized banks is often the government, which does not always use the funds wisely.

We have seen that government regulation can increase the amount of information in financial markets to make them work more efficiently. Many developing and ex-communist countries have an underdeveloped regulatory apparatus that retards the provision of adequate information to the marketplace. For example, these countries often have weak accounting standards, making it very hard to ascertain the quality of a borrower's balance sheet. As a result, asymmetric information problems are more severe, and the financial system is severely hampered in channeling funds to the most productive uses.

The institutional environment of a poor legal system, weak accounting standards, inadequate government regulation, and government intervention through directed credit programs and nationalization of banks all help explain why many countries stay poor while others grow richer.

FINANCIAL CRISES AND AGGREGATE ECONOMIC ACTIVITY

Our theoretical analysis of the effects of adverse selection and moral hazard can help us understand **financial crises,** major disruptions in financial markets that are characterized by sharp declines in asset prices and the failures of many financial and nonfinancial firms. Financial crises have been common in most countries throughout modern history. The United States experienced major financial crises in 1819, 1837, 1857, 1873, 1884, 1893, 1907, and 1930–1933 but has not had full-scale financial crises since then.[6] Studying financial crises is worthwhile because they have led to severe economic downturns in the past and have the potential for doing so in the future.

Financial crises occur when there is a disruption in the financial system that causes such a sharp increase in adverse selection and moral hazard problems in financial markets that the markets are unable to channel funds efficiently from savers to people with productive investment opportunities. As a result of this inability of financial markets to function efficiently, economic activity contracts sharply.

Factors Causing Financial Crises

To understand why banking and financial crises occur and more specifically how they lead to contractions in economic activity, we need to examine the factors that cause them. Four categories of factors can trigger financial crises: increases in interest rates, increases in uncertainty, asset market effects on balance sheets, and bank panics.

Increases in Interest Rates As we saw earlier, individuals and firms with the riskiest investment projects are exactly those who are willing to pay the highest interest rates. If market interest rates are driven up sufficiently because of increased demand for credit or because of a decline in the money supply, good credit risks are less likely to want to borrow while bad credit risks are still willing to borrow. Because of the resulting increase in adverse selection, lenders will no longer want to make loans. The substantial decline in lending will lead to a substantial decline in investment and aggregate economic activity.

Increases in Uncertainty A dramatic increase in uncertainty in financial markets, due perhaps to the failure of a prominent financial or nonfinancial institution, a recession, or a stock market crash, makes it harder for lenders to screen good from bad credit risks. The resulting inability of lenders to solve the adverse selection problem makes them less willing to lend, which leads to a decline in lending, investment, and aggregate activity.

Asset Market Effects on Balance Sheets The state of firms' balance sheets has important implications for the severity of asymmetric information problems in the financial system. A sharp decline in the stock market is one factor that can cause a serious deterioration in firms' balance sheets that can increase adverse selection and moral hazard problems in financial markets and provoke a financial crisis. A

[6]Although we in the United States have not experienced any financial crises since the Great Depression, we have had several close calls—the October 1987 stock market crash, for example. An important reason why we have escaped financial crises is the timely action of the Federal Reserve to prevent them during episodes like that of October 1987. The Fed's role in preventing financial crises is discussed in Chapter 7.

decline in the stock market means that the net worth of corporations has fallen because share prices are the valuation of a corporation's net worth. The decline in net worth as a result of a stock market decline makes lenders less willing to lend because, as we have seen, the net worth of a firm plays a role similar to that of collateral. When the value of collateral declines, it provides less protection to lenders, meaning that losses on loans are likely to be more severe. Because lenders are now less protected against the consequences of adverse selection, they decrease their lending, which in turn causes investment and aggregate output to decline. In addition, the decline in corporate net worth as a result of a stock market decline increases moral hazard by providing incentives for borrowing firms to make risky investments, as they now have less to lose if their investments go sour. The resulting increase in moral hazard makes lending less attractive—another reason why a stock market decline and hence a decline in net worth leads to decreased lending and economic activity.

In economies in which inflation has been moderate, which characterizes most industrialized countries, many debt contracts are typically of fairly long maturity with fixed interest rates. In this institutional environment, unanticipated declines in the aggregate price level also decrease the net worth of firms. Because debt payments are contractually fixed in nominal terms, an unanticipated decline in the price level raises the value of firms' liabilities in *real* terms (increases the burden of the debt) but does not raise the real value of firms' assets. The result is that net worth in *real* terms (the difference between assets and liabilities in *real* terms) declines. A sharp drop in the price level therefore causes a substantial decline in real net worth and an increase in adverse selection and moral hazard problems facing lenders. An unanticipated decline in the aggregate price level thus leads to a drop in lending and economic activity.

Because of uncertainty about the future value of the domestic currency in developing countries (and in some industrialized countries), many nonfinancial firms, banks, and governments in these countries find it easier to issue debt denominated in foreign currencies. This can lead to a financial crisis in a fashion similar to an unanticipated decline in inflation. With debt contracts denominated in foreign currency, when there is an unanticipated depreciation or devaluation of the domestic currency, the debt burden of domestic firms increases. Since assets are typically denominated in domestic currency, there is a resulting deterioration in firms' balance sheets and a decline in net worth, which then increases adverse selection and moral hazard problems along the lines just described. The increase in asymmetric information problems leads to a decline in investment and economic activity.

Although we have seen that increases in interest rates have a direct effect on increasing adverse selection problems, increases in interest rates also play a role in promoting a financial crisis through their effect on both firms' and households' balance sheets. A rise in interest rates and therefore in households' and firms' interest payments decreases firms' **cash flow,** the difference between cash receipts and cash expenditures. The decline in cash flow causes a deterioration in the balance sheet because it decreases the liquidity of the household or firm and thus makes it harder for lenders to know whether the firm or household will be able to pay its bills. As a result, adverse selection and moral hazard problems become more severe for potential lenders to these firms and households, leading to a decline in lending and economic activity. There is thus an additional reason why sharp increases in interest rates can be an important factor leading to financial crises.

Problems in the Banking Sector Banks play a major role in financial markets since they are well positioned to engage in information-producing activities that facilitate productive investment for the economy. The state of banks' balance sheets has an important effect on bank lending. If banks suffer a deterioration in their balance sheets and so have a substantial contraction in their capital, they will have fewer resources to lend, and bank lending will decline. The contraction in lending then leads to a decline in investment spending, which slows economic activity.

If the deterioration in bank balance sheets is severe enough, banks will start to fail, and fear can spread from one bank to another, causing even healthy banks to go under. The multiple bank failures that result are known as a **bank panic.** The source of the contagion is again asymmetric information. In a panic, depositors, fearing the safety of their deposits (in the absence of deposit insurance) and not knowing the quality of banks' loan portfolios, withdraw their deposits from other banks to the point that the banks fail. The disappearance of a large number of banks in a short period of time means that there is a loss of information production in financial markets and hence a direct loss of financial intermediation by the banking sector. The decrease in bank lending during a financial crisis also decreases the supply of funds to borrowers, which leads to higher interest rates. The outcome is an increase in adverse selection and moral hazard problems in credit markets; this produces an even sharper decline in lending to facilitate productive investments and a strong contraction in economic activity.

Application Financial Crises in the United States

As mentioned, the United States has a long history of banking and financial crises, such crises having occurred every 20 years or so in the nineteenth and early twentieth centuries—in 1819, 1837, 1857, 1873, 1884, 1893, 1907, and 1930–1933. Our analysis of the factors that lead to a financial crisis can explain why these crises took place and why they were so damaging to the U.S. economy.

Study Guide To understand fully what took place in a U.S. financial crisis, make sure that you can state the reasons why each of the factors—increases in interest rates, increases in uncertainty, asset market effects on balance sheets, and bank panics—increases adverse selection and moral hazard problems, which in turn lead to a decline in economic activity. To help you understand these crises, you might want to refer to Figure 3, a diagram that traces the sequence of events in a U.S. financial crisis.

As shown in Figure 3, most financial crises in the United States have begun with a deterioration in banks' balance sheets, a sharp rise in interest rates (frequently stemming from increases in interest rates abroad), a steep stock market decline, and an increase in uncertainty resulting from a failure of major financial or nonfinancial firms (the Ohio Life Insurance & Trust Company in 1857, the Northern Pacific Railroad and Jay Cooke & Company in 1873, Grant & Ward in 1884, the National Cordage Company in 1893, the Knickerbocker Trust Company in 1907, and the Bank of the United States in 1930). During these crises, deterioration in banks' balance sheets, the increase in uncertainty, the rise in interest rates, and the stock market decline increased the severity of adverse selection problems in credit markets; the stock market decline, the deterioration in banks'

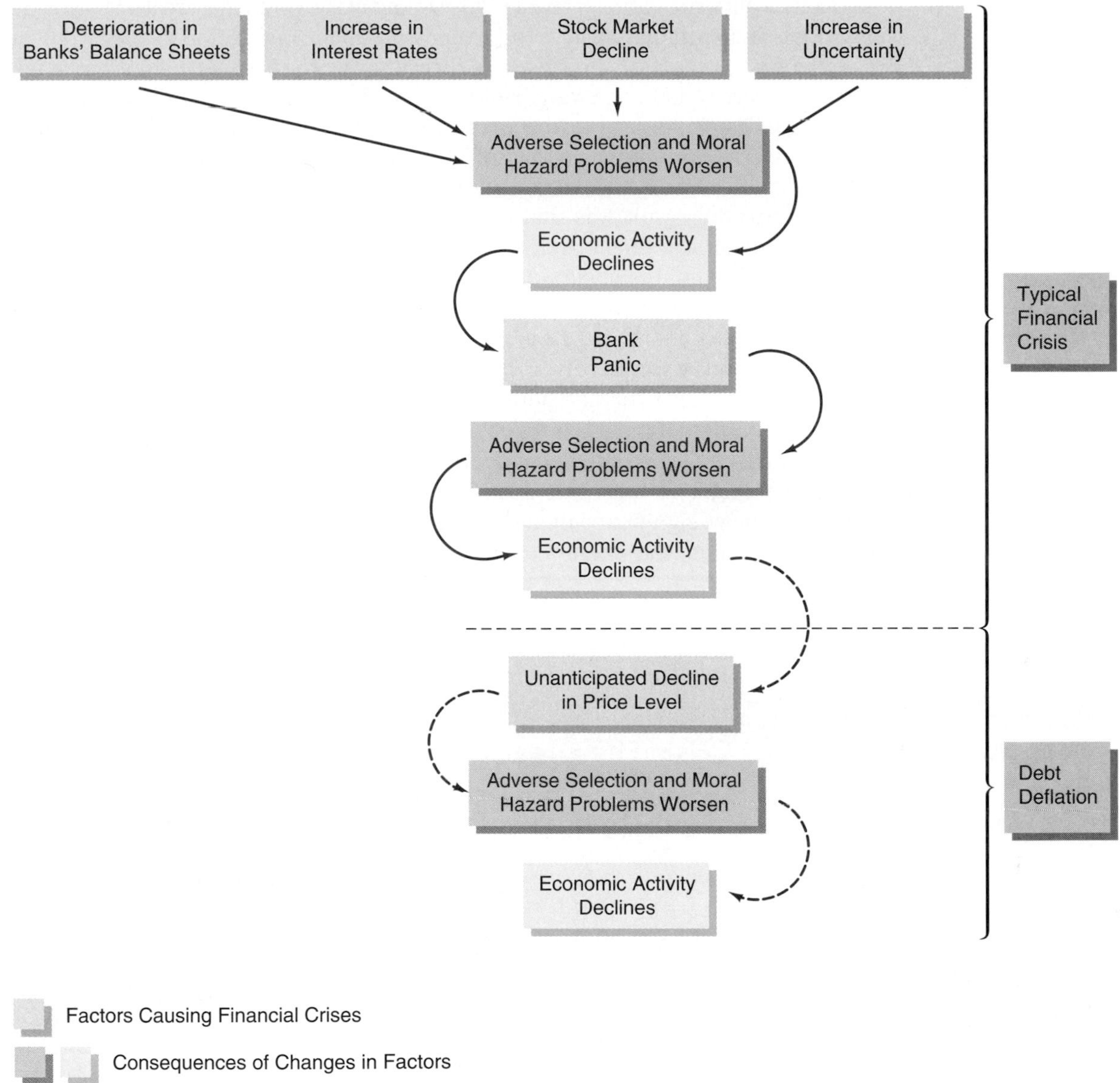

FIGURE 3 Sequence of Events in U.S. Financial Crises

The solid arrows trace the sequence of events in a typical financial crisis; the dotted arrows show the additional set of events that occurs if the crisis develops into a debt deflation.

balance sheets, and the rise in interest rates, which decreases firms' cash flow, also increased moral hazard problems. The rise in adverse selection and moral hazard problems then made it less attractive for lenders to lend and led to a decline in investment and aggregate economic activity.

Because of the worsening business conditions and uncertainty about their bank's health (perhaps banks would go broke), depositors began to withdraw their funds from banks, and the massive withdrawal of deposits led to bank failures, which, if they snowballed, led to a full-scale bank panic. The resulting decline in the number of banks raised interest rates even further and decreased the amount of financial intermediation by banks. Worsening of the problems created by adverse selection and moral hazard led to further economic contraction.

Finally, there was a sorting out of firms that were **insolvent** (that had a negative net worth and hence were bankrupt) from healthy firms by bankruptcy proceedings. The same process occurred for banks, often with the help of public and private authorities. Once this sorting out was complete, uncertainty in financial markets declined, the stock market underwent a recovery, and interest rates fell. The overall result was that adverse selection and moral hazard problems diminished and the financial crisis subsided. With the financial markets able to operate well again, the stage was set for the recovery of the economy.

If, however, the economic downturn led to a sharp decline in prices, the recovery process was short-circuited. In this situation, shown in Figure 3, a process called **debt deflation** occurred, in which a substantial decline in the price level set in, leading to a further deterioration in firms' net worth because of the increased burden of indebtedness. When debt deflation set in, the adverse selection and moral hazard problems continued to increase so that lending, investment spending, and aggregate economic activity remained depressed for a long time. The most significant financial crisis that included debt deflation was the Great Depression, the worst economic contraction in U.S. history (see Box 3).

BOX 3

Case Study of a Financial Crisis: The Great Depression

Federal Reserve officials viewed the stock market boom of 1928 and 1929, during which stock prices doubled, as excessive speculation. To curb it, they pursued a tight monetary policy to raise interest rates. The Fed got more than it bargained for when the stock market crashed in October 1929.

Although the 1929 crash had a great impact on the minds of a whole generation, most people forget that by the middle of 1930, more than half of the stock market decline had been reversed. What might have been a normal recession turned into something far different, however, with adverse shocks to the agricultural sector, a continuing decline in the stock market after the middle of 1930, and a sequence of bank collapses from October 1930 until March 1933 in which over one-third of the banks in the United States went out of business.

The continuing decline in stock prices after mid-1930 (by mid-1932 stocks had declined to 10% of their value at the 1929 peak) and the increase in uncertainty from the unsettled business conditions created by the economic contraction made adverse selection and moral hazard problems worse in the credit markets. The loss of one-third of the banks reduced the amount of financial intermediation. This intensified adverse selection and moral hazard problems, thereby decreasing the ability of financial markets to channel funds to firms with productive investment opportunities. As our analysis predicts, the amount of outstanding commercial loans fell by half from 1929 to 1933, and investment spending collapsed, declining by 90% from its 1929 level.

The short-circuiting of the process that kept the economy from recovering quickly, which it does in most recessions, occurred because of a fall in the price level by 25% in the 1930–1933 period. This huge decline in prices triggered a debt deflation in which net worth fell because of the increased burden of indebtedness borne by firms. The decline in net worth and the resulting increase in adverse selection and moral hazard problems in the credit markets led to a prolonged economic contraction in which unemployment rose to 25% of the labor force. The financial crisis in the Great Depression was the worst ever experienced in the United States, and it explains why this economic contraction was also the most severe one ever experienced by the nation.*

*See Ben Bernanke, "Nonmonetary Effects of the Financial Crisis in the Propagation of the Great Depression," *American Economic Review* 73 (1983): 257–276, for a discussion of the role of asymmetric information problems in the Great Depression period.

Application Financial Crises in Emerging-Market Countries: Mexico, 1994–1995, and East Asia, 1997–1998

Find out about the East Asian financial crisis at www.worldbank.org/data, which provides background information, speeches and articles, and press releases.

In recent years, many emerging-market countries have experienced financial crises, the most dramatic of which were the Mexican crisis, which started in December 1994, and the East Asian crisis, which started in July 1997. An important fact is how a developing country can shift dramatically from a path of high growth before a financial crisis—as was true for Mexico and particularly the East Asian countries of Thailand, Malaysia, Indonesia, the Philippines, and South Korea—to a sharp decline in economic activity, damaging both the economy and the social fabric of the country. We can again apply our asymmetric information analysis of financial crises to explain this fact and to understand the Mexican and East Asian situations.

Because of the different institutional features of emerging-market countries' debt markets, the sequence of events in the Mexican and East Asian crises is different from what occurred in the United States in the nineteenth and early twentieth centuries. Figure 4 diagrams the sequence of events that occurred in Mexico and East Asia.

An important factor leading up to both financial crises was the deterioration in banks' balance sheets because of increasing loan losses. When financial markets were deregulated, a lending boom ensued in which bank credit to the private nonfinancial business sector accelerated sharply. Because of weak supervision by bank regulators and a lack of expertise in screening and monitoring borrowers at banking institutions, losses on the loans began to mount, causing an erosion of banks' net worth (capital). As we have seen, this would mean that the banks would have fewer resources to lend, and this lack of lending would eventually lead to a contraction in economic activity.

Consistent with the U.S. experience in the nineteenth and early twentieth centuries, another precipitating factor to the Mexican (but not East Asian) financial crisis was a rise in interest rates abroad. Beginning in February 1994, the Federal Reserve began to raise the federal funds rate to head off inflationary pressures. Although the policy was quite successful in keeping inflation in check in the United States, it put upward pressure on Mexican interest rates, thereby increasing asymmetric information problems in the Mexican financial system. Furthermore, the Mexican central bank, the Banco de Mexico, raised interest rates to protect the value of the peso in the foreign exchange market. The rise in interest rates directly added to increased adverse selection in Mexican financial markets because, as discussed earlier, it made it more likely that the parties willing to take on the most risk would seek loans.

Also consistent with the U.S. experience in the nineteenth and early twentieth centuries, stock market declines and increases in uncertainty were additional factors precipitating the full-blown crises in Mexico, Thailand, and South Korea. (The stock market declines in Malaysia, Indonesia, and the Philippines occurred simultaneously with the onset of the crisis.) The Mexican economy in 1994 was hit by political shocks that created uncertainty, specifically the assassination of Luis Donaldo Colosio, the ruling party's presidential candidate, and an uprising in the southern state of Chiapas. By the middle of December 1994, stock prices on the Bolsa (stock exchange) had fallen nearly 20% from their September 1994 peak. In January 1997, a major Korean *chaebol* (conglomerate), Hanbo Steel, collapsed; it was the first bankruptcy of a *chaebol* in a decade. Shortly thereafter, Sammi

Steel and Kia Motors also declared bankruptcy. In Thailand, Samprosong Land, a major real estate developer, defaulted on its foreign debt in early February 1997, and financial institutions that had lent heavily in the real estate market began to encounter serious difficulties, requiring over $8 billion of loans from the Thai central bank to prop them up. Finally, in June, the failure of a major Thai finance company, Finance One, imposed substantial losses on both domestic and foreign creditors. These events increased general uncertainty in the financial markets of Thailand and South Korea, and both experienced substantial declines in their securities markets. From peak values in early 1996, Korean stock prices fell by 25% and Thai stock prices fell by 50%.

As we have seen, an increase in uncertainty and a decrease in net worth as a result of a stock market decline increase asymmetric information problems. It becomes harder to screen out good from bad borrowers, and the decline in net

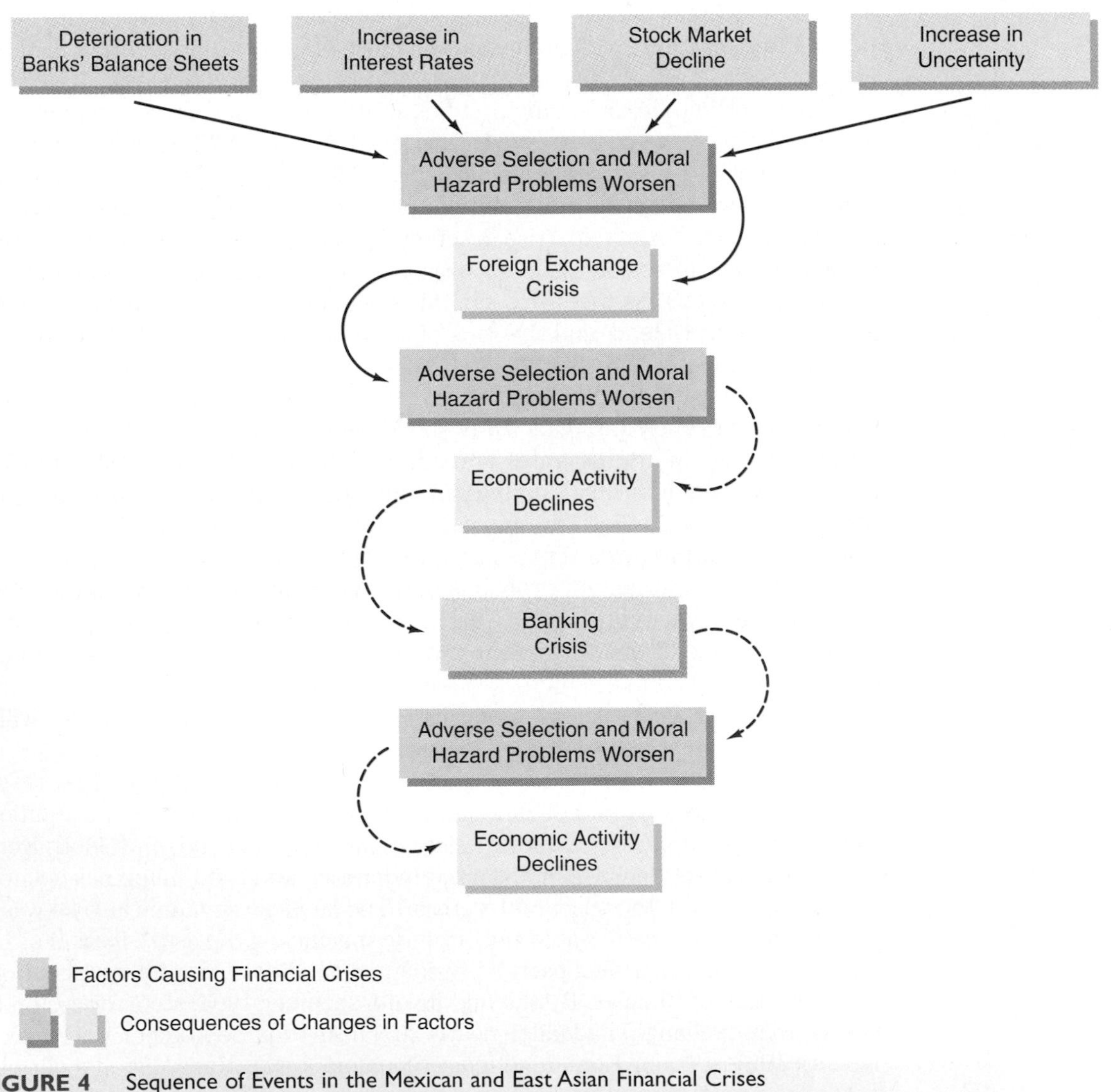

FIGURE 4 Sequence of Events in the Mexican and East Asian Financial Crises

The arrows trace the sequence of events during the Mexican and East Asian financial crises.

worth decreases the value of firms' collateral and increases their incentives to make risky investments because there is less equity to lose if the investments are unsuccessful. The increase in uncertainty and stock market declines that occurred before the crisis, along with the deterioration in banks' balance sheets, worsened adverse selection and moral hazard problems (shown at the top of the diagram in Figure 4) and made the economies ripe for a serious financial crisis.

At this point, full-blown speculative attacks developed in the foreign exchange market, plunging these countries into a full-scale crisis. With the Colosio assassination, the Chiapas uprising, and the growing weakness in the banking sector, the Mexican peso came under attack. Even though the Mexican central bank intervened in the foreign exchange market and raised interest rates sharply, it was unable to stem the attack and was forced to devalue the peso on December 20, 1994. In the case of Thailand, concerns about the large current account deficit and weakness in the Thai financial system, culminating with the failure of Finance One, a large finance company, led to a successful speculative attack that forced the Thai central bank to allow the baht to float downward. Soon thereafter, speculative attacks developed against the other countries in the region, leading to the collapse of the Philippine peso, the Indonesian rupiah, the Malaysian ringgit, and the South Korean won.

The institutional structure of debt markets in Mexico and East Asia now interacted with the currency devaluations to propel the economies into full-fledged financial crises. Because so many firms in these countries had debt denominated in foreign currencies like the dollar and the yen, depreciation of their currencies resulted in increases in their indebtedness in domestic currency terms, even though the value of their assets remained unchanged. When the peso lost half its value by March 1995 and the Thai, Philippine, Malaysian, and South Korean currencies lost between a third and half of their value by the beginning of 1998, firms' balance sheets took a big negative hit, which caused a dramatic increase in adverse selection and moral hazard problems. This negative shock was most severe for Indonesia, which saw the value of its currency fall by an astronomical 80%, resulting in insolvency for any firm with substantial amounts of debt denominated in foreign currencies.

The collapse of currencies also led to a rise in actual and expected inflation in these countries, and market interest rates rose sky high (to over 100% in Mexico). The resulting increase in interest payments caused reductions in households' and firms' cash flow, which led to further deterioration in their balance sheets. A feature of debt markets in emerging-market countries, like those in Mexico and East Asia, is that debt contracts have very short durations, typically less than one month. Thus the rise in short-term interest rates in these countries meant that the effect on cash flow and hence on balance sheets was substantial. As our asymmetric information analysis suggests, this deterioration in households' and firms' balance sheets increased adverse selection and moral hazard problems in the credit markets, making lenders even less willing to lend.

In addition, in the aftermath of the currency crises, stock markets crashed. The Mexican market declined 50% from its peak value, and the Thai, Philippine, Malaysian, Indonesian, and South Korean markets declined 50% to 80%. The collapse of stock market values further worsened adverse selection and moral hazard problems.

These asymmetric information problems were severe not only for domestic lenders but for foreign lenders as well because they had difficulty obtaining information regarding these economies. Foreign lenders were thus eager to pull their funds out of Mexico and the East Asian crisis countries, and that is what they did. Foreign portfolio investment inflows to Mexico, which had been on the order of $20 billion a year in 1993, reversed course, and the outflows exceeded $10 billion a year by the fourth quarter of 1994. Similarly in East Asia, capital flows for Thailand, Malaysia, the Philippines, Indonesia, and South Korea reversed from an inflow of close to $100 billion in 1996 to an outflow of more than $10 billion in 1997. Consistent with the theory of financial crises outlined in this chapter, the sharp decline in lending helped lead to a collapse of economic activity, with real GDP growth falling sharply.

As shown in Figure 4, further deterioration in the economy occurred because the collapse in economic activity and the deterioration in the cash flow and balance sheets of both firms and households led to a worsening banking crisis. The problems of firms and households meant that many of them were no longer able to pay off their debts, resulting in substantial losses for the banks. Even more problematic for the banks was that they had many short-term liabilities denominated in foreign currencies, and the sharp increase in the value of these liabilities after the devaluation led to a further deterioration in the banks' balance sheets. Under these circumstances, the banking system would have collapsed in the absence of a government safety net—as it did in the United States during the Great Depression. But with the assistance of the International Monetary Fund, these countries were in some cases able to protect depositors and avoid a bank panic. However, given the loss of bank capital and the need for the government to intervene to prop up the banks, the banks' ability to lend was nevertheless sharply curtailed. As we have seen, a banking crisis of this type hinders the ability of the banks to lend and also makes adverse selection and moral hazard problems worse in financial markets because banks are less capable of playing their traditional financial intermediation role. The banking crisis, along with other factors that increased adverse selection and moral hazard problems in the credit markets of Mexico and East Asia, explains the collapse of lending and hence economic activity in the aftermath of the crisis.

In the aftermath of their crises, Mexico began to recover in 1996, while the crisis countries in East Asia saw the glimmer of recovery in 1999. In all these countries, the economic hardship caused by the financial crises was tremendous. Unemployment rose sharply, poverty increased substantially, and even the social fabric of the society was stretched thin. For example, Mexico City has become one of the most crime-ridden sites in the world, while Indonesia has experienced waves of ethnic violence.

SUMMARY

1. There are eight basic facts about our financial structure. The first four emphasize the importance of financial intermediaries and the relative unimportance of securities markets for the financing of corporations; the fifth recognizes that financial markets are among the most heavily regulated sectors of the economy; the sixth states that only large, well-established corporations have access to securities markets; the seventh indicates that collateral is an important feature of debt contracts; and the eighth presents debt contracts as complicated legal documents that place substantial restrictions on the behavior of the borrower.
2. Transaction costs freeze many small savers and borrowers out of direct involvement with financial markets. Financial intermediaries can take advan-

tage of economies of scale and are better able to develop expertise to lower transaction costs, thus enabling their savers and borrowers to benefit from the existence of financial markets.

3. Asymmetric information results in two problems: adverse selection, which occurs before the transaction, and moral hazard, which occurs after the transaction. Adverse selection refers to the fact that bad credit risks are the ones most likely to seek loans, and moral hazard refers to the risk of the borrower's engaging in activities that are undesirable from the lender's point of view.

4. Adverse selection interferes with the efficient functioning of financial markets. Tools to help reduce the adverse selection problem include private production and sale of information, government regulation to increase information, financial intermediation, and collateral and net worth. The free-rider problem occurs when people who do not pay for information take advantage of information that other people have paid for. This problem explains why financial intermediaries, particularly banks, play a more important role in financing the activities of businesses than securities markets do.

5. Moral hazard in equity contracts is known as the principal-agent problem because managers (the agents) have less incentive to maximize profits than stockholders (the principals). The principal-agent problem explains why debt contracts are so much more prevalent in financial markets than equity contracts. Tools to help reduce the principal-agent problem include monitoring, government regulation to increase information, and financial intermediation.

6. Tools to reduce the moral hazard problem in debt contracts include net worth, monitoring and enforcement of restrictive covenants, and financial intermediaries.

7. Financial crises are major disruptions in financial markets. They are caused by increases in adverse selection and moral hazard problems that prevent financial markets from channeling funds to people with productive investment opportunities, leading to a sharp contraction in economic activity. The four types of factors that lead to financial crises are increases in interest rates, increases in uncertainty, asset market effects on balance sheets, and bank panics.

KEY TERMS

bank panic, *p. 392*
cash flow, *p. 391*
collateral, *p. 374*
costly state verification, *p. 384*
creditor, *p. 389*
debt deflation, *p. 394*
equity capital, *p. 382*
financial crisis, *p. 390*
free-rider problem, *p. 379*
incentive-compatible, *p. 386*
insolvent, *p. 394*
net worth, *p. 382*
principal-agent problem, *p. 383*
restrictive covenants, *p. 374*
secured debt, *p. 374*
unsecured debt, *p. 374*
venture capital firm, *p. 385*

QUESTIONS AND PROBLEMS

1. How can economies of scale help explain the existence of financial intermediaries?

*2. Describe two ways in which financial intermediaries help lower transaction costs in the economy.

3. Would moral hazard and adverse selection still arise in financial markets if information were not asymmetric? Explain your answer.

*4. How do standard accounting principles required by the government help financial markets work more efficiently?

5. Do you think the lemons problem would be more severe for stocks traded on the New York Stock Exchange or for those traded over-the-counter? Explain your answer.

*6. Which firms are most likely to use bank financing rather than to issue bonds or stocks to finance their activities? Why?

7. How can the existence of asymmetric information provide a rationale for government regulation of financial markets?

*8. Would you be more willing to lend to a friend if she put all of her life savings into her business than you would if she had not done so? Why?

9. Rich individuals often worry that people will seek to marry them only for their money. Is this a problem of adverse selection?

*10. "The more collateral there is backing a loan, the less the lender has to worry about adverse selection." Is this statement true, false, or uncertain? Explain your answer.

11. How does the free-rider problem aggravate adverse selection and moral hazard problems in financial markets?

*12. Explain how the separation of ownership and control in American corporations might lead to poor management.

13. Is a financial crisis more likely to occur when the economy is experiencing deflation or inflation? Explain your answer.

*14. How can a stock market crash provoke a financial crisis?

15. How can a sharp rise in interest rates provoke a financial crisis?

WEB EXERCISES

Theory of Financial Structure

1. In this chapter we discuss the lemons problem and its effect on the efficient functioning of a market. This theory was initially developed by George Akerlof. Go to http://www.nobel.se/economics/laureates/2001/public.html. This site reports that Akerlof, Michael Spence, and Joseph Stiglitz were awarded the Nobel Prize in Economics in 2001 for their work. Read this report down through the section on George Akerlof. Summarize his research ideas in a one-page report.

2. This chapter discusses how an understanding of adverse selection and moral hazard can help us better understand financial crises. The greatest financial crisis faced by the United States was during The Great Depression from 1929 to 1933. Go to http://www.korpios.org/resurgent/THE_GREAT_DEPRESSION.htm. This site contains a brief discussion of the factors that led to this Depression. Write a one-page summary explaining how adverse selection and moral hazard were responsible for the Depression.

Chapter 15 The Banking Firm and Bank Management

Preview

Because banks (depository institutions) play such a major role in channeling funds to borrowers with productive investment opportunities, they are important in ensuring that the financial system and the economy run smoothly and efficiently. In the United States, banks supply over $5 trillion of credit annually. They provide loans to businesses, help us finance our college educations or the purchase of a new car or home, and provide us with services such as checking and savings accounts.

In this chapter we examine how banks, the most important of all the financial intermediaries, operate to earn the highest profits possible: how and why they make loans, how they acquire funds and manage their assets and liabilities (debts), and how they earn income. Although we focus on commercial banks because they hold over two-thirds of the assets in the banking system, the principles are equally applicable to other types of banking institutions, such as savings and loans, mutual savings banks, and credit unions. Furthermore, many of the principles of bank management discussed here also apply to many other financial institutions.

THE BANK BALANCE SHEET

To understand how a bank operates, first we need to examine its **balance sheet,** a list of the bank's assets and liabilities. As the name implies, this list balances; that is, it has the characteristic that

A sample bank balance sheet is available at www.bankofamerica.com/annualreport/cons_balance.cfm

$$\text{Total assets} = \text{total liabilities} + \text{capital}$$

Furthermore, a bank's balance sheet lists *sources* of bank funds (liabilities) and *uses* to which they are put (assets). Banks obtain funds by borrowing and by issuing other liabilities such as deposits. They then use these funds to acquire assets such as securities and loans. Banks make profits by charging an interest rate on their holdings of securities and loans that is higher than the expenses on their liabilities. The balance sheet of all commercial banks at the end of 2001 appears in Table 1.

Liabilities

A bank acquires funds by issuing (selling) liabilities, which are consequently also referred to as *sources of funds.* The funds obtained from issuing liabilities are used to purchase income-earning assets.

Checkable Deposits Checkable deposits are bank accounts that allow the owner of the account to write checks to third parties. Checkable deposits include all accounts on which checks can be drawn: non-interest-bearing checking accounts (demand deposits), interest-bearing NOW (negotiable order of withdrawal) accounts, and money market deposit accounts (MMDAs). Introduced with the Depository Institutions Act in 1982, MMDAs have features similar to money market mutual funds and are included in the checkable deposits category. However, MMDAs differ from checkable deposits in that they are not subject to reserve requirements (discussed later in the chapter) like checkable deposits. Table 1 shows that the category of checkable deposits is an important source of bank funds, making up 10% of bank liabilities. Once checkable deposits were the most important source of bank funds (over 60% of bank liabilities in 1960), but with the appearance of new, more attractive financial instruments such as money market mutual funds, the share of checkable deposits in total bank liabilities has shrunk over time.

Checkable deposits and money market deposit accounts are payable on demand; that is, if a depositor shows up at the bank and requests payment by making a withdrawal, the bank must pay the depositor immediately. Similarly, if a person who receives a check written on an account from a bank presents that

TABLE 1 Balance Sheet of All Commercial Banks (items as a percentage of the total, end of 2001) Amounts in Billions of Dollars

Assets (Uses of Funds)*		Liabilities (Sources of Funds)	
Reserves and cash items	1	Checkable deposits	10
Securities		Nontransaction deposits	
U.S. government and agency	15	Small-denomination time deposits	
State and local government and other securities	7	(<$100,000) + savings deposits	48
Loans		Large-denomination time deposits	11
Commercial and industrial	18	Borrowings	23
Real estate	35	Bank capital	8
Consumer	6		
Interbank	11		
Other	2		
Other assets (for example, physical capital)	5		
Total	100	Total	100

*In order of decreasing liquidity.

Source: http://www.federalreserve.gov/releases/Z1/Current/z1r-4.pdf

check at the bank, it must pay the funds out immediately (or credit them to that person's account).

A checkable deposit is an asset for the depositor because it is part of his or her wealth. Conversely, because the depositor can withdraw funds from an account that the bank is obligated to pay, checkable deposits are a liability for the bank. They are usually the lowest-cost source of bank funds because depositors are willing to forgo some interest in order to have access to a liquid asset that can be used to make purchases. The bank's costs of maintaining checkable deposits include interest payments and the costs incurred in servicing these accounts—processing and storing canceled checks, preparing and sending out monthly statements, providing efficient tellers (human or otherwise), maintaining an impressive building and conveniently located branches, and advertising and marketing to entice customers to deposit their funds with a given bank. In recent years, interest paid on deposits (checkable and time) has accounted for around 45% of total bank operating expenses, while the costs involved in servicing accounts (employee salaries, building rent, and so on) have been approximately 50% of operating expenses.

Nontransaction Deposits Nontransaction deposits are the primary source of bank funds (59% of bank liabilities in Table 1). Owners cannot write checks on nontransaction deposits, but the interest rates are usually higher than those on checkable deposits. There are two basic types of nontransaction deposits: savings accounts and time deposits (also called certificates of deposit, or CDs).

Savings accounts were once the most common type of nontransaction deposit. In these accounts, to which funds can be added or from which funds can be withdrawn at any time, transactions and interest payments are recorded in a monthly statement or in a small book (the passbook) held by the owner of the account.

Time deposits have a fixed maturity length, ranging from several months to over five years, and have substantial penalties for early withdrawal (the forfeiture of several months' interest). Small-denomination time deposits (deposits of less than $100,000) are less liquid for the depositor than passbook savings, earn higher interest rates, and are a more costly source of funds for the banks.

Large-denomination time deposits (CDs) are available in denominations of $100,000 or over and are typically bought by corporations or other banks. Large-denomination CDs are negotiable; like bonds, they can be resold in a secondary market before they mature. For this reason, negotiable CDs are held by corporations, money market mutual funds, and other financial institutions as alternative assets to Treasury bills and other short-term bonds. Since 1961, when they first appeared, negotiable CDs have become an important source of bank funds (11%).

Borrowings Banks obtain funds by borrowing from the Federal Reserve System, the Federal Home Loan Banks, other banks, and corporations. Borrowings from the Fed are called **discount loans** (also known as *advances*). Banks also borrow reserves overnight in the federal (fed) funds market from other U.S. banks and financial institutions. Banks borrow funds overnight in order to have enough deposits at the Federal Reserve to meet the amount required by the Fed. Other sources of borrowed funds are loans made to banks by their parent companies (bank holding companies), loan arrangements with corporations (such as repurchase agreements), and borrowings of Eurodollars (deposits denominated in U.S. dollars residing in foreign banks or foreign branches of U.S. banks). Borrowings have become a more important source of bank funds over time: In 1960, they made up only 2% of bank liabilities; currently, they are 23% of bank liabilities.

Bank Capital The final category on the liabilities side of the balance sheet is bank capital, the bank's net worth, which equals the difference between total assets and liabilities (8% of total bank assets in Table 1). The funds are raised by selling new equity (stock) or from retained earnings. Bank capital is a cushion against a drop in the value of its assets, which could force the bank into insolvency (when the value of bank assets falls below its liabilities, meaning that the bank can be forced into liquidation). One important component of bank capital is *loan loss reserves,* which are described in Box 1.

Assets

A bank uses the funds that it has acquired by issuing liabilities to purchase income-earning assets. Bank assets are thus naturally referred to as *uses of funds,* and the interest payments earned on them are what enable banks to make profits.

Reserves All banks hold some of the funds they acquire as deposits in an account at the Fed. **Reserves** are these deposits plus currency that is physically held by banks (called **vault cash** because it is stored in bank vaults overnight).

BOX 1

Understanding Loan Loss Reserves

Perhaps you have seen headlines in the press about a bank's large increase in loan loss (bad debt) reserves. Often there is confusion about loan loss reserves, perhaps because they have a similar-sounding name to the "reserves" item on a bank's balance sheet. Actually, loan loss reserves have nothing to do with the reserves shown on the assets side of the balance sheet; rather, they are a component of the liabilities item known as bank capital.

To see how loan loss reserves work, suppose that a bank suspects that some of its loans, say, $1 million worth, might prove to be bad debts that will have to be written off (valued at zero) in the future. The bank can set aside $1 million of its earnings and put it into its loan loss reserves account. Because the $1 million is now retained earnings, it adds to the difference between the bank's assets and liabilities and so increases bank capital. The fact that adding to loan loss reserves increases bank capital explains why loan loss reserves are counted as a component of capital. As a result of adding to loan loss reserves, the bank reduces its reported earnings by $1 million, even though it has not yet actually lost the $1 million—in effect, taking its lumps even before the bad debt is written off.

If the bank eventually determines that the $1 million loan will never be paid back and formally writes it off, it reduces the value of its assets by $1 million. The resulting $1 million decline in bank capital is reflected as a decrease in the loan loss reserves account by $1 million. At this time, however, reported earnings are unaffected by the loan write-off because they were reduced earlier when the bank set aside $1 million of earnings as loan loss reserves.

Banks add to loan loss reserves before some loans have to be written off because it is better for them to allow for potential losses when they have plenty of earnings rather than to wait and find that they must take the loss when they have little in earnings to write the loan off against. In addition, adding to loan loss reserves, which reduces reported earnings, can reduce the amount of taxes a bank has to pay and is also a way of informing the bank's stockholders, depositors, and regulators of potential future losses on loans.

Although reserves currently do not pay any interest, banks hold them for two reasons. First, some reserves, called **required reserves,** are held because, by law, the Fed requires that for every dollar of checkable deposits at a bank, a certain fraction (10 cents, for example) must be kept as reserves. This fraction (10% in the example) is called the **required reserve ratio.** Banks hold additional reserves, called **excess reserves,** because they are the most liquid of all bank assets and can be used by a bank to meet its obligations when funds are withdrawn, either directly by a depositor or indirectly when a check is written on an account.

Cash Items in Process of Collection Suppose that a check written on an account at another bank is deposited in your bank and the funds for this check have not yet been received (collected) from the other bank. The check is classified as a cash item in process of collection, and it is an asset for your bank because it is a claim on another bank for funds that will be paid within a few days.

Securities A bank's holdings of securities are an important income-earning asset: Securities (made up entirely of debt instruments for commercial banks because banks are not allowed to hold stock) account for 22% of bank assets in Table 1, and they provide commercial banks with about 10% of their revenue. These securities can be classified into three categories: U.S. government and agency securities, state and local government (municipal) securities, and other securities. U.S. government and agency securities are the most liquid because they can be easily traded and converted into cash with low transaction costs. Because of their high liquidity, short-term U.S. government securities are called **secondary reserves.**

State and local government securities are desirable for banks to hold primarily because state and local governments are more likely to do business with banks that hold their securities. In addition, state and local government securities purchased before August 1986 have substantial tax advantages for banks because their interest payments are deductible from income taxes, and 80% of the interest costs associated with the funding of their purchase is deductible. State and local government and other securities are less marketable (hence less liquid) and are also riskier than U.S. government securities, primarily because of default risk: There is some possibility that the issuer of the securities may not be able to make its interest payments or pay back the face value of the securities when they mature.

Loans Banks make their profits primarily by issuing loans. In Table 1, some 72% of bank assets are in the form of loans, and in recent years they have generally produced more than half of bank revenues. A loan is a liability for the individual or corporation receiving it but an asset for a bank because it provides income to the bank. Loans are typically less liquid than other assets because they cannot be turned into cash until the loan matures. If the bank makes a one-year loan, for example, it cannot get its funds back until the loan comes due in one year. Loans also have a higher probability of default than other assets. Because of the lack of liquidity and higher default risk, the bank earns its highest return on loans.

As you can see in Table 1, the largest categories of loans for commercial banks are commercial and industrial loans made to businesses and real estate loans.

Commercial banks also make consumer loans and lend to each other. The bulk of these interbank loans are overnight loans lent in the federal funds market. The major difference in the balance sheets of the various depository institutions is primarily in the type of loan in which they specialize. Savings and loans and mutual savings banks, for example, specialize in residential mortgages, while credit unions tend to make consumer loans.

Other Assets The physical capital (bank buildings, computers, and other equipment) owned by the banks is included in this category.

BASIC OPERATION OF A BANK

Before proceeding to more detailed study of how a bank manages its assets and liabilities in order to make the highest profit, you should understand the basic operation of a bank.

In general terms, banks make profits by selling liabilities with one set of characteristics (a particular combination of liquidity, risk, size, and return) and using the proceeds to buy assets with a different set of characteristics. This process is often referred to as *asset transformation.* Instead of making a mortgage loan directly to a neighbor, a person can hold a savings deposit that enables a bank to use the funds provided by the deposit to make the loan to the neighbor. The bank has, in effect, transformed the savings deposit (an asset held by the depositor) into a mortgage loan (an asset held by the bank). Another way this process of asset transformation is described is to say that the bank "borrows short and lends long" because it makes long-term loans and funds them by issuing short-dated deposits.

The process of transforming assets and providing a set of services (check clearing, record keeping, credit analysis, and so forth) is like any other production process in a firm. If the bank produces desirable services at low cost and earns substantial income on its assets, it earns profits; if not, the bank suffers losses.

To make our analysis of the operation of a bank more concrete, we use a tool called a **T-account.** A T-account is a simplified balance sheet, with lines in the form of a T, that lists only the changes that occur in balance sheet items starting from some initial balance sheet position. Let's say that Jane Brown has heard that the First National Bank provides excellent service, so she opens a checking account with a $100 bill. She now has a $100 checkable deposit at the bank, which shows up as a $100 liability on the bank's balance sheet. The bank now puts her $100 bill into its vault so that the bank's assets rise by the $100 increase in vault cash. The T-account for the bank looks like this:

First National Bank

Assets		Liabilities	
Vault cash	+$100	Checkable deposits	+$100

Since vault cash is also part of the bank's reserves, we can rewrite the T-account as follows:

Assets		Liabilities	
Reserves	+$100	Checkable deposits	+$100

Note that Jane Brown's opening of a checking account leads to *an increase in the bank's reserves equal to the increase in checkable deposits.*

If Jane had opened her account with a $100 check written on an account at another bank, say, the Second National Bank, we would get the same result. The initial effect on the T-account of the First National Bank is as follows:

Assets		Liabilities	
Cash items in process of collection	+$100	Checkable deposits	+$100

Checkable deposits increase by $100 as before, but now the First National Bank is owed $100 by the Second National Bank. This asset for the First National Bank is entered in the T-account as $100 of cash items in process of collection because the First National Bank will now try to collect the funds that it is owed. It could go directly to the Second National Bank and ask for payment of the funds, but if the two banks are in separate states, that would be a time-consuming and costly process. Instead, the First National Bank deposits the check in its account at the Fed, and the Fed collects the funds from the Second National Bank. The result is that the Fed transfers $100 of reserves from the Second National Bank to the First National Bank, and the final balance sheet positions of the two banks are as follows:

First National Bank				**Second National Bank**			
Assets		Liabilities		Assets		Liabilities	
Reserves	+$100	Checkable deposits	+$100	Reserves	−$100	Checkable deposits	−$100

The process initiated by Jane Brown can be summarized as follows: When a check written on an account at one bank is deposited in another, the bank receiving the deposit gains reserves equal to the amount of the check, while the bank on which the check is written sees its reserves fall by the same amount. Therefore, ***when a bank receives additional deposits, it gains an equal amount of reserves; when it loses deposits, it loses an equal amount of reserves.***

Study Guide T-accounts are used to study various topics throughout this text. Whenever you see a T-account, try to analyze what would happen if the opposite action were taken; for example, what would happen if Jane Brown decided to close her $100 account at the First National Bank by writing a $100 check and depositing it in a new checking account at the Second National Bank?

Now that you understand how banks gain and lose reserves, we can examine how a bank rearranges its balance sheet to make a profit when it experiences a change in its deposits. Let's return to the situation when the First National Bank has just received the extra $100 of checkable deposits. As you know, the bank is obliged to keep a certain fraction of its checkable deposits as required reserves. If the fraction (the required reserve ratio) is 10%, the First National Bank's required reserves have increased by $10, and we can rewrite its T-account as follows:

First National Bank

Assets		Liabilities	
Required reserves	+$10	Checkable deposits	+$100
Excess reserves	+$90		

Let's see how well the bank is doing as a result of the additional checkable deposits. Because reserves pay no interest, it has no income from the additional \$100 of assets. But servicing the extra \$100 of checkable deposits is costly because the bank must keep records, pay tellers, return canceled checks, pay for check clearing, and so forth. The bank is making a loss! The situation is even worse if the bank makes interest payments on the deposits, as with NOW accounts. If it is to make a profit, the bank must put to productive use all or part of the \$90 of excess reserves it has available.

Let us assume that the bank chooses not to hold any excess reserves but to make loans instead. The T-account then looks like this:

Assets		Liabilities	
Required reserves	+\$10	Checkable deposits	+\$100
Loans	+\$90		

The bank is now making a profit because it holds short-term liabilities such as checkable deposits and uses the proceeds to buy longer-term assets such as loans with higher interest rates. As mentioned earlier, this process of asset transformation is frequently described by saying that banks are in the business of "borrowing short and lending long." For example, if the loans have an interest rate of 10% per year, the bank earns \$9 in income from its loans over the year. If the \$100 of checkable deposits is in a NOW account with a 5% interest rate and it costs another \$3 per year to service the account, the cost per year of these deposits is \$8. The bank's profit on the new deposits is then \$1 per year (a 1% return on assets).

GENERAL PRINCIPLES OF BANK MANAGEMENT

Now that you have some idea of how a bank operates, let's look at how a bank manages its assets and liabilities in order to earn the highest possible profit. The bank manager has four primary concerns. The first is to make sure that the bank has enough ready cash to pay its depositors when there are **deposit outflows,** that is, when deposits are lost because depositors make withdrawals and demand payment. To keep enough cash on hand, the bank must engage in **liquidity management,** the acquisition of sufficiently liquid assets to meet the bank's obligations to depositors. Second, the bank manager must pursue an acceptably low level of risk by acquiring assets that have a low rate of default and by diversifying asset holdings (**asset management**). The third concern is to acquire funds at low cost (**liability management**). Finally, the manager must decide the amount of capital the bank should maintain and then acquire the needed capital (**capital adequacy management**).

To understand bank management fully, we must go beyond the general principles of bank asset and liability management described next and look in more detail at how a bank manages its assets. In Chapter 22 we look at how managers of financial institutions such as banks manage risk, specifically, **credit risk,** the risk arising because borrowers may default, and **interest-rate risk,** the riskiness of earnings and returns on bank assets that results from fluctuations in interest rates.

Liquidity Management and the Role of Reserves

Let us see how a typical bank, the First National Bank, can deal with deposit outflows that occur when its depositors withdraw cash from checking or savings accounts or write checks that are deposited in other banks. In the example that follows, we assume that the bank has ample excess reserves and that all deposits have the same required reserve ratio of 10% (the bank is required to keep 10% of its time and checkable deposits as reserves). Suppose that the First National Bank's initial balance sheet is as follows:

Assets		Liabilities	
Reserves	$20 million	Deposits	$100 million
Loans	$80 million	Bank capital	$ 10 million
Securities	$10 million		

The bank's required reserves are 10% of $100 million, or $10 million. Since it holds $20 million of reserves, the First National Bank has excess reserves of $10 million. If a deposit outflow of $10 million occurs, the bank's balance sheet becomes

Assets		Liabilities	
Reserves	$10 million	Deposits	$90 million
Loans	$80 million	Bank capital	$10 million
Securities	$10 million		

The bank loses $10 million of deposits *and* $10 million of reserves, but since its required reserves are now 10% of only $90 million ($9 million), its reserves still exceed this amount by $1 million. In short, ***if a bank has ample reserves, a deposit outflow does not necessitate changes in other parts of its balance sheet.***

The situation is quite different when a bank holds insufficient excess reserves. Let's assume that instead of initially holding $10 million in excess reserves, the First National Bank makes loans of $10 million, so that it holds no excess reserves. Its initial balance sheet would be

Assets		Liabilities	
Reserves	$10 million	Deposits	$100 million
Loans	$90 million	Bank capital	$ 10 million
Securities	$10 million		

When it suffers the $10 million deposit outflow, its balance sheet becomes

Assets		Liabilities	
Reserves	$ 0	Deposits	$90 million
Loans	$90 million	Bank capital	$10 million
Securities	$10 million		

After $10 million has been withdrawn from deposits and hence reserves, the bank has a problem: It has a reserve requirement of 10% of $90 million, or $9 million, but it has no reserves! To eliminate this shortfall, the bank has four basic options. One is to acquire reserves to meet a deposit outflow by borrowing them from other banks in the federal funds market or by borrowing from corporations.[1] If the First National Bank acquires the $9 million shortfall in reserves by borrowing it from other banks or corporations, its balance sheet becomes

Assets		Liabilities	
Reserves	$ 9 million	Deposits	$90 million
Loans	$90 million	Borrowings from other banks or corporations	$ 9 million
Securities	$10 million	Bank capital	$10 million

The cost of this activity is the interest rate on these loans, such as the federal funds rate.

A second alternative is for the bank to sell some of its securities to help cover the deposit outflow. For example, it might sell $9 million of its securities and deposit the proceeds with the Fed, resulting in the following balance sheet:

Assets		Liabilities	
Reserves	$ 9 million	Deposits	$90 million
Loans	$90 million	Bank capital	$10 million
Securities	$ 1 million		

The bank incurs some brokerage and other transaction costs when it sells these securities. The U.S. government securities that are classified as secondary reserves are very liquid, so the transaction costs of selling them are quite modest. However, the other securities the bank holds are less liquid and the transaction costs can be appreciably higher.

A third way that the bank can meet a deposit outflow is to acquire reserves by borrowing from the Fed. In our example, the First National Bank could leave its security and loan holdings the same and borrow $9 million in discount loans from the Fed. Its balance sheet would be

Assets		Liabilities	
Reserves	$ 9 million	Deposits	$90 million
Loans	$90 million	Discount loans from the Fed	$ 9 million
Securities	$10 million	Bank capital	$10 million

There are two costs associated with discount loans. First is the interest rate that must be paid to the Fed (called the **discount rate**). The second is a nonexplicit cost resulting from the Fed's discouragement of too much borrowing from it. If a bank takes out too many discount loans, the Fed may refuse to let it borrow further. In popular parlance, the Fed can "close down the discount window" for that bank.

[1]One way that the First National Bank can borrow from other banks and corporations is by selling negotiable certificates of deposit. This method for obtaining funds is discussed in the section on liability management.

Finally, a bank can acquire the $9 million of reserves to meet the deposit outflow by reducing its loans by this amount and depositing the $9 million it then receives with the Fed, thereby increasing its reserves by $9 million. This transaction changes the balance sheet as follows:

Assets		Liabilities	
Reserves	$ 9 million	Deposits	$90 million
Loans	$81 million	Bank capital	$10 million
Securities	$10 million		

The First National Bank is once again in good shape because its $9 million of reserves satisfies the reserve requirement.

However, this process of reducing its loans is the bank's costliest way of acquiring reserves when there is a deposit outflow. If the First National Bank has numerous short-term loans renewed at fairly short intervals, it can reduce its total amount of loans outstanding fairly quickly by *calling in* loans—that is, by not renewing some loans when they come due. Unfortunately for the bank, this is likely to antagonize the customers whose loans are not being renewed because they have not done anything to deserve such treatment. Indeed, they are likely to take their business elsewhere in the future, a very costly consequence for the bank.

A second method for reducing its loans is for the bank to sell them off to other banks. Again, this is very costly because other banks do not personally know the customers who have taken out the loans and so may not be willing to buy the loans at their full value.

The foregoing discussion explains why banks hold excess reserves even though loans or securities earn a higher return. When a deposit outflow occurs, holding excess reserves allows the bank to escape the costs of (1) borrowing from other banks or corporations, (2) selling securities, (3) borrowing from the Fed, or (4) calling in or selling off loans. ***Excess reserves are insurance against the costs associated with deposit outflows. The higher the costs associated with deposit outflows, the more excess reserves banks will want to hold.***

Just as you and I would be willing to pay an insurance company to insure us against a casualty loss such as the theft of a car, a bank is willing to pay the cost of holding excess reserves (the opportunity cost, which is the earnings forgone by not holding income-earning assets such as loans or securities) in order to insure against losses due to deposit outflows. Because excess reserves, like insurance, have a cost, banks also take other steps to protect themselves; for example, they might shift their holdings of assets to more liquid securities (secondary reserves).

Study Guide Bank management is easier to grasp if you put yourself in the banker's shoes and imagine what you would do in the situations described. To understand a bank's possible responses to deposit outflows, imagine how you as a banker might respond to two successive deposit outflows of $10 million.

Asset Management

Now that you understand why a bank has a need for liquidity, we can examine the basic strategy a bank pursues in managing its assets. To maximize its profits, a bank must simultaneously seek the highest returns possible on loans and securities, reduce risk, and make adequate provisions for liquidity by holding liquid assets. Banks try to accomplish these three goals in four basic ways.

First, banks try to find borrowers who will pay high interest rates and are unlikely to default on their loans. They seek out loan business by advertising their borrowing rates and by approaching corporations directly to solicit loans. It is up to the bank's loan officer to decide if potential borrowers are good credit risks who will make interest and principal payments on time. Typically, banks are conservative in their loan policies; the default rate is usually less than 1%. It is important, however, that banks not be so conservative that they miss out on attractive lending opportunities that earn high interest rates.

Second, banks try to purchase securities with high returns and low risk. Third, in managing their assets, banks must attempt to lower risk by diversifying. They accomplish this by purchasing many different types of assets (short- and long-term, U.S. Treasury, and municipal bonds) and approving many types of loans to a number of customers. Banks that have not sufficiently sought the benefits of diversification often come to regret it later. For example, banks that had overspecialized in making loans to energy companies, real estate developers, or farmers suffered huge losses in the 1980s with the slump in energy, property, and farm prices. Indeed, many of these banks went broke because they had "put too many eggs in one basket."

Finally, the bank must manage the liquidity of its assets so that it can satisfy its reserve requirements without bearing huge costs. This means that it will hold liquid securities even if they earn a somewhat lower return than other assets. The bank must decide, for example, how much excess reserves must be held to avoid costs from a deposit outflow. In addition, it will want to hold short-term U.S. government securities as secondary reserves so that even if a deposit outflow forces some costs on the bank, these will not be terribly high. Again, it is not wise for a bank to be too conservative. If it avoids all costs associated with deposit outflows by holding only excess reserves, losses are suffered because reserves earn no interest, while the bank's liabilities are costly to maintain. The bank must balance its desire for liquidity against the increased earnings that can be obtained from less liquid assets such as loans.

Liability Management

Before the 1960s, liability management was a staid affair: For the most part, banks took their liabilities as fixed and spent their time trying to achieve an optimal mix of assets. There were two main reasons for the emphasis on asset management. First, over 60% of the sources of bank funds was obtained through checkable (demand) deposits that by law could not pay any interest. Thus banks could not actively compete with one another for these deposits, and so their amount was effectively a given for an individual bank. Second, because the markets for making overnight loans between banks were not well developed, banks rarely borrowed from other banks to meet their reserve needs.

Starting in the 1960s, however, large banks (called **money center banks**) in key financial centers, such as New York, Chicago, and San Francisco, began to explore ways in which the liabilities on their balance sheets could provide them with reserves and liquidity. This led to an expansion of overnight loans markets, such as the federal funds market, and the development of new financial instruments such as negotiable CDs (first developed in 1961), which enabled money center banks to acquire funds quickly.[2]

This new flexibility in liability management meant that banks could take a different approach to bank management. They no longer needed to depend on checkable deposits as the primary source of bank funds and as a result no longer treated their sources of funds (liabilities) as given. Instead, they aggressively set target goals for their asset growth and tried to acquire funds (by issuing liabilities) as they were needed.

For example, today, when a money center bank finds an attractive loan opportunity, it can acquire funds by selling a negotiable CD. Or if it has a reserve shortfall, funds can be borrowed from another bank in the federal funds market without incurring high transaction costs. The federal funds market can also be used to finance loans.

The emphasis on liability management explains some of the important changes over the past three decades in the composition of banks' balance sheets. While negotiable CDs and bank borrowings have greatly increased in importance as a source of bank funds in recent years (rising from 2% of bank liabilities in 1960 to 34% by the end of 2001), checkable deposits have decreased in importance (from 61% of bank liabilities in 1960 to 10% by the end of 2001). Newfound flexibility in liability management and the search for higher profits have also stimulated banks to increase the proportion of their assets held in loans, which earn higher income (from 46% of bank assets in 1960 to 72% by the end of 2001).

Capital Adequacy Management

Banks have to make decisions about the amount of capital they need to hold for three reasons. First, bank capital helps prevent *bank failure,* a situation in which the bank cannot satisfy its obligations to pay its depositors and other creditors and so goes out of business. Second, the amount of capital affects returns for the owners (equity holders) of the bank. And third, a minimum amount of bank capital (bank capital requirements) is required by regulatory authorities.

How Bank Capital Helps Prevent Bank Failure Let's consider two banks with identical balance sheets, except that the High Capital Bank has a ratio of capital to assets of 10% while the Low Capital Bank has a ratio of 4%.

High Capital Bank			
Assets		Liabilities	
Reserves	$10 million	Deposits	$90 million
Loans	$90 million	Bank capital	$10 million

Low Capital Bank			
Assets		Liabilities	
Reserves	$10 million	Deposits	$96 million
Loans	$90 million	Bank capital	$ 4 million

Suppose that both banks got caught up in the euphoria of the real estate market in the 1980s, only to find that $5 million of their real estate loans became worthless in the 1990s. When these bad loans are written off (valued at zero), the total value of assets declines by $5 million, and so bank capital, which equals

[2]Because small banks are not as well known as money center banks and so might be a higher credit risk, they find it harder to raise funds in the negotiable CD market. Hence they do not engage nearly as actively in liability management.

total assets minus liabilities, also declines by $5 million. The balance sheets of the two banks now look like this:

High Capital Bank				**Low Capital Bank**			
Assets		Liabilities		Assets		Liabilities	
Reserves	$10 million	Deposits	$90 million	Reserves	$10 million	Deposits	$96 million
Loans	$85 million	Bank capital	$ 5 million	Loans	$85 million	Bank capital	−$1 million

The High Capital Bank takes the $5 million loss in stride because its initial cushion of $10 million in capital means that it still has a positive net worth (bank capital) of $5 million after the loss. The Low Capital Bank, however, is in big trouble. Now the value of its assets has fallen below its liabilities, and its net worth is now − $1 million. Because the bank has a negative net worth, it is insolvent: It does not have sufficient assets to pay off all holders of its liabilities (creditors). When a bank becomes insolvent, government regulators close the bank, its assets are sold off, and its managers are fired. Since the owners of the Low Capital Bank will find their investment wiped out, they would clearly have preferred the bank to have had a larger cushion of bank capital to absorb the losses, as was the case for the High Capital Bank. We therefore see an important rationale for a bank to maintain a high level of capital: ***A bank maintains bank capital to lessen the chance that it will become insolvent.***

How the Amount of Bank Capital Affects Returns to Equity Holders Because owners of a bank must know whether their bank is being managed well, they need good measures of bank profitability. A basic measure of bank profitability is the **return on assets (ROA),** the net profit after taxes per dollar of assets:

$$ROA = \frac{\text{net profit after taxes}}{\text{assets}}$$

The return on assets provides information on how efficiently a bank is being run because it indicates how much profits are generated on average by each dollar of assets.

However, what the bank's owners (equity holders) care about most is how much the bank is earning on their equity investment. This information is provided by the other basic measure of bank profitability, the **return on equity (ROE),** the net profit after taxes per dollar of equity capital:

$$ROE = \frac{\text{net profit after taxes}}{\text{equity capital}}$$

There is a direct relationship between the return on assets (which measures how efficiently the bank is run) and the return on equity (which measures how well the owners are doing on their investment). This relationship is determined by the so-called **equity multiplier (EM),** which is the amount of assets per dollar of equity capital:

$$EM = \frac{\text{assets}}{\text{equity capital}}$$

To see this, we note that

$$\frac{\text{Net profit after taxes}}{\text{Equity capital}} = \frac{\text{net profit after taxes}}{\text{assets}} \times \frac{\text{assets}}{\text{equity capital}}$$

which, using our definitions, yields

$$ROE = ROA \times EM \quad (1)$$

The formula in Equation 1 tells us what happens to the return on equity when a bank holds a smaller amount of capital (equity) for a given amount of assets. As we have seen, the High Capital Bank initially has \$100 million of assets and \$10 million of equity, which gives it an equity multiplier of 10 (= \$100 million/\$10 million). The Low Capital Bank, by contrast, has only \$4 million of equity, so its equity multiplier is higher, equaling 25 (= \$100 million/\$4 million). Suppose that these banks have been equally well run so that they both have the same returns on assets of 1%. The return on equity for the High Capital Bank equals 1% × 10 = 10%, while the return on equity for the Low Capital Bank equals 1% × 25 = 25%. The equity holders in the Low Capital Bank are clearly a lot happier than the equity holders in the High Capital Bank because they are earning more than twice as high a return. We now see why owners of a bank may not want it to hold a lot of capital. ***Given the return on assets, the lower the bank capital, the higher the return for the owners of the bank.***

Trade-Off Between Safety and Returns to Equity Holders We now see that bank capital has benefits and costs. Bank capital benefits the owners of a bank in that it makes their investment safer by reducing the likelihood of bankruptcy. But bank capital is costly because the higher it is, the lower will be the return on equity for a given return on assets. In determining the amount of bank capital, managers must decide how much of the increased safety that comes with higher capital (the benefit) they are willing to trade off against the lower return on equity that comes with higher capital (the cost).

In more uncertain times, when the possibility of large losses on loans increases, bank managers might want to hold more capital to protect the equity holders. Conversely, if they have confidence that loan losses won't occur, they might want to reduce the amount of bank capital, have a high equity multiplier, and thereby increase the return on equity.

Bank Capital Requirements Banks also hold capital because they are required to do so by regulatory authorities. Because of the high costs of holding capital for the reasons just described, bank managers often want to hold less bank capital than is required by the regulatory authorities. In this case, the amount of bank capital is determined by the bank capital requirements. We discuss the details of bank capital requirements and why they are such an important part of bank regulation in Chapter 18.

THE PRACTICING FINANCIAL INSTITUTION MANAGER

Strategies for Managing Bank Capital

Mona, the manager of the First National Bank, has to make decisions about the appropriate amount of bank capital. Looking at the balance sheet of the bank, which has a ratio of bank capital to assets of 10% (\$10 million of capital and \$100 million of assets), Mona is concerned that the large amount of bank capital is causing the return on equity to be too low. She concludes that the bank has a capital surplus and should increase the equity multiplier to increase the return on equity. To lower the amount of capital relative to assets and raise the equity multiplier, she can do any of three things: (1) She can reduce the amount of bank capital by buying back some of the bank's stock. (2) She can reduce the bank's capital by paying out higher dividends to its stockholders, thereby reducing the bank's retained earnings. (3) She can keep bank capital constant but increase the bank's assets by acquiring new funds, say, by issuing CDs, and then seeking out loan business or purchasing more securities with these new funds. Because the bank manager feels that she will enhance her position with the stockholders, she decides to pursue the second alternative and raises the dividends on First National Bank stock.

Now suppose that the First National Bank is in a situation similar to that of the Low Capital Bank and has a ratio of bank capital to assets of 3%. The bank manager now might worry that the bank is short on capital relative to assets because it does not have a sufficient cushion to prevent bank failure. To raise the amount of capital relative to assets, she now has the following three choices: (1) She can raise capital for the bank by having it issue equity (common stock). (2) She can raise capital by reducing the bank's dividends to shareholders, thereby increasing retained earnings that it can put into its capital account. (3) She can keep capital at the same level but reduce the bank's assets by making fewer loans or by selling off securities and then using the proceeds to reduce its liabilities. Suppose that raising bank capital is not easy to do at the current time because capital markets are tight or because shareholders will protest if their dividends are cut. Then Mona might have to choose the third alternative and decide to shrink the size of the bank.

In recent years, many banks have experienced capital shortfalls and have had to restrict asset growth, as Mona did, when the bank is short of capital. The important consequences of this for the credit markets are discussed in the application that follows.

Application Did the Capital Crunch Cause a Credit Crunch in the Early 1990s?

During the 1990–1991 recession and the year following, there occurred a slowdown in the growth of credit that was unprecedented in the post-World War II era. Many economists and politicians have claimed that there was a "credit crunch" during this period in which credit was hard to get, and as a result the performance of the economy in 1990–1992 was very weak. Was the slowdown in credit growth a manifestation of a credit crunch, and if so, what caused it?

Our analysis of how a bank manages bank capital suggests that a credit crunch was likely to have occurred in 1990–1992 and that it was caused at least in part by the so-called capital crunch in which shortfalls of bank capital led to slower credit growth.

The period of the late 1980s saw a boom and then a major bust in the real estate market that led to huge losses for banks on their real estate loans. As our example on how bank capital helps prevent bank failures demonstrates, the loan losses caused a substantial fall in the amount of bank capital. At the same time, regulators were raising capital requirements (a subject we will discuss in Chapter 18). The resulting capital shortfalls meant that banks had either to raise new capital or to restrict their asset growth by cutting back on lending. Because of the weak economy at the time, raising new capital was extremely difficult for banks, so they chose the latter course. Banks did restrict their lending, and borrowers found it harder to obtain loans, leading to complaints from banks' customers.[3] Only with the stronger recovery of the economy in 1993, helped by a low-interest-rate policy at the Federal Reserve, did these complaints subside.

OFF-BALANCE-SHEET ACTIVITIES

Although asset and liability management has traditionally been the major concern of banks, in the more competitive environment of recent years banks have been aggressively seeking out profits by engaging in off-balance-sheet activities. **Off-balance-sheet activities** involve trading financial instruments and generating income from fees and loan sales, activities that affect bank profits but do not appear on bank balance sheets. Indeed, off-balance-sheet activities have been growing in importance for banks: The income from these activities as a percentage of assets has nearly doubled since 1980.

Loan Sales

One type of off-balance-sheet activity that has grown in importance in recent years involves income generated by loan sales. A **loan sale,** also called a *secondary loan participation,* involves a contract that sells all or part of the cash stream from a specific loan and thereby removes the loan from the bank's balance sheet. Banks earn profits by selling loans for an amount slightly greater than the amount of the original loan. Because the high interest rate on these loans makes them attractive, institutions are willing to buy them even though the higher price means that they earn a slightly lower interest rate than the original interest rate on the loan, usually on the order of 0.15 percentage point.

Generation of Fee Income

Another type of off-balance-sheet activity involves the generation of income from fees that banks receive for providing specialized services to their customers, such as making foreign exchange trades on a customer's behalf, servicing a mortgage-backed security by collecting interest and principal payments and then paying them out, guaranteeing debt securities such as banker's acceptances (the bank promises to make interest and principal payments if the party issuing the security cannot), and providing backup lines of credit. There are several types of backup lines of credit. The most important is the **loan commitment,** under which for a fee the bank agrees to provide a loan at the customer's request, up to a given dollar amount, over a specified period of time. Credit lines are also now available to bank depositors with "overdraft privileges"—these bank customers can write checks in excess of their deposit balances and, in effect, write themselves a loan. Other lines of credit for which banks get fees include standby letters of credit to back up issues of

---

[3]As we will see in Chapter 18, not only were capital requirements raised, but also risk-based capital requirements were imposed that required even more capital if loans were made but not if banks bought government securities. The risk-based capital requirements thus encouraged banks to switch out of loans and into government securities, and this was an additional factor that led to a decline in bank lending. For a discussion of the evidence on how the capital crunch caused the credit crunch of 1990–1992, see "The Role of the Credit Slowdown in the Recent Recession," *Federal Reserve Bank of New York Quarterly Review,* Spring 1993.

commercial paper and other securities, and credit lines—called **note issuance facilities (NIFs)** and **revolving underwriting facilities (RUFs)**—for underwriting Euronotes, which are medium-term Eurobonds.

Off-balance-sheet activities involving guarantees of securities and backup credit lines increase the risk a bank faces. Even though a guaranteed security does not appear on a bank balance sheet, it still exposes the bank to default risk: If the issuer of the security defaults, the bank is left holding the bag and must pay off the security's owner. Backup credit lines also expose the bank to risk because the bank may be forced to provide loans when it does not have sufficient liquidity or when the borrower is a very poor credit risk.

Available at www.federalreserve.gov/boarddocs/SupManual/default.htm#trading, the Federal Reserve Bank "Trading and Capital Market Activities Manual" offers an in-depth discussion of a wide range of risk management issues encountered in trading operations.

Trading Activities and Risk Management Techniques

Banks' attempts to manage interest-rate risk led them to trading in financial futures, options for debt instruments, and interest-rate swaps. Banks engaged in international banking also conduct transactions in the foreign exchange market. All transactions in these markets are off-balance-sheet activities because they do not have a direct effect on the bank's balance sheet. Although bank trading in these markets is often directed toward reducing risk or facilitating other bank business, banks also try to outguess the markets and engage in speculation. This speculation can be a very risky business and indeed has led to bank insolvencies, the most dramatic being the failure of Barings, a British bank, in 1995.

Trading activities, although often highly profitable, are dangerous because they make it easy for financial institutions and their employees to make huge bets both easily and quickly. A particular problem for management of trading activities is that the principal-agent problem, discussed in Chapter 14, is especially severe. Given the ability to place large bets, a trader (the agent), whether she trades in bond markets, in foreign exchange markets, or in financial derivatives, has an incentive to take on excessive risks: If her trading strategy leads to large profits, she is likely to receive a high salary and bonuses, but if she takes large losses, the financial institution (the principal) will have to cover them. As the Barings Bank failure in 1995 so forcefully demonstrated, a trader subject to the principal-agent problem can take a bank that is quite healthy and drive it into insolvency very fast (see Box 2).

To reduce the principal-agent problem, bank management must set up internal controls to prevent debacles like the one at Barings. Such controls include the complete separation of the people in charge of trading activities and those in charge of the bookkeeping for trades. In addition, bank management must set limits on the total amount of traders' transactions and on the bank's risk exposure. Bank management must also scrutinize risk assessment procedures using the latest computer technology. One such method involves the so-called value-at-risk approach. In this approach, the bank develops a statistical model with which it can calculate the maximum loss that its portfolio is likely to sustain over a given time interval, dubbed the value at risk, or VAR. For example, a bank might estimate that the maximum loss that it would be likely to sustain over one day with a probability of 1 in 100 is $1 million; the $1 million figure is the bank's calculated value at risk. Another approach is called "stress testing." In this approach, the bank asks models what would happen if a doomsday scenario occurs; that is, it looks at the losses it would sustain if an unusual combination of bad events occurred. With the value-at-risk approach and stress testing, a bank can assess its risk exposure and take steps to reduce it.

BOX 2

Barings, Daiwa, and Sumitomo: Rogue Traders and the Principal-Agent Problem

The demise of Barings, a venerable British bank over a century old, is a sad morality tale of how the principal-agent problem operating through a rogue trader can take a financial institution that has a healthy balance sheet one month and turn it into an insolvent tragedy the next.

In July 1992, Nick Leeson, Barings's new head clerk at its Singapore branch, began to speculate on the Nikkei, the Japanese version of the Dow Jones index. By late 1992, Leeson had suffered losses of $3 million, which he hid from his superiors by stashing the losses in a secret account. He even fooled his superiors into thinking he was generating large profits, thanks to a failure of internal controls at his firm, which allowed him to execute trades on the Singapore exchange *and* oversee the bookkeeping of those trades. (As anyone who runs a cash business, such as a bar, knows, there is always a lower likelihood of fraud if more than one person handles the cash. Similarly for trading operations, you never mix management of the back room with management of the front room; this principle was grossly violated by Barings management.) Things didn't get better for Leeson, who by late 1994 had losses exceeding $250 million. In January and February 1995, he bet the bank. On January 17, 1995, the day of the Kobe earthquake, he lost $75 million, and by the end of the week had lost more than $150 million. When the stock market declined on February 23, leaving him with a further loss of $250 million, he called it quits and fled Singapore. Three days later, he turned himself in at the Frankfurt airport. By the end of his wild ride, Leeson's losses, $1.3 billion in all, ate up Barings's capital and caused the bank to fail.

Our asymmetric information analysis of the principal-agent problem explains Leeson's behavior and the danger of Barings's management lapse. By letting Leeson control both his own trades and the back room, it increased asymmetric information because it reduced the principal's (Barings's) knowledge about Leeson's trading activities. This lapse increased the moral hazard incentive for him to take risks at the bank's expense, as he was now less likely to be caught. Furthermore, once he had experienced large losses, he had even greater incentives to take on even higher risk because if his bets worked out, he could reverse his losses and keep in good standing with the company, whereas if his bets soured, he had little to lose since he was out of a job anyway. Indeed, the bigger his losses, the more he had to gain by bigger bets, which explains the escalation of the amount of his trades as his losses mounted. If Barings's managers had understood the principal-agent problem, they would have been more vigilant in learning what Leeson was up to, and the bank might still be here today.

Unfortunately, Nick Leeson is no longer a rarity in the rogue traders' billionaire club, those who have lost more than $1 billion. Over 11 years, Toshihide Iguchi, an officer in the New York branch of Daiwa Bank, also had control of both the bond trading operation and the back room, and he racked up $1.1 billion in losses over the period. In July 1995, Iguchi disclosed his losses to his superiors, but the management of the bank did not disclose them to its regulators. The result was that Daiwa was slapped with a $340 million fine and the bank was thrown out of the country by U.S. bank regulators. Yasuo Hamanaka is the latest member of the billionaire club. In July 1996, he topped Leeson's and Iguchi's record, losing $2.6 billion for his employer, the Sumitomo Corporation, one of Japan's top trading companies. The moral of these stories is that management of firms engaged in trading activities must reduce the principal-agent problem by closely monitoring their traders' activities.

Because of the increased risk that banks are facing from their off-balance-sheet activities, U.S. bank regulators have become concerned about increased risk from banks' off-balance-sheet activities and, as we will see in Chapter 18, are encouraging banks to pay increased attention to risk management. In addition, the Bank for International Settlements is developing additional bank capital requirements based on value-at-risk calculations for a bank's trading activities.

MEASURING BANK PERFORMANCE

To understand how well a bank is doing, we need to start by looking at a bank's income statement, the description of the sources of income and expenses that affect the bank's profitability.

Bank's Income Statement

The end of year 2000 income statement for all federally insured commercial banks appears in Table 2.

Operating Income **Operating income** is the income that comes from a bank's ongoing operations. Most of a bank's operating income is generated by interest on its assets, particularly loans. As we see in Table 2, in 2000 interest income represented 73.5% of commercial banks' operating income. Interest income fluctuates with the level of interest rates, and so its percentage of operating income is highest when interest rates are at peak levels. That is exactly what happened in 1981, when interest rates rose above 15% and interest income rose to 93% of total bank operating income.

Noninterest income, which made up 26.5% of operating income in 2000, is generated partly by service charges on deposit accounts, but the bulk of it comes from the off-balance-sheet activities mentioned earlier, which generate fees or trading profits for the bank. The importance of these off-balance-sheet activities to bank profits has been growing in recent years. Whereas in 1980 other noninterest income from off-balance-sheet activities represented only 5% of operating income, it reached 22.3% in 2000.

TABLE 2 Income Statement for All Federally Insured Commercial Banks, 2000

	Amount ($ billions)		Share of Operating Income or Expenses (%)	
Operating Income				
Interest income		427.5		73.5
Interest on loans	319.0		54.9	
Interest on securities	68.5		11.8	
Other interest	40.0		6.9	
Noninterest income		153.5		26.5
Service charges on deposit accounts	23.8		4.2	
Other noninterest income	129.7		22.3	
Total operating income		581.0		100.0
Operating Expenses				
Interest expenses		224.4		47.7
Interest on deposits	115.0		24.4	
Interest on fed funds and repos	27.5		5.8	
Other	81.9		17.4	
Noninterest expenses		216.1		45.9
Salaries and employee benefits	88.6		18.8	
Premises and equipment	26.8		5.7	
Other	100.7		21.4	
Provisions for loan losses		29.9		6.4
Total operating expense		470.4		100.0
Net Operating Income		110.6		
Gains (losses) on securities		–2.3		
Extraordinary items, net		0.0		
Income taxes		–37.9		
Net Income		70.4		

Source: www.fdic.gov/banks/statistical/statistics/0106/cbr

Operating Expenses **Operating expenses** are the expenses incurred in conducting the bank's ongoing operations. An important component of a bank's operating expenses is the interest payments that it must make on its liabilities, particularly on its deposits. Just as interest income varies with the level of interest rates, so do interest expenses. Interest expenses as a percentage of total operating expenses reached a peak of 74% in 1981, when interest rates were at their highest, and fell to 47.7% in 2000 as interest rates moved lower. Noninterest expenses include the costs of running a banking business: salaries for tellers and officers, rent on bank buildings, purchases of equipment such as desks and vaults, and servicing costs of equipment such as computers.

The final item listed under operating expenses is provisions for loan losses. When a bank has a bad debt or anticipates that a loan might become a bad debt in the future, it can write up the loss as a current expense in its income statement under the "provision for loan losses" heading. Provisions for loan losses are directly related to loan loss reserves (discussed in Box 1 earlier in the chapter). When a bank wants to increase its loan loss reserves account by, say, $1 million, it does this by adding $1 million to its provisions for loan losses. Loan loss reserves rise when this is done because by increasing expenses when losses have not yet occurred, earnings are being set aside to deal with the losses in the future.

Provisions for loan losses have been a major element in fluctuating bank profits in recent years. The 1980s brought the third-world debt crisis mentioned in Chapter 18; a sharp decline in energy prices in 1986, which caused substantial losses on loans to energy producers; and a collapse in the real estate market. As a result, provisions for loan losses were particularly high in the late 1980s, reaching a peak of 13% of operating expenses in 1987. Since then, losses on loans have begun to subside, and in 2000 provisions for loan losses dropped to only 6.4% of operating expenses.

Income Subtracting the $470.4 billion in operating expenses from the $581.0 billion of operating income in 2000 yields net operating income of $110.6 billion. Net operating income is closely watched by bank managers, bank shareholders, and bank regulators because it indicates how well the bank is doing on an ongoing basis.

Two items, gains (or losses) on securities sold by banks (–$2.3 billion) and net extraordinary items, which are events or transactions that are both unusual and infrequent (insignificant), are added to the $110.6 billion net operating income figure to get the $108.3 billion figure for net income before taxes. Net income before taxes is more commonly referred to as profits before taxes. Subtracting the $37.9 billion of income taxes then results in $70.4 billion of net income. Net income, more commonly referred to as profits after taxes, is the figure that tells us most directly how well the bank is doing because it is the amount that the bank has available to keep as retained earnings or to pay out to stockholders as dividends.

Measures of Bank Performance

Although net income gives us an idea of how well a bank is doing, it suffers from one major drawback: It does not adjust for the bank's size, thus making it hard to compare how well one bank is doing relative to another. A basic measure of bank profitability that corrects for the size of the bank is the return on assets *(ROA)*, mentioned earlier in the chapter, which divides the net income of the bank by the amount of its assets. *ROA* is a useful measure of how well a bank manager is doing on the job because it indicates how well a bank's assets are being used to generate profits. At the beginning of 2001, the assets of all federally insured commercial banks amounted to $5,915.9 billion, so using the $70.4 billion net income figure from Table 2 gives us a return on assets of

$$ROA = \frac{\text{net income}}{\text{assets}} = \frac{70.4}{5915.9} = 0.0119 = 1.19\%$$

Although *ROA* provides useful information about bank profitability, we have already seen that it is not what the bank's owners (equity holders) care about most. They are more concerned about how much the bank is earning on their equity investment, an amount that is measured by the return on equity (*ROE*), the net income per dollar of equity capital. At the beginning of 2001, equity capital for all federally insured commercial banks was $502.14 billion, so the *ROE* was therefore

$$ROE = \frac{\text{net income}}{\text{capital}} = \frac{70.4}{502.14} = 0.1402 = 14.02\%$$

Another commonly watched measure of bank performance is called the **net interest margin** (*NIM*), the difference between interest income and interest expenses as a percentage of total assets:

$$NIM = \frac{\text{interest income} - \text{interest expenses}}{\text{assets}}$$

As we have seen earlier in the chapter, one of a bank's primary intermediation functions is to issue liabilities and use the proceeds to purchase income-earning assets. If a bank manager has done a good job of asset and liability management such that the bank earns substantial income on its assets and has low costs on its liabilities, profits will be high. How well a bank manages its assets and liabilities is affected by the spread between the interest earned on the bank's assets and the interest costs on its liabilities. This spread is exactly what the net interest margin measures. If the bank is able to raise funds with liabilities that have low interest costs and is able to acquire assets with high interest income, the net interest margin will be high, and the bank is likely to be highly profitable. If the interest cost of its liabilities rises relative to the interest earned on its assets, the net interest margin will fall, and bank profitability will suffer.

Recent Trends in Bank Performance Measures

Table 3 provides measures of return on assets (*ROA*), return on equity (*ROE*), and the net interest margin (*NIM*) for all federally insured commercial banks from 1980 to 2001. Because the relationship between bank equity capital and total assets for all commercial banks remained fairly stable in the 1980s, both the *ROA* and *ROE* measures of bank performance move closely together and indicate that from the early to the late 1980s, there was a sharp decline in bank profitability. The rightmost column, net interest margin, indicates that the spread between interest income and interest expenses remained fairly stable throughout the 1980s and even improved in the late 1980s and early 1990s, which should have helped bank profits. The *NIM* measure thus tells us that the poor bank performance in the late 1980s was not the result of interest-rate movements.

TABLE 3 Measures of Bank Performance, 1980–2001

Year	Return on Assets *(ROA)* (%)	Return on Equity *(ROE)* (%)	Net Interest Margin *(NIM)*(%)
1980	0.77	13.38	3.33
1981	0.79	13.68	3.31
1982	0.73	12.55	3.39
1983	0.68	11.60	3.34
1984	0.66	11.04	3.47
1985	0.72	11.67	3.62
1986	0.64	10.30	3.48
1987	0.09	1.54	3.40
1988	0.82	13.74	3.57
1989	0.50	7.92	3.58
1990	0.49	7.81	3.50
1991	0.53	8.25	3.60
1992	0.94	13.86	3.89
1993	1.23	16.30	3.97
1994	1.20	15.00	3.95
1995	1.17	14.66	4.29
1996	1.19	14.45	4.27
1997	1.23	14.69	4.21
1998	1.18	13.30	3.47
1999	1.31	15.31	4.07
2000	1.19	14.02	3.95
2001*	1.17	13.42	3.84

*Projected by FDIC

Source: http://www2.fdic.gov/qbp

The explanation of the weak performance of commercial banks in the late 1980s is that they had made many risky loans in the early 1980s that turned sour. The resulting huge increase in loan loss provisions in that period directly decreased net income and hence caused the fall in *ROA* and *ROE*. (Why bank profitability deteriorated and the consequences for the economy are discussed in Chapters 16 and 18.)

Beginning in 1992, bank performance improved substantially. The return on equity rose to nearly 14% in 1992 and remained above 13% in the 1993–2001 period. Similarly, the return on assets rose from the 0.5% level in the 1990–1991 period to around the 1.2% level in 1993–2001. The performance measures in Table 3 suggest that the banking industry has returned to health.

FINANCIAL INNOVATION

Like other industries, the financial industry is in business to earn profits by selling its products. If a soap company perceives that there is a need in the marketplace for a laundry detergent with fabric softener, it develops a product to fit the need. Similarly, in order to maximize their profits, financial institutions develop new products to satisfy their own needs as well as those of their customers; in other words, innovation—which can be extremely beneficial to the economy—is driven by the desire to get (or stay) rich. This view of the innovation process leads to the following simple analysis: ***A change in the financial environment will stimulate a search by financial institutions for innovations that are likely to be profitable.***

Center for the Study of Financial Innovation, www.csfi.fsnet.co.uk, is an independent think tank formed in 1993 to stimulate research into the future of the financial services industry.

Starting in the 1960s, individuals and financial institutions operating in financial markets were confronted with drastic changes in the economic environment: Inflation and interest rates climbed sharply and became harder to predict, a situation that changed demand conditions in financial markets. Computer technology advanced rapidly, which changed supply conditions. In addition, financial regulations became more burdensome. Financial institutions found that many of the old ways of doing business were no longer profitable; the financial services and products they had been offering to the public were not selling. Many financial intermediaries found that they were no longer able to acquire funds with their traditional financial instruments, and without these funds they would soon be out of business. To survive in the new economic environment, financial institutions had to research and develop new products and services that would meet customer needs and prove profitable, a process referred to as **financial engineering.** In their case, necessity was the mother of innovation.

Our discussion of why financial innovation occurs suggests that there are three basic types of financial innovations: responses to changes in demand conditions, responses to changes in supply conditions, and avoidance of regulations. Now that we have a framework for understanding why financial institutions such as banks produce innovations, let's look at examples of how financial institutions in their search for profits have produced financial innovations of the three basic types.

Responses to Changes in Demand Conditions

The most significant change in the economic environment that altered the demand for financial products in recent years has been the dramatic increase in the volatility of interest rates. In the 1950s, the interest rate on three-month Treasury bills fluctuated between 1.0% and 3.5%; in the 1970s, it fluctuated between 4.0% and 11.5%. This volatility became even more pronounced in the 1980s, during which the three-month T-bill rate ranged from 5% to over 15%. We have seen in Chapter 3 (Table 2) that a rise in the interest rate from 10% to 20% would result in a capital loss of nearly 50% on a 30-year bond and a negative return of almost 40%. Large fluctuations in interest rates lead to substantial capital gains or losses and greater uncertainty about returns on investments. Recall that the risk that is related to the uncertainty about interest-rate movements and returns is called *interest-rate risk,* and high volatility of interest rates, such as we saw in the 1970s and 1980s, leads to a higher level of interest-rate risk.

We would expect the increase in interest-rate risk to increase the demand for financial products and services that could reduce that risk. This change in the economic environment would thus stimulate a search for profitable innovations by financial institutions that meet this new demand and would spur the creation of new financial instruments that help lower interest-rate risk. One financial innovation in the banking industry that appeared in the 1970s confirms this prediction: the development of adjustable-rate mortgages.

Adjustable-Rate Mortgages Like other investors, financial institutions find that lending is more attractive if interest-rate risk is lower. They would not want to make a mortgage loan at a 10% interest rate and two months later find that they could obtain a 12% interest rate on the same mortgage. To reduce interest-rate risk, in 1975 savings and loans in California began to issue adjustable-rate mortgages, mortgage loans on which the interest rate changes when a market interest rate (usually the Treasury bill rate) changes. Initially, an adjustable-rate mortgage might have a 5% interest rate. In six months, this interest rate might increase or decrease by the amount of the increase or decrease in, say, the six-month Treasury bill rate, and the mortgage payment would change. Because adjustable-rate mortgages allow mortgage-issuing institutions to earn higher interest rates on mortgages when rates rise, profits are kept higher during these periods.

This attractive feature of adjustable-rate mortgages has encouraged mortgage-issuing institutions to issue adjustable-rate mortgages with lower initial interest rates than on conventional fixed-rate mortgages, making them popular with many households. However, because the mortgage payment on a variable-rate mortgage can increase, many households continue to prefer fixed-rate mortgages. Hence both types of mortgages are widespread.

Responses to Changes in Supply Conditions

The most important source of the changes in supply conditions that stimulate financial innovation has been the improvement in computer and telecommunications technology. These changes have made it profitable for financial institutions to create new financial products and services to supply to the public. When computer technology that substantially lowered the cost of processing financial transactions became available, financial institutions conceived new financial products and instruments dependent on this technology that might appeal to the public, including the bank credit card and electronic banking facilities.

Bank Credit and Debit Cards Credit cards have been around since well before World War II. Many individual stores (Sears, Macy's, Goldwater's) institutionalized charge accounts by providing customers with credit cards that allowed them to make purchases at these stores without cash. Nationwide credit cards were not established until after World War II, when Diners Club developed one to be used in restaurants all over the country (and abroad). Similar credit card programs were started by American Express and Carte Blanche, but because of the high cost of operating these programs, cards were issued only to selected persons and businesses who could afford expensive purchases.

A firm issuing credit cards earns income from loans it makes to credit card holders and from payments made by stores on credit card purchases (a percentage of the purchase price, say, 5%). A credit card program's costs arise from loan defaults, stolen cards, and the expense involved in processing credit card transactions.

Bankers saw the success of Diners Club, American Express, and Carte Blanche and wanted to share in the profitable credit card business. Several commercial banks attempted to expand the credit card business to a wider market in the 1950s, but the cost per transaction when running these programs was so high that their early attempts failed.

In the late 1960s, improved computer technology, which lowered the transaction costs for providing credit card services, made it more likely that bank credit card programs would be profitable. The banks tried to enter this business again, and this time their efforts led to the creation of two successful bank credit card programs: BankAmericard (originally started by the Bank of America but now an independent organization called Visa) and MasterCharge (now MasterCard, run by the Interbank Card Association). These programs have become phenomenally successful; more than 200 million of their cards are in use. Indeed, bank credit cards have been so profitable that nonfinancial institutions such as Sears (which launched the Discover card), General Motors, and AT&T have also entered the credit card business. Consumers have benefited because credit cards are more widely accepted than checks when paying for purchases (particularly abroad), and they allow consumers to take out loans more easily.

The success of bank credit cards has led these institutions to come up with a new financial innovation, *debit cards*. Debit cards often look just like credit cards and can be used to make purchases in an identical fashion. However, in contrast to credit cards, which extend the purchaser a loan that does not have to be paid off immediately, a debit card purchase is immediately deducted from the card holder's bank account. Debit cards depend even more on low costs of processing transactions, since their profits are generated entirely from the fees paid by merchants on debit card purchases at their stores. Debit cards have been growing increasingly popular in recent years.

Electronic Banking The wonders of modern computer technology have also enabled banks to lower the cost of bank transactions by having the customer interact with an electronic banking facility rather than with a human being. One important form of an e-banking facility is the **automated teller machine (ATM),** an electronic machine that allows customers to get cash, make deposits, transfer funds from one account to another, and check balances. The ATM has the advantage that it does not have to be paid overtime and never sleeps, thus being available for use 24 hours a day. Not only does this result in cheaper transactions for the bank, but it also provides more convenience for the customer. Furthermore, because of its low cost, ATMs can be put at locations other than a bank or its branches, further increasing customer convenience. The low cost of ATMs has meant that they have sprung up everywhere and now number over 250,000 in the United States alone. Furthermore, it is now as easy to get foreign currency from an ATM when you are traveling in Europe as it is to get cash from your local bank. In addition, transactions with ATMs are so much cheaper for the bank than ones conducted with human tellers that some banks charge customers less if they use the ATM than if they use a human teller.

With the drop in the cost of telecommunications, banks have developed another financial innovation, home banking. It is now cost-effective for banks to set up an electronic banking facility in which the bank's customer is linked up with the bank's computer to carry out transactions by using either a telephone or a personal computer. Now a bank's customers can conduct many of their bank transactions without ever leaving the comfort of home. The advantage for the customer is the convenience of home banking, while banks find that the cost of transactions is substantially less than having the customer come to the bank. The success of ATMs and home banking has led to another innovation, the **automated banking machine (ABM),** which combines in one location an ATM, an Internet connection to the bank's website, and a telephone link to customer service.

With the decline in the price of personal computers and their increasing presence in the home, we have seen a further innovation in the home banking area, the appearance of a new type of banking institution, the **virtual bank,** a bank that has no physical location but rather exists only in cyberspace. In 1995, Security First Network Bank, based in Atlanta but now owned by Royal Bank of Canada, became the first virtual bank, planning to offer an array of banking services on the Internet—accepting checking account and savings deposits, selling certificates of deposits, issuing ATM cards, providing bill-paying facilities, and so on. The virtual bank thus takes home banking one step further, enabling the customer to have a full set of banking services at home 24 hours a day. In 1996, Bank of America and Wells Fargo entered the virtual banking market, to be followed by many others, with Bank of America now being the largest Internet bank in the United States. Will virtual banking be the predominant form of banking in the future (see Box 3)?

Electronic Payment The development of inexpensive computers and the spread of the Internet now makes it very cheap for banks to allow their customers to make bill payments electronically. Where in the past you had to pay your bills by mailing a check, now banks provide a website in which you just log on, make a few clicks, and your payment is transmitted electronically. You not only save the cost of the stamp, but paying bills now becomes (almost) a pleasure, requiring little effort. Electronic payment systems provided by banks now even allow you to avoid the step of having to log on to pay the bill. Instead, recurring bills can be automatically deducted from your bank account without your having to do a thing. Providing these services increases profitability for banks in two ways. First, payment of a bill electronically means that banks don't need people to process what would have otherwise been a paper transaction. Estimates of the cost savings for banks when a bill is paid electronically rather than by a check exceed one dollar. Second, the extra convenience for you, the customer, means that you are more likely to open an account with the bank. Electronic payment is thus becoming far more common in the United States, but Americans are far behind Europeans, particularly Scandinavians, in their use of electronic payments (see Box 4).

BOX 3: E-FINANCE

Will "Clicks" Dominate "Bricks" in the Banking Industry?

With the advent of virtual banks ("clicks") and the convenience they provide, a key question is whether they will become the primary form in which banks do their business, eliminating the need for physical bank branches ("bricks") as the main delivery mechanism for banking services. Indeed, will stand-alone Internet banks be the wave of the future?

The answer seems to be no. Internet-only banks such as Wingspan (owned by Bank One), First-e (Dublin-based), and Egg (a British Internet-only bank owned by Prudential) have had disappointing revenue growth and profits. The result is that pure on-line banking has not been the success that proponents had hoped for. Why has Internet banking been a disappointment?

There have been several strikes against Internet banking. First, bank depositors want to know that their savings are secure, so are reluctant to put their money into new institutions without a long track record. Second, customers worry about the security of their on-line transactions and whether their transactions will truly be kept private. Traditional banks are viewed as being more secure and trustworthy in terms of releasing private information. Third, customers may prefer services provided by physical branches. For example, banking customers seem to prefer to purchase long-term savings products face-to-face. Fourth, Internet banking still has run into technical problems—server crashes, slow connections over phone lines, mistakes in conducting transactions—that will probably diminish over time as technology improves.

The wave of the future thus does not appear to be pure Internet banks. Instead it looks like "clicks and bricks" will be the predominant form of banking, in which on-line banking is used to complement the services provided by traditional banks. Nonetheless, the delivery of banking services is undergoing massive changes, with more and more banking services delivered over the Internet and the number of physical bank branches likely to decline in the future.

BOX 4: E-Finance

Why Are Scandinavians so Far Ahead of Americans in Using Electronic Payments and On-Line Banking?

Americans are the biggest users of checks in the world. Close to 100 billion checks are written every year in the United States, and over three-quarters of noncash transactions are conducted with paper. In contrast, in most countries of Europe, over two-thirds of noncash transactions are electronic, with Finland and Sweden having the greatest proportion of on-line banking customers of any countries in the world. Indeed, if you were Finnish or Swedish, instead of writing a check, you would be far more likely to pay your bills on-line, not only through a personal computer, but even with your mobile phone. Why are Europeans and especially Scandinavians so far ahead of Americans in the use of electronic payments and on-line banking?

First, Europeans got used to making payments without checks, even before the advent of the personal computer. Europeans have made use of so-called *giro* payments for a long time, in which banks and post offices transfer funds for customers to pay bills. Second, Europeans, and particularly Scandinavians, are much greater users of mobile phones and the Internet than are Americans. Finland has the highest per capita use of mobile phones in the world, while Finland and Sweden lead the world in the percentage of the population that accesses the Internet. Maybe this is because of the low population densities of their countries and the fact that it is so cold and dark during the winter that Scandinavians prefer to stay inside at their PCs. Scandinavians would rather take the view that the reason for their being more high-tech is their good education systems and the resulting high degree of computer literacy, the presence of top technology companies such as Finland's Nokia and Sweden's Ericsson, and government policies to increase the use of personal computers, such as Sweden's giving companies tax incentives to provide their employees with home computers. The result of their wired population is that the Finns (and to a lesser extent Swedes) are percentagewise the biggest users of on-line banking in the world.

Americans are clearly behind the curve in their use of electronic payments, and this has imposed a high cost on the economy. Switching from checks to electronic payments might save the U.S. economy tens of billions of dollars per year, according to some estimates. Indeed, the U.S. federal government is trying to switch all its payments to electronic ones by directly depositing them into bank accounts in order to reduce its expenses. Can Americans be weaned from paper checks in the future and fully embrace the world of high-tech banking?

E-Money Electronic payments technology can not only substitute for checks but can, in the form of **electronic money** (or **e-money**), money that exists only in electronic form, substitute for cash as well. The first form of e-money is a stored-value card. The simplest form of stored-value card is purchased for a preset dollar amount that the consumer spends down. The more sophisticated stored-value card is known as a **smart card.** It contains its own computer chip so that it can be loaded with digital cash from the owner's bank account whenever needed. Smart cards can be loaded either from ATM machines, personal computers with a smart card reader, or from specially equipped telephones.

A second form of electronic money is often referred to as **e-cash,** and it is used on the Internet to purchase goods or services. A consumer gets e-cash by setting up an account with a bank that has links to the Internet and then has the e-cash transferred to her PC. When she wants to buy something with e-cash, she surfs to a store on the Web, clicks the "buy" option for a particular item, whereupon the e-cash is automatically transferred from her computer to the merchant's computer. The merchant can then have the funds transferred from the consumer's bank account to his before the goods are shipped.

Given the convenience of e-money, you might think that we would move quickly to the cashless society in which all payments were made electronically. However, this hasn't happened, as discussed in Box 5.

BOX 5: E-FINANCE

Are We Headed for a Cashless Society?

Predictions of a cashless society have been around for decades, but they have not come to fruition. For example, *Business Week* predicted in 1975 that electronic means of payment "would soon revolutionize the very concept of money itself," only to reverse itself several years later. Pilot projects in recent years with smart cards to convert consumers to the use of e-money have not been a success. Mondex, one of the widely touted, early stored-value cards that was launched in Britain in 1995, is only used on a few British university campuses. In Germany and Belgium, millions of people carry bank cards with computer chips embedded in them that enable them to make use of e-money, but very few use them. Why has the movement to a cashless society been so slow in coming?

Although e-money might be more convenient and may be more efficient than a payments system based on paper, several factors work against the disappearance of the paper system. First, it is very expensive to set up the computer, card reader, and telecommunications networks necessary to make electronic money the dominant form of payment. Second, electronic means of payment may raise security and privacy concerns. We often hear media reports that an unauthorized hacker has been able to access a computer database and to alter information stored there. The fact that this is not an uncommon occurrence means that unscrupulous persons might be able to access bank accounts in electronic payments systems and steal funds by moving them from someone else's accounts into their own. The prevention of this type of fraud is no easy task, and a whole new field of computer science is developing to cope with security issues. A further concern is that the use of electronic means of payment leaves an electronic trail that contains a large amount of personal data on buying habits. There are worries that government, employers, and marketers might be able to access these data, thereby encroaching on our privacy.

The conclusion from this discussion is that although the use of e-money will surely increase in the future, to paraphrase Mark Twain, "the reports of cash's death are greatly exaggerated."

Avoidance of Existing Regulations

The process of financial innovation we have discussed so far is much like innovation in other areas of the economy: It occurs in response to changes in demand and supply conditions. However, because the financial industry is more heavily regulated than other industries, government regulation is a much greater spur to innovation in this industry. Government regulation leads to financial innovation by creating incentives for firms to skirt regulations that restrict their ability to earn profits. Edward Kane describes this process of avoiding regulations as "loophole mining."[4] The economic analysis of innovation suggests that when the economic environment changes such that regulatory constraints are so burdensome that large profits can be made by avoiding them, loophole mining and innovation are more likely to occur.

Because banking is one of the most heavily regulated industries in America, loophole mining is especially likely to occur. The rise in inflation and interest rates from the late 1960s to 1980 made the regulatory constraints imposed on this industry even more burdensome. Under these circumstances, we would expect the pace of financial innovation in banking to be rapid, and, indeed, it has been.

Two sets of regulations have seriously restricted the ability of banks to make profits: reserve requirements that force banks to keep a certain fraction of their deposits as reserves (deposits in the Federal Reserve System) and restrictions on the interest rates that can be paid on deposits. For the following reasons, these

[4]"Banking Takes a Beating," *Time*, December 3, 1984, p. 49.

regulations have been among the major forces behind financial innovation in recent years.

Reserve Requirements The key to understanding why reserve requirements affect financial innovation is to recognize that they act, in effect, as a tax on deposits. Because the Fed does not pay interest on reserves, the opportunity cost of holding them is the interest that a bank could otherwise earn by lending the reserves out. For each dollar of deposits, reserve requirements therefore impose a cost on the bank equal to the interest rate i that could be earned if the reserves could be lent out times the fraction of deposits required as reserves r_D. The cost of $i \times r_D$ imposed on the bank is just like a tax on bank deposits of $i \times r_D$.

It is a great tradition to avoid taxes if possible, and banks also play this game. Just as taxpayers look for loopholes to lower their tax bills, banks seek to increase their profits by mining loopholes and by producing new financial innovations that allow them to escape the tax on deposits imposed by reserve requirements.

Restrictions on Interest Paid on Deposits Until 1980, legislation prohibited banks in most states from paying interest on checking account deposits, and through Regulation Q, the Fed set maximum limits on the interest rate that could be paid on time deposits. The desire to avoid these **deposit rate ceilings** also led to financial innovations.

If market interest rates rose above the maximum rates that banks paid on time deposits under Regulation Q, depositors withdrew funds from banks to put them into higher-yielding securities. This loss of deposits from the banking system restricted the amount of funds that banks could lend (called **disintermediation**) and thus limited bank profits. Banks had an incentive to get around deposit rate ceilings because by so doing, they could acquire more funds to make loans and earn higher profits.

We can now look at how the desire to avoid restrictions on interest payments and the tax effect of reserve requirements led to several important financial innovations.

Eurodollars and Bank Commercial Paper In the late 1960s, inflation was accelerating, and (as we would expect from our analysis of the Fisher effect in Chapter 4) interest rates began to rise. The tax on deposits from reserve requirements $i \times r_D$ also began to rise, and the incentives to avoid this tax increased. In addition, higher interest rates meant that market interest rates exceeded the maximum rate payable on time deposits under Regulation Q, and as market interest rates climbed to then record highs in 1969, investors reduced their time deposits to invest in higher-yielding securities. By the late 1960s, commercial banks had a strong incentive to search for new funds that would not be subject to reserve requirements and so escape the tax of $i \times r_D$ and not be subject to the interest rate ceiling set by Regulation Q.

As the economic analysis of innovation predicts, the banks began to mine loopholes and discovered two sources of funds that avoided both reserve requirements and deposit rate ceilings: Eurodollars and bank commercial paper. Because Eurodollars (deposits abroad denominated in dollars) were borrowed from banks outside the United States, they were not subject to reserve requirements or to Regulation Q. Similarly, commercial paper issued by a bank's parent holding company was not treated as deposits and so was also exempt from these regulations.

Not surprisingly, the markets for Eurodollars and bank commercial paper began to expand rapidly in the late 1960s.

NOW Accounts, ATS Accounts, and Overnight Repos The rise in interest rates in the late 1960s, which made the avoidance of restrictions on deposit rates profitable, stimulated the development of new types of checking accounts. Because of Regulation Q ceilings, savings and loans and mutual savings banks were hit especially hard by the rise in interest rates in the late 1960s. They lost large amounts of funds to financial instruments that paid higher interest rates, and they needed to find new sources of funds to continue to make profitable loans.

In 1970, as a result of diligent loophole mining, a mutual savings bank in Massachusetts struck gold by discovering a loophole in the prohibition of interest payments on checking accounts. In effect, by calling a check a "negotiable order of withdrawal" (NOW), accounts on which these NOWs could be written were not legally checking accounts. Hence NOW accounts were not subject to regulations on checking accounts and could pay interest. In May 1972, after two years of litigation, mutual savings banks in Massachusetts were allowed to issue NOW accounts that paid interest. Subsequently, in September 1972, the courts approved NOW accounts in New Hampshire.

NOW accounts were immediately successful in Massachusetts and New Hampshire, and they enabled savings and loans and mutual savings banks in those states to earn higher profits because they were able to attract more funds that could be loaned out. Since commercial banks did not want competition from other financial intermediaries for checking account deposits (at the time only commercial banks were legally allowed to issue checking accounts), they mounted a campaign to prevent the spread of these accounts to other states. The result was congressional legislation enacted in January 1974 that limited NOW accounts to New England. Legislation in 1980 finally authorized NOW accounts nationwide for savings and loans, mutual savings banks, and commercial banks, and similar accounts (**share draft accounts**) were authorized for credit unions.

Another innovation that enables banks to pay interest on checking accounts is the ATS (automatic transfer from savings) account. Balances above a certain amount in a checking account are automatically transferred into a savings account that pays interest. When a check is written on the ATS account, the necessary funds to cover the check are automatically transferred from the savings account into the checking account. Thus balances earning interest in a savings account are effectively part of the depositor's checking account because they are available for writing checks. Legally, however, it is the savings account and not the checking account that pays interest to the depositor.

Commercial banks provide a variant of the ATS account to their corporate depositors, which involves the use of a so-called *sweep account* to engage in overnight repurchase agreements (repos). In this type of arrangement, any balances above a certain amount in a corporation's checking account at the end of a business day are "swept out" of the account and invested in overnight repos that pay the corporation interest. (As you may recall from Chapter 2, the repo is an agreement whereby a corporation purchases Treasury bills that the bank agrees to repurchase the next day at a slightly higher price.) Again, although the checking account does not legally pay interest, in effect the corporation is receiving interest on balances that are available for writing checks.

The financial innovations of ATS accounts and overnight repo arrangements were stimulated not only by deposit rate ceilings but also by new technology. Without low-cost computers to process inexpensively the additional transactions required by these accounts, neither of these innovations would be profitable and therefore would not have been developed. Technological factors often combine with other incentives, such as the desire to get around restrictions on deposit rates, to produce financial innovation.

Conclusion Our discussion of financial innovation and the challenges that are facing managers of banks indicates that banking is no longer the staid profession it once was, prompting one banker to state, "Despite all the dark suits worn by its leaders, banking is a very dynamic industry."[5]

THE PRACTICING FINANCIAL INSTITUTION MANAGER

Profiting from a New Financial Product: A Case Study of Treasury Strips

We have seen that the advent of high-speed computers, which lowered the cost of processing financial transactions, led to such financial innovations as bank credit and debit cards. Because there is money to be made from financial innovation, it is important for managers of financial institutions to understand the thinking that goes into producing new, highly profitable financial products that take advantage of computer technology. To illustrate how financial institution managers can figure out ways to increase profits through financial innovation, we look at Treasury strips, a financial instrument first developed in 1982 by Salomon Brothers and Merrill Lynch. (Indeed, this innovation was so successful that the U.S. Treasury copied it when they issued STRIPS in 1985, as discussed in Chapter 9.)

One problem for investors in long-term coupon bonds, even when investors have a long holding period, is that there is some uncertainty in their returns arising from what is called *reinvestment risk.* Even if an investor holding a long-term coupon bond has a holding period of ten years, the return on the bond is not certain. The problem is that coupon payments are made before the bond matures in ten years, and these coupon payments must be reinvested. Because the interest rates at which the coupon payments will be reinvested fluctuate, the eventual return on the bond fluctuates as well. In contrast, long-term zero-coupon bonds have no reinvestment risk because they make no cash payments before the bond matures. The return on a zero-coupon bond if it is held to maturity is known at the time of purchase. The absence of reinvestment risk is an attractive feature of zero-coupon bonds, and as a result, investors are willing to accept a slightly lower interest rate on them than on coupon bonds, which do bear some reinvestment risk.

The fact that zero-coupon bonds have lower interest rates, along with the ability to use computers to create so-called hybrid securities, which are securities derived from other underlying securities, gave employees of Salomon Brothers and Merrill Lynch a brilliant idea for making profits. They could use computers to separate ("strip") a long-term Treasury coupon bond into a set of zero-coupon bonds. For example, a $1 million ten-year Treasury bond might be stripped into ten $100,000 zero-coupon bonds, which, naturally enough, are called *Treasury strips*. The lower interest rates on the more desirable Treasury strip zero-coupon bonds would mean that the value of these bonds would exceed the price of the

[5]Ibid.

underlying long-term Treasury bond, allowing Salomon Brothers and Merrill Lynch to make a profit by purchasing the long-term Treasury bond, separating it into Treasury strips, and selling them off as zero-coupon bonds.

To see in more detail how their thinking worked, let's look more closely at a $1 million ten-year Treasury bond with a coupon rate of 10% whose yield to maturity is also 10%, so it is selling at par. The cash payments for this bond are listed in the second column of Table 4. To make things simple, let's assume that the yield curve is absolutely flat so that the interest rate used to discount all the future cash payments is the same. Because zero-coupon bonds, which have no reinvestment risk, are more desirable than the ten-year Treasury coupon bond, the interest rate on the zero-coupon bonds is 9.75%, a little lower than the 10% interest rate on the coupon bond.

How would Fran, a smart and sophisticated financial institution manager, figure out if she could make a profit from creating and selling the Treasury strips? Her first step is to figure out what the zero-coupon Treasury strips would sell for. She would find this easy to do if she had read Chapter 3 of this book: Using Equation 1 in that chapter, she would figure out that each of the Treasury strip zero-coupon bonds would sell for its present discounted value:

$$\frac{\text{Cash payment in year } n}{(1 + 0.0975)^n}$$

The results of this calculation for each year are listed in column (4) of Table 4. When Fran adds up the values of the collection of the Treasury strip zero-coupon bonds, she gets a figure of $1,015,528, which is greater than the $1 million purchase price of the Treasury bond. As long as it costs less than $15,528 to collect the payments from the Treasury and then pass them through to the owners of the zero-coupon strips, which is likely to be the case since computer technology makes the cost of conducting these financial transactions low, the zero-coupon strips will be profitable for her financial institution. Fran would thus recommend that her firm go ahead and market the new financial product. Because the financial institution can now generate much higher profits by selling substantial numbers of Treasury strips, it would amply reward Fran with a spanking new red BMW and a $100,000 bonus!

TABLE 4 Market Value of Treasury Strip Zero-Coupon Bonds Derived from a $1 Million Ten-Year Treasury Bond with a 10% Coupon Rate and Selling at Par

(1)	(2)	(3)	(4)
Year	Cash Payment ($)	Interest Rate on Zero-Coupon Bond (%)	Present Discounted Value of Zero-Coupon Bond ($)
1	100,000	9.75	91,116
2	100,000	9.75	83,022
3	100,000	9.75	75,646
4	100,000	9.75	68,926
5	100,000	9.75	62,802
6	100,000	9.75	57,223
7	100,000	9.75	52,140
8	100,000	9.75	47,508
9	100,000	9.75	43,287
10	100,000	9.75	39,442
10	1,000,000	9.75	394,416
Total			$1,015,528

SUMMARY

1. The balance sheet of commercial banks can be thought of as a list of the sources and uses of bank funds. The bank's liabilities are its sources of funds, which include checkable deposits, time deposits, discount loans from the Fed, borrowings from other banks and corporations, and bank capital. The bank's assets are its uses of funds, which include reserves, cash items in process of collection, deposits at other banks, securities, loans, and other assets (mostly physical capital).
2. Banks make profits through the process of asset transformation: They borrow short (accept deposits) and lend long (make loans). When a bank takes in additional deposits, it gains an equal amount of reserves; when it pays out deposits, it loses an equal amount of reserves.
3. Although more liquid assets tend to earn lower returns, banks still desire to hold them. Specifically, banks hold excess and secondary reserves because they provide insurance against the costs of a deposit outflow. Banks manage their assets to maximize profits by seeking the highest returns possible on loans and securities while at the same time trying to lower risk and making adequate provisions for liquidity. Although liability management was once a staid affair, large (money center) banks now actively seek out sources of funds by issuing liabilities such as negotiable CDs or by actively borrowing from other banks and corporations. Banks manage the amount of capital they hold to prevent bank failure and to meet bank capital requirements set by the regulatory authorities. However, they do not want to hold too much capital because by so doing they will lower the returns to equity holders.
4. Off-balance-sheet activities consist of trading financial instruments and generating income from fees and loan sales, all of which affect bank profits but are not visible on bank balance sheets. Because these off-balance-sheet activities expose banks to increased risk, bank management must pay particular attention to risk assessment procedures and internal controls to restrict employees from taking on too much risk.
5. A bank's net operating income equals operating income minus operating expenses. Adding gains (or losses) on securities and net extraordinary items to net operating income and then subtracting taxes yields net income (profits after taxes). Additional measures of bank performance include the return on assets *(ROA),* the return on equity *(ROE),* and the net interest margin *(NIM).*
6. A change in the economic environment will stimulate financial institutions to search for financial innovations that are likely to be profitable. Changes in demand conditions, especially the rise in interest-rate risk, have stimulated a search for profits that has resulted in financial innovations such as adjustable-rate mortgages, while changes in supply conditions because of advances in computer technology have led to financial innovations such as bank credit cards and electronic banking facilities. Regulation leads to financial innovation at banks by encouraging loophole mining. Starting in the late 1960s, for example, higher interest rates (resulting from higher inflation) combined with deposit rate ceilings and the "tax" on deposits to limit bank profits. The desire to avoid these regulations encouraged financial innovations, including NOW accounts, ATS accounts, and overnight repos.

KEY TERMS

asset management, *p. 408*
automated banking machine (ABM) *p. 426*
automated teller machine (ATM) *p. 426*
balance sheet, *p. 401*
capital adequacy management, *p. 408*
credit risk, *p. 408*
deposit outflows, *p. 408*
deposit rate ceiling, *p. 430*
discount loans, *p. 403*
discount rate, *p. 410*
disintermediation, *p. 430*
electronic money (e-money), *p. 428*
equity multiplier *(EM), p. 414*
excess reserves, *p. 404*
financial engineering, *p. 424*
interest-rate risk, *p. 408*
liability management, *p. 408*
liquidity management, *p. 408*
loan commitment, *p. 417*
loan sale, *p. 417*
money center banks, *p. 412*
net interest margin (NIM), *p. 422*
note issuance facilities (NIFs), *p. 418*
off-balance-sheet activities, *p. 417*
operating expenses, *p. 421*
operating income, *p. 420*
required reserve ratio, *p. 404*
required reserves, *p. 404*
reserves, *p. 404*

return on assets (ROA), *p. 414*
return on equity (ROE), *p. 414*
revolving underwriting facilities (RUFs), *p. 418*
secondary reserves, *p. 405*
share draft account, *p. 431*
smart card, *p. 428*
T-account, *p. 406*
vault cash, *p. 404*
virtual bank, *p. 426*

QUESTIONS AND PROBLEMS

1. Why might a bank be willing to borrow funds from other banks at a higher rate than it can borrow from the Fed?

***2.** Rank the following bank assets from most to least liquid:

a. Commercial loans
b. Securities
c. Reserves
d. Physical capital

3. Using the T-accounts of the First National Bank and the Second National Bank, describe what happens when Jane Brown writes a $50 check on her account at the First National Bank to pay her friend Joe Green, who in turn deposits the check into his account at the Second National Bank.

***4.** What happens to reserves at the First National Bank if one person withdraws $1000 of cash and another person deposits $500 of cash? Use T-accounts to explain your answer.

5. The bank you own has the following balance sheet:

Assets		Liabilities	
Reserves	$75 million	Deposits	$500 million
Loans	$525 million	Bank capital	$100 million

If the bank suffers a deposit outflow of $50 million with a required reserve ratio on deposits of 10%, what actions must you take to make sure that your bank meets its reserve requirements?

***6.** If a deposit outflow of $50 million occurs, which balance sheet would a bank rather have initially, the balance sheet in Problem 5 or the following balance sheet? Why?

Assets		Liabilities	
Reserves	$100 million	Deposits	$500 million
Securities	$500 million	Bank capital	$100 million

7. If the president of a bank told you that the bank was so well run that it has never had to call in loans, sell securities, or borrow as a result of a deposit outflow, would you be willing to buy stock in that bank? Why or why not?

***8.** If the bank you own has no excess reserves and a sound customer comes in asking for a loan, should you automatically turn the customer down, explaining that you don't have any excess reserves to loan out? Why or why not? What options are available for you to provide the funds your customer needs?

9. Why has the development of overnight loan markets made it more likely that banks will hold fewer excess reserves?

***10.** If you are a banker and expect interest rates to rise in the future, would you want to make short-term or long-term loans?

11. "Bank managers should always seek the highest return possible on their assets." Is this statement true, false, or uncertain? Explain your answer.

***12.** "Banking has become a more dynamic industry because of more active liability management." Is this statement true, false, or uncertain? Explain your answer.

13. Why has noninterest income been growing as a source of bank operating income?

***14.** Which components of operating expenses experience the greatest fluctuations? Why?

15. Why do equity holders care more about *ROE* than about *ROA*?

***16.** What does the net interest margin measure, and why is it important to bank managers?

17. If a bank doubles the amount of its capital and *ROA* stays constant, what will happen to *ROE*?

***18.** If a bank finds that its *ROE* is too low because it has too much bank capital, what can it do to raise its *ROE*?

19. What are the benefits and costs for a bank when it decides to increase the amount of its bank capital?

***20.** If a bank is falling short of meeting its capital requirements by $1 million, what three things can it do to rectify the situation?

The Banking Firm and Bank Management

1. Table 1 reports the balance sheet of all commercial banks based on aggregate data found in the Federal Reserve website. Compare this table to the balance sheet reported by Wachovia found at http://www.wachovia.com/investor/annualfinancials.asp. Does Wachovia have more or less of its portfolio in loans than the average bank? What types of loans does it hold the most of?
2. It is relatively easy to find up-to-date information on banks because of their extensive reporting requirements. Go to http://www2.fdic.gov/qbp/. Sponsored by the Federal Deposit Insurance Corporation, this site offers summary data on financial institutions. Go to the most recent Quarterly Banking Profile. Scroll to the bottom and open Table 1-A.
   a. Have banks' return on assets been increasing or decreasing over the last few years?
   b. Has the core capital been increasing, and how does it compare to the capital ratio reported in Table 1 in the text?
   c. How many institutions are currently reporting to the FDIC?

Chapter 16

Commercial Banking Industry: Structure and Competition

Preview

The operations of individual banks (how they acquire, use, and manage funds to make a profit) are roughly similar throughout the world. In all countries, banks are financial intermediaries in the business of earning profits. When you consider the structure and operation of the banking industry as a whole, however, the United States is in a class by itself. In most countries, four or five large banks typically dominate the banking industry, but in the United States there are on the order of 9,000 commercial banks.

Is more better? Does this diversity mean that the American banking system is more competitive and therefore more economically efficient and sound than banking systems in other countries? What in the American economic and political system explains this large number of banking institutions? In this chapter we try to answer these questions by examining the historical trends in the commercial banking industry and its overall structure.

We start by examining the industry in detail. In addition to looking at our domestic banking system, we also examine the forces behind the growth in international banking to see how it has affected us in the United States. Finally, we examine how financial innovation has increased the competitive environment for the banking industry and is causing fundamental changes in it.

HISTORICAL DEVELOPMENT OF THE BANKING SYSTEM

The modern commercial banking industry began when the Bank of North America was chartered in Philadelphia in 1782. With the success of this bank, other banks opened for business, and the American banking industry was off and running. (As a study aid, Figure 1 provides a time line of the most important dates in the history of American banking before World War II.)

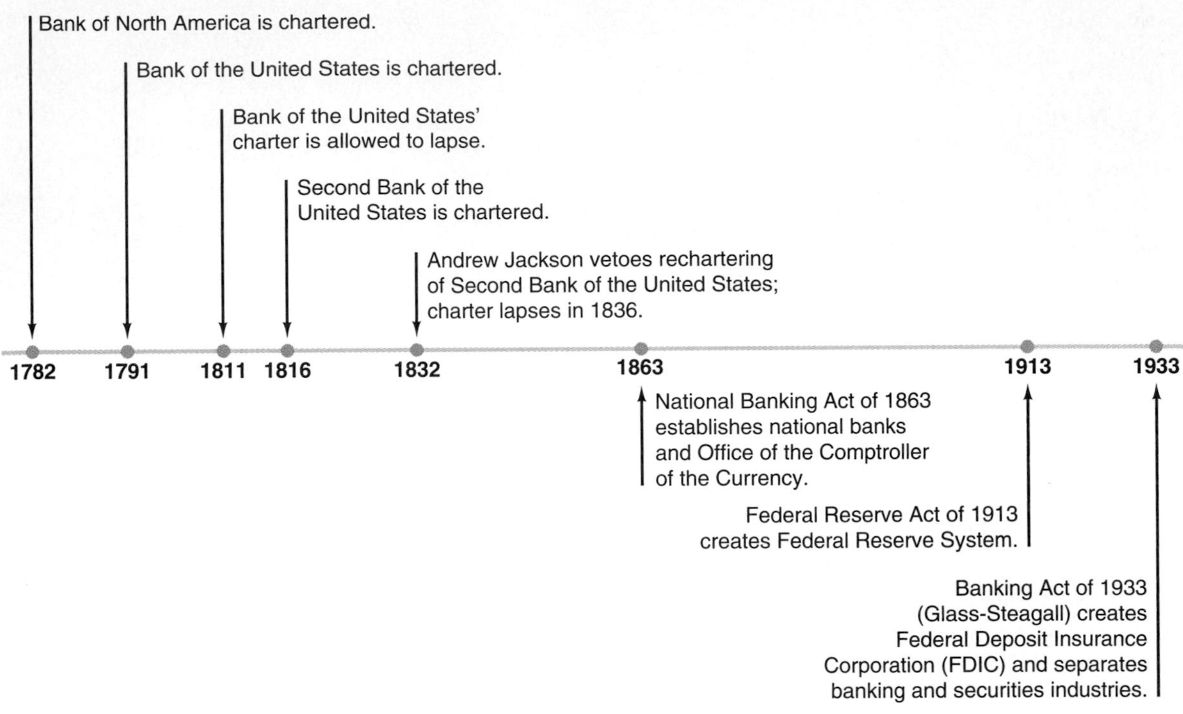

FIGURE 1 Time Line of the Early History of Commercial Banking in the United States

A major controversy involving the industry in its early years was whether the federal government or the states should charter banks. The Federalists, particularly Alexander Hamilton, advocated greater centralized control of banking and federal chartering of banks. Their efforts led to the creation in 1791 of the Bank of the United States, which had elements of both a private and a central bank, a government institution that has responsibility for the amount of money and credit supplied in the economy as a whole. Agricultural and other interests, however, were quite suspicious of centralized power and hence advocated chartering by the states. Furthermore, their distrust of moneyed interests in the big cities led to political pressures to eliminate the Bank of the United States, and in 1811 their efforts met with success when its charter was not renewed. Because of abuses by state banks and the clear need for a central bank to help the federal government raise funds during the War of 1812, Congress was stimulated to create the Second Bank of the United States in 1816. The tensions between advocates and opponents of centralized banking power were a recurrent theme during the operation of this second attempt at central banking in the United States, and with the election of Andrew Jackson, a strong advocate of states' rights, the fate of the Second Bank was sealed. After the election in 1832, Jackson vetoed the rechartering of the Second Bank of the United States as a national bank, and its charter lapsed in 1836.

Until 1863, all commercial banks in the United States were chartered by the banking commission of the state in which each operated. No national currency existed, and banks obtained funds primarily by issuing *banknotes* (currency circulated by the banks that could be redeemed for gold). Because banking regulations were extremely lax in many states, banks regularly failed due to fraud or lack of sufficient bank capital; their banknotes became worthless.

To eliminate the abuses of the state-chartered banks (called **state banks**), the National Banking Act of 1863 (and subsequent amendments to it) created a new banking system of federally chartered banks (called **national banks**), supervised by the Office of the Comptroller of the Currency, a department of the U.S. Treasury. This legislation was originally intended to dry up sources of funds to state banks by imposing a prohibitive tax on their banknotes while leaving the banknotes of the federally chartered banks untaxed. The state banks cleverly escaped extinction by acquiring funds by offering checking accounts. As a result, today the United States has a **dual banking system** in which banks supervised by the federal government and banks supervised by the states operate side by side.

Central banking did not reappear in this country until the Federal Reserve System (the Fed) was created in 1913 to promote an even safer banking system. All national banks were required to become members of the Federal Reserve System and became subject to a new set of regulations issued by the Fed. State banks could choose (but were not required) to become members of the system, and most did not because of the high costs of membership stemming from the Fed's regulations.

During the Great Depression years 1930–1933, some 9000 bank failures wiped out the savings of many depositors at commercial banks. To prevent future depositor losses from such failures, banking legislation in 1933 established the Federal Deposit Insurance Corporation (FDIC), which provided federal insurance on bank deposits. Member banks of the Federal Reserve System were required to purchase FDIC insurance for their depositors, and non-Federal Reserve commercial banks could choose to buy this insurance (almost all of them did). The purchase of FDIC insurance made banks subject to another set of regulations imposed by the FDIC.

The FDIC gathers data about individual financial institutions and the banking industry that you can access at www.fdic.gov/bank/

Because investment banking activities of the commercial banks were blamed for many bank failures, provisions in the banking legislation of 1933 (also known as the Glass-Steagall Act) prohibited commercial banks from underwriting or dealing in corporate securities (commercial banks were allowed to sell new issues of government securities, however) and limited banks to the purchase of debt securities approved by the bank regulatory agencies. Likewise it prohibited investment banks from engaging in commercial banking activities. In effect, the Glass-Steagall Act separated the activities of commercial banks from those of the securities industry.

Under the conditions of the Glass-Steagall Act, commercial banks had to sell off their investment banking operations. The First National Bank of Boston, for example, spun off its investment banking operations into the First Boston Corporation, now one of the most important investment banking firms in America. Investment banking firms typically discontinued their deposit business, although J. P. Morgan discontinued its investment banking business and reorganized as a commercial bank; however, some senior officers of J. P. Morgan went on to organize Morgan Stanley, another one of the largest investment banking firms today.

Multiple Regulatory Agencies

Commercial bank regulation in the United States has developed into a crazy-quilt system of multiple regulatory agencies with overlapping jurisdictions. The Office of the Comptroller of the Currency has the primary supervisory responsibility for the 3000 national banks that own more than half of the assets in the commercial banking system. The Federal Reserve and the state banking authorities have joint primary responsibility for the 1000 state banks that are members of the Federal Reserve System. The Fed also has sole regulatory responsibility over companies that own one or more banks (called **bank holding companies**) and secondary responsibility for the national banks. The FDIC and the state banking authorities jointly supervise the 6000 state banks that have FDIC insurance but are not members of the Federal Reserve System. The state banking authorities have sole jurisdiction over the fewer than 500 state banks without FDIC insurance. (Such banks hold less than 0.2% of the deposits in the commercial banking system.)

If you find the U.S. bank regulatory system confusing, imagine how confusing it is for the banks, which have to deal with multiple regulatory agencies. Several proposals have been raised by the U.S. Treasury to rectify this situation by centralizing the regulation of all depository institutions under one independent agency. However, none of these has been successful in Congress, and whether there will be regulatory consolidation in the future is highly uncertain.

STRUCTURE OF THE U.S. COMMERCIAL BANKING INDUSTRY

There are around 8200 commercial banks in the United States, far more than in any other country in the world. As Table 1 indicates, we have an extraordinary number of small banks. 31.6 percent of the banks have less than $50 million in assets. Far more typical is the size distribution in Canada or the United Kingdom, where five or fewer banks dominate the industry. In contrast, the five largest commercial banks in the United States (listed in Table 2) together hold just 45% of the assets in their industry.

Most industries in the United States have far fewer firms than the commercial banking industry; typically, large firms tend to dominate these industries to a greater extent than in the commercial banking industry. (Consider the computer software industry, which is dominated by Microsoft, or the automobile industry, which is dominated by General Motors, Ford, Chrysler, Toyota, and Honda.) Does the large number of banks in the commercial banking industry and the absence of a few dominant firms suggest that commercial banking is more competitive than other industries?

TABLE 1 Size Distribution of Insured Commercial Banks, June 30, 2001

Assets	Number of Banks	Share of Banks (%)	Share of Assets Held (%)
Less than $25 million	967	11.8	0.3
$25–$50 million	1620	19.8	1.0
$50–$100 million	2098	25.7	2.4
$100–$300 million	2303	28.2	6.1
$300–$500 million	474	5.8	2.8
$500 million–$1 billion	324	4.0	3.5
$1–$3 billion	220	2.7	5.8
$3–$10 billion	93	1.1	8.3
$10 billion or more	79	1.0	69.9
Total	8178	100.1	100.1

Source: http://www.fdic.gov/bank/statistical/statistics/0109/allstru.html

TABLE 2 Ten Largest U.S. Banks, 2001

Bank	Assets ($ billions)	Share of All Commercial Bank Assets (%)
1. Citicorp, New York	902.20	14.2
2. Chase, New York	715.30	11.2
3. Bank of America, Charlotte, NC	642.20	10.1
4. Wachovia/First Union, Charlotte, NC	328.20	5.2
5. Wells Fargo, San Francisco	272.40	4.3
6. Bank One, Columbus, OH	269.30	4.2
7. FleetBoston Financial Corp., Boston, MA	219.20	3.4
8. Washington Mutual, Seattle, WA	188.60	3.0
9. U.S. Bancorp/Firstar, Minneapolis, MN	164.90	2.6
10. Sun Trust Bank, Atlanta, GA	103.50	1.6
Total	3,805.80	59.8

Source: http://www.onlinebankingreport.com/resources/100.html

Restrictions on Branching

The presence of so many commercial banks in the United States actually reflects past regulations that restricted the ability of these financial institutions to open **branches** (additional offices for the conduct of banking operations). Each state had its own regulations on the type and number of branches that a bank could open. Regulations on both coasts, for example, tended to allow banks to open branches throughout a state; in the middle part of the country, regulations on branching were more restrictive. The McFadden Act of 1927, which was designed to put national banks and state banks on an equal footing (and the Douglas Amendment of 1970, which closed a loophole in the McFadden Act) effectively prohibited banks from branching across state lines and forced all national banks to conform to the branching regulations in the state of their location.

The result of the McFadden Act and the state branching regulations was that many small banks stayed in existence because a large bank capable of driving them out of business was often restricted from opening a branch nearby. Indeed, it was often easier for a U.S. bank to open a branch in a foreign country than to open one in another state!

Advocates of restrictive state branching regulations argue that these regulations foster competition by keeping so many banks in business. But the existence of large numbers of banks in the United States must be seen as an indication of a *lack* of competition, *not* the presence of vigorous competition. Inefficient banks have been able to remain in business because their customers could not find a conveniently located branch of another bank in which to conduct their business.

The McFadden Act and state branching regulations constituted strong anticompetitive forces in the commercial banking industry. If competition is beneficial to society, why have regulations restricting branching arisen in America? The simplest explanation is that the American public has historically been hostile to large banks. States with the most restrictive branching regulations were typically ones in which populist antibank sentiment was strongest in the nineteenth century. (These states usually had large farming populations whose relations with banks periodically became tempestuous when banks would foreclose on farmers who couldn't pay their debts.) The legacy of nineteenth-century politics was a banking system with restrictive branching regulations and hence an inordinate number of small banks. However, as we will see later in this chapter, branching restrictions are being eliminated, and we are heading toward nationwide banking.

Response to Branching Restrictions

An important feature of the U.S. banking industry is that competition can be repressed by regulation but not completely quashed. As we saw in Chapter 15, the existence of restrictive regulation will stimulate banking institutions to go "loophole mining," coming up with financial innovations that get around these regulations in the banks' search for profits. Regulations restricting branching have stimulated similar economic forces and have promoted the development of three financial innovations: bank holding companies, nonbank banks, and automated teller machines.

Bank Holding Companies A holding company is a corporation that owns several different companies. This form of corporate ownership has important advantages for banks in that (1) it has allowed them to circumvent restrictive branching regulations, because the holding company can own a controlling interest in several banks even if branching is not permitted; (2) a bank holding company can engage in other activities related to banking, such as the provision of investment advice, data processing and transmission services, leasing, credit card services, and servicing of loans in other states; and (3) the holding company can issue commercial paper, allowing the bank to tap into nondeposit sources of funds.

At the current time, bank holding companies are restricted to owning businesses that are "closely related to banking." Permissible activities, which are specified by the Federal Reserve's Regulation Y, include the activities mentioned here as well as others, ranging from providing courier services to real estate appraisal. In the past, the Fed and congressional legislation have prohibited bank holding companies from engaging in activities such as brokering real estate, underwriting securities, operating travel agencies, and offering general management consulting. However, in their continuing search for profits, bank holding companies have been seeking ways to get around these regulations and have been entering previously prohibited areas.

Bank holding companies also have the advantage that many states would allow bank holding companies headquartered in other states to purchase banks in their state. In addition, starting in 1982, banks were permitted to purchase out-of-state banks that were failing. For example, bank holding companies headquartered in New York, Ohio, North Carolina, Michigan, and California gained entry into the Texas market by purchasing failing institutions in that state. The result was that the McFadden Act's restrictions on branching no longer prevented these companies from providing banking services in other states.

The growth of the bank holding companies has been dramatic over the past three decades. Today bank holding companies own almost all large banks, and over 90% of all commercial bank deposits are held in banks owned by holding companies.

Nonbank Banks Another way banks could avoid branching restrictions was through a loophole in the Bank Holding Company Act of 1956, which defined a bank as a financial institution that accepts deposits *and* makes loans. Once bank holding companies recognized this loophole, they realized that if they opened limited-service banks that either took deposits but did not make commercial loans or did not take deposits but made commercial loans, these so-called **nonbank banks** would not be subject to branching regulations. Thus the bank holding companies discovered a way of branching across state lines. However, the Competitive Equality Bank Act passed in 1987 placed a moratorium on new nonbank banks, thus closing this loophole.

Automated Teller Machines Another financial innovation that avoided the restrictions on branching is the electronic banking facility known as the automated teller machine (ATM). Banks realized that if they did not own or rent the ATM, but instead let it be owned by someone else and paid for each transaction with a fee, the ATM would probably not be considered a branch of the bank and thus would not be subject to branching regulations. This is exactly what the regulatory agencies and courts in most states concluded. Because they enable banks to widen their markets, a number of these shared facilities (such as Cirrus and NYCE) have been established nationwide. Furthermore, even when an ATM is owned by a bank, states typically have special provisions that allow wider establishment of ATMs than is permissible for traditional "brick and mortar" branches.

As we saw in Chapter 15, avoiding regulation was not the only reason for the development of the ATM. The advent of cheaper computer and telecommunications technology enabled banks to provide ATMs at low cost, making them a profitable innovation. This further illustrates that technological factors often combine with incentives such as the desire to avoid restrictive regulations like branching restrictions to produce financial innovation.

BANK CONSOLIDATION AND NATIONWIDE BANKING

As we can see in Figure 2, after a remarkable period of stability from 1934 to the mid-1980s, the number of commercial banks has begun to fall dramatically. Why is this sudden decline taking place?

The banking industry hit some hard times in the 1980s and early 1990s, with bank failures running at a rate of over 100 per year from 1985 to 1992 (more on this in Chapter 18). But bank failures are only part of the story. In the years 1985–1992, the number of banks declined by 3000—more than double the number of failures. And in the period 1992–2001, when the banking industry returned to health, the number of commercial banks declined by over 3000, less than 5 percent of which were bank failures, and most of those were of small banks. Thus we see that bank failures played an important, though not predominant, role in the decline in the number of banks in the 1985–1992 period and an almost negligible role in the decline in the number of banks since then.

So what explains the rest of the story? The answer is bank consolidation. Banks have been merging to create larger entities or have been buying up other banks. This gives rise to a new question: Why has bank consolidation been taking place in recent years?

As we have seen, loophole mining by banks has reduced the effectiveness of branching restrictions, with the result that many states have recognized that it would be in their best interest if they allowed ownership of banks across state lines. The result has been the formation of reciprocal and regional compacts in which banks in one state are allowed to own banks in other states in the region. In 1975, Maine enacted the first interstate banking legislation that allowed out-of-state bank holding companies to purchase banks in that state. In 1982, Massachusetts enacted

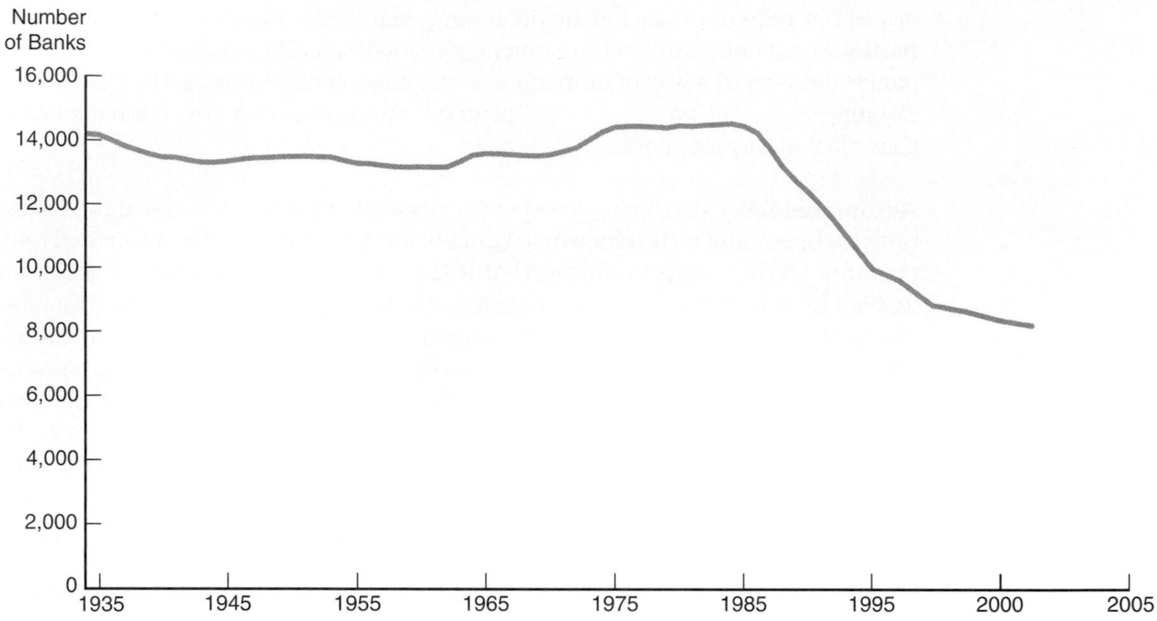

FIGURE 2 Number of Insured Commercial Banks in the United States, 1934–2001

Source: http://www.fdic.gov/bank/statistical/statistics/sectionb.html

a regional compact with other New England states to allow interstate banking, and many other regional compacts were adopted thereafter until, by the early 1990s, almost all states allowed some form of interstate banking.

With the barriers to interstate banking breaking down in the early 1980s, banks recognized that they could gain the benefits of diversification because they would now be able to make loans in many states rather than in just one. This gave them the advantage that if one state's economy was weak, another in which they operated might be strong, thus decreasing the likelihood that loans in different states would default at the same time. In addition, allowing banks to own banks in other states meant that they could take advantage of economies of scale by increasing their size through out-of-state acquisition of banks or by merging with banks in other states. Mergers and acquisitions explain the first phase of banking consolidation which has played such an important role in the decline in the number of banks since 1985. Another result of the loosening of restrictions on interstate branching is the development of a new class of bank, the so-called **superregional banks,** bank holding companies that have begun to rival the money center banks in size but whose headquarters are not based in one of the money center cities (New York, Chicago, and San Francisco). Examples of these superregional banks are NationsBank of Charlotte, North Carolina, and Banc One of Columbus, Ohio.

Riegle-Neal Interstate Banking and Branching Efficiency Act of 1994

Banking consolidation has been given further stimulus by the passage in 1994 of the Riegle-Neal Interstate Banking and Branching Efficiency Act. This legislation expands the regional compacts to the entire nation and overturns the McFadden Act and Douglas Amendment's prohibition of interstate banking. Not only does this act allow bank holding companies to acquire banks in any other state, notwithstanding any state laws to the contrary, but it allows interstate branching by allowing bank holding companies to merge the banks they own into one bank with branches in different states beginning June 1, 1997. States do have the option of allowing interstate branching to occur earlier than this date, and several have done so; they also have the option of opting out of interstate branching, a choice only Texas has made.

The Riegle-Neal Act finally establishes the basis for a true nationwide banking system. Although interstate banking was accomplished previously by out-of-state purchase of banks by bank holding companies, up until 1994 interstate branching was virtually nonexistent because very few states had enacted interstate branching legislation. Allowing banks to conduct interstate banking through branching is especially important because many bankers feel that economies of scale cannot be fully exploited through the bank holding company structure; they can be fully exploited only through branching networks in which all of the bank's operations are fully coordinated.

Nationwide banks are now beginning to emerge. With the merger in 1998 of BankAmerica and NationsBank, which created the first bank with branches on both coasts, consolidation in the banking industry should eventually lead to banking organizations with operations in almost all of the 50 states.

What Will the Structure of the U.S. Banking Industry Look Like in the Future?

With true nationwide banking becoming a reality, the benefits of bank consolidation for the banking industry have increased substantially, thus driving the next phase of mergers and acquisitions and accelerating the decline in the number of commercial banks. Great changes are occurring in the structure of this industry, and the natural question arises: What will the industry look like in, say, ten years?

One view is that the industry will become more like that in many other countries (see Box 1) and we will end up with only a couple of hundred banks. A more extreme view is that it will look like that of Canada or the United Kingdom with a few large banks dominating the industry. Research on this question, however, comes up with a different answer. The structure of the U.S. banking industry will still be unique, but not as unique as it once was. Most experts predict that the consolidation surge will settle down as the U.S. banking industry approaches several thousand, rather than several hundred, banks. One simple way of seeing why the number of banks will continue to be substantial is to recognize that California, which has unrestricted branching throughout the state, has close to 400 commercial banks. Blowing up the number of banks by the share of banking assets in California relative to the whole country produces an estimate of the number of banks with unrestricted nationwide branching on the order of 4000. More sophisticated research suggests that the number of banks in the United States will ultimately be somewhat fewer than this, but not much.[1]

---

[1]For example, see Allen N. Berger, Anil K. Kashyap, and Joseph Scalise, "The Transformation of the U.S. Banking Industry: What a Long, Strange Trip It's Been," *Brookings Papers on Economic Activity* 2 (1995): 55–201, and Timothy Hannan and Stephen Rhoades, "Future U.S. Banking Structure, 1990–2010," in *Antitrust Bulletin* 37 (1992): 737–798. For a more detailed treatment of the bank consolidation process taking place in the United States, see Frederic S. Mishkin, "Bank Consolidation: A Central Banker's Perspective," National Bureau Working Paper No. 5849, December 1996.

BOX 1: GLOBAL

Comparison of Banking Structures in the United States and Abroad

The structure of the commercial banking industry in the United States is radically different from that in other industrialized nations. The United States is the only country that is just now developing a true national banking system in which banks have branches throughout the country. One result is that there are many more banks in the United States than in other industrialized countries. In contrast to the United States, which has on the order of 8100 commercial banks, every other industrialized country has well under 1000. Japan, for example, has fewer than 100 commercial banks—a mere fraction of the number in the United States, even though its economy and population are half the size of the United States. Another result of the past restrictions on branching in the United States is that our banks tend to be much smaller than those in other countries.

Banking consolidation will result in not only a smaller number of banks, but as the mergers between Chase Manhattan Bank and Chemical Bank and between BankAmerica and NationsBank suggest, a shift in assets from smaller banks to larger banks as well. Within ten years, the share of bank assets in banks with less than $100 million in assets is expected to halve, while the amount at the so-called megabanks, those with over $100 billion in assets, is expected to more than double. Indeed, some analysts have predicted that we won't have long to wait before the first trillion-dollar bank emerges.

Are Bank Consolidation and Nationwide Banking Good Things?

Advocates of nationwide banking believe that it will produce more efficient banks and a healthier banking system less prone to bank failures. However, critics of bank consolidation fear that it will eliminate small banks, referred to as *community banks,* and that this will result in less lending to small businesses. In addition, they worry that a few banks will come to dominate the industry, making the banking business less competitive.

Most economists are skeptical of these criticisms of bank consolidation. As we have seen, research indicates that even after bank consolidation is completed, the United States will still have plenty of banks. Furthermore, megabanks will not dominate the banking industry. This research suggests that there will be more than ten banks with assets over $100 billion, and their collective share of bank assets will be less than 50%. The banking industry will thus remain highly competitive, probably even more so than now considering that banks that have been protected from competition from out-of-state banks will now have to compete with them vigorously to stay in business.

It also does not look as though community banks will disappear. When New York State liberalized branching laws in 1962, there were fears that community banks upstate would be driven from the market by the big New York City banks. Not only did this not happen, but some of the big boys found that the small banks were able to run rings around them in the local markets. Similarly, California, which has had unrestricted statewide branching for a long time, continues to have a thriving collection of community banks.

Economists see some important benefits of bank consolidation and nationwide banking. The elimination of geographic restrictions on banking will increase competition and drive inefficient banks out of business, thus raising the efficiency of

BOX 2: E-FINANCE

Technology and Bank Consolidation

The advent of the Web and improved computer technology is another factor driving bank consolidation. To achieve low costs, huge investments in technology are necessary, requiring that a business line be of very large scale. This has been particularly true in the credit card business in recent years. Huge technology investments have been made to provide customers with convenient websites and to develop better systems to handle processing and risk analysis for both credit and fraud risk. The result has been substantial consolidation: As recently as 1995, the top five banking institutions issuing credit cards held less than 40% of total credit card debt, while today this number is above 60%.

Technology has also led to increasing consolidation of the bank custody business. Banks hold the actual certificate for investors when they purchase a stock or bond and provide data on the value of these securities and how much risk an investor is facing. Because this business is also computer intensive, it also requires very large scale investments in computer technology in order for the bank to offer these services at competitive rates. The percentage of assets at the top 10 custody banks has therefore risen from 40% in 1990 to over 90% today.

The increasing importance of e-finance, in which the computer is becoming more important in delivering financial services, is leading to tremendous changes in the structure of the banking industry. Although banks are more than willing to offer a full range of products to their customers, they no longer find it profitable to produce all of them. Instead, they are contracting out the business, which will lead to further consolidation of technology-intensive banking businesses in the future.

the banking sector. The move to larger banking organizations is also being driven by advances in computer technology (see Box 2), and it also means that there will be some increase in efficiency because of economies of scale. The increased diversification of banks' loan portfolios may lower the probability of a banking crisis in the future. In the 1980s and early 1990s, bank failures were often concentrated in states with weak economies. For example, after the decline in oil prices in 1986, all the major commercial banks in Texas, which had been very profitable, now found themselves in trouble. At that time, banks in New England were doing fine. However, when the 1990–1991 recession hit New England hard, New England banks started failing. With nationwide banking, a bank could make loans in both New England and Texas and would thus be less likely to fail because when the loans were going sour in one location, they would likely be doing well in the other. Thus nationwide banking is seen as a major step toward creating a healthy banking system that is less prone to banking crises.

The two potential negatives to bank consolidation are that it might lead to a reduction in lending to small businesses because of the reduction in assets at small banks that specialize in small business lending and that the rush of banks to expand into new geographic markets might lead them into increased risk taking, which might lead to bank failures. The jury is still out on these concerns, but most economists see the benefits of bank consolidation and nationwide banking as outweighing the costs.

SEPARATION OF THE BANKING AND OTHER FINANCIAL SERVICE INDUSTRIES

Another important feature of the structure of the banking industry in the United States until recently was the separation of the banking and other financial services industries—such as securities, insurance, and real estate—mandated by the

Glass-Steagall Act of 1933. Glass-Steagall allowed commercial banks to sell new offerings of government securities but prohibited them from underwriting corporate securities or from engaging in brokerage activities. It also prevented banks from engaging in insurance and real estate activities. In turn, it prevented investment banks and insurance companies from engaging in commercial banking activities, and thus protected banks from competition.

Erosion of Glass-Steagall

Despite the Glass-Steagall prohibitions, the pursuit of profits and financial innovation stimulated both banks and other financial institutions to bypass the intent of the Glass-Steagall Act and encroach on each other's traditional territory. Brokerage firms engaged in the traditional banking business of issuing deposit instruments with the development of money market mutual funds and cash management accounts. After the Federal Reserve used a loophole in Section 20 of the Glass-Steagall Act in 1987 to allow bank holding companies to underwrite previously prohibited classes of securities, banks began to enter this business. The loophole allowed affiliates of approved commercial banks to engage in underwriting activities as long as the revenue didn't exceed a specified amount, which started at 10% but was raised to 25%, of the affiliates' total revenue. After the U.S. Supreme Court validated the Fed's action in July 1988, the Federal Reserve allowed J.P. Morgan, a commercial bank holding company, to underwrite corporate debt securities (in January 1989) and to underwrite stocks (in September 1990), with the privilege extended to other bank holding companies. The regulatory agencies later allowed banks to engage in some real estate and some insurance activities.

The Gramm-Leach-Bliley Financial Services Modernization Act of 1999: Repeal of Glass-Steagall

Because restrictions on commercial banks' securities and insurance activities put American banks at a competitive disadvantage relative to foreign banks, bills to overturn Glass-Steagall appeared in almost every session of Congress in the 1990s. With the Citicorp-Travelers merger in 1998 (see Box 3), the pressure to abolish Glass-Steagall became overwhelming, and legislation to eliminate Glass-Steagall finally came to fruition in 1999. This legislation, the Gramm-Leach-Bliley Financial Services Modernization Act of 1999, allows securities firms and insurance companies to purchase banks, and allows banks to underwrite insurance and securities and engage in real estate activities. Under this legislation, states retain regulatory authority over insurance activities while the Securities and Exchange Commission will continue oversight of securities activities. The Office of the Comptroller of the Currency has the authority to regulate bank subsidiaries engaged in securities underwriting, but the Federal Reserve continues to have the authority to oversee bank holding companies under which all real estate and insurance activities and large securities operations will he housed.

Implications for Financial Consolidation

As we have seen, the Riegle-Neal Interstate Banking and Branching Efficiency Act of 1994 has stimulated consolidation of the banking industry. The financial consolidation process will be even further speeded up by the Gramm-Leach-Bliley Act

BOX 3

The Citicorp-Travelers Merger

On April 6, 1998, the financial world was rocked by the announcement of what was expected to be the largest corporate merger ever, between Citicorp, the second-largest bank in the United States, and the Travelers Group, which was in the insurance business and also owned the third-largest securities firm in the country, Salomon Smith Barney. (Because of a decline in the value of Citicorp by the time the merger actually took place, it turned out only to be the second-largest corporate merger in history; the Bank of America and NationsBank merger around the same time edged it out slightly.) The merged bank holding company, called Citigroup, would be one of the largest financial services firms in the world, with 100 million customers in 100 countries, over 150,000 employees, and $700 billion in assets.

The merger was remarkable not only for its size but also because under the Glass-Steagall Act of 1933 and the Bank Holding Company Act of 1956, the combination of these two corporations would be illegal. However, the marriage was approved by the Federal Reserve in September 1998 and was consummated in early October. As part of the approval process, the Federal Reserve produced a waiver giving Citigroup two to five years to sell off prohibited businesses like insurance underwriting. However, Citicorp and Travelers were betting that by the time the five-year period was up, Congress would pass legislation eliminating the restrictions imposed by Glass-Steagall and the Bank Holding Company Act, thereby enabling Citigroup to engage in all financial service activities. The Citigroup and Travelers bet was a good one—Congress finally did pass the Gramm-Leach-Bliley Act overturning Glass-Steagall in 1999.

of 1999, because the way is now open to consolidation in terms not only of the number of banking institutions but also across financial service activities. Mergers of banks with other financial service firms like that of Citicorp and Travelers should become increasingly common, and more mega-mergers are likely to be on the way. Banking institutions will become not only larger but increasingly complex organizations, engaging in the full gamut of financial service activities.

Separation of Banking and Other Financial Services Industries Throughout the World

Not many other countries in the aftermath of the Great Depression followed the lead of the United States in separating the banking and other financial services industries. In fact, in the past this separation was the most prominent difference between banking regulation in the United States and in other countries. Around the world, there are three basic frameworks for the banking and securities industries.

The first framework is *universal banking,* which exists in Germany, the Netherlands, and Switzerland. It provides no separation at all between the banking and securities industries. In a universal banking system, commercial banks provide a full range of banking, securities, and insurance services, all within a single legal entity. Banks are allowed to own sizable equity shares in commercial firms, and often they do.

The British-style universal banking system, the second framework, is found in the United Kingdom and countries with close ties to it, such as Canada and Australia. The British-style universal bank engages in securities underwriting, but it differs from the German-style universal bank in three ways: Separate legal subsidiaries are more common, bank equity holdings of commercial firms are less common, and combinations of banking and insurance firms are less common.

The third framework features legal separation of the banking and securities industries, as in the United States and Japan. A major difference between the U.S.

and Japanese banking systems is that Japanese banks are allowed to hold substantial equity stakes in commercial firms, whereas American banks cannot. In addition, most American banks use a bank-holding-company structure, but bank holding companies are illegal in Japan. Although the banking and securities industries are legally separated under the Glass-Steagall Act in the United States and Section 65 of the Japanese Securities Act, in both countries commercial banks are increasingly being allowed to engage in securities activities and are thus becoming more like British-style universal banks.

INTERNATIONAL BANKING

In 1960, only eight U.S. banks operated branches in foreign countries, and their total assets were less than $4 billion. Currently, around 100 American banks have branches abroad, with assets totaling over $500 billion. The spectacular growth in international banking can be explained by three factors.

First is the rapid growth in international trade and multinational (worldwide) corporations that has occurred since 1960. When American firms operate abroad, they need banking services in foreign countries to help finance international trade. For example, they might need a loan in a foreign currency to operate a factory abroad. And when they sell goods abroad, they need to have a bank exchange the foreign currency they have received for their goods into dollars. Although these firms could use foreign banks to provide them with these international banking services, many of them prefer to do business with the U.S. banks with which they have established long-term relationships and which understand American business customs and practices. As international trade has grown, international banking has grown with it.

Second, when American banks go abroad, they are allowed to pursue activities that are prohibited in the United States under the Glass-Steagall Act. American banks are very active in global investment banking, in which they underwrite foreign securities. They also sell insurance abroad, and they derive substantial profits from these investment banking and insurance activities. The desire to escape burdensome regulations, an important factor that has stimulated financial innovations, has therefore also been a major spur to international banking.

Third, American banks have wanted to tap into the large pool of dollar-denominated deposits in foreign countries known as Eurodollars. To understand the structure of U.S. banking overseas, let us first look at the Eurodollar market, an important source of growth for international banking.

Eurodollar Market

Eurodollars are created when deposits in accounts in the United States are transferred to a bank outside the country and are kept in the form of dollars. For example, if Rolls-Royce PLC deposits a $1 million check, written on an account at an American bank, in its bank in London—specifying that the deposit is payable in dollars—$1 million in Eurodollars is created.[2] Over 90% of Eurodollar deposits are time deposits, more than half of them certificates of deposit with maturities of 30 days or more. The total amount of Eurodollars outstanding exceeds $2 tril-

[2]Note that the London bank has acquired the deposit at the American bank formerly owned by Rolls-Royce, so the creation of Eurodollars has not caused a reduction in the amount of bank deposits in the United States.

lion, making the Eurodollar market one of the most important financial markets in the world economy.

Why would companies like Rolls-Royce want to hold dollar deposits outside the United States? First, the dollar is the most widely used currency in international trade, so Rolls-Royce might want to hold deposits in dollars to conduct its international transactions. Second, Eurodollars are "offshore" deposits—they are held in countries that will not subject them to regulations such as reserve requirements or restrictions (called *capital controls*) on taking the deposits outside the country.[3]

The main center of the Eurodollar market is London, a major international financial center for hundreds of years. Eurodollars are also held outside of Europe in locations that provide offshore status to these deposits—for example, Singapore, the Bahamas, and the Cayman Islands.

The minimum-sized transaction in the Eurodollar market is typically $1 million, and approximately 75% of Eurodollar deposits are held by banks. Plainly, you and I are unlikely to come into direct contact with Eurodollars. The Eurodollar market is, however, an important source of funds to U.S. banks, whose borrowing of these deposits is over $100 billion. Rather than using an intermediary and borrowing all the deposits from foreign banks, American banks decided that they could earn higher profits by opening their own branches abroad to attract these deposits. Consequently, the Eurodollar market has been an important stimulus to U.S. banking overseas.

Structure of U.S. Banking Overseas

U.S. banks have most of their foreign branches in Latin America, the Far East, the Caribbean, and London. The largest volume of assets is held by branches in London because it is a major international financial center and the central location for the Eurodollar market. Latin America and the Far East have many branches because of the importance of U.S. trade with these regions. Parts of the Caribbean (especially the Bahamas and the Cayman Islands) have become important as tax havens, with minimal taxation and few restrictive regulations. In actuality, the bank branches in the Bahamas and the Cayman Islands are "shell operations" because they function primarily as bookkeeping centers and do not provide normal banking services.

An alternative corporate structure for U.S. banks that operate overseas is the **Edge Act corporation,** which is a special subsidiary engaged primarily in international banking. This corporate structure, created by the Edge Act of 1919, allows American banks to compete more effectively against foreign banks by exempting Edge Act corporations from certain U.S. banking regulations. For example, Edge Act corporations are exempt from the prohibition on branching across state lines; they can have branches in different states to facilitate the financing of trade with different parts of the world—an office on the West Coast to handle the financing of trade with Japan, an office in Miami to handle the financing of trade with Latin America, and so forth.

---

[3]Although most offshore deposits are denominated in dollars, some are also denominated in other currencies. Collectively, these offshore deposits are referred to as Eurocurrencies. A German mark–denominated deposit held in London, for example, is called a Euromark, and a French franc–denominated deposit held in London is called a Eurofranc.

U.S. banks (through their holding companies) can also own a controlling interest in foreign banks and in foreign companies that provide financial services, such as finance companies. The international activities of member banks of the Federal Reserve System, bank holding companies, and Edge Act corporations (which account for almost all international banking conducted by U.S. banks) are governed by the Federal Reserve's Regulation K. As in the case of bank holding companies, these international activities must be "closely related to banking."

In late 1981, the Federal Reserve approved the creation of **international banking facilities (IBFs)** within the United States that can accept time deposits from foreigners but are not subject to either reserve requirements or restrictions on interest payments. IBFs are also allowed to make loans to foreigners, but they are not allowed to make loans to domestic residents. States have encouraged the establishment of IBFs by exempting them from state and local taxes. In essence, IBFs are treated like foreign branches of U.S. banks and are not subject to domestic regulations and taxes. The purpose of establishing IBFs is to encourage American and foreign banks to do more banking business in the United States rather than abroad. From this point of view, IBFs have been a success: Their assets climbed to nearly $200 billion in the first two years and currently exceed that amount.

Foreign Banks in the United States

The growth in international trade has not only encouraged U.S. banks to open offices overseas but also encouraged foreign banks to establish offices in the United States. Foreign banks have been extremely successful in the United States. Over the past 20 years, foreign banks have more than doubled their market share in the United States. Currently, they hold more than 20% of total U.S. bank assets and do almost as much commercial lending as U.S.-owned banks, with nearly a 50% share of the market lending to U.S. corporations.

Foreign banks engage in banking activities in the United States by operating an agency office of the foreign bank, a subsidiary U.S. bank, or a branch of the foreign bank. An agency office can lend and transfer funds in the United States, but it cannot accept deposits from domestic residents. Agency offices have the advantage of not being subject to regulations that apply to full-service banking offices (such as requirements for FDIC insurance and restrictions on branching). A subsidiary U.S. bank is just like any other U.S. bank (it may even have an American-sounding name) and is subject to the same regulations, but it is owned by the foreign bank. A branch of a foreign bank bears the foreign bank's name and is usually a full-service office. Foreign banks may also form Edge Act corporations and IBFs.

Before 1978, foreign banks were not subject to many regulations that applied to domestic banks: They could open branches across state lines and were not expected to meet reserve requirements, for example. The passage of the International Banking Act of 1978, however, put foreign and domestic banks on a more equal footing. Now foreign banks may open new full-service branches only in the state they designate as their home state or in states that allow the entry of out-of-state banks. Limited-service branches and agency offices in any other state are permitted, however, and foreign banks are allowed to retain any full-service branches opened before ratification of the International Banking Act of 1978.

The internationalization of banking, both by U.S. banks going abroad and by foreign banks entering the United States, has meant that financial markets throughout the world have become more integrated. As a result, there is a growing trend toward international coordination of bank regulation, one example of which is the 1988 Basel agreement to standardize minimum capital requirements in industrialized countries, discussed in Chapter 18. Financial market integration has also encouraged bank consolidation abroad, culminating in the creation of the first trillion-dollar bank with the proposed merger of the Industrial Bank of Japan, Dai-Ichi Kangyo Bank, and Fuji Bank, announced in August 1999, but to take place in 2002. Another development has been the importance of foreign banks in international banking. As shown in Table 3, in 2001, eight of the ten largest banks in the world were foreign.

FINANCIAL INNOVATION AND THE DECLINE OF TRADITIONAL BANKING

The traditional financial intermediation role of banking has been to make long-term loans and fund them by issuing short-dated deposits, a process of asset transformation commonly referred to as "borrowing short and lending long." Earlier in the chapter, we saw that changes in regulations restricting bank branching have been increasing the competitive environment in the banking industry in the United States. Another source of increasing competition for this industry is coming from financial innovations. Here we examine how the same economic forces we examined in Chapter 15 have generated financial innovations that present the banking industry with competitive challenges that are causing traditional banking business to decline. The decline in traditional banking has important implications for the future of the banking industry and creates new challenges for regulators.

Behind the Decline: Four Financial Innovations

Four financial innovations have played an important role in the decline of traditional banking: money market mutual funds, junk bonds, the rise of the commercial paper market, and securitization.

Money Market Mutual Funds As we saw in Chapter 15, the desire to avoid regulations such as deposit rate ceilings and the restrictions on interest paid on deposits resulted in innovations developed by banks such as NOW and ATS accounts. These same forces produced a new financial institution, the money

TABLE 3 Ten Largest Banks in the World, 2001

Bank	Assets (U.S. $ billions)
1. Deutsche Bank (Germany)	955,579
2. Bank of Tokyo-Mitsubishi (Japan)	726,286
3. Citigroup (U.S.)	716,937
4. BNP Paribas (France)[1]	703,091
5. Bank of America (U.S.)	632,574
6. UBS (Switzerland)	616,798
7. HSBC Holdings (U.K./Hong Kong)	601,847
8. Fuji Bank (Japan)	561,345
9. Bayerische Hypo Bank (Germany)	559,860
10. Sumitomo Bank (Japan)	519,153

Source: http://interactive.wsj.com/public/resources/documents/wb00-100-fpublic-2000-09-25.htm

The world's 20 largest banks by assets as of 1998 and 1999 are listed at www.financialservicefacts.org/international/fr.html

market mutual fund, discussed in Chapter 8, that now competes with banks for deposits.

Money market mutual funds issue shares that are redeemable at a fixed price (usually $1) by writing checks. For example, if you buy 5000 shares for $5000, the money market fund uses these funds to invest in short-term money market securities (Treasury bills, certificates of deposit, commercial paper) that provide you with interest payments. In addition, you are able to write checks up to the $5000 held as shares in the money market fund. Although money market fund shares effectively function as checking account deposits that earn interest, they are not legally deposits and so are not subject to reserve requirements or prohibitions on interest payments. For this reason, they can pay higher interest rates than deposits at banks.

The first money market mutual fund was created by two Wall Street mavericks, Bruce Bent and Henry Brown, in 1971. However, the low market interest rates from 1971 to 1977 (which were just slightly above Regulation Q ceilings of 5.25% to 5.5%) kept them from being particularly advantageous relative to bank deposits. In early 1978, the situation changed rapidly as market interest rates began to climb over 10%, well above the 5.5% maximum interest rates payable on savings accounts and time deposits under Regulation Q. In 1977, money market mutual funds had assets under $4 billion; in 1978, their assets climbed to close to $10 billion; in 1979, to over $40 billion; and in 1982, to $230 billion. Currently, their assets are around $1.845 trillion. To say the least, money market mutual funds have been a successful financial innovation, which is exactly what we would have predicted to occur in the late 1970s and early 1980s when interest rates soared beyond Regulation Q ceilings.

Junk Bonds Before the advent of computers and advanced telecommunications, it was difficult to acquire information about the financial situation of firms that might want to sell securities. Because of the difficulty in screening out bad from good credit risks, the only firms that were able to sell bonds were very well established corporations that had high credit ratings.[4] Before the 1980s, then, only corporations that could issue bonds with ratings of Baa or above could raise funds by selling newly issued bonds. Some firms that had fallen on bad times, so-called *fallen angels,* had previously issued long-term corporate bonds that now had ratings that had fallen below Baa, bonds that were pejoratively dubbed "junk bonds."

With the improvement in information technology in the 1970s, it became easier for investors to screen out bad from good credit risks, thus making it more likely that they would buy long-term debt securities from less well-known corporations with lower credit ratings. With this change in supply conditions, we would expect that some smart individual would pioneer the concept of selling new public issues of junk bonds, not for fallen angels but for companies that had not yet achieved investment-grade status. This is exactly what Michael Milken of Drexel Burnham, an investment banking firm, started to do in 1977. Junk bonds, discussed in Chapter 9, became an important factor in the corporate bond market, with the amount outstanding exceeding $200 billion by the late 1980s. Although there was a sharp slowdown in activity in the junk bond market after Milken was indicted for securities law violations in 1989, it has heated up again in the 1990s.

[4]The discussion of adverse selection problems in Chapter 14 provides a more detailed analysis of why only well-established firms with high credit ratings were able to sell securities.

Commercial Paper Market Recall that *commercial paper* is a short-term debt security issued by large banks and corporations. As we saw in Chapter 8, the commercial paper market has undergone tremendous growth since 1970, when there was $33 billion outstanding, to over $1.16 trillion outstanding at the end of 2001. Indeed, commercial paper has been one of the fastest-growing money market instruments.

Improvements in information technology also help provide an explanation for the rapid rise of the commercial paper market. We have seen that the improvement in information technology made it easier for investors to screen out bad from good credit risks, thus making it easier for corporations to issue debt securities. Not only did this make it easier for corporations to issue long-term debt securities as in the junk bond market, but it also meant that they could raise funds by issuing short-term debt securities like commercial paper more easily. Many corporations that used to do their short-term borrowing from banks now frequently raise short-term funds in the commercial paper market instead.

The development of money market mutual funds has been another factor in the rapid growth in the commercial paper market. Because money market mutual funds need to hold liquid, high-quality, short-term assets such as commercial paper, the growth of assets in these funds to around $1.845 trillion has created a ready market in commercial paper. The growth of pension and other large funds that invest in commercial paper has also stimulated the growth of this market.

Securitization An important example of a financial innovation arising from improvements in both transaction and information technology is securitization, one of the most important financial innovations in the past two decades. **Securitization** is the process of transforming otherwise illiquid financial assets (such as residential mortgages), which have typically been the bread and butter of banking institutions, into marketable capital market securities. As we have seen, improvements in the ability to acquire information have made it easier to sell marketable capital market securities. In addition, with low transaction costs because of improvements in computer technology, financial institutions find that they can cheaply bundle together a portfolio of loans (such as mortgages) with varying small denominations (often less than $100,000), collect the interest and principal payments on the mortgages in the bundle, and then "pass them through" (pay them out) to third parties. By dividing the portfolio of loans into standardized amounts, the financial institution can then sell the claims to these interest and principal payments to third parties as securities. The standardized amounts of these securitized loans make them liquid securities, and the fact that they are made up of a bundle of loans helps diversify risk, making them desirable. The financial institution selling the securitized loans makes a profit by servicing the loans (collecting the interest and principal payments and paying them out) and charging a fee to the third party for this service. Securitization of mortgages has expanded enormously; two-thirds of all residential mortgages are now securitized, and over $1 trillion of securitized mortgages are currently outstanding (see Chapter 11).

Securitization has not stopped with mortgages, however: Securitization of automobile loans, credit card receivables, and commercial and computer leases began in the mid-1980s. Securitized credit card receivables have been particularly successful: By 1989, the amount outstanding of these so-called plastic bonds had surpassed $30 billion and is currently over $150 billion.

Computer technology has also enabled financial institutions to tailor securitization to produce securities that have payment streams considered especially desirable by the market. Collateralized mortgage obligations (CMOs), which are bonds that pass through the payments from a portfolio of mortgages, are a good example of such tailoring; they first appeared in 1983. Computerization enables a CMO to be split into several classes known as *tranches.* The first tranches receive interest payments according to the coupon rate on the CMO, with class 1 first receiving all principal payments and prepayments from the collateralized pool of mortgages. After the class 1 bonds have been paid off, the principal payments and prepayments are used to retire the remaining classes sequentially. The last class, called *accrual* or *Z bonds,* receives interest and principal payments only after the other classes have been paid off. The basic CMO described here has the advantage of containing bonds of both short maturity (class 1) and long maturity (the later classes or the accrual bond), thus increasing its potential market. Indeed, the financial innovation process has led to even more complicated CMOs that fit additional niches in the marketplace.

Although securitization could not take place without modern computer technology (think of the cost of collecting payments and paying them out by hand), technology is not the only factor encouraging it; the government has played an important role too. Securitization first started with GNMA guarantees of mortgage payments and even today involves mostly assets directly or indirectly guaranteed by the government. Tax rules have also stimulated new securitized instruments. A change in IRS regulations made possible real estate mortgage investment conduits (REMICs), which are essentially CMOs with a more favorable tax treatment.

Decline of Traditional Banking

In the United States, the importance of commercial banks as a source of funds to nonfinancial borrowers has shrunk dramatically. As we can see in Figure 3, in 1974 commercial banks provided 35% of these funds; yet by 2001, their market share was down to near 25%. The decline in market share for thrift institutions has been even more precipitous: from over 20% in the late 1970s to below 10% today. Another way of viewing the declining role of banking in traditional financial inter-

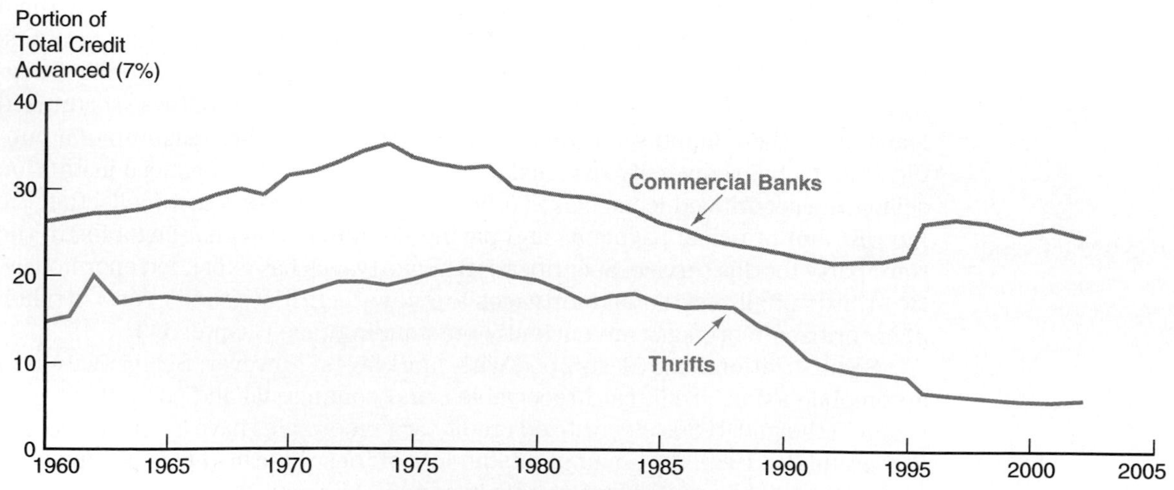

FIGURE 3 Bank Share of Total Nonfinancial Borrowing, 1960–2001

Source: FRB Table 1.59 Line 5 and 1.26 Line 5.

mediation is to look at the size of banks' balance sheet assets relative to those of other financial intermediaries. Commercial banks' share of total financial intermediary assets has fallen from around 40% in the 1960–1980 period to below 25% by the end of 2001. Similarly, the share of total financial intermediary assets held by thrift institutions has declined even more from the 20% level of the 1960–1980 period to below 10% by 2001.

Clearly, the traditional financial intermediation role of banking, whereby banks make loans that are funded with deposits, is no longer as important in our financial system. However, the decline in the market share of banks in total lending and total financial intermediary assets does not necessarily indicate that the banking industry is in decline. If we look at bank profitability relative to GDP, there is no evidence of a declining trend. As we can see in Figure 4, after a dismal performance in the late 1980s and early 1990s, bank profits have rebounded sharply, with strong profits posted every year since 1992. It seems as though the worst is over for the American banking industry and that predictions of its demise may have been exaggerated.[5]

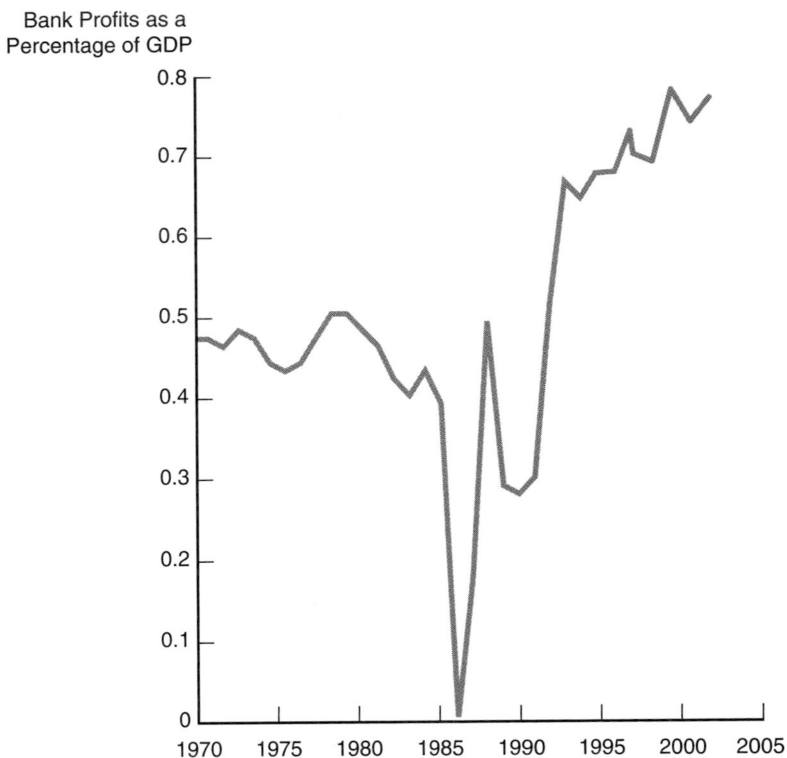

FIGURE 4 Commercial Bank Profitability, 1970–2001

Sources: http://w3.access.gpo.gov/usbudget/fy2001/sheets/b_01b.xls and http://www2.fdic.gov/qbp/2001sep/cniqb1.html

[5]For a further discussion of whether the banking industry is in decline, see John H. Boyd and Mark Gertler, "Are Banks Dead? Or Are the Reports Greatly Exaggerated?" in *The Declining(?) Role of Banking* (Chicago: Federal Reserve Bank of Chicago, 1994), pp. 85–117; Gary Gorton and Richard Rosen, "Corporate Control, Portfolio Choice, and the Decline in Banking," *Journal of Finance* (1995; vol 50, pp. 1377–1420); and Franklin Edwards and Frederic S. Mishkin, "The Decline of Traditional Banking: Implications for Financial Stability and Regulatory Policy," *Federal Reserve Bank of New York Economic Policy Review,* July 1995, pp. 27–45.

However, overall bank profitability is not a good indicator of the profitability of traditional banking because it includes an increasing amount of income from nontraditional off-balance-sheet activities discussed in Chapter 15. As you can see in Figure 5, noninterest income derived from off-balance-sheet activities, as a share of total bank income, increased from around 19% in the 1960–1980 period to more than 40% of total bank income by 2001. Given that the overall profitability of banks has not risen, the increase in income from off-balance-sheet activities implies that the profitability of traditional banking business has declined. This decline in profitability then explains why banks have been reducing their traditional business.

Reasons for the Decline

To understand why traditional banking business has declined in both size and profitability, we need to look at how the financial innovations described earlier have caused banks to suffer declines in their cost advantages in acquiring funds, that is, on the liabilities side of their balance sheet, while at the same time they have lost income advantages on the assets side of their balance sheet. The simultaneous decline of cost and income advantages has resulted in reduced profitability of traditional banking and an effort by banks to leave this business and engage in new and more profitable activities.

Decline in Cost Advantages in Acquiring Funds (Liabilities) Until 1980, banks were subject to deposit rate ceilings that restricted them from paying any inter-

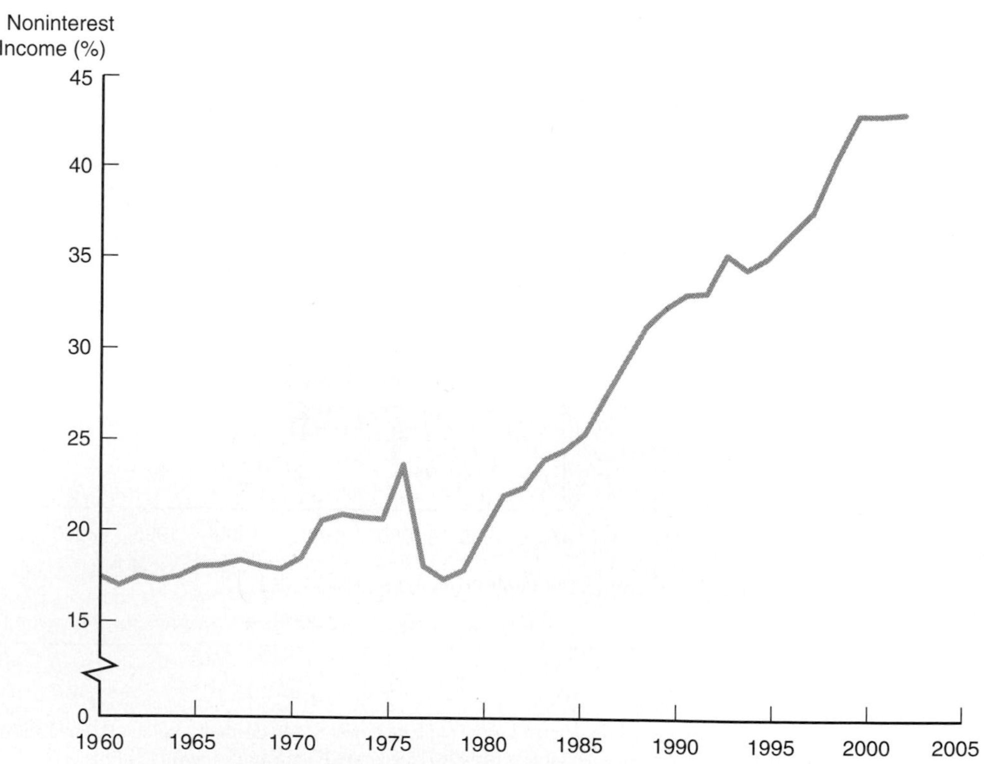

FIGURE 5 Share of Noninterest Income in Total Bank Income, 1960–2001

Source: http://www.fdic.gov/bank/statistical/statistics/sectionb.html

est on checkable deposits and (under Regulation Q) limited them to paying a maximum interest rate of a little over 5% on time deposits. Until the 1960s, these restrictions worked to the banks' advantage because their major source of funds (over 60%) was checkable deposits, and the zero interest cost on these deposits meant that the banks had a very low cost of funds. Unfortunately, this cost advantage for banks did not last. The rise in inflation from the late 1960s on led to higher interest rates, which made investors more sensitive to yield differentials on different assets. The result was the so-called disintermediation process in which people began to take their money out of banks, with their low interest rates on both checkable and time deposits, and began to seek out higher-yielding investments. Also, as we have seen, at the same time, attempts to get around deposit rate ceilings and reserve requirements led to the financial innovation of money market mutual funds, which put the banks at an even further disadvantage because depositors could now obtain checking account-like services while earning high interest on their money market mutual fund accounts. One manifestation of these changes in the financial system was that the low-cost source of funds, checkable deposits, declined dramatically in importance for banks, falling from over 60% of bank liabilities to 10% today.

The growing difficulty for banks in raising funds led to their supporting legislation in the 1980s that eliminated Regulation Q ceilings on time deposit interest rates and allowed checkable deposits like NOW accounts that paid interest. Although these changes in regulation helped make banks more competitive in their quest for funds, it also meant that their cost of acquiring funds had risen substantially, thereby reducing their earlier cost advantage over other financial institutions.

Our discussion of international banking earlier in the chapter documented the encroachment of foreign (particularly Japanese) banks in U.S. financial markets. The loss of cost advantages of American banks helps explain this trend. With the high savings by the Japanese public, Japanese banks were able to tap a large savings pool and thus had access to a cheaper source of funds than American banks. This cost advantage for Japanese banks meant that they could more aggressively seek out loan business in the United States, which is exactly what they did. As a result, they grew at the expense of American banks. This explains why only two of the top ten banks are U.S.

Decline in Income Advantages on Uses of Funds (Assets) The loss of cost advantages on the liabilities side of the balance sheet for American banks is one reason that they have become less competitive, but they have also been hit by a decline in income advantages on the assets side from the financial innovations we discussed earlier, junk bonds, securitization, and the rise of the commercial paper market.

We have seen that improvements in information technology have made it easier for firms to issue securities directly to the public. This has meant that instead of going to banks to finance short-term credit needs, many of the banks' best business customers now find it cheaper to go to the commercial paper market for funds instead. The loss of this competitive advantage for banks is evident in the fact that before 1970, nonfinancial commercial paper equaled less than 5% of commercial and industrial bank loans, whereas the figure has risen to over 20% today. In addition, this growth in the commercial paper market has allowed finance companies, which depend primarily on commercial paper to acquire funds, to expand their operations at the expense of banks. Finance companies, which lend to many of the same businesses that borrow from banks, have increased their market share relative to banks: Before 1980, finance company loans to business equaled around 30% of commercial and industrial bank loans; currently, they are 60%.

The rise of the junk bond market has also eaten into banks' loan business, as the following headline from the *Wall Street Journal* indicated: "Wall Street Is Using Junk Bonds to Take Another Slice of Banks' Lending Pie."[6] Improvements in information technology have made it easier for corporations to sell their bonds to the public directly, thereby bypassing banks. Although Fortune 500 companies started taking this route in the 1970s, now lower-quality corporate borrowers are using banks less often because they have access to the junk bond market.

We have also seen that improvements in computer technology have led to securitization, whereby illiquid financial assets such as bank loans or mortgages are transformed into marketable securities. Computers enable other financial institutions to originate loans because they can now accurately evaluate credit risk with statistical methods, while computers have lowered transaction costs, making it possible to bundle these loans and sell them as securities. As a result, banks no longer have an advantage in making loans when default risk can be easily evaluated with computers. Without their former advantages, banks have lost loan business to other financial institutions even though the banks themselves are involved in the process of securitization. Securitization has been a particular problem for mortgage-issuing institutions such as S&Ls because most residential mortgages are now securitized.

Banks' Responses

In any industry, a decline in profitability usually results in exit from the industry (often due to widespread bankruptcies) and a shrinkage of market share. This occurred in the banking industry in the United States during the 1980s via consolidations and bank failures. As we see in Figure 6, in the 1945–1980 period, bank failures in the United States averaged fewer than ten per year, but during the 1980s bank failures soared, exceeding 200 a year by the end of the decade.

In the attempt to survive and maintain adequate profit levels, many U.S. banks face two alternatives. First, they can attempt to maintain their traditional lending activity by expanding into new and riskier areas of lending. For example, U.S. banks have increased their risk taking by placing a greater percentage of their total funds in commercial real estate loans, traditionally a riskier type of loan. In addition, they have increased lending for corporate takeovers and leveraged buyouts, which are highly leveraged transaction loans. The decline in the profitability of banks' traditional business may thus have helped lead to the crisis in banking that we discuss in Chapter 18.

The second way banks have sought to maintain former profit levels is to pursue new off-balance-sheet activities that are more profitable. As we saw in Figure 5, U.S. commercial banks did this during the early 1980s, nearly doubling the share of their income coming from off-balance-sheet, noninterest-income activities.[7] This strategy, however, has generated concerns about what are proper activ-

[6]May 18, 1993, p. C1.

[7]Note that some off-balance-sheet activities, such as loan commitments and letters of credit, which produce fee income, can be classified as being in the category of traditional banking business. The data in Figure 5 overstate somewhat the importance of nontraditional banking business.

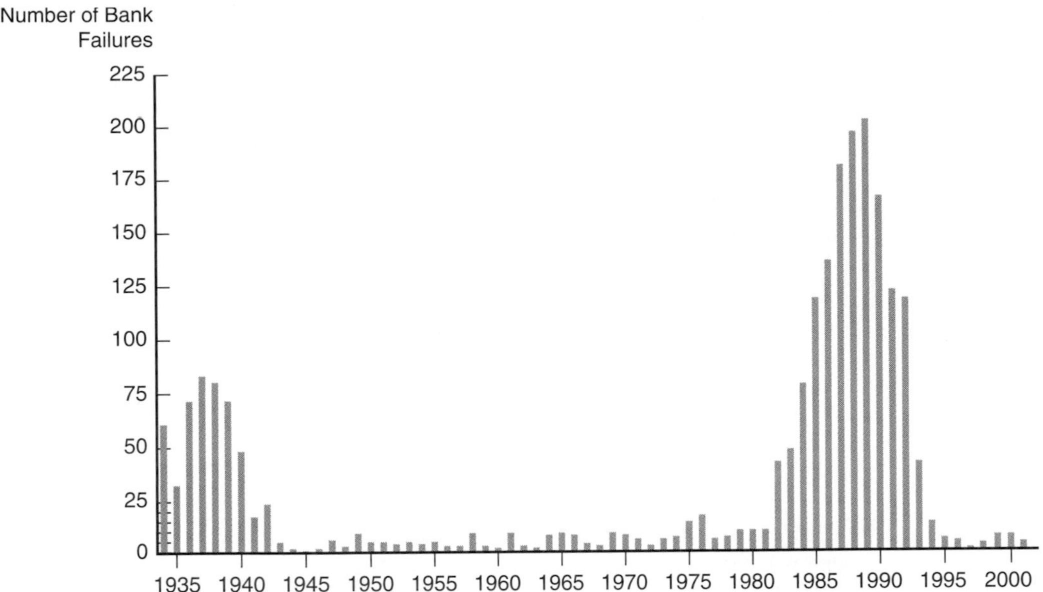

FIGURE 6 Bank Failures in the United States, 1934–2001

Source: http://www.fdic.gov/bank/historical/bank/index.html

ities for banks and about whether nontraditional activities might be riskier and result in banks' taking excessive risks.

The decline of banks' traditional business has thus meant that the banking industry has been driven to seek out new lines of business. This could be beneficial because by so doing, banks can keep vibrant and healthy. Indeed, bank profitability has been high in recent years, and nontraditional, off-balance-sheet activities have been playing an important role in the resurgence of bank profits. However, there is a danger that the new directions in banking could lead to increased risk taking, and thus the decline in traditional banking requires regulators to be more vigilant. It also poses new challenges for bank regulators, who, as we will see in Chapter 18, must now be far more concerned about banks' off-balance-sheet activities.

Decline of Traditional Banking in Other Industrialized Countries

Forces similar to those in the United States have been leading to the decline of traditional banking in other industrialized countries. The loss of banks' monopoly power over depositors has occurred outside the United States as well. Financial innovation and deregulation are occurring worldwide and have created attractive alternatives for both depositors and borrowers. In Japan, for example, deregulation has opened a wide array of new financial instruments to the public, causing a disintermediation process similar to that in the United States. In European countries, innovations have steadily eroded the barriers that have traditionally protected banks from competition.

In other countries, banks have also faced increased competition from the expansion of securities markets. Both financial deregulation and fundamental economic forces in other countries have improved the availability of information in securities markets, making it easier and less costly for firms to finance their activities by issuing securities rather than going to banks. Further, even in countries where securities markets have not grown, banks have still lost loan business because their best corporate customers have had increasing access to foreign and offshore capital markets, such as the Eurobond market. In smaller economies, like Australia, which still do not have well-developed corporate bond or commercial paper markets, banks have lost loan business to international securities markets. In addition, the same forces that drove the securitization process in the United States are at work in other countries and will undercut the profitability of traditional banking in these countries as well. Thus although the decline of traditional banking has occurred earlier in the United States than in other countries, the same forces are resulting in competitive problems for banks in these countries as well.

The increase in the competitive environment for foreign banks has meant that some of them have found themselves in financial difficulties. Return on assets and return on equity have fallen in Japan and many European countries, and banks in these countries have sometimes been finding themselves in financial difficulties. France's largest bank, Crédit Lyonnais, required a $10 billion bailout in 1995, with additional infusions of over $1 billion in 1996 and 1997, and in 1996, the Italian government injected over $1 billion to help keep the Banco di Napoli afloat. Even in countries like Switzerland and Germany, banks have been running into trouble. For example, in January 1993, BfG Bank, a German bank, needed a capital infusion from its parent company, Crédit Lyonnais, because it suffered huge losses in 1992. In Chapter 18, we will discuss the extensive problems in the Japanese banking industry. The United States is not unique in seeing its banks face a more difficult competitive environment.

SUMMARY

1. The history of banking in the United States has left us with a dual banking system, with commercial banks chartered by the states and the federal government. Multiple agencies regulate commercial banks: the Office of the Comptroller, the Federal Reserve, the FDIC, and the state banking authorities.
2. Restrictive state branching regulations and the McFadden Act, which prohibits branching across state lines, have led to a large number of small commercial banks. The large number of commercial banks in the United States reflects the past *lack* of competition, not the presence of vigorous competition. Bank holding companies, nonbank banks, and ATMs were important responses to branching restrictions that have weakened the restrictions' anticompetitive effect.
3. Since the mid-1980s, bank consolidation has been occurring at a rapid pace. The first phase of bank consolidation was the result of bank failures and the reduced effectiveness of branching restrictions. The second phase has been stimulated by the Riegle-Neal Interstate Banking and Branching Efficiency Act of 1994, which establishes the basis for a nationwide banking system. Once banking consolidation has settled down, we are likely to be left with a banking system with several thousand banks. Most economists believe that the benefits of bank consolidation and nationwide banking will outweigh the costs.
4. The Glass-Steagall Act separated commercial banking from the securities industry. With competitive forces causing bypass of the intent of the act, the Gramm-Leach-Bliley legislation of 1999 repealed

Glass-Steagall and removed the separation of these industries.

5. With the rapid growth of world trade since 1960, international banking has grown dramatically. U.S. banks engage in international banking activities by opening branches abroad, owning controlling interests in foreign banks, forming Edge Act corporations, and operating international banking facilities (IBFs) located in the United States. Foreign banks operate in the United States by owning a subsidiary American bank or by operating branches or agency offices in the United States.

6. Financial innovation has caused banks to suffer declines in cost advantages in acquiring funds and in income advantages on their assets. The resulting squeeze has hurt profitability in banks' traditional lines of business and has led to a decline in traditional banking.

KEY TERMS

bank holding companies, *p. 440*
branches, *p. 441*
dual banking system, *p. 439*
Edge Act corporation, *p. 451*
international banking facilities (IBFs), *p. 452*
national banks, *p. 439*
nonbank banks, *p. 443*
securitization, *p. 455*
state banks, *p. 439*
superregional banks, *p. 444*

QUESTIONS AND PROBLEMS

1. Why was the United States one of the last of the major industrialized countries to have a central bank?

*2. Which regulatory agency has the primary responsibility for supervising the following categories of commercial banks?
   a. National banks
   b. Bank holding companies
   c. Non-Federal Reserve member state banks
   d. Federal Reserve member state banks

3. "The commercial banking industry in Canada is less competitive than the commercial banking industry in the United States because in Canada only a few large banks dominate the industry, while in the United States there are around 8,175 commercial banks." Is this statement true, false, or uncertain? Explain your answer.

*4. Why has new technology made it harder to enforce limitations on bank branching?

5. Why has there been such a dramatic increase in bank holding companies?

*6. What incentives have regulatory agencies created to encourage international banking? Why have they done this?

7. How could the approval of international banking facilities (IBFs) by the Fed in 1981 have reduced employment in the banking industry in Europe?

*8. If the bank at which you keep your checking account is owned by Saudi Arabians, should you worry that your deposits are less safe than if the bank were owned by Americans?

9. If reserve requirements were eliminated in the future, as some economists advocate, what effects would this have on the size of money market mutual funds?

*10. Why have banks been losing cost advantages in acquiring funds in recent years?

11. "If inflation had not risen in the 1960s and 1970s, the banking industry might be healthier today." Is this statement true, false, or uncertain? Explain your answer.

*12. Why have banks been losing income advantages on their assets in recent years?

13. "The invention of the computer is the major factor behind the decline of the banking industry." Is this statement true, false, or uncertain? Explain your answer.

*14. How did competitive forces lead to the repeal of the Glass-Steagall Act's separation of the banking and the securities industries?

15. What will be the likely effect of the Gramm-Leach-Bliley Act on financial consolidation?

WEB EXERCISES

Commercial Banking Industry: Structure and Competition

1. Go to http://www.fdic.gov/bank/statistical/statistics/index.html. Select "highlights and trends." Choose "Number of FDIC-Insured Commercial Banks and Trust Companies." Looking at the trend in bank branches, does the public appear to have more or less access to banking facilities? How many banks were there in 1934, and how many are there now? Does the graph indicate that the trend toward consolidation is continuing?
2. Despite the regulations that protect banks from failure, some do fail. Go to http://www2.fdic.gov/hsob/. Select the tab labeled "Bank and Thrift Failures." How many bank failures occurred in the United States during the most recent complete calendar year? What were the total assets held by the banks that failed? How many banks failed in 1937?

Chapter 17 Savings Associations and Credit Unions

Preview

Suppose that you are a typical middle-class worker in New York in 1820. You work hard and earn fair wages as a craftsman. You are married and about to have a child, so you decide that you would like to own your own home. There are many commercial banks in the city, but as their name implies, these institutions exist to serve commerce, not the working class, because that is where the profits are. Where could you go to borrow the money to buy a home? Your options at that time are very limited. Later in the century, however, a new institution emerged that opened the possibility of home ownership to more than the very wealthy. That institution was the savings and loan association.

The middle class also had problems finding financial institutions willing to offer small consumer-type loans. Again, banks had determined that loans to these customers were not profitable. Another type of institution, the credit union, emerged at about the same time as savings and loans to service the borrowing needs of this segment of the economy.

In Chapters 15 and 16 we discussed commercial banks, the largest of the depository institutions. Though smaller, savings and loan associations, mutual savings banks, and credit unions, collectively called thrift institutions or thrifts, are important to the servicing of consumer borrowing needs. Thrifts are primarily concerned with lending to individuals and households, as opposed to banks, which still tend to be more concerned with lending to businesses. We begin our discussion by reviewing the history of the thrift industry. We then describe the nature of the industry today and project where it might be in the future.

MUTUAL SAVINGS BANKS

The first pure savings banks were established by philanthropists in Scotland and England to encourage saving by the poor. The founders of the institutions would often provide subsidies that allowed the institution to pay interest rates above the current market level. Because of the nature of the savings banks' customers, the institutions were very conservative with their funds and placed most of them in commercial banks. The first savings banks in the United States were chartered by Congress and founded in the Northeast in 1816. These institutions quickly lost their distinction of being strictly for the poor and instead became a popular place for members of the middle class to store their excess money.

Savings banks were originally organized as **mutual banks,** meaning that the depositors were the owners of the firm. This form of ownership led to a conservative investment posture, which prevented many of the mutual savings banks from failing during the recession at the end of the nineteenth century or during the Great Depression in the 1930s. In fact, between 1930 and 1937, deposits in mutual savings banks grew while those in commercial banks actually shrank. Following World War II, savings banks made mortgage lending their primary business. This focus made them similar to savings and loans.

Mutual ownership means that no stock in the bank is issued or sold; the depositors own a share of the bank in proportion to their deposits. There are currently 815 mutual savings banks operating in 17 states, primarily concentrated on the eastern seaboard. Most are state chartered (federal chartering of savings banks did not begin until 1978.) Because they are state chartered, they are regulated and supervised by the state as well as the federal government.

The mutual form of ownership has both advantages and disadvantages. On the one hand, since the capital of the institution is contributed by the depositors, more capital is available because all deposits represent equity. This leads to greater safety in that mutual savings banks have far fewer liabilities than other banking organizations. On the other hand, the mutual form of ownership accentuates the principal-agent problem that exists in corporations. In corporations, managers are hired by the board of directors, who are in turn elected by the shareholders. Because most shareholders do not own a very large percentage of the firm, when there is a disagreement with management, it makes more sense to sell shares than to try to change policy. This problem also exists for the mutual form of ownership. Most depositors do not have a large enough stake in the firm to make it cost-effective for them to monitor the firm's managers closely.

The corporation, however, has alternative methods of aligning managers' goals with those of shareholders. For example, managers can be offered a stake in the firm, or stock options can be part of their compensation package. Similarly, managers of corporations are always under the threat of takeover by another firm if they fail to manage effectively. These alternatives are not available in the mutual form of ownership. As a result, there may be less control over management.

An advantage to the mutual form of ownership is that managers are more risk-averse than in the corporate form. This is because mutual managers gain nothing if the firm does very well, since they do not own a stake in the firm, but they lose everything if the firm fails. This incentive arrangement appeals to the very risk-averse investor, but its importance has diminished now that the government provides deposit insurance.

SAVINGS AND LOAN ASSOCIATIONS

In the early part of the nineteenth century, commercial banks focused on short-term loans to businesses, so it was very difficult for families to obtain loans for the purchase of a house. In 1816, Congress decided that home ownership was part of the American dream, and to make that possible, Congress passed regulations creating savings and loans and mutual savings institutions. Congress chartered the first savings and loans 15 years after the first mutual savings banks received their charters. The original mandate to the industry was to provide a source of funds for families wanting to buy a home.

Information about savings institutions is available on-line; for example, the Wisconsin Department of Financial Institutions website, www.wdfi.org/fi/saving_institutions/, gives lists of savings institutions, statues, rules and financial data of the institutions.

These institutions were to aggregate depositors' funds and use the money to make long-term mortgage loans. The institutions were not to take in demand deposits but instead were authorized to offer savings accounts that paid slightly higher interest than that offered by commercial banks.

www2.fdic.gov/qbp/ provides a source of tools and charts related to savings and loans. Most current data in this chapter comes from this source.

There were about 12,000 savings and loans in operation by the 1920s. Mortgages accounted for about 85% of their total assets. The rest of their assets were usually deposited in commercial banks. One of every four mortgages in the country was held by a savings and loan institution, making S&Ls the single largest provider of mortgage loans in the country.

Despite the large number of separate savings and loan institutions, they were not an integrated industry. Each state regulated its own S&Ls, and regulations differed substantially from state to state. In 1913, Congress created the Federal Reserve System to regulate and help commercial banks. No such system existed for savings and loans.

Before any significant legislation could be passed, the Great Depression caused the failure of thousands of thrift institutions. In response to the problems facing the industry and to the loss of $200 million in savings, Congress passed the **Federal Home Loan Bank Act of 1932.** This act created the **Federal Home Loan Bank Board (FHLBB)** and a network of regional home loan banks, similar to the organization of the Federal Reserve System. The act gave thrifts the choice of being state or federally chartered. In 1934, Congress continued its efforts to support savings and loans by establishing the **Federal Savings and Loan Insurance Corporation (FSLIC),** which insured deposits in much the same way as the FDIC did for commercial banks.

Savings and loans were successful, low-risk businesses for many years following these regulatory changes (see Chapter 18). Their main source of funds was individual savings accounts, which tended to be stable and low-cost, and their primary assets (about 60% of their total assets) were mortgage loans (see Figure 1). Since real estate secured virtually all of these loans and since real estate values increased steadily through the mid–1970s, loan losses were very small. Thrifts provided the fuel for the home-building boom that for almost half a century, from 1934 to 1978, was the centerpiece of America's domestic economy.

Mutual Savings Banks and Savings and Loans Compared

Mutual savings banks and savings and loan associations are similar in many ways; however, they do differ in ways other than ownership structure.

- Mutual savings banks are concentrated in the northeastern United States; savings and loans are located throughout the country.
- Mutual savings banks may insure their deposits with the state or with the Federal Deposit Insurance Corporation; S&Ls may not.

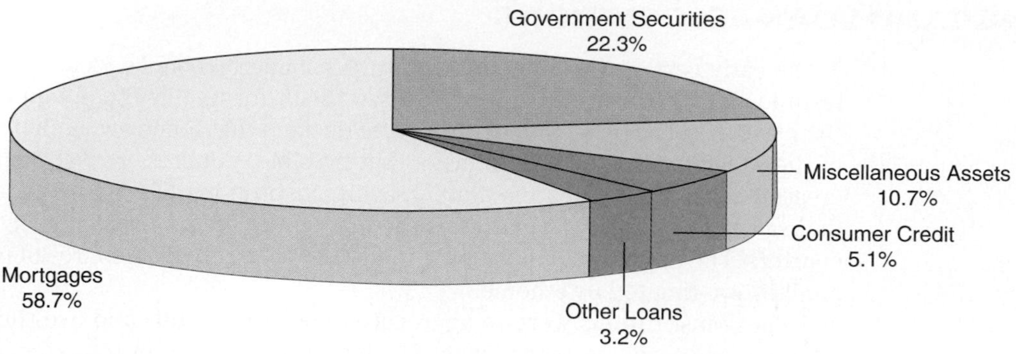

FIGURE 1 Distribution of Savings and Loan Assets, 2001

Source: http://www.2.fdic.gov/qbp/2001mar/sav2.html

- Mutual savings banks are not as heavily concentrated in mortgages and have had more flexibility in their investing practices than savings and loans.

Because the similarities between mutual savings banks and savings and loans are more important than the differences, the focus of this chapter will be more on savings and loans.

SAVINGS AND LOANS IN TROUBLE: THE THRIFT CRISIS

As part of the regulatory changes following the Great Depression, Congress imposed a cap on the rate of interest that savings and loans could pay on savings accounts. The theory was that if S&Ls obtained funds at a low cost, they could make loans to home borrowers at a low cost. The interest-rate caps became a serious problem for savings and loans in the 1970s when inflation rose. Chapters 15 and 16 provide an in-depth discussion of the capital adequacy and interest-rate problems depository institutions faced at that time.

By 1979, inflation was running at 13.3%, but savings and loans were restricted to paying a maximum of 5.5% on deposits. These rates were far from even maintaining depositors' purchasing power with inflation running almost 8% higher than their interest return—in effect, the real interest rate they were earning was –7.8%. They were actually losing money leaving it in savings and loans.

At this same time, securities houses began offering a new product that circumvented interest-rate caps. *Money market accounts* paid market rates on short-term funds (see Chapters 16 and 21 for details). Though not insured, the bulk of the cash placed in money market funds was in turn invested in Treasury securities or commercial paper. Because the savings and loan customers were not satisfied with the low returns they were earning on their funds, they left S&Ls in droves for the high returns these accounts offered.

Financial innovation and deregulation in the permissive atmosphere of the Reagan years led to expanded powers for the S&L industry that led to several problems. First, many S&L managers did not have the required expertise to manage risk appropriately in these new lines of business. Second, the new expanded powers meant that there was a rapid growth in new lending, particularly to the real estate sector. Even if the required expertise was available initially, rapid credit growth might outstrip the available information resources of the banking institution, resulting in excessive risk taking. Third, these new powers of the S&Ls and lending boom meant that their activities were expanding in scope and were becoming more complicated, requiring an expansion of regulatory resources to monitor these activities appropriately. Unfortunately, regulators of the S&Ls at the Federal Savings and Loan Insurance Corporation (FSLIC) had neither the expertise nor the resources that would have enabled them to monitor these new activities sufficiently. Given the lack of expertise in both the S&L industry and the FSLIC, the weakening of the regulatory apparatus, and the moral hazard incentives provided by deposit insurance, it is no surprise that S&Ls took on excessive risks, which led to huge losses on bad loans.

In addition, the incentives of moral hazard were increased dramatically by a historical accident: the combination of the sharp increases in interest rates from late 1979 until 1981 and a severe recession in 1981–1982, both of which were engineered by the Federal Reserve to bring down inflation. The sharp rises in interest rates produced rapidly rising costs of funds for the savings and loans that were not matched by higher earnings on the S&Ls' principal asset, long-term residential mortgages (whose rates had been fixed at a time when interest rates were far lower). The 1981–1982 recession and a collapse in the prices of energy and farm products hit the economies of certain parts of the country such as Texas very hard. As a result, there were defaults on many S&Ls' loans. Losses for savings and loan institutions mounted to $10 billion in 1981–1982, and by some estimates over half of the S&Ls in the United States had a negative net worth and were thus insolvent by the end of 1982.

Later Stages of the Crisis: Regulatory Forbearance

At this point, a logical step might have been for the S&L regulators—the Federal Home Loan Bank Board and its deposit insurance subsidiary, the Federal Savings and Loan Insurance Fund (FSLIC), both now abolished—to close the insolvent S&Ls. Instead, these regulators adopted a stance of **regulatory forbearance:** They refrained from exercising their regulatory right to put the insolvent S&Ls out of business. To sidestep their responsibility to close ailing S&Ls, they adopted irregular regulatory accounting principles that in effect substantially lowered capital requirements. For example, they allowed S&Ls to include in their capital calculations a high value for intangible capital, called *goodwill.*

There were three main reasons why the Federal Home Loan Bank Board and FSLIC opted for regulatory forbearance. First, the FSLIC did not have sufficient funds in its insurance fund to close the insolvent S&Ls and pay off their deposits. Second, the Federal Home Loan Bank Board was established to encourage the growth of the savings and loan industry, so the regulators were probably too close to the people they were supposed to be regulating. Third, because bureaucrats do not like to admit that their own agency is in trouble, the Federal Home Loan Bank Board and the FSLIC preferred to sweep their problems under the rug in the hope that they would go away.

Regulatory forbearance increases moral hazard dramatically because an operating but insolvent S&L (nicknamed a "zombie S&L" by Edward Kane of Ohio State University because it is the "living dead") has almost nothing to lose by taking on great risk and "betting the bank": If it gets lucky and its risky investments pay off, it gets out of insolvency. Unfortunately, if, as is likely, the risky investments don't pay off, the zombie S&L's losses will mount, and the deposit insurance agency will be left holding the bag.

This strategy is similar to the "long bomb" strategy in football. When a football team is almost hopelessly behind and time is running out, it often resorts to a high-risk play: the throwing of a long pass to try to score a touchdown. Of course, the long bomb is unlikely to be successful, but there is always a small chance that it will work. If it doesn't, the team has lost nothing, since it would have lost the game anyway.

Given the sequence of events we have discussed here, it should be no surprise that savings and loans began to take huge risks: They built shopping centers in the desert, bought manufacturing plants to convert manure to methane, and purchased billions of dollars of high-risk, high-yield junk bonds. The S&L industry was no longer the staid industry that once operated on the so-called *3–6–3 rule:* You took in money at 3%, lent it at 6%, and played golf at 3 P.M. Although many savings and loans were making money, losses at other S&Ls were colossal.

Another outcome of regulatory forbearance was that with little to lose, zombie S&Ls attracted deposits away from healthy S&Ls by offering higher interest rates. Because there were so many zombie S&Ls in Texas pursuing this strategy, above-market interest rates on deposits at Texas S&Ls were said to have a "Texas premium." Potentially healthy S&Ls now found that to compete for deposits, they had to pay higher interest rates, which made their operations less profitable and frequently pushed them into the zombie category. Similarly, zombie S&Ls in pursuit of asset growth made loans at below-market interest rates, thereby lowering loan interest rates for healthy S&Ls, and again made them less profitable. The zombie S&Ls had actually taken on attributes of vampires—their willingness to pay above-market rates for deposits and take below-market interest rates on loans was sucking the lifeblood (profits) out of healthy S&Ls.

Competitive Equality in Banking Act of 1987

Toward the end of 1986, the growing losses in the savings and loan industry were bankrupting the insurance fund of the FSLIC. The Reagan administration sought $15 billion in funds for the FSLIC, a completely inadequate sum considering that many times this amount was needed to close down insolvent S&Ls. The legislation passed by Congress, the Competitive Equality in Banking Act (CEBA) of 1987, did not even meet the administration's requests. It allowed the FSLIC to borrow only $10.8 billion through a subsidiary corporation called Financing Corporation (FICO) and, what was worse, included provisions that directed the Federal Home Loan Bank Board to continue to pursue regulatory forbearance (allow insolvent institutions to keep operating), particularly in economically depressed areas such as Texas.

The failure of Congress to deal with the savings and loan crisis was not going to make the problem go away, and consistent with our analysis, the situation deteriorated rapidly. Losses in the savings and loan industry surpassed $10 billion in 1988 and approached $20 billion in 1989. The crisis was reaching epidemic proportions. The collapse of the real estate market in the late 1980s led to additional huge loan losses that greatly exacerbated the problem.

POLITICAL ECONOMY OF THE SAVINGS AND LOAN CRISIS

Although we now have a grasp of the regulatory and economic forces that created the S&L crisis, we still need to understand the political forces that produced the regulatory structure and activities that led to it. The key to understanding the political economy of the S&L crisis is to recognize that the relationship between voter-taxpayers and the regulators and politicians creates a particular type of moral hazard problem, discussed in Chapter 14: the *principal-agent problem,* which occurs when representatives (agents) such as managers have incentives that differ from those of their employer (the principal) and so act in their own interest rather than in the interest of the employer.

Principal-Agent Problem for Regulators and Politicians

Regulators and politicians are ultimately agents for voter-taxpayers (principals) because in the final analysis, taxpayers bear the cost of any losses by the deposit insurance agency. The principal-agent problem occurs because the agent (a politician or regulator) does not have the same incentives to minimize costs to the economy as the principal (the taxpayer).

To act in the taxpayer's interest and lower costs to the deposit insurance agency, regulators have several tasks, as we have seen. They must set tight restrictions on holding assets that are too risky, must impose high capital requirements, and must not adopt a stance of regulatory forbearance, which allows insolvent institutions to continue to operate. However, because of the principal-agent problem, regulators have incentives to do the opposite. Indeed, as our sad saga of the S&L debacle indicates, they have at times loosened capital requirements and restrictions on risky asset holdings and pursued regulatory forbearance. One important incentive for regulators that explains this phenomenon is their desire to escape blame for poor performance by their agency. By loosening capital requirements and pursuing regulatory forbearance, regulators can hide the problem of an insolvent bank and hope that the situation will improve. Edward Kane characterizes such behavior on the part of regulators as "bureaucratic gambling."

Another important incentive for regulators is that they want to protect their careers by acceding to pressures from the people who most influence their careers. These people are not the taxpayers but the politicians who try to keep regulators from imposing tough regulations on institutions that are major campaign contributors. Members of Congress have often lobbied regulators to ease up on a particular S&L that contributed large sums to their campaigns (as we see in the following application). Regulatory agencies that have little independence from the political process are more vulnerable to these pressures.

In addition, both Congress and the presidential administration promoted banking legislation in 1980 and 1982 that made it easier for savings and loans to engage in risk-taking activities. After the legislation passed, the need for monitoring the S&L industry increased because of the expansion of permissible activities. The S&L regulatory agencies needed more resources to carry out their monitoring activities properly, but Congress (successfully lobbied by the S&L industry) was unwilling to allocate the necessary funds. As a result, the S&L regulatory agencies became so shortstaffed that they actually had to cut back on their on-site examinations just when these were needed most. In the period from January 1984 to July 1986, for example, several hundred S&Ls were not examined even once. Worse yet, spurred on by the intense lobbying efforts of the S&L industry, Congress passed the Competitive Equality in Banking Act of 1987, which provided inadequate funding to close down the insolvent S&Ls and also hampered the S&L regulators from doing their job properly by including provisions encouraging regulatory forbearance.

As these examples indicate, the structure of our political system has created a serious principal-agent problem; politicians have strong incentives to act in their own interests rather than in the interests of taxpayers. Because of the high cost of running campaigns, American politicians must raise substantial contributions. This situation may provide lobbyists and other campaign contributors with the opportunity to influence politicians to act against the public interest, as we see in the following application.

Application Principal-Agent Problem in Action: Charles Keating and the Lincoln Savings and Loan Scandal

We see that the principal-agent problem for regulators and politicians creates incentives that may cause excessive risk taking on the part of banking institutions, which then cause substantial losses to the taxpayer. The scandal associated with Charles H. Keating Jr. and the Lincoln Savings and Loan Association provides a graphic example of the principal-agent problem at work. As Edwin Gray, a former chairman of the Federal Home Loan Bank Board, stated, "This is a story of incredible corruption. I can't call it anything else."[1]

Charles Keating was allowed to acquire Lincoln Savings and Loan of Irvine, California, in early 1984, even though he had been accused of fraud by the SEC less than five years earlier. For Keating, whose construction firm, American Continental, planned to build huge real estate developments in Arizona, the S&L was a gold mine: In the lax regulatory atmosphere at the time, controlling the S&L gave his firm easy access to funds without being scrutinized by outside bankers. Within days of acquiring control, Keating got rid of Lincoln's conservative lending officers and internal auditors, even though he had promised regulators he would keep them. Lincoln then plunged into high-risk investments such as currency futures, junk bonds, common stock, hotels, and vast tracts of desert land in Arizona.

Because of a shortage of savings and loan examiners at the time, Lincoln was able to escape a serious examination until 1986, whereupon examiners from the Federal Home Loan Bank of San Francisco discovered that Lincoln had exceeded the 10% limit on equity investments by $600 million. Because of these activities and some evidence that Lincoln was deliberately trying to mislead the examiners, the examiners recommended federal seizure of the bank and all its assets. Keating was not about to take this lying down; he engaged hordes of lawyers—eventually 77 law firms—and accused the bank examiners of bias. He also sued unsuccessfully to overturn the 10% equity limit. Keating is said to have bragged that he spent $50 million fighting regulators.

Lawyers were not Keating's only tactic for keeping regulators off his back. After receiving $1.3 million of contributions to their campaigns from Keating, five senators—Dennis De Concini and John McCain of Arizona, Alan Cranston of California, John Glenn of Ohio, and Donald Riegle of Michigan (subsequently nicknamed the "Keating Five")—met with Edwin Gray, the chairman of the Federal Home Loan Board, and later with four top regulators from San Francisco in April 1987. They complained that the regulators were being too tough on Lincoln and urged the regulators to quit dragging out the investigation. After Gray was replaced by M. Danny Wall, Wall took the unprecedented step of removing the San Francisco examiners from the case in September 1987 and transferred the investigation to the bank board's headquarters in Washington. No examiners called on Lincoln for the next ten months, and as one of the San Francisco examiners described it, Lincoln dropped into a "regulatory black hole."

---

[1]Quoted in Tom Morganthau, Rich Thomas, and Eleanor Clift, "The S&L Scandal's Biggest Blowout," *Newsweek*, November 6, 1989, p. 35.

Lincoln Savings and Loan finally failed in April 1989, with estimated costs to taxpayers of $2.6 billion, making it possibly the most costly S&L failure in history. Keating was convicted for abuses (such as having Lincoln pay him and his family $34 million), but after serving four and a half years in jail, his conviction was overturned in 1996. Wall was forced to resign as head of the Office of Thrift Supervision because of his involvement in the Keating scandal. As a result of their activities on behalf of Keating, the Keating Five senators were made the object of a congressional ethics investigation, but given Congress's propensity to protect its own, they were subjected only to minor sanctions.

SAVINGS AND LOAN BAILOUT: FINANCIAL INSTITUTIONS REFORM, RECOVERY, AND ENFORCEMENT ACT OF 1989

Immediately after taking office, the Bush administration proposed new legislation to provide adequate funding to close down the insolvent S&Ls. The resulting legislation, the **Financial Institutions Reform, Recovery, and Enforcement Act (FIRREA),** was signed into law on August 9, 1989. It was the most significant legislation to affect the thrift industry since the 1930s. FIRREA's major provisions were as follows: The regulatory apparatus was significantly restructured without the Federal Home Loan Bank Board and the FSLIC, both of which had failed in their regulatory tasks. The regulatory role of the Federal Home Loan Bank Board was relegated to the Office of Thrift Supervision (OTS), a bureau within the U.S. Treasury Department, whose responsibilities are similar to those that the Office of the Comptroller of the Currency has over the national banks. The regulatory responsibilities of the FSLIC were given to the FDIC, and the FDIC became the sole administrator of the federal deposit insurance system with two separate insurance funds: the Bank Insurance Fund (BIF) and the Savings Association Insurance Fund (SAIF). Another new agency, the **Resolution Trust Corporation (RTC),** was established to manage and resolve insolvent thrifts placed in conservatorship or receivership. It was made responsible for selling more than $450 billion of real estate owned by failed institutions. After seizing the assets of about 750 insolvent S&Ls, over 25% of the industry, the RTC sold over 95% of them, with a recovery rate of over 85%. After this success, the RTC went out of business on December 31, 1995.

The Office of Thrift Supervision website, www.ots.treas.gov, contains quarterly industry information, statistical reports, and laws and regulations. The OTS 2000 Fact Book, www.ots.treas.gov/docs/48080.pdf, offers a statistical profile of the thrift industry.

Initially, the total cost of the bailout was estimated to be $159 billion over the ten-year period through 1999, but more recent estimates indicated that the cost would be far higher. Indeed, the General Accounting Office placed a cost for the bailout at more than $500 billion over 40 years. However, as pointed out in Chapter 3, this estimate was misleading because, for example, the value of a payment 30 years from now is worth much less in today's dollars. The present value of the bailout cost actually ended up being on the order of $150 billion. The funding for the bailout came partly from capital in the Federal Home Loan Banks (owned by the S&L industry) but mostly from the sale of government debt by both the Treasury and the Resolution Funding Corporation (RefCorp).

To replenish the reserves of the Savings Association Insurance Fund, insurance premiums for S&Ls were increased from 20.8 cents per $100 of deposits to 23 cents and can rise as high as 32.5 cents. Premiums for banks immediately rose from 8.3 cents to 15 cents per $100 of deposits and were raised further to 23 cents in 1991.

FIRREA also imposed new restrictions on thrift activities that in essence reregulated the S&L industry to the asset choices it had before 1982. S&Ls can no longer purchase junk bonds and had to sell their holdings by 1994. Commercial real estate loans are restricted to four times capital rather than the previous limit of 40% of assets, and so this new restriction is a reduction for all institutions whose capital is less than 10% of assets. S&Ls must also hold at least 70%—up from 60%—of their assets in investments that are primarily housing-related. Among the most important provisions of FIRREA was the increase in the core capital leverage requirement from 3% to 8% and the eventual adherence to the same risk-based capital standards imposed on commercial banks.[2]

FIRREA also enhanced the enforcement powers of thrift regulators by making it easier for them to remove managers, issue cease and desist orders, and impose civil penalties. The Justice Department was also given $75 million per year for three years to uncover and prosecute fraud in the banking industry, and maximum fines rose substantially.

As a result of the failure of savings and loans and the passage of FIRREA, the total assets of savings and loans fell between 1988 and 1998. Figure 2 shows the total assets of savings and loans between 1979 and 2001; note the rapid decrease between 1988 and 1992. Since 1992, the assets of S&Ls have remained relatively constant.

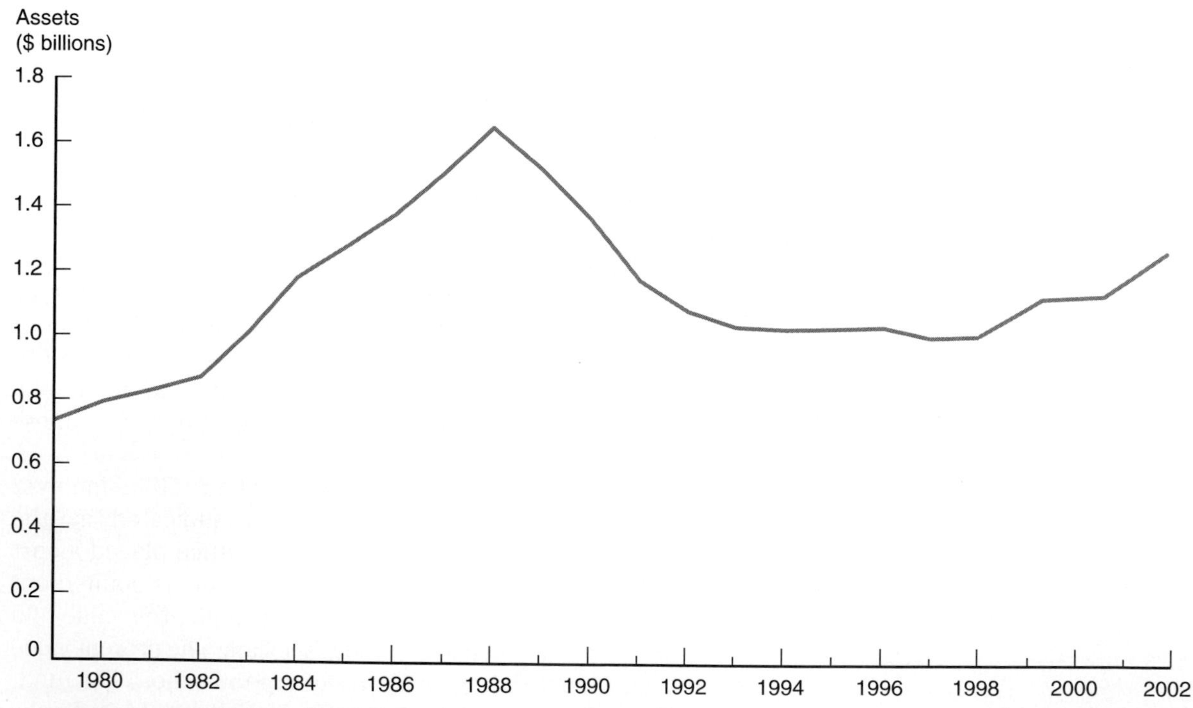

FIGURE 2 Total Assets of Savings and Loan Associations, 1979–2001

Source: http://www2.fdic.gov/qbp

[2]Thrifts are now prohibited from accepting brokered deposits, short-term large-denomination deposits placed in thrifts by funds managers. Brokered deposits are discussed further in Chapter 18.

THE SAVINGS AND LOAN INDUSTRY TODAY

Despite the problems and turmoil surrounding the industry in the 1980s, the savings and loan industry managed to survive, although somewhat changed. In this section we review the current state of the industry.

Number of Institutions

The savings and loan industry has witnessed a substantial reduction in the number of institutions. Many failed or were taken over by the RTC; others merged with stronger institutions to avoid failure. The number of S&Ls declined by more than half between the end of 1986, when there were 3600 of them, and 2001, when there were only 1584. As shown in Figure 3, the number of savings institutions continues to decline. Although new S&Ls continue to open, existing ones convert to commercial banks or credit unions or merge with other savings banks. It is interesting to note that consolidation in the savings industry has not been as dramatic as in commercial banking in recent years.

S&L Size

Figure 4 shows the average total assets for savings and loans since 1984. The graph indicates that the industry has consolidated in recent years. Between 1988 and 1991, the average size of S&Ls fell. This was likely due to the 1989 passage of

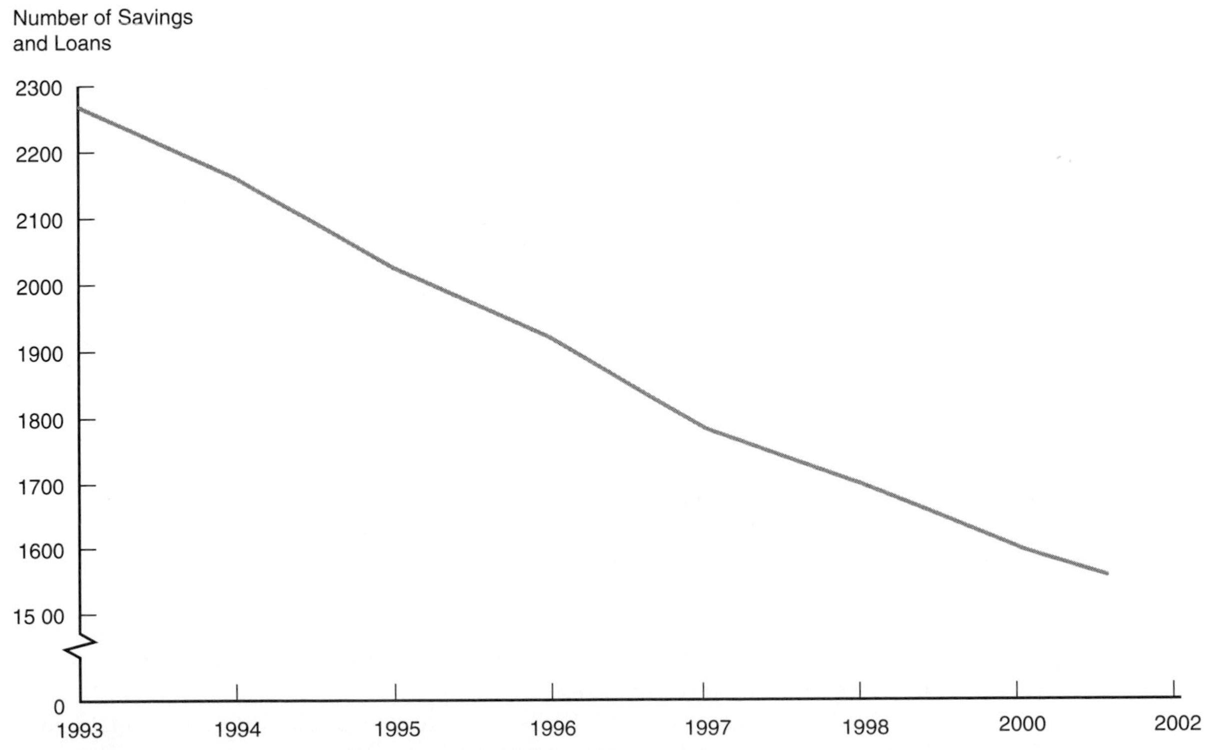

FIGURE 3 Number of Savings and Loans in the United States, 1993–2001

Source: http://www2.fdic.gov/qbp/2001mar/sav1.html

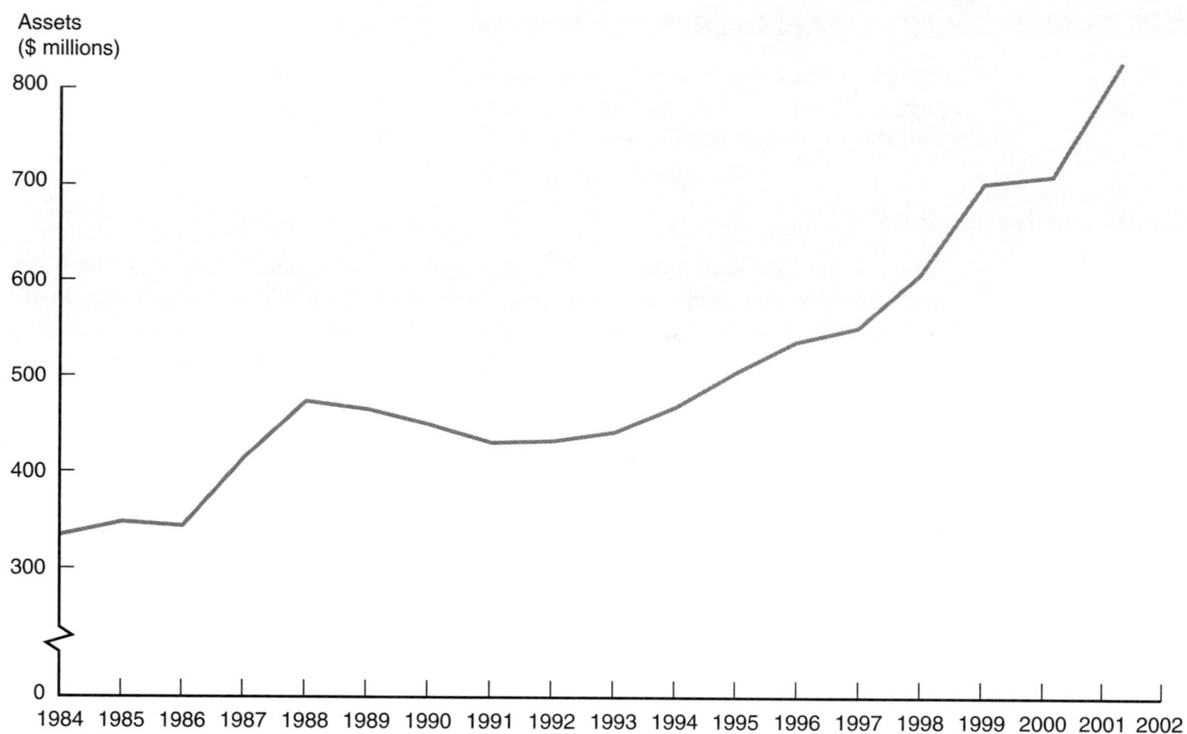

FIGURE 4 Average Assets per Savings and Loan Association, 1984–2001

Source: http://www2.fdic.gov/qbp/2001sep/sav3.html

FIRREA, which required S&Ls to increase their capital-to-asset ratio. Many institutions met the new standard by decreasing their assets rather than by increasing their capital. From 1992 to 2001, total S&L assets increased, even though the number of institutions has decreased. The result is fewer but larger institutions.

A second point to note about Figure 4 is that the average size of savings and loans is substantially greater than that of commercial banks. Recall from Chapter 16 that the growth of commercial banks was often constrained by restrictive banking regulations. As a result, the average size of commercial banks at the end of 2001 was about $800 million in assets. Thus the size of the average commercial bank is less than that of the average savings and loan. Now that Congress has removed most of the restrictions on interstate branching by commercial banks, many industry observers expect a period of rapid consolidation in that industry.

S&L Assets

Figure 5 provides a consolidated balance sheet for the savings and loan industry. Let us first discuss the assets side.

The 1982 reforms allowed S&Ls to make consumer and commercial loans. The intent of this legislation was to give S&Ls a source of assets with short maturities. The problem was that commercial loans are far riskier and require lending expertise that many S&Ls did not possess. FIRREA severely curtailed S&Ls'

Savings and Loan Associations

Assets		Liabilities	
Cash and reserves	47.1	Deposits	755.5
Securities	255.3	Other borrowed funds	289.7
Mortgage loans	751.7	All other liabilities	121.7
Commercial loans	43.8	Equity	107.0
Consumer credit	65.3	Total liabilities and equities	1273.9
Corporate equities	25.6		
Miscelleneous	85.1		
Total assets	1273.9		

FIGURE 5 Consolidated Balance Sheet for Savings and Loan Associations ($ billions, second quarter, 2001)

Sources: Flow of Funds, Table L114 and www.federalreserve.gov/releases/z1

commercial lending. In the four years following passage of the law, the number of loans made for commercial purposes dropped by about 50%. Currently, nearly 90% of all S&L loans are secured by real estate, and 69% are for residential mortgages. Clearly, the industry has returned to its original mandate of financing home ownership.

Savings and loans are subject to reserve requirements, just like banks. Recall from Chapter 15 that reserve requirements are cash deposits that must be held in the vault or at the Federal Reserve in non-interest-bearing accounts. The purpose of reserve requirements is to limit the expansion of the money supply and to ensure adequate liquidity for the institutions. About 4% of total S&L assets are kept in cash.

In addition to cash, savings and loans hold securities, such as corporate, Treasury, and government agency bonds. Unlike reserve deposits, these assets earn interest. The 1982 legislation allowed savings and loans to hold up to 11% of their assets in junk bonds. S&Ls were a major source of funds during the mid–1980s for corporations looking for capital to use in acquiring other firms. In 1989, the FIRREA required that savings and loans divest themselves of these high-risk securities. Currently, only relatively safe securities can be purchased.

S&L Liabilities and Net Worth

Now let's look at the right-hand side of the balance sheet in Figure 5. The primary liabilities of savings and loans are deposits and borrowed funds.

The largest liability of savings and loans are customer funds held on deposit. In the past, the bulk of the deposits were from **passbook savings accounts,** interest-bearing savings accounts. In the past, banks issued small books to savers to use for keeping track of their savings balances. The customer would present this book to the teller every time a deposit or withdrawal was made, and the teller would validate the entry. The physical passbook has almost been phased out over the years and replaced with computerized record keeping.

The second major liability is *borrowings,* funds obtained in either the money or capital markets. Since savings and loan deposits are typically short-term, one way to lengthen their average maturity is to borrow long-term funds. Borrowed funds have become a major source of funds for savings and loans, now accounting for over 28% of total assets, up from 11% in 1990.

Capital

The capital of financial institutions is often measured by the *net worth ratio,* total equity (also known as *net worth*) divided by total assets. This figure is closely watched by regulators for indications that a financial institution may be undercapitalized. The average net worth-to-assets ratio was about 3% in 1984. Many institutions had a negative net worth at this time. Since 1989, the average net worth ratio has improved. At the end of 2000, it stood at 8.4%. This is now about the same as the 8.5% average net worth ratio for commercial banks. One reason for the improvement in the capital of savings and loans is that FIRREA mandated that it be increased. (We discussed the importance of capital in the functioning of a financial institution in Chapter 15.)

The accounting for savings and loans permitted extensive use of goodwill, an asset account on the balance sheet that supposedly reflects the value of a firm's good name and reputation. For example, in 1987, goodwill accounted for $29.6 billion of savings and loan assets. This represented more than half of the $53.8 billion in total capital. If we removed goodwill from capital before calculating the net worth-to-assets ratio in 1987, we find that the ratio is only 1.6%, not the 3.7% it was when including goodwill. The value of goodwill fell steadily since its high that year. Listing large amounts of goodwill as an asset was another way that savings and loans were able to hide the fact that they were insolvent.

Profitability and Health

One indication that the health of savings and loans has improved in recent years is that their earnings have increased. From 1987 through 1990, the industry suffered net losses. But in 1991, net after-tax income for the industry was $859 million, and by 2000, it had reached $10.7 billion (see Figure 6).

A better measure of a firm's health than net income is its return on equity *(ROE).* Figure 7 shows that there was a steady increase in S&Ls' *ROE* from 1993 to 2001, when it was nearly 12%. S&L profits for 1999 were the highest ever reported by the industry. Over 94% of all S&Ls were profitable. Part of this income was due to the sale of mortgage loans that had increased in value when interest rates fell.

Only four S&Ls have failed since 1995. Furthermore, the number of "problem" thrifts is down to 13, compared to 146 in 1993. The percentage of loans being charged off as losses is also at a low 0.25%.

In summary, savings institutions, which were in grave condition a decade ago, have returned to robust health. They are providing fair returns to their shareholders and are not in any danger of causing additional taxpayer losses. The industry's equity-to-capital ratio is now the highest it has ever been.

The Future of the Savings and Loan Industry

One issue that has received considerable attention in recent years is whether the savings and loan industry is still needed. Observers who favor eliminating S&L charters altogether point out that there is now a large number of alternative mortgage loan outlets available for home buyers. In Chapter 11 we introduced the securitized mortgage. This new instrument has provided the majority of the funds needed by the mortgage market. A reasonable question to ask is whether there

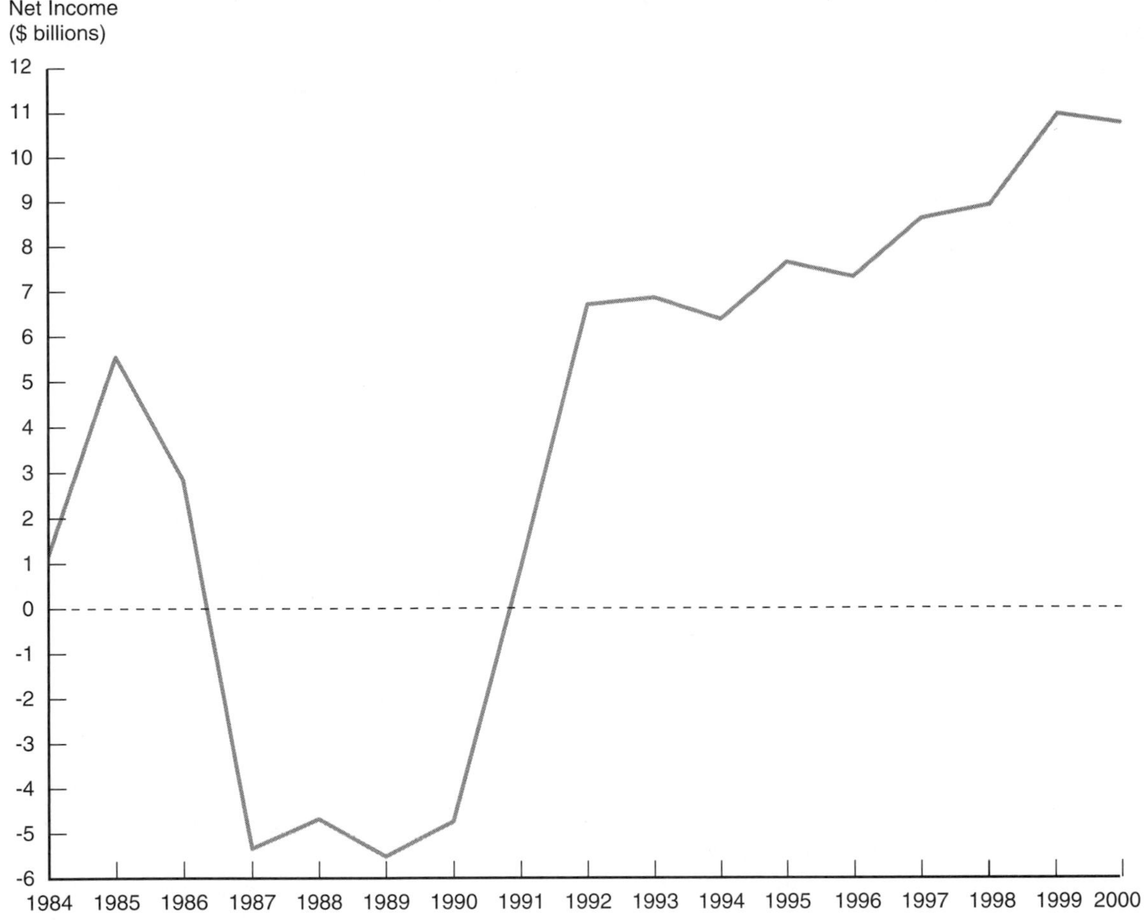

FIGURE 6 Net Income of Savings and Loan Associations, 1984–2000

Source: http://www2.fdic.gov/qbp/

is a need for an industry dedicated exclusively to providing a service efficiently provided elsewhere in the financial system.

Let us review the history of the savings and loan industry for a moment. S&Ls were established to provide mortgages to home buyers. The industry was healthy until interest rates increased and they were stuck holding low-interest fixed-rate mortgages financed with high-cost funds. Congress attempted to provide relief by giving S&Ls a great deal of flexibility in their capital structure and lending functions. Due to abuses, poor market conditions, inadequate supervision by FSLIC, and fraud, tremendous losses accrued. Finally, Congress reregulated the industry and again required that its primary business be mortgage lending. The only trouble now is that mortgage loans are available from many other sources (see Chapter 11).

Just as efficient markets develop new securities and services when the need for them arises, efficient markets should eliminate unneeded institutions when they are no longer required. Many industry analysts expect the savings and loan

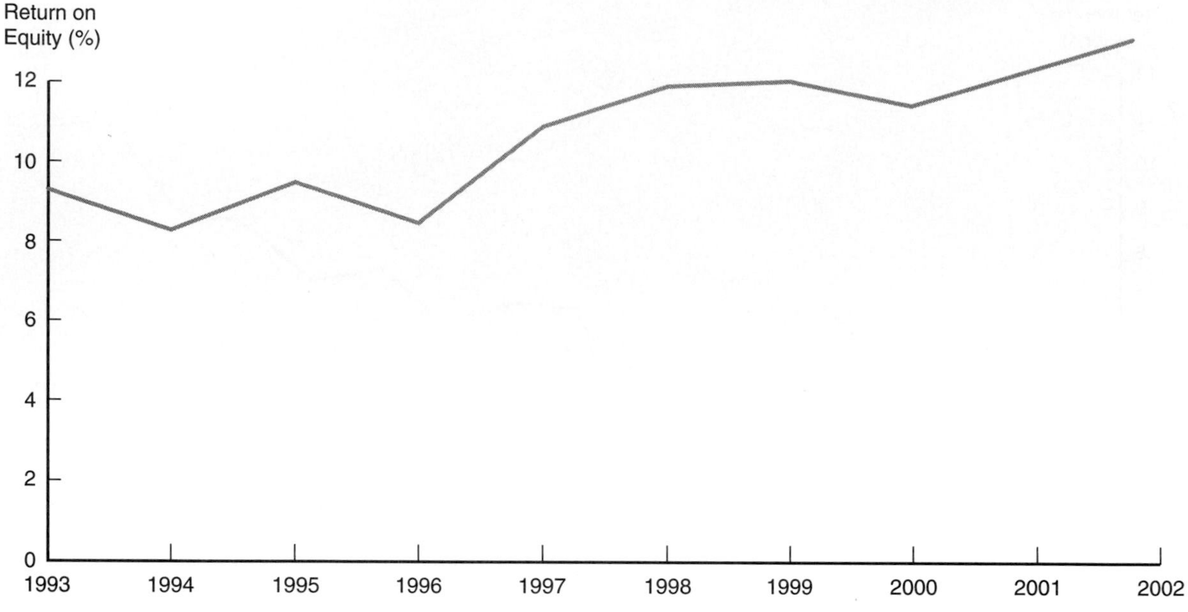

FIGURE 7 Average Return on Equity for Savings and Loan Institutions, 1993–2001

Source: http://www2.fdic.gov/qbp/2001mar/sav1.html

industry to disappear, perhaps by existing savings and loans being acquired by other institutions or by commercial banks. We can examine the evidence to see if this is beginning to happen.

We noted earlier that the number of savings and loans has decreased by 56% since its high in 1986. There were fewer S&Ls in 2001 than in 1994. However, the drop in the number of institutions could be due to consolidation within the industry, much like what is happening in commercial banking. A better indication of the future of the industry may be provided by the trend in total assets. Figure 2 shows that the total assets of savings and loans have increased since 1993. This suggests that there is at least not a rapid trend to eliminate these institutions. It may be that they will continue to be a provider of mortgage loans along with a number of other sources.

Congress will be pressured again to deregulate the industry to allow S&Ls to perform more of the functions allowed by commercial banks. Although this may happen, the losses sustained as a result of the last attempt at deregulation are still fresh in the minds of regulators. It is unlikely that we will again witness an attempt at rapid deregulation. Instead, we can expect to see gradual changes in the industry that will continue to blur the distinction between savings and loans and commercial banks.

CREDIT UNIONS

The third type of thrift institution is the **credit union,** a financial institution that focuses on servicing the banking and lending needs of its members. These institutions are also designed to service the needs of consumers, not businesses, and are distinguished by their ownership structure and their "common bond" membership requirement. Most credit unions are relatively small.

History and Organization

In the early 1900s, commercial banks focused most of their attention on the business borrower. This left the small consumer without a ready source of funds. Because Congress was concerned that commercial banks were not meeting the needs of consumers, it established savings banks and savings and loan associations to help consumers obtain mortgage loans. In the early 1900s, the credit union was established to help consumers with *other* types of loans. A secondary purpose was to provide a place for small investors to place their savings.

The concept behind credit unions originated in Germany in the nineteenth century. A group of consumers would pool their assets as collateral for a loan from a bank. The funds so raised were then loaned to the members of the group, and each member of the group was personally liable for repayment of the loan. Defaults were very rare because members knew one another well.

The first two credit unions in the United States were established in Massachusetts in 1910. The Massachusetts Credit Union (MCU) was organized in 1914 as a functioning credit union but with the additional purpose of encouraging the formation of additional credit unions. The MCU evolved into a kind of central credit union facility. In 1921, the MCU was reorganized as the **Credit Union National Extension Bureau (CUNEB),** which worked to have credit unions established in every state. In 1935, CUNEB was replaced by the **Credit Union National Association (CUNA).**

In 1934, Congress passed the **Federal Credit Union Act,** which allowed federal chartering of credit unions in all states. Prior to this, most credit unions were chartered by the state in which they operated. Currently, about 40% of credit unions have state charters and 60% have federal charters.

One reason for the growth of credit unions has been the support they received from employers. They realized that employee morale could be raised and time saved if banking-type facilities were readily available. In many cases, employers donated space on business property for the credit union to operate. The convenience of this institution soon attracted a large number of customers.

Mutual Ownership Credit unions are organized as *mutuals;* that is, they are owned by their depositors. A customer receives shares when a deposit is made. Rather than earning interest on deposited funds, the customer earns dividends. The amount of the dividend is not guaranteed, like the interest rate earned on accounts at banks. Instead, the amount of the dividend is estimated in advance and is paid if at all possible.

Each depositor has one vote, regardless how much money he or she may have with the institution. Depositors vote for directors, who in turn hire managers to run the credit union.

Because credit unions are cooperative businesses, they are managed somewhat differently from other businesses. For example, many credit unions make extensive use of volunteer help to reduce their costs. Since any cost reductions are passed on to the depositors, volunteers feel that they are working for the common good. Similarly, as noted, operating facilities may be donated.

Common Bond Membership The single most important feature of credit unions that distinguishes them from other depository institutions is the common bond member rule. The idea behind **common bond membership** is that only members of a particular association, occupation, or geographic region are permitted to join the credit union. A credit union's common bonds define its field of membership.

The most frequent type of common bond applies to employees of a single occupation or employer. For example, most state employees are eligible to join their state credit union. Similarly, the Navy Credit Union is open to all U.S. Navy personnel. Other credit unions accept members from the same religious or professional background.

One problem with the common bond membership rule is that it prevents credit unions from diversifying their risk. If most of a credit union's members are employed by one business and that business is forced to lay off workers, it is likely that the credit union will have high default rates on loans. A recent trend among credit unions has been for several to merge, a move that helps reduce the risk of having all members linked by a single bond. To make mergers easier, regulators have interpreted the common bond requirement less strictly. For example, most credit unions now let members of the immediate family of an eligible member join, and many credit unions have adopted a "once a member, always a member" policy. In 1982, regulators ruled that credit unions could accept members from several employee groups instead of just one. In 1988, regulators determined that the bond between members of the American Association of Retired People was sufficient and authorized the organization to open its own credit union. The American Automobile Association, however, was rejected.

The commercial bank lobby violently disagrees with relaxed membership rules for credit unions that in some instances have allowed them to admit virtually everyone in a community. Commercial banks view credit unions as unfair competitors due to the government support they receive in the form of tax advantages (to be discussed shortly). Many bankers feel that the threat posed by credit unions could cause more vulnerable banks to fail.

To curb this threat, a group of Tennessee bankers sued to change the regulators' stance that federal law allows multiple occupational groups, each of which independently shares a common bond, to join a single credit union. In April 1997, an appeals court ruled in favor of the bankers, saying that the restrictions on common bond membership should be left intact.

On February 24, 1997, the U.S. Supreme Court reviewed a different lower court ruling on the AT&T Family Federal Credit Union that placed sharp limits on membership in federally chartered credit unions. It ruled that bankers have the right to sue about the field-of-membership issue and that the credit union regulator, the National Credit Union Administration, can no longer allow federal credit unions to expand outside of their original memberships.

This ruling resulted in intense congressional lobbying by credit union supporters that led to the passage of the Credit Union Membership Access Act on August 7, 1998. The intent of this law was to preserve the right of all consumers to choose the credit union alternative. It maintains the concept of common bond membership but allows for the combining of groups with different common bonds in a single credit union. This act became effective on January 1, 1999.

Nonprofit, Tax-Exempt Status The Federal Credit Union Act of 1934 contained the provision that credit unions were to be nonprofit and consequently exempt from federal taxation. All of the income earned by the institutions is to be spent on their members. Credit unions are currently the only financial institutions that are tax-exempt. This makes it easier for them to accumulate retained earnings than it is for other institutions. Banks and S&Ls are questioning this tax-exempt status as credit unions become larger and more significant competitors. Savings and loans lost their tax-exempt status in 1951. The American Bankers Association estimates that the subsidy reduces the cost of funds to credit unions by almost 2.5% and gives them a cost advantage of $1 billion per year. The credit unions themselves dispute this number and assign their cost advantage to their use of volunteer help. It remains a question how long the favorable tax treatment for credit unions can be maintained.

Partly as a result of being nonprofit and partly due to the cost advantage of being tax-exempt, credit union fees tend to be lower than those of banks.

Regulation and Insurance The **National Credit Union Act of 1970** established the **National Credit Union Administration (NCUA).** This independent federal agency is charged with the task of regulating and supervising federally chartered credit unions and state-chartered credit unions that receive federal deposit insurance. The remaining credit unions are regulated by state credit union or banking departments, which generally follow federal practices.

The National Credit Union Administration site, www.ncua.gov, includes general information about credit unions and credit union data.

The National Credit Union Act of 1970 also established the **National Credit Union Share Insurance Fund (NCUSIF),** to be controlled by the NCUA. This fund insures the deposits of all nationally chartered credit unions and most state-chartered credit unions for up to $100,000 per account. The remaining state-chartered credit unions are insured by one of the state insurance systems. Since the savings and loan crisis, most states are eager to get out of the insurance business. It is likely that in the future, all credit union deposit insurance will be provided by the NCUSIF.

Central Credit Unions Because many credit unions are small and have very little diversification, they are often susceptible to seasonal cash flow problems. Most credit unions also lack the size needed to support large administrative staffs. One way they overcome these problems is with "state central" or "corporate" credit unions, which service the credit unions in their area by providing computer and financial assistance. There are currently 44 state central credit unions, which provide a number of valuable services, including these:

- They may help with member institutions' credit needs. The state central can invest excess funds and make loans to cover short-term shortages.
- They can invest excess funds with the **U.S. Central Credit Union,** which in turn can invest in the financial markets.
- They can hold clearing balances.
- They can provide educational services.

The U.S. Central Credit Union was organized in 1974 to act as a central bank for credit unions. It is chartered as a commercial bank in Kansas, and its primary function is to provide banking services to the 44 state central credit unions. It allows these institutions access to the money markets and to long-term capital markets. Most individual credit unions and even most state central credit unions lack sufficient size and transaction volume to operate efficiently in these wholesale markets.

In 1978, the **Financial Institutions Reform Act** created the **Central Liquidity Facility (CLF)** as the lender of last resort for credit unions. This agency provides many of the same functions for credit unions that the Federal Reserve provides for commercial banks. Although most day-to-day liquidity needs of credit unions are met by the state central organizations, in the event of a national liquidity crisis, a federal agency can raise far more funds. For example, in a crisis, the CLF can borrow directly from the Federal Reserve.

Membership in the CLF is voluntary, and any state or federally chartered credit union may join the CLF by pledging 0.5% of capital. Most of the funds in the CLF are borrowed from the federal government.

Credit Union Size Credit unions are small relative to other depository financial institutions. The industry accounts for only about 10% of all consumer deposits and about 15% of all consumer loans. One reason for credit unions' limited size is the common bond restraint. Because credit unions can enroll only members who satisfy the common bond, their growth potential is severely restricted. Nevertheless, some credit unions have grown quite large. The Navy Credit Union dwarfs the others, with nearly $14 billion in total assets. However, most credit unions have less than $1 billion in assets, and many have less than $5 million. Table 1 lists the largest credit unions.

As discussed earlier, mergers between credit unions help them capture economies of scale and diversify their risk. This trend has resulted in fewer but larger credit unions. Figure 8 reports the number of credit unions active from 1933 to 2001. The number has fallen steadily since 1970 as credit unions merged.

Trade Associations Because credit unions are so small, they often lack the economies of scale necessary to service their customers at competitive costs. For example, a credit union with only $5 million of deposits cannot afford the costs of maintaining a computer center for processing checks and sending out statements. Similarly, most credit unions cannot afford to maintain their own automated teller machine network. One solution to this problem is the use of **trade associations,** groups of credit unions that have organized together. These associations provide services to large numbers of credit unions.

The largest of the trade associations is the Credit Union National Association. CUNA has a number of affiliations that provide specific services:

- CUNA Service Group provides new products for credit unions.
- CUNA Supply, Inc., provides for bulk purchases of supplies to lower supply costs.
- ICU Services, Inc., provides various investment options, automated payment services, credit card programs, and IRA plans.

TABLE 1 10 Largest Federal Credit Unions, June 30, 2001

Current Rank	Name of Credit Union	Rank 1 Year Ago	City	State	Year Chartered	Assets
1	Navy	1	Merrifield	VA	1947	13,939,149,524
2	State Employees'	2	Raleigh	NC	1937	7,521,903,954
3	Pentagon	4	Alexandria	VA	1935	4,053,066,861
4	Boeing Employees	3	Tukwila	WA	1935	3,690,940,744
5	The Golden 1	6	Sacramento	CA	1933	3,481,521,237
6	United Airlines Employees'	5	Chicago	IL	1935	3,309,626,503
7	Orange County Teachers	8	Santa Ana	CA	1934	3,147,805,363
8	American Airlines	7	DFW Airport	TX	1982	3,029,185,902
9	Suncoast Schools	9	Tampa	FL	1978	2,757,357,987
10	Hughes Aircraft Employees	10	Manhattan Beach	CA	1940	2,369,167,757

Source: http://www.ncua.gov/ref/statistics/midyear2001.pdf

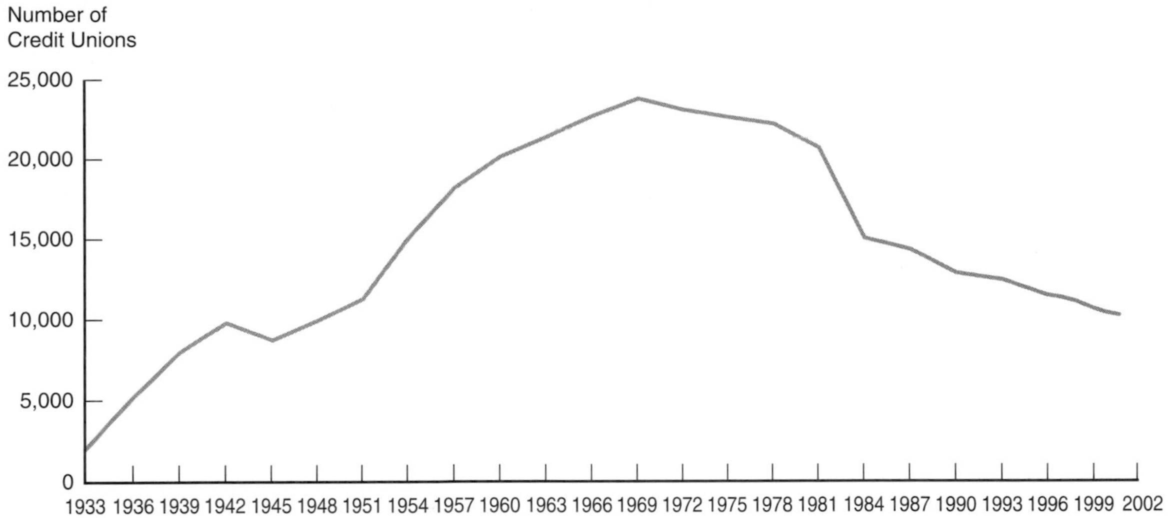

FIGURE 8 Number of Credit Unions, 1933–2001

Source: http://ncua.gov/ref/statistics/midyear2001.pdf

- CUNA Mortgage provides a liquidity facility for mortgage lending by credit unions.

In addition to using trade associations, many credit unions contract with commercial banks for data processing services. Checks written by credit union customers are automatically routed to the bank, which takes the funds out of a credit union account. The bank then provides a transaction history in electronic form that is given to the credit union. The tie-in with the servicing bank may be so close that the credit union's teller terminals are linked to the bank's computer system, just like the bank's own teller terminals. The credit union customer may never be aware that a bank is involved in the process.

Sources of Funds

Over 87% of credit union funds come from customer savings and share draft accounts. Unlike commercial banks, credit unions seldom purchase funds in the capital or money markets. Four main types of accounts are offered by credit unions: regular share accounts, share certificates, share draft accounts, and money market accounts. Figure 9 shows the distribution of funds among the share accounts.

Regular Share Accounts Regular share accounts are savings accounts. Customers cannot write checks against these accounts, although they can withdraw funds without giving prior notice or incurring any penalties. These accounts make up about 34% of total deposits. Customers do not receive interest on these accounts. Instead they receive dividends that are not guaranteed in advance but are estimated. The credit union tries to pay the estimated amount.

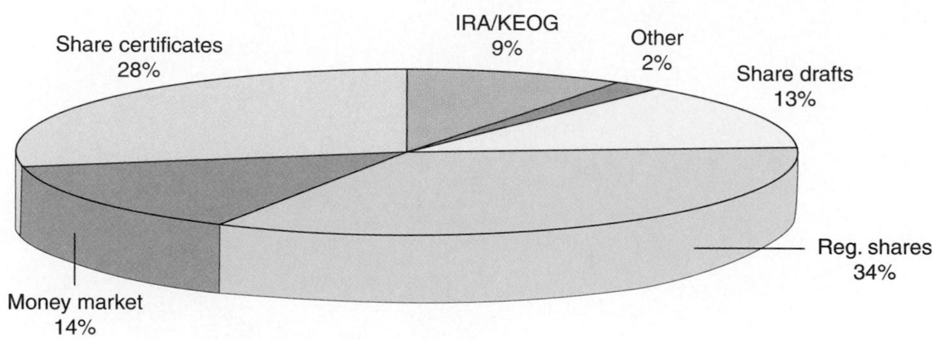

FIGURE 9 Share Distribution

Source: http://www.ncua.gov/ref/statistics/midyear2001.pdf

Share Certificates Share certificates are comparable to CDs offered by commercial banks. The customer agrees to leave the funds on deposit with the credit union for a specified length of time and in exchange receives a higher return.

Share Draft Accounts Share drafts were first developed in 1974 and made legal nationally in 1980. They are virtually identical to the checks written by customers of commercial banks. Share draft accounts usually pay interest and permit depositors to write share drafts against them. These accounts represent about 13% of credit union liabilities.

Capital Credit union capital cannot be measured in the usual way because credit union share accounts are in fact equity accounts. A more meaningful approach is to measure capital as the difference between total assets and total liabilities where liabilities include all share accounts. Using this approach, the average capital-to-asset ratio was 11.4% in December 2000. One reason for this strong capital position is that regulations require a capital-to-loan ratio of at least 10% for credit unions.

Uses of Funds

In December 2000, 68.6% of credit union assets were invested in loans. Most credit union loans are relatively small. For example, the average credit union loan in 2000 was $3750. This is in keeping with the mission of credit unions to provide loans to small borrowers. Credit union loan losses are usually quite small. The average ratio of delinquent loans to total loans was under .75% in 2000, the lowest rate ever. This compares favorably to the loan loss ratio for commercial banks. The rate of charged off loans was .42% in 2000.

The mix of loans made by credit unions demonstrates that credit unions are indeed providing a service directed at consumers. Figure 10 shows the loan distribution of the industry. We see that auto loans make up 40% of the total loans volume.

The balance of credit union assets are in cash, government securities, deposits at other institutions, and fixed assets. Credit unions tend not to make risky investments and are limited by regulations to certain types of investment securities that assure low risk.

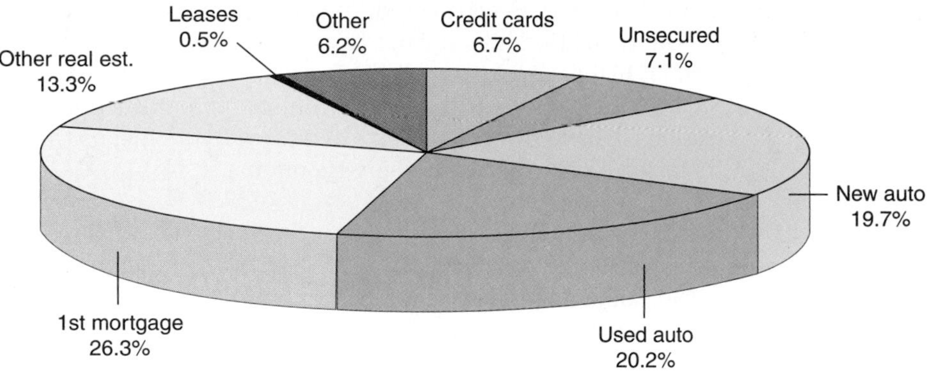

FIGURE 10 Loan Distribution

Source: http://www.ncua.gov/ref/statistics/midyear2001.pdf

Advantages and Disadvantages of Credit Unions

Figure 11 traces the membership in credit unions from 1933 to 2002. The steady increase is expected to continue because credit unions enjoy several advantages over other depository institutions. These advantages have contributed toward their growth and popularity.

- *Employer support.* Many employers recognize that it is in their own best interest to help their employees manage their funds. This motivates the firm to support the employee credit union. Businesses will frequently provide free office space, utilities, and other help to the credit unions.

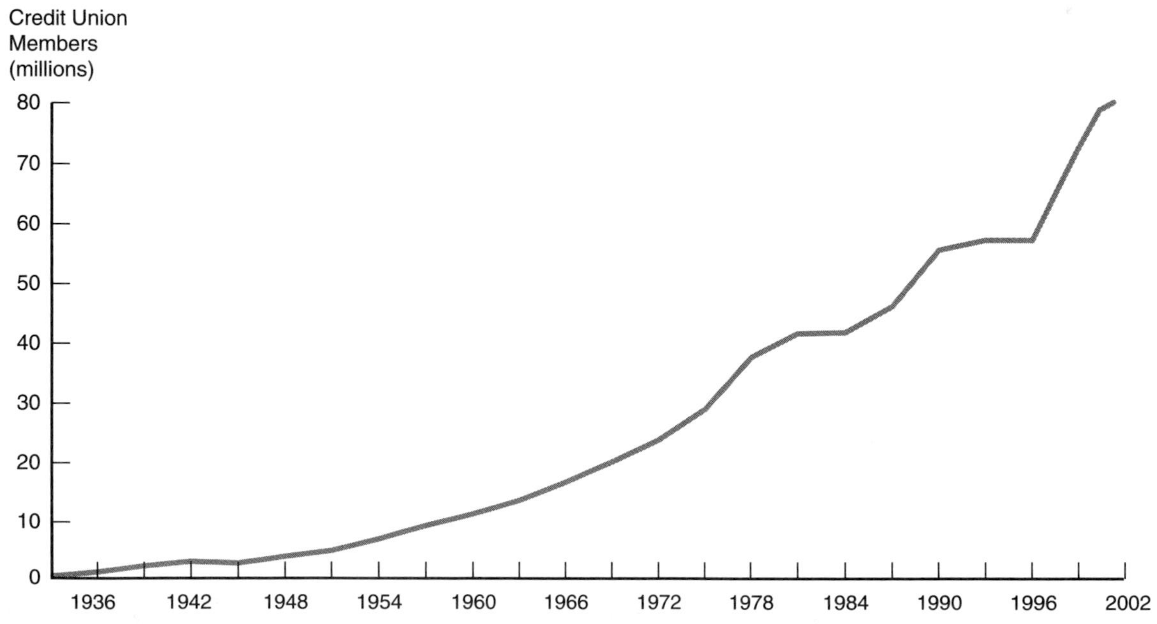

FIGURE 11 Credit Union Membership, 1933–2002

Source: http://www.ncua.gov/ref/statistics/midyear2001.pdf

- *Tax advantage.* Because credit unions are exempt from paying taxes by federal regulation, this savings can be passed on to the members in the form of higher dividends or lower account-servicing costs.
- *Strong trade associations.* Credit unions have formed many trade associations, which lower their costs and provide the means to offer services the institutions could not otherwise offer.

The main disadvantage of credit unions is that the common bond requirement keeps many of them very small. The cost disadvantage can prevent them from offering the range of services available from larger institutions. This disadvantage is not entirely equalized by the use of trade associations.

The Future of Credit Unions

Credit unions are well positioned to continue their growth as a significant provider of financial services to consumers. Figure 12 shows that credit union assets

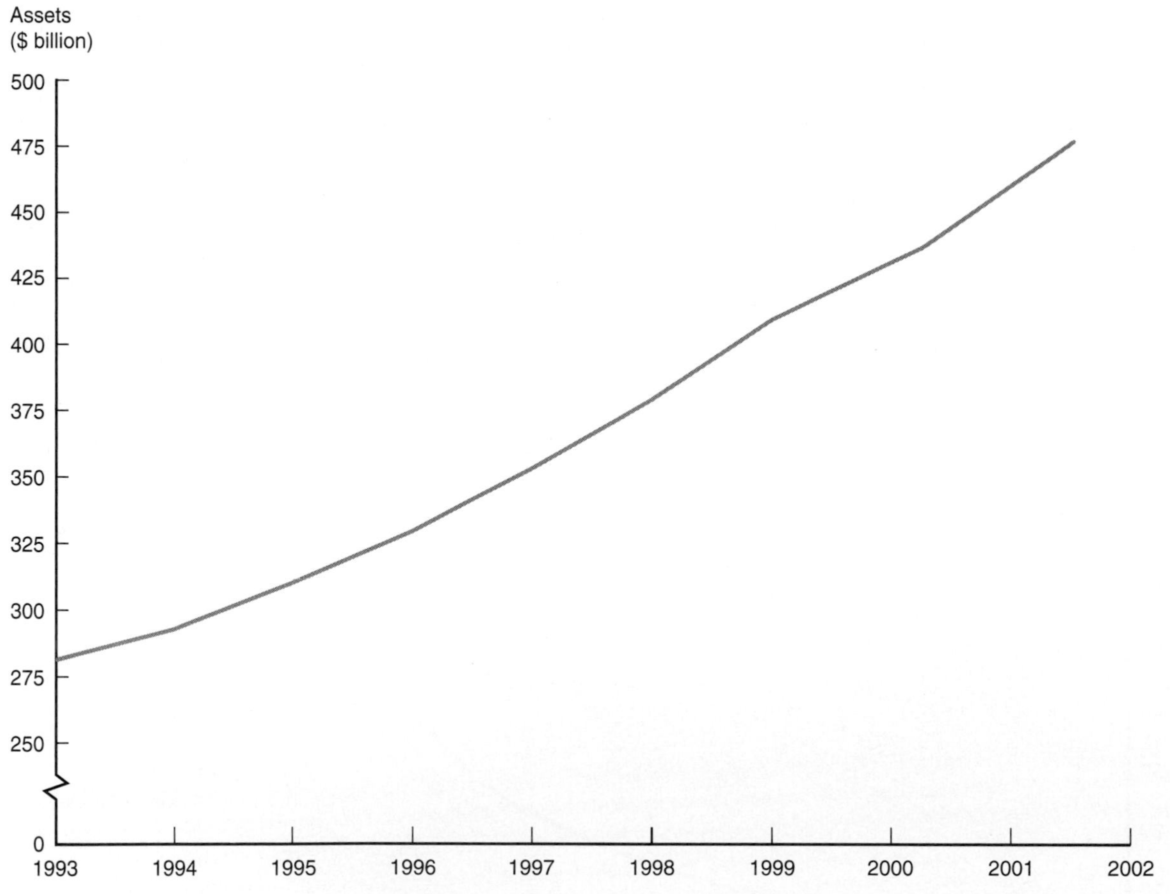

FIGURE 12 Credit Union Assests, 1993–2002

Source: http://www.ncua.gov/ref/statistics/midyear2001.pdf

increased from $282 billion to $477.2 billion over an eight-year period, a 6.8% compounded annual growth rate. Though credit unions are likely to remain small compared to other financial institutions, their cost advantages give them a competitive edge that will continue to attract consumer business.

SUMMARY

1. Congress mandated that savings and loans and mutual savings banks provide mortgage loan opportunities for consumers. For most of the twentieth century, they profitably satisfied this need.
2. In the late 1970s and the 1980s, savings and loans lost money because interest rates on their deposits rose while the return on their mortgage portfolios was fixed. These losses initially led to deregulation. Savings and loans continued to lose money despite regulatory reform.
3. Due to mounting losses among savings and loans the industry was reregulated in 1987. It has since recovered in terms of both profitability and net worth. The industry continues to consolidate, though total assets are remaining about constant. It is too early to determine whether the industry will simply merge with commercial banks or remain independent.
4. Credit unions were established to serve the public's demand for consumer-type loans. They are unique because members must satisfy a common bond requirement to join. This common bond requirement has restricted the growth of credit unions. Most are small compared to savings and loans and commercial banks.
5. Because of their small size, credit unions have benefited by forming cooperative organizations. These coops, such as CUNA, provide technical, liquidity, mortgage, and insurance services that would be impossible for the individual credit unions to have otherwise.
6. Credit unions enjoy several advantages that should keep them viable in the future. First, as nonprofit organizations, they are exempt from federal taxation. Second, many have strong support from a sponsoring company or business, which lowers the operating cost of the institution. The use of volunteers also helps keep costs low.

KEY TERMS

Central Liquidity Facility (CLF), *p. 483*
common bond membership, *p. 481*
credit union, *p. 480*
Credit Union National Association (CUNA), *p. 481*
Credit Union National Extension Bureau (CUNEB), *p. 481*
Federal Credit Union Act, *p. 481*
Federal Home Loan Bank Act of 1932, *p. 467*
Federal Home Loan Bank Board (FHLBB), *p. 467*
Federal Savings and Loan Insurance Corporation (FSLIC), *p. 467*
Financial Institutions Reform Act, *p. 483*
Financial Institutions Reform, Recovery, and Enforcement Act (FIRREA), *p. 473*
mutual bank, *p. 466*
National Credit Union Act of 1970, *p. 483*
National Credit Union Administration (NCUA), *p. 483*
National Credit Union Share Insurance Fund (NCUSIF), *p. 483*
passbook savings account, *p. 477*
regulatory forbearance, *p. 469*
Resolution Trust Corporation (RTC), *p. 473*
trade association, *p. 484*
U.S. Central Credit Union, *p. 483*

QUESTIONS AND PROBLEMS

*1. How does the mutual form of ownership differ from the typical corporate form of ownership?

2. What is the primary disadvantage of the mutual form of ownership?

*3. What are the primary assets of savings and loan institutions?

4. Name three factors that led to the thrift crisis.

*5. Why did depositors not object to the risky loans and investments made by savings and loans in the early and mid–1980s?

6. How was the thrift crisis ended?

*7. What is the most common measure of the capital adequacy of a financial institution?

8. What has been the trend in S&L net income since the mid–1990s?

*9. What type of customers are credit unions focused on servicing?

10. What is the purpose of the Credit Union National Association (CUNA)?

*11. Describe the common bond membership rule.

12. Why does the commercial banking lobby object to the nonprofit, tax-exempt status enjoyed by credit unions?

*13. Are most credit unions larger or smaller than commercial banks? Why?

14. What are share accounts, share certificates, and share drafts?

*15. What are the primary advantages enjoyed by credit unions?

16. Why is regulatory forebearance a dangerous strategy for a deposit insurance agency?

*17. Why did the S&L crisis not occur unitl the 1980s?

18. The FIRREA legislation in 1989 is the most comprehensive thrift legislation since the 1930s. Describe its major features.

*19. Some advocates of campaign finance reform believe that government funding of political campaigns and restrictions on campaign financing might reduce the principal-agent problem in our political system. Do you agree?

20. How can the S&L crisis be blamed on the principal-agent problem?

WEB EXERCISES

Thrifts: Savings and Loans and Credit Unions

1. Like banks, thrifts provide a great deal of summary information to the public. One of the most extensive sites for thrift information is at http://www.ots.treas.gov. Select "Industry Performance" under "Data and Research" on the left margin of the site. Now go to "Select Indicator" on the site to answer the following questions.
   - **a.** What is the return on average assets for the most recent time period?
   - **b.** What is the return on average equity for the most recent time period?
   - **c.** How many thrift institutions are reporting to the OTS during the most recent time period?

2. Go to http://www.ncua.gov/. This is the home page of the National Credit Union Administration. Click on the history of the credit union industry.
   - **a.** According to the NCUA, what features definc a credit union?
   - **b.** What was the name of the first credit union opened in the United States in 1909?
   - **c.** In what year was the Federal Credit Union Act signed into law?

Chapter 18

Banking Regulation

Preview

As we have seen in earlier chapters, the financial system is among the most heavily regulated sectors of the economy, and banks are among the most heavily regulated of financial institutions. In this chapter we develop an economic analysis of why regulation of banking takes the form it does.

Unfortunately, the regulatory process may not always work very well, as evidenced by recent crises in the banking systems, not only in the United States but in many countries throughout the world. Here we also use our analysis of banking regulation to explain the worldwide crises in banking and how the regulatory system can be reformed to prevent future disasters.

ASYMMETRIC INFORMATION AND BANK REGULATION

Bank regulation information is available at www.ny.frb.org/Pihome/regs.html. You can access regulatory publications of the Federal Reserve Board at www.federalreserve.gov/Regulations/default.htm

In earlier chapters we have seen how asymmetric information, the fact that different parties in a financial contract do not have the same information, leads to adverse selection and moral hazard problems that have an important impact on our financial system. The concepts of asymmetric information, adverse selection, and moral hazard are especially useful in understanding why government has chosen the form of banking regulation we see in the United States and in other countries. There are seven basic categories of banking regulation: the government safety net, restrictions on bank asset holdings and capital requirements, chartering and bank examination, disclosure requirements, consumer protection, restrictions on competition, and separation of the banking and securities industries.

Government Safety Net: Deposit Insurance and the FDIC

As we saw in Chapter 14, banks are particularly well suited to solving adverse selection and moral hazard problems because they make private loans that help avoid the free-rider problem. However, this solution to the free-rider problem creates another asymmetric information problem because depositors lack information about the quality of these private loans. This asymmetric information problem leads to two reasons why the banking system might not function well.

First, before the FDIC started operations in 1934, a bank failure (in which a bank is unable to meet its obligations to pay its depositors and other creditors and so must go out of business) meant that depositors would have to wait to get their deposit funds until the bank was liquidated (until its assets had been turned into cash); at that time, they would be paid only a fraction of the value of their deposits. Unable to learn if bank managers were taking on too much risk or were outright crooks, depositors would be reluctant to put money in the bank, thus making banking institutions less viable. Second is that depositors' lack of information about the quality of bank assets can lead to bank panics, which, as we saw in Chapter 14, can have serious harmful consequences for the economy. To see this, consider the following situation. There is no deposit insurance, and an adverse shock hits the economy. As a result of the shock, 5% of the banks have such large losses on loans that they become insolvent (have a negative net worth and so are bankrupt). Because of asymmetric information, depositors are unable to tell whether their bank is a good bank or one of the 5% that are insolvent. Depositors at bad *and* good banks recognize that they may not get back 100 cents on the dollar for their deposits and will want to withdraw them. Indeed, because banks operate on a "sequential service constraint" (a first-come, first-served basis), depositors have a very strong incentive to show up at the bank first because if they are last in line, the bank may run out of funds and they will get nothing. Uncertainty about the health of the banking system in general can lead to runs on banks both good and bad, and the failure of one bank can hasten the failure of others (referred to as the *contagion effect*). If nothing is done to restore the public's confidence, a bank panic can ensue.

Indeed, bank panics were a fact of American life in the nineteenth and early twentieth centuries, with major ones occurring every 20 years or so in 1819, 1837, 1857, 1873, 1884, 1893, 1907, and 1930–1933. Bank failures were a serious problem even during the boom years of the 1920s, when the number of bank failures averaged around 600 per year.

A government safety net for depositors can short-circuit runs on banks and bank panics, and by providing protection for the depositor, it can overcome reluctance to put funds in the banking system. One form of the safety net is deposit insurance, a guarantee such as that provided by the Federal Deposit Insurance Corporation (FDIC) in the United States in which depositors are paid off in full on the first $100,000 they have deposited in the bank no matter what happens to the bank. With fully insured deposits, depositors don't need to run to the bank to make withdrawals—even if they are worried about the bank's health—because their deposits will be worth 100 cents on the dollar no matter what. From 1930 to 1933, the years immediately preceding the creation of the FDIC, the number of bank failures averaged over 2000 per year. After the establishment of the FDIC in 1934, bank failures averaged fewer than 15 per year until 1981.

The FDIC uses two primary methods to handle a failed bank. In the first, called the *payoff method,* the FDIC allows the bank to fail and pays off deposits up to the $100,000 insurance limit (with funds acquired from the insurance premiums paid by the banks that have bought FDIC insurance). After the bank has been liquidated, the FDIC lines up with other creditors of the bank and is paid its share of the proceeds from the liquidated assets. Typically, when the payoff method is used, account holders with deposits in excess of the $100,000 limit get back more than 90 cents on the dollar, although the process can take several years to complete.

In the second method, called the *purchase and assumption method,* the FDIC reorganizes the bank, typically by finding a willing merger partner who assumes (takes over) all of the failed bank's deposits so that no depositor loses a penny. The FDIC may help the merger partner by providing it with subsidized loans or by buying some of the failed bank's weaker loans. The net effect of the purchase and assumption method is that the FDIC has guaranteed *all* deposits, not just those under the $100,000 limit. The purchase and assumption method was the FDIC's most common procedure for dealing with a failed bank before new banking legislation in 1991.

Deposit insurance is not the only way in which governments provide a safety net for depositors. In other countries, governments have often stood ready to provide support to domestic banks when they face runs even in the absence of explicit deposit insurance. This support is sometimes provided by lending from the central bank to troubled institutions and is often referred to as the "lender of last resort" role of the central bank. In other cases, funds are provided directly by the government to troubled institutions, or these institutions are taken over by the government and the government then guarantees that depositors will receive their money in full. However, in recent years, government deposit insurance has been growing in popularity and has spread to many countries throughout the world. Whether this trend is desirable is discussed in Box 1.

Moral Hazard and the Government Safety Net Although a government safety net has been successful at protecting depositors and preventing bank panics, it is a mixed blessing. The most serious drawback of the government safety net stems

BOX 1: GLOBAL

The Spread of Government Deposit Insurance Throughout the World: Is This a Good Thing?

For the first 30 years after federal deposit insurance was established in the United States, only 6 countries emulated the United States and adopted deposit insurance. However, this began to change in the late 1960s, with the trend accelerating in the 1990s, when the number of countries adopting deposit insurance doubled to over 70. Government deposit insurance has taken off throughout the world because of growing concern about the health of banking systems, particularly after the increasing number of banking crises in recent years (documented at the end of the chapter). Has this spread of deposit insurance been a good thing? Has it helped improve the performance of the financial system and prevent banking crises?

The answer seems to be no under many circumstances. Research at the World Bank has found that on average, the adoption of explicit government deposit insurance is associated with less banking sector stability and a higher incidence of banking crises.* Furthermore, on average it seems to retard financial development. However, the negative effects of deposit insurance appear only in countries with weak institutional environments: an absence of rule of law, ineffective regulation and supervision of the financial sector, and high corruption. This is exactly what might be expected because, as we will see later in this chapter, a strong institutional environment is needed to limit the incentives for banks to engage in excessively risky behavior created by deposit insurance. The problem is that developing a strong institutional environment may be very difficult to achieve in many emerging market countries. This leaves us with the following conclusion: Adoption of deposit insurance may be exactly the wrong medicine for promoting stability and efficiency of banking systems in emerging market countries.

*See World Bank, *Finance for Growth: Policy Choices in a Volatile World* (World Bank and Oxford University Press: Oxford 2001.

from moral hazard, the incentives of one party to a transaction to engage in activities detrimental to the other party. Moral hazard is an important concern in insurance arrangements in general because the existence of insurance provides increased incentives for taking risks that might result in an insurance payoff. For example, some drivers with automobile collision insurance that has a low deductible might be more likely to drive recklessly because if they get into an accident, the insurance company pays most of the costs for damage and repairs.

Moral hazard is a prominent concern in government arrangements to provide a safety net. Because with a safety net depositors know that they will not suffer losses if a bank fails, they do not impose the discipline of the marketplace on banks by withdrawing deposits when they suspect that the bank is taking on too much risk. Consequently, banks with a government safety net have an incentive to take on greater risks than they otherwise would.

Adverse Selection and the Government Safety Net A further problem with a government safety net like deposit insurance arises because of adverse selection, the fact that the people who are most likely to produce the adverse outcome insured against (bank failure) are those who most want to take advantage of the insurance. For example, bad drivers are more likely than good drivers to take out automobile collision insurance with a low deductible. Because depositors protected by a government safety net have little reason to impose discipline on the bank, risk-loving entrepreneurs might find the banking industry a particularly attractive one to enter—they know that they will be able to engage in highly risky activities. Even worse, because protected depositors have so little reason to monitor the bank's activities, without government intervention outright crooks might also find banking an attractive industry for their activities because it is easy for them to get away with fraud and embezzlement.

"Too Big to Fail" The moral hazard created by a government safety net and the desire to prevent bank failures have presented bank regulators with a particular quandary. Because the failure of a very large bank makes it more likely that a major financial disruption will occur, bank regulators are naturally reluctant to allow a big bank to fail and cause losses to its depositors. Indeed, consider Continental Illinois, one of the ten largest banks in the United States when it became insolvent in May 1984. Not only did the FDIC guarantee depositors up to the $100,000 insurance limit, but it also guaranteed accounts exceeding $100,000 and even prevented losses for Continental Illinois bondholders. Shortly thereafter, the Comptroller of the Currency (the regulator of national banks) testified to Congress that the FDIC's policy was to regard the 11 largest banks as "too big to fail"—in other words, the FDIC would bail them out so that no depositor or creditor would suffer a loss. The FDIC would do this by using the purchase and assumption method, giving the insolvent bank a large infusion of capital and then finding a willing merger partner to take over the bank and its deposits. As Box 1 indicates, the too-big-to-fail policy has been extended to big banks that are not even among the 11 largest. (Note that "too big to fail" is somewhat misleading because when a bank is closed or merged into another bank, the managers are usually fired, and the stockholders in the bank lose their investment.)

One problem with the too-big-to-fail policy is that it increases the moral hazard incentives for big banks. If the FDIC were willing to close a bank using the alternative payoff method, paying depositors only up to the $100,000 limit, large depositors with more than $100,000 would suffer losses if the bank failed. Thus they would have an incentive to monitor the bank by examining the bank's activities closely and pulling their money out if the bank was taking on too much risk. To prevent such a loss of deposits, the bank would be more likely to engage in less risky activities. However, once large depositors know that a bank is too big to fail, they have no incentive to monitor the bank and pull out their deposits when it takes on too much risk: No matter what the bank does, large depositors will not suffer any losses. The result of the too-big-to-fail policy is that big banks might take on even greater risks, thereby making bank failures more likely.[1]

Another serious problem with the too-big-to-fail policy is that it is basically unfair. Small banks are put at a competitive disadvantage because they will be allowed to fail, creating potential losses for their large depositors, while big banks' large depositors are immune from losses. The unfairness of the too-big-to-fail doctrine came to a head with the different FDIC treatment of two insolvent banks in late 1990 and early 1991 described in Box 2.

Financial Consolidation and the Government Safety Net With the passage of the Riegle-Neal Interstate Banking and Branching and Efficiency Act of 1994 and the Gramm-Leach-Bliley Financial Services Modernization Act in 1999, financial consolidation has been proceeding at a rapid pace, leading to both larger and more complex banking organizations. Financial consolidation poses two challenges to banking regulation because of the existence of the government safety net. First, the increased size of banks as a result of financial consolidation increases the too-big-to-fail problem because there will now be more large institutions whose failure exposes the financial system to systemic (systemwide) risk. Thus, more banking institutions are likely to be treated as too big to fail, and the increased moral hazard incentives for these large institutions to take on greater risk can then increase the fragility of the financial system. Second, financial consolidation of banks with other financial service firms means that the government safety net may be extended to new activities such as securities underwriting, insurance, or real estate activities, thereby increasing incentives for greater risk taking in these activities, which can also weaken the fabric of the financial system. Limiting the moral hazard incentives for larger, more complex, financial organizations that are resulting from recent changes in legislation will be one of the key issues facing banking regulators in the future.

Restrictions on Asset Holdings and Bank Capital Requirements

As we have seen, the moral hazard associated with a government safety net encourages too much risk taking on the part of banks. Bank regulations that restrict asset holdings and bank capital requirements are directed at minimizing this moral hazard, which can cost the taxpayers dearly.

Even in the absence of a government safety net, banks still have the incentive to take on too much risk. Risky assets may provide the bank with higher earnings when they pay off; but if they do not pay off and the bank fails, depositors are left holding the bag. If depositors were able to monitor the bank easily by acquiring information on its risk-taking activities, they would immediately withdraw their

[1]Recent evidence reveals, as our analysis predicts, that large banks have taken on riskier loans than smaller banks and that this has led to higher loan losses for big banks; see John Boyd and Mark Gertler, "U.S. Commercial Banking: Trends, Cycles and Policy," *NBER Macroeconomics Annual,* 1993, pp. 319–368.

BOX 2

A Tale of Two Bank Collapses: Bank of New England and Freedom National Bank

The FDIC's procedures for handling two bank collapses, those of the Bank of New England and Freedom National Bank, illustrate how the too-big-to-fail policy works.

The Bank of New England, based in Boston, was the thirty-third-largest bank holding company in the United States, with over $20 billion of assets. In the 1980s, it was the region's most aggressive real estate lender; over 30% of its loan portfolio was in commercial real estate. With the collapse of real estate prices in New England beginning in the late 1980s (commercial real estate values dropped by more than 25%), many of the bank's loans went sour. On Friday, January 4, 1991, the bank announced a projected $450 million fourth-quarter loss that exceeded the bank's capital of $255 million. Expecting the failure of the bank, in the next 48 hours depositors lined up at the bank and withdrew over $1 billion in funds, much of it from automated teller machines.

The chairman of the FDIC, William Seidman, expressed his concern over the ramifications of the potential failure: "Given the condition of the financial system in New England, it would be unwise to send a signal that large depositors weren't going to be protected."* The FDIC invoked its too-big-to-fail policy. Sunday night, January 6, the FDIC moved in to stop the run on the bank and agreed to guarantee all Bank of New England deposits, including those in excess of the $100,000 insurance limit. To keep the bank in operation until a buyer could be found and the purchase and assumption method could be used to make sure that no depositors would suffer any loss, the FDIC created what is called a *bridge bank*. In this arrangement, the FDIC creates a new corporation to run the bank and immediately injects capital ($750 million in the case of the Bank of New England). The FDIC and the buyer of the bank then put additional capital into the bank over time, and eventually the acquirer buys out the FDIC's share. The net result of these transactions was that the FDIC spent $2.3 billion bailing out the Bank of New England, the third-costliest bailout in the FDIC's history. However, when all was said and done and spent, none of the depositors lost a penny.

The very different FDIC treatment of a small insolvent bank in Harlem several months earlier raised serious questions of fairness. The Freedom National Bank was founded in 1964 by baseball great Jackie Robinson and other minority investors. Despite its small size (under $100 million of deposits), it was one of the most prominent black-owned banks.

As a result of numerous speculative loans that went bad, the bank became insolvent in November 1990. Because of the bank's small size, the FDIC was not concerned that the failure of the bank would have serious repercussions for the rest of the banking system, so it decided to close the bank on November 9 using the payoff method. The Freedom National Bank was liquidated, and large depositors were paid only 50 cents on the dollar for deposits in excess of $100,000. Not only fat cats suffered losses when this bank failed. Charitable organizations like the United Negro College Fund, the National Urban League, and several churches were among the large depositors at the bank. Seidman described the unfairness of the treatment of the Freedom National Bank to Congress: "My first testimony when I came to this job was that it's unfair to treat big banks in a way that covers all depositors but not small banks. I promised to do my best to change that. Five years later, I can report that my best wasn't good enough."**

---

*Quoted in John Meehan, "A Shock to the System: How Far Will Banking's Crisis of Confidence Spread?" *Business Week*, January 21, 1991, p. 26.

**Quoted in Kenneth H. Bacon, "Failures of a Big Bank and a Little Bank Bring Fairness of Deposit-Security Policy into Question," *Wall Street Journal*, December 5, 1990, p. A18.

Source: Reprinted from January 24, 1991 issue of *Business Week* by special permission, Copyright © 1991 by the McGraw-Hill Companies, Inc.

deposits if the bank was taking on too much risk. To prevent such a loss of deposits, the bank would be more likely to reduce its risk-taking activities. Unfortunately, acquiring information on a bank's activities to learn how much risk the bank is taking can be a difficult task. Hence most depositors are incapable of imposing discipline that might prevent banks from engaging in risky activities. A strong rationale for government regulation to reduce risk taking on the part of banks therefore existed even before the establishment of federal deposit insurance.

Bank regulations that restrict banks from holding risky assets such as common stock are a direct means of making banks avoid too much risk. Bank regulations also promote diversification, which reduces risk by limiting the amount of loans in particular categories or to individual borrowers. Requirements that banks have sufficient bank capital are another way to change the bank's incentives to take on less risk. When a bank is forced to hold a large amount of equity capital, the bank has more to lose if it fails and is thus more likely to pursue less risky activities.

Bank capital requirements take three forms. The first type is based on the so-called **leverage ratio,** the amount of capital divided by the bank's total assets. To be classified as well capitalized, a bank's leverage ratio must exceed 5%; a lower leverage ratio, especially one below 3%, triggers increased regulatory restrictions on the bank. Throughout most of the 1980s, minimum bank capital in the United States was set solely by specifying a minimum leverage ratio.

In the wake of the Continental Illinois and savings and loans bailouts, regulators in the United States and the rest of the world have become increasingly worried about banks' holdings of risky assets and about the increase in banks' **off-balance-sheet activities**, activities that involve trading financial instruments and generating income from fees, which do not appear on bank balance sheets but nevertheless expose banks to risk. An agreement among banking officials from industrialized nations has set up the **Basel Committee on Banking Supervision** (because it meets under the auspices of the Bank for International Settlements in Basel, Switzerland), which has implemented the so-called **Basel Accord** on risk-based capital requirements. The Basel Accord, which required that banks hold as capital at least 8% of their risk-weighted assets, has been adopted by over 100 countries, including the United States. Assets and off-balance-sheet activities were allocated into four categories, each with a different weight to reflect the degree of credit risk. The first category carried a zero weight and included items that have little default risk, such as reserves and government securities in the OECD (industrialized) countries. The second category had a 20% weight and included claims on banks in OECD countries. The third category had a weight of 50% and included municipal bonds and residential mortgages. The fourth category had the maximum weight of 100% and included debts to consumers and corporations. Off-balance-sheet activities are treated in a similar manner by assigning a credit-equivalent percentage that converts them to on-balance-sheet items to which the appropriate risk weight applies. The 1996 Market Risk Amendment to the Accord set minimum capital requirements for risks in banks' trading accounts.

Over time, limitations of the Accord have become apparent because the regulatory measure of bank risk as stipulated by the risk weights can differ substantially from the actual risk the bank faces. This has resulted in what is known as **regulatory arbitrage**, in which banks keep on their books assets that have the same risk-based capital requirement but are relatively risky, such as a loan to a company with a very low credit rating, while taking off their books low-risk assets such as a loan to a company with a very high credit rating. The Basel Accord could thus lead to increased risk taking, the opposite of its intent. To address these limitations, the Basel Committee on Bank Supervision has released proposals for a new capital accord, often referred to as Basel 2, but it is not clear if it is workable and when it will be implemented (see Box 3).

The Basel Committee's work on bank capital requirements is never ending. As the banking industry changes, the regulation of bank capital must change with it to ensure the safety and soundness of the banking institutions.

Bank Supervision: Chartering and Examination

Overseeing who operates banks and how they are operated, referred to as **bank supervision** or more generally as **prudential supervision,** is an important method for reducing adverse selection and moral hazard in the banking business.

BOX 3

Basel 2: Is it Spinning Out of Control?

Starting in June 1999, the Basel Committee on Banking Supervision has released several proposals to reform the original 1988 Basel Accord. Basel 2 is based on three pillars.

Pillar 1 intends to link capital requirements more closely to actual risk. It does this by specifying many more categories of risk with different weights in its so-called standardized approach and allows sophisticated banks to instead pursue an internal ratings-based approach that allows banks to use their own models of credit risk. Pillar 2 focuses on strengthening the supervisory process, particularly in assessing the quality of risk management in banking institutions and whether these institutions have adequate procedures to determine how much capital they need. Pillar 3 focuses on improving market discipline by increased disclosure such as details about the bank's credit exposures, its amount of reserves and capital, who controls the bank, and how a well a bank's internal ratings system operates.

Although Basel 2 makes great strides in the direction of limiting excessive risk taking by banking institutions, it has come at a cost of greatly increasing the complexity of the Accord. The document describing the original Basel Accord was 26 pages, while the second draft of Basel 2 issued in January 2001 is over 500 pages long. The original timetable was for the final round of consultation to be finished by the end of May 2001, with the new rules taking effect by 2004. However, criticism from banks, trade associations and national regulators has led to a one-year postponement, with the final draft to be finished by January 2002 and the Accord to be implemented by 2005. Will the increasing complexity of the Basel Accord lead to further postponements, raising the question of whether Basel 2 will actually be put into operation?

Because banks can be used by crooks or overambitious entrepreneurs to engage in highly speculative activities, such undesirable people would be eager to run a bank. (Charles Keating Jr., discussed in Chapter 17, was one such person.) Chartering banks is one method for preventing this adverse selection problem; through chartering, proposals for new banks are screened to prevent undesirable people from controlling them.

Regular on-site bank examinations, which allow regulators to monitor whether the bank is complying with capital requirements and restrictions on asset holdings, also function to limit moral hazard. Bank examiners give banks a so-called *CAMELS rating* (the acronym is based on the six areas assessed: capital adequacy, asset quality, management, earnings, liquidity, and sensitivity to market risk). With this information about a bank's activities, regulators can enforce regulations by taking such formal actions as *cease and desist orders* to alter the bank's behavior or even close a bank if its CAMELS rating is sufficiently low. Actions taken to reduce moral hazard by restricting banks from taking on too much risk help reduce the adverse selection problem further because with less opportunity for risk taking, risk-loving entrepreneurs will be less likely to be attracted to the banking industry.

Note that the methods regulators use to cope with adverse selection and moral hazard have their counterparts in private financial markets (see Chapter 14). Chartering is similar to the screening of potential borrowers, regulations restricting risky asset holdings are similar to restrictive covenants that prevent borrowing firms from engaging in risky investment activities, bank capital requirements act like restrictive covenants that require minimum amounts of net worth for borrowing firms, and regular bank examinations are similar to the monitoring of borrowers by lending institutions.

A commercial bank obtains a charter either from the Comptroller of the Currency (in the case of a national bank) or from a state banking authority (in the case of a state bank). To obtain a charter, the people planning to organize the bank must submit an application that shows how they plan to operate the bank. In evaluating the application, the regulatory authority looks at whether the bank is likely to be sound by examining the quality of the bank's intended management, the likely earnings of the bank, and the amount of the bank's initial capital. Before 1980, the chartering agency typically explored the issue of whether the community needed a new bank. Often a new bank charter would not be granted if existing banks in a community would be severely hurt by its presence. Today this anticompetitive stance (justified by the desire to prevent bank failures of existing banks) is no longer as strong in the chartering agencies.

Once a bank has been chartered, it is required to file periodic (usually quarterly) *call reports* that reveal the bank's assets and liabilities, income and dividends, ownership, foreign exchange operations, and other details. The bank is also subject to examination by the bank regulatory agencies to ascertain its financial condition at least once a year. To avoid duplication of effort, the three federal agencies work together and usually accept each other's examinations. This means that, typically, national banks are examined by the Office of the Comptroller of the Currency, the state banks that are members of the Federal Reserve System are examined by the Fed, and nonmember state banks are examined by the FDIC.

Bank examinations are conducted by bank examiners, who sometimes make unannounced visits to the bank (so that nothing can be "swept under the rug" in anticipation of their examination). The examiners study a bank's books to see whether it is complying with the rules and regulations that apply to its holdings of assets. If a bank is holding securities or loans that are too risky, the bank examiner can force the bank to get rid of them. If a bank examiner decides that a loan is unlikely to be repaid, the examiner can force the bank to declare the loan worthless (to write off the loan). If, after examining the bank, the examiner feels that it does not have sufficient capital or has engaged in dishonest practices, the bank can be declared a "problem bank" and will be subject to more frequent examinations.

A New Trend in Bank Supervision: Assessment of Risk Management

Traditionally, on-site bank examinations have focused primarily on assessment of the quality of the bank's balance sheet at a point in time and whether it complies with capital requirements and restrictions on asset holdings. Although the traditional focus is important for reducing excessive risk taking by banks, it is no longer felt to be adequate in today's world in which financial innovation has produced new markets and instruments that make it easy for banks and their employees to make huge bets easily and quickly. In this new financial environment, a bank that is quite healthy at a particular point in time can be driven into insolvency extremely rapidly from trading losses, as forcefully demonstrated by the failure of Barings in 1995 (discussed in Chapter 15). Thus an examination that focuses only on a bank's position at a point in time, may not be effective in indicating whether a bank will in fact be taking on excessive risk in the near future.

This change in the financial environment for banking institutions has resulted in a major shift in thinking about the bank supervisory process throughout the world. Bank examiners are now placing far greater emphasis on evaluating the soundness of a bank's management processes with regard to controlling risk. This shift in thinking was reflected in a new focus on risk management in the Federal Reserve System's 1993 guidelines to examiners on trading and derivatives activities. The focus was expanded and formalized in the Trading Activities Manual issued early in 1994, which provided bank examiners with tools to evaluate risk management systems. In late 1995, the Federal Reserve and the Comptroller of the Currency announced that they would be assessing risk management processes at the banks they supervise. Now bank examiners give a separate risk management rating from 1 to 5 that feeds into the overall management rating as part of the CAMELS system. Four elements of sound risk management are assessed to come up with the risk management rating: (1) The quality of oversight provided by the board of directors and senior management, (2) the adequacy of policies and limits for all activities that present significant risks, (3) the quality of the risk measurement and monitoring systems, and (4) the adequacy of internal controls to prevent fraud or unauthorized activities on the part of employees.

This shift toward focusing on management processes is also reflected in recent guidelines adopted by the U.S. bank regulatory authorities to deal with interest-rate risk. At one point, U.S. regulators were contemplating requiring banks to use a standard model to calculate the amount of capital a bank would need to have to allow for the interest-rate risk it bears. Because coming up with a one-size-fits-all model that would work for all banks has proved difficult, the regulatory agencies have instead decided to adopt guidelines for the management of interest-rate risk, although bank examiners will continue to consider interest-rate risk in deciding on the bank's capital requirements. These guidelines require the bank's board of directors to establish interest-rate risk limits, appoint officials of the bank to manage this risk, and monitor the bank's risk exposure. The guidelines also require that senior management of a bank develop formal risk management policies and procedures, to ensure that the board of directors' risk limits are not violated and to implement internal controls to monitor interest-rate risk and compliance with the board's directives.

Disclosure Requirements

The free-rider problem described in Chapter 14 indicates that individual depositors and other bank creditors will not have enough incentive to produce private information about the quality of a bank's assets. To ensure that there is better information for depositors and the marketplace, regulators can require that banks adhere to certain standard accounting principles and disclose a wide range of information that helps the market assess the quality of a bank's portfolio and the amount of the bank's exposure to risk. More public information about the risks incurred by banks and the quality of their portfolio can better enable stockholders, creditors, and depositors to evaluate and monitor banks and so act as a deterrent to excessive risk taking. This view is consistent with a recent position paper issued by the Eurocurrency Standing Committee of the G–10 Central Banks, which recommends that estimates of financial risk generated by firms' own internal risk management systems be adapted for public disclosure purposes.[2] Such information would supplement disclosures based on traditional accounting conventions by providing information about risk exposure and risk management that is not normally included in conventional balance sheet and income statement reports. Dis-

[2]See Eurocurrency Standing Committee of Central Banks of Group of Ten Countries (Fisher Group), "Discussion Paper on Public Disclosure of Markets and Credit Risks by Financial Intermediaries," September 1994, and a companion piece to this report, Federal Reserve Bank of New York, "A Discussion Paper on Public Disclosure of Risks Related to Market Activity," September 1994.

closure requirements can also be the primary focus of a bank regulatory system, as with a new approach recently implemented in New Zealand (see Box 4).

Consumer Protection

The existence of asymmetric information also suggests that consumers may not have enough information to protect themselves fully. Consumer protection regulation has taken several forms. First is "truth in lending," mandated under the Consumer Protection Act of 1969, which requires all lenders, not just banks, to provide information to consumers about the cost of borrowing including a standardized interest rate (called the annual percentage rate, or APR) and the total finance charges on the loan. The Fair Credit Billing Act of 1974 requires creditors, especially credit card issuers, to provide information on the method of assessing finance charges and requires that billing complaints be handled quickly. Both of these acts are administered by the Federal Reserve System under Regulation Z.

BOX 4: GLOBAL

New Zealand's Disclosure-Based Experiment in Bank Regulation

Until 1995, New Zealand took a conventional approach to bank regulation that relied on regular examinations by the central bank to ensure that the banks complied with capital requirements and asset restrictions and followed good management practices. At the start of 1996, this system was scrapped for one based on disclosure requirements that uses the market to police the behavior of the banks.

As part of this new system, every bank in New Zealand must supply a comprehensive, quarterly financial statement that provides information on the quality of its assets, its lending activities, and its ratings from private credit-rating agencies, among other things. These financial statements must be audited two times a year, and not only must they be provided to the central bank, which will monitor them, but they must also be made public, with a two-page summary posted in all bank branches. In addition, bank directors are required to validate these statements and state publicly that their bank's risk management systems are adequate and being properly implemented. A most unusual feature of this system is that a bank's directors now face unlimited liability—that is, they can lose all their assets, not just their holdings in the bank—if they are found to have made false or misleading statements. Directors are thus in the dangerous position that they can be sued by creditors for everything they are worth if the bank goes bust.

The rationale for this approach is that the market will now provide the necessary discipline to prevent bankers from taking excessive risks because it will have sufficient information about banks' activities—depositors have the incentive to monitor the banks because there is no deposit insurance in New Zealand. Furthermore, banks will now have the incentive to improve their financial health in order to acquire good credit ratings. The system also has the advantage that it reduces regulatory costs for the banks because it will eliminate examination fees and burdensome rules on management procedures.

Critics of New Zealand's new approach point out that even with the new disclosure requirements, the asymmetric information problem may still not be solved. Banks may be less willing to admit to problems if the information has to be made public. In addition, depositors may not have the sophistication to understand the information provided and thus may not impose the necessary discipline on the banks. Furthermore, unlimited liability for directors might discourage top people from taking these positions, thereby weakening the management of the banks.

Although advocates of the New Zealand system think that it may prove to be a model for the rest of the world, skeptics point out that it might work only because of the peculiar features of the New Zealand banking system. Almost all New Zealand banks are foreign-owned, and around 90% of deposits are at foreign-owned banks. Thus these skeptics contend that in effect, bank regulation has been outsourced to the regulators of the foreign banks that own the New Zealand banks—central banks such as the Bank of England and the Reserve Bank of Australia that supervise the banks with subsidiaries in New Zealand.

Congress has also passed legislation to reduce discrimination in credit markets. The Equal Credit Opportunity Act of 1974 and its extension in 1976 forbid discrimination by lenders based on race, gender, marital status, age, or national origin. It is administered by the Federal Reserve under Regulation B. The Community Reinvestment Act (CRA) of 1977 was enacted to prevent "redlining," a lender's refusal to lend in a particular area (marked off by a hypothetical red line on a map). The Community Reinvestment Act requires that banks show that they lend in all areas in which they take deposits, and if banks are found to be in noncompliance with the act, regulators can reject their applications for mergers, branching, or other new activities. The increased enforcement of CRA provisions in recent years has been controversial (see Box 5).

Restrictions on Competition

Increased competition can also increase moral hazard incentives for banks to take on more risk. Declining profitability as a result of increased competition could tip the incentives of bankers toward assuming greater risk in an effort to maintain former profit levels. Thus governments in many countries have instituted regulations to protect banks from competition. These regulations have taken two forms in the United States. First are restrictions on branching, such as those described in Chapter 16, which reduce competition between banks. The second form involves preventing nonbank institutions from competing with banks by engaging in banking business.

Although restricting competition may prop up the health of banks, restrictions on competition can also have serious disadvantages: They can lead to higher charges to consumers and can decrease the efficiency of banking institutions,

BOX 5

Political Hot Button: The Community Reinvestment Act

The Community Reinvestment Act (CRA) has become more controversial recently because of the strengthening of its provisions in recent years and increased enforcement by bank regulators. Banks now have new reporting requirements on such items as small business lending and community involvement, and they complain that the increased paperwork is both burdensome and costly. The CRA has also received more attention recently because of increased merger activity in the banking industry, which raises its importance because meeting its provisions affects the merger approval process.

Many congressional Republicans regard the act as a heavy-handed affirmative action program that increases the burden of regulation unnecessarily and have strongly advocated its abolishment or at least the exemption of many banks and savings and loans from its provisions. Advocates of the act, who feel just as strongly, have pointed out that in the past minorities have been discriminated against by banks, and it has increased lending to minorities, which has recently begun to rise at a much faster rate than lending to whites.

The controversy over the Community Reinvestment Act came to a head during the passage of the Gramm-Leach-Bliley Act of 1999. Senator Phil Gramm, the Republican chairman of the Senate Banking Committee, blocked the legislation until provisions were added to the bill to require disclosure of CRA deals with community groups who receive bank funds for low-income lending programs. However, Gramm-Leach-Bliley did extend CRA rules to bank holding companies that are merging or entering new areas of business, although it reduced the frequency that small banks have to show regulators that they are complying with CRA requirements. Given that affirmative action remains a hot political topic, the controversy over the Community Reinvestment Act is likely to continue.

BOX 6: E-FINANCE

Electronic Banking: New Challenges for Bank Regulation

The advent of electronic banking has raised new concerns for banking regulation, specifically about security and privacy.

Worries about the security of electronic banking and e-money are an important barrier to their increased use. With electronic banking, you might worry that criminals might access your bank account and steal your money by moving your balances to someone else's account. Indeed, a notorious case of this happened in 1995, when a Russian computer programmer got access to Citibank's computers and moved funds electronically into his and his conspirators' accounts. Private solutions to deal with this problem have arisen with the development of more secure encryption technologies to prevent this kind of fraud. However, because bank customers are not knowledgeable about computer security issues, there is a role for the government to regulate electronic banking to make sure that encryption procedures are adequate. Similar encryption issues apply to e-money, so requirements that banks make it difficult for criminals to engage in digital counterfeiting make sense. To meet these challenges, bank examiners in the United States assess how a bank deals with the special security issues raised by electronic banking and also oversee third-party providers of electronic banking platforms. Also, because consumers want to know that electronic banking transactions are executed correctly, bank examiners also assess the technical skills of banks in setting up electronic banking services and the bank's capabilities for dealing with problems. Another security issue of concern to bank customers is the validity of digital signatures. The Electronic Signatures in Global and National Commerce Act of 2000 makes electronic signatures as legally binding as written signatures in most circumstances.

Electronic banking also raises serious privacy concerns. Because electronic transactions can be stored on databases, banks are able to collect a huge amount of information about their customers—their assets, creditworthiness, what they purchase, and so on—that can be sold to other financial institutions and businesses. This potential invasion of our privacy rightfully makes us very nervous. To protect customers' privacy, the Gramm-Leach-Bliley Act of 1999 has limited the distribution of these data, but it does not go as far as the European Data Protection Directive, which prohibits the transfer of information about on-line transactions. How to protect consumers' privacy in our electronic age is one of the great challenges our society faces, so privacy regulations for electronic banking are likely to evolve over time.

which do not have to compete as hard. Thus although the existence of asymmetric information provides a rationale for anticompetitive regulations, it does not mean that they will be beneficial. Indeed, in recent years, the impulse of governments in industrialized countries to restrict competition has been waning. Electronic banking has raised a new set of concerns for regulators to deal with. See Box 6 for a discussion of this challenge.

Study Guide Because so many laws regulating banking have been passed in the United States, it is hard to keep track of them all. As a study aid, Table 1 lists the major banking legislation in the twentieth century and its key provisions.

INTERNATIONAL BANKING REGULATION

Because asymmetric information problems in the banking industry are a fact of life throughout the world, bank regulation in other countries is similar to that in the United States. Banks are chartered and supervised by government regulators, just as they are in the United States. Deposit insurance is also a feature of the regulatory systems in most other developed countries, although its coverage is often smaller than in the United States and is purposely not advertised. We have also

The most important laws that have affected the banking industry in the United States are described at www.fdic.gov/regulations/laws/important/

TABLE 1 Major Banking Legislation in the United States in the Twentieth Century

Federal Reserve Act (1913)
Created the Federal Reserve System

McFadden Act of 1927
Put national and state banks on equal footing regarding branching
Effectively prohibited banks from branching across state lines

Banking Acts of 1933 (Glass-Steagall) and 1935
Created the FDIC
Separated commercial banking from the securities industry
Prohibited interest on checkable deposits and restricted such deposits to commercial banks
Put interest-rate ceilings on other deposits

Bank Holding Company Act (1956) and Douglas Amendment (1970)
Clarified the status of bank holding companies (BHCs)
Gave the Federal Reserve regulatory responsibility for BHCs

Depository Institutions Deregulation and Monetary Control Act (DIDMCA) of 1980
Gave thrift institutions wider latitude in activities
Approved NOW and ATS accounts nationwide
Phased out interest rate ceilings on deposits
Imposed uniform reserve requirements on depository institutions
Eliminated usury ceilings on loans
Increased deposit insurance to $100,000 per account

Depository Institutions Act of 1982 (Garn–St Germain)
Gave the FDIC and the FSLIC emergency powers to merge banks and thrifts across state lines
Allowed depository institutions to offer money market deposit accounts (MMDAs)
Granted thrifts wider latitude in commercial and consumer lending

Competitive Equality in Banking Act (CEBA) of 1987
Provided $10.8 billion to the FSLIC
Made provisions for regulatory forbearance in depressed areas

Financial Institutions Reform, Recovery, and Enforcement Act (FIRREA) of 1989
Provided funds to resolve S&L failures
Eliminated the FSLIC and the Federal Home Loan Bank Board
Created the Office of Thrift Supervision to regulate thrifts
Created the Resolution Trust Corporation to resolve insolvent thrifts
Raised deposit insurance premiums
Reimposed restrictions on S&L activities

Federal Deposit Insurance Corporation Improvement Act (FDICIA) of 1991
Recapitalized the FDIC
Limited brokered deposits and the too-big-to-fail policy
Set provisions for prompt corrective action
Instructed the FDIC to establish risk-based premiums
Increased examinations, capital requirements, and reporting requirements
Included the Foreign Bank Supervision Enhancement Act (FBSEA), which strengthened the Fed's authority to supervise foreign banks

Riegle-Neal Interstate Banking and Branching Efficiency Act of 1994
Overturned prohibition of interstate banking
Allowed branching across state lines

Gramm-Leach-Bliley Financial Services Modernization Act of 1999
Repeals Glass-Steagall separation of the banking and securities industry
Allows security firms and insurance companies to purchase banks
Allows banks to underwrite securities and insurance and engage in real estate activities

seen that bank capital requirements are in the process of being standardized across countries with agreements like the Basel accord.

Problems in Regulating International Banking

Particular problems in bank regulation occur when banks are engaged in international banking and thus can readily shift their business from one country to another. Bank regulators closely examine the domestic operations of banks in their country, but they often do not have the knowledge or ability to keep a close watch on bank operations in other countries, either by domestic banks' foreign affiliates or by foreign banks with domestic branches. In addition, when a bank operates in many countries, it is not always clear which national regulatory authority should have primary responsibility for keeping the bank from engaging in overly risky activities. The difficulties inherent in regulating international banking were highlighted by the BCCI scandal discussed in Box 7. Cooperation among regulators in different countries and standardization of regulatory requirements provide potential solutions to the problems of regulating international banking. The world has been moving in this direction through agreements like the Basel accord on capital requirements in 1988 and the new regulatory oversight procedures announced by the Basel Committee in July 1992. However, whether agreements of this type will solve the problem of regulating international banking in the future is an open question.

BOX 7: GLOBAL
The BCCI Scandal

The Bank of Credit and Commerce International (BCCI) was chartered in Luxembourg in 1972 by a Pakistani businessman, Agha Hasan Abedi. The bank grew rapidly to $20 billion in assets and by 1991 was operating in more than 70 countries. Unfortunately, the bank was siphoning off funds to secret accounts in the Cayman Islands, where much of this money was stolen. Indeed, estimates suggest that nearly half of the bank's assets may have "disappeared." Fraud was not the only shady activity BCCI engaged in. BCCI supposedly helped dictators such as Saddam Hussein of Iraq, Manuel Noriega of Panama, and Ferdinand Marcos of the Philippines steal huge sums from their countries, helped the CIA channel funds to the *contra* rebels in Nicaragua, and acted as a banker for the notorious Abu Nidal terrorist group. Not surprisingly, BCCI has been dubbed the "Bank of Crooks and Criminals, Inc."

How did BCCI get away with these fraudulent activities for so long? The answer illustrates the difficulties of regulating banks with operations in many countries. Although BCCI's headquarters were in London, regulatory oversight fell to the chartering country, Luxembourg, whose tiny bank regulator, the Institut Monétaire Luxembourgeois (IML), was not up to the task. As a result, BCCI effectively operated free of government regulatory oversight for 15 years. In 1987, the IML reached an agreement with seven other countries' regulators to oversee BCCI jointly, but even this larger group was unable to keep track of the bank's activities. Only in spring 1990 did these regulators uncover some evidence of fraud, and not until July 1991 did the Price Waterhouse accounting firm document the pervasiveness of the fraud to the Bank of England, which then closed BCCI down.

The losses to depositors and stockholders from the BCCI collapse were immense, and national regulators, particularly the Bank of England, have been severely criticized for their slowness in uncovering the scandal. A year after the BCCI collapse, in July 1992, the Basel Committee announced an agreement to standardize further the regulation of international banks. Now a bank's worldwide operations will be under the scrutiny of a single home-country regulator with enhanced powers to acquire information on the bank's activities. Furthermore, regulators in other countries will have the right to restrict operations of a foreign bank if they feel that it lacks effective oversight. Despite this improvement in the regulation of international banks, fears remain that a BCCI-like scandal could happen again.

Summary

Asymmetric information analysis explains what types of banking regulations are needed to reduce moral hazard and adverse selection problems in the banking system. However, understanding the theory behind regulation does not mean that regulation and supervision of the banking system are easy in practice. Getting bank regulators and supervisors to do their job properly is difficult for several reasons. First, as we learned in the discussion of financial innovation in Chapter 15, in their search for profits, financial institutions have strong incentives to avoid existing regulations by loophole mining. Thus regulation applies to a moving target: Regulators are continually playing cat and mouse with financial institutions—financial institutions think up clever ways to avoid regulations, which then causes regulators to modify their regulation activities. Regulators continually face new challenges in a dynamically changing financial system, and unless they can respond rapidly to change, they may not be able to keep financial institutions from taking on excessive risk. This problem can be exacerbated if regulators and supervisors do not have the resources or expertise to keep up with clever people in financial institutions who think up ways to hide what they are doing or ways to get around the existing regulations.

Bank regulation and supervision are difficult for two other reasons. In the regulation and supervision game, the devil is in the details. Subtle differences in the details may have unintended consequences; unless regulators get the regulation and supervision just right, they may be unable to prevent excessive risk taking. In addition, regulators and supervisors may be subject to political pressure not to do their jobs properly. For all these reasons, there is no guarantee that bank regulators and supervisors will be successful in promoting a healthy financial system. Indeed, as we will see, bank regulation and supervision have not always worked well, leading to banking crises in the United States and throughout the world.

THE 1980s U.S. BANKING CRISIS

Before the 1980s, federal deposit insurance seemed to work exceedingly well. In contrast to the pre–1934 period, when bank failures were common and depositors frequently suffered losses, the period from 1934 to 1980 was one in which bank failures were a rarity, averaging about 15 a year for commercial banks. After 1981, this rosy picture changed dramatically. Failures of commercial banks climbed to levels more than ten times greater than in earlier years. Why did this happen? How did a deposit insurance system that seemed to be working well for half a century find itself in so much trouble?

The story starts with the burst of financial innovation in the 1960s, 1970s, and early 1980s: NOW accounts, money market mutual funds, junk bonds, securitization, and the rise of the commercial paper market (discussed in Chapters 15 and 16). Financial innovation decreased the profitability of certain traditional business for commercial banks. Banks now faced increased competition for their sources of funds from new financial institutions such as money market mutual funds while they were losing commercial lending business to the commercial paper market and securitization.

With the decreasing profitability of their traditional business, by the mid 1980s commercial banks were forced to seek out new and potentially risky business to keep their profits up, by placing a greater percentage of their total loans in real estate and in credit extended to assist corporate takeovers and leveraged buyouts (called *highly leveraged transaction loans*).

The existence of deposit insurance increased moral hazard for banks because insured depositors had little incentive to keep the banks from taking on too much risk. Regardless of how much risk banks were taking, deposit insurance guaranteed that depositors would not suffer any losses.

Adding fuel to the fire, financial innovation produced new financial instruments that widened the scope for risk taking. New markets in financial futures, junk bonds, swaps, and other instruments made it easier for banks to take on extra risk—making the moral hazard problem more severe.

In addition, the Depository Institutions Deregulation and Monetary Control Act of 1980 increased the mandated amount of federal deposit insurance from $40,000 per account to $100,000 and phased out Regulation Q deposit-rate ceilings. Banks that wanted to pursue rapid growth and take on risky projects could now attract the necessary funds by issuing larger-denomination insured certificates of deposit with interest rates much higher than those being offered by their competitors. Without deposit insurance, high interest rates would not have induced depositors to provide the high-rolling banks with funds because of the realistic expectation that they might not get the funds back. But with deposit insurance, the government was guaranteeing that the deposits were safe, so depositors were more than happy to make deposits in banks with the highest interest rates.

A financial innovation that made it even easier for high-rolling banks to raise funds is known as **brokered deposits,** which enable depositors to circumvent the $100,000 limit on deposit insurance. Brokered deposits work as follows: A large depositor with $10 million goes to a broker, who breaks the $10 million into 100 packages of $100,000 each and then buys $100,000 CDs at 100 different banks. Because the amount of each CD is within the $100,000 limit for deposits at each bank, the large depositor has in effect obtained deposit insurance on all $10 million. The federal deposit insurance agencies passed a regulation to ban brokered deposits in 1984, but a federal court judgment overturned the ban.

As a result of these forces, commercial banks did take on excessive risks and began to suffer substantial losses. The outcome was that bank failures rose to a level of 200 per year by the late 1980s. The resulting losses for the FDIC meant that it would have depleted its Bank Insurance Fund by 1992, requiring that this fund be recapitalized. Although the Financial Institutions Reform, Recovery, and Enforcement Act (FIRREA) of 1989 (described in Chapter 17) did not focus on the underlying adverse selection and moral hazard problems created by deposit insurance, it did, however, mandate that the U.S. Treasury produce a comprehensive study and plan for reform of the federal deposit insurance system. After this study appeared in 1991, Congress passed the Federal Deposit Insurance Corporation Improvement Act (FDICIA), which engendered major reforms in the bank regulatory system.

FEDERAL DEPOSIT INSURANCE CORPORATION IMPROVEMENT ACT OF 1991

FDICIA's provisions were designed to serve two purposes: to recapitalize the Bank Insurance Fund of the FDIC and to reform the deposit insurance and regulatory system so that taxpayer losses would be minimized.

FDICIA recapitalized the Bank Insurance Fund by increasing the FDIC's ability to borrow from the Treasury to $30 billion (up from $5 billion). FDICIA also allowed the FDIC to borrow $45 billion for working capital—money that would be repaid as the FDIC sold the assets of failed banks. FDICIA also mandated that the FDIC assess higher deposit insurance premiums until it could pay back its loans and achieve a level of reserves in its insurance funds that would equal 1.25% of insured deposits within 15 years, a goal that was reached for the Bank Insurance Fund (BIF) more than ten years early in 1995 because of the return to health of the commercial banking industry.

The bill reduced the scope of deposit insurance in several ways. First, the FDIC is allowed to insure brokered deposits or accounts only if they are established under pension plans at well-capitalized banks. Second, and more important, the too-big-to-fail doctrine has been substantially limited: The FDIC must now close failed banks using the least-costly method, thus making it far more likely that uninsured depositors will suffer losses. An exception to this provision, whereby a bank would be declared too big to fail so that all depositors, both insured and uninsured, would be fully protected, would be allowed only if not doing so would "have serious adverse effects on economic conditions or financial stability." Furthermore, to invoke the too-big-to-fail policy, a two-thirds majority of both the Board of Governors of the Federal Reserve System and the directors of the FDIC, as well as the approval of the secretary of the Treasury, would be required. Furthermore, FDICIA requires that the Fed share in the FDIC's losses if long-term Fed lending to a bank that fails increases the FDIC's losses.

Probably the most important feature of FDICIA is its prompt corrective action provisions, which require the FDIC to intervene earlier and more vigorously when a bank gets into trouble. Banks are now classified into five groups based on bank capital. Group 1, classified as "well capitalized," are banks that significantly exceed minimum capital requirements and are allowed privileges such as insurance on brokered deposits and the ability to do some securities underwriting. Banks in group 2, classified as "adequately capitalized," meet minimum capital requirements and are not subject to corrective actions but are not allowed the privileges of the well-capitalized banks. Banks in group 3, "undercapitalized," fail to meet capital requirements. Banks in groups 4 and 5 are "significantly undercapitalized" and "critically undercapitalized," respectively, and are not allowed to pay interest on their deposits at rates that are higher than average. In addition, for group 3 banks, the FDIC is required to take prompt corrective actions such as requiring them to submit a capital restoration plan, restrict their asset growth, and seek regulatory approval to open new branches or develop new lines of business. Banks that are so undercapitalized as to have equity capital less than 2% of assets fall into group 5, and the FDIC must take steps to close them down.

FDICIA also instructed the FDIC to come up with risk-based insurance premiums. The system the FDIC has put in place uses the bank capital classifications just outlined and other supervisory criteria to assess these premiums. However, deposit insurance premiums have not been very risk-based in practice. Although insurance premiums range from zero for well-capitalized banks that have a high supervisory rating to 27 cents per $100 of insured deposits for undercapitalized banks with a low supervisory rating, well over 90% of commercial banks and savings institutions are classified in the least risky category and therefore all pay the same insurance premium, zero.

Other provisions of FDICIA require regulators to perform annual on-site examinations, restrict real estate lending, and mandate stricter and more burdensome reporting requirements. The act also requires that the existing risk-based capital standards, which focus solely on credit risk, be modified to take account of interest-rate risk as well. FDICIA also provides securities firms with access to Federal Reserve discount lending during a financial crisis.

FDICIA also includes the Foreign Bank Supervision Enhancement Act (FBSEA), which in the wake of the BCCI scandal gives supervisory responsibility for foreign banks to the Federal Reserve and gives the Fed increased powers to acquire information on the foreign banks' activities. In addition, the Fed now has the right to prevent the operation of a foreign bank in the United States if it feels that the home country's supervision is not adequate or if the foreign bank is engaging in unsound banking practices.

Application Evaluating FDICIA and Other Proposed Reforms of the Banking Regulatory System

FDICIA is a major step in reforming the banking regulatory system. How well will it work to solve the adverse selection and moral hazard problems of the bank regulatory system? Let's use the analysis in the chapter to evaluate the most important provisions of this legislation to answer this question.

Study Guide Before looking at the evaluation for each set of provisions and proposals in this application, try to reason out how well they will solve the current problems with banking regulation. This exercise will help you develop a deeper understanding of the material in this chapter.

Limits on the Scope of Deposit Insurance

FDICIA's reduction of the scope of deposit insurance by limiting insurance on brokered deposits and restricting the use of the too-big-to-fail policy might have increased the incentives for uninsured depositors to monitor banks and to withdraw funds if the bank is taking on too much risk. Because banks might now fear the loss of deposits when they engage in risky activities, they might have less incentive to take on too much risk. Limitations on the use of the too-big-to-fail policy starting in 1992 have resulted in increased losses to uninsured depositors at failed banks as planned.

Although the cited elements of FDICIA strengthen the incentive of depositors to monitor banks, some critics of FDICIA would take these limitations on the scope of deposit insurance even further. Some suggest that deposit insurance should be eliminated entirely or should be reduced in amount from the current \$100,000 limit to, say, \$50,000 or \$20,000. Another proposed reform would institute a system of **coinsurance** in which only a percentage of a deposit, say, 90%, would be covered by insurance. In this system, the insured depositor would suffer a percentage of the losses along with the deposit insurance agency. Because depositors facing a lower limit on deposit insurance or coinsurance would suffer losses if the bank goes broke, they will have an incentive to monitor the bank's activities. Other critics believe that FDICIA still provides too much support for the too-big-to-fail policy. Because under FDICIA the Fed, the Treasury, and the FDIC can still agree to implement too-big-to-fail and thus bail out uninsured as well as insured depositors, big banks will not be subjected to enough discipline by uninsured depositors. These critics advocate eliminating the too-big-to-fail policy entirely, thereby decreasing the incentives of big banks to take on too much risk.

However, other experts do not believe that depositors are capable of monitoring banks and imposing discipline on them. The basic problem with reducing the scope of deposit insurance even further as proposed is that banks would be subject to runs, sudden withdrawals by nervous depositors. Such runs could by themselves lead to bank failures. In addition to protecting individual depositors, the purpose of deposit insurance is to prevent a large number of bank failures, which would lead to an unstable banking system and an unstable economy as occurred periodically before the establishment of federal deposit insurance in 1934. From this perspective, federal deposit insurance has been a resounding success. Bank panics, in which there are simultaneous failures of many banks and consequent disruption of the financial system, have not occurred since federal deposit insurance was established.

On the one hand, evidence that the largest banks benefiting from the de facto too-big-to-fail policy before 1991 were also the ones that took on the most risk suggests that limiting its application, as FDICIA does, may substantially reduce risk taking. On the other hand, eliminating the too-big-to-fail policy altogether would also cause some of the same problems that would occur if deposit insurance were eliminated or reduced: The probability of bank panics would increase. If a big bank were allowed to fail, the repercussions in the financial system might be immense. Other banks with a correspondent relationship with the failed bank (those that have deposits at the bank in exchange for a variety of services) would suffer large losses and might fail in turn, leading to a full-scale panic. In addition, the problem of liquidating the big bank's loan portfolio might create a major disruption in the financial market.

Prompt Corrective Action

The prompt corrective action provisions of FDICIA should also substantially reduce incentives for bank risk taking and reduce taxpayer losses. FDICIA uses a carrot-and-stick approach to get banks to hold more capital. If they are well capitalized, they receive valuable privileges; if their capital ratio falls, they are subject to more and more onerous regulation. Increased bank capital reduces moral hazard incentives for the bank because the bank now has more to lose if it fails and so is less likely to take on too much risk.

In addition, encouraging banks to hold more capital reduces potential losses for the FDIC because increased bank capital is a cushion that makes bank failure less likely. Furthermore, forcing the FDIC to close banks once their net worth is less than 2% (group 5) rather than waiting until net worth has fallen to zero makes it more likely that when a bank is closed, it will still have a positive net worth, thus limiting FDIC losses.

Prompt corrective action, which requires regulators to intervene early when bank capital begins to fall, is a serious attempt to reduce the principal-agent problem for politicians and regulators. With prompt corrective action provisions, regulators no longer have the option of regulatory forbearance, which, as we have seen, can greatly increase moral hazard incentives for banks.

Some critics of FDICIA feel that there are too many loopholes in the bill that still allow regulators too much discretion, thus leaving open the possibility of regulatory forbearance. However, an often overlooked part of the bill increases the accountability of regulators. FDICIA requires a mandatory review of any bank failure that imposes costs on the FDIC. The resulting report must be made available to any member of Congress and to the general public upon request, and the General Accounting Office must do an annual review of these reports. Opening up the actions of the regulators to public scrutiny will make regulatory forbearance less attractive to them, thereby reducing the principal-agent problem. It will also reduce the incentives of politicians to lean on regulators to relax their regulatory supervision of banks.

Risk-Based Insurance Premiums

Under FDICIA, banks deemed to be taking on greater risk, in the form of lower capital or riskier assets, will be subjected to higher insurance premiums. Risk-based insurance premiums will consequently reduce the moral hazard incentives for banks to take on higher risk because if they do so, they will have to pay higher premiums. In addition, the fact that risk-based premiums drop as the bank's capital increases encourages the bank to hold more capital, which has the benefits already mentioned.

One problem with risk-based premiums is that the scheme for determining the amount of risk the bank is taking may not be very accurate. For example, it might be hard for regulators to determine when a bank's loans are risky. Some critics have also pointed out that the classification of banks by such measures as the Basel risk-based capital standard solely reflects credit risk and does not take sufficient account of interest-rate risk. The regulatory authorities, however, are encouraged by FDICIA to modify existing risk-based standards to include interest-rate risk and, as we have seen earlier in this chapter, have proposed guidelines to encourage banks to manage interest-rate risk.

Other FDICIA Provisions

FDICIA's requirements that regulators perform bank examinations at least once a year are necessary for monitoring banks' compliance with bank capital requirements and asset restrictions. As the S&L debacle illustrates, frequent supervisory examinations of banks are necessary to keep them from taking on too much risk or committing fraud. Similarly, beefing up the ability of the Federal Reserve to monitor foreign banks might help dissuade international banks from engaging in these undesirable activities.

The stricter and more burdensome reporting requirements for banks have the advantage of providing more information to regulators to help them monitor bank activities. However, these reporting requirements have been criticized by banks, which claim that the requirements make it harder to lend to small businesses.

Other Proposed Changes in Banking Regulations

Regulatory Consolidation The current bank regulatory system in the United States has banking institutions supervised by four federal agencies: the FDIC, the Office of the Comptroller of the Currency, the Office of Thrift Supervision, and the Federal Reserve. Critics of this system of multiple regulatory agencies with

Information on bank regulations and the monthly interpretation from the Office of the Comptroller of the Currency are available at www.occ.treas.gov/interp/monthly.htm

overlapping jurisdictions believe that it creates a system that is too complex and too costly because it is rife with duplication. The Clinton administration proposed a consolidation in which the duties of the four regulatory agencies would be given to a new Federal Banking Commission governed by a five-member board with one member from the Treasury, one from the Federal Reserve, and three independent members appointed by the president and confirmed by the Senate. The Federal Reserve strongly opposed this proposal because it believed that it needed to have hands-on supervision of the largest banks through their bank holding companies (as is the case currently) in order to have the information that would enable the Fed to respond sufficiently quickly in a crisis. The Fed also pointed out that a monolithic regulator might be less effective than two or more regulators in providing checks and balances for regulatory supervision. The Clinton administration's proposal was not passed by Congress, but the issue of regulatory consolidation is sure to come up again.

Market-Value Accounting for Capital Requirements We have seen that the requirement that a bank have substantial equity capital makes the bank less likely to fail. The requirement is also advantageous because a bank with high equity capital has more to lose if it takes on risky investments and so will have less incentive to hold risky assets. Unfortunately, capital requirements, including new risk-based measures, are calculated on a historical-cost (book value) basis in which the value of an asset is set at its initial purchase price. The problem with historical-cost accounting is that changes in the value of assets and liabilities because of changes in interest rates or default risk are not reflected in the calculation of the firm's equity capital. Yet changes in the market value of assets and liabilities and hence changes in the market value of equity capital are what indicate if a firm is truly insolvent. Furthermore, it is the market value of capital that determines the incentives for a bank to hold risky assets.

Market-value accounting when calculating capital requirements is another reform that receives substantial support. All assets and liabilities could be updated to market value periodically, say, every three months, to determine if a bank's capital is sufficient to meet the minimum requirements. This market-value accounting information would let the deposit insurance agency know quickly when a bank was falling below its capital requirement. The bank could then be closed down before its net worth fell below zero, thus preventing a loss to the deposit insurance agency. The market-value-based capital requirement would also ensure that banks would not be operating with negative capital, thereby preventing the bet-the-bank strategy of taking on excessive risk.

Objections to market-value-based capital requirements center on the difficulty of making accurate and straightforward market-value estimates of capital. Historical-cost accounting has an important advantage in that accounting rules are easier to define and standardize when the value of an asset is simply set at its purchase price. Market-value accounting, by contrast, requires estimates and approximations that are harder to standardize. For example, it might be hard to assess the market value of your friend Joe's car loan, whereas it would be quite easy to value a government bond. In addition, conducting market-value accounting would prove costly to banks because estimation of market values requires the collection of more information about the characteristics of assets and liabilities. Nevertheless, proponents of market-value accounting for capital requirements point out that although market-value accounting involves some estimates and approximations, it would still provide regulators with more accurate assessment of bank equity capital than historical-cost accounting does.

Overall Evaluation

FDICIA appears to be an important step in the right direction because it increases the incentives for banks to hold capital and decreases their incentives to take on excessive risk. However, more could be done to improve the incentives for banks to limit their risk taking. Yet eliminating deposit insurance and the too-big-to-fail policy altogether may be going too far because these proposals might make the banking system too prone to a banking panic.

BANKING CRISES THROUGHOUT THE WORLD

Because misery likes company, it might make you feel better to know that the United States has by no means been alone in suffering a banking crisis. Indeed, as Figure 1 and Table 2 illustrate, banking crises have struck a large number of countries throughout the world, and many of them have been substantially worse than ours. We will examine what took place in several of these other countries and see that the same forces that produced a banking crisis in the United States have been at work elsewhere too.

Scandinavia

As in the United States, an important factor in the banking crises in Norway, Sweden, and Finland was the financial liberalization that occurred in the 1980s. Before the 1980s, banks in the Scandinavian countries were highly regulated and subject to restrictions on the interest rates they could pay to depositors and on the interest rates they could earn on loans. In this noncompetitive environment, and with artificially low rates on both deposits and loans, these banks lent only to the best credit risks, and both banks and their regulators had little need to develop expertise in screening and monitoring borrowers. With the deregulated environment, a lending boom ensued, particularly in the real estate sector. Given the lack of expertise in both the banking industry and its regulatory authorities in keeping risk taking in check, banks engaged in risky lending. When real estate prices collapsed in the late 1980s, massive loan losses resulted. The outcome of this process was similar to what happened in the savings and loan industry in the United States. The government was forced to bail out almost the entire banking industry in these countries in the late 1980s and early 1990s on a scale that was even larger relative to GDP than in the United States (see Table 2).

Latin America

The Latin American banking crises show a similar pattern to those in the United States and in Scandinavia. Before the 1980s, banks in many Latin American countries were owned by the government and were subject to interest-rate restrictions as in Scandinavia. Their lending was restricted to the government and other low-risk borrowers. With the deregulation trend that was occurring worldwide, many

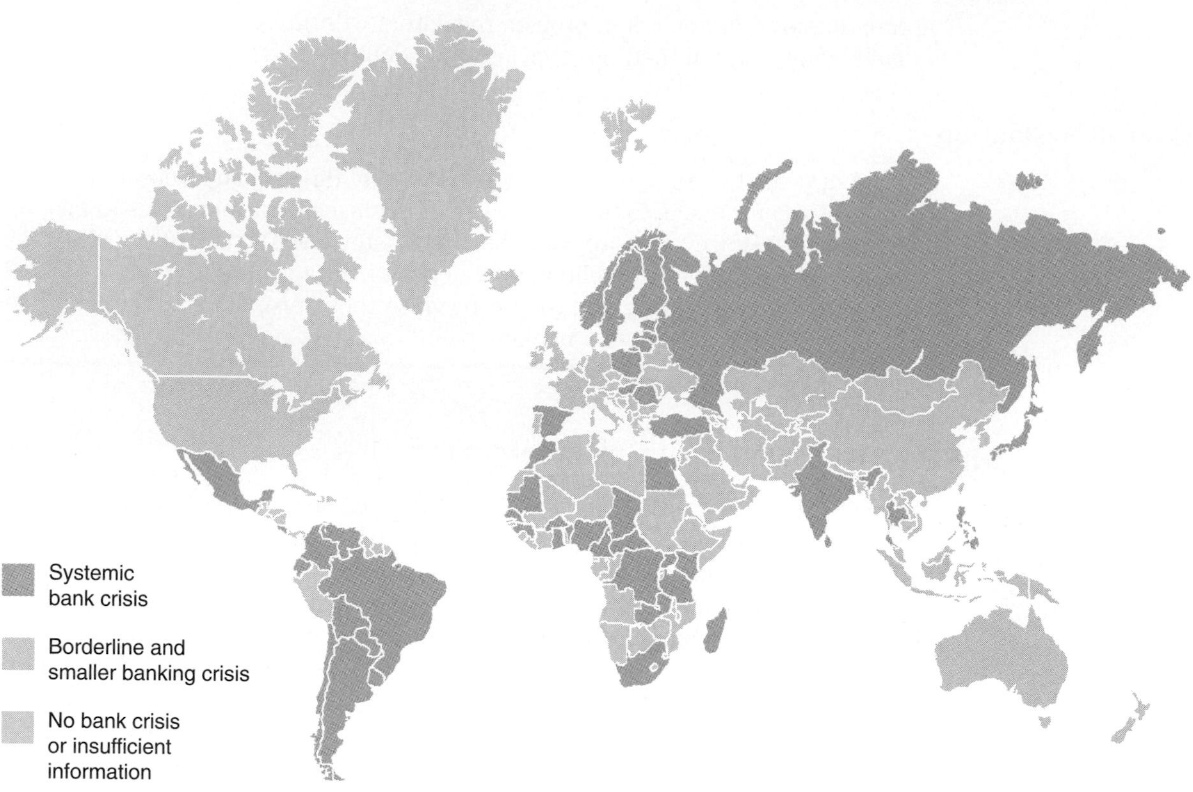

FIGURE 1 Banking Crises Throughout the World Since 1970

Source: Gerard Caprio Jr. and Daniela Klingbiel, "Bank Insolvency: Bad Luck, Bad Policy, or Bad Banking?" paper prepared for the World Bank's Annual Bank Conference on Development Economics, Washington, D.C., April 25–26, 1996.

TABLE 2 The Cost of Rescuing Banks in Several Countries

Date	Country	Cost as a Percentage of GDP
1980–1982	Argentina	55
1997–	Indonesia	50–55
1981–1983	Chile	41
1997–	Thailand	33
1997–	South Korea	27
1997–	Malaysia	21
1994–ongoing	Venezuela	20+
1995	Mexico	20
1990's	Japan	12+
1989–ongoing	Czech Republic	12+
1991–1994	Finland	11
1991–1995	Hungary	10
1994–1995	Brazil	5–10
1987–1993	Norway	8
1998	Russia	5–7
1991–1994	Sweden	4
1984–1991	United States	3

Source: Gerard Caprio Jr. and Daniela Klingbiel, "Episodes of Systemic and Borderline Financial Crises" mimeo., World Bank, October 1999.

of these countries liberalized their credit markets and privatized their banks. We then see the same pattern we saw in the United States and Scandinavia, a lending boom in the face of inadequate expertise on the part of both bankers and regulators. The result was again massive loan losses and the inevitable government bailout. What is particularly striking about the Latin American experience is that the cost of the bailout relative to GDP dwarfs that in the United States. For example, in the recent banking crises in Mexico and Venezuela, the cost to the taxpayer of the government bailouts exceeded 10% of GDP.

Russia and Eastern Europe

Before the end of the Cold War, in the communist countries of Eastern Europe and the Soviet Union, banks were owned by the state. When the downfall of communism occurred, banks in these countries had little expertise in screening and monitoring loans. Furthermore, bank regulatory and supervisory apparatus that could rein in the banks and keep them from taking on excessive risk barely existed. Given the lack of expertise on the part of regulators and banks, not surprisingly, substantial loan losses ensued, resulting in the failure or government bailout of many banks. For example, in the second half of 1993, eight banks in Hungary with 25% of the financial system's assets were insolvent, and in Bulgaria, an estimated 75% of all loans in the banking system were estimated to be substandard in 1995. On August 24, 1995, a bank panic requiring government intervention occurred in Russia when the interbank loan market seized up and stopped functioning because of concern about the solvency of many new banks. This was not the end of troubles in the Russian banking system. On August 17, 1998, the Russian government announced that Russia would impose a moratorium on the repayment of foreign debt because of insolvencies in the banking system. In November, the Russian central bank announced that nearly half of the country's 1500 commercial banks were likely to go under and that the cost of the bailout would be on the order of $15 billion.

Japan

Japan was a latecomer to the banking crisis game. Before 1990, the vaunted Japanese economy looked unstoppable. Unfortunately, it has recently experienced many of the same pathologies that we have seen in other countries. Before the 1980s, Japan's financial markets were among the most heavily regulated in the world, with very strict restrictions on the issuing of securities and interest rates. Financial deregulation and innovation produced a more competitive environment that set off a lending boom, with banks lending aggressively in the real estate sector. As in the other countries we have examined here, financial disclosure and monitoring by regulators did not keep pace with the new financial environment. The result was that banks could and did take on excessive risks, and when property values collapsed in the early 1990s, the banks were left holding massive amounts of bad loans. For example, Japanese banks decided to get into the mortgage lending market by setting up the so-called *jusen*, home mortgage lending companies that raised funds by borrowing from banks and then loaned these funds out to households. Seven of these *jusen* became insolvent, leaving banks with $60 billion or so of bad loans.

As a result, the Japanese have experienced their first bank failures since World War II. In July 1995, Tokyo-based Cosmo Credit Corporation, Japan's fifth-largest credit union, failed and on August 30, the Osaka authorities announced the imminent closing of Kizu Credit Cooperative, Japan's second-largest credit union. (Kizu's story is remarkably similar to that of many U.S. savings and loans. Kizu, like many American S&Ls, began offering high rates on large time deposits and grew at a blistering pace, with deposits rising from $2.2 billion in 1988 to $12 billion by 1995 and real estate loans growing by a similar amount. When the property market collapsed, so did Kizu.) On the same day, the Ministry of Finance announced that it was liquidating Hyogo Bank, a midsize Kobe bank that was the first commercial bank to fail. Larger banks now began to follow the same path. In late 1996, the Hanwa Bank, a large regional bank, was liquidated, and this was followed in 1997 by a government-assisted restructuring of the Nippon Credit Bank, Japan's seventeenth-largest bank. In November 1997, Hokkaido Takushoku Bank was forced to go out of business, making it in the first city bank (a large commercial bank) to be closed during the crisis.

The Japanese have been going through the same cycle of regulatory forbearance as occurred in the United States in the 1980s. The Japanese regulators in the Ministry of Finance enabled banks to meet capital standards and to keep operating by allowing them to inflate the value of their assets. For example, they were allowed to value their large holdings of equities at historical value, rather than market value, which was much lower. Inadequate amounts were allocated for recapitalization of the banking system, and the extent of the problem was grossly underestimated by government officials. Furthermore, until the closing of the Hokkaido Takushoku Bank, the bank regulators in the Ministry of Finance were unwilling to close down city banks and impose any losses on stockholders or uninsured creditors.

By the middle of 1998, the Japanese government began to take some steps to clean up the banking mess. In June, the supervision authority over financial institutions was taken away from the Ministry of Finance and transferred to the Financial Supervisory Agency (FSA), which reports directly to the prime minister. This was the first instance in half a century in which the all-powerful Ministry of Finance was stripped of some of its authority. In October, the parliament passed a bailout package of $500 billion. However, disbursement of the funds depended on the voluntary cooperation of the banks: The law did not require insolvent banks to close or to accept the funds if they were insolvent. Indeed, acceptance of the funds required the bailed-out bank to open its books and reveal its true losses, and thus many banks remain very undercapitalized. The banking sector in Japan thus remains in very poor shape: It is burdened with bad loans and poor profitability. Indeed, in April 2001, new data from the Financial Supervisory Agency (FSA) indicates that bad loans had reached a level of 150 trillion yen (over $1 trillion), almost double the previous amount estimated by the FSA.

There has been some progress in cleaning up the banking mess: Immediately after the 1998 banking law was passed, one of the ailing city banks, Long-Term Credit Bank of Japan, was taken over by the government and declared insolvent, and in December 1998, the Nippon Credit Bank was finally put out of its misery and closed down by the government. Since then, the cleanup process has stalled and the economy has remained weak, with a growth rate from 1991–2001 averaging an anemic 1%. However, the election in 2001 of a new, reform-oriented prime minister, Junichiro Koizumi, who has pledged to clean up the banking system, may lead to more progress in the future.

East Asia

The banking and financial crisis in the East Asian countries (Thailand, Malaysia, Indonesia, the Philippines, and South Korea) was discussed in Chapter 14. Due to inadequate supervision of the banking system, the lending booms that arose in the aftermath of financial liberalization led to substantial loan losses, which became huge after the currency collapses that occurred in the summer of 1997. An estimated 15% to 35% of all bank loans are now nonperforming in Thailand, Indonesia, and South Korea, and estimates of the cost of the bailout for the banking system in these countries is more than 20% of GDP. The cost of the bailout in Malaysia may also exceed 20%; the Philippines are expected to fare somewhat better.

"Déjà Vu All Over Again"

What we see in banking crises in these different countries is that history has kept on repeating itself. The parallels between the banking crisis episodes in all these countries are remarkably similar, leaving us with a feeling of déjà vu. Although financial liberalization is generally a good thing because it promotes competition and can make a financial system more efficient, as we have seen in the countries examined here, it can lead to an increase in moral hazard risk taking on the part of banks if there is lax regulation and supervision; the result can then be banking crises. However, these episodes do differ in that deposit insurance has not played an important role in many of the countries experiencing banking crises. For example, the size of the Japanese equivalent of the FDIC, the Deposit Insurance Corporation, was so tiny relative to the FDIC that it did not play a prominent role in the banking system and exhausted its resources almost immediately with the first bank failures. This means that deposit insurance is not to blame for some of these banking crises. However, what is common to all the countries discussed here is the existence of a government safety net, in which the government stands ready to bail out banks whether deposit insurance is an important feature of the regulatory environment or not. It is the existence of a government safety net, and not deposit insurance per se, that increases moral hazard incentives for excessive risk taking on the part of banks.

SUMMARY

1. The concepts of asymmetric information, adverse selection, and moral hazard help explain the seven types of banking regulation that we see in the United States and other countries: the government safety net, restrictions on bank asset holdings and capital requirements, bank supervision, disclosure requirements, consumer protection, restrictions on competition, and the separation of the banking and securities industries.
2. Because asymmetric information problems in the banking industry are a fact of life throughout the world, bank regulation in other countries is similar to that in the United States. It is particularly problematic to regulate banks engaged in international banking because they can readily shift their business from one country to another.
3. Because of financial innovation and deregulation, adverse selection and moral hazard problems increased in the 1980s and resulted in a banking crisis in the United States.
4. The Federal Deposit Insurance Corporation Improvement Act (FDICIA) of 1991 recapitalized the Bank Insurance Fund of the FDIC and included reforms for the deposit insurance and regulatory system so that taxpayer losses would be minimized. This legislation limited brokered deposits and the use of the too-big-to-fail policy, mandated prompt corrective action to deal with troubled banks, and instituted risk-based deposit insurance premiums. These provisions have helped reduce the incentives of banks to take on excessive risk and so should help reduce taxpayer exposure in the future.

5. Proposals for reforming the banking regulatory system include elimination of deposit insurance, lower limits on the amount of deposit insurance, outright elimination of the too-big-to-fail policy, coinsurance, risk-based insurance premiums, regulatory consolidation, and market-value accounting for capital requirements.
6. The parallels between the banking crisis episodes that have occurred in other countries are striking, indicating that similar forces are at work.

KEY TERMS

bank supervision, *p.497*
Basel Accord, *p.497*
Basel Committee on Banking Supervision, *p.497*
brokered deposits, *p.507*
coinsurance, *p.509*
leverage ratio, *p.497*
off-balance-sheet activities, *p.497*
prudential supervision, *p.497*
regulatory arbitrage, *p.497*

QUESTIONS AND PROBLEMS

1. Give one example each of moral hazard and adverse selection in private insurance arrangements.
*2. If casualty insurance companies provided fire insurance without any restrictions, what kind of adverse selection and moral hazard problems might result?
3. What bank regulation is designed to reduce adverse selection problems for deposit insurance? Will it always work?
*4. What bank regulations are designed to reduce moral hazard problems created by deposit insurance? Will they completely eliminate the moral hazard problem?
5. What are the costs and benefits of a too-big-to-fail policy?
*6. What special problem do off-balance-sheet activities present to bank regulators, and what have they done about it?
7. Why does imposing bank capital requirements on banks help limit risk taking?
*8. What forms does bank supervision take, and how does it help promote a safe and sound banking system?
9. What steps were taken in the FDICIA legislation of 1991 to improve the functioning of federal deposit insurance?
*10. Why has the trend in bank supervision moved away from a focus on capital requirements to a focus on risk management?
11. How do disclosure requirements help limit excessive risk taking by banks?
*12. Do you think that eliminating or limiting the amount of deposit insurance would be a good idea? Explain your answer.
13. Do you think that removing the impediments to a nationwide banking system will be beneficial to the economy? Explain.
*14. How could higher deposit insurance premiums for banks with riskier assets benefit the economy?
15. How could market-value accounting for bank capital requirements benefit the economy? How difficult would it be to implement?

WEB EXERCISES

Banking Regulation

1. Go to http://www.fdic.gov/regulations/laws/important/. This site reports on the most significant pieces of legislation affecting banks since the 1800s. Summarize the most recently enacted bank regulation on this site.
2. The Office of the Comptroller of the Currency is responsible for many of the regulations affecting bank operations. Go to http://www.occ.treas.gov/. Click on "Regulatory Information." Now click on the 12 CFR Parts 1 to 199. What does Part 1 cover? How many parts are there in 12 CFR? Open Part 18. What topic does it cover? Summarize its purpose.

Chapter 19

Insurance Companies and Pension Funds

Preview

In this chapter we continue our discussion of financial institutions by looking at two nonbank institutions: insurance companies and pension funds. Insurance is an important industry in the United States. Most people hold one or more types of insurance policies (health, life, homeowners, automobile, disability, and so on), and the annual revenues of insurance companies exceed $600 billion. Insurance companies are also a major employer, especially of business majors. Figure 1 shows the number of persons employed by the insurance industry between 1960 and 2000. The numbers rose rapidly during the 1960s, 1970s, and early 1980s. (Currently, well over 2 million Americans are employed in the insurance industry.) In recent years, the rate of growth has slowed however. There are a couple of possible explanations for this. First, technology has streamlined claims processing so that fewer back-office workers are needed. Second, competition by other financial institutions such as commercial banks and brokerage houses may be cutting into some of the business traditionally reserved for insurance companies.

One major competitor to insurance has been the private, company-sponsored pension plan. Better-educated and longer-lived workers are putting more money into pension funds than ever before. Over 65 million individuals are now invested in a private pension fund. These plans are also reviewed in this chapter.

Insurance companies and pension funds are considered financial intermediaries for several reasons. First, they receive investment funds from their customers. For example, when a person buys a whole life insurance policy, the person receives a life insurance benefit and accumulates a cash balance. Many people use insurance companies as their primary investment avenue. Similarly, private pension

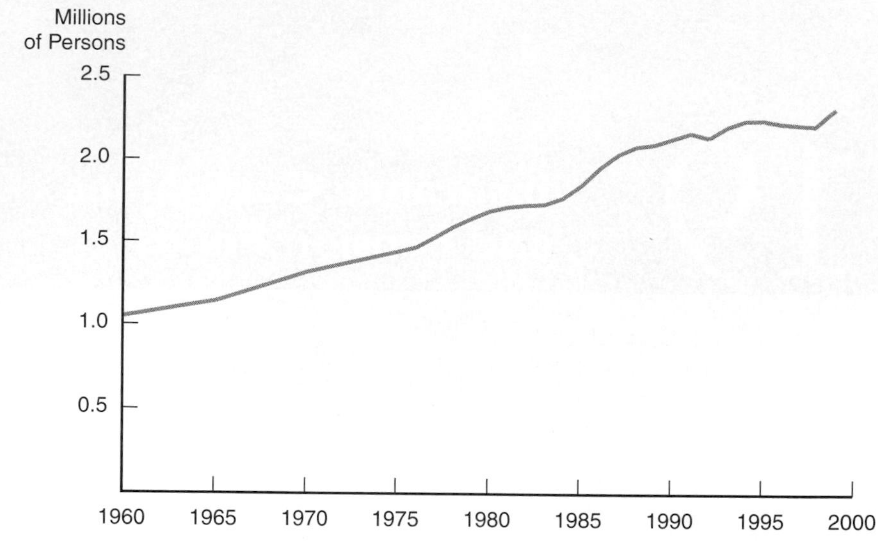

FIGURE 1 Number of Persons Employed in the U.S. Insurance Industry, 1960–2000

Source: Insurance Company Fact Book, 2001.

funds also take in investment dollars from their customers. Second, both of these institutions place their money in a variety of money-earning investments. Insurance companies and pension funds make large commercial mortgage loans, invest in stocks, and buy bonds. Thus these institutions are financial intermediaries in that they take in funds from one sector and invest it in another.

INSURANCE COMPANIES

Insurance companies are in the business of assuming risk on behalf of their customers in exchange for a fee, called a *premium*. Insurance companies make a profit by charging premiums that are sufficient to pay the expected claims to the company plus a profit. Why do people pay for insurance when they know that over the lifetime of their policy, they will probably pay more in premiums than the expected amount of any loss they will suffer? Because most people are risk averse: They would rather pay a **certainty equivalent** (the insurance premium) than accept the gamble that they will lose their house or their car. Thus it is because people are risk-averse that they prefer to buy insurance and know with certainty what their wealth will be (their current wealth minus the insurance premium) than to incur the risk and run the chance that their wealth may fall.

Consider how people's lives would change if insurance were not available. Instead of knowing that the insurance company would help if an emergency occurred, everyone would have to set aside reserves. These reserves could not be invested long-term but would have to be kept in an extremely liquid form. Furthermore, people would be constantly worried that their reserves would be inadequate to pay for catastrophic events such as the loss of their house to fire, the theft of their car, or the death of the family breadwinner. Insurance allows us the peace of mind that a single event can have only a limited impact on our lives.

FUNDAMENTALS OF INSURANCE

Although there are many types of insurance and insurance companies, all insurance is subject to several basic principles.

1. There must be a relationship between the *insured* (the party covered by insurance) and the *beneficiary* (the party who receives the payment should a loss occur). In addition, the beneficiary must be someone who may suffer potential harm. For example, you could not take out a policy on your neighbor's teenage driver because you are unlikely to suffer harm if the teenager gets into an accident. The reason for this rule is that insurance companies do not want people to buy policies as a way of gambling.
2. The insured must provide full and accurate information to the insurance company.
3. The insured is not to profit as a result of insurance coverage.
4. If a third party compensates the insured for the loss, the insurance company's obligation is reduced by the amount of the compensation.
5. The insurance company must have a large number of insureds so that the risk can be spread out among many different policies.
6. The loss must be quantifiable. For example, an oil company could not buy a policy on an unexplored oil field.
7. The insurance company must be able to compute the probability of the loss occurring.

The purpose of these principles is to maintain the integrity of the insurance process. Without them, people may be tempted to use insurance companies to gamble or speculate on future events. Taken to an extreme, this behavior could undermine the ability of insurance companies to protect persons in real need. In addition, these principles provide a way to spread the risk among many policies and to establish a price for each policy that will provide an expectation of a profitable return. Despite following these guidelines, insurance companies suffer greatly from the problems of asymmetric information that we first described in Chapter 2.

Adverse Selection and Moral Hazard in Insurance

Recall that adverse selection occurs when the individuals most likely to benefit from a transaction are the ones who most actively seek out the transaction and are thus most likely to be selected. In Chapter 2 we discussed adverse selection in the context of borrowers with the worst credit being the ones who most actively seek loans. The problem also occurs in the insurance market. Who is more likely to apply for health insurance, someone who is seldom sick or someone with chronic health problems? Who is more likely to buy flood insurance, someone who lives on a mountain or someone who lives in a river valley? In both cases, the party more likely to suffer a loss is the party likely to seek insurance. The implication of adverse selection is that loss probability statistics gathered for the entire population may not accurately reflect the loss potential for the persons who actually want to buy policies.

The adverse selection problem raises the issue of which policies an insurance company should accept. Because someone in poor health is more likely to buy a supplemental health insurance policy than someone in perfect health, we might predict that insurance companies should turn down anyone who applies.

Since this does not happen, insurance companies must have found alternative solutions. For example, most insurance companies require physical exams and may examine previous medical records before issuing a health or life insurance policy. If some previous illness is found to be a factor in the person's health, the company may issue the policy but exclude this preexisting condition. Insurance firms often offer better rates to insure groups of people, such as everyone working at a particular business, because the adverse selection problem is then avoided.

In addition to the adverse selection problem, moral hazard plagues the insurance industry. Moral hazard occurs when the insured fails to take proper precautions to avoid losses because losses are covered by insurance. For example, moral hazard may cause you not to lock your car doors if you will be reimbursed by insurance if the car is stolen. When Hurricane Fran approached the North Carolina coast in 1996, many yacht owners did not take down their old canvas covers because they hoped the covers would be destroyed by the hurricane, in which case the owners could file a claim with the insurance company and get money to buy new covers.

One way that insurance companies combat moral hazard is by requiring a **deductible.** A deductible is the amount of any loss that must be paid by the insured before the insurance company will pay anything. For example, if new canvas yacht covers cost $5000 and the yacht owner has $1000 deductible, the owner will pay the first $1000 of the loss and the insurance company will pay $4000. In addition to deductibles, there may be other terms in the insurance contract aimed at reducing risk. For example, a business insured against fire may be required to install and maintain a sprinkler system on its premises to reduce the loss should a fire occur.

Although contract terms and deductibles help with the moral hazard problem, these issues remain a constant difficulty for insurance companies. The insurance industry's reaction to moral hazard and adverse selection are discussed in greater detail in "The Practicing Financial Institutional Manager" later in this chapter.

Selling Insurance

Another problem common to insurance companies is that people often fail to seek as much insurance as they actually need. Human nature tends to cause people to ignore their mortality, for example. For this reason, insurance, unlike many banking services, does not sell itself. Instead, insurance companies must hire large sales forces to sell their products. The expense of marketing may account for up to 20% of the total cost of a policy. A good sales force can convince people to buy insurance coverage that they never would have pursued on their own yet may have a need for.

Insurance is unique in that agents sell a product that commits the company to a risk. The relationship between the agent and the company varies: *Independent agents* may sell insurance for a number of different companies. They do not have any particular loyalty to any one firm and simply try to find the best product for their customer. There are in excess of 60,000 independent agents in the United States. *Exclusive agents* sell the insurance products for only one insurance company.

Most agents, whether independent or exclusive, are compensated by being paid a commission. The agents themselves are usually not at all concerned with the level of risk of any one policy because they have little to lose if a loss occurs. (Rarely are commissions influenced by the claims submitted by an agent's customers.) To keep control of the risk that agents are incurring on behalf of the company, insurance companies employ **underwriters,** people who review and sign off on each policy an agent writes and who have the authority to turn down a policy if they deem the risk unacceptable. If underwriters have questions about the quality of customers, they may order an independent inspector to review the property being insured or request additional medical information. A final decision to accept the policy may depend on the inspector's report (see Box 1).

GROWTH AND ORGANIZATION OF INSURANCE COMPANIES

Figure 2 shows the number of life insurance companies from 1950 to 1999. There was a steady increase in the number until 1988. Since then the number has fallen steadily. Another interesting point to note about Figure 2 is that insurance companies can

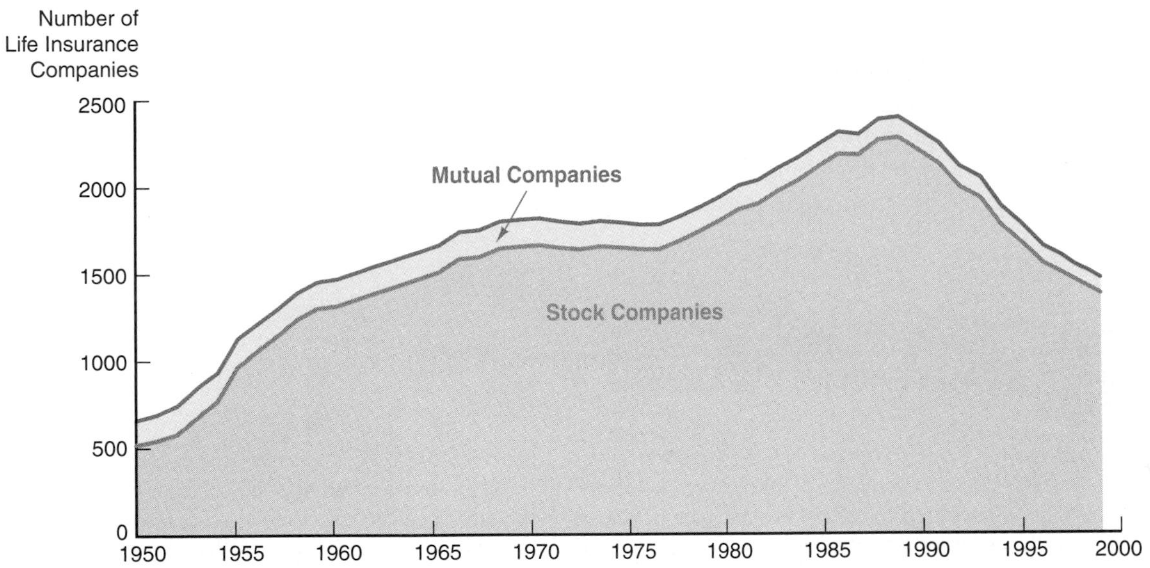

FIGURE 2 Number of Life Insurance Companies in the United States, 1950–1999

Source: Life Insurance Fact Book, 2000, Table 5.1

BOX 1

Insurance Agent: The Customer's Ally

An underwriter working for Prudential Insurance was responsible for a number of agents selling property insurance in Southern California in 1985. One agent sold a large number of fire insurance policies and was always careful to document clearly when a fire hydrant was on the property by including it in a photograph attached to the policy application. The agent made a mistake on one policy, however, when he included his car in a picture of a different view of the property. The picture showed a plastic fire hydrant lying in the open trunk of his car. He had been putting this fire hydrant on property for years when he needed to give a low quote to get business.

The agent was neither fired nor sued. He was simply advised to halt the practice, and his policies continued to be accepted by the company.

be organized as either *stock* or *mutual* firms. A **stock company** is owned by stockholders and has the objective of making a profit.

Mutual insurance companies are owned by the policyholders. The objective of mutual insurance firms is to provide insurance at the lowest possible cost to the insured. Policyholders are paid dividends that reflect the surplus of premiums over costs. Because the policyholders share in reducing the cost of insurance, there may be some reduction in the moral hazard that most insurance companies face. A unique feature of mutual insurance dividends is that they are not taxed like dividends received from other types of corporations. The Internal Revenue Service regards the dividends as refunds of overcharges on insurance premiums.

Most new insurance companies organize as stock corporations. As Figure 2 shows, at the end of 1999, only 106 of 1462 insurance companies were organized as mutuals. (See Box 2 for a description of a unique form of insurance ownership.)

TYPES OF INSURANCE

Insurance is classified by which type of undesirable event is insured. The most common types are life insurance and property and casualty insurance. In its simplest form, life insurance provides income for the heirs of the deceased. Many insurance companies offer policies that provide retirement benefits as well as life insurance. In this case, the premium combines the cost of the life insurance

BOX 2: GLOBAL
The Woes of Lloyd's of London

In June 1993, Lloyd's of London announced the biggest loss in its history, $4.33 billion for the year 1990 (Lloyd's waits three years to allow all claims to be processed before reporting profits or losses). The chairman of Lloyd's stated that the 1990 deficit "represents in every way the low point of Lloyd's history in the last 305 years."* Things continued to get worse for Lloyd's, with losses continuing until 1992, for a cumulative amount of more than $12 billion over the five-year period 1988–1992.

Lloyd's began in 1688 in a London coffeehouse owned by Edward Lloyd, which was a meeting place for merchants, shipowners, and sea captains. Lloyd's became a marketplace in which members, known as "names," trade pieces of insurance policies in order to spread the risk, a process called *reinsurance*. An unusual feature of Lloyd's is that names are directly exposed to losses because they accept unlimited personal liability for any claims they have to pay. Many of those participating in Lloyd's have come to regret it in recent years, having lost their entire personal fortunes. Indeed, the average loss per name was over $150,000 in 1990. The losses at Lloyd's have also resulted in a slew of lawsuits, with members suing each other right and left over who should be responsible for paying claims.

To survive, the basic structure of Lloyd's has had to change. Lloyd's has opened itself up to corporate capital with only limited liability, has taken measures to lower central spending by the organization, and has altered the way it is governed. In 1996, Lloyd's was able to announce record profits for the year 1993. However, to settle its lawsuits, Lloyd's offered a $4.8 billion rescue package to its 34,000 names, including the creation of a new corporation called Equitas that took over Lloyd's liabilities incurred before 1993, and profits were high for the next few years.

Lloyds is by no means out of the woods yet. It still has antiquated technology and high central operating costs and has experienced losses in recent years. While it had high profits in the mid-1990s, in March 2001, it announced that it lost over 1 billion pounds ($1.4 billion) in 1999, after suffering a loss of over a billion pounds in 1998. Additionally, it may sustain losses exceeding $1.5 billion in the aftermath of the terrorist attack on the World Trade Center in New York. A victim of the worldwide woes of the property and casualty insurance industry, Lloyd's of London, after three centuries, will never be the same.

*"Lloyd's of London Posts Big Loss, Raising Fears on Market's Viability," *Wall Street Journal*, June 23, 1993, p. A10.

with a savings program. The cost of life insurance depends on such factors as the age of the insured, average life expectancies, the health and lifestyle of the insured (whether the insured smokes, engages in a dangerous hobby such as skydiving, and so on), and the insurance company's operating costs.

Property and casualty insurance protects property (houses, cars, boats, and so on) against losses due to accidents, fire, disasters, and other calamities. Marine insurance, for example, which insures against the loss of a ship and its cargo, is the oldest form of insurance, predating even life insurance. Property and casualty policies tend to be short-term contracts subject to frequent renewal. Another significant distinction between life insurance policies and property and casualty policies is that the latter do not have a savings component. Property and casualty premiums are based simply on the probability of sustaining the loss. That is why car insurance premiums are higher if a driver has had speeding tickets, has caused accidents, or lives in a high-crime area. Each of these events increases the likelihood that the insurance company will have to pay a claim.

Life Insurance

Life is assumed to unfold in a predictable sequence: You work for a number of years while saving for retirement; then you retire, live off the fruits of your earlier labor, and die at a ripe old age. The problem is that you could die too young and not have time to provide for your loved ones, or you could live too long and run out of retirement assets. Either option is very unappealing to most people. The purpose of life insurance is to relieve some of the concern associated with either eventuality. Although insurance cannot make you comfortable with the idea of a premature death, it can at least allow you the peace of mind that comes with knowing that you have provided for your heirs. Life insurance companies also want to help people save for their retirement. In this way, the insurance company provides for the customer's whole life.

The basic products of life insurance companies are life insurance proper, disability insurance, annuities, and health insurance. Life insurance pays off if you die, protecting those who depend on your continued earnings. As mentioned, the person who receives the insurance payment after you die is called the *beneficiary* of the policy. Disability insurance replaces part of your income should you become unable to continue working due to illness or an accident. An **annuity** is an insurance product that will help if you live longer than you expect. For an initial fixed sum or stream of payments, the insurance company agrees to pay you a fixed amount for as long as you live. If you live a short life, the insurance company pays out less than expected. Conversely, if you live unusually long, the insurance company may pay out much more than expected.

Notice one curiosity among these various types of insurance: Although predicting any one individual's life expectancy or probability of being disabled is very difficult, when many people are insured, the actual amount to be paid out by the insurance company can be predicted very accurately. Insurance companies collect and analyze statistics on life expectancies, health claims, disability claims, and other relevant matters.

For example, a life insurance company can predict with a high degree of accuracy when death benefits must be paid by using *actuarial tables* that predict life expectancies. Table 1 lists the expected life of persons at various ages. A 25-year-old female can expect to live another 55.4 years; a 25-year-old male, however, can expect to live only another 50.1 years.

TABLE 1 Life Expectancy at Various Ages in the United States, 1997

Age	Male	Female	Total Population
0	73.6	79.4	76.5
15	59.4	65.1	62.3
25	50.1	55.4	52.8
35	40.8	45.7	43.4
45	31.8	36.3	34.1
55	23.3	27.3	25.4
65	15.9	19.2	17.7
75	9.9	12.1	11.2
85	5.5	6.6	6.3

Source: Life Insurance Fact Book, 2000, Table 13.4.

The **law of large numbers** says that when many people are insured, the probability distribution of the losses will assume a normal probability distribution, a distribution that allows accurate predictions. This distribution is important: Because insurance companies insure so many millions of people, the law of large numbers tends to make the company's predictions quite accurate and allows companies to price the policies so that they can earn a profit.

Life insurance policies protect against an interruption in the family's stream of income. The broad categories of life insurance products are *term, whole life,* and *universal life.*

Term Life The simplest form of life insurance is the *term insurance policy,* which pays out if the insured dies while the policy is in force. This form of policy contains no savings element. Once the policy period expires, there are no residual benefits.

As the insured ages, the probability of death increases, so the cost of the policy rises. For example, Table 2 shows the estimated premiums for a 40-year-old male nonsmoker for $100,000 of term life insurance from a major insurance company. The premium for the first year is $134. This rises to $147 when the insured is 41 years old, $153 when the insured is 42, and so on. By the time the insured is 60 years old, $100,000 of life insurance costs $810 per year. Of course, rates vary among insurance companies, but these sample rates demonstrate how the annual cost of a term policy rises with the age of the insured.

Some term policies fix the premiums for a set number of years, usually five or ten. Alternatively, *decreasing term policies* have a constant premium, but the amount of the insurance coverage declines each year.

TABLE 2 Typical Annual Premiums on a $100,000 Term Policy for a 40-Year-Old Male Nonsmoker

Age of Insured	Cost ($)
40	134
41	147
42	153
45	192
50	286
55	461
60	810

Term policies have been historically hard to sell because once they expire, the policyholder has nothing to show for the premium paid. This problem is solved with whole life policies.

Whole Life A *whole life insurance* policy pays a death benefit if the policyholder dies. Whole life policies usually require the insured to pay a level premium for the duration of the policy. In the beginning, the insured pays more than if a term policy had been purchased. This overpayment accumulates as a cash value that can be borrowed by the insured at reasonable rates.

Survivorship benefits also contribute to the accumulated cash values. When members of the insured pool die, any remaining cash values are divided among the survivors. If the policyholder lives until the policy matures, it can be surrendered for its cash value. This cash value can be used to purchase an annuity. In this way, the whole life policy is advertised as covering the insured for the duration of his or her life.

Universal Life In the late 1970s, whole life policies fell into disfavor because the rates of return earned on the policy premiums were well below rates available on other investments. For example, say that an investor bought a term policy instead of a whole life policy and invested the difference in the premiums. If she did this each year for the term of the whole life policy, she would be able to pay for term insurance and still have a much greater amount in her investment account than if she had initially purchased the whole life policy. Investment advisers and insurance agents began steering customers away from whole life policies. The sales pitch became "buy term and invest the difference." Because the agents were also selling other investments, they did not suffer from this change in insurance plans. To combat the flow of funds out of their companies, insurance firms introduced the *universal life policy.*

Universal life policies combine the benefits of the term policy with those of the whole life policy. The major benefit of the universal life policy is that the cash value accumulates at a much higher rate.

The universal life policy is structured to have two parts, one for the term life insurance and one for savings. One important advantage that universal life policies have over many alternative investment plans is that the interest earned on the savings portion of the account is tax-exempt until withdrawn. To keep this favorable tax treatment, the cash value of the policy cannot exceed the death benefit.

Universal life policies were introduced in the early 1980s when interest rates were at record high levels. They immediately became very popular and by 1984 accounted for 32% of the volume of life insurance sold. Later, as interest rates fell, their popularity ebbed.

Annuities If we think of term life insurance as insuring against death, the annuity can be viewed as insuring against life. As we noted earlier, one risk people have is outliving their retirement funds. If they live longer than they projected when they initially retired, they could spend all of their money and end up in poverty. One way to avoid this outcome is by purchasing annuities. Once an annuity has been purchased for a fixed amount, it makes payments as long as the beneficiary lives.

Annuities are particularly susceptible to the adverse selection problem. When people retire, they know more about their life expectancy than the insurance company knows. People who are in good health, have a family history of longevity, and have attended to their health all of their lives are more likely to live longer and hence to want to buy an annuity than people in poor or average health. To avoid this problem, insurance companies tend to price individual annuities expensively. Most annuities are sold to members of large groups where all employees covered by a particular pension plan automatically receive their benefit distribution by purchasing an annuity from the insurance company. Because the annuity is automatic, the adverse selection problem is eliminated.

Assets and Liabilities of Life Insurance Companies Life insurance companies derive funds from two sources. First, they receive premiums that represent future obligations that must be met when the insured dies. Second, they receive premiums paid into pension funds managed by the life insurance company. These funds are long-term in nature.

Since life insurance liabilities are predictable and long-term, life insurance companies can invest in long-term assets. Figure 3 shows the distribution of assets of the average life insurance company at the beginning of 2000. Most of the assets are in long-term investments such as corporate stocks and bonds.

Insurance companies have also invested heavily in mortgages and real estate over the years. In 2000, about 7.7% of life insurance assets were invested either in mortgage loans or directly in real estate. This percentage is down substantially from historic levels. Figure 4 displays the percentage of assets invested in mortgages from 1920 to 2001. The decline in mortgage investment, which represents a shift to lower-risk assets, has been offset by increased investment in corporate bonds and government securities.

The shift to less risky securities may be the result of losses suffered by some insurance companies in the late 1980s. As insurance companies competed against mutual funds and money market funds for retirement dollars, they found that they needed higher-return investments. This led some insurance companies to invest in real estate and junk bonds. Deteriorating real estate values brought on by overbuilding during the 1980s caused some firms to suffer large losses. The combination of large real estate losses and junk bond investment contributed to the failure of several large firms in 1991, including Executive Life, with assets of $15 billion, and Mutual Benefit Life, with assets of $14 billion.

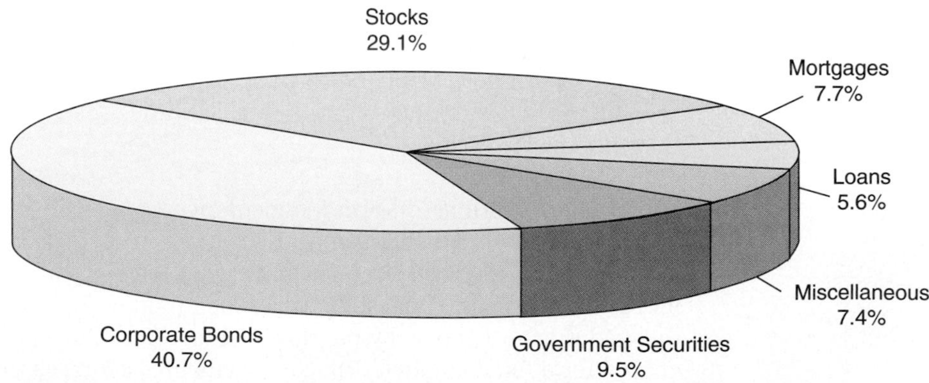

FIGURE 3 Distribution of Life Insurance Company Assets (beginning of 2000)

Source: Federal Reserve Flow of Funds Accounts.

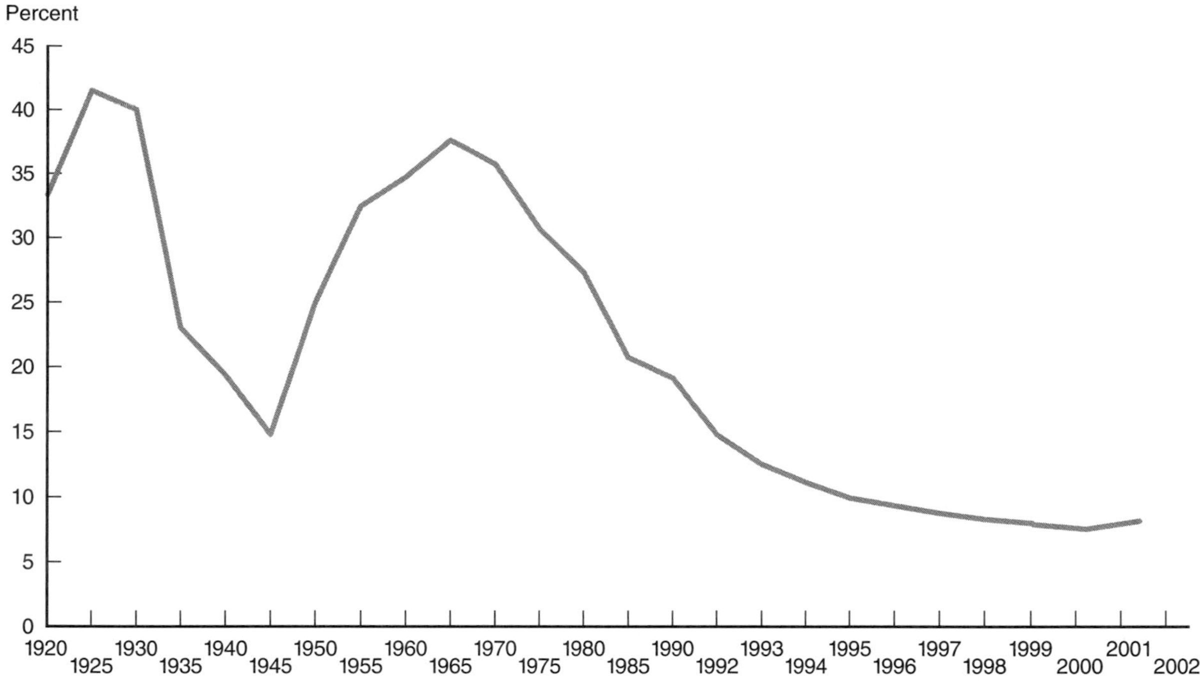

FIGURE 4 Percentage of Life Insurance Company Assets Invested in Mortgages, 1920–2001

Source: Federal Reserve Flow of Funds Accounts.

Health Insurance

Individual health insurance coverage is very vulnerable to adverse selection problems. People who know that they are likely to get ill are the most likely to seek health insurance coverage. This causes individual health insurance to be very expensive. Most policies are offered through company-sponsored programs in which the company pays all or part of the employee's policy premium.

Most life insurance companies also offer health insurance. Health insurance premiums account for about 25% of total premium income. Life insurance companies compete with Blue Cross and Blue Shield organizations, nonprofit firms that are sponsored by hospitals. Blue Cross usually covers hospital care and Blue Shield, doctors' services. One national agency coordinates and monitors the 73 Blue Cross/Blue Shield organizations.

The government is also involved in health insurance through Medicare and Medicaid. Medicare provides medical coverage for the elderly, and Medicaid provides coverage for people on welfare.

Health insurance was a major political issue in the 1992 presidential election and continues to be the subject of regulation. In 1996, Congress passed legislation making it more difficult for insurance companies to refuse to insure a person with a preexisting medical problem.

One reason for the extensive debate over medical insurance has been the spiraling costs of health care. For most of the past decade, the cost of health care has risen much faster than the cost of living and real wages. One factor contributing to this increase is the more sophisticated and expensive treatments constantly being offered. For example, studies have shown that cholesterol-reducing drugs can reduce the likelihood of cardiovascular trouble across a broad portion of the population. These drugs cost about $3 per day and did not even exist 15 years ago. Insurance companies have dealt with these rising costs in a number of ways. For example, today the risk of most company-sponsored plans is borne by the company, with the insurance company administering the plan and covering catastrophic expenses. This increases the sponsoring company's incentive to maintain a healthy workforce and to encourage responsible use of medical facilities by its employees. For example, many large firms have found it cost-effective to employ physician assistants on site to reduce medical fees and absenteeism.

Another way that insurance companies are attempting to deal with increased medical costs is by controlling them. This is done by negotiating contracts with physician groups to provide services at reduced cost and through *managed care,* where approval is required before services can be rendered. *Health maintenance organizations (HMOs)* shift the risk from the insurance company to the provider. The insurance company pays the HMO a fixed payment per person covered in exchange for medical services. One problem many people find with the HMO form of health care is that the provider has an incentive to limit medical services. Recent regulation was required, for example, to ensure mothers at least 48 hours in the hospital following a delivery.

Though it appears that a national health insurance overhaul is not going to come out of Congress, the attention focused on the problem has prompted many changes at the state and local levels. These changes are likely to continue in the future, due largely to pressure from insurance companies.

Property and Casualty Insurance

Property and casualty insurance was the earliest form of insurance. It began in the Middle Ages when merchants sent ships off to foreign ports to trade. A merchant, though willing to accept the risk that the trading might not turn a profit, was often unwilling to accept the risk that the ship might sink or be captured by pirates. To reduce such risks, merchants began to band together and insure each other's ships against loss. The process became more sophisticated as time went on, and insurance policies were written that were then traded in the major commercial centers of the time.

In 1666, the Great Fire of London did much to advance the case for fire insurance. The first fire insurance company was founded in London in 1680. In the United States, the first fire insurance company was formed by a group led by Benjamin Franklin in 1752. By the beginning of the nineteenth century, the assets of property and casualty insurance firms exceeded even those of commercial banks, making these firms the most important financial intermediary. The invention of the automobile did a great deal to spur the growth of property and casualty insurance companies during the twentieth century.

Property and Casualty Insurance Today Property and casualty insurance protects against losses from fire, theft, storm, explosion, and even neglect. **Property insurance** protects businesses and owners from the impact of risk associated with owning property. This includes replacement and loss of earnings from income-producing property as well as financial losses to owners of residential property. **Casualty insurance** (or **liability insurance**) protects against liability for harm the insured may cause to others as a result of product failure or accidents. For example, part of your car insurance is property insurance (which pays if your car is damaged), and part is casualty insurance (which pays if you cause an accident).

Property and casualty insurance is different from life insurance. First, policies tend to be short-term, usually for one year or less. Second, whereas life insurance is limited to insuring against one event, property and casualty companies insure against many different events. Finally, the amount of the potential loss is much more difficult to predict than for life insurance. These characteristics cause property and casualty companies to hold more liquid assets than those of life insurance companies. Figure 5 reports total losses per year between 1991 and 2000. The wide range of losses means that property and casualty firms must maintain substantial liquidity.

Property insurance can be provided in either **named-peril policies** or **open-peril policies.** Named-peril policies insure against loss only from perils that are specifically named in the policy, whereas open-peril policies insure against all perils except those specifically excluded by the policy. For example, many homeowners in low-lying areas are required to buy flood insurance. This insurance covers only losses due to flooding, so it is a named-peril policy. A homeowner's insurance policy, which protects the house from fire, hurricane, tornado, and other damage, is an example of an open-peril policy.

Casualty or liability insurance protects against financial losses because of a claim of negligence. Liability insurance is bought not only by manufacturers who might be sued because of product defects but also by many types of professionals, including physicians, lawyers, and building contractors. Whereas the risk exposure in property insurance policies is relatively easy to predict, since it is usually limited to the value of the property, liability risk exposure is much more difficult to determine.

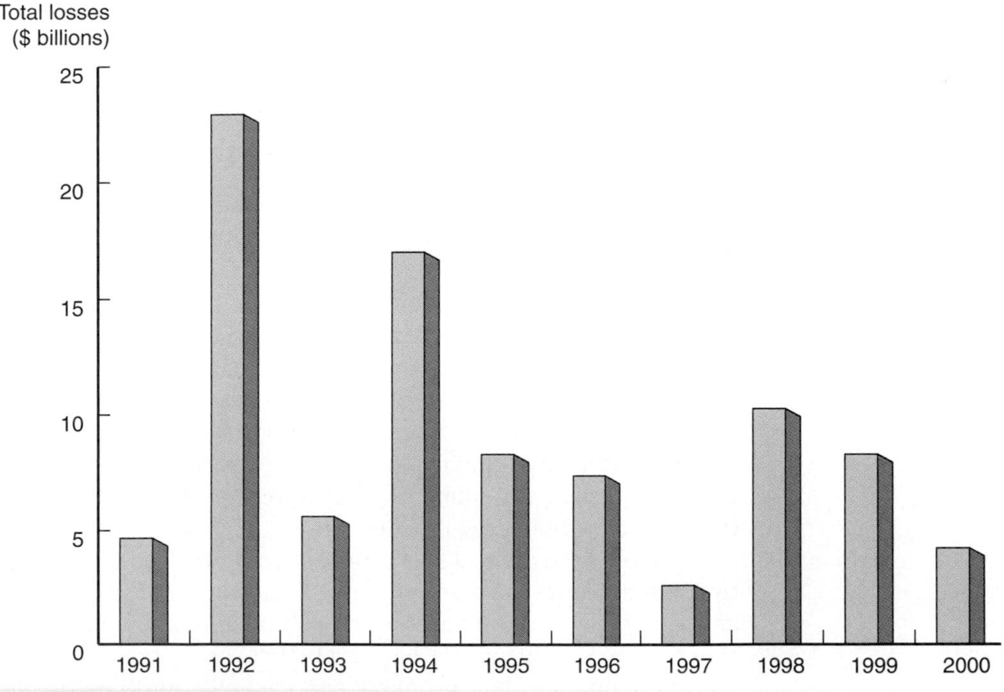

FIGURE 5 Annual Catastrophic Losses to Property and Casualty Insurance Companies, 1991–2000

Source: *IAMagazine,* Published by IIAA Membership Services Inc.

Liability risk exposure can have long lag times (often referred to as "tails"). This means that a liability claim may be filed long after the policy expires. Consider liability claims filed against the manufacturers of light airplanes. In the 1950s, 1960s, and 1970s, Cessna and Piper produced airplanes that are still being used today. The companies often get sued when one of these 30- or 40-year-old planes crashes. Insurance premiums grew so large in the 1980s due to the extensive lag time that both Cessna and Piper had to stop producing private airplanes. The cost of the liability insurance put the price of the planes out of reach of most private pilots.

There has been extensive publicity about high liability awards given by juries. These awards have often been well above what the insurance companies could have predicted. Liability insurance premiums continue to rise as a result. Some states have attempted to limit liability awards in an effort to contain these insurance costs.

Reinsurance One way that insurance companies may reduce their risk exposure is to obtain **reinsurance**. Reinsurance allocates a portion of the risk to another company in exchange for a portion of the premium. Reinsurance allows insurance companies to write larger policies because a portion of the policy is actually held by another firm.

About 10% of all property and casualty insurance is reinsured. Smaller insurance firms obtain reinsurance more frequently than large firms. You can think of it as insurance for the insurance company.

Since the originator of the policy usually has more to lose than the reinsurer, the moral hazard and adverse selection problems are small. This means that little specific information about the risk being reinsured is required. As a result of the simplified information requirements, the reinsurance market consists of relatively standardized contracts. One problem with the market is the risk that the reinsurer can fail. For example, in 1990, insurance firms were owed about $20 billion in unrecovered reinsurance.

Insurance Regulation

Insurance companies are subject to less federal regulation than many other financial institutions. In fact, the McCarran-Ferguson Act of 1945 explicitly exempts insurance from federal regulation. The primary federal regulator is the Internal Revenue Service, which administers special taxation rules.

Most insurance regulation occurs at the state level. Not only must an insurance company follow the standards set by the state in which it is chartered, but it must also comply with the regulations set in any state in which it does business. New York requires that any insurance company doing business in the state comply with its investment standards. Because New York is such a big market, virtually every company complies. This makes the New York State regulations almost the same as national regulations.

The purpose of most regulations is to protect policyholders from losses due to the insolvency of the company. To accomplish this, insurance companies are restricted as to their asset composition and minimum capital ratio. All states also require that insurance agents and brokers obtain state licenses to sell each kind of insurance: life, property and casualty, and health. These licenses are to ensure that all agents have a minimum level of knowledge about the products they sell.

THE PRACTICING FINANCIAL INSTITUTION MANAGER

Insurance Management

Insurance companies, like banks, are in the financial intermediation business of transforming one type of asset into another for the public. Insurance companies use the premiums paid on policies to invest in assets such as bonds, stocks, mortgages, and other loans; the earnings from these assets are then used to pay out claims on the policies. In effect, insurance companies transform assets such as bonds, stocks, and loans into insurance policies that provide a set of services (for example, claim adjustments, savings plans, friendly insurance agents). If the insurance company's production process of asset transformation efficiently provides its customers with adequate insurance services at low cost and if it can earn high returns on its investments, it will make profits; if not, it will suffer losses.

In Chapters 2 and 14 the concepts of adverse selection and moral hazard allowed us to understand why financial intermediaries like insurance companies are important in the economy. Here we use the adverse selection and moral hazard concepts to explain many management practices specific to the insurance industry.

In the case of an insurance policy, moral hazard arises when the existence of insurance encourages the insured party to take risks that increase the likelihood of an insurance payoff. For example, a person covered by burglary insurance might not take as many precautions to prevent a burglary because the insurance company will reimburse most of the losses if a theft occurs. Adverse selection holds that the people most likely to receive large insurance payoffs are the ones who will want to purchase insurance the most. For example, a person suffering from a terminal disease would want to take out the biggest life and medical insurance policies possible, thereby exposing the insurance company to potentially large losses. Both adverse selection and moral hazard can result in large losses to insurance companies because they lead to higher payouts on insurance claims. Minimizing adverse selection and moral hazard to reduce these payouts is therefore an extremely important goal for insurance companies, and this goal explains the insurance practices we discuss here.

Screening

To reduce adverse selection, insurance companies try to screen out poor insurance risks from good ones. Effective information collection procedures are therefore an important principle of insurance management.

When you apply for auto insurance, the first thing your insurance agent does is ask you questions about your driving record (number of speeding tickets and accidents), the type of car you are insuring, and certain personal matters (age, marital status). If you are applying for life insurance, you go through a similar grilling, but you are asked even more personal questions about such things as your health, smoking habits, and drug and alcohol use. The life insurance company even orders a medical evaluation (usually done by an independent company) that involves taking blood and urine samples. The insurance company uses the information you provide to allocate you to a risk class—a statistical estimate of how likely you are to have an insurance claim. Based on this information, the insurance company can decide whether to accept you for the insurance or to turn you down because you pose too high a risk and thus would be an unprofitable customer for the insurance company.

Risk-Based Premium

Charging insurance premiums on the basis of how much risk a policyholder poses for the insurance company is a time-honored principle of insurance management. Adverse selection explains why this principle is so important to insurance company profitability.

To understand why an insurance company finds it necessary to have risk-based premiums, let's examine an example of risk-based insurance premiums that at first glance seems unfair. Harry and Sally, both college students with no accidents or speeding tickets, apply for auto insurance. Normally, Harry will be charged a much higher premium than Sally. Insurance companies do this because young males have a much higher accident rate than young females. Suppose, though, that one insurance company did not base its premiums on a risk classification but rather just charged a premium based on the average combined risk for males and females. Then Sally would be charged too much and Harry too little. Sally could go to another insurance company and get a lower rate, while Harry would sign up for the insurance. Because Harry's premium isn't high enough to cover the accidents he is likely to have, on average the company would lose money on Harry. Only with a premium based on a risk classification, so that Harry is charged more, can the insurance company make a profit.[1]

Restrictive Provisions

Restrictive provisions in policies are another insurance management tool for reducing moral hazard. Such provisions discourage policyholders from engaging in risky activities that make an insurance claim more likely. One type of restrictive provision keeps the policyholder from benefiting from behavior that makes a claim more likely. For example, life insurance companies have provisions in their policies that eliminate death benefits if the insured person commits suicide. Restrictive provisions may also require certain behavior on the part of the insured that makes a claim less likely. A company renting motor scooters may be required to provide helmets for renters in order to be covered for any liability associated with the rental. The role of restrictive provisions is not unlike that of restrictive covenants on debt contracts described in Chapter 14: Both serve to reduce moral hazard by ruling out undesirable behavior.

Prevention of Fraud

Insurance companies also face moral hazard because an insured person has an incentive to lie to the company and seek a claim even if the claim is not valid. For example, a person who has not complied with the restrictive provisions of an insurance contract may still submit a claim. Even worse, a person may file claims for events that did not actually occur. Thus an important management principle for insurance companies is conducting investigations to prevent fraud so that only policyholders with valid claims receive compensation.

Cancellation of Insurance

Being prepared to cancel policies is another insurance management tool. Insurance companies can discourage moral hazard by threatening to cancel a policy when the insured person engages in activities that make a claim more likely. If your

[1]You may recognize that the example here is in fact the lemons problem described in Chapter 14.

auto insurance company makes it clear that if a driver gets too many speeding tickets, coverage will be canceled, you will be less likely to speed.

Deductibles

The deductible is the fixed amount by which the insured's loss is reduced when a claim is paid off. A $250 deductible on an auto policy, for example, means that if you suffer a loss of $1000 because of an accident, the insurance company will pay you only $750. Deductibles are an additional management tool that helps insurance companies reduce moral hazard. With a deductible, you experience a loss along with the insurance company when you make a claim. Because you also stand to lose when you have an accident, you have an incentive to drive more carefully. A deductible thus makes a policyholder act more in line with what is profitable for the insurance company; moral hazard has been reduced. And because moral hazard has been reduced, the insurance company can lower the premium by more than enough to compensate the policyholder for the existence of the deductible.

Another function of the deductible is to eliminate the administrative costs of small losses by forcing the insured to bear these losses.

Coinsurance

When a policyholder shares a percentage of the losses along with the insurance company, their arrangement is called **coinsurance.** For example, some medical insurance plans provide coverage for 80% of medical bills, and the insured person pays 20% after a certain deductible has been met. Coinsurance works to reduce moral hazard in exactly the same way that a deductible does. A policyholder who suffers a loss along with the insurance company has less incentive to take actions, such as going to the doctor unnecessarily, that involve higher claims. Coinsurance is thus another useful management tool for insurance companies.

Limits on the Amount of Insurance

Another important principle of insurance management is that there should be limits on the amount of insurance provided, even though a customer is willing to pay for more coverage. The higher the insurance coverage, the more the insured person can gain from risky activities that make an insurance payoff more likely and hence the greater the moral hazard. For example, if Zelda's car were insured for more than its true value, she might not take proper precautions to prevent its theft, such as making sure that the key is always removed or putting in an alarm system. If her car were stolen, she comes out ahead because the excessive insurance payoff would allow her to buy an even better car. By contrast, when the insurance payment is lower than the value of her car, she will suffer a loss if it is stolen and will thus take the proper precautions to prevent this from happening. Insurance companies must always make sure that their coverage is not so high that moral hazard leads to large losses.

Summary

Effective insurance management requires several practices: information collection and screening of potential policyholders, risk-based premiums, restrictive provisions, prevention of fraud, cancellation of insurance, deductibles, coinsurance, and limits on the amount of insurance. All of these practices reduce moral hazard and adverse selection by making it harder for policyholders to benefit from engaging in activities that increase the amount and likelihood of claims. With smaller benefits available, the poor insurance risks (those who are more likely to engage in the activities in the first place) see less benefit from the insurance and are thus less likely to seek it out.

PENSIONS

A **pension plan** is an asset pool that accumulates over an individual's working years and is paid out during the nonworking years. Pension plans represent the fastest-growing financial intermediary. There are a number of reasons for this rapid growth.

As the United States became more urban, people realized that they could not rely on their children to care for them in their retirement. In a rural culture, families tend to stay together on the farm. The property passes from generation to generation with an implicit understanding that the younger generations will care for the older ones. When families became more dispersed and moved off farms, both the opportunity for and the expectation of extensive financial support of the older generations declined.

A second factor contributing to the growth of pension plans is that people are living longer and retiring younger. Again, in the rural setting, people often remained productive well into their retirement years. Many companies in urban America, however, encourage older workers to retire. They are often earning high wages as a result of seniority, yet may be less productive than younger workers. The result of this trend toward younger retirement and longer lives is that the average person can expect to spend more years in retirement. These years must be funded somehow, and the pension plan is often the vehicle of choice.

TYPES OF PENSIONS

Pension plans can be categorized in several ways. They may be defined-benefit or defined-contribution plans, and they may be public or private.

Defined-Benefit Pension Plans

Under a **defined-benefit plan,** the plan sponsor promises the employees a specific benefit when they retire. The payout is usually determined with a formula that uses the number of years worked and the employee's final salary. For example, a pension benefit may be calculated by the following formula:

$$\text{Annual payment} = 2\% \times \text{average of final 3 years' income} \times \text{years of service}$$

In this case, if a worker had been employed for 35 years and the average wages during the last three years were \$50,000, the annual pension benefit would be

$$0.02 \times \$50{,}000 \times 35 = \$35{,}000 \text{ per year}$$

The defined-benefit plan puts the burden on the employer to provide adequate funds to ensure that the agreed payments can be made. External audits of pension plans are required to determine whether sufficient funds have been contributed by the company. If sufficient funds are set aside by the firm for this purpose, the plan is **fully funded.** If more than enough funds are available, the plan is **overfunded.** Often, insufficient funds are available and the fund is **underfunded.** For example, if Jane Brown contributes $100 per year into her pension plan and the interest rate is 10%, after ten years, the contributions and their interest earnings would be worth \$1753.[2] If the defined benefit on her pension plan is \$1753 or less after ten years, the plan is fully funded because her contributions and earnings will cover this payment in full. But if the defined benefit is \$2000, the plan is underfunded because her contributions and earnings do not cover this amount. Underfunding is most common when the employer fails to contribute adequately to the plan. Surprisingly, it is not illegal for a firm to sponsor an underfunded plan. The General Motors Corporation pension plan was underfunded by billions of dollars for most of the 1990s. The degree of funding does not affect the sponsor's responsibility to pay its obligations under the plan. Difficulties arise, however, when firms go bankrupt. If the pension fund is underfunded, retirees may not receive their benefits.

Defined-Contribution Pension Plans

As the name implies, instead of defining what the pension plan will pay, **defined-contribution plans** specify only what will be contributed into the fund. The retirement benefits are entirely dependent on the earnings of the fund. Corporate sponsors of defined-contribution plans usually put a fixed percentage of each employee's wages into the pension fund each pay period. In some instances, the employee also contributes to the plan. An insurance company or fund manager acts as trustee and invests the fund's assets. Frequently, employees are allowed to specify how the funds in their individual accounts will be invested. For example, an employee who is a conservative investor may prefer government securities, while one who is a more aggressive investor may prefer to have her retirement funds invested in corporate stock. When the employee retires, the balance in the pension account can be transferred into an annuity or some other form of distribution.

Defined-contribution pension plans are becoming increasingly popular. Many existing defined-benefit plans are converting to this form, and virtually all new plans are established as defined-contribution. One reason the defined-contribution plan is becoming so popular is that the onus is put on the employee rather than the employer to look out for the pension plan's performance. This reduces the liability of the employer.

Another problem is that plan participants may not understand the need to diversify their holdings. For example, many firms actively encourage employees to invest in company stock. The firm's motivation is to better align employee interest with that of stockholders. The downside is that employees suffer twice should the firm fail. First, they lose their jobs, and second, their retirement portfolios evaporate. The recent collapse of Enron Inc. has brought this issue forcibly to public attention.

One problem with defined-contribution plans is that many employees are not familiar enough with investments to make wise long-term choices. For example, only 3.7% of plan participants choose to put any more than half of their investment in stocks, even though long-term growth potential is greatest in the stock market.

Private and Public Pension Plans

Private pension plans, sponsored by employers, groups, and individuals, have grown rapidly as people have become more concerned about the viability of Social

[2]The \$100 contributed in year 1 would become worth $\$100 \times (1 + 0.10)^{10} = \$259.37$ at the end of ten years; the \$100 contributed in year 2 would become worth $\$100 \times (1 + 0.10)^{9} = 235.79$; and so on until the \$100 contributed in year 10 would become worth $\$100 \times (1 + 0.10) = \$110$. Adding these together, we get the total value of these contributions and their earnings at the end of ten years as \$1753.

Security and more sophisticated about preparing for retirement (see Figure 6). In the past, private pension plans invested mostly in government securities and corporate bonds. Although these instruments are still important pension plan assets, corporate stocks, mortgages, open market paper, and time deposits now play a significant role. Figure 7 shows the distribution of private pension plan assets. They are now the largest institutional investor in the stock market. This makes pension plan managers a potentially powerful force if they choose to exercise control over firm management (see Box 3).

An alternative to privately sponsored pension plans is the public plans, though in many cases there is very little difference between the two. A **public pension plan** is one that is sponsored by a governmental body.

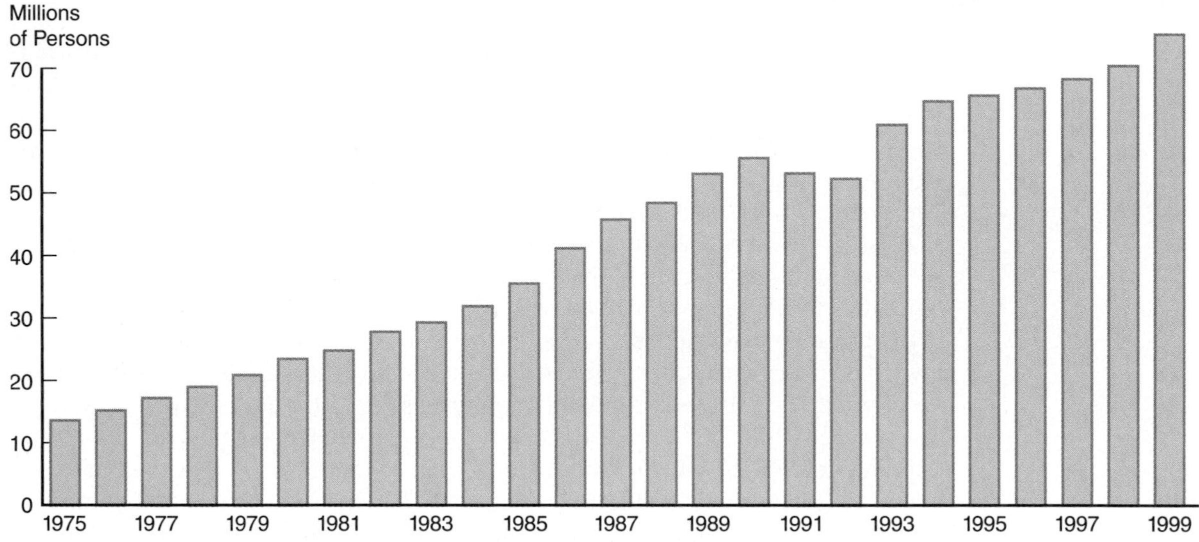

FIGURE 6 Number of Americans Covered by Private Pension Plans, 1975–1999

Source: Life Insurance Fact Book, 2000.

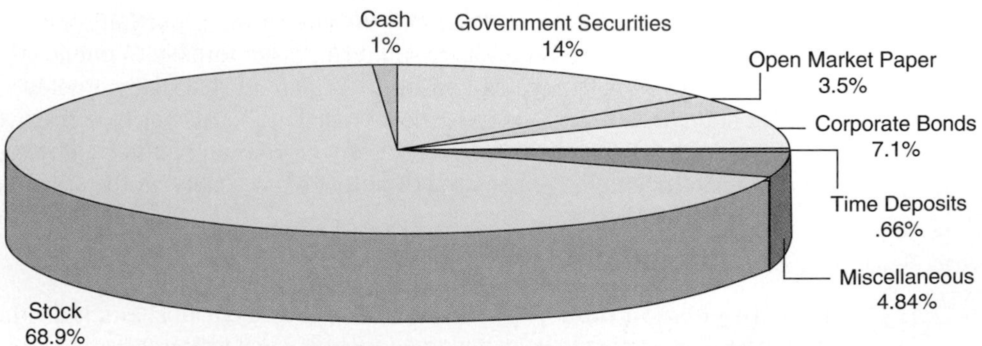

FIGURE 7 Distribution of Private Pension Plan Assets (end of 1999)

Source: Life Insurance Fact Book, 2000.

BOX 3

Power to the Pensions

One ramification of the growth of pension plans and other institutional investors is that the managers of these funds have the ability to exercise substantial control over corporate management. Clearly, when a pension fund manager, who controls many thousands of shares, calls a corporate officer, the officer is going to listen. Evidence suggests that fund managers actively apply the power they have to influence corporate management. For example, pension funds recently defeated management-sponsored antitakeover proxy proposals at Honeywell. And Texaco agreed to name a director from candidates submitted by the huge California Public Employees Retirement System. In addition, the stated mission of the Council of Institutional Investors is to "encourage trustees to take an active role in assuring that corporate actions are not taken at the expense of shareholders." It is possible that these actions will work to benefit shareholders, who do not individually wield enough clout to exert control. However, the clout shareholders wield when their shares are placed into a fund manager's hands may be sufficient to improve corporate management significantly.

The largest of the public plans is the Federal Old Age and Disability Insurance Program (often called simply Social Security). This pension plan was established in 1935 to provide a safety net for aging Americans and is a "pay-as-you-go" system—money that workers contribute today pays benefits to current recipients. Future generations will be called on to pay benefits to the individuals who are currently contributing. Many people fear that the fund will be unable to meet its obligations by the time they retire. This fear is based on problems that the fund encountered in the 1970s and on the realization that a large number of people from the baby boom generation (born between 1946 and 1964) will swell the ranks of retirees in the rapidly approaching future.

Information on your Social Security benefits is available at www.ssa.gov/

The amount of the Social Security benefits a retiree receives is based on the person's earnings history. Workers contribute 6.2% of wages up to a current maximum wage of $84,900 (as of 2001). Employers contribute the same amount. There is a certain amount of redistribution in the benefits, with low-income workers receiving a relatively larger return on their investment than high-income workers. One way to evaluate the amount of the benefits of a pension plan is to determine how the monthly benefits compare to preretirement income. This replacement ratio ranged from 49% for someone earning $15,000 a year to 24% for someone earning $53,400.

Figure 8 shows that the total assets in the Social Security fund decreased in the late 1970s and 1980s at the same time that the number of insured people was increasing. This situation led to a restructuring that included raising the program's contributions and reducing the program's benefits. To build public confidence, the Social Security system has started accumulating reserves to be used when the baby boom generation begins retiring.

The problem is that the 77 million baby boomers born between 1946 and 1964 will begin reaching their normal retirement ages in 2011. Meanwhile, the number of workers supporting each one of those retirees will fall from 3.3 to 2 by 2038. The government predicts that the Social Security trust fund, built up over the years with excess payroll taxes, will be depleted by that date (see Figure 9). After that, taxes would cover only 75% of benefits. Some experts argue that the crisis will arrive much earlier, as soon as 2013. This is because in 2013 the program will have to start redeeming the trust fund's special Treasury bonds that represent the Social

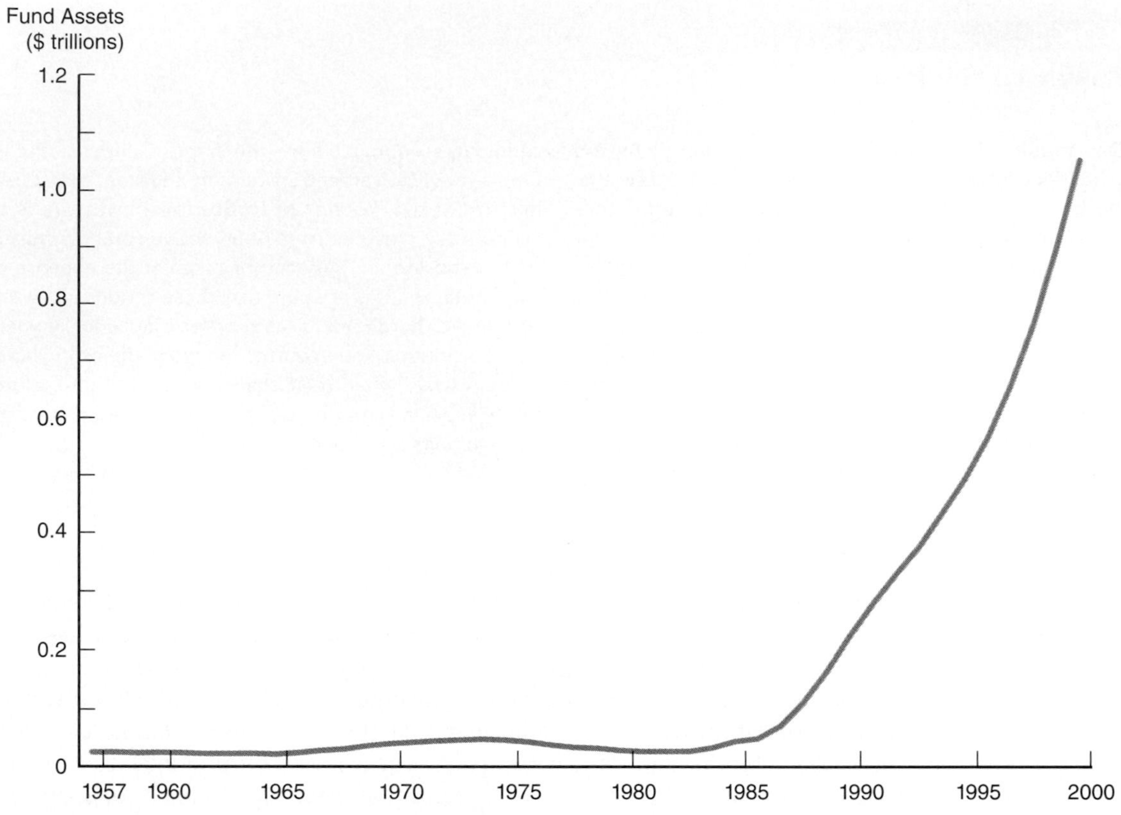

FIGURE 8 Social Security Fund Assets, 1957–2000

Source: www.ssa.gov/OACT/STATS/table4a3.html

www.ssab.gov is the website for the Social Security advisory board. This site will report the most current estimates for when the trust fund will be depleted.

Security surplus. The trouble is that money to redeem these bonds is being spent to run the federal government. By 2030, Social Security will have to redeem $750 billion worth of bonds. "Whether that's a crisis for Social Security, it certainly is a crisis for whoever is around trying to come up with $750 billion," says Michael Tanner, director of the Cato Institute's Project on Social Security Privatization.

The government began holding hearings in 1999 to address the problems. The question likely to get the most attention is whether the system should be reformed by investing in the private securities markets. Privatization could take the form of one of several options being proposed:

- *Individual accounts financed by a portion of payroll taxes.* This has the potential to provide higher rates of return on investments. This option is more risky than the current system and would result in some retirees receiving much less than others. This option is strongly supported by the securities industry and strongly opposed by organized labor and Democrats.
- *Government investment of the surplus in private markets.* This could improve the system's overall rate of return while minimizing the risk to individuals. Critics warn that this option could result in government control of business through stock ownership.

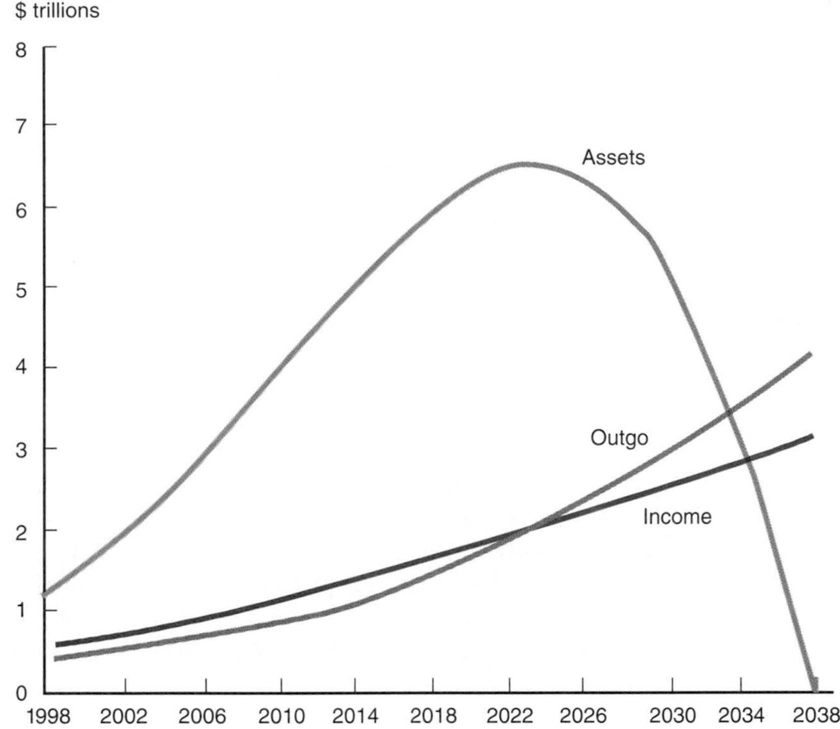

FIGURE 9 Projected Social Security Trust Fund Assets

Source: http://www.ssab.gov/actionshouldbetaken.pdf

- *Personal accounts in addition to the payroll tax.* This option may give people more funds at retirement but would require greater current withholding in the form of an added tax. Critics say this is already possible through the private markets.

The biggest obstacle to privatization is that funds diverted into private accounts would not be available to pay current retirees' benefits. This exacerbates the looming problem rather than solving it. Analysts estimate that the cost of transitioning to a fully funded privatized plan would be enormous—about $100 billion. Over time, analysts argue, privatization would gradually transform Social Security from an unfunded, pay-as-you-go system to a fully funded pension with real assets. Workers who retired 20 years ago received all that they paid in, plus interest and much more. But those who retire today will get only about a 2.2% return, adjusted for inflation. A 30-year-old worker will lose money in absolute terms upon retirement. However, falling stock prices in 2000–2002 have reduced support for all privatization options.

In the short term, Social Security reform is more likely to take the form of an increase in tax, a reduction in benefits, or both. For example, the age at which benefits begin is already scheduled to increase from 65 to 67. Some plans suggest delaying benefits until age 70 or accelerating the timetable for the change to paying benefits at age 67. It is also possible that the $84,900 cap (in 2001) on wages subject to Social Security tax could be raised.

www.socialsecurity.org/calc/calculator.html lets you estimate your future Social Security benefits.

If no funding reforms take place and the current estimates regarding the depletion of the Social Security fund are accurate, the payroll tax rate would have to be increased from 12.4% to 18%.

We must remember that these estimates are based on current facts as they are known. Many factors can change to cause the estimates to change. For example, research on cures for cancer has received a great deal of publicity recently. If a cure for any major cause of death is found, the fund will be in greater trouble than currently thought.

REGULATION OF PENSION PLANS

For many years, pension plans were relatively free of government regulation. Many companies provided pension benefits as rewards for long years of good service and used the benefits as an incentive. Frequently, pension benefits were paid out of current income. When the firm failed or was acquired by another firm, the benefits ended. During the Great Depression, widespread pension plan failures led to increased regulation and to the establishment of the Social Security system.

A major U.S. Supreme Court decision in 1949 established that pension benefits were a legitimate part of collective bargaining, the negotiation of contracts by unions. This decision led to a great increase in the number of plans in existence as unions pressured employers to establish such plans for union members.

Employee Retirement Income Security Act

The most important and most comprehensive legislation affecting pension funds is the **Employee Retirement Income Security Act (ERISA),** passed in 1974. ERISA set certain standards that must be followed by all pension plans. Failure to follow the provisions of the act may cause a plan to lose its advantageous tax status. The motivation for the act was that many workers who had contributed to plans for many years were losing their benefits when plans failed. The principal features of the act are the following:

- ERISA established guidelines for funding.
- It provided that employees switching jobs may transfer their credits from one employer plan to the next.
- It said that plans must have minimum vesting requirements. *Vesting* refers to how long an employee must work for the company to be eligible for pension benefits. The maximum permissible vesting period is seven years, though most plans allow for vesting in less time. Employee contributions are always immediately vested.
- It increased the disclosure requirements for pension plans, providing employees with more ample information about the health and investments of their pension plans.
- It assigned the responsibility of regulatory oversight to the Department of Labor.

ERISA also established the **Pension Benefit Guarantee Corporation** (called **Penny Benny**), a government agency that performs a role similar to that of the FDIC. It insures pension benefits up to a limit (currently just over $40,700 per year per person) if a company with an underfunded pension plan goes bankrupt or is unable to meet its pension obligations for other reasons. Penny Benny charges pension plans a premium to pay for this insurance, but it can also borrow funds up to $100 million from the U.S. Treasury.

Individual Retirement Plans

The Pension Reform Act of 1978 updated the Self-Employed Individuals Tax Retirement Act of 1962 to authorize **individual retirement accounts (IRAs).** IRAs permitted people (such as those who are self-employed) who are not covered by other pension plans to contribute into a tax-deferred savings account. Legislation in 1981 and 1982 expanded the eligibility of these accounts to make them available to almost everyone. IRAs proved extremely popular, to the extent that their use resulted in significant losses of tax revenues to the government. That led Congress to include provisions in the Tax Reform Act of 1986 sharply curtailing eligibility.

Keogh plans are a retirement savings option for the self-employed. Funds can be deposited with a depository institution, life insurance company, or securities firm. The owner of the Keogh is often allowed some discretion as to how the funds will be invested.

On January 1, 1997, the Small Business Protection Act of 1996 went into effect. This act created simplified retirement plans with so-called SIMPLE IRAs and 401(k) plans for businesses with 100 or fewer employees. SIMPLE retirement plans are becoming significantly more popular, especially among the smallest businesses.

THE FUTURE OF PENSION FUNDS

We can expect that pension funds will continue their growth and popularity as the population continues to grow and age. Workers in their early years of employment often find discussions of retirement investing creeping into their conversations. This heightened attention to providing for the future will result in an increased number of pension funds as well as a greater variety of pension fund options to choose among. We can also expect to see pension funds gain increased power over corporations as they control increasing amounts of stock.

SUMMARY

1. Insurance companies exist because people are risk-averse and prefer to transfer risk away from themselves. Insurance benefits people's lives by reducing the size of reserves they would have to maintain to cover possible loss of life or property.
2. Adverse selection and moral hazard are problems inherent to the insurance business. Many of the provisions of insurance policies—including deductibles, application screening, and risk-based premiums—are aimed at reducing their effects.
3. Insurance is usually divided into two primary types, life insurance and property and casualty insurance. Many life insurance products also serve as savings vehicles. Property and casualty insurance usually has a much shorter term than most life insurance.
4. Because life insurance liabilities are very predictable, these insurers are able to invest in long-term assets. Property and casualty insurance companies must keep their assets more liquid to pay out on unexpected losses.

5. Pension plans are rapidly growing as a longer-lived generation plans for early retirement.
6. There are two primary types of pension plans: defined-benefit and defined-contribution. Defined-benefit plans pay benefits according to a formula that is established in advance. Defined-contribution plans specify only how much is to be saved; benefits depend on the returns generated by the plans.
7. The largest public pension plan is Social Security, which is a pay-as-you-go system. Current retirees receive payments from current workers. Many people are concerned that as the number of retirees increases, the amount paid in to the Social Security system will not be sufficient to cover the sums being paid out.
8. Most private pension plans are insured by the Pension Benefit Guarantee Corporation, which pays benefits when a plan's sponsor goes bankrupt or is otherwise unable to make payments.

KEY TERMS

annuity, *p. 525*
casualty (liability) insurance, *p. 530*
certainty equivalent, *p. 520*
coinsurance, *p. 535*
deductible, *p. 522*
defined-benefit plan, *p. 536*
defined-contribution plan, *p. 537*
Employee Retirement Income Security Act (ERISA), *p. 542*
fully funded, *p. 537*
individual retirement account (IRA), *p. 543*
law of large numbers, *p. 526*
mutual insurance company, *p. 524*
named-peril policy, *p. 531*
open-peril policy, *p. 531*
overfunded, *p. 537*
Penny Benny, *p. 542*
Pension Benefit Guarantee Corporation, *p. 542*
pension plan, *p. 536*
private pension plan, *p. 537*
property insurance, *p. 530*
public pension plan, *p. 538*
reinsurance, *p. 532*
stock company, *p. 524*
underfunded, *p. 537*
underwriter, *p. 523*

QUESTIONS AND PROBLEMS

***1.** Why do people choose to buy insurance even if their expected loss is less than the payments they will make to the insurance company?

2. Why do insurance companies not allow people to buy insurance on personally unrelated risks?

***3.** What is information asymmetry, and how does it affect insurance companies?

4. Distinguish between adverse selection and moral hazard as they relate to the insurance industry.

***5.** How do insurance companies protect themselves against losses due to adverse selection and moral hazard?

6. Distinguish between independent agents and exclusive agents.

***7.** Are most insurance companies organized as mutuals or stock companies?

8. How are insurance companies able to predict their losses from claims accurately enough to let them price their policies such that they will make a profit?

***9.** What is the difference between term life insurance and whole life insurance?

10. What risk do property and casualty insurance policies protect against?

***11.** What is the purpose behind reinsurance?

12. Distinguish between defined-benefit and defined-contribution pension plans.

***13.** Why have private pension plans grown rapidly in recent years?

14. What is a pay-as-you-go pension plan?

***15.** Why is Social Security in danger of eventually going bankrupt?

WEB EXERCISES

Insurance Companies and Pension Funds

1. There are many sites on the Web to help you compute whether you are properly preparing for your retirement. One of the better is offered by Quicken. You will find it at http://www.quicken.com/retirement/planner/.

   Have you set aside enough retirement money to last your lifetime? The earlier you start, the easier it will be.

   In general, your retirement funds will come from four sources:
   - Pension plans
   - Social Security
   - Tax-deferred savings
   - Basic (taxable) savings

   Use the Retirement Planner to predict the income from the first two, and to determine how much you will need to save to make up the balance for your retirement goals.

2. An alternative to the financial goals calculation in problem 1 is sites that offer calculators that let you input figures to compute your goals. Go to http://library.thinkquest.org/10326/other_features/calc.html. Use the financial calculator provided to answer the following questions.

   Solve for the length of time and total gains in the following problems (do not input $ or ,) by plugging in each number in the following sequence:
   1. Your goals = $1,000,000; Initial capital = $1000; Monthly invested = $400; ROI = 12%.
   2. Your goals = $2,000,000; Initial capital = $1000; Monthly invested = $600; ROI = 15%.
   3. Your goals = $1,500,000; Initial capital = $10,000; Monthly invested = $0; ROI = 15%.

3. The Internet offers many calculators to help consumers estimate their needs for various financial services. When using these tools, you must remember that they are usually sponsored by financial intermediaries that hope to sell you products. Visit one such site at www.finaid.org/calculators/lifeinsuranceneeds.phtml and calculate how much life insurance you need. Are you the beneficiary of any life insurance policies? Use the calculator to see if that policy is large enough.

Chapter 20 Venture Capital Firms, Finance Companies, and Financial Conglomerates

Preview

Suppose that you are graduating from college and about to start work at that high-paying job you were offered. You may decide that your first purchase must be a car. If you are not mechanically inclined, you may opt to buy a new one. The problem, of course, is that you do not have the $20,000 needed for the purchase. A finance company may come to your rescue. Most automobile financing is provided by finance companies owned by the automobile companies.

Now suppose that you have gone to work and your first assignment is to acquire a new piece of equipment. After doing some math, you may decide that the company should lease the equipment. Again, you may find yourself dealing with another type of finance company.

Later, you are asked to see what you can do to increase your company's liquidity. You may again find that finance companies can help by purchasing your accounts receivable in a transaction called *factoring*.

Finally, you decide to develop and market a new process that you think has a great chance of being a success. However, since it is new and unproven, you cannot get funding from conventional sources. Instead you appeal to the venture capital industry for financial support.

It is clear that finance companies are an important intermediary to many segments of the economy. In this chapter we discuss the different types of finance companies and describe what they do. A specialized firm that provides start-up financing is the venture capital firm. We begin our discussion with this industry.

VENTURE CAPITAL FIRMS

Description of Industry

Venture capital is usually defined as money supplied to young, start-up firms. This money is most frequently raised by limited partnerships and invested by the general partner in firms showing promise of high returns in the future.

Since the mid 1940s venture capital firms have nurtured the growth of America's high-technology and entrepreneurial communities. Their activities have resulted in job creation, economic growth, and international competitiveness. Venture capitalists backed many of the most successful high-technology companies during the 1980s and 1990s, including Apple Computer, Cisco Systems, Genetech, Microsoft, Netscape, and Sun Microsystems. A number of service firms, such as Staples, Starbucks, and TCBY, also benefited from venture financing. Indeed, much of the growth experienced through the 1980s and 1990s can be traced back to the funding provided by the venture capital industry. Table 1 shows the explosive growth in venture capital funding witnessed during the 1990s.

Venture Capitalists Reduce Asymmetric Information

Uncertainty and information asymmetries frequently accompany start-up firms, especially in high-technology communities. Managers of these firms may engage in wasteful expenditures, such as leasing expensive office space, since the manager may benefit disproportionately from them but does not bear their entire cost. The difficulty outside investors have of tracking early-stage high-technology companies leads to other types of costs. For example, a biotechnology company founder may invest in research that brings personal acclaim but little chance for significant returns to investors. As a result of these informational asymmetries, external financing may be costly, difficult, or even impossible to obtain.

Venture capital firms can alleviate the information gap and thus allow firms to receive financing they could not obtain elsewhere. First, as opposed to bank loans or bond financing, venture capital firms hold an equity interest in the firm. The firms are usually privately held, so the stock does not trade publicly. Equity interests in privately held firms are very illiquid. As a result, venture capital invest-

Year	Number of Companies Funded	Investment Total ($millions)
1990	1317	3,376.21
1991	1088	2,511.43
1992	1294	5,177.56
1993	1151	4,962.87
1994	1191	5,351.18
1995	1327	5,608.30
1996	2004	11,277.67
1997	2696	17,207.05
1998	3155	22,576.49
1999	3956	59,163.93
2000	5458	103,848.59

TABLE 1 Venture Capital Investments Made From 1990–2000

Source: http://www.NVCA.com/ffax.html

ment horizons are long-term. The partners do not expect to earn any return for a number of years, often as long as a decade. In contrast, most investors in stocks are anxious to see annual returns through either stock appreciation or dividend payouts. They are often unwilling to wait years to see if a new idea, process, innovation, or invention will yield profits. Similarly, most investors in bonds are not going to wait years for revenues to grow to a point where interest payments become available. Venture capital financing thus fills an important niche left vacant by alternative sources of capital.

As a second method of addressing the asymmetric information problem, venture capital usually comes with strings attached, the most noteworthy being that the partners in a venture capital firm take seats on the board of directors of the financed firm. Venture capital firms are not passive investors. They actively attempt to add value to the firm through advice, assistance, and business contacts. Venture capitalists may bring together two firms that can complement each other's activities. Venture capital firms will apply their expertise to help the firm solve various financing and growth-related problems. The venture capital partners on the board of directors will carefully monitor expenditures and management to help safeguard the investment in the firm.

One of the most effective ways venture capitalists have of controlling managers is to disburse funds to the company in stages only as the firm demonstrates progress toward its ultimate goal. If development stalls or markets change, funds can be withheld to cut losses.

Implicit to venture capital financing is an expectation of high risk and large compensating returns. Venture capital firms will search very carefully among hundreds of companies to find a few that show real growth potential. Despite this exhaustive search effort, the selected firms usually have little to show initially other than a unique and promising idea. Venture capitalists mitigate the risk by developing a portfolio of young companies within a single fund. Additionally, many venture capital partnerships will manage multiple funds simultaneously. By diversifying the risk among a number of start-up firms, the risk of loss is significantly lowered.

Origins of Venture Capital

The first true venture capital firm was American Research and Development (ARD), established in 1946 by MIT president Karl Compton and local business leaders. The bulk of their success can be traced to one $70,000 investment in a new firm, the Digital Equipment Company. This seed money grew in value to $355 million over the next three decades.[1]

During the 1950s and 1960s most venture capital funding was for the development of real estate and oil fields. By the late 1960s a shift occurred toward financing technology start-ups. High technology remains the dominant area for venture capital funding. Table 2 shows the breakdown of the venture capital disbursements by industry. About 88% of venture dollars were spent on technology in 2000.

The source of venture capital funding has shifted from wealthy individuals to pension funds and corporations. In 1979, the U.S. Department of labor clarified the **prudent man rule,** which restricted pension funds from making risky investments, to explicitly allow investment in some high-risk assets. This resulted in a surge of pension fund dollars going into venture projects.

[1]Part of this discussion is based on "The Venture Capital Revolution," by Paul Gompers and Josh Lerner, *Journal of Economic Perspectives,* Number 2, Spring 2001, pages 145–168.

Industry Group	Number of Companies	Sum Invested ($millions)
Internet specific	2484	48424.85
Communications	573	17377.79
Computer software and services	979	14874.57
Semiconductors/Other electric	249	6415.24
Other products	305	5263.42
Medical/Health	341	3671.98
Biotechnology	183	2780.22
Computer hardware	149	2330.49
Consumer related	141	1617.22
Industrial/Energy	73	1337.94
Total	5477	104093.72

TABLE 2 U.S. Company Venture Capital Disbursements by Industry in 2000

Source: http://www.NVCA.com

Corporate funding of venture capital projects increased when many companies reduced their investment in their own in-house R&D in favor of outside start-up companies. If the project was successful, the company could acquire the start-up. This change was fueled by evidence that many of the best ideas from in-house centralized R&D languished unused or were commercialized in new firms started by defecting employees. Salaried employees tend not to be as motivated as entrepreneurs who stand to capture a large portion of the profits a new idea may generate. By investing in start-up firms, corporations can benefit from new discoveries while supporting the entrepreneurial spirit.

Structure of Venture Capital Firms

Most early venture capital firms were organized as closed-end mutual funds. A closed-end mutual fund sells a fixed number of shares to investors. Once all of the shares have been sold, no additional money can be raised. Instead, a new venture fund is established. The advantage of this organizational structure is that it provides the long-term money required for venture investing. Investors cannot pull money out of the investment as they could from an open-end mutual fund.

In the 1970s and 1980s venture capital firms began organizing as limited partnerships. This organizational structure is exempt from securities regulations, including the burdensome disclosure requirements of the Investment Security Act of 1940. While both organizational forms continue to be used, currently most venture capital firms are limited partnerships.

Many of the largest venture capital firms have ties to established brokerage houses. Table 3 lists the 20 largest venture capital firms in order by amount invested.

The Life of a Deal

Most venture capital deals follow a similar life cycle that begins when a limited partnership is formed and funds are raised. In the second phase, the funds are invested in start-up companies. Finally, the venture firm exits the investment.

Next, we take a more detailed look at this process.

Firm	Number of Companies	Sum Invested ($millions)
J.P. Morgan Partners (FKA: Chase Capital Partners)	220	1230.27
New Enterprise Associates	133	1045.03
Madison Dearborn Partners, LLC	21	963.03
Morgan Stanley Dean Witter Capital Partners, LLC	88	903.23
SOFTBANK Venture Capital	95	863.19
Goldman, Sachs & Co.	107	808.42
GE Equity	94	767.76
Accel Partners	87	666.97
J&W Seligman & Company	89	651.39
Sprout Group	81	638.24
Crosspoint Venture Partners	64	627.17
Oak Investment Partners	84	614.28
First Union Capital Partners	54	607.79
Norwest Venture Partners	72	593.95
J.P. Morgan Capital Corp.	44	560.62
Intel Corp.	133	556.97
Mayfield Fund	88	547.65
Columbia Capital Corporation	23	513.47
Warburg, Pincus & Co., LLC	43	508.26
BancBoston Capital/BancBoston Ventures	91	502.77

TABLE 3 Top 20 Venture Capital Firms Listed by Amount Invested in 2000

Source: http://www.NVCA.com

Fundraising A venture firm begins by soliciting commitments of capital from investors. As discussed above, these investors are typically pension funds, corporations, and wealthy individuals. Venture capital firms usually have a portfolio target amount that they attempt to raise. The average venture fund will have from just a few investors up to 100 limited partners. Because the minimum commitment is usually so high, venture capital funding is generally out of reach of most average individual investors.

Once the venture fund begins investing, it will "call" its commitments from the limited partners. These capital calls from the limited partners to the venture fund are sometimes called "takedowns" or "paid-in-capital." Venture firms typically call their capital on an as-needed basis.

The limited partners understand that investments in venture funds are long-term. It may be several years before the first investment starts to pay. In many cases, the capital may be tied up for seven to ten years. The illiquidity of the investment must be carefully considered by the potential investor.

Investing Once commitments have been received, the venture fund can begin the investment phase. Venture funds may either specialize in one or two industry segments or may generalize, looking at all available opportunities. It is not uncommon for venture funds to focus investments in a limited geographical area to make it easier to review and monitor the firms' activities.

Frequently, venture capitalists invest in a firm before it has a real product or is even clearly organized as a company. This is called "seed investing." Investing in a firm that is a little further along in its life cycle is known as "early stage investing." Finally, some funds focus on "later stage investing" by providing funds to help the company grow to a critical mass to attract public financing.

In 2000, about 56% of venture capital funds went into seed investments, 24% went into early-stage investments, and 20% went into later-stage investments.

Exiting The goal of a venture capital investment is to help nurture a firm until it can be funded with alternative capital. Venture firms hope that an exit can be made in no more than seven to ten years. Later-stage investments may take only a few years. Once an exit is made, the partners receive their share of the profits and the fund is dissolved.

There are a number of ways for a venture fund to successfully exit an investment. The most glamorous and visible is through an initial public offering. At the public stock offering, the venture firm is considered an insider and receives stock in the company, but the firm is regulated and restricted in how that stock can be sold or liquidated for several years. Once the stock is freely tradable, usually after two years, the venture fund distributes the stock to its limited partners, who may then hold the stock or sell it. Over the last 25 years, over 3000 companies financed by venture funds have had initial public offerings. There were 258 venture-backed initial public offerings in 2000 alone.

While not as visible, an equally common type of successful exit for venture investments is through mergers and acquisitions. In these cases, the venture firm receives stock or cash from the acquiring company. These proceeds are then distributed to the limited partners. There were 269 venture-backed merger and acquisition deals in 2000.

Venture Fund Profitability Venture investing is extremely high-risk. Most start-up firms do not succeed. Despite the careful monitoring and advice provided by the venture capital firm, there are innumerable hurdles that must be jumped before a new concept or idea yields profits. If venture investing is high-risk then there must also be the possibility of a high return to induce investors to continue supplying funds.

Historically, venture capital firms have been very profitable, despite their high risk. The 20-year average return is 20.3%. Seed investing is the most profitable, with a 20-year average return of 24.5% compared to about 18% for later-stage investing. The 1990s were a wonderful time to be a venture capitalist. The ten-year average return was 30%. From 1995 to 2000, the average return soared to over 50%.

In the late 1990s, venture capital returns continued to be extraordinary. For example, returns exceeded 165% in 1999. Unfortunately, as the market cooled to technology, so to did venture capital returns. By 2000, average returns were 37.5%, and in 2001, venture firms reported a first quarter loss of 8.9%. These losses are likely to extend for a number of years while venture capital firms recover from excessive investment in Web-based technology companies. Box 1 discusses possible explanations for the losses suffered by venture capital firms.

HISTORY OF FINANCE COMPANIES

The earliest examples of finance companies date back to the beginning of the 1800s when retailers offered **installment credit** to customers. With an installment credit agreement, a loan is made that requires the borrower to make a series of equal payments over some fixed length of time. Prior to installment credit agreements, loans were usually of the single-payment or balloon type. A **balloon loan**

BOX 1: E-FINANCE

Venture Capitalists Lose Focus with Internet Companies

Figure 1 shows that there was a tremendous surge in funds available for venture capitalists in the last half of the 1990s. Much of the investing focus was on the financing of dot-com companies. There are two serious ramifications that result. First, it is likely that there are only a certain number of worthy projects to finance at any one time. When too much money is chasing too few deals, firms are going to obtain financing that would be rejected at other times. As result, the average quality of venture fund portfolios falls.

A second problem caused by the surge of money into venture funds is that the ability of the partners to provide quality monitoring is reduced. Consider the case of Webvan, an Internet grocer that received more than *$1 billion* in venture financing. Even though it was backed by a group of experienced financiers, including Goldman Sachs and Sequoia Capital, its business plan was fundamentally flawed. In its short life, Webvan spent more than $1 billion building automated warehouses and pricey tech gear. This high overhead made it impossible to compete in the grocery business, where average margins are about 1%. Had the investment bankers been actively monitoring the activities of Webvan, they might have balked at developing an infrastructure that required 4000 orders per day per warehouse just to break even. Not surprisingly, Webvan declared bankruptcy in July 2001.

requires the borrower to make a single large payment at the loan's maturity to retire the debt. Installment loans appealed to consumers because they allowed them to make small payments on the loan out of current income.

Finance companies came into their own when automobile companies began mass marketing. In the early 1900s, banks did not offer car loans because cars were considered consumer purchases rather than productive assets. Many people wanted to buy cars but found it difficult to raise the purchase price. The automobile companies established subsidiaries, called *finance companies,* to provide installment loans to car buyers.

Soon many other retailers adopted the idea of providing financing for consumers who wanted to buy their goods. They found not only that sales increased but also the subsidiary finance company was profitable.

Eventually, banks recognized the value of consumer loans and began offering them too. By offering lower interest rates, banks rapidly gained the larger part of the consumer credit market. By the end of 2001, banks held $540.7 billion in consumer loans, compared to $191.1 billion by finance companies.[2]

As the proportion of credit offered by finance companies to consumers declined, the proportion offered to businesses in the form of sales and leasing increased. At the end of 2001, for example, finance companies held $540.2 billion of business loans.

PURPOSE OF FINANCE COMPANIES

Finance companies are money market intermediaries. Recall from Chapter 8 that the money markets are wholesale markets. This means that most securities that trade there have very large denominations. The minimum investment of $100,000 makes it impossible for individuals and most small companies to trade in this market. A second obstacle is that consumers and small companies lack the credit

[2]*Source: Federal Reserve Bulletin,* Table 1.55.

standing necessary to borrow in the money markets. These factors exclude consumers and small businesses from being able to take advantage of the low interest rates available on money market securities.

Finance companies allow smaller participants access to this market by selling commercial paper and using the proceeds to make loans. (In Chapter 8 we noted that finance companies were the largest sellers of commercial paper.)

The financial intermediation process of finance companies can be described by saying that they borrow in large amounts but often lend in small amounts—a process quite different from that of commercial banks, which collect deposits in small amounts and then often make large loans.

A key feature of finance companies is that although they lend to many of the same customers that borrow from banks, they are virtually unregulated compared to commercial banks and thrift institutions. States regulate the maximum amount they can loan to individual consumers and the terms of the debt contract, but there are no restrictions on branching, the assets they hold, or how they raise their funds. The lack of restrictions enables finance companies to tailor their loans to customer needs better than banking institutions can.

Finance companies exist to service both individuals and businesses. Consumer finance companies that focus on loans to individuals differ from banks in significant ways. First, consumer finance companies often accept loans with much higher risk than banks would. These high-risk customers may not have any source of loans other than the consumer finance company. Second, consumer finance companies are often wholly owned by a manufacturer who uses the company to make loans to consumers interested in purchasing the manufacturer's products. For example, all U.S. automobile companies own consumer finance companies that fund auto loans. Often these loans are made on very favorable terms to encourage product sales.

Business finance companies exist to fill financing needs not served by banks, such as lease financing. Manufacturers of business products often own finance companies for the same reasons as automobile companies: Sales can be increased if attractive financing terms are available.

RISK IN FINANCE COMPANIES

Like other financial institutions, finance companies face several types of risk. The greatest is **default risk,** the chance that customers will fail to repay their loans. As mentioned earlier, many consumer finance companies lend to borrowers who are unable to obtain credit from other sources. Naturally, these borrowers tend to default more frequently. Finance company delinquency rates are usually higher than those for banks or thrifts. Finance companies recoup the losses they suffer from bad loans by charging higher interest rates, often as much as twice that charged by banks. When economic conditions deteriorate, finance company customers are often the first to be unemployed, and defaults cause losses.

Another type of risk finance companies face is **liquidity risk.** Liquidity risk refers to problems that arise when a firm runs short of cash. For example, a bank may have a liquidity problem if many depositors withdraw their funds at once. Finance companies run the risk of liquidity problems because their assets, consumer and business loans, are not easily sold in the secondary financial markets. Thus if they are in need of cash, they must borrow. This is not difficult for larger finance companies because they have access to the money markets and can sell commercial paper, but borrowing may be more difficult for smaller firms.

Offsetting the lack of a secondary market for finance company assets is the fact that none of the firm's funds come from deposits, so unexpected withdrawals do not occur. The greater problem is that a change in the perceived risk of the finance company may make it difficult to **roll over** its short-term debt instruments. The term *roll over* means to renew the debt each time it matures.

Interest-rate risk is a major problem for banks and thrifts but not of great concern to finance companies. Recall that interest-rate risk refers to a decline in value of fixed-rate loans when market interest rates rise. Banks and thrifts hold more long-term loans than finance companies do and hence are subject to greater interest-rate risk. Finance companies can be affected by changing interest-rate levels because their assets (loans) are not as interest-rate sensitive as their liabilities (borrowings). We discuss risk management in financial institutions and in finance companies in particular in greater detail in Chapter 22.

TYPES OF FINANCE COMPANIES

Federal Reserve releases of financial companies are available at www.federalreserve.gov/Releases/G20/current/default.htm

There are three types of finance companies: business, sales, and consumer. Figure 1 shows the distribution of loans for finance companies. Business loans are the most common type. Note that loans secured by real estate can be made to both businesses and consumers but more often result when consumers obtain second mortgages on their homes. (Second mortgage loans are discussed in Chapter 11.)

Business (Commercial) Finance Companies

In the early 1900s, commercial banks were reluctant to lend money secured by a company's accounts receivable (funds owed to the company by other businesses and individuals) because the Federal Reserve discounted or bought only promissory notes that were related to productive purposes, such as financing for a factory. Not until after the Great Depression did commercial banks begin competing for loans secured by accounts receivable. By this time, finance companies were offering to make loans that were secured by equipment and inventory to businesses as well. Finance companies gained the reputation of being more innovative

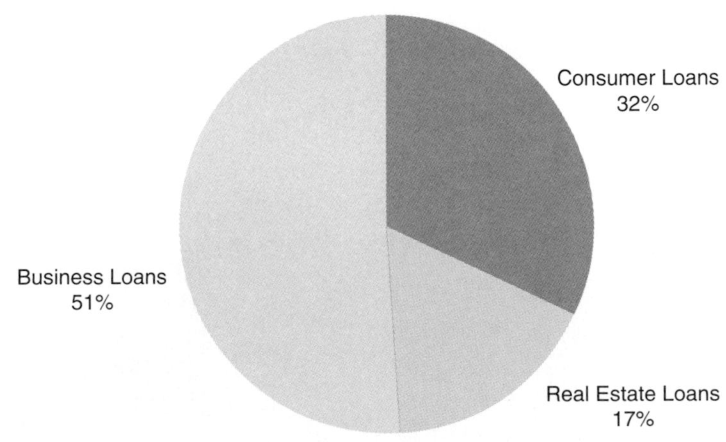

FIGURE 1 Types of Loans Made by Finance Companies, 2001

Source: Federal Reserve Bulletin, Table 1.51.

than banks at finding ways to finance small businesses. One reason they could be more flexible was their near-total absence of regulation. Because there are no depositors to protect, the government has never found the need to restrict the activities of these types of firms. Figure 2 reports the different types of business loans made by finance companies. Equipment financing is the most prevalent. Loans secured by motor vehicles, which include loans to buy autos for business use and for resale, are also common.

Factoring Business finance companies provide specialized forms of credit to businesses by making loans and purchasing accounts receivable at a discount; this provision of credit is called **factoring.** For example, a dressmaking firm might have outstanding bills (accounts receivable) of $100,000, due from the retail stores that have bought its dresses. If this firm needs cash to buy 100 new sewing machines, it can sell its accounts receivable for, say, $90,000 to a finance company, which is now entitled to collect the $100,000 owed to the firm.

Factoring is a very common practice in the apparel industry. One advantage of factoring is that the finance company (called a *factor* in this situation) usually assumes responsibility for collecting the debt. If the debt becomes uncollectable, the factor suffers the loss. This removes the need for the apparel company to have a credit department or be involved in the collection effort.

Factors usually check the credit of the firm's receivables before accepting them. The factoring arrangement works well because the factor is able to specialize in bill processing and collections and to take advantage of economies of scale. Besides the cost savings from reduced salary expenses, many firms like to use factors because they do not want their relationship with their customers spoiled by having to collect money from them.

Finance companies also provide financing of accounts receivable without taking ownership of the accounts receivable. In this case, the finance company receives documents from the business giving it the right to collect and keep the accounts receivable should the business fail to pay its debt to the finance company. Many firms prefer this arrangement over factoring because it leaves them in con-

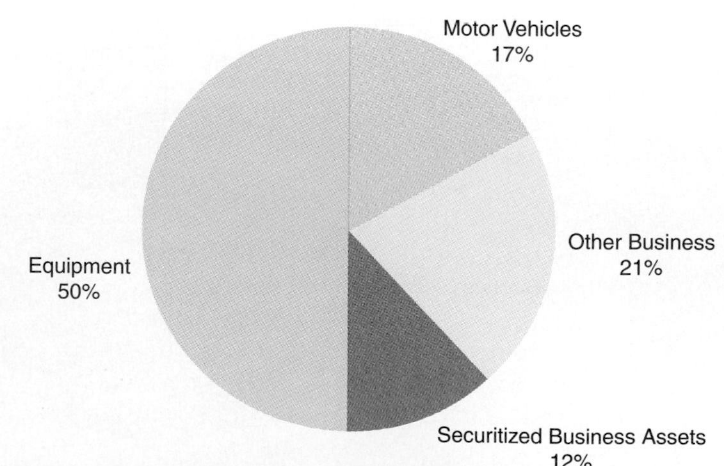

FIGURE 2 Types of Business Loans Made by Finance Companies (end of 2001)

Source: Federal Reserve Bulletin, Table 1.52.

trol of their accounts receivable. They can work with their customers if special arrangements are required to assure payment.

Leasing Business finance companies also specialize in **leasing** equipment (such as railroad cars, jet planes, and computers), which they purchase and then lease to businesses for a set number of years. Indeed, much of the growth in finance companies in recent years has come from business leasing. Under a lease, the finance company buys the asset and then leases it back to the business. One advantage of leasing is that **repossession** of the asset is easier. Repossession occurs when the finance company takes the asset back when the lessee (the firm that is leasing the asset) fails to make the payments on time. Lenders can repossess an asset under loans and lease contracts, but it is easier under a lease because the finance company already owns the asset, so no transfer of title of ownership is required.

Finance companies that are subsidiaries of equipment manufacturers have an additional advantage over banks. When a piece of equipment must be repossessed, the manufacturer is in a better position to re-lease or resell the asset.

The owner of an asset is able to depreciate the asset over time and to capture a tax savings as a result. If the firm that plans to use the asset does not have income to offset with the depreciation, the tax saving may be more valuable to the finance company. Part of this tax benefit can be passed on to the lessee in the form of lower payments than on a straight loan. In effect, the government is supporting the equipment purchase in the amount of the tax savings. This support is lost unless a firm earning income actually owns the asset.

A final advantage to leasing is that the lessee is often not required to make as large an up-front payment as is usually required on a straight loan. This conserves valuable working capital and is often the critical factor in leasing decisions.

Floor Plan Loans Some auto manufacturers require that dealers accept auto deliveries throughout the year, even though sales tend to be seasonal. To help dealers pay for their inventories of cars, finance companies began offering **floor plans.** In a floor plan arrangement, the finance company pays for the car dealership's inventory of cars received from the manufacturer and puts a lien on each car on the showroom floor. When a car is sold, the dealer must pay off the debt owed on that car before the finance company will provide a clear title of ownership. The dealer must pay the finance company interest on the floor loans until the inventory has been sold. Floor plan financing is most common in the auto industry because cars have titles that the finance company can hold to secure its loans. Floor plan financing exists in other industries where assets with titles are involved, such as construction equipment and boats.

A close relationship usually evolves between the finance company and the dealer. Consider that each sale requires correspondence between the firms. As a result of the close relationship, it is common to find that the same finance company also provides retail financing for the dealer's customers. The help that an aggressive finance company can provide by financing weak credit customers also helps the finance company's floor loans get paid.

Note that banks also provide floor plan financing; however, such loans tend to be high-maintenance. The unregulated, lower-cost structure of finance companies often makes them the preferred intermediaries.

Finance companies have enjoyed continued growth in business loans (see Figure 3). This trend is likely to continue due to the regulatory advantages such loans enjoy.

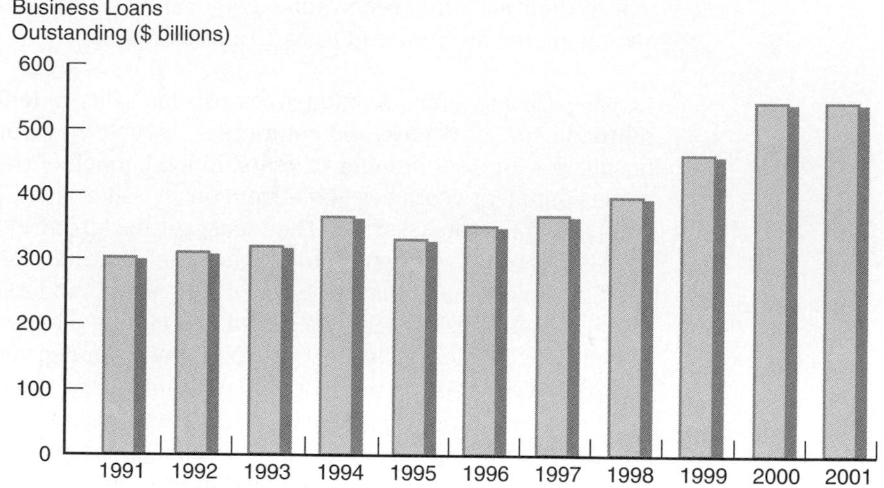

FIGURE 3 Finance Company Business Loans, 1991–2001

Source: Federal Reserve Bulletin, Table 1.52.

Consumer Finance Companies

Consumer finance companies make loans to consumers to buy particular items such as furniture or home appliances, to make home improvements, or to help refinance small debts. Consumer finance companies are separate corporations (like Household Finance Corporation) or are owned by banks (Citicorp owns Person-to-Person Finance Company, which operates offices nationwide). Typically, these companies make loans to consumers who cannot obtain credit from other sources due to low income or poor credit history. Finance companies will often accept items for security, such as old cars or old mobile homes, that would be unacceptable to banks. Because these loans are often high in both risk and maintenance, they usually carry high interest rates.

There are two exceptions: Finance companies are becoming more active in making home equity loans, loans secured by a second mortgage on the borrower's home. The Tax Reform Act of 1986 ended the ability to deduct most consumer interest from income when computing taxes. Unchanged, however, was the right to deduct interest paid on loans against a principal residence.[3] This lowers the effective interest rate by 1 minus the tax rate.

EXAMPLE 1: Consumer Finance Companies

Suppose that the interest rate on a home equity loan is 8% and that the marginal tax is 28%. What is the effective after-tax cost of the loan?

[3]Interest on loans made against a second home is also deductible.

Solution

The effective after-tax cost of the loan would be 5.76%

$$\text{Effective interest rate} = \text{interest rate} \times (1 - \text{marginal tax rate})$$

where

Interest rate = 0.08

Marginal tax rate = 0.28

Thus

$$\text{Effective interest rate} = 0.08 \times (1 - 0.28) = 0.0576 = 5.76\%$$

The reduced effective interest rates have made home equity loans very popular. Most consumers continue to obtain home equity loans through banks. However, lower-income consumers and those with poor credit histories obtain them from finance companies.

The disadvantage to home equity lending is that the lender will usually be in second position on the title. This requires the lender to pay off the first mortgage before taking ownership of the property. We discussed second mortgages in detail in Chapter 11.

Another growth area for consumer finance companies is in retail credit cards. Many retailers like to offer their customers a "private label" credit card to increase sales. Many large retailers operate their own credit card programs either in-house or through finance subsidiaries, but smaller retailers may contract with a finance company. When the retailers accept applications for credit cards, they pass them on to the finance company for approval. The finance company then sends the retailer's card to the customer. The finance company provides billing and collection services for the account. The consumer may never be aware that a finance company is involved in these transactions. Finance companies allow smaller retailers to provide a service that only larger retailers could offer otherwise.

Sales Finance Companies

Sales finance companies make loans to consumers to purchase items from a particular retailer or manufacturer. Sears, Roebuck Acceptance Corporation, for example, finances consumer purchases of all goods and services at Sears stores, and General Motors Acceptance Corporation (GMAC) finances purchases of GM cars. Sales finance companies compete directly with banks for consumer loans and are used by consumers because loans can frequently be obtained faster and more conveniently at the location where an item is purchased.

A sales finance company, also called a **captive finance company,** is owned by the manufacturer to make loans to consumers to help finance the purchase of the manufacturer's products (GMAC is the largest of these). These captive finance companies often offer interest rates below those of banks and other finance companies to increase sales. Profits made on the sale offset any losses made on the loans. Other major manufacturers also own captive finance companies (Box 2 profiles Ford Motor Credit).

BOX 2

The Expansion of Ford Motor Credit

In December 1996, Ford Motor Credit announced its intention to expand its lending operations to include subprime loans, loans to individuals with poor credit records. The lure to make these types of loans is that $100 billion is lent to people with flawed credit each year to buy new and used cars. Most of this business now goes to a number of smaller finance companies that specialize in high-risk lending, often charging very high rates to compensate for the risk. Ford Motor Credit thinks it can compete effectively for these loans.

Ford is very interested in the income generated by its finance operations. Its credit program began in 1923 when customers were permitted to pay $5 per week toward the purchase of a $265 Ford. Only when the full amount had been paid was the customer allowed to drive the car home. In 2000, credit operations had expanded to the point where Ford earned $442 million from financial services, compared to $1 billion from its automotive operations. Ford's financial service operations consists of the Ford Motor Credit Company, which is primarily an auto lender; the Associates, which is the second-biggest independent finance company in the United States; and International Businesses, which makes auto loans internationally.

Ford's entry into high-risk lending is a departure from the usual lending practices of the major automotive finance companies. Ford admits that it will be difficult to balance the need to protect its assets by repossessing cars while they can still be located against protecting Ford's reputation. The new subsidiary, to be named Fairlane Credit, hopes to identify customers who have once had problems but have recovered, such as college students who overextended on credit cards or people who unexpectedly lost their jobs but are now employed. Whereas a normal, high-credit loan is usually approved in less than an hour, Fairlane expects to spend several days evaluating its subprime customers. It hopes to be rewarded for its effort with loyal, long-term Ford customers and high profits due to the high interest rates these types of loans command.

REGULATION OF FINANCE COMPANIES

As noted, because there are no depositors to protect and no government deposit insurance is involved, finance companies are far less regulated than banks and thrifts. The exception to this is when a finance company is acting as a bank holding company or is a subsidiary of a bank holding company. (Recall from Chapter 16 that bank holding companies are firms that own the stock of one or more banking institutions.) In these cases, federal regulations are imposed. Finance companies without a direct relationship to a bank are regulated by the state.

What regulations do affect finance companies are aimed at protecting unsophisticated customers. **Regulation Z** (the "truth in lending" regulation) requires that banks and finance companies disclose the annual percentage rate charged on loans in a prominent and understandable fashion. The lender must also disclose what the total interest cost of the credit will be over the life of the loan.

Federal bankruptcy laws were revised in 1979 to increase the protection provided to consumers who declare bankruptcy. The homestead exemption in the revised law allows consumers to declare bankruptcy, thereby eliminating their debts, while still retaining ownership of many of their assets. Because many finance company customers have few assets to begin with, they lose little if they declare bankruptcy. This is a serious concern for finance companies and is one reason they usually demand adequate security before making a loan.

The level of interest rates that finance companies can charge customers is limited by **usury** statutes. Usury is charging an excessive or inordinate interest rate on a loan. The permissible interest-rate ceiling depends on the size and maturity of the loan, with small, short-term loans having the highest rates. The usury limits vary by state, but most are sufficiently high not to be a limiting factor to reputable finance companies.[4]

State and federal government regulations impose restrictions on finance companies' ability to collect on delinquent and defaulted loans. For example, many states restrict how aggressive a finance company can be when calling customers and prohibit them from calling late at night or at work. Regulations also require that certain legal procedures be followed and that the lender bear the expense of collecting on the bad debt.

In contrast to consumer lending, few regulations limit finance companies in the business loan market. Regulators feel that businesses should be financially sophisticated enough to protect themselves without government intervention.

FINANCE COMPANY BALANCE SHEET

Table 4 presents the aggregate balance sheet for finance companies.

Assets

The primary asset of finance companies is their loan portfolio, consisting of consumer, business, and real estate loans. The largest category of loans is to businesses, currently representing 36% of total assets and 51% of all loans made.

Because of the high risk of loans made to consumers, more loans default. To protect their income against these defaults, finance companies allocate a portion of income each period to an account to be used to offset losses, called the **reserve for loan losses.** The reason for having a reserve for loan losses is to smooth losses over time. By recognizing a set amount of loss each period, different losses in

Assets	Billions of dollars	Percent of Total
Consumer loans	293	22
Business loans	472	36
Real estate loans	152	12
Less reserve for loan losses	−76	−6
Other assets	475	36
Total Assets	1,316	100
Liabilities		
Bank loans	41	3
Commercial paper	178	14
Owed to parent	138	10
Debt not elsewhere	502	38
Other liabilities	300	23
Equity	157	12
Total Liabilites and Equity	1,316	100

TABLE 4 Consolidated Finance Company Balance Sheet ($ billions, 2001)

Source: Federal Reserve Bulletin, 2001, Table 1.51.

[4]Some critics of usuary laws counter that these laws do not protect consumers, but instead prevent marginal or high-risk borrowers from obtaining credit.

one period over another do not show up on the bottom line. Banks and thrifts also maintain a reserve for loan losses; however, it does not need to be as large as that for finance companies.

Liabilities

Because finance companies do not accept deposits, they must raise funds from other sources to fund their loans. An important source of funds is commercial paper (discussed in detail in Chapter 8). Recall that commercial paper is unsecured, short-term debt issued by low-risk companies. Its advantage over bank loans and other sources of funds is that it carries a low interest rate. Finance companies also obtain funds by borrowing from other money market sources and occasionally from banks (about 3% of assets). Captive finance companies have the option of borrowing directly from their parent corporation. Figure 4 shows that the use of commercial paper by finance companies has increased dramatically in recent years as this market has continued to develop.

On average, finance companies have a 12% capital-to-total-assets ratio. This is relatively strong when compared to the 9% to 10% usually observed for banks and savings and loans.

Income

Finance company income derives from several sources. The primary source, of course, is interest income from its loan portfolio. Finance companies also earn income from loan origination fees. These are fees they charge borrowers for making a loan. These fees cover the processing costs involved. Many finance companies also sell credit insurance, which pays off any balance due on a loan if the borrower should die or become disabled. Credit insurance tends to generate very high profits compared to other types of life insurance coverage. Some finance companies earn additional income from expanding their operations to include income tax preparation services.

Finance Company Growth

Finance companies grew rapidly in the late 1980s and, after a pause, the 1990s. This growth was fueled by the expansive economy, which caused the demand for finance company business loans to increase. The recession of the early 1990s caused a dip in the demand for business loans, as did the growth in assets, but growth soon resumed. Figure 5 traces the growth in finance company assets from 1979 to 2001.

FINANCIAL CONGLOMERATES

A **financial conglomerate** is a firm that owns and manages a number of different types of financial intermediaries. For example, in 1981, Sears—in addition to its ownership of consumer finance subsidiaries Allstate Insurance Company and Allstate Life Insurance Company—acquired Coldwell Banker Real Estate and Dean Witter (a brokerage firm). It also introduced its Discover card and acquired a $6 billion California-based savings bank.

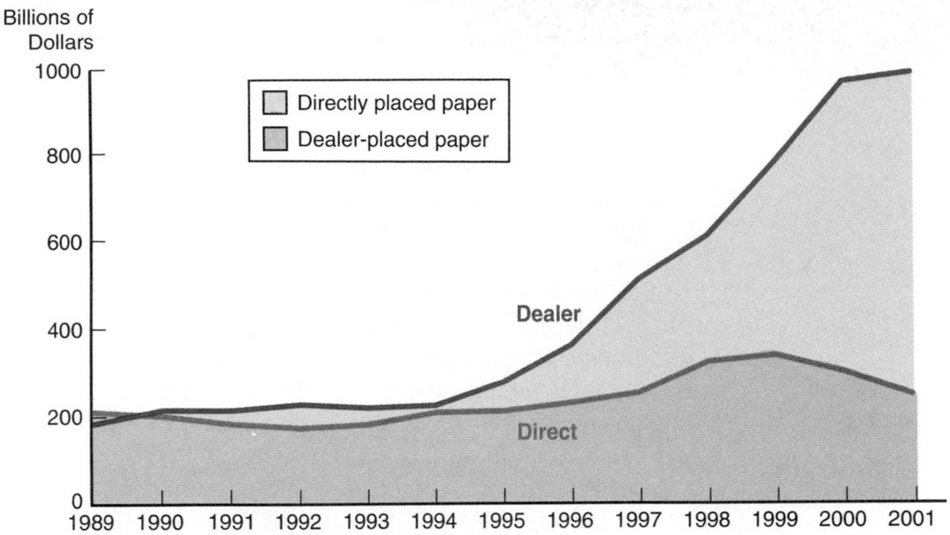

FIGURE 4 Commercial Paper Placed by Finance Companies, 1989–2001

Source: Federal Reserve Bulletin, various issues, Table 1.32.

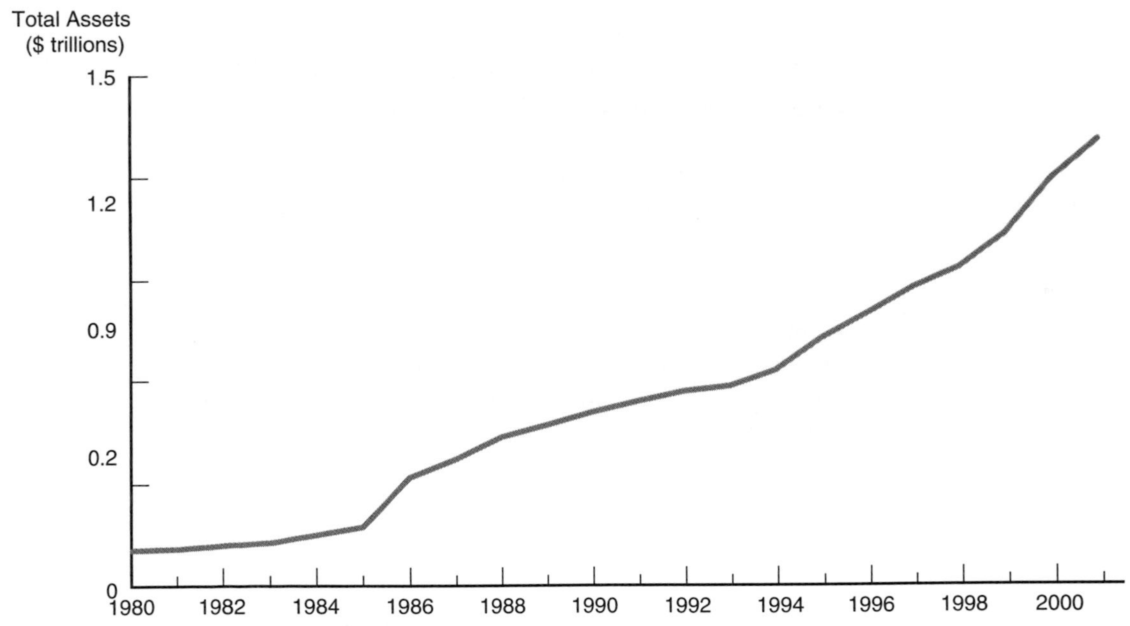

FIGURE 5 Growth of Finance Company Assets, 1980–2001

Source: www.federalreserve.gov/releases/G20/hist

Financial conglomerates began in the early 1970s when Merrill Lynch made a cash management account available to its customers. This account allowed investors to transfer money conveniently into and out of various securities. Many customers began using these accounts as substitutes for checking accounts. Securities firms have historically offered margin loans, which are used to pay a portion of the cost of security purchases. Thus by the late 1970s, we saw securities firms offering the equivalent of checking accounts, loans, and brokerage services.

Mutual fund families are another type of financial conglomerate that offer a wide variety of investment options under one corporate umbrella. For example, Vanguard offers over 50 separate investment funds, each with its own management, to meet the needs of a wide variety of consumers. We discuss securities firms more extensively in Chapter 21.

Insurance companies have also entered the financial conglomerate fray. Many of their customers were already trusting insurance agents to help them plan for retirement when they bought whole life policies (see Chapter 19 for a discussion of the different types of insurance policies offered). It was an easy step to offer additional investor services, including mutual funds, IRA accounts, Keogh account management, and lease financing. Prudential Insurance Company led the way into expansion by acquiring Bache Securities in 1981. Prudential Securities now offers a wide range of financial services.

More recently, we have seen many banks combine with security firms, such as the 1998 merger of Citicorp with Travelers Group, the parent of Travelers Insurance and Salomon Smith Barney. This megafirm, now called Citigroup, employs 160,000 people and serves 100 million customers in 100 countries. The impetus for its formation was the desire to take advantage of the synergies of a financial superstore. Analysts expect the firm to trim expenses by at least $1 billion in two years. (The Citicorp-Travelers merger is discussed in Box 3 in Chapter 16.)

By putting these businesses under one roof, the goal is to achieve economies of scale and scope. **Economies of scale** reflect the savings that can be achieved through increased size. For example, one computer system or warehouse could provide service to several different subsidiaries. Similarly, existing management could oversee operations for a number of similar firms. **Economies of scope** reflect increased business from offering many products in one easy-to-reach location. For example, a customer wanting auto insurance could also be sold a life insurance policy and shares in a mutual fund. Sears, as well as other large retailers, felt that customers would rather deal with one well-known and trusted business than with a variety of smaller firms. Xerox, for example, owned a securities business and an insurance company. Ford, Chrysler, Westinghouse, AT&T, and Kodak all established or expanded their finance company subsidiaries to compete for retail business. The various divisions of Citigroup plan to sell to each other's customers.

Though the concept of a one-stop-shopping financial conglomerate may seem reasonable, it has often not been successful. The types of businesses tackled by these conglomerates are very competitive. Consumers generally do not perceive any great benefit from dealing with a single firm for all of their financial needs and instead continue to shop for the best deals available.

By 1989, Sears recognized that in-store offices of Coldwell Banker and Dean Witter were losing money. In response, it sold off the Coldwell Banker group. In 1992, Sears announced its intent to dispose of its securities and real estate business, the Discover card, and 20% of its interest in Allstate. Other financial conglomerates are doing the same. Many of those named in this discussion have either sold or announced plans to sell all or part of their financial intermediary holdings.

On the other hand, the Citigroup merger appears to have been successful. When the merger was initially announced, the stocks of the two firms rose to a combined market value of $165 billion. By year-end, the market cap had fallen to $107 billion—a 35% drop. By 2001, the market cap had risen to $241 billion. Citigroup reported net income of $3.8 billion for 2000.

Another exception to the rule that financial conglomerates tend to fail is General Electric Capital Services. It purchased a $1 billion finance subsidiary from Eastman Kodak. It also owns Kidder Peabody, a major investment bank, and Employers Reinsurance, one of the largest property and casualty reinsurers. GEFSCO, a subsidiary, is a leading supplier of private-label credit cards to retailers as well a major servicer of home mortgages. Earnings from this conglomerate account for up to one-third of General Electric's total income.

Despite the success of General Electric Capital Services and Citigroup, the luster has apparently vanished from the conglomerate concept. Companies have learned that it is more important to be flexible than to be big and it is better to be an expert at one business than a dabbler in many. Although finance companies continue to grow and prosper, the future of financial conglomerates is not at all assured.

SUMMARY

1. Venture capital firms are intermediaries that typically invest in start-up firms with good prospects for growth. They are usually organized as limited partnerships or closed-end mutual funds. The investors are pension funds, corporations, and wealthy individuals.
2. Venture capital firms act as intermediaries to reduce asymmetric information between firm insiders and investors. They closely monitor firm management, often taking seats on the board of directors. They usually fund a firm in stages as progress is demonstrated.
3. Venture funds may invest in very new firms that have little more than a good idea to sell. These are called "seed investments." Alternatively, they may invest in firms that have made some progress or in firms that are nearly ready to go public but just need some help in getting to that level. These are called early-stage investments and later-stage investments, respectively.
4. The goal of the venture fund is to successfully exit the company once the company has matured to a point where traditional financing is available. The exit is usually made through an initial public offering or through a merger or acquisition.
5. Finance companies were initially owned by manufacturers who wanted to provide easy financing to help the sales of their products. The concept rapidly expanded when automobile financing became more commonplace.
6. Finance companies sell short-term securities in the money markets and use the proceeds to make small consumer and business loans. In this way, they act as intermediaries in the money markets. They typically borrow in large amounts and lend in small.
7. Another purpose served by consumer finance companies is servicing higher-risk customers. As a result of making these high-risk loans, default is the primary risk finance companies face. Finance companies compensate for default risk by charging higher interest rates. Finance companies also make business loans and offer leases.
8. The three types of finance companies are business, consumer, and sales. Business finance companies finance accounts receivable (often through an arrangement called factoring) and provide inventory loans and leases. Consumer finance companies make loans to high-risk customers for the purchase of autos and appliances and to refinance other debt. Sales finance companies finance a firm's sales, often through in-house credit or credit cards.
9. Because there are no deposits at risk, finance companies are less regulated than banks and thrifts. They are subject, however, to consumer regulations that limit interest rates and require disclosure of the cost of loans.
10. Financial conglomerates are firms offering a variety of financial services under one umbrella. These services may include consumer loans, credit cards, insurance, real estate sales, and brokerage services. Most of the efforts to provide a one-stop financial superstore have not fared well. Many early efforts are being dismantled.

KEY TERMS

QUESTIONS AND PROBLEMS

1. What factors distinguish venture capital financing from other types of capital market financing?

***2.** Why would a pension fund be more likely to invest in a venture capital fund than would a property and casualty insurance company?

3. Why is a start-up high-technology firm more subject to asymmetric information than a mature company?

***4.** How can venture capital firm intermediation reduce the asymmetric information problem?

5. How can a venture capital investment be exited?

***6.** What is the difference between an installment loan and a balloon loan?

7. What caused finance companies to grow rapidly in the early 1900s?

***8.** Who are the typical customers of consumer finance companies, and why do they not go to commercial banks, where interest rates are lower?

9. How do consumer finance companies maintain their income in the face of high default rates on their loans?

***10.** Do finance companies face liquidity risk? Why?

11. Do finance companies face interest-rate risk? Why?

***12.** What is factoring?

13. What is the advantage of leasing assets to the lessor? To the lessee?

***14.** Many auto dealers finance their inventory using floor plan loans advanced by finance companies. What is a floor plan loan?

15. Many manufacturers own finance companies that finance the purchase of the manufacturers' products. What are these finance companies called?

***16.** Why are home equity loans popular?

17. Why are finance companies so concerned that their customers may file bankruptcy?

***18.** What does Regulation Z require of finance companies?

19. What types of statutes limit the interest rates that finance companies can charge their customers?

***20.** Have financial conglomerates been successful at providing one-stop shopping for financial services?

WEB EXERCISES

Venture Capital Firms Finance Companies and Financial Conglomerates

1. Initial Public Offerings (IPOs) are where securities are sold to the public for the very first time. Go to http://ipo.com. This site lists various statistics regarding the IPO market.
   a. What is the largest IPO year-to-date ranked by amount raised?
   b. What is the next IPO to be offered to the public?
   c. How many IPOs were priced this year?

2. The Federal Reserve maintains extensive data on finance companies. Go to http://www.federalreserve.gov/releases and scroll down until you find G.20 Finance Companies. Click on "Releases" and find the current release.
   a. Review the terms of credit for new car loans. What is the most recent average interest rate, and what is the term to maturity? How much is the average new car loan offered by finance companies?
   b. Do finance companies make more consumer loans, real estate loans, or business loans?
   c. Which type of loan has grown most rapidly over the last five years?

Chapter 21

Investment Banks, Brokerage Firms, and Mutual Funds

Preview

If you decide to take advantage of that hot stock tip you just heard about from your roommate or if you want to earn more than 1.5% on funds you have on deposit at your bank, you will need to interact with one of many securities companies. Similarly, as the new CFO of WWCF, a candy manufacturer, you may need a securities company if you are asked to coordinate a bond sale or to issue additional stock. If your grandfather decides to sell his firm to the public, you may need to help him by working with investment bankers at that securities company. Finally, if you are looking for a high-paying job, your next stop may be a securities firm.

The smooth functioning of securities markets, in which bonds and stocks are traded, involves several financial institutions, including securities brokers and dealers, investment banks, and organized exchanges. None of these institutions were included in our list of financial intermediaries in Chapter 12 because they do not perform the intermediation function of acquiring funds by issuing liabilities and then using the funds to acquire financial assets. Nonetheless, they are important in the process of channeling funds from savers to spenders.

To begin our look at how securities markets work, recall the distinction between primary and secondary securities markets discussed in Chapter 2. In a **primary market,** new issues of a security are sold to buyers by the corporation or government agency ultimately using the funds. A **secondary market** then trades the securities that have been sold in the primary market (and so are secondhand). Investment banks assist in the initial sale of securities in the primary market; securities brokers and dealers assist in the trading of securities in the secondary markets, some of which are organized into exchanges.

INVESTMENT BANKS

Investment bankers were called "Masters of the Universe" in Tom Wolfe's *The Bonfire of the Vanities.* They are the elite on Wall Street. They have earned this reputation from the types of financial services they provide. Investment banks are best known as intermediaries that help corporations raise funds. However, this definition is far too narrow to accurately explain the many valuable and sophisticated services these companies provide. (Despite its name, an investment bank is not a bank in the ordinary sense; that is, it is not a financial intermediary that takes in deposits and then lends them out.). In addition to underwriting the initial sale of stocks and bonds, **investment banks** also play a pivotal role as deal makers in the mergers and acquisitions area, as intemediaries in the buying and selling of companies, and as private brokers to the very wealthy. Some well-known investment banking firms are Morgan Stanley, Merrill Lynch, Salomon Brothers, First Boston Corporation, and Goldman, Sachs.

One feature of investment banks that distinguishes them from stockbrokers and dealers is that they usually earn their income from fees charged to clients rather than from commissions on stock trades. These fees are often set as a fixed percentage of the dollar size of the deal being worked. Because the deals frequently involve huge sums of money, the fees can be substantial. The percentage fee will be smaller for large deals, in the neighborhood of 3%, and much larger for smaller deals, sometimes exceeding 10%.

Background

In the early 1800s, most American securities had to be sold in Europe. As a result, most securities firms developed from merchants who operated a securities business as a sideline to their primary business. For example, the Morgans built their initial fortune with the railroads. To help raise the money to finance railroad expansion, J. P. Morgan's father resided in London and sold Morgan railroad securities to European investors. Over time, the profitability of the securities businesses became evident and the securities industry expanded.

Prior to the Great Depression, many large, money center banks in New York sold securities and simultaneously conducted conventional banking activities. During the Depression about 10,000 banks failed (about 40 percent of all commercial banks). This led to the passage of the **Glass-Steagall Act,** which separated commercial banking from investment banking.

The Glass-Steagall Act made it illegal for a commercial bank to buy or sell securities on behalf of its customers. The original reasoning behind this legislation was to insulate commercial banks from the greater risk inherent in the securities business. There were also concerns that conflicts of interest might arise that would subject commercial banks to increased risk. For example, suppose that an investment banker working at a commercial bank makes a mistake pricing a new stock offering. After promising the customer that he can sell the stock for $20, no sales materialize. The investment banker might be tempted to go down the hall to the commercial bank's investment department and talk them into bailing him out. This would subject depositors to the risk that the bank could lose money on poor investments.

Regulators thought another problem existed. Suppose the investment banker still cannot sell all of that $20 stock issue. He could call up bank customers and offer to loan them 100% of the funds needed to buy a portion of the stock issue.

This would not cause a problem if the stock price rose in the future, but if it fell, the value of the securities would be less than the amount of the loan and the customer might not feel a great obligation to repay the loan. Many industry observers felt that this practice was partially to blame for some of the bank failures that occurred during the Depression. However, bank lobbyists currently argue that although only large banks were involved in issuing securities, most banks that actually failed were small. There is no evidence that security abuses led directly to any bank failures.

When the Glass-Steagall Act separated commercial banking from investment banking, new securities firms were created, many of which currently offer both investment banking services (selling new securities to the public) as well as brokerage services (selling existing securities to the public).

The legal barriers between commercial and investment banks have been decaying rapidly since the 1980s. One significant trend has been the acquisition of investment banks by commercial banks. For example, in 1997, Bankers Trust acquired Alex Brown, the oldest investment bank in the nation. Bankers Trust was subsequently acquired by Deutsche Banks, which has been spending enormous amounts of money establishing its own investment banking arm. Bank of America bought Roberson Stephens & Co., while NationsBank acquired Montgomery Securities. Subsequent mergers among banks are continuing the consolidation.

Underwriting Stocks and Bonds

When a corporation wants to borrow or raise funds, it may decide to issue long-term debt or equity instruments. It then usually hires an investment bank to facilitate the issuance and subsequent sale of the securities. The investment bank may underwrite the issue. The process of underwriting a stock or bond issue requires that the securities firm *purchase* the entire issue at a predetermined price and then resell it in the market. There are a number of services provided in the process of underwriting.

Giving Advice Most firms do not issue capital market securities very frequently. Over 80% of all corporate expansion is financed using profits retained from prior-period earnings. As a result, the financial managers at most firms are not familiar with how to proceed with a new security offering. Investment bankers, since they participate in this market daily, can provide advice to firms contemplating a sale. For instance, a firm may not know if it should raise capital by selling stocks or by selling bonds. The investment bankers may be able to help by pointing out, for example, that the market is currently paying high prices for stocks in the firm's industry (historically high PE ratios), while bonds are currently carrying relatively high interest rates (and therefore low prices).

Firms may also need advice as to *when* securities should be offered. If, for example, competitors have recently released earnings reports that show poor profits, it may be better to wait before attempting a sale: Firms want to time the market to sell stock when it will obtain the highest possible price. Again, because of daily interaction with the securities markets, investment bankers should be able to advise firms on the timing of their offerings.

Possibly the most difficult advice an investment banker must give a customer concerns at what *price* the security should be sold. Here the investment banker and the issuing firm have somewhat differing motives. First, consider that the firm wants to sell the stock for the highest price possible. Suppose you started a firm and ran it well for 20 years. You now wish to sell it to the public and retire to Tahiti. If 500,000 shares are to be offered and sold at $10 each, you will receive $5 million for your company. If you can sell the stock for $12, you will receive $6 million.

Investment bankers, however, do not want to overprice the stock because in most underwriting agreements, they will buy the entire issue at the agreed price and then resell it through their brokerage houses. They earn a profit by selling the stock at a slightly higher price than they paid the issuing firm. If the issue is priced too high, the investment bank will not be able to resell, and it will suffer a loss.

Pricing securities is not too hard if the firm has prior issues currently selling in the market, called **seasoned issues.** When a firm issues stock for the first time, called an **initial public offering (IPO),** it is much more difficult to determine what the correct price should be. All of the skill and expertise of the investment banking firm will be used to determine the most appropriate price. If the issuing firm and the investment banking firm can come to agreement on a price, the investment banker can assist with the next stage, filing the required documents.

Filing Documents In addition to advising companies, investment bankers will assist with making the required **Securities and Exchange Commission (SEC)** filings. The activities of investment banks and the operation of primary markets are heavily regulated by the SEC, which was created by the Securities and Exchange Acts of 1933 and 1934 to ensure that adequate information reaches prospective investors. Issuers of new securities to the general public (for amounts greater than $1.5 million in a year and with a maturity longer than 270 days) must file a **registration statement** with the SEC. This statement contains information about the firm's financial condition, management, competition, industry, and experience. The firm also discloses what the funds will be used for and management's assessment of the risk of the securities. The issuer must then wait 20 days after the registration statement is filed with the SEC before it can sell any of the securities. The SEC will review the registration statement, and if it does not object during a 20-day waiting period, the securities can then be sold.

The SEC review in no way represents an endorsement of the offering by the SEC. Their approval merely means that all of the required statements and disclosures are included in the statement. Nor does SEC approval mean that the information is accurate. Inaccuracies in the registration statement open the issuing firm's management up to lawsuits if it incurs losses. In extreme cases, inaccuracies could result in criminal charges.

A portion of the registration statement is reproduced and made available to investors for review. This widely circulated document is called a **prospectus** (see Figure 1). By law, investors must be given a prospectus before they can invest in a new security.

While the registration document is in the process of being approved, the investment banker has other chores to attend to. For issues of debt, the investment banker must:

- Secure a credit rating from one or more of the credit review companies, such as Standard and Poor's or Moody's.
- Hire a bond counsel who will issue a statement attesting to the legality of the issue.
- Select a trustee who is responsible for seeing that the issuer fulfills its obligations as stated in the security's contract.
- Have the securities printed and prepared for distribution.

PROSPECTUS

3,750,000 Shares

The E-Business and Internet Technology Network

Common Stock

internet.com Corporation is selling 1,750,000 shares of common stock. Penton Media, Inc., one of our stockholders, is selling 2,000,000 shares of common stock. We will not receive any proceeds from the sale of shares by Penton Media. Our common stock is traded on the Nasdaq National Market under the symbol "INTM." On January 26, 2000 the last reported sales price for our common stock on the Nasdaq National Market was $63.00 per share.

	Per Share	Total
Public offering price	$ 60.00	$225,000,000
Underwriting discounts	$ 3.45	$ 12,937,500
Proceeds to internet.com Corporation before expenses	$ 56.55	$ 98,962,500
Proceeds to selling stockholder	$ 56.55	$113,100,000

The selling stockholder has granted the underwriters an option for a period of 30 days to purchase up to 562,500 additional shares of common stock.

Investing in our common stock involves a high degree of risk.
See "Risk Factors" beginning on page 5.

Neither the Securities and Exchange Commission nor any state securities commission has approved these securities or passed upon the adequacy or accuracy of this prospectus. Any representation to the contrary is a criminal offense.

CHASE H&Q **ROBERTSON STEPHENS**

U.S. BANCORP PIPER JAFFRAY

WILLIAM BLAIR & COMPANY

January 27, 2000

FIGURE 1 Front Page of a Prospectus

For equity issues, the investment banker may arrange for the securities to appear on one of the stock exchanges. Clearly, the investment banker can be of great assistance to an issuer well before any securities are actually offered for sale.

Underwriting Once all of the paperwork has been completed, the investment banker can proceed with the actual underwriting of the issue. At a prespecified time and date, the issuer will sell all of the stock or bond issue to the investment banking firm at the agreed price. The investment banker must now distribute this issue to the public at a greater price to earn its fee. (The ten largest underwriters in the United States are listed in Table 1.)

By agreeing to underwrite an issue, the investment banking firm is certifying the qualify of the issue to the public. We again see how asymmetric information helps justify the need for an intermediary. Investors do not want to put in weeks and weeks of hard technical study of a firm before buying its stock. Nor can they trust the firm's insiders to accurately report its condition. Instead, they rely on the ability of the investment bank to collect information about the firm in order to accurately establish the firm's value. They trust the investment bank's assessment, since it is backing up its opinion by actually purchasing securities in the process of underwriting them. Investment bankers recognize the responsibility they have to report information accurately and honestly, since once they lose investors' confidence, they will no longer be able to market their deals.

The investment banking firm is clearly taking a huge risk at this point. One way that they can reduce the risk is by forming a **syndicate.** A syndicate is a group of investment banking firms each of which buys a portion of the security issue. Each firm in the syndicate is then responsible for reselling its share of the securities. Most securities issues are sold by syndicates because it is such an effective way to spread the risk among many different firms.

Investment banks advertise upcoming securities offerings with ads in the *Wall Street Journal.* The traditional advertisement is a large block ad in the financial section of the paper. These ads are called **tombstones** because of their shape and they list all of the investment banking firms included in the syndicate. Review the tombstone reproduced in the Following the Financial News box. Notice the prominent statement that this "is neither an offer to sell nor a solicitation, but only an announcement." The actual offer to sell can only be made in the prospectus. Also note the number of different investment banking firms involved in the syndicate.

TABLE 1 Top Ten Underwriters of U.S. Debt and Equity Issues, 2001

Underwriter	Market Share (%)
1. Citigroup/Salomon Smith Barney	12.0
2. Merrill Lynch	10.6
3. Credit Suisse First Boston	8.5
4. J.P. Morgan Chase	7.7
5. Goldman Sachs	7.4
6. Morgan Stanley	6.8
7. Lehman Brothers	6.4
8. UBS Warburg	6.2
9. Deutsche Bank	5.5
10. Banc of America Securities	4.0
Total for top ten	75.1

Source: Wall Street Journal, January 2, 2002, p. R19.

FOLLOWING THE FINANCIAL NEWS

New Securities Issues

Information about new securities being issued is presented in distinctive advertisements published in the *Wall Street Journal* and other newspapers. These advertisements, called "tombstones" because of their appearance, are typically found in the "Money and Investing" section of the *Journal.*

The tombstone shown here indicates the number of shares of stock being issued (2,300,000 shares for WPS Resources Corporation) and the investment banks involved in selling them.

This announcement is neither an offer to sell nor a solicitation of offers to buy any of these securities. The offering is made only by the Prospectus Supplement and the related Prospectus.

New Issue

December 19, 2001

2,300,000 Shares

WPS Resources Corporation

Common Stock

Price $34.36 Per Share

Copies of the Prospectus Supplement and the related Prospectus may be obtained from such of the undersigned and other dealers or brokers as may lawfully offer these securities in such State.

A.G. Edwards & Sons, Inc.

Robert W. Baird & Co.

Edward D. Jones & Co., L.P.

Legg Mason Wood Walker
Incorporated

Source: Wall Street Journal, December 20, 2001 p. C5.

The longer the investment banker holds the securities before reselling them to the public, the greater the risk that a negative price change will cause losses. One way that the investment banking firm speeds the sale is to solicit offers to buy the securities from investors prior to the date the investment bankers actually take ownership. Then, when the securities are available, the orders are filled and the securities are quickly transferred to the final buyers.

Most investment bankers are attached to larger brokerage houses (multifunction securities firms) that have nationwide sales offices. Each of these offices will be contacted prior to the issue date, and the sales agents will contact their customers to see if they would like to review a prospectus on the new security. The goal is to **fully subscribe** the issue. A fully subscribed issue is one where all of the securities available for sale have been spoken for before the issue date. Security issues may also be **undersubscribed.** In this case, the sales agents have been unable to generate sufficient interest in the security among their customers to sell all of the securities by the issue date. An issue may also be **oversubscribed,** in which case there are more offers to buy than there are securities available.

It is tempting to assume that the best alternative is for an issue to be oversubscribed, but in fact this will alienate the investment banker's customers. Suppose you were issuing a security for the first time and had negotiated with your investment banker to sell the issue of 500 thousand shares of stock at $20. Now you find out that the issue is oversubscribed. You would feel that the investment banker had set the price too low and that you had lost money as a result. Maybe the stock could have sold for $25 and you could have collected an extra $2.5 million ($25 – $20 × 500,000 = $2,500,000). You, as well as other issuing firms, would be unlikely to use this investment banker in the future.

It is equally serious for an issue to be undersubscribed, since it may be necessary to lower the price below the price the investment bankers paid to the issuer in order to sell all of the securities to the public. The investment banking firm stands to lose extremely large amounts of money because of the volume of securities involved. For example, review the tombstone shown in the Following the Financial News box once more. There are 2.3 million shares being offered for sale. If the price must be lowered by even $.25 per share, $575,000 would be lost. The high risk taken by investment bankers explains why they tend to be the most elite and highest paid professionals on Wall Street, many earning in the millions of dollars per year.

Best Efforts An alternative to underwriting a securities offering is to offer the securities under a *best efforts agreement*. In a best efforts agreement the investment banker sells the securities on a commission basis with no guarantee regarding the price the issuing firm will receive. The advantage to the investment banker of a best efforts transaction is that there is no risk of mispricing the security. There is also no need for the time-consuming task of establishing the market value of the security. The investment banker simply markets the security at the price the customer asks. If the security fails to sell, the offering can be canceled.

Private Placements An alternative method of selling securities is called the *private placement.* In a private placement, securities are sold to a limited number of investors rather than to the public as a whole. The advantage of the private placement is that the security does not need to be registered with the SEC as long as certain restrictive requirements are satisfied. Investment bankers are also often involved in private placement transactions. While investment bankers are not required for a private placement, they often facilitate the transaction by advising the issuing firm on the appropriate terms for the issue and by identifying potential purchasers.

The buyers of private placements must be large enough to purchase large amounts of securities at one time. This means that the usual buyers are insurance companies, commercial banks, pension funds, and mutual funds. Private placements are more common for the sale of bonds than for stocks. Goldman Sachs is the most active investment banking firm in the private placement market.

The process of taking a security public is summarized in Figure 2.

Equity Sales

Another service offered by investment banks is to help with the sale of companies or corporate divisions. For example, in 1984, Mattel was dangerously close to having its bank loans called when its electronics subsidiary incurred significant losses. Mattel enlisted the help of the investment banking firm Drexel Burnham Lambert. The first step in the firm's restructuring was to sell of all of its nontoy businesses. Mattel returned to health until it again ran into problems in 1999 due to the acquisition of a software company. In 2000, Mattel again used the services of investment bankers to sell this subsidiary.

The first step in any equity sale will be the seller's determination of the business's worth. The investment banker will provide a detailed analysis of the current market for similar companies and apply various sophisticated models to establish company value. Unlike a box of detergent or bar of candy, a going concern has no set price. The company value is based on the use the buyer intends to make of it. If a buyer is only interested in the physical assets, the firm will be worth one amount. A buyer who sees the firm as an opportunity to take advantage of synergies between this firm and another will have a very different price. Despite the elasticity of the yardstick, investment bankers have developed a number of tools to give business owners a range of values for their firms.

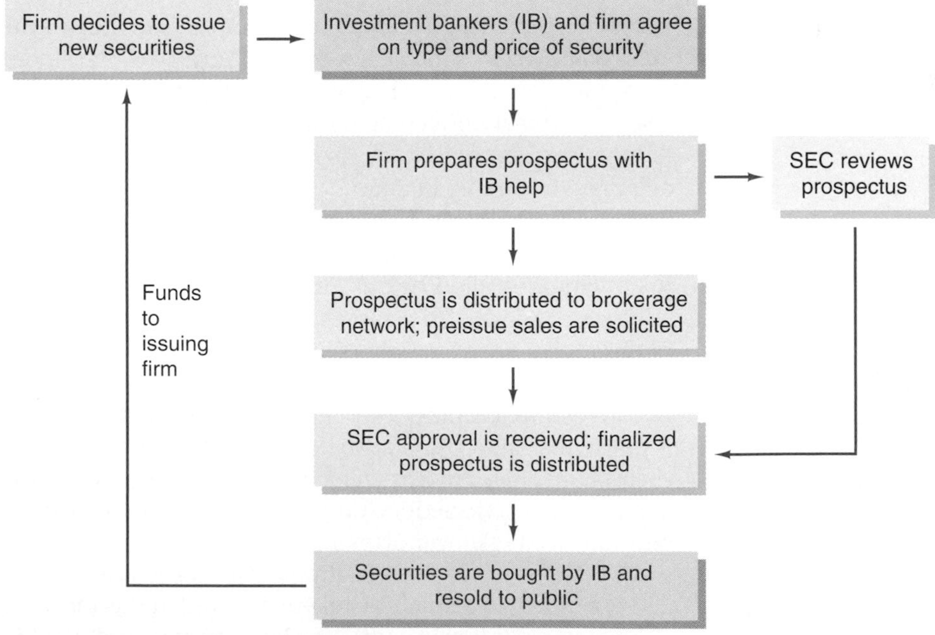

FIGURE 2 Using Investment Bankers to Distribute Securities to the Public

How much cash flows will have to be discounted depends very much on who will be bidding on the firm. Again, investment bankers help. They may make discreet inquiries to feel out who in the market may be interested. Additionally, they will prepare a **confidential memorandum** that presents the detailed financial information required by prospective buyers to make an offer for the company. All prospective buyers must sign a confidentiality agreement stipulating that they will not use the information to compete or share it with third parties. The investment bank will screen prospects to ensure that the information goes only to qualified buyers.

The next step in an equity sale will be the **letter of intent** issued by a prospective buyer. This document signals a desire to go forward with a purchase and outlines preliminary terms. The investment banker will negotiate the terms of the sale on the seller's behalf and will help to analyze and rank competing offers. The investment banker may even help structure financing in order to obtain a better offer.

Once the letter of intent has been accepted by the seller, the **due diligence** period begins. This 20- to 40-day period is used by the buyer to verify the accuracy of the information contained in the confidential memorandum. The findings shape the terms of the **definitive agreement.** This agreement converts information gathered during the due diligence period and the results of subsequent negotiations into a legally binding contract.

As this discussion demonstrates, a wide variety of skills are required to move a typical corporate sale forward. To meet these needs, investment banks often send in multidisciplined teams of experts to work with clients on their projects. These teams include attorneys, financial analysts, accountants, and industry experts.

Mergers and Acquisitions

Investment banks have been active in the **mergers and acquisitions** market since the 1960s. A merger occurs where two firms combine to form one new company. Both firms support the merger, and corporate officers are usually selected so that both companies contribute to the new management team. Stockholders turn in their stock for stock in the new firm. In an acquisition, one firm acquires ownership of another by buying its stock. Often this process is friendly, and the firms agree that certain economies can be captured by combining resources. At other times, the firm being purchased may resist. Resisted takeovers are called *hostile.* In these cases, the acquirer attempts to purchase sufficient shares of the target firm to gain a majority of the seats on the board of directors. Board members are then able to vote to merge the target firm with the acquiring firm.

Investment bankers serve both acquirers and target firms. Acquiring firms require help in locating attractive firms to pursue, soliciting shareholders to sell their shares in a process called a *tender offer* and raising the required capital to complete the transaction. Target firms may hire investment bankers to help ward off undesired takeover attempts.

The mergers and acquisitions markets requires very specialized knowledge and expertise. Investment bankers involved in this market are highly trained (and, not incidentally, highly paid). The best known investment banker involved in mergers and acquisitions was Michael R. Milken who worked at Drexel Burnham Lambert, Inc. Milken is credited with inventing the junk bond market which we discussed in Chapter 9. *Junk bonds* are high-risk, high-return debt securities that were used primarily to finance takeover attempts. By allowing companies to raise large amounts of capital, even small firms could pursue and take over large ones. During the 1980s, when Milken was most active in this market, merger and acquisition activity peaked. On February 13, 1990, Drexel Burnham Lambert filed for bankruptcy due to rising default rates on its portfolio of junk bonds, a slow economy, and regulations that forced the savings and loan industry out of the junk bond market. Milken pled guilty to securities fraud and was sent to prison.

As a result of the collapse of Drexel and the junk bond market, merger and acquisitions activity slowed during the early 1990s. A healthy economy and regulatory changes caused a resurgence, especially among commercial banks, in the mid and late 1990s. Mergers and acquisitions again slowed during the recession in 2001.

SECURITIES BROKERS AND DEALERS

Securities brokers and dealers conduct trading in secondary markets. *Brokers* are pure middlemen who act as agents for investors in the purchase or sale of securities. Their function is to match buyers with sellers, a function for which they are paid brokerage commissions.

In contrast to brokers, dealers link buyers and sellers by standing ready to buy and sell securities at given prices. Therefore, dealers hold inventories of securities and make their living by selling these securities for a slightly higher price than they paid for them—that is, on the *spread* between the *bid price,* the price that the broker pays for securities they buy for their inventory, and the *ask price,* the price they receive when they sell the securities. This is a high-risk business because dealers hold securities that can rise or fall in price; in recent years, several firms specializing in bonds have collapsed. Brokers, by contrast, are not as exposed to risk because they do not own the securities involved in their business dealings.[1]

Brokerage Services

Securities brokers offer several types of services.

Securities Orders If you call a securities brokerage house to buy a stock, you will speak with a broker who will take your order. You have three primary types of transactions available: market orders, limit orders, and short sells.

The two most common types of securities orders are the market order and the limit order. When you place a **market order,** you are instructing your agent to buy or sell the security at the current market price. When placing a market order, there is a risk that the price of the security may have changed significantly from what it was when you made your investment decision. If you are buying a stock and the price falls, no harm is done, but if the price goes up, you may regret your decision. The most notable occasion when prices changed between when orders were placed and when they were filled was during the October 19, 1987, stock crash. Panicked investors told their brokers to sell their stocks, but the transaction

[1]It is easy to remember the distinction between dealers and brokers if you relate to auto dealers and real estate brokers. Auto *dealers* take ownership of the cars and resell them to the public. Real estate *brokers* do not take ownership of the property; they just act as go-betweens.

volume was so great that day that many orders were not filled until hours after they were placed. By the time they were filled, the price of the stocks had often fallen far below what they were at the time the original orders were placed.

An alternative to the market order is the **limit order.** Here buy orders specify a *maximum* acceptable price and sell orders specify a *minimum* acceptable price. For example, you could place a limit order to sell your 100 shares of IBM at $100. If the current market price of IBM is less than $100, the order will not be filled. Unfilled limit orders are reported to the stock specialist who works that particular stock on the exchange. When the stock price moves in such a way that limit orders are activated, the stock specialist initiates the trade.

When investors believe that the price of a stock will rise in the future, they buy that stock and hold it until the increase occurs. They can then sell at a profit and capture a gain for their effort. What can be done if an investor is convinced that a stock will *fall* in the future? The solution is to sell short. A **short sell** requires that the investor borrow stocks from a brokerage house and sell them today, with the promise of replacing the borrowed stocks by buying them in the future. Suppose that you just tried out the new Apple notebook computer and decided that it would sell poorly (in fact, in 1995, Apple had to recall all of its Powerbook computers to fix problems). You might believe that as the rest of the market learned of the poor product, the price of Apple's stock could decline. To take advantage of this situation, you might instruct your broker to short Apple 100 shares. The broker would then borrow 100 shares from another investor on your behalf and sell them at current market prices. You do not own those shares, of course. They are borrowed and at some point in the future, you would be required to purchase those 100 shares at the new market price to replace them. If you were right and the price of Apple declined, you would buy the shares at a lower price than you received for their earlier sale and would earn a profit. Of course, if you are wrong and the price rises, you will suffer a loss.

Market and limit orders allow you to take advantage of stock price *increases,* and short sells allow you to take advantage of stock price *decreases.* Analysts track the number of short positions taken on a stock as an indicator of the number of investors who feel that a stock's price is likely to fall in the future. Box 1 presents an example of how a stock specialist responds to various types of orders.

Other Services In addition to trading in securities, stockbrokers provide a variety of other services. Investors typically leave their securities in storage with the broker for safekeeping. If the securities are left with the broker, they are insured against loss by the Securities Investor Protection Corporation (SIPC), an agency of the federal government. This guarantee is not against loss in value, only against loss of the securities themselves.

Brokers also provide **margin credit.** Margin credit refers to loans advanced by the brokerage house to help investors buy securities. For example, if you are certain that Intel Corporation stock is going to rise rapidly when its latest computer chip is introduced, you could increase the amount of stock you can buy by borrowing from the brokerage house. If you had $5000 and borrowed an additional $5000, you could buy $10,000 worth of stock. Then if the price goes up as you predict, you could earn nearly twice as much as without the loan. The Federal Reserve sets the percentage of the stock purchase price that brokerage houses can lend. Interest rates on margin loans are usually 1 or 2 percentage points above the prime interest rate (the rate charged large, creditworthy corporate borrowers).

BOX 1

Using the Limit-Order Book

Suppose that a trader on the New York Stock Exchange is a specialist responsible for Circuit City stock. The limit-order book might look like the following:

Unfilled Circuit City Limit Orders

Buy Orders		Sell Orders	
37	100		
37 1/8	300		
37 1/4	100		
		37 3/8	200
		37 1/2	500
		37 5/8	100

Listed under "Buy Orders" are the highest prices investors are willing to pay to buy the stock. Listed under "Sell Orders" are the lowest prices investors holding Circuit City stock are willing to accept to sell. Currently, no transactions occur because there are no crossover or common prices. In other words, no one is currently willing to sell Circuit City stock at a price anyone is willing to pay.

Now suppose that the specialist receives a new 200-share market order to buy, an order to be filled at the best market price currently available. The specialist consults the "Sell Orders" column and fills the order at 37 3/8.

Next the specialist receives a 300-share limit order to sell at 37 1/8. Again, the specialist consults the book but this time looks in the "Buy Orders" column. The limit order is filled with 100 shares at 37 1/4 and 200 shares at 37 1/8.

Next suppose that a limit order to buy 500 shares at 36 7/8 is received. Because there is no sell order for this amount, the order is added to the book, which now looks like this:

Unfilled Circuit City Limit Orders

Buy Orders		Sell Orders	
36 7/8	500		
37	100		
37 1/8	100		
		37 1/2	500
		37 5/8	100

As noted in Chapter 16, the forces of competition have led brokerage firms to offer services and engage in activities traditionally conducted by commercial banks. In 1977, Merrill Lynch developed the cash management account (CMA), which provides a package of financial services that includes credit cards, immediate loans, check-writing privileges, automatic investment of proceeds from the sale of securities in a money market mutual fund, and unified record keeping. CMAs were adopted by other brokerage firms and spread rapidly. Many of these accounts allow check-writing privileges and offer ATM and debit cards. In these ways, they compete directly with banks.

As a result of CMAs, the distinction between banking activities and the activities of nonbank financial institutions has become blurred. Walter Wriston, former head of Citicorp (the largest bank holding company in the country), has been quoted as saying, "The bank of the future already exists, and it's called Merrill Lynch."[2]

The advantage of brokerage-based cash management accounts is that they make it easier to buy and sell securities. The stockbroker can take funds out of the account when an investor buys a security and put the money into the account when the investor sells securities.

Full-Service Versus Discount Brokers Prior to May 1, 1975, virtually all brokerage houses charged the same commissions on trades. Brokerage houses distinguished

[2]"Banking Takes a Beating," *Time,* December 3, 1984, p. 50.

themselves primarily on the basis of their research and customer relations. In May 1975, Congress determined that fixed commissions were anticompetitive and passed the Securities Acts Amendment of 1975, which abolished fixed commissions. Now brokerage houses may charge whatever fees they choose. This has resulted in two distinct types of brokerage firms: full-service and discount.

Full-service brokers provide research and investment advice to their customers. Full-service brokers will often mail weekly and monthly market reports and recommendations to their customers in an effort to encourage them to invest in certain securities. For example, when the investment banking department of the brokerage house has an initial public offering available, brokers will contact customers they feel may be interested and offer to send a prospectus. Full-service brokers attempt to establish long-term relationships with their customers and to help them assemble portfolios that are consistent with their financial needs and risk preferences. Of course, this extra attention is costly and must be paid for by requiring higher fees for initiating trades. Merrill Lynch is the biggest of the full-service brokers.

Discount brokers simply execute trades on request. If you want to buy a particular security, you call the discount broker and place your request. No advice or research is typically provided. Because the cost of operating a discount brokerage firm is significantly less than the cost of operating a full-service firm, lower transaction costs are charged. These fees may be as little as half the fees charged by a full-service broker. Charles Schwab & Company is the best-known discount broker. Many discount brokerage firms are owned by large commercial banks, which have historically been prohibited from offering full-service brokerage services.

Regardless of which type of brokerage firm you choose, it will own seats on the major exchanges and have computer links to the NASDAQ (National Association of Security Dealers Automated Quotation System). Suppose that you place an order for 100 shares of IBM with your local Merrill Lynch office. Your broker will send an electronic message to the Merrill Lynch traders who work on the floor of the New York Stock Exchange (NYSE) to buy 100 shares of IBM in your name. (Merrill Lynch will have purchased a number of seats on the exchange for its traders, as discussed in Chapter 9.) On the floor of the NYSE, there are circular work areas where specialists in each security that is traded on the exchange stand. Each specialist is responsible for several stocks. The Merrill Lynch floor trader will know where the IBM specialist is and will approach that person to fill your buy order. Confirmation of the purchase will then be communicated back to your local broker, who will inform you that the trade has been completed.

Securities Dealers

Securities dealers hold inventories of securities, which they sell to customers who want to buy. They also hold securities purchased from customers who want to sell.

It is impossible to overemphasize the importance of dealers to the smooth functioning of the U.S. financial markets. Consider what an investor demands before buying a security. In addition to requiring a fair return, the investor wants to know that the investment is *liquid*—that it can be sold quickly if it no longer fits into the investor's portfolio. Consider a small, relatively unknown firm that is trying to sell securities to the public. An investor may be tempted to buy the firm's securities, but if these securities cannot be resold easily, it is unlikely that the investor will take a chance on them. This is where the dealers become crucial. They stand ready to make a market in the security at any time—that is, they make sure that an investor can always sell or buy a security. For this reason, dealers are also called **market makers.** When an investor wishes to sell a thinly traded stock (one without an active secondary market), it is unlikely that another investor is simultaneously seeking to buy that security. This nonsynchronous trading problem is solved when the dealer buys the security from the investor and holds it in inventory until another investor is ready to buy it. The knowledge that dealers will provide this service encourages investors to buy securities that would be otherwise unacceptable. In countries with less well developed financial markets, where dealers will not make a market for less popular securities, it is extremely difficult for small, new, or regional firms to raise funds. Securities market dealers are largely responsible for the health and growth of small businesses in the United States.

REGULATION OF SECURITIES FIRMS

Many financial firms engage in all three securities market activities, acting as brokers, dealers, and investment bankers. The largest in the United States is Merrill Lynch; other well-known firms include Paine Webber, Morgan Stanley Dean Witter, and Salomon Smith Barney. The SEC not only regulates the firms' investment banking operations but also restricts brokers and dealers from misrepresenting securities and from trading on *insider information,* unpublicized facts known only to the management of a corporation.

When discussing regulation, it is important to recognize that the public's confidence in the integrity of the financial markets is critical to the growth of our economy and the ability of firms to continue using the markets to raise new capital. If the public believes that there are other powerful players with superior information who can take advantage of smaller investors, the market will be unable to attract funds from these smaller investors. Ultimately, the markets could fail entirely.

The lemons problem introduced in Chapter 14 also applies to the securities markets. Due to asymmetric information, investors will not know as much about securities being offered for sale by firms as firm insiders will. If an average price is set for all securities based on this lack of information, good securities would be withdrawn and only poor and overpriced securities would remain for sale. With only these securities offered, the average price would fall. Now any securities worth more than this new average would be withdrawn. Eventually, the market would fail as the average security offered drops in quality and market prices fall as a result. One solution to the lemons problem is for the government to regulate full disclosure so that asymmetric information is reduced.

The securities laws were designed with two goals: to protect the integrity of the markets and to restrict competition among securities firms so that they would be less likely to fail. Two acts passed in 1933 and 1934 provide the primary basis for regulation of today's securities markets. These acts were passed shortly after the Great Depression and were largely responding to abuses that many people at the time felt were partly responsible for the economic troubles the country was suffering. The principal provisions of the 1933 and 1934 acts are as follows:

The Securities and Exchange Commission website, www.sec.gov, contains regulatory actions, concept releases, interpretive releases, and more.

- To establish the Securities and Exchange Commission (SEC), which is charged with administering securities laws
- To require that issuers register new securities offerings and that they disclose all relevant information to potential investors

- To require that all publicly held corporations file annual and semiannual reports with the SEC; publicly held corporations must also file a report whenever any event of "significant interest" to investors occurs
- To require that insiders file reports whenever shares are bought or sold
- To prohibit any form of market manipulation

Prior to the passage of these acts, the market was subject to much abuse. For example, a study conducted in 1933 showed evidence of 127 "investment pools" operating during 1932 alone. An investment pool is formed to manipulate the market. A group of investors band together and spread false but damaging rumors about the health of a firm. These rumors drive the price of the firm's stock down. When the price is depressed, the members of the pool buy the stock. Once they all hold shares purchased at artificially low prices, the members of the pool release good news about the company so that the price of the stock rises. Obviously, the members of the pool stand to earn huge profits. Small, uninformed investors lose. Practices such as these were outlawed by the securities acts of 1933 and 1934.

As noted in our discussion of private placements, not all securities issues are subject to SEC oversight. SEC registration is not required if less than $1.5 million in securities is issued per year, if the securities mature in less than 270 days, or if the securities are issued by the U.S. government or most municipalities.

Other legislation of significance to securities firms include the Glass-Steagall Act of 1933, which separated commercial and investment banking (mostly repealed by Gramm-Leach-Bliley Act); the Investment Advisers Act of 1940, which required investment advisers to register with the SEC; and the Securities Protection Corporation Act of 1970, which established the Securities Investor Protection Corporation, which insures customers of securities firms from losses to their cash accounts up to $100,000 and from losses of securities documents up to $500,000. Other regulations related specifically to banks but of interest to securities firms are discussed in Chapter 18.

RELATIONSHIP BETWEEN SECURITIES FIRMS AND COMMERCIAL BANKS

For many years, commercial banks have lobbied for legislative relief to enable them to compete with securities firms. Consider how the business of banking has been eroded. Prior to the introduction of cash management accounts at Merrill Lynch, the only source of checking accounts was a bank. The Merrill Lynch account not only provided low-cost checking but also paid interest that was higher than the law permitted banks to pay. Securities firms were allowed to make loans, offer credit and debit cards, provide ATM access, and, most important, sell securities. In addition, securities firms could sell some types of insurance. It is not hard to understand why bankers were frustrated. Regulations prevented them from competing with securities firms, but no laws restricted securities firms from competing with banks.

Commercial banks clamored on Capitol Hill for a "level playing field." As noted in Chapter 18, regulatory relief in 1980 and 1982 substantially slowed the movement of funds from commercial banks to securities firms; however, banks were still not permitted to sell securities. This is gradually changing.

MUTUAL FUNDS

The major brokerage houses, independent securities firms, and banks all offer a wide variety of mutual funds. Mutual funds pool the resources of many small investors by selling them shares and using the proceeds to buy securities. Through the asset transformation process of issuing shares in small denominations and buying large blocks of securities, mutual funds can take advantage of volume discounts on brokerage commissions and can purchase diversified portfolios of securities. Mutual funds allow the small investor to obtain the benefits of lower transaction costs in purchasing securities and to take advantage of the reduction of risk by diversifying the portfolio of securities held.

Access the *Mutual Fund Fact Book*, which is published by Investment Company Institute, at www.ici.org./facts_figures/factbook_toc.html to find information about the mutual funds industry's history, regulation, taxation, and share holders.

Despite the fact that research discussed in Chapter 10 has consistently demonstrated that mutual funds do not outperform the market, even when fees are not considered, many investors prefer to rely on professional money managers to select their stocks. The failure of mutual funds to post greater-than-average returns should not come as a surprise given our discussion of market efficiency. Still, the financial markets remain something of a mystery to a large number of investors. These investors are willing to pay fees that can often be very high to let someone else choose their stocks.

Another reason investors purchase mutual funds is that they provide a low-cost way of diversifying into foreign stocks. It can be difficult and expensive to invest in foreign stocks not listed on U.S. exchanges. Annual net flows into world equity funds totaled $50 billion in 2000, up from $11 billion in 1999. This unusually large surge was likely due to the weak U.S. stock market during that period.

Mutual funds have had a large increase in total proportion of stocks held since 1980 (see Figure 4). The primary source of this growth has been the booming stock market during the 1990s; another has been the appearance of mutual funds that specialized in debt instruments (which first appeared in the 1970s). Before 1970, mutual funds invested almost solely in common stocks. Funds that purchase common stocks may specialize even further and invest solely in foreign securities or in specialized industries, such as energy or high technology. Funds that purchase debt instruments may specialize further in corporate, U.S. government or tax-exempt municipal bonds or in long-term or short-term securities.[3] There are currently over 8200 separate mutual funds available to investors. This means there are more distinct funds than there are stocks listed on the New York Stock Exchange and the American Stock Exchange combined.

Mutual fund companies frequently offer a number of separate mutual funds. They are called complexes and are defined as a group of funds under substantially common management (or distributorship), composed of one or more families of funds. Table 2 reports the total fund assets, number of funds, number of share holder accounts, and number of complexes since 1970. We can see that the number of funds offered per complex has increased dramatically since they were first reported in 1979. The advantage to investors of fund complexes is that investments can usually be transferred among different funds within a family very easily and quickly. Additionally, account information can be summarized by the complex to help investors keep their assets organized.

Most mutual funds require a minimum investment before an account may be opened. For example, 14% of funds require an initial deposit of at least $500. About 37% of funds require a minimum initial deposit of $1000. Most funds waive their minimum deposit requirement when an investor is opening an IRA or automatic investment plan.

[3]Tax-exempt bond funds did not appear until after 1976, when a change in the tax law allowed mutual funds to pass through to shareholders the tax exemption on the interest income from municipal bonds.

TABLE 2 Total Industry Net Assets, Number of Funds, Shareholder Accounts, and Complexes

Year	Net Assets (millions)	Number of Funds	Number of Accounts (thousands)	Number of Complexes
1970	47,618.10	361	10,690.30	N/A
1971	55,045.30	392	10,901.00	N/A
1972	59,830.60	410	10,635.30	N/A
1973	46,518.50	421	10,330.90	N/A
1974	35,776.80	431	10,074.20	N/A
1975	45,874.40	426	9,876.10	N/A
1976	51,276.60	452	9,060.10	N/A
1977	48,936.90	477	8,692.60	N/A
1978	55,837.70	505	8,658.40	N/A
1979	94,511.30	524	9,790.00	119
1980	134,760.90	564	12,087.60	123
1981	241,365.40	665	17,499.00	134
1982	296,678.10	857	21,448.40	150
1983	292,985.10	1,026	24,604.70	164
1984	370,680.00	1,241	28,268.30	189
1985	495,385.10	1,527	34,762.30	217
1986	715,667.80	1,835	46,012.80	261
1987	769,171.90	2,312	54,421.20	314
1988	809,370.50	2,708	54,676.90	349
1989	980,671.10	2,900	58,135.00	357
1990	1,065,194.10	3,081	61,948.60	361
1991	1,393,189.30	3,405	68,334.80	361
1992	1,642,543.00	3,826	79,932.80	364
1993	2,070,023.50	4,538	93,217.30	375
1994	2,155,396.00	5,330	114,388.30	398
1995	2,811,484.00	5,728	131,231.10	401
1996	3,526,270.00	6,254	150,176.50	417
1997	4,468,200.60	6,684	170,521.10	424
1998	5,525,209.30	7,314	193,854.00	419
1999	6,846,339.20	7,791	226,872.90	433
2000	6,965,249.10	8,171	243,518.90	431

Source: Mutual Fund Fact Book, 2001.

Types of Investment Funds

There are four basic types of mutual funds available to investors. These are (1) stock funds (also called equity funds), (2) bond funds, (3) hybrid funds (composed of both stocks and bonds), and (4) money market funds. About 57% of the total investment in mutual funds is invested in stock funds, 27% in money market funds, 12% in bond funds, and the rest in hybrid funds.

In addition to being classified by the types of securities held in the fund, mutual funds are also separated by their published investment objective. The Investment Company Institute classifies mutual funds into investment objective categories. These categories are summarized in Figure 3.

The simplest types of funds to manage are called **index funds.** The managers of index funds simply buy the securities that are included in some popular stock index, such as the S&P 500. Rebalancing occurs only when a stock enters or leaves the index or when price changes make it necessary. Since no research or aggressive management is required of these funds, lower fees are charged. Research suggests that due to the lower fees, these funds usually outperform the more actively managed funds.

Equity Funds
- Capital appreciation funds
- Aggressive growth
- Growth funds
- Sector funds

Total Return Funds
- Growth-and-income funds
- Income-equity funds
- World equity funds
- Emerging market funds
- Global equity funds
- International equity funds
- Regional equity funds

Hybrid Funds
- Asset allocation funds
- Balanced funds invest
- Flexible portfolio
- Income-mixed funds

Taxable Bond Funds
- Corporate bond funds (short, intermediate and long term funds)
- High-yield bond funds
- World bond funds
- Global bond funds
- Government bond funds
- Mortgage-backed securities
- Strategic income funds

Tax-Free Bond Funds
- State municipal bond funds
- National municipal bond funds

Money Market Funds
- Taxable money market funds
- National tax-exempt money market
- State tax-exempt money market funds

FIGURE 3 Mutual Fund Classes by Investment Objectives

Figure 4 shows the distribution of assets by type of fund in 1986 and 2001. We can observe that the proportion of funds invested in mmmFs has increased. This is because the stock market performance in 2000–2001 prompted investors to seek safe havens and money market securities.

Ownership of Mutual Funds

An estimated 50.6 million households or 49.0% now own the majority of the mutual funds industry's assets. At the end of 2000, they held 80% of mutual fund shares, with the rest owned by fiduciaries and other business organizations. This represents a tremendous increase since 1980, when only 5.7% of U.S. households held mutual fund shares (see Figure 5). According to the Investment Company Institute, the average mutual fund investor is middle-class, 44 years old, married, and employed and possesses financial assets of $80,000. Shareholders are fairly evenly distributed among age groups, and only 18% of shareholders are retired. Fully 84%

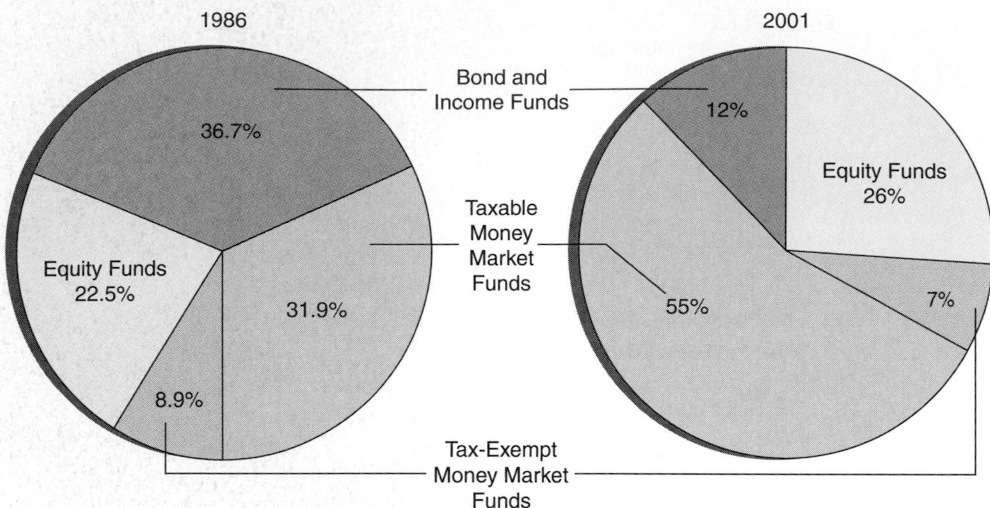

FIGURE 4 Distribution of Mutual Fund Assets, 1986 and 2001

Source: Investment Company Institute

cite preparing for retirement as one of their main reasons for holding shares, and 26% cite saving for a child's college education.

Generation X (consisting of individuals aged 18 to 30) is very interested in mutual fund investing. This group has the lowest level of household assets but the second-highest portion of financial assets in mutual funds (38%), after those aged 50 to 70. Among the age groups, Generation X also has the highest tolerance for investment risk. Generation X is also leading the way in Internet access to mutual funds (see Box 2).

Fee Structure of Investment Funds

Mutual funds are structured in two ways. The most common structure is an **open-end fund,** from which shares can be redeemed at any time at a price that is

BOX 2: E-FINANCE
Mutual Funds and the Internet

The Investment Company Institute estimates that as of 2000, 68% of households owning mutual funds use the Internet, and nearly half of those on-line shareholders visit fund-related websites. The Internet increases the attractiveness of mutual funds because it enables shareholders to review performance information, share prices and personal account information.

Of all U.S. households that conducted mutual funds transactions between April 1999 and March 2000, 18% bought or sold fund shares on-line. The median number of funds transactions conducted over the Internet during the 12-month period was four, while the average number was eight, indicating that a high volume of on-line transactions were conducted by a small number of shareholders.

On-line shareholders were typically younger, had greater household income, and were better educated than those not using the Internet. The median on-line shareholder was 42 years old, had a household income of $100,900, and was college educated. The median shareholder not using the Internet was 51 years old, had a household income of $41,000, and did not have a college degree.

The use of the Internet to track and trade mutual funds is rapidly increasing. The number of shareholders who visited websites offering fund shares nearly doubled between April 1999 and March 2000.

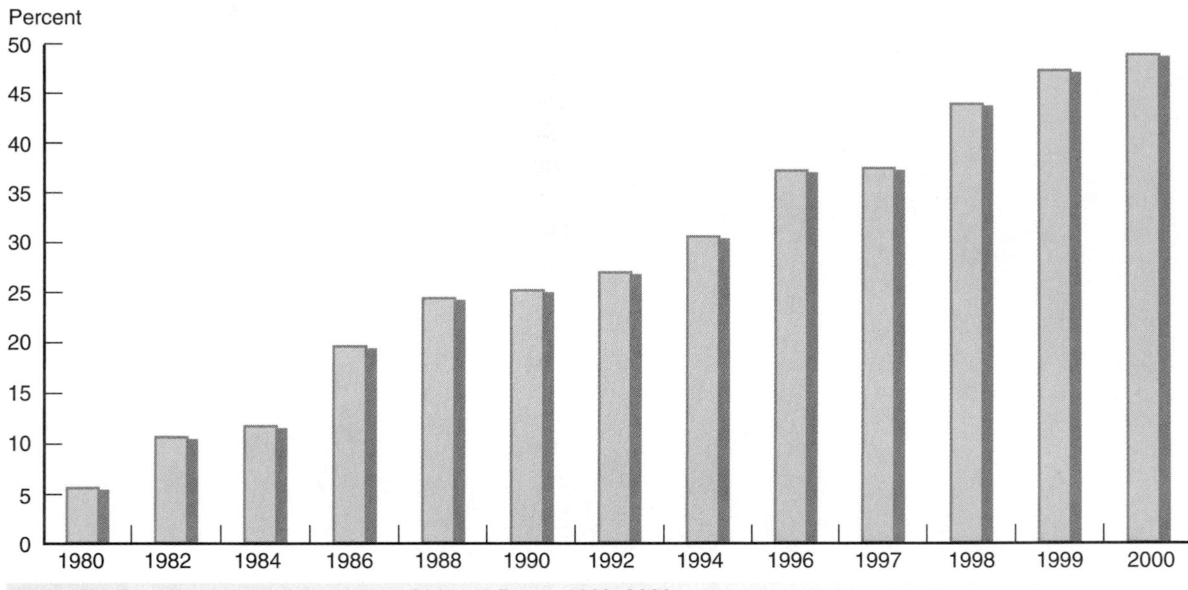

FIGURE 5 Household Ownership of Mutual Funds, 1980–2000

Source: Mutual Fund Fact Book.

tied to the asset value of the fund. A mutual fund can also be structured as a **closed-end fund,** in which a fixed number of nonredeemable shares are sold at an initial offering and are then traded in the over-the-counter market like common stock. The market price of these shares fluctuates with the value of the assets held by the fund. In contrast to the open-end fund, however, the price of the shares may be above or below the value of the assets held by the fund, depending on factors such as the liquidity of the shares or the quality of the management. The greater popularity of the open-end funds is explained by the greater liquidity of their redeemable shares relative to the nonredeemable shares of closed-end funds.

Application Calculating a Mutual Fund's Net Asset Value

If you invest in a mutual fund, you will receive periodic statements summarizing the activity in your account. The statement will show funds that were added to your investment balance, funds that were withdrawn, and any earnings that have accrued. One term on the statement that is critical to understanding the investment's performance is the **net asset value (NAV)**. The net asset value is the total value of the mutual fund's stocks, bonds, cash, and other assets minus any liabilities such as accrued fees, divided by the number of shares outstanding. An example will make this clear.

Suppose that a mutual fund has the following assets and liabilities:

Stock (at current market value)	\$20,000,000
Bonds (at current market value)	\$10,000,000
Cash	\$ 500,000
Total value of assets	\$30,500,000
Liabilities	–\$ 300,000
Net worth	\$30,200,000

The net asset value is computed by dividing the net worth by the number of shares outstanding. If 10 million shares are outstanding, the net asset value is $3.02 ($30,200,000/10,000,000 = $3.02).

The net asset value rises and falls as the value of the underlying assets change. For example, suppose that the value of the stock portfolio held by the mutual fund rises by 10% and the value of the bond portfolio falls by 2% over the course of a year. If the cash and liabilities are unchanged, the new net asset value will be

Stock (at current market value)	$22,000,000
Bonds (at current market value)	$9,800,000
Cash	$ 500,000
Total value of assets	$32,300,000
Liabilities	–$ 300,000
Net worth	$32,000,000

$$NAV = \frac{\$32{,}000{,}000}{10{,}000{,}000} = \$3.20$$

The yield on your investment in the mutual fund is then

$$\text{Yield} = \frac{\$3.20 - \$3.02}{\$3.02} = \frac{\$0.18}{\$3.02} = 5.96\%$$

When you buy and sell shares in the mutual fund, you do so at the current *NAV.*

Originally, shares of most open-end mutual funds were sold by salespeople (usually brokers) who were paid a commission. Because this commission is paid at the time of purchase and is immediately subtracted from the redemption value of the shares, these funds are called **load funds.** Most mutual funds are currently **no-load funds;** the funds sell directly to the public (bypassing brokers) with no sales commissions.

Fees in addition to sales commissions may be charged:

- A *contingent deferred sales charge* imposed at the time of redemption is an alternative way to compensate financial professionals for their services. This fee typically applies for the first few years of ownership and then disappears.
- A *redemption fee* is a back-end charge for redeeming shares. It is expressed as a dollar amount or a percentage of the redemption price.
- An *exchange fee* may be charged when transferring money from one fund to another within the same fund family.
- An *account maintenance fee* is charged by some funds to maintain low-balance accounts.
- *12b-1 fees,* if any, are deducted from the fund's assets to pay marketing and advertising expenses or, more commonly, to compensate sales professionals. By law, 12b-1 fees cannot exceed 1% of the fund's average net assets per year. The 12b-1 fee may include a service fee of up to 0.25% of average net assets per year to compensate sales professionals for providing services or maintaining shareholder accounts.

Clearly, there are many opportunities for mutual fund managers to charge investors for the right to invest. Investors should very carefully evaluate a mutual fund's fee structure before investing, since these fees can range from 0.5% to as much as 8% per year. No research supports the argument that investors get better returns by investing in funds that charge higher fees. On the contrary, most high-fee mutual funds fail to do as well, after expenses, as low-fee funds.

Over the last 20 years, competition within the mutual fund industry has produced substantially lower costs. Between 1980 and 2000, the average total shareholder cost of equity mutual funds decreased by 40%. The cost of bond and money market funds dropped by 29% and 24% respectively. One factor undoubtedly contributing to this reduction is the requirement by the SEC that mutual funds clearly disclose all fees and costs investors will incur. The SEC further requires mutual funds to include in their prospectus a standardized sample account where $10,000 is invested for 1, 3, 5, and 10 years. The analysis shows investors exactly what fees they will be subject to if they choose the fund. This fee disclosure requirement makes it very easy for investors to compare funds.

Regulation of Mutual Funds

Mutual funds are regulated under four federal laws designed to protect investors. The Securities Act of 1933 mandates that funds make certain disclosures. The Securities Exchange Act of 1934 set out antifraud rules covering the purchase and sale of fund shares. The Investment Company Act of 1940 requires all funds to register with the SEC and to meet certain operating standards. Finally, the Investment Advisers Act of 1940 regulates fund advisers.

As part of this government regulation, all funds must provide two types of documents free of charge: a prospectus and a shareholder report. A mutual fund's prospectus describes the fund's goals, fees and expenses, and investment strategies and risks; it also gives information on how to buy and sell shares. The SEC requires a fund to provide a full prospectus either before an investment or together with the confirmation statement of an initial investment.

Annual and semiannual shareholder reports discuss the fund's recent performance and include other important information, such as the fund's financial statements. By examining these reports, an investor can learn if a fund has been effective in meeting the goals and investment strategies described in the fund's prospectus.

In addition, investors are sent a yearly statement detailing the federal tax status of distributions received from the fund. Mutual fund shareholders are taxed on the fund's income directly, as if the shareholders held the underlying securities themselves. Similarly, any tax-exempt income received by a fund is generally passed on to the shareholders as tax-exempt.

Investment funds are run by brokerage houses and by institutional investors, who now control over 50% of the outstanding stock in the United States. Over 70% of the total daily volume in stocks is due to institutions initiating trades. Many of the mutual funds are run by brokerage houses; others are run by independent investment advisers. Because of the volume of stock controlled by these investors, there is tremendous competition for their business. This has led to significant cost cutting and to the proliferation of alternative methods of trading. For example, computerized trading that eliminates the broker from the transaction accounts for a growing percentage of the activity in stocks.

Mutual funds are the only companies in America that are required by law to have independent directors. The SEC believes that independent directors play a critical role in the governance of mutual funds. In January 2001, the SEC adopted substantive rule amendments designed to enhance the independence of investment company directors and provide investors with more information to assess directors' independence. These rules require that:

- Independent directors constitute at least a majority of the fund's board of directors,
- Independent directors select and nominate other independent directors, and
- Any legal counsel for the fund's independent directors be an independent legal counsel.

In addition, SEC rules require that mutual funds publish extensive information about directors, including their business experience and fund shares held. This system of overseeing the interests of mutual fund shareholders has helped the industry avoid systemic problems and contributed significantly to public confidence in mutual funds.

Mutual Funds and the Retirement Market

Mutual funds accounted for $2.5 trillion, or 20%, of the $12.3 trillion U.S. retirement market at year-end 2000. The remaining $9.8 trillion of assets in the retirement market are managed by pension funds, insurance companies, banks, and brokerage firms. This $2.5 trillion in mutual fund retirement plan assets represented 35% of all mutual fund assets at year-end 2000.

Deposits into retirement mutual funds come from two sources: employer-sponsored defined contribution plans, especially 401(k) plans, and individual retirement accounts (IRAs). The mutual funds' share of the 401(k) market has increased during the 1990s from 9% in 1990 to an estimated 45% at year-end 2000. A similar increase in mutual fund IRA accounts occurred.

Figure 6 shows the average asset allocation for all 401(k) plan balances. The bulk of retirement assets are in equity funds, followed by company stock. Younger investors tend to put a greater percentage of their retirement dollars into stock funds (63%) while workers in their sixties invest 44% in stock funds.

Hedge Funds

Hedge funds are a special type of mutual fund that have received considerable attention recently due to the near collapse of Long Term Capital Management. In Chapter 22 we discuss how financial markets can use hedges to reduce risk in a wide variety of situations. These risk-reducing strategies should not be confused with hedge funds. Although hedge funds often attempt to be market-neutral, protected from changes in the overall market, they are not riskless.

To illustrate a typical type of transaction conducted by hedge funds, consider a trade made by Long Term Capital Management in 1994. The fund managers noted that $29\frac{1}{2}$ year U.S. Treasury bonds seemed cheap relative to 30-year Treasury securities. The managers figured that the value of the two bonds would converge over time. After all, these securities have nearly identical risk since the maturity risk difference between $29\frac{1}{2}$-year securities and 30-year securities is insignificant. To make money from the temporary divergence of the bond prices, the fund bought $2 billion of the $29\frac{1}{2}$-year bonds and sold short $2 billion of the 30-year bonds. (Selling short means that the fund borrowed bonds it did not own and sold them. Later the fund must cover its short position by buying the bonds back,

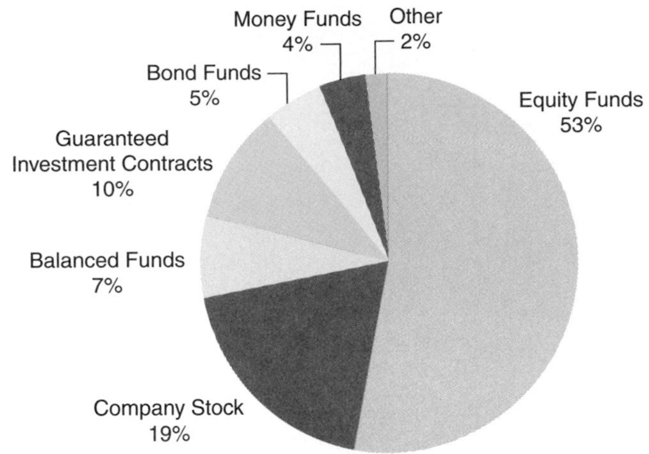

FIGURE 6 Average Asset Allocation for All 401(k) Plan Balances

Source: Mutual Fund Fact Book (http://www.ici.org/aboutfunds/factbook_toc.html).

hopefully at a lower price.) The net investment by Long Term Capital was $12 million. Six months later, the fund covered its short position by buying 30-year bonds and sold its $29\frac{1}{2}$-year bonds. This transaction yielded a $25 million profit.[4]

In the transaction, the managers did not care whether the overall bond market rose or fell. In this sense, the transaction was market-neutral. All that was required for a profit was that the prices of the bonds converge, an event that occurred as predicted. Hedge fund managers scour the world in their search for pricing anomalies between related securities. Figure 7 shows a situation where hedge funds could invest. Securities A and B move in lockstep over time. At some point they diverge, creating an opportunity. The hedge fund would buy security B, because it is expected to increase relative to A, and would sell A short. The fund managers hope that the gain on security B will be greater than the loss on security A. At times, the search for opportunities leads hedge funds to adopt exotic approaches that are not easily available elsewhere, from investing in distressed securities to participating in venture-capital financing.

In addition to investing money contributed by individuals and institutions, hedge funds often set up lines of credit to use to leverage their investments. For instance, in our example, Long Term Capital earned $25 million on an investment of $12 million, a 108% return [($25 million – $12 million)/$12 million = 1.08 = 108%]. Suppose that half of the $12 million had been borrowed funds. Ignoring interest cost, the return on invested equity would then be 317% ($25 million – $6 million/$6 million = 3.17 = 317%). Long Term Capital advertised that it was leveraged 20 to 1; however, by the time of the crisis, the figure was actually closer to 50 to 1. Box 3 discusses how Long Term Capital eventually required a private rescue plan to prevent its failure.

Hedge funds accumulate money from many people and invest on their behalf, but several features distinguish them from traditional mutual funds. First, hedge

[4]*Wall Street Journal,* November 16, 1998, p. A18.

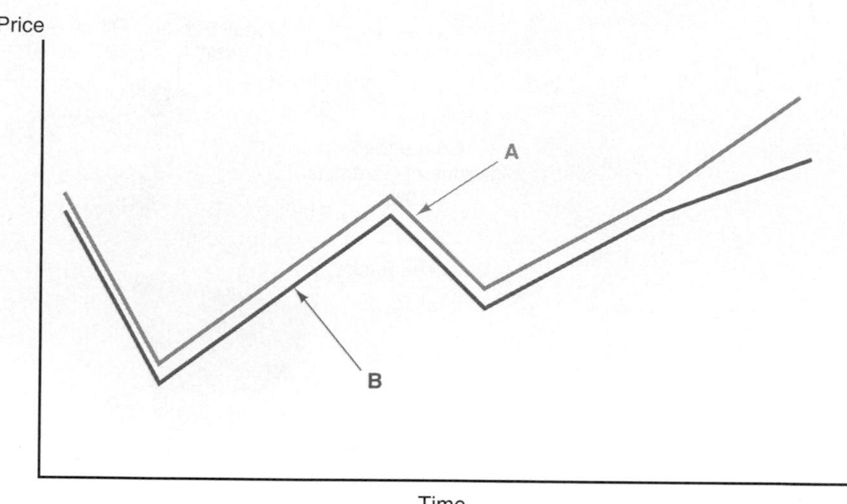

FIGURE 7 The Price of Two Similar Securities

Hedge funds search for related securities that historically move in lockstep but have temporarily diverted. In this example, the hedge fund would sell security A short and buy security B.

funds have a minimum investment requirement of between $100,000 and $20 million, with the typical minimum investment being $1 million. Long Term Capital Management required a $10 million minimum investment. Most hedge funds are set up as limited partnerships. Federal law limits hedge funds to no more than 99 limited partners with steady annual incomes of $200,000 or more or a

BOX 3

The Long Term Capital Debacle

Long Term Capital Management is a hedge fund managed by a group that included two Nobel Prize winners and 25 other Ph.D.s. It made headlines in September 1998, because it required a private rescue plan organized by the Federal Reserve Bank of New York.

The experience of Long Term Capital Management demonstrates that hedge funds are not risk-free, despite their being market-neutral. Long Term Capital expected that the spread between long-term Treasury bonds and long-term corporate bonds would narrow. Many stock markets around the world plunged, causing a flight to quality. Investors bid up the price of Treasury securities while the price of corporate securities fell. This is exactly the opposite of what Long Term Capital Management had predicted. As losses mounted, Long Term Capital's lenders required that the fund increase its equity position.

By mid-September, the fund was unable to raise sufficient equity to meet the demands of its creditors. Faced with the potential collapse of the fund, together with its highly leveraged investment portfolio consisting of nearly $80 billion in equities and over $1 trillion of notional value in derivatives, the Federal Reserve stepped in to prevent the fund from failing. The Fed's rationale was that a sudden liquidation of the Long Term Capital Management portfolio would create unacceptable systemic risk. Tens of billions of dollars worth of illiquid securities would be dumped on an already jittery market, causing potentially huge losses to numerous lenders and other institutions. A group consisting of banks and brokerage firms contributed $3.6 billion to a rescue plan that prevented the fund's failure.

The Fed's involvement in organizing the rescue of Long Term Capital is controversial, despite no public funds being expended. Some critics argue that the intervention increases moral hazard by weakening the discipline imposed by the market on fund managers. However, others say that the tremendous economic damage the fund's failure would have caused was unacceptable. This debate is likely to rage for some time.

net worth of $1 million, excluding their homes. Funds may have up to 499 limited partners if each has $5 million in invested assets. All of these restrictions are aimed at allowing hedge funds to exist largely unregulated, on the theory that the rich can look out for themselves. Many of the 4000 funds are domiciled offshore to escape all regulatory restrictions.

Second, hedge funds are unique in that they usually require that investors commit their money for long periods of time, often several years. The purpose of this requirement is to give managers breathing room to attempt long-range strategies.

Hedge funds often charge large fees to investors. The typical fund charges a 1% annual asset management fee plus 20% of profits. Some charge significantly more. For example, Long Term Capital Management charged investors a 2% management fee and took 25% of profits.

SUMMARY

1. Investment banks are firms that assist in the initial sale of securities in the primary market and, as securities brokers and dealers, assist in the trading of securities in the secondary markets, some of which are organized into exchanges. The Securities and Exchange Commission regulates the financial institutions in the securities markets and ensures that adequate information reaches prospective investors.
2. Underwriting involves the investment banking firm's taking ownership of the stock issue by purchasing all of the shares from the issuer and then reselling them in the market. Issues may be oversubscribed, undersubscribed, or fully subscribed, depending on whether the price is set correctly.
3. Investment bankers assist issuing firms by providing advice, filing documents, and marketing issues. Investment bankers often assist in mergers and acquisitions and in private placements as well.
4. Securities brokers act as go-betweens and do not usually own securities. Securities dealers do buy and sell securities and by doing so make a market. By always having securities to sell and by always being willing to purchase securities, dealers guarantee the liquidity of the market.
5. Investors may place an order, called a *market order,* to buy a security at the current market price. They may also set limits to the lowest price at which they will sell their security or the highest price they will pay for a security. Orders of this type are called *limit orders.*
6. Some brokerage houses provide research and investment advice in addition to conducting trades on behalf of customers. These are called *full-service brokers. Discount brokers* simply place orders. Brokerage houses also store securities, advance loans to buy securities, and offer cash management accounts.
7. Investment funds pool the funds of many small investors and purchase large quantities of securities. These funds offer a wide variety of funds designed to appeal to most investment strategies.

KEY TERMS

closed-end fund, *p. 587*
confidential memorandum, *p. 576*
definitive agreement, *p. 576*
due diligence, *p. 576*
fully subscribed, *p. 574*
Glass-Steagall Act, *p. 568*
hedge fund, *p. 590*
index fund, *p. 584*
initial public offering (IPO), *p. 570*
investment banks, *p. 568*
letter of intent, *p. 576*
limit order, *p. 578*
load fund, *p. 588*
margin credit, *p. 578*
market maker, *p. 581*
market order, *p. 577*
mergers and acquisitions market, *p. 576*
net asset value (NAV), *p. 587*
no-load fund, *p. 588*
open-end fund, *p. 587*
oversubscribed, *p. 574*
prospectus, *p. 570*
registration statement, *p. 570*
seasoned issues, *p. 570*
short sell, *p. 578*
syndicate, *p. 572*
tombstone, *p. 572*
undersubscribed, *p. 574*

QUESTIONS AND PROBLEMS

*1. What was the motivation behind legislation separating commercial banking from investment banking?

2. What law separated investment banking from commercial banking?

*3. What does it mean to say that investment bankers *underwrite* a security offering? How is this different from a best-efforts offering?

4. What are the primary services that an investment banker will provide a firm issuing securities?

*5. Does the fact that a security has passed an SEC review mean that investors can buy the security without having to worry about taking a loss on the investment?

6. Why do investment banking firms often form syndicates for selling securities to the public?

*7. Is it better for a security issue to be fully subscribed or oversubscribed?

8. Why would an investment banker advise a firm to issue a security using best efforts rather than underwriting?

*9. What is the difference between a hostile takeover and a merger?

10. What valuable service do dealers provide that facilitates transaction trading and keeping the markets liquid?

*11. What is the difference between a market order and a limit order?

12. Is it possible to make money if you know that the price of a security will *fall* in the future? How?

*13. Why do commercial banks object to brokerage houses' being allowed to offer many of the same services traditionally reserved for banks?

14. What is an index fund? Why are index funds increasingly popular?

*15. What is the difference between a load fund and a no-load fund?

WEB EXERCISES

Investment Banks, Brokerage Firms and Mutual Funds

1. Morningstar is the best-known company that specializes in analysis and review of mutual funds. There are a number of websites that report Morningstar's results. Go to www.quicken.com/investments/mutualfunds/finder/. Perform the EasyStep Search according to your own preferences for investment. Can you find funds that provide the return you want with the expense ratio you are willing to pay?

2. The mutual fund industry publishes a fact book containing exhaustive data on the historic and current state of mutual funds. Go to http://www.ici.org/aboutfunds/factbook_toc.html.
   a. According to Chapter 3, did the terrorist attack in September 2001 cause an obvious decrease in mutual funds assets?
   b. According to Chapter 4, what percentage of mutual funds assets are currently owned by households?
   c. According to Chapter 4, what is the average annual income of an investor in mutual funds?

Part 6

The Management of Financial Institutions

Chapter 22 Risk Management in Financial Institutions

Preview

The website of the Risk Management Association, www.rmahq.org, offers useful information such as annual statement studies, on-line publications, and more.

Managing financial institutions has never been an easy task, but in recent years it has become even more difficult because of greater uncertainty in the economic environment. Interest rates have become much more volatile, resulting in substantial fluctuations in profits and in the value of assets and liabilities held by financial institutions. Furthermore, as we have seen in Chapter 5, defaults on loans and other debt instruments have also climbed dramatically, leading to large losses at financial institutions. In light of these developments, it is not surprising that financial institution managers have become more concerned about managing the risk their institutions face as a result of greater interest-rate fluctuations and defaults by borrowers.

In this chapter we examine how managers of financial institutions cope with credit risk, the risk arising because borrowers may default on their obligations, and with interest-rate risk, the risk arising from fluctuations in interest rates. We will look at the tools that these managers use to measure risk and the strategies that they employ to reduce it.

MANAGING CREDIT RISK

A major part of the business of financial institutions such as banks, insurance companies, pension funds, and finance companies is making loans. In order for these institutions to earn high profits, they must make successful loans that are paid back in full (and so have low credit risk). The concepts of adverse selection and moral hazard (introduced in Chapter 2) provide a framework for understanding the principles that financial institution managers must follow to minimize credit risk and make successful loans.

Adverse selection is problematic in loan markets because bad credit risks (borrowers most likely to default) are the ones who usually line up for loans—in other words, those who are most likely to produce an *adverse* outcome are the most likely to be *selected*. Borrowers with very risky investment projects in mind have much to gain if their projects are successful, and so they are the most eager to obtain loans. Clearly, however, they are the least desirable borrowers because of the greater possibility that they will be unable to pay back their loans.

Moral hazard is a problem in loan markets because borrowers may have incentives to engage in activities that are undesirable from the lender's point of view. In such situations, it is more likely that the lender will be exposed to the *hazard* of default. Once borrowers have obtained a loan, they are more likely to invest in high-risk investment projects—projects that pay high returns to the borrowers if successful. The high risk, however, makes it less likely that the loan will be paid back.

To be profitable, financial institutions must overcome the adverse selection and moral hazard problems that make loan defaults more likely. The attempts of financial institutions to solve these problems help explain a number of principles for managing credit risk: screening and monitoring, establishment of long-term customer relationships, loan commitments, collateral, compensating balance requirements, and credit rationing.

Screening and Monitoring

Asymmetric information is present in loan markets because lenders have less information about the investment opportunities and activities of borrowers than borrowers do. This situation leads to two information-producing activities by financial institutions: screening and monitoring.

Screening Adverse selection in loan markets requires that financial institutions screen out the bad credit risks from the good ones so that loans will be profitable. To accomplish effective screening, financial institutions must collect reliable information from prospective borrowers. Effective screening and information collection together form an important principle of credit risk management.

When you go into a bank or a finance company to apply for a consumer loan (such as a car loan or a mortgage to purchase a house), the first thing you are asked to do is fill out forms that elicit a great deal of information about your personal finances. You are asked about your salary, bank accounts, other assets (such as cars, insurance policies, and furnishings), and outstanding loans; your record of loan, credit card, and charge account repayments; and the number of years you've worked and who your employers have been. You also are asked personal questions such as your age, marital status, and number of children. The bank or finance company uses this information to evaluate how good a credit risk you are by calculating your "credit score," a statistical measure derived from your answers that predicts whether you are likely to have trouble making your loan payments. Deciding on how good a risk you are cannot be entirely scientific, so the bank or finance company must also use judgment. A loan officer, whose job is to decide whether you should be given the loan, might call your employer or talk to some of the personal references you supplied. The officer might even make a judgment based on your demeanor or your appearance.

The process of screening and collecting information is similar when a financial institution makes a business loan. The loan officer needs to collect information about the company's profits and losses (income) and about its assets and liabilities. The officer also has to evaluate the likely future success of the business. So in addition to obtaining information such as sales figures, the loan officer might ask questions about the company's future plans, how the loan will be used, and the competition in the industry and might even visit the company to obtain a firsthand look at its operations. The bottom line is that, be it for personal or business loans, financial institutions need to be nosy.

One puzzling feature of lending by financial institutions is that they often specialize in lending to local firms or to firms in particular industries, such as energy. In one sense, this behavior appears surprising because it means that the financial institution is not diversifying its portfolio of loans and is therefore exposing itself to more risk. But from another perspective, such specialization makes perfect sense. Recall that the adverse selection problem requires that financial institutions screen out bad credit risks. It is easier for a financial institution to collect information about local firms and determine their creditworthiness than to collect similar information on firms that are far away. Similarly, by specializing in lending to firms in specific industries, the financial institution becomes more knowledgeable about these industries and is therefore better able to predict whether the firms it lends to will be able to make timely payments on their debt.

Monitoring After a loan has been obtained, the borrower may have an incentive to take on risky activities that make it less likely that the loan will be paid off. To reduce this moral hazard, financial institution managers must adhere to the principle for managing credit risk of writing provisions (restrictive covenants) into loan contracts that prevent borrowers from engaging in overly risky activities. By monitoring borrowers' activities to see whether they are complying with the restrictive covenants and by enforcing the covenants if they are not, financial institution managers can make sure that borrowers are not taking on risks at the institution's expense. The need for financial institutions to engage in screening and monitoring explains why successful financial institutions spend so much money on auditing and information-collecting activities.

Long-Term Customer Relationships

An additional way for financial institution managers to obtain information about borrowers is to establish long-term customer relationships, another important principle of credit risk management.

If a prospective borrower has had a checking or savings account or loans with the financial institution over a long period of time, a loan officer can look at past activity in the accounts and learn quite a bit about the borrower. The balances in the checking and savings accounts tell the loan officer how liquid the potential borrower is and at what times of the year the borrower has a strong need for cash. A review of the checks the borrower has written reveals the borrower's suppliers. If the borrower has borrowed previously from the financial institution, the institution has a record of the loan payments. Thus long-term customer relationships reduce the costs of information collection and make it easier to screen out bad credit risks.

The need for monitoring by financial institutions adds to the importance of long-term customer relationships. If the borrower has borrowed from the financial institution before, the institution has already established procedures for monitoring that customer. Therefore, the costs of monitoring long-term customers are lower than those for new customers.

Long-term relationships benefit the customers as well as the financial institution. A firm with a previous relationship will find it easier to obtain a loan at a low interest rate because the financial institution has an easier time determining if the prospective borrower is a good credit risk and incurs fewer costs in monitoring the borrower.

A long-term customer relationship has another advantage for the financial institution. No financial institution manager can think of every contingency when the institution writes restrictive covenants into a loan contract; there will always be risky borrower activities that are not ruled out. However, what if a borrower wants to preserve a long-term relationship with the financial institution to make it easier to get future loans at low interest rates? The borrower then has the incentive to avoid risky activities that would upset the financial institution, even if these risky activities are not specifically addressed in the loan contract. Indeed, if the financial institution manager doesn't like what a borrower is doing even when the borrower isn't violating any restrictive covenants, the manager has some power to discourage the borrower from such activity by threatening to refuse new loans in the future. Long-term customer relationships therefore enable financial institution managers to deal with even unanticipated moral hazard contingencies.

Loan Commitments

Banks have a special vehicle for institutionalizing long-term relationships called a **loan commitment.** A loan commitment is a bank's commitment (for a specified future period of time) to provide a firm with loans up to a given amount at a fixed interest rate or, more commonly, at a rate that is tied to some market interest rate. The majority of commercial and industrial loans from banks are made under the loan commitment arrangement. The advantage for the firm is that it has a source of credit when it needs it. The advantage for the bank is that the loan commitment promotes a long-term relationship, which in turn facilitates information collection. In addition, provisions in the loan commitment agreement require that the firm continually supply the bank with information about the firm's income, asset and liability position, business activities, and so on. A loan commitment arrangement is a powerful method for reducing the bank's costs for screening and information collection.

Collateral

Collateral requirements for loans are important credit risk management tools. Loans with these collateral requirements are often referred to as **secured loans.** Collateral, which is property promised to the lender as compensation if the borrower defaults, lessens the consequences of adverse selection because it reduces the lender's losses in the case of a loan default. If a borrower defaults on a loan with collateral, the lender can sell the collateral and use the proceeds to make up for its losses on the loan. Collateral requirements thus offer important protection for financial institutions making loans, and that is why they are extremely common in loans made by financial institutions.

Compensating Balances

One particular form of collateral required when a bank makes commercial loans is called **compensating balances:** A firm receiving a loan must keep a required minimum amount of funds in a checking account at the bank. For example, a business getting a $10 million loan may be required to keep compensating balances of at least $1 million in its checking account at the bank. If the borrower defaults, this $1 million in compensating balances can be taken by the bank to make up some of the losses on the loan.

Besides serving as collateral, compensating balances help increase the likelihood that a loan will be paid off. They do this by helping the bank monitor the borrower and consequently minimize moral hazard. Specifically, by requiring the borrower to use a checking account at the bank, the bank can observe the firm's check payment practices, which may yield a great deal of information about the borrower's financial condition. For example, a sustained drop in the borrower's checking account balance may signal that the borrower is having financial trouble, or account activity may suggest that the borrower is engaging in risky activities; perhaps a change in suppliers means that the borrower is pursuing new lines of business. Any significant change in the borrower's payment procedures is a signal to the bank that it should make inquiries. Compensating balances therefore make it easier for banks to monitor borrowers more effectively and are consequently another important credit risk management tool.

Credit Rationing

Another way in which successful financial institution managers deal with adverse selection and moral hazard is through **credit rationing:** Lenders refuse to make loans even though borrowers are willing to pay the stated interest rate or even a higher rate. Credit rationing takes two forms. The first occurs when a financial institution refuses to make a loan of *any amount* to a borrower, even if the borrower is willing to pay a higher interest rate. The second occurs when the financial institution is willing to make a loan but restricts the size of the loan to less than the borrower would like.

At first you might be puzzled by the first type of credit rationing. After all, even if the potential borrower is a credit risk, why doesn't the financial institution just extend the loan but at a higher interest rate? The answer is that adverse selection rules out this solution. Individuals and firms with the riskiest investment projects are precisely the ones that are willing to pay the highest interest rates. If a borrower took on a high-risk investment and succeeded, the borrower would become extremely rich. But a financial institution wouldn't want to make such a loan precisely because the investment risk is high; the likely outcome is that the borrower will *not* succeed and the financial institution will not be paid back. Charging a higher interest rate just makes adverse selection worse for the financial institution; that is, it increases the likelihood that the financial institution is lending to a bad credit risk. The financial institution would therefore rather not make any loans at a higher interest rate; instead, it would engage in the first type of credit rationing and would turn down loans.

Financial institutions engage in a second type of credit rationing to guard against moral hazard: They grant loans to borrowers, but not loans as large as the borrowers want. Such credit rationing is necessary because the larger the loan, the greater the benefits from moral hazard. For example, if a financial institution gives you a $1000 loan, you are likely to take actions that enable you to pay it back because you don't want to hurt your credit rating for the future. However, if the financial institution lends you $10 million, you are more likely to fly off to Rio to celebrate. The larger your loan, the greater your incentives to engage in activities that make it less likely that you will repay the loan. Because more borrowers repay their loans if the loan amounts are small, financial institutions ration credit by providing borrowers with smaller loans than they seek.

MANAGING INTEREST-RATE RISK

As the volatility of interest rates increased in the 1980s, financial institution managers became more concerned about their exposure to interest-rate risk, the riskiness of earnings and returns that is associated with changes in interest rates. Indeed, the S&L debacle, described in Chapter 17, made clearer the dangers of interest-rate risk when many S&Ls went out of business because they had not managed interest-rate risk properly. To see what interest-rate risk is all about, let's take a look at the balance sheet of the First National Bank:

First National Bank

Assets		Liabilities	
Reserves and cash items	$5 million	Checkable deposits	$15 million
Securities		Money market deposit accounts	$5 million
Less than 1 year	$5 million	Savings deposits	$15 million
1 to 2 years	$5 million	CDs	
Greater than 2 years	$10 million	Variable-rate	$10 million
Residential mortgages		Less than 1 year	$15 million
Variable-rate	$10 million	1 to 2 years	$5 million
Fixed-rate (30-year)	$10 million	Greater than 2 years	$5 million
Commercial loans		Fed funds	$5 million
Less than 1 year	$15 million	Borrowings	
1 to 2 years	$10 million	Less than 1 year	$10 million
Greater than 2 years	$25 million	1 to 2 years	$5 million
Physical capital	$5 million	Greater than 2 years	$5 million
		Bank capital	$5 million
Total	$100 million	Total	$100 million

The first step in assessing interest-rate risk is for the bank manager to decide which assets and liabilities are rate-sensitive, that is, which have interest rates that will be reset (repriced) within the year. Note that rate-sensitive assets or liabilities can have interest rates repriced within the year either because the debt instrument matures within the year or because the repricing is done automatically, as with variable-rate mortgages.

For many assets and liabilities, deciding whether they are rate-sensitive is straightforward. In our example, the obviously rate-sensitive assets are securities with maturities of less than one year ($5 million), variable-rate mortgages ($10 million), and commercial loans with maturities less than one year ($15 million), for a total of $30 million. However, some assets that look like fixed-rate assets whose interest rates are not repriced within the year actually have a component that is rate-sensitive. For example, although fixed-rate residential mortgages may have a maturity of 30 years, homeowners can repay their mortgages early by selling their homes or repaying the mortgage in some other way. This means that within the year, a certain percentage of these fixed-rate mortgages will be paid off, and interest rates on this amount will be repriced. From past experience the bank manager knows that 20% of the fixed-rate residential mortgages are repaid within a year, which means that $2 million of these mortgages (20% of $10 million) must be considered rate-sensitive. The bank manager adds this $2 million to the

\$30 million of rate-sensitive assets already calculated, for a total of \$32 million in rate-sensitive assets.

The bank manager now goes through a similar procedure to determine the total amount of rate-sensitive liabilities. The obviously rate-sensitive liabilities are money market deposit accounts (\$5 million), variable-rate CDs and CDs with less than one year to maturity (\$25 million), federal funds (\$5 million), and borrowings with maturities of less than one year (\$10 million), for a total of \$45 million. Checkable deposits and savings deposits often have interest rates that can be changed at any time by the bank, although banks often like to keep their rates fixed for substantial periods. Thus these liabilities are partially but not fully rate-sensitive. The bank manager estimates that 10% of checkable deposits (\$1.5 million) and 20% of savings deposits (\$3 million) should be considered rate-sensitive. Adding the \$1.5 million and \$3 million to the \$45 million figure yields a total for rate-sensitive liabilities of \$49.5 million.

Now the bank manager can analyze what will happen if interest rates rise by 1 percentage point, say, on average from 10% to 11%. The income on the assets rises by \$320,000 (= 1% × \$32 million of rate-sensitive assets), while the payments on the liabilities rise by \$495,000 (= 1% × \$49.5 million of rate-sensitive liabilities). The First National Bank's profits now decline by \$175,000 = (\$320,000 – \$495,000). Another way of thinking about this situation is with the net interest margin concept described in Chapter 15, which is interest income minus interest expense divided by bank assets. In this case, the 1% rise in interest rates has resulted in a decline of the net interest margin by 0.175% (= –\$175,000/\$100 million). Conversely, if interest rates fall by 1%, similar reasoning tells us that the First National Bank's income rises by \$175,000 and its net interest margin rises by 0.175%. This example illustrates the following point: ***If a financial institution has more rate-sensitive liabilities than assets, a rise in interest rates will reduce the net interest margin and income, and a decline in interest rates will raise the net interest margin and income.***

Income Gap Analysis

One simple and quick approach to measuring the sensitivity of bank income to changes in interest rates is **gap analysis** (also called **income gap analysis**), in which the amount of rate-sensitive liabilities is subtracted from the amount of rate-sensitive assets. This calculation, *GAP,* can be written as

$$GAP = RSA - RSL \tag{1}$$

where RSA = rate-sensitive assets
RSL = rate-sensitive liabilities

In our example, the bank manager calculates *GAP* to be

$$GAP = \$32 \text{ million} - \$49.5 \text{ million} = -\$17.5 \text{ million}$$

Multiplying *GAP* times the change in the interest rate immediately reveals the effect on bank income:

$$\Delta I = GAP \times \Delta i \tag{2}$$

where ΔI = change in bank income
Δi = change in interest rates

EXAMPLE 1: Income Gap Analysis

Using the –$17.5-million gap calculated using Equation 1, what is the change in income if interest rates rise by 1%?

Solution

The change in income is −$175,000.

$$\Delta I = GAP \times \Delta i$$

where

$GAP = RSA - RSL \qquad = -\$17.5$ million

$\Delta i =$ change in interest rate $= 0.01$

Thus

$$\Delta I = -\$17.5 \text{ million} \times 0.01 = -\$175{,}000$$

The analysis we just conducted is known as *basic gap analysis,* and it suffers from the problem that many of the assets and liabilities that are not classified as rate-sensitive have different maturities. One refinement to deal with this problem, the *maturity bucket approach,* is to measure the gap for several maturity subintervals, called maturity buckets, so that effects of interest-rate changes over a multiyear period can be calculated.

EXAMPLE 2: Income Gap Analysis

The manager of First National Bank notices that the bank balance sheet produces a more refined maturity bucket that allows him to estimate the potential change in income over the next one to two years. Rate-sensitive assets in this period consist of $5 million of securities maturing in one to two years, $10 million of commercial loans maturing in one to two years, and an additional $2 million (20% of fixed-rate mortgages) that the bank expects to be repaid. Rate-sensitive liabilities in this period consist of $5 million of one- to two-year CDs, $5 million of one- to two-year borrowings, $1.5 million of checkable deposits (the 10% of checkable deposits that the bank manager estimates are rate-sensitive in this period), and an additional $3 million of savings deposits (the 20% estimate of savings deposits). For the next one to two years, calculate the gap and the change in income if interest rates rise by 1%.

Solution

The gap calculation for the one- to two-year period is $2.5 million.

$$GAP = RSA - RSL$$

where

$RSA =$ rate-sensitive assets $\qquad = \$17$ million

$RSL =$ rate-sensitive liabilities $= \$14.5$ million

Thus

$$GAP = \$17 \text{ million} - \$14.5 \text{ million} = \$2.5 \text{ million}$$

If interest rates remain 1% higher, then in the second year income will improve by $25,000.

$$\Delta I = GAP \times \Delta i$$

where

$GAP = RSA - RSL \quad = \$2.5$ million

Δi = change in interest rate $= 0.01$

Thus

$$\Delta I = \$2.5 \text{ million} \times 0.01 = \$25{,}000$$

By using the more refined maturity bucket approach, the bank manager can figure out what will happen to bank income over the next several years when there is a change in interest rates.

Duration Gap Analysis

The gap analysis we have examined so far focuses only on the effect of interest-rate changes on income. Clearly, owners and managers of financial institutions care not only about the effect of changes in interest rates on income but also about the effect of changes in interest rates on the market value of the net worth of the financial institution.[1]

An alternative method for measuring interest-rate risk, called **duration gap analysis,** examines the sensitivity of the market value of the financial institution's net worth to changes in interest rates. Duration analysis is based on Macaulay's concept of *duration,* which measures the average lifetime of a security's stream of payments (described in Chapter 3). Recall that duration is a useful concept because it provides a good approximation, particularly when interest-rate changes are small, of the sensitivity of a security's market value to a change in its interest rate using the following formula:

$$\%\Delta P \approx -DUR \times \frac{\Delta i}{1 + i} \tag{3}$$

where

$\%\Delta P = (P_{t+1} - P_t)/P_t$ = percent change in market value of the security
DUR = duration
i = interest rate

After having determined the duration of all assets and liabilities on the bank's balance sheet, the bank manager could use this formula to calculate how the

[1]Note that accounting net worth is calculated on a historical-cost (book-value) basis, meaning that the value of assets and liabilities is based on their initial price. However, book-value net worth does not give a complete picture of the true worth of the firm; the market value of net worth provides a more accurate measure. This is why duration gap analysis focuses on what happens to the market value of net worth, and not on book value, when interest rates change.

market value of each asset and liability changes when there is a change in interest rates and then calculate the effect on net worth. There is, however, an easier way to go about doing this, derived from the basic fact about duration we learned in Chapter 3: Duration is additive; that is, the duration of a portfolio of securities is the weighted average of the durations of the individual securities, with the weights reflecting the proportion of the portfolio invested in each. What this means is that the bank manager can figure out the effect that interest-rate changes will have on the market value of net worth by calculating the average duration for assets and for liabilities and then using those figures to estimate the effects of interest-rate changes.

To see how a bank manager would do this, let's return to the balance sheet of the First National Bank. The bank manager has already used the procedures outlined in Chapter 3 to calculate the duration of each asset and liability, as listed in Table 1. For each asset, the manager then calculates the weighted duration by multiplying the duration times the amount of the asset divided by total assets, which in this case is \$100 million. For example, in the case of securities with maturities less than one year, the manager multiplies the 0.4 year of duration times \$5 million divided by \$100 million to get a weighted duration of 0.02. (Note that

TABLE 1 Duration of the First National Bank's Assets and Liabilities

	Amount (\$ millions)	Duration (years)	Weighted Duration (years)
Assets			
Reserves and cash items	5	0.0	0.00
Securities			
Less than 1 year	5	0.4	0.02
1 to 2 years	5	1.6	0.08
Greater than 2 years	10	7.0	0.70
Residential mortgages			
Variable-rate	10	0.5	0.05
Fixed-rate (30-year)	10	6.0	0.60
Commercial loans			
Less than 1 year	15	0.7	0.11
1 to 2 years	10	1.4	0.14
Greater than 2 years	25	4.0	1.00
Physical capital	5	0.0	0.00
Average duration			2.70
Liabilities			
Checkable deposits	15	2.0	0.32
Money market deposit accounts	5	0.1	0.01
Savings deposits	15	1.0	0.16
CDs			
Variable-rate	10	0.5	0.05
Less than 1 year	15	0.2	0.03
1 to 2 years	5	1.2	0.06
Greater than 2 years	5	2.7	0.14
Fed funds	5	0.0	0.00
Borrowings			
Less than 1 year	10	0.3	0.03
1 to 2 years	5	1.3	0.07
Greater than 2 years	5	3.1	0.16
Average duration			1.03

physical assets have no cash payments, so they have a duration of zero years.) Doing this for all the assets and adding them up, the bank manager gets a figure for the average duration of the assets of 2.70 years.

The manager follows a similar procedure for the liabilities, noting that total liabilities excluding capital are $95 million. For example, the weighted duration for checkable deposits is determined by multiplying the 2.0-year duration by $15 million divided by $95 million to get 0.32. Adding up these weighted durations, the manager obtains an average duration of liabilities of 1.03 years.

EXAMPLE 3: Duration Gap Analysis

The bank manager wants to know what happens when interest rates rise from 10% to 11%. The total asset value is $100 million, and the total liability value is $95 million. Use Equation 3 to calculate the change in the market value of the assets and liabilities.

Solution

With a total asset value of $100 million, the market value of assets falls by $2.5 million ($100 million × 0.025 = $2.5 million).

$$\%\Delta P = -DUR \times \frac{\Delta i}{1 + i}$$

where

DUR = duration = 2.70
Δi = change in interest rate = 0.11 − 0.10 = 0.01
i = interest rate = 0.10

Thus

$$\%\Delta P \approx -2.70 \times \frac{0.01}{1 + 0.10} = -0.025 = -2.5\%$$

With total liabilities of $95 million, the market value of liabilities falls by $0.9 million ($95 million × 0.009 = –$0.9 million).

$$\%\Delta P \approx -DUR \times \frac{\Delta i}{1 + i}$$

where

DUR = duration = 1.03
Δi = change in interest rate = 0.11 − 0.10 = 0.01
i = interest rate = 0.10

Thus

$$\%\Delta P \approx -1.03 \times \frac{0.01}{1 + 0.10} = -0.009 = -0.9\%$$

The result is that the net worth of the bank would decline by $1.6 million (–$2.5 million – (–$0.9 million) = –$2.5 million + $0.9 million = –$1.6 million).

The bank manager could have gotten to the answer even more quickly by calculating what is called a *duration gap,* which is defined as follows:

$$DUR_{gap} = DUR_a - \left(\frac{L}{A} \times DUR_l\right) \tag{4}$$

where
DUR_a = average duration of assets
DUR_l = average duration of liabilities
L = market value of liabilities
A = market value of assets

EXAMPLE 4: Duration Gap Analysis

Based on the information provided in Example 3, use Equation 4 to determine the duration gap for First National Bank.

Solution

The duration gap for First National Bank is 1.72 years.

$$DUR_{gap} = DUR_a - \left(\frac{L}{A} \times DUR_l\right)$$

where

DUR_a = average duration of assets = 2.70
L = market value of liabilities = 95
A = market value of assets = 100
DUR_l = average duration of liabilities = 1.03

Thus

$$DUR_{gap} = 2.70 - \left(\frac{95}{100} \times 1.03\right) = 1.72 \text{ years}$$

To estimate what will happen if interest rates change, the bank manager uses the DUR_{gap} calculation in Equation 3 to obtain the change in the market value of net worth as a percentage of total assets. In other words, the change in the market value of net worth as a percentage of assets is calculated as

$$\frac{\Delta NW}{A} \approx -DUR_{gap} \times \frac{\Delta i}{1+i} \tag{5}$$

EXAMPLE 5: Duration Gap Analysis

What is the change in the market value of net worth as a percentage of assets if interest rates rise from 10% to 11%? (Use Equation 5.)

Solution

A rise in interest rates from 10% to 11% would lead to a change in the market value of net worth as a percentage of assets of –1.6%

$$\frac{\Delta NW}{A} = -DUR_{gap} \times \frac{\Delta i}{1 + i}$$

where

$$\begin{aligned} DUR_{gap} &= \text{duration gap} &&= 1.72 \\ \Delta i &= \text{change in interest rate} = 0.11 - 0.10 &&= 0.01 \\ i &= \text{interest rate} &&= 0.10 \end{aligned}$$

Thus

$$\frac{\Delta NW}{A} = -1.72 \times \frac{0.01}{1 + 0.10} = -0.016 = -1.6\%$$

With assets totaling \$100 million, Example 5 indicates a fall in the market value of net worth of \$1.6 million, which is the same figure that we found in Example 3.

As our examples make clear, both income gap analysis and duration gap analysis indicate that the First National Bank will suffer from a rise in interest rates. Indeed, in this example, we have seen that a rise in interest rates from 10% to 11% will cause the market value of net worth to fall by \$1.6 million, which is one-third the initial amount of bank capital. Thus the bank manager realizes that the bank faces substantial interest-rate risk because a rise in interest rates could cause it to lose a lot of its capital. Clearly, income gap analysis and duration gap analysis are useful tools for telling a financial institution manager the institution's degree of exposure to interest-rate risk.

Study Guide To make sure that you understand income gap and duration gap analysis, you should be able to verify that if interest rates fall from 10% to 5%, the First National Bank will find its income increasing and the market value of its net worth rising. For even more practice with these concepts, do some of the problems at the end of this chapter.

Example of a Nonbanking Financial Institution

So far we have focused on an example involving a banking institution that has borrowed short and lent long so that when interest rates rise, both income and the net worth of the institution fall. It is important to recognize that income and duration gap analysis applies equally to other financial institutions. Furthermore, it is important for you to see that some financial institutions have income and duration gaps that are opposite in sign to those of banks, so that when interest rates rise, both income and net worth rise rather than fall. To get a more complete picture of income and duration gap analysis, let us look at a nonbank financial institution, the Friendly Finance Company, which specializes in making consumer loans.

The Friendly Finance Company has the following balance sheet:

Friendly Finance Company

Assets		Liabilities	
Cash and deposits	$3 million	Commercial paper	$40 million
Securities		Bank loans	
Less than 1 year	$5 million	Less than 1 year	$3 million
1 to 2 years	$1 million	1 to 2 years	$2 million
Greater than 2 years	$1 million	Greater than 2 years	$5 million
Consumer loans		Long-term bonds and	
Less than 1 year	$50 million	other long-term debt	$40 million
1 to 2 years	$20 million	Capital	$10 million
Greater than 2 years	$15 million		
Physical capital	$5 million		
Total	$100 million	Total	$100 million

The manager of the Friendly Finance Company calculates the rate-sensitive assets to be equal to the $5 million of securities with maturities less than one year plus the $50 million of consumer loans with maturities of less than one year, for a total of $55 million of rate-sensitive assets. The manager then calculates the rate-sensitive liabilities to be equal to the $40 million of commercial paper, all of which has a maturity of less than one year, plus the $3 million of bank loans maturing in less than a year, for a total of $43 million. The calculation of the income gap is then

$$GAP = RSA - RSL = \$55 \text{ million} - \$43 \text{ million} = \$12 \text{ million}$$

To calculate the effect on income if interest rates rise by 1%, the manager multiplies the *GAP* of $12 million times the change in the interest rate to get the following:

$$\Delta I = GAP \times \Delta i = \$12 \text{ million} \times 1\% = \$120{,}000$$

Thus the manager finds that the finance company's income will rise by $120,000 when interest rates rise by 1%. The reason that the company has benefited from the interest-rate rise, in contrast to the First National Bank, whose profits suffer from the rise in interest rates, is that the Friendly Finance Company has a positive income gap because it has more rate-sensitive assets than liabilities.

Like the bank manager, the manager of the Friendly Finance Company is also interested in what happens to the market value of the net worth of the company when interest rates rise by 1%. So the manager calculates the weighted duration of each item in the balance sheet, adds them up as in Table 2, and obtains a duration for the assets of 1.16 years and for the liabilities, 2.77 years. The duration gap is then calculated to be

$$DUR_{gap} = DUR_a - \left(\frac{L}{A} \times DUR_l\right) = 1.16 - \left(\frac{90}{100} \times 2.77\right) = -1.33 \text{ years}$$

Since the Friendly Finance Company has a negative duration gap, the manager realizes that a rise in interest rates by 1 percentage point from 10% to 11% will increase the market value of net worth of the firm. The manager checks this

TABLE 2 Duration of the Friendly Finance Company's Assets and Liabilities

	Amount ($ millions)	Duration (years)	Weighted Duration (years)
Assets			
Cash and deposits	3	0.0	0.00
Securities			
Less than 1 year	5	0.5	0.05
1 to 2 years	1	1.7	0.02
Greater than 2 years	1	9.0	0.09
Consumer loans			
Less than 1 year	50	0.5	0.25
1 to 2 years	20	1.5	0.30
Greater than 2 years	15	3.0	0.45
Physical capital	5	0.0	0.00
Average duration			1.16
Liabilities			
Commercial paper	40	0.2	0.09
Bank loans			
Less than 1 year	3	0.3	0.01
1 to 2 years	2	1.6	0.04
Greater than 2 years	5	3.5	0.19
Long-term bonds and other long-term debt	40	5.5	2.44
Average duration			2.77

by calculating the change in the market value of net worth as a percentage of assets:

$$\Delta NW = -DUR_{gap} \times \frac{\Delta i}{1+i} = -(-1.33) \times \frac{0.01}{1+0.10} = 0.012 = 1.2\%$$

With assets of $100 million, this calculation indicates that net worth will rise in market value by $1.2 million.

Even though the income and duration gap analysis indicates that the Friendly Finance Company gains from a rise in interest rates, the manager realizes that if interest rates go in the other direction, the company will suffer a fall in income and market value of net worth. Thus the finance company manager, like the bank manager, realizes that the institution is subject to substantial interest-rate risk.

Some Problems with Income and Duration Gap Analysis

Although you might think that income and duration gap analysis is complicated enough, further complications make a financial institution manager's job even harder.

One assumption that we have been using in our discussion of income and duration gap analysis is that when the level of interest rates changes, interest rates on all maturities change by exactly the same amount. That is the same as saying that we conducted our analysis under the assumption that the slope of the yield curve remains unchanged. Indeed, the situation is even worse for duration gap analysis because the duration gap is calculated assuming that interest rates for all maturities are the same—in other words, the yield curve is assumed to be flat. As our discussion of the term structure of interest rates in Chapter 5 indicated, however, the yield curve is not flat, and the slope of the yield curve fluctuates and has a tendency to change when the level of the interest rate changes. Thus to get a truly accurate assessment of interest-rate risk, a financial institution manager has to assess what might happen to the slope of the yield curve when the level of the interest rate changes and then take this information into account when assessing interest-rate risk. In addition, duration gap analysis is based on the approximation in Equation 3 and thus only works well for small changes in interest rates.

A problem with income gap analysis is that as we have seen, the financial institution manager must make estimates of the proportion of supposedly fixed-rate assets and liabilities that may be rate-sensitive. This involves estimates of the likelihood of prepayment of loans or customer shifts out of deposits when interest rates change. Such guesses are not easy to make, and as a result, the financial institution manager's estimates of income gaps may not be very accurate. A similar problem occurs in calculating durations of assets and liabilities because many of the cash payments are uncertain. Thus the estimate of the duration gap might not be accurate either.

Do these problems mean that managers of banks and other financial institutions should give up on gap analysis as a tool for measuring interest-rate risk? Financial institutions do use more sophisticated approaches to measuring interest-rate risk, such as scenario analysis and value-at-risk analysis, which make greater use of computers to more accurately measure changes in prices of assets when interest rates change. Income and duration gap analyses, however, still provide simple frameworks to help financial institution managers to get a first assessment of interest-rate risk, and they are thus useful tools in the financial institution managers' toolkit.

THE PRACTICING FINANCIAL INSTITUTION MANAGER

Strategies for Managing Interest-Rate Risk

Once financial institution managers have done the duration and income gap analysis for their institutions, they must decide which alternative strategies to pursue. If the manager of the First National Bank firmly believes that interest rates will fall in the future, he or she may be willing to take no action knowing that the bank has more rate-sensitive liabilities than rate-sensitive assets and so will benefit from the expected interest-rate decline. However, the bank manager also realizes that the First National Bank is subject to substantial interest-rate risk because there is always a possibility that interest rates will rise rather than fall, and as we have seen, this outcome could bankrupt the bank. The manager might try to shorten the duration of the bank's assets to increase their rate sensitivity either by purchasing assets of shorter maturity or by converting fixed-rate loans into adjustable-rate loans. Alternatively, the bank manager could lengthen the duration of the liabilities. With these adjustments to the bank's assets and liabilities, the bank would be less affected by interest-rate swings.

For example, the bank manager might decide to eliminate the income gap by increasing the amount of rate-sensitive assets to $49.5 million to equal the $49.5 million of rate-sensitive liabilities. Or the manager could reduce rate-sensitive liabilities to $32 million so that they equal rate-sensitive assets. In either case, the income gap would now be zero, so a change in interest rates would have no effect on bank profits in the coming year.

Alternatively, the bank manager might decide to immunize the market value of the bank's net worth completely from interest-rate risk by adjusting assets and liabilities so that the duration gap is equal to zero. To do this, the manager can set DUR_{gap} equal to zero in Equation 4 and solve for DUR_a:

$$DUR_a = \frac{L}{A} \times DUR_l = \frac{95}{100} \times 1.03 = 0.98$$

These calculations reveal that the manager should reduce the average duration of the bank's assets to 0.98 year. To check that the duration gap is set equal to zero, the calculation is

$$DUR_{gap} = 0.98 - \left(\frac{95}{100} \times 1.03\right) = 0$$

In this case, as in Equation 5, the market value of net worth would remain unchanged when interest rates change. Alternatively, the bank manager could calculate the value of the duration of the liabilities that would produce a duration gap of zero. To do this would involve setting DUR_{gap} equal to zero in Equation 4 and solving for DUR_l:

$$DUR_l = DUR_a \times \frac{A}{L} = 2.70 \times \frac{100}{95} = 2.84$$

This calculation reveals that the interest-rate risk could also be eliminated by increasing the average duration of the bank's liabilities to 2.84 years. The manager again checks that the duration gap is set equal to zero by calculating

$$DUR_{gap} = 2.70 - \left(\frac{95}{100} \times 2.84\right) = 0$$

Study Guide To see if you understand how a financial institution manager can protect income and net worth from interest-rate risk, first calculate how the Friendly Finance Company might change the amount of its rate-sensitive assets or its rate-sensitive liabilities to eliminate the income gap. You should find that the income gap can be eliminated either by reducing the amount of rate-sensitive assets to \$43 million or by raising the amount of rate-sensitive liabilities to \$55 million. Also do the calculations to determine what modifications to the duration of the assets or liabilities would immunize the market value of Friendly Finance's net worth from interest-rate risk. You should find that interest-rate risk would be eliminated if the duration of the assets were set to 2.49 years or if the duration of the liabilities were set to 1.29 years.

One problem with eliminating a financial institution's interest-rate risk by altering the balance sheet is that doing so might be very costly in the short run. The financial institution may be locked into assets and liabilities of particular durations because of its field of expertise. Fortunately, recently developed financial instruments, such as financial futures, options, and interest-rate swaps, help financial institutions manage their interest-rate risk without requiring them to rearrange their balance sheets. We discuss these instruments and how they can be used to manage interest-rate risk in the next chapter.

SUMMARY

1. The concepts of adverse selection and moral hazard explain the origin of many credit risk management principles involving loan activities, including screening and monitoring, development of long-term customer relationships, loan commitments, collateral, compensating balances, and credit rationing.

2. With the increased volatility of interest rates that occurred in recent years, financial institutions became more concerned about their exposure to interest-rate risk. Income gap and duration gap analyses tell a financial institution if it has fewer rate-sensitive assets than liabilities (in which case a rise in interest rates will reduce income and a fall in interest rates will raise it) or more rate-sensitive assets than liabilities (in which case a rise in interest rates will raise income and a fall in interest rates will reduce it). Financial institutions can manage interest-rate risk by modifying their balance sheets and by making use of new financial instruments.

KEY TERMS

compensating balance, *p. 600*
credit rationing, *p. 601*
duration gap analysis, *p. 605*
gap analysis (income gap analysis), *p. 603*
loan commitment, *p. 600*
secured loan, *p. 600*

QUESTIONS AND PROBLEMS

1. Can a financial institution keep borrowers from engaging in risky activities if there are no restrictive covenants written into the loan agreement?

***2.** Why are secured loans an important method of lending for financial institutions?

3. "If more customers want to borrow funds at the prevailing interest rate, a financial institution can increase its profits by raising interest rates on its loans." Is this statement true, false, or uncertain? Explain your answer.

***4.** Why is being nosy a desirable trait for a banker?

5. A bank almost always insists that the firms it lends to keep compensating balances at the bank. Why?

***6.** "Because diversification is a desirable strategy for avoiding risk, it never makes sense for a financial institution to specialize in making specific types of loans." Is this statement true, false, or uncertain? Explain your answer.

For Problems 7–14, assume that the First National Bank initially has the balance sheet shown on page 602 and that interest rates are initially at 10%.

7. If the First National Bank sells $10 million of its securities with maturities greater than two years and replaces them with securities maturing in less than one year, what is the income gap for the bank? What will happen to profits next year if interest rates fall by 3 percentage points?

***8.** If the First National Bank decides to convert $5 million of its fixed-rate mortgages into variable-rate mortgages, what happens to its interest-rate risk? Explain with gap analysis.

9. If the manager of the First National Bank revises the estimate of the percentage of fixed-rate mortgages that are repaid within a year from 20% to 10%, what will be the revised estimate of the interest-rate risk the bank faces? What will happen to profits next year if interest rates fall by 2 percentage points?

***10.** If the manager of the First National Bank revises the estimate of the percentage of checkable deposits that are rate-sensitive from 10% to 25%, what will be the revised estimate of the interest-rate risk the bank faces? What will happen to profits next year if interest rates rise by 5 percentage points?

11. Given the estimates of duration in Table 1, what will happen to the bank's net worth if interest rates rise by 10 percentage points? Will the bank stay in business? Why or why not?

***12.** If the manager of the First National Bank revises the estimates of the duration of the bank's assets to four years and liabilities to two years, what is the effect on net worth if interest rates rise by 2 percentage points?

13. Given the estimates of duration in Problem 12, how should the bank alter the duration of its assets to immunize its net worth from interest-rate risk?

***14.** Given the estimates of duration in Problem 12, how should the bank alter the duration of its liabilities to immunize its net worth from interest-rate risk?

For Problems 15–20, assume that the Friendly Finance Company initially has the balance sheet shown on page 610 and that interest rates are initially at 8%.

15. If the manager of the Friendly Finance Company decides to sell off $10 million of the company's consumer loans, half maturing within one year and half maturing in greater than two years, and uses the resulting funds to buy $10 million of Treasury bills, what is the income gap for the company? What will happen to profits next year if interest rates fall by 5 percentage points? How could the Friendly Finance Company alter its balance sheet to immunize its income from this change in interest rates?

***16.** If the Friendly Finance Company raises an additional $20 million with commercial paper and uses the funds to make $20 million of consumer loans that mature in less than one year, what happens to its interest-rate risk? In this situation, what additional changes could it make in its balance sheet to eliminate the income gap?

17. Given the estimates of duration in Table 2, what will happen to the Friendly Finance Company's net worth if interest rates rise by 3 percentage points? Will the company stay in business? Why or why not?

***18.** If the manager of the Friendly Finance Company revises the estimates of the duration of the company's assets to two years and liabilities to four years, what is the effect on net worth if interest rates rise by 3 percentage points?

19. Given the estimates of duration found in Problem 18, how should the Friendly Finance Company alter the duration of its assets to immunize its net worth from interest-rate risk?

***20.** Given the estimates of duration in Problem 18, how should the Friendly Finance Company alter the duration of its liabilities to immunize its net worth from interest-rate risk?

WEB EXERCISES

Risk Management in Financial Institutions

1. This chapter discussed the need financial institutions have to control credit risk by lending to creditworthy borrowers. If you allow your credit to deteriorate, you may find yourself unable to borrow when you need to. Go to http://www.quicken.com/cms/viewers/article/banking/39654 and assess your own creditworthiness. What can you do to improve your appeal to lenders?

2. The FDIC is extremely concerned with risk management in banks. High-risk banks are more likely to fail and cost the FDIC money. The FDIC regularly examines banks and rates them using a system called CAMELS. Go to http://www.fdic.gov/regulations/safety/manual/index.html. What does the acronym CAMELS stand for? Go to Part VII. 7.1 and review the discussion of Market Risk. Summarize the FDIC interest-rate risk-measurement methods.

Chapter 23 Hedging with Financial Derivatives

Preview

Starting in the 1970s and increasingly in the 1980s and 1990s, the world became a riskier place for financial institutions. Swings in interest rates widened, and the bond and stock markets went through some episodes of increased volatility. As a result of these developments, managers of financial institutions have become more concerned with reducing the risk their institutions face. Given the greater demand for risk reduction, the process of financial innovation described in Chapter 15 came to the rescue by producing new financial instruments that help financial institution managers manage risk better. These instruments, called **financial derivatives,** have payoffs that are linked to previously issued securities and are extremely useful risk reduction tools.

In this chapter we look at the most important financial derivatives that managers of financial institutions use to reduce risk: forward contracts, financial futures, options, and swaps. We examine not only how markets for each of these financial derivatives work but also how each can be used by financial institution managers to reduce risk.

HEDGING

Financial derivatives are so effective in reducing risk because they enable financial institutions to **hedge**, that is, engage in a financial transaction that reduces or eliminates risk. When a financial institution has bought an asset, it is said to have taken a **long position**, and this exposes the institution to risk if the returns on the asset are uncertain. On the other hand, if it has sold an asset that it has agreed to deliver to another party at a future date, it is said to have taken a **short position**, and this can also expose the institution to risk. Financial derivatives can be used to reduce risk by invoking the following basic principle of hedging: ***Hedging risk involves engaging in a financial transaction that offsets a long***

position by taking an additional short position, or offsets a short position by taking an additional long position. In other words, if a financial institution has *bought* a security and has therefore taken a long position, it conducts a hedge by contracting to *sell* that security (take a short position) at some future date. Alternatively, if it has taken a short position by *selling* a security that it needs to deliver at a future date, then it conducts a hedge by contracting to *buy* that security (take a long position) at a future date. We first look at how this principle can be applied using forward contracts.

FORWARD MARKETS

Forward contracts are agreements by two parties to engage in a financial transaction at a future (forward) point in time. Here we focus on forward contracts that are linked to debt instruments, called **interest-rate forward contracts;** later in the chapter we discuss forward contracts for foreign currencies.

Interest-Rate Forward Contracts

Interest-rate forward contracts involve the future sale of a debt instrument and have several dimensions: (1) specification of the actual debt instrument that will be delivered at a future date, (2) amount of the debt instrument to be delivered, (3) price (interest rate) on the debt instrument when it is delivered, and (4) date on which delivery will take place. An example of an interest-rate forward contract might be an agreement for the First National Bank to sell to the Rock Solid Insurance Company, one year from today, $5 million face value of the 8s of 2023 Treasury bonds (coupon bonds with an 8% coupon rate that mature in 2023) at a price that yields the same interest rate on these bonds as today's, say, 8%. Because Rock Solid will buy the securities at a future date, it has taken a long position, while the First National Bank, which will sell the securities, has taken a short position.

THE PRACTICING FINANCIAL INSTITUTION MANAGER

Hedging Interest-Rate Risk with Forward Contracts

To understand why the First National Bank might want to enter into this forward contract, suppose that you are the manager of the First National Bank and have previously bought $5 million of the 8s of 2023 Treasury bonds, which currently sell at par value and so their yield to maturity is also 8%. Because these are long-term bonds, you recognize that you are exposed to substantial interest-rate risk and worry that if interest rates rise in the future, the price of these bonds will fall, resulting in a substantial capital loss that may cost you your job. How do you hedge this risk?

Knowing the basic principle of hedging, you see that your long position in these bonds must be offset by a short position with a forward contract. That is, you need to contract to sell these bonds at a future date at the current par value price. As a result you agree with another party, in this case, Rock Solid Insurance Company, to sell them the $5 million of the 8s of 2023 Treasury bonds at par one year from today. By entering into this forward contract, you have locked in the future price and so have eliminated the price risk First National Bank faces from interest-rate changes. In other words, you have successfully hedged against interest-rate risk.

Why would the Rock Solid Insurance Company want to enter into the forward contract with the First National Bank? Rock Solid expects to receive premiums of $5 million in one year's time that it will want to invest in the 8s of 2023 but worries that interest rates on these bonds will decline between now and next year. By using the forward contract, it is able to lock in the 8% interest rate on the Treasury bonds (which will be sold to it by the First National Bank).

Pros and Cons of Forward Contracts

The advantage of forward contracts is that they can be as flexible as the parties involved want them to be. This means that an institution like the First National Bank may be able to hedge completely the interest-rate risk for the exact security it is holding in its portfolio, just as it has in our example.

However, forward contracts suffer from two problems that severely limit their usefulness. The first is that it may be very hard for an institution like the First National Bank to find another party (called a *counterparty*) to make the contract with. There are brokers to facilitate the matching up of parties like the First National Bank with the Rock Solid Insurance Company, but there may be few institutions that want to engage in a forward contract specifically for the 8s of 2023. This means that it may prove impossible to find a counterparty when a financial institution like the First National Bank wants to make a specific type of forward contract. Furthermore, even if the First National Bank finds a counterparty, it may not get as high a price as it wants because there may not be anyone else to make the deal with. A serious problem for the market in interest-rate forward contracts, then, is that it may be difficult to make the financial transaction or that it will have to be made at a disadvantageous price; in the parlance of the financial world, this market suffers from a *lack of liquidity*. (Note that this use of the term *liquidity* when it is applied to a market is somewhat broader than its use when it is applied to an asset. For an asset, liquidity refers to the ease with which the asset can be turned into cash, whereas for a market, liquidity refers to the ease of carrying out financial transactions.)

The second problem with forward contracts is that they are subject to default risk. Suppose that in one year's time, interest rates rise so that the price of the 8s of 2023 falls. The Rock Solid Insurance Company might then decide that it would like to default on the forward contract with the First National Bank because it can now buy the bonds at a price lower than the agreed price in the forward contract. Or perhaps Rock Solid may not have been rock solid and will have gone bust during the year and so is no longer available to complete the terms of the forward contract. Because there is no outside organization guaranteeing the contract, the only recourse is for the First National Bank to go to the courts to sue Rock Solid, but this process will be costly. Furthermore, if Rock Solid is already bankrupt, the First National Bank will suffer a loss; the bank can no longer sell the 8s of 2023 at the price it had agreed with Rock Solid but instead will have to sell at a price well below that because the price of these bonds has fallen.

The presence of default risk in forward contracts means that parties to these contracts must check each other out to be sure that the counterparty is both financially sound and likely to be honest and live up to its contractual obligations. Because this is a costly process and because all the adverse selection and moral hazard problems discussed in earlier chapters apply, default risk is a major barrier to the use of interest-rate forward contracts. When the default risk problem is combined with a lack of liquidity, we see that these contracts may be of limited usefulness to financial institutions. Although there is a market for interest-rate forward contracts, particularly in Treasury and mortgage-backed securities, it is not nearly as large as the financial futures market, to which we turn next.

FINANCIAL FUTURES MARKETS

Given the default risk and liquidity problems in the interest-rate forward market, another solution to hedging interest-rate risk was needed. This solution was provided by the development of financial futures contracts by the Chicago Board of Trade starting in 1975.

Financial Futures Contracts

Find information about financial futures contract specifications at http://home.teleport.com/~rpotts/fincontr.html

A **financial futures contract** is similar to an interest-rate forward contract in that it specifies that a financial instrument must be delivered by one party to another on a stated future date. However, it differs from an interest-rate forward contract in several ways that overcome some of the liquidity and default problems of forward markets.

To understand what financial futures contracts are all about, let's look at one of the most widely traded futures contracts, that for Treasury bonds, which are traded on the Chicago Board of Trade. (An illustration of how prices on these contracts are quoted can be found in the "Following the Financial News" box.) The contract value is for $100,000 face value of bonds. Prices are quoted in points, with each point equal to $1000, and the smallest change in price is one thirty-second of a point ($31.25). This contract specifies that the bonds to be delivered must have at least 15 years to maturity at the delivery date (and must also not be callable, that is, redeemable by the Treasury at its option, in less than 15 years). If the Treasury bonds delivered to settle the futures contract have a coupon rate different from the 8% specified in the futures contract, the amount of bonds to be delivered is adjusted to reflect the difference in value between the delivered bonds and the 8% coupon bond. In line with the terminology used for forward contracts, parties who have bought a futures contract and thereby agreed to buy (take delivery) of the bonds are said to have taken a *long position*, and parties who have sold a futures contract and thereby agreed to sell (deliver) the bonds have taken a *short position*.

To make our understanding of this contract more concrete, let's consider what happens when you buy or sell one of these Treasury bond futures contracts. Let's say that on February 1, you sell one $100,000 June contract at a price of 115 (that is, $115,000). By selling this contract, you agree to deliver $100,000 face value of the long-term Treasury bonds to the contract's counterparty at the end of June for $115,000. By buying the contract at a price of 115, the buyer has agreed to pay $115,000 for the $100,000 face value of bonds when you deliver them at the end of June. If interest rates on long-term bonds rise so that when the contract matures at the end of June the price of these bonds has fallen to 110 ($110,000 per $100,000 of face value), the buyer of the contract will have lost $5000 because he or she paid $115,000 for the bonds but can sell them only for the market price of $110,000. But you, the seller of the contract, will have gained $5000 because you can now sell the bonds to the buyer for $115,000 but have to pay only $110,000 for them in the market.

It is even easier to describe what happens to the parties who have purchased futures contracts and those who have sold futures contracts if we recognize the

FOLLOWING THE FINANCIAL NEWS

Financial Futures

The prices for financial futures contracts for debt instruments are published daily. In the *Wall Street Journal,* these prices are found in the "Commodities" section under the "Interest Rate" heading of the "Futures Prices" columns. An excerpt is reproduced here.

Interest Rate

TREASURY BONDS (CBT)-$100,000; pts. 32nds of 100%

	OPEN	HIGH	LOW	SETTLE	CHANGE	LIFETIME HIGH	LIFETIME LOW	OPEN INTEREST
Mar	100-17	101-19	100-17	101-17	+ 32	111-16	97-11	418,017
June	99-15	100-13	99-15	100-12	+ 33	110-00	96-30	32,522

Est vol 48,000; vol Fri 85,703; open int 450,604, −7,806.

Information for each contract is presented in columns, as follows. (The Chicago Board of Trade's contract for delivery of long-term Treasury bonds in March 2002, is used as an example.)

Open: Opening price; each point corresponds to $1000 of face value—100 17/32 is $100,531 for the March contract

High: Highest traded price that day—101 19/32 is $101,594 for the March contract

Low: Lowest traded price that day—100 17/32 is $100,531 for the March contract

Settle: Settlement price, the closing price that day—101 17/32 is $101,531 for the March contract

Chg: Change in the settlement price from the previous trading day—+32/32 is + $1000 for the March contract

Lifetime High: Highest price ever—111 16/32 is $111,500 for the March contract

Lifetime Low: Lowest price ever—97 11/32 is $97,344 for the March contract

Open Interest: Number of contracts outstanding—418,017 for the March contract, with a face value of $41.8 billion (418,017 × $100,000)

Source: Wall Street Journal, January 2, 2002, p. C16. Republished by permission of Dow Jones, Inc. via Copyright Clearance Center, Inc.

following fact: ***At the expiration date of a futures contract, the price of the contract is the same as the price of the underlying asset to be delivered.*** To see why this is the case, consider what happens on the expiration date of the June contract at the end of June when the price of the underlying $100,000 face value Treasury bond is 110 ($110,000). If the futures contract is selling below 110, say, at 109, a trader can buy the contract for $109,000, take delivery of the bond, and immediately sell it for $110,000, thereby earning a quick profit of $1000. Because earning this profit involves no risk, it is a great deal that everyone would like to get in on. That means that everyone will try to buy the contract, and as a result, its price will rise. Only when the price rises to 110 will the profit opportunity cease to exist and the buying pressure disappear. Conversely, if the price of the futures contract is above 110, say, at 111, everyone will want to sell the contract. Now the sellers get $111,000 from selling the futures contract but have to pay only $110,000 for the Treasury bonds that they must deliver to the buyer of the contract, and the $1000 difference is their profit. Because this profit involves no risk, traders will continue to sell the futures contract until its price falls back down to 110, at which price there are no longer any profits to be made. The elimination of riskless profit opportunities in the futures market is referred to as **arbitrage,** and it guarantees that the price of a futures contract at expiration equals the price of the underlying asset to be delivered.[1]

Armed with the fact that a futures contract at expiration equals the price of the underlying asset makes it even easier to see who profits and loses from such a contract when interest rates change. When interest rates have risen so that the price of the Treasury bond is 110 on the expiration day at the end of June, the June Treasury bond futures contract will also have a price of 110. Thus if you bought the contract for 115 in February, you have a loss of 5 points, or $5000 (5% of $100,000). But if you sold the futures contract at 115 in February, the decline in price to 110 means that you have a profit of 5 points, or $5000.

THE PRACTICING FINANCIAL INSTITUTION MANAGER

Hedging with Financial Futures

As the manager of the First National Bank, you can also use financial futures to hedge the interest-rate risk on its holdings of $5 million of the 8s of 2023.

To see how to do this, suppose that in March 2003, the 8s of 2023 are the long-term bonds that would be delivered in the Chicago Board of Trade's T-bond futures contract expiring one year in the future, in March 2004. Also suppose that the interest rate on these bonds is expected to remain at 8% over the next year so that both the 8s of 2023 and the futures contract are selling at par (i.e., the $5 million of bonds is selling for $5 million and the $100,000 futures contract is selling for $100,000). The basic principle of hedging indicates that you need to offset the long position in these bonds with a short position, so you have to sell the futures contract. But how many contracts should you sell? The number of contracts required to hedge the interest-rate risk is found by dividing the amount of the asset to be hedged by the dollar value of each contract, as is shown in Equation 1 below.

$$NC = VA/VC \tag{1}$$

where

NC = number of contracts for the hedge
VA = value of the asset
VC = value of each contract

EXAMPLE 1: Hedging with Interest-Rate Futures

The 8s of 2023 are the long-term bonds that would be delivered in the CBT T-bond futures contract expiring one year in the future in March 2004. The interest rate on these bonds is expected to remain at 8% over the next year so that both the 8s of 2023 and the futures contract are selling at par. How many contracts must First National sell to remove its interest-rate exposure from its $5 million holdings of the 8s of 2023?[2]

[1] In actuality, futures contracts sometimes set conditions for delivery of the underlying assets that cause the price of the contract at expiration to differ slightly from the price of the underlying assets. Because the difference in price is extremely small, we ignore it in this chapter.

[2] In the real world, designing a hedge is somewhat more complicated than the example here because the bond that is most likely to be delivered might not be an 8s of 2023.

Solution

$$VA = \$5 \text{ million}$$
$$VC = \$100{,}000$$

Thus

$$NC = \$5 \text{ million}/\$100{,}000 = 50$$

You therefore hedge the interest-rate risk by selling 50 of the Treasury Bond futures contracts.

Now suppose that over the next year, interest rates increase to 10% due to an increased threat of inflation. The value of the 8s of 2023 the First National Bank is holding will then fall to \$4,163,508 in March 2004.[3] Thus, the loss from the long position in these bonds is \$836,492 as shown below:

Value on March 2004 @10% interest rate	\$4,163,508
Value on March 2003 @8% interest rate	−\$5,000,000
Loss	−\$ 836,492

However, the short position in the 50 futures contracts that obligate you to deliver \$5 million of the 8s of 2023 on March 2004 has a value equal to the \$5 million of these bonds on that date, after the interest rate has risen to 10%. This value is \$4,163,568, as we have seen above. Yet when you sold the futures contract, the buyer was obligated to pay you \$5 million on the maturity date. Thus the gain from the short position on these contracts is also \$836,492, as shown below:

Amount paid to you on March 2004, agreed in March 2003	\$5,000,000
Cost of bonds delivered on March 2004 @10% interest rate	−\$4,163,508
Gain	\$ 836,492

Therefore the net gain for the First National Bank is zero, showing that the hedge has been conducted successfully.

The hedge just described is called a **micro hedge** because the financial institution is hedging the interest-rate risk for a specific asset it is holding. A second type of hedge that financial institutions engage in is called a **macro hedge,** in which the hedge is for the institution's entire portfolio. For example, if a bank has more rate-sensitive liabilities than assets, we have seen in Chapter 22 that a rise in interest rates will cause the value of the bank to decline. By selling interest-rate future contracts that will yield a profit when interest rates rise, the bank can off-set the losses on its overall portfolio from an interest-rate rise and thereby hedge its interest-rate risk.

Organization of Trading in Financial Futures Markets

Financial futures contracts are traded in the United States on organized exchanges such as the Chicago Board of Trade, the Chicago Mercantile Exchange, the New York Futures Exchange, the MidAmerica Commodity Exchange, and the Kansas City Board of Trade. These exchanges are highly competitive with one another,

[3]The value of the bonds can be calculated using a financial calculator as follows: FV = \$5,000,000, PMT = \$400,000, I = 10%, N = 19, PV = \$4,163,508.

and each organization tries to design contracts and set rules that will increase the amount of futures trading on its exchange.

The futures exchanges and all trades in financial futures in the United States are regulated by the Commodity Futures Trading Commission (CFTC), which was created in 1974 to take over the regulatory responsibilities for futures markets from the Department of Agriculture. The CFTC oversees futures trading and the futures exchanges to ensure that prices in the market are not being manipulated, and it also registers and audits the brokers, traders, and exchanges to prevent fraud and to ensure the financial soundness of the exchanges. In addition, the CFTC approves proposed futures contracts to make sure that they serve the public interest. The most widely traded financial futures contracts listed in the *Wall Street Journal* and the exchanges where they are traded (along with the number of contracts outstanding, called **open interest,** on January 2, 2002) are listed in Table 1.[4]

Given the globalization of other financial markets in recent years, it is not surprising that increased competition from abroad has been occurring in financial futures markets as well.

Globalization of Financial Futures Markets

Because American futures exchanges were the first to develop financial futures, they dominated the trading of financial futures in the early 1980s. For example, in 1985, all of the top ten futures contracts were traded on exchanges in the United States. With the rapid growth of financial futures markets and the resulting high profits made by the American exchanges, foreign exchanges saw a profit opportunity and began to enter this business. By the 1990s, Eurodollar contracts traded on the London International Financial Futures Exchange, Japanese government bond contracts and Euroyen contracts traded on the Tokyo Stock Exchange, French government bond contracts traded on the Marché à Terme International de France, and Nikkei 225 contracts traded on the Osaka Securities Exchange. All became among the most widely traded futures contracts in the world. Even developing countries are getting into the act. In 1996, seven developing countries (also referred to as *emerging-market countries*) established futures exchanges, and this number is expected to double within a few years.

Foreign competition has also spurred knockoffs of the most popular financial futures contracts initially developed in the United States. These contracts traded on foreign exchanges are virtually identical to those traded in the United States and have the advantage that they can be traded when the American exchanges are closed. The movement to 24-hour-a-day trading in financial futures has been further stimulated by the development of the Globex electronic trading system, which allows traders throughout the world to trade futures even when the exchanges are not officially open. Financial futures trading is thus well on the way to being completely internationalized, and competition between U.S. and foreign exchanges will continue to be intense in the future.

Explaining the Success of Futures Markets

The tremendous success of the financial futures market in Treasury bonds is evident from the fact that the total open interest of Treasury bond contracts was 418,017 on

[4]For a more detailed treatment of financial futures and option markets, see Franklin R. Edwards and Cindy W. Ma, *Futures and Options* (New York: McGraw-Hill, 1992).

TABLE 1 Widely Traded Financial Futures Contracts

Type of Contract	Contract Size	Exchange*	Open Interest (January 2, 2002)
Interest-Rate Contracts			
Treasury bonds	$100,000	CBT	418,017
Treasury notes	$100,000	CBT	538,391
Five-year Treasury notes	$100,000	CBT	447,337
Two-year Treasury notes	$200,000	CBT	69,559
Thirty-day Fed funds	$5 million	CBT	31,714
Treasury bills	$1 million	CME	533
One-month LIBOR	$3 million	CME	14,497
Municipal Bond Index	$1000	CBT	7,736
Eurodollar	$1 million	CME	4,229,780
Euroyen	100 million	CME	30,207
Sterling	£500,000	LIFFE	732,345
Long Gilt	£50,000	LIFFE	58,147
Three-month Euribar	1,000,000 euros	LIFFE	1,714,847
Euroswiss franc	SF 1 million	LIFFE	141,856
Ten-year Euronational bonds	100,000 euros	MATIF	12,316
Canadian banker's acceptance	C$1,000,000	ME	504,056
Ten-year German Euro bonds	E100,000	ME	54,300
Stock Index Contracts			
Standard & Poor's 500 Index	$250 × index	CME	482,048
Standard & Poor's MIDCAP 400	$500 × index	CME	14,780
NASDAQ 100	$100 × index	CME	47,412
Nikkei 225 Stock Average	$5 × index	CME	12,587
Financial Times–Stock Exchange 100-Share Index	£10 per index point	LIFFE	356,840
Currency Contracts			
Yen	¥ 12,500,000	CME	111,232
Euro	E125,000	CME	93,058
Canadian dollar	C$100,000	CME	58,305
British pound	£ 62,500	CME	23,591
Swiss franc	SF 125,000	CME	35,097
Mexican peso	N$ 500,000	CME	26,902

*Exchange abbreviations: CBT, Chicago Board of Trade; CME, Chicago Mercantile Exchange; LIFFE, London International Financial Futures Exchange; MATIF, Marché à Terme International de France; ME, Montreal Exchange.

Source: Wall Street Journal, January 2, 2002, p. C11. Republished by permission of Dow Jones, Inc. via Copyright Clearance Center, Inc.

January 2, 2002, for a total value of over $41 billion (418,017 × $100,000). There are several differences between financial futures and forward contracts and in the organization of their markets that help explain why financial futures markets, like those for Treasury bonds have been so successful.

Several features of futures contracts were designed to overcome the liquidity problem inherent in forward contracts. The first feature is that, in contrast to forward contracts, the quantities delivered and the delivery dates of futures contracts are standardized, making it more likely that different parties can be matched up in the futures market, thereby increasing the liquidity of the market. In the case of the Treasury bond contract, the quantity delivered is $100,000 face value of bonds, and the delivery dates are set to be the last business day of March, June, September, and December. The second feature is that after the futures contract has been bought or sold, it can be traded (bought or sold) again at any time until the delivery date. In contrast, once a forward contract is agreed on, it typically cannot be traded. The third feature is that in a futures contract, not just one specific type of Treasury bond is deliverable on the delivery date, as in a forward contract. Instead, any Treasury bond that matures in more than 15 years and is not callable for 15 years is eligible for delivery. Allowing continuous trading also increases the liquidity of the futures market, as does the ability to deliver a range of Treasury bonds rather than one specific bond.

Another reason why futures contracts specify that more than one bond is eligible for delivery is to limit the possibility that someone might corner the market and "squeeze" traders who have sold contracts. To corner the market, someone buys up all the deliverable securities so that investors with a short position cannot obtain from anyone else the securities that they contractually must deliver on the delivery date. As a result, the person who has cornered the market can set exorbitant prices for the securities that investors with a short position must buy to fulfill their obligations under the futures contract. The person who has cornered the market makes a fortune, but investors with a short position take a terrific loss. Clearly, the possibility that corners might occur in the market will discourage people from taking a short position and might therefore decrease the size of the market. By allowing many different securities to be delivered, the futures contract makes it harder for anyone to corner the market because a much larger amount of securities would have to be purchased to establish the corner. Corners are more than a theoretical possibility, as Box 1 indicates, and are a concern to both regulators and the organized exchanges that design futures contracts.

Trading in the futures market has been organized differently from trading in forward markets to overcome the default risk problems arising in forward contracts. In both types, for every contract there must be a buyer who is taking a long position and a seller who is taking a short position. However, the buyer and seller of a futures contract make their contract not with each other but with the clearinghouse associated with the futures exchange. This setup means that the buyer of the futures contract does not need to worry about the financial health or trustworthiness of the seller, or vice versa, as in the forward market. As long as the clearinghouse is financially solid, buyers and sellers of futures contracts do not have to worry about default risk.

To make sure that the clearinghouse is financially sound and does not run into financial difficulties that might jeopardize its contracts, buyers or sellers of futures contracts must put an initial deposit, called a **margin requirement,** of perhaps $2000 per Treasury bond contract into a margin account kept at their brokerage firm. Futures contracts are then **marked to market** every day. What this means is that at the end of every trading day, the change in the value of the futures contract is added to or subtracted from the margin account. Suppose that after buying the Treasury bond contract at a price of 115 on Wednesday morning, its closing price at the end of the day, the *settlement price*, falls to 114. You now have a loss of 1 point, or $1000, on the contract, and the seller who sold you the contract has a gain of 1 point, or $1000. The $1000 gain is added to the seller's margin account, making a total of $3000 in that account, and the $1000 loss is subtracted from your account, so you now only have $1000 in your account. If the amount in this margin account falls below the maintenance margin requirement (which can be the same as the initial requirement but is usually a little less), the trader is required to add money to the account. For example, if the maintenance margin requirement is also $2000, you would have to add $1000 to your

BOX 1

The Hunt Brothers and the Silver Crash

In early 1979, two Texas billionaires, W. Herbert Hunt and his brother, Nelson Bunker Hunt, decided that they were going to get into the silver market in a big way. Herbert stated his reasoning for purchasing silver as follows: "I became convinced that the economy of the United States was in a weakening condition. This reinforced my belief that investment in precious metals was wise . . . because of rampant inflation." Although the Hunts' stated reason for purchasing silver was that it was a good investment, others felt that their real motive was to establish a corner in the silver market. Along with other associates, several of them from the Saudi royal family, the Hunts purchased close to 300 million ounces of silver in the form of either actual bullion or silver futures contracts. The result was that the price of silver rose from $6 an ounce to over $50 an ounce by January 1980.

Once the regulators and the futures exchanges got wind of what the Hunts were up to, they decided to take action to eliminate the possibility of a corner by limiting to 2000 the number of contracts that any single trader could hold. This limit, which was equivalent to 10 million ounces, was only a small fraction of what the Hunts were holding, and so they were forced to sell. The silver market collapsed soon afterward, with the price of silver declining back to below $10 an ounce. The losses to the Hunts were estimated to be in excess of $1 billion, and they soon found themselves in financial difficulty. They had to go into debt to the tune of $1.1 billion, mortgaging not only the family's holdings in the Placid Oil Company but also 75,000 head of cattle, a stable of thoroughbred horses, paintings, jewelry, and even such mundane items as irrigation pumps and lawn mowers. Eventually both Hunt brothers were forced into declaring personal bankruptcy, earning them the dubious distinction of declaring the largest personal bankruptcies ever in the United States.

Nelson and Herbert Hunt paid a heavy price for their excursion into the silver market, but at least Nelson retained his sense of humor. When asked right after the collapse of the silver market how he felt about his losses, he said, "A billion dollars isn't what it used to be."

Source: G. Christian Hill, "Dynasty's Decline: The Current Question About the Hunts of Dallas: How Poor Are They?" *Wall Street Journal*, November 14, 1984, p. C28. Republished by permission of Dow Jones, Inc. via Copyright Clearance Center, Inc.

account to bring it up to $2000. Margin requirements and marking to market make it far less likely that a trader will default on a contract, thus protecting the futures exchange from losses.

A final advantage that futures markets have over forward markets is that most futures contracts do not result in delivery of the underlying asset on the expiration date, whereas forward contracts do. A trader who sold a futures contract is allowed to avoid delivery on the expiration date by making an offsetting purchase of a futures contract. Because the simultaneous holding of the long and short positions means that the trader would in effect be delivering the bonds to itself, under the exchange rules the trader is allowed to cancel both contracts. Allowing traders to cancel their contracts in this way lowers the cost of conducting trades in the futures market relative to the forward market in that a futures trader can avoid the costs of physical delivery, which is not so easy with forward contracts.

THE PRACTICING FINANCIAL INSTITUTION MANAGER

Hedging Foreign Exchange Risk with Forward and Futures Contracts

As we discussed in Chapter 12, foreign exchange rates have been highly volatile in recent years. The large fluctuations in exchange rates subject financial institutions and other businesses to significant foreign exchange risk because they generate substantial gains and losses. Luckily for financial institution managers, the financial derivatives discussed in this chapter—forward and financial futures contracts—can be used to hedge foreign exchange risk.

To understand how financial institution managers manage foreign exchange risk, let's suppose that in January, the First National Bank's customer Frivolous Luxuries, Inc., is due a payment of 10 million euros in two months for $10 million worth of goods it has just sold in Germany. Frivolous Luxuries is concerned that if the value of the euro falls substantially from its current value of $1, the company might suffer a large loss because the 10 million euro payment will no longer be worth $10 million. So Sam, the CEO of Frivolous Luxuries, calls up his friend Mona, the manager of the First National Bank, and asks her to hedge this foreign exchange risk for his company. Let's see how the bank manager does this using forward and financial futures contracts.

Hedging Foreign Exchange Risk with Forward Contracts

Forward markets in foreign exchange have been highly developed by commercial banks and investment banking operations that engage in extensive foreign exchange trading and so are widely used to hedge foreign exchange risk. Mona knows that she can use this market to hedge the foreign exchange risk for Frivolous Luxuries. Such a hedge is quite straightforward for her to execute. Because the payment of euros in two months means that at that time Sam would hold a long position in euros, Mona knows that the basic principle of hedging indicates that she should offset this long position by a short position. Thus, she just enters a forward contract that obligates her to sell 10 million euros two months from now in exchange for dollars at the current forward rate of $1 per euro.[5]

In two months, when her customer receives the 10 million euros, the forward contract ensures that it is exchanged for dollars at an exchange rate of $1 per euro, thus yielding $10 million. No matter what happens to future exchange rates, Frivolous Luxuries will be guaranteed $10 million for the goods it sold in Germany. Mona calls up her friend Sam to let him know that his company is now protected from any foreign exchange movements, and he thanks her for her help.

Hedging Foreign Exchange Risk with Futures Contracts

As an alternative, Mona could have used the currency futures market to hedge the foreign exchange risk. In this case, she would see that the Chicago Mercantile Exchange has a euro contract with a contract amount of 125,000 euros and a price of $1 per euro. To do the hedge, Mona must sell euros as with the forward contract, to the tune of 10 million euros of the March futures.

[5]The forward exchange rate will probably differ slightly from the current spot rate of $1 per euro because the interest rates in Europe and the United States may not be equal. In that case, as we saw in Equation 2 in Chapter 12, the future expected exchange rate will not equal the current spot rate and neither will the forward rate. However, since interest differentials have typically been less than 6% at an annual rate (1% bimonthly), the expected appreciation or depreciation of the euro over a two-month period has always been less than 1%. Thus the forward rate is always close to the current spot rate, and so our assumption in the example that the forward rate and the spot rate are the same is a reasonable one.

EXAMPLE 2: Hedging with Foreign Exchange Futures Contracts

How many of the Chicago Mercantile Exchange March euro contracts must Mona sell in order to hedge the 10 million euro payment due in March?

Solution

Using Equation 1:

$$VA = 10 \text{ million euros}$$
$$VC = 125{,}000 \text{ euros}$$

Thus

$$NC = 10 \text{ million}/125{,}000 = 40$$

Mona does the hedge by selling 40 of the CME euro contracts.

Given the $1 per euro price, the sale of the contract yields 40 × 125,000 euros = $10 million. The futures hedge thus again enables her to lock in the exchange rate for Frivolous Luxuries so that it gets its payment of $10 million.

One advantage of using the futures market is that the contract size of 125,000 euros, worth $125,000, is quite a bit smaller than the minimum size of a forward contract, which is usually $1 million or more. However, in this case, the bank manager is making a large enough transaction that she can use either the forward or the futures market. Her choice depends on whether the transaction costs are lower in one market than in the other. If the First National Bank is active in the forward market, that market would probably have the lower transaction costs, but if First National rarely deals in foreign exchange forward contracts, the bank manager may do better by sticking with the futures market.

STOCK INDEX FUTURES

More detailed information about stock index futures is available at www.usafutures.com/stockindexfutures.htm

As we have seen, financial futures markets can be useful in hedging interest-rate risk. However, financial institution managers, particularly those who manage mutual funds, pension funds, and insurance companies, also worry about **stock market risk,** the risk that occurs because stock prices fluctuate. Stock index futures were developed in 1982 to meet the need to manage stock market risk, and they have become among the most widely traded of all futures contracts. The futures trading in stock price indexes is now controversial (see Box 2) because critics assert that it has led to substantial increases in market volatility, especially in such episodes as 1987's stock market crash.

Stock Index Futures Contracts

To understand stock index futures contracts, let's look at the Standard & Poor's 500 Index futures contract (shown in the "Following the Financial News" box), the most widely traded stock index futures contract in the United States. (The S&P 500 Index measures the value of 500 of the most widely traded stocks.) Stock index futures contracts differ from most other financial futures contracts in that they are settled with

BOX 2

Program Trading and Portfolio Insurance: Were They to Blame for the Stock Market Crash of 1987?

In the aftermath of the Black Monday crash on October 19, 1987, in which the stock market declined by over 20% in one day, trading strategies involving stock price index futures markets have been accused (especially by the Brady Commission, which was appointed by President Reagan to study the stock market) of being culprits in the market collapse. One such strategy, called program trading, involves computer-directed trading between the stock index futures and the stocks whose prices are reflected in the stock price index. Program trading is a form of arbitrage conducted to keep stock index futures and stock prices in line with each other. For example, when the price of the stock index futures contract is far below the prices of the underlying stocks in the index, program traders buy index futures, thereby increasing their price, and sell the stocks, thereby lowering their price. Critics of program trading assert that the sharp fall in stock index futures prices on Black Monday led to massive selling in the stock market to keep stock prices in line with the stock index futures prices.

Some experts also blame portfolio insurance for amplifying the crash because they feel that when the stock market started to fall, uncertainty in the market increased, and the resulting increased desire to hedge stocks led to massive selling of stock index futures. The resulting large price declines in stock index futures contracts then led to massive selling of stocks by program traders to keep prices in line.

Because they view program trading and portfolio insurance as causes of the October 1987 market collapse, critics of stock index futures have advocated restrictions on their trading. In response, certain brokerage firms, as well as organized exchanges, have placed limits on program trading. For example, the New York Stock Exchange has curbed computerized program trading when the Dow Jones Industrial Average moves by more than 50 points in one day. However, some prominent finance scholars (among them Nobel laureate Merton Miller of the University of Chicago) do not accept the hypothesis that program trading and portfolio insurance provoked the stock market crash. They believe that the prices of stock index futures primarily reflect the same economic forces that move stock prices—changes in the market's underlying assessment of the value of stocks.

a cash delivery rather than with the delivery of a security. Cash settlement gives these contracts the advantage of a high degree of liquidity and also rules out the possibility of anyone's cornering the market. In the case of the S&P 500 Index contract, at the final settlement date, the cash delivery due is $250 times the index, so if the index is at 1000 on the final settlement date, $250,000 would be the amount due. The price quotes for this contract are also quoted in terms of index points, so a change of 1 point represents a change of $250 in the contract's value.

To understand what all this means, let's look at what happens when you buy or sell this futures contract. Suppose that on February 1, you sell one June contract at a price of 1000 (that is, $250,000). By selling the contract, you agree to a delivery amount due of $250 times the S&P 500 Index on the expiration date at the end of June. By buying the contract at a price of 1000, the buyer has agreed to pay $250,000 for the delivery amount due of $250 times the S&P 500 Index at the expiration date at the end of June. If the stock market falls so that the S&P 500 Index declines to 900 on the expiration date, the buyer of the contract will have lost $25,000 because he or she has agreed to pay $250,000 for the contract but has a delivery amount due of the $225,000 (900 × $250). But you, the seller of the contract, will have a profit of $25,000 because you agreed to receive a $250,000 purchase price for the contract but have a delivery amount due of only $225,000. Because the amount payable and due are netted out, only $25,000 will change hands; you, the seller of the contract, receive $25,000 from the buyer.

FOLLOWING THE FINANCIAL NEWS

Stock Index Futures

The prices for stock index futures contracts are published daily. In the *Wall Street Journal*, these prices are found in the section "Futures Prices" under the "Index" heading. An excerpt from this listing is reproduced here.

Index

S&P 500 INDEX (CME) $250 times index

						LIFETIME		OPEN
	OPEN	HIGH	LOW	SETTLE	CHANGE	HIGH	LOW	INTEREST
Mar	115950	116250	114100	114920	−10.10	134960	94100	479,906
June	....	....	....	115140	−10.40	170550	95030	12,645
Sept	115000	116950	115000	115470	−10.80	165670	95530	2,114

Est vol 31,660; vol Fri 35,552; open int 496,439, −2,076.
Idx prl: High 1161.16; Low 1148.04; Close 1148.08, −12.94.

Information for each contract is given in columns, as follows. (The March S&P 500 Index contract is used as an example.)

Open: Opening price; each point corresponds to $250 times the index—1159.50; that is, 1159.50 × $250 = $289,875 per contract

High: Highest traded price that day—1162.50, or $290,625 per contract

Low: Lowest traded price that day—1141.00, or $285,250 per contract

Settle: Settlement price, the closing price that day—1149.20, or $287,300 per contract

Chg: Change in the settlement price from the previous trading day— −10.10 points, or $2,525 per contract

High: High price for the year—1349.60, or $337,400 per contract

Low: Low price for the year—941.00, or $235,250 per contract

Open Interest: Number of contracts outstanding—479,906, or a total value of $137 billion (= 479,906 × $287,300).

Source: Wall Street Journal, January 2, 2002, p. C11. Republished by permission of Dow Jones, Inc. via Copyright Clearance Center, Inc.

THE PRACTICING FINANCIAL INSTITUTION MANAGER

Hedging with Stock Index Futures

Financial institution managers can use stock index futures contracts to reduce stock market risk.

EXAMPLE 3: Hedging with Stock Index Futures

Suppose that in March 2004, Mort, the portfolio manager of the Rock Solid Insurance Company, has a portfolio of stocks valued at $100 million that moves percentagewise one-for-one with the S&P Index. Suppose also that the March 2005 S&P 500 Index contracts are currently selling at a price of 1000. How many of these contracts should Mort sell so that he hedges the stock market risk of this portfolio over the next year?

Solution

Because Mort is holding a long position, using the basic principle of hedging, he must offset it by taking a short position in which he sells S&P futures. To calculate the number of contracts he needs to sell, he uses Equation 1.

$$VA = \$100 \text{ million}$$

$$VC = \$250 \times 1000 = \$250{,}000$$

Thus

$$NC = \$100 \text{ million}/\$250{,}000 = 400$$

Mort's hedge therefore involves selling 400 S&P March 2005 futures contracts.

If the S&P Index falls 10% to 900, the $100 million portfolio will suffer a $10 million loss. At the same time, however, Mort makes a profit of 100 × $250 = $25,000 per contract because he agreed to be paid $250,000 for each contract at a price of 1000, but at a price of 900 on the expiration date he has a delivery amount of only $225,000 (900 × $250). Multiplied by 400 contracts, the $25,000 profit per contract yields a total profit of $10 million. The $10 million profit on the futures contract exactly offsets the loss on Rock Solid's stock portfolio, so Mort has been successful in hedging the stock market risk.

Why would Mort be willing to forego profits when the stock market rises? One reason is that he might be worried that a bear market was imminent, so he wants to protect Rock Solid's portfolio from the coming decline (and so protect his job).

OPTIONS

Another vehicle for hedging interest-rate and stock market risk involves the use of options on financial instruments. **Options** are contracts that give the purchaser the option, or *right,* to buy or sell the underlying financial instrument at a specified price, called the **exercise price** or **strike price,** within a specific period of time (the *term to expiration*). The seller (sometimes called the *writer*) of the option is *obligated* to buy or sell the financial instrument to the purchaser if the owner of the option exercises the right to sell or buy. These option contract features are important enough to be emphasized: The *owner* or buyer of an option does not have to exercise the option; he or she can let the option expire without using it. Hence the *owner* of an option is *not obligated* to take any action but rather has the *right* to exercise the contract if he or she so chooses. The *seller* of an option, by contrast, has no choice in the matter; he or she *must* buy or sell the financial instrument if the owner exercises the option.

Because the right to buy or sell a financial instrument at a specified price has value, the owner of an option is willing to pay an amount for it called a **premium.** There are two types of option contracts: **American options** can be exercised *at any time up to* the expiration date of the contract, and **European options** can be exercised only *on* the expiration date.

Option contracts are written on a number of financial instruments (an example of which is shown in the "Following the Financial News" box). Options on individual stocks are called **stock options,** and such options have existed for a long time. Option contracts on financial futures called **financial futures options,**

FOLLOWING THE FINANCIAL NEWS

Futures Options

The prices for financial futures options are published daily. In the *Wall Street Journal,* they are found in the section "Futures Options Prices" under the "Interest Rate" heading. An excerpt from this listing is reproduced here.

Information for each contract is reported in columns, as follows. (The Chicago Board of Trade's option on its Treasury Notes futures contract is used as an example.)

Interest Rate
T-Notes (CBT)
$100,000; points and 64ths of 100%

STRIKE	CALLS-SETTLE			PUTS-SETTLE		
PRICE	Feb	Mar	Jun	Feb	Mar	Jun
103	2-31	2-55	2-52	0-22	0-46	2-06
104	1-47	2-12	2-19	0-38	1-03	2-37
105	1-09	1-39	1-55	1-00	1-30	3-08
106	0-45	1-10	1-31	1-36	2-01	. . . .
107	0-25	0-51	1-11	2-16	2-42	. . . .
108	0-13	0-34	. . . .	. . . .	3-24	5-11

Est. vol. 36,000; Fr 40,482 calls; 14,532 puts
Op. Int. Fri 636,432 calls; 436,838 puts

Strike Price: Strike (exercise) price of each contract, which runs from 103 to 108

Calls-Settle: Premium (price) at settlement for call options on the Treasury bond futures expiring in the month listed, with each full point representing $1000 and sixty-fourths of a point listed to the right of the hyphen; at a strike price of 104, the February call option's premium is 1-47, or $1,734.38 per contract

Puts-Settle: Premium (price) at settlement for put options on the Treasury bond futures expiring in the month listed, with each full point representing $1000 and sixty-fourths of a point listed to the right of the hyphen; at a strike price of 104, the February put option's premium is 0-38, or $593.75 per contract

Source: Wall Street Journal, January 2, 2002, p. C12. Republished by permission of Dow Jones, Inc. via Copyright Clearance Center, Inc.

or, more commonly, **futures options,** were developed in 1982 and have become the most widely traded option contracts.

You might wonder why option contracts are more likely to be written on financial futures than on underlying debt instruments such as bonds or certificates of deposit. As you saw earlier in the chapter, at the expiration date, the price of the futures contract and of the deliverable debt instrument will be the same because of arbitrage. So it would seem that investors should be indifferent about having the option written on the debt instrument or on the futures contract. However, financial futures contracts have been so well designed that their markets are often more liquid than the markets in the underlying debt instruments. Investors would rather have the option contract written on the more liquid instrument, in this case the futures contract. That explains why the most popular futures options are written on many of the same futures contracts listed in Table 1.

The regulation of option markets is split between the Securities and Exchange Commission (SEC), which regulates stock options, and the Commodity Futures Trading Commission (CFTC), which regulates futures options. Regulation focuses on ensuring that writers of options have enough capital to make good on their contractual obligations and on overseeing traders and exchanges to prevent fraud and ensure that the market is not being manipulated.

Option Contracts

A **call option** is a contract that gives the owner the right to *buy* a financial instrument at the exercise price within a specific period of time. A **put option** is a contract that gives the owner the right to *sell* a financial instrument at the exercise price within a specific period of time.

Study Guide Remembering which is a call option and which is a put option is not always easy. To keep them straight, just remember that having a *call* option to *buy* a financial instrument is the same as having the option to *call in* the instrument for delivery at a specified price. Having a *put* option to *sell* a financial instrument is the same as having the option to *put up* an instrument for the other party to buy.

Profits and Losses on Option and Futures Contracts

To understand option contracts more fully, let's first examine the option on the June Treasury bond futures contract that we looked at earlier. Recall that if you buy this futures contract at a price of 115 (that is, $115,000), you have agreed to pay $115,000 for $100,000 face value of long-term Treasury bonds when they are delivered to you at the end of June. If you sold this futures contract at a price of 115, you agreed, in exchange for $115,000, to deliver $100,000 face value of the long-term Treasury bonds at the end of June. An option contract on the Treasury bond futures contract has several key features: (1) It has the same expiration date as the underlying futures contract, (2) it is an American option and so can be exercised at any time before the expiration date, and (3) the premium (price) of the option is quoted in points that are the same as in the futures contract, so each point corresponds to $1000. If, for a premium of $2000, you buy one call option contract on the June Treasury bond contract with an exercise price of 115, you have purchased the right to buy (call in) the June Treasury bond futures contract for a price of 115 ($115,000 per contract) at any time through the expiration date of this contract at the end of June. Similarly, when for $2000 you buy a put option on the June Treasury bond contract with an exercise price of 115, you have the right to sell (put up) the June Treasury bond futures contract for a price of 115 ($115,000 per contract) at any time until the end of June.

Futures option contracts are somewhat complicated, so to explore how they work and how they can be used to hedge risk, let's first examine how profits and losses on the call option on the June Treasury bond futures contract occur. In February, our old friend Irving the Investor buys, for a $2000 premium, a call option on the $100,000 June Treasury bond futures contract with a strike price of 115. (We assume that if Irving exercises the option, it is on the expiration date at the end of June and not before.) On the expiration date at the end of June, suppose that the underlying Treasury bond for the futures contract has a price of 110. Recall that on the expiration date, arbitrage forces the price of the futures contract to be the same as the price of the underlying bond, so it too has a price of 110 on the expiration date at the end of June. If Irving exercises the call option and buys the futures contract at an exercise price of 115, he will lose money by buying at 115 and selling at the lower market price of 110. Because Irving is smart, he will not exercise the option, but he will be out the $2000 premium he paid. In such a situation, in which the price of the underlying financial instrument is below the exercise price, a call option is said to be "out of the money." At the price of 110 (less than the exercise price), Irving thus suffers a loss on the option contract of the $2000 premium he paid. This loss is plotted as point A in panel (a) of Figure 1.

On the expiration date, if the price of the futures contract is 115, the call option is "at the money," and Irving is indifferent whether he exercises his option

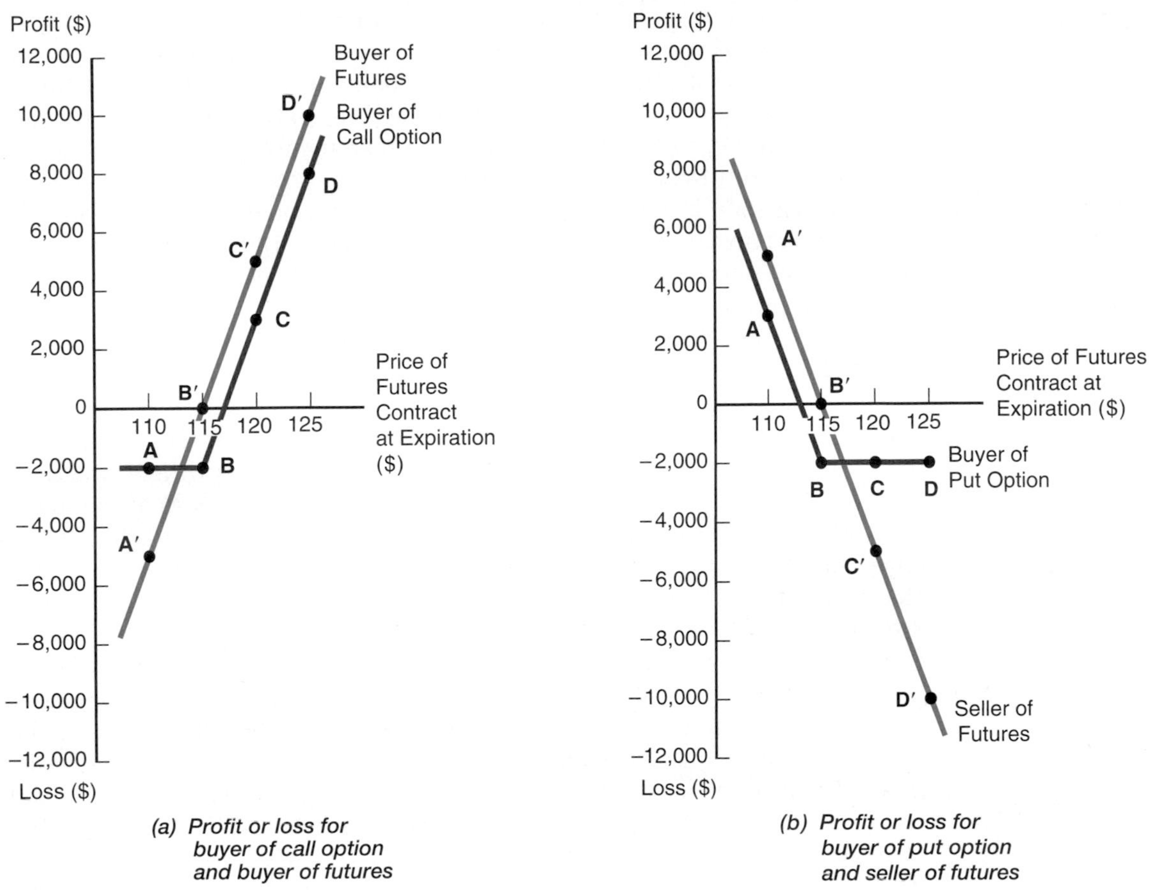

FIGURE 1 Profits and Losses on Options Versus Futures Contracts

The futures contract is the $100,000 June Treasury bond contract, and the option contracts are written on this futures contract with an exercise price of 115. Panel (a) shows the profits and losses for the buyer of the call option and the buyer of the futures contract, and panel (b) shows the profits and losses for the buyer of the put option and the seller of the futures contract.

to buy the futures contract or not, since exercising the option at 115 when the market price is also at 115 produces no gain or loss. Because he has paid the $2000 premium, at the price of 115 his contract again has a net loss of $2000, plotted as point B.

If the futures contract instead has a price of 120 on the expiration day, the option is "in the money," and Irving benefits from exercising the option: He would buy the futures contract at the exercise price of 115 and then sell it for 120, thereby earning a 5% gain ($5000 profit) on the $100,000 Treasury bond contract. Because Irving paid a $2000 premium for the option contract, however, his net profit is $3000 ($5000–$2000). The $3000 profit at a price of 120 is plotted as point C. Similarly, if the price of the futures contract rose to 125, the option contract would yield a net profit of $8000 ($10,000 from exercising the option minus the $2000 premium), plotted as point D. Plotting these points, we get the kinked profit curve for the call option that we see in panel (a).

Suppose that instead of purchasing the futures *option* contract in February, Irving decides instead to buy the $100,000 June Treasury bond *futures* contract at the price of 115. If the price of the bond on the expiration day at the end of June declines to 110, meaning that the price of the futures contract also falls to 110, Irving suffers a loss of 5 percentage points, or $5000. The loss of $5000 on the futures contract at a price of 110 is plotted as point A′ in panel (a). At a price of 115 on the expiration date, Irving would have a zero profit on the futures contract, plotted as point B′. At a price of 120, Irving would have a profit on the contract of 5 percentage points, or $5000 (point C′), and at a price of 125, the profit would be 10 percentage points, or $10,000 (point D′). Plotting these points, we get the linear (straight-line) profit curve for the futures contract that appears in panel (a).

Now we can see the major difference between a futures contract and an option contract. As the profit curve for the futures contract in panel (a) indicates, the futures contract has a linear profit function: Profits grow by an equal dollar amount for every point increase in the price of the underlying financial instrument. By contrast, the kinked profit curve for the option contract is highly nonlinear, meaning that profits do not always grow by the same amount for a given change in the price of the underlying financial instrument. The reason for this nonlinearity is that the call option protects Irving from having losses that are greater than the amount of the $2000 premium. In contrast, Irving's loss on the futures contract is $5000 if the price on the expiration day falls to 110, and if the price falls even further, Irving's loss will be even greater. This insurance-like feature of option contracts explains why their purchase price is referred to as a premium. Once the underlying financial instrument's price rises above the exercise price, however, Irving's profits grow linearly. Irving has given up something by buying an option rather than a futures contract. As we see in panel (a), when the price of the underlying financial instrument rises above the exercise price, Irving's profits are always less than that on the futures contract by exactly the $2000 premium he paid.

Panel (b) plots the results of the same profit calculations if Irving buys not a call but a put option (an option to sell) with an exercise price of 115 for a premium of $2000 and if he sells the futures contract rather than buying one. In this case, if on the expiration date the Treasury bond futures have a price above the 115 exercise price, the put option is "out of the money." Irving would not want to exercise the put option and then have to sell the futures contract he owns as a result of exercising the put option at a price below the market price and lose money. He would not exercise his option, and he would be out only the $2000 premium he paid. Once the price of the futures contract falls below the 115 exercise price, Irving benefits from exercising the put option because he can sell the futures contract at a price of 115 but can buy it at a price below this. In such a situation, in which the price of the underlying instrument is below the exercise price, the put option is "in the money," and profits rise linearly as the price of the futures contract falls. The profit function for the put option illustrated in panel (b) of Figure 1 is kinked, indicating that Irving is protected from losses greater than the amount of the premium he paid. The profit curve for the sale of the futures contract is just the negative of the profit for the futures contract in panel (a) and is therefore linear.

Panel (b) of Figure 1 confirms the conclusion from panel (a) that profits on option contracts are nonlinear but profits on futures contracts are linear.

Study Guide To make sure you understand how profits and losses on option and futures contracts are generated, calculate the net profits on the put option and the short position in the futures contract at prices on the expiration day of 110, 115, 120, and 125. Then verify that your calculations correspond to the points plotted in panel (b) of Figure 1.

Two other differences between futures and option contracts must be mentioned. The first is that the initial investment on the contracts differs. As we saw earlier in the chapter, when a futures contract is purchased, the investor must put up a fixed amount, the margin requirement, in a margin account. But when an option contract is purchased, the initial investment is the premium that must be paid for the contract. The second important difference between the contracts is that the futures contract requires money to change hands daily when the contract is marked to market, whereas the option contract requires money to change hands only when it is exercised.

Factors Affecting the Prices of Option Premiums

If we again look closely at the *Wall Street Journal* entry for Treasury bond futures options in the "Following the Financial News" box, we learn several interesting facts about how the premiums on option contracts are priced. The first thing you might have noticed is that when the strike (exercise) price for a contract is set at a higher level, the premium for the call option is lower and the premium for the put option is higher. For example, in going from a contract with a strike price of 103 to one with 108, the premium for the February call option falls from 2 31/64 to 13/64, and the premium for the February put option rises from 22/64 to 2 16/64.

Our understanding of the profit function for option contracts illustrated in Figure 1 helps explain this fact. As we saw in panel (a), a higher price for the underlying financial instrument (in this case a Treasury bond futures contract) relative to the option's exercise price results in higher profits on the call (buy) option. Thus the lower the strike price, the higher the profits on the call option contract and the greater the premium that investors like Irving are willing to pay. Similarly, we saw in panel (b) that a higher price for the underlying financial instrument relative to the exercise price lowers profits on the put (sell) option, so that a higher strike price increases profits and thus causes the premium to increase.

The second thing you might have noticed in the *Wall Street Journal* entry is that as the period of time over which the option can be exercised (the term to expiration) gets longer, the premiums for both call and put options rise. For example, at a strike price of 104, the premium on the call option increases from 1 47/64 in February to 2 12/64 in March and to 2 19/64 in June. Similarly, the premium on the put option increases from 38/64 in February to 1 3/64 in March and to 2 37/64 in June. The fact that premiums increase with the term to expiration is also explained by the nonlinear profit function for option contracts. As the term to expiration lengthens, there is a greater chance that the price of the underlying financial instrument will be very high or very low by the expiration date. If the price becomes very high and goes well above the exercise price, the call (buy) option will yield a high profit, but if the price becomes very low and goes well below the exercise price, the losses will be small because the owner of the call option will simply decide not to exercise the option. The possibility of greater variability of the underlying financial instrument as the term to expiration lengthens raises profits on average for the call option.

Similar reasoning tells us that the put (sell) option will become more valuable as the term to expiration increases because the possibility of greater price variability of the underlying financial instrument increases as the term to expiration increases. The greater chance of a low price increases the chance that profits on the put option will be very high. But the greater chance of a high price does not produce substantial losses for the put option because the owner will again just decide not to exercise the option.

Another way of thinking about this reasoning is to recognize that option contracts have an element of "heads, I win; tails, I don't lose too badly." The greater variability of where the prices might be by the expiration date increases the value of both kinds of options. Since a longer term to the expiration date leads to greater variability of where the prices might be by the expiration date, a longer term to expiration raises the value of the option contract.

The reasoning that we have just developed also explains another important fact about option premiums. When the volatility of the price of the underlying instrument is great, the premiums for both call and put options will be higher. Higher volatility of prices means that for a given expiration date, there will again be greater variability of where the prices might be by the expiration date. The "heads, I win; tails, I don't lose too badly" property of options then means that the greater variability of possible prices by the expiration date increases average profits for the option and thus increases the premium that investors are willing to pay.

Summary

Our analysis of how profits on options are affected by price movements for the underlying financial instrument leads to the following conclusions about the factors that determine the premium on an option contract:

1. The higher the strike price, everything else being equal, the lower the premium on call (buy) options and the higher the premium on put (sell) options.
2. The greater the term to expiration, everything else being equal, the higher the prémiums for both call and put options.
3. The greater the volatility of prices of the underlying financial instrument, everything else being equal, the higher the premiums for both call and put options.

The results we have derived here appear in more formal models, such as the Black-Scholes model, which analyze how the premiums on options are priced. You might study such models in other finance courses.

THE PRACTICING FINANCIAL INSTITUTION MANAGER

Hedging with Futures Options

Earlier in the chapter, we saw how a financial institution manager like Mona, the manager of the First National Bank, could hedge the interest-rate risk on its $5 million holdings of 8s of 2023 by selling $5 million of T-bond futures (50 contracts). A rise in interest rates and the resulting fall in bond prices and bond futures contracts would lead to profits on the bank's sale of the futures contracts that would exactly offset the losses on the 8s of 2023 the bank is holding.

As panel (b) of Figure 1 suggests, an alternative way for the manager to protect against a rise in interest rates and hence a decline in bond prices is to buy \$5 million of put options written on the same Treasury bond futures. Because the size of the options contract is the same as the futures contract (\$100,000 of bonds), the number of put options contracts bought is the same as the number of futures contracts sold, that is, 50. As long as the exercise price is not too far from the current price as in panel (b), the rise in interest rates and decline in bond prices will lead to profits on the futures and the futures put options, profits that will offset any losses on the \$5 million of Treasury bonds.

The one problem with using options rather than futures is that the First National Bank will have to pay premiums on the options contracts, thereby lowering the bank's profits in order to hedge the interest-rate risk. Why might the bank manager be willing to use options rather than futures to conduct the hedge? The answer is that the option contract, unlike the futures contract, allows the First National Bank to gain if interest rates decline and bond prices rise. With the hedge using futures contracts, the First National Bank does not gain from increases in bond prices because the profits on the bonds it is holding are offset by the losses from the futures contracts it has sold. However, as panel (b) of Figure 1 indicates, the situation when the hedge is conducted with put options is quite different: Once bond prices rise above the exercise price, the bank does not suffer additional losses on the option contracts. At the same time, the value of the Treasury bonds the bank is holding will increase, thereby leading to a profit for the bank. Thus using options rather than futures to conduct the micro hedge allows the bank to protect itself from rises in interest rates but still allows the bank to benefit from interest-rate declines (although the profit is reduced by the amount of the premium).

Similar reasoning indicates that the bank manager might prefer to use options to conduct the macro hedge to immunize the entire bank portfolio from interest-rate risk. Again, the strategy of using options rather than futures has the disadvantage that the First National Bank has to pay the premiums on these contracts up front. By contrast, using options allows the bank to keep the gains from a decline in interest rates (which will raise the value of the bank's assets relative to its liabilities) because these gains will not be offset by large losses on the option contracts.

In the case of a macro hedge, there is another reason why the bank might prefer option contracts to futures contracts. Profits and losses on futures contracts can cause accounting problems for banks because such profits and losses are not allowed to be offset by unrealized changes in the value of the rest of the bank's portfolio. Consider the case when interest rates fall. If First National sells futures contracts to conduct the macro hedge, then when interest rates fall and the prices of the Treasury bond futures contracts rise, it will have large losses on these contracts. Of course, these losses are offset by unrealized profits in the rest of the bank's portfolio, but the bank is not allowed to offset these losses in its accounting statements. So even though the macro hedge is serving its intended purpose of immunizing the bank's portfolio from interest-rate risk, the bank would experience large accounting losses when interest rates fall. Indeed, bank managers have lost their jobs when perfectly sound hedges with interest-rate futures have led to large accounting losses. Not surprisingly, bank managers might shrink from using financial futures to conduct macro hedges for this reason.

Futures options, however, can come to the rescue of the managers of banks and other financial institutions. Suppose that First National conducted the macro hedge by buying put options instead of selling Treasury bond futures. Now if interest rates fall and bond prices rise well above the exercise price, the bank will not have large losses on the option contracts because it will just decide not to exercise its options. The bank will not suffer the accounting problems produced by hedging with financial futures. Because of the accounting advantages of using futures options to conduct macro hedges, option contracts have become important to financial institution managers as tools for hedging interest-rate risk.

INTEREST-RATE SWAPS

In addition to forwards, futures, and options, financial institutions use one other important financial derivative to manage risk. **Swaps** are financial contracts that obligate each party to the contract to exchange (swap) a set of payments it owns for another set of payments owned by another party. There are two basic kinds of swaps: **Currency swaps** involve the exchange of a set of payments in one currency for a set of payments in another currency. **Interest-rate swaps** involve the exchange of one set of interest payments for another set of interest payments, all denominated in the same currency. We focus on interest-rate swaps.

Interest-Rate Swap Contracts

Interest-rate swaps are an important tool for managing interest-rate risk, and they first appeared in the United States in 1982 when, as we have seen, there was an increase in the demand for financial instruments that could be used to reduce interest-rate risk. The most common type of interest-rate swap (called the *plain vanilla swap*) specifies (1) the interest rate on the payments that are being exchanged; (2) the type of interest payments (variable or fixed-rate); (3) the amount of **notional principal,** which is the amount on which the interest is being paid; and (4) the time period over which the exchanges continue to be made. There are many other more complicated versions of swaps, including forward swaps and swap options (called *swaptions*), but here we will look only at the plain vanilla swap. Figure 2 illustrates an interest-rate swap between the Midwest Savings Bank and the Friendly Finance Company. Midwest Savings agrees to pay Friendly Finance a fixed rate of 7% on $1 million of notional principal for the

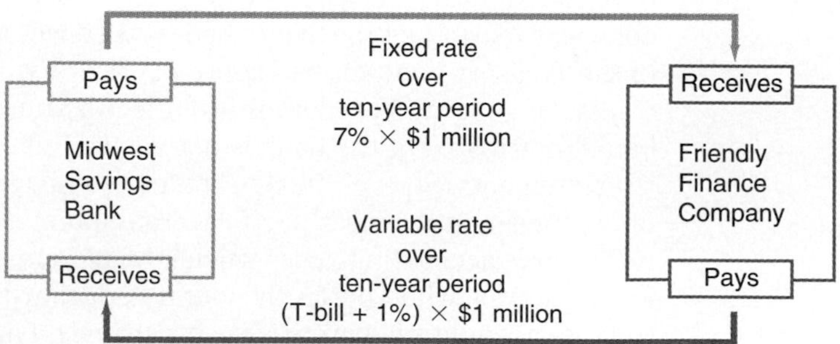

FIGURE 2 Interest-Rate Swap Payments

In this swap arrangement, with a notional principal of $1 million and a term of ten years, the Midwest Savings Bank pays a fixed rate of 7% × $1 million to the Friendly Finance Company, which in turn agrees to pay the one-year Treasury bill rate plus 1% × $1 million to the Midwest Savings Bank.

next ten years, and Friendly Finance agrees to pay Midwest Savings the one-year Treasury bill rate plus 1% on $1 million of notional principal for the same period. Thus as shown in Figure 2, every year, the Midwest Savings Bank would be paying the Friendly Finance Company 7% on $1 million while Friendly Finance would be paying Midwest Savings the one-year T-bill rate plus 1% on $1 million.

THE PRACTICING FINANCIAL INSTITUTION MANAGER

Hedging with Interest-Rate Swaps

You might wonder why the managers of the two financial institutions find it advantageous to enter into this swap agreement. The answer is that it may help both of them hedge interest-rate risk.

Suppose that the Midwest Savings Bank, which tends to borrow short-term and then lend long-term in the mortgage market, has $1 million less of rate-sensitive assets than it has of rate-sensitive liabilities. As we learned in Chapter 22, this situation means that as interest rates rise, the rise in the cost of funds (liabilities) is greater than the rise in interest payments it receives on its assets, many of which are fixed-rate. The result of rising interest rates is thus a shrinking of Midwest Savings' net interest margin and a decline in its profitability. As we saw in Chapter 22, to avoid this interest-rate risk, the manager of the Midwest Savings would like to convert $1 million of its fixed-rate assets into $1 million of rate-sensitive assets, in effect making rate-sensitive assets equal to rate-sensitive liabilities, thereby eliminating the gap. This is exactly what happens when she engages in the interest-rate swap. By taking $1 million of its fixed-rate income and exchanging it for $1 million of rate-sensitive Treasury bill income, she has converted income on $1 million of fixed-rate assets into income on $1 million of rate-sensitive assets. Now when interest rates increase, the rise in rate-sensitive income on its assets exactly matches the rise in the rate-sensitive cost of funds on its liabilities, leaving the net interest margin and bank profitability unchanged.

The manager of the Friendly Finance Company, which issues long-term bonds to raise funds and uses them to make short-term loans, finds that he is in exactly the opposite situation to Midwest Savings: He has $1 million more of rate-sensitive assets than of rate-sensitive liabilities. He is therefore concerned that a fall in interest rates, which will result in a larger drop in income from its assets than the decline in the cost of funds on its liabilities, will cause a decline in profits. By doing the interest-rate swap, the manager eliminates this interest-rate risk because he has converted $1 million of rate-sensitive income into $1 million of fixed-rate income. Now the manager of the Friendly Finance Company finds that when interest rates fall, the decline in rate-sensitive income is smaller and so is matched by the decline in the rate-sensitive cost of funds on its liabilities, leaving profitability unchanged.

Advantages of Interest-Rate Swaps

To eliminate interest-rate risk, both the Midwest Savings Bank and the Friendly Finance Company could have rearranged their balance sheets by converting fixed-rate assets into rate-sensitive assets, and vice versa, instead of engaging in an interest-rate swap. However, this strategy would have been costly for both financial institutions for several reasons. The first is that financial institutions incur substantial transaction costs when they rearrange their balance sheets. Second, different financial institutions have informational advantages in making loans to certain customers who may prefer certain maturities. Thus, adjusting the balance sheet to eliminate interest-rate risk may result in a loss of these informational advantages, which the financial institution is unwilling to give up. Interest-rate swaps solve these problems for financial institutions because in effect they allow the institutions to convert fixed-rate assets into rate-sensitive assets without affecting the balance sheet. Large transaction costs are avoided, and the financial institutions can continue to make loans where they have an informational advantage.

We have seen that financial institutions can also hedge interest-rate risk with other financial derivatives such as futures contracts and futures options. Interest-rate swaps have one big advantage over hedging with these other derivatives: They can be written for very long horizons, sometimes as long as 20 years, whereas financial futures and futures options typically have much shorter horizons, not much more than a year. If a financial institution needs to hedge interest-rate risk for a long horizon, financial futures and option markets may not do it much good. Instead it can turn to the swap market.

Disadvantages of Interest-Rate Swaps

Although interest-rate swaps have important advantages that make them very popular with financial institutions, they also have disadvantages that limit their usefulness. Swap markets, like forward markets, can suffer from a lack of liquidity. Let's return to looking at the swap between the Midwest Savings Bank and the Friendly Finance Company. As with a forward contract, it might be difficult for the Midwest Savings Bank to link up with the Friendly Finance Company to arrange the swap. In addition, even if the Midwest Savings Bank could find a counterparty like the Friendly Finance Company, it might not be able to negotiate a good deal because it couldn't find any other institution to negotiate with.

Swap contracts also are subject to the same default risk that we encountered for forward contracts. If interest rates rise, the Friendly Finance Company would love to get out of the swap contract because the fixed-rate interest payments it receives are less than it could get in the open market. It might then default on the contract, exposing Midwest Savings to a loss. Alternatively, the Friendly Finance Company could go bust, meaning that the terms of the swap contract would not be fulfilled.

It is important to note that the default risk of swaps is not the same as the default risk on the full amount of the notional principal because the notional principal is never exchanged. If the Friendly Finance Company goes broke because $1 million of its one-year loans default and it cannot make its interest payment to Midwest Savings, Midwest Savings will stop sending its payment to Friendly Finance. If interest rates have declined, this will suit Midwest Savings just fine because it would rather keep the 7% fixed-rate interest payment, which is at a higher rate, than receive the rate-sensitive payment, which has declined. Thus a default on a swap contract does not necessarily mean that there is a loss to the other party. Midwest Savings will suffer losses from a default only if interest rates have risen when the default occurs. Even then, the loss will be far smaller than the amount of the notional principal because interest payments are far smaller than the amount of the notional principal.[6]

[6]The actual loss will equal the present value of the difference in the interest payments that the bank would have received if the swap were still in force as compared to interest payments it receives otherwise.

Financial Intermediaries in Interest-Rate Swaps

As we have just seen, financial institutions do have to be aware of the possibility of losses from a default on swaps. As with a forward contract, each party to a swap must have a lot of information about the other party to make sure that the contract is likely to be fulfilled. The need for information about counterparties and the liquidity problems in swap markets could limit the usefulness of these markets. However, as we saw in Chapter 14, when informational and liquidity problems crop up in a market, financial intermediaries come to the rescue. That is exactly what happens in swap markets. Intermediaries such as investment banks and especially large commercial banks have the ability to acquire information cheaply about the creditworthiness and reliability of parties to swap contracts and are also able to match up parties to a swap. Hence large commercial banks and investment banks have set up swap markets in which they act as intermediaries.

Application Are Financial Derivatives a Worldwide Time Bomb?

With the bankruptcies of Orange County in 1994 (see Box 3) and the Barings Bank in 1995 (discussed in Chapter 15)—both of which involved trades in financial derivatives—politicians, the media, and regulators have become very concerned about the dangers of derivatives. This concern is international and has spawned a slew of reports issued by such organizations as the Bank for International Settlements (BIS), the Bank of England, the Group of Thirty, the Office of the U.S. Comptroller of the Currency (OCC), the Commodity Futures Trading Commission (CFTC), and the Government Accounting Office (GAO). Particularly scary are the notional amounts of derivatives contracts—tens of trillions of dollars worldwide—and the fact that banks, which are subject to bank panics, are major players in the derivatives markets. As a result of these fears, some politicians have called for restrictions on banks' involvement in the derivatives markets. Are financial derivatives a time bomb that could bring down the world financial system?

There are three major concerns about financial derivatives. First is that financial derivatives allow financial institutions to increase their leverage; that is, they can in effect hold an amount of the underlying asset that is many times greater than the amount of money they have had to put up. Increasing their leverage enables them to take huge bets on currency and interest-rate movements, which if they are wrong can bring down the bank, as was the case for Barings in 1995. This concern is valid. As we saw earlier in the chapter, the amount of money placed in margin accounts is only a small fraction of the price of the futures contract, meaning that small movements in the price of a contract can produce losses that are many times the size of the initial amount put in the margin account. Thus although financial derivatives can be used to hedge risk, they can also be used by financial institutions to take on excessive risk.

The second concern is that financial derivatives are too sophisticated for managers of financial institutions because they are so complicated. Although it is true that some financial derivatives can be so complex that some financial managers are not sophisticated enough to use them—a possibility in the Orange County case—this seems unlikely to apply to the big international financial institutions that are the major players in the derivatives markets. Indeed, in the Barings case, the bank was brought down not by trades in complex derivatives but rather by trades in one of the simplest of derivatives, stock index futures. (Recall from Chapter 15 that

BOX 3

The Orange County Bankruptcy

Orange County, California, one of the richest counties in the United States, was forced to declare bankruptcy on December 6, 1994, in the largest municipal bankruptcy filing ever. Orange County's downfall was the investment activities of its treasurer, Robert Citron, who was in charge of the $7.8 billion investment fund, which had not only $4.7 billion of funds from Orange County agencies but also $3.1 billion from 180 other municipalities and local government agencies. For years, the Orange County fund looked like a good investment, with the annual returns averaging 10% over the 15-year period to 1994. Unfortunately, these high returns were obtained with a highly leveraged strategy in which the fund purchased amounts of medium- to long-term bonds several times the value of the fund by borrowing with repurchase agreements. Everything was fine until interest rates began to rise in late 1993 and early 1994 and bond prices declined, leaving the fund with large losses.

We have already seen in our discussion of the Barings collapse how the principal-agent problem becomes especially severe once a trader or a manager of a fund starts to experience sizable losses. Once in the hole, the manager of the fund knows that his or her future depends on reversing these losses promptly. In this situation, the fund manager has a strong moral hazard incentive to take excessive risks. This is exactly what Citron did in late 1993 and early 1994 when he began buying large amounts of "inverse floaters," highly risky derivative securities that have high payoffs if long-term bond rates decline. Unfortunately for Citron, interest rates continued to rise, and the fund slipped deeper in the hole. When Peter Swan, the president of the Irvine Ranch Water District, became suspicious about the financial situation of the fund in November 1994 and asked to redeem $400 million, the jig was up for Citron because the fund did not have the cash to meet this redemption. Finally, on December 5, Citron was forced to resign, and the following day, Orange County declared bankruptcy. When bankruptcy was declared, the fund had estimated losses of $1.5 billion, and was found to have $20 billion of securities, $8.5 billion of which were derivatives, a risky portfolio indeed.

Although the role of derivatives in the Orange County debacle has often been emphasized, the problem here was really one of leverage and the principal agent problem at work. Indeed, an important reason that Citron was able to get away with such a risky strategy, particularly after the fund sustained large losses, was that disclosure requirements were not as strong as they could be for municipal investment funds in the state of California. In contrast to other states, which require monthly or even daily disclosure of the market value of their municipal investment funds, California required this disclosure only once a year. If California had stricter disclosure requirements, investors in Citron's fund would have found out more quickly the risks he was taking, making it more likely that they would have pulled out their funds. This might have prevented Citron from taking on the risks that he did, and the Orange County bankruptcy would have been avoided.

Barings's problem was more a lack of internal controls at the bank than a problem with derivatives per se.)

A third concern is that banks have holdings of huge notional amounts of financial derivatives, particularly swaps, that greatly exceed the amount of bank capital, and so these derivatives expose the banks to serious risk of failure. Banks are indeed major players in the financial derivatives markets, particularly the swaps market, where our earlier analysis has shown that they are the natural market-makers because they can act as intermediaries between two counterparties who would not make the swap without their involvement. However, looking at the notional amount of swaps at banks gives a very misleading picture of their risk exposure. First is that because banks act as intermediaries in the swap markets, they are typically exposed only to credit risk—a default by one of their counterparties. Furthermore, swaps, unlike loans, do not involve payments of the notional amount but rather the much smaller interest payments based on the notional amounts. For example, in the case of a 7% interest rate, the payment is only $70,000 for the $1 million swap. Estimates of the credit exposure from swap contracts indicate that they are on the order of only 1% of the notional value of the contracts and that credit exposure at banks from derivatives is generally less than a quarter of their total credit exposure from loans. Banks' credit exposure from their derivatives activities are thus not out of line with other credit exposures they face. Furthermore, an analysis by the GAO indicates that actual credit losses incurred by banks in their derivatives contracts have been very small, on the order of 0.2% of their gross credit exposure.

The conclusion is that financial derivatives do have their dangers for financial institutions, but some of these dangers have been overplayed. The biggest danger occurs in trading activities of financial institutions, and as discussed in Chapter 18, regulators have been paying increased attention to this danger and have issued new disclosure requirements and regulatory guidelines for how derivatives trading should be done. The credit risk exposure posed by derivatives, by contrast, seems to be manageable with standard methods of dealing with credit risk, both by managers of financial institutions and their regulators.

SUMMARY

1. Interest-rate forward contracts, which are agreements to sell a debt instrument at a future (forward) point in time, can be used to hedge interest-rate risk. The advantage of forward contracts is that they are flexible, but the disadvantages are that they are subject to default risk and their market is illiquid.
2. A financial futures contract is similar to an interest-rate forward contract in that it specifies that a debt instrument must be delivered by one party to another on a stated future date. However, it has advantages over a forward contract in that it is not subject to default risk and is more liquid. Forward and futures contracts can be used by financial institutions to hedge against (protect) interest-rate risk.
3. Stock index futures are financial futures whose underlying financial instrument is a stock market index like the Standard and Poor's 500 Index. Stock index futures can be used to hedge stock market risk by reducing systematic risk in portfolios or by locking in stock prices.
4. An option contract gives the purchaser the right to buy (call option) or sell (put option) a security at the exercise (strike) price within a specific period of time. The profit function for options is nonlinear—profits do not always grow by the same amount for a given change in the price of the underlying financial instrument. The nonlinear profit function for options explains why their value (as reflected by the premium paid for them) is negatively related to the exercise price for call options, positively related to the exercise price for put options, positively related to the term to expiration for both call and put options, and positively related to the volatility of the prices of the underlying financial instrument for both call and put options. Financial institutions use futures options to hedge interest-rate risk in a similar fashion to the way they use financial futures and forward contracts. Futures options may be preferred for macro hedges because they suffer from fewer accounting problems than financial futures.
5. Interest-rate swaps involve the exchange of one set of interest payments for another set of interest payments and have default risk and liquidity problems similar to those of forward contracts. As a result, interest-rate swaps often involve intermediaries such as large commercial banks and investment banks that make a market in swaps. Financial institutions find that interest-rate swaps are useful ways to hedge interest-rate risk. Interest-rate swaps have one big advantage over financial futures and options: They can be written for very long horizons.
6. There are three concerns about the dangers of derivatives: They allow financial institutions to more easily increase their leverage and take big bets (by effectively enabling them to hold a larger amount of the underlying assets than the amount of money put down), they are too complex for managers of financial institutions to understand, and they expose financial institutions to large credit risks because the huge notional amounts of derivative contracts greatly exceed the capital of these institutions. The second two dangers seem to be overplayed, but the danger from increased leverage using derivatives is real.

KEY TERMS

American option, *p. 632*
arbitrage, *p. 622*
call option, *p. 633*
currency swap, *p. 640*
European option, *p. 632*
exercise price (strike price), *p. 632*
financial derivatives, *p. 617*
financial futures contract, *p. 620*
financial futures option (futures option), *p. 632*
hedge, *p. 617*
interest-rate forward contract, *p. 618*
interest-rate swap, *p. 640*
long position, *p. 617*
macro hedge, *p. 623*
margin requirement, *p. 626*
marked to market, *p. 626*
micro hedge, *p. 623*
notional principal, *p. 640*
open interest, *p. 624*
option, *p. 632*
premium, *p. 632*
put option, *p. 633*
short position, *p. 617*
stockmarket risk, *p. 629*
stock option, *p. 632*
swap, *p. 640*

QUESTIONS AND PROBLEMS

1. If the pension fund you manage expects to have an inflow of $120 million six months from now, what forward contract would you seek to enter into to lock in current interest rates?

***2.** If the portfolio you manage is holding $25 million of 8s of 2023 Treasury bonds with a price of 110, what forward contract would you enter into to hedge the interest-rate risk on these bonds over the coming year?

3. If at the expiration date, the deliverable Treasury bond is selling for 101 but the Treasury bond futures contract is selling for 102, what will happen to the futures price? Explain your answer.

***4.** If you buy a $100,000 June Treasury bond contract for 108 and the price of the deliverable Treasury bond at the expiration date is 102, what is your profit or loss on the contract?

5. Suppose that the pension you are managing is expecting an inflow of funds of $100 million next year and you want to make sure that you will earn the current interest rate of 8% when you invest the incoming funds in long-term bonds. How would you use the futures market to do this?

***6.** How would you use the options market to accomplish the same thing as in Problem 5? What are the advantages and disadvantages of using an options contract rather than a futures contract?

7. If you buy a put option on a $100,000 Treasury bond futures contract with an exercise price of 95 and the price of the Treasury bond is 120 at expiration, is the contract in the money, out of the money, or at the money? What is your profit or loss on the contract if the premium was $4000?

***8.** Suppose that you buy a call option on a $100,000 Treasury bond futures contract with an exercise price of 110 for a premium of $1500. If on expiration the futures contract has a price of 111, what is your profit or loss on the contract?

9. Explain why greater volatility or a longer term to maturity leads to a higher premium on both call and put options.

***10.** Why does a lower strike price imply that a call option will have a higher premium and a put option a lower premium?

11. If the finance company you manage has a gap of +$5 million (rate-sensitive assets greater than rate-sensitive liabilities by $5 million), describe an interest-rate swap that would eliminate the company's income gap.

***12.** If the savings and loan you manage has a gap of −$42 million, describe an interest-rate swap that would eliminate the S&L's income risk from changes in interest rates.

13. If your company has a payment of 200 million euros due one year from now, how would you hedge the foreign exchange risk in this payment with 125,000 euros futures contracts?

***14.** If your company has to make a 10 million euros payment to a German company in June, three months from now, how would you hedge the foreign exchange risk in this payment with a 125,000 euros futures contract?

15. Suppose that your company will be receiving 30 million euros six months from now and the euro is currently selling for 1 euro per dollar. If you want to hedge the foreign exchange risk in this payment, what kind of forward contract would you want to enter into?

WEB EXERCISES

Hedging with Financial Derivatives

1. We have discussed various stock markets in detail throughout this text. Another market that is less well known is the New York Mercantile Exchange. Here contracts on a wide variety of commodities are traded on a daily basis. Go to http://www.nymex.com/welcome/info_01.htm and read the discussion explaining the origin and purpose of the mercantile exchange. Write a one-page summary discussing this material.

2. We leave the details of pricing option contracts to another course. However, the following site can be used to demonstrate how the features of an option affect the option's prices. Go to http://www.intrepid.com/~robertl/option-pricer4.html. Indicate what happens to the price of an option under each of the following situations:
   a. The strike price increases.
   b. Interest rates increase.
   c. Volatility increases.
   d. The time until the option matures increases.

Glossary

advances: See *discount loans.*

adverse selection: The problem created by asymmetric information before a transaction occurs: the people who are the most undesirable from the other party's point of view are the ones who are most likely to want to engage in the financial transaction. 24

American depository receipts (ADR): A receipt for foreign stocks held by a trustee. The receipts trade on U.S. stock exchanges instead of the actual stock. 263

American option: An option that can be exercised at any time up to the expiration date of the contract. 632

amortized: Paid off in stages over a period of time. Each payment on a loan consists of the accrued interest and an amount that is applied to repay the principal. When all of the payments have been made, the loan is paid off (fully amortized). 292

annuity: An insurance product that provides a fixed stream of payments. 525

appreciation: Increase in a currency's value. 313

arbitrage: Elimination of a riskless profit opportunity in a market. 622

asset: A financial claim or piece of property that is a store of value. 4, 75

asset management: The acquisition of assets that have a low rate of default and diversification of asset holdings to increase profits. 408

asset market approach: Determining asset prices using stocks of assets rather than flows. 84

asymmetric information: The inequality of knowledge that each party to a transaction has about the other party. 24

automated banking machine (ABM): An electronic machine that combines in one location an ATM, an Internet connection to the bank's website, and a telephone link to customer service. 426

automated teller machine (ATM): An electronic machine that allows customers to get cash, make deposits, transfer funds from one account to another, and check balances. 426

balance of payments: A bookkeeping system for recording all payments that have a direct bearing on the movement of funds between a country and all other countries. 344

balance-of-payments crisis: A foreign exchange crisis stemming from problems in a country's balance of payments. 356

balance sheet: A list of the assets and liabilities of a bank (or firm) that balances: total assets equal total liabilities plus capital. 401

balloon loan: A loan on which the payments do not fully pay off the principal balance, meaning that the final payment must be larger than the rest. 292, 552

bank failure: A situation in which a bank cannot satisfy its obligations to pay its depositors and other creditors and thus goes out of business. 413, 492

bank holding companies: Companies that own one or more banks. 440

bank panic: The simultaneous failure of many banks, as during a financial crisis. 392

bank supervision: Overseeing who operates banks and how they are operated. 497

banker's acceptance: A short-term promissory note drawn by a company to pay for goods on which a bank guarantees payment at maturity. Usually used in international trade. 230

banks: Financial institutions that accept deposits and make loans (such as commercial banks, savings and loan associations, and credit unions). 8

Basel Accord: An agreement by the Basel Committee on Banking Supervision to implement risk-based capital requirements. 497

Basel Committee on Banking Supervision: A committee that meets under the auspices of the Bank for International Settlements in Basel, Switzerland and that sets bank regulatory standards. 497

basis point: One one-hundredth of a percentage point. 55

bearer instrument: A security payable to the holder or "bearer" when presented. No proof of ownership is required. 227

best-effort underwriting: An approach to underwriting in which the underwriter does not take ownership of the security issue and does not commit to sell the issue at a given price. Instead, the underwriter solicits, offers, and attempts to market the security for the best price possible. 574

beta: A measure of sensitivity of an asset's return to changes in the value of the market portfolio, which is also a measure of the asset's marginal contribution to the risk of the market portfolio.

Board of Governors of the Federal Reserve System: A board with seven governors (including the chairman) that plays an essential role in decision making within the Federal Reserve System. 151

bond: A debt security that promises to make payments periodically for a specified period of time. 4

bond indenture: Document accompanying a bond that spells out the details of the bond issue, such as covenants and sinking fund provisions. It states the lender's rights and privileges and the borrower's obligations. 252

book entry: A system of tracking securities ownership where no certificate is issued. Instead, the security issuer keeps records, usually electronically, of who holds outstanding securities. 223

branches: Additional offices of banks that conduct banking operations. 441

Bretton Woods system: The international monetary system in use from 1945 to 1971 in which exchange rates were fixed and the U.S. dollar was freely convertible into gold (by foreign governments and central banks only). 348

brokered deposits: Deposits that enable depositors to circumvent the $100,000 limit at each bank so that the total amount deposited is fully insured. 507

brokers: Agents for investors who match buyers with sellers. 19

bubble: A situation in which the price of an asset differs from its fundamental market value. 288

call option: An option contract that provides the right to buy a security at a specified price. 633

call provision: A right, usually included in the terms of a bond, that gives the issuer the ability to repurchase outstanding bonds before they mature. 253

capital account: An account that describes the flow of capital between the United States and other countries. 346

capital adequacy management: Managing the amount of capital the bank should maintain and then acquiring the needed capital. 408

capital call: A requirement of limited partners in a venture capital agreement to supply funds per their commitment with the partnership. 551

capital market: A financial market in which longer-term debt (maturity of greater than one year) and equity instruments are traded. 20

capital mobility: A situation in which foreigners can easily purchase a country's assets and the country's residents can easily purchase foreign assets. 322

captive finance company: A finance company that is owned by a retailer and makes loans to finance the purchase of goods from the retailer. 559

cash flow: The difference between cash receipts and cash expenditures. 268, 391

casualty (liability) insurance: Protection against financial losses because of a claim of negligence. 530

central bank: The government agency that oversees the banking system and is responsible for the amount of money and credit supplied in the economy; in the United States, the Federal Reserve System. 8

Central Liquidity Facility (CLF): The lender of last resort for credit unions, created in 1978 by the Financial Institutions Reform Act. 483

certainty equivalent: An amount that will be received or spent with certainty. An insurance payment is a certainty equivalent since it removes the risk that unexpected amounts will need to be spent. 520

closed-end fund: A fund that sells a fixed number of shares of stock and does not continue to accept investments. 587

coinsurance: An insurance policy under which the policyholder bears a percentage of the loss along with the insurance company. 509, 535

collateral: Property that is pledged to the lender to guarantee payment in the event that the borrower should be unable to make debt payments. 374

collateralized mortgage obligation (CMO): Securities classified by when prepayment is likely to occur. Investors may buy a group of CMOs that are likely to mature at a time that meets the investors' needs. 306

common bond membership: A requirement that all members of credit unions share some common bond, such as working for the same employer. 481

common stock: A security that gives the holder an ownership interest in the issuing firm. This ownership interest includes the right to any residual cash flows and the right to vote on major corporate issues. 259

compensating balance: A required minimum amount of funds that a firm receiving a loan must keep in a checking account at the bank. 600

competitive bidding: Competing in an auction against other potential buyers of Treasury securities. 223

confidential memorandum: A document that presents detailed financial information required by prospective buyers prior to making an offer to acquire a firm. 576

conventional mortgages: Mortgage contracts originated by banks and other mortgage lenders that are not guaranteed by the FHA or the VA. They are often insured by private mortgage insurance. 299

costly state verification: Monitoring a firm's activities, an expensive process in both time and money. 384

coupon bond: A credit market instrument that pays the owner a fixed interest payment every year until the maturity date, when a specified final amount is paid. 38

coupon rate: The dollar amount of the yearly coupon payment expressed as a percentage of the face value of a coupon bond. 38

credit rationing: A lender's refusing to make loans even though borrowers are willing to pay the stated interest rate or even a higher rate or restricting the size of loans to less than the amount being sought. 601

credit risk: The risk arising from the possibility that the borrower will default. 408

credit union: A financial institution that focuses on servicing the banking and lending needs of its members, who must be linked by a common bond. 480

Credit Union National Association (CUNA): A central credit union facility that encourages establishing credit unions and provides information to its members. 481

Credit Union National Extension Bureau (CUNEB): A central credit union facility established in 1921 that was later replaced by the Credit Union National Association. 481

creditor: A holder of debt. 389

currency swap: A swap that involves the exchange of a set of payments in another currency. 640

current account: An account that shows international transactions involving currently produced goods and services. 344

current yield: An approximation of the yield to maturity that equals the yearly coupon payment divided by the price of a coupon bond. 50

dealers: People who link buyers with sellers by buying and selling securities at stated prices. 19

debt deflation: A situation in which a substantial decline in the price level sets in, leading to a further deterioration in firms' net worth because of the increased burden of indebtedness. 394

deductible: An amount of any loss that must be paid by the insured before the insurance company will pay anything. 522

deep markets: Markets where there are many participants and a great deal of activity, thus ensuring that securities can be sold rapidly at fair prices. 222

default: A situation in which the party issuing a debt instrument is unable to make interest payments or pay off the amount owed when the instrument matures. 120

default-free bonds: Bonds with no default risk, such as U.S. government bonds. 120

default risk: The risk that a loan customer may fail to repay a loan as promised. 120, 554

defined-benefit plan: A pension plan in which the benefits are stated up front and are paid regardless how the investments perform. 536

defined-contribution plan: A pension plan in which the contributions are stated up front but the benefits paid depend on the performance of the investments. 537

definitive agreement: A legally binding contract that details the terms and conditions for an acquisition of one firm by another. 576

demand curve: A curve depicting the relationship between quantity demanded and price when all other economic variables are held constant. 81

demand deposit: A deposit held by a bank that must be paid to the depositor on demand. Demand deposits are more commonly called *checking accounts*. 227

deposit outflows: Losses of deposits when depositors make withdrawals or demand payment. 408

deposit rate ceilings: Restrictions on the maximum interest rates payable on deposits. 430

depreciation: Decrease in a currency's value. 313

devaluation: Resetting of the par value of a currency at a lower level. 351

direct placement: An issuer's bypassing the dealer and selling the security directly to the investor. 230

discount bond: A credit market instrument that is bought at a price below its face value and whose face value is repaid at the maturity date; it does not make any interest payments. Also known as a *zero-coupon bond*. 38

discount loans: A bank's borrowings from the Federal Reserve System. Also known as *advances*. 403

discount points: Percentage of the total loan paid back immediately when a mortgage loan is obtained. Payment of discount points lowers the annual interest rate on the debt. 294

discount rate: The interest rate that the Federal Reserve charges banks on discount loans. 173, 410

discount window: The Federal Reserve facility at which discount loans are made to banks. 180

discount yield: See *yield on a discount basis.*

discounting: Reduction in the value of a security at purchase such that when it matures at full value, the investor receives a fair return. 221

disintermediation: A reduction in the flow of funds into the banking system that causes the amount of financial intermediation to decline. 430

diversification: The holding of many risky assets. 79

dividends: Periodic payments made by equities to shareholders. 18, 268

dollarization: A monetary strategy in which a country abandons its currency altogether and adopts that of another country, typically the U.S. dollar. 352

down payment: A portion of the original purchase price that is paid by the borrower so that the borrower will have equity (ownership interest) in the asset pledged as collateral. 295

dual banking system: The system in the United States in which banks supervised by the federal government and banks supervised by the states operate side by side. 439

due diligence period: A 20–40 day period used by the buyer of a firm to verify the accuracy of the information contained in the confidential memorandum. 576

duration: The average lifetime of a debt security's stream of payments. 65

duration gap analysis: A measurement of the sensitivity of the market value of a bank's assets and liabilities to changes in interest rates. 605

early stage investing: Investment by a venture capital firm in a company that is in the very beginning stage of its development. 551

e-cash: A second form of electronic money used on the Internet to pay for goods and services. 428

econometric model: A model whose equations are estimated using statistical procedures. 109

economies of scale: Savings that can be achieved through increased size. 23, 564

economies of scope: Increased business that can be achieved by offering many products in one easy-to-reach location. 564

Edge Act corporation: A special subsidiary of a U.S. bank that is engaged primarily in international banking. 451

effective exchange rate index: An index reflecting the value of a basket of representative foreign currencies. 333

efficient market hypothesis: The hypothesis that prices of securities in financial markets fully reflect all available information. 267

electronic money (or e-money): Money that exists only in electronic form and substitutes for cash as well. 428

Employee Retirement Income Security Act (ERISA): A comprehensive law passed in 1974 that set standards that must be followed by all pension plans. 542

equities: Claims to share in the net income and assets of a corporation (such as common stock). 18

equity capital: See *net worth.*

equity multiplier: The amount of assets per dollar of equity capital. 414

Eurobonds: Bonds denominated in a currency other than that of the country in which they are sold. 21

Eurocurrencies: Foreign currencies deposited in banks outside the home country. 21

Eurodollars: U.S. dollars that are deposited in foreign banks outside of the United States or in foreign branches of U.S. banks. 21

European option: An option that can be exercised only at the expiration date of the contract. 632

excess demand: A situation in which quantity demanded is greater than quantity supplied. 83

excess reserves: Reserves in excess of required reserves. 172, 404

excess supply: A situation in which quantity supplied is greater than quantity demanded. 83

exchange rate: The price of one currency in terms of another. 6, 311

exchange rate overshooting: A phenomenon whereby the exchange rate changes by more in the short run than it does in the long run when the money supply changes. 332

exchanges: Secondary markets in which buyers and sellers of securities (or their agents or brokers) meet in one central location to conduct trades. 19

exercise price: The price at which the purchaser of an option has the right to buy or sell the underlying financial instrument. Also known as the *strike price*. 632

expected return: The return on an asset expected over the next period. 75

factoring: The sale of accounts receivable to another firm, which takes responsibility for collections. 556

Federal Credit Union Act: Law passed in 1934 that allowed federal chartering of credit unions in all states. 481

federal funds: Short-term deposits bought or sold between banks. 224

federal funds rate: The interest rate on overnight loans of deposits at the Federal Reserve. 174

Federal Home Loan Bank Act of 1932: Law that created the Federal Home Loan Bank Board and a network of regional home loan banks. 467

Federal Home Loan Bank Board (FHLBB): Agency responsible for regulating and controlling savings and loan institutions, superseded by FIRREA in 1989. 467

Federal Open Market Committee (FOMC): The committee that makes decisions regarding the conduct of open market operations; composed of the seven members of the Board of Governors of the Federal Reserve System, the president of the Federal Reserve Bank of New York, and the presidents of four other Federal Reserve banks on a rotating basis. 151

Federal Reserve banks: The 12 district banks in the Federal Reserve system. 151

Federal Reserve System (the Fed): The central banking authority responsible for monetary policy in the United States. 8

Federal Savings and Loan Insurance Corporation (FSLIC): An agency that provided deposit insurance to savings and loan similar to the Federal Deposit Insurance Corporation which insured banks. FSLIC was eliminated in 1989. 467

financial conglomerate: A firm that owns and manages a number of different types of financial intermediaries. 562

financial crisis: A major disruption in financial markets, characterized by sharp declines in asset prices and the failures of many financial and non-financial firms. 390

financial derivatives: Instruments that have payoffs that are linked to previously issued securities and are extremely useful risk reduction tools. 617

financial engineering: The process of researching and developing new financial products and services that would meet customer needs and prove profitable. 424

financial futures contract: A futures contract in which the standardized commodity is a particular type of financial instrument. 620

financial futures options: Options in which the underlying instrument is a futures contract. Also called *futures options*. 632

financial guarantee: A contract that guarantees that bond purchasers will be paid both principal and interest in the event the issuer defaults on the obligation. 257

Financial Institutions Reform Act: Law passed in 1978 that created the Central Liquidity Facility as the lender of last resort for credit unions. 483

Financial Institutions Reform, Recovery, and Enforcement Act: Law passed in 1989 to stop losses in the savings and loan industry. It reversed much of the deregulation included in the Garn–St Germain Act of 1982. 473

financial instrument: See *security*.

financial intermediaries: Institutions (such as banks, insurance companies, mutual funds, pension funds, and finance companies) that borrow funds from people who have saved and then make loans to others. 8

financial intermediation: The process of indirect finance whereby financial intermediaries link lender-savers and borrower-spenders. 22

financial markets: Markets in which funds are transferred from people who have a surplus of available funds to people who have a shortage of available funds. 3

financial panic: The widespread collapse of financial markets and intermediaries in an economy. 30

firm-commitment underwriting: Underwriting in which the underwriter agrees to buy the entire security issue at a prespecified price and then to resell it. This method ensures that the entire issue will be marketed. 569

Fisher effect: The outcome that when expected inflation occurs, interest rates will rise; named after economist Irving Fisher. 93

fixed exchange rate regime: Policy under which central banks buy and sell their own currencies to keep their exchange rates fixed at a certain level. 348

fixed-payment loan: A credit market instrument that provides a borrower with an amount of money that is repaid by making a fixed payment periodically (usually monthly) for a set number of years. 38

floor plan: A type of loan for which inventory is pledged as security and a portion of the loan is repaid each time an item of inventory is sold. 557

foreign bonds: Bonds sold in a foreign country and denominated in that country's currency. 20

foreign exchange intervention: An international financial transaction in which a central bank buys or sells currency to influence foreign exchange rates. 339

foreign exchange market: The market in which exchange rates are determined. 6, 311

foreign exchange rate: See *exchange rate*.

forward contract: An agreement by two parties to engage in a financial transaction at a future (forward) point in time. 618

forward exchange rate: The exchange rate for a forward transaction. 313

forward rate: The interest rate predicted by pure expectations theory of the term structure of interest rates to prevail in the future. 141

forward transaction: An exchange rate transaction that involves the exchange of bank deposits denominated in different currencies at some specified future date. 313

free reserves: Excess reserves in the banking system minus the volume of discount loans. 197

free-rider problem: The problem that occurs when people who do not pay for information take advantage of the information that other people have paid for. 379

fully funded: Describing a pension plan in which the contributions to the plan and their earnings over the years are sufficient to pay out the defined benefits when they come due. 537

fully subscribed: Describing a security issue for which all of the securities available have been spoken for before the issue date. 574

futures options: See *financial futures options*.

gap analysis: A measurement of the sensitivity of bank profits to changes in interest rates, calculated by subtracting the amount of rate-sensitive assets. Also called *income gap analysis*. 603

general obligation bonds: Bonds that are secured by the full faith and credit of the issuer, which includes the taxing authority of municipalities. 250

Glass-Steagall Act: Law that made it illegal for commercial banks to underwrite securities for sale to the public. 568

gold standard: A regime under which a currency is directly convertible into gold. 347

hedge: To protect oneself against risk. 617
hybrid funds: A mutual fund that is composed of both stocks and bonds. 584

incentive-compatible: Aligning the incentives of both parties to a contract. 386
income gap analysis: See *gap analysis*.
index fund: A mutual fund that is composed only of securities that are included in some popular stock index, such as the S&P 500. The fund is designed to mimic the returns generated by the underlying index. 584
indexed bonds: Bonds whose interest and principal payments are adjusted for changes in the price level and whose interest rate thus provides a direct measure of a real interest rate. 59
individual retirement account (IRA): Retirement account in which pretax dollars can be invested by individuals not covered by some other retirement plan. 543
initial public offering (IPO): A corporation's first sale of securities to the public. 570
insolvent: In a situation in which the value of a firm's or bank's assets have fallen below its liabilities; bankrupt. 394
installment credit: A loan that requires the borrower to make a series of equal payments over some fixed length of time. 552
insured mortgage: Mortgages guaranteed by either the Federal Housing Administration or the Veterans Administration. These agencies guarantee that the bank making the loan will not suffer any losses if the borrower defaults. 299
interest parity condition: The observation that the domestic interest rate equals the foreign interest rate plus the expected appreciation in the foreign currency. 323
interest rate: The cost of borrowing or the price paid for the rental of funds (usually expressed as a percentage per year). 4
interest-rate forward contracts: Forward contracts that are linked to debt instruments. 618
interest-rate risk: The possible reduction in returns that is associated with changes in interest rates. 62, 408
interest-rate swap: A financial contract that allows one party to exchange (swap) a set of interest payments for another set of interest payments owned by another party. 640
intermediate target: Any number of variables, such as monetary aggregates or interest rates, that have a direct effect on employment and the price level and that the Fed seeks to influence. 189
intermediate-term: With reference to a debt instrument, having a maturity of between one and ten years. 18
international banking facilities (IBFs): Banking establishments in the United States that can accept time deposits from foreigners but are not subject to either reserve requirements or restrictions on interest payments. 452
International Monetary Fund (IMF): The international organization created by the Bretton Woods agreement whose objective is to promote the growth of world trade by making loans to countries experiencing balance-of-payments difficulties. 348
international policy coordination: Agreements among countries to enact policies cooperatively. 202
international reserves: Central bank holdings of assets denominated in foreign currencies. 339
inverted yield curve: A yield curve that is downward-sloping. 128
investment banker: A securities dealer who facilitates the transfer of securities from the original issuer to the public. 568
investment banks: Firms that assist in the initial sale of securities in the primary market. 19, 568

January effect: An abnormal rise in stock prices from December to January. 282
junk bonds: Bonds rated lower than BBB by bond-rating agencies. Junk bonds are not investment grade and are considered speculative. They usually have a high yield to compensate investors for their high risk. 122, 255

later stage investing: Investment by a venture capital firm in a company to help the firm grow to a critical mass needed to attract public financing. 551
law of large numbers: The observation that when many people are insured, the probability distribution of the losses will assume a normal probability distribution. 526

law of one price: The principle that if two or more countries produce an identical good, the price of this good should be the same no matter which country produces it. 316

leasing: An arrangement whereby one party obtains the right to use an asset for a fee paid to another party for a predetermined length of time. 557

letter of intent: A document issued by a prospective buyer that signals a desire to go forward with a purchase and that outlines the preliminary terms of the purchase. 576

leverage ratio: A bank's capital divided by its assets. 497

liabilities: IOUs or debts. 16

liability management: The acquisition of funds at low cost to increase profits. 408

lien: A legal claim against a piece of property that gives a lender the right to foreclose or seize the property if a loan on the property is not repaid as promised. 295

limit order: An order placed by a customer to buy stock that specifies a maximum price or an order to sell stock that places a minimum acceptable price. 578

liquid: Easily converted into cash. 19

liquidity: The relative ease and speed with which an asset can be converted into cash. 75

liquidity management: The decision made by a bank to maintain sufficient liquid assets to meet the bank's obligations to depositors. 408

liquidity preference framework: A model developed by John Maynard Keynes that predicts the equilibrium interest rate on the basis of the supply of and demand for money. 96

liquidity premium theory: The theory that the interest rate on a long-term bond will equal an average of short-term interest rates expected to occur over the life of the long-term bond plus a positive term (liquidity) premium. 135

liquidity risk: The risk that a firm may run out of cash needed to pay bills and to keep the firm operating. 554

load fund: A mutual fund that charges a fee when money is added to or withdrawn from the fund. 588

loan commitment: A bank's commitment (for a specified future period of time) to provide a firm with loans up to a given amount at an interest rate that is tied to some market interest rate. 417, 600

loan sale: The sale under a contract (also called a *secondary loan participation*) of all or part of the cash stream from a specific loan, thereby removing the loan from the bank's balance sheet. 417

loanable funds: The quantity of loans. 84

loanable funds framework: Determining the equilibrium interest rate by analyzing the supply of and demand for bonds (loanable funds). 84

London interbank bid rate (LIBID): The rate of interest large international banks charge on overnight loans among themselves. 233

London interbank offer rate (LIBOR): The interest rate charged on short-term funds bought or sold between large international banks. 233

long position: A contractual obligation to take delivery of an underlying financial instrument. 617

long-term: With reference to a debt instrument, having a maturity of ten years or more. 18

macro hedge: A hedge of interest-rate risk for a financial institution's entire portfolio. 623

managed float regime: The current international financial environment in which exchange rates fluctuate from day to day, but central banks attempt to influence their countries' exchange rates by buying and selling currencies. Also known as a *dirty float*. 339

margin credit: Loans advanced by a brokerage house to help investors buy securities. 578

margin requirement: A sum of money that must be kept in an account (the margin account) at a brokerage firm. 626

marked to market: Repriced and settled in the margin account at the end of every trading day to reflect any change in the value of the futures contract. 626

market equilibrium: A situation occurring when the quantity that people are willing to buy (demand) equals the quantity that people are willing to sell (supply). 83

market fundamentals: Items that have a direct impact on future income streams of the security. 278

market maker: Dealers who buy or sell securities from their own inventories, thereby ensuring that there is always a market in which investors can buy or sell their securities. 581

market order: An order placed by a customer to buy stock at the current market price. 577

market segmentation theory: A theory of the term structure that sees markets for different-maturity bonds as completely separated and segmented such that the interest rate for bonds of a given maturity is determined solely by supply and demand for bonds of that maturity. 133

maturity: Time to the expiration date (maturity date) of a debt instrument. 18

mean reversion: The phenomenon that stocks with low returns today tend to have high returns in the future, and vice versa. 283

mergers and acquisitions market: An informal and unorganized market where firms are bought, sold, or merged with other firms. 576

micro hedge: A hedge for a specific asset. 623

monetary base: The sum of the Fed's monetary liabilities (currency in circulation and reserves) and the U.S. Treasury's monetary liabilities (Treasury currency in circulation, primarily coins). 172

monetary neutrality: A proposition that in the long run, a percentage rise in the money supply is matched by the same percentage rise in the price level, leaving unchanged the real money supply and all other economic variables such as interest rates. 332

monetary policy: The management of the money supply and interest rates. 8

money: Anything that is generally accepted in payment for goods or services or in the repayment of debts. Also called *money supply*. 8

money center banks: Large banks in key financial centers. 412

money market: A financial market in which only short-term debt instruments (maturity of less than one year) are traded. 20

money market mutual funds: Funds that accumulate investment dollars from a large group of people and then invest in short-term securities such as Treasury bills and commercial paper. 29, 235

money market securities: Securities that have an original maturity of less than one year, such as Treasury bills, commercial paper, banker's acceptances, and negotiable certificates of deposit. 221

money supply: See *money*.

moral hazard: The risk that one party to a transaction will engage in behavior that is undesirable from the other party's point of view. 24

mortgage: A long-term loan secured by real estate. 292

mortgage-backed security: A security that is collateralized by a pool of mortgage loans. Also called a *securitized mortgage*. 304

mortgage pass-through: A security that has the multiple borrower's mortgage payments pass through a trustee before being disbursed to the investors. 305

mutual bank: A bank owned by the depositors. 466

mutual insurance company: An insurance company that is owned by the policyholders and has the objective of providing insurance for the lowest possible price. 524

named-peril policy: Insurance policy that protects against loss from perils that are specifically named in the policy. 531

National Association of Securities Dealers Automated Quotation System (NASDAQ): A computerized network that links dealers around the country together and provides price quotes on over-the-counter securities. 244

national banks: Federally chartered banks. 439

National Credit Union Act of 1970: Law that established the National Credit Union Administration (NCUA), an independent agency charged with the task of regulating and supervising federally chartered credit unions and state-chartered credit unions that receive federal deposit insurance. 483

National Credit Union Share Insusrance Fund (NCUSIF): Agency established by the National Credit Union Act of 1970 that is controlled by the National Credit Union Administration and insures the deposits in credit unions for $100,000 per account. 483

natural rate of unemployment: The rate of unemployment consistent with full employment at which the demand for labor equals the supply of labor. 186

negotiable certificates of deposit: A bank-issued short-term security that documents a deposit and specifies the interest rate and the maturity date. 227

net asset value: The total value of a mutual fund's assets minus any liabilities, divided by the number of shares outstanding. 587

net interest margin (NIM): The difference between interest income and interest expense as a percentage of assets. 422

net worth: The difference between a firm's assets (what it owns or is owed) and its liabilities (what it owes). Also called *equity capital*. 382

no-load fund: A mutual fund that does not charge a fee when funds are added to or withdrawn from the fund. 588

nominal interest rate: An interest rate that does not take inflation into account. 56

nonbank banks: Limited-service banks that either do not make commercial loans or do not take in deposits. 443

noncompetitive bidding: Offering to buy Treasury securities without specifying a price; the securities are ultimately sold at the weighted average of the competitive bids accepted at the same auction. 223

notional principal: The amount on which interest is being paid in a swap arrangement. 640

off-balance-sheet activities: Bank activities that involve trading financial instruments and the generation of income from fees and loan sales, all of which affect bank profits but are not visible on bank balance sheets. 417, 497

official reserve transactions balance: The current account balance plus items in the capital account. 346

open-end fund: A mutual fund that accepts investments and allows investors to redeem shares at any time. The value of the shares is tied to the value of investment assets of the fund. 587

open interest: The number of contracts outstanding. 624

operating expenses: The expenses incurred from a bank's ongoing operations. 421

operating income: The income earned on bank's ongoing operations. 420

operating target: Any of a set of variables, such as reserve aggregates or interest rates, that the Fed seeks to influence and that are responsive to its policy tools. 189

opportunity cost: The amount of interest (expected return) sacrificed by not holding an alternative asset. 99

options: Contracts that give the purchaser the option (right) to buy or sell the underlying financial instrument at a specified price, called the *exercise price* or *strike price*, within a specific period of time (the *term to expiration*). 632

overfunded: Describing a pension plan that has assets greater than needed to make the projected benefit payments owed by the plan. 537

oversubscribed: Having received more offers to buy than there are securities available for sale. 574

over-the-counter (OTC) market: A secondary market in which dealers at different locations who have an inventory of securities stand ready to buy and sell securities to anyone who comes to them and is willing to accept their prices. 19

passbook savings account: An interest-bearing savings account held at a commercial bank. 477

Pension Benefit Guarantee Corporation (Penny Benny): A government agency that performs a role similar to that of the FDIC, insuring pension benefits up to a limit if a company with an underfunded pension plan goes bankrupt. 542

pension plan: An asset pool that accumulates over an individual's working years and is paid out during the nonworking years. 536

perpetuity: A perpetual bond with no maturity date and no repayment of principal that makes periodic fixed payments forever. 47

political business cycle: A business cycle caused by expansion policies before an election. 166

preferred habitat theory: The theory that the interest rate on a long-term bond will equal the average of the short-term interest rates expected to occur over the life of the long-term bond plus a term premium that responds to supply and demand conditions for that bond. 133

preferred stock: Stock on which a fixed dividend must be paid before common dividends are distributed. It often does not mature and usually does not give the holder voting rights in the company. 259

premium: The amount paid for an option contract. 632

present discounted value: See *present value*.

present value: Today's value of a payment to be received in the future when the interest rate is i. Also called *present discounted value*. 39

primary market: A financial market in which new issues of a security are sold to initial buyers. 18, 567

principal-agent problem: A moral hazard problem that occurs when the managers in control (the agents) act in their own interest rather than in the interest of the owners (the principals) due to differing sets of incentives. 383

private mortgage insurance (PMI): Insurance that protects the lender against losses from defaults on mortgage loans. 296

private pension plan: A pension plan sponsored by an employer, group, or individual. 537

property insurance: Insurance that protects against losses from fire, theft, storm, explosion, and neglect. 530

prospectus: A portion of a security registration statement that is filed with the Securities and Exchange Commission and made available to potential purchasers of the security. 570

public pension plan: A pension plan sponsored by a government body. 538

pure expectations theory: The theory that the interest rate on a long-term bond will equal the average of the short-term interest rates that people expect to occur over the life of the bond. 129

put option: An option contract that provides the right to sell a security at a specified price. 633

quotas: Restrictions on the quantity of foreign goods that can be imported. 318

random walk: The movements of a variable whose future changes cannot be predicted because, given today's value, the variable is just as likely to fall as to rise. 280

rate of capital gain: The change in a security's price relative to the initial purchase price. 61

rate of return: See *return.*

rational expectations: Expectations that reflect optimal forecasts (the best guess of the future) using all available information. 275

real bills doctrine: A guiding principle (now discredited) for the conduct of monetary policy that states that as long as loans are made to support the production of goods and services, providing reserves to the banking system to make these loans will not be inflationary. 194

real interest rate: The interest rate adjusted for expected changes in the price level (inflation) so that it more accurately reflects the true cost of borrowing. 56

real terms: Terms reflecting actual goods and services one can buy. 57

registered bonds: Bonds requiring that their owners register with the company to receive interest payments. Registered bonds have largely replaced bearer bonds, which did not require registration. 253

registration statement: Information about a firm's financial condition, management, competition, industry, and experience that must be filed with the Securities and Exchange Commission prior to the sale to the public of any security with a maturity of more than 270 days. 570

Regulation Q: The regulation under which the Federal Reserve System has the power to set maximum interest rates that banks can pay on savings and time deposits. 32

Regulation Z: The requirement that lenders disclose the full cost of a loan to the borrower; also known as the "truth in lending" regulation. 560

regulatory arbitrate: An attempt to avoid regulatory capital requirements by keeping assets on banks' books that have the same risk-based capital requirement but are relatively risky, while taking off their books low-risk assets. 497

regulatory forbearance: Refraining from exercising a regulatory right to put insolvent savings and loans out of business. 469

reinsurance: Allocating a portion of the risk to another company in exchange for a portion of the premium. 532

reinvestment risk: The interest-rate risk associated with the fact that the proceeds of short-term investments must be reinvested at a future interest rate that is uncertain. 63

repossession: The taking of an asset that has been pledged as collateral for a loan when the borrower defaults. 557

repurchase agreement: A form of loan in which the borrower simultaneously contracts to sell securities and contracts to repurchase them, either on demand or on a specified date. 180

required reserve ratio: The fraction of deposits that the Fed requires be kept as reserves. 172, 404

required reserves: Reserves that are held to meet Fed requirements that a certain fraction of bank deposits be kept as reserves. 172, 404

reserve account: An account used to make insurance and tax payments due on property securing a mortgage loan. A portion of each monthly loan payment goes into the reserve account. 303

reserve currency: A currency such as the U.S. dollar that is used by other countries to denominate the assets they hold as international reserves. 349

reserve for loan losses: An account that offsets the loan accounts on a lender's books that reflects the lender's projected losses due to default. 561

reserve requirements: Regulations making it obligatory for depository institutions to keep a certain fraction of their deposits in accounts with the Fed. 32, 174

reserves: Banks' holding of deposits in accounts with the Fed, plus currency that is physically held by banks (vault cash). 172, 404

Resolution Trust Corporation (RTC): A temporary agency created by FIRREA that was responsible for liquidating the assets of failed savings and loans. 473

restrictive covenants: Provisions that specify certain activities that a borrower can and cannot engage in. 253, 374

return: The payments to the owner of a security plus the change in the security's value, expressed as a fraction of its purchase price; more precisely called the *rate of return*. 59

return on assets (ROA): Net profit after taxes per dollar of assets. 414

return on equity (ROE): Net profit after taxes per dollar of equity capital. 414

revaluation: Resetting of the par value of a currency at a higher level. 351

revenue bonds: Bonds for which the source of income that is used to pay the interest and to retire the bonds is from a specific source, such as a toll road or an electric plant. If this revenue source is unable to make the payments, the bonds can default, despite the issuing municipality's being otherwise healthy. 250

risk: The degree of uncertainty associated with the return on an asset. 75

risk premium: The spread between the interest rate on bonds with default risk and the interest rate on default-free bonds. 120

risk structure of interest rates: The relationship among the various interest rates on bonds with the same term to maturity. 119

roll over: To renew a debt when it matures. 555

seasoned issues: Securities that have been trading publicly long enough to have let the market clearly establish their value. 570

secondary market: A financial market in which securities that have previously been issued can be resold. 18, 567

secondary reserves: U.S. government and agency securities held by banks. 405

secured debt: Debt guaranteed by collateral. 374

secured loan: A loan guaranteed by collateral. 600

securitization: The process of transforming illiquid financial assets into marketable capital market instruments. 455

securitized mortgage: See *mortgage-backed security*. 308

security: A claim on the borrower's future income that is sold by the borrower to the lender. Also called a *financial instrument*. 4

seed investing: Investment by a venture capital firm in a company before it has a real product or is even clearly organized as a company. 551

Separate Trading of Registered Interest and Principal Securities (STRIPS): Securities that have their periodic interest payments separated from the final maturity payment and the two cash flows are sold to different investors. 248

share draft account: Accounts at credit unions that are similar to checking accounts at banks. 431

shelf registration: An arrangement with the Securities and Exchange Commission that allows a single registration document to be filed that permits multiple securities issues. 570

short position: A contractual obligation to deliver an underlying financial instrument. 617

short sell: An arrangement with a broker to borrow and sell securities. The borrowed securities are replaced with securities purchased later. Short sells let investors earn profits from falling securities prices. 578

short-term: With reference to a debt instrument, having a maturity of one year or less. 18

simple loan: A credit market instrument providing the borrower with an amount of funds that must be repaid to the lender at the maturity date along with an additional payment (interest). 38

sinking fund: Fund created by a provision in many bond contracts that requires the issuer to set aside each year a portion of the final maturity payment so that investors can be certain that the funds will be available at maturity. 253

smart card: A more sophisticated stored-value card that contains its own computer chip so that it can be loaded with digital cash from the owner's bank account whenever needed. 428

special drawing rights (SDRs): A paper substitute for gold issued by the International Monetary Fund that functions as international reserves. 354

spot exchange rate: The exchange rate at a given moment. 141, 313

spot transaction: The immediate exchange of bank deposits denominated in different currencies. 313

state banks: Banks chartered by the state. 439

sterilized foreign exchange intervention: A foreign exchange intervention with an offsetting open market operation that leaves the monetary base unchanged. 342

stock: A security that is a claim on the earnings and assets of a corporation. 5

stock company: A firm that issues stock and has the objective of making a profit for its shareholders. 524

stock market risk: The risk associated with fluctuations in stock prices. 629

stock option: An option on an individual stock. 632

strike price: See *exercise price*.

superregional banks: Bank holding companies similar in size to money center banks whose headquarters are not based in one of the money center cities (New York, Chicago, San Francisco). 444

supply curve: A curve depicting the relationship between quantity supplied and price when all other economic variables are held constant. 83

swap: A financial contract that obligates one party to exchange (swap) a set of payments it owns for a set of payments owned by another party. 640

syndicate: A group of investment banks that come together for the purpose of issuing a security. The syndicate spreads the risk of the issue among the members. Each participant attempts to market the security and shares in losses. 572

systematic risk: The component of an asset's risk that cannot be eliminated by diversification.

T-account: A simplified balance sheet with lines in the form of a T that lists only the exchanges that occur in balance sheet times starting from some initial balance sheet position. 340, 406

tariffs: Taxes on imported goods. 318

term security: A security with a specified maturity date. 227

term structure of interest rates: The relationship among interest rates on bonds with different terms to maturity. 119

theory of efficient capital markets: The theory that prices of securities in financial markets fully reflect all available information. 275

theory of purchasing power parity (PPP): The theory that exchange rates between any two currencies will adjust to reflect changes in the price levels of the two countries. 316

thrift institutions (thrifts): Savings and loan associations, mutual savings banks, and credit unions. 26

tombstone: A large notice placed in financial newspapers announcing that a security will be offered for sale by an underwriter or group of underwriters. 572

trade association: A group of credit unions organized to provide a variety of services to a large number of credit unions. 484

trade balance: The difference between merchandise exports and imports. 344

transaction costs: The time and money spent trying to exchange financial assets, goods, or services. 22

Treasury bills (T-bills): Securities sold by the federal government with initial maturities of less than one year. They are often considered the lowest-risk security available. 221

underfunded: Describing a pension plan in which the contributions and their earnings are insufficient to pay out the defined benefits when they come due. 537

undersubscribed: Having received fewer offers to buy than there are securities available for sale. 574

underwriters: Investment banks that guarantee prices on securities to corporations and then sell the securities to the public. 523

underwriting: Guaranteeing prices on securities to corporations and then selling the securities to the public. 19, 264

unexploited profit opportunity: A situation in which an investor can earn a higher-than-normal return. 277

unsecured debt: Debt not guaranteed by collateral. 374

unsterilized foreign exchange intervention: A foreign exchange intervention in which a central bank allows the purchase or sale of domestic currency to affect the monetary base. 341

U.S. Central Credit Union: A central bank for credit unions that was organized in 1974 and provides banking services to the state central credit unions. 483

usury: Charging an excessive or inordinate interest rate on a loan. 560

vault cash: Currency that is physically held by banks and stored in vaults overnight. 404

venture capital firm: A financial intermediary that pools the resources of its partners and uses the funds to help entrepreneurs start up new businesses. 385

wealth: All resources owned by an individual, including all assets. 75

wholesale market: Market where extremely large transactions occur, as for money market funds or foreign currency. 216

World Bank: The International Bank for Reconstruction and Redevelopment, an international organization that provides long-term loans to assist developing countries in building dams, roads, and other physical capital that would contribute to their economic development. 349

yield curve: A plot of the interest rates for particular types of bonds with different terms to maturity. 128

yield on a discount basis: The measure of interest rates by which dealers in bill markets quote the interest rate on U.S. Treasury bills. Also known as the *discount yield.* 51

yield to maturity: The interest rate that equates the present value of payments received from a credit market instrument with its value today. 41

zero-coupon bond: See *discount bond.*

Answers to Selected Questions and Problems

Chapter 1

2. Businesses would cut investment spending because the cost of financing this spending is now higher, and consumers would be less likely to purchase a house or a car because the cost of financing their purchase is higher.

4. No. People who borrow to purchase a house or a car are worse off because it costs them more to finance their purchase; however, savers benefit because they can earn higher interest rates on their savings.

6. Higher stock prices mean that consumers' wealth is higher and so they will be more likely to increase their spending.

8. It makes British goods more expensive relative to American goods. American businesses will find it easier to sell their goods in the United States and abroad, and the demand for their products will rise.

10. In the mid- to late 1970s and the late 1980s and early 1990s, the value of the dollar was low, making travel abroad relatively more expensive; that would have been a good time to vacation in the United States and see the Grand Canyon. As the dollar's value rose in the early 1980s, travel abroad became relatively cheaper, making it a good time to visit the Tower of London.

12. Savings and loan associations, mutual savings banks, credit unions, insurance companies, mutual funds, pension funds, and finance companies.

14. The profitability of financial institutions is affected by changes in interest rates, stock prices, and foreign exchange rates; fluctuations in these variables expose these institutions to risk.

Chapter 2

1. The share of IBM stock is an asset for its owner because it entitles the owner to a share of the earnings and assets of IBM. The share is a liability for IBM because it is a claim on its earnings and assets by the owner of the share.

3. Yes, because the absence of financial markets means that funds cannot be channeled to people who have the most productive use for them. Entrepreneurs then cannot acquire funds to set up businesses that would help the economy grow rapidly.

5. This statement is false. Prices in secondary markets determine the prices that firms issuing securities receive in primary markets. In addition, secondary markets make securities more liquid and thus easier to sell in the primary markets. Therefore, secondary markets are, if anything, more important than primary markets.

7. Because you know your family member better than a stranger, you know more about the borrower's honesty, propensity for risk taking, and other traits. There is less asymmetric information than with a stranger and less likelihood of an adverse selection problem, with the result that you are more likely to lend to the family member.

9. Loan sharks can threaten their borrowers with bodily harm if borrowers take actions that might jeopardize paying off the loan. Hence borrowers from a loan shark are less likely to engage in moral hazard.

11. Yes, because even if you know that a borrower is taking actions that might jeopardize paying off the loan, you must still stop the borrower from doing so. Because that may be costly, you may not spend the time and effort to reduce moral hazard, and so moral hazard remains a problem.

13. Because the costs of making the loan to your neighbor are high (legal fees, fees for a credit check, and so on), you will probably not be able to earn 5% on the loan after your expenses even though it has a 10% interest rate. You are better off depositing your savings with a financial intermediary and earning 5% interest. In addition, you are likely to bear less risk by depositing your savings at the bank rather than lending them to your neighbor.

15. Increased discussion of foreign financial markets in the U.S. press and the growth in markets for international financial instruments such as Eurodollars and Eurobonds.

Chapter 3

1. Less. It would be worth $1/(1 + 0.20) = \$0.83$ when the interest rate is 20%, rather than $1/(1 + 0.10) = \$0.91$ when the interest rate is 10%.

3. $\$1100/(1 + 0.10) + \$1210/(1 + 0.10)^2 + \$1331/(1 + 0.10)^3 = \$3000$.

5. $\$2000 = \$100/(1 + i) + \$100/(1 + i)^2 + \ldots + \$100/(1 + i)^{20} + \$1000/(1 + i)^{20}$.

7. 14.9%, derived as follows: The present value of the \$2 million payment five years from now is $\$2/(1 + i)^5$ million, which equals the \$1 million loan. Thus $1 = 2/(1 + i)^5$. Solving for i $(1 + i)^5 = 2$, so that $i = \sqrt[5]{2} - 1 = 0.149 = 14.9\%$.

9. If the one-year bond did not have a coupon payment, its yield to maturity would be $(\$1000 - \$800)/\$800 = \$200/\$800 = 0.25 = 25\%$. Since it does have a coupon payment, its yield to maturity must be greater than 25%. But because the current yield is a good approximation of the yield to maturity for a 20-year bond, we know that the yield to maturity on this bond is approximately 15%. Therefore, the one-year bond has a higher yield to maturity.

11. You would rather own the Treasury bill because it has a higher yield to maturity. As the example in the text indicates, the discount yield's understatement of the yield to maturity for a one-year bond is substantial, exceeding 1 percentage point. Thus the yield to maturity on the one-year bill would be greater than 9%, the yield to maturity on the one-year Treasury bond.

13. No. If interest rates rise sharply in the future, long-term bonds may suffer such a sharp fall in price that their return might be quite low, possibly even negative.

15. The observers are right. They reason that nominal interest rates were below expected rates of inflation in the late 1970s, making real interest rates negative. The expected inflation rate, however, fell much faster than nominal interest rates in the mid–1980s, so nominal interest rates were above the expected inflation rate and real rates became positive.

17. The present value of the five \$80 coupon payments plus the \$1000 face value of the bond are, respectively, \$77.67, \$75.41, \$73.21, \$71.08, \$69.01, and \$862.61, which sum to a total present value of \$1228.99. The weights for these payments are, respectively, 0.0631982, 0.0613593, 0.0595692, 0.0578361, 0.0561518, and 0.7018853. The duration is then the sum of the weighted maturities: $(1 \times 0.0631982) + (2 \times 0.0613593) + (3 \times 0.0595692) + (4 \times 0.0578361) + (5 \times 0.0561518 + (5 \times 0.7018853) = 4.3861543$ years.

19. The approximate percentage change in the price is $-DUR \times \Delta i/(1 + i) = -8 \times 0.01/1.07 = -0.075 = -7.5\%$.

Chapter 4

2. (a) More, because your wealth has increased; (b) more, because it has become more liquid; (c) less, because its expected return has fallen relative to Polaroid stock; (d) more, because it has become less risky relative to stocks; (e) less, because its expected return has fallen.

4. Purchasing shares in the pharmaceutical company is more likely to reduce my overall risk because the correlation of returns on my investment in a football team with the returns on the pharmaceutical company shares should be low. By contrast, the correlation of returns on an investment in a football team and an investment in a basketball team are probably pretty high, so in this case there would be little risk reduction if I invested in both.

6. When the Fed sells bonds to the public, it increases the supply of bonds, thus shifting the supply curve B^s to the right. The result is that the intersection of the supply and demand curves B^s and B^d occurs at a higher equilibrium interest rate, and the interest rate rises. With the liquidity preference framework, the decrease in the money supply shifts the money supply curve M^s to the left, and the equilibrium interest rate rises. The answer from the loanable funds framework is consistent with the answer from the liquidity preference framework.

8. When the price level rises, the quantity of money in real terms falls (holding the nominal supply of money constant); to restore their holdings of money in real terms to their former level, people will want to hold a greater nominal quantity of money. Thus the money demand curve M^d shifts to the right, and the interest rate rises.

11. Interest rates would rise. A sudden increase in people's expectations of future real estate prices raises the expected return on real estate relative to bonds, so the demand for bonds falls. The demand curve B^d shifts to the left, and the equilibrium interest rate rises.

13. In the loanable funds framework, the increased riskiness of bonds lowers the demand for bonds. The demand curve B^d shifts to the left, and the equilibrium interest rate rises. The same answer is found in the liquidity preference framework. The increased riskiness of bonds relative to money increases the demand for money. The money demand curve M^d shifts to the right, and the equilibrium interest rate rises.

15. Yes, interest rates will rise. The lower commission on stocks makes them more liquid than bonds, and the demand for bonds will fall. The demand curve B^d will therefore shift to the left, and the equilibrium interest rate will rise.

17. The interest rate on the AT&T bonds will rise. Because people now expect interest rates to rise, the expected return on long-term bonds such as the $8\frac{1}{8}$s of 2022 will fall, and the demand for these bonds will decline. The demand curve B^d will therefore shift to the left, and the equilibrium interest rate will rise.

19. Interest rates will rise. When bond prices become volatile and bonds become riskier, the demand for bonds will fall. The demand curve B^d will shift to the left, and the equilibrium interest rate will rise.

Chapter 5

2. U.S. Treasury bills have lower default risk and more liquidity than negotiable CDs. Consequently, the demand for Treasury bills is higher, and they have a lower interest rate.

4. True. When bonds of different maturities are close substitutes, a rise in interest rates for one bond causes the interest rates for others to rise because the expected returns on bonds of different maturities cannot get too far out of line.

6. (a) The yield to maturity would be 5% for a one-year bond, 6% for a two-year bond, 6.33% for a three-year bond, 6.5% for a four-year bond, and 6.6% for a five-year bond. (b) The yield to maturity would be 5% for a one-year bond, 4.5% for a two-year bond, 4.33% for a three-year bond, 4.25% for a four-year bond, and 4.2% for a five-year bond. The upward-sloping yield curve in (a) would be even steeper if people preferred short-term bonds over long-term bonds because long-term bonds would then have a positive risk premium. The downward-sloping yield curve in (b) would be less steep and might even have a slight positive upward slope if the long-term bonds have a positive risk premium.

8. The flat yield curve at shorter maturities suggests that short-term interest rates are expected to fall moderately in the near future, while the steep upward slope of the yield curve at longer maturities indicates that interest rates further into the future are expected to rise. Because interest rates and expected inflation move together, the yield curve suggests that the market expects inflation to fall moderately in the near future but to rise later on.

10. The reduction in income tax rates would make the tax-exempt privilege for municipal bonds less valuable, and they would be less desirable than taxable Treasury bonds. The resulting decline in the demand for municipal bonds and increase in demand for Treasury bonds would raise interest rates on municipal bonds while causing interest rates on Treasury bonds to fall.

12. Lower brokerage commissions for corporate bonds would make them more liquid and thus increase their demand, which would lower their risk premium.

14. The expected one-year interest rate two years from now is $i^e_{t+2} = [(1 + i_{3t} - k_{3t})^3/(1 + i_{2t} - k_{2t})^2] - 1 = [(1 + 0.06 - 0.0035)^3/(1 + 0.05 - 0.0025)^2] - 1 = 0.075 = 7.5\%$.

Chapter 6

1. Because of traditional American hostility to a central bank and centralized authority, the system of 12 regional banks was set up to diffuse power along regional lines.

3. Like the U.S. Constitution, the Federal Reserve System, originally established by the Federal Reserve Act, has many checks and balances and is a peculiarly American institution. The ability of the 12 regional banks to affect discount policy was viewed as a check on the centralized power of the Board of Governors, just as states' rights are a check on the centralized power of the federal government. The provision that there be three types of directors (A, B, and C) representing different groups (professional bankers, businesspeople, and the public) was again intended to prevent any group from dominating the Fed. The Fed's independence of the federal government and the setting up of the Federal Reserve banks as incorporated institutions were further intended to restrict government power over the banking industry.

5. The Board of Governors sets reserve requirements and the discount rate; the FOMC directs open market operations. In practice, however, the FOMC helps make decisions about reserve requirements and the discount rate.

7. The Board of Governors has clearly gained power at the expense of the regional Federal Reserve banks. This trend toward ever more centralized power is a general one in American government, but in the case of the Fed it was a natural outgrowth of the Fed's having been given the responsibility for promoting a stable economy. This responsibility has required greater central direction of monetary policy, the role taken over the years by the Board of Governors and by the FOMC, which the board controls.

9. The threat that Congress will acquire greater control over the Fed's finances and budget.

11. False. Maximizing one's welfare does not rule out altruism. Operating in the public interest is clearly one objective of the Fed. The theory of bureaucratic behavior only points out that other objectives, such as maximizing power, also influence Fed decision making.

13. False. The Fed is still subject to political pressure because Congress can pass legislation limiting the Fed's power. If the Fed is performing badly, Congress can therefore make the Fed accountable by passing legislation that the Fed does not like.

15. The argument for not releasing the FOMC directives immediately is that it keeps Congress off the Fed's back, thus enabling the Fed to pursue an independent monetary policy that is less subject to inflation and political business cycles. The argument for releasing the directive immediately is that it would make the Fed more accountable.

Chapter 7

1. Disagree. Some unemployment is beneficial to the economy because the availability of vacant jobs makes it more likely that a worker will find the right job and that the employer will find the right worker for the job.

3. True. In such a world, hitting a monetary target would mean that the Fed would also hit its interest target, or vice versa. Thus the Fed could pursue both a monetary target and an interest-rate target at the same time.

5. The Fed can control the interest rate on three-month Treasury bills by buying and selling them in the open market. When the bill rate rises above the target level, the Fed would buy bills, which would bid up their price and lower the interest rate to its target level. Similarly, when the bill rate falls below the target level, the Fed would sell bills to raise the interest rate to the target level. The resulting open market operations would of course affect the money supply and cause it to change. The Fed would be giving up control of the money supply to pursue an interest-rate target.

7. Disagree. Although nominal interest rates are measured more accurately and more quickly than the money supply, the interest rate variable that is of more concern to policymakers is the *real* interest rate. Because the measurement of real interest rates requires estimates of inflation, it is not true that real interest rates are necessarily measured more accurately and more quickly than the money supply. Interest-rate targets are therefore not necessarily better than money supply targets.

9. False. The FDIC would not be effective in eliminating bank panics without Fed discounting to troubled banks in order to keep bank failures from spreading.

11. The rise in the discount rate caused a sharp drop in discount borrowing on the part of the banks. The resulting sharp drop in the monetary base then led to a sharp drop in the money supply.

13. Because the Fed did not lend to troubled banks during this period, massive bank failures occurred, leading to a decline in the money supply when depositors increased their holdings of currency relative to deposits and banks increased their excess reserves to protect themselves against runs. As our money supply model indicates, these decisions by banks and depositors led to a sharp contraction of the money supply.

15. When the Federal Reserve was concerned that the dollar had risen too much by the mid–1980s, it pursued expansionary monetary policy in the 1985–1987 period to bring the value of the dollar back down again. When it felt that the dollar had fallen far enough by 1987, it pursued more contractionary policy to keep the dollar from falling further.

17. When the economy enters a recession, interest rates usually fall. If the Fed is targeting interest rates, it tries to prevent a decline in interest rates by selling bonds, thereby lowering their prices and raising interest rates to the target level. The open market sale would then lead to a decline in the monetary base and in the money supply. The decline in interest rates would also cause excess reserves to rise and the volume of discount loans to fall, thereby raising free reserves. With a free reserve target, the Fed would find monetary policy easy and would pursue contractionary policy. Therefore, neither interest-rate nor free reserve targets are very satisfactory because both can lead to a slower rate of money supply growth during a recession, just when the Fed would not want to slow money supply growth.

19. A borrowed reserves target will produce smaller fluctuations in the federal funds rate. In contrast to when there is a nonborrowed reserves target, when the federal funds rate rises with a borrowed reserves target, the Fed prevents the tendency of discount borrowings to rise by buying bonds to lower interest rates. The result is smaller fluctuations in the federal funds rate with a borrowed reserves target.

Chapter 8

1. The money markets can be characterized as having securities that trade in one year or less, are of large denomination, and are very liquid.

3. Banks have higher costs than the money markets owing to the need to maintain reserve requirements. The lower cost structure of the money markets, coupled with the economies of scale resulting from high volume and large-denomination securities, allows for higher interest rates.

5. Following the Great Depression, regulators were primarily concerned with stopping banks from failing. By removing interest-rate competition, bank risk was substantially reduced. The problem with these regulations was that when market interest rates rose above the established interest-rate ceiling, investors withdrew their funds from banks.

7. Businesses both invest and borrow in the money markets. They borrow to meet short-term cash flow needs, often by issuing commercial paper. They invest in all types of money market securities as an alternative to holding idle cash balances.

9. Life insurance companies can invest for the long term because the timing for their liabilities is known with reasonable accuracy. Property and casualty insurance companies cannot predict the natural disasters that cause large payouts on policies.

11. In competitive bidding for securities, buyers submit bids. A noncompetitive bidder accepts the average of the rate paid by the competitive bidders.

13. The Federal Reserve cannot directly set the federal funds rate of interest. It can influence the interest rate by adding funds to or withdrawing reserves from the economy.

15. Banker's acceptances substitute the creditworthiness of a bank for that of a business. When a company sells a product to a company it is unfamiliar with, it often prefers to have the promise of a bank that payment will be made.

Chapter 9

1. Investors use capital markets for long-term investment purposes. They use money markets, which have lower yields, primarily for temporary or transaction purposes.

3. The primary market is for securities being issued for the very first time, and the issuer receives the funds paid for the security. The secondary market is for securities that have been issued previously but are being traded among investors.

5. NASDAQ is a computer network that allows traders to monitor stocks traded on the over-the-counter market. It provides current bid and ask prices on about 4000 actively traded securities.

7. Treasury bills mature in less than 1 year, Treasury notes mature in 1 to 10 years, and Treasury bonds mature in 10 to 30 years.

9. Agencies that issue securities include Ginnie Mae (formerly the Government National Mortgage Association), the Federal Housing Administration, the Veterans Administration, the Federal National Mortgage Association, and the Student Loan Marketing Association. The first four fund mortgage loans and the last funds college student loans.

11. A sinking fund contains funds set aside by the issuer of a bond to pay for the redemption of the bond when it matures. Because a sinking fund increases the likelihood that a firm will have the funds to pay off the bonds as required, investors like the feature. As a result, interest rates are lower on securities with sinking funds.

13. Stocks do not mature, do not pay a fixed amount every period, and often give holders the right to vote on management issues.

15. At least 7 of the 30 firms are involved in high-technology products or services. This has increased the volatility of the Dow index in recent years as these firms were added.

Chapter 10

2. There are two cash flows from stock, periodic dividends, and a future sales price. Dividents are frequently changed when firm earnings either rise or fall. The future sales price is also difficult to estimate, since it depends on the dividends that will be paid at some date even farther in the future. Bond cash flows also consist of two parts, periodic interest payments and a final maturity payment. These payments are established in writing at the time the bonds are issued and cannot be changed without the firm defaulting and being subject to bankruptcy. Stock prices tend to be more volatile, since their cash flows are more subject to change.

4. $P_0 = \dfrac{\$3 \times (1.07)}{.18 - .07} = \$29.18$

6. False. Expectations can be highly inaccurate and still be rational because optimal forecasts are not necessarily accurate: A forecast is optimal if it is the best possible even if the forecast errors are large.

8. No, because he could improve the accuracy of his forecasts by predicting that tomorrow's interest rates will be identical to today's. His forecasts are therefore not optimal, and he does not have rational expectations.

10. No, you shouldn't buy stocks because the rise in the money supply is publicly available information that will be already incorporated into stock prices. Hence you cannot expect to earn more than the equilibrium return on stocks by acting on the money supply information.

12. No, because this is publicly available information and is already reflected in stock prices. The optimal forecast of stock returns will equal the equilibrium return, so there is no benefit from selling your stocks.

14. No, if the person has no better information than the rest of the market. An expected price rise of 10% over the next month implies over a 100% annual return on IBM stock, which certainly exceeds its equilibrium return. This would mean that there is an unexploited profit opportunity in the market, which would have been eliminated in an efficient market. The only time that the person's expectations could be rational is if the person had information unavailable to the market that allowed him or her to beat the market.

16. False. The people with better information are exactly those who make the market more efficient by eliminating unexploited profit opportunities. These people can profit from their better information.

18. True in principle. Foreign exchange rates are a random walk over a short interval such as a week because changes in the exchange rate are unpredictable. If a change were predictable, large unexploited profit opportunities would exist in the foreign exchange market. If the foreign exchange market is efficient, these unexploited profit opportunities cannot exist and so the foreign exchange rate will approximately follow a random walk.

20. False. Although human fear may be the source of stock market crashes, that does not imply that there are unexploited profit opportunities in the market. Nothing in rational expectations theory rules out large changes in stock prices as a result of fears on the part of the investing public.

Chapter 11

1. Securities in the mortgage markets are collateralized by real estate.

3. The global market for loans results in competition that keeps the rates low.

5. A lien is a publicly recorded claim on a piece of real property that has been pledged as collateral. Mortgage lenders file liens to secure loans.

7. Lenders may require private mortgage insurance.

9. The Veterans Administration and the Federal Housing Administration guarantee lenders against losses from loans insured by them. Conventional loans do not have this guarantee, so the lender usually requires private mortgage insurance.

11. The goal of the graduated-payment loan is to let the borrower qualify by reducing the first few years' payments, whereas the goal of the growing-equity loan is to let the borrower pay off early.

13. The bank accepts the home as security and advances money each month. When the borrower dies, the borrower's estate sells the property to retire the debt.

15. The payments on a pool of mortgages are sent by the borrowers to a trustee, who then passes the payments through to holders of securities that are backed by the pass-through.

Chapter 12

2. False. Although a weak currency has the negative effect of making it more expensive to buy foreign goods or to travel abroad, it may help domestic industry. Domestic goods become cheaper relative to foreign goods, and the demand for domestically produced goods increases. The resulting higher sales of domestic products may lead to higher employment, a beneficial effect on the economy.

4. It predicts that the value of the euro will fall 5% in terms of dollars.

6. Even though the Japanese price level rose relative to the American, the yen appreciated because the increase in Japanese productivity relative to American productivity made it possible for the Japanese to continue to sell their goods at a profit at a high value of the yen.

8. The pound depreciates but overshoots, declining by more in the short run than in the long run. Consider Britain the domestic country. The rise in the money supply leads to a higher domestic price level in the long run, which leads to a lower expected future exchange rate. The resulting expected depreciation of the pound raises the expected return on foreign deposits, shifting R^F to the right. The rise in the money supply lowers the interest rate on pound deposits in the short run, which shifts R^D to the left. The short-run outcome is a lower equilibrium exchange rate. However, in the long run, the domestic interest rate returns to its previous value, and R^D shifts back to its original position. The exchange rate rises to some extent, although it still remains below its initial position.

10. The dollar will depreciate. A rise in nominal interest rates but a decline in real interest rates implies a rise in expected inflation that produces an expected depreciation of the dollar that is larger than the increase in the domestic interest rate. As a result, the expected return on foreign deposits rises by more than the expected return on domestic deposits. R^F shifts rightward more than R^D, so the equilibrium exchange rate falls.

12. The dollar will depreciate. An increased demand for imports would lower the expected future exchange rate and result in an expected appreciation of the foreign currency. The higher resulting expected return on foreign deposits shifts the R^F schedule to the right, and the equilibrium exchange rate falls.

14. The contraction of the European money supply will increase European interest rates and raise the future value of the euro, both of which will shift R^F (with Europe as the foreign country) to the right. The result is a decline in the value of the dollar.

Chapter 13

2. The purchase of dollars involves a sale of foreign assets, which means that international reserves fall and the monetary base falls. The resulting fall in the money supply causes interest rates to rise and R^D to shift to the right while it lowers the future price level, thereby raising the future expected exchange rate, causing R^F to shift to the left. The result is a rise in the exchange rate. However, in the long run, the R^D curve returns to its original position, and so there is overshooting.

4. Because other countries often intervene in the foreign exchange market when the United States has a deficit so that U.S. holdings of international reserves do not change. By contrast, when the Netherlands has a deficit, it must intervene in the foreign exchange market and buy guilders, which results in a reduction of international reserves for the Netherlands.

6. Two euros per dollar.

8. A large balance-of-payments surplus may require a country to finance the surplus by selling its currency in the foreign exchange market, thereby gaining international reserves. The result is that the central bank will have supplied more of its currency to the public, and the monetary base will rise. The resulting rise in the money supply can cause the price level to rise, leading to a higher inflation rate.

10. Countries may implement a contractionary monetary policy when they decide to intervene in the foreign exchange market and buy domestic currency to finance the deficit. The result is that they sell off international reserves and their monetary base falls, leading to a decline in the money supply.

12. When other countries buy U.S. dollars to keep their exchange rates from changing vis-à-vis the dollar because of the U.S. deficits, they gain international reserves and their monetary base increases. The outcome is that the money supply in these countries grows faster and leads to higher inflation throughout the world.

14. There are no direct effects on the money supply because there is no central bank intervention in a pure flexible exchange rate regime; therefore, changes in international reserves that affect the monetary base do not occur. However, monetary policy can be affected by the foreign exchange market because monetary authorities may want to manipulate exchange rates by changing the money supply and interest rates.

16. Although capital outflows can harm a country when they lead to a devaluation of the domestic currency, controls in capital outflows are generally not thought to be a good idea. They are seldom effective in a crisis because the private sector figures out ways to get around them; they may even stimulate further capital outflows because they weaken confidence in the government. They also can lead to corruption and may also encourage governments to procrastinate and not take the steps necessary to reform their financial systems.

18. Engaging in a lender-of-last resort operation is likely to weaken the credibility of the central bank and lead to inflation and an even larger depreciation of the domestic currency. Because debt is short-term and denominated in foreign currency in emerging-market countries, the depreciation would lead to a deterioration of balance sheets; thus, the lender-of-last resort operation is likely to make the financial crisis even worse.

20. The international lender of last resort needs to make it clear that it will extend liquidity only to governments that take measures to prevent excessive risk taking. It can also reduce moral hazard by restricting the ability of governments to bail out stockholders and large uninsured creditors of domestic financial institutions.

Chapter 14

2. Financial intermediaries develop expertise in such areas as computer technology so that they can inexpensively provide liquidity services such as checking accounts that lower transaction costs for depositors. Financial intermediaries can also take advantage of economies of scale and engage in large transactions that have a lower cost per dollar of investment.

4. Standard accounting principles make profit verification easier, thereby reducing adverse selection and moral hazard problems in financial markets and hence making them operate better. Standard accounting principles make it easier for investors to screen out good firms from bad firms, thereby reducing the adverse selection problem in financial markets. In addition, they make it harder for managers to understate profits, thereby reducing the principal-agent (moral hazard) problem.

6. Smaller firms that are not well known are the most likely to use bank financing. Since it is harder for investors to acquire information about these firms, it will be hard for the firms to sell securities in the financial markets. Banks that specialize in collecting information about smaller firms will then be the only outlet these firms have for financing their activities.

8. Yes. The person who is putting her life savings into her business has more to lose if she takes on too much risk or engages in personally beneficial activities that don't lead to higher profits. So she will act more in the interest of the lender, making it more likely that the loan will be paid off.

10. True. If the borrower turns out to be a bad credit risk and goes broke, the lender loses less because the collateral can be sold to make up any losses on the loan. Thus adverse selection is not as severe a problem.

12. The separation of ownership and control creates a principal-agent problem. The managers (the agents) do not have as strong an incentive to maximize profits as the owners (the principals). Thus the managers might not work hard, might engage in wasteful spending on personal perks, or might pursue business strategies that enhance their personal power but do not increase profits.

14. A stock market crash reduces the net worth of firms and so increases the moral hazard problem. With less of an equity stake, owners have a greater incentive to take on risky projects and spend corporate funds on items that benefit them personally. A stock market crash, which increases the moral hazard problem, thus makes it less likely that lenders will be paid back. So lending and investment will decline, creating a financial crisis in which financial markets do not work well and the economy suffers.

Chapter 15

2. The rank from most to least liquid is (c), (b), (a), (d).

4. Reserves drop by $500. The T-account for the First National Bank is as follows:

First National Bank

Assets		Liabilities	
Reserves	−$500	Checkable deposits	−$500

6. The bank would rather have the balance sheet shown in this problem because after it loses $50 million due to deposit outflow, the bank would still have excess reserves of $5 million: $50 million in reserves minus required reserves of $45 million (10% of the $450 million of deposits). Thus the bank would not have to alter its balance sheet further and would not incur any costs as a result of the deposit outflow. By contrast, with the balance sheet in Problem 5, the bank would have a shortfall of reserves of $20 million ($25 million in reserves minus the required reserves of $45 million). In this case the bank will incur costs when it raises the necessary reserves through the methods described in the text.

8. No. When you turn a customer down, you may lose that customer's business forever, which is extremely costly. Instead, you might go out and borrow from other banks, corporations, or the Fed to obtain funds so that you can make the customer's loan. Alternatively, you might sell negotiable CDs or some of your securities to acquire the necessary funds.

10. You would want to make short-term loans. Then, when these loans mature, you will be able to make loans at higher interest rates, which will generate more income for the bank.

12. True. Banks can now pursue new loan business much more aggressively than in the past because when they see profitable loan opportunities, they can use liability management to acquire new funds and expand the bank's business.

14. Interest expenses have large fluctuations because interest rates fluctuate so much; provisions for loan losses fluctuate a lot because when the economy turns down or a particular sector of the economy deteriorates, the potential for loan losses rises dramatically.

16. The net interest margin measures the difference between interest income and expenses. It is important because it indicates whether asset and liability management is being done properly so that the bank earns substantial income on its assets and has low costs on its liabilities.

18. To lower capital and raise *ROE,* holding its assets constant, it can pay out more dividends or buy back some of its shares. Alternatively, it can keep its capital constant but increase the amount of its assets by acquiring new funds and then seeking out new loan business or purchasing more securities with these new funds.

20. It can raise $1 million of capital by issuing new stock. It can cut its dividend payments by $1 million, thereby increasing its retained earnings by $1 million. It can decrease the amount of its assets so that the amount of its capital relative to its assets increases, thereby meeting the capital requirements.

Chapter 16

2. (a) Office of the Controller of the Currency; (b) the Federal Reserve; (c) state banking authorities and the FDIC; (d) the Federal Reserve.

4. New technologies such as electronic banking facilities are frequently shared by several banks, so these facilities are not classified as branches. Thus they can be used by banks to escape limitations to offering services in other states and, in effect, to escape limitations from restrictions on branching.

6. International banking has been encouraged by giving special tax treatment and relaxed branching regulations to Edge Act corporations and to international banking facilities (IBFs); this was done to make American banks more competitive with foreign banks. The hope is that it will create more banking jobs in the United States.

8. No, because the Saudi-owned bank is subject to the same regulations as the American-owned bank.

10. The rise of inflation and the resulting higher interest rates on alternatives to checkable deposits meant that banks had a big shrinkage in this low-cost way of raising funds. The innovation of money market mutual funds also meant that the banks lost checking account business. The abolishment of Regulation Q and the appearance of NOW accounts did help decrease disintermediation but raised the cost of funds for American banks, which now had to pay higher interest rates on checkable and other deposits. Foreign banks were also able to tap a large pool of domestic savings, thereby lowering their cost of funds relative to American banks.

12. The growth of the commercial paper market and the development of the junk bond market meant that corporations were now able to issue securities rather than borrow from banks, thus eroding the competitive advantage of banks on the lending side. Securitization has enabled other financial institutions to originate loans, again taking away some of the banks' loan business.

14. Brokerage firms began to engage in the traditional banking business of issuing deposit instruments, while foreign bank activities in the United States further eroded the competitive position of U.S. banks. This led to the Federal Reserve's allowing bank holding companies to enter the underwriting business through a loophole in Glass-Steagall in order to keep them competitive. Finally, legislation in 1999 was passed to repeal Glass-Steagall.

Chapter 17

1. All of the depositors at a mutual bank are owners of the firm. Instead of receiving interest payments, they receive dividend income.

3. The primary assets of S&Ls are loans, for the most part mortgage loans.

5. Because depositors were insured by the government against losses, they had no incentive to monitor bank management.

7. The net worth ratio is the most common measure of capital adequacy.

9. Credit unions are mandated to provide financial services to consumers rather than corporate customers.

11. Only people living in a certain geographic area or employed in a specific business or by a particular employer are eligible for membership in a credit union.

13. The common bond membership rule restricts membership in any particular credit union so that the average size of credit unions is substantially lower than for commercial banks.

15. The main advantages of credit unions are employer support, tax-exempt status, and strong trade associations.

17. The S&L crisis did not occur until the 1980s because interest rates stayed low before then, so S&Ls were not subjected to losses from high interest rates. Also, the opportunities for risk taking were not available until the 1980s, when legislation and financial innovation made it easier for S&Ls to take on more risk, thus greatly increasing the adverse selection and moral hazard problems.

19. If political candidates receive campaign funds from the government and are restricted in the amount they spend, they will have less need to satisfy lobbyists to win elections. As a result, they may have greater incentives to act in the interest of taxpayers (the principals), and so the political process might improve.

Chapter 18

2. There would be adverse selection because people who might want to burn their property for some personal gain would actively try to obtain substantial fire insurance policies. Moral hazard could also be a problem because a person with a fire insurance policy has less incentive to take measures to prevent a fire.

4. Regulations that restrict banks from holding risky assets directly decrease the moral hazard of risk taking by the bank. Requirements that force banks to have a large amount of capital also decrease the banks' incentives for risk taking because banks now have more to lose if they fail. Such regulations will not completely eliminate the moral hazard problem because bankers have incentives to hide their holdings of risky assets from the regulators and to overstate the amount of their capital.

6. Because off-balance-sheet activities do not appear on bank balance sheets, they cannot be dealt with by simple bank capital requirements, which are based on bank assets, such as a leverage ratio. Banking regulators have dealt with this problem by imposing an additional risk-based bank capital requirement that requires banks to set aside additional bank capital for different kinds of off-balance-sheet activities.

8. Bank supervision involves bank examinations in which bank examiners assess six areas of the bank represented in the CAMELS rating (capital adequacy, asset quality, management, earnings, liquidity, and sensitivity to market risk). A low score on the CAMELS rating allows the supervisors to declare a bank to be a "problem bank," making it more subject to frequent examinations and to sanctions to reduce the amount of risk taking it is engaged in. Bank examiners also check that the bank is following the rules and regulations and is not holding securities or loans that are too risky. All of these measures help ensure that banks are not taking on too much risk, and thus promote a safer and sounder banking system.

10. With the advent of new financial instruments, a bank that is quite healthy at a particular point in time can be driven into insolvency extremely rapidly from risky trading in these instruments. Thus, a focus on bank capital at a point in time may not be effective in indicating whether a bank will be taking on excessive risk in the near future. Therefore, to make sure that banks are not taking on too much risk, bank supervisors now are focusing more on whether the risk-management procedures in banks keep them from excessive risk taking that might make a future bank failure more likely.

12. Eliminating or limiting the amount of deposit insurance would help reduce the moral hazard of excessive risk taking on the part of banks. It would, however, make bank failures and panics more likely, so it might not be a very good idea.

14. The economy would benefit from reduced moral hazard; that is, banks would not want to take on too much risk because doing so would increase their deposit insurance premiums. The problem is, however, that it is difficult to monitor the degree of risk in bank assets because often only the bank making the loans knows how risky they are.

Chapter 19

1. People carry insurance because they are risk-averse and prefer to know their wealth with certainty.

3. Information asymmetry exists when one party to a transaction knows more about the situation than the other does. Often the person buying insurance knows more about the risk than the insurance company knows.

5. Insurance companies protect themselves by requiring inspections and medical examinations, insuring groups rather than individuals, and insisting on a deductible.

7. Most are stock companies.

9. Term life insurance pays a death benefit if the policyholder dies; no other benefit is paid. Whole policies pay a death benefit but also include a savings program that pays out if the policyholder lives.

11. Reinsurance allocates a portion of the risk to another company in exchange for a portion of the premium.

13. A more sophisticated public, greater awareness of providing for retirement, and a lack of confidence in Social Security have led to growth in private pension plans.

15. The demographics suggest that more people will be retiring than will be entering the workforce in the future. With fewer people paying into the plan and more taking out, it could go bankrupt.

Chapter 20

2. Venture financing is long-term. Pension funds hold long-term funds and can predict very accurately when the funds will be needed. The illiquidity of the investment is not a problem for them. Property and casualty insurance companies need access to their funds if there are a large number of claims, say from a hurricane. They could not tolerate the illiquidity of the investment.

4. Ventures firms provide screening of potential investments. They monitor firm activities and participate in management decision making. They also require firms to demonstrate progress in order to obtain continuing funding.

6. A balloon loan requires that a single large payment be made when the loan matures, whereas on an installment loan, the borrower makes a series of small, equal payments.

8. They often have poor credit records, low incomes, or inferior security. All of these factors make them unacceptable to banks.

10. Yes, because there is no well-established secondary market for their loans.

12. Factoring is selling accounts receivable to a finance company. The selling firm gets immediate cash for its sales and avoids having to go after its customers for collections.

14. Under a floor plan, the finance company holds the inventory as security and releases its lien on the inventory only when the items are sold and the loan is paid.

16. The tax code allows the interest paid on loans secured by homes to be deducted from taxes. This lowers the effective cost of the debt.

18. Regulation Z requires that the company disclose the annual percentage rate charged on loans in a prominent and understandable fashion.

20. No, consumers did not perceive any great benefit to dealing with a single firm for all of their financial needs.

Chapter 21

1. Regulators felt that investment banking was riskier and had led to bank failures during the Great Depression.

3. When an offering is underwritten, the investment banker purchases the issue at a prespecified price. In a best-efforts issue, the investment banker does not take ownership.

5. No, an SEC review simply determines if the proper documents have been filed.

7. It is better to be fully subscribed because oversubscription indicates that the investment bankers priced the security too low.

9. In a hostile takeover, the target firm does not want control to pass to the acquiring firm, and so its management makes every effort to prevent the takeover from happening. In a merger, both sides work together to expedite the union of the firms.

11. A market order has the broker buy or sell the security at the current market price. A limit order sets a maximum price for buying the security and a minimum price for selling the security.

13. Banks object because legislation prevents banks from entering the brokerage business but does not prevent brokers from entering the banking business.

15. Load funds charge sales commissions; no-load funds do not.

Chapter 22

2. Secured loans are an important method of lending for financial institutions because if the borrower defaults, the financial institution can take title to the collateral, sell it off, and use the proceeds to offset any losses on the loan. Thus the financial institution can worry less about the adverse selection problem because it has some protection even if the borrower was a bad credit risk.

4. To reduce adverse selection, a banker needs to screen out bad credit risks by learning as much as possible about potential borrowers. Similarly, to minimize moral hazard, the banker must continually monitor borrowers to see that they are complying with restrictive loan covenants. Hence it pays for the banker to be nosy.

6. False. Although diversification is a desirable strategy for a bank, it may still make sense for a bank to specialize in certain types of lending. For example, a bank may have developed expertise in screening and monitoring a particular kind of loan, thereby improving its ability to handle problems of adverse selection and moral hazard.

8. Rate-sensitive assets increase by \$4 million, so *GAP* goes from –\$17.5 million to –\$13.5 million. (Of the \$5 million of fixed-rate mortgages, \$1 million is rate-sensitive because 20% are repaid within a year, so converting the \$5 million of fixed-rate mortgages into variable-rate mortgages produces a net increase of rate-sensitive assets of \$4 million.) Because *GAP* falls in absolute value, the effect of changes in interest rates on its profits and hence on its interest-rate risk is smaller.

10. The manager raises the estimate of rate-sensitive liabilities by \$2.25 million so that *GAP* goes from –\$17.5 million to –\$19.75 million. Because *GAP* rises in absolute value, the effect of changes in interest rates on its profits and hence its interest-rate risk is larger. If interest rates rise by 5 percentage points, profits next year change by $\Delta I = GAP \times \Delta i = -\$19.75$ million $\times\ 0.05 = -\$0.9875$ million.

12. The duration gap is now $DUR_{gap} = DUR_A - (L/A \times DUR_L) = 4 - (95/100 \times 2) = 2.1$ years. The change in net worth as a percentage of assets is $\%\Delta NW = -DUR_{GAP} \times \Delta i/(1 + i) = -2.1 \times 0.02/(1 + 0.10) = -0.038 = -3.8\%$. With \$100 million of assets, net worth declines by \$3.8 million, from \$5 million to \$1.2 million.

14. It should solve the following equation: $0 = 4 - (95/100 \times DUR_L)$. This yields a duration of liabilities DUR_L of 4.2 years.

16. Interest-rate risk stays the same because rate-sensitive assets and rate-sensitive liabilities increase by an equal amount, leaving the income gap the same. The Friendly Finance Company still has an income gap of \$12 million, and to eliminate it, it could either reduce its rate-sensitive assets to \$43 million or increase its rate-sensitive liabilities to \$55 million.

18. The duration gap is now $DUR_{GAP} = DUR_A - (L/A \times DUR_L) = 2 - (90/100 \times 4) = -1.6$ years. The change in net worth as a percentage of assets is $\%\Delta NW = -DUR_{GAP} \times \Delta i/(1 + i) = -(-1.6) \times 0.03/(1 + 0.08) = 0.044 = 4.4\%$. With \$100 million of assets, net worth increases by \$4.4 million, from \$10 million to \$14.4 million.

20. It should solve the following equation: $0 = 2 - (90/100 \times DUR_L)$. This yields a duration of liabilities DUR_L of 2.22 years.

Chapter 23

2. You would enter into a contract that specifies that you will sell the \$25 million of 8s of 2015 at a price of 110 one year from now.

4. You have a loss of 6 points, or \$6000, per contract.

6. You would buy \$100 million worth (1000 contracts) of the call long-term bond option with a delivery date of one year in the future and with a strike price that corresponds to a yield of 8%. This means that you would have the option to buy the long bond with the 8% interest rate, thereby making sure that you can earn the 8%. The disadvantage of the options contract is that you have to pay a premium that you would not have to pay with a futures contract. The advantage of the options contract is that if the interest rate rises and the bond price falls during the next year, you do not have to exercise the option and so will be able to earn a higher rate than 8% when the funds come in next year, whereas with the futures contract, you have to take delivery of the bond and will only earn 8%.

8. You have a profit of 1 point (\$1000) when you exercise the contract, but you have paid a premium of \$1500 for the call option, so your net profit is –\$500, a loss of \$500.

10. Because for any given price at expiration, a lower strike price means a higher profit for a call option and a lower profit for a put option. A lower strike price makes a call option more desirable and raises its premium and makes a put option less desirable and lowers its premium.

12. It would swap interest on $42 million of fixed-rate assets for the interest on $42 million of variable-rate assets, thereby eliminating its income gap.

14. You would hedge the risk by buying 80 euro futures contracts that mature 3 months from now.

Index

Note: Page numbers followed by letters *f, n,* and *t* refer to figures, notes, and tables, respectively.

C

Guide to Commonly Used Symbols

Symbol	Page Where Introduced	Term
Δ	69	change in a variable
π^e	57	expected inflation
σ	77	standard deviation
B^d	83	demand for bonds
B^s	83	supply of bonds
C	45	yearly coupon payment
D	125	demand curve
DUR	67	duration
DUR_{GAP}	608	duration gap
E	321	exchange (spot) rate
$(E^e_{t+1} - E_t)/E_t$	321	expected appreciation of domestic currency
EM	414	equity multiplier
GAP	603	income gap
i	39	interest rate (yield to maturity)

Symbol	Page Where Introduced	Term
i^D	321	interest rate on dollar assets
i^F	321	interest rate on foreign assets
i_r	57	real interest rate
M	100	quantity of money
M^d	98	demand for money
M^s	98	supply of money
P_t	60	price of a security at time t
R	60	return
R^D	322	expected return on dollar deposits
R^F	322	expected return on foreign deposits
ROA	414	return on assets
ROE	414	return on equity
RSA	603	rate-sensitive assets
RSL	603	rate-sensitive liabilities
S	125	supply curve